9780873520188
AF130008

# FIRST-LINE INDEX OF ENGLISH POETRY

## 1500–1800

IN MANUSCRIPTS OF
THE BODLEIAN LIBRARY
OXFORD

# FIRST-LINE INDEX OF ENGLISH POETRY
# 1500–1800
## IN MANUSCRIPTS OF THE BODLEIAN LIBRARY OXFORD

EDITED BY

MARGARET CRUM

VOLUME I

INDEX COMMITTEE OF
THE MODERN LANGUAGE ASSOCIATION
OF AMERICA
1969

Published and distributed in America
by the Modern Language Association of America
62 Fifth Avenue, New York, New York, 10011

Library of Congress Card Number: 68-11313



PRINTED IN GREAT BRITAIN

# PREFACE

THE originator of the first-line index of English verse in Bodleian manuscripts was Percy Simpson, who was anxious that the library's poetical holdings should be made accessible by a tool similar to the MS. Index of First and Last Lines in the Department of Manuscripts at the British Museum. Even from the fullest of descriptive catalogues, to learn what poems are present in manuscripts is laborious, and much of the poetry in the Bodleian collections is described in the *Summary Catalogue of Western Manuscripts*, from which detail was excluded. Dr. Simpson saw that this material would remain virtually buried until an index of first lines could be provided. In 1932 it was settled, after consultation with members of the English faculty, that a card-index should be formed. It was hoped that the task of writing the cards might be shared amongst those students working for post-graduate degrees in English literature to whom experience in reading manuscripts would be valuable. The Malone manuscripts were taken first, and were finished within two years. Rawlinson poetry was taken next, but was finished only in 1951.

Professor F. P. Wilson gave fresh impetus to the work, and in 1950, at his instigation, funds were made available so that progress need no longer depend on voluntary effort and I was appointed to carry out the work. Happily Dr. Simpson, who from the first had supervised all that was done, continued his part, checking each entry both against the manuscripts and against the British Museum index, for as long as his health allowed. Subsequently, through the kindness of the Keeper of Manuscripts, a microfilm of the British Museum index was obtained, which greatly facilitated checking.

The card-index was completed in April 1961, and poetry acquired after that date is not included.

The first writers of cards in 1931–2 were Miss M. A. Beese, R. K. Black, H. F. Brooks, Miss M. M. E. Fletcher, Miss A. M. Morton, W. J. Paylor, Miss I. H. Robinson, E. E. Sandeen, H. B. Spencer, and A. Tillotson. In 1932–3 E. R. Brown, Miss H. A. Buchan, and J. Williams continued. Later contributions were made by H. T. Cunningham, who indexed state poems in MSS. Firth c. 15 and 16; H. F. Brooks again (John Oldham's MS. Rawl. poet. 123); E. Davis; Miss B. Geary; Miss Clare Kirchberger (the collection of religious poetry in MS. Eng. poet. b. 5); and G. M. Storey (Alabaster's MS. Eng. poet. e. 57). Members of staff, notably J. R. Liddell, who indexed sixteen Rawl. poet. manuscripts, assisted. Amongst those engaged on research involving Bodleian poetical manuscripts who have given information are L. G. Black, W. J. Cameron, Mrs. Herbert Davis, T. R. Davis, Margaret Forey, D. F. Foxon, C. B. Gullans, H. D. Johnstone, Dr. C. H. Josten, Robert Krueger, Rosamond McGuinness, the Revd. F. McKay, Paul Morgan, Brian Morris, Anne Pratt, Professor William A. Ringler, Professor Eleanor Withington, and F. B. Zimmerman. Help from Professor F. P. Wilson, Professor J. A. W. Bennett, David Ogg, and John Crow must also be acknowledged, and so must that of the Keeper of Western Manuscripts. The task of giving references in support of Dr. Simpson's attributions to Francis Quarles was lightened by Miss S. R. Broughton, who made an index of his printed poems. Miss M. E. Wheeler laboriously and accurately numbered the cards and entries. Other members of staff who contributed to the index were Mrs. C. Campbell, Mrs. D. Gardiner, Mrs. C. Allen, and Mrs. A. Ward, who with much skill prepared copy for the printer from cards; and D. H. Merry and Bernard Robinson, who read through the typescript.

The publication of the index is due to the exertions of Professor J. M. Osborn, who brought it before the Index Committee of the Modern Language Association of America. It was agreed that the Modern Language Association and the Delegates of the Oxford University Press should be jointly responsible for publication. We are very grateful to both these bodies for taking on so large a work.

MARGARET CRUM

## STATEMENT FOR THE INDEX COMMITTEE OF THE MODERN LANGUAGE ASSOCIATION OF AMERICA

THE Index Committee joins Miss Crum in rejoicing that this index, after more than thirty-five years of devoted labour by members of the Bodleian staff and numerous volunteers, has been brought to completion and can be made available to scholars. We are happy that we can be responsible for its distribution in the United States of America because we are confident that present and future generations of American scholars will find these volumes invaluable.

One point which Miss Crum's modesty prevents her from stressing in her preface, the Committee would like to emphasize, namely that completion of this index is due primarily to her own efforts. Although many members of the Bodleian staff, and other volunteers have participated, for nearly twenty years Miss Crum has devoted a large portion of her time to this project. In this she has had the constant encouragement and advice of Dr. Richard Hunt, Keeper of Western Manuscripts in the Bodleian. Let users of this index direct their gratitude to them.

We join with all those concerned in the publication of this book in dedicating it to the memory of its instigator and prime mover, Dr. Percy Simpson.

BENJAMIN C. NANGLE

# CONTENTS

# ABBREVIATIONS AND SHORT TITLES

Allison and Rogers: *A Catalogue of Catholic Books in English . . . 1558–1640*, A. F. Allison and D. M. Rogers.

*Athenae*: *Athenae Oxonienses*, Anthony à Wood, ed. Philip Bliss, 1813–20.

*B.L.R.*: *Bodleian Library Record.*

*B.Q.R.*: *Bodleian Quarterly Record.*

Brown–Robbins Index: *The Index of Middle English Verse*, Carleton Brown and R. Hope Robbins, 1943.

*C.S.P.D.*: *Calendar of State Papers, Domestic Series.*

Case: *A Bibliography of English Poetical Miscellanies, 1521–1750*, by Arthur E. Case, O.B.S., 1935.

*Contents and Contributors*: W. P. Courtney, *Dodsley's Collection of Poetry: Its Contents and Contributors*, 1910.

*Dodsley's Collection of Poems*: Collations, lists, and indexes by R. W. Chapman (*O.B.S. Proceedings and Papers*, iii, 1933, pp. 269–316).

*Fasti*: *Fasti Oxonienses*, Anthony à Wood, ed. Philip Bliss, 1815–20.

G.E.C.: *The Complete Peerage*, by G. E. Cokayne, new ed. Vicary Gibbs, etc., 1910–59.

H. Gardner, *The Elegies*, etc.: *John Donne: The Elegies and the Songs and Sonnets*, 1965.

Greg: *A Bibliography of the Printed Drama to the Restoration*, by W. W. Greg, 1939–59.

*M. & L.*: *Music and Letters.*

*M.L.R.*: *Modern Language Review.*

O.B.S.: Oxford Bibliographical Society.

*O.B.S. P. & P.*: *Oxford Bibliographical Society Proceedings and Papers.*

O.H.S.: Oxford Historical Society.

*P.M.L.A.*: *Publications of the Modern Language Association of America.*

*P.Q.*: *Philological Quarterly.*

*Poems*: printed works of the poet named in entry.

*Purcell*: *Henry Purcell: an analytical catalogue of his music*, by F. B. Zimmerman, 1963.

*R.E.S.*: *Review of English Studies.*

*Roxburghe Ballads*: published by the Ballad Society, 1871–97.

*S.C. of W. MSS.*: *A Summary Catalogue of Western MSS. in the Bodleian Library.*

*S.T.C.*: *Short Title Catalogue of Books printed in England, Ireland, and Scotland, 1475–1640*, by A. W. Pollard and G. R. Redgrave, 1926.

Vieth: *Attribution in Restoration Poetry: A study of Rochester's Poems of 1680*, by David M. Vieth (Yale Studies in English, vol. 153, 1963).

Wing: *Short-Title Catalogue of Books printed . . . 1641–1700*, by Donald Wing, Index Society, 1945.

| | | |
|---|---|---|
| attr.: attributed | brds.: broadside | matr.: matriculated |
| autogr.: autograph | d.: died | pr.: printed |
| b.: born | m.: married | tr.: translated |

# NOTE ON THE ARRANGEMENT OF ENTRIES

THE entries are arranged as follows:

1. First line of the poem, in modernized spelling except for names. Variants in wording of the first line are given in brackets, e.g.

   A fitter match hath never [could ne'er, would never have] been [seen].

   For different versions of the first line separated in the alphabetical sequence, cross-references are given. Other variants are not mentioned.

   Copies of parts of poems are indexed under the first line of the complete poem.

   Contractions such as I'll, We'll are placed in their alphabetical order ignoring the apostrophe) to avoid the doubtful use of 'homonym'.)

2. Last line of the usual version of the poem.

3. Author's name, if known; title of the poem; other information derived from the manuscript.

   The author's name is enclosed in square brackets when it is not derived from one or more of the manuscripts.

   Titles and notes in inverted commas are quoted exactly from the manuscript. Information derived from the manuscripts, but not quoted literally, is given without inverted commas.

4. Editorial notes, chiefly references to printed versions of a poem.

5. List of Bodleian manuscripts in which the poem is found, with folio or page references.

   Autograph manuscripts are set out on a separate line followed by the abbreviation '(autogr.)'.

   Other manuscripts are enumerated in alphabetical order of shelf-mark. The full shelf-mark is not repeated where there is a string of manuscripts from the same collection. e.g.

   MSS. Eng. poet. e. 14, fol. 90$^{v}$; e. 40. fol. 114; e. 97, p. 68.

   Manuscripts preceded by an asterisk (*) are those which contain the work of a single author (or of two authors), e.g.:

   Alas, poor Death: Where is now thy glory
   Thou so much worse, that thou shalt be no more.
   Herbert, George, 'A dialogue Anthem: Christian, Death'.
   Pr. *The Temple*, 1633, p. 164.
   MSS. Rawl. poet. 90, fol. 138; *Tanner 307, fol. 124$^{v}$.

   MS. Tanner 307 is the licensed copy of *The Temple*, probably copied at Little Gidding from Herbert's own 'little book' bequeathed to Nicholas Ferrar.

   Manuscripts with shelf-mark Mus. and Mus. Sch. include musical settings. Music appearing in other manuscripts is mentioned, usually after the shelf-mark.

# A

ENTRIES 1–1978

1 A baker once there was
And broke his neck again.
MS. Eng. poet. f. 9, p. 1.

2 A ballad late was made
And came again in May.
'Answer' to I1841, I1844, I1853.
Pr. *Ignoramus*, ed. Hawkins, 1787, and *Poems of Corbet*, ed. Gilchrist, 1807.
MSS. Douce f. 5, fol. 25; Firth d. 7, fol. 76; Rawl. poet. 26, fol. 28$^{v}$; Tanner 465 fol. 77; Top. Oxon. e. 344, fol. 134.

3 A banished man long barred from his desire
A bait most fit for hungry minded guest.
Sidney, Sir Philip, from the *Arcadia*.
MS. *e Mus. 37, fol. 108.

4 A bashful man begets himself disgrace
Bold face speeds best, where s'ere he comes in place.
Robinson, Robert.
MS. *Rawl. poet. 218, p. 69 (autogr.).

5 A battle amongst the bees
The lion and dragon set up again.
'Prophesy, 1656'.
MSS. Rawl. D. 317, fol. 211$^{v}$; 397, fol. 317.

6 A bear of a wife
And deserves to have his fill.
Williams, John.
MS. *Rawl. poet. 184, fol. 92$^{v}$ (autogr.).

7 A beard thick or thin
His land is well manured.
'A song of the beards'.
MS. CCC. 328, fol. 38$^{v}$.

8 A beauteous lady being newly wed
Let's to't each night for health, each morn for pleasure.
MS. Ashmole 38, p. 152; see also A213, A216, A218, A220, A260.

9 A beauteous lady sitting in a muse
Sir lock it if you please, you keep the keys.
[Harington, Sir John].
MS. Rawl. poet. 172, fol. 2; see also A151, A155, A526.

A beautiful girl of true catholic breed 10
Though three times alas! it went out in the socket.
Parsons, William, 'Song written at Paris'.
MS. *Don. d. 123, p. 115 (autogr.).

A beauty smoother than an ivory plain 11
Those hearts are double slain it shines so bright.
Strode, William, 'On a gentlewoman who escaped the marks of the pox'.
Pr. *Parnassus Biceps*, 1656.
MS. CCC. 325, fol. 88 (autogr.).
MSS. Ashmole 47, fol. 51$^{v}$; CCC. 328, fol. 82; Eng. poet. c. 50, fol. 129$^{v}$; f. 25, fol. 19; Rawl. poet. 84, fol. 85.

A beggar asked a penny once, and swore 12
So that I gave; yet both our oaths were kept.
MS. Rawl. poet. 209, fol. 33$^{v}$.

A beggar once, exceeding poor 13
Yet both of us our oaths did save.
'A Quibble'.
MS. Eng. misc. e. 183, fol. 71.

A bird that hath an angel's plume 14
A thievish pace, a hellish tune.
'On the peacock', couplet translated from Latin.
MSS. Rawl. D. 954, fol. 42; Rawl. poet. 209, fol. 34$^{v}$.

A blameless soul, and spotless beauty join'd 15
Weak to support the blaze of such a light.
Barton, [Henry, Warden of Merton, 1759–90 (?)], 'On Miss Wallop Daughter of Ld. Lymington'.
MS. Ballard 47, fol. 66.

A bleeding heart lo made a sacrifice 16
Destined t'enjoy so sweet a she as she.
Burton, Francis, 'On the author's heart'.
MS. *Add. A.267, fol. 152 (autogr.).

A blest confession, for which expect 17
Not to suppress the flame but raise it higher.
Tatham, John, 'Ostella confessing she loved me'.
Pr. *Ostella*, 1650, p. 22.
Pr. bk. 27980 e. 86, opposite p. 56.

18 A boat, a boat, bring to the ferry
And every blade his whore.
'A catch'.
MS. Rawl. poet. 152, fol. 23.

19 A boat, a boat haste to the ferry
And laugh and quaff and drink old sherry.
MS. Rawl. poet. 65, fol. 32.

20 A body and a coat I have
Be worse then, thou shalt have more.
'Of the matter and practice of the Philosopher's stone'.
MS. Ashmole 204, fol. 144.

21 A body chaste, a virtuous mind
A spotless maid, a matchless wife.
Epitaph on Dorothy Busfeild of Leeds, 1669.
MSS. Rawl. poet. 84, fol. 45.
Top. Yorks c. 26, fol. 121;

22 A body sound and healthful, free from pain
Of that which shall eternally endure.
MS. Rawl. poet. 66, fol. 33.

23 A bonny lad of noble race
Will welcome him that's far away.
'A Scotch Song'.
MS. Rawl. poet. 155, p. 176.

24 A bonny northern lad
Sweet death come end the strife.
'Lovesick Jockey. A Scotch song to a tune of Wm. Crofts'.
MS. Mus. Sch. C. 95, p. 67.

25 A bottle and friend the delight of my life
In mirth and good humour with bottle and friend.
'A Social Companion . . . composed by Mr. Blewitt'.
MS. Mus. e. 19, p. 80.

26 A branch I wear, which makes me memorize
A living death, which hope may ease, not cure.
MS. Rawl. poet. 148, fol. 66$^{v}$.

27 A bridegroom to be met, five virgins trim
But these stand, knock and call; yet all in vain.
'The Ten Virgins'.
MS. Rawl. poet. 154, fol. 111.

28 A British Trojan great by his worthy birth
Her coffin stinks Hub Bub 'tis time to bury her.
'Epitaphium scriptum et infixum super magnum stercus'.
MS. Rawl. poet. 120, fol. 30.

29 A British youth to an Italian dame
'Caro! come home, and lie with me to-night'.
Parsons, William.
MS. *Don. d. 123, p. 123 (autogr.).

A brittle gem, bubble is beauty pale 30
A rose, dew, snow, smoke, wind air naught at all.
Translation of Latin epigram, couplet.
MS. Rawl. D. 1372, fol. 33.

A broader streak of crimson light 31
Flames the bright sun of steady joy.
R. L., 'Ode to a lady on her Birth-Day 1779'.
MS. *Eng. poet. e. 16, fol. 17.

A broken altar, Lord, thy servant rears 32
And sanctify this altar to be thine.
Herbert, George, 'The Church. The Altar'.
Pr. *The Temple*, 1633, p. 18.
MS. *Tanner 307, fol. 15$^{v}$.

A brook whose stream so great, so good 33
The muses with their tears supply.
Crashaw, R[ichard], 'In obitum D$^{ris}$ Brooke'.
MS. Tanner 465, fol. 65$^{v}$, attr. to Mr. Crashaw on fol. 1*a*.

A building rare, of strange device, in Egypt first was framed 34
And on the middle a steeple stood, a pillar long likewise That . . . (incomplete).
Price, E., 'Lemnos'.
MS. Douce 290, fol. 129 (autogr.).

A buxom lass of London town 35
The finest sausage in my shop.
'The Disappointment'.
MS. Rawl. poet. 152, fol. 179$^{v}$.

A camp of soldiers late was seen 36
And on each shoulder muskets seven, God save the Queen.
'Riddle'.
MS. Rawl. D. 833, fol. 170.

A captain bold in Halifax, that dwelt in county quarters 37
Oh! Miss Bailey, that wicked ghost Miss Bailey, etc.
'Unfortunate Miss Bailey'.
MS. Eng. poet. c. 51, p. 263.

A captive slave of Satan 38
The praise of my salvation.
Kenton, James.
MS. *Eng. poet. e. 20, p. 190 (autogr.).

A careful wit with late repentance taught 39
Were better never had than so dear bought.
Couplet.
MS. Rawl. poet. 117, fol. 274 rev.

A carol a carol of glory and praise 40
'Cause Christmas is come we sing hallelujah.
Tune: 'Jacob & Esau'.
MS. Rawl. poet. 37, p. 61.

41 A certain feme tenant in general tail
If the cow, calf, and horns go not all to the cook.
[Libel on Edward Coke and his second wife Lady Hatton].
MS. Don. c. 54, fol. 7.

42 A certain king married a son
And make no long delay.
MS. Eng. poet. b. 5, p. 38.

43 A certain man four children had
William and Mary, George and Ann.
'The four children'.
MS. Firth d. 13, fol. 67.

44 A certain man upon a time
You may see what fortune is.
[Res]houlde, James.
MS. Rawl. poet. 85, fol. 64.

45 A certain man who was named
Whose name was Manahene.
Tye, Christopher, 'Acts of the Apostles', chapters 5–13, first stanza only of each chapter.
MS. Mus. d. 12, fol. 18.

46 A certain old cook called his dog cuckold
To call a dog after a Christian's name.
'Cuckold'.
Pr. *Modus Salium*, 1751.
MSS. Don. d. 58, fol. 37; Eng. poet. e. 14, fol. 80v rev.; Tanner 466, fol. 66v; Wood E. 32 (Modus Salium), fol. 12.

47 A certain priest had hoarded up [there was that had]
Your God is risen and gone.
MSS. Douce f. 5, fol. 34; Add. B. 105, fol. 25v; see also A81, A177, A294.

48*a* A certain Welshman, 'twixt St. Taffy's day and Easter
What toes her think her knows not chalk from cheese.
'On a Welshman'.
MS. Eng. poet. f. 10, fol. 89v; see also A275.

48*b* A certain young cook called his dog cuckold
To call a dog after a Christian's name.
'On Allsoules under-cook'.
MS. Douce f. 5, fol. 17v.

49 A chaise and four horses, my lord at full gallop
What wishes can give you amen and amen.
Macdonald, Sir Alexander, 'A letter extempore written to Lord George Sutton, 1768'.
MS. Eng. poet. e. 28, p. 153.

A change in all ensues, the winter's cold 50
And for his sake forgive my heinous crimes. Thus I conclude.
'Sweden's Lamentation'.
MS. Rawl. poet. 195, fol. 154*b*.

A change there is, and why it is I prithee tell 51
Which to resolve in rhyme do not neglect.
Meddus, Joseph.
MS. Rawl. D. 929, fol. 25 (autogr.).

A chapel of the riding-house is made 52
The laymen bridled and the clergy ride.
Farquhar, George, 'An epigram on the riding house in Dublin, made into a chapel'.
Pr. *Love and Business*, 1702.
MSS. Rawl. poet. 116, fol. 90; 172, fol. 132v, attr. to Mr. Farquhar.

A cheerful spirit acts a noble part 53
Drives away sorrow makes a merry heart.
Robinson, Robert, couplet.
MS. *Rawl. poet. 218, p. 105 (autogr.).

A cheerful swain as e'er Arcadia bred 54
Take care oh swain you don't your own neglect.
Walsh, Octavia, 'A dialogue between Strephon & Claius'.
MS. *Eng. poet. e. 31, fol. 140v rev. (autogr.).

A child, and a stranger Christ in Egypt came 55
Of joy and glory come to th' full perfection.
MS. *Rawl. poet. 97, fol. 40v (autogr.).

A child with a chaplet shall array him right [be in array] 56
To heaven mote bring both you and me.
'The prophecy of Sir Thomas of Astledowne'.
MSS. Ashmole 1835, fol. 19v; North c. 80, fol. 14v.

A chine of beef (God bless us all!) 57
A trophy and a sacrifice.
Pr. *Wits Interpreter*, 1655, p. 268.
MS. Sancroft 53, p. 46.

A choir of bright beauties in spring did appear 58
When Pan, little Daphnis, and Syrinx return.
Dryden, John, 'A Song, 1691'.
Pr. *Poetical Miscellanies*, v, 1704.
Answered by H1483.
MSS. Don. c. 55, fol. 18v, attr. to Dryden; Firth d. 13, fol. 44.

A chosen privacy a cheap content 59
Be virtuous, is the great immortal man.
Philips, Katherine, 'A Revery'.
Pr. *Poems*, 1667, p. 86.
MSS. Rawl. poet. 65, fol. 15v, attr. to K.P.O.; 90, fol. 77.

60 A Christian true doth love
He says and lives, 'God's will be done'.
'The portraiture of a Christian', tune, 'The Gipsies'.
MSS. Rawl. poet. 37, p. 98; 172, fol. 173.

61 A Christian turned Turk, a saint to rebel
Their impudence hates to acknowledge their shame.
Robinson, Robert.
MS. *Rawl. poet. 218, p. 32 (autogr.).

62 A Christian's like a fig-tree, that does bear
Fig trees are always dead, where no figs be.
[Quarles, Francis], 'On a figg-tree'.
Pr. *Divine Fancies*, 1632, iv. 16.
MS. Rawl. poet. 90, fol. 73.

63 A clown in Flanders once there was
I might have lost my life.
'A Ballad', attr. to Thomas Western of Rivenhall, Essex, in B.M. Add. MS. 5832, fol. 126ᵛ.
MS. Eng. poet. e. 8, fol. 18.

64 A coal on fire not long doth hold
By silver flames and blaze of gold.
Robinson, Robert, 'Hot love soon cold'.
MS. *Rawl. poet. 218, p. 15 (autogr.).

65 A coal on fire not long on fire doth hold
Of the white silver, and the yellow gold.
Robinson, Robert, 'Hot love soon cold'.
MS. *Rawl. poet. 218, p. 15 (autogr.).

66 A cobbler and a curate once disputed
But if you will we'll make them cobblers both.
[Harington, Sir John], 'On a curate and a cobbler'.
Pr. *Epigrams*, 1618, i. 67.
MS. Malone 19, p. 55.

67 A cobbler there was and he liv'd in a stall
That love brings us all to an end at the last, Derry down, etc.
'The Cobler's end'.
MSS. Montagu e. 13, fol. 69ᵛ; Top. Oxon. b. 170, fol. 12ᵛ.

68 A cobbler there was and he lived in a stall
Nay perhaps in a stall, but by Jove not a kitchen.
'On Dr. Bentham, Reg. Prof. of Divin. Ox.'
MS. Eng. misc. e. 241, fol. 107.

69 A college life! I hate the odious phrase
But live and die devoted to the graces.
'A College Life'.
MS. Montagu c. 5, fol. 58.

A constant heart within a woman's breast 70
For thou hast such a heart in such a chest.
'To his Mistresse' and 'Her Answer'.
Pr. *Wits Recreations*, 1663, Sig. Q3.
MS. Eng. poet. d. 152, fol. 107.

A constant man is like a true cut die 71
Or stroke, or strike him, still he's on his guard.
Wake, William, of Cambridge.
MS. Eng. misc. d. 1, fol. 36ᵛ.

A couchant husband and a rampant wife 72
Are copulatives disjunctive all their life.
Couplet.
MS. Rawl. D. 1372, fol. 16 from end.

A country client who had waited 73
I'm glad your stomach's so much stronger.
Taylor, William, 'Potage, a Tale'.
MS. Eng. poet. e. 40, fol. 133.

A country fellow coarser clothed than witted 74
Why Sir, because I think you have no law.
'Necessitas non habet legem'.
MS. Rawl. poet. 153, fol. 14.

A country pair were walking all alone 75
Then kiss me Kate, and so an end.
Pr. in T. Weelkes' *Madrigals*, 1597, no. v.
MS. Mus. d. 8, fol. 53.

A country swain that loved a lass 76
The forked cuckold's crown.
'A Cuckold by Desert'.
MS. Rawl. poet. 172, fol. 4.

A county that's far off I seek 77
Will last eternally.
Tipping, William, 'Peregrinus sum In Terra'.
MS. *Rawl. poet. 101, fol. 29ᵛ (autogr.).

A courteous dame, who saw a lawyer roam 78
To hear your wife for want should twelve pence borrow.
MS. Rawl. poet. 26, fol. 2.

A courtier profess'd, much esteem'd by the great 79
And depend on my service to tell my Lord Bute.
'To the Gentlemen Freeholders of the County of Gloucester . . . ? 1753'.
MS. Firth b. 22, fol. 64.

A courting I went to my love 80
Oh what a dull booby was I.
[Lepipre, Gabriel (?)], 'Young Lolpoope's Courtship to fair Carbonia. 1747. A Ballad'.
MS. Eng. poet. e. 40, fol. 129 (in Lepipre's hand).

81 A covetous priest did lay in store.
Your gold is rose and gone.
'On a covetous priest'.
MS. Eng. poet. e. 14, fol. 20$^{v}$; see also A47, A177, A294.

82 A crabbed shrew, a husband's woe
Not as he would, he can.
Robinson, Robert.
MS. *Rawl. poet. 218, p. 167 (autogr.).

83 A cripple born that crept on ground
That loving friend did overthrow.
MS. Rawl. poet. 217, fol. 77.

84 A crowned king, a complete knight
Whose shrill voice makes the thief to shake.
[Scot, Thomas], 'On a Cock'.
Pr. *Philomythie*, 1616, sig. H2$^{v}$.
MS. Sancroft 98, p. 228.

85 A cuckold I can't say, but bull you be,
For you had lately by your wife calves three.
[Owen's Epigram] '156. In D. Vitum' translated.
MS. *Rawl. poet. 197, fol. 9$^{v}$ (autogr.).

86 A cuckold is an animal bicorned
The cause is this, he never knew his maker.
'The description of a Cuckold'.
MSS. Firth e. 4, p. 6; Rawl. D. 1092, fol. 271.

87 A cuckold once as stories says
Were only crowned *in ordine ad sacrificandum.*
'Vocativo' on George I.
MS. Rawl. poet. 155, p. 33.

88 A curious artist, that doth want.
Like knighthood without lands.
Robinson, Robert.
MS. *Rawl. poet. 218, p. 116 (autogr.).

89 A curious workman works at 's pleasure;
So money comes to him at leisure.
Robinson, Robert, couplet.
MS. *Rawl. poet. 218, p. 132 (autogr.).

90 A curse on such representatives
By this old White-Hall pump.
'A supplement to the Chequer-Inne'.
Pr. *Poems on Affairs of State*, iii, 1704, p. 64.
MS. Don. b. 8, p. 539.

91 A cutter's wife with cutting looks hath cut my heart in twain
I vow and swear I'll cut and slash but in her cut I'll be.
'On a Cutter's Wife'.
MS. Ashmole 38, p. 148.

92 A cypress grove whose melancholy shade
For what is life without the nymph I love.
Cantata, 'Martillo'.
MS. Mus. Sch. B. 8*, fol. 21.

A damsel, I'm told 93
Now do what you will with my twitcher.
'The Twitcher, a Song'. [pr. 1721]
MS. Eng. misc. b. 48, fol. 93.

A damsel late a secretary took 94
The times are turned and you must turn your arse.
'The Mistaken Lass'.
MS. Rawl. poet. 155, p. 81.

A damsel was threading 95
And draw us in tune to agree.
Roach, Richard, 'Matching and Scratching. A Riddle'.
MS. Rawl. D. 832, fol. 171 (autogr.).

A damsel young if she have known, 96
It sparkles fire suspiciously.
MS. Rawl. D. 431, fol. 86$^{v}$.

A dance by death the holy Baptist paid 97
Since maids in dancing have such power to kill.
'Epigram', with Latin version.
MS. Eng. poet. d. 22, fol. 27.

A dead man and in the land of mor brettayne 98
When that this time come is and gone.
'Prophecy'.
MS. Rawl. C. 813, fol. 116$^{v}$.

A dean and prebendary 99
And ne'er was heard on since.
'The battle royal, 1698'.
Pr. William King's *Works*, 1776, i. 221; attr. to W. Pittis, *D.N.B. sub verbo* William Sherlock.
MSS. Eng. poet. e. 87, p. 80; Locke c. 32, fol. 41; Rawl. D. 108, fol. 30.

A deer when by the hunter chased is 100
It is a case well known, no notion new.
Tipping, William.
MS. *Rawl. poet. 101, fol. 117$^{v}$ (autogr.).

A delicate and tender thought 101
Within the soul as more divine and pure.
Traherne, Thomas, 'Thoughts II'.
MS. *Eng. poet. c. 42, fol. 13$^{v}$ (autogr.).

A desperate hazard courage does create 102
As he plays frankly, who has least estate.
MS. Sancroft 85, p. 281 rev.

A devil there was, a few years ago 103
You need not look up, the Devil's within.
'The Devil over Lincoln College', 1797.
MS. Top. Oxon. a. 29, fol. 72.

104 A dialogue happened at Burford of late
He'd be glad to come off half so well at the Bar: Derrydown etc.
Luttrell, J., 'Ballad made upon the Bashaw of Burford'.
MS. Ballard 47, fol. 165.

105 A distant friend I mourn, whose high desert
Such friendship's use, and such its sweet employ.
'On an absent Friend a Fragment'.
MS. Eng. poet. c. 9, p. 70.

106 A dizzard late skipp'd out upon our stage
I'll never leave, till I have rhymed thee dead.
Pr. *A Whip for an Ape*, 1589.
MS. Douce 309, fol. 13.

107 A doctor riding once before his wife
To ride before, and kiss his wife behind.
'On a doctor riding before his wife'.
MS. Eng. poet. f. 10, fol. 94; see also D388, O1006.

108 A doctor told his patient Omphida
Mistaking, cries, oh my certificate.
MS. Tanner. 465, fol. 94ᵛ.

109*a* A doleful song in dismal rhyme
Your wives will quickly learn her practice.
Barnes, Joshua, 'On Judith Minikin in Bury Jayle', 1692.
MS. Hearne's diaries 11, p. 88.

109*b* A Dorsetshire stream, and the banks where it runs
Makes the name of the maid for whom my heart burns.
'Rebus on Miss Laetitia Weyland Nov. 23. 1748'. Couplet.
MS. Eng. poet. e. 40, fol. 85.

110 A dragon with a red rose that is of great fame
God bring his soul to heaven Amen.
'Prophecy'.
MS. Rawl. C. 813, fol. 118.

111 A dreadful fire, beholders daily gaze
Chastised England, ah cruel fatal blaze.
'A line to find out what day of the week every month falls on'.
MS. Rawl. poet. 213, fol. 2ᵛ.

112 A drop, one drop, how sweetly one fair drop
Spare this one jewel, I'll be Dives still.
Crashaw, Richard, 'On Dives asking a drop of water'.
Pr. *Steps to the Temple*, 1646.
MSS. Eng. misc. e. 241, fol. 24, attr. to Crashaw; Tanner 465, fol. 36.

113 A duchess dowager one day
Will put 'em to severer labour.
Boswell, James, 'The Dutchess Dowager'.
MS. *Douce 193, fol. 25 (autogr.).

A dying latinist of great renown 114
With female gender the case masculine.
'Lipsius dying bequeathd his gown to the Virgin Mary'. Translated from Latin.
MS. Rawl. poet. 246, fol. 5ᵛ.

A fabric is the subject of my verse 115
The house is, all, King Philip's monument.
Fanshawe, Sir Richard, 'On the Escurial, built by King Philip II of Spain'.
MS. *Firth c. 1, p. 93.

A fair tongued hypocrite full easy can 116
Deceive an honest, true, plain dealing man.
Robinson, Robert, couplet.
MS. *Rawl. poet. 218, p. 90 (autogr.).

A falcon once I do behold 117
The higher still she did prevail.
MS. Rawl. poet. 217, fol. 75.

A false surmise is a forging of lies: 118
This no man denies, if surely he's wise.
Robinson, Robert.
MS. *Rawl. poet. 218, p. 98 (autogr.).

A faltering tongue, a twinkling eye 119
For neither; would you have no woe.
MS. Rawl. poet. 66, fol. 21.

A famous assembly was summon'd of late 120
So walk'd out triumphant, and singing of psalms.
Sheffield, John, 'The choosing a Poet Laureate at the death of Mr. Row'.
MS. Ballard 50, two copies, fols. 84, 100ᵛ.

A farmer whose lewd wife to lust was bent 121
The children which thou hast are scarce thine own.
'Upon a certain farmer'.
MS. Douce f. 5, fol. 2ᵛ.

A feigned friend by proof I find 122
Than false deceit hid under trust.
MS. Mus. f. 20, fol. 109ᵛ.

A fellow rid by the green wood-side 123
Why stand you so and do not go?
MS. Rawl. D. 1372, fol. 38ᵛ.

A female author once again appears 124
But wish your feelings may pronounce 'em true.
Boswell, James, prologue to [Frances Sheridan's *The Discovery*].
MS. *Douce 193, fol. 54 (autogr.).

A field I have (God knows) a barren one 125
Be kept, for else I labour to be poor.
'Spiritual Husbandry'.
MS. *Eng. poet. e. 51, p. 39 (autogr.).

126 A fig for Thales' watery element
Liœus' wine we crave wit's adamant.
Couplet.
MS. Rawl. poet. 117, fol. 276 rev.

127 A fine compliment sent by a man that is hired
And acknowledge the favour with patience perforce.
Williams, John, 'The Visiter's coming'.
MS. *Rawl. poet. 184, fol. 40 (autogr.).

128 A fine tongued knave (deny it who can)
Will pass for an honest, an honest good man.
Robinson, Robert, couplet.
MS. *Rawl. poet. 218, p. 159 (autogr.).

129 A fine young priest akin to Friar Frapper
Your children and your wife only these twain.
'Ludicrum of Marriage'.
MS. Add. B. 97, fol. 38$^{v}$.

130 A fitter match hath never [could ne'er, would never have] been [seen]
The flesh is married to the skin.
Strode, William, 'On a Butcher marrying a Tanner's daughter', couplet.
Pr. Camden's *Remaines*, 1637, p. 413.
MS. *CCC. 325, fol. 71 (autogr.).
MSS. Ballard 50, fol. 196; CCC. 328, fol. 4$^{v}$; Douce f. 5, fol. 2$^{v}$; Eng. poet. e. 14, fol. 90$^{v}$; e. 40, fol. 114; e. 97, p. 68, attr. to Will Stroad; f. 10, fol. 89; Rawl. D. 1372, fol. 10 from end; Rawl. poet. 116, fol. 56$^{v}$; Sancroft 53, p. 61; see also F343.

131 A fool being bit with fleas put out the light
And said; so now you cannot see to bite.
'Epigram', couplet.
MS. Ashmole 38, p. 82.

132 A fool hath knowledge, and hath wit
As hath a bear that's loose.
Robinson, Robert.
MS. *Rawl. poet. 218, p. 150 (autogr.).

133 A fool with his money, money will gain
Where tools are not had, the work must lie still.
Robinson, Robert.
MS. *Rawl. poet. 218, p. 77 (autogr.).

134 A fool's say is first, I'll do as I list
The fool's cry at last is, oh had I wist.
Robinson, Robert, couplet.
MS. *Rawl. poet. 218, p. 10 (autogr.).

135 A foul mouthed fool, a fair tongued knave
Let me not be their mate nor slave.
Robinson, Robert, couplet.
MS. *Rawl. poet. 218, p. 140 (autogr.).

A freeman yet no man 136
The like was never seen.
'Dr. King and his wife whose name was Freeman'.
MS. Malone 19, p. 98.

A friar an hayward a fox and a fulmar 137
The best is a screw.
MS. Tanner 407, fol. 52.

A friar died the other day; 138
Below, no doubt, you'd eat the devil.
'Epigram on the Death of a Friar. From the French'; cf. A330.
MS. *Eng. poet. d. 47, fol. 47.

A friar got a nun to put she says 139
Look you yourself to that at the back door.
MS. Rawl. poet. 84, fol. 43.

A friar pressed a nun she groaning says 140
Lest that the soul slip out at postern gate.
MS. Rawl. poet. 84, fol. 43$^{v}$.

A friend did ask me when I would 141
I told that friend then would I come.
MS. Rawl. poet. 217, fol. 78.

A friend in words where deeds be dead 142
Make words and works alike to be.
By F. Th.
MS. Rawl. poet. 108, fol. 9$^{v}$.

A friend of his this for the Author says 143*a*
His plays are works when thy best works are lays.
Reply to M344.
MS. CCC. 328, fol. 43$^{v}$.

A friend of mine, pitying my hopeless love 143*b*
A goddess thou shalt prove, and happy I.
[Constable, Henry], sonnet, pr. *Diana*, 1592, Sig. B4.
MS. Ashmole 38, p. 53.

A friend of mine, suppose 'twas John a Stile 144
The question is whether the cup be mine.
'A Case'. Subscribed 'Solvat Apollo'.
MS. Rawl. poet. 212, fol. 117$^{v}$.

A friend that is a friend, 145
Of friends and friendship too.
MS. Eng. misc. c. 292, fol. 99.

A friend that is sincere and free 146
And all my faults resist.
Williams, John.
MS. *Rawl. poet. 184, fol. 40$^{v}$ (autogr.).

A friend that's eke my hateful foe 147
Yet, being gone, I draw him back.
MS. Rawl. poet. 217, fol. 78.

148 A friend's reproof is good, though it be smart:
But flattering words proceed from no good heart.
Robinson, Robert.
MS. *Rawl. poet. 218, p. 87 (autogr.).

149 A froward wife; and a rebellious child
If Christ, who all things is, be lodged there.
MS. Rawl. poet. 66, fol. 60.

150 A fruitful branch of Jesse's blissful stem
Blessed be the Lamb, blessed eternally.
MS. Rawl. poet. 23, p. 137, reference to setting by E. Hooper.

151 A gallant lady sitting in a muse
My key will open but will not shut the lock.
'Sr. John Keys to his Lady'.
MS. Eng. poet. f. 10, fol. 89; see also A9, A155, A526.

152 A gallant lass out of a window saw
Oh nose, thou didst me wrong.
'On a Long Nose'.
MS. Rawl. poet. 153, fol. 14.

153 A gallant man you were and courtier true
A quiet soul in life or death was thee.
Cavendish, Lady Jane, 'On my Grandfather Mr. Basset'.
MS. *Rawl. poet. 16, p. 32.

154 A gallant ship from England came,
Who made the Frenchman quickly fly.
'A Gallant Sea-Fight'.
MS. Firth c. 18, fol. 88.

155 A gentle lady sitting in a muse
Then lock it if you please, you keep the keys.
[Harington, Sir John].
MS. Eng. poet. d. 152, fol. 96; see also A9, A151, A526.

156 A gentle miss whom mother's care
A butterfly is all thy gains.
'Miss and the Butterfly, a Tale'.
MS. Add. D. 79, fol. 89$^{v}$ rev.

157 A german princess once this isle did grace [graced this isle]
And may they share in equal fate.
'Upon the Duchess of Marlborough'.
Pr. Hearne's *Collections*, ed. C. E. Doble, ii, O.H.S. vii, 1886, p. 26.
MSS. Hearne's diaries 15, p. 35; Rawl. D. 383, fol. 118; Smith 23, p. 111.

158 A giant's tongue and pigmy hands
Which ne'r perform'd will be.
Robinson, Robert.
MS. *Rawl. poet. 218, p. 158 (autogr.).

A glorious branch from France did haply spring 159
From th' fury of factious spirits world without end, Amen.
Hanson, R., 'Upon the Queen's safe return from Holland', Feb. 1643.
MS. Malone 21, fol. 29.

A glorious figure did I once make 160
Crown not your head, with British bays.
'On I and O', James II and William of Orange, 1690.
MSS. Eng. poet. c. 18, fol. 17$^{v}$; e. 50, p. 65; see also A318.

A glow-worm, who with tiny lamp 161
Like Wells's glow worm imitation!
Parsons, William, 'The Eagle and the Glow-worm . . . Occasion'd by Mr. Wells's imitation of Mrs. Siddons', 27 Apr. 1788.
MS. *Don. d. 123, p. 176 (autogr.).

A god, and yet a man? 162
Believe and leave to wonder.
See *Reliquiae Antiquae*, T Wright and J. O. Halliwell, 1841, i. 127, 207; in *Religious Lyrics of the XV Cent.*, W. Carleton Brown, 1939, no. 120.
MS. Rawl. B. 332, before fol. 1.

A godly maid by [with] one of her society 163
Like to the mother, so the daughter shared.
'On a maid got with child'.
MSS. Don. d. 58, fol. 35; Eng. poet. e. 14, fol. 89$^{v}$ rev.; Rawl. poet. 31, fol. 3$^{v}$; see also A389, A412.

A godly speech doth oft times stir up factions. 164
And holy words do lead to evil actions.
Robinson, Robert, couplet.
MS. *Rawl. poet. 218, p. 119 (autogr.).

A gold- and silver-laden silly ass 165
In his exploits will find himself much fading.
Robinson, Robert.
MS. *Rawl. poet. 218, p. 160 (autogr.).

A good and wise man, such Apollo when 166
Condemns the wrong, commends and crowns the right.
J. F., 'Ausonii, Vir Bonus'.
MS. *Eng. poet. f. 17, p. 133 (autogr.).

A good man cannot act a dirty knave. 167
Be he a Christian, Jew, Pagan, or Turk.
Robinson, Robert.
MS. *Rawl. poet. 218, p. 123 (autogr.).

A good man keeps the laws, but oh, who can 168
Give them and keep them too? Lo! here's the man.
'Law books'. Translation from Latin; couplet.
MS. Rawl. poet. 246, fol. 35$^{v}$.

169 A good-man labours day by day:
Then comes a knave takes all away.
Robinson, Robert, couplet.
MS. *Rawl. poet. 218, p. 8 (autogr.).

170 A good thought, as a garment bright,
Bedaubs, and spots it all.
Robinson, Robert.
MS. *Rawl. poet. 218, p. 39 (autogr.).

171 A good wife is a crown of gold
To scratch him, till he's dead.
Robinson, Robert.
MS. *Rawl. poet. 218, p. 22 (autogr.).

172 A grave discourse to utter I intend
With heart sincere and hand discreet did show.
Herbert, Mary (*née* Sidney), Countess of Pembroke, Psalm lxxviii.
MSS. *Rawl. poet. 24, p. 113; *25, fol. 71ᵛ.

173 A great contest, I with a spirit had
And me condemn, as I myself now do.
Tipping, William, 'Thursday night May 4th, 1699'.
MS. *Rawl. poet. 101, fol. 71ᵛ (autogr.).

174 A great estate oh never prize
Where in the breast the bird sings sweetly.
Robinson, Robert, 'Dulcissima avis in pectore cantat'.
MS. *Rawl. poet. 218, p. 28 (autogr.).

175 A great French king having his face
To all the world's astonishment.
'Prophecy' of the death of Henry IV, from Howell's *Life . . . of Lewis XIII*, 1646, p. 4.
MS. Rawl. D. 1110, fol. 99.

176 A great prince, whilst he stands alive
He then shall have no more than I.
Robinson, Robert.
MS. *Rawl. poet. 218, p. 59 (autogr.).

177 A greedy minded griping clerk
Your god is risen and gone.
'On a covetous priest'.
MS. CCC. 328, fol. 90ᵛ; see also A47, A81, A294.

178 A gulf of great grief,
All sinners do run.
Meddus, Joseph, 'The description of hell'.
MS. Rawl. D. 929, fol. 27 (autogr.).

179 A half blind boy born of a half blind mother
The queen of beauty, you the god of love.
'Upon a one-eyed boy born of a one-eyed mother'.
MS. CCC. 328, fol. 31; Rawl. poet. 84, fol. 85; see also A324, F53, H142, T2227.

A handsome woman when she's young 180
With wicked man nor whore.
Tipping, William.
MS. *Rawl. poet. 101, fol. 96 (autogr.).

A harmless game raised merely [only] for delight 181
'Tis but removing of one man that's me.
'The petition of poet Middleton, Author of the Game at Chess, to King James'.
See *Works of Tho. Middleton*, ed. Bullen, 1885, i, p. lxxxiii, and *A Game at Chesse*, ed. R. C. Bald, 1929, p. 166.
MSS. Douce f. 5, fol. 22ᵛ; Rawl. poet. 152, fol. 3.

A hateful cure with hate to heal 182
Who hath saved all that is even I.
Sidney, Sir Philip, from the *Arcadia*.
MS. *e Mus. 37, fol. 77ᵛ.

A head he has, with face of brass 183
For when that moves, all shakes below.
'Wood's Picture'.
MS. Rawl. D. 214, fol. 80ᵛ.

A health to jolly Bacchus 184
And bring more liquor hither.
MS. Rawl. D. 377, fol. 23ᵛ.

A healthy world we soon might hope to see 185
True love takes seat, and harmless mirth goes round.
Williams, John.
MS. *Rawl. poet. 191, fol. 43ᵛ (autogr.).

A heart I have a heart I crave 186
Till proof thereof I see.
MS. Rawl. poet. 85, fol. 105ᵛ.

A heart not once debauched with love 187
'Tis you I idolize.
MS. Rawl. poet. 196, fol. 41.

A heavy hap, that Adam's own wife, Eve 188
Is not to be excused no not his heart.
MS. *Rawl. poet. 97, fol. 10 (autogr.).

A heavy purse makes a light heart ('tis said) 189
But a light purse makes a most heavy head.
Robinson, Robert.
MS. *Rawl. poet. 218, p. 84 (autogr.).

A heavy spectacle for every eye 190
Henry the Prince of men and Mars of arms.
G. B., 'Epitaph' on Prince Henry, 1612.
MS. *Rawl. poet. 116, fol. 11.

A herd, a swain, a martial knight 191
With bows, with ploughs, with manly might.
MS. Rawl. poet. 85, fol. 83ᵛ.

192 A hermit's house beside a stream
To triumph not to die.
'Retirement—Written in America by a Native Bard. M[orning] Herald 1789'.
MS. Montagu e. 14, fol. 56v.

193 A hero of no small renown
For all is lost, when that is ended.
'A Ballad in praise of a certain Commander'.
MS. Rawl. poet. 173, fol. 147v.

194 A hero's noble merits to rehearse
And whilst this lasts far be all strife and fray.
'A pindarique ode on the 10th of June 1715'.
MS. Rawl. poet. 155, p. 136.

195 A hideous hag, with visage stern appears,
Which shows her words, wherewith the good she wounds.
Whitney, Geoffrey, 'Invidiae descriptio'.
MS. *Rawl. poet. 56, fol. 55v.

196 A holy cheat a hellish feat
With scourge of scorpions shall be beat.
Robinson, Robert, couplet.
MS. *Rawl. poet. 218, p. 136 (autogr.).

197 A homely face will make herself as gay
The gentle spirit is the woman's grace.
Robinson, Robert.
MS. *Rawl. poet. 218, p. 93 (autogr.).

198 A Hoope by birth, a hermit's wight
When hence he parts away.
Verses in York Minster on Mrs. Gibson, *née* Hoope, d. 21 April 1608.
MS. Dodsworth 161, fol. 27v.

199 A house that was not made with hands
Whom I have always found so kind to me.
Tipping, William, 'The Triumph of Faith'.
MS. *Rawl. poet. 101, fol. 48 (autogr.).

200 A housewife neat, I've seen of homely cut,
And a nice dame prove oft a nasty slut.
Robinson, Robert, couplet.
MS. *Rawl. poet. 218, p. 59 (autogr.).

201 [A husband sil]enc'd by a nipping frost
I speak; silence best shows a woman's wit.
MS. Tanner 306, fol. 420v.

202 A husband sooner may be had,
Than a well-pleasing wife.
Robinson, Robert.
MS. *Rawl. poet. 218, p. 161 (autogr.).

203 A jailor's wife and bawd, and witch and whore
In Lifland exiles and this Russian bawd.
James, Richard, 'An execration on Marie of Colmogorod'.
MSS. James 13, p. 250; *35, p. 10 (both autogr.).

A king of British blood, in cradle crowned 204
Restore the cross and make this isle renowned.
'Marlyns verses of our kinge', 1607.
MS. Tanner 169, fol. 62v.

A king out of the north shall come 205
Shall take away his aged breath.
'Merlin's Prophecy'.
MSS. Eng. poet. c. 50; fol. 26v; Rawl. poet. 26, fol. 67; Tanner 88, fol. 252v; see also A378.

A king's a worm, I'm another, 206
And subjects ought to obey: 'tis God's decree.
Robinson, Robert.
MS. *Rawl. poet. 218, p. 166 (autogr.).

A knave is good, a fool is wise, 207
No man is still the same.
Robinson, Robert.
MS. *Rawl. poet. 218, p. 95 (autogr.).

A knave thus railed at an old scrub 208
But you the wealth of others.
Boswell, James, 'Epigram'.
MS. *Douce 193, fol. 46 (autogr.).

A knife dear girl cuts love they say 209
Save only, cut and come again.
[Bishop, Samuel], 'Verses with a present of a knife'.
Pr. *Poetical Works*, 1796, ii. 16.
MSS. Eng. misc. e. 241, fol. 30v; Eng. poet. c. 51, p. 240.

A knight of Cales, a Shentleman of Wales 210
Will buy them out all three.
MSS. Firth e. 4, p. 13; Malone 19, p. 150.

A knowing man full as a tun 211
Who thinks he's wise, is no wise such.
Robinson, Robert, 'Homo verbosus stultus gloriosus'.
MS. *Rawl. poet. 218, p. 139 (autogr.).

A lad thus addressed an old man of four-score 212
Is a crime too enormous for words to express.
'The Witlings and the Beggar'.
MS. Eng. misc. e. 219, fol. 8.

A lady fair being newly married 213
Each night for pleasure.
MS. Firth d. 7, fol. 161; see also A8, A216, A218, A220, A260.

A lady fair with the green sickness late 214
Keep the first letters of these several lines.
'A cure for the green sickness'.
MSS. Ashmole 38, p. 149; Rawl. poet. 172, fol. 2v; see also A263, A266.

A lady gave me a gift she had n[ot] 215
For I am fast sworn I may not.
'A riddle'.
MS. Rawl. poet. 172, fol. 3v.

216 A lady lately that was fully sped
We'll to't each night for health each morn for pleasure.
'On a jolly lady'.
MSS. Eng. poet. e. 14, fol. 81 rev.; f. 25, fol. 13; see also A8, A213, A218, A220, A260.

217 A lady once did ask of me
Then give it me for sure you may.
'A Riddle'.
MS. Rawl. poet. 172, fol. 3ᵛ.

218 A lady once that newly was besped
We'll take the morn for health, the night for pleasure.
'On a Lady'.
MSS. Ashmole 47, fol. 52; CCC. 328, fol. 44; Don. d. 58, fol. 36ᵛ; see also A8, A213, A216, A220, A260.

219 A lady once two suitors had
No music to the stroke of a pricket in a course.
'A proper old and new Ballad'. At end, heavily crossed out, 'finis per franciscus [Montagu (?)]'.
MS. Rawl. poet. 120, fol. 23.

220 A lady that was newly wed
Let's to't all night for health, all day for pleasure.
MS. Rawl. poet. 172, fol. 11; see also A8, A213, A216, A218, A260.

221 A lady wise as well as fair
The living lustre of your eyes.
'An apology to Lady Carteret made by Dean Swift'.
MS. Ballard 50, fol. 93.

222 A land tax and poll is lately come forth,
For fear of the charge of maintaining our poor. Which nobody can deny.
'A Song', *c.* 1692.
MS. Rawl. D. 361, fol. 216.

223 A landlord of Bath put upon me a queer turn
I called for some punch, the dog gave me merum.
'A Literal Translation'.
MS. Eng. poet. c. 51, p. 217.

224 A late expedition to Oxford was made
They'd marched more nimble without their music. Which nobody can deny.
Smith, John, of Magdalen (see MS. Firth d. 13, fol. 1), 'On the Lord Lovelace's Triumphant March into Oxford', 1688.
Pr. *Poems on Affairs of State*, ii, 1703, p. 268.
MSS. Eng. poet. c. 18, fol. 57ᵛ; Firth e. 6, fol. 21.

A lean, yet fat recusant being confin'd 225
Marry, quoth he, I say it is well fed.
[Davies, John of Hereford].
Pr. *Scourge of Folly*, 1611, 90.
MS. Eng. poet. c. 50, fol. 34.

A learned and a happy ignorance 226
The glorious wonders of the Deity.
Traherne, Thomas, 'Eden'.
MS. *Eng. poet. c. 42, fol. 3ᵛ (autogr.).

A learned bishop of [in] this [the] land 227
That scruple troubles all the rest.
[Andrewes, Francis], on Archbishop Bancroft.
For attribution see B.M. MS. Harl. 4955, fol. 83, and Donne's *Poems*, ed. Grierson, 1912, ii. 83.
MSS. Don. d. 58, fol. 38; Malone 23, p. 118; Rawl. poet. 26, fol. 9; 62, fol. 54; see also A229, A289.

A learned prelate late disposed to laugh 228
Call him Lord Aff, for all the land is gone.
[Harington, Sir John], 'Of the Bishop of Landaffe'.
Pr. *Epigrams*, 1618, ii. 2.
MS. Firth d. 7, fol. 163.

A learned prelate of this land 229
The scruple troubled all the rest.
[Andrewes, Francis], on Archbishop Bancroft.
MSS. Don. e. 6, fol. 31; Rawl. poet. 84, fol. 108; see also A227, A289.

A liar Satan from beginning was 230
Enter in glory; and give gifts to men.
MS. *Rawl. poet. 97, fol. 71 (autogr.).

A lie deserves the stab, *ergo* take heed 231
For women when they lie are stabbed indeed.
Couplet.
MS. CCC. 328, fol. 48.

A life of sabbaths here beneath! 232
A root of bliss; a pearl each tear.
Traherne, Thomas, 'The Third Century. 47'.
MS. Eng. th. e. 50, fol. 56 (autogr.).

A light young man lay with a lighter woman 233
A yard of holland for an ell of cotton.
'On the marriage of Th. Holland to Nell Cotton'.
MSS. CCC. 328, fol. 26ᵛ; Eng. poet. f. 10, fol. 95.

A like dissembler, a dissembler raises 234
They'll saint a knave, they'll knave an honest man.
Robinson, Robert, 'Upon a flatterer highlie commending an unworthie person'.
MS. *Rawl. poet. 218, p. 106 (autogr.).

235 A lion gracious, wise and bold
And each to th' public slander adds his private lie.
'A Fable' [William III].
MS. Eng. poet. e. 17, fol. $20^v$.

236 A little earth, a little dusty ground
But was the means him to renew and save.
MS. *Rawl. poet. 97, fol. 17 (autogr.).

237 A little fire doth make the faggot burn
The smallest blowing makes the greatest fire.
MS. Rawl. poet. 85, fol. $114^v$.

238 A little hole will serve a little mouse:
A great rich man must have a great rich house.
Robinson, Robert, couplet.
MS. *Rawl. poet. 218, p. 89 (autogr.).

239 A little mushroom table spread
Grac'd by his priest, the feast is ended.
Herrick, Robert, 'King Oberon's Feast'.
Pr. *Hesperides*, 1648, and *Description of the King and Queene of Fayries*, 1635, p. 4.
MSS. Ashmole 38, p. 100, attr. to Robt. Hericke; Eng. poet. c. 50, two copies, fol. 46 and, attr. to Sir Simon Stewarde, fol. $63^v$; Firth e. 4, p. 23; Malone 16, p. 3, attr. to Rich. Hiericke of Clare Hall; Rawl. poet. 160, fol. $169^v$, attr. to Rob. Herrick.

240 A little stock doth rise to much,
By vain expence abus'd.
Robinson, Robert, 'Pecunia radix divitiarum'.
MS. *Rawl. poet. 218, p. 78 (autogr.).

241 A little ta'en from many fleeces,
Adds but little to the stock.
Robinson, Robert.
MS. *Rawl. poet. 218, p. 49 (autogr.).

242 A little week, I leave, with anxious heart
Dim apparition there—and bitter is my tear!
Seward, Anna, 'Egam', 1788.
MS. *Pigott d. 12, fol. $6^v$ (autogr.).

243 A little wit, two grains of common sense
When join'd together make our modern beaux.
'Cottile, bellus homo es', Oct. 25 1734.
MS. Eng. misc. e. 240, p. 71.

244 A lofty heart, a lifted eye,
Such endless trust, on God to place.
Herbert, Mary (*née* Sidney), Countess of Pembroke, Psalm cxxxi.
MS. *Rawl. poet. 24, p. 198.

245 A log that in the chimney, thus,
Beaus often are but logs of wood.
'A Dialogue at the Fireside . . . Harrison's Miscellanies, p. 299'.
MS. Eng. poet. c. 6, fol. 104.

A long adieu to all that's fair 246
But curse your stars too late.
Chatwin, John, 'The cheat. Song'.
MS. *Rawl. poet. 94, p. 176 (autogr.).

'A long farewell!' the courtier said 247
They tend—and never swerve from you.
Skinner, John, 'Letters from Oxford', 8, 25 Oct. 1793.
MS. *Top. Oxon. e. 41, p. 233.

A Lord Baron Bish 248
A hierarchy not worth a louse.
'No Lord Bishops'.
MS. Firth e. 6, fols. 140, $144^v$ rev.–$142^v$ rev.

A lord in this land 249
Who made his horse a consul.
Ballad 'Upon the Election of knight for the shire in Norfolk . . . April 1675', Sir Robert Kempe.
MS. Tanner 306, fol. 395.

A lord that spake in way of scorn 250
I hope sweet heart you learned have to swim.
'On a Lord that cursed Cuckolds'.
MS. Ashmole 47, fol. 55.

A louse without licence a man did molest 251
And there must he [word omitted] the crush of the nail.
'Upon a Louse'.
MS. Malone 19, p. 57.

A love more tormenting than mine 252
A headache for that of the heart.
Boswell, James, 'The Amorous Milksop's Complaint. A Pastoral Ballad'.
MS. *Douce 193, two copies, fols. $5^v$ and 34 (autogr.).

A lovely lass that had a roman nose 253
Kiss where is none there freely take your fill.
'In Tindarum'.
MS. Don. d. 58, fol. 38.

A lover I'm born and a lover I'll be 254
How they kiss and embrace and can never have done.
Pr. *Choice Ayres, Songs & Dialogues*, 2nd ed. 1675, p. 14.
MSS. Mus. Sch. F. 572, p. 90 (melody by Pelham Humphrey); G. 637, fol. 3.

A lover once I did espy 255
Some sparks of love though not a lover.
[Grange, John].
Pr. Playford's *Select Musicall Ayres and Dialogues*, 1652, i. 12.
MS. Don. c. 57, fol. 69, music by Henry Lawes.

256 A loyal loving wife, a mother dear
Your happy welcome, or my sad farewell.
Epitaph on Katherine Chewney (d. 1650), St. Nicholas at Wade, Kent.
MS. Rawl. D. 376, fol. 223.

257 A lusty lass but loose, not worth the naming
Yet she performed her oath imagine how.
'On a young wanton'.
MS. CCC. 328, fol. 26$^v$.

258 A lusty squire in an assembly brave
Fain would I know, how this could be.
MS. Rawl. poet. 217, fol. 76$^v$.

259 A lusty swain was cleaving of a block
For when I hum I cleave, but now I bore.
MS. Malone 19, p. 74; see also A408.

260 A lusty young wife that was lately sped
We'll to't each morn for health, each night for pleasure.
MS. Rawl. poet. 142, fol. 40; see also A8, A213, A216, A218, A220.

261 A maceless mayor, never known before
Though now thy ruler's sceptre is not seen.
[William Powell] Bilston [of Magdalen Hall], 'On the Mayor and Bailiffs of Oxford not attending the City Church during their year of Office 1762–3'.
MS. Top. Oxon. b. 116, fol. 121.

262 A maid, a wife, she lived, a widow died
And join each to his own, himself to all.
'An Epitaph upon the Lady Markham'.
MS. Rawl. poet. 31, fol. 30.

263 A maid of the green sickness [I of] late
Keep the first letter of these several lines.
MS. Rawl. poet. 260, p. 74; Eng. poet. e. 14, fol. 87 rev.; see also A214, A266.

264 A maid, yet willing to become a mother.
Well born, yet not so high to set me low.
'A wife'.
MS. Rawl. poet. 153, fol. 14$^v$.

265 A maiden fair I dare not [will not] wed
Some fault remains amongst them all!
'How to choose a wife'.
MSS. Don. d. 58, fol. 14; Douce f. 5, fol. 16, attr. to John Pe: of Glo[ucester] hall; Eng. poet e. 14, fol. 74; f. 10, fol. 94$^v$; Sancroft 53, p. 58; see also A567.

266 A maiden fair of the green sickness late [laid]
Keep the first letters of these several lines.
'A cure for the green sickness'.
MSS. CCC. 328, fol. 47$^v$; Rawl. poet. 152, fol. 23; see also A214, A263.

A maiden head is so unsound 267
That it is lost when first 'tis found.
Couplet.
MS. Eng. poet. e. 97, p. 28.

A major and a captain gone: good troth 268
From two more horrid. Manchester and thee.
Weaver, Thomas, 'An Epigram to the under-Marshal of Manchester, upon the Escape of 2 Prisoners'.
Not pr. in *Songs and Poems*, 1654.
MS. *Rawl. poet. 211, fol. 7$^v$ (autogr.).

A man and a wife when once they marry 269
The other should a conquest see.
Cavendish, Lady Jane, 'A Song'.
MS. *Rawl. poet. 16, p. 26.

A man had need be resolute and bold 270
Who never give the fair the least offence.
Williams, John, 'The Prologue new' to 'The Fudling Husbands and The Furious Wives'.
MS. *Rawl. poet. 193, fol. 1 (autogr.).

A man in power shall never want 271
To greatness of unhappy fate.
Robinson, Robert.
MS. *Rawl. poet. 218, p. 74 (autogr.).

A man in words and not in deeds 272
Then thank thy self, and blame not me.
MS. Rawl. poet. 148, inside front cover.

A man may many friends retain 273
He may true friendship want.
Copy by Wiman Ramsey, *c.* 1595.
MS. Rawl. D. 649, fol. 26.

A man of sorrow born 274
Absorb'd in all the depths of love.
Kenton, James.
MS. *Eng. poet. e. 20, p. 322 (autogr.).

A man of Wales between [twixt] St. David's [day] and Easter 275
What does her think her knows not chalk from cheese.
'On a welsh-man'.
MSS. CCC. 328, fol. 26; Douce f. 5, fol. 34; Hearne's diaries 30, p. 214; Rawl. poet. 116, fol. 57; see also A48.

A man that speaks but now and then 276
Attentive fools adore.
Williams, John, 'Satyr upon Idle words'.
MS. *Rawl. poet. 193, fol. 54$^v$ (autogr.).

A man, that's born into this world, 277
From death to life to rise.
Robinson, Robert.
MS. *Rawl. poet. 218, p. 54 (autogr.).

278 A man, that's neither high nor low
It shall be no objection.
Amherst, Elizabeth, 'The choice of a husband for Miss Monk . . . 1762'.
MSS. Eng. poet. e. 28, p. 52; *e. 109, p. 10.

279 A man to kill his Lord is an offence
For love of money an Apostle's place.
MS. *Rawl. poet. 97, fol. 59 (autogr.).

280 A man with expence and wonderful toil
There was nothing but weeds what was garden before.
'A Tale of A Nettle', *cf.* Swift's Poems, ed. Williams, p. 1084.
MSS. Rawl. D. 376, fol. 199v; D. 383, fol. 61.

281 A man with three feet with the eagle shall meet
And hunger in divers places, within this a while.
Prophecy, continued in prose.
MS. Rawl. C. 813, fol. 147v.

282 A maxim this among the wise;
Love will be love do what you will.
'Free thinker'.
MS. Rawl. poet. 116, fol. 105*c*.

283 A measure for cloth and a vessel for wine
Is the name of the girl, that I wish to be mine.
'Rebus of Miss Elton'. Couplet.
MS. Eng. poet. e. 40, fol. 159.

284 A memory great for much discourse is fit:
That has not in his memory.
Robinson, Robert.
MS. *Rawl. poet. 218, p. 172 (autogr.).

285 A mermaid flesh above and fish below
I pray let's taste your lower parts this lent.
'On a maid'.
MS. Ashmole 47, fol. 52v.

286 A merry jest sometimes doth come in season;
The head from plotting, tongue from speaking treason.
Robinson, Robert.
MS. *Rawl. poet. 218, p. 65 (autogr.).

287 A mighty great fleet, the like was ne'er seen
With the loss of some ships, but in battle none slain.
'England's Triumph, in the year 1691—To the Tune of, the Blacksmith'.
MSS. Ballard 29, fol. 135; Rawl. poet. 169, fol. 19.

288 A mighty pain to love it is,
Gold, alas, does love beget.
Cowley, Abraham, 'Gold, or Love become mercenary'.
Pr. *Works*, 1668, 'Miscellanies', vii.
MS. Rawl. poet. 173, fol. 159.

A mighty prelate in this land 289
The scruple troubled all the rest.
[Andrewes, Francis].
MS. Eng. poet. e. 97, p. 182; see also A227, A229.

A milk white hind, immortal and unchang'd 290
With glorious visions of her future state.
Dryden, John, 'The Hind and the Panther'.
MS. Rawl. poet. 115, fol. 5.

A mine of gold some say there's found 291
And yet to find some under.
Pr. Hearne's *Collections*, ed. C. E. Doble, iii, O.H.S. xiii, 1889, p. 224.
MSS. Douce f. 5, fol. 34v; Hearne's diaries 30, p. 214; Malone 23, p. 120.

A mingled form where two strange shapes combined 292
And different natures bull and man were joined.
'Minotaurus'; translation of Greek verses in Dryden's Plutarch, Life of Theseus.
MS. Rawl. D. 1372, fol. 24 from end.

A mirror of your self oh king 293
Doth shut your shadow in.
Draft of dedicatory verses to James I (?).
MS. Bodl. 176, p. v (autogr. (?)).

A miser man did hoard up gold 294
Your god is risen and gone.
MS. Rawl. poet. 219, fol. 16v; see also A47, A81, A177.

A mistress begun 295
Of the kingdom.
'The Mistresses. A Ballad to the tune of the Pudding'.
MS. Don. c. 55, fol. 10.

A mistress i' faith is a fine thing 296
For by Jove I'll say her no.
'A Song'.
MS. Rawl. poet. 214, fol. 84.

A *mittimus*, a warrant, a release 297
Is formal too, the final is the fee.
Pestell, Thomas, 'A country Justice'.
MS. *Malone 14, p. 35.

A modern tete of jaunty air. 298
And plainess is the dress of use.
'The Tete and the Tobacco Pipe, a fable'.
MS. Eng. misc. e. 241, fol. 19v.

A monster in a course of vice grown old 299
Pity a wretch like him should ever live.
'Verses on Epitaphs in general'.
MS. Eng. poet. e. 40, fol. 162.

300 A monster in this land and no mankin
As neuter Antrim is by Scottish swains.
'A true description of the Malignant party in England'.
MS. Rawl. poet. 71, p. 114.

301 A month! prohibited to see
Lengthen each moment to a day.
'Damon's desired to defer his Visit for a Month: A Soliloquy'.
MS. *Eng. poet. d. 47, fol. 170.

302 A morning fair, as the first looks of May
For what we love, should never please too much.
Cowley, Abraham, on the death of G. Creswell of Oxford.
MS. Rawl. poet. 117, fol. 169$^{v}$.

303 A mother, and a virgin, bear a son,
Whose taste doth us from beasts to men renew.
H. W., 'Divine Meditations of Christ's Birth, life and death: 1. The Mystery of Christs Incarnation'.
MS. Tanner 466, fol. 103 (autogr.).

304 A mother dead! and am I from the throne
Let Kendal at her peril mourn for thee.
'On the Prince not going in mourning for the Queen', 1726.
MSS. Ballard 47, fol. 63; Top. Oxon. c. 220, p. 14.

305 A multitude of weighty reasons may
Of all that can be said or hath been done.
MS. *Rawl. poet. 97, fol. 3$^{v}$ (autogr.).

306 A muse unknown her feeble voice would raise
His glorious end but one, his country's good.
'To the Rt. Hon. G. Lyttelton, Esq. G(entlemen's] M[agazine]
MS. Eng. poet. e. 39, p. 183.

307 A muse's power (though fate has stopped his breath)
To have my verse approved—by nobody.
'In Praise of No body. 1698'.
MS. Eng. poet. e. 50, p. 92.

308 A naked beauty here I stand forlorn
To have your infamy upon record.
'The New Mercate House at Bedford Addressing herself to the Mayor and Aldermen . . . 1682'.
MS. Don. c. 55, fol. 16.

309 A nation, that has not abroad to offend,
And then they're all lost; their power's at an end.
Robinson, Robert.
MS. *Rawl. poet. 218, p. 112 (autogr.).

310 A needless thing no doubt it were
For lack of food be dead.
MS. Rawl. D. 986, fol. 34.

A neighbour mine not long ago there was 311
Whereto two parties once be content.
Sidney, Sir Philip, from the *Arcadia*.
MS. *e Mus. 37, fol. 139$^{v}$.

A new and well composed song 312
To make the melody.
'A Hymn to be sung at the Sacrament'.
MS. Rawl. C. 580, fol. 18$^{v}$.

A new droll made by a new quibbling pate 313
And the time's new turncoat.
'The old Roundhead. And the new turncoat'.
MS. Rawl. poet. 84, fol. 47.

A new song anew 314
Changeable as the wind.
MS. Rawl. C. 813, fol. 14$^{v}$.

A new war has a new cause, 315
New religion and new laws.
Robinson, Robert, couplet.
MS. *Rawl. poet. 218, p. 16 (autogr.).

A nice young dame, that longed for dainty cates 316
Mine arse, quoth t' other, may your kitchen be.
MS. Tanner 465, fol. 94.

A nine day's wonder made by good feeding 317
And all he slighted are bold to spurn him.
Williams, John.
MS. *Rawl. poet. 184, fol. 41$^{v}$ (autogr.).

A noble figure did I once make [once I sate] 318
Crown not your heads with British bays!
'J. & O.', James II and William of Orange.
MSS. Firth e. 6, fol. 15; Rawl. poet. 181, fol. 4; see also A160.

A northern pair, we waive the name, 319
Give nature vent, and shed it here.
'The Power of Innocence. 1762'.
MS. Eng. poet. e. 28, p. 46.

A noted magpie of renown 320
And so my liege adieu.
I. W., 'The Magpyes Song', on Bishop Burnet.
MS. Rawl. poet. 155, p. 52.

A nymph and a swain to Apollo once prayed, 321
And the nymph may be chaste who has never been tried.
MS. Ballard 47, fol. 6.

A nymph of forty, who 'tis said 322
Half a loaf's better than no bread.
Parsons, William, 'A Proverb Written at Bilboa in Biscay. 15 Aug. 1788'.
MS. *Don. d. 123, p. 182 (autogr.).

323 A nymph, when as the summer beams,
I know and you may think.

'On a Nymph bathing'.

MSS. Ashmole 38, p. 153; CCC. 328, fol. 42v; Rawl. poet. 116, fol. 56.

324 A one eyed boy born of a half blind mother
The queen of beauty, thou the god of love.

'On a Mother and her sonn haveing on eye apeyce'.

Pr. Camden's *Remaines*, 1637, p. 414; *Wits Recreations*, 1640, Sig. L1.

MSS. Ashmole 38, p. 155; Eng. poet. f. 10, fol. 114v; Tanner 465, fol. 96v; see also A179, F53, H142, T2227.

325 A page, a knight [squire] a viscount [lord], and an earl
A wife, a witch, a murderess, and a whore.

On Sir Robert Carr and Lady Frances Howard, married 26 Dec. 1613.

MSS. Ashmole 38, p. 116; Don. c. 54, fol. 23; Malone 19, p. 38; Rawl. D. 1048, fol. 64; Rawl. poet. 160, fol. 163; Tanner 465, fol. 96v.

326 A painter if he should adjoin
But having sucked her fill.

'The art of Poetry', translation from Horace.

MS. e Mus. 57, fol. 69.

327 A painter once there lived (as stories say)
At least a Titian or a Veronese.

Webb, Foster, 'A Fable'.

MS. Eng. poet. c. 9, p. 130.

328 A painter there was in London town
'To be sold by the great Christie!'

Parsons, William, 'The Fate of the Villa', Sir Joshua Reynolds's House at Richmond.

MS. *Don. d. 123, p. 204 (autogr.).

329 A pale consumption gave the fatal blow
Pitied my sighs, and kindly brought me rest.

On Mary Bailey, 1772, Eartham Church Yard, Essex.

MS. Top. gen. e. 32, fol. 117.

330 A papist died, as 'twas Jehovah's will,
Should you come in you'd eat the Devil here.

'The Ghost'.

Pr. *The Muses Farewel to Popery and Slavery*, 1689, p. 58, and *A Collection of the Newest Songs against Popery*, 1689, i. 7. Cf. A138.

MSS. Add. B. 105, fol. 26; Don. e. 23, fol. 56; Eng. poet. d. 53, p. 31; Rawl. poet. 173, fol. 123v.

A parish priest was of the pilgrim train: 331
He needs no foil: but shines by his own proper light.

Dryden, John, 'The Character of A Good Parson; Imitated from Chaucer, and Inlarg'd'.

Pr. *Fables*, 1700.

MSS. Add. B. 105, fol. 49; Rawl. D. 697, fol. 13.

A parley with my love I fain would pray 332
Thy favour save, or thy disfavour drown me.

Burton, Francis.

MS. *Add. A. 267, fol. 80 (autogr.).

A parson having a tithe pig or two 333
For spirit-like it had no flesh at all.

MS. Eng. poet. f. 10, fol. 95.

A pattern of the active life she reigned; 334
With her, secur'd and blest our happy isle.

'On the Death of the Queen', Caroline, 1737.

MS. Eng. misc. b. 48, fol. 51.

A peer, God knows, unworthily, I'm made 335
God knows it well enough, and so do I.

MS. Don. c. 81, fol. 148.

A peer of Great Britain, as fame does report 336
She thinks to herself, Sir, I will if I can.

'Momus Ridens . . . on the Weekely Reports, Feb. 4th, 1691. No. 15'.

MS. Eng. poet. d. 53, p. 146.

A peerless matron pride of female life 337
She lived a phoenix and expired in flame.

'An Epitaph on Lady Molesworth', 6 May 1763.

MS. Montagu e. 13, fol. 176.

A penny doth a shilling bring, 338
And more doth more abound.

Robinson, Robert.

MS. *Rawl. poet. 218, p. 77 (autogr.).

A penny I daily give to the poor 339
Help, Help, that men beg not from door to door.

Robinson, Robert, 'A charitable mans gift and his well wishing to the poor'.

MS. *Rawl. poet. 218, p. 141 (autogr.).

A penny with hard labour yields a pound: 340
A small seed brings forth much in fruitful ground.

Robinson, Robert, couplet.

MS. *Rawl. poet. 218, p. 77 (autogr.).

A perfect and true prognostication 341
Do no more but give us a little leave to lie.

'Prognostication'.

MS. Rawl. poet. 26, fol. 128.

342 A pillar of the church some Lee do call
He's gone to Rome, there's room for such as he . . . (last line missing).
'Upon Lee a papist'.
MS. Firth e. 4, p. 19.

343 [A] pity 'tis so generous a soul
T'hereditary sweetness, love, and wit.
Astley, —, 'Edmunde Woodehouse. She done wounded me'.
MS. Tanner 306, fol. 411$^{v}$ (autogr.).

344 A place there is remote, in furthest east
Gaining by gift of death eternal life.
J. F., 'Lactantius his Phoenix'.
MS. *Eng. poet. f. 17, p. 40 (autogr.).

345 A place there is, 'twas purchased cheap
Miss V——ne, and all about it.
'The Queens Hermitage', on Queen Caroline's 'Hermitage' and 'Merlins Cave' at Richmond, *c.* 1735.
MSS. Eng. poet. f. 12, p. 10; Rawl. poet. 172, fol. 129.

346 A placed alone is but an idle word
Not A, nor E, nor O, but, I and U.
Breton, Nicholas, 'I and U . . . Theis . . . verses weare made and geaven me by Mr. Nic. Bretton . . . 1617: oct. 17'.
Pr. Grosart, *Breton* (Chertsey Worthies Library), 1879, i. 24.
MS. Tanner 169, fol. 173$^{v}$.

347 A plain and faithful minister
It's fit the Christian faith he taught.
Robinson, Robert.
MS. *Rawl. poet. 218, p. 175 (autogr.).

348 A plain good man without deceit
Pleas'd in himself, and praised by all.
Hammond, Anthony, 'The Happy Man'.
Pr. *Miscellany of Original Poems*, 1720, p. 62.
MS. Rawl. D. 360, fol. 73 (autogr.).

349 A plant I was which grew in fertile soil
And thou shalt find, that I great wonders tell.
MS. Rawl. poet. 217, fol. 73$^{v}$.

350 A plant of noble stem, forward, and fair
Oh, do thou water it with one kind tear.
Cr[ashaw], R[ichard], 'On Mr. Herris'.
MS. Tanner 465, fol. 69$^{v}$.

351 A pleasant new ditty
That's otherwise called the wag wanton.
Weaver, Thomas, 'A Roundelay', prelude to 'Once I a curious Eye did fix'.
Not pr. in *Songs and Poems*, 1654.
MS. *Rawl. poet. 211, fol. 78 (autogr.).

A pleasant plant I once plucked up 352
Except ye do reward me well.
MS. Rawl. poet. 217, fol. 74.

A pleasing flattery soothes me with such art 353
(My hearts' own home) shall there find joy and rest.
'Aboard my Lord Duffus's Ship in Port-Mahon'.
MS. Rawl. D. 360, fol. 80.

A pleasing form, a firm yet cautious mind 354
At length enjoys that liberty he lov'd.
[Pope, Alexander], 'Epitaph' on Sir William Trumbull.
Pr. *Works*, 1717, etc.
MS. Rawl. poet. 153, fol. 54.

A pleasing freedom with a smile forbid 355
For us that love, it is no shame to kiss.
Williams, John, 'Of a kiss denied'.
MS. *Rawl. poet. 191, fol. 92 (autogr.).

A poet once the Spartans led, to fight 356
Let Caesar live, and Carthage be subdued.
[Dryden, John], 'The Epilogue' to the 'play of Amboyna'.
MS. Don. b. 8, p. 464.

A poet? you'll say; that's right: true head of block 357
No: truncheon in their hand that clod-pates down can knock.
Roach, Richard (?), couplet.
MS. Rawl. D. 833, fol. 183, in Roach's hand.

A poor helpless wanderer the wide world before me 358
When the soft tear of pity can sooth her distress.
'Bess The Beggar Girl'.
MS. Percy d. 9, fol. 18$^{v}$.

A poor hydroptic creature, whose disease 359
No time amiss, when works of mercy call.
'The nice Pharisee'.
MS. Rawl. poet. 154, fol. 112.

A poor man proud, is still in want 360
Gets much, but spendeth not.
Robinson, Robert.
MS. *Rawl. poet. 218, p. 104 (autogr.).

A poor man's counsel let not men despise 361
Where want of art affords not other skill.
Robinson, Robert.
MS. *Rawl. poet. 218, p. 89 (autogr.).

A potent, grave, and reverend Signor I! 362
The life of pleasure and the soul of whim.
Parsons, William, 'To the Honble. Mrs. Villiers'.
MS. *Don. d. 123, p. 236 (autogr.).

363 A pox of the troubles men make in the world
I'll be here in a trice I read a good trot.
Drinking song, *temp.* Charles II.
MS. Douce 357, fol. 77.

364 A pox of this fooling and plotting of late
This is the profession, that never will alter.
Oldham, [John], 'The Careless Good-Fellow . . . 9th March 1660' [*sic*, for 1680].
Pr. Oldham's *Compositions in Prose and Verse*, ed. E. Thompson, 1770, iii. 38.
MS. Rawl. D. 1480, fol. 200$^{v}$.

365 A pox on whigs we'll now grow wise
Such cursed rogues are we.
*Temp.* James II.
MS. Tanner 306, fol. 407.

366 A pox take ye all from you my sorrows swell
May they more debtors have and all like me.
'[Thomas] Randolph to his Creditors'.
Pr. *Poems*, 2nd ed., 1640, p. 116.
MS. CCC. 328, fol. 36; see also P306.

367 A pox, who'd be a poet in our days?
There's no spare fop now left amongst you all.
'The Intended prologue for a Duke & no Duke' [by N. Tate, 1683].
MS. Add. B. 8, fol. 52$^{v}$ rev.

368 A practic life, led by a knowing mind
Once the elect lady, now the Jezabel.
'Authore Incerto: The Christian Warning-piece'.
MS. Add. B. 106, fol. 12.

369 A prayer on Sygionoth
He will make me to see.
Fleming, Robert, 'Habakkuk's prayer, 1674'.
MS. Rawl. poet. 213, fol. 76 rev. (autogr.).

370 A preface in verse! What a task you impose!
Such solid good sense in such beautiful binding.
Parsons, William, 'Written in a MSS. Journal of a Tour through England . . . the author Mrs. D[awso]n'.
MS. *Don. d. 123, p. 212 (autogr.).

371 A prelate hurled
Went hand in hand together.
'Burnett & Wharton welcome to Pluto's Shades', 1715.
MSS. Ballard 47, fol. 72; Rawl. poet. 155, p. 148.

372 A presbyterian parson had a carriage
And this last meanness never be forgotten.
Gough, Richard, 'Aug. 17. 1772. sent to St. James's Evening Post'.
MS. *Eng. poet. c. 5, fol. 215 (autogr.).

A pretty little lass, with a round ear'd cap 373
But at night I do nothing but roar.
MS. Montagu c. 5, fol. 51$^{v}$.

A pretty seal of virgin wax 374
That nothing but impression lacks.
'On a Maiden', couplet.
MSS. Ashmole 36, 37, fol. 143$^{v}$; see also A1370.

A priest for penance one enjoined to take 375
His wit did serve him first to boil the peas.
'Epigrams: In sacrificum quendam'.
MS. Don. d. 58, fol. 35$^{v}$.

A priest ranging the park did find 376
That so no way her soul should find.
'On a Parson's Swiveing a zealous whore'.
MS. Add. A. 301, fol. 3$^{v}$.

A prince doth sit a slippery seat, 377
Bring us both great and small.
'A proper new Ballad entitled. The merry Life of the Countryman'.
MS. Rawl. poet. 185, fol. 19$^{v}$.

A prince out of the north shall come 378
Shall take away his aged breath.
'Mr. Ball's Prophecy', 'Merlin's Prophecy'.
MSS. Ashmole 423, fol. 263; Tanner 88, fol. 253; see also A205.

A prison is in all things like a grave 379
Two prisons quits, the body and the jail.
King, Henry, 'An Essay on Death, and a Prison'.
Pr. *Poems*, 1657, p. 130.
MSS. *Eng. poet. e. 30, fol. 10; *Malone 22, fol. 6$^{v}$.

A prison's but the emblem of a grave 380
Return to his first principles again.
'A Satyr on a Gaoler'.
MS. Add. A. 301, fol. 71$^{v}$ rev.

A private shower of tears, wept from those eyes 381
Secured of state and hid him from a grave.
Dutton, William, 'An Elegy on the Honourable Thomas Coventry Lord Keeper of the greate Seale of England', d. 13 Jan. 1639/40.
MS. Ashmole 38, p. 162.

A proper maid that bears sweet beauty's prize 382
Either none so fair or else she's wondrous rare.
MS. Eng. poet. f. 10, fol. 122.

A proper squire in lands as most men say 383
He sold his land to die a merry death.
'On Mr. Amery Death commonly called Amery Day'.
MS. Eng. poet. e. 14, fol. 86 rev.

384 A prophet to an harlot joined?
The sinner whom he came to save.
Kenton, James.
MS. *Eng. poet. e. 20, p. 21 (autogr.).

385 A prophet while denouncing God's decrees
He set up molten calves and they adored.
'The Withered Hand'.
MS. Rawl. poet. 154, fol. 108.

386 A pure white lily, like a silver cup
God, part of her inheritance and cup.
Pr. *Parthenia Sacra*, ed. I. Fletcher, 1633, p. 35.
MS. Eng. poet. b. 5, p. 107.

387 A puritan is like a poet's purse
For both do hate the cross, what cross is worse.
MS. Rawl. poet. 172, fol. 12.

388 A puritan is such a monstrous thing
Each seems a saint and either proves a knave.
'A true Puritan without disguise'. Answer to T260.
MSS. Eng. hist. e. 28, p. 577; Malone 23, p. 213; Rawl. poet. 26, fol. 109.

389 A puritan, with one of her society
She hath a pulpit, where a preacher may be.
MS. Rawl. poet. 26, fol. 8$^{v}$; see also A163.

390 A quiet silent person may possess
Like God himself, and heaven and earth was there.
Traherne, Thomas, 'Silence'.
MS. *Eng. poet. c. 42, fol. 6$^{v}$ (autogr.).

391 A rare and precious pearl is hardly found
Such was the virgin mother paragon.
Pr. *Parthenia Sacra*, ed. I. Fletcher, 1633, p. 195.
MS. Eng. poet. b. 5, p. 106.

392 A resident is (when rightly understood)
One sent to lie abroad for the public good.
Couplet, 'Legatus est Vir bonus peregre missus ad mentiendum (to lie abroad) Reipublicae causa. Sir H. Wotton'.
MS. Sancroft 98, p. 173.

393 A reverend dame late sick did lie,
Who called for a physician.
'On "the Church is in no danger"'.
MS. Rawl. poet. 81, fol. 43.

394 A reverend dean
He handled it more than his text
'On Dr. Corbet', 1621. Extract from T844.

395 A rich man, like a fox, a wolf, a bear
To flesh himself, and his own cubs to rear.
Robinson, Robert, couplet.
MS. *Rawl. poet. 218, p. 139 (autogr.).

A rich man to a poor man gives a nod 396
But keeps his money: oh, it is his God.
Robinson, Robert, couplet.
MS. *Rawl. poet. 218, p. 105 (autogr.).

A rich man wants his health 397
The better is or worse.
Robinson, Robert.
MS. *Rawl. poet. 218, p. 46 (autogr.).

A rich man's many pennies gained 398
To keep him up from ground.
Robinson, Robert.
MS. *Rawl. poet. 218, p. 155 (autogr.).

A riddle, a riddle me neighbour John 399
Chil hold in great indudgeon.
[Strode, William].
MSS. Ashmole 36, 37, fol. 114; see also R207, T2225.

A riddle now to you I do describe 400
My mind shall fully unfold to you.
Meddus, Joseph (?).
MS. Rawl. D. 929, fol. 24, in the hand of Meddus.

A ring for any one to wear 401
To me, the latter's none.
Tipping, William.
MS. *Rawl. poet. 101, fol. 2$^{v}$ (autogr.)

A romanist is one that knows a way 402
Resolve to put a period to their state.
MS. Eng. poet. c. 50, fol. 31.

A rope for parrot, what strange fustian this, 403
Fame carbonadoed, is a dish for Jove.
N.C., 'fame carbonaded is a dish for Jove'.
MS. Ashmole 38, p. 44.

A rose that hung on Julia's breast 404
Th'immortal power sustains!
Parsons, William, 'The faded Rose'.
Pr. *Fidelity* etc., 1798, p. 52, and *Travelling Recreations*, 1807.
MS. *Don. d. 123, p. 162 (autogr.).

A Royston horse, and a Cambridge Master of Arts, 405
*Nulli mortalium cedent de via.*
MS. Malone 19, p. 1.

A rumour from the Lord we hear 406
And to the God of mercy turn.
Kenton, James.
MS. *Eng. poet. e. 20, p. 100 (autogr.).

A rural squire, to crowds and courts unknown, 407
Might plan new schemes, and draw their swords in vain.
Somervile, William, 'The Country Gentleman'. Not in *Poems*, 1727.
MS. Ballard 47, fol. 13.

408 A rustic swain was cleaving [at] of a block
For when I hemmed I cleft, but now I bore.
'An Epigram'.
MSS. CCC. 328, fol. 48; Douce f. 5, fol. 18; Top. London e. 9, p. 35; see also A259.

409 A safe and common way it is
'Tis knavery by your leave.
Translation of Latin couplet.
MSS. Rawl. poet. 117, fol. 273v rev.; 212, fol. 85v.

410 A sage archdeacon, wondrous man!
Prisoner within the wire . . . (incomplete).
Gough, Richard, 'On the Society of Antiquaries and their Library'.
MS. *Eng. poet. c. 5, fol. 145 (autogr.).

411 A saint in church, a sinner great abroad
Zealous in faith, more ready to defraud.
Robinson, Robert.
MS. *Rawl. poet. 218, p. 41 (autogr.).

412 A saintlike sister hath turned votary
It hath a pulpit where a preacher may be.
MS. Rawl. poet. 172, fol. 12; see also A163, A389.

413 A Salop's Ouseley I
Did here my lodging take.
On Richard Ouseley, Courtenhall Church, Northamptonshire, 1598.
MS. Top. gen. e. 32, fol. 118.

414 A satyr once did run away for dread
Who burnt his lips to kiss fair shining fire.
Sidney, Sir Philip.
Pr. *Arcadia*, 1598, p. 478.
MSS. *e Mus. 37, fol. 237v; Rawl. poet. 85, fol. 8v, attr. to S. P. S.

415 A scoffing mate passing along Cheapside
To buy quoth he; or else shut up your shop.
[Parrot, Henry], 'Upon a gentlewoman that went bare breasted'.
Pr. *Epigrams*, 1608, Sig. G1v.
MS. Ashmole 38, p. 115.

416 A secret fire consumes my heart
The joys of heaven, or pains of hell.
'A Song'.
MS. Rawl. poet. 222, fol. 37v.

417 A secret murther hath been done of late
At whose sweet sight my wound doth bleed anew.
'Goss'.
Pr. *The Phoenix Nest*, 1593, p. 70, amongst poems by Sir Walter Ralegh.
MS. Rawl. poet. 85, fol. 108v.

A secret seldom seen, that women counsel keep 418
Unless they wake their wits, and lull their tongues asleep.
'Woman prattlers'.
MSS. Don. d. 58, fol. 43; Eng. poet. e. 14, fol. 68; Malone 19, p. 150; see also A435.

A senseless blockhead very soon 419
. . . (incomplete) . . .
'The Picture of a Glutton'.
MS. Mus. e. 19, p. 25.

A serpent shall rise in the north ugly 420
And bring it into christian men's hand.
'Prophecy'.
MS. North c. 80, fols. 3v, 3r, 10, 11.

A servant gracious Lord of Thine 421
My every work shall please.
Kenton, James.
MS. *Eng. poet. e. 20, p. 46 (autogr.).

A servant—no—an unassuming friend 422
In zeal a Martha, with a Mary's heart.
Madan, Spencer, Bp. of Peterborough (?), 'Memorial verse to Sarah Jackson', d. 1796.
MS. Eng. poet. c. 51, p. 111.

A session of ladies was held on the stage 423
Since the goddess had made so equal a choice.
'The Session of Ladies. 1688'.
MSS. Firth c. 15, p. 292; c. 16, p. 269; see also T433.

A session of lovers was held t'other day 424
He had left being a man she would make him a beast.
'The Lovers' Session, 1687'.
Pr. *Poems on Affairs of State*, ii, 1703, p. 156.
MSS. Douce 357, fol. 118; Firth c. 15, p. 277.

A sessions was held the other day 425
When he lends any poet about the town.
[Suckling, Sir John], 'The Wits'.
Pr. *Fragmenta Aurea*, 1646.
MSS. Eng. poet. c. 53, fol. 18; Malone 13, p. 31.

A set of phrases learnt by rote 426
So, holla boys; God save the King.
Swift, Jonathan, 'The Furniture of a Woman's Mind'.
MS. Eng. poet. c. 9, p. 113.

A sheep and boy, a boy, wife, husband, by 427
The knife, the water, rope and grief doth die.
Couplet, translating preceding Latin.
MS. Rawl. poet. 213, fol. 1.

A shepherd in a shade his plaining made 428
Fie, fie on love, it is a foolish thing.
Pr. John Dowland's *Second Booke of Songs or Ayres*, 1600, xvii.
MS. Douce 280, fol. 69.

429 A shepherd wholly blest with Pastora's sight
I pardon beg for lines, I hastily have penned.
MS. Montagu e. 13, fol. 130.

430 A shining star, that glist'ned far
His soul in heaven is crowned.
On Edward Mershell, Gamlinghay Church, d. 1625.
MS. Top. Camb. c. 1, fol. 113.

431 A ship, and so a bird are flying things,
To their wished havens, oh, with what joy they sing.
Robinson, Robert.
MS. *Rawl. poet. 218, p. 68 (autogr.).

432 A ship with soldiers ready prest
That thus much water hath to drink.
Molle, Henry, 'Witt in a Tempest: a translation'.
MSS. Ashmole 36, 37, fol. 173$^{v}$, attr. to Hen. Molle; Rawl. poet. 147, p. 2, attr. to H. Molle; 210, fol. 49, attr. to H. Molle.

433 A sickness sore, that doth in secret wound,
She unawares, was prey unto his bow.
Whitney, Geoffrey, 'Zelotypia', translation from Ovid, *Metamorphoses* vii.
MS. *Rawl. poet. 56, fol. 120$^{v}$.

434 A sickness wastes my love; Sol show thy skill
Since th' fates can't act on immortality.
Edwards, Thomas, St. John's, Oxford, 'A prayer to Apollo for his Mistresses health'.
MS. Rawl. poet. 65, fol. 63.

435 A silence seldom seen
And lulled her tongue asleep.
MS. Rawl. poet. 85, fol. 91; see also A418.

436 A silent tree I was, and mute did stand
Art after death a life to me did give.
'On a harp'.
MS. Rawl. poet. 210, fol. 52$^{v}$.

437 A silent unlamented death I hate
Let sighs of friends and tears attend my fate.
Couplet in Dryden's translation of Plutarch.
MS. Rawl. D. 1372, fol. 29 from end.

438 A silly child, seeing his shadow move
Wishing to play with shadows, like to them.
'The Shadow-Catcher'.
MS. Rawl. poet 66, fol. 56.

439 A silly John surprised with joy
But aim for John's good hap.
MS. Jones 27*, fol. 18$^{v}$; Malone 19, p. 80, attr. to J[ohn] Deane; see also A810.

A silly shepherd wooed and wist not 440
When he will he shall have nay.
'A Song'.
MS. CCC. 327, fol. 13.

A silly swain long time had loved a lass 441
Blushed, ran away and scorned him ever after.
MS. Eng. poet. e. 14, fol. 9.

A singing man and yet not sing 442
My voice is in another county.
Mansel, Dr. [William Lort, Master of Trinity College 1798–1820], 'Epigram on a Chorister of Peterborough'.
MS. Eng. poet. c. 51, p. 114.

A single Church not large but neat 443
An easy exit and eternal life.
'The Parson's Wish'.
MS. Top. London e. 9, p. 165.

A sinking state he's likely to uphold 444
In counsel cool, but in performance bold.
Couplet.
MS. Sancroft 85, p. 282 rev.

A sister once I had which always saw 445
Thus in her quiet rest, myself was crossed.
Cavendish, Lady Jane, 'On my sweete Sister the Lady Harpur'.
MS. *Rawl. poet. 16, p. 32.

A skilful orator in prose or rhyme, 446
A saint a devil, a devil a saint to make.
Robinson, Robert.
MS. *Rawl. poet. 218, p. 107 (autogr.).

A slaughtered bull appeaseth angry Jove 447
That burnt the temple where she was adored.
'To his cruell mistress'.
MS. CCC. 328, fol. 21.

A slow [soft] tongue betokens modesty 448
Both worse than fiends, both fit to live in hell.
'Of a talking woman'.
MSS. Eng. poet. e. 14, fol. 83$^{v}$ rev.; Malone 19, p. 77.

A slut was our dam, a sloven our sire 449
In all cleanly manner, to serve each degree.
MS. Rawl. poet. 217, fol. 77.

A small fault is soon amended, 450
'Tis money makes a man befriended.
Robinson, Robert.
MS. *Rawl. poet. 218, p. 71 (autogr.).

A smiling lawyer now lies here 451
Happy, could he lie for ever.
Vyse, William, Archdeacon of Salop, 'Epitaph upon a Lawyer'.
MS. Eng. poet. c. 51, p. 86.

452 A smoke, a storm, and a contentious wife,
When children cry for hunger, wanting bread.
MS. Rawl. poet. 209, fol. 32v.

453 A snarling cur, did in the manger lie,
Yet are they like, the dog, in ox's stall.
Whitney, Geoffrey, '*Nec sibi, nec alteri*'.
MS. *Rawl. poet. 56, fol. 113v.

454 A soft pate has tender heels.
In equipage they never meet.
Robinson, Robert.
MS. *Rawl. poet. 218, p. 159 (autogr.).

455 A soldier and a sailor
Which won this fair maid's heart.
Congreve, William, from *Love for Love*.
MSS. Eng. poet. f. 13, fol. 74v, attr. to Mr. Congreve; Mus. Sch. C. 95, p. 237, music by Eccles.

456 A soldier once, on whom god Morpheus' charms
He swore a prayer or two and so he slept.
'The Swearing Soldiers Dream'.
MS. Firth d. 7, fol. 186.

457 A soldier's oratory's great;
He'll fetch it by his sword.
Robinson, Robert, 'Facundia militis in ense est militis'.
MS. *Rawl. poet. 218, p. 138 (autogr.).

458 A soldier's oratory's in his sword;
Deliver quickly, down down else you go.
Robinson, Robert.
MS. *Rawl. poet. 218, p. 138 (autogr.).

459 A sole old woman keeps Sir William's door,
Or majesty mistake thee for a pig!
Parsons, William, 'Epigram written at Naples on Sir William H[amilton]'.
MS. *Don. d. 123, p. 139 (autogr.).

460 A solid body makes but little sound
In hollow vessels greatest noise is found.
Robinson, Robert, couplet.
MS. *Rawl. poet. 218, p. 161 (autogr.).

461 A span in age and growth of two years might
That won a race as soon as she could go.
Strode, William, 'On a child dying at 2 years of age'.
MS. *CCC. 325, fol. 124v (autogr.).

462 A spark, by its own nature taught to aspire
Light on her breast, and true love kindle there.
Bacon, Phanuel, 'To Mira. Occasiond by a spark's flying into her Eye'.
MS. Eng. poet. e. 45, fol. 43 (autogr.).

A spot there is say traveller? where it lies 463
Eat with content—and leave the rest to heaven.
Fox, Charles, 'Enigma . . . on a table'.
MS. Eng. letters d. 103, p. 149 rev.

A sprightly maid as I did once appear 464
(page torn) . . . rivulets to a deluge come.
'Being disturb'd in thought I wright thies'.
MS. Eng. poet. e. 17, fol. 8v (autogr.).

A sprightsome heart doth make a lightsome body: 465
A dullsome spirit makes a dolesome noddy.
Robinson, Robert, couplet.
MS. *Rawl. poet. 218, p. 164 (autogr.).

A stands for artifice, B for a buzzard 466
Whom you have acted up to the very life.
Roach, Richard, 'The Correction, and Reverse of Mr. Craftsmans Alphabet'.
See *The Craftsman*, 20 Jan. 1728.
MS. Rawl. D. 833, fols. 192v, 191v, 192 (autogr.).

A star [did late arise] of late appeared in Virgo's train 467
Charles sit thou fast and look unto thy wain.
'On the blazing star', *c.* 1623.
MSS. Eng. poet. c. 50, fol. 129; e. 14, fol. 76v rev., attr. to Dr. Lapworth; e. 97, p. 11; Rawl. D. 1048, fol. 50v; D. 1092, fol. 272; Rawl. poet. 116, fol. 57.

A steady follower of a gracious God 468
And in his kind embraces ever rest.
Kenton, James, epitaph on Mrs. Anne Holloway, d. 1776, dated Aug. 1782.
MS. *Eng. poet. e. 19, p. 257 (autogr.).

A steady virtue formed for self-command 469
To steal through life, and bless a world around.
'On the Death of Sir Jo. James, Bart.', d. 1741.
MS. Eng. poet. e. 39, p. 104.

A story I'll tell and no title enlarge 470
For he is out of their debt as he owed them a shame.
On George I.
MS. Top. Oxon. c. 108, p. 98.

A story strange I shall unfold, fa la 471
Begotten when he lay alone, fa la.
Pr. *Wit and Drollery*, 1661, p. 64.
MS. Rawl. B. 35, fol. 56 rev.

A strange mishapen monster 472
Shall keep another fifth day of November.
By I. C.
MS. Rawl. poet. 142, fol. 21.

473 A stranger coming to the town
The french men's harms within.
'On the flower de luce'.
MSS. Don. d. 58, fol. 36; Douce f. 5, fol. 16; Eng. poet. e. 14, fol. 20$^{v}$; Malone 19, p. 52.

474 A stranger here, as all my fathers were
And teach me how I may thy dwelling find.
Pr. J. Amner's *Sacred Hymns*, 1615, xxiv.
MSS. Mus. f. 20–24: f. 20, fol. 74$^{v}$.

475 A strong man being in chamber high
Tell me, good friend, how this could be?
MS. Rawl. poet. 217, fol. 73.

476 A studious mind must needs be vex'd
Than when from coxcombs I am free.
'The Recluse and the Impertinent. A Fable'.
MS. *Eng. poet. d. 47, fol. 99.

477 A sturdy friar nor old nor young
And stink as much as I.
'The Way to Tame', endorsed 'Verses to a Fox-Hunter found in N[ew] C[ollege] Cloysters'.
MS. Eng. poet. d. 10, fol. 8.

478 A sumptuous house, with tenants of great choice
Good friend, if thou canst, I pray thee me show.
MS. Rawl. poet. 217, fol. 74$^{v}$.

479 A sunny bank in shade hath seldom been
But they will prate and nothing secret keep.
'On one Sunnybank taken by Parret the proctor', Oxford [1545–6].
MS. Eng. poet. e. 14, fol. 79 rev.

480 A swain, long tortured with disdain
As you grow daring we grow kind.
'A Song'.
MSS. Eng. poet. d. 152, fol. 85 rev.; Montagu e. 13, fol. 46.

481 A swearing drunking whoring saint
Contentious, covetous devil.
Robinson, Robert.
MS. *Rawl. poet. 218, p. 120 (autogr.).

482 A sycophant is like the satyr old:
As you will have him he'll blow hot or cold.
Robinson, Robert, couplet.
MS. *Rawl. poet. 218, p. 84 (autogr.).

483 A tablet stood of that abstersive tree
[Nor rudely skips o'er bishops' heads like knights].
Denham, J[ohn], 'Chesse'.
Pr. *Poems*, 1668, p. 126, 'An occasional Invitation of a Modern Author [i.e. Davenant] upon the Game of Chess'.
MS. CCC. 309, fol. 57$^{v}$.

A tabour and a shepherd's reed 484
When they might dance or tumble.
MS. Jones 27*, fol. 17$^{v}$.

A taylor, [held, ta'en] thought [to be] a man of upright dealing 485
Of such a coloured shred; in all the flag.
H[arington], Sir J[ohn], 'On a Taylour'.
Pr. *Epigrams*, 1618, i. 20.
MSS. Ashmole 38, p. 85, attr. to Sir J. H.; Rawl. poet. 26, fol. 3$^{v}$; 31, fol. 4; 172, fol. 12; 212, fol. 101, attr. to Sir I. H.

A tenant which I loved well 486
Until the tenant won the field.
MS. Rawl. poet. 217, fol. 78.

A tender heart dear Lord I want 487
Form both my heart and life anew.
Beddome, Benjamin.
MS. *Eng. misc. e. 227, fol. 3 (autogr.).

A tender loving wife and what's more rare 488
Desiring to be good not minding to be great.
On Elizabeth Millechamp, d. 1700. Gloucester Cathedral.
MS. Willis 71, p. 306.

A term of life is set to every man. 489
Which is but short and pass it no one can.
MS. Add. B. 8, fol. 63.

A Thais? no Diana thou didst wed 490
And she hath given to thee Actaeon's head.
'Upon a Cuckold'.
MS. CCC. 328, fol. 26.

A thief condemned to die, 491
For giving them such scope.
Whitney, Geoffrey, 'Indulgentia parentum filiorum pernicies'.
MSS. *Rawl. poet. 56, fol. 100; 85, fol. 46$^{v}$.

A thief that bravely bears away his prize 492
Let Heer Van Brush, or Tyburn be his doom.
'Made upon the Lord Chancellor when he carried the charter home' [Lord Jeffreys (?)].
MSS. Eng. poet. c. 18, fol. 67; e. 49, p. 45.

A thin ill natured ghost that haunts the king 493
Should e're be thus condem'd to counselling.
'The Nine'. 1690.
Pr. *Poems, on Affairs of State*, ii, 1703, p. 211.
MSS. Eng. poet. c. 18, fol. 82$^{v}$; d. 53, p. 53; Firth e. 6, fol. 146$^{v}$; Malone 41, fol. 24; Rawl. poet. 159, fol. 188.

A thing of small price which all men know 494
This is the material of our stone.
'A Riddle'.
Pr. *Theatrum Chemicum Britannicum*, 1652.
MS. Ashmole 972, fol. 282$^{v}$.

495 A thing there is maids blush to tell't
Each lass would have't or put fair for't.
'Content'.
MS. Rawl. poet. 120, fol. 35.

496 A thing was lost, which money cost
Till they it found. Then brought it.
MS. Rawl. poet. 217, fol. 75$^{v}$.

497 A third upon his quiver wreaks his hate
Then thou must sigh, then thou must weep again.
Oldham, John, 'The Lamentation of Adonis', dated 'June 2 [16]81'.
MS. *Rawl. poet. 123, p. 217 (autogr.).

498 A thousand martyrs I have made
Despise the fools that die for love.
'The vaunting, false Courtier'.
MS. Rawl. poet. 173, fol. 87.

499 A thousand times, hath my enamoured eye,
Than your commands he holds his life less dear.
Burton, Francis.
MS. *Add. A. 267, fol. 147$^{v}$ (autogr.).

500*a* A thousand times I have resolved and swore
But for my life and blood I cannot hold.
Walsh, William, '206' [from Greek Anthology].
MS. Malone 9, fol. 28$^{v}$ (autogr.).

500*b* A thousand times I've heard base calumnies
And swear to any thing that she'll stand by.
Barnes, Joshua, 'My Defence', to Mrs. Mary Honywood Cotton.
MS. Hearne's diaries 11, p. 144.

501 A tired ox more firm his hoof doth beat;
A wearied man doth seek a resting seat.
Robinson, Robert, couplet.
MS. *Rawl. poet. 218, p. 171 (autogr.).

502 A title of barrister on every wench
That only suretyship hath brought them there.
'A Lawyers wooing'.
MS. Rawl. poet. 172, fol. 10$^{v}$.

503 A torrent is a sudden flowing stream
Eternal are pain, hell, joys, God's presence.
F. W., 'Why the joys of heaven are called torrens Voluptatis'.
MS. *Rawl. C. 639, p. 63.

504 A tower is fallen and it lies
Lo here lies murther's complement.
Quarles, John, 'An Epitaph upon the right honourable Arthur Lord Capell'. Acrostic, copied from *A Kingly Bed*, 2nd ed., 1649, p. 94.
MS. Rawl. B. 165, fol. 141.

A towering kite in pomp arose 505
And shattered, torn, disjointed, fell.
Skinner, John, 'The kite . . . 1789'.
MS. *Eng. poet. d. 22, fol. 22.

A treasurer too, they chose most fit 506
And had a double tongue.
P. O., 'L[or]d of Ox[for]d's' character [Harley.]
MS. Firth b. 4, fol. 15 (autogr.).

A treaty's on foot look about English boys 507
As half a loaf's better than no bread at all.
Pr. 1711 as a second part to . . . Lilliburlero.
MS. Rawl. D. 992, fol. 23$^{v}$.

A tree grown old, but a dead trunk is found 508
A man grown aged sapless falls to the ground.
Robinson, Robert, couplet.
MS. *Rawl. poet. 218, p. 44 (autogr.).

A trifling song you shall hear 509
The song is a trifle to boot.
'The Triffle', 1703.
Attr. to Farquhar in B.M. Add. MS. 28101, fol. 186. Cf. B.M. MS. Lansd. 852, p. 40.
MSS. Eng. misc. c. 292, fol. 101; e. 183, fol. 18$^{v}$; Eng. poet. e. 87, p. 26.

A true blue priest, a linsey-woolsey brother, 510
For anything entirely but an ass.
MS. Add. B. 106, fol. 52.

A true friend's love must like a chimney be, 511
Warm in the winter of adversity.
'Mr. Dawson's chimney at the Blue Boar, Oxford'.
Pr. *Modius Salium*, ed. T. Warton (?), 1751, p. 17.
MSS. Malone 19, p. 100; Tanner 466, fol. 66$^{v}$; Wood E. 32 (Modius Salium), fol. 12.

A true friend's love must [should] like a [his] privy be 512
To ease his friend at his necessity.
'On a house of office'.
MSS. CCC. 328, fol. 44; Malone 19, p. 100.

A true saint's ashes, if this marble lid 513
Don't cover, surely then no stone e'er did.
Couplet on Anne, eldest daughter of Sir Charles Scarburgh, d. June 3, 1707, buried in Acton church.
MS. Rawl. D. 896, fol. 15.

A trumpeter the captains captive led, 514
Yet with thy wind, thou others did'st provoke.
Whitney, Geoffrey, 'Agentes, et consentientes, pari poena puniendi'.
MS. *Rawl. poet. 56, fol. 30$^{v}$.

515 A tyrant priest upon the throne?
He'd make God all his mischiefs own.
Robinson, Robert.
MS. *Rawl. poet. 218, p. 111 (autogr.).

516 A valiant man, that stoutly fights in evil
O he's a worthy of his prince the devil.
Robinson, Robert, couplet translating 'In malo fortissimus Daemonis Domini sui dignissimus'.
MS. *Rawl. poet. 218, p. 126 (autogr.).

517 A vapour's life! My sands are almost run;
Since joy eternal must be had through death.
'A Thought in Sickness. W. P. B.'
MS. *Eng. poet. d. 47, fol. 69.

518*a* A verse may take him who a sermon flies
And turn delight into a sacrifice.
Couplet.
MS. Rawl. poet. 117, two copies, fols. 247 and 168 rev.

518*b* A vintner from fair London would ride,
And say that you met with a right honest man.
'The Broken Vintner of London'.
MS. Firth d. 14, fol. 70.

519 A virgin blossom in her May
She'll rise a star, that fell a flower.
'Eleanor Freeman, 1650, Tewkesbury Church Gloucestershire'.
MS. Top. gen. e. 32, fol. 72$^v$.

520 A virgin came to me in bed last night
Believe me as I hope for grace it's true.
Tipping, William. Dated: 'Munday decemb' 13. 1695'; see also S1295.
MS. *Rawl. poet. 101, fol. 69 (autogr.).

521 A virgin full of spotless innocence
Ne'er then deny but tell me that I am, etc.
'On a Lady's name an Acrostick' (Anna Maria Thompson).
MS. Rawl. poet. 152, fol. 165.

522 A virgin most perfect, for beauty renowned
Whoever beholds her, must 'suredly love her.
[Lepipre, Gabriel (?)], 'The Innoxious Maid', Sarah Carbonnel.
MS. *Eng. poet. e. 40, fol. 96 (in Lepipre's hand).

523 A virgin, mother was unto a son, how can we show it?
Faith mounts aloft, and reason doth come under.
MS. Eng. poet. c. 50, fol. 33$^v$.

524 A virtue self denial once was thought
Then when they might their name as well disown.
Williams, John, 'Of Self Denial'.
MS. *Rawl. poet. 191, fol. 152$^v$ (autogr.).

A virtuoso had a mind to see 525
Pray let me just step home, and fetch you mine.
King, Dr. [William], 'The Incurious'.
MS. Rawl. poet. 153, fol. 54.

A virtuous lady sitting in a muse 526
Sir lock it if you please, you keep the key.
[Harington, Sir John], 'On a Lady'.
Pr. *Alcilia*, 1613. Cf. B636.
MSS. Ashmole 47, fol. 53$^v$; CCC. 328, fol. 44; Eng. poet. e. 14, fol. 81$^v$ rev.; f. 25, fol. 15$^v$; Malone 19, p. 75; Rawl. poet. 116, fol. 53; 142, fol. 40; see also A9, A151, A155.

A virtuous wife, be she of homely feature, 527
Excels a bad wife, though a comely creature.
Robinson, Robert, couplet.
MS. *Rawl. poet. 218, p. 25 (autogr.).

A virtuous wife is glory's precious crown 528
Since all the glory of her life's to please.
Samber, Robert, 'To my Mistresses' from 'The Bellman's Verses'.
MS. *Rawl. poet. 134*b*, fol. 156 (autogr.).

A viscount, proud of his late-purchased coat 529
You should a cap of the same making wear.
Oldisworth, Nicolas, 'On Heraldry'.
MS. *Don. c. 24, fol. 20$^v$ (autogr.).

A voice by tender grief subdued 530
Is lasting cordial to the soul.
'On being desired by Sir J[ohn] D[oyle] to go and speak comfort to a beloved sister to whom he had just bid a long adieu'.
MS. North. b. 7, fol. 30.

A vote lately passed in the Parliament house 531
They're both coming over as soon as they can.
F. G., 'The Slip', i.e. the flight of Bolingbroke and the Duke of Ormonde, 1715.
MS. Rawl. poet. 155, p. 196.

A Vulcane and a Venus seldom part 532
Have like the watch one pulse, one sympathy.
Strode, William, 'On a watch made by a blacksmith'.
MS. *CCC. 325, fol. 95 (autogr.).
MS. Eng. poet. e. 97, p. 30.

A wanton art thou mistress [four] in 533
And then our [trey] will work apace.
Verse in which some words are represented by dice symbols.
MS. Rawl. poet. 172, fol. 3.

534 **A wanton wench sitting on bed**
**Let me have morning's health.**
Poule, Sir Stephen (translator). 'Ould Mr. Ked gave me thiese verses . . . which he sayed weare made by a learned woman in Latin: but Dr. Franke my tenant sayed he made at the request of a fine Lady . . . 12 Maii. 1606'.
MS. Tanner 169, fol. 68v (autogr.).

535 **A watch a jewel is, if it speak right;**
**A bad watch still is bad, though often mended.**
Robinson, Robert.
MS. *Rawl. poet. 218, p. 22 (autogr.).

536 **A watch lost in a tavern, that's ['twas] a crime:**
**Pocket your watch, and watch your pocket too.**
'On a Watch lost in a Tavern'.
MSS. Ashmole 36, 37, fol. 159; Rawl. poet. 116, fol. 59v.

537 **A watery pit received my parting breath**
**I rest forever happy in his love's embrace.**
Kenton, James, 'Epitaph for Mr. James Rodwell of Deptford', 1786.
MS. *Eng. poet. e. 19, p. 269 (autogr.).

538 **A wealthy farm sometime I did possess**
**Sweet comfort yields, in great distress.**
MS. Rawl. poet. 217, fol. 72v.

539 **A wealthy island which no help desires**
**And surfeit great Augustus with her treasures.**
Translation of Latin, 'De Anglia duo Disticha'.
MS. Lat. misc. c. 19, p. 425.

540 **A wealthy man, that to his back**
**A fool; he is no better.**
Robinson, Robert.
MS. *Rawl. poet. 218, p. 140 (autogr.).

541 **A well timed pregnancy her titles gained**
**A faithful clue to Rosamonda's bower.**
'Countess of Rochford' (d. 1773).
MS. Eng. poet. e. 28, p. 29.

542 **A Welshman coming late into an inn**
**I' th' morning he took his heels and run away.**
MS. Tanner 465, fol. 95.

543 **A wheel that turneth a wheel that turneth ever**
**Oh Lord keep us in thine eternal favour.**
'Eternity compared to wheel'.
MS. Rawl. D. 1334, fol. 29 rev.

544 **A wholesome drink, and what needs cultivation**
**Denotes the fairest lady in the nation.**
'Rebus of Miss Weyland of Tottenham'; see Y29.
MS. Eng. poet. e. 40, fol. 131.

**A wholesome sentence, safely kept in mind,** 545
**The next words coming put the last words out.**
Robinson, Robert.
MS. *Rawl. poet. 218, p. 34 (autogr.).

**A whore that nightly did through Fleet Street trapes** 546
**H'as a good token left to do it by.**
Walsh, William.
MS. Malone 9, fol. 29v (autogr.).

**A whorish wife, is she a pleasant frow?** 547
**Woe to the husband, woe oh grievous woe.**
Robinson, Robert.
MS. *Rawl. poet. 218, p. 10 (autogr.).

**A wicked old peer** 548
**Will bring in the House of Hanover.**
'Wharton and Burnet', satire, 1715.
MSS. Eng. poet. e. 87, p. 57; Rawl. poet. 155, p. 101; 181, fol. 22; Top. Oxon. b. 170, fol. 6.

**A widow kept a favourite cat** 549
**Here, Towzer! do him justice.**
'The Widow and her Cat. A Fable', on Queen Anne and the Duke of Marlborough, Dec. 1711.
MS. Eng. poet. e. 87, p. 90.

**A widow rich ne much in years** 550
**Your chant may well be pricked.**
'A Roman Catholick story upon what happend at Bristol 1742 in old English'.
MS. Gough Gen. Top. 29, fol. 258.

**A widower who is once become** 551
**Good fortune may him save.**
'Of widdowers'.
Pr. *British Bibliographer*, ii, 1812, p. 611, with original by Sir Thomas More.
MS. Rawl. poet. 108, fol. 17v.

**A wife although most wise and chaste** 552
**Are women small and tender.**
'Three Genders'.
Pr. *Wits Recreations*, 1663, Ep. 29.
MS. Eng. poet. d. 152, fol. 104v.

**A wife domestic, good and pure** 553
**An echo, clock and snail.**
'Three things a good wife should be like; which three things she should not be like'.
MS. Eng. poet. c. 51, p. 288.

**A wife endowed, credit, and friends** 554
**Is speech and Venus due.**
Lines from a moral dialogue in prose.
MS. Rawl. D. 1092, fol. 36v.

555 A wife is like a garment used and torn
Selling at second hand like broker's ware.
'A degree of faemalls'.
MS. Eng. poet. e. 14, fol. 33.

556 A wife or a whore, none can love more
But to deceive me.
MS. Eng. poet. d. 152, fol. 97.

557 A wife who never did [to] her husband [ne'er laid] claim
This wife this mother, still remains a maid.
'A Riddle'.
MSS. Add. B. 105, fol. 102$^{v}$; Eng. misc. b. 48, fol. 104.

558 A wilful man advise you may,
And then cries, had I wist.
Robinson, Robert.
MS. *Rawl. poet. 218, p. 145 (autogr.).

559 A willow garland thou didst send
Come forth and sweetly die.
Herrick, Robert.
Pr. Playford's *Select Musicall Ayres and Dialogues*, 1652, i. 35.
MS. Don. c. 57, fol. 72$^{v}$, music by Henry Lawes.

560 A windmill fair, that all things had to grind,
And fortune seldom, the wisher's turn doth serve.
Whitney, Geoffrey, 'Otium sortem exspectat'.
MS. *Rawl. poet. 56, fol. 12.

561 A wise man laughed to see an ass
That cost so many tears and sighs.
'On the South Sea'.
MS. Rawl. poet. 116, fol. 101.

562 A wise man may a fool beget
A wise and gracious son.
Robinson, Robert.
MS. *Rawl. poet. 218, p. 158 (autogr.).

563 A wise man poor is like a sacred book that's never read
Than of a threadbare saint in wisdom's school.
'A 5. Voc. Geo. Kirbye'.
Not printed.
MSS. Mus. f. 20–24: f. 20, fol. 4.

564 A wise man shuns a knave: because he knows,
To catch a fool wise in his own conceit.
Robinson, Robert.
MS. *Rawl. poet. 218, p. 48 (autogr.).

565 A wolf had stole a harmless lamb
Justice not force does them adorn... (incomplete)
Williams, John, 'An answer to a Challenge'.
MS. *Rawl. poet. 192, fol. 79$^{v}$ (autogr.).

A woman always called her husband dear 566
That she may live and make her dear a buck.
MS. Eng. poet. e. 14, fol. 87 rev.

A woman fair I dare not wed 567
I find some faults among them all.
'A second Charge. From a News-paper'.
MS. Eng. poet. c. 5, fol. 35; see also A265.

A woman is a book, and often found 568
Above all things, to study in the night.
'On Woman'.
Pr. *Wits Recreations*, 1663, Epig. 70.
MS. Eng. poet. 152, fol. 104.

A woman may be fair, yet her mind 569
Yet she's a planet, not a fixed star.
'On the inconstancy of women'.
MS. Rawl. poet. 153, fol. 22.

A woman that in beauty far 570
Continually doth wear.
MS. Gough Norfolk 43, fol. 50$^{v}$.

A woman to define I think no pen 571
But blessed is that man can live without them.
'Invect[ive]'.
MS. Rawl. poet. 117, fol. 23.

A woman's an exquisite creature 572
Her lover grows cruelly kind.
'Song'.
MS. Rawl. poet. 152, fol. 164$^{v}$.

A woman's love is like a [the] Syrian flower 573
That buds and spreads and withers in an hour.
'On women's love'.
Pr. *Wits Recreations*, 1640, Epig. 397.
MSS. CCC. 327, fol. 27; Douce f. 5, fol. 15$^{v}$; Eng. poet. d. 152, fol. 104; e. 14, fol. 84$^{v}$ rev.

A woman's rule should be in such a fashion 574
Obeying husbands, or commanding wives.
MS. Rawl. poet. 209, fol. 44.

A woman's tongue that is as swift as thought, 575
Queans of their tongue are most queans of their tail.
MS. Rawl. poet. 172, fol. 83$^{v}$.

A woman's worse, than ever was the Devil: 576
For man whom God made good, woman made evil.
Couplet.
MS. Rawl. poet. 153, fol. 21$^{v}$.

A wonder once I did behold 577
Tell me, good friend, I thee entreat.
MS. Rawl. poet. 217, fol. 74.

578 A wond'rous fabric in this British nation
Baffles their open force, and secret arts Oft . . . (incomplete).
MS. Eng. misc. e. 183, fol. 76*b*.

579 A wondrous wight I am, of power great
Yet man never saw me by night nor by day.
MS. Rawl. poet. 217, fol. 76ᵛ.

580 A word there is of sacred age
For she in secrets most delights.
Mervall, Alphonso, 'Licoris'. Subscribed 'Coridon'.
MS. *Rawl. poet. 166, p. 47 (autogr.).

581 A word in your ear: these unmerciful times
'Twould be God bless the rhyming, but de'il pay the Mayor.
'The Welshman's Petition to a Mercer then Mayor of Oxford', and 'Answer'.
MS. Eng. poet. d. 47, fol. 34.

582 A word to the wise is too little
Than to monopolize Euxinus.
Gough, Richard, 'Addressed to Edw. Haistwell at Bath. Nov. 15. 1769'.
MS. *Eng. poet. c. 5, fol. 171.

583 A word was said
And now I have told you how.
Pr. *Epitaphs*, 1604 (see Allison and Rogers, no. 293).
Variant of a poem in B.M. Add. MS. 15225, fol. 10. Cf. H. E. Rollins, *Old English Ballads*, 1920, p. 203.
MS. Eng. poet. b. 5, p. 5.

584 A work out-lasting brass, and higher
Crown, crown me (willing Muse) with bays.
F[anshawe], Sir R[ichard], translator, Horace, *Odes* III. XXX.
Pr. *Poems of Horace*, A. Brome etc., 2nd ed., 1671, p. 129.
MS. Rawl. D. 261, p. 17.

585 A workman good I did espy
Where it was placed fine and neat.
MS. Rawl. poet. 217, fol. 74ᵛ.

586 A world of stories find we writ
I take it though the Captain's paid his farewell.
Bulteel, John, 'A country Scuffle'.
MS. *Rawl. poet. 159, fol. 216.

587 A world of wonder 'tis and argument
So many as are natures in their kind.
James, Richard, 'A translation of Lucretius or Ritterhusius in his Notes uppon Isidore Pelusiota', 1605, IV, cxiv, Sig. $\gamma$4.
MS. *James 35, pp. 23, 24, 3 and 4 (autogr.).

A wreathed garland of deserved praise, 588
For this poor wreath, give thee a crown of praise.
Herbert, George, 'A wreath'.
Pr. *The Temple*, 1633, p. 179.
MS. *Tanner 307, fol. 136ᵛ.

A wretch had committed all manner of evil 589
But all yesterday I was drunk with October.
'The Church Builder'.
MS. Montagu e. 13, fol. 103.

A year of wonder to the world was 88 590
But thy anagram with it is direful.
'Georgius Villerus. Regis, Vulgi, Elusor'.
MS. Eng. poet. f. 10, fol. 96ᵛ.

A young cook married was, on Monday last 591
And he grew old ere Tuesday night was past.
'A cuckold', couplet.
Pr. *Modius Salium*, ed. T. Warton (?), 1751, p. 17.
MSS. Ashmole 38, p. 148; CCC. 328, fol. 43; Douce f. 5, fol. 15ᵛ; Malone 19, p. 51; Tanner 466, fol. 66ᵛ; Wood E. 32 (Modius Salium), fol. 12.

A young knight out of England shall ride 592
With great plenty mirth and solace.
Prophecy.
MS. Rawl. C. 813, fol. 157ᵛ.

A young man lazing in his bed 593
While such a lazy man's alive.
Robinson, Robert.
MS. *Rawl. poet. 218, p. 93 (autogr.).

A young man may die, but an old man must 594
His swaddling clouts, nurse, mother, cradle, tomb.
'Youth cannot protect us from the stroke of death'.
MS. Rawl. poet. 90, fol. 44ᵛ.

A young man seldom wise doth prove, 595
When folly hath him smitten.
Robinson, Robert.
MS. *Rawl. poet. 218, p. 18 (autogr.).

A young man wanteth but a wife, 596
That makes him weary of his life.
Robinson, Robert.
MS. *Rawl. poet. 218, p. 64 (autogr.).

A youth adorned with ev'ry art 597
No cries awake the dead.
[Mallet, David], 'A Song In the Masque of Alfred'.
Printed in a revised form in *Alfred: a masque*, 1751, p. 5.
MS. Montagu e. 14, fol. 37.

598 A youth of pregnant parts and wit
Through which the living Homer begged his bread.
'Poetry its Cure'.
MS. Eng. misc. c. 116, fol. 4.

599 A youthful lad, but in his language blunt
Did give to Venus, 'tis a good long —.
MS. Rawl. poet. 153, fol. 29.

600 A zealous [blacksmith] lock-smith died of late
Because he meant to pick the lock.
'Uppon A Smith'.
Pr. Camden's *Remaines*, 1637, p. 408, and *Wits Recreations*, 1640, Epit. 22.
MSS. Ashmole 38, p. 169; CCC. 328, fol. 14; Eng. poet. c. 50, fol. 128v; Rawl. D. 1372, fol. 9v from end; see also T1750, T2034.

601 Aaron thus proposed to Moses
Then whip off this bottle and call for another.
'Mr. Hen. Purcell'.
Pr. *Vinculum Societatis*, ii, 1688. F. B. Zimmerman, *Purcell*, 1963, no. 351.
MS. Mus. Sch. C. 95, p. 133.

602 Abel, why droop'st thou? why stands thou so aloof,
Crying a rope a rope best fits *A Bell*.
'Of Alderman Abell'.
Dated 1640 in B.M. Add. MS. 30982, fol. 117.
MS. Rawl. poet. 209, fol. 27.

603–4 Abel with sacrifice appears
Accepted through his sacrifice.
Kenton, James.
MS. *Eng. poet. e. 20, p. 377 (autogr.).

605 About in masking robes goeth mischief muffled now
And subtle sleights with snakish stings do lodge in smiting brow.
MS. Gough Norfolk 43, fol. 50v.

606 About the sweet bag of a bee
And gave the bag between them.
[Herrick, Robert].
Pr. *Select Musicall Ayres and Dialogues*, 1652, i. 33.
MS. Don. c. 57, fol. 95v, music by H. Lawes.

607*a* About the time that one shall be
The fox shall ride the goose the goose the ass.
'Part of a Prophisy which has been in manuscript in the Ld. Powes family about 60 yrs', *temp.* James II.
Pr. *Poems on Affairs of State*, ii, 1703, p. 213.
MSS. Ballard 1, fol. 70; Douce 357, fol. 116.

[About the time when I shall be] 607*b*
And discord in religion cease.
'A Prophesy, or Merlin's Riddle . . . of 73. Vide Nostre Dame', T351.
In B.M. MS. Burney 390, fol. 10v; *Poems on Affairs of State*, ii, 1703, p. 214.
MS. Don. b. 8, p. 456.

About the time, when Vesper in the west 608
*Stirps rudis urtica est: stirps generosa rosa.*
'The Honour of the Garter. Displaied in a Poeme gratulatory to . . . Sir Robert Karre install'd att Windsore . . . 1611'.
Adapted from George Peele's verses on the installation of the Earl of Northumberland, 1593.
MS. Rawl. B. 30.

About the world Diana's honour ring 609
And all the Britons from his land expelling.
W. A., Horace, *Odes* I. xxi.
MS. *Rawl. poet. 104, fol. 8 (autogr.).

About three hours after the sun gan spring 610
With a great huge cross on his shoulders laid.
'Howers of our Lady Engl. and Lat. ad usum Sarum, the hymne for the third hower of the Crosse'.
MS. Eng. poet. e. 56, p. 9.

Above in Heaven where God reigns, 611
There I will love and never change.
Ashe, Betty.
MS. Rawl. poet. 191, fol. 105v.

Above my head the lonely turtle mourns 612
Lies here; whose name doth only now remain.
Mervall, Alphonso, 'Regreets': 'upon the infidelity of A freind B: E' added later.
MS. *Rawl. poet. 166, p. 16 (autogr.).

Above the earth are many hills conveyed 613
And what was heavenly heaven doth invest.
Beaumont, Thomas, 'Beau-mont/A fayr hill'.
MS. *Malone 18, p. 44 (autogr.).

Above the mighty powers of earth 614
Are all thy heritage.
Psalm lxxxii.
MS. *Rawl. C. 113, fol. 59.

Above the stars my saviour dwells 615
Come Lord Jesu come away.
Pr. in *Musica Deo Sacra*, Tomkins, 1668.
MSS. Mus. Sch. D. 213, fol. 83v and D. 216, fol. 56, music by Thomas Tomkins; Rawl. poet. 23, p. 103, reference to Tomkins's setting.

616 Above the subtle foldings of the sky,
And with fixed eyes drink in immortal rays.
Cowley, Abraham, 'The Throne of God'.
Pr. *Poems and Davideis*, 1656, p. 11.
MS. Tanner 466, fol. 24.

617 Abra'm the second time being called on heard
And in thy seed I will all nations bless.
'Phrophecyes of the old Testament concerning Christ'. Genesis XXII. 15.
MS. *Rawl. C. 113, fol. 1$^{v}$ (autogr.).

618 Abra'm to Canaan called
And make our way to God.
Beddome, Benjamin.
MS. *Eng. misc. e. 227, fol. 58.

619 Absalom hang'd on a tree
And put a spear in his arsie.
Boyd, Zacharie (?).
MS. Eng. poet. e. 48, p. x.

620 Absence and death have but this difference
Since only death can from that torment free.
MS. Malone 13, p. 86.

621 Absence, hear [thou] my protestation
And so enjoy and so miss her.
[Hoskins, John (?)], 'A Poem upon Absence'. See Grierson's *Poems of John Donne*, 1912, i. 428.
MSS. Eng. poet. e. 14, fol. 39$^{v}$, attr. to D. Dun; Eng. poet. f. 9, p. 43.

622 Absence, thou tort'rer of my heart
Maria's sight expels the pain.
'Absence'.
MS. Rawl. poet. 153, fol. 43.

623 Abusive words are like a stormy wind,
Nor hear, nor see, nor do their mischiefs bear.
Williams, John.
MS. *Rawl. poet. 192, fol. 157 (autogr.).

624*a* Accept dear girl these simple lays
A sister and a friend.
Skinner, John, 'To — on her birthday March 17 1798'.
MS. *Eng. poet. d. 22, fol. 47$^{v}$.

624*b* Accept, most noble Promo, don't refuse
At least be pardoned, for one better will.
Elstob, William, 'Verses on Mr. Prickett Butler of University College'. Copied by Hearne 30 Nov. 1705.
Pr. Hearne's *Collections*, ed. C. E. Doble, i, O.H.S. ii, 1885, p. 107.
MS. Hearne's diaries 5, p. 351.

Accept my Elinor! these faithful lines, 625
Sincerely prays your brother and your friend.
Peart, Joshua, 'A Poetic Letter to his Sister Elea: Peart written the 19th of Jan: 1768'.
MS. *Eng. poet. e. 28, p. 158.

Accept my Lord of this poor glittering thing 626
And when the Arch-Duke's King you an Arch Duke shall be.
'The Arch Duke to the Duke of Marlbro' with his picture and a sword', October, 1703.
MS. Smith 23, p. 113; pr. bk. Firth b. 21, fol. 61$^{v}$.

Accept my prayers. Nor to the cries 627
And when I call, with speed reply.
Psalm lxvii, 3-part setting by H. Lawes.
Pr. H. and W. Lawes, *Choice Psalmes*, 1648.
MS. Mus. Sch. E. 451, p. 42.

Accept oh Eglinton, the rural lays 628
T'enjoy that innocence the world has lost.
[Ramsay, Allan], 'An Epistle to the Countess of Eglinton with the gentle Shepherd'.
Pr. 1728.
MS. Add. D. 79, fol. 88 rev.

Accept, sweet maid, a gift, that friendship sends 629
What friendship penned to friendship must be dear.
Jessop, William, 'To Miss Mary Baggs'.
MS. Percy b. 1, fol. 20 (autogr.).

Accept these for my verse, my verse for me, 630
Thy virtue, beauty, grace and courtesy.
Burton, Francis.
MS. *Add. A. 267, fol. 139 (autogr.).

Accept this lay, whilst mid intestine woe, 631
And show what British admirals ought to be.
'To Admiral Townshend, on his destroying the Martinico Fleet', 1762.
MS. Montagu e. 13, fol. 88.

Accept this trifle from an absent friend 632
And smile upon it, for the giver's sake.
Amherst, Elizabeth, 'With a ring to my Friend'.
MS. *Eng. poet. e. 109, p. 30.

633 Accept thou shrine of my dead [dear] saint
Till we shall meet and never part.
King, Henry, 'An Exequy'.
Pr. *Poems*, 1657, p. 52.
MSS. Ashmole 36, 37, fol. 253, attr. to Dr. Harry Kinge; CCC. 328, fol. 93, attr. to Dr. Kinge; Don. d. 58, fol. 1, attr. to Henry Kinge; *Eng. poet. e. 30, fol. 27; e. 37, p. 87, attr. to Dr. H. Kinge; *Malone 22, fol. 17$^{v}$; Rawl. D. 398, fol. 175; Rawl. poet. 26, fol. 149, attr. to Dr. Henry King; 160, fol. 41$^{v}$, attr. to Dr. Kinge.

634 Accepted for Jesus's sake
Nor stray from the fold of thy sheep.
Kenton, James.
MS. *Eng. poet. e. 20, p. 44 (autogr.).

635 Accepted in Jesus's name
Safe sheltered in him I abide.
Kenton, James.
MS. *Eng. poet. e. 20, p. 214 (autogr.).

636 Accepted in the saviour's name
Meet to remove to Paradise.
Kenton, James.
MS. *Eng. poet. e. 20, p. 94 (autogr.).

637 Access, my friend, to honours' fame
And ope the way to love and you.
Temple, R. G.
MS. Don. c. 81, fol. 142 (autogr.).

638 Accomplish now the word
And everlasting rest.
Kenton, James.
MS. *Eng. poet. e. 20, p. 308 (autogr.).

639 Accomplish thy all-gracious words
Pursue my way to heaven.
Kenton, James.
MS. *Eng. poet. e. 20, p. 367 (autogr.).

640 Accursed be those streams from whence did flow
For thou hast taken all his part away.
Guil. de Riv., 'Epitaphium in obitum Mri. [Ralph] Flood. Coll. regii', 1624.
MS. *Rawl. poet. 104, fol. 63$^{v}$ (autogr.).

641 Accursed for ever be the baleful morn
And now the angry fates have crown'd them all.
'The third Chapter of Job attempted in verse'.
MS. Top. London e. 9, p. 17.

642 Accursed the man, whom fate ordains, in spite
And will, though poor without, have peace within.
Churchill, Charles, 'The Author'.
MS. *Eng. poet. d. 113, p. 117.

[Achilles Peleus' son's destructive rage] 643
'Gainst sovereign power, and majesty of kings.
Ogilby, John, translation of the *Iliad*, brief extract.
Pr. 1660 (p. 39).
MS. Sancroft 98, p. 103.

Achilles' tomb, upon Sigeia shore, 644
Their famous acts, do pierce the azure sky.
Whitney, Geoffrey, 'Strenuorum immortale nomen'.
MS. *Rawl. poet. 56, fol. 115$^{v}$.

Achilles was with grief possessed 645
And various thoughts did bustle in his breast.
Lines from Homer quoted in Plutarch's Life of Coriolanus, not North's translation, nor Dryden's.
MS. Rawl. D. 1372, fol. 54$^{v}$ from end.

Achitophel to Absolom adheres 646
Goes home and hangs himself to be at ease.
'Ahithophell'.
MS. Rawl. poet. 154, fol. 107.

Acon and Leonella twins did either want one eye 647
So he shall eyeless Cupid be, and thou the queen of love.
[Translation from Hier. Amaltheus, 'de gemellis'], 'Lumine Acon caret dextro, Leonella sinistro'.
Latin pr. *Trium Fratrum Amaltheorum Carmina*, 1627.
MS. Rawl. poet. 117, fol. 269$^{v}$ rev.

Acquaint thyself most narrowly 648
And so rejoice you here for ever.
'An A.B.C. as followeth'.
MS. Eng. poet. b. 5, p. 28.

Acrisius' daughter a well guarded tower 649
(Blest is the man contented) asketh more.
W. A., Horace, *Odes* III. xvi.
MS. *Rawl. poet. 104, fol. 30 (autogr.).

Actaeon here, as in a glass behold 650
Shall them devour and all their deeds deface.
Whitney, Geoffrey, 'Voluptas ærumnosa'.
MS. *Rawl. poet. 56, fol. 65.

Actaeon's dogs devoured his flesh, bones, skin, 651
But still his horns at London may be seen.
[Owen's Epigram] 'on Actaeon', couplet.
MS. *Rawl. poet. 197, fol. 10 (autogr.).

Actions alike should bear an equal shame 652
Hang but the last the parallel's complete.
'The Paralel', Judas and the first Duke of Marlborough.
MS. Rawl. poet. 155, p. 173.

653 Active and passive duties for man's sake
He's equal God from all eternity.
MS. *Rawl. poet. 97, fol. 74v (autogr.).

654 Adam and Eve being in Paradise
God's love to lineate insufficient be.
MS. *Rawl. poet. 97, fol. 16 (autogr.).

655 Adam by his offence sans comfort left,
Enwrapped them and all their offspring in.
MS. *Rawl. poet. 97, fol. 15 (autogr.).

656 Adam in earth's fair fruit did seek content,
Of sin, when vice is now but made a sport.
MS. *Rawl. poet. 97, fol. 22 (autogr.).

657 Adam that lived so many years ago
No living with them, nor no life without them.
Stone, B[enjamin], of New College, 'On women's tempting'.
MSS. Douce f. 5, fol. 29v, attr. to New Coll. Stone; Eng. poet. c. 50, fol. 36v; Rawl. poet. 212, fol. 154 rev., attr. to B. Stone.

658 Adam, the highest pitch of perfect nature,
To one: when one slew a world of men.
[Quarles, Francis], 'On Miserable Man'. Pr. *Divine Fancies*, 1632, ii. 53.
MS. Rawl. poet. 90, fol. 68.

659 Adam told old Kit today
If her old tricks spoil not his boasting.
'Cupid's delight . . . to the tune of Amaryllis'.
MS. CCC. 318, fol. 199.

660 Adam was made the head; God did proceed
As much as in thee lieth, now defact.
MS. *Rawl. poet. 97, fol. 14v (autogr.).

661 Adam was placed on earth to be a Lord,
First cleanseth, then gives life eternally.
MS. *Rawl. poet. 97, fol. 61v (autogr.).

662 Adam's sin darkness did on earth induce
All people shall be blessed in thy seed.
MS. *Rawl. poet. 97, fol. 38 (autogr.).

663 Addresses of thanks and addresses of praise
Themselves they destroy and all other men wrong.
Williams, John.
MS. *Rawl. poet. 184, fol. 59v (autogr.).

664 Adepts in nature lay this down for truth;
Without one tooth I'd take thee to my arms.
'On Delia's Loss of a Tooth'.
MS. *Eng. poet. d. 47, fol. 102.

665 Adieu, adieu my heartès lust,
Until I die alas alas.
MS. Ashmole 176, fol. 100.

Adieu adieu my only life 666
To watch me in the battle.
'The Soldier's adieu'.
MS. Mus. e. 19, p. 6.

Adieu blest soul! yet take my tears with thee 667
Left here to wail, and which is worse to live.
Radclyffe, E., 'Upon the death of Sir Thomas Bamburghe Barront.', 1624.
MS. Don. d. 58, fol. 7v.

Adieu dear sufferer, 'scap'd from earth and gone 668
And clasp thee in my arms to part no more.
Kenton, James, 'On the Death of Miss Frances Harley, d. Feby. 23 1773 Aged 2 yrs. 6 mths.'.
MS. *Eng. poet. e. 19, p. 228 (autogr.).

Adieu deceitful world, thy pleasures I detest: 669
Now others with thy shows delude, my hope in heaven doth rest.
Whitney, Geoffrey, 'Superest quod supra est'. 'Inlarged' in E145.
MS. *Rawl. poet. 56, fol. 125.

Adieu deluding hope, adieu 670
Shall all but drive me thither.
Melton, Richard, 'Banish'd hope recald'.
MS. Rawl. poet. 65, fol. 97v.

Adieu, departed spirit! 671
His utmost power of love.
Kenton, James, 'On the Death of Mrs. Deborah Harley', wife of Peter John Harley, 1787.
MS. *Eng. poet. e. 19, p. 274 (autogr.).

Adieu fair fickle one adieu 672
I have lost possession.
Weaver, Thomas, 'The fruit of ficklnes'. Not pr. in *Songs and Poems*, 1654.
MS. *Rawl. poet. 211, fol. 62 (autogr.).

Adieu fond love too late I find 673
And resolve ne'er to think of love more.
Pavey, Wm., 'Song'.
MS. Rawl. poet. 116, fol. 109v.

Adieu! fond visions of domestic life! 674
And live to reason and thyself alone!
Parsons, William, 'Palinode . . . Dec. 1792'.
MS. *Don. d. 123, p. 209 (autogr.).

Adieu fond world and all thy gilded charms 675
Without the least regret or cause of fear.
Walsh, Octavia (?).
MS. *Eng. poet. e. 31, fol. 163 rev., in the hand of O. Walsh.

Adieu my pretty pussy 676
Remember me among.
MS. Ashmole 48, fol. 137.

677 Adieu pleasure welcome mourning
Doth not consider my true heart.
MS. Ashmole 176, fol. 99.

678 Adieu sad prospect, of that sacred shrine
Which dost his bones enclose, and shalt do mine.
Pr. bk. Wood 460, after *Threnodia in obitum E. Lewkenor*, 1606.

679 Adieu this is no cheap air
The house to give that soul more room in it.
G[odolphin], S[idney].
MS. Malone 13, p. 91.

680 Adieu thou cold companion of my bed adieu
So none are loosers by it.
Stevens, Thomas, of Bury, 'A Farewell to Virginitie'.
MS. Rawl. poet. 147, p. 91.

681 Adieu to all that's great, or high
And smiling bid the world adieu.
Bromley, Henry, 'The Farewell'.
MS. *Don. e. 19, fol. 17ᵛ (autogr.).

682 Adieu to Hanover, long Parliament's over
And let Shimeis rail as they can.
MS. Rawl. poet. 207, p. 17.

683 Adieu to the village delights
We may meet again never to part.
'Glee—[Joseph] Baildon'.
MS. Mus. d. 177, fol. 47ᵛ.

684 Adieu to winter's cloudy days
In the chaste joys of nuptial love.
Sidney, William, 'To Mr. Flemming . . . occasioned By His Happy Marriage With Mrs. Grey', 1 April 1730.
MS. Rawl. poet. 154, fol. 135 (autogr.).

685 Adieu unhappy fatal cell; and since
To all successors cursed; as to me.
'One writ his bill over his door to let his house'.
MS. Ashmole 38, p. 117.

686 Adieu vain world and all thy wiles
But Heaven, and my own breast alone.
'The World's Adieu'.
MS. Rawl. poet. 90, fol. 146ᵛ.

687 Adieu whate'er seduced my vagrant aim
And fix the wandering Arab to a home!
Parsons, William, 'Sonnet given Miss V—s—t when I thought I was soon to be married to her . . .' Sept. 1792.
MS. *Don. d. 123, p. 208 (autogr.).

688 Adieu? why so? dear Castaminda stay
The way to speed is by this harmless folly.
MS. Don. c. 57, fol. 62ᵛ, with music.

Admire-all weakness, wrongs the right 689
They that cannot see are blind.
'A Libell' on the enemies of the Earl of Essex, dated in B.M. Add. MS. 5956, fol. 23, 20 Dec. 1599.
MSS. Don. c. 54, fol. 7; Eng. hist. c. 272, p. 41; Rawl. poet. 26, fol. 20ᵛ.

Admired lady: your sweet vacant hours 690
Yields such a work no not the Vatican.
Beesley, John, verses to Lady Elizabeth Poulett on her present of an embroidered representation of six scenes from the Life of Christ to Oxford University, 9 July 1636.
MS. Bodl. 22, fol. 8.

Admired of every heart and eye 691
The cause thereof God best doth know.
G. B., Epitaph on Prince Henry, 1612, in 'Cestria Lugens'.
MS. *Rawl. poet. 116, fol. 10.

Admiring readers look on tombs to know 692
How short the time betwixt the grave and them.
On Mary Wooten, 22 Nov. 1744, St. Mary Magdalene Church, Oxford.
MS. Top. Oxon. c. 299, fol. 266ᵛ.

Admit I pray, my daughter here to be 693
Will, while he breathes this air, be always your devoted servant.
Briggs, Samson, 'The Dedication' of 'Danäe' to Mrs. A. Darill.
MSS. Rawl. poet. 116, fol. 71ᵛ rev.; 147, p. 253 rev., attr. to S. Briggs.

Adonis' death Venus could but lament 694
And pearly crystal dew does fade away.
Marshall, Stephen, Verses 'fixed to [the] Herse cloth' of John Freind, d. 1672.
MS. Top. Oxon. f. 31, p. 283.

Adore no other Gods but only me 695
Court not, what may others damnify.
Endorsed 'Copies for Schollers to Write'.
MS. Rawl. poet. 152, fol. 232.

Adored ghost or what doth yet remain 696
Must still add tears to thy blest memory.
'On the death of Sr. Henry Savill', 19 Feb. 1622.
MS. Ashmole 47, fol. 30.

Adorned with princely choice again, the year 697
Honour deserves. No meaner stream to' have bred . . . (incomplete).
I. H., translator, 'Claudian his Panegyrick upon the ffourth Consulshipp of Honorius, 1665'.
MS. Rawl. poet. 154, fol. 49*b*.

698 Adorned with sweetness, courtesy, and wit
Your bloom are these 'tis that completes the belle.
Williams, John, 'An Anagram to Miss Anne Gooddy youngest daughter to — Gooddy Esq. of Hatton Garden made upon St. Stephen's Day anno 1710 being the day when we were contracted'.
MS. *Rawl. poet. 192, fol. 31v (autogr.).

699 Advance my soul, unto that heavenly pitch,
Therefore sweet saviour, heal me with thy blood.
Spour, Edmund, 'Three Petitionary Penitentiall Anthems, I'.
MS. *Eng. poet. c. 52, fol. 40v (autogr.).

700 Advance thou Jove to entertain thy guests
His grout-head being overset hangs down.
Cratinus: verses on Pericles in *Nemesis*; and Teleclides on the same, quoted in Plutarch's Life of Pericles. Not North's translation nor 'Dryden's'.
MS. Rawl. D. 1372, fol. 43v from end.

701 Advance thy voice in mournful moans
Is now the Church, and laymen's books.
Lilliat, John, 'Against cold devotion'.
MS. Rawl. poet. 148, fol. 76 (autogr.).

702 Advance ye British fair, a wonder see
See there! they cry, see there! a beast! a beast!
Riddle.
MS. Ballard 29, fol. 146v.

703 Advise a young fool all you can,
This evil I had missed.
Robinson, Robert.
MS. *Rawl. poet. 218, p. 154 (autogr.).

704 Advise with gentleness and rather show
Only by chance is safe from doing ill.
Williams, John.
MS. *Rawl. poet. 191, fol. 102 (autogr.).

705 A'e day a bonny lass and braw
Your loaf is bread enough for that.
Ramsay, Allan, 'The hand Preferd to the Hat. An Epigram'.
MS. Eng. poet. e. 8, fol. 21.

706 Aeneas bears his father out of Troy,
Who oft despise the stock whereof they came.
Whitney, Geoffrey, 'Pietas filiorum in parentes'.
MS. *Rawl. poet. 56, fol. 102.

707 Affected wisdom has a woman made
Though marble is the thing that's next her heart.
'Countess of Pomfret' (d. 1761).
MS. Eng. poet. e. 28, p. 31.

Affecting Venus gives me strait command 708
That unto Venus sacrifice I may.
W. A., Horace, *Odes* I. xix.
MS. *Rawl. poet. 104, fol. 7v.

Affection set not upon things that fade, 709
The safest in short time may see a dreadful change.
Williams, John, 'The 3ds [i.e. 3rd words] are I wait for You'.
MS. *Rawl. poet. 184, fol. 52 (autogr.).

Afflicted widows and the fatherless 710
The port whereto they others guide themselves have missed.
MS. Ashmole 383, fol. 10.

Afflictions sore, long they bore 711
And ease them of their pain.
On Henrietta Maria and William Hitchcock, d. 1789, 1791, St. Peter-in-the-East, Oxford.
MS. Top. Oxon. c. 299, fol. 103.

Afflictions to the heaven-born soul 712–13
Thy will not mine be done.
Beddome, Benjamin.
MS. *Eng. misc. e. 227, fol. 80v.

After a prayer to the muse 714
Ye'll be advertised by the next.
Colvill, S[amuel], 'Mock Poem or Whiggs Supplication'.
Part first, pr. 1681.
MS. Eng. poet. e. 48; see also A722.

After a pretty amorous discourse, 715
You'd been more happy had you been less fair.
Etherege, Sir George, 'The imperfect Enjoyment'.
Translated from Charles Beys, 'Le Iovissance Imparfaite'; cf. *P.Q.*, xlii, 1963, p. 190.
MSS. Rawl. D. 1171, fol. 40, attr. to Sir George Etherege; Rawl. poet. 173, fol. 97, attr. to Sir Geo. Etherege.

After a tedious conflict had within me 716
I shall beware to trust a young man's love.
Burton, Francis.
MS. *Add. A. 267, fol. 32 (autogr.).

After Christ's baptism in the desert he 717
God's blessing only prospers all, may see.
MS. *Rawl. poet. 97, fol. 50v (autogr.).

After death nothing is, and nothing death 718
Dreams, whimsies, and no more.
[Wilmot, John, Earl of Rochester], 'Seneca's Troas. Act 2, Chorus'.
See Vieth, p. 397.
MS. Don. b. 8, p. 498.

719 **After fourteen days thinking of Whig and of Tory**
**The fools might be Whigs, none but knaves should be Tories.**
'My opinion', on George I, George, Prince of Wales, and Ernest Augustus, Duke of York.
MS. Rawl. poet. 152, fol. 186; see also A734.

720 **After great pains and many matters fell**
**I have risen clarified without spot or wrinkle.**
Translation from Dutch in *Rosarium Philosophorum*, 1550.
MS. Ashmole 1459, p. 465.

721 **After his resurrection forty days**
**Then first he made him; hence appears most plain.**
MS. *Rawl. poet. 97, fol. $67^{v}$ (autogr.).

722 **After invoking of the muse**
**Ye'll be advertised by the next.**
C[olvill], S[amuel], 'Mock Poem . . . Part First'.
Pr. 1681.
MS. Eng. poet. e. 41, p. 1; see also A714.

723 **After like manner as first Adam fell**
**In His great acts is God omnipotent!**
MS. *Rawl. poet. 97, fol. $38^{v}$ (autogr.).

724 **After long dangerous travail wearied I**
**Where equal lustre with the stars I get.**
Strode, William, translation of Latin verse on Sir Edwin Sandy's death, 1629.
MS. *CCC. 325, fol. 108 (autogr.).

725 **After long penance of a nine year Lent**
**For we'll no longer drudge to be your cuckold makers.**
Smith, [Thomas (?)], University College, Oxford, 'The Musick-Speech . . . July 8 1693'.
See Wood's *Life and Times*, iii, ed. A. Clarke, O.H.S. xxvi, 1894, p. 427.
MSS. Eng. poet. f. 13, fol. $61^{v}$, attr. to Smith of University College; Top. Oxon. c. 326, two copies, fols. 52 and 54; e. 280, p. 672 rev., attr. to Smith of University College.

726 **After man had broken the precepts of the Lord**
**And alway to remember our gracious new year's gift.**
'A carol for new year's day'.
MS. Ashmole 48, fol. 3.

727 **After midnight when dreams doth fall**
**Be said to me arise I say.**
MS. Ashmole 48, fol. $21^{v}$.

**After pangs and after cares** 728
**I'll be satisfied with this.**
Walsh, William.
MS. Malone 9, fol. 63 (autogr.).

**After so many concurring [complying] petitions** 729
**Already you have had too much of his prose.**
[Denham, Sir John], 'The Humble Petition of the Poets to the 5 Members'. Satire after the Kentish Petition, March 1642.
Pr. *Rump Songs*, 1662, Sig. $C3^{v}$, and Denham's *Poems*, 1668, p. 101.
MSS. Ashmole 36, 37, fol. 97; Rawl. D. 398, fol. 233; Rawl. poet. 62, fol. 51.

**After so many sad mishaps,** 730
**Full fair and soft, he made her arse lie.**
Denham, Sir John, 'To Sir W. Davenant', on *Gondibert*.
Pr. *Certain Verses . . . to be reprinted with . . . Gondibert*, 1653, p. 5.
MSS. CCC. 309, fol. $50^{v}$; Rawl. poet. 152, fol. 203; Sancroft 53, p. 33, attr. to Sr. John Denham.

**After that sort of academic wit** 731
**Like mighty muses there inspiring it.**
'To the Country Ladies', verse from prevaricator speech at Cambridge, probably 1680; cf. A820.
MS. Rawl. D. 1026, fols. 8 and $7^{v}$ (autogr.).

**After the duty of a verse** 732*a*
**If you be pleased I have my pay.**
Cavendish, Lady Jane, dedication of a pastoral to the Earl of Newcastle.
MS. *Rawl. poet. 16, p. 49.

**[After the feast (my Shapcot)] see** 732*b*
**He'll do no doubt this yarn is spun.**
Herrick, Robert, 'King Oberon's Pallace'.
MSS. Ashmole 38, two copies, p. 101; Firth e. 4, p. 52, attr. to Mr. Hearick; Rawl. poet. 160, fol. 167, attr. to R. Herick.

**After the soul with swelling sails of light** 733
**What's then to love, that love, all love did frame.**
F. W., 'Sonnet. 50'.
MS. *Rawl. C. 639, p. 228.

**After thinking a [this] fortnight of Whig and of Tory** 734
**The fools should be Whigs, none but knaves should be Tories.**
'My Opinion: Or the nine pins'.
Pr. Buckingham's *Works*, 1705, ii. 14, headed 'The . . . E. of D-rs-t's Opinion'.
MSS. Douce 357, fol. $116^{v}$; Firth c. 16, p. 29, attr. to Dk. B.; see also A719.

735 After two sittings, now our lady state
Give us this court, and rule without a guard.
Marvell, Andrew, 'The last Instructions to a Painter. London September 4th 1667'.
M. T. Osborne, *Advice-to-a-Painter Poems*, 1949, no. 14.
MS. *Eng. poet. d. 49, p. 193.

736 Again imperial winter's sway
Let our great cement be the public good.
[Whitehead, William], New Year Ode, 1777. Music by Boyce.
Pr. *Poems*, 1790, ii. 125.
MS. Mus. Sch. D. 336.

737 Again man's forming had not profited
But next Christ's blood a better life doth give.
MS. *Rawl. poet. 97, fol. 17 (autogr.).

738 Again returns the circling year
Thrones, independence, laws and liberty.
[Whitehead, William], New Year Ode, 1771. Music by Boyce.
Pr. *Poems*, 1790, ii. 103.
MS. Mus. Sch. D. 325.

739 Again returns the genial day
Say 'twas an honest man.
Skinner, John, 'Verses written in Holland on the Birthday of a Friend Feb. 14. 1789'.
MS. *Eng. poet. d. 22, fol. 21.

740 Again the blushful May returns
But sorrow's solitary sigh.
Wolcot, John (Peter Pindar), 'Sonnet'.
MS. Montagu d. 3, fol. 73 (autogr.).

741 Again the sun's revolving sphere
And man enjoy the birthright of his kind.
[Whitehead, William], New Year Ode, 1760. Music by Boyce.
Pr. *Poems*, 1774, ii. 270.
MS. Mus. Sch. D. 307.

742 Against Great Britain, and her royal line
The churchyard Semlin's Plain, and Temeswar their tomb.
[Roach, Richard], 'On Prince Eugene's Beating the Turks, as the Last Hope and Refuge of the Tories'. August 1716, August 1717.
MS. Rawl. D. 832, fol. 167 (autogr.).

743 Against us in vain
Under our feet.
Kenton, James.
MS. *Eng. poet. e. 20, p. 260 (autogr.).

Age, age will break us: death will give's a fall: 744
Rich poor, high low; stern death will down with all.
Robinson, Robert, couplet.
MS. *Rawl. poet. 218, p. 162 (autogr.).

Age and death slew Grandy Day; 745
His feet lie close at Grandy's head.
'Grandy Day, Eddy Reed. All Saints Church Newcastle'.
MS. Top. gen. e. 32, fol. 59$^{v}$.

Age is deformed, youth's unkind: 746
We scorn their bodies, they our mind.
'Senectus iuventus'.
Pr. *Wits Recreations*, 1641, no. 159.
MSS. Ashmole 36, 37, fol. 142.

Agree'd we change, the male [I'm grown] 747
To Lady Jemmy dwindles.
'The double Metamorphosis', 4 Jun 175[3].
Pr. *The Oxfordshire Contest*, 1753, p. 52.
MS. Mus. e. 20, fol. 25*c*.

Ah, Anna; thy new friends and prick-eared court 748
Lest thy white neck be made to bleed.
'On the New Promotions made by the Queen', 1705.
MS. Rawl. D. 383, fol. 89$^{v}$.

Ah! beauteous maid, to pluck my stem, forbear 749
But lo! a wondering universe is thine.
Wolcot, John, (Peter Pindar), 'The Rose's Petition'.
MS. Montagu d. 3, fol. 84 (autogr.).

Ah Calista did you know 750
And light you in, or light me out.
'Plain Dealing to Calista'.
MS. Don. c. 55, fol. 6$^{v}$.

Ah, Cambridge! famous for unlucky hits! 751
A recantation makes all whole again.
'Hermaphroditus or Good Friday falling upon a Wednesday as it is in the Cambridg Almanack Printed for the Year 1687'.
MS. Don. e. 23, fol. 61$^{v}$.

Ah, cannot sighs, nor tears, nor ought else move thee? 752
Was never grief like mine, nor death more painful.
Madrigal.
Pr. Wilbye's *Second Set*, 1609, no. xxx.
MSS. Mus. Sch. D. 233–6; D. 236, fol. 103$^{v}$ rev.

Ah Celia while with studious care 753
Since its beauties ever last.
'To Caelia'.
MS. Eng. poet. c. 9, p. 233.

754 Ah Celia! would the powers above
For fear I stay and see it die.
'The Departure to Celia'.
MS. Rawl. poet. 87, p. 43.

755 Ah Chloris would the gods allow
Its vertues lost, and cures no more.
'Of Love's Inconstancy'.
MSS. Rawl. poet. 65, fol. 31; 90, fol. 133.

756 Ah cruel bloody fate
There needs no second blow.
[Lee, Nathaniel], song in *Theodosius*, act v; pr. 1680.
MS. Rawl. poet. 196, fol. 16.

757*a* Ah cruel death my being to destroy
Or you will make a ghost with every bill.
'A letter from Holmes's Ghost to the Dr.', Cary Butt, Lichfield.
MS. Top. Staffs. c. 1, fol. 76ᵛ.

757*b* Ah, cruel death! that hast bereaved me
As oldest soldier to bring up the rear.
Corbet, W., 'On the Death of my Brother and Sister'.
MS. *Rawl. poet. 210, fol. 24ᵛ.

758*a* Ah cruel death! thou dost no good
What shall we do for faggots?
'On John Underwood', in Bideford Churchyard.
MS. Eng. poet. c. 51, p. 45.

758*b* Ah cruel death to make three meals of one
He'll find his feet to stand when thou dost fall.
'Epitaph in Banbury Church Yard'.
MS. Hearne's diaries 98, p. 26.

759 Ah cruel death! What could more cruel be?
Death shall not kill me; here's the fatal wound!
Morrice, John, 'An Elegy, upon the Death of a young Lady', 16 Jan. 1707.
MS. *Rawl. poet. 114, fol. 172 (autogr.).

760 Ah Damon dear shepherd adieu
Ah Damon dear shepherd farewell.
Elegy on Frederick, Prince of Wales, 1751.
MS. Eng. poet. d. 10, fol. 39.

761 Ah! Damon how unhappy is old age
And wish you both eternally content.
Williams, John, 'A Dialogue between an old Maid and a Young man she was in Love with'.
MS. *Rawl. poet. 188, fol. 65 (autogr.).

762 Ah dear heart, why do you rise
And perish in their infancy.
Pr. Orlando Gibbons' *First Set of Madrigals*, 1612, xv; cf. L353.
MSS. Mus. f. 20, 23–24: f. 20, fol. 56ᵛ; see also S1149.

Ah! dearest Jocky, woot you now leave me 763
And Jockey with my charms.
MS. Mus. Sch. C. 95, p. 65.

Ah! Delia see the fatal hour! 764
Wilt ever think on me?
'Translated from the Italian by Miss [Elizabeth] Carter'.
Pr. *Poems*, 1762, p. 51.
MS. Montagu e. 14, fol. 24ᵛ.

Ah fading joy [joys] how quickly art thou [are you] past! 765
To gentle slumbers call.
Head, Thomas, 'A Song'.
MSS. Rawl. poet. 65, fol. 38ᵛ; 214, fol. 84ᵛ rev., attr. to Tho. Head.

Ah few and full of sorrows are the days 766
And answer at thy call.
[Sandys, George], *A Paraphrase of the Divine Poems*, 1638, Job, xiv. i, p. 19. Music by H. Purcell. Cf. *Purcell*, F. B. Zimmerman, 1963, no. 130 (1).
MS. Mus. c. 28, fol. 115ᵛ.

Ah friend, if love had booted, care, or cost, 767
Heaven had not won, nor earth so timely lost.
Couplet.
MS. Sancroft 59, p. 296 rev.

Ah, friend, the posting years how fast they fly: 768
Shall flow, and make the drunken pavement shine.
Potenger, John, 'On Death', Horace, *Odes* II. xiv.
Pr. J. Nichols's *Select Collection of Poems*, i, 1780, p. 213.
MSS. *Eng. poet. d. 161, p. 99; Rawl. poet. 90, fol. 177ᵛ.

Ah gentle friends, forbear to tire my ears 769
Which grov'ling in the mud your glories show.
Walsh, Octavia.
MS. *Eng. poet. e. 31, fol. 24ᵛ (autogr.).

Ah gentle wind if e'er thou didst suspire 770
Or slake the hot flames of my old desire.
MS. Eng. poet. c. 50, fol. 83.

Ah great shepherd for that thou art dead 771
Missing a full dear foster-father for their souls.
'In obitum literatissimi sanctissimique viri magistri Gulielmi Perkins', d. 1602.
MS. Ashmole 781, p. 163.

Ah had she not been fair, and so unkind 772
My muse had slept, and none had known my mind.
Daniel, Samuel, Delia, vi, ll. 13–14.]
MS. Rawl. poet. 116, fol. 53ᵛ.

773 **Ah happy grove, dark and secure retreat,**
**They speak their passion in repeated vows.**
[Roscomman, Wentworth Dillon, Earl of] 'Part of the fifth scene of Guarini's Pastor Fido Act the 2d.'
Pr. *Works of . . . Rochester and Roscommon*, 1709, Roscommon, p. 33.
MS. Eng. poet. e. 47, p. 71.

774 **Ah helpless wretch what shall I do**
**And grant me rest amongst thy saints.**
'A sinners complaint'.
MSS. Mus. f. 11–15: f. 11, fol. 51$^{v}$, set by Ravenscroft; Rawl. poet. 23, p. 126, reference to setting by W. Mundye.

775 **Ah! hills beloved! where once a happy child**
**There's no oblivion but in death alone!**
Smith, Charlotte, 'Sonnett. To the South Downs'.
MS. Montagu e. 14, fol. 26.

776 **Ah, how dull it is to love,**
**Rather die, than conquered be.**
'The Maid['s] Precaution. A Song'.
MS. Rawl. poet. 173, fol. 87.

777 **Ah! how her picture charms the eager sight**
**When from his glorious bed the mounting sun comes on.**
Hammond, Antony, 'Occasion'd by looking on Clarinda's Picture'.
Pr. *Miscellany of Original Poems*, 1720, p. 106.
MS. Rawl. D. 360, fol. 78 (autogr.).

778 **Ah how lovely sweet and dear**
**Be blest my love be mine to day.**
[Motteux, Peter], song from 'The Mad Lover'.
Pr. *Mercurius Musicus*, 1700.
Ms. Mus. Sch. E. 397, p. 87 rev.

779 **Ah how sweet are the cooling breeze**
**When into his bower Love guides Musidora.**
Durfey, Thomas, 'An Ode on Musidora walking in Spring Garden. Tune by Mr. Croft'.
MS. Mus. Sch. C. 95, p. 68.

780 **Ah idle fear! Ah foolish man!**
**Who keeps his servant day by day.**
Kenton, James.
MS. *Eng. poet. e. 20, p. 217 (autogr.).

781 **Ah is it then great Henry so fam'd**
**To crown his tomb or else him homage do.**
Fairfax, Thomas, Lord (translator), 'The teares of France for the deplorable death of Henry 4 surnamed the Great', from Anne de Rohan's Elegy, pr. in part in Agrippa d'Aubigné's *Histoire Universelle*. See *Connecticut Academy of Arts and Sciences*: *Transactions*, xiv. 246.
MS. *Fairfax 40, p. 641 (autogr.).

**Ah lead me Genius to the roar** 782
**Or lightnings blast can ne'er devour.**
Jackson, —, 'Invocation'.
MS. Eng. misc. e. 241, fol. 61.

**Ah let the cloud be quickly drawn aside** 783
**Must droop, sleep, weep, and mourn till you come by.**
H. S.
MS. *Rawl. poet. 120, fol. 18 (autogr.).

**Ah! let the melancholy muse attend.** 784
**For all the living suffer in the dead.**
'Epitaph on the Rev. Mr. A—, Rector of B—, in the county of G— lately deceased, &c. G[entleman's] Mag.'
MS. Eng. poet. e. 39, p. 66.

**Ah lovely Amoret the care** 785
**And haste to catch the flying game.**
Waller, Edmund, 'A La Malade'.
Pr. *Poems*, 1645, p. 78.
MSS. *Don. d. 55, fol. 23$^{v}$; Eng. poet. c. 50, fol. 123; *Rawl. poet. 174, p. 45.

**Ah lovely Lichfield! that so long hast shone** 786
**And heedless of herself, for others live.**
Seward, Anna, 'The Anniversary', 1769.
MS. *Pigott d. 12, fol. 3 (autogr.).

**Ah lovely sweet snatch'd from the earth away** 787
**And fall at last into the arms divine.**
Kenton, James, 'On the Death of Miss Deborah Harley', d. 25 Aug. 1756.
MS. *Eng. poet. e. 19, p. 136 (autogr.).

**Ah! lovely youth! than Adonis more fair;** 788
**Since thou art gone to fill the heavenly choir.**
Morrice, John, 'An Epitaph upon a Quirister, a fair Youth'.
MS. *Rawl. poet. 114, fol. 176 (autogr.).

**Ah me! I have a wife my heart will break** 789
**Then since you are reveng'd your heart pray never break.**
[Owen's] 'Epigram 38 Husband & Cuckold-maker'.
MS. *Rawl. poet. 197, fol. 9 (autogr.).

**Ah me! where shall I wander to** 790
**Makes but a penitent loses her lover.**
Goldsmith, [Oliver,] 'To the tune of Langolee'.
A different version pr. *London Magazine*, xliii, 1774, p. 295.
MS. Eng. misc. e. 241, fol. 3$^{v}$.

791 **Ah mighty prince! By too great birth betray'd**
**The crown of conquest, and the crown of wit.**
Turner, John, of Christ's College, Cambridge, 'On the Election of the Duke of Monmouth to be Chancellor of the University of Cambridge', 1674.
MSS. Don. b. 8, p. 506; Rawl. poet. 19, fol. 68, attr. to Mr. Turner of Christ's Coll.

792 **Ah modest shentle, when her see**
**Py Griffin ap Shones, ap Morgan, ap Rice, ap Vaughan, ap Powell.**
'A Loving Welshman to his Mrs.'
MSS. Ashmole 38, p. 147, with a postscript; Rawl. poet. 153, fol. 12ᵛ.

793 **Ah my dear angry Lord:**
**I will lament, and love.**
Herbert, George, 'Bitter Sweet'.
Pr. *The Temple*, 1633, p. 165.
MSS. Rawl. poet. 90, fol. 138; 213, fol. 57ᵛ, attr. to Herbert; *Tanner 307, fol. 126.

794 **Ah! my dear Celia did you know**
**'Twill never punish what it does approve.**
Chatwin, John, 'To Celia'.
MS. *Rawl. poet. 94, p. 210 (autogr.).

795 **Ah my heart ah this is my song**
**Ah my heart ah.**
MS. Ashmole 176, fol. 99ᵛ.

796 **Ah my too dear Myrtillo how severe**
**You'd be so kind to close her dying eyes.**
MS. Montagu e. 13, fol. 147.

797 **Ah, never more shall these sad eyes**
**Its shade best suits my mourn.**
M[iddleton], L[ady] E[lizabeth]. Music (autograph) by W. Davis.
MS. Mus. c. 16, fol. 118ᵛ.

798 **Ah! no 'tis all in vain, believe me, 'tis,**
**Themselves outdone in luxury.**
Congreve, William, 'Horace, Lib: II Ode 14 Imitated'.
Pr. Gildon's *Miscellany*, 1692, p. 12.
MSS. Add. B. 105, fol. 23, attr. to Mr. Congreve; Rawl. D. 1095, fol. 124; Rawl. poet. 173, fol. 30, attr. to Mr. Congreve.

799 **Ah! once I thought my Kitty,**
**With hearts more hard than Kitty's.**
Skinner, John, from Molière's *Bourgeois Gentilhomme*, '1792'.
MS. *Eng. poet. d. 22, fol. 30 (autogr.).

**Ah! parent excellent adieu** 800
**By grace eternally is thine.**
Kenton, James, 'Epitaph . . . for Mrs. Anne Holloway . . . 1776'.
MS. *Eng. poet. e. 19, p. 256 (autogr.).

**Ah poor Dorante! now thy fortune's crossed** 801
**But to the wedding I must haste away.**
'Epilogue to be spoken by Dorante at acting part of [Susan Centlivre's play] the Gamester'.
MS. *Rawl. poet. 197, fol. 11 (autogr.).

**Ah poor Olinda never boast** 802
**He like a God is every where.**
'The Answer' to F375.
MS. Rawl. poet. 196, fol. 12.

**Ah Posthumus our years hence fly** 803
**Far more than night bewearied.**
[Herrick, Robert], 'His ould age to Mr. Weeks'.
Pr. *Hesperides*, 1648.
MSS. Eng. poet. c. 50, fol. 89; Firth e. 4, p. 7.

**Ah, Posthumus, the years of man** 804
**Which makes our bishops fat.**
Fanshawe, Sir Richard (translator), 'To Posthumus', Horace, *Odes* II. xiv.
MS. *Firth c. 1, p. 48.

**Ah! Rawleigh, when thou didst thy breath resign** 805
**No poisonous tyrants on thy earth shall live.**
[Marvell, Andrew (?)], 'A Dialogue. Brittannia and Rawleigh', 1676.
Pr. *Poems on Affairs of State*, 1689, p. 7; see also *Poems of Marvell*, ed. Margoliouth, 1952, i. 305.
MSS. Don b. 8, p. 535; Douce 357, fol. 113ᵛ; *Eng. poet. d. 49, p. 277, attr. to Mr. [John] Aylof; Rawl. D. 924, fol. 312ᵛ; Rawl. poet. 19, fol. 64; 159, fol. 102, attr. to Marvel.

**Ah Robin, dear Robin, adieu!** 806
**Ah Robin, dear Robin, adieu!**
C[hapman], E[lizabeth], 'On the death of a Favourite Robin'. June 1793.
MS. Montagu e. 14, fol. 8 (autogr.).

**Ah! sad effects of ignorance and pride** 807
**When with old Niobe turn all to stone!**
Cromwell, Edward, 'Anniversary Wedding Day Sept. 29. 1[71]6'.
MS. *Rawl. poet. 165, fol. 40 (autogr.).

**A[h] senseless heart, to take no rest,** 808
**Thrust out, ill-used by all, but by none slain.**
'Upon the parting with the heart again'.
MS. Rawl. poet. 90, fol. 122.

809 Ah silly bashful tim'rous swain
And make the poor soul stark mad.
'The Encouragement', music by J. E. Galliard.
MS. Mus. c. 107, fol. 8.

810 Ah silly John surpriz'd with joy
Joan whiter than the lily.
MS. Eng. poet. f. 9, p. 50; see also A439.

811 Ah silly soul [how are thy thoughts confounded]
[Whilst looking through false love thine eyes are blind].
Pr. Byrd's *Psalms Songs & Sonnets*, 1611.
MSS. Mus. f. 20–24: f. 20, fol. 23.

812 Ah silly wretch, how trim a man art thou
At those young years for to be married now.
'The Poet saith of Philoctetes'.
Pr. North's *Plutarch*, 1603, Life of Solon, p. 92.
MS. Rawl. D. 1372, fol. 26$^{v}$ from end.

813 Ah sinners they are very fools
They leave the party dead.
Creswell, Robert, 'No merry song, But a song of good Life. To the Tune of Nemo Laeditur nisi a seipso'.
MS. *Eng. poet. f. 24, fol. 17 (autogr.).

814 Ah, Son of David help: What sinful cry
Thy soul shall neither languish, bleed, nor die.
[Quarles, Francis], 'A Dialogue betwixt Jesus and a Sin-sick Soule'.
Pr. *Emblemes*, 1635, III. iii.
MS. Rawl. poet. 90, fol. 99.

815 Ah Sylvia 'tis a cruel law
And in my veins infused the charms.
MS. Montagu e. 13, fol. 142.

816 Ah that well tuned breath is dead, my lord.
Oh! ever spare our well tuned chorister.
T. B. [Bonham, Thomas (?)], 'Upon a Nightingale ravish'd & devour'd by a Catt'.
MS. Rawl. poet. 147, p. 127; see also A818.

817 Ah the sighs that come from my heart
Farewell my joy for evermore.
3-part song by W. Cornysshe, transcribed from B.M. Add. MS. 31922.
MSS. Mus. d. 183, fol. 5; d. 184, fol. 8.

818 Ah the well tuned breath is dead my Lord
Unbedded it betimes, and took no nod . . . (incomplete)
'Upon a Nightingale devourd by a Catt'.
MS. Firth d. 7, fol. 191; see also A816.

819 Ah! 'tis more fading than the peach's bloom
For as it's rising, so it's setting's sure!
Maitland, Penelope, 'On Beauty'.
MS. Eng. poet. c. 51, p. 180*b*.

Ah! to what sorrows am I led 820
I rest thine, lamentable Obadiah.
Lines supposed to have been written by the Junior Proctor at Cambridge, 'quoted' in prevaricator speech (probably 1680, when Obadiah Collinson of Queens' College was Junior Proctor); cf. A731.
MS. Rawl. D. 1026, fol. 6 (autogr.).

Ah! what advice can I receive? 821
Of cutting through a flame.
Cowley, Abraham, 'Counsell'.
Pr. *Works*, 1668, 'The Mistress', p. 68.
MS. Rawl. poet. 173, fol. 80$^{v}$.

Ah! what avails it to become the slave 822
To know that fortune favours but the brave.
'A Halloween Contemplation'.
MS. Montagu c. 5, fol. 44.

Ah; where with every soothing charm arrayed 823
And taste true bliss, amidst the realms of day.
'Ode to Felicity'.
MS. Eng. poet. e. 47, p. 103.

Ah! wherefore grieve! can evil men 824
I saw, and heav'd a sigh.
Skinner, John, Psalm xxxvii.
MS. *Eng. poet. d. 22, fol. 144.

Ah wherefore, tyrant passion with thy rage 825
And lov'd Eliza's bliss be all my grateful care!
'Scriblerus', 'Sonnet . . . 4 June 1789'.
MS. Montagu e. 14, fol. 49$^{v}$.

Ah whither whither would Achilles flee 826*a*
For with Achilles Deidamia dies.
'Deidamia's Parting with Achilles', music by W. Boyce.
MS. Mus. c. 3, fol. 70.

[Ah who can tell how hard it is to climb] 826*b*
Bright through th'eternal year of love's triumphant reign.
Beattie, James, 'The Minstrel', I. xxiii-xxvii.
MS. Montagu e. 14, fol. 27.

Ah who is she, whose pensive face 827
To dwell with her in bliss for ever.
'My Mother'.
MS. Percy d. 9, fol. 56$^{v}$.

Ah why around the social blaze 828
Kneels at the throne of love.
R. L., 'Ode. 1780'.
MS. *Eng. poet. e. 16, fol. 25.

Ah! why didst thou desire of me, 829
Then I can leave thee; only thee I love.
MS. Montagu e. 13, fol. 139$^{v}$.

830 Ah why should love still seek to bind
Round gentlest hearts to last forever.
Translation from 'Il Pastor fido'.
MS. Eng. misc. e. 241, fol. 19.

831 Ah wondrous prince! who a true friend couldst be,
There have been fewer friends on earth than kings.
'On Jonathan'.
MS. Rawl. poet. 213, fol. 4v.

832 Ah! would my Mira from the muse
When you gave me but one.
[Bacon, Phanuel], 'To [Mira], upon her desiring the Author to make a Song upon Three Feathers and a Broomstick'.
MS. Eng. poet. e. 45, fol. 43 (autogr.).

833 Ah wretch in thy Corinna's love unblest
His and her breast or his and hers a-cold.
[Randolph, Thomas], 'In Coridonem et Corinnam . . . Paraphrased'.
Pr. *Poems*, 1638.
MS. Eng. poet. c. 50, fol. 104v.

834 Ah wretched Israel! once a bless'd, and happy state,
For every life a myriad, every drop a flood.
Oldham, John, 'David's Lamentation for . . . Saul and Jonathan, 1692'.
MS. Rawl. poet. 12, fol. 61.

835 Ah! wretched world! how hard the task, to plant
And lose my sorrows in the clay cold grave!
Walker, W.
MSS. Don. c. 81, fol. 1; d. 123, p. 54.

836 Aid, Clio, aid, assist my infant quill,
Assaults, march forth the least may conquer so.
Dyve, Lewis, of King's School, Sherborne, on Robert Whetcombe, 'Antientest Governour of the King's Schoole of Sherebourne', d. 24 Oct. 1656.
MS. Gough Dorset 35 (1), fol. 22.

837 Aid me Bellona while the dreadful fight
Much blood the monsters lost, and they their arms.
[Waller, Edmund], 'The Battaile of the Summer Islands'.
Pr. *Poems*, 1645, p. 95.
MS. *Don. d. 55, fol. 29.

838 Aid me, ye muses, on Parnassus' hill
And he became most healthy, good and wise.
Percy, Henry, son of the Bp. of Dromore, 'Æsculapius, a Tale . . . finished at Easter 1777'.
MS. Percy c. 8, fol. 27 (autogr.).

Aid me ye poets of the ancient age 839
Under a cart-house, then my heroes fly.
Gough, Richard, aged about 10.
MS. *Eng. poet. c. 5, fol. 25 (autogr.).

Aid me, ye sacred muses nine, 840
Their servile subjects thought no sin [incomplete (?)]
Gough, Richard, 'The twelve Caesars'.
MS. *Eng. poet. c. 5, fol. 36 (autogr.).

Aider of the poor, and punisher of trespass 841
Oppressor of all wrong; and of justice guardian.
MS. Rawl. poet. 66, fol. 5v.

Ajax had made an end, and all the rout 842
For Pallas' sake, whose image here you see.
Strode, William, 'Ulysses his speech translated out of the 13th booke of Ovids Metamorph:'
MS. *CCC. 325, fol. 52 (autogr.).

Alack Alack what shall I do 843
And true love locked thereto.
3-part song by 'The kyng H. viii' copied from B.M. Add. MS. 31922, fol. 35v.
MS. Mus. d. 198, fol. 3v.

Alack when I look back 844
The follies of my youth.
MS. Rawl. poet. 23, p. 114, reference to setting by W. Bird.

Alarming call! hence giddy mortals know, 845
Nor lodge a wish to loiter long behind.
'On the Death of a Gentleman who died suddenly'.
MS. *Eng. poet. e. 28, p. 337.

Alas! Alas! Alas! 'tis so, 846
Oh happy change unto her native light.
Poole, James, 'A Paraphrase upon Horace', *Odes* II. xiv, with preface, 1709.
MS. Eng. poet. c. 25, fol. 88.

Alas! alas! All flesh is grass 847
And neither worth a T-d.
'An irregular Ode on the Death of her late Majesty Queen Caroline: by a Boy, Son to the Earl of Northampton's Gardener'. 1737.
MS. Ballard 47, fol. 163.

Alas! Alas! my Pegasus is dead, 848
Upon thy grave this epitaph shall lie.
'The lame [Wiltshire] Paritor's Verses on his Horse', copied 1700–1703 (?). See T166.
MS. Tanner 306, fol. 409.

849 **Alas, alas, poor gentry small avails**
**And virtue less, if land, and riches fail[s].**
Couplet.
MS. Rawl. poet. 117, fol. 274 rev.

850 **Alas! Alas! Young man your case**
**Who rhiming heads bewitch.**
A846, 'answer'd by Mrs. Judith Wild, &c.'
MS. Ballard 47, fol. 163.

851 **Alas at Rome nothing there but money reigns**
**As neither God, man heaven or hell thou fears.**
Fairfax, Thomas, Lord, translator, 'Mantua Ecloga 5'.
MS. *Fairfax 40, p. 608 (autogr.).

852 **Alas Britannia that thou liv'st to know**
**Like that which now's possess'd by Britain's Queen.**
Sidney, William, 'A Poem on the Death of Her most Sacred Majesty Queen Caroline inscrib'd to the Dutchess of Kent', 1737.
MS. Rawl. poet. 70, fol. 1 (autogr.).

853 **Alas! dear G— in this our world below**
**I'll sport my bows, and flash my frill no more.**
Parsons, William, 'The Climax of Misfortune'.
MS. *Don. d. 123, p. 76 (autogr.).

854 **Alas fair face why doth that smoothed brow**
**That by his beams, my beams to thine may run.**
Pr. Pilkington's *First Book of Songs*, 1605, iv.
MSS. Mus. f. 7–10: f. 10, fol. 19.

855 **Alas fond man, how are thy thoughts beguil'd.**
**Where gain's uncertain, and the pain is sure.**
[Quarles, Francis], 'The World compar'd to a Hive of Waspes'.
Pr. *Emblemes*, 1635, I. iii.
MS. Rawl. poet. 90, fol. 18v.

856 **Alas for poor St. James' Park**
**'Tis thought he had lost his life.**
'A Court Satyr, 1682', and 'Answer'.
MSS. Eng. poet. d. 53, p. 13; Firth c. 16, p. 7.

857 **Alas! how devious from their course**
**And know the real good.**
Skinner, John, translator, Boethius, *Consolations* III. viii.
MS. *Eng. poet. d. 22, fol. 97.

858 **Alas how dull's the mind, when it is drown'd**
**Is forc'd (alas), dully to view the ground.**
Bacon, Sir Nicholas, translator, Boethius, *Consolations* I. ii (1664).
MS. Tanner 306, fol. 348v (autogr.).

**Alas how folly maketh wretches stray** 859
**The true ones to discern.**
Bacon, Sir Nicholas, translator, Boethius, *Consolations* III. viii (1664).
MS. Tanner 306, fol. 329 (autogr.).

**Alas! how sad and desolate** 860
**Inexorable grown.**
'Jeremiah's Lamentations', translated in five elegies.
MS. *Eng. poet. e. 51, p. 154.

**Alas! how soon are pleasures done** 861
**And cure his own deceit.**
'On short-liv'd joyes: or, on a Friends death'.
MS. Rawl. poet. 90, fol. 165v.

**Alas how soon the wisest are deceiv'd** 862
**This girl, the perfect hypocrite can play.**
MS. Eng. poet. e. 47, p. 61.

**Alas how sorrowful am I** 863
**In God's name to follow nature.**
'The Complaint of Nature against the erronius Alchymist by John de Mehung', with prefatory quatrain *beg.* Here Nature her complaint doth show. Answered by M271.
MS. Ashmole 58, fol. 27.

**Alas, how transient a scene** 864
**That life which saints and angels live above.**
Bromley, Henry, 'Mortality'.
MS. *Don. e. 19, fol. 7 (autogr.).

**Alas I am in love and cannot speak it** 865
**..(incomplete)...**
'Hide Park'.
MS. Mus. d. 184, fol. 58v.

**Alas I cannot love, nor will I wrong** 866
**Whereby we over-value things, though good.**
North, Dudley, 3rd Baron.
Pr. *A Forest of Varieties*, 1645.
MS. *North e. 41, fol. 53, corrected by the author.

**Alas in this poor heart of mine** 867
**Can all my foes subdue.**
Beddome, Benjamin, 'Hymn'.
MS. *Eng. misc. e. 227, fol. 55v.

**Alas mine eye why dost thou bring** 868
**Why art thou thus my mortal foe.**
MS. Ashmole 176, fol. 99.

**Alas my sins have found me out** 869
**Have mercy Lord on me.**
Beddome, Benjamin.
MS. *Eng. misc. e. 227, fol. 175.

870 Alas our day, is forc'd to fly by night
Your ditty death, and blood in lieu of words.
[Southwell, Robert,] 'Of the Blessed Saviour's flight into Egypt'.
Pr. *Mæoniæ*, 1595, p. 9.
MS. Eng. poet. b. 5, p. 80.

871 Alas our loss and grief, that we should say
We lost too much because too much we lov'd.
Strode, William, 'On Mrs. Withypoll an Epitaph'.
MS. *CCC. 325, fol. 124^v (autogr.).

872 Alas poor Cupid art thou blind
And all you shoot at surely dies.
Ascribed to Dr. Henry Hughes in the index to H. Lawes' *Third Book of Ayres*, 1669.
MSS. Rawl. poet. 65, fol. 33^v; 214, fol. 85, attr. to Tho[mas] H[ead].

873 Alas, poor Death: Where is thy glory:
Thou so much worse, that thou shalt be no more.
Herbert, George, 'A Dialogue Anthem: Christian, Death'.
Pr. *The Temple*, 1633, p. 164.
MSS. Rawl. poet. 90, fol. 138; *Tanner 307, fol. 124^v.

874 Alas poor face!
She's pinked to last, indented to endure.
'Uppon the best face that ever was most injuried by the Poxe'.
MSS. Malone 19, p. 47, attr. to John Deane; Rawl. poet. 199, p. 43.

875 Alas! poor Lion—What a dog was he!
Gone, like a Frenchman, to eternal sleep.
Madan, Spencer, 'Elegy on poor little Lion . . . about 1792'.
MS. Eng. poet. c. 51, p. 115.

876 Alas poor muse, what wast thou only born
Hath chang'd this frail life for eternity.
Leigh, Peter, 'An Elegy on Mr. Thomas Yale son to Dr. Yale Chauncellor [1587–1608] to the Bp. of Chester'.
MS. Dodsworth 61, fol. 74^v.

877 Alas sweet youth and [what] is thy blood so staid
And then a lower but a higher bliss.
'On a bashfull youth'.
MSS. CCC. 328, fol. 76; Eng. poet. e. 14, fol. 54^v.

878 Alas! 'tis done the time's far slipp'd away
Unto those joys which shall for ever last.
Bromley, Henry, 'Time'.
MS. *Don. e. 19, fol. 1 (autogr.).

Alas to men in years, how small 879
A part of life is left in all.
Couplet, 'Heu senibus vitae portio quanta manet?'
MS. Rawl. D. 986, fol. 109^v.

Alas to whom should I complain 880
And am exiled remediless.
MS. Ashmole 176, fol. 100.

Alas what grief is this 881
May flourish in our realm.
'A Complaynte agaynst the wicked enemies of Christ'. Licensed 4 September 1564.
MS. Firth d. 14, fol. 91.

Alas! what murtherers have been here? What's this 882
Religion's born with him but dies with these.
'An Elegie . . . uppon Sir Charles Lucas and Sir George Lisle . . . murthered in Colchester Aug. 28, 1648'.
MS. Rawl. poet. 172, fol. 35.

Alas what news is this 883
Farewell sweet Christmas.
Twelfth day carol; tune, 'To ride to Rumford'.
MS. Eng. poet. b. 5, p. 67.

Alas what shall I do for love 884
To keep you me unto. Alas.
Transcript of 4-part song by 'The kynge H. viii' from B.M. Add. MS. 31922.
MS. Mus. d. 198, fol. 2.

Alas what take you pepper in your noses 885
I'll wear my sovereign's colours in my soul.
Pr. *Rump Songs*, 1662, Sig. K3.
MSS. Ashmole 36, 37, fol. 82.

Alas what thing can be more grievous pain 886
Then I which am yours unto my life's end.
MS. Rawl. C. 813, fol. 13^v.

Alas! what trust is in these earthly things 887
Sorrow and doleful sighings fly away.
Freind, Nathaniel, on his son John, d. 1672.
MS. Top. Oxon. f. 31, p. 301 (autogr.).

Alas! what's man? who knows but this did bear 888
Will be the same when death for her does call.
'On A Human skull'.
MS. Add. B. 105, fol. 106.

Alas, where is my love, where is my sweeting 889
To be reveng'd of all her deep disdaining.
Pr. Tho. Bateson's *First set of English Madrigales*, 1604, xviii.
MSS. Mus. f. 20–24: f. 20, fol. 46^v.

890 Alas where is the man,
Unto her noble grace.
Markant or Marquannt, John, 1559.
MS. Firth d. 14, fol. 142.

891 Alas; why lived I so long?
A doleful deadly end.
[Price, E. (?)], 'The lamentacion of Thisbe when her love pirramus slewe him selfe'.
MS. *Douce 290, fol. 97 (autogr. (?) *cf.* fol. 86[v]).

892 Alas! with wha' assiduous errors driven
To the world's machine prove a funeral pyre.
J. F., translator of 'Milton, against Nature's Senescency' [Naturam non pati senium].
MS. *Eng. poet. f. 17, p. 83 (autogr.).

893 Alas would you have me conceal
That which your self could not but needs reveal.
Couplet.
MS. Rawl. poet. 117, fol. 275 rev.

894 Albeit I well hoped sweet coz the times
Thy wishes always gentle coz I end.
Burton, Francis.
MS. *Add. A. 267, fol. 123 (autogr.).

895 Albion, where's thy champions gone?
Take up a pistol, and fling off a fan.
MS. Firth d. 13, fol. 43.

896*a* Alexander Ward his corps here doth lie
Thus greater than Alexander the great could be.
Epitaph, 1663, in Shenstone Church, nr. Lichfield.
MS. Rawl. D. 377, fol. 68.

896*b* Alexander's [Necke (?)] can teach us this
The school and court by greatness fashioned is.
Couplet.
MS. Rawl. poet. 117, fol. 164[v] rev.

897 Alexis! dear Alexis! lovely boy!
For what my sighs and prayers can ne'er retrieve!
Flatman, Thomas, 'Coridon, on the Death of his deare Alexis', his son, d. 28 Jan. 1681/2.
Pr. *Poems*, 4th ed., 1686, p. 199.
MS. Tanner 306, fol. 392 (autogr.).
MS. Eng. poet. d. 53, p. 20, attr. to Mr. Flatman.

898 Alexis do not slight me so
And would not from you part.
'A Song' and 'The Answer'.
MS. Montagu e. 13, fol. 48.

899 Alexis shunn'd his fellow swains
He bow'd obey'd and died.
'A Song'.
MS. Montagu e. 13, fol. 52.

Algernon Sidney fills this tomb 900
Where neither Pope, nor Devil hath to do.
'An Epitaph on Algernoon Sydney who was murdred on Tower Hill', 7 Dec. 1683.
MSS. Don. e. 23, fol. 48; Douce 357, fol. 142.

All after pleasures as I rid one day 901
Till even his beams sing and my music shine.
Herbert, George, 'Christmas'.
Pr. *The Temple*, 1633, p. 72.
MS. *Tanner 307, fol. 55[v].

All, all must die; the poor, the rich, the great ones; 902
The old, the young: men, children, babes, the small bones.
Robinson, Robert, couplet.
MS. *Rawl. poet. 218, p. 158 (autogr.).

All, all my trust Lord have I put in thee 903
Be strong in hope his strength shall you supply.
Sidney, Sir Philip, Psalm xxxi.
MS. *Rawl. poet. 25, fol. 23; see also A994.

All attendants apart 904
And do penance in shape of a wife.
Miss Soaper, 'Repentance', 11 July 1730.
Pr. Dodsley's *Collection of Poems*, 1758, vi. 232.
MS. Eng. poet. c. 9, p. 224.

All-beard stood upon a stick 905
All-beard had all his beard again.
MS. Rawl. D. 859, fol. 97.

All blessed Jesus, to thy holy name 906
That I with him in Heav'n might live and reign.
Williams, John, 'A Prayer at recieving the Cup'.
MS. *Rawl. poet. 192, fol. 180 (autogr.).

All blessing and praise 907
And victoriously follow my Lord to the skies.
Kenton, James.
MS. *Eng. poet. e. 20, p. 7 (autogr.).

All bliss 908
With greedier eyes, more boys though men.
Traherne, Thomas, 'Blisse'.
MS. *Eng. poet. c. 42, fol. 13[v] (autogr.).

All bliss have they that in Jehova's love 909
And thy commands I never shall forget.
Harington, Sir John, Psalm cxix.
MS. *Douce 361, fol. 74.

All blots I cannot from my memory wipe 910
My love will find a tally for them all.
Dryden, John, translator, Ovid, *Amores* II. iv, 'That he loves women of all sorts and Sizes'.
MS. Rawl. poet. 173, fol. 45.

911 All, (brother Gallio) blessedness would find
And after hurried down again as fast?
Seneca, *De vita beata.*
MS. Rawl. poet. 103, fol. 3.

912 All bruised man [*sic*] why should'st thou take such care
Are but as tears shed at thy funeral.
[King, Henry], 'On the life of man'.
MS. CCC. 328, fol. 26; see also I1095.

913 All christian men in my behalf,
And at his father's years have worn fair horns.
'On Sir John Calfe, Anglice', from Latin distich.
MSS. Eng. poet. e. 14, fol. 94v rev.; e. 40, fol. 123; see also A940.

914 All christian men that walk me by
All christian men beware by me.
MS. Rawl. C. 813, fol. 4v.

915 All Christ's obedience, all his suffering pain
By it, hence rise to bliss perpetual.
MS. *Rawl. poet. 97, fol. 66 (autogr.).

916 All cold beneath this mould'ring heap
Revive the verdure with her tears.
'On Mrs. Wren'.
MS. Eng. misc. e. 241, fol. 103v.

917 All conquering gold who can thy power withstand?
It turns the strictest love, to bitter hate.
'Auri sacra fames quid non mortalia pectora coges? Exercise for a breaking up'.
MS. *Rawl. poet. 197, fol. 5 (autogr.).

918 All creatures else on earth that are
Who with their wives contend and jar.
Fairfax, Thomas, Lord, 'Upon an ill Husband'.
MS. *Fairfax 40, p. 571 (autogr.).
MS. *Fairfax 38, p. 319.

919 All cuckolds now or married folk
May pay for Privy Seal.
'On Dr. Jo. Wall', Canon of Christ Church, d. 20 Oct. 1666.
MS. Tanner 306, fol. 374; formerly in Wood E. 31, now lost.

920 All dainty meats I do defy, yet feed men fat as swine,
Who hath his kitchen in a box, his roast meat in a pipe.
'On Tobacco'.
MSS. Ashmole 36, 37, fol. 144.

All day alas I languish in despair 921
Iris! what doom awaits thine enemies?
Skinner, John, translator, from Molière's *Bourgeois Gentilhomme*, 1792.
MS. *Eng. poet. d. 22, fol. 30.

All day I debauch without musing or thinking 922
Our lives much too short are for drinking and whoring.
'A Catch'.
MS. Rawl. poet. 194, fol. 27.

All die, no fixed inheritance we have 923
And raise it up much better, yet the same.
Nalson, Robert, 'An Elegy upon the death of Mr. J. Hopkinson of Lofthouse', 29 Feb. 1680.
MS. Top. Cheshire c. 6, fol. 241 (autogr.).

All Dutch and English that are left 924
Would act fair, and stand neuter.
'The Dutch-mens Reasons For a Dutch Sunday to be Observ'd once a Month'.
MS. Firth d. 13, fol. 57.

All earthly creatures chiefest pomp and glory 925
So is his glory suitable to it.
MS. *Rawl. poet. 97, fol. 26v (autogr.).

All earthly things are in a waning state 926
It shall to all eternity extend.
MS. *Rawl. poet. 97, fol. 61 (autogr.).

All earthly wealth that each wight here doth gain 927
As fainting flowers, that vanish like a shade.
Dudley, Richard, 'A praise of vertue'.
MS. Rawl. poet. 148, fol. 113v.

All evil from the north saith proverb old 928
It's good to us that sends us such a king.
On James I, translated from the Latin.
MS. Wood D. 13, p. 191.

All factions cease, on earth's all peace; 929
If with himself he can agree.
Robinson, Robert, 'Cum sacerdotes concordent pax erit per totum orbem confirmata'.
MS. *Rawl. poet. 218, p. 6 (autogr.).

All flesh is grass; and withereth like the hay 930
For to prepare, they cannot death delay.
Whitney, Geoffrey, 'Omnis caro foenum'.
MS. *Rawl. poet. 56, fol. 123.

All flesh is grass our life time draweth on 931
To this frail world, ne'er to be known again.
Bulkeley, Rich[ard], 'An Elegie upon the death of Mrs. Anne Greenewell', 26 April, 1633.
MSS. Ashmole 36, 37, fol. 34.

932 All fleshly religion of what sort soever
Though it have been accounted a bare and vain thing.
Tune, 'Blew cap'.
MS. Rawl. poet. 37, p. 56.

933 All friends and neighbours, so good and jolly
God bless you assist us—so God save the King.
Amherst, Elizabeth, 'The humble petition of the Weavers Shoe Makers and Taylors of the Parish of Welford'.
MS. *Eng. poet. e. 109, p. 99.

934 All from the rising sun
His truth's for ever sure.
Fairfax, Thomas, Lord, Psalm c.
MS. *Fairfax 40, p. 243 (autogr.); see also A972*b*.

935 All generous hearts are best by kindness gain'd
And they are fast and loose alternately.
MS. Rawl. D. 174, fol. 86v,r.

936 All gladness gladdest hearts can hold
Filled had, yea over filled.
Herbert, Mary (*née* Sidney), Countess of Pembroke, Psalm lxxxi.
MSS. *Rawl. poet. 24, p. 121; *25, fol. 77.

937 All glorious God! how long wilt veil thy face?
Because, with me, he'th dealt so lovingly.
Morrice, John, Psalm xiii, 1707.
MS. *Rawl. poet. 114, fol. 158 (autogr.).

938 All glory be to God on high
And we will sing, as well as you, Hosanna.
MS. Rawl. poet. 23, fol. 43, reference to setting by Thomas Ford.

939 All glory, laud and praise to thee
Thou reignst above in heavenly throne.
Huish, Alexander, 'Gloria, laus et honor, &c. In die Palmarum', translated 24 Jan. 1634.
MS. *Eng. poet. e. 56, p. 126 (autogr.).

940 All good people in God's behalf
And with his fathers have worn long horns.
'Epitaphium Johannis Calfe'.
MSS. Ashmole 36, 37, fol. 142; see also A913.

941 All grow inquisitive, and ask what news?
The laughing stock, and scoff of Christendom.
[Dec. 1640–May 1641].
MS. Ballard 50, fol. 14.

942 All hail all hail thou Munster prince
The halters yours, the axe is mine.
On the Bishop of Munster's peace with Holland, April 1666, and Edward Hyde. See *English Historical Review*, xxi, 1906, p. 686.
MS. Add. A. 48, fol. 12.

[A]ll hail! brave Duke, whose soul, not whiffling fate 943
May drowsy Lethe never view the hearse.
Baskerville, J[ohn] (1641–81), translation from Latin verse, possibly on the Duke of Buck[ingham], sent to Nathaniel Johnston at Pontefract, 167[?].
MS. Eng. poet. c. 25, fol. 74 (autogr.).

All hail (great sir) your city's glorious light, 944
Wish you long to enjoy prosperity.
Perkins, T[homas], translation of Latin verses addressed to Sir John Ireton, Lord Mayor 1658–9, 'on Mathewes day . . . 1659' at Christ's Hospital.
MS. Rawl. D. 1041, fol. 122v.

All hail inexorable lord 945
Within thy cold embrace?
Burns, Robert, 'To Ruin'.
Pr. *Poems*, 1787, p. 249.
MS. Montagu e. 14, fol. 11v.

All hail Maria full of grace! 946
And bless'd the fruit thy womb contains.
'Ave Maria', 18th cent.
MS. Eng. poet. e. 56, p. 67.

All hail (my masters!) I must now implore 947
Seleucus-like, an anchor on my thigh.
[Wharton, George], 'Verses for 1659'.
MS. Ashmole 423, fol. 275 (autogr.).

All hail oh Virgin crowned with stars 948
When unto thee we call.
'To our Blessed Lady the Advocate of Sinners', by a Benedictine Nun (?), prefacing a book of 'Confessions'.
MS. Rawl. C. 581, fol. 10v.

All hail sweet poet full of more [strange] strong fire 949
All the world's lion, though I be thy ape.
Donne, John, 'To Mr. T. W.'
MSS. Don. c. 54, fol. 9*a*; *Eng. poet. f. 9, p. 55, attr. to J. D.

All hail the morn! that with auspicious ray 950
And call you from the earth to mount the skies.
'Epithalamium 1748'.
MS. Eng. poet. e. 40, fol. 73.

All hail! thou blest incarnate God 951
And save me from my sins.
Kenton, James.
MS. *Eng. poet. e. 20, p. 318 (autogr.).

All happiness shall thee betide, 952
But gifts of peace shall grace.
Herbert, Mary (*née* Sidney), Countess of Pembroke, Psalm cxxviii.
MSS. *Rawl. poet. 24, p. 195; *25, fol. 130v.

953 All health fair nymph pride of the college shades
Down falls my pen my dissolution's near.
H[ammond], A[nthony].
MS. Rawl. D. 360, fol. 59.

954 All hearty love my Lord I bear
To sing with me oh praise the Lord.
Harington, Sir John, Psalm cxvi.
MS. *Douce 361, fol. 72.

955 All heaven he sold whilst he lived here
All hell you know is left him.
'On a late Pope'. Translation from George Buchanan, *Franciscanus*, etc., 1584, Sig. C6$^{v}$.
MS. Eng. misc. e. 241, fol. 19.

956 All his just praise in her life may be read
The true wife of his worth, as of his bed.
Couplet.
MS. Sancroft 59, p. 293 rev.

957*a* All, howsoe'er bound, vexed, or possess'd
God gives to all; all must confess Him, good.
MS. *Rawl. poet. 97, fol. 56$^{v}$ (autogr.).

957*b* [All human race would fain be wits]
Like prudent Fabius by delay.
Swift, Jonathan, 'On Poetry. A Rhapsody'.
Pr. Dublin, 1733.
MS. Eng. misc. f. 79, p. 103.

958 All human things are subject to decay
With doubled portion of his father's art.
[Dryden, John], 'Mac Fleckno. A Satyr. A°. 1678.' In John Oldham's hand.
MS. Rawl. poet. 123, pp. 232–5 and 214.

959 All Hybla's honey, all that sweetness can
It is too sweet to be a long-lived one.
[Crashaw, Richard], [On our Lord's last comfortable discourse with his Disciples].
Pr. *Steps to the Temple*, 1646.
MS. Tanner 465, two copies, fols. 38 and 65$^{v}$.

960 All in a melancholy study
Oh thither thither thither will I go.
[Wild, Robert], 'The schollers complaint in these latter ages'.
MS. Malone 21, fol. 33; see also I1219.

961 All in a morning fair,
And there is an end of the story.
'The Fox Chace or the Huntsman's Harmony by the noble Duke of Buckingham's Hounds &c.'
MS. Ballard 47, fol. 173$^{v}$.

962 All in a sunshine day withouten cloud
Where ever since remains he out of sight.
Subscribed, 'Incertus author'.
MS. Rawl. poet. 85, fol. 85$^{v}$.

All in amaze at what is done I stood, 963
And let the world turn which way 'twill for me.
'The opinion of one who wore for his motto *Semper Idem.* 1609'.
MS. Rawl. poet. 173, fol. 128.

All in the city of Westminster 964*a*
But I will save my soul.
'A dialogue between the Ld. Bp. of Ely, Dr. Moore, and Tom Negroe . . . To the Tune of Chevy Chase'.
Pr. Hearne's *Collections*, ed. C. E. Doble, ii, O.H.S. vii, 1886, p. 110.
MS. Hearne's diaries 17, p. 42.

All in the downs the fleet was moor'd 964*b*
Adieu she cries and waves her lily hand.
'A Song'.
MS. Montagu e. 13, fol. 12.

All in the king's name 965
But himself and Baron de Bartue.
'A Libell on the Coffee-Houses'.
Proclamation for their suppression, 29 Dec. 1675; additional proclamation, allowing their continuation subject to certain conditions, 8 Jan. 1675/6.
MS. Don. b. 8, p. 557.

All in the land of cider 966
Himself a bed to lie on.
[Hall, Henry], 'A Ballad in Imitation of All in the Land of Essex'; verses against Sir Edward Harley, on an incident at Brampton Bryan.
Included in MS. of Hall's poems, Brotherton Collection, University of Leeds.
MS. Eng. poet. e. 87, p. 36.

All in the land of Essex 967
Shall pass at least for a martyr.
[Denham, Sir John], 'Newes from Colchester'.
Pr. *Rump Songs*, 1662, Sig. Aa1$^{v}$, and Denham's *Poems*, 1668, p. 109.
MSS. Ashmole, 36, 37, fol. 88.

All in the town of London 968
And give him th' Extreme Unction.
'To the Tune of the loyall Tinker'.
MS. Don. b. 8, p. 185.

All in the town of Oxon 969
Go seek a convenient stopple.
Lennard, Francis (?), of All Souls, 'The Philosopher without a Stone', 1668.
MS. Gough misc. antiq. 11, fol. 82.

All is performed, all is brought to pass 970
The profit doth to Hevah's seed remain.
MS. *Rawl. poet. 97, fol. 38 (autogr.).

971 All kings, and all their favourites
To write threescore, this is the second of our reign.
Donne, John, 'The Anniversary'.
Pr. *Poems*, 1633.
MSS. *Eng. poet. e. 99, fol. 112; *f. 9, p. 99, attr. to J. D.

972*a* All lands extol our Lord with laud
His truth from age to age endureth.
Harington, Sir John, Psalm c.
MS. *Douce 361, fol. 60.

972*b* All lands from rising sun
His truth's for ever sure.
Fairfax, Thomas, Lord, Psalm c.
MS. *Fairfax 38, p. 370; see also A934.

973 All lands the limbs of earthy round
My hopeful help, his mercy's aid.
Herbert, Mary (*née* Sidney), Countess of Pembroke, Psalm lxvi.
MSS. *Rawl. poet. 24, p. 91; *25, fol. 55$^{v}$.

974 All languid and pale
And then sing no more.
Copied 2 Oct. 1751.
MS. Mus. e. 20, fol. 22$^{v}$.

975 All laud and praise with heart and voice
Give laud and thanks always.
[Hopkins, John], Psalm xxx.
MSS. Rawl. poet. 23, p. 33; 112, fol. 63$^{v}$ rev.

976 All letters even at head and feet must stand
Zealously strive your fellows to excel.
'Copies for Schollers to Write'.
MS. Rawl. poet. 152, fol. 231.

977 All living men are worms, 'tis a true ditty;
In Christ who do trust, their souls He will save.
Robinson, Robert.
MS. *Rawl. poet. 218, p. 73 (autogr.).

978 All love and thanksgiving
May mount to the sky.
Kenton, James.
MS. *Eng. poet. e. 20, p. 396 (autogr.).

979 All lovers (sweet) are husbandmen, that yield
Some piece of earth that bears a richer mould.
[Beaumont, Thomas], 'Love like husbandry'.
MS. *Malone 18, p. 17.

980 All mankind hath but one original
Quitting their own original.
Bacon, Sir Nicholas, translation of Boethius, *Consolations* III. vi, 1664.
MS. Tanner 306, fol. 328$^{v}$ (autogr.).

All mankind upon earth 981
The original.
Polwhele, John, Boethius, *Consolations* III. vi.
MS. *Eng. poet. f. 16, fol. 28$^{v}$ (autogr.).

All manner of men that lust for to hear 982
In a fair new tomb here buried is he.
'A Copy of the table that was hanging in the Priorye of Stone [Staffordshire], at the time of the suppression', 1536.
MS. Dugdale 20, fol. 144$^{v}$.

All men are now with greedy minds possess'd 983
And say gain's sweet however it be had.
MS. Rawl. poet. 120, fol. 36*a*.

All men for certain have their faults 984
Or help we shall have none.
Robinson, Robert.
MS. *Rawl. poet. 218, p. 81 (autogr.).

All men have gifts, though not alike, they say, 985
So saving some, the belly food doth last.
Robinson, Robert.
MS. *Rawl. poet. 218, p. 43 (autogr.).

All men have sure their vanities, 986
And thou (no doubt) hast thine.
Robinson, Robert.
MS. *Rawl. poet. 218, p. 40 (autogr.).

All men in me are found to take delight 987–8
And yet I am what all men hate or slight.
Williams, John, 'A Riddle. it is Pride'. Couplet.
MS. *Rawl. poet. 193, fol. 81$^{v}$ (autogr.).

All men the[y] do wish unto them self all good 989
And would that all my friends of that wish should have part.
Morley, Henry, Lord.
Pr. Wood's *Athenae*, ed. Bliss, i, 1813, 117, and E. Flügel, *Neuenglisches Lesebuch*, 1895, p. 37.
MS. Ashmole 48, fol. 10.

All men would rule, none by their wills obey 990
This breaks all peace; this causeth many a fray.
Robinson, Robert, couplet.
MS. *Rawl. poet. 218, p. 112 (autogr.).

All my belief and confidence is in the lord of might: 991
To whom be all dominion and praise for evermore.
'The Creed', Old Version.
MS. Rawl. poet. 112, fol. 24$^{v}$ rev.

992 **All my past [joys are] life is mine no more**
**'Tis all that heaven allows.**
[Wilmot, John, Earl of] Roch[ester], 'Love and Life, a Song'.
See Vieth, p. 425.,
MSS. Add. B. 106, fol. $45^v$, attr. to Roch.; Rawl. poet. 90, fol. $132^v$.

993 **All my sense thy sweetness gain**
**The less I love I live the less.**
Sidney, Sir Philip, 'To the tune of Napolitan Villan'.
Pr. *Arcadia*, 1598, p. 486.
MS. *e Mus. 37, fol. 242.

994 **All my whole trust, Lord I have put in thee**
**And he shall your establishment renew.**
Sidney, Sir Philip, Psalm xxxi.
MS. *Rawl. poet. 24, p. 39; see also A903.

995 **All nations of the earth, and all**
**O magnify his praise.**
Psalm cxvii.
MS. *Rawl. C. 113, fol. 81.

996 **All nature, and its laws lay hid in night**
**God said, let Newton be, And all was light.**
Pope, Alexander, couplet on Newton.
Pr. *Minor Poems*, ed. N. Ault and J. Butt, 1954, p. 317.
MS. Top. Oxon. c. 108, p. 47.

997 **All noble men take heed**
**A dawcock ye be and so shall be still.**
[Skelton, John], introductory and concluding sections of 'Why come ye not to Court'.
Pr. *Pithy Pleasant and Profitable workes*, 1568, Sigg. Liv, Niii$^v$–Oiii.
MS. Rawl. C. 813, fol. 36.

998 **All on a day as we set sail**
**All in the ocean main.**
'The Jovial Mariner's Resolution'.
Pr. *The New Years Garland* (pr. bk. Douce PP. 183).
MS. Firth c. 18, fol. 1.

999 **All our men has been merry merry**
**All our men has been a-drinking.**
Mrs. Anne E., 'A catch'.
MS. Rawl. poet. 214, fol. $71^v$.

1000 **All people hearken and give ear, to that that I shall tell**
**But like brute beasts so doth he live, which turn to dust and powder.**
[Sternhold, Thomas], Psalm xlix.
MS. Rawl. poet. 112, fol. $57^v$ rev.

**All people listen and give ear** 1001
**His head, hands and his gear.**
'A Song'.
MS. CCC. 328, fol. 38.

**All people that on earth do dwell** 1002
**And shall from age to age endure.**
[Kethe, William], Psalm c.
Pr. John Daye's *Psalmes*, 1561.
MSS. Don. c. 20, fol. 1, music by Tallis; Montagu e. 10, fol. $76^v$; Rawl. poet. 112, fol. 42 rev.

**All people to Jehovah bring** 1003
**Princes the shields, that earth defend.**
Herbert, Mary (*née* Sidney), Countess of Pembroke, Psalm xlvii.
MSS. *Rawl. poet. 24, p. 68; *25, fol. $40^v$.

**All pleasure hath this property** 1004
**With a too long-enduring smart.**
Bacon, Sir Nicholas, translation of Boethius, *Consolations* III. vii. 1664.
MS. Tanner 306, two copies, fols. $312^v$ and 329 (autogr.).

**All pleasures have one common toy** 1005
**Eat their own death with sweet delight.**
Polwhele, John, translation of Boethius, *Consolations* III. vii.
MS. *Eng. poet. f. 16, fol. 29 (autogr.).

**All private [quarrels] wranglings and intestine jars** 1006
**My knowledge is no larger, than my faith.**
Translation from Latin 'Epitaph upon Bp. [Samuel] Parker made by himself'.
Pr. *Poems on Affairs of State*, iii, 1698, p. 102.
MSS. Eng. poet. c. 18, fol. $42^v$; Rawl. D. 316 fol. 110.

**All prosperous stars, though absent to the sense** 1007
**Bless those they shine for by their influence.**
Couplet.
MS. Add. B. 8, fol. 75.

**All sacred gold! whose mighty power** 1008
**Struggles, kicks, winces groans and dies.**
'The Power of Gold'.
MS. *Eng. poet. d. 47, fol. 111.

**All see, Amphialus, the sun hath motes** 1009
**T'have made her wife; when you made her a mother.**
Epigram, 'Ad Amphialum'.
MS. Don. d. 58, fol. $31^v$.

**All sin is of the devil, this we see** 1010
**Of Satan, can divert the Lord's decree.**
MS. *Rawl. poet. 97, fol. $12^v$ (autogr.).

1011 All sorrow we'll banish and troublesome care
What tomorrow may bring we'll till then keep away.
Williams, John, 'The 3ds [i.e. third words] are—We'll come to Morrow'.
MS. *Rawl. poet. 191, fol. 14 (autogr.).

1012 All thanks to thee my God this night
Praise Father, Son, and Holy Ghost.
[Ken, Thomas, Bp. of Bath and Wells], 'An Evening Hymn'.
Pr. *Manual of Prayers*, 1695, p. 145, in a different version.
MS. Rawl. D. 361, fol. 325v.

1013 All that are born and cry
Live they or far or nigh.
Robinson, Robert.
MS. *Rawl. poet. 218, p. 126 (autogr.).

1014 All that Christ's questions and his answers hear
No petty matter could astonish them.
MS. *Rawl. poet. 97, fol. 46v (autogr.).

1015 All that draw breath
Until the quiet grave our bodies cover.
Robinson Robert.
MS. *Rawl. poet. 218, p. 138 (autogr.).

1016 All that have eyes [awake] now wake and weep
James the peaceful and the just.
'On the death of King James', 1625.
MSS. CCC. 328, fol. 7; Eng. poet. c. 50, fol. 23v; e. 14, fol. 10; e. 97, p. 10; Rawl. poet. 199, p. 62; see also H421.

1017 All that hither chance to come
The French man's harms within.
'On the Flour de luce in Oxford'.
MS. Eng. poet. e. 14, fol. 86 rev.; see also A1070.

1018 All that I have, all that I am
A temper so divine.
Beddome, Benjamin.
MS. *Eng. misc. e. 227, fol. 10.

1019 All that was good and truly just,
As he did truly lengthen his.
'To the . . . Memory of Thomas Crutch', d. 15 July 1711; copied by Hearne in Binsey church-yard and included in his notes to *Guilelmus Neubrigensis*, 1719, ii. 767.
MS. Rawl. D. 1164, fol. 247.

1020 All that's sweet and soft attend
Locked in one another's arms.
'An Epithalamium'.
MS. Rawl. poet. 173, fol. 91v.

All the chief talk is now 1021
Besides us will be merry.
'To the tune of Virginia'.
MS. Rawl. poet. 160, fol. 177v.

All the day I waste in weeping 1022
And see thy wretched lover die.
Pr. Thomas Bateson's *Second set of Madrigales*, 1618, xxii–xxiii.
MSS. Mus. f. 20–24: f. 20, fol. 40.

All the day long, extolling God 1023
Our guard and guide will be.
Psalm xliv.
MS. Montagu c. 5, fol. 24.

All the earth's fullness is the Lord's 1024*a*
Who hath on high his throne.
Psalm xxiv.
MS. *Rawl. C. 113, fol. 23v.

All the maids in Sunningwell 1024*b*
You may put in a nutshell.
Couplet.
MS. Hearne's diaries 91, p. 71.

All the materials are the same 1025
[That can at once be chaste and fair].
MS. Mus. b. 1, fol. 134v, music by John Wilson.

All the news that's [now in town] stirring now 1026
As now poor french folks do.
'On the Spanish Match', 1623.
MSS. Don. b. 8, p. 117; Malone 19, p. 32; Rawl. D. 1048, fol. 76; Rawl. poet. 26, fol. 24v.

All the nuns in Holywell 1027
Pray for the soul of Sir Thomas Lovell.
Epitaph. 25 May 1524, 'written on a Window in the old Nunnery of Holywell in old London', couplet.
MS. Eng. poet. e. 40, fol. 163.

All the perfection of both sexes joined, 1028
Reader, there is not, Huntington lies here.
[Cary, Sir Henry, first Viscount] Falkland, 'An Epitaph on the Lady Huntington', [Elizabeth, *née* Stanley, d. 1632/3(?)].
MS. Malone 13, p. 14.

All the town so [lewd] is grown 1029
And all mankind must excuse me.
MS. Rawl. poet. 196, fol. 39.

All the welshmen cry out oh 1030
For the death of Davy Gough.
'On the death of David Gough a Welchman', 'Anglice', couplet translating Latin distich.
MS. Eng. poet. e. 14, fol. 94 rev.; see also O232.

1031 All the world can't afford
To pull himself down.
'Upon King James (1686)'.
MS. Eng. poet. e. 49, p. 22.

1032 All the world's a stage, and all the women like the men but players,
Sans teeth, sans eyes, sans taste, sans everything.
Parsons, Williams, 'Parody on Shakespeare's Seven Ages'.
MS. *Don. d. 123, p. 216 (autogr.).

1033 All they which with thy bonds on earth shall fast'ned be.
Through ages infinite, beyond the count of days.
'English Primer of our Ladie, 1631 . . . p. 19'.
MS. Eng. poet. e. 56, p. 43.

1034 All things are changed in court and state,
In spite of her nose of wax Sir.
'A Ballad by Mr. Manwaring upon Mr. Secretary Harley & Mrs. Massam'. Answered, A1045.
Pr. *Pill to Purge State-Melancholy*, 1715, p. 35. Dated July 1708 in B.M. Add. MS. 40060.
MS. Eng. poet. e. 87, p. 28.

1035 All things are dust and laughter all things naught
For out of senseless things were all things wrought.
James, Richard, couplet, translating Greek epigram.
MS. *James 35, p. 16 (autogr.).

1036 All things are preappointed, neither can
Sustain some grief, or are a little crossed.
MS. *Rawl. poet. 97, fol. 35$^v$ (autogr.).

1037 All things at all times mayn't be spoke
Must make his tongue to's thoughts a stranger.
MS. Rawl. poet. 116, fol. 99.

1038 All things created must obedient stand
Ascribed to Christ, which with none else agree.
MS. *Rawl. poet. 97, fol. 20 (autogr.).

1039 All things, desires, and loves are vain
Sanctus, Sanctus to thee.
G. M.
MS. Rawl. poet. 200, fol. 39.

1040 All things improve in this aspiring age
And sense and taste are with our bullion fled.
Sheridan, R. B., 'On Waltzing'.
MS. Eng. lett. d. 103, p. 150 rev.

All things lay hush'd as when the drawers tread 1041
No link nor coaches heard.
Radcliffe, [Alexander], of Gray's Inn. Parody of lines by Dryden from *The Indian Emperor*, III. ii, beg. All things lay hush'd.
Pr. *The Ramble*, Alexander Radcliffe, 1682, p. 31.
MS. Eng. poet. c. 25, fol. 75$^v$ rev.

All things must yield to time nought can withstand, 1042
Witness where Troy stood now's an open field.
'Tempus edax rerum. A translation from my Latin Verses'.
MS. *Rawl. poet. 197, fol. 3 (autogr.).

All things seem hard when we do begin 1043*a*
I can say no more to thee if thou wert my brother.
Forman, Simon, 'compositor huius libri ad lectorem 1597'.
MS. Ashmole 1472, fol. 6 (autogr.).

[All things submit themselves to our command] 1043*b*
Forgoing sense for a fantastic name.
'The feminine Monarchy', from *A Collection of Poems . . . upon several Occasions, by several Persons*, 1672.
MS. Sancroft 53, p. 2.

All things that are or ever were, or shall hereafter be 1044
Whom we so highly honour here come all of one alone.
MS. Rawl. D. 1372, two copies, fols. 57$^v$ and 68$^v$.

All things went well in court and state 1045
But have at her head, or so Sir.
An answer to A1034.
MS. Eng. poet. e. 87, p. 30.

All this night shrill Chanticleer 1046
Hail oh sun of righteousness.
A[ustin], W[illiam], '1st hymn for Christmas-day'.
Pr. *Certain . . . Meditations*, 1635, p. 52.
MS. Rawl. poet. 61, fol. 79.

All trees, all leafy groves confess the spring 1047
A sweetly temper'd mean, nor hot, nor cold.
Cr[ashaw], R[ichard], 'E. Virg. Georg: particula In laudem Veris'.
MS. Tanner 465, fol. 51$^v$.

All vices cure themselvs as some folks think 1048
But drink first or he'll not leave a sup.
'On the Drunken Dutch Parsons'; see O462.
MS. Douce 357, fol. 132$^v$.

1049 All we have is God's: and yet
So long as Caesar's self is God's.
[Crashaw, Richard], 'Upon paying tribute to Caesar'.
Pr. *Steps to the Temple*, 1646.
MS. Tanner 465, fol. 33.

1050 All weakness, pain, and sorrow have
Their general *quietus* in the grave.
'An epitaph in Tottenham Church Yard', couplet.
MS. Eng. poet. e. 40, fol. 1.

1051 All what our saviour Christ here underwent
A servant was, such much more His should be.
MS. *Rawl. poet. 97, fol. 58v (autogr.).

1052 All wisdom surely parted is between
The Chaldees and the Hebrews, as is seen.
Couplet, translation from Greek: 'The oracle of Apollo'.
MS. Rawl. D. 1293, fol. 69.

1053 All wonder, how this cushion came to slide
They cannot say, justice the cushion missed.
Peart, R., 'On Mr. Cushion officiating in a Surplice and Cope'.
MS. Rawl. poet. 26, fol. 15.

1054 All worthy eyes, read this, that hither come
Ready to crown that life a laurel tree.
'On [Sir Walter Waller's] Lady'.
MS. Eng. poet. e. 14, fol. 96 rev.

1055 All would be blest, but most
By their false course, with it and them for e'er shall perish.
J. F., Psalm i.
MS. *Eng. poet. f. 17, p. 168 (autogr.).

1056 All ye that are to mirth inclined
Became a saviour to us all.
Pr. Deloney, *Garland of Good Will*, [*c.* 1700], Sig. D2v; see also Percy Society Publications, xxx, 1852, p. ix; *Old Castleton Christmas Carols*, ed. W. H. Shawcross, 1904, p. 4; H. W. Husk, *Song of the Nativity*, 1867, p. 20; and *Roxburghe Ballads*, ii. 486.
MS. Eng. poet. b. 5, p. 50.

1057 All ye that fear the Lord
And still maintains it there.
Beddome, Benjamin, Psalm cxxxv. 20.
MS. *Eng. misc. e. 227, fol. 1v.

1058 All ye that know men, and for virgins would pass,
By concealing a brat, and a pox are undone.
'The Lady's Mistake . . . 1686'.
MS. Firth c. 15, p. 226.

All ye that lovers be 1059
Their thing is made of felt.
Pr. *Poems* [by John Eliot], 1658, Sig. H4.
MS. CCC. 328, fol. 89v; see also A1071 and A1076.

All ye that serve Jehovah blaze his fame 1060
Of joyful babes to prove a fruitful nest.
Harington, Sir John, Psalm cxiii.
MS. *Douce 361, fol. 70v.

All ye the Lord that serve 1061
That heaven and earth did frame.
Harington, Sir John, Psalm cxxxiv.
MS. *Douce 361, fol. 83v.

All ye whose rambling thoughts are bent to please 1062
You need no more, although I worse could tell.
'Cordial Advice . . . Shewing the many Dangers and Hardships that Sailors endure'.
MS. Firth c. 18, fol. 168.

All ye, with fair prosperity glide smooth along! 1063
Be not deceived, it is not thee, but death.
Wake, William, of Cambridge, 'Porto debiles. Protego flebiles'.
Verses in shape of wings; see M118.
MS. Eng. misc. d. 1, fol. 36v.

All you divided peoples, all 1064
As like a beast he lives, he like a beast shall perish.
J. F., Psalm xlix.
MS. *Eng. poet. f. 17, p. 104 (autogr.).

All you good men, who are 1065
To blow up the church and the state.
'Daughter Church's Advice To her Sons on Occasion of the Wardmotes of London June 10 1690'.
MS. Rawl. poet. 159, fol. 50.

All you that are elect to deal in this high Parliament 1066
The ears of thine Elizabeth our Queen, Amen, we say.
'The cry of the poor to the Parliament', on the deficiency of parish priests (*c.* 1588).
MS. Rawl. C. 849, fol. 395.

All you that do desire 1067
In the last Christmas.
MS. Eng. poet. b. 5, p. 56.

All you that do desire to know 1068
For the King no longer waits on me.
'A true Relation of the Escape of the King of Scots from London to France', Charles II.
MS. Firth c. 20, fol. 82.

1069 All you that have protestant ears to hear
Then broke all their swords, and cried vive le Roy.

Haynes, Jos., 'Ballad on the blew Guards alias The Inniskilling Regimt.', 1689.
MSS. Eng. poet. c. 18, fol. 70$^{v}$, attr. to Jo. Haynes; d. 53, p. 50, attr. to Jos. Haynes; e. 49, p. 55, attr. to Jo. Haynes; Firth e. 6, fol. 66$^{v}$, attr. to Jo. Haynes.

1070 All you that hither [chance to] come
The Frenchman's harms within.

'On the Fleur de luce, an Inne', at Oxford.
MSS. Tanner 466, fol. 66$^{v}$; Rawl. poet. 212, fol. 87$^{v}$, with Latin by R. L.; see also A1017.

1071 All you that lovers be
Their things are made of felt.

'A description of women'.
Pr. John Eliot's *Poems*, 1658, Sig. H4; *Cupids Master-Piece*, [1670 (?)], Sig. A7.
MSS. Eng. poet. e. 14, fol. 80 rev.; Malone 19, p. 45; Rawl. poet. 216, fol. 92; see also A1059, A1076.

1072 All you that now do here pass by
Therefore prepare to follow me.

'An Epitaph in Tottenham Church Yard'.
MS. Eng. poet. e. 40, fol. 3.

1073 All you that seek Christ, let your sight
And to the Holy Ghost for aye.

'On the Transfiguration of our Lord . . . English Primer of our Lady, 1631 . . . p. 26'.
MS. Eng. poet. e. 56, p. 50.

1074 All you that standeth near me,
For my unlawful swearing.

'Perjury Punish'd with equal Justice; or, Miles France his Sorrowful Lamentation for his foul Offence'.
MS. Firth d. 14, fol. 14.

1075 All you that will no longer
Come come away, etc.

[Weaver, Thomas], 'Come a way &c.'
MS. Rawl. poet. 71, p. 26; see also A1077.

1076 All you that women love,
Their things are made of felt.

'Of women'. Answered by W2749.
MSS. Ashmole 38, p. 146, attr. to Sir Thomas Gansforde; 47, fol. 104; CCC. 327, fol. 32; Eng. poet. f. 10, fol. 121; Rawl. poet. 117, fol. 189$^{v}$ rev.; 147, p. 82; 172, fol. 74; see also A1059, A1071.

All you that would no longer 1077
[Five Members and Kimbolton]

Weaver, Thomas, 'A Song', 1642.
Pr. *Poems*, 1654, p. 28; see also Firth, in *Transactions of the Royal Hist. Soc.*, 3rd Ser., vi, 1912, p. 48.
MS. *Rawl. poet. 211, fol. 73$^{v}$ (autogr.).
MSS. Ashmole 36, 37, fol. 76; Douce 357, fol. 20$^{v}$; see also A1075.

All you this emblem that behold or must 1078
By them he's conquered and his death's enrolled.

Darcie, Abraham(?), Emblem. See T665.
MS. Top. Yorks. c. 26, fol. 140$^{v}$.

All you who on the Lord do wait 1079
You out of Zion shall bless and aid.

Fairfax, Thomas, Lord, Psalm cxxxiv.
MS. *Fairfax 40, p. 347 (autogr.).
MS. *Fairfax 38, p. 437.

All you whose better thoughts are newly born, 1080
Heav'n's never deaf, but when man's heart is dumb.

[Quarles, Francis], 'The Entertainment'.
Pr. *Emblemes*, 1635, p. 125.
MS. Rawl. poet. 90, fol. 37$^{v}$.

All's cheap to rich men: they no money want; 1081
All's dear to poor men; Oh their money's scant.

Robinson, Robert, couplet.
MS. *Rawl. poet. 218, p. 64 (autogr.).

All's come but mine, each Corydon hath brought 1082–3
Your bedesman and your bondsman by being free.

[Dalby, Edward, of New College], 'Ad [Dr. Robert Pinke] on New years day'.
MS. Ashmole 47, fol. 119$^{v}$.

Allen of Rome by title Cardinal 1084
Let such, oh Lord, thy church nor people rack.

On Cardinal Allen and James I, translated from the Latin.
MS. Wood D. 13, p. 197.

Almighty everlasting power 1085
Shall bring us to our heavenly home.

Kenton, James.
MS. *Eng. poet. e. 20, p. 230 (autogr.).

Almighty God dost thou require 1086
And practice what I know.

Beddome, Benjamin.
MS. *Eng. misc. e. 227, fol. 2.

Almighty God eternal prince, judge of justice right, 1087
And come to thee oh mighty God, which judgest best.

'A prayer to be said towards bed'.
MS. Gough Norfolk 43, fol. 46$^{v}$.

1088 Almighty God is a consuming fire.
'Cause they their comforter incensed had.
MS. *Rawl. poet. 97, fol. 13$^{v}$ (autogr.).

1089 Almighty God maker of heaven
Now sweet Jesu have mercy on me.
Brown-Robbins *Index*, 253, no. 9 stanzas with refrain, i.e. a fuller version than either of those recorded in Brown-Robbins.
MS. Lat. liturg. e. 17, fol. 51.

1090 Almighty God to whom the right
Will blast and consume all.
Psalm xciv.
MS. *Rawl. C. 113, fol. 66*a*$^{v}$.

1091 Almighty God uncreate and without measure
Amongst all manner of men measure we may use.
Wallys, John.
MS. Ashmole 48, fol. 93.

1092 Almighty Jove great architect of all
While Alban's shrine her stones for relics keeps.
Shrimpton, John, 'The spoiles of Tyme', History of Verulam.
MS. Gough Herts. 3, fol. 5 (autogr.).

1093 Almighty Judge, how shall poor wretches brook
There thou shalt find, my faults are thine.
Herbert, George, 'Judgement'.
Pr. *The Temple*, 1633, p. 182.
MS. *Tanner 307, fol. 138$^{v}$.

1094 Almighty King thy boundless reign
Ten thousand blessings on its wings.
'From the Reading Mercury, on the Earth Quake at Lisbon'.
MS. Eng. misc. e. 227, fol. 30.

1095 Almighty Lord, who from thy glorious throne
Who may with thee compare?
Herbert, George, 'The Church Militant'.
Pr. *The Temple*, 1633, p. 184.
MS. *Tanner 307, fol. 141.

1096 Almighty love, I love the stripes, which thou
When shall my thirsty soul be fill'd with love!
'"Ετλην οἷ οὔπω τις ἐπιχθόνιος βροτὸς ἄλλος' 'Die Secundo Post Festum Paschae' 68 Sic Cecinit πολύτλας E. E.'
MS. Tanner 306, fol. 405.

1097 Almighty love! 'tis in thy power to make
The proud submissive, and the brisk man sad.
'Love's strong effects'.
MS. Rawl. poet. 173, fol. 79.

1098 Almighty lowness, whose free power
Rise what thou wouldst thou shouldst not go away.
Paman, Clement, 'Good Friday'.
MS. Rawl. poet. 147, p. 157.

Almighty power! amazing are thy ways 1099
How far above our knowledge and our praise.
'Hymn from the 8th Psalm'.
MS. Percy d. 9, fol. 31$^{v}$.

Almighty power my father and my friend, 1100
Oh! let us meet, and bless thy name at last.
'Scriblerus', 'A Prayer', 'Vide Spectator N° Vol. ' (*sic.*).
MS. Montagu e. 14, fol. 15.

Almighty universal Lord 1101
In all the majesty of love.
Kenton, James.
MS. *Eng. poet. e. 20, p. 240 (autogr.).

Along this lonely unfrequented plain, 1102
Than I'm her namesake and admiring friend.
Maitland, Charlotte, 'Lines . . . to Mrs. Charlotte Smith Authoress of Rural Walks &c.', Oct. 1798.
MS. Eng. poet. c. 51, p. 104.

Alpha nor omega will Coa espy 1103
Till she ascend up to the cornered pi.
Pr. *Wits Recreations*, 1640, no. 381.
MS. Rawl. poet. 153, fol. 28.

Alpha the priests' prayers, host's plague, prince's wrath 1104
Omega Priam's gifts dead Hector buy.
J. F., 'The Argument of Homer's Iliad translated'.
MS. *Eng. poet. f. 17, p. 99 (autogr.).

Alphonsor boasting of his yard 1105
Before the top of it by chance was fired.
Epigram.
MS. Rawl. poet. 172, fol. 7$^{v}$.

Also this lesson son I thee lere 1106
And evermore beware of Had I wist.
'Anonimous'.
MS. Ashmole 972, fol. 304$^{v}$.

Although a speech penn'd by abusive wit 1107
Add to the glories of next morning sun.
[Lawrence, Thomas, of University College], dedication to a lady of a music speech, 1669. See Wood's *Fasti*, ii. 302 (where the date is given as 1671).
MS. Top. Oxon. e. 202, p. 29.

Although Christ all His time in innocence 1108
God's love to man is most of all expressed.
MS. *Rawl. poet. 97, fol. 57$^{v}$ (autogr.).

Although fair gems proud Nero had 1109
Which are bestowed by wicked men.
Bacon, Sir Nicholas, translation of Boethius, *Consolations* III. iv, 1664.
MS. Tanner 306, fol. 328 (autogr.).

1110 Although I be an honest Laird
The rich and gallant Knight Sir Sawney.
'A Crambo Song on losing my mistress'.
MS. Douce 193, fol. 62.

1111 Although it rack my heart I will bereave
Unto that part which time nor death can touch.
Beaumont, Thomas, 'Of his intent to leave her after so many crosses in their affection'.
MS. *Malone 18, p. 58 (autogr.).

1112 Although it was of weakness that Eve sinned
Them more, who for small trifles will offend.
MS. *Rawl. poet. 97, fol. 9$^{v}$ (autogr.).

1113 Although men's hearts were hardened so, that when
To be partaker of corruption.
MS. *Rawl. poet. 97, fol. 65 (autogr.).

1114 Although my muse sweet mistress oftentimes
Though grief remain with me joy reign with you.
Burton, Francis.
MS. *Add. A. 267, fol. 98 (autogr.).

1115 Although no art the fire of love can tame
'Tis oft extinguished by an equal flame.
'Distich on Love—Sed potes igne pari'.
Pr. *Poems on Several Occasions, by several Persons*, 1672, p. 32.
MS. Sancroft 53, p. 1.

1116 Although of Israel the major part
And cried a God, alive yet worms him ate.
MS. *Rawl. poet. 97, fol. 65$^{v}$ (autogr.).

1117 Although the French king [yclept] most Christian be
His crowns be circumcised most Jewishly.
Couplet, 'Of French Crowns'.
MSS. Malone 19, p. 150; 23, p. 220.

1118 Although the speaking word have life,
When the spoken word is fled.
MS. Rawl. D. 954, fol. 44$^{v}$.

1119 Although thy hand, and faith, and good works too
Of music, joy, life and eternity.
Donne, John, Elegy III.
Pr. *Poems*, 1633.
MSS. *Eng. poet. e. 99, fol. 16$^{v}$; *f. 9, p. 62; Rawl. poet. 117, two copies attr. to Mr. Dunne, fols. 248 and 201$^{v}$ rev.

1120 Although thy store be small, for to begin
And heaps are made of many little things.
Whitney, Geoffrey, 'De Parvis, grandis acervus erit'.
MS. *Rawl. poet. 56, fol. 52$^{v}$.

Although what might within God's heart resides, 1121
Whose love is life, whose lack eternal pain.
F. W., 'Sonnet 36. The manner how the holy ghost procedeth'.
MS. *Rawl. C. 639, p. 186.

Although you now are in great state 1122
I wish you, to prevent the blow.
'Left in the Chamber-Window of the Duke of Lauderdail, at his being in Scotland in the Summer. 1672'.
MS. Don. b. 8, p. 370.

Always irresolute, loose and fast, 1123
And if you can't get her mind her not.
Williams, John, 'Love Character'.
MS. *Rawl. poet. 184, fol. 94$^{v}$ (autogr.).

Always love me as I love you 1124
No time shall my firm love subdue.
Williams, John.
MS. *Rawl. poet. 184, fol. 53 (autogr.).

Am I despised because you say 1125
By these true tears y' are weeping.
[Herrick, Robert], 'An old man to his young Mrs.'
Pr. *Hesperides*, 1648, and in Henry Lawes' *Ayres and Dialogues*, 1653, i. 19.
MSS. Don. c. 57, fol. 28$^{v}$, with music by H. Lawes; Rawl. poet. 147, p. 14, attr. to Herricke.

Am I Jove's sister? is't the only name 1126
Which heretofore gave mighty gods content.
'Hercules Furens a Tragaedy translated out of Seneca'.
MS. Rawl. poet. 76, p. 1.

Am I mad, oh noble Festus 1127
That he favoured superstition.
[Corbett, Richard], 'The distracted Puritan'.
Pr. *Poëtica Stromata*, 1648.
MSS. Rawl. poet. 26, fol. 121; 212, fol. 149$^{v}$ rev.

Am I so soon forgot, too well I see 1128
Since love's all false on earth there's no true love.
Beaumont, Thomas, 'On her Wavering'.
MS. *Malone 18, p. 56 (autogr.).

Amarillis by a spring's 1129
He chirped for joy to see himself deceived.
[Herrick, Robert].
Pr. *Hesperides*, 1648, beg. Sweet Amaryllis.
MS. Don. c. 57, fol. 94$^{v}$, with music.

Amarillis o' late 1130
Revived in her heart.
Godolphin, Sidney, 'A Ballet'.
MS. Malone 13, p. 21.

1131 Amarillis tear thy hair
Canst thou sleep when I am here.
Pr. Henry Lawes' *Select Ayres and Dialogues*, 1669, p. 25, and in *New Ayres and Dialogues*, 1678, p. 75, with music by W. Lawes.
MS. Don. c. 57, fol. 59, a different setting from those printed.

1132 Amarillis told her swain
For I do love thee dearly.
[Porter, Thomas], song in 'The Villain', 1663, Act. II.
MS. Rawl. poet. 65, fol. 31ᵛ.

1133 Amarillis was full fair
Are warned to take heed.
Dyer, Sir Edward.
Pr. from MS. Tanner 306, R. M. Sargent, *At the court of Queen Elizabeth*, 1935.
MSS. Rawl. poet. 85, fol. 98ᵛ, attr. to E. Dyer; Tanner 306, fol. 174.

1134 Amazing, condescending love
And never, never thence depart.
Kenton, James.
MS. *Eng. poet. e. 20. p. 266 (autogr.).

1135 Ambition ventures highly for a crown,
And subjects, children-like, should him obey.
Robinson, Robert.
MS. *Rawl. poet. 218, p. 31 (autogr.).

1136 Ambitious man, to gain a crown,
Then they die: so ends the story.
Robinson, Robert.
MS. *Rawl. poet. 218, p. 54 (autogr.).

1137 Ambitious to be known in deathless verse.
And with it is the thought of Merlin gone.
'Via prima salutis Nate Dea, Graia pandetur ab urbe', Virgil, 1735.
MS. Eng. misc. e. 240, p. 337.

1138 Amend, Eliza, candidly attend
And with immortal radiance gild the skies.
Mr. M[erric]k, 'Letter to a Friend On Love'.
MS. Eng. poet. e. 39, p. 157.

1139 Amid the press of men of might
To take them as thy right.
[Hopkins, John], Psalm lxxxii.
MS. Rawl. poet. 112, fol. 46ᵛ.

1140 Amid the purple clouds, the glitt'ring sun
Oh! wretched life, how weary is thy stay!
'Scriblerus', 'On Sun-Set. Vide opening to Marmontel's Shepherdess of the Alps'.
MS. Montagu e. 14, fol. 26.

Amidst a herd of learned fools 1141
Amid the blaze of day.
Webb, Foster, Horace, *Odes* I. xxxiv.
Subscribed 'Telarius' in *Gentleman's Magazine*, xii, 1742, p. 46.
MS. Eng. poet. c. 9, p. 80.

Amidst my joys I will accord 1142
Above the high heavens that doth dwell.
Forman, Simon, 'A Rehearsal of his first trouble . . . 1576'.
Pr. *A Brief Description of the Ancient and Modern manuscripts . . . [at] Plymouth*, J. O. Halliwell Phillipps, 1853, p. 39.
MS. Ashmole 802, fol. 123 (autogr.).

Amidst my mirth and pleasantness 1143
It comes in mind to wait the wanton wight.
'Tempore quo fodiebat'. Six stanzas, with a refrain 'So often warned', etc.
MS. Ashmole 48, fol. 1.

Amidst our cups, have we no other talk. 1144
Dispute religion, so make none at all.
Robinson, Robert.
MS. Rawl. poet. 218, p. 19 (autogr.).

Amidst the blinder rage 1145
Thy memory must be our kindest influence.
Dugard, Samuel, 'On the Death of his Honourd Uncle Mr. William DuGard, Head Master of Merchant Taylors School'.
MS. Rawl. poet. 19, fol. 32.

Amidst the fairest mountain tops 1146
But yet a woman's heart.
Dyer, Sir Edward. At end, crossed out, 'The Earle Essex, vel, L. Mountioy'.
See *Writings of Sir E. Dyer*, ed. Grosart, 1872, p. 58.
MS. Rawl. poet. 148, fol. 65, attr. to Mr. Dier; another copy of one verse with music, fol. 112ᵛ.

Amidst the throng of poets which do strive 1147
Spout fresh, and from his ashes new tears rise.
Unfinished mourning verse.
MS. Add. B. 109, fol. 98ᵛ.

Amidst those volumes of conceited mirth 1148
Who is light's son, and not the son of lightness.
Langewoorth, Dr. [John, D.D. 1579 (?)], 'The Proeme' to verses on the Trinity and on the fall of Adam.
MS. Rawl. poet. 148, fol. 104.

Amidst variety of means 1149
I'm only on the road.
Beddome, Benjamin.
MS. *Eng. misc. e. 227, fol. 173.

1150 Among the High Church men I find there are several
It may be Hoadly the high and Sacheverell the low.
Pr. Hearne's *Collections*, ed. C. E. Doble, ii, O.H.S. vii, 1886, p. 352. Winter 1709/10.
MSS. Eng. poet. c. 41, fol. 23; Hearne's diaries 23, p. 187.

1151 Among the little pages, who were sent
Or mother church espouse her bully's cause.
Endorsed, 'Dr B[irch]' i.e. Dr. Peter Birch, D.D. 1688, d. 1710(?).
MS. Tanner 306, fol. 469.

1152 Among the myrtles as I walked
Like those short sweets are knit together.
[Herrick, Robert].
MS. Don. c. 57, fol. 97, with music; see also A1166.

1153 Among the pots, where I
Receive her groans, and bottle every tear.
'Desertion'.
MS. *Eng. poet. e. 51, p. 42.

1154 Among the princes of the earth
To thine inheritance.
Psalm lxxxii, 'Oct. 18, 1747'.
MS. *Montagu e. 10, fol. $34^v$.

1155 Among the sheep was I
Shepherd and bishop of my soul.
Kenton, James.
MS. *Eng. poet. e. 20, p. 234 (autogr.).

1156 Among the woes of those unhappy wights
That all the world may read of thy renown.
Briton, [Nicholas], 'Amoris lachrimæ on the death of Sr. P. Sidney'.
Pr. *Brittons Bowre of Delights*, 1591; see *Poems by Nicholas Breton*, ed. J. Robertson, 1952, p. xxv.
MS. Rawl. poet. 85, fol. 27.

1157 Among us mortals oft we're truly told
And prov'd thee once an infant, twice a man.
[Madan, Martin], 'Englished' epitaph on William Earl of Mansfield, d. 1793.
MS. Eng. poet. c. 51, p. 23.

1158 Amongst a thousand books (what fitter place?)
He was a greater library than they.
Sancroft, William, translator of H. Grotius, 'In Effigiem Jos. Scaligeri in Bibliotheca Leidensi'.
MS. Sancroft 48, fol. $32^v$ (autogr.).

Amongst all the hard names that denote reproach 1159
A Scotchman's greatest plague, God send him home.
'Dr. Bur[ne]ts Character in Jacobite Satyr'.
MS. Eng. poet. d. 53, p. 83.

Amongst Antonius mounted ships with speed 1160
Of him that spends and wasteth all his days.
W. A., Horace *Epodes* i.
MS. *Rawl. poet. 104, fol. 47 (autogr.).

Amongst black crimes, and foremost of the train 1161
Besotted into such credulity . . .
'Ambition, a vision, 1685', first 17 lines only.
MS. Sancroft 53, p. 51.

Amongst men, none more happy is than he, 1162
That can his own by others' harms forsee.
Couplet.
MS. Rawl. D. 431, fol. 99.

Amongst much inward profound perpending 1163
So grant the lord that highest sitteth in throne.
Forrest, William, 'To the Queen's majesty, An Oration Consolatory . . .' i.e. to Queen Mary, with 'Griselde the Second'.
MS. Wood empt. 2, fol. 71.

Amongst our sex sweet Pursland pure you are 1164
'Tis Frances Cavendish, and no other she.
Cavendish, Lady Jane, 'On my sweet Sister Fraunces'.
MS. *Rawl. poet. 16, p. 11.

Amongst the Dutch, this for a proverb's spoken 1165
That glass and drink, and friends, shall all be broken.
'Epigram in Belgarum [proverbium]'.
MS. Ashmole 38, p. 82.

Amongst the myrtles as I walked 1166
Like those short sweets are knit together.
[Herrick, Robert].
MS. Rawl. poet. 65, fol. $30^v$; see also A1152.

Amongst the number in despair poor silly man 1167
And make her wander with her commander in all misery.
MS. Eng. poet. f. 10, fol. 88.

Amongst the poets Dacus numbered is 1168
Among the poets Dacus numbered is.
Davis, John, of Gray's Inn, 'In Dacum'.
MS. *Rawl. poet. 212, fol. 60 rev.; see also D3.

Amongst the sons of men how few are known 1169
Reynolds in time, may be like Hogarth now.
Churchill, Charles, 'An Epistle to William Hogarth'.
MS. *Eng. poet. d. 113, p. 80.

1170 Amongst the thousands who your glories sing
And glad mankind till time shall be no more.
Samber, Robert, 'To the Marquis of Caermarthen on his Lordship's Marriage with Lady Anne Seymour . . . 1719'.
MSS. Rawl. poet. 11, fol. 18; *134*a*, fol. 207 (both autogr.).

1171 Amongst the writing race of modern wit
By gentle doctors, and by small commander.
'A small Satire'.
Answer to 'Among the Race of England's modern peers'. Both pr. *Poems on Affairs of State*, iii. 1704, p. 144.
MS. Don. b. 8, p. 653.

1172 Amongst your pots leave off to brawl and scold
Of this Chimæra thee in freedom place.
W. A., Horace, *Odes* I. xxvii.
MS. *Rawl. poet. 104, fol. 9ᵛ (autogr.).

1173 Amoret, the milky way
And powerful too as either God.
[Waller, Edmund], 'To Amoret'.
Pr. *Poems*, 1645, p. 137.
MS. *Don. d. 55, fol. 35ᵛ.

1174 Amount my soul from earth awhile
And there my dwelling have.
See H. E. Rollins, *Old English Ballads*, 1920, p. 152, and L. I. Guiney, *Recusant Poets*, 1938, pp. 269, 278.
MS. Eng. poet. b. 5, p. 18.

1175 Amphion well skill'd
For Handel can work them as well.
'Upon a piece of Music composed by Mr. Handel and performed at Oxford to make Money for a Music Room building there'.
MS. Top. Oxon. b. 116, fol. 121.

1176 Amstrother all men she comes near, she engages
But she then for a place at court did tarry.
'A Lampoon'.
MS. Don. b. 8, p. 483.

1177 Amyntas, I am come alone,
She answer'd with a kiss.
Sedley, Sir Charles, 'Amyntas courting Cælia for her last Favour'.
MS. Rawl. poet. 173, fol. 76.

1178 An aged man is cold; doth heat require;
In depth of winter, be it frost or snow.
Robinson, Robert.
MS. *Rawl. poet. 218, p. 177 (autogr.).

1179 An aged swan, when death drew nigh
Sings and rejoices at his fate.
'The Swan and the Stork'.
MS. *Eng. poet. d. 47, fol. 141.

An angel to Tortosa flies, enjoin'd, 1180
And their usurper startle at the news.
T[albot], Sir G[ilbert], 'Argument' of Tasso's Holy War, canto I.
MS. Rawl. poet. 4, fol. 8.

An ant was nimbly tripping in the shade 1181
Is rich in her sepulchre, and precious made.
Sancroft, Archbishop William (?), Martial, *Epigrams* VI. XV.
MS. Sancoft 48, fol. 31ᵛ (in Sancroft's hand).

An ape, a lion, a fox, and an ass, 1182
Then birds of ill omen, and women no more.
See F. B. Zimmerman, *Purcell*, 1963, no. 241.
MS. Montagu e. 13, fol. 96ᵛ.

An ape which had twins, like a foolish fond mother, 1183
To those they indulge most, are cruelly kind.
'The Ape and her Cubs'.
MS. Eng. misc. e. 219, fol. 7ᵛ.

An assignation is an amorous zeal 1184
Next with a catalogue we'll stock the town.
'The Assignation'.
MS. Firth e. 6, fol. 80ᵛ.

An atheist now must a monster be, 1185
Oh wicked Parliament.
Kennett, White, 'To Mr. E[dward] L[isle] on his Majesty's dissolving the late Parliament at Oxford. March 28, 1681'.
Pr. *Wood's Life and Times*, ed. Clarke, ii, O.H.S. xxi, 1892, p. 534. Brds., pr. bk. Wood 276A, no. 524, attr. to White Kennett in Wood's hand.
MSS. Rawl. D. 398, fol. 119, attr. to White Kennett; Wood F. 34, fol. 177.

An eagle and a crow, by chance unknown 1186
He, who gilds o'er his precepts, best succeeds.
'The young Eagles and Crows'.
MS. Eng. misc. e. 219, fol. 7.

An eagle shall come flee forth of the aerie 1187
With many a sore dent.
'Marlyn and Ambrisse'.
MS. Rawl. C. 813, fol. 137.

An ear, ye youthful fair ones lend, 1188
And peace, and honour, shall thy soul possess.
Bate, S[ally], 'The Introduction to the Whole Duty of Woman versified . . . 1768'.
MS. *Eng. poet. e. 28, p. 246.

An early blossom in its prime 1189
To strangle hope, by blasting thee.
On Joseph Barker.
MS. Rawl. poet. 210, fol. 61.

1190 An earthen vessel's thrown away
Only fit for the ground.
Robinson, Robert.
MS. *Rawl. poet. 218, p. 131 (autogr.).

1191 An easy thing to keep off death
It is but keeping one in breath.
Pestell, Thomas, 'Receipt against death'. Couplet.
MS. *Malone 14, p. 35.

1192 An eighty-eight brought in Spain's Armado,
France lies entombed with Spain i' th' British seas.
Translation of Latin, 'Epitaphium Tryumphale—De victoria navali in Gallos Anno 1692', [La Hogue].
MS. Add. A. 301, fol. vii.

1193 An eloquent knight in the height of his speech
Though himself be a joke, yet his whore must be spared.
'Sir Wm. Windham and Lord Peterborough', Spring 1715.
MS. Eng. poet. e. 87, p. 103; see also W884.

1194 An emblem of the giddy world I stand
And innocently thine's th' admired ground.
Amherst, Elizabeth, 'Inscriptions intended for Newbold, 1771'.
MS. *Eng. poet. e. 109, p. 64.

1195 An empty purse doth nothing gain;
Money gets money with might and main.
Robinson, Robert, couplet.
MS. *Rawl. poet. 218, p. 38 (autogr.).

1196 An English lad long wooed a lass of Wales
Have digged already I can dig no more.
[Harington, Sir John], 'Nil refert loqui dum uti liceat'.
In Harington's autograph, Folger MS. 4455 (indexed in pr. bk. Thorn-Drury d. 43; for description see *Census of Medieval and Renaissance MSS. in U.S. and Canada*, S. de Ricci, 1937, p. 2267). Pr. Henry Parrot's *Laquei Ridiculosi*, 1613, ii. 195.
MSS. Eng. poet. f. 9, p. 18, attr. to J. D.; Firth d. 7, fol. 162; Rawl. poet. 160, fol. 158v.

1197 An esquire he was right hardy to the field
Where body and soul shall ever praise his name.
On William Skeffington of Whiteladies, 1550, Tonge Church, Salop.
MS. Ashmole 854, fol. 226v.

1198 An evening with its sweeter light
Renew the pleasures, of the day.
'The fountain of Verity, in the Gardens of Beau-plaine'.
MS. Rawl. A. 176, fol. 82.

An evil wife, a daily strife, 1199
Is a good wife, in weal or woe.
Robinson, Robert.
MS. *Rawl. poet. 218, p. 176 (autogr.).

An exorcist who no small income gain'd 1200
The rulers fear, while Paul and Silas sing.
'The Exorcist'.
MS. Rawl. poet. 154, fol. 115.

An eye in a corner who useth to have 1201
More dainties who catcheth than dainty fed mouse.
MS. Rawl. poet. 108, fol. 9v.

An harlot to her husband poison gave, 1202
More cruel grows to save her husband's life.
'An Epigram translated from Martial'.
MS. Eng. poet. f. 12, p. 71.

An hogshead never broached possess I now 1203
Let pleasing notes from care turn back thy face.
W. A., Horace, *Odes* IV. ii.
MS. *Rawl. poet. 104, fol. 43v (autogr.).

An honest careful and ingenuous child 1204
And being dead, she lives eternally.
Freind, John, 'Verses in Praise of my Sister Sarah who d. 31 Dec. 1670', aged 5.
MS. *Top. Oxon. f. 31, p. 305.

An honest cause that has no money by, 1205
There's no withstanding of a man of might.
Robinson, Robert.
MS. *Rawl. poet. 218, p. 73 (autogr.).

An honest German had for years 1206
And leave them just as nature meant!
Parsons, William, 'A Caution to Ladies who use white paint', Oct. 1785.
MS. *Don. d. 123, p. 130 (autogr.).

An honest miller and a gracious king, 1207
Forget the livery slave and give the wit his due.
Somervile, William, 'The King and Miller of Mansfield. An Epilogue', endorsed 'never printed'.
MS. Ballard 47, fol. 16.

An honourable sail of Dunkirk was made 1208
Would allay the distemper that makes us so mad.
Satire during the Dutch War, 'all things done by honour'; dated 19 July 1667 in B.M. Add. MS. 18220, fol. 20v.
MS. Add. A. 48, fol. 13.

An humble lad, whose young and simple thought 1209
It might not be in lake of Lethe drowned.
'On the death of the Lady Poole of Saperton, 1611'.
MS. Malone 19, p. 69.

1210 An humble spirit better is allow'd,
Pride doth most commonly preambulate.
[Jordan, Thomas], 'On Pride'.
Pr. *Divinity and Morality*, Sig. §§3ᵛ.
MS. Rawl. poet. 90, fol. 102.

1211 An humble worshipper
Till I all thy glory see.
Kenton, James.
MS. *Eng. poet. e. 20, p. 83 (autogr.).

1212 An hundred years now past and gone,
The round earth far and near.
Robinson, Robert.
MS. *Rawl. poet. 218, p. 5 (autogr.).

1213 An I were a maiden as many one is
I would not do amiss.
4-part song transcribed from B.M. Add. MS. 31922. Cf. John Stevens, *Music and Poetry in the Early Tudor Court*, 1961.
MS. Mus. d. 183, fol. 11ᵛ.

1214 An ill stomach and the word of disgrace
Is the name of the man with the flattering face.
[Nowell, Alexander (?)], 'On Sir Walter Rawleigh's shame', couplet.
MS. Rawl. poet. 84, fol. 72ᵛ; see also T1100.

1215 An ill year, of a Good-year us bereft
Wise, comely, learned, eloquent, and kind.
'Upon Sir Henry Goodyer of Powleworth'.
Pr. Camden's *Remaines*, 1605, p. 55.
MSS. Ashmole 38, p. 178; Eng. poet. e. 40, fol. 123.

1216 An imposter of late
To the health of the right Mr. Wickham.
MS. Mus. Sch. C. 95, p. 101.

1217 An indian nymph invited had of yore
From whence the woods record them o'er and o'er.
T[ofte], R[obert].
MS. Malone 16, p. 40.

1218 An inundation, says the fable,
To nourish vermin, may be bit.
Swift, Jonathan, 'On the word, brother Protestants, and Fellow Christians', so used by the Advocates for the the Repeal of the Test Act in Ireland, 1733.
First printed in the *Gentleman's Magazine*, Supplement, 1733, iii. 710. See Swift's *Poems*, ed. H. Williams, 1937, iii. 809.
MS. Eng. poet. c. 41, fol. 41.

An it, An't . . .
See A1355.

An oaken broken elbow chair 1219
Why not as well as Doctor Swift.
'A True and faithfull Inventory of the Goods belonging to Doctor Swift'.
MS. Montagu e. 13, fol. 95.

An old man his old house props up. 1220
Down down to th' ground it falls.
Robinson, Robert.
MS. *Rawl. poet. 218, p. 108 (autogr.).

An old man poor is wretched without doubt: 1221
A young man poor in time may work it out.
Robinson, Robert, couplet.
MS. *Rawl. poet. 218, p. 67 (autogr.).

An old man's character is hit with ease 1222
And fond of no man's humour—but his own.
'The Old Man in Horace'.
MS. Eng. poet. e. 40, fol. 35.

An old man's pike, most women dislike 1223
It doubles like a rush, when it comes to the push.
Couplet.
MS. Wood E. 32, fol. 10.

An old stale widower loving a young wench 1224
You shall not thatch my new house with old straw.
MS. Eng. poet. f. 10, fol. 114.

An old wicked seer and a bishop revered 1225
Will bring in the house of Hanover.
'On the death of Bishop Burnet and the Marquess of Wharton', 1715.
Pr. bk. Firth b. 22, fol. 17.

An open heart, a generous mind 1226
Who love, lament him—but despise.
'The Rake'.
Pr. Dodsley's *Collection of Poems*, iv, 1755, p. 325, attr. to 'a Lady in New England'.
MS. *Eng. poet. d. 47, fol. 174.

An ounce of pleasure's worth a pound of profit 1227
And beggary at last shall be thy gain.
Robinson, Robert.
MS. *Rawl. poet. 218, p. 34 (autogr.).

An ox and ass together yoked 1228
An ox and angel in one plough.
Boswell, James, 'Epigram'.
Pr. *A Collection of Original Poems by Scotch Gentlemen*, ii, 1762, p. 79.
MS. *Douce 193, fol. 84.

1229 An ox in Lancashire was bred.
And Æsop's toad spits in his face.
Somervile, W[illiam], 'The Ox and the Toad. A Fable . . . in respect to himself and Mr. Jon Parker of Kineton Farm . . . July 31 1729'; endorsed 'never printed'.
MS. Ballard 47, fol. 2.

1230 An Oxon lass did take her coats up high
And yet betwixt them both I swear a man was born.
'On an Oxon lasse'.
MS. CCC. 328, fol. 21; see also B102, F28, M411.

1231 An undefiled course who leadeth
O leave me not then quite forsaken.
Herbert, Mary (*née* Sidney), Countess of Pembroke, Psalm cxix, A, 'Beati immaculati'.
MSS. *Rawl. poet. 24, p. 174; *25, fol. 118.

1232 An unmarried man [vicar] in the nominative case
Brought them both to an ablative danger.
'On an unmarried man'.
MSS. Douce f. 5, fol. 10; Eng. poet. e. 14, fol. 79v.

1233 An usurer, whose idol was his gold.
For god will waste your stock, and make you starve.
Whitney, Geoffrey, 'Male parta male dilabuntur'.
MS. *Rawl. poet. 56, fol. 104.

1234 And all the greatest praises I can give
Are found too small whilst you beyond 'em live.
Williams, John, couplet.
MS. *Rawl. poet. 191, fol. 50 (autogr.).

1235 And am I sworn a dunghill slave for ever
And Heav'n's blest kingdom find, with heav'n's blest king Jehovah.
[Quarles, Francis], 'The Miserable Man's desire to be at rest'.
Pr. *Emblemes*, 1635, v. xiii.
MS. Rawl. poet. 90, fol. 30.

1236 And are these all the rites that must be done,
Till he return i'th resurrection.
[Wild, Dr. Robert], 'An Epitaph upon Robert E: of Essex', buried 19th October 1646.
Pr. *Iter Boreale with . . . other Poems*, 1668, p. 36.
MSS. Ashmole 36, 37, fol. 4v.

And are we thus transform'd by fate? 1237
Which none but saints, like thee, have trod.
'Upon seeing some Verses of a Lady's written upon a Scull, in continuation of the same', 18th cent.
MS. Top. Oxon. c. 220, p. 21.

And are you sure the news is true? 1238
Or trust the rude seas more.
'The Husband's return'.
MS. Percy d. 9, fol. 9.

And are you there old Pas in faith I ever thought 1239
Let cat and dog fight which shall have both you.
Sidney, Sir Philip, from the *Arcadia*.
MS. *e Mus. 37, fol. 82.

And art return'd [thou back] again [great Duke] with all thy faults, 1240
Thy treachery, neglect, and cowardice.
'On the Duke of Buckingham', at his return from Rhé, November 1627.
Pr. *Poems and Songs* on the Duke of Buckingham, Percy Society Publications, xxix (5), 1850, p. 19.
MSS. Ashmole 36, 37, fol. 50v; 38, p. 133, attr. to Mr. [John] Heappe; Malone 21, fol. 56v; 23, p. 106; Tanner 306, fol. 264; Tanner 465, fol. 98v; see also A1247, A1422.

And art thou born, brave babe? blest be the day [thy birth] 1241
Sol will re-shine; if not, Charles hath a son.
Jonson, Ben., 'Epigram on the Prince's birth', 29 May, 1630.
MSS. Eng. poet. e. 14, fol. 48; Rawl. poet. 26, fol. 10v, attr. to Ben Jhonson; 84, fol. 61; 147, p. 232 rev., attr. to Ben Johnson; 160, fol. 12v; 206, p. 57, attr. to Johnson.

And art thou come, dear Saviour? hath thy love 1242
Will make the stall a court, the cratch a throne.
Judge Hale, [Sir Matthew], 'Christmas-day, 1659'.
Pr. *Contemplations*, 1676, p. 116, '1649'.
MS. Montagu c. 5, fol. 13; see also B631.

And art thou dead dear child, and laid in grave 1243
Joy in that lot, thou dost precede thy sire.
[Burghe, Nicholas (?)] translator of Latin verses by Sir Peter Frechvill on the death of his daughter, 17 Sept. 1626.
MS. Ashmole 38, p. 189.

And art thou dead who whilom thought'st thy state 1244
Where our creator, and redeemer is.
On the Duke of Buckingham, 1628.
MS. Malone 23, p. 198.

1245 And art thou grieved, sweet and sacred dove,
My want of tears with store of blood.
Herbert, George, '4 Ephes. 30, Greive not the h. spirit &c.'
Pr. *The Temple*, 1633, p. 128.
MS. *Tanner 307, fol. 97ᵛ.

1246 And art thou not the same
Thy goodness to adore.
Kenton, James.
MS. *Eng. poet. e. 20, p. 7 (autogr.).

1247 And art thou return'd again with all thy faults
Thy swollen ambition made his carcase swell . . .
'On the duke's return from the Ile of Ree', incomplete.
MS. Douce f. 5, fol. 5ᵛ; see also A1240, A1422.

1248 And as in prisons mean rogues beat
Hemp for the service of the great.
Couplet.
MS. Rawl. poet. 153, fol. 30ᵛ.

1249 And call ye this, to utter what is just
There is a God, that carves to each his own.
Herbert, Mary (*née* Sidney), Countess of Pembroke, Psalm lviii.
MS. *Rawl. poet. 24, p. 81.

1250 And can I e'er forget
To dwell with him on high.
Kenton, James.
MS. *Eng. poet. e. 20, p. 178 (autogr.).

1251 And can I even dare to claim
Humbly to serve thy church below.
Kenton, James.
MS. *Eng. poet. e. 20, p. 81 (autogr.).

1252 And can I of his goodness doubt
In realms of everlasting day.
Kenton, James.
MS. *Eng. poet. e. 20, p. 249 (autogr.).

1253 And can it be that a dull motley group
'Tis true 'tis pity, pity 'tis 'tis true.
'On the French Players at Clifden'.
Pr. bk. Firth b. 22, fol. 43.

1254 And can we e'er forget
And on our Jesus gaze.
Kenton, James.
MS. *Eng. poet. e. 20, p. 74 (autogr.).

1255 And can ye so ungrateful prove
Darkness is light ye fondly dream.
Kenton, James.
MS. *Eng. poet. e. 20, p. 144 (autogr.).

And can you Doris think the world to cheat 1256
He's crown'd that is victorious in war.
Bromley, Henry, 'To Doris against Privacy'.
MS. *Don. e. 19, fol. 2 (autogr.).

And can you then, dear Miss, resolve to hide 1257
It is sincere, and never shall have end.
Williams, John, 'To Miss Ashe'.
MS. *Rawl. poet. 191, fol. 106ᵛ (autogr.).

And can your kindness pain disarm 1258
But aggravate despair.
Skinner, John, 'To Miss —, . . . Verses addressed to Delia'.
MS. *Eng. poet. d. 22, two copies, fols. 47, 63.

And canst then leave thy Nancy? 1259
So may conclude me here.
'The Parting Lovers a Song'.
MS. Montagu e. 13, fol. 62ᵛ.

And could he in his last, even impious breath, 1260
Should in one day be lost.
Roach, Richard. Translation for *The Postman* [?] of poem by Augustus Caesar, on Virgil's commanding his poems to be burnt.
MS. Rawl. D. 833, fol. 165ᵛ rev. (autogr.).

And dar'st thou venture still to live in sin, 1261
Jesus forgive us, we know not what we do.
[Quarles, Francis], 'On Man's Cruelty'.
Pr. *Divine Fancies*, 1632, i. 51.
MS. Rawl. poet. 90, fol. 63.

And did the love of pontiff sway 1262
And thus the simple souls enslave.
Kenton, James.
MS. *Eng. poet. e. 20, p. 177 (autogr.).

And dost thou live? We stand amaz'd, to read 1263
Nature will put her whole freehold to cost.
Oldisworth, Nicolas, 'To his Friend beyond Sea'.
MS. *Don. c. 24, fol. 11 (autogr.).

And hast thou left me then? can nothing stay 1264
To you, and follies all, Adieu, Adieu.
Mervall, Alphonso, 'To Lycoris adieu'. Subscribed 'Daphnis'.
MS. *Rawl. poet. 166, p. 30 (autogr.).

And has[t] thou left old Jemmy in the lurch? 1265
And may all christian people say Amen to 't.
[Brown, Thomas], 'A Satyr upon the French King writ after the Peace was concluded at Reswick anno 1679'.
Pr. *Poems on Affairs of State*, ii, 1703, p. 258, and Brown's *Works*, 1730, i. 59.
MS. Rawl. poet. 173, fol. 127.

1266 And hast thou left us [so] then dear soul? must we
In death undarkened by the night of sin.

[Radcliffe, Edward, of University College], on the death of John, eldest son of Philip Lord Stanhope (later 1st Earl of Chesterfield), Oxford, 1625.

MSS. Ashmole 47, fol. 93$^{v}$; CCC. 327, fol. 33$^{v}$; 328, fol. 70; Don. d. 58, fol. 7, attr. to E. Radclyffe; Douce f. 5, fol. 4.

1267 And hast thou then, in the gay spring of life,
With modest independency to dwell!

Parsons, William, 'On a friend'.

MS. *Don. d. 123, p. 18 (autogr.).

1268 And hast thou thus oh more than cruel death
Henceforth of mirth, my muse shall sing no more.

G. B., 'Epitaph 17' on Prince Henry in 'Cestria Lugens', 1612.

MS. *Rawl. poet. 116, fol. 9.

1269 And have I found you then (dread majesties)
We will be chang'd transform'd to any thing.

[Wilde, George], 'Prologus' to the *Hospitall of Lovers*, acted before Charles I and the Queen at St. John's College, Oxford, August 1636.

MS. Rawl. poet. 172, fol. 27.

1270 And have I heard her say oh cruel pain
Where her who should rule pain false pain abuseth.

Sidney, Sir Philip, Sonnet, 'made when his lady had pain in her face'.

Pr. *Arcadia*, 1598, p. 476, and in Henry Constable's *Diana*, 1594, Third Decade, Sonnet V.

MSS. *e Mus. 37, fol. 245$^{v}$; Rawl. poet. 85, fol. 56, attr. to Sir Philip Sidney.

1271 And here the precious dust is laid
Frail as our flesh, crumble to dust.

Carew, Thomas, 'The Inscription on the Tomb of the Lady Mary Wentworth . . . 1632'.

See *Poems*, ed. R. Dunlap, 1949, p. 243.

MSS. *Don. b. 9, fol. 31; Rawl. D. 682, fol. 4$^{v}$, copied from the tomb in Toddington Church, Beds.

1272 And I warn you workmen win while you may
And ere this king come kame shall ane.

Alliterative prophetical verses.

MS. Rawl. C. 813, two copies, fols. 140$^{v}$, 142.

1273 And I was sent in all haste to you here
If hate the poet's happy in this night.

Cavendish, Lady Jane, epilogue to 'The Concealed Fancies'.

MS. *Rawl. poet. 16, p. 155.

And if from Clout you take this letter C 1274
The Clout is Lout and that I send to thee.

Couplet, 'An answer in a handkerchief', to I964.

MS. Douce f. 5, fol. 16$^{v}$.

And if men's fingers cannot make the wheat 1275
For where he is there must his ser[vants be].

'A Meditation how to discern the Lord's Body in the Blessed Sacrament'.

MS. Rawl. C. 986, fol. 38.

And if our music cannot please your ears 1276
Great Jove shall fetch you music from the spheres.

'Of Musick', couplet.

MS. Rawl. poet. 148, fol. 3.

And if thou wo'st what thing it were 1277
Be merry honest and liberal.

Alphabetical sequence of aphorisms.

MS. Gough Norfolk 43, fol. 52$^{v}$.

And in our day have we not seen 1278
Till thou bestow the eternal crown.

Kenton, James.

MS. *Eng. poet. e. 20, p. 134 (autogr.).

And is death naught but sleep, I fear the dead 1279*a*
To lie one hour's the way to sit up three.

Southwell, Sir Robert, 'Mors nihil est nisi somnus'.

MS. *Eng. poet. f. 6, fol. 45$^{v}$ (autogr.).

And is he dead indeed? Is virtue so forset 1279*b*
I wiped mine eyes, and thanked God, and clapped my hands for joy.

'A briefe of the lyfe and deathe of Sir Edmunde Campian'.

See *Recusant Poets*, L. I. Guiney, 1939, p. 177.

MS. Laud misc. 755 (roll).

And is he gone, whom these arms held but now? 1280
Thy heaven to thee?

Crashaw, Richard, 'Luke 2. Quærit Jesum suum Maria'.

MS. Tanner 465, fol. 32; attr. to Mr. Crashaw fol. 1*a*.

And is it so, that after Hydra's slain 1281
Breathing her last, thus died Creed, thus I.

Owen, Corbett, 'On the death of Dr. Creed'.

MS. Eng. misc. e. 255, fol. 25.

And is it true? has then our Charles his grace 1282
Can't choose but both the king and people please.

Wright, Abraham, on the birth of James, Duke of York, 1633.

MS. Eng. misc. e. 82, fol. 38 (autogr.).

1283 **And is my Harley caught away**
**Forever love and gaze.**
Kenton, James, 'Further Thoughts on the Death of Mrs. Deborah Harley', 1787–8.
MS. *Eng. poet. e. 19, p. 314 (autogr.).

1284 **And is my little sprightly friend**
**My little friend above.**
Kenton, James, 'On the Death of Richard Field; who died 1789 Aged 5 yrs. and three months'.
MS. *Eng. poet. e. 19, p. 338 (autogr.).

1285 **And is the lovely shadow fled?**
**To give a child to God.**
'To a Lady on the death of her only Child, an Infant'.
MS. Eng. poet. e. 39, p. 49.

1286 **And is the sufferer gone?**
**In the smile of Jesu's face.**
Kenton, James, 'On the Death of Mrs. Frances Revill', 1783.
MS. *Eng. poet. e. 19, p. 261 (autogr.).

1287 **And is this all thou great Baboon in wit**
**And come with birch and thunder in thy rear.**
'For Mr. John Kay, alias Poet Ninny a Defiance'.
MS. Eng. poet. c. 25, fol. 81.

1288 **And is this all? will you but thus pass by?**
**And oft'ner we'll express our grateful piety.**
To Queen Anne on her visit to Oxford, September, 1617.
MS. Rawl. D. 1048, fol. 69.

1289 **And lives there one, by cankered malice led**
**And scorns to tear the unresisting prey!**
Mrs. Madan of Stafford Row, 'in reply to an invidious Epistle', N251.
MSS. Eng. poet. c. 51, p. 309, attr. to Mrs. Madan of Stafford Row; e. 40, fol. 82.

1290 **And may at last my weary age**
**That heart-felt joy which none can tell . . .** (incomplete)
'The Cave of Morar, The man of Sorrows'.
MS. Percy c. 8, fol. 133.

1291 **And must I go? and must I be no more**
**A curse to be immortal, and not here.**
Norris, [John, of Bemerton, 'The complaint of Adam Turn'd out of Paradise'], the first three stanzas only.
Pr. *A Collection of Miscellanies*, 1687, p. 112.
MS. Rawl. D. 868, fol. 50v.

**And must I needs depart then** 1292
**Oh break asunder heart to satisfy her.**
Pr. Thomas Bateson's *First set of English Madrigales*, 1604, xiv.
MSS. Mus. f. 20–24: f. 20, fol. 47v.

**And must I still be guilty, still untrue,** 1293
**I am not guilty, I've not broke my vow.**
Creech, Thomas, translator: Ovid, *Amores*, II. vii, 'He protest's he had never anything to do with the Chambermaid'.
MS. Rawl. poet. 173, fol. 47.

**And must I then a loathsome carcass be** 1294
**I shall awake again the blest.**
'On sight of a Grave Stone on which was Written As I am So shalt thou be'.
MS. Eng. poet. e. 40, fol. 163.

**And must I then forsake my native shore** 1295
**England and Germany are just the same.**
On Baroness von Walmoden's leaving for England, 1738.
MS. Eng. misc. b. 48, fol. 1.

**And must perfection be attain'd** 1296
**But diligence is ours.**
Beddome, Benjamin.
MS. *Eng. misc. e. 227, fol. 83.

**And must we, dear Belinda, bid adieu,** 1297
**And from their souls, exclude each glimpse of joy.**
'The Farewell to the Spring-Gardens'.
MS. Eng. poet. c. 9, p. 141.

**And must we part with thee, dear Lambert! now?** 1298
**Translate to greater happiness above.**
Cromwell, Edward, 'On Mr. Joseph Lambert's death' dated 'Jan. 21. 1716–17'.
MS. *Rawl. poet. 165, fols. 35v, 36v (autogr.).

**And now all nature seem'd in love,** 1299
**To welcome the new-liveried year.**
Wotton, Sir Henry, 'On the spring'.
Pr. *Reliquiae Wottonianae*, 1651, p. 524.
MSS. Rawl. poet. 147, p. 47, attr. to Sir H. Wotton; Tanner 465, fol. 61v, attr. to Sir H. Wotton.

**And now cow-hearts look to the shop** 1300
**Cuckolds all a row.**
MS. Rawl. poet. 26, fol. 160.

**And now God bless our gracious king** 1301
**Nor ever did a wise one.**
[Wilmot, John, Earl of Rochester], 'Writ on the Glass'.
Pr. in 'Miscellany Poems' appended to *Miscellaneous Works of Rochester and Roscommon*, 1707, p. 135.
MS. North b. 24, fol. 146v.

1302 And now, John Shaw, why so uneasy?
Prithee sing. May the king—
Drake, S.: 'Teste G. Smith' is added to the note on the authorship.
MS. Rawl. poet 207, p. 179.

1303 And now Lord what remaineth? but that we
With heart and voice for ever, sing Amen.
MS. *Rawl. poet. 97, fol. 76 (autogr.).

1304 And now more great than when you were
A churchman 'scape and a Lord Treasurer.
[Wright, Abraham], 'The temper', on Bishop Juxon, continued from T2065.
Attr. to Wright by Wood, *Athenae* iv. 277.
MS. Malone 21, fol. 54.

1305 And now, my muse, 'tis time we should have done
Not for what others say, or critics dare.
Samber, Robert, 'The Epilogue', to 'the Bellman's Verses'.
MS. *Rawl. poet. 134*b*, fol. 158 (autogr.).

1306 And now the bleating flocks for shelter run
Do stretch and fill the air with notes.
Percy, Thomas, nephew of the Bishop of Dromore: 'Summer, . . . about Nov. 1776'.
MS. Percy c. 8, fol. 49 (autogr.).

1307 And now the earth on its vast axle rolls,
And thence, displeas'd, the wrathful goddess flew.
'Paradise'.
MS. Rawl. poet. 173, fol. 176ᵛ.

1308 And now the net wide spreading in its arms
And on them is his chief rely.
Percy, Thomas, nephew of the Bp. of Dromore: 'Autumn', 1776.
MS. Percy c. 8, two copies. fols. 45 (autogr.) and 90.

1309 And now the night's dim tragedies are done
He like the sun, in his meridian dwell.
Ashmole, Elias, 'Caesaris arma canant alii: nos Caesaris aras', on Charles II.
Pr. as *Sol in Ascendente*, 1660, MSS. Ashmole 36, 37, fol. 17.
MS. Ashmole 38, fol. 230 (autogr. corrected draft).

1310 And now thou art set wide ope: the spear's sad art
Thus set them ope.
Crashaw, Richard, 'I am the door'.
MS. Tanner 465, fol. 36, attr. to Mr. Crashaw fol. *1a*.

And now 'tis time for their officious haste 1311
Where piety and valour jointly go.
Dryden, John, 'On the Death of Oliver Cromwell'.
Pr. *Three Poems upon the Death of . . . [the] Lord Protector*, 1659.
MSS. Eng. misc. e. 147, fol. 88, attr. to John Dryden; Eng. poet. e. 4, p. 92, attr. to Dryden; Rawl. D. 260, fol. 41ᵛ; Sancroft 53, p. 9, verse 10 on p. vi, attr. to John Dryden; Top. Oxon. e. 202, fol. 66.

And say you so? I by experience find 1312
She'd ne'er have done what now she 's forc't to do.
Southwell, Sir Robert,' Volenti nihil difficile: ad Tutorem'.
MS. *Eng. poet. f. 6, fol. 36ᵛ (autogr.).

[And shall great Halifax resign to fate] 1313
And Halifax in those recesses thought.
Extract from 'An Epistle to Joseph Addison Esqr. occasion'd by the death of the Right Honourable Charles late Earl of Halifax. Lond. 1715 fol. pag. 8'.
Also pr. *Works and Life of Halifax*, 1715, p. 75.
MS. Rawl. D. 896, fol. 38.

And shall I yet persist to grieve 1314
That Thou and Love art one.
Kenton, James.
MS. *Eng. poet. e. 20, p. 115 (autogr.).

And shall thy furious anger burn 1315
Shall thy devouring vengeance prove.
Kenton, James.
MS. *Eng. poet. e. 20, p. 109 (autogr.).

And since our Phoebus hath his throne 1316
The proud usurping charioteer.
'Of a bad prince'.
MS. Eng. poet. e. 14, fol. 57.

And there is magic in her eye 1317
I'll scorn the scorn of all the wise.
Clarke, Captain Thomas.
MS. Eng. misc. e. 241, fol. 50.

And think you I have not a load 1318
So enter free; pass may the slouch.
Buckley, Thomas, of All Souls, 'The libell of Oxenforde', *c.* 1564.
Pr. *Athenae*, ed. Bliss, i, 1813, col. 610; see also *Fasti*, ed. Bliss, i, 1815, 171.
MSS. Rawl. poet. 85, fol. 72ᵛ; 212, fol. 118, attr. to Mr. Buckley; Tanner 465, fol. 105, attr. to Mr. Buckley; see also W631.

1319 **And this firm line in brazen leaves enroll**
**The conscience is the hell that dooms the soul.**
Couplet.
MS. Rawl. poet. 117, fol. 272 rev.

1320 **And those which gain all with this curse receive it**
**From fools they get it, to their sons they leave it.**
Couplet.
MS. Rawl. poet. 117, fol. 276 rev.

1321 **And thou my son? such inhumanity**
**No sooner open'd be, than made thy grave.**
Southwell, Sir Robert, 'Oratio Caesaris ad Brutum mortem ei miniantem'.
MS. *Eng. poet. f. 6, fol. 34 rev. (autogr.).

1322–3 **And to thy mercy, Lord and Father dear**
**For Christ's sake, sweet father let me have it.**
Prayer in 6-line stanzas, incomplete.
MSS. Ashmole 36, 37, fol. 61.

1324 **And truth (sweet virgins) 'twere a vile miscarriage**
**And scandal never blast the lady's joy.**
Price, H[owell, M.A. 1696], T[rinity] C[ollege] So[cius], 'Epilogue after the Music Act', at Cambridge.
MS. Rawl. D. 1164, fol. 306.

1325 **And were the sunbeams of that eye too fierce**
**To save this beauty, and have struck us blind.**
'Upon the eyeblemish of a beautiful Lady'.
Attr. to F. Quarles in B.M. Add. MS. 22602, fol. 31ᵛ and MS. Egerton 923, fol. 46.
MS. Tanner 465, fol. 59ᵛ.

1326 **And wert thou doomed thus wretchedly to close**
**Which her sweet pity drops upon a brute?**
Homer, Philip Bracebridge, 'On the death of a favourite Cat'.
MS. *Add. C. 282, p. 4.

1327 **And who can the power of the city withstand.**
**When the sword bearer's hilt is in the sword-bearer's hand.**
Couplet.
MS. Rawl. D. 431, fol. 100.

1328 **And why all this, (my Sam) turn votary**
**Of moisture radical, the vital sack.**
MS. Eng. poet. c. 53, fols. 4ᵛ, 6.

1329 **And why should I not share my tears and be**
**Have wept, let those that know more weep the rest.**
'On the [death] of Toby Mathew, Archbishop of York'. 29 March 1628.
MSS. CCC. 328, fol. 67ᵛ; Eng. poet. e. 97, p. 50, attr. to John Earles.

1330 **And why so coy? what is your rose**
**I hope will give me leave to till.**
MS. Mus. b. 1, fol. 117ᵛ, music by John Wilson.

**And why so neat? you virgins have an art** 1331
**Men love your body, for thy beauty sake.**
Oldisworth, Robert or Giles, 'Satyricall against Womens Vanity', in 'The Pattern of Piety'.
MS. *Rawl. C. 422, fol. 6ᵛ (in the hand of Giles Oldisworth).

**And why this vault and tombs alive we must** 1332
**There would not need an epitaph at all.**
[Philips, Katherine], 'Wiston Vault'.
Pr. *Poems*, 1664, p. 68.
MS. Rawl. poet. 65, fol. 20.

**And why to me do you stand bare** 1333
**Ev'n so much as our littleness.**
Oldisworth, Nicolas, 'On complements . . . given to a Courtier, 1630'.
MS. *Don. c. 24, fol. 10ᵛ (autogr.).

**And why to me this letter of complaint** 1334
**A husband's prudence you will soon excuse.**
'An Answer to J. Poultney's letter. Why I do not let my wife keep some sort of company. 1698'.
MS. Eng. poet. e. 50, p. 94.

**And why to me this [thus] thou lame god [lord] of fire?** 1335
**Thy wife's pox on thee, and Bess Broughton's too.**
Jonson, Ben., 'An Execration upon Vulcan'. *The Underwood*, xliii.
Pr. *Ben Jonson*, Herford and Simpson, viii, 1947, p. 202.
MSS. Eng. poet. e. 14, two copies, fols. 22ᵛ, attr. to Ben Johnson, and 78 rev., attr. to Johnson; e. 97, p. 71, attr. to Ben Johnson, Regis Professor.

**And will these prodigies never be gone?** 1336
**She's a man and no man, as he king and no king.**
Creswell, Robert, 'A Drum Major brought to bed of a Manchild. June 1655'.
MS. *Eng. poet. f. 24, fol. 11 (autogr.).

**And wilt thou gi'e me all that** 1337
**There's room enough for all that.**
MS. Wood F. 34, fol. 175.

**And wilt thou go brave duke and leave us here** 1338
**That we may think't a happy victory.**
'Verses on the duke [of Buckingham] setting forth to Spain', 1627.
Pr. *Poems and Songs* on the Duke of Buckingham, Percy Society, xxix (5), 1850, p. 9.
MSS. Douce f. 5, fol. 21ᵛ; Eng. poet. c. 50, fol. 13ᵛ; Malone 23, p. 105; Rawl. poet. 26, fol. 80ᵛ; 160, fol. 198.

1339 And with Pope's genius is all genius fled?
And only Robin-Hood lamenting grieved.
'The Age of Dullness. A Satire . . . By a natural son of the late Mr. Pope. 1756'.
MS. Douce 201, fol. 45.

1340 And you, auspicious prince, our other care,
To you return the vigour they receive.
Cowslade, [Thomas], 'To the Prince . . . 1702'.
MS. Eng. poet. f. 13, fol. 182$^{v}$.

1341 And you have offered too methinks, your pleasure
Just so you have showed no wit but proffered.
Answer to C229.
MS. Eng. poet. e. 14, fol. 57.

1342 And you shall find the greatest enemy
That man can have is his prosperity.
Couplet subscribed 'Daniell'.
MS. Rawl. poet. 117, fol. 275 rev.

1343 Andrew and Maudlin, Rebecca and Will
Till their bills and their bellies went a pintle a pantle.
D'Urfey, Thomas, 'Song. The Country-Dance'.
Pr. D'Urfey's *Pills to Purge Melancholy*, 1719, ii. 19.
MS. Rawl. poet. 147, p. 89.

1344 Andrew by Christ call'd on Tiberias lake
Since he was ours we must not be our own.
Clifford, Henry, Earl of Cumberland, 'Saint Andrew'.
MS. *Rawl. poet. 95, fol. 36.

1345 Andrew is called, but his readiness
That all thy blessing and thy love may gain.
Cromwell, Edward, paraphrase of Latin verses 'in Festum Sancti Andrææ' dated 30 Nov. 1715.
MS. *Rawl. poet. 165, fol. 29 (autogr.).

1346 Anellus sends his corn unto the mill,
And of thy wife, too prodigal and plain.
Whitney, Geoffrey, 'Præpostera fides'.
MS. *Rawl. poet. 56, fol. 47.

1347 Angels in bright attire
Accept dear Lord this little all.
Beddome, Benjamin, 2. Cor. ix. 15.
Pr. *Hymns . . . of B. Beddome*, 1818, 44.
MS. *Eng. misc. e. 227, fol. 175.

1348 Angels, Saints, nor the fiends of Hell
And the king's heart he searcheth too.
'Deus videt', *temp.* James I.
MS. Eng. poet. c. 50, fol. 41$^{v}$.

Anger in hasty words, or blows 1349
And wing'd with fear, outflies the wind.
Waller, Edmund, 'Of Love'.
Pr. *Poems*, 1645, p. 116. Answered by U79.
MSS. *Don. d. 55, fol. 17; Malone 13, p. 47, attr. to Waller; *Rawl. poet. 174, p. 67; Top. Oxon. e. 380, fol. 177$^{v}$, attr. to N. L.

Anna her anagram holds still one name 1350
A queen on earth in heaven now the same.
On Queen Anne, wife of James I, 1619, couplet.
MS. Malone 19, p. 5.

Anna, to you these artless lines I send 1351
And health combine to make your joys complete.
Bate, Sally, 'To a friend', 1764.
MS. *Eng. poet. e. 28, p. 71.

Anne is an angel. True; what though [which and if] she be? 1352
Yet is an angel but a lawyer's fee.
'On Anne Angell, wooed by a lawyer'.
Pr. *Wits Recreations*, 1640, p. 485.
MSS. Eng. poet. f. 25, fol. 10; Tanner 465, fol. 95.

Another passing year is flown 1353
And none but the tyrant and faithless shall fear.
[Mr. Havard], Birthday Ode 'for Ranelagh—For Mr. Beard and Mrs. Stover'. Music by Wm. Boyce. Text printed *London Magazine*, 1752, p. 241.
MS. Mus. Sch. C. 105.

Another's faults we soon espy 1354
We in our selves see none.
Robinson, Robert.
MS. *Rawl. poet. 218, p. 24 (autogr.).

An't please your worship we thee present 1355
[Senatal (?)] Metamorphosis.
'Three Publicans petition to Sr R. S. Cotton to make Audlem a Market-Town'.
MS. Top. Cheshire c. 9, fol. 150.

Antæus was a mighty lord 1356
Turn'd a poor venal, abject slave.
'Antæus and Alcides. Pultney and Walpole'. 1742.
MS. Ballard 47, fol. 40.

Apelles' curious eye must gaze upon 1357
[That chastely lives and dies in a perfume].
R[andolph,] T[homas], 'The character of a perfect Woman'.
Not pr. in early editions: see G. Thorn-Drury's ed., 1929, pp. 165 and 214.
MS. Firth e. 4, p. 35.

1358 Apelles prince of painters never drew
No copy like the right original.
'Upon the woes pronounced by our Saviour against the scribes and pharisees'.
MS. Rawl. poet. 116, fol. 131.

1359 Aper with bibbing sack hath such a nose
His lips being dry his nose will fire his beard.
MS. Rawl. poet. 172, fol. 7v.

1360 Apollo concerned to see the transgressions
And leave them together by the ears for the bays.
'The Sessions of the Poets'.
Pr. *Poems on Affairs of State*, 1697, p. 206. See postscript, I1699.
MSS. Don. b. 8, p. 175; Douce 357, fol. 139; Locke c. 17, p. 153; Rawl. poet. 84, fol. 52*a*v rev.; Sancroft 53, p. 64.

1361 Apollo great whose beams the greater world do light
That nothing wins the heaven but what doth earth forsake.
Sidney, Sir Philip, from the *Arcadia*.
MS. *e Mus. 37, fol. 78v.

1362 Apollo help me to rehearse
For Prick is buried beneath these stones.
'On Mr. Pricke, M.A. in Christs College Cambridge', i.e. Edmund Pricke, d. 1618 (?).
MSS. Ashmole 38, p. 169; Eng. poet. d. 152, fol. 18.

1363 Apollo of old on Britannia did smile
Sprung from the fair and to the fair returns.
[Williams, Sir Charles Hanbury], 'To a Lady at Bath' [Mrs. Bindon], *Whitehall Evening Post*, 2 Feb. 1737/8, 'The Lady's Answer', and 'Reply to the Lady's Answer'.
Pr. Dodsley's *Collection of Poems*, v, 1758, p. 156.
MS. Eng. misc. e. 183, fol. 72v.

1364 Apollo's servant here now scales the sky
He purged was, t'ascend to heaven more pure.
[Freind, Nathaniel (?)], translator of verses by John Oldham on the death of John Freind. 1672.
MS. Top. Oxon. f. 31, p. 288, in Nathaniel Freind's hand.

1365 Apostate spirit vile
And bless him day by day.
Kenton, James.
MS. *Eng. poet. e. 20, p. 340 (autogr.).

Appear 1366
Or take its rest, till it hath found out thee.
Oldisworth, Nicolas, 'For a lover, whose mistress concealed her self from him'.
MS. *Don. c. 24, fol. 66v (autogr.).

Appear oh James; approach thy native shore 1367
And James shall James succeed with better fate.
'The Invitation', 30 Jan. 1714/15.
MSS. Eng. poet. e. 87, p. 161; Rawl. poet. 155, p. 227.

Appear thou mighty bard to open view 1368
Though thou'rt the only proof how interest can prevail.
[Gould, Robert], 'The Laureate or Jack Squab's History in little', on Dryden, 1687.
Pr. *A Collection of the Newest Poems . . . against Popery*, 1689, i. 17, and as a broadside.
MSS. Firth c. 16, p. 197; Rawl. poet. 159, fol. 22.

Approach you poor survivors of her sex 1369
Such sweets as will requite you with perfume.
Manwaring, D., on Mrs. Sarah Manwaring.
MS. Ashmole 47, fol. 88.

April's seal of virgin wax 1370
Which nothing but impression lacks.
'A maiden', couplet.
MS. Eng. poet. e. 14, fol. 70; see also A374.

*Arabia faelix*. So thou art to me 1371
To follow him, who gives eternal rest.
Astley, —, 'Barbara Astleii, Bear stil, Arabia, Anagram, To my wife. Epigram'.
MS. Tanner 306, fol. 412 (autogr.).

*Arbiter elegantiarum* 1372
Each miss cries 'that's the man for me'.
Parsons, William, 'Spoken extempore'.
MS. *Don. d. 123, p. 159 (autogr.).

Archeanassa now delights my eyes 1373
Whose ashes burn us what would her flame do.
Walsh, William, translator of Antipater Sidonius, 'Asclepiadus p. 337'. [Greek Anthology].
MS. Malone 9, fol. 26v (autogr.).

Arch-miracle of men, in whom we see 1374
When all his hopes and fortunes were o'erthrown.
Ayton, Ro[bert], letter to the Duke of Buckingham, beginning and ending in verse, concerning a monopoly of Sea coal; probably before 26 July 1620. See *C.S.P.D.* 1619–23, p. 168.
MS. Tanner 306, fol. 262 (autogr.).

1375 Are all diseases dead? or will death say
Nor time, nor death, could ever celebrate.
'Upon the Death of the Duke of Richmond and Lennox'.
Ludovick Stuart, buried 17 Feb. 1623/4; opening of parliament, 19 Feb.
Pr. Camden's *Remaines*, 1637, p. 400.
MSS. Ashmole 38, p. 173; 47, fol. 59; Eng. poet. c. 50, fol. 59, attr. to Sir John Eliott; e. 14, fol. 24; f. 10, fol. 116ᵛ; Rawl. poet. 147, p. 42; 160, fol. 23ᵛ; Tanner 465, fol. 73ᵛ.

1376 Are all men mortal? and all born to die?
'Twas not that man should think his haven's here.
MS. Rawl. poet. 209, fol. 43ᵛ.

1377 Are all our hopes but this? did we expect
For others thou dost fight, for thyself die.
[Gomersall, Robert], 'An Elegy on the death of Gustavus Adolphus the victorious king of Sweden'.
Pr. *Poems*, 1633, Sig. O2.
MS. Malone 21, fol. 15.

1378 Are lovers full of fire
To freeze the tongue and fire the heart.
[Davison, Francis].
Pr. Robert Jones's *First set of Madrigals*, 1607, xxv–vi.
MSS. Mus. f. 25–28: f. 25, fols. 6ᵛ–7, 10ᵛ.

1379 Are not the ravens, great God, sustained by Thee;
Whilst lilies flourish, and the raven's fed.
[Quarles, Francis], 'On Ravens and Lilies'.
Pr. *Divine Fancies*, 1632, iv. 65.
MS. Rawl. poet. 90, fol. 75.

1380 Are robbers with good workmen poor?
That thrusts the workman out of door.
Robinson, Robert.
MS. *Rawl. poet. 218, p. 117 (autogr.).

1381 Are saints distinguished by their fruits,
Thyself my constant guide.
Beddome, Benjamin.
MS. *Eng. misc. e. 227, fol. 6ᵛ.

1382 Are these the choice dishes the doctor has sent us?
Heaven sends us good meat, but the devil sends cooks.
Garrick, David, 'On Dr. G[oldsmith] Characteristical Cookery. a Jeu d'Esprit'.
Pr. bk. Vet. A5 d. 569, added at end.

Are these the strings that [which] poets feign 1383
So I've but scratched these notes of mine.
Masters, T[homas] of New College, 'On Lute strings Catt-bitten'.
MSS. Ashmole 47, fol. 24, attr. to T. M. of New College; Malone 21, fol. 85, attr. to Mr. Masters; Rawl. poet. 147, p. 104; 206, p. 59, attr. to Master; Sancroft 53, p. 30.

Are these two sisters twins pray stand and view, 1384
For nothing went betwixt them but the shears.
'Of one Mr. Sheires that lay with two sisters'.
MS. Firth d. 7, fol. 181.

Are wise men mad? are good men fools? Oh then 1385
God help us all: we all are wretched men.
Robinson, Robert, couplet.
MS. *Rawl. poet. 218, p. 136 (autogr.).

Are women fair? [Ay] yea passing fair to [look] see to. 1386
And yet so needful few can live without them.
'Women'.
MSS. CCC. 328, fol. 77ᵛ; Eng. poet. e. 14, fol. 72; Rawl. poet. 172, fol. 2.

Are women so named 1387
Beshrew me then.
The initials 'J. F.' are crossed out at the foot of the poem.
MS. Rawl. poet. 85, fol. 84.

Are wretched men in want? they're at hell's brink; 1388
But money not well used, their souls may sink.
Robinson, Robert, couplet.
MS. *Rawl. poet. 218, p. 144 (autogr.).

Argus of old we greatly prize 1389
Who seest an hundred ways with two.
'Epigram upon . . . a man who squinted'.
MS. Eng. poet. c. 51, p. 217.

Ariodant reigned, and yet (perhaps) doth reign 1390
His legs and feet by Mors were umbrated.
Sheppard, Samuel, 'The Faerie King Fashioning Love and Honour'.
MS. Rawl. poet. 28, fol. 4.

Arion's fame each wondering nation knows, 1391
And nine refulgent stars adorn his scales.
'The Story of Arion . . . From a News-paper'.
MS. Eng. poet. c. 5, fol. 30ᵛ, ʳ.

1392 **Arise and shine,**
**Of all-commanding George, all-charming Caroline.**
Roach, Richard, 'Carmen Coronarium To the Queen', 1727.
MS. Rawl. D. 832, fol. 263v (autogr.).

1393 **Arise and wake for Christis sake**
**With loud voice say the same.**
MS. Ashmole 48, fol. 101v.

1394 **Arise, arise, immortal Shakespeare rise**
**Their hearts are all courage their souls are all fire.**
Ode to Shakespeare; autograph music of Wm. Boyce.
MS. Mus. d. 14, fol. 16.

1395 **Arise, arise the glorious sun**
**O'ertake, outdo the industrious sun.**
'A call to rise'.
MS. *Don. f. 5, fol. 4.

1396*a* **Arise bright Phœbus, make no stay**
**'Twill please my ghost it has no cause to grieve.**
Chatwin, John, 'To the Morning'.
MS. *Rawl. poet. 94, p. 8 (autogr.).

1396*b* **Arise Britannia! see around thy head**
**Resum'd his seat, and shone more awful than before.**
'To the King on his landing in Scotland' 1715.
MS. Hearne's diaries 61, p. 87.

1397 **Arise my glad soul, and praise thou the Lord.**
**And swift on the wings of the wind doth he ride . . . (unfinished).**
Psalm civ.
MS. *Montagu e. 10, fol. 81v.

1398 **Arise my muse: and to thy tuneful lyre**
**Go on great prince go on.**
D'Urfey, Tom, 'set to Music by Mr. H. Purcell on the Queens Birthday April 30 1690'.
Pr. *Poems on Affairs of State,* 1698, p. 63; in F. B. Zimmerman, *Purcell,* 1963, no. 320.
MS. Mus. c. 26, fol. 71.

1399 **Arise my soul [all] my inward frame**
**His works all praise him in their spheres.**
Fairfax, Thomas, Lord, Psalm ciii.
MS. *Fairfax 40, p. 252 (autogr.).
MS. *Fairfax 38, p. 190.

1400 **Arise oh [George] from stupid sleep awake,**
**Take heart and like the ministers resign.**
Satire addressed to George II during Walpole's ministry.
MS. Eng. misc. b. 48, fol. 23.

**Arise, shine: for, thy light is come:** 1401
**Whom once we saw less in himself than story.**
'New-Year's Day'.
MS. Rawl. poet. 23, p. 184.

**Arithmetic nine digits and no more** 1402
**How soon mischance hath made a hand of thee.**
Randolph, Thomas, 'on the loss of his little finger cut off'.
Pr. *Poems,* 1638, p. 41.
MSS. Ashmole 47, fol. 93, attr. to Mr. Randolph; CCC. 328, fol. 75v, attr. to Randolph; Eng. poet. e. 97, p. 25; Firth e. 4, p. 29, attr. to T. R.; Malone 19, p. 121, attr. to Randolph of Cambridge; Rawl. poet. 209, fol. 8, attr. to Randol.

**Arm arm in heaven there is faction** 1403
**To see how they can gull him.**
On Jove (James I) and Ganymede (Buckingham), 1623.
MSS. Eng. poet. c. 50, fol. 41v; Rawl. poet. 160, fol. 174; Tanner 306, fol. 261.

**Arm, neighbours at length** 1404
**When old Nick wants a rasher of Bacon. Fol de Rol.**
R. T., 'From the St. James Chronicle of May 1st 1798'.
MS. Eng. poet. c. 51, p. 48*b*.

**Armed with a ferula, the flying troop** 1405
**Had but one fly been left to draw him home.**
Southwell, Sir Robert, 'Carmina Emanuelis The[sauri]: in [Domitianum Captantem Muscas]'.
MS. *Eng. poet. f. 6, fol. 52 (autogr.).

**Armed with her native force, behold** 1406
**Which gave such monarchs birth.**
[Whitehead, William], Birthday Ode, 1778. Music by Boyce.
Pr. *Poems,* 1790, ii. 131.
MS. Mus. Sch. D. 339.

**Arms and a doughty knight I sing** 1407
**And in they toss both devil and pope.**
F. G., 'On Marlborough's Triumphant Entry', 4 Aug. 1714.
MS. Rawl. poet. 155, p. 193.

**Arms and arts have long contended** 1408
**That first taught universal grace.**
D[arell], Sir S[amson], 'On his Lady making a pen'.
MS. Rawl. poet. 210, fol. 52v.

**Arms and the boy I sing, whose slighted dart** 1409*a*
**Nature in you has prov'd the art divine.**
Acrostic on 'Arabella Deighton'.
MS. Ballard 47, fol. 75.

1409b [Arms and the man I sing, who forced by fate]
Of full desire, and sunk to pleasing rest.
Dryden, John, translator, Virgil's *Aeneid*; extract from book VIII.
MS. Rawl. poet. 173, fol. 25.

1410 Around me as I turn my wandering eyes
And view again the long extinguished day.
'A Soliloquy in a Church-Yard'.
MS. *Eng. poet. d. 47, fol. 177ᵛ.

1411 Arraign'd and guilty found of such a crime
If in the spending she might reap content.
Mervall, Alphonso, 'To Cloris', subscribed 'Tettix'.
MS. *Rawl. poet. 166, p. 8 (autogr.).

1412 Art had done well, if in a subject meet
May say that heavenly hue is thine of right.
Mervall, Alphonso. 'To Cloris of her picture', subscribed 'Tettix'.
MS. *Rawl. poet. 166, p. 38 (autogr.).

1413 *Art in few places* hath thus shown her skill
Had she but what was framed not kept so ill.
Anagram on 'Francis (sic) Paulet'. Couplet.
MS. Rawl. poet. 84, fol. 1.

1414 Art not ashamed that those that seem to be
In humble, patient holy poverty.
MS. *Don. f. 5, fol. 11ᵛ.

1415 Art thou a king? look well unto thy state.
Now live to god, and bid the world, adieu.
MS. Rawl. poet. 66, fol. 45.

1416 Art thou a sinner, and wouldst merit Heaven
So, of all curses, tyrants are the worst.
'Tyrannicidium', endorsed 1689. James II and Louis XIV.
MS. Rawl. poet. 159, fol. 148.

1417 Art thou a teacher? teach peace and good will;
And we are brethren, whether great or small.
Robinson, Robert.
MS. *Rawl. poet. 218, p. 64 (autogr.).

1418 Art thou advanc'd to thy supreme desire?
And a painful earnest of a heaven to come.
[Quarles, Francis], *Iob Militant*, 1624, 5, 'In re-advancement'.
MS. Rawl. poet. 127, fol. 17ᵛ.

1419 Art thou ascended, blessed Lord, on high,
Till I ascend to thee, and joys above.
'On Ascension day'.
MS. Rawl. poet. 200, fol. 124.

Art thou gone too (thou great and gallant mind) 1420
Leave on thy stone: here lies the ministry.
Wild, R[obert], 'Upon the death of Mr. Vines'.
Pr. *Iter Boreale, with . . . other Poems*, 1668, p. 29.
MS. Lat. misc. c. 19, p. 146.

Art: thou most glorious of temporal acquisitions 1421
Consigned to judgement: to receive their due.
'The Excellence of Art. Or an Encomium on Painting', 13 March 1732.
MS. Rawl. poet. 158, fol. 2.

Art thou returned [again] great duke with all thy faults 1422
Thy treachery, neglect and cowardice.
On the Duke of Buckingham's voyage to Rhé, 1627.
MSS. Eng. poet. c. 50, fol. 27ᵛ; Rawl. poet. 26, fol. 79; 160, fol. 198; see also A1240, A1247.

Art thou sick? the way to health 1423
'Till from thee I've purchased peace.
Colman, Henry, on prayer.
MS. *Rawl. poet. 204, fol. 15 (autogr.).

Art thou then gone, thou sweet and humble mind 1424
Expect to see them to eternity.
Fleming, Robert, 'To the Memory of the truly Religious Mrs. Susanna Soame, 1691/2'.
MS. *Rawl. poet. 202, fol. 11ᵛ (autogr.).

Arthur o'Bower has broken his band 1425
Cannot turn Arthur of the Bower.
MS. Douce d. 59, fol. 52.

Artist, that underneath my table 1426
Ends both the spider and the poet.
Littleton, Edward, of King's College, Cambridge, 'On a Spider'.
Pr. Anthony Hammond's *Miscellany*, 1720, p. 147; *The Vocal Miscellany*, ii. 144 (2nd ed., 1738, ii. 334).
MSS. Eng. poet. f. 12, p. 91; Rawl. poet. 116, fol. 107ᵛ, attr. to Edwd. Littleton; Top. Oxon. e. 379, fol. 7ᵛ.

Artists, who with true hearts, do true arts love, 1427
Deign (for their sakes) these artless lines t'approve.
Cheyney, William, 'To the learned Readers'.
MS. *Rawl. poet. 86, fol. 32ᵛ.

As a friend, friendlike, to a friend far absent 1428
Till we do meet. (Echo) Meet.
Reshoulde, James, 'Amico suo T.M.'.
MS. Rawl. poet. 85, fol. 53ᵛ.

1429 As a louse as we crack, hath a list on his back
No badge of his reading.
Hoskins, [John], 'on a dull Lawyer'.
Pr. from this MS., *Life*, etc. of Hoskyns, L. B. Osborn, 1937, p. 211.
MS. Malone 19, p. 148.

1430 As a love token by her dear heart sent
When mother comes up starts, and forth it rolls.
Creswell, Robert, 'Ex Catull[o] . . . ut mittum sponsi furtivo . . .'
MS. *Eng. poet. f. 24, fol. 63v (autogr.).

1431 As a poor traveller, that hath to go
Say shall I die disdained or live beloved.
Burton, Francis.
MS. *Add. A. 267, fol. 68v (autogr.).

1432 As a sad turtle sits alone,
You to unfaithfulness or scorn persuade.
MS. Montagu e. 13, fol. 141v.

1433 As a small bird who by a Timon's care
Dispel his darkness and enlarge his day.
Earbery, Matthias, 'David's flight from the Court of Saul . . . Psalm XI', sent to Charles Trimnell, Bp. of Norwich 1708–21.
MS. Tanner 306, fol. 464 (autogr.).

1434 As a stately vessel o'er the ocean sweeps
Quit its clay prison, and with angels join.
Bate, S[ally], 'On the Death of the Duke of Cumberland . . . 1765'.
MS. *Eng. poet. e. 28, p. 76.

1435 As a student in college
[Cussa Sheny (?)] old port's our bride.
Lampoon, late 18th cent.
MS. Top. Oxon. a. 29, fol. 69.

1436 As abroad in the gardens and meadow I range
Of showing my friendship at th' expense of my sense.
Truesdale, Frances, 'To her friend Miss Elea: Peart . . . Harefield-Place May. 1768'.
MS. Eng. poet. e. 28, p. 174.

1437 As after pride a fall will ever be
So before honour is humility.
Beaumont, Thomas, 'The Motto to his Escutchion'.
MS. *Malone 18, p. 98 (autogr.).

1438 As all between yon aged oaks I strayed
'Come, Mortal, come away'.
Bampfylde, J[ohn Codrington]. Not pr. in his *Poetical Works*, Routledge's British Poets, 1881.
MS. Eng. misc. e. 241, fol. 60v.

As all the lesser planets by the force 1439
It will appear I did but set to rise.
Beaumont, Thomas, 'Upon his goinge from his Mrs.'.
MS. *Malone 18, p. 55 (autogr.).

As all things else, so do these senseless gloves, 1440
The time will come you'll be as base as I.
H. S.
MS. *Rawl. poet. 120, fol. 13v (autogr.).

As Anstis was trotting away from the chapter, 1441
So the king saves his money, and God save the king.
'An excellent new Ballad, April [21st] 1741'. On the installing as Knights of the Garter the Dukes of St. Albans, Marlborough, Kingston-upon-Hull, and Portland.
MS. Eng. misc. b. 48, fol. 10; pr. bk. Firth b. 22, fol. 39.

As at a banquet some meats have sweet, some sour taste 1442
Even so the doublet is too short in the waist.
The second line is by [John] Hoskins, as a 'reply' to the first.
MS. Malone 19, p. 149.

As at a mark so may I aim, 1443
On thy statutes to talk.
Psalm cxix. 15, not W. Whittingham's version. Set for 6 bells.
MS. Rawl. D. 886, fol. 26.

As at a window in my court I stood 1444
Struck through his liver and transfixed his heart.
Proverbs vii. 6–24.
MS. Don. c. 55, fol. 14.

As banish'd Ovid (if so great a name as he 1445
To which he by ungrateful Rome was sent.
Oldham, John, 'In Answer to Mr. Spencer'. Draft of 'A letter from the Country'.
MS. *Rawl. poet. 123, p. 87 (autogr.).

As beauteous flowers openly display 1446
To him even him a full reward in Heaven. Amen.
E. P.,' On Hen Smythe, Esqr. an Eligie 1706'.
MS. Eng. poet. c. 41, fol. 59.

As beautiful Jenny, ah, who was so witty? 1447
And left her to mourn on the plains of Coleraine.
'Song Adapted to the favourite Air of Kitty of Coleraine'.
MS. Malone 41, fol. 49.

As bees and flies unto the honey pot, 1448
So merchants to th' Exchange where's money got.
Robinson, Robert, couplet.
MS. *Rawl. poet. 218, p. 127 (autogr.).

1449 As bees in meadows thick do swarm
Thy friends will all be gone.
'Of feigned friends'.
Pr. *British Bibliographer*, ii, 1812, p. 611.
MS. Rawl. poet. 108, fol. 16.

1450 As Bisset modest be, as Suffield wise,
And with his reverence your God address.
'Advice to Mr. Maydman when Mayor of Portsmouth'.
MS. Eng. misc. c. 116, fol. 14v.

1451 As books, and of the lighter kind,
Of what the poet owes to thee.
Pratt, Samuel Jackson, 'To Col. Thornton —with the author's Works in 22 Volumes'.
MS. Montagu d. 3, fol. 55 (autogr.).

1452 As books imprinted sheweth right as we find
That now in our English tongue this book is printed in.
'Bartholmeus de proprietate Rerum printed by Winken de Word . . . at the latter end of the Book ther is found verses in praise of the printer and likewise of him that made the paper.'
MS. Rawl. D. 398, fol. 1v.

1453 As bright as flame, as swift as wind
All proud to serve their sovereign's will.
Tate, [Nahum], and Brady, [Nicholas], part of Psalm civ, the altered version, 1698.
MS. Rawl. D. 868, fol. 18v.

1454 As Britain's monarch guards our favour'd isle,
To bless his subjects, and adorn his throne.
'Twelfth-day Character—King'.
MS. Montagu e. 14, fol. 8v.

1455 As Butler's Cupid took his stand
And till you're married wear your breeches!
Parsons, William, 'The unfortunate Whist-player'.
MS. *Don. d. 123, p. 81 (autogr.).

1456 As by some tyrant's stern command,
Thus calmly to the grave descend!
[Blackstone, William], 'The Lawyer to his Muse', dated 1 May 1744.
Pr. Dodsley's *Collection of Poems*, iv, 1755, p. 228. For attribution see *O.B.S. P. & P.*, iii, 1931–3, p. 285.
MS. Eng. misc. c. 292, fol. 102.

1457 As by Tajo's wavy bed
Madden, madden in thy chains!
Wiffen, Jeremiah Holmes, translator, 'The Prophecy of Tagus. From the Spanish of Luis de Leon'.
MS. Montagu d. 5, fol. 286 (autogr.).

As by the fruit the tree is known, 1458
So by man's works his work is shown.
Robinson, Robert, couplet.
MS. *Rawl. poet. 218, p. 64 (autogr.).

As by the Jews, Christ to his cross was led 1459
What e'er of Shiloh prophets have foretold.
MS. *Rawl. poet. 97, fol. 64 (autogr.).

As, by the rigid laws of Rome 1460
Portend his lordship's fate is near.
'An Epigram on the Lord Lovelace's being beaten'.
MS. Firth e. 6, fol. 66.

As by the rivers we lay down 1461
And none shall pity their despair.
Godolphin, Sidney, Psalm cxxxvii.
MS. Malone 13, p. 18.

As by the Templars' holds you go 1462
And law without delay.
MS. Eng. misc. e. 241, fol. 66.

As captive mice into close prison betrayed 1463
In the same flames with them to burn.
Creswell, Robert, 'Love and Necessity'.
MS. *Eng. poet. f. 24, fol. 47 (autogr.).

As careful mothers [nurses] [do (*or* will *or* that) to sleep (*or* sleeping) lay] to [in *or* on] their beds do lay 1464
Nature my nurse laid me to bed betimes.
'On the death of a child'.
Pr. Camden's *Remaines*, 1637, p. 411, and *Wit's Recreations*, 1640, Sig. Bb4.
MSS. Ashmole 38, two copies, pp. 168 and 198; 47, fol. 52v; CCC. 328, fol. 49v; Eng. poet. c. 50, fol. 130v; e. 14, fol. 99 rev.; e. 40, fol. 116; Rawl. poet. 84, fol. 85; 116, fol. 52v; 117, fol. 196v rev., attr. to Sr. Joh. Davis; 206, p. 65; Sancroft 53, p. 45; see also A1613.

As Celia near a fountain lay 1465
And rifled all her charms.
'A Song'.
MS. Montagu e. 13, fol. 30.

As chafed hart for thirst doth seek 1466
Thou cause shalt have to thank him ever.
Harington, Sir John, Psalm xlii.
MS. *Douce 361, fol. 25v.

As Chloe o'er the meadow passed 1467
The parts disclos'd you ne'er shall touch.
Sedley, Sir Charles, 'The Fall'.
MS. Rawl. poet. 222, fol. 29v.

1468 As Chloris full of harmless thoughts
And yielded to the swain.
Wilmot, John, Earl of Rochester, 'The Yielding Nymph'.
See Vieth, p. 407.
MS. Rawl. poet. 173, fol. 71.

1469 As Chloris warm'd her by the fire
Repentant ashes left behind.
[Philipott, Thomas].
Pr. *Poems*, 1646, p. 33.
MS. Firth e. 4, p. 116, attr. to T. R.

1470 As Christ commands the earth, so must the sea
Have them but for a curse, or punishment.
MS. *Rawl. poet. 97, fol. 54$^{v}$ (autogr.).

1471 As Christ His sufferings were sans parallel
To all the elect in the last agony!
MS. *Rawl. poet. 97, fol. 73 (autogr.).

1472 As Christ the scripture making mention
With power to heal lepers and renew youth.
4 verses on the philosopher's stone, part of a diagram accompanying 'The power of divers things'.
MS. Rawl. poet. 121, fol. 70.

1473 As Christ willed it and spake it
In earth to live no more.
Lines on the Eucharist.
MSS. Ballard 72, fol. 104$^{v}$; Rawl. poet. 219, fol. 15; see also C268, T3371, T3378.

1474 As cities, that to the fierce conqueror yield
Yet we'd better by far have him, than his brother.
[Marvell, Andrew (?)], 'Upon Sir Robert Viner's setting up the king's statue on horseback, and &c.' [unveiled 29 May 1672].
See Margoliouth, Marvell's *Poems*, 2nd ed., 1952, p. 179 and note.
MSS. Don. b. 8, p. 368; *Eng. poet. d. 49, p. 250; Rawl. poet. 181, fol. 49.

1475 As Colon drove his sheep along
Blither girls, than any there.
'A Satyre', in B.M. MS. Harl. 6913 attr. to Lord Buckhurst, 'on the Duchess of Portsmouth's place being exposed to sale', 1679.
Pr. *Poems on Affairs of State*, i, 1703, p. 132. Not in *Works of Rochester* etc., 1721.
MSS. Don. b. 8, p. 598; Douce 357, fol. 66$^{v}$; Eng. poet. d. 152, fols. 52, 54–58$^{v}$.

1476 As Cupid took his bow and bolts
Who could not see to shoot.
'On Cupid and a Clown'.
MSS. Malone 19, p. 104; Rawl. poet. 142, fol. 41.

As Cupid took his bow some birding sport to find 1477
Then they should prove unto his heart the conduits to his woe.
MS. Malone 16, p. 33.

As Cynthia on her downy pillow lay 1478
Then of its joys bereave me.
'Song'.
MS. Rawl. poet. 152, fol. 171$^{v}$.

As Damon that unhappy swain 1479
The body flies and leaves the soul behind.
T. B., 'The Parting'.
MS. Rawl. poet. 222, fol. 5.

As dogs for bones, so men for money fight. 1480
The dog loves bones, and money is man's delight.
Robinson, Robert, couplet.
MS. *Rawl. poet. 218, p. 77 (autogr.).

As doth the root itself and branches feed, 1481
And faith from God's grace; so hath God decreed.
Robinson, Robert.
MS. *Rawl. poet. 218, p. 96 (autogr.).

As down in the meadow one morning I passed 1482
But if men are all false why should women prove true.
'A Ballad'.
MSS. Eng. poet. e. 8, fol. 19$^{v}$; Mus. Sch. D. 261, fol. 37.

As down the torrent of an angry flood 1483
For know that you are clay and they are brass.
'The Fable of the Pot and Pitcher, as it was told by Col. Titus the night before he kissed the King's hand'.
Pr. *A Collection of the Newest Songs against Popery*, 1689, ii. 18. See 'Morall', L96.
MSS. Ballard 22, fol. 47; Douce 357, fol. 153$^{v}$; Firth c. 16, p. 262; Rawl. poet. 173, fol. 120; Smith 27, fol. 5.

As due by many tithes (*sic*), I resign 1484
And Satan hates me, yet is loth to lose me.
Donne, John, 'Sonnett'.
Pr. *Poems*, 1633.
MS. *Eng. poet. e. 99, fol. 43.

As duty does command and prudence does advise 1485
Strive that both they and you may happy die and live.
Williams, John, 'Love thy neighbour as thy self'.
MS. *Rawl. poet. 184, fol. 123 (autogr.).

As dying saints who sweetly pass away 1486
My heart is wax . . . steel my integrity.
[Donne, John], version of 'A Valediction forbidding Mourning', A1711.
Pr. *Poems*, 1633, p. 193.
MS. Ashmole 38, p. 121, attr. to S. Butterris.

1487 As eastern princes when friends came or went
You give me the Præadamite.
Creswell, Robert, 'The Suit and the Book, . . . To Mr. R. B.'. *Praeadamitae*, I. de la Peyrère, 1655, English translation 1656.
MS. *Eng. poet. f. 24, fol. 27 (autogr.).

1488 As e'en Mars was by Pallas o'ercome
For myrtle that grows in the hedges!
Parsons, William.
MS. *Don. d. 123, p. 145 (autogr.).

1489 As Eloquence upon a trotting nag
Who had no leader nor shall have a follower.
H. S., 'In Laudem Libri et itineris primi Thome Coriati'.
MS. *Rawl. poet. 120, fol. 31v (autogr.).

1490 As Eve to Adam did in paradise
Most by fair shows (as Eva) are undone.
MS. *Rawl. poet. 97, fol. 10 (autogr.).

1491 As executioners can mercy show
To leave her, in compassion seemed unkind.
Reresby, Sir John, 'On Celia's petting when I was to go a Journey. Epigram'.
MS. *Rawl. D. 204, fol. 96v rev. (autogr.).

1492 As fades the blushing rose: so speeds
Her beauty in one day.
MS. Rawl. B. 14, fol. 53v.

1493 As fair ideas from the sky,
And all it doth receive returns again.
Traherne, Thomas, 'The Circulation'.
MS. *Eng. poet. c. 42, fol. 10 (autogr.).

1494 As fair Olinda sat beneath a shady tree,
Oh kill me, stick me, stick me, kill me, kill me quite, my dear.
'Cure for Green Sickness'.
Pr. *Poems on Affairs of State*, ii, 1703, p. 266.
MS. Rawl. poet. 173, fol. 82.

1495 As falcons are by nature fair of flicht.
That nature quhilk into your sex so hantis.
James I.
MS. *Bodl. 165, fol. 43 (autogr.).

1496 As first I went out in the morning
That it ne'r shall undo us again.
'All Men Madd. To the Tune of old Sr. Simon the king' [*c*. 1710].
MS. Rawl. poet. 169, fol. 12.

1497 As first it season'd is with good or ill.
The vessel doth retain the same scent still.
Robinson, Robert, translator, Horace, *Epistles* I. ii. 60.
MS. *Rawl. poet. 218, p. 175 (autogr.).

As first the doleful news, That he was gone 1498
Compar'd to which, all worldly wealth is nought.
C[hafe (?)], T[homas (?)], of King's School Sherborne, on the death of Robert Whetcombe, 'Antientest Governour of the King's Schoole of Sherebourne', 24 Oct. 1656.
MS. Gough Dorset 35(1), fol. 25.

As flowers fade and soon decay 1499
The wheel of time turns in one day.
Robinson, Robert, couplet.
MS. *Rawl. poet. 218, p. 71 (autogr.).

As flying Parthian shoots his piercing dart, 1500
So Celia flying wounds the follower's heart.
[Owen's Epigram] '98 Upon Caelia', couplet.
MS. *Rawl. poet. 197, fol. 9 (autogr.).

As Foot from Lombard's rich though dark abode 1501
And swifter sought the shades of his own Cray.
Parsons, William, 'The Centaur not fabulous'.
MS. *Don. d. 123, p. 207 (autogr.).

As for my part I do nor hurt nor good 1502
Stupid and senseless whilst they guide my hand.
'The King's speech' [George I].
Pr. bk. Firth b. 22, fol. 20.

As for my solace on a summer's day 1503
Even Venus self would wish to be my debtor.
Burton, Francis, acrostic, 'Anne Brocke that Lovelie mayde and Venus darlinge'.
MS. *Add. A. 267, fol. 28 (autogr.).

As for the lady which you name much heard I of her praise 1504*a*
So blinded th'are in their dark ways they cannot see the light.
MS. Ashmole 204, fol. 141v.

As from Italia's fragrant shore 1504*b*
And they like matchless Celia fair.
'Ode . . . caelum non Animum mutant qui trans mare currunt'.
MS. Eng. misc. c. 399, fol. 78.

As full of virtues as of royal blood 1505
Else had it sung thy praise in higher strain.
G. B., epitaph on Prince Henry in 'Cestria Lugens', 1612.
MS. *Rawl. poet. 116, fol. 5v.

As gasping Strephon on his death-bed lay, 1506
Live not like Strephon, but like Strephon die.
Flatman, Thomas, translation of lines by Nat. Hanbury, of Trinity College, Cambridge, 'In obitum Poenitentissimum Joannis Wilmott nuper Comitis Roffensis
Pr. *Poems and Songs*, 3rd ed., 1682, p. 146.
MS. Add. B. 105, fol. 20; see also A1621.

1507 As gentle Strephon sung and played
While Clois this blest clime shall grace.
'Song'.
MS. Firth e. 6, fol. 107v.

1508 As G[eorg]e essayed the royal ship to move
And would not launch in a pretender's right.
'On the Launching of a Ship called the Royal George', [*temp.* George I].
MS. Rawl. poet. 181, fol. 65v.

1509 As glorious scenes in masques our senses take,
He by example may in us survive.
'On the Death of Mr. Fran. Usher, Senior Fellow of Trin. Coll. Dub., Sep. 4 [16]71'.
MS. Rawl. poet. 127, fol. 4.

1510 As good men grow, so knaves do likewise spring.
Fruit, herbs, weeds, poisonous things earth forth doth bring.
Robinson, Robert, couplet.
MS. *Rawl. poet. 218, p. 69 (autogr.).

1511 As happy a palm sir, as most in this land
The man that you are, for God and the King.
[Jonson, Ben.], 'The Lord Keeper's fortune' in *The Gypsies Metamorphosed.*
MSS. Rawl. poet. 172, fol. 78; Tanner 306, fol. 252.

1512 As he lay on the plain his arm under his head,
And our eyes tell each other, what neither dare name.
'A Song'.
MS. Montagu e. 13, fol. 58v.

1513 As he, that sees a dark and shady grove,
Your first acquaintance might discredit all.
Herbert, George, 'H. Baptisme'.
Pr. *The Temple*, 1633, p. 36.
MS. *Tanner 307, fol. 27v.

1514 As Hell of old did the swine retire
And all her pains was—*Bury'd in a hog.*
Coley, Henry, 'John Gadbury. Anagramiz'd. Bury'd in a Hog'.
MS. *Add. B. 8, fol. 10v (autogr.).

1515 As Hervey sat smoking alone in his hall
I dismiss you at present, because my pipe's out.
'The Interlogue . . . Writ when the Bill against Occasional Conformity was on foot. 1704'.
MS. Don. c. 55, fol. 25v.

1516 As his worm-eaten volumes old Time tumbled o'er
Made the record authentic, and gave it to—Fame.
'On William Duke of Cumberland's defeating the Rebels at the Battle of Culoden . . . 15 April, 1747'.
MS. Montagu e. 13, fol. 92v.

As Homer sings on some great holy day 1517
For know thy pen is feebler than thy prick.
Somervile, William, 'On Sr. Dicky Wimble, i.e. Sr. R[ichard] Cocks', endorsed 'never printed'.
MS. Ballard 47, fol. 18.

As honest Tom Snip from counter broke loose 1518
To my old cribbing master, long bill'd Tommy Harper.
Skinner, John, 'The honest Taylor. Oxford 1792'.
MSS. *Eng. poet. d. 22, fol. 30v; *Top. Oxon. e. 41, p. 165.

As I a sweet rose in pleasant spring 1519
Where angels sing continually.
'Of St. Wenefrede'.
MS. Eng. poet. b. 5, p. 98.

As I a walking was the other day 1520
And when I more do hear, I more will tell you.
'The Fancy, Or The Duke of York's last Farewell', on the King's speech, 6 March 1678/9.
Pr. *The Third Collection of Songs against Popery*, 1689, p. 22, and *The Muse's Farewell*, 2nd ed., 1690, p. 180.
MSS. Don. b. 8, p. 629; e. 23, fol. 39.

As I about the town do walk 1521
His son brought the petition.
'A song of the times. June 1641'.
MS. Douce 357, fol. 36v.

As I alone 1522
They would not last one day.
'On a Gentlewoman seen naked'.
MS. Eng. poet. e. 14, fol. 65.

As I behind a bush did sit 1523
But hoarse and dry my pipes I now must spare.
Sidney, Sir Philip, from the *Arcadia.*
MS. *e Mus. 37, fol. 85.

As I came by a bower so fair 1524
And asked mercy for our lady's sake.
MS. Rawl. C. 813, fol. 1v.

As I came in by Mussle B'rough Fisher 'raw was near me 1525
And that's the way of doing o't for poor folk has na siller.
'A Ballad'.
MS. Eng. poet. e. 8, fol. 24.

As I grow an old maid and I find I go down, 1526
And good nature attended her very last day.
'The Old Maid's Wish'.
MS. Ballard 47, fol. 145v.

1527 **As I have oftentimes and long since too.**
**If thou e'er lov'st me, break not my command.**
B[rome], A[lexander], translator, Horace, *Epistles* I. xiii.
Pr. *Poems of Horace*, A. Brome, etc., 2nd ed., 1671, p. 337.
MS. Rawl. D. 261, p. 55.

1528 **As I have walked Lord entire with thee**
**And bless the Lord when in his house I pray.**
Fairfax, Thomas, Lord, Psalm xxvi.
MS. *Fairfax 40, p. 54 (autogr.).
MS. *Fairfax 38, p. 162.

1529 **As I in hoary winter's night**
**That it was Christmas day.**
[Southwell, Robert, 'The burning Babe'].
First pr. *Saint Peters Complaint*, 1602, p. 74.
MS. Eng. poet. b. 5, p. 52.

1530 **As I lay half asleep in bed this night**
**But wicked women I do dread the most.**
Tipping, William. Dated 'This Friday night Feb: 17th 1699'.
MS. *Rawl. poet. 101, fol. 73 (autogr.).

1531 **As I lay musing in my bed / Full warm . . .**
**From any dangerous ground.**
'The Praise of Sailors'.
MS. Firth c. 18, fol. 207.

1532 **As I lay musing in my bed / I heard**
**From whores all o' row.**
'Whores'.
MS. Rawl. poet. 142, fol. 47$^{v}$.

1533 **As I lay musing in my bed / No creature**
**To be so near and miss so sweet a turn.**
'A Maiden's dreame'.
MSS. Ashmole 36, 37, fol. 53; see also A1536.

1534 **As I lay of late musing in my bed**
**Make me as perfect when I am waking.**
Headed 'Jhc'; at end, 'quothe t.s.p'.
MS. Ashmole 48, fol. 39$^{v}$.

1535 **As I lay slumbering in manner of a trance**
**And not to strain courtesy who shall first begin.**
Sponar, Henry.
MS. Ashmole 48, fol. 55.

1536 **As I lay slumbering [in my naked] once within my bed**
**To be so nigh, and miss so good a turn.**
'A Maiden's Dream'.
MSS. Ashmole 38, p. 85; Eng. poet. e. 97, p. 184; Rawl. poet. 160, fol. 157; see also A1533.

**As I my flocks lay keeping, mine eyes fell asleeping** 1537
**[In sorrows all alone].**
Strode, William, 'Song'. 7 verses, the first pr. by Dobell in *Works of Strode*, 1907, p. 130.
MS. *CCC. 325, fol. 65$^{v}$ (autogr.).

**As I my little flock on Ister bank** 1538
**Sure shepherd's sign that morn would soon fetch day.**
Sidney, Sir Philip, from the *Arcadia*.
MS. *e Mus. 37, fol. 142.

**As I one evening sat before my cell** 1539
**I am but finite yet thine infinitely.**
Herbert, George, 'Artillery'.
Pr. *The Temple*, 1633, p. 132.
MS. *Tanner 307, fol. 100$^{v}$.

**As I out of a casement sent** 1540
**For fear of some idolatry.**
Strode, William, 'Song'.
MS. *CCC. 325, fol. 63$^{v}$ (autogr.).
MS. Rawl. poet. 84, fol. 60.

**As I read in a time another than this,** 1541
**Us thyself feed in thy worthy feast.**
Prophecy, with a prayer.
MS. Rawl. C. 813, fol. 144$^{v}$.

**As I saw fair Clora walk alone** 1542
**To deck her froze into a gem.**
'Song by Mr. [George] Hayden', [words by W. Strode].
MS. Ballard 50, fol. 111$^{v}$; see also I430.

**As I stood in a park straight up by a tree** 1543*a*
**I may no more speak my breath is all gone.**
[Lacy, John], 'The testament of the buck'.
Pr. by William Copland, n.d. [1548–68], *S.T.C.* 4001 (Bodl. pr. bk. S. Seld. d. 45(24).
MS. Rawl. C. 813, fol. 30.

**[As I stroll through the city, oft I]** 1543*b*
**All the soul in every face.**
[Swift, Jonathan], 'Legion Club'. 1736.
Pr. *S—t contra omnes. An Irish miscellany.* 1736.
MS. Eng. misc. f. 79, p. 102.

**As I through one churchyard did pass** 1544
**It's all our Saviour doth require.**
MS. Eng. poet. b. 5, p. 98.

**As I walked by myself** 1545
**The self-same thing will be.**
'W[illiam] P[rince of] O[range]'.
MS. Sancroft 53, p. 59.

1546 **As I walked in the woods one evening of late**
**And languish for ever for want of a man.**
Song with tune.
MS. Mus. Sch. G. 637, fol. 9v.

1547*a* **As I walked out one May morning down by a river's side,**
**Since the raging seas and stormy winds have parted my love and I.**
'Maiden's Complaint for the Loss of her Sailor'.
MS. Firth c. 18, fol. 154.

1547*b* **As I wandered on my walking**
**This world is but a vanity.**
Subscribed 'Explicit cantus qd de Thomas Peny of Houghton'.
Another copy in MS. Porkington 10.
MS. Lat. misc. e. 85, fol. 81.

1548 **As I wandered up Ratcliffe Highway,**
**He will make a good soldier for his Queen and country.**
'The New Deserter'.
MSS. Firth c. 17, fol. 68; c. 20, fol. 43.

1549 **As I was at a merry meeting**
**True blue will never stain.**
'The Loyal British fighting in Flanders'.
Pr. *Roxburghe Ballads*, vii. 752.
MS. Firth c. 17, fol. 22.

1550 **As I was going last night to Whitehall**
**Or else you should have had 'em this end of September.**
'News from Whitehall'.
MS. Firth c. 16, p. 215.

1551 **As I was going to sell my eggs**
**I tripped up his heels and 'fell on his nose.**
MS. Douce d. 59, fol. 52v.

1552 **As I was pondering one evening late**
**Usurp Hell's royal throne, and me should abdicate.**
'The Rivals. December 8th 1690'.
MS. Firth d. 13, fol. 62.

1553 **As I was, so be ye**
**That I left, that I lost.**
Epitaph in St. Olave's, Hart Street.
Pr. Camden's *Remaines*, 1605, p. 53.
MSS. Ashmole 38, p. 178, attr. to Mr. William Lambe; Eng. poet. e. 40, two copies, fols. 122 and 163.

1554 **As I was walking out to take the air**
**And make the show as fine as e'er you can.**
'The Hawkers upon their Prohibition to Summon to Horn Fair'.
MS. Rawl. poet. 207, p. 36.

**As I was wandering the wood** 1555
**In true humility I bow.**
'A new new song concerning preregrination and anihilation', Tune, 'if God be god as all agree'.
MS. Rawl. poet. 37, p. 16.

**As I went by St. James's I heard a bird sing** 1556
**There was no other way for the mending the breed.**
'The Prince of Darkness'. [1688].
Pr. *Poems on Affairs of State*, iv, 1707, supplement, p. 16.
MSS. Firth c. 16, p. 300; Rawl. poet. 159, fol. 95*b*.

**As I went down by one wood side** 1557
**And good houses will be kept, each where out of hand.**
'A song of conscience making of mone'.
MS. Eng. poet. b. 5, p. 32.

**As I went to Westminster Abbey** 1558
**And bid her speak well of the court.**
MS. Rawl. B. 35, fol. 36 rev.

**As if the storm meant him?** 1559
**And he, that here fears danger, does deserve his fear.**
Crashaw, Richard, 'Upon the disciples awaking Christ in the storme'.
MS. Tanner 465, fol. 33, attr. to Mr. Crashaw on fol. 1*a*.

**As I'm inform'd, on Monday last you sat,** 1560
**Instead of fulsome A— use wholesome C—.**
'Advice to Dr. Oates . . . 1685'.
MS. Firth c. 15, p. 182.

**As in a dream our thinking monarch lay** 1561
**Puffing to find himself, so far outdone.**
'K. Charles II's Ghost', 1691.
Pr. *Poems on Affairs of State*, ii, 1703, p. 317.
MSS. Eng. poet. c. 18, fol. 106v; Rawl. poet. 159, fol. 86*b*.

**[As] in a feast so in a comedy** 1562
**So wish we you, what you may give us, rest.**
'Epilogus' to *Sicelides*, by Phineas Fletcher.
MS. Rawl. poet. 214, fol. 67v.

**As in a ship-wreck some poor sailor tossed** 1563
**And all my life be suited to my theme.**
Dryden, Charles, 'On the happiness of a retird Life'.
Pr. Dryden's *Miscellany*, 1716, iv. 292.
MSS. Add. B. 105, fol. 15, attr. to Charles Dryden; Rawl. poet. 173, fol. 166, attr. to Dryden junior.

1564 As in an Ellinge Lane I took my way
So never be like this sad beetle found.
Amherst, Elizabeth, 'The sorrowfull story of a Beetle'. Imitation of Spencer.
MS. *Eng. poet. e. 109, p. 80.

1565 As in my bed distressed wretch I lay
And more than that what more him seemeth best.
Burton, Francis.
MS. Add. A. 267, fol. 22ᵛ (autogr.).

1566 As in old chaos, heaven with earth confused
At once receives of pleasure, and excuse.
Waller, Edmund, 'Of her passing through a Crowd of People'.
Pr. *Poems*, 1645, p. 48.
MSS. *Don. d. 55, fol. 6ᵛ; Rawl. poet. 173, fol. 96.

1567 As in the days of yore was odds
He turned the parliament out of door.
'The Busse Royall, or Proroguation', [1674 (?)].
Pr. *Poems on Affairs of State*, i, 1703, ii. 41.
MSS. Don. b. 8, p. 535; Douce 357, fol. 71; also pr. bk. Vet. A 3c. 123, fol. 3.

1568 As in the flowery bank of Isis gay
Where earth can pay no better sacrifice.
Couldry, William, 'To the mayor of Oxford, on Oxford's new charter', [2] Oct. 1684.
See Wood's *Life and Times*, ed. A. Clark, iii, O.H.S. xxvi, 1894, p. 112.
MS. Wood D. 19(2), fol. 102.

1569 As in the garden of my father
Vent some kind rhyme that may my pardon get.
Walsh, Octavia.
MS. *Eng. poet. e. 31, fol. 160ᵛ rev. (autogr.).

1570 As in the groves I walked alone
But thanks the gods that him restore.
'Occasioned by a Report of the Queen's being a dying' [Queen Anne].
MS. Rawl. poet. 155, p. 1.

1571 As in the new moon we behold
The old man dying in the new.
MS. Eng. poet. e. 17, fol. 22.

1572 As in the nozzle works the taper's flame,
So man doth die, so flies his life away.
Robinson, Robert.
MS. *Rawl. poet. 218, p. 125 (autogr.).

As in those nations where they yet adore 1573
And beauty's a disease where 'tis unkind.
Sedley, Sir Charles, 'To Mris Mary Napp'.
Pr. *Poems on Several Occasions, By several Persons*, 1672, p. 43.
MSS. Eng. poet. e. 4, p. 169, attr. to Sir Charles Sedley; Rawl. C. 556, fol. 31ᵛ; Rawl. poet. 173, fol. 74, attr. to Sr. Ch. Sedley; Sancroft 53, p. 1.

As in times past the rustic shepherds sent 1574
So shall you show, my friendship you affect.
Cornwaleys, William, verses endorsed 'to . . . Mr. John Done Secretary to my Lorde Keeper', [1596–1600].
Pr. *Life and Letters of John Donne*, E. Gosse, 1899, i. 91.
MS. Tanner 306, fol. 237 (autogr.).

As is your beauty by your thoughts divine 1575
There is no truth in truthless womankind.
'Lovs exclamation'.
MS. Rawl. poet. 172, fol. 6.

As it befell [fell out] on a Pentecost day 1576
And with that he shook his sword Excalaber.
'Out of the Acts of K. Arthur', copied, 17th cent., from 'MS. in Lord Windsor's library'; 18th cent., from 'MS. at Bristol'.
MSS. Ballard 50, fol. 10; Gough Gen. Top. 29, fol. 256.

As Jack above a draper's shop 1577
For modesty—departed.
'Epigram'.
MS. Eng. poet. c. 51, p. 38.

As Killigrew came t'other day 1578
Than half the time extremely sore.
Satire on Charles II and Tom Killigrew.
MS. Douce 357, fol. 127ᵛ.

As Lambeth pray'd, so prov'd [was] the dire event 1579
The bishop and his clerks replied Amen.
'The Archbishop in a printed form of prayer for success at sea, pray'd that God would be a Rock unto our ships, on which for the loss of Sir C. Shovell, was made what follows', 1707.
Pr. Hearne's *Collections*, ed. C. E. Doble, ii, O.H.S. vii, 1886, p. 146.
MSS. Hearne's diaries 17, p. 218; Rawl. D. 383, fol. 146; Rawl. poet. 81, fol. 44.

As lambs and wolves by nature disagree 1580
Whilst he is tribune of the martial band.
W. A., translator, Horace, *Epode* iv.
MS. *Rawl. poet. 104, fol. 49 (autogr.).

1581 As late at funeral pomp I sat
Should thus have all's old scores made even.
'The Mourners, 1695'.
MS. Eng. poet. e. 50, p. 71.

1582 As late at night a bankrupt spied
I've in vain search'd here by day-light.
'An Epigram', 1735.
MS. Eng. misc. e. 240, p. 232.

1583 As late the spot I sought with ardour keen
My spirit seek that lives in Montague.
Parsons, William.
Pr. *Travelling Recreations*, 1807, ii. 135.
MS. Don. c. 81, fol. 7 (autogr.).

1584 As lately I, on silver Thames did ride
But naming her grief lets me say no more.
Waller, Edmund, 'Thirsis and Galatea'. On the death of the Duchess of Hamilton, 10 May 1638.
Pr. *Poems*, 1645, p. 90.
MSS. *Don. d. 55, fol. 28; *Rawl. poet. 174, p. 48.

1585 As lately I was reading the common news letter
And the English be masters once more of the sea.
'Introduction' to 'The Weekely Lampoon . . . on the last weeks Public News Letters and Observator', [pr. and sold by Randall Taylor], 1690.
MS. Eng. poet. d. 53, p. 101.

1586 As lately through London I rambled along
Than the box of Pandora could ever enclose.
'On the 3 per cent Scheme 1737'.
Pr. bk. Firth b. 22, fol. 35.

1587 As life is wasting, so death is hasting,
To all eternity.
Robinson, Robert.
MS. *Rawl. poet. 218, p. 4 (autogr.).

1588*a* As life's a voyage sages say
In copious draughts of college ale.
Skinner, John, 'Letters from Oxford. 6. To [William] — Esq. June 15. 1793'.
Extracts pr. O.H.S. xxii, 1892, p. 199.
MS. *Top. Oxon. e. 41, p. 185.

1588*b* [As like a hermit abroad I walked]
Yet on my Phyllis my mind is still.
Teonge, Henry, 'Song . . . composed in the Downs', 26 July 1678.
Pr. *Diary, 1675–9*, 1825.
MS. Firth c. 18, fol. 166.

1589 As listening to the wild waves' solemn roar,
The vision vanished in the shades of night.
Parsons, William, 'On hearing that Admiral Keppel was acquitted', 12 Feb. 1779.
MS. *Don. d. 123, p. 48 (autogr.).

As long as Moco's happy tree shall grow, 1590
So long her honour, name, and praise shall last.
Pope, Alexander, lines in a letter to Henry Cromwell, 15 July 1711.
Pr. Curll's *Miscellanea*, 1727, i. 59.
MS. Rawl. letters 90, fol. 39 (autogr.).

As long as there is goose or gander 1591
We shall remember Alexander.
'Scimus Alexandrum post sæcula commemorandum'. Couplet.
MS. Lat. misc. c. 19, p. 427.

As Lycidas sat rapt, inspired, 1592
The buskin and the sock.
Parsons, William, 'The Poet disturb'd, an Epigram'.
MS. *Don. d. 123, p. 153 (autogr.).

As man in Westminster to each that comes 1593*a*
Their Lordships only and the Lord does know.
Hall, Hen[ry], of Hereford, 'A farther Explanation of the Oxford Almanack', 1706.
Pr. Hearne's *Collections*, ed. C. E. Doble, i, O.H.S. ii, 1885, p. 205.
MS. Hearne's diaries 9, p. 27.

As man at first in gardening was employed 1593*b*
And rise again to meet our heavenly king.
'An Epitaph on a gardener buried in Shoreditch Church yard'.
MS. Rawl. D. 1334, fol. 28 rev.

As many a mighty potentate, doth grudge to view and see, 1594
And so let every Christian do, which thinks this life will end.
Wodwall, William, 'The Acts of Queen Elizabeth Allegorized'.
MS. Eng. hist. e. 198, fol. 5.

As Martial's life was grave and sad, 1595
What e'er we want, our book has nose.
[Denham, John], 'Upon the Preface of [Davenant's] Gondibert. Martial Epigr., Lasciva est nobis Pagina, vita proba est'.
Pr. *Certain Verses . . . to be reprinted with . . . Gondibert*, 1653, p. 4. See *T.L.S.*, 1 Sept. 1966, p. 788.
MS. CCC. 309, fol. 50.

As Mary mourned, to find the stone removed 1596
Upon her best beloved husband gone.
Epitaph on Wm. Hampton, d. 16 April 1624, Lee Church, Essex.
MS. Rawl. D. 682, fol. 3v.

As men, for fear the stars should sleep and nod, 1597
To heaven alone both go, and lead.
Herbert, George, 'Divinity'.
Pr. *The Temple*, 1633, p. 127.
MS. *Tanner 307, fol. 97.

1598 As moody Job in shirtless case
'Twill ease thee of thy anguish.
MS. Firth d. 13, fol. 50.

1599 As mortals languish when the rays of light
With angels, who in charms she equalled here.
'On a young lady taken ill at a Ball'.
MS. *Eng. poet. d. 47, fol. 32.

1600 As Mortimer lay pensive and with pains
And left the J—r to his thoughts alone.
'The Apparition'. Endorsed 'Queens Statue at St. Pauls 1712'.
Pr. bk. Firth b. 21, fol. 114.

1601 As Moses once and Joshua
And councils without sense.
'The Miracle'.
Dated January 1709/10 in B.M. MS. Lansd. 852, fol. 30.
MS. Eng. poet. e. 87, p. 85.

1602 As mother Cook went t'other day
And squitter squatter gilt his bays.
'Old Gammer Cook: A Ballad' [on *The Observator*].
Pr. in *The Muses Farewell to Popery*, 1690, p. 191.
MS. Firth c. 16, p. 104.

1603 As much as fairest lilies does surpass
Adorn'd with graces, more than half divine.
'. . . Salomon's Songs' translated 'by a Gentleman'.
MS. Eng. poet. c. 9, p. 89.

1604 As musing I ranged
And she pierc'd both the air and my heart with the cries . . . (incomplete).
Song.
MS. Mus. e. 20, fol. 7.

1605 As musing in long winter nights I lie
That when thou knock'st, I be not found asleep.
Corbet, W., 'Nocturna Visio'.
MS. *Rawl. poet. 210, fol. 20.

1606 As mute as fishes till we come to land,
They'll all run fast about the walking pot.
Williams, John.
MS. *Rawl. poet. 184, fol. 41v (autogr.).

1607 As nature hath an inclination
To rest perpetual we may ascend.
Forrest, William, 'The Seconde Griselde', i.e. Catherine of Arragon, 'fynyshed the 25 daye of June 1558'.
Pr. for the Roxburghe Club, 1875.
MS. Wood empt. 2, fol. 1 (autogr.); see also MS. Wood D. 18 (101), fols. 67–77v.

As nature yields no breath and life 1608
God send to them his heavenly grace to end this mortal life.
[Glover, Richard] On Richard Mellow, d. 1574, Aldborough, Norfolk.
MS. Top. Norf. c. 1, fol. 5.

As near Porto-Bello lying 1609
And for England sham'd in me.
'Admiral Hosier's Ghost'.
MS. Montagu e. 13, fol. 63.

As needy gallants in the scriveners' hands 1610
As much improper, as would honesty.
[Dryden, John], 'Prologue to . . . Amboyna'. See *R.E.S.*, July, 1925.
MS. Don. b. 8, p. 463.

As Nero laughing saw fierce fires [flames] consume 1611
And speedily call King James from exile home.
'Nero II', on George I and a fire in Thames Street, 13 Jan. 1714/15.
Pr. *Hearne's Collections*, v, ed. D. W. Rannie, 1901, O.H.S. xlii, p. 43.
MSS. Eng. poet. e. 87, p. 8; Hearne's diaries 53, p. 116; Rawl. D. 383, fol. 111; Rawl. poet. 155, p. 18; 181, fol. 21; pr. bk. Firth b. 22, fol. 14(a)v.

As now the shades of eve embrown 1612
But sweeter friendship's solemn theme.
Glee for 4 voices, by Benjamin Cooke II, Mus. Doc.
MS. Mus. d. 177, fol. 20v.

As nurses strive their babes in bed to lay 1613
Nature my nurse put me to bed betimes.
'On an infants death'.
MSS. Sancroft 59, p. 286 rev.; Tanner 465, fol. 62; see also A1464.

As o'er my solitary tea 1614
The poet laughed at the physician.
'An Epistle to an Apothecary', 1735.
MS. Eng. misc. e. 240, p. 239.

As o'er the varied meads I stray 1615
And pleasure to devotion turns.
Glee by Webb.
MS. Mus. d. 177, fol. 52v.

As oft we see before a sudden shower 1616
She lifts aloft, from whence he soon may slide.
Pr. from this MS. by R. W. Bond, *John Lyly*, 1902, iii. 498.
MS. Rawl. poet. 148, fol. 86v.

As old ones out the world do go, 1617
And so hath ever been.
Robinson, Robert.
MS. *Rawl. poet. 218, p. 41 (autogr.).

1618 As on a day Sabina was asleep
And still [Sabina] . . . (leaf torn).
'Sabina'.
MS. Rawl. poet. 172, fol. 2.

1619 As on a window late I cast mine eye,
The man replied: it figures Jesus Christ.
Herbert, George, 'Love-Joy'.
Pr. *The Temple*, 1633, p. 109.
MSS. Rawl. poet. 90, fol. 139[v]; *Tanner 307, fol. 82.

1620 As on Euphrates banks we stood
The marble with your infants' brains.
Beaumont, Thomas, 'The 139th Psalm paraphrased'.
MS. *Malone 18, p. 102 (autogr.).

1621 As on his deathbed gasping Strephon lay
Live not like Strephon, but like Strephon die.
Flatman, Thomas, 'On the Death of my Lord Rochester, Pastorall'.
Pr. in Flatman's *Poems*, 3rd ed., 1682, p. 146.
MSS. Aubrey 6, fol. 56, attr. to T. Flatman; Rawl. poet. 19, fol. 82, attr. to Mr. Flatman; Smith 11, p. 9, attr. to Mr. Flatman; see also A1506.

1622 As on some mountain's brow a lofty pine
Nor been the mark of spiteful destiny.
Mervall, Alphonso, 'An Allegory'.
MS. *Rawl. poet. 166, p. 65 (autogr.).

1623 As on the beach sad Ariadne lay
Beguile my sorrows, and my cares compose.
Adams, —, translator, Propertius, Elegy I. 3, 'from D[ryden's] Miscellany Poems', 1684, p. 215.
MS. Rawl. poet. 222, fol. 36.

1624 As once a twelvemonth to the priest
And wreaths round William's glorious head.
Prior, Matthew, 'An epistle to Fleetwood Shephard, Esq[r]; Burleigh, 14 May 1689'.
MS. Rawl. poet. 152, fol. 123[v].

1625 As once Euripus with ambiguous flows
Seems to have lost its metal in the flame.
Townely, Zouch, 'Domine si non capio te, tu capias me'.
MS. Rawl. poet. 170, fol. 44.

1626 As once on earth almighty ire
Thou envoy of Gomorrha!
Parsons, William, on Sir Horace Mann.
MS. *Don. d. 123, p. 126 (autogr.).

1627 As one that's naked and fortunately finds
Live in my heart his worth in streamy plenty.
H. S., 'In amicum Johannem Mynne praecharissimum defunctum'.
MS. *Rawl. poet. 120, fol. 28 (autogr.).

As one who mounts Vesuvius steepy height 1628
And Godfroy's pious aims, and Petrarch's hapless love!
Parsons, William, 'Sonnet to Mrs. N. on her beginning to learn Italian'.
Pr. *Fidelity*, etc. 1798, p. 80, and in *Travelling Recreations*.
MS. *Don. d. 123, p. 198 (autogr.).

As one who strives being sick and sick to death 1629
I'll think on you, and by you think on heaven.
[Carew, Thomas]. First printed in *Poems*, 3rd ed., 1651.
MS. Eng. poet. c. 50, fol. 73[v].

As other men hath in land 1630
Me thought I had great wrong.
MS. Laud. misc. 23, fol. 114[v].

As our peace must end in a war 1631
How easily Holland's turned up.
'Prophesy', corrected draft.
MS. Eng. poet. c. 11, fol. 15 (autogr.).

As our saint patron with his eagle's eye 1632
While all the Worcester angels clap their wings.
Villiers, Edward, Earl of Jersey, 'Speech to the King in St. John's College Library, at Cambr: Octob: 4. 1671'.
MS. Rawl. poet. 19, fol. 60.

As panting hinds the water seek, 1633
My low estate will raise.
Psalm xlii.
MS. *Rawl. C. 113, fol. 34.

As pants the hart for cooling steams 1634
Thou majesty divine.
[Tate, Nahum, and Brady, Nicholas], 'Anthem', Psalm xlii. 1. Music by Charles King.
MS. Mus. c. 1, fol. 22.

As Paris home through seas was tumbling 1635
Will burn to ashes poor Troy town!
Horace, *Odes* I. xv. 'Imitated'. 1735.
MS. Eng. misc. e. 240, p. 271.

As plundering bands of savage thieves 1636
But yield—to the divine.
Maitland, Charlotte Mary, 'Opening the Will [of Col. Augustus Maitland] Decem. 1799'.
MS. Eng. poet. c. 51, p. 176.

As Polyphemus drunk in's cave doth lie 1637
He cannot give him sight can drown his foe.
Translating 'Primi Dialogi Luciani Argumentum'.
MS. Rawl. poet. 194, fol. 32.

1638 As poor Ophelia dying lay
Her soul upon the wing . . . (incomplete).
Song with music.
MS. Mus. c. 26, fol. 112$^{v}$.

1639 As proud as a beggar, as lazy and lousy,
When King Coxcomb thinks fit shall be made his Queen Bess.
Williams, John, 'Love-Character'.
MS. *Rawl. poet. 184, fol. 94$^{v}$ (autogr.).

1640 As Quin and Foote one day went out
One shilling in the pound.
'Dialogue'.
MS. Eng. poet. c. 51, p. 151.

1641 As rare to hear as seldom to be seen
To have his will yet ever to require.
Dyer, [Sir Edward].
Pr. *The Phœnix Nest*, 1593, p. 75.
MS. Rawl. poet. 85, fol. 7$^{v}$.

1642 As ravens, crows, and other birds of prey
Only to swallow their estate.
Williams, John, 'Upon Rich men's Friends'.
MS. *Rawl. poet. 193, fol. 63$^{v}$ (autogr.).

1643 As Roger and Harry were trudging along
Tho' humble, I'm yet in the secrets below.
Boswell, James, 'Epigram'.
MS. *Douce 193, fol. 47 (autogr.).

1644 As Roger with his Jug was walking
He'd gone with Jug a little farther.
[Whaley, John], 'The kiss repay'd; A Tale'.
Pr. *Poems*, 1732, p. 119.
MS. Rawl. poet. 222, fol. 16.

1645 As roll the rivers to the sea
Lost in the vast abyss of love.
Kenton, James.
MS. *Eng. poet. e. 20, p. 267 (autogr.).

1646 As round the venerable pile I stray'd
And to the world tranquillity afford.
'A Vision in Westminster Abbey', 1759.
Pr. bk. Firth b. 22, fol. 60.

1647 As rudely nipt by winter's lagging rear
And all is Delia, love, and ecstacy.
R. L., 'Sonnet. 1776'.
MS. *Eng. poet. e. 16, fol. 6.

1648 As sage sowgelder roves the country round
That here at leisure, they may all forget.
Verses from 'terrae filius's speech, Oxon, 1703'.
MS. Rawl. D. 697, fol. 1.

As Sampson's lion honey gave 1649
That mighty state till now had stood.
'Of The Lady Mary', on her marriage to William of Orange, 1677.
MS. Douce 357, fol. 70$^{v}$.

As Satan first the serpent conquered: 1650
Would not content him, till he knew that too.
MS. *Rawl. poet. 97, fol. 10$^{v}$ (autogr.).

As Satan o'er Lincoln was looking [was looking o'er Lincoln] one day 1651
He'd be glad to come off half so well at Cambray.
'Upon King G[eorge I's] effigy plac'd on the Top of Bloomsbury Steeple', 1723.
MSS. Ballard 50, fol. 49; Eng. misc. c. 292, fol. 104; Eng. poet. f. 12, p. 95, attr. to Mr. Bartie; Top. Oxon. b. 170, fol. 21$^{v}$.

As seamen shipwrackt on some happy shore 1652
I had a smile from Beauty's general heir.
Dryden, John, 'To the Countess of Castlemaine, for procuring a Play of his might be printed'.
Pr. *A New Collection of Poems and Songs*, John Bulteel, 1674, p. 71; and *Examen Poeticum*, 1693.
MSS. Eng. poet. e. 4, p. 173, attr. to John Dryden; Top. Oxon. e. 202, fol. 72, attr. to John Dryden.

As Sengreene takes his name of that, 1653
And lusty always seen.
'On Young'.
MSS. Ashmole 36, 37, fol. 210.

As several cities made their claim 1654
Had stil'd himself D'aphne D'avenantigo.
'Upon the Author's writing his Name (as in the Title of his Book) D'avenant'.
Pr. *Certain Verses . . . to be published with . . . Gondibert*, 1653, p. 24.
MS. CCC. 309, fol. 57.

As sin makes gross the soul, and thickens it 1655
Asleep in dust, dream of eternity.
Strode, William, 'An Epitaph on Mrs. Mary Nedham'.
MS. *CCC. 325, fol. 96$^{v}$ (autogr.).

As Sion standeth very firmly steadfast 1656
Peace be for ever.
Herbert, Mary (*née* Sidney), Countess of Pembroke, Psalm cxxv.
MSS. *Rawl. poet. 24, p. 193; *25, fol. 129$^{v}$.

As sleeps the hoary lion on the field 1657
Nor timid caution draw the veil.
Gough, Richard.
MS. *Eng. poet. c. 5, fol. 138 (autogr.).

1658 As smoke from trembling flames ascends
When dead, to that where live the yet unborn.
MS. Malone 13, p. 94.

1659 As some at gnats most sadly strain,
To serve me break their necks.
Williams, John.
MS. *Rawl. poet. 184, fol. 91[v] (autogr.).

1660 As some brave admiral in former war
And now grown good for nothing else be wise.
Wilmot, John, Earl of Rochester, 'The disabled Debauchee'.
See Vieth, p. 384.
MSS. Don. b. 8, p. 409, attr. to the Earle of Rochester; Rawl. poet. 81, fol. 22, attr. to My Ld. Rochester; see also A1663.

1661 As some brave knight who once with spear and shield,
And hang his consecrated buskin here.
Rowe, [Nicholas], 'Epilogue to the Comedy of Love for Love represented in the Spring of 1709 for the benefit of Mr. Thos. Betterton'.
See *D.N.B.* on Betterton.
MS. Montagu e. 14, fol. 34.

1662 As some lone redbreast urged by beating storms
Then to grow weary, turn aside, and die.
Dyer, George, 'Elegy written at night in Emanuel College Cambridge'.
Pr. *Poems*, 1801, p. 155.
MS. *Eng. poet. c. 21, fol. 49.

1663 As some old admiral in former war
And now grown good for nothing else, be wise.
Wilmot, John, Earl of Rochester, 'The disabled Debauchee'.
MS. Eng. poet. e. 4, p. 187; see also A1660.

1664 As some poor mariner, if chance a rock
And launch anew on love's tempestuous main?
Parsons, William, 'Sonnet to a Lady who advised me to marry'.
MS. *Don. d. 123, p. 260 (autogr.).

1665*a* As some raw lad from country school brought down
And kindly on us all bestow their claps.
Lawrence, Thomas, of St. John's and University College, Oxford. 'Epilogue at Parting'; music speech, 1669.
MSS. Add. A. 368, fol. 12; Top. Oxon. e. 202, fol. 28.

1665*b* [As some raw youth in country bred]
She ne'er inspires against conviction.
Swift, Jonathan, 'To Dr. Delaney'.
Pr. as pamphlet, 'To Doctor D—l—y, on the Libels writ against him'. 1730.
MS. Eng. misc. f. 79, p. 91.

As some too timid traveller whose way 1666*a*
Hopeless I live, nor can to peace return!
Parsons, William, 'Sonnet, the idea from the Italian of March. Gio. Gioseffo Corsi'.
MS. *Don. d. 123, p. 268 (autogr.).

As soon as blest with your salute 1666*b*
The golden legend of your beauty.
[Creswell, Robert (?)]. 'To one that askt him why he was dumb'.
MS. *Eng. poet. f. 24, fol. 31[v] (on an inserted leaf).

As soon as I was dead, the world began 1667*a*
Only the copy of translated me.
Oldisworth, Nicolas, 'On Sir B. R.'
MS. *Don. c. 24, fol. 34[v] (autogr.).

As soon as mild Augustus could assuage 1667*b*
They stoop for ease, and pitch upon the ground.
Potenger, John. 'On the king's house then building at Winchester'.
Pr. *Sylvae*, 1685, p. 475.
MS. *Eng. poet. d. 161, p. 103.

As soon as new year was begun 1668
Examine them together.
MS. Ashmole 383, fol. 23.

As soon as the porter had done Sir 1669
Our Abram an Isaac must have.
[Roach, Richard], fragment.
MS. Rawl. D. 832, fol. 199 (autogr.).

As soon as the wind it came kindly about 1670
For the De'll wo'nt take if I turn ye away. Derry down.
'A Ballad. May 1719'.
Pr. bk. Firth b. 22, fol. 20.

As Stoics teach mankind should firmly bear 1671
'Twas Warren at my door, who call'd to tea.
Skinner, John, 'Letters from Oxford. 5. To [J. Page]. 1793'.
MS. Eng. poet *d. 22, fol. 15 (autogr.).
MSS. Eng. poet. *d. 22, fol. 38[v]; *Top. Oxon. e. 41, p. 175.

As Sylvia near a purling stream 1672
But blessed the welcome boy.
MS. Rawl. poet. 152, fol. 155.

As tender lambs with wolves agree; 1673
Is best at cutting purses.
Baker, Sir James. 'Horace. Epod IV. Imitated . . . To Lord Cad-n'.
MS. Firth c. 20, fol. 55.

As the blest indians hug themselves and play 1674
None court the waters, now the angel's gone.
'On the departure of the Lady Victoria Vuedall from Wickham 1672/3'.
MS. *Rawl. poet. 87, p. 13.

1675 **As the bold visitant who could presume**
**And love's bright lamp is dash'd by rough disdain!**
Parsons, William, 'On . . . a story of [Mrs. Inchbald] having taken up a poker to defend herself'.
MS. *Don. d. 123, p. 245 (autogr.).

1676 **As the brave Rook, Tholous did beat,**
**The quite contrary way.**
On the battle off Gibraltar, August 1704.
MS. Montagu e. 13, fol. 104$^{v}$.

1677 **As the chafed hart which brayeth**
**Thy true God, and will be ever.**
Sidney, Sir Philip, Psalm xlii.
MSS. *Rawl. poet. 24, p. 61; *25, fol. 35.

1678 **As the late character of godlike men**
**Here lies the only prince who left all evil ways.**
'The Man of No Honour'.
Pr. *The Muses Farewell to Popery*, 1690, p. 5.
MS. Firth c. 16, p. 155.

1679 **As the pale moon the sun's bright orb o'ershades**
**So let the cuckold to the king give way.**
'On the Eclipse, [22 Apr.] 1715'.
MSS. Eng. misc. c. 116, fol. 7, marked 'R. C.'; Rawl. poet. 155, p. 110.

1680 **As the pelican with her own blood**
**Thee my redeemer see.**
Tipping, William, 'None But Christ'.
MS. *Rawl. poet. 101, fol. 52 (autogr.).

1681 **As the prophetic swan before**
**Whose life was tune, whose death keeps time.**
H. B., C.O.S. [Fellow of Oriel (?)] 'Octaves on Jacob's death the Lutinist'.
MS. Add. B. 109, fol. 108$^{v}$.

1682 **As the sun in heaven and as its splendid light,**
**Or else your beauty does his heart control.**
'Owens Epigrams', '5. To The Lady Mary Neville'.
MS. *Rawl. poet. 197, fol. 8$^{v}$ (autogr.).

1683 **As the sun once lift up his burning lamp**
**Finding instead of sea a sea of blood.**
Holland, Abraham, 'Naumachia, or The Description of a cruell Sea fight'.
Pr. 1622.
MS. Rawl. poet. 83, fol. 5 (autogr.).

1684 **As the sweet sweat of roses in a still**
**She and comparisons are odious.**
Donne, John, Elegy viii, 'The Comparison'.
Pr. *Poems*, 1633.
MSS. CCC. 327, fol. 28$^{v}$, attr. to Donne; Eng. poet. e. 14, fol. 60$^{v}$; *f. 9, p. 54; Rawl. poet. 117, fol. 206 rev. as part of N49, attr. to Dunne; 142, fol. 18$^{v}$.

**As the three children late in council sate** 1685
**But,—Gad! She'll get no reputation by us.**
Pope, Alexander, or Cromwell, Henry, 'Epigram Papal. On the female Canticle'.
Pr. Curll's *Miscellanea*, 1727, i. 87.
MS. Rawl. letters 90, fol. 50, in the hand of H. Cromwell.

**As the young rural maid, brought up at home** 1686
**Than all the bays that crown the strutting bard!**
Parsons, William, 'To my Aunt R . . . copies of . . . my verses'.
MS. *Don. d. 123, p. 28 (autogr.).

**As they who draw by copies still come short** 1687
**For others' good and your own ill.**
Creswell, Robert, 'The Poetasters'.
MS. *Eng. poet. f. 24, fol. 45$^{v}$ (autogr.).

**As those we love decay, we die in part** 1688
**Till dying, all he can resign is breath!**
Thomson, [James], 'Epitaph'.
MS. Montagu e. 14, fol. 25$^{v}$.

**As those, which for a while in heaven have been** 1689
**When they might fare well, and pay nothing here.**
Oldisworth, Nicolas, 'On the Christmas at C'osham in Wilt-shire. 1632' [Sir Edward Hungerford's house].
MS. *Don. c. 24, fol. 61 (autogr.).

**As thou hast said so Lord pray I** 1690
**Of Israel's sons to be the praise.**
Fairfax, Thomas, Lord, '[Songs of the old and New Testament.] Simeon's Song'.
MS. *Fairfax 40, p. 431 (autogr.).
MS. *Fairfax 38, p. 467.

**As thou in might excels Lord be thou praised** 1691
**This god's our god till death our guide unto.**
Fairfax, Thomas, Lord, Psalm xlviii.
MS. *Fairfax 40, p. 107 (autogr.).
MS. *Fairfax 38, p. 207.

**As though a second deluge was approaching** 1692
**But 'tis so dry, I fear the conflagration.**
T[rist, John, of Exeter College, Oxford], 'On books lying in a window in the rain', 12 Oct. 1734.
MS. Eng. misc. e. 240, p. 59.

**As threatening storms insult the skies** 1693
**Return triumphant to our hemisphere.**
'On Bolingbrokes going over' to France, 1715.
MS. Rawl. poet. 155, p. 112.

**As through the thickets of a shady wood** 1694
**And send the fatal arrow to your heart.**
'An Idyllium from the Greek'.
MS. Eng. poet. f. 12, p. 60.

1695 As through the Zodiac yearly rides the sun;
Or live contented, or unpitied die.
'Cuckoldom'.
MS. Ballard 47, fol. 28.

1696 As time creeps on, and brings in age,
That now have vital breath.
Robinson, Robert.
MS. *Rawl. poet. 218, p. 136 (autogr.).

1697 As 'tis appointe[d] men should die
Your heart with filial fear.
[Bunyan, John], 'Of Judgment'.
Pr. *One Thing is Needful*, 3rd ed., 1683.
MS. Rawl. poet. 58, fol. 6$^v$.

1698 As 'tis observed the rhyming race
The reason of this huge offence.
Boswell, James.
MS. *Douce 193, fol. 90 (autogr.).

1699 As to the chace with opening hounds
. . . (crossed out) . . .
4 stanzas on Adonis, 1735.
MS. Eng. misc. e. 240, p. 270.

1700 As to the eternal ever [often] in anguishes,
Faster I find to the war, they arm them.
Herbert, Mary (*née* Sidney), Countess of Pembroke, Psalm cxx.
MSS. *Rawl. poet. 24, p. 191; *25, fol. 128.

1701 As to the pole the lily bends
In the true centre of her bliss.
MS. Eng. poet. b. 5, p. 3.

1702 As t'other day milking I sat in the vale
Though he frightened my cow and my milk was kicked down.
MS. Mus. e. 19, p. 38.

1703 As t'other night in bed I thinking lay
'Tis ten to one but we shall dream again.
'A dream of the Cabal', 1672/3.
Pr. *Poems on Affairs of State*, i, 1703, p. 137.
MSS. Add. A. 48, fol. 19; Don. b. 8, p. 411; Rawl. poet. 159, fol. 204*b*, attr. to Marvel.

1704 As toyish as apes till twenty and one
And after as asses we counted shall be.
MS. Malone 19, p. 139.

1705 As truth directs, so only shall we act,
Pure and unmixed on thee the holy drops shall fall.
[Mason, William], 'Ode from Elfrida': set by Philip Hayes, and 'Perform'd as a lecture May 6 1785'.
MS. Mus. d. 68, fol. 34.

As Tully erst an orator, a Wife 1706
She could not equal such a husband yet.
Sylvester, Joshua, 'To the maker of this wife', Sir Thomas Overbury.
MS. Don. c. 54, fol. 4.

As tuned harp-strings sad notes take 1707
Alas for pity and so die.
MS. Mus. b. 1, fol. 35$^v$, music by John Wilson.

As unthrifts [grieve] mourn in straw, for their pawned beds 1708
Dead, all her faults are on her forehead writ.
'On the lady Markham', 1609.
See Donne's *Poems*, ed. Grierson, 1912, vol. ii, p. cii.
MSS. Ashmole 38, p. 76, attr. to F[rancis] B[eaumont]; *Eng. poet. f. 9, p. 199, attr. to J. D.; Rawl. poet. 117, fol. 193 rev.; 160, fol. 27$^v$.

As Venus in a myrtle grove 1709
For now my kingdom's of a piece.
'Venus pleased', 24 Oct. 1734.
MS. Eng. misc. e. 240, p. 71.

As verily as Christ was born in Bethl'em 1710
As verily as the flood stood, staunch thou blood.
'How to staunch blode a perfect saying'.
MS. Gough Norfolk 43, fol. 31$^v$.

As virtuous men pass mildly away 1711
And makes me end where I begun.
Donne, John, 'A valediction'.
Pr. *Poems*, 1633, p. 193.
MSS. Ashmole 51, fol. 7; Eng. poet. e. 14, fol. 39, attr. to D: Dun; Eng. poet. e. 37, p. 33; *e. 99, fol. 102$^v$; *f. 9, p. 39; Rawl. poet. 142, fol. 18$^v$; see also A1486.

As walking forth to take the air, 1712
Or I die for Kath'rine Ogie.
'A Song'.
MS. Montagu e. 13, fol. 37$^v$.

As Watkine walked by the way 1713
I thank Watkinge for his good ale.
'A new ballad of mother watkins ale'.
MS. Rawl. poet. 185, fol. 14$^v$.

As we esteem the greatest princess blest 1714
I could almost believe Pythagoras.
May, T[homas, on Sir Kenelm Digby].
MS. Malone 16, p. 39.

As we lay musing in our beds, 1715
Whilst the landsmen lies below.
'The Seaman's Distress'.
Pr. J. Ashton, *Real Sailor Songs*, 1891, p. 42.
MS. Firth c. 18, fol. 125.

1716 As we walked Westminster, a barge we spied
Ye sup assunder, or ye sup together.
Oldisworth, Nicolas, 'Iter Australe, 1632. Or, A journey southwards'.
MS. *Don. c. 24, fol. 45 (autogr.).

1717 As we went o'er the clan my boys
And the seventh beshit his trousers.
MS. Wood D. 19 (2), fol. 114.

1718 As wearied kings, that quit the throne
And think thy self like Hercules.
'Advice to the poor king of Hearts on his being turn'd out'.
MS. Firth e. 6, fol. 40v.

1719 As weary travellers, when the night is come,
From singing Holy, Holy, Three in One.
'A Pilgrim's Thought'.
MS. Rawl. poet. 213, fol. 52.

1720 As well tuned music sweetly seize
Virtue alone to heaven ascends.
Fairfax, Thomas, Lord, 'Of Vertue'.
MS. *Fairfax 40, p. 577 (autogr.); see also V60*b*.

1721 As when a bully draws his sword
Mongrels will serve to keep him down.
A[shton], E[dmund], 'On the British Princes', by Edward Howard.
Pr. Dryden's *Miscellany Poems*, 4th ed. 1716, iii. 71. See Vieth, p. 445.
MSS. Add. B. 105, fol. 74; Eng. poet. e. 4, p. 197, attr. to E. A.

1722 As when a chased deer
For favours which my God hath timely shown to me.
Knollys, Fra., Psalm xlii.
MS. *Rawl. poet. 60, p. 37 (autogr.).

1723 As when a fox or wolf too long doth fleece
Because they got it all, by selling you.
'A welcome home to the Parlamt. Men'.
MS. Rawl. poet. 181, fol. 11.

1724 As when a maid fearing her love to lose
'Twill please my wand'ring ghost when I am dead. Farewell for ever.
'Phillis to Damon'.
MS. *Rawl. poet. 197, fol. 47v (autogr.).

1725 As when a mighty monarch with renown
Who with him doth both grace and glory bring.
[E. S.], 'On Christ's Advent'.
MS. Rawl. poet. 65, fol. 80v.

1726 As when a miser circled in with gold
Not to destroy the thing you newly did create.
'The Departure; to Philoclea'.
MS. *Rawl. poet. 87, p. 41.

As when a sort of wolves infest the night 1727
Those painted clouds, which form Thaumantia's bow.
Waller, Edmund, 'Of the misreport of her being Painted'.
Pr. *Poems*, 1645, p. 47.
MS. *Don. d. 55, fol. 3.

As when a tempest rages in the air 1728
A grief that equals our unhappiness.
Spinedge, Anthony, of Jesus Coll., Cambridge, on the death of John Sherman, [1 May 1667, in Jesus College(?)].
MS. Tanner 306, fols. 386v and 385 (autogr.).

As when of old heroic story tells 1729
Bright flames arise, which never can expire.
Congreve, William, 'To Mr. Dryden, on his Translations of Persius'.
Pr. Gildon's *Miscellany*, 1692, p. 12.
MS. Rawl. poet. 152, fol. 116.

As when of old some bright and heavenly dame 1730
Nor think a higher blessing in the gift of fate.
Oldham, John, 'Upon the Marriage of the Prince of Orange with the Lady Mary', 1677.
MS. *Rawl. poet. 123, p. 27 (autogr.).

As when proud Lucifer aimed at the throne 1731
For though pride's as great his cunning's less.
'The Paralell on the banishing the Lord Mulgrave', [on his courtship of the Princess Anne, 1682].
Pr. *Poems on Affairs of State*, i, 1703, p. 254.
MSS. Douce 357, fol. 134; Firth c. 16, p. 11.

As when the chiefest priest ascends alone, 1732
To that most virtuous mind that shines in you.
Trotter, —, to Archbishop Sancroft, 1688(?)
MS. Tanner 306 .fol. 401.

As when the labouring sun hath wrought his track 1733
Be as the sun to this poor orb of mine.
'Hymn to the Holy Ghost', *c*. 1720–5.
MS. Rawl. C. 17, fol. 23 rev.

As when the queen of love engaged in war 1734
While she the goddess is, and you the saint.
'On the Recovery of Mrs. Mohun from the Small Pox'.
MS. Eng. poet. c. 18, fol. 136.

As when to Heaven a soul is newly flown 1735
So sweet a sacrifice to God, their king.
Bludder, Sir Thomas, 'Upon the death of the Lady Anne Rich'.
MS. Eng. misc. e. 262, fol. 42.

1736 As Willy went they said
That never till death decayed.
Markham, Robert, 'Songe'.
MS. Ashmole 38, p. 118.

1737 As winds and seas obey our saviour so
Dev'ls out of many, which increase His fame.
MS. *Rawl. poet. 97, fol. 54v (autogr.).

1738 As wise as Pallas, fair without design,
Though more inviting than the Cyprian Queen.
'Countess of Plimouth' (d. 1790).
MS. Eng. poet. e. 28, p. 28.

1739 As wise men set all things to right,
Not laws to please, but such laws, as are fit.
[Robinson, Robert], 'Difficile est regnare'.
MS. Ashmole 826, fol. 110, and copied in a secret character, fol. 113 (autogr.).

1740 As wrapped in death-like sleep Xantippe lay
Nor make a toil of that which gives us pleasure.
'From the London Mag: Sept. 1740 Xantippe Redivia'.
MS. Eng. poet. c. 9, p. 33.

As you came from . . . see A1742.

1741 As you expect that men should deal by you
Our thoughts must mount on contemplation's wing.
'Copies for Schollers to Write'.
MS. Rawl. poet. 152, fol. 231v.

1742 As you went to Walsingham
From itself never turning.
R[alegh], Sr. W[alter].
MS. Rawl. poet. 85, fol. 123.

1743 As youth and courage hath the eagle prest
Whom wit forbids in bloody fights to swerve.
W. A., translator, Horace, *Odes* IV. iv.
MS. *Rawl. poet. 104, fol. 39 (autogr.).

1744 As zealous farriers use t'employ
On ragged colts that have the farcy . . . (incomplete).
'On the new Miracle wrought by the Duke of Monmouth curing a Young Wench of the King's Evill'.
MS. Rawl. poet. 19, fol. 38v.

1745 Ascend that mount whose top is crowned with light,
Nor look behind till thou hast gained the top.
MS. *Don. f. 5, fol. 7.

1746 Ascend three gibbets, other right th' hast none
Whilst all the people cry Go kisse mine arse.
'The Answer to' A1747.
MS. Rawl. poet. 246, fol. 15v.

Ascend three thrones great captain, and divine 1747
And all bare-headed cry God save the king.
'The General [Cromwell]'s picture was hung upon one of the pillars of the Exchange, and under the picture was written as followeth', 1653.
MSS. Rawl. poet. 246, fol. 15; Tanner 52, fol. 13.

Ascending to his glory 1748
Our all redeeming Jesus.
Kenton, James.
MS. *Eng. poet. e. 20, p. 103 (autogr.).

Ascribe unto the lord of light 1749
Which blessed by him in peace remains.
Sidney, Sir Philip, Psalm xxix.
MSS. *Rawl. poet. 24, p. 37; *25, fol. 22.

Ask and have says Apostle James by name, 1750
I would King James to me would say the same.
[Owen's Epigram] '170 . . . made in King James I's time'. Couplet.
MS. *Rawl. poet. 197, fol. 9v (autogr.).

Ask if yon damask rose be sweet 1751
If dear Susanna's fair.
MS. Mus. c. 107, fol. 55v.

Ask me no more my Quintius, whether I 1752
First, death is the last scene of misery.
[R. T.], translator, Horace, *Epistles* I. xvi.
Pr. *Poems of Horace*, A. Brome, etc., 2nd ed., 1671, p. 342.
MS. Rawl. D. 261, p. 61.

Ask me no more the cause why Oxford wind 1753
That tyrannous disease, and cleared the town.
Oldisworth, Nicolas, 'On a Bag of Perfumes given him by a Friend'.
MS. *Don. c. 24, fol. 52 (autogr.).

Ask me no more whither do [doth] stray 1754
And in thy fragrant bosom dies.
[Carew, Thomas], 'In praise of his Mrs.'
Pr. with verses in different order, *Poems*, 1642, p. 180; and as here in *Poems of Pembroke and Ruddier*, 1660, p. 92, and in *Cheerfull Ayres or Ballads*, by John Wilson, 1660, p. 42. Another version in *Wit Restor'd*, 1658, p. 114.
MSS. Ashmole 38, p. 137; 47, fol. 53; CCC. 325, fol. 100v; 328, fol. 80v; Don. c. 57, fol. 36v, music anon.; d. 58, fol. 30v; Eng. poet. f. 25, fol. 63; Firth e. 4, p. 86; Mus. b. 1, fol. 113v, music by John Wilson; Tanner 465, fol. 60, attr. to Sir H. Wootton.

1755 Ask me no more whither doth stray
Be, and we two could ne'er agree.
Parody of Thomas Carew's A1754. See *Poems of Thomas Carew*, ed. A. Vincent, 1899, pp. 141 and 255 n.
MS. Firth e. 4, p. 87.

1756 Ask me not where the spring retires
Since flowers can spring from ice, and fire from snow.
Mr. D—d, 'On Colonel L—'s Lady'.
MS. Eng. poet. e. 40, fol. 7.

1757 Ask me why I send you here
What fainting hopes are in a lover.
Herrick, [Robert], 'The Primrose'.
Pr. bk. 27980 e. 86, opposite p. 50.

1758 Ask not divines, what, where, or whence, is hell
Court waiting weary suitors, best can till.
Couplet.
MS. Ashmole 38, p. 154.

1759 Ask not fair ladies, ask not why
I know you're too too ready to conceive.
'A song'.
MS. Rawl. poet. 84, fol. 25 rev.

1760 Ask not if nature's varying face
And answering joy in beauty's eye.
Wiffin, Jeramiah Holmes, 'To . . .'.
MS. Montagu d. 5, fol. 292 (autogr.).

1761 Ask not the cause that makes one cuckold ride
For making infidels to turn their backs.
'An Epigram', on George I.
MS. Rawl. poet. 155, p. 50.

1762 Ask not to know this woman? she is worse
The Devil, and be the damning of us all.
[Jonson, Ben., *Underwood* xx.]
MS. Ashmole 38, p. 155.

1763 Ask Tiscus how his luck doth go
For all men know 'tis longer ebb than flood.
'Epigram'.
MS. Rawl. poet. 172, fol. 7v.

1764 Ask what you will ask right and ye shall have it
Good Lord we pray thee teach us how to pray.
'A meditation upon prayer'.
MS. Rawl. poet. 142, fol. 81.

1765 Aslumbering as I lay last night,
And then we would be gone to Hell,
MSS. Ashmole 36, 37, fol. 117v.

1766 Assemble now you people all
Thy power and name always.
Forman, Simon, composed '1604 January 19 to be songe at his burialle'.
MS. Ashmole 802, fols. 135–40v, imperfect between fols. 136/7 (autogr.).

Asses milk, half a pint, take at seven or before. 1767
And those you may end, when you please to prove kind.
Chesterfield, Philip Dormer Stanhope, Earl of, 'Verses . . . to the Lady Fanny Shirley'.
MS. Eng. poet. e. 40, fol. 41.

Assist me, muse divine! to sing the morn, 1768
When time, and sin, and death shall be no more!
'On Christmas Day'.
MS. Eng. poet. e. 39, p. 121.

Assist me, muse, my infant genius raise 1769
Jove's thunder shakes the earth, but she shakes Jove.
'A Christmas Entertainment'.
MS. Eng. poet. f. 12, p. 48.

Assist me now you doleful dames 1770
Oh pain sorrowful pain—pain that nips me sore.
'To the tune of Hobbinoble and Iohn a side'.
MS. Rawl. poet. 185, fol. 9.

Assist me, oh my God, to Thee to seek 1771
Let all Thy works Thy wondrous praise confess.
Williams, John, 'A prayer for Miss Betty Ashe being ill of the meazles', 11 Jan. 1709/10.
MS. *Rawl. poet. 184, fol. 69 (autogr.).

Assist me satire since I find 'tis grown 1772
To adjourn satire till another season.
Satire on 'Bladness Towne'.
MS. Eng. poet. e. 50, p. 8.

Assist me, some auspicious muse, to tell 1773
Subdue the prowess of one poor old man.
'On the death of a Beadle in a fight with the Dukes of Albermarle and Monmouth' [1670/1].
MS. Don. b. 8, p. 208.

Assist me, some good spirit with a hi with a hi, 1774
And like ravens cry, York, york, with a hi tra, etc.
'The Magpye, or the song against the Bishops sung by Aaron Smyth at the Feast of the Lords at the Gunn at Mile-end-Green'.
Exclusion Bill, November 1680.
MS. Don. b. 8, p. 621.

Assist me, Stanhope, while I sing 1775
In prose, or else in rhyme.
'Chevy Chace. 2 Part'.
Dated 1682 in B.M. MS. Harl. 7319, fol. 89v.
MS. Rawl. poet. 159, fol. 167v.

1776 Assist my muse!—assist to sing
Of Johnny Wilkes's brother.
'A Burlesque Ode to the Memory of B[ra]ss C[rosb]y Esq. Lord Mayor of London in 1771'.
MS. *Eng. poet. e. 28, p. 322.

1777 Assist sweet muse to celebrate the morn
And bless the lovely Harriet's natal morn
'. . . sent by Miss G— to Miss [Harriet] L— on her Birth-Day'.
MS. Eng. poet. e. 39, p. 225.

1778 Assist ye muses nine and graces three
But yet believe me 'tis no trivial thing.
'In veru Tricusp'.
MS. Rawl. poet. 194, fol. 29.

1779 Assist you mighty sons of art
By which we taste of Heaven below.
Ode for St. Cecilia's day, set by W. Davis.
MS. Mus. c. 16, fol. 2, composer's autograph.

1780 Assured by the unerring word
To full fruition there.
Kenton, James.
MS. *Eng. poet. e. 20, p. 115 (autogr.).

1781 Asterie, why dost thou mourn
Th'art hard; still hard remain.
Fanshawe, Sir Richard, translator, Horace, *Odes* III. vii.
MS. *Firth c. 1, p. 50.

1782 Astonished at thy wondrous love
Then look me to thy paradise.
Kenton, James.
MS. *Eng. poet. e. 20, p. 316 (autogr.).

1783 Astonishment and strange surprise
Shall gain eternal life through him.
Kenton, James.
MS. *Eng. poet. e. 20, p. 19 (autogr.).

1784 Astrea when will you pity my anguish,
In this fixed resolve . . . I'll die.
M[iddleton], L[ady] Eliz[abeth], 'A Dialogue between Celadon and Astrea', set by W. Davis.
MS. Mus. c. 16, fol. 116$^{v}$, composer's autograph.

1785 Astrologers say Venus the same star
With every year a new Epiphany.
[Cleveland, John], 'On Princesse Elizabeth borne the night before new yeares dayes', i.e. Elizabeth, daughter of Charles I, born 28 Dec. 1635.
Pr. *Clievelandi Vindiciæ*, 1677, p. 74.
MS. Rawl. poet. 84, fol. 83$^{v}$.

Astrology is high, Theology is deep: 1786
And honesty let's keep.
Robinson, Robert.
MS. *Rawl. poet. 218, p. 92 (autogr.).

At all religions present, and all past 1787
Rail at all women, and then wed an whore.
'To Mr. Dryden upon the change of his Religion', 1686.
MSS. Ashmole 36, 37, fol. 324; Sancroft 53, p. 58.

At all times I will bless the Lord 1788*a*
In complete ruin ends.
Psalm xxxiv.
MS. *Rawl. C. 113, fol. 28$^{v}$.

At Anna's call the Austrian eagle flies 1788*b*
Leaves the true monarch to command the world.
Stepney, [George], 'The Austrian Eagle'.
MS. Rawl. poet. 173, fol. 129$^{v}$.

At Ashby was a wedding 1789
And so they all went to 't.
'A Song to the Tune of a Soldier and a Sailor'.
MS. Ballard 47, fol. 162.

At beauty's bar where I did stand 1790
It was in too much praising you.
[Gascoigne, George]. Pr. *A Hundreth Sundrie Flowres*, [1573].
MS. Ashmole 48, fol. 139.

At Cana's feast great Heaven's [our blessed] Lord 1791
But turned their claret into water.
'On it's raining on George I's Birthday . . . 28 May, 1723, at Edinburgh'.
MSS. Ballard 47, fol. 63; Rawl. D. 383, fol. 128.

At certain hours unto God for to pray 1792
Such praying was received in the Church Christian.
'Howers of the B. Virgin Engl. and lat. ad usum Sarum. At the end of Mattins of the Crosse'.
MS. Eng. poet. e. 56, p. 90.

At Christmas last as did appear 1793
Desiring God to stand my friend.
'This is Richard Adams ditty / And very true though nothing witty'.
MS. Rawl. D. 398, fol. 194.

At church I heard the parson say 1794
When he got home—with knife and fork.
Maitland, Penelope, 'Epigram'.
MS. Eng. poet. c. 51, p. 106.

1795 At commerce we met, by my cards you were slain
And try to engage in a commerce of hearts.
Parsons, William, 'Extempore on playing Commerce with a Lady'.
MS. *Don. d. 123, p. 200 (autogr.).

1796 At compline time this mother of mercy
To her son most exalted in glory.
'Howers of the B. Virgin, Eng. and lat. ad usum Sarum, Hymne for Complyn of the Compassion of our Lady'.
MS. Eng. poet. e. 56, p. 83.

1797 At Compline's latest hour
My mind's continual care.
'Engl. Primer of our Ladie, 1631, Office of the Crosse at Compline, p. 319'.
MS. Eng. poet. e. 56, p. 13.

1798 At court? Alas what should I do
Attract court-eyes to insides ne'er so gross.
In B.M. Harl. MS. 7319, fol. 105$^{v}$, headed, 'Scotch Royalty, Or Remarks upon the Instalment, 1682'.
MS. Rawl. poet. 206, p. 28.

1799 At court I met it, in clothes brave enough
For I will dare none: good Lord walk dead still.
[Jonson, Ben.], 'On something that walks somewhere'.
*Epigrammes* xi.
MS. Ashmole 47, fol. 45$^{v}$.

1800 At dead at night, after an evening ball,
Leaving the trembling princess drowned in tears.
'Dutchess of Yorks Ghost', 1690/1.
MSS. Eng. poet. c. 18, fol. 171; e. 50, p. 38.

1801 At Delphos' shrine one did a doubt propound
While Spencer is alive, it is no question.
'On Edmund Spencer'.
Pr. Camden's *Remaines*, 1637, p. 401.
MSS. Eng. poet. e. 40, fol. 128; Sancroft 53, p. 69.

1802 At dice who plays in this conceit may enter
My hope, my health, my life, my wealth I venture.
Couplet, from Latin distich.
MS. Rawl. D. 954, fol. 42$^{v}$.

1803 At Down-Patrick in one tomb doth lie
Bridget, Patrick, and a pigeon pie.
'An Epitaph in Ireland . . . English'd by the Parish Priest'.
MS. Eng. poet. e. 40, fol. 3.

1804 At eight o'clock at night
And in her best attire / A little (last six lines crossed out).
'A riddle'.
MS. Rawl. poet. 172, fol. 3.

At first, apart from woman woman's mind 1805
Man than a good wife, none worse than a bad.
J. F., on 'Simonides of Women, interpreted by Buchanan'.
MS. *Eng. poet. f. 17, p. 51 (autogr.).

At first oh! Rome how sacred was your fame! 1806
Whilst faith and virtue wept, but wept in vain.
'In Nonas Novembris'.
MS. Top. London e. 9, p. 111.

At first, on observing the tea chest was fast 1807
It's proper to carry the key.
Madan, Martin, 'On the Tea being locked up . . . viz: the Lock Chapel', *c.* 1775.
See *The Madan Family*, F. Madan, 1933, p. 112.
MS. Eng. poet. c. 51, p. 39.

At five i'th' morn when Phoebus rais'd his head 1808
Did seem to me by much the wiser creature.
[Wilmot, John, Earl of] R[ochester], 'Tunbridge Wells', 'L$^{d}$ R. fecit Sept. 20: 81'.
MS. Douce 357, fol. 136$^{v}$.

At four o'clock this morn I bid adieu 1809
Thine whilst my own. Yet hear'st? I do but jest.
Ashmole, Elias, 'Upon my riding post from London to Bradfield. To Mr. [William] Hutchinson'. 15 May 1648.
MSS. Ashmole 36, 37, fol. 230$^{v}$ (autogr.).

At Hampton Court I pleaded 1810
From Turk and Pope defend us.
'The Second part [of the distracted Puritan] to the tune of Tom of Bedlam'.
MS. Rawl. poet. 212, fol. 149 rev.

At Hatfield near Hertford there [is a] lies in a coffin 1811
And therefore had reason to keep it to his end.
On Sir Robert Cecil, first Earl of Salisbury, 1612.
MSS. Firth d. 7, fol. 156; Tanner 299, fol. 11.

At home abroad, most willingly I will 1812
Unbounded bides, no time can it define.
Herbert, Mary (*née* Sidney), Countess of Pembroke, Psalm cxi.
MSS. *Rawl. poet. 24, p. 166; *25, fol. 113.

At Katherine's dock [there] was launched a pink 1813
God mend her mast, that's all I crave.
'Upon the earl of Somerset's marriage with the earl of Essex' wife her husband being alive', 1613.
MSS. Don. c. 54, fol. 23; Rawl. poet. 84, fol. 68 rev.

1814 At Knoll the air, and entertain
And therefore I'll come home.
'Lady Constantia's Answer' to Y508.
MSS. Rawl. A. 175, fol. 167; 176, fol. 109.

1815 At last the glorious mystery's revealed
And are yourselves to seek, though we poor mortals more.
'Mrs. Randolph's poem on Christmas day'.
Pr. bk. Gough London 143 (7*).

1816 At length by work of wondrous fate
As for the great rapping and oft coming in.
'On the Porter at Winchester'.
MSS. Don. d. 58, fol. 17v; Eng. poet. e. 14, fol. 94v rev.; Malone 19, p. 77.

1817 At length comes oft too late
Amends for every wrong.
'Upon the poesy Tandem si'.
MSS. Eng. poet. c. 50, fol. 126; Rawl. poet. 85, fol. 113.

1818 At length I trust the conflict's o'er
For female softness, you, and mild attractive grace!
Parsons, William, 'Ode on the Prospect of Peace. To a Lady born in America, 2 Jan. 1783'.
MS. *Don. d. 123, p. 71 (autogr.).

1819 At length kind heaven has the enchantment broke
That saved the state from France, the Church from Rome.
'On the Death of the Queen', Anne, 1 Aug. 1714.
Pr. bk. Fol. $\theta$ 665, fol. 219v.

1820 At length my soul the fatal union finds
And on my head let the old cottage fall.
Walsh, Octavia.
MS. *Eng. poet. e. 31, fol. 26 (autogr.).

1821 At length the fleeting year is o'er
And awe th' aspiring nations into peace.
[Whitehead, William], New Year Ode, 1772.
Pr. *Poems*, 1790, ii. 107.
MS. Mus. Sch. D. 327, music by Boyce.

1822 At length the gods propitious to our prayers
Worse is an evil fame, much worse than known.
Glanvill, [John], 'A private Condition Securest', imitation of Seneca, *Thyestes*, ii. 339–403.
MS. Rawl. poet. 173, fol. 57v.

1823 At length th' imperious lord of war
His throne each Briton's heart.
[Whitehead, William], New Year Ode, 1763.
Pr. *Poems*, 1774, ii. 279.
MS. Mus. Sch, D. 312, music by Boyce.

At length too soon dear creature 1824
With love's soft tumult beat.
MS. Mus. c. 107, two copies, fols. 38 and 41.

At length with age exhausted Fountain's dead 1825
'Till wide expanded thou becom'st a sea.
'On Mr. Brook, succeeding to the Living of Mr. Fountain'.
MS. Eng. poet. c. 51, p. 51.

At length with vengeance bursts my raging vein 1826
And lost in transport, beg to wake no more.
[Amhurst, Nicholas], 'Strephon's Revenge—A Satire on the Oxford Toasts Inscrib'd to the Author of Merton Walks'.
Pr. 1718.
MS. Top. Oxon. e. 167, fol. 4.

At London Town there was a wedding 1827
The Squire will shoe his horse round.
[Roach, Richard], 'Marriage a la Mode . . . A Ballad'.
MS. Rawl. D. 832, two copies, fols. 192 and 200 (autogr.).

At lowest ebb of fortune when you lay 1828
And wonted happiness returns no more.
'Harv. Juvenal'.
MS. Eng. poet. c. 9, p. 151.

At midnight when the fever rag'd 1829
And charmed my soul to rest.
'An Ode . . . Jany. 22 1732'.
MS. Eng. poet. c. 9, p. 56.

At monstrous births which do the mother fright 1830
Their raised swords dropped when they heard the lash.
'A translation of Claudian's first Booke against Eutropius A° 1664'.
MS. Rawl. poet. 154, two copies, fols. 27 and 38*b*v (autogr.).

At my beginning Christ me speed 1831
Shalt find default in time of need.
Stanzas of moral advice.
MS. Rawl. C. 813, fol. 9.

At my heart there is a pain 1832
Love both took his life and death.
Subscribed 'S. P. S.' [Sir Philip Sidney] at a later time.
MS. Rawl. poet. 85, fol. 25v.

At night uprising let us watch and pray 1833
In every coast.
Huish, Alexander, translator, *Nocte surgentes vigilemus omnes*: 'Elucidat Ecclesiast, fol. 3 . . . Brev. Rom. p. 3, Brev. Sar. fol. 1, Diebus Dominicus, ad nocturnam matutinum', translated 27 Jan. 1634.
MS. Eng. poet. e. 56, p. 130 (autogr.).

1834 At noon the youthful Corydon
And their warm souls together fled.
Chatwin, John, 'Song'.
MS. *Rawl. poet. 94, p. 195 (autogr.).

1835 At once, from hence my lines, and I depart
Merit of love, bestow that love on me.
Donne, John, 'An Old Letter'.
Pr. *Poems*, 1633.
MSS. *Eng. poet. e. 99, fol. 29; Rawl. poet. 116, fol. 52v.

1836 At Osney Abbey you may find
To cure all those with love oppressed.
'Whitsunale . . . at Osney. Notice by the Cryer'.
MS. Top. Oxon. a. 29, fol. 73.

1837 At our creation but the word was said
He 's made and lost.
[Quarles, Francis], 'On man'.
Pr. *Divine Fancies*, 1632, iii. 67.
MS. Don. d. 58, fol. 13.

1838 At Polwart on the Green
To take a part of mine.
'A Song'.
MS. Montagu e. 13, fol. 9v.

1839 At Portsmouth, duke, I [can] will no longer stay
Adieu, I have no title to a tittle.
'Charon and the Duke of Buckingham', 1628.
Pr. *Poems and Songs . . . relating to . . . Buckingham*, Percy Soc. Publications, xxix (5), 1850, p. 56.
MSS. Douce f. 5, fol. 13v; Eng. poet. e. 14, fol. 19; Rawl. poet. 26, fol. 14; Tanner 465, fol. 103.

1840*a* At Rome a time of liberty and sin
What we must first give thanks and then repent.
'Shrove Tuesday at Dublin'.
MS. Rawl. poet. 155, p. 174.

1840*b* At St. James's of late
That you'd pull an old house on your head.
'1717'. 'See the Frontispiece', i.e. an engraving pasted to a fly-leaf.
Pr. bk. Linc. B. 26. 75 (12).

1841 At St. Osyth by the mill
And grant it all in her.
'The Lass of St. Osyth'.
MS. Montagu e. 13, fol. 65v.

1842 At Sarra in the land of Tartary
Her bounteous groats, in empty palms to shed.
Lane, John, 'Chaucer's Piller, being . . . the Squier's Tale . . . now found out . . . 1630'.
Pr. by the Chaucer Society, 1888.
MS. Ashmole 53, fol. 1.

At scribblers poor who write to eat 1843
That ever try to part ye.
'On Sir R. Walpole's writing a pamphlet, 1728'.
Pr. bk. Firth b. 22, fol. 33.

At Se'noke so famed for virginity old, 1844
The Justice desisted, and here ends my tale.
Amherst, Elizabeth, 'Se'noke Nunnery; to the tune of Packington's pound', 1745.
MSS. Eng. poet. c. 41, fol. 73; *e. 109, p. 38.

At seventy years Tom Kestel's silver hairs 1845
Hide the one's fault, the other's worth display.
'On Kestell and Fortescue'.
MS. Eng. poet. e. 4, p. 43.

At several hopes wisely to fly 1846
A thing that always flees from you.
MS. Rawl. poet. 213, fol. 66.

At Shiloh's suffering the sun in sable cloud 1847
Who Shiloh slew, yet did the scripture know.
MS. *Rawl. poet. 97, fol. 57 (autogr.).

At Taundean lond I woz a-bore and a bred 1848
To vaither and mother an ziztar Kaite.
'A West country song'.
Pr. J. O. Halliwell, *Collection of Pieces in the Dialect of Zummerset*, 1843, p. 3, from this MS.
MSS. Ashmole 36, 37, fol. 112.

At Temple's hospitable table 1849
Bring Burney's rods to pay their b—ms!
Parsons, William, 'To R. G. Temple'.
MS. *Don. d. 123, p. 228 (autogr.).

At the brow of a hill a fair shepherdess dwelt 1850
But remember the lass at the brow of the hill.
Copied 13 Sept. 1751.
MS. Mus. e. 20, fol. 22v.

At the close of the day as we drive to the fold 1851
Such sounds to hear, such sports to see.
Glee by [Henry] Harington [M.D., 1727–1816].
MS. Mus. d. 177, fol. 38v.

At the close of the day 1852
And trifled no more with the rest.
Gay, John, 'A Ballad'.
MS. Eng. poet. e. 8, fol. 30*a*.

At the close of the day, when the hamlet is still 1853
And beauty immortal awakes from the tomb.
Beattie, James, 'The Hermit'.
MS. Montagu e. 14, fol. 15v.

1854 At the conqueror's feet he stood, and whilst that he
'Cause I think Caesar worthy life to give.
Thomas Weaver (?), translator, 'Luc[an] li. 4. v. 340'.
Not pr. in *Songs and Poems by T. W.*, 1654.
MS. *Rawl. poet. 211, fol. 59$^{v}$, in Weaver's hand.

1855 At the great Jehovah's word
Thy glorious name to praise.
Kenton, James.
MS. *Eng. poet. e. 20, p. 183 (autogr.).

1856 At the heavenly herald's cry
Grace below, and Heaven above.
Kenton, James.
MS. *Eng. poet. e. 20, p. 377 (autogr.).

1857 At the large foot of a fair hollow tree,
With peace, let tares and acorns be my food.
Cowley, Abraham, 'The Country-Mouse'.
Paraphrased from Horace, *Satires* II. vi. 79–117. Pr. *Works*, 1668, 'Essays in Verse and Prose', p. 109.
MSS. Rawl. poet. 90, fol. 95; 173, fol. 37$^{v}$, attr. to Mr. Cowley.

1858 At the nativity of Christ our Lord
And keep this feast with joy and civil mirth.
'Copies for Schollers to Write'.
MS. Rawl. poet. 152, fol. 232.

1859 At the ninth hour, his life
The sun no light forth sends.
'Engl. Primer of o$^{r}$ Lady, 1631, p. 317'.
MS. Eng. poet. e. 56, p. 11.

1860 At the posts of wisdom's door.
The work of faith and love.
Kenton, James.
MS. *Eng. poet. e. 20, p. 102 (autogr.).

1861 At the round earth's imagined corners, blow
As if thou hadst seal'd my pardon, with thy blood.
Donne, John, 'Sonnett 4'.
Pr. *Poems*, 1633.
MS. *Eng. poet. e. 99, fol. 44.

1862 At the sight of bright Celia, I lay down my arms
That burns up my heart.
'A Song'.
MS. Montagu e. 13, fol. 23$^{v}$.

1863 At the sight of my Phyllis from every part
T' live sober all day, and chaste all the night.
[Wilmot, John, Earl of Rochester (?)].
See Prinz, *Rochester* (Palaestra cliv), 1927, p. 141.
MS. Don. b. 8, p. 429.

At [the sign of St. James's] de sine of St. James at de nort side de park 1864
Yet for oat and rebellion he vil give ye de dispensasho.
'The High Dutch Show', the court of George I.
MS. Rawl. poet. 155, p. 181.

At the sweet hour when mortals here below 1865
Blest the approach of the delightful morn.
Chatwin, John, 'On his not Sleeping one Night by reason of the Tooth-Ache'.
MS. *Rawl. poet. 94, p. 100 (autogr.).

At the temple gate see this poor sinner stand, 1866
Thou'lt enter in, and find God nigher hand.
Sancroft, Abp. William, translation of Crashaw's epigram on Luke xviii. 13 from *Epigrammata Sacra*, 1634.
MS. Sancroft 48, fol. 12$^{v}$ (autogr.).

At the third hour they cry 1867
Unto the place of pain.
'Eng. Primer of o$^{r}$ Lady 1631 . . . p. 315'.
MS. Eng. poet. e. 56, p. 9.

At the town of Lyn in Norfolk 1868
As the good folks at Lyn.
'The merry Tales of Lyn'.
MS. Douce 193, fol. 88.

At this calm silent hour of Morpheus' reign 1869
Must needs arise, if ye take him / Take all.
Bulteel, John, 'Upon Sir Percy Smith's sudden sickness'.
MS. *Rawl. poet. 159, fol. 215.

At this glad triumph when most poets use 1870
Heir to himself through all posterity.
King, Henry, 'By Occasion of the young Prince's happy Birth', Charles II, 'May 29, 1630'.
Pr. *Poems*, 1657, p. 40.
MSS. *Eng. poet. e. 30, fol. 49; *Malone 22, fol. 25.

At this unwonted hour, behold 1871
Of Heaven's free, vast benevolence to man.
'A Christmas Ode. G[entleman's] Mag.'
MS. Eng. poet. e. 39, p. 193.

At this vain season when each flippant fool 1872
To claim your fair possessions in the skies!
Parsons, William, 'Verses to my Mother'.
MS. *Don. d. 123, p. 25 (autogr.).

At threescore winter's end I died 1873
And wish my father never had.
Cowper, William, translator, 'On a discontented man'.
MS. Eng. poet. c. 51, p. 238.

1874 At thy approach each new-born joy appeared
From the possession of such heavenly joy?
Whaley, John, 'To Caelia Absent'.
Pr. *Poems*, 1732, p. 99.
MS. Rawl. poet. 222, fol. 13v.

1875 At Thy command I rise
I shall see my Jesus there.
Kenton, James.
MS. *Eng. poet. e. 20, p. 57 (autogr.).

1876 At Thy gracious throne we bow
Thy saving mercy prove.
Kenton, James.
MS. *Eng. poet. e. 20, p. 139 (autogr.).

1877 At twelve years' age Christ's disputation
All were to hear on pain of punishment.
MS. *Rawl. poet. 97, fol. 57v (autogr.).

1878 At Westminster warehouse are now to be sold
Be pleased to enquire of Zach'ry and Co.
'Advertisment', satire on Zachary Pearce, Dean of Westminster 1756–68.
MS. Eng. poet. c. 51, p. 19.

1879 At what late happen'd in th' Antipodes
First to take thieves away, then bishops too.
J. S., translator of 'Jocosum Antipodianum', by A. G., which precedes.
MS. Rawl. poet. 26, fol. 135v.

1880 At what time Jacob's race, did leave of Egypt take
And purling springs, from flint to flow.
Herbert, Mary (*née* Sidney), Countess of Pembroke, Psalm cxiv.
MSS. *Rawl. poet. 24, p. 168; *25, fol. 114.

1881 At Whitehall sits a High Commission
Not long since led a better king to France.
MS. Top. Oxon. c. 108, p. 87; see also B511, B620.

1882 At York the Lords have stayed for
You hear no more of me.
'On the Lords mustering their forces at York', 1642.
MS. Rawl. poet. 71, p. 89.

1883 At your request I here have made a shift
Good words are something, though they nothing cost.
'To a Gentlewoman that desired nothing to her New-years gift'.
MS. Rawl. poet. 26, fol. 3.

1884 At your request these lines I sends
For nothing can surpass their innocency.
'To Mr. Morland'.
MS. Eng. poet. e. 17, fol. 6v.

Atheist, be dumb or blind: lift but an eye 1885
That my strength and redeemer art.
J. F., Psalm xix.
MS. *Eng. poet. f. 17, p. 147 (autogr.).

Attend all mortals high and low 1886
When he comes to descend into the pit below.
Fleming, Robert, 'Thoughts upon the Forty Ninth Psalm in Pindariques'.
MS. *Rawl. poet. 202, fol. 17v.

Attend all ye curious, and to your own fate 1887
She begs a stiff coral to rub her old gums.
'Cupid's Post Boy. 1697'.
MS. Eng. poet. e. 50, p. 76.

Attend and list awhile 1888
Ay that it would.
'1660?'.
Pr. bk. Firth b. 20, fol. 141.

Attend and prepare for a cargo from Dover 1889
Whores cuckolds and fools bawds bullies and beaux.
'The Merchant Alamode . . . on the Duke D'Amont the french Ambassador who came to England after the peace 1713'.
MSS. Eng. misc. c. 116, fol. 5v; Rawl. C. 986, fol. 25; see also A1903.

Attend awhile, 1890
And say, the crow is white.
Lilliat, John, 'his Malecontent'.
MS. Rawl. poet. 148, fol. 90 (autogr.).

Attend British boys 1891
By St. George but another Convention.
On the victory at Porto Bello, Nov. 1740, opposition ballad.
MS. Eng. poet. c. 41, fol. 20.

Attend good Christian people to my story 1892
And now I pray you sing the lamentation.
'The penitent Traytor. Or the humble Confession of a Devonshire gentleman Condemn'd for High Treason and executed at Tyburne. A. D., 1264' (*sic*).
See *Loyal songs*, 1662, p. 53; and W. Chappell, *Old English Popular Music*, 2nd ed., 1893, i. 78.
MS. Rawl. poet. 152, fol. 5.

Attend good people and give ear 1893
Both head, hands face and gear.
'Song'.
MS. Ashmole 38, p. 119.

Attend, good people, and to me give ear 1894
To light their fleet home through the Northern passage.
'A new Ballad . . . on the late Comet so much talked of. 1664'.
MS. Don. b. 8, p. 345.

1895 **Attend good people, lay by scoffs and scorns**
**Mine only is Strange-Lee and his Le-Strange.**
[Wild, Robert], 'The Recantation of a penitent Proteus, or the Changeling, as it was acted with good applause in St. Maries in Cambridge and St. Pauls in London. 1663'. Answered by Y76.
Pr. as a broadsheet, 1664 (MS. Tanner 306, fol. 394) and in *Iter Boreale with large additions*, 1668, p. 93.
MS. Don. b. 8, p. 437.

1896 **Attend harmonious saint and see**
**In joy and harmony and love.**
Addision, Joseph, 'Ode in Praise of Musick, Perform'd for [John Alcock's] Bachelor's Degree in Music in Act Term 1755'.
MS. Mus. Sch. C. 49.

1897 **Attend mine humble prayer Lord.**
**And stand before thee clear.**
Byrd's 3-part setting of Psalm cxliii.
Pr. *Songs of Sundrie natures*, 1589, vii.
MSS. Mus. f. 11–15: f. 14, fol. 6$^{v}$.

1898 **Attend my brethren every one**
**You'ld wish you were but luke-warm.**
[Weaver, Thomas], 'Zeale over heated', 'To the tune of Chieffy Chase'.
MS. Ballard 50, fol. 4; see also A1905, A1907.

1899 **Attend, my friends, the cheerful glass**
**Ye trumpets horns and shrill hautboys.**
Gough, Richard, translator, 'An Ode to the Prince of Orange from the French'.
MS. Eng. poet. c. 5, fols. 34$^{v}$–33$^{v}$ (autogr.).

1900 **Attend my people and give ear;**
**Or any thing which is not thine.**
W[hittingham], W[illiam], 'The x commaundementes'.
MS. Rawl. poet. 112, fol. 25 rev.

1901 **Attend my people to my law**
**Did govern them indeed.**
[Sternhold, Thomas], Psalm lxxviii.
MS. Rawl. poet. 112, fol. 48$^{v}$ rev.

1902 **Attend my people, to the law**
**He ruled the chosen seed.**
Psalm lxxviii.
MS. *Montagu e. 10, fol. 28.

1903 **Attend to prepare for a cargo from Dover**
**Whores, cuckolds and fools, bawds bullies and beaux.**
'The Merchant Alamode', on the Peace of Utrecht, March 1713.
MS. Eng. poet. c. 41, fol. 48; see also A1889.

**Attend with due regard** 1904
**Will out of Sion bless.**
Psalm cxxxiv.
MS. *Rawl. C. 113, fol. 95$^{v}$.

**Attend ye brethren every one** 1905
**'Gainst clubs of reformation.**
Weaver, Thomas, 'Zeal over-heated'.
Pr. *Songs and Poems . . . by T. W.*, 1654, p. 21.
MS. *Rawl. poet. 211, fol. 80$^{v}$ rev. (autogr.).
MSS. Ashmole 36, 37, fol. 160; see also A1898, A1907.

**Attend ye nymphs whilst I impart** 1906
**Devoted all to love and me.**
'Song'.
MS. Percy d. 9, fol. 11$^{v}$.

**Attend you brethren every one** 1907
**Of the furious element.**
[Weaver, Thomas], 'Zeale over-heated'.
MS. Rawl. poet. 26, fol. 142; see also A1898, A1905.

**Attention to th' advice I give** 1908
**To give thee all my thankful heart.**
Kenton, James.
MS. *Eng. poet. e. 20, p. 233 (autogr.).

**Attentive to the promise given** 1909
**To make a wife of grace his choice.**
Kenton, James.
MS. *Eng. poet. e. 20, p. 387 (autogr.).

**Aubrey! whom heaven's extended bounties bless,** 1910
**His sovereign's glory with the people's rights.**
'By the Revd. Mr. Cooke, of Thame', 'Address'd to John Aubrey Esq$^{r}$ . . . On his glorious Triumph at Aylesbury', in the election, 6 May 1784.
MS. Rawl. poet. 172, fol. 159.

**Audacious painters have nine worthies made** 1911
**Which termed his love a giant for her wit.**
Davies, Sir John, 'In Decium',
Pr. amongst 'Epigrames', in *Ovids Elegies*, trans. C. M., *c*. 1600.
MSS. *Add. B. 97, fol. 44; *Rawl. poet. 212, fol. 63 rev.

**Augustus with the senate, people all** 1912
**[A]ll things are under his authority.**
Translation of Latin, which precedes.
MSS. Ashmole 36, 37, fol. 185$^{v}$.

**Aulon a sorry tale thou toldst last day** 1913
**Aulon good night; would I thy sorrows could allay.**
Pipe, Richard, 'Satirical eclogues', 1617, 'Eglogue ii'.
MS. *Don. e. 22, fol. 8 (autogr.).

1914 Aulon, I promised thee last night to bring
Sure he and Pimblemeer are cuffing.
Pipe, Richard, 'Satirical eclogues', 1617, 'Eglogue iii'.
MS. *Don. e. 22, fol. 10v (autogr.).

1915 Aulon, 'tis strange thou wouldst not stay to hear
We anniversal tears for thanks will give.
Pipe, Richard, 'Satirical eclogues', 1617, 'Eglogue ix'.
MS. *Don. e. 22, fol. 35 (autogr.).

1916 Aurelia bloomed the sweetest maid
Princes, that glittered on a throne.
Jessop, William, ballad.
MS. Percy b. 1, fol. 14v (autogr.).

1917 Aurelia! Oh that name does vigour give!
And clasp, and twine, and clasp t' eternity.
Chatwin, John, 'Concerning Aurelia'.
MS. *Rawl. poet. 94, p. 87 (autogr.).

1918 Aurora now had left Ithorus' bed
Knowing whatever is, is best.
Bate, S[ally], 'A Dialogue between Amoret and Lisette, 1767'.
MS. *Eng. poet. e. 28, p. 133.

1919 Aurora now thou showest thy blushing light
Make me still fear thy fair appearing show.
Sidney, Sir Philip, from the *Arcadia*.
MS. *e Mus. 37, fol. 123.

1920 Aurora shines not with so sweet a grace
Let your light shine towards us; God's light towards you.
Oldisworth, Giles, 'The good morrow'.
MS. *Rawl. C. 422, fol. 30 (autogr.).

1921 Auspicious day! the best in all the year!
But drink a jolly health to good old Puss.
'On the 30th of January' 1687.
MSS. Eng. poet. c. 18, fol. 77; e. 49, p. 70; Rawl. poet. 159, fol. 14.

1922 Auspicious morn, whose chiefest pride,
Nor Haistwell happy be alone.
Gough, Richard, 'Epithalamium on the marriage of Edward Haistwell. printed in [Nichols'] Literary Anecdotes', vi, 1812, p. 338.
MS. *Eng. poet. c. 5, fol. 191 (autogr.).

1923 Authors write that in Hibernian sand
Religion wrote his epitaph in brass.
'On Thomas Earl of Strafford', 1641.
MS. Dodsworth 79, fol. 160.

1924 Autumn's frost had on each tree
See; the lad himself complains.
Mervall, Alphonso, 'To Cloris', subscribed 'Tettix'.
MS. *Rawl. poet. 166, p. 12 (autogr.).

Avaunt ye smooth-tongued flatterers of the age 1925
That these black patches stick upon her face.
'On ignorant and scandalous Ministers'.
MS. Rawl. poet. 65, fol. 83v.

Avaunt you giddy-headed multitude, 1926
I'll smile on them that can but bark at me.
'Rhodomantados . . . from None-such June 21 [1628] The copie of his Grace [the Duke of Buckingham]'s . . . Rhodomantados sent . . . to the Lower House'.
Pr. *Poems and Songs . . . relating to . . . Buckingham*, ed. F. W. Fairholt, Percy Soc., xxix (5), 1850, p. 28. Quoted in part by S. R. Gardiner, *History of England . . . 1603–1642*, vi, 1886, p. 321.
MSS. Ashmole 36, 37, fol. 57; 38, p. 44, attr. to I. S.; Locke c. 32, fol. 1; Malone 23, p. 113.

Averse to pampered and unruly steeds 1927
What vast ideas they must have of corn.
Nares, [Robert], of Christ Church, Oxford, 1774, 'omne ignotum pro Magnifico'.
Pr. 'among Geo: Huddesford's poems on Salmigundi' [1801, p. 128].
MS. Eng. misc. e. 241, fol. 107.

Avoid profaneness come not here 1928
May at his peril further go.
Herbert, George, 'Superliminare'.
Pr. *The Temple*, 1633, p. 17.
MS. *Tanner 307, fol. 15.

Awake, adored saint, and show 1929
And, makes them like himself.
'A Song to a Lady sleeping'.
MS. Rawl. poet. 31, fol. 21v.

Awake all faithful hearts awake 1930
To live for aye.
Sponar, [Henry].
MS. Ashmole 48, fol. 62v.

Awake and with attention hear, 1931
They in the dens shall lurk, beasts in the palaces shall reign.
Cowley, A[braham], Isaiah xxxiv. 'Poëm p. 48 et seq.', reference to *Poems and Davideis*, 1656, iii, 'Pindarique Odes'.
MS. Tanner 466, fol. 13.

Awake, awake, Æolian lyre 1932
To do the deed.
Gough, Richard, 'On the River Wye . . . to Edward Haistwell Esq. of Bloomsbury Square, and Sir Joseph Andrews of Shaw Place Berks. Sept. 3, 1765'.
MS. *Eng. poet. c. 5, fol. 117 (autogr.).

1933 Awake awake, let not sleep bind,
Begone dark night, 'tis day, 'tis day.
'An alarm from sleep'.
MS. *Don. f. 5, fol. 4.

1934 Awake awake our drowsy powers
Salvation doth belong.
Beddome, Benjamin.
MS. *Eng. misc. e. 227, fol. 56v.

1935 Awake, awake, rouse up thyself my muse,
Cut off: they shall not in God's holy city stand.
Knollys, Fra[ncis], Psalm ci.
MS. *Rawl. poet. 60, p. 47 (autogr.).

1936 Awake, awake the morn will never rise
Till she can dress her beauties at thine eyes.
[Davenant, Sir William], song, music by John Wilson.
Pr. Wilson's *Cheerfull Ayres or Ballads*, 1660, p. 54.
Adapted from 'The lark now leaves his watery nest'.
MS. Mus. b. 1, fol. 128v.

1937 Awake Britannia, rouse thyself and say
And round thy temples, wind the verdant bays.
[Philips, Katherine (?)], 'Upon his Majesties most happy restauration . . .', 1660, subscribed 'Cecinit Domina Phillips agro Pembrokiæ'.
Pr. bk. Firth b. 20, fol. 136.

1938 Awake, dull muse, the sun appears
And Phoebus now assumes his state.
Ford, Thomas, 'On the King's Return, May 29 166[0]'.
MS. Eng. poet. e. 4, p. 167.

1939 Awake my heart awake my tongue
But Jesus be my only joy.
Beddome, Benjamin, 'An Hymn'.
MS. *Eng. misc. e. 227, fol. 174.

1940 Awake my lute, daughters of music come
And afterwards for ever blest.
M.A.
MS. Rawl. poet. 154, fol. 91.

1941 Awake my lyre and tell thy silent master's humble tale
Sleep again my lyre and let thy master die.
[Cowley, Abraham], song from *Davideis*, III. Act song composed by Dr. John Blow, 1678, performed 1679.
Pr. with Bowman's setting in *Songs for 1, 2 and 3 voices . . .* by Henry Bowman, 1678; Blow's setting in *Choice Ayres, and Songs. The Third Book*, 1681, p. 46.
MS. Mus. Sch. C. 122.

Awake my lyre thy vocal strings prepare 1942
To sing his praise who taught us here to love.
Stukeley, William, 'Sonnet'.
MS. *Eng. misc. e. 386, fol. 1v.

Awake my muse for shame oh raise thy drowsy head 1943
Have summoned all the force they can.
Walsh, Octavia.
MS. *Eng. poet. e. 31, fol. 28v (autogr.).

Awake my silent long reserved muse, 1944
She absent, thou, alone my mind must please.
North, Dudley, 3rd Baron, Sonnet i.
Pr. *A Forest of Varieties*, 1645.
MS. *North e. 41, fol. 7.

Awake my soul and come away 1945
Peace upon earth glory to God on high.
'A Him for Christmas Day', setting for 3 voices by Dr. [W.] Childe.
MS. Mus. Sch. C. 32–37: C. 32, fol. 4v.

Awake my soul and higher climb 1946
Oh come Lord Jesus quickly come.
Bromley, Henry, 'The Antidote'.
MS. *Don. e. 19, fol. 9v (autogr.).

Awake (my soul) and in the incestuous bed 1947
Conscience thy company and heaven thy end.
MS. Ashmole 381, p. 139.

Awake my soul and with the sun 1948
Praise father, son and holy ghost.
Ken, Thomas, Bp. of Bath and Wells, 'his Morning Hymn', first and last verses only as pr. in Winchester *Manual of Prayers*, 1695, p. 141.
MS. Rawl. D. 361, fol. 324.

Awake my soul why dost so fondly dote 1949
Help thou to clothe me, ere I'm called away.
Corbet, W., 'Statutum est omnibus semel mori'.
MS. *Rawl. poet. 210, fol. 36.

Awake oh England wail and weep 1950
Our souls may depart with a conscience clear.
'To the tune, when the King enjoys his owne again'.
See note by H. E. Rollins, *Old English Ballads*, 1920, p. 233.
MS. Eng. poet. b. 5, p. 120.

Awake oh soul and look abroad, 1951
Yet grace shall more than sin abound.
Smyth, Richard, 'The Sinners Counsell to his soule'.
Pr. *Munition against mans misery and mortality*, 2nd ed., 1612, Sig. A7v.
MS. Rawl. D. 1323, fol. 18.

1952 Awake, oh wretched man, awake;
And cheerfully like her thy task pursue.

'Ne sis tantus cessatur, ut calcaribus indigeas. Exercise at Trinity College, Cambridge'.
MS. Eng. poet. c. 9, p. 11.

1953 Awake, (respond) awake!
To bid thy Lord's anointed welcome home.

'A Hymn upon the Nativity'.
MS. Add. A. 301, fol. 32ᵛ rev.

1954 Awake rich men for shame and hear
To see his glorious face.

Sponar, Henry.
MS. Ashmole 48, fol. 67ᵛ.

1955 Awake rouse up my dull theorbo; join
To thy broke slumbers; and repose ye.

Quarles, Francis, [invocation to his lute].
Pr. from this MS., *Works*, ed. Grosart, Chertsey Worthies Libr., 1880, i, p. lxxiii.
MSS. Ashmole 36, 37, fol. 23ᵛ.

1956 Awake sad Britain and advance at last
Treason, ambition, murder, pride and lust.

On the murder of the Duke of Buckingham, 1628.
MSS. Dodsworth 79, fol. 158; Douce 357, fol. 18; Malone 23, p. 195.

1957 Awake, sad heart, whom sorrow ever drowns,
Draws tears, or blood, not want a handkerchief.

Herbert, George, 'The Dawning'.
Pr. *The Temple*, 1633, p. 104.
MS. *Tanner 307, fol. 78ᵛ.

1958 Awake thou stupid world, how dar'st thou say
Great changes in your state yet without blood.

[Vernon, John (?)]. With Latin verses on the same subject, i.e. William III's arrival in England, 1688, signed 'I.V.Xt Church'.
MS. Top. Oxon. c. 326, fol. 58 (autogr. (?)).

1959 Awaked from nature's sleep
Then lifts me up to Heaven.

Kenton, James.
MS. *Eng. poet. e. 20, p. 362 (autogr.).

1960 Away, away, vex me no more
And thine ne'er wanted fuel.

Song.
MS. Mus. b. 1, fol. 71ᵛ, music by John Wilson.

1961 Away! Away! we've crown'd the day,
Have not disdained to wear the horn.

Hunting song.
MS. Ballard 47, fol. 4ᵛ.

Away despair, my gracious Lord doth hear, 1962
Any thing to me. Hark, despair away.

Herbert, George, 'The Bag'.
Pr. *The Temple*, 1633, p. 145.
MSS. Rawl. C. 580, p. 314, copied from George Swinnock's *Christian-Man's Calling*, 1668, p. 228; Rawl. poet. 90, fol. 141ᵛ; *Tanner 307, fol. 110.

Away fear with thy projects, no false fire 1963
Now bid me into flame from smoke to run.

Alabaster, William, 'Sonnet 18'.
Pr. J. P. Collier, *Hist. of Eng. Dram. Poetry*, 1831, ii. 432 note; *Bibliographical and Critical Account of the Rarest Books in the English Language*, 1865, i. 16; B. Dobell, *Athenaeum*, no. 3974, 26 Dec. 1903.
MS. *Eng. poet. e. 57, fol. 4.

Away fond men, away! give o'er, leave to dispute, 1964
Ascend from death, and reign with Him, there's no dispute.

Wake, William, of Cambridge, verses on the epiphany star, written in the shape of wings. See M118.
MS. Eng. misc. d. 1, fol. 36.

Away, let naught to love displeasing, 1965
And I go wooing in my boys.

[Cooper, J. G.], 'The Rational Lover'.
Pr. Dodsley's *Collection of Poems*, iv, 1755, p. 282; for ascription see *O.B.S. P. & P.*, iii, 1931–3, p. 285.
MS. *Eng. poet. d. 47, fol. 175.

Away now controversy, filth and dung 1966
As has this second John Divine, at least to me.

E. H., M. D., 'A Rhapsodie, [on a] Trinitarian Tract, . . . The Tripple Crown of Glorie', 1688.
MS. Rawl. C. 548, fol. 19ᵛ.

Away she went so sweet a thing is gold 1967
That maugre can invade the strongest hold.

Couplet.
MS. Rawl. poet. 172, fol. 10ᵛ.

Away, these forced embraces; amorous arms 1968
More care, than on the soul, which knows no end.

Oldisworth, Robert or Giles, 'The uncivil Court fashions, laid open', from an Arcadian romance, *The Pattern of Piety*.
MS. *Rawl. C. 422, fol. 7, in the hand of Giles Oldisworth.

Away thou changeling motley humourist 1969
And constantly awhile must keep his bed.

Donne, John, 'Satyre 1'.
Pr. *Poems*, 1633.
MSS. *Eng. poet. e. 99, fol. 1; *f. 9, p. 172.

1970 Away thou foolish devil get thee gone
Toads, vipers, serpents, though without they shine.
MS. *Don. f. 5, fol. 16.

1971 Away with these self-loving lads
That love likes no laws but his own.
Pr. Dowland's *Songs or Ayres*, 1597, xxi.
MSS. Mus. f. 7–10: f. 7, fol. 12v.

1972 Away ye brave fox-hunting race
And jolly huntsman blow poor Reynard's knell.
Somervile, William, Hunting song.
MS. Ballard 47, fol. 4v.

1973 Awhile dear sir, from busy life withdraw,
And each true Briton drops a tender tear.
'On the Death of Mr. Pope [to] A Lawyer in the Temple'.
MS. *Eng. poet. e. 28, p. 4.

1974 Ay me—my mistress scorns my love
To weep for her, that laughs at thee.
Pr. Thomas Bateson's *First Set of Madrigales*, 1604, iv.
MSS. Mus. f. 17–19: f. 19, fol. 22v.

Ay me poor earth why am I made receiver 1975
Alas I was not able to resist him.
'Upon the death of prince Henry: the Earths Complaint', 1612.
MS. Rawl. poet. 160, fol. 36.

Ay me, she frowns, my mistress is offended 1976
Let's dally and embrace.
Pr. Pilkington's *First Book of Songs*, 1605, vii.
MSS. Mus. f. 7–10: f. 7, fol. 25.

Ay me that thorns his royal head should wound 1977*a*
What pleasure 'tis to smart for other's pain.
Alabaster, William, 'Sonnet 6. upon the crowne of Thornes'.
MS. *Eng. poet. e. 57, fol. 2.

Ay we are merry cobblers, and we lead merry lives 1977*b*
And drink and merrily sing, and make a jovial end.
'Cant. 9.'
MS. Don. d. 58, fol. 23v.

Ayloffe when thou seest this platter 1978
Because there's none. I'll send no beef.
Vintner, [Henry, Fellow of King's Coll., Camb., 1626–49, or Edmund, Fellow 1643–89], 'The Answer' to Ayloffe's lines V46.
MS. Rawl. poet. 62, fol. 13v.

# B

ENTRIES 1–781

1 **B—! if thou wouldst gain the fair**
**One squeeze all Milton's strain sublime!**
Parsons, William, 'To a friend in Love'.
Pr. *Travelling Recreations*, 1807, i. 206.
MS. *Don. d. 123, p. 265 (autogr.).

2 **B—! if you would take a wife**
***Memento mori* there's inscribed!**
Parsons, William, 'To a friend who said he should prefer to marry a Maid'.
MS. *Don. d. 123, p. 263 (autogr.).

3 **B—! who now in love's fierce flame dost broil**
**To serve like him three 'prenticeships in vain!**
Parsons, William, 'Sonnet'.
Pr. *Travelling Recreations*, 1807, i. 207.
MS. *Don. d. 123, p. 265 (autogr.).

4 **Baal's priests pretend thy soul to save,**
**Gold is their God, their godliness is gain.**
Robinson, Robert.
MS. *Rawl. poet. 218, p. 121 (autogr.).

5 **Bacchus instructing I my self did see**
**Against thy face not able to prevail.**
W. A., translator, Horace, *Odes* II. xix.
MS. *Rawl. poet. 104, fol. 20v (autogr.).

6 **Bacchus Jaccus fill our brains**
**[Wherefore give us the cheer in bowls].**
'A song', with a tune.
MS. Eng. poet. f. 10, fol. 98.

7 **Bacchus smiles when Sylvia flushes**
**We leave those mighty bowls we loved before.**
'To Sylvia at the Tavern'.
MS. Rawl. D. 361, fol. 335.

8 **Backed with confederate force the Austrian goes**
**You're king of Spain as Anne is Queen of France.**
'On Queen Anne's sending assistance to the Arch Duke', Charles III of Spain, 1703–4.
MS. Rawl. poet. 81, fol. 42; pr. bk. Firth b. 21, fol. 61v; see also H1455.

9 **Bacon, thou hardly wilt believe that we**
**Our comely sister thee we will enstile.**
Oldisworth, Nicolas, 'To his Friend beyond sea', Richard Bacon.
MS. *Don. c. 24, fol. 28v (autogr.).

**Bad commentators spoil the best of books** 10
**So God gives meat, the Devil sends the cooks.**
Couplet.
MS. Sancroft 53, p. 368 rev.

**Baldus the painter in a monstrous rage** 11
**Against the nose that burns his mistress' face.**
'Epigram . . . Aper with bibbing sack hath such a nose'.
MS. Rawl. poet. 172, fol. 7v.

**Baldwin awake, thy pen hath slept too long** 12
**Eternized by immortality.**
Life of Mary Queen of Scots. Note by P. Bliss 'This has been printed by Mr. [John] Fry of Bristol [1810] from a MS. written by Tho. Wenman'.
MS. Rawl. B. 161, fol. 60.

**Balls of this metal slack'd Atlanta's pace** 13
**Unto my wish, and die creating gold.**
Waller, Edmund, 'The Miser's Speech in a Maske'.
Pr. *Poems*, 1645, p. 68.
MSS. *Don. d. 55, fol. 2; Eng. poet. c. 50, fol. 122v; *Rawl. poet. 174, p. 59.

**Balm of my cares, sweet solace of my toils** 14
**And sing his favourite theme in kindred strains.**
Warton, Thomas (1728–90), 'A Panegyric on Ale. By an Oxford Scholar'.
Pr. *The Student*, Oxford, 1750, i. 65 (*recte* 105).
MS. Don. c. 75, fol. 64 (autogr.).

**Banbury, Lantoni, Carlegeon; (Esseca stand by)** 15
**Mares-milk, and slices, strong stink-breath; fie o' thy cheese [pie (?)].**
'Of Cheese'.
MS. Rawl. poet. 26, fol. 61.

**Bancroft was for plays; leave Lent and holy-days** 16
**To let in the strumpet of Rome.**
[On Archbishop Bancroft].
MS. Ashmole 1463, p. 13.

17–18 Banished from life, to seek out death I go
A diamond love can pierce a diamond heart.
Fanshawe, Sir Richard, translator, 'A Cupid of Diamonds sent to a Ladie . . . in her disdaine' from the Spanish.
MS. *Firth c. 1, p. 80.

19 Bank feels no lameness of his knotty gout
He toils to be at hell as soon as they.
[Jonson, Ben.], 'On Bank the usurer', *Epigrammes*, xxxi.
MS. Ashmole 47, fol. $45^{v}$.

20 Baptized with the external sign
Then soar to meet him in the skies.
Kenton, James.
MS. *Eng. poet. e. 20, p. 140 (autogr.).

21 Baptizing, speaks Christ an indulgent lord
Are out of's ark and may the flood expect.
E. S., 'On Baptisme'.
MS. Rawl. poet. 65, fol. $80^{v}$.

22 Barbary has beaten Rutland think you so
*Cuius contrarium* Barbary was beaten.
MS. Eng. poet. c. 50, fol. 43.

23 Barbus hath sworn and often hath said
He wanted money and therefore meant to sell it.
'On one Barbus'.
MS. Eng. poet. e. 14, fol. 88 rev.

24 Barce though old, ill-natured, ugly, dull
For any man that will have you, is one.
Walsh, William, 'On Barce'.
MS. Malone 9, fol. 31 (autogr.).

25 Bark foul-mouthed carping Momus, if thou durst:
What I have writ is bad; now speak thy worst.
Couplet.
MS. Rawl. D. 1372, fol. $26^{v}$.

26 Barnabas full of th' Holy Ghost and power
Were honoured first with name of Christians.
Clifford, Henry, Earl of Cumberland, 'Saint Barnabas'.
MS. *Rawl. poet. 95, fol. 34.

27 Barnaby's dead and laid in his tomb
But tumble down Dick is come in his room.
'A motto on a signe, A catch for four voices', couplet.
MS. Mus. Sch. C. 95, p. 59.

28 Barren, and airy name! Thee fortune flies
And while she long consults the prize is gone.
'Vertu'.
MS. Sancroft 85, p. 281 rev.

29 Base and imperious, very sluttish and proud
A house full of noise and a heart full of care.
Williams, John, 'An odious woman'.
MS. *Rawl. poet. 193, fol. $54^{v}$ (autogr.).

Base coward eyes, to run away 30
And not pry into mysteries.
Paman, Clement, 'The Vision'.
MS. Rawl. poet. 147, p. 68.

Base excrement of earth which dost confound 31
Because you were burnt, not that they loved the smell.
'Of Perfume'.
MS. Douce f. 5, fol. 12.

Base metal hanger by thy master's thigh 32
Else I'll nere draw thee but against a post.
MS. Eng. poet. d. 152, fol. 9, attr. to Lord Rochester.

Bathed I have too long (sweet friend) my lady Thalia 33
Thou mayst live there above partaker of heavenly Venite.
Mills, Robert, 'To his freend: J. Finnett: Car: Hex'. Subscribed 'from Stamforde'.
MS. Rawl. poet. 85, fol. $77^{v}$.

Batter my heart, three person'd God; for you 34
Nor ever chaste, except you ravish me.
Donne, John, 'Sonnett 10'.
Pr. *Poems*, 1633.
MS. *Eng. poet. e. 99, fol. $45^{v}$.

Bawds, fiddlers, whores, buffoons o' th' age 35
Smirk Darnel be my judge in this.
Horace, *Satires* I. ii.
MS. Rawl. poet. 159, fol. 66.

Be a good husband in thy youth 36
In age, when strength is past.
Robinson, Robert.
MS. *Rawl. poet. 218, p. 163 (autogr.).

Be all your senses blest with harmony 37
Diffusive, great, and in their truth, secure.
Godolphin, Sidney, 'To the King and Queen'.
MS. Malone 13, p. 9.

Be as wise as thou canst; wantest thou silver and gold? 38
What then? what then? oh then the worms will eat us.
Robinson, Robert.
MS. *Rawl. poet. 218, p. 97 (autogr.).

Be blithe Fopdoudells, for our author knows 39
And our endeavours with your love be crowned.
Bucksteed, William, 'A prologue to a play to the Cuntry people'.
Pr. *Wit and Drollery*, 1661, p. 236.
MS. Ashmole 38, p. 145

40 Be dark oh sun! or hide at least thy light
Obedience always meets a just reward.
'In Caroli primi decollationem'.
MS. Rawl. poet. 116, fol. 87.

41 Be drowned all eyes in tears for drowned he lies
Admired Prince would I had died for thee.
'On the Death of the Prince Palatines eldest Son', 1629.
MS. Rawl. poet. 84, fol. 74^v rev.

42 Be dumb unhallowed oracles, and more
To be our sacrifice and Paschal Lamb.
Blagrave, John, 'On the Nativity of Christ'.
MSS. Eng. poet. e. 4, p. 110; Rawl. poet. 65, fol. 55^v, attr. to Johan: Blagrave A. M. Joan.

43 Be dumb ye [you] infant chimes; thump not the [your] metal
We'll all be glad (great Tom) to see thee hanged.
Corbet, Richard, 'On Tom of Christ Church'.
Pr. *Poems*, 1647, p. 28. Attr. to Corbet, B.M. Add. MS. 30982, fol. 3^v; to Jer. Terrent, B.M. MS. Harl. 6931, fol. 73^v; and to Gervase Warmstry in two Folger MSS. See Corbett's *Poems*, ed. J. A. W. Bennett and H. R. Trevor-Roper, 1955, p. 149.
MSS. Ashmole 36, 37, fol. 260; CCC. 328, fol. 35^v; Douce f. 5, two copies, fol. 10 and, attr. to Mr. Dr. Corbet, fol. 27; Engl. poet. c. 50, fol. 131; e. 14, fol. 46^v; Rawl. D. 1092, fol. 268, attr. to Jer. Terrent; Tanner 466, fol. 67^v.

44 Be every heart and tongue employed
The growing honours of his name.
Beddome, Benjamin, Hymn.
MS. *Eng. misc. e. 227, fol. 54^v.

45 Be faithful: Lord, what's that
Thou givest us faith: and faith, a crown of life.
[Quarles, Francis], 'Be thou faithfull unto death, and I will give thee, the Crowne of Life. Revel. 11. 9'.
'The Farewell', *Emblemes*, 1635.
MS. Rawl. poet. 90, fol. 31.

46 Be frugal; save; so have a stock in store.
And that (be sure) will keep him poor.
Robinson, Robert.
MS. *Rawl. poet. 218, p. 50 (autogr.).

47 Be glad in the Lord
And honour his name.
Kenton, James.
MS. *Eng. poet. e. 20, p. 187 (autogr.).

Be gone, fantastic whimsies, hence be gone; 48
We'll hoise up sail and touch the wished shore.
Mr. Cleveland, 'Another [Antiplatonick]'.
Attributed to John Cleveland in print only in the 1687 edition of his *Works*, p. 211.
MS. Rawl. poet. 173, fol. 83.

Be grieved you vainer beauties that express 49
Turn that to an embrace me to a man.
'On a Gentlewoman in a bath'.
MS. Rawl. poet. 199, p. 15.

Be hushed each sigh, whose murm'ring moan 50
To meet thy will resign'd.
'Lines in the Hermit of Snowden', [by Elizabeth Ryves, 1789].
MS. Percy d. 9, fol. 33^v.

Be hushed my griefs! 'Tis his almighty will 51
Just are the ways, thou king of saints and true.
'On the Divine Veracity'.
MS. Top. Oxon. c. 220, p. 17.

Be in my house as busy as a bee 52
But be as wanton, toying as an ape.
8 lines, advice to a wife.
MS. Rawl. D. 1372, fol. 29^v.

Be light and glad in God rejoice which is our strength and stay: 53
And made the rock with honey drop that they their fills should eat.
[Hopkins John], Psalm lxxxi.
MS. Rawl. poet. 112, fol. 47 rev.

Be meek and mild of heart and tongue 54
And leaden a man the ways to heaven.
'The seven deadly sins, and the contrary vertues, . . . Ex MS. *c. temp*. Henry V', B.M. MS. Harl. 1706, fol. 206.
MS. Eng. poet. e. 56, p. 116.

Be merciful to me oh Lord 55
The Heav'ns exalted high.
Psalm lvii.
MS. *Rawl. C. 113, fol. 42^v.

Be merciful to us, oh Lord! 56
Your sure defence he is.
Psalm lvii.
MS. Montagu c. 5, fol. 25.

Be merry brave English boys 57
Pox put in doctor Ducke.
Verses on the Long Parliament, *c*. 1640.
MS. Tanner 76, fol. 118^v.

Be merry in heart, and give God praise 58
For that sufficeth to anger the envious.
MS. Rawl. poet. 148, fol. 113^v.

59 Be mild still
It is honour to forgive those you could kill.
Couplet.
MS. Rawl. poet. 117, fol. 276 rev.

60 Be never discontented, never grudge
God is a loving Father, a just judge.
Barksdale, Clement, 'Content', distich.
MS. Autog. c. 9, fol. 154 (autogr.).

61 Be not aggrieved, my humorous lines afford
You can not blame him, if his broom do stink.
MS. Sancroft 53, p. 367 rev.

62 Be not austere to him, whose heart's intent
Take my advice be freely kind.
Bulteel, John, acrostic on 'Bridget Tynte'.
MS. *Rawl. poet. 159, fol. 224.

63 Be not fairest nymph mistook
Gives a value where there's none.
'Sent with a pair of gloves. To his Mrs. G. L.'.
MS. Rawl. poet. 147, p. 230 rev.

64 Be not offended at our sad complaint
We mourn our loss, but we commend your choice.
[Wren (?)], —, 'On Mr. Steevens fellow of St. Johns in Oxon, an excellent Musitian'.
Attr. to Mr. Wren, B.M. Add. MS. 30982, fol. 53$^{v}$.
MSS. Eng. poet. e. 14, fol. 97$^{v}$ rev.; Rawl. poet. 160, fol. 37$^{v}$.

65 Be not, oh be not, silent still
High placed above all earthly place.
Herbert, Mary (*née* Sidney), Countess of Pembroke, Psalm lxxxiii.
MSS. *Rawl. poet. 24, p. 123; *25, fol. 78$^{v}$.

66 Be not overbold in
And Bisset have been beshit on.
'The Squabble', satire on Wm. Bisset, d. 1747.
MS. Ballard 47, fol. 37$^{v}$.

67*a* Be not proud, pretty one
Die in the story.
Glee by William Lawes.
MS. Mus. c. 5, fol. 4.

67*b* Be not secure, none sooner are oppress'd
Than they whom confidence betrays to rest.
Couplet.
MS. Rawl. poet. 117, fol. 164 rev.

68 Be not so foolish nice
Come bill and kiss and I'll show you.
Pr. with music by J. Wilson in *Cheerfull Ayres*, 1660.
MS. Eng. poet. c. 50, fol. 36$^{v}$.

Be not too daring painter, 'tis 69
Leave off: or paint her with a voice.
Shirley, James, 'To the Painter upon his preparation to draw Mrs. M[ary] H[ammond's] Picture'.
Recast, *Poems*, 1646. Pr. Anthony Hammond's *Miscellany*, 1720, p. 150, headed 'To the Painter preparing to draw Mrs. Mary Hammond Sister to Sir William Hammond of St. Alban's in Kent. . . . 1634'. In Jauncy's *New Miscellany*, 1720, p. 150, dated 1634; *Advice-to-a-Painter Poems*, M. T. Osborne, 1949, no. 2.
MS. *Rawl. poet. 88, p. 66.

Be not too forward thy money to lend 70
But never intend thy money to pay.
Robinson, Robert.
MS. *Rawl. poet. 218, p. 74 (autogr.).

Be not unwilling my request to grant 71
Which only can preserve what time would kill.
North, Dudley, 3rd Baron, Sonnet 8.
Pr. *A Forest of Varieties*, 1645.
MS. *North e. 41, fol. 12$^{v}$, with author's correction.

Be of Christ's army, of free Israel's stem, 72
Himself no more Hell's vassal to remain.
MS. *Don. f. 5, fol. 7.

Be pleased to hear this English Homer cant 73
And plainly read poor London's tragedy.
Milne, John, 'To the Reverend and most learned Thomas Barlow, D.D.'
On the fire, 1666, in a copy of Simon Ford's *The Conflagration*, 1667.
Pr. bk. C. 13. 10. Linc. (autogr.).

Be prudent and ware to know by skill 74
That should rule men both great and small.
'Virtutes morales, . . . ex MS. . . . . *c. temp.* Henry V', B.M. MS. Harl. 1706, fol. 208.
MS. Eng. poet. e. 56, p. 119.

Be rich in divers graces, ever true 75–76
Trust you not time, for time will not trust you.
Bulteel, John, acrostic on 'Bridget Tynte'.
MS. *Rawl. poet. 159, fol. 224.

Be saving, when thou 'ginnest the world: 77
Who were at first but poor.
Robinson, Robert.
MS. *Rawl. poet. 218, p. 161 (autogr.).

Be she fair as lilies be 78
Of nature's good that shows it least.
MSS. Don. c. 57, fol. 20, with music; Mus. b. 1, fol. 44$^{v}$, with music by John Wilson.

79 Be silent [ye] you still music of the spheres
To die with such an anthem on my tomb.
Strode, William, 'On a gentlewoman which sung and played on a lute'.
Pr. *Parnassus Biceps*, 1656, p. 82.
MSS. Ashmole 47, fol. 92v, attr. to B[en] John[son]; CCC. 328, two copies, fols. 14, attr. to W. S., and 28; Don. d. 58, fol. 44*b*; Rawl. poet. 84, fol. 38v; 199, p. 12.

80 Be still oh ye winds, and attentive ye swains
Gives joy to the night and enlivens the day.
'Colin and Phebe'.
MS. Eng. misc. b. 48, fol. 102.

81 Be still sweet babe refrain thy tears
Be still sweet babe with lullabie.
'Our Blessed Lady's lullabie'.
MS. Eng. poet. b. 5, p. 83.

82 Be still thou rebel thought
The herald of thy glorious works to be.
J. F., Psalm lxxiii.
MS. *Eng. poet. f. 17, p. 85 (autogr.).

83 Be still ye soft murmurs, be silent awhile
And you bless him with more than a little flirtation!
Parsons, William, 'To a Lady', 1783.
MS. *Don. d. 123, p. 69 (autogr.).

84 Be sure that slipper time, so slide not slyly his way
The just and only pay, of her that blessed is.
'A praise of vertue'.
MS. Rawl. poet. 148, fol. 113v.

85 Be sure thou grave thou faithful prove
They're all recorded in the register above.
On Sarah Loombe, 1727, St. Andrew's Church, Norwich.
MS. Top. gen. e. 32, fol. 28.

86 Be sure you ne'er your breakfast do forget
To be a simple and a rustic clown.
Brader, John, 'The translation of [F. Dedekind] Grobian[us]', academic verse exercise, 1660–4.
MS. Locke b. 7, fol. 126 (autogr.).

87 Be thankful and rejoice
As we do place our trust in thee.
Harington, Sir John, Psalm xxxiii.
MS. *Douce 361, fol. 18v.

88 Be thou Marcellus, with a length of days;
The only happy is the self approv'd.
'From an Elegy to Lord Villiers', possibly William FitzGerald, Lord Villiers 1732–9.
MS. Eng. poet. e. 47, p. 140.

Be thou my judge, oh God, and plead 89
For favours which my God hath timely shown to me.
Knollys, Fra., Psalm xliii.
MS. *Rawl. poet. 60, p. 76 (autogr.).

Be thou oh God my light and strength 90
And happy be my end.
Beddome, Benjamin, Psalm xxxi. 3.
MS. *Eng. misc. e. 227, fol. 31.

Be thou oh Lord my cause's pleader 91
Of thy great goodness all my days.
Harington, Sir John, Psalm xxxv.
MS. *Douce 361, fol. 20.

Be virtuous and assure thy self 92
That hath her in his eye.
MS. Ashmole 51, fol. 6v.

Be wary (good man) in choice of thy wife; 93
And so come to live a wearisome life.
Robinson, Robert.
MS. *Rawl. poet. 218, p. 76 (autogr.).

Be wise as Somerset, as Somers brave 94
Will make ye for an able statesman fit.
Brown[e, Joseph], 'The Country Parson's advice to my Ld. Keeper [William] Cooper. . . . By Brown who was Pillory'd for this', 1706.
Pr. Hearne's *Collections*, ed. C. E. Doble, i, O.H.S. ii, 1885, p. 178.
MSS. Eng. misc. c. 116, fol. 6, attr. to Brown; Hearne's diaries 8, p. 51, attr. to Dr. Brown; pr. bk. Vet. A3 c. 123 (5), fol. 2.

Be wise my friend whilst in your prime, 95
In winter must expect to die.
Peart, Joshua, 'Be mindful of the future', School Exercise.
MS. *Eng. poet. e. 28, p. 316.

Beam of thy father's glory bright 96
The father like in Christ together.
Huish, Alexander, translator, 'Splendor paternae gloriae', 29 Jan. 1634.
MS. Eng. poet. e. 56, p. 139 (autogr.).

Bear me, oh muse, to Sustead's mild retreat 97
And sleep to all the world; to Sally wake.
Watson, John, Rector of Woodrising, near Thetford, 'A Ramble to Mattishal [Norfolk] In the Spring, 1721. Inscribed to Mrs. Sarah Chamberlain'.
MS. Tanner 306, fol. 484 (autogr.).

[Bear up, Sarissa, through the ruffling storms] 98
And shout their boisterous joys.
Watts, Isaac, Epistle to Sarissa (lines 7–28).
Pr. *Horae Lyricae*, 1743, p. 155.
MS. Rawl. D. 868, fol. 55v.

99 Bear witness all you powers above
Lies not in wealth nor lands.
Subscribed 'Ignot'.
MS. Rawl. poet. 65, fol. 23v.

100 Beat on proud billows, Boreas blow
My king can only captivate my mind.
L'Estrange, Roger, 'The liberty of an imprisoned Royalist'.
See *N. & Q.*, 26 March 1904, p. 250.
MSS. Add. B. 106, fol. 45v; Don c. 57, fol. 34, with music; Rawl. poet. 142, fol. 46v, attr. to Mr. L'Estrange.

101 Beat up a drum
Frolicked with a new.
'Christmas Carol' with a tune.
MSS. Ashmole 36, 37, fol. 25.

102 Beatrice did something high advance her coat
But yet betwixt them both a man was born.
'On Beatrice'.
MS. Douce f. 5, fol. 2v; see also A1230, F28, M411.

103 Beaumont and Fletcher (that exalted pair)
You'll find him fooling in the Tiring Room.
MS. Sancroft 53, p. 50.

104 Beaumont lies here and where now shall we have
Thou shalt not share, but take up all his room.
'On the death of Mr. Francis Beaumont', 1616.
Pr. *Poems by Francis Beaumont*, 1640, Sig. K1; and in the folio *Comedies and Tragedies*, 1647.
MSS. Ashmole 47, fol. 44v; CCC. 328, fol. 66v; Eng. poet. e. 97, p. 55, attr. to John Earles.

105 Beauteous girl whose milk white hue
Kill me not half-dead before.
'The Lyrick of Cor. Gallus'.
MS. Rawl. B. 165, fol. 99.

106 Beauteous machine! let love thy movement guide
That Cupid nicks with nicer art than Quare.
Warton, Thomas (1688–1745), 'Written in the Case of Her Watch'.
Pr. *Poems on several occasions*, 1748, p. 136.
MS. Don. c. 75, fol. 6 (autogr.).

107 Beauty alone how frail! it blows to-day
Her presence too shall crown the blessing there.
'On Miss D—n of Camberwell — London Mag: Octr. 1744'.
MS. Eng. poet. c. 9, p. 160.

108 Beauty and empire, sacred rays from heav'n,
Your daughters, Madam, ought to shine at court.
'To the Lady Lawrence that she would permit her Daughters to come to Court'.
MS. Rawl. D. 360, fol. 169.

Beauty and innocence, distressed 109
And o'er the ruined land laments.
'A Song'.
MS. Rawl. poet. 153, fol. 40v.

Beauty and lechery are things attractive 110
Does beat men's balls into the women's plackets.
'Lust'.
MS. Eng. poet. e. 14, fol. 35v.

Beauty and love once fell at odds 111
'Gainst Cupid and his power.
'Song'.
MS. Rawl. poet. 147, p. 133.

Beauty and love once fell at odds 112*a*
Do court deformity.
'Mock-song' to B111.
MS. Rawl. poet. 147, p. 134.

Beauty and wit are near allied 112*b*
A sun of wit and beauty from her breaks.
Barnes, Joshuah.
MS. Hearne's diaries 11, p. 116.

Beauty hath force to catch the human sight 113
Things rightly prized love is the band of love.
Sidney, Sir Philip, from the *Arcadia*.
MS. *e Mus. 37, fol. 125.

Beauty is a lovely sweet 114
It would more delight the eyne.
Pr. Thomas Bateson's *First set of . . . Madrigals*, 1604, i.
MSS. Mus. f. 17–19: f. 19, fol. 21v.

Beauty like ice, our footing doth betray 115
And see the dangers, which we can not shun.
MS. Sancroft 85, p. 282 rev.

Beauty might long to take her place 116
And so forbear once quits the scores.
'Manicotta or The Janezary Mistresse In 5 Canto's'. On fol. 2, 'Licensed June 22 1671 Roger L'estrange'.
MS. Rawl. poet. 205.

Beauty, more than mortal, 117
Nor takes she pride to know them.
[Jonson, Ben.], 'To L[ucy] C[ountess] off B[edford]'.
MS. Rawl. poet. 31, fol. 20v.

Beauty sat bathing by a spring 118
As when I fell a sleeping.
[Munday, Anthony].
Pr. Pilkington's *First Book of Songs*, 1605, xviii.
MSS. Don. d. 58, fol. 29; Mus. f. 7–10, with music by Pilkington: f. 7, fol. 16.

119 Beauty, thou active passive ill
When thou, alas dost in the fancy lie . . . (unfinished).
MS. Add. B. 105, fol. 98.

120 Beauty thou vain imaginary good
And one eternal spring of love goes round.
Samber, Robert, 'In Praise of Witt before Beauty and Riches', a paradox translated from Bernardo Morando.
MS. *Rawl. poet. 11, fol. 50v (autogr.).

121 Beauty, thou vain, thou gaudy flower
That very time, would add unto the soil.
Bate, Sally, 'On Beauty. 1764'.
MS. *Eng. poet. e. 28, p. 73.

122 Beauty which all men admire
For such vile use to us they're born.
MSS. Eng. poet. c. 50, fol. 118; Mus. b. 1, fol. 122, with music by John Wilson.

123 Beauty which leads the captive world in chains
May you neglected godly virgins die.
Hammond, Anthony, 'A Prologue to Theodosius or the Force of Love', [by Nathaniel Lee].
MS. Rawl. D. 360, fol. 72 (autogr.).
MS. *Rawl. poet. 129, fol. 6v, dated 1687.

124 Beauty's a frail and brittle good
Th' incendiary of strife of passions magazine.
Fairfax, Thomas, Lord, 'Of Beauty'.
MS. *Fairfax 40, p. 568 (autogr.).
MS. *Fairfax 38, p. 318.

125 Beauty's a gaudy sign, no more
Be hid, to be revered the more.
'The Curious Maid'.
MSS. Ballard 50, fol. 109; Eng. poet. f. 13, fol. 71v.

126 Beauty's bright emblem of the powers above
Pressed by myself I gazed and was undone.
MS. Eng. poet. e. 47, p. 70.

127 Beauty's no other but a lovely grace,
Of lively colours, flowing from the face.
'On Beauty', couplet.
Pr. *Wits Recreations*, 1663, Epigram 498.
MS. Eng. poet. d. 152, fol. 106v.

128*a* Because a servant does not understand
In serving thy immortal praise.
Williams, John, 'Of Providence'.
MS. *Rawl. poet. 192, fol. 177 (autogr.).

Because his days be short 128*b*
Himself he means to give.
Symse, Richard, 1605.
Pr. Hearne's *Collections*, ed. C. E. Doble, iii, O.H.S. xiii, 1889, p. 369.
MSS. Hearne's diaries 36, p. 33; Laud misc. 299 at end.

Because I find, I wisdom have transgressed 129
To the enjoying joys eternity.
Burton, Francis.
MS. *Add. A. 267, fol. 151v (autogr.).

Because if 'tis of any body true, 130
For you have pinched me till I'm black and blue.
Williams, John, 'The Reason . . .'.
MS. *Rawl. poet. 184, fol. 95 (autogr.).

Because men want the eyes to see 131
They'd see his glories with surprise.
Williams, John, 'Of Love, Justice, Fate and Fortune being represented blind'.
MS. *Rawl. poet. 191, fol. 103 (autogr.).

Because my master and friend good 132
And me to forgive, if I have offended.
Parkyn, Robert, Life of Christ, copied 1548–54.
MS. Eng. poet. e. 59 (autogr.).

Because my whilom mistress changed desire 133
Or else her tedious love will hurt thee worse.
Beaumont, Thomas, 'Her constant inconstancie'.
MS. *Malone 18, p. 24 (autogr.).

Because old Dryden's more sublime 134
Sir H[orace] reads nor one nor t'other.
Parsons, William, 'On Sir H[orace] M[ann] . . . on the Florence miscellany'.
MS. *Don. d. 123, p. 125 (autogr.).

Bede, Merlin, Astledon, with Thomas of Canterbury 135*a*
Clean without conscience both far and near.
Prophecy.
MS. North c. 80, fol. 9.

Beef and bacon 135*b*
To parch my peasen.
Shrove-Tuesday verses, Sunningwell, near Abingdon.
MS. Hearne's diaries 106, p. 106.

Bees fetch and bring into the hive: 136
The shopman gets the greatest gains.
Robinson, Robert.
MS. *Rawl. poet. 218, p. 81 (autogr.).

137 Befalls there to man a shortness of breath?
Doth breathing once cease? Oh life is no more.
Robinson, Robert.
MS. Rawl. poet. 218, p. 58 (autogr.).

138 Before a thief returning clients sing
For from the city they no money bring.
'[Owen's Epigram] 102, On Clients. Cantabat vacuus coram latrone viator', translated.
MS. *Rawl. poet. 197, fol. 11 (autogr.).

139 Before creating nature willed
Fools read, and take me for your pains.
'Guess and Take me', riddle on Nothing.
MSS. Eng. poet. d. 47, fol. 25; Montagu e. 13, fol. 163.

140 Before I do begin to love
How to serve you, and you trust me.
'An Epode', during the great Rebellion.
MSS. Ashmole 36, 37, fol. 217.

141 Before I enter, with my Sophoclean quill
Vengeance do find me, nuzzling in my crimes.
'Solitary Ejaculations . . .', (1) Prologue, (2) Colloquy, (3) Raptures.
MS. Rawl. poet. 172, fol. 118.

142 Before I lay with other men's wives
I will lie at rack and manger.
MS. Rawl. B. 35, fol. 49$^{v}$ rev.

143 Before I sigh my last gasp, let me breathe
T'invent and practise this one way to annihilate all three.
Donne, John, 'The Will'.
Pr. *Poems*, 1633, p. 283.
MSS. CCC. 327, fol. 5$^{v}$; *Eng. poet. e. 99, fol. 126$^{v}$; *f. 9, p. 31, attr. to J. D.; Malone 19, p. 83; Rawl. poet. 117, fol. 215 rev., attr. to Dunne.

144 Before Jehovah's awful throne
When rolling years shall cease to move.
Madan, the Revd. Martin (1725–90), Psalm c.
MS. Eng. poet. c. 51, p. 313*a*.

145 Before man was created, he had done
Him from that pleasant place, he first him gave.
MS. *Rawl. poet. 97, fol. 5 (autogr.).

146 Before my face the picture hangs
My life may mend sith I must die.
[Southwell, Robert], verses upon the image of death.
Pr. *Mæoniae*, 1595; also in *Microbiblion*, S. Wastell, 1629, Sig. Z3$^{v}$.
MS. Eng. poet. b. 5, p. 21.

Before my faith's enlightened eyes 147
To bring his servant home.
Kenton, James.
MS. *Eng. poet. e. 20, p. 122 (autogr.).

Before swift time had tried its trusty wings 148
To sing creation with excessive joy.
'On the Creation'.
MS. Rawl. poet. 173, fol. 175$^{v}$.

Before the clergy did of marriage taste 149
Till a new prick's raised out of St. Paul's old stones.
MS. Douce 357, fol. 36.

Before the eleven, Peter, the Pope prefers, 150
Else would I name him though here he be not nameless.
H. S., Acrostic on 'Bartholomewe'.
MS. *Rawl. poet. 120, fol. 11$^{v}$ (autogr.).

Before the first day of the next year 151
And so all flesh shall go to rest.
'Haxbeyes Riddle'.
MS. Rawl. poet. 246, fol. 4$^{v}$.

Before the glance of new born freedom 152
Who survives, will taste the fruits.
'The Charter of Brother Hood. Tune viva la —'.
On the society of United Irishman, etc. *c.* 1796–7.
MS. North e. 34, fol. 1$^{v}$.

Before the lord God with my voice I did send out my cry: 153
When thou art good to me the just shall press me round about.
[Norton, Thomas], Psalm cxlii.
MS. Rawl. poet. 112, fol. 30 rev.

Before the rosy dawn of day 154
Thy lofty praises sing.
'Hymn'.
MS. Eng. poet. e. 39, p. 92.

Before the sixth day of this next new year 155–6
Whose head is made of flesh and mouth of horn.
Ralegh, Sir Walter, 'A Prognostication upon cards and dice'.
See *Poems of Ralegh*, ed. Agnes Latham, 1951, p. 138.
MSS. Eng. poet. e. 14, fol. 77 rev.; Malone 19, p. 55, attr. to Sir Wal. R.; Rawl. poet. 84, fol. 68.

Before the sun had gild' the morn of silver day 157
As Mars or Jove or Sol or Love enamoured do.
Transcript from B.M. Add. MS. 29481.
MS. Mus. d. 184, fol. 40$^{v}$.

158 Before the world was drowned
For Noy has't all in's ark.
'Sent by Ben Johnson to Attorney Noy, who was feasting with venison in another Roo[m]'.
See *Ben Jonson*, ed. Herford and Simpson, i, 1925, p. 187; viii, 1947, p. 447.
MS. Rawl. poet. 26, fol. 143; see also W1549.

159 Before we come unto the history
And more becoming far than my gray hairs.
Shrimpton, John, preliminary verses to a history of Verulam.
MS. Gough Herts. 3, fol. 3$^{v}$ (autogr.).

160 Before world's vast goodly frame begun
His life shall be preserved and's soul secure.
Fairfax, Thomas, Lord, 'Wisdom's Antiquity', from *Proverbs* viii. 22–35.
MS. *Fairfax 40, p. 471 (autogr.).
MS. *Fairfax 38, p. 29.

161 Before your friendly note I got,
And my good name outstruck scholar!
Bishop, Samuel, rhymed letter to Dickins. 5 June 1777.
MS. Montagu d. 2, fol. 59 (autogr.).

162 Before you're at your tedious page's end
But is I fear an atheist in his heart.
'The Court Diversion. 1685'.
MS. Eng. poet. d. 152, fol. 74.

163 Beggars must [should] be no choosers, hence I muse
So many beg at court that well may choose.
Epigram 'Beggars', couplet.
MSS. Ashmole 36, 37, fol. 143$^{v}$; CCC. 327, fol. 32$^{v}$.

164 Beggars (the proverb's still extant)
The blows you got from Heath, Sir.
'On the late Welch assault. July 30. 1796'.
MS. Eng. poet. c. 51, p. 213*b*.

165 Begin, be bold, and venture to be wise,
That runs and as it runs, for ever will run on.
MS. Add. B. 105, fol. 97$^{v}$.

166 Begin high, a poor man die:
That you may rest, when you are old.
Robinson, Robert.
MS. *Rawl. poet. 218, p. 51 (autogr.).

167 Begin high, end low: too fast at first
Not far will go.
Robinson, Robert, couplet.
MS. *Rawl. poet. 218, p. 172 (autogr.).

Begin my muse and sadly tell 168
When God can die what is't that Nature must not do.
Chatwin, John, 'A Pindaric Ode upon the Passion of our Blessed Saviour'.
MS. *Rawl. poet. 94, p. 256 (autogr.).

Begin my muse, assume thy wing 169
Of whom at present—*Ignoramus*.
'The Tunbridge Ladies'.
MS. Eng. misc. b. 48, fol. 105.

Begin, my song, from the immortal nine, 170
For unrelenting is the hand of Death.
'Hesiod's Thegonia translated', 1735.
MS. Eng. misc. e. 240, pp. 63 *et passim*.

Begin not high, lest highness bring thee low: 171
Quick shooting willows soon receive their fall.
Robinson, Robert.
MS. *Rawl. poet. 218, p. 144 (autogr.).

Begin the gladsome shout, the loud acclaim 172
In splendours pure and majesty of might.
Hawkins, William, 'The Song of Deborah', with music in the hand of Philip Hayes, dated 21 Jan.–15 Feb. 1782.
MS. Mus. d. 66, p. 1.

Begin the high celestial strain 173
To heaven's almighty king.
'Hymn 2 Collect. Poems'.
MS. Eng. poet. e. 39, p. 84.

Begin the noble song, 174
Think she is gone to earth again.
'Ode on St. Cecilia's Day set to music by Mr. Norris'.
MS. Mus. c. 28, fol. 40.

Begin the song, all your instruments sound 175
To raise the powers of the votive choir.
Oldham, John, 'Ode for St. Cecilia's Day', set by Philip Hayes, 1779: partly in his hand.
MS. Mus. d. 68, fol. 61.

Begin the song—ye subject quires. 176
By whom all nature smiles, and beauteous order reigns.
[Whitehead, William], Birthday Ode, 1759. Music by Boyce.
Pr. *Poems*, 1790, ii. 62.
MS. Mus. Sch. D. 306.

177 Begin the song, your instruments advance;
With tongue and fingers bears a part.

[Oldham, John], 'A song performed on St. Cecilia's Day', 22 Nov. 1684.
Pr. *A Second Musical Entertainment*, H. Playford, 1685.
MS. *Rawl. poet. 123, p. 240 (autogr. draft of chorus).
MS. Mus. c. 26, fol. 103$^{v}$, with music by Dr. John Blow.

178 Begone all fruitless joys,
To make amends for all my troubles past.

'Fruitless joys'.
MS. Rawl. poet. 90, fol. 147$^{v}$.

179 Begone from me thou stranger to all joy,
In silence only, and the shades of night.

Chatwin, John, 'A Sigh'.
MS. *Rawl. poet. 94, p. 269 (autogr.).

180 Begone from me, ye vulgar throng
And happiness I there shall find.

'Odi profanum vulgus etc. imitated'.
MS. *Eng. poet. d. 47, fol. 132.

181 Begone I say; fly thou from my calm breast,
One breeds distraction, t'other makes debate.

'Ira furor brevis est', for a school's breaking up.
MS. *Rawl. poet. 197, fol. 3$^{v}$ (autogr.).

182 Begone infernal fiend be gone
Thine own confusion end.

Beddome, Benjamin.
MS. *Eng. misc. e. 227, fol. 59.

183 Begone thou fatal fiery fever [fury]
Do never wake again.

MSS. Eng. poet. f. 25, fol. 68$^{v}$; Rawl. poet. 116, fol. 39$^{v}$; 142, fol. 48$^{v}$, headed 'Gerards gentall Mistris'; 199, p. 59.

184 Begone, thou Stoic, and on no pretence
Then by reluctancy new griefs create.

Hammond, Antony, 'Horace, Lib. I. Ode 24 Imitated. On the Death of my Uncle Will: Hammond, Esq.' Endorsed 'Not Printed'.
MS. Rawl. D. 174, fol. 101 (autogr.).

185 Begone vain world my thoughts ascend
And taste of pleasures so divine.

Beddome, Benjamin, 'An Hymn'.
MS. *Eng. misc. e. 227, fol. 173$^{v}$.

186 Begotten by the sacred Word
The fulness of redeeming love.

Kenton, James.
MS. *Eng. poet. e. 20, p. 114 (autogr.).

Behind a figtree great, himself did Adam hide, 187
For none but God can thee forgive, who all thy ways doth see.

Whitney, Geoffrey, 'Dominus vivit et videt'.
MS. *Rawl. poet. 56, fol. 128.

Behold a cluster to itself a vine 188
Where the only danger is to keep a measure.

Alabaster, William, 'Sonnet 5: upon the Crucifix'.
MS. *Eng. poet. e. 57, fol. 1$^{v}$.

Behold a joy that doth excel 189
With endless bliss his people fill.

Harington, Sir John, Psalm cxxxiii.
MS. *Douce 361, fol. 83.

Behold a little tender babe 190
Which he from heaven doth bring.

[Southwell, Robert, 'New prince, new pompe'].
Pr. *St. Peters Complaint*, 1602, p. 73.
MS. Eng. poet. b. 5, p. 51.

Behold a maid of a pale envious hue 191
Like crocodiles or sirens o'er their prey.

Pavey, William, 'A Description of an envious young Lady'.
MS. Rawl. poet. 116, fol. 107.

Behold a new thing under sun 192
If much amiss heaven's grant it mended.

'Occasionall Meditations upon the present Plague of Protections'.
MS. Douce 357, fol. 112$^{v}$.

Behold a nymph with every virtue graced 193
To charm the lover and his thoughts refine.

Williams, —, 'On a young Lady (Mrs. Rooke)'.
Pr. *British Magazine*, 1765, subscribed A. B.
MS. *Eng. poet. e. 7, fol. 16 (autogr.).

Behold a rich man dead: oh 'tis a woe thing! 194
He left great wealth did carry with him nothing.

Robinson, Robert, 'Upon the death of a rich man', couplet.
MS. *Rawl. poet. 218, p. 14 (autogr.).

Behold a virgin free from any spot 195
That to be born is cause enough to die.

Strode, William, on Ursula Sadlier.
MS. *CCC. 325, fol. 41 (autogr.).

Behold a wonder such as hath not been 196
For I'm resolved that mine shall teach me wit.

'Elegia'.
MS. Rawl. poet. 160, fol. 170$^{v}$.

197 Behold an obsequy without annoy
The grave of all our fears, and birth of joy.
'Upon the Duke of Buck: Funerall'. 1628.
MS. Rawl. poet. 84, fol. 74.

198 Behold and have regard ye servants of the lord:
Doth Sion bless and will conserve for evermore the same.
[Kethe, William], Psalm cxxxiv.
MS. Rawl. poet. 112, fol. 32 rev.

199 Behold and listen, while the fair
Men strive not, but deplore the fire.
Waller, Edmund, 'Of Mrs. Arden'.
Pr. *Poems*, 1645, p. 59.
MSS. *Don. d. 55, fol. 4$^{v}$; Eng. poet. c. 50, fol. 124; *Rawl. poet. 174, p. 56; Smith 27, p. 43, with a Latin translation by Sir John Cotton.

200 Behold and see lo here's a wondrous change
And work salvation for this sinking land.
'Roger Le-strange and Harry Care good Friends', etc.
Pr. bk. Firth b. 20, fol. 135.

201 Behold, dear Lord, amongst the populous row
As you a second being are to me.
Williams, Richard, 'To the Lord Treasurer Weston'.
MS. Rawl. poet. 147, p. 235 rev.

202 Behold! He comes to make thy people groan,
To stem by force his madness and despair.
'Pasquin to the Queen [Anne]'s Statue at St. Pauls, during the procession'. 20 Jan. 1714/15.
MSS. Eng. poet. e. 87, p. 99; Hearne's diaries 62, p. 7*c*; Rawl. poet. 155, p. 128; 173, fol. 3; Top. Oxon. c. 108, p. 159.

203 Behold her skin, her teeth, her hair all swan
Must first go equal this in every part.
Gibbs, H., translator, *Alba cutis, nives dentes, albisque capilli.*
MS. Ashmole 788, fol. 18$^{v}$.

204 Behold him here to dust and ashes turned
Will serve thy turn, take one more, witness bliss.
Oldisworth, Nicolas, 'An epitaph on Mr. Little of Abingdon'.
MS. *Don. c. 24, fol. 47$^{v}$ (autogr.).

205 Behold him whom I uphold, and ordain
And all the herbs that grow upon them blast.
Isaiah xlii, from a 'Paraphrased collection of some Prophecyes of the old Testament concerning Christ'.
MS. *Rawl. C. 113, fol. 7 (autogr.).

Behold how excellently good 206
Those keep their bond of love.
Psalm cxxxiii.
MS. *Rawl. C. 113, fol. 95.

Behold how God-like heroes deck the signs 207
There Taurus-like to shake your awful face.
'On George' [I].
MS. Rawl. poet. 155, p. 175.

Behold how good a thing it is 208
God life and peace doth ever send.
Fleming, Robert, Psalm cxxxiii.
Pr. *The Mirrour of Divine Love*, 1691, 'Poems', p. 81.
MS. Rawl. poet. 213, fol. 46$^{v}$ (autogr.).

Behold how Marius, from Minturnus lake 209
Thy beauty was a tyrant soon deposed.
Fanshawe, Sir Richard, translator from Spanish, Sonnet 7.
MS. *Firth c. 1, p. 75.

Behold how masters worthiest of praise 210
Their owner looked they should some fruit produce.
Williams, John, Matthew xxv. 29.
MS. *Rawl. poet. 188, fol. 75$^{v}$ (autogr.).

Behold how Papal Wright with lordly pride 211
At once to charm the ear and mend the heart.
'On the Presbyterian Clergy, 1736'.
MSS. Eng. misc. c. 116, fol. 14; Eng. poet. c. 9, pp. 150, 152, and 271–2, attr. to Baker.

Behold I here unfold to mortal sight 212
Because he got by wisdom substance all.
F. W., Sonnet 33.
MS. *Rawl. C. 639, p. 173.

Behold my fair! that loaded be 213
With care each forward youth repel.
Unnamed author 'having offended a Lady . . . wrote . . . verses to excuse himself'. Answered by William Parsons.
Pr. *Travelling Recreations*, 1807, i. 40.
MS. *Don. d. 123, p. 164 (in the hand of Parsons).

Behold my friend the rosy fingered morn 214
With wine cheer the night, as sports bless the day.
Somervile, William, 'A Hunting song'.
Pr. *Poems*, 1727, p. 141.
MS. Ballard 47, two copies, fols. 3 and 12.

Behold my young friends in a riddle comprised 215
Those who court her the least have the most of her smiles.
'A Logogriphe . . . To Mr. John and Mr. Percy Meade'.
MS. Percy c. 8, fol. 120 (autogr.).

216 **Behold now give heed such as be the lords servants faithful and true**
**Give to you and your nation his blessing mercy and favour.**
'. . . Exhortacion to be songe before Eveninge prayer'.
MS. Rawl. poet. 112, fol. 25.

217 **Behold now hoary winter is no more**
**Nor pity'll move them nor will words.**
Percy, Thomas, nephew of Bp. of Dromore, 'Spring', written autumn 1776.
MS. Percy c. 8, fol. 44 (autogr.); see also W2497.

218 **Behold oh God IN RIvers of my tears**
**To live with thee sweet Jesus say Amen.**
[Browne, William of Tavistock], acrostic poem 'On the crucifiction of Our Saviour and the two Theives'.
Pr. among Browne's poems, ed. Gordon Goodwin, 1894, ii. 310.
MSS. Eng. misc. c. 35, fol. 56ᵛ; Eng. poet. b. 5, p. viii (incomplete).

219 **Behold oh God the sad and heavy case**
**Thy servant Charles [*sic*] our king, our peace and wealth.**
MS. Rawl. poet. 23, p. 35, reference to setting by Byrd.

220 **Behold (oh God) with thy all-prospering eye**
**Of blessed James, great king of Britanny.**
MS. Rawl. poet. 23, p. 170, reference to setting by Byrd.

221 **Behold (oh Lord) thy servant offers thee**
**The precious incense to be cast away.**
Colman, Henry, poem in shape of an altar.
MS. *Rawl. poet. 204, fol. 1ᵛ (autogr.).

222 **Behold, oh mortal man what is thy end,**
**For as I am, so all of you shall be.**
'A Memento drawne from the view of a Deaths head' subscribed 'Gate house 14 Marcij 1615, E. H.'
MSS. Ashmole 36, 37, fol. 284.

223 **Behold our crimes ye foreign shores and see**
**With thunder Jove strike the blasphemer down.**
'On the Thanksgiving', 20 Jan. 1714/15, anniversary of the beginning of Charles I's trial.
MS. Rawl. poet. 155, p. 76.

224 **Behold th'ambitious man,**
**Receives his corpse like others, vile.**
Gough, Richard, 'On Alexander . . . Aug. 21. 1754'.
MS. *Eng. poet. c. 5, fol. 40ᵛ (autogr.).

**Behold the bleating flocks for shelter run** 225
**Do stretch and fill the air with notes.**
Percy, Thomas, nephew of the Bp. of Dromore, 'Summer', written Autumn, 1776.
MS. Percy c. 8, fol. 89.

**Behold the brand of beauty tossed** 226
**Moves with the numbers, which she hears.**
Waller, Edmund, 'Song'.
Pr. *Poems*, 1645, p. 52.
MSS. *Don. d. 55, fol. 4ᵛ; Eng. poet. c. 50, fol. 124; *Rawl. poet. 174, p. 75.

**Behold the burning bush** 227
**Nor reigns above the skies.**
Beddome, Benjamin.
MS. *Eng. misc. e. 227, fol. 85.

**Behold the circle forms! Prepare!** 228
**No people so blessed, no monarch so great.**
[Cibber, Colley], New Year Ode, 1758.
MS. Mus. Sch. D. 303. Music by Boyce.

**Behold the covenant and the kingdom quit,** 229
**Like a God-damme to a faith-and-troth.**
'On burning the Covenant', 1661.
MS. Eng. poet. e. 4, p. 113.

**Behold! the democratic host!** 230
**But now they have lost their Arsenal.**
Madan, Spencer, 1758–1836, 'Extempore . . . on the Burning of the Sans Culottes Fleet and Arsenal at Toulon'.
MS. Eng. poet. c. 51, p. 185.

**Behold the dove ascending to inspire** 231
**For to discard the knaves from out the pack.**
Bolton, —, 'Upon the feast of Pentecost'.
MS. Add. B. 109, fol. 112ᵛ, attr. to Bolton on fol. 138.

**Behold the father is the daughter's son** 232
**Whose taste doth us from beasts to men renew.**
[Southwell, Robert], 'Upon Christ'.
Pr. *St. Peters Complaint*, 1595, p. [44].
MSS. CCC. 328, fol. 46; Douce 280, fol. 180ᵛ; Eng. poet. b. 5, p. 78; Rawl. D. 954, fol. 40ᵛ.

**Behold the grave turned wedding bed! a pair** 233
**This makes the dead to live eternally.**
Strode, William, 'An Epitaph on Mr. Blacknoll, and his Wife'.
MS. *CCC. 325, fol. 99ᵛ (autogr.).

234 Behold the happy day again!
And may thy life be lasting as thy name.
Sedley, Sir Charles, 'To King Wm. upon his Birth Day', 4 Nov. 1700.
Pr. *Miscellaneous Works*, pubd. by Ayloffe, 1702.
MS. Rawl. D. 361, fol. 56.

235 Behold the hour, the boat arrive
Oh tell me, does she muse on me?
Burns, Robert, 'Song'.
MS. Percy d. 9, fol. 46$^{v}$.

236 Behold the king that in his cradle got
Prove a good steward both to us and thee.
'An Elagie. Kinge James'.
MS. Eng. poet. c. 50, fol. 24.

237 Behold the Lamb of God lift up on high
Love to the death, for him loved us no less.
Colman, Henry, written within the outline of an altar inscribed 'I.N.R.I.'
MS. Rawl. poet. 204, fol. 40$^{v}$ (autogr.).

238 Behold the model of your sullen fate
(But to future ages) whate'er was good.
Mason, C[harles], 'To the famous sisters, both the Universityes On the death of . . . The Lady Theophila Cooke'.
MS. Rawl. poet. 246, fol. 20$^{v}$.

239 Behold the morn with cheerful countenance
Nought but content be thine dear friend. Good-morrow.
Burton, Francis, 'A Sundayes Good-morrowe to a freinde', acrostic, 'Bridgett Vernon'.
MS. *Add. A. 267, fol. 16 (autogr.).

240 Behold the muses' gallants who do lead on
A double sacrifice, burnt by a double ray.
Creswell, Robert, 'An ode Pindarick—of Strong Lines'.
MS. *Eng. poet. f. 24, fol. 50 (autogr.).

241 Behold the place, whence England's woes proceed
The villain's refuge and the woman's lust.
'A conventicle'.
MS. Rawl. poet. 207, p. 19.

242 Behold the portrait of fair virtue's queen
Shall propagated be by sounding fame.
Vicars, John, 'On the Picture of Queene Eliza'.
MS. Ashmole 38, p. 24.

243 Behold the prince of princes so renowned
Henry alas your prince, here buried lies.
G. B., 'Epitaph 32' on Prince Henry in 'Cestria Lugens', 1612.
MS. *Rawl. poet. 116, fol. 14.

Behold the promised land where pleasure flows 244
So blushed Adonis in the seat of bliss.
T. B., 'On Flowers in a Lady's Bosom'.
MS. Rawl. poet. 222, fol. 5$^{v}$.

Behold the seal!—My promise saved 245
So keep it for the giver's sake.
Peart, Joshua, 'To Miss Bell on presenting her with a Seal'.
MS. *Eng. poet. e. 28, p. 342.

Behold the virgin Mary and condole 246
Well might she weep, when she her saviour missed.
MS. *Rawl. poet. 97, fol. 44 (autogr.).

Behold the woman and the tree 247
The woman worst, drive on the cart.
'In Connubium: worse then hanginge', translation of Latin verses.
MS. Add. B. 97, fol. 39$^{v}$.

Behold the wonder of her sex, and time 248
The force of nature could no further go.
'Countess of Coventry'.
MS. Eng. poet. e. 28, p. 30.

Behold these two whom Death hath equal made: 249
Dives athirst in Hell for water cries.
Robinson, Robert, 'Upon Dives and Lazarus'.
MS. *Rawl. poet. 218, p. 50 (autogr.).

Behold these woods, and mark (my sweet) 250
Unless you'll meet again to morrow.
Randolph, Thomas, 'A pastorall Courtshipp'.
Pr. *Poems*, 1638, p. 103.
MSS. Ashmole 38, p. 157, attr. to Tho. Randolph; CCC. 328, fol. 16$^{v}$, attr. to Tho. Randolph; Firth e. 4, p. 43, attr. to T. R.; Rawl. poet. 142, fol. 16$^{v}$.

Behold this little volume here enrolled 251
The legible and written Deity.
Strode, William, 'On the Bible'.
MS. *CCC. 325, fol. 78 (autogr.).
MSS. CCC. 328, fol. 91, attr. to Str.; Eng. poet. e. 50, p. 14, attr. to W. S.; e. 97, p. 141, attr. to W.S.

Behold this obsequy: but without tears 252
The birth of all our joy, and grave of fears.
'Upon [the Duke of Buckingham's] Funerall'. 1628.
MS. Malone 23, p. 197.

253 Behold we come, dear Lord, to thee
Till time itself be done.
[Austin, John], 'The Introit upon the Lord's-Day'.
Hymn I in *Devotions in the Ancient Way of Offices*, 1668, p. 4.
MS. Rawl. poet. 200, fol. 126$^{v}$.

254 Behold ye Protestants! behold the day
Of Protestants with greater lustre shine.
Cromwell, Edward, 'On the Fifth of November 1715. To all Protestants'.
MS. *Rawl. poet. 165, fol. 22$^{v}$ (autogr.).

255 Behold ye wretched sons of mortal men
Because for you these things he underwent.
Endorsed 'Copies for Schollers to write'.
MS. Rawl. poet. 152, fol. 232.

256 Behold yon mountain's hoary height
These, these are joys, the gods for youth ordain.
Dryden, John, translator, Horace, *Odes* I. ix. Pr. *Sylvae*, 1685.
MS. Rawl. poet. 173, fol. 27$^{v}$.

257 Behold yon plain with blended colours gay.
May these fair banks like Paradise appear.
Irwin, Eyles, 'Epistles to William Hayley', translation of 'a motto from Ferdusi'.
MS. Eng. poet. d. 37, fol. 22.

258 Behold yon tree that once appeared
And slaves no more opprest.
Walsh, Octavia, 'The Emblem'.
MS. *Eng. poet. e. 31, fol. 5 (autogr.).

259 Being entered, and the bed with all things fit
She what she feared, he hath what he desires.
'The Brides goeing to Bed'.
MSS. Don. d. 58, fol. 53$^{v}$; Rawl. poet. 214, fol. 71 rev., attr. to W. C.

260 Being here brought forth to view earth's stage,
Their doom must now be told.
Robinson, Robert.
MS. *Rawl. poet. 218, p. 95 (autogr.).

261 Being in shops of sadness now I cry
Of ladies customers to haunt my door.
Cavendish, Lady Jane, song in 'The Concealed Fancies'.
MS. *Rawl. poet. 16, p. 132.

262 Being one day at my window all alone
Yet think that death shall spoil your goodly features.
Spenser, Edmund, 'The visions of Petrarche'.
MS. Douce 280, fol. 44.

Being weary of eating good beef and plum pudding 263
And an eunuch become; for want of my stones.
Hulse, Thomas, 'The Trooper turn'd Poet; The Poet's Voyage to Amsterdam'.
MS. *Rawl. poet. 152, fol. 60 (autogr.).

Beldam brought forth my grand-dam dear, 264
Which oft do cause the strong to stagger.
Riddle.
MS. Rawl. poet. 217, fol. 78.

Believe in God that all hath wrought 265
That been most highest of all.
'Divinae virtutes', copied from B.M. MS. Harl. 1706, fol. 208.
MS. Eng. poet. e. 56, p. 119.

Believe it (Dick) it is no fable 266
They would have eat the parlour up.
Proby, Henry, 'A letter from Colchester, relating theire Dyet', 1648.
MS. Rawl. poet. 62, fol. 21.

Believe it Flaccus sweet odes shall be sung 267
Dares for dear friends, or country die.
Polwhele, John, translator, Horace, *Odes* IV. ix.
MS. *Eng. poet. f. 16, fol. 59 (autogr.).

Believe it I'll never be governed by gain, 268
To purchase consent will be labour in vain.
Williams, John, 'The 3$^{d}$ [word]s are—Ile never consent'.
MS. *Rawl. poet. 184, fol. 52$^{v}$ (autogr.).

Believe me, ladies, I'm no cheat. 269
You have me at your fingers' ends.
Bacon, Phanuel, 'A Riddle'.
MS. Eng. poet. e. 45, fol. 45 (autogr.).

Believe me Ma'am 'twas sad 'twas shocking news 270
To the feelings of a mind, that's racked with pain.
'A Fragment dedicated to a Lady on the Sickness of a Friend'.
MS. Eng. poet. e. 28, p. 55.

Believe me nymph whilst you contend 271
Both life and heart his own.
'Wm. Tunstal to Mrs. M. M. in Answer to a Song she sent him'.
MS. Rawl. poet. 155, p. 254.

Believe me, Will, that they that have least sense 272
Lies in the more, or less degree of sense.
'A Satyr on Mankind out of Boileau by Mr. W. R.'
Pr. *A New Collection of Poems relating to State Affairs*, 1705, p. 238, as 'The Fourth Satyr of Boileau to W. K. 1687'.
MS. Rawl. poet. 173, fol. 60.

273 Believe me, young man! for I tell you truth
Of upstart poets, let me slip, adieu.

Potenger, John, 'A letter to a young man addicted to Poetry'.
MS. *Eng. poet. d. 161, p. 154.

274 Believe not him whom Love hath left so wise
But pity him that lives and must endure.

[Felltham, Owen], 'By a Gentlewoman' and 'His Answer'.
Pr. *Resolves*, 1661, 'Lusoria', p. 29; cf. Donne's *Poems*, ed. Grierson, 1912, i. 447, last 6 lines.
MS. Rawl. D. 737, fol. 17 rev.

275 Believe on God, gainst whom no oath commence
Thy neighbour's wife, and all to him doth 'long.

Lilliat, John, 'x Comaundements'.
MS. Rawl. poet. 148, fol. 110$^{v}$ (autogr.).

276 Believe you not yourself; need I declare
Saints I'll compare to you, but you to none.

Oldisworth, Robert or Giles, 'Verses to my Aunt Overbury. New Years day. 1636'.
MS. *Rawl. C. 422, fol. 8, in the hand of Giles Oldisworth.

277 Belinda, see from yonder flowers
Which you inhumanly would starve.

'On snatching a kiss'.
MS. Eng. poet. c. 9, p. 91.

278 Belinda, while with skill divine
More fragrant were their smell.

MS. Eng. poet. e. 45, fol. 30.

279 Belinda's charms by Pope have well been sung
Your lovely form, and stile you patroness.

'On the Lady Patroness written extempore'. Acrostic to Miss Betty Tracy of Oxford.
MS. Eng. misc. b. 48, fol. 78.

280 Belinda's pretty pleasing form
She panting lies.

'In the Farce . . . Women will have their Wills . . . set by Mr. John Eccles'.
MS. Mus. Sch. C. 95, p. 133.

281 Bell and the dragon too! give leave to say
The one Tom Godwin, the other Robin Neve.

Mr. Evington, 'To Elizabeth and Mary Bell, 1650'.
MS. Rawl. poet. 246, fol. 29$^{v}$.

282 Bellona's red chariot and smoking hot steeds
And give it all back—and—who could ask more!

Gough, Richard, 'To Sylvanus Urban Gent. From back of Title to' *Gentleman's Magazine*, 1801, i.
MS. *Eng. poet. c. 5, fol. 303.

Beloved she lived and when in death she slept 283
Grief sigh'd around, and all yon village wept.

Couplet, 'In Long Wittenham Ch: yd. Berks. on Ruth Prowse'.
MS. Eng. misc. e. 241, fol. 103.

Beloved sirs and prisoners 284
Be to him evermore.

MS. Rawl. poet. 58, fol. 65$^{v}$.

Ben do not leave the stage 285
Thou that can soar so high can stoop so low.

Randolph, Thomas, answer to Ben Jonson's Ode, B288, *q.v.*
Pr. *Poems*, 1638, p. 71.
MSS. Ashmole 47, fol. 110, attr. to Mr. Randoll; CCC. 328, fol. 48$^{v}$, attr. to Tho: Randolph; Eng. poet. c. 50, fol. 101, attr. to T. R.; see also B 288.

Ben Hoadly, Julian, Johnson, Titus Oats, 286
That thou mayst be impeached and he preferred.

'To Dr. Hoadley . . . 2 Jan. 1710'.
On a resolution passed by the Commons, 14 Dec. 1709. Pr. *Collection of poems for and against Dr. Sacheverille*, 1712, iv. 6.
MS. Eng. poet. c. 41, fol. 23$^{v}$; pr. bk. Firth b. 21, fol. 73.

Ben Jonson's womb was great; and we 287
And lo, an infant crowned with bays.

Oldisworth, Nicolas, 'On Abraham Cowley the yong poet laureat'.
MS. *Don. c. 24, fol. 63$^{v}$ (autogr.).

Ben leave the [loathed] stage 288
Thou that canst sing so high, canst reach as low.

'Ben Jonson: his discontented soliloquye upon the censure of his Play called the new Inne, answered by Thomas Randolph'. See B 285.
MSS. Firth e. 4, p. 30, attr. to B. J. and T. R.; Rawl. poet. 62, fol. 38$^{v}$, attr. to Ben Johnson and Tho. Randall.

Ben, thou art the muses' friend 289
Sings, the chorus must be thine.

Polw[hele], J[ohn], 'To the admired Ben: Johnson . . . after his farewel to the stage. 1631. Alluding to Horace ode' I. xxvi.
MS. *Eng. poet. f. 16, fol. 10 (autogr.).

Beneath a dismal yew whose baleful shade, 290
With him I'll gladly die and make my end.

Chatwin, John, 'A Coppy of Verses made under the Yew Tree in The Honourable Mr. Finch's Orchard in Ashby Magna'.
MS. *Rawl. poet. 94, p. 265 (autogr.).

291*a* Beneath a drooping willow tree
And plead thy cause in Heaven.
'The Wretched Mother'.
MS. Percy d. 9, fol. 53.

291*b* Beneath a gloomy yew's unhealthy shade.
And let me have the pleasure to obey.
Potenger, John, 'A Pastoral Reflection on Death'.
Pr., 1691.
MS. *Eng. poet. 161, p. 134.

292 Beneath a melancholy shade
Rages and groans, and still submits.
'The Murmur'.
MS. Don. c. 55, fol. 5*a*v.

293 Beneath a myrtle shade
Asleep or waking you must ease my pain.
[Dryden, John], song in *The Conquest of Granada*, Part I, Act III.
MS. Rawl. poet. 65, fol. 37v.

294 Beneath a sleeping infant lies;
Had been as short as thine.
Wesley, Samuel, epitaph at Wisbech, Cambridgeshire.
MS. Top. gen. e. 32, fol. 101.

295 Beneath in the dust
In hopes that her crust will be raised.
'An Epitaph upon Ellen Batchelor the old Pye Woman at Cambridge'.
MS. Eng. poet. c. 51, p. 2.

296 Beneath some aged oak the swains of old
To th' archives of blest immortality.
Chatwin, John, 'On Mr. Wanley's . . . Poem, the Witch of Endor'.
MS. *Rawl. poet. 94, p. 115 (autogr.).

297 Beneath that stone, lies buried one,
The same as at my birth.
T[raherne], T[homas], 'Job. XIX, 25–27, Memento mori'.
MS. Lat. misc. f. 45, p. 207 (autogr.).

298 Beneath the arch there sat a man
To feel the force of stone than cut of knife.
MS. Eng. poet. e. 40, fol. 119v.

299 Beneath the covert of a grove
Think on thy own mortality.
'An anacreontique . . . in Dryden's miscellany', [vi, 1716, p. 127].
MS. Eng. misc. e. 241, fol. 85.

300 Beneath the fir-tree's mournful shade
As spotless as her own.
'Scriblerus', 'Epitaph On a Canary-bird and Blackbird Buried in Eliza's Garden March 1790'.
MS. Montagu e. 14, fol. 71.

Beneath the horrors of a grave 301
To pluck the fairest flower first.
'An Epitaph on a Monument at Kinsale in Ireland'.
MS. Eng. poet. e. 40, fol. 63.

Beneath the shadow of a beaver hat, 302
The billing dove and fondling lamb to thee.
Song about the Quakers.
MS. Mus. d. 10, fol. 81 rev.

Beneath these honours of a tomb 303
To aid the triumphs of the day.
Watts, Isaac, epitaph on William III.
Pr. *Horae Lyricae*.
MS. Rawl. D. 868, fol. 53v.

Beneath these moss-grown roots this rustic cell 304
What drawing room can boast so fair a train.
'Father Francis his Prayer. . . . Inscription for the cell'.
MS. Eng. poet. c. 41, fol. 25v.

Beneath this brazen plate those ashes lie 305
Their rays shall burn without consumption.
Strode, William, 'An Epitaph'.
MS. *CCC. 325, fol. 95v (autogr.).

Beneath this covering, innocence shall sleep, 306
Thy spirit join its kindred spirits there.
[Chapman], Eliza[beth], 'Lines from Eliza to her God-daughter . . . May 1789'.
MS. Montagu e. 14, fol. 49v (autogr.).

Beneath this marble stone doth lie 307
For tree and fruit shall spring again.
Wither, Ge[orge], 'Upon a mother and her Child buried In one grave'.
MSS. Ashmole 38, fol. 179, attr. to Ge. Wither; Eng. poet. e. 97, p. 117.

Beneath this marble stone there lies 308
Is only griev'd—there's nothing left.
'Epitaph on a spend-thrift'.
MS. Eng. misc. e. 219, fol. 10.

Beneath this modest marble lies 309
Best pattern of eternal love.
On Anne Stuart, 20 June 1738.
MSS. Ballard 50, fol. 187; Eng. misc. e. 183, fol. 17v.

Beneath this monumental shrine is laid 310
And life burns brightest in the shortest space.
'Monument in a Parish-Church in London', 1735.
MS. Eng. misc. e. 240, p. 261.

311 Beneath this sculptured arch with roses spread
In aught save beauty, to resemble mine.
Mrs. [Martha] P[eckard], 'Inscription for the Tomb of Mary Queen of Scots removed from the Cathedral to the Garden of the Dean of Peterborough'.
MS. Eng. poet. c. 51, p. 21.

312 Beneath this sculptured, pompous marble stone
What you, and all the sons of earth, shall be.
'On viewing the Tomb of Florio'.
MS. Eng. poet. d. 47, fol. 8$^{v}$.

313 Beneath this silent stone is laid
Because she hates a place of rest.
'On an old Maid. Pitton Churchyard Bedfordshire'.
MS. Top. gen. e. 32, fol. 46$^{v}$.

314 Beneath this stone, a lump of clay
Began to hold her tongue.
'On a Violent Scold'.
MS. Eng. poet. c. 51, p. 4.

315 Beneath this stone as cold as ice
Was ev'ry beauty in epitome.
Chatwin, John, 'An Epitaph on Camilla'.
MS. *Rawl. poet. 94, p. 172 (autogr.).

316 Beneath this stone Biberio's dust is laid,
For there's a dreadful reckoning still to pay.
'Man remarkable for excessive Drinking'.
MS. Top. gen. e. 32, fol. 59.

317 Beneath this stone doth lie
Was not she a lovely maid.
MS. Eng. poet. e. 40, fol. 105$^{v}$.

318 Beneath this stone lies Flavia's sad remains,
At fifty-four unasked, she died a maid.
'An Epitaph on an Old Maid'.
MS. Montagu e. 13, fol. 93$^{v}$.

319 Beneath this stone lies Katherine Gray
She in her shop may be again.
'Katherine Gray, an Old Woman, seller of Pots in Chester'.
MS. Top. gen. e. 32, fol. 64$^{v}$.

320 Benign Creator of the stars
Whilst time lasts, and when time is done.
'Engl. Primer of our Ladie. 1631 . . . p. 1'.
MS. Eng. poet. e. 56, p. 24.

321 Bentinck the goblet holds, Caermarthen fills,
But none regards the writing on the wall.
'Mene, Mene Tekel, Upharsin'.
MSS. Firth d. 13, fol. 77; Rawl. poet. 81, fol. 33$^{v}$.

Bereft of all my comfort here 322
I shall eternal life secure.
Kenton, James.
MS. *Eng. poet. e. 20, p. 146 (autogr.).

Beside a hill, by nature formed 323
Cast a faint light to guide their homeward way.
Bate, Sally, 'Delia . . . 1768'.
MS. *Eng. poet. e. 28, p. 213.

Beside a mountain's venerable seat, 324
Th' Almighty's goodness is equal to his power.
Bate, S[ally], 'The Hermit . . . 1760; from Esops Fables'.
MS. *Eng. poet. e. 28, p. 195.

Besides the devil, who for's presumptuous pride 325
Which at time's fulness fell on his own pate.
MS. *Rawl. poet. 97, fol. 7 (autogr.).

Besides those two in nature there's another 326
Sir Robert's gallantry James Sherly's wit.
Blackman, John, on the birth of Sir R. Sherley's son Seymour, 23 Jan. 1646/7.
MS. Rawl. poet. 65, fol. 53$^{v}$, subscribed Joan: Blackman A. B. [1 Feb. 1647/8] Joann:'.

Bess for abuses offered [me] meet me at six o'clock 327
Look to your self, my ward is sure, my hour I'll keep.
'A challenge' and 'answer'.
MSS. Eng. poet. f. 10, fol. 122$^{v}$; f. 25, fol. 8.

Bess she was sick: Burnett prescribes a vomit 328
For Burnett, fits the mouth, and Birch the tail.
Barrett, William, epigram headed 'Mris E. H. being sicke was by Dr. Burnett appoynted' etc.
MS. Ashmole 38, p. 146.

Best is that man, that best may be 329
Nor loved of God or man.
'A. 5 voc. Ravenscroft', 'Æolian'.
MSS. Mus. f. 11–15: f. 11, fol. 49$^{v}$.

Best Majesties: lest that your eyes should lose 330
Written, Long live the King, Long live the Queen.
'Epilogus, Cupid presents St. Johns new-building in the Scene', 1636.
MS. Rawl. poet. 172, fol. 27$^{v}$.

Best of gifts the gods bestow 331
Bella's goodness truth and sense.
'Soliloquy on Friendship, 1767'.
MS. Eng. poet. e. 28, p. 121.

Best pleased is he when as he wished him worst 332
As still the fox fares best, when he's most curst.
Couplet.
MS. Rawl. poet. 117, fol. 274 rev.

333 Bestir the wits Oh muse awake
My mistress bears the bell away.
'A flattering Comendation of a nastie mistris'.
MS. Rawl. poet. 172, fol. 4v.

334 Bestir your stump good Story now,
With us to live and reign.
Cornet, John, minister, *Admonysson of Doctour Storye*, pr. 1571; see *A Transript of the Stationers' Register*, E. Arber, i, 1875, p. 443.
MS. Firth d. 14, fol. 100.

335 Bestow what pains and cost you can
The house will down to th' ground.
Robinson, Robert.
MS. *Rawl. poet. 218, p. 121 (autogr.).

336 Bethesdah's porches filled, with weak and lame
Propitious prove; but Christ much more than they.
'The hospitall'.
MS. Rawl. poet. 154, fol. 113.

337 Betime when sleep is sweet,
That same would take his rest.
Whitney, Geoffrey, 'Garrulitas'.
MS. *Rawl. poet. 56, fol. 28.

338 Better a little hungry be,
A heavy head is dull.
Robinson, Robert.
MS. *Rawl. poet. 218, p. 154 (autogr.).

339 Better than others I may mean
And form my soul for heaven and thee.
Beddome, Benjamin.
MS. *Eng. misc. e. 227, fol. 30.

340 Better to be rich man, than so deemed,
Of what they are not, nor will e'er be so.
Robinson, Robert.
MS. *Rawl. poet. 218, p. 91 (autogr.).

341 Better to die a thousand deaths and more
Than live contemned, who honoured was before.
Couplet.
MS. Malone 19, p. 46.

342 Betty, who yet had looked on man
Fair Proserpine away.
'On the nuptials of Joseph Smith L.L.D. formerly of Queen's College, Oxford, with Miss Bourchier of Long Hanborough'.
MSS. Eng. poet. d. 47, fol. 108; Rawl. poet. 172, fol. 107.

Between Father Patrick and's Highness of late 343
He managed this matter, as he did his sea-fight.
[Wilmot, John, Earl of Rochester (?)], 'His Highnesse Conversion by Father Patricke'. 1673.
See J. Prinz, *Rochester, his Life and Writings* (Palaestra cliv), 1927, p. 134.
MS. Don. b. 8, p. 419; see also B348.

Between two brethren civil war [wars] and worse 344
And either to have conquerd other, sad.
Translation, 'Bella inter geminos . . .', on John and William Rainolds by William Alabaster.
MSS. CCC. 309, fol. 10v; Rawl. D. 399, fol. 199; Tanner 306, fol. 138v, attr. by Sancroft to Dr. Alabaster; Top. Cheshire c. 6, fol. 458; see also B353.

Between two hills of driven snow 345
T'other as Love shall it depose.
R. B., translator, 'Ænigm. ex Ital.'
MS. Eng. poet. f. 24, fol. 37.

Between two suitors sits a lady fair 346
She doth most honour, she most love doth bear.
Rhymed conundrum.
MS. Ashmole 781, p. 144; see also B355.

Between your sheets you soundly sleep 347
Between your sheets.
Wortley Montagu, Lady Mary.
MS. Don. c. 56, fol. 36 (autogr.).

Betwixt father Patrick and his Highness of late 348
He managed the matter as he did the sea-fight.
'1673. On the Duke of Yorks changing his Religion'.
MS. Top. Oxon. e. 202, fol. 129; see also B343.

Betwixt pot and poet there is but a letter 349
Which makes the poet love the pot the better.
Couplet.
MS. Douce f. 5, fol. 10.

Betwixt St. George and Mark the Gospeller 350
To one of George his knights in holy bands.
Strode, William, 'On Mrs. Jane Hele borne on the 24 of Aprill betwixt St. George's Day and St. Markes. 1637. A Calculation'.
MS. *CCC. 325, fol. 126 (autogr.).

Betwixt the chief of summer, and the said winter 351
Though I write as it was, I wist it not.
'The Prophesies of Beade'.
MS. Ashmole 1835, fol. 43v.

352 Betwixt the hours of twelve and one
Not writ yet.
Evans, A., 'An Epistolary Ode from Dr. Ch[arlet]t to Mr. P[erci]val of Xt. Ch'. Latin on fol. 153. Answered by N403.
MS. Lat. misc. e. 19, fol. 174.

353 Betwixt two brothers civil wars and worse
And either to have conquered other, sad.
'In duas Reginaldos fratres inter se de religione certantes et in Contrarium versos'.
MS. Ashmole 38, p. 74, subscribed 'per Guilemum Alablaster'; see also B344.

354 Betwixt two knights beyond the sea
Pray we all for charity.
Subscribed 'Amen qd. Rate'.
MS. Ashmole 61, fol. 26ᵛ.

355 Betwixt two suitors sat a lady fair
She most doth honour she most love doth bear.
Riddle and 'Reply'.
Pr. *Wits Recreations*, 1641, Sig. T7ᵛ.
MS. Eng. misc. f. 49, fol. 28ᵛ; see also B346.

356 Betwixt you and me, such perfections we boast
I should grieve to see such a post put in the ground.
Verses exchanged between Dr. Pinnel and Lady Bathurst.
MS. Eng. misc. e. 241, fol. 87ᵛ.

357 Beware fair maid of musky courtiers' oaths
From lords to lackeys, and at last to all.
[Sylvester, Joshuah], 'To yonge gentlewomen at Court'.
Pr. *Du Bartas his divine Weekes and Workes*, etc., 1641, p. 651.
MSS. Eng. poet. f. 9, p. 25; f. 25, fol. 69; Rawl. poet. 117, fol. 28ᵛ; Tanner 169, fol. 199ᵛ.

358–9 Beware Glyceria [Lucelia] lest you be
And miss thy miseries.
'The answere' to N192.
MSS. Rawl. poet. 65, fol. 24ᵛ; 116, fol. 40ᵛ.

360 Beware of a fool: a fool is mischievous;
Love still a good man: he ne'er will o'erreach thee.
Robinson, Robert.
MS. *Rawl. poet. 218, p. 154 (autogr.).

361–2 Beware of him that solemn sits
The river is the deeper.
MS. Rawl. poet. 172, fol. 11.

Beware thy wife too much thou trust 363
So well I e'er them loved.
Tipping, William, 'If thou hast a wife'.
MS. *Rawl. poet. 101, fol. 80 (autogr.).

Beware tread gently 364
Here lies Dr. Bently.
Couplet.
MS. Wood D. 19 (2), fol. 109ᵛ.

Beware ye Christian doctrines all. 365
Was Antichristian self denial.
See I1366.
MSS. Add. A. 301, fol. xvᵛ; Firth e. 6, fol. 24ᵛ.

Bewildered in imaginations, we 366
Coveting nothing I can nothing want.
'Virtus repulsae nescia sordidae Intaminatis fulget honoribus'.
MS. Top. London e. 9, p. 51.

Beza why bides thou, why does tho[u stay] 367
I shall her [laiche (?)] kiss again.
'Theodori Bezae epigramma', translated. Original in *Poemata*, 1548, p. 94.
MS. Tanner 306, fol. 145.

Bibax that while he lived, would often say 368
For he has drunk himself as dry as dust.
On a drunkard.
MS. Eng. poet. e. 14, fol. 93 rev.

Bid all who build their hopes on towers of air 369
The ruins of a rotten inward side.
MS. Rawl. poet. 84, fol. 81 rev.

Bid me go reason with the wind 370
Than of a rope to hang a thief.
Bulteel, John, 'Ode'.
MS. *Rawl. poet. 159, fol. 211.

Bid me not go where neither suns nor showers 371
And lovers live by thinking on their loss.
Cartwright, [William], 'a valediction'.
Pr. *Poems*, 1651, p. 245.
MS. Eng. misc. e. 241, fol. 24ᵛ.

Bid not farewell for fate can ne'er divorce 372
To crown corruption with eternity.
Answer to F156.
MS. Don. c. 57, fol. 50ᵛ, with music.

Big with the thoughts of pleasure down I came 373
Whose humours are as crooked as Miss Scott.
'Tunbridge Lampoon. Sept. 1683'.
MSS. Firth c. 16, p. 93; Rawl. poet. 159, fol. 150.

374 Birth, breeding, beauty; grace, and carriage sweet,
To see her match't, with an eternal king.

'Upon the second daughter of Sir Thomas Puckering' in Warwick, 13 April 1636.
MSS. Ashmole 38, p. 196; Don. e. 6, fol. 62.

375 Birth of Pandora's box thou female sex
Rocked with the murmur of the river slept.

'Phillis Tiranny translated out of Ariosto'.
MSS. Don. d. 58, fol. 45; Eng. poet. e. 14, fol. 63ᵛ; Malone 21, fol. 82ᵛ.

376 Birth-noble friend Maecenas hither approach
Castor and Pollux shall me safe defend.

W. A., translator, Horace, *Odes*, III. xxix.
MS. *Rawl. poet. 104, fol. 35ᵛ (autogr.).

377 Black boy complain not that I fly,
And I'll bequeath my self to thee.

[King, Henry], answer to S1385.
MSS. CCC. 328, fol. 16; Rawl. D. 1092, fol. 271ᵛ; see B379, B382.

378 Black cypress veils [cypresses] are shrouds [types] of night
You may be censured we go free.

'Answer' to L18.
Pr. *Wits Recreations*, 1640, no. 469; *Parnassus Biceps*, 1656, p. 66; and *Poems of Corbet*, ed. Gilchrist, 1807, p. 233. Attr. to John Grange in MS. Folger 1669. 2. Answered by I903.
MSS. Ashmole 36, 37, fol. 174; 38, p. 65; 47, fol. 111ᵛ; Eng. poet. c. 50, fol. 26; e. 14, fol. 78 rev.; Malone 21, fol. 47; Rawl. poet. 117, fol. 177ᵛ rev.; 260, p. 76; Tanner 465, fol. 58ᵛ.

379 Black girl complain not that I fly
And I'll bequeath myself to thee.

[King, Henry], 'The answer' to F30.
MSS. Ashmole 47, fol. 48ᵛ; Malone 21, fol. 63; Rawl. poet. 199, p. 5; see also B377, B382.

380 Black, grizzly death did nick his arrow right
When leaving rovers, he did hit the white.

'On one White'.
MS. Firth e. 4, p. 110.

381 Black is too dark, and dulls the eye.
There is no beauty but in Browne.

'Uppon the Ladye B[rowne]'.
MSS. Firth d. 7, fol. 182; Rawl. poet. 117, fol. 179 rev.

Black maid complain not that [why] I fly 382
And then I will bequeath myself to thee.

King, Henry, answer to S1145, W2373.
Pr. *Poems*, 1657, and H. Lawes' *Select Ayres and Dialogues*, 1669, p. 49.
MSS. CCC. 325, fol. 127ᵛ, copied by W. Strode; Don. c. 57, fol. 46, with music by John Wilson; Eng. misc. e. 13, fol. 24; Eng. poet. e. 14, fol. 20ᵛ; *e. 30, fol. 23ᵛ; f. 16, fol. 8ᵛ; f. 25, fol. 19; Firth e. 4, p. 111; *Malone 22, fol. 14; Mus. b. 1, fol. 91ᵛ, with music by John Wilson; Rawl. poet. 84, fol. 86; 116, fol. 48; 206, p. 64; see also B377, B379.

Blame me not, if unkind I prove 383
Your stars are cruel, and not I.

Weaver, Thomas, 'To a Lady desiring his Love'.
Not pr. in *Songs & Poems*, 1654.
MS. *Rawl. poet. 211, fol. 7ᵛ (autogr.).

Blame me not (muses) 'cause I often play 384
He'll teach you wit; for that is the thing you want.

'Newes from Cambridge' on B. Holiday's play, 1621.
MS. Douce f. 5, fol. 6ᵛ.

Blame me not reader though 385
I know not how soon my time will be past.

'A commendation & exhortat[ion] to his frends wyth his last [testament]. to the Read[er]', [Testament of Heresy], mentioning T. Garrat, J. Lambert, W. Jerome, T. Bilney.
MS. Lat. misc. e. 85, fol. 75ᵛ.

Blame nature only for it, blame not me 386
Would she permit, I then should virtuous be.

Couplet.
MS. Add. B. 8, fol. 47.

Blame not, my friend, that to the muse resigned 387*a*
For that high object 'Man's eternal weal!'

Parsons, William, 'To the revᵈ Mr. [W.] W[alker]', his answer, and W. Parsons's answer in return.
MS. *Don. d. 123, p. 52, in the hand of W. Parsons.

Blame not my heart for flying up too high 387*b*
My love a fire, and so ascends above.

[Constable, Henry], sonnet, pr. *Diana*, 1592, Sig. B2.
MS. Ashmole 38, p. 52.

388 Blame not the times, nor doom this age for ill
Thus made the subject of my barren pen.
Wharton, G[eorge], 'On the present flourishing Estate of the Sciences Mathematicall'.
MS. Ashmole 423, fol. 274 (autogr.).

389 Blame not ye sages of the bar
The law is all mine arse.
MS. Eng. poet. d. 152, fol. 123.

390 Blame not your Armida nor call her your grief
But all my kind wishes I straw on your hearse.
MS. Rawl. poet. 65, fol. 36v.

391*a* Blame not your fate ye hawkers shrill
With pamphlet proclamations.
'Comfort to the Hawkers'.
MS. Rawl. poet. 155, p. 71.

391*b* Blandusia's spring! more bright than glass,
From whence thy prattling waters fall.
'My Cousin [Ant.] Hammond's Translation of Horace', *Odes* III. xiii.
MS. Rawl. D. 360, fol. 61.

392 Blasted with sighs and surrounded [furrowed] with [cares] tears
Who's therefore true, because her truth kills me.
Donne, John, 'Twickenham garden'.
Pr. *Poems*, 1633.
MSS. Eng. poet. c. 50, fol. 64, attr. to Herricke; *e. 99, fol. 115; *f. 9, p. 37; Rawl. poet. 117, fol. 214v rev., ref. to Donne's *Poems*.

393 Bless God my soul, and magnify his name;
Bless thou oh praise ye him with one accord.
Fleming, Robert, 'The CIV Psalm paraphrased, In Heroicks'.
Pr. *The Mirrour of Divine Love*, 1691, 'Poems', p. 74.
MS. Rawl. poet. 213, fol. 42v (autogr.).

394 Bless God my soul with all thy might
Soul Hallelujahs sing Jehovah's praise.
Fairfax, Thomas, Lord, Psalm civ.
MS. *Fairfax 40, p. 255 (autogr.).
MS. *Fairfax 38, p. 376.

395 Bless Lord Jehovah my blessed child
Upon sweet symphony aye singing.
Lilliat, John, 'A Ditie, upon his beloved Daughter Priscilla: 1599'.
MS. Rawl. poet. 148, fol. 103v (autogr.).

Bless me! what sight is this invades my eyes? 396
Your crimes the offspring which she shall produce.
Lawrence, Thomas, of St. John's and University College, Oxford, Prologue to Music Speech, 1669.
MSS. Add. A. 368, fol. 7, attr. to Mr. Lawrence of University Coll:; Top. Oxon. e. 202, fol. 15, attr. to Mr. Lawrence of University Coll:; e. 344, fol. 148v rev., attr. to Mr. Laurence of Univ: Coll:.

Bless me! with wonder I'm confounded 397
Women amongst the men among the [ ].
'The Hermaphrodite'.
Pr. bk. Vet. A3 c. 123, fol. 21.

Bless the good ladies and good food 398
Men may obey and women rule the helm.
'A Grace before meat at a Christ'ning Dinner'.
Pr. *Poems on Affairs of State*, iv, 1707, p. 428.
MS. Rawl. poet. 173, fol. 141v.

Bless us good Lord from that dull sect that say 399
The contrary, to Tyburn be their way. Amen.
'The Antibrownest', introducing the words of the Lord's Prayer to conclude each couplet.
MS. Douce 357, fol. 31v.

Bless you, bless you, Bunney Bee. 400
Take your wings and fly away.
MS. Douce d. 59, fol. 51.

Blessed and happy are all those that find 401
What he intends can be by none withstood.
Williams, John, Psalm xxxii.
MS. *Rawl. poet. 191, fol. 56v.

Blessed are they that perfect are 402
Like a lost sheep have strayed.
Psalm cxix.
MS. *Rawl. C. 113, fol. 82.

Blessed are they that perfect are 403
From thy statutes to slide.
[Whittingham, William], Psalm cxix.
MSS. Rawl. D. 886, verses 9 and 10 set for 6 bells, fols. 28 and 30; Rawl. poet. 112, fol. 36v rev.

Blessed art thou that fearest God 404
Prosperity and peace.
[Sternhold, Thomas], Psalm cxxviii.
MS. Rawl. poet. 23, p. 25, reference to setting by Dr. Giles; Rawl. poet. 112, fol. 32v rev.

405 Blessed be God, father almight
And take us from this heaviness.
'Primer of Hen. 8. Eng. and Lat. 1536. The hymne for Complyn of our Lady. fol. 79$^{v}$'.
MS. Eng. poet. e. 56, p. 115.

406 Blessed be the Father's love
I shall live to die no more.
Kenton, James.
MS. *Eng. poet. e. 20, p. 127 (autogr.).

407 Blessed be the God of love
Of our victorious King.
Kenton, James.
MS. *Eng. poet. e. 20, p. 89 (autogr.).

408 Blessed forever may he be,
That doth confess in Persons Three / The Unity.
Corbett, Richard, 'For Trinity Sunday an Anthymne'.
MSS. CCC. 315*b*, fol. 352, attr. to 'R. Norv.'; 325, fol. 49$^{v}$, attr. to 'R. Norv.' in the hand of W. Strode.

409 Blessed is he regards the poor
From age to age Amen.
Psalm xli.
MS. *Rawl. C. 113, fol. 33$^{v}$.

410 Blessed is he whose filthy stain
Your hearts with clearness armed.
Sidney, Sir Philip, Psalm xxxii.
MSS. *Rawl. poet. 24, p. 41; *25, fol. 24.

411 Blessed is he whose sins are purged,
Their shouts of praise to him.
Psalm xxxii.
MS. *Rawl. C. 113, fol. 27$^{v}$.

412 Blessed is he whose wickedness
That are in heart upright.
Psalm xxxii.
MS. *Montagu e. 10, fol. 51$^{v}$.

413 Blessed is the man God directs
In their destruction ends.
Psalm i.
MS. *Rawl. C. 113, fol. 11, with author's correction.

414 Blessed St. Peter hath his fetters which him bound
The cruel ravenous wolf drives from his wished prey.
Huish, Alexander, 'Petrus beatus . . . Brev. Rom. Prop. Sanct. p. 909', translated Decemb. 1635.
MS. Eng. poet. e. 56, p. 49 (autogr.).

Blessed Saviour, Lord of all 415
Ever and ever to inherit.
[Cosin, John], 'Salvator mundi Domine . . . Collection of privat devotions . . . 1627 . . . p. 150'.
MS. Eng. poet. e. 56, p. 73.

Blessed spirit, thy infant breath 416
Since what is thy fate now, must once be mine.
King, John, 'Upon the untimely death of J[ohn] K[ing] first borne of H[enry] K[ing]'.
See *B.Q.R.* v, March 1929, p. 329, and *B.L.R.* iv, 1953, p. 208.
MS. Rawl. D. 317, fol. 175 (autogr.).

Blessed the man that fears the Lord 417
The peace of Israel.
Psalm cxxviii.
MS. *Rawl. C. 113, fol. 93$^{v}$.

Blessed the man, that hath not gone astray 418
Tend to destruction and shall [ ] perish.
Samber, Robert, Psalm i.
MS. *Rawl. poet. 134*b*, fol. 178 (autogr.).

Blessed the man who fears the Lord, 419
Frustrate in all designs.
Psalm cxii.
MS. *Rawl. C. 113, fol. 78$^{v}$.

Blessing, and thanks, and love 420
In the Jerusalem above.
Kenton, James.
MS. *Eng. poet. e. 20, p. 352 (autogr.).

Blessings crown the lovely pair 421
Round the bride her *cestus* ties.
'Epithalamium'.
MS. Ballard 47, fol. 142.

Blest are the pure in heart who are sincere 422
And thy strayed sheep back to the pastures lead.
Fairfax, Thomas, Lord, Psalm cxix.
MS. *Fairfax 40, p. 310 (autogr.).
MS. *Fairfax 38, p. 412.

Blest as the immortal gods is he 423
I fainted sank and died away.
'A Song'.
MS. Montagu e. 13, fol. 43.

Blest be that heavenly power that brought to light 424
Those that contemn them most with shame would perish.
'An answer to' O486.
MS. Rawl. poet. 84, fol. 69$^{v}$ rev.; see also B432.

425 Blest be the God of love
And in this love more, than in bed I rest.
Herbert, George. 'Evensong'.
Pr. *The Temple*, 1633, p. 55.
MS. *Tanner 307, fol. 42v.

426 Blest be the lord my strength
Whose god is God the lord.
[Norton, Thomas], Psalm cxliv.
MS. Rawl. poet. 112, fol. 29v rev.

427 Blest be the man (and blest be he) whoe'er
Let my life sleep, and learn to know her end.
Cowley, Abraham, 'The Country Life, the happyest'.
Pr. *Works*, 1668, 'Essays in Verse and Prose', p. 113.
MS. Rawl. poet. 173, fol. 169v.

428 Blest be the man! his memory at least
Nor her soft heart in chains of pearls been tied.
[Winchilsea, Anne, Countess of], 'Lines in Praise of the invention of Writing . . . by a Lady'.
Pr. *Poems on Several Occasions*, 1713, p. 215.
MSS. Eng. poet. c. 9, p. 57; Rawl. poet. 116, fol. 98.

429 Blest be the youth, (if such there can be found)
And every Joseph meets a Joseph's fate.
'Upon Joseph and Potiphars Wife', Genesis xxxix.
MS. Eng. poet. e. 28, p. 5.

430 Blest be thy friendly light which o'er the plain
Confide in him my father and my God.
'Scriblerus', 'Sonnet To the Moon. Composed . . . 1788'.
MS. Montagu e. 14, fol. 11.

431 Blest be thy name, my gracious God
Once were my sweetest meat.
Tipping, William.
MS. *Rawl. poet. 101, fol. 3 (autogr.).

432 Blest be you heavenly powers that brought to light
No devil's factor, unless man's the devil.
'An answer to' O486.
MS. Rawl. poet. 214, fol. 81 rev.; see also B424.

433 Blest creature, laugh at my mistake. When I
Any thus doubly happy, besides you?
Oldisworth, Nicolas, 'To Mrs. Thorold of Arborvill'.
MS. *Don. c. 24, fol. 50 (autogr.).

Blest happy night! more blest my happy dreams! 434
'Cause had I dreamt of parting too, I'd died.
Ashmole, Elias, 'Dreaming that I enioyed my first wife againe', 3 Aug. 1648.
MSS. Ashmole 36, 37, fol. 234v (autogr.).

Blest in thy presence mighty king 435
To hope for bliss above.
Skinner, John, Psalm xv.
MS. *Eng. poet. d. 22, fol. 123.

Blest is he that spotless stands 436
Which hath filled the world's wide space.
Carew, Thomas, Psalm cxix, vv. 1–64.
MS. *Don. b. 9, fol. 11v.

Blest is the man, beyond all thought, ne'er knew 437
Or add to me, I'm happier far than you.
Chatwin, John, 'The Country Life'.
MS. *Rawl. poet. 94, p. 20 (autogr.).

Blest is the man in walking daily shuns 438
Or 'mongst the just who in sins way do trudge.
Fairfax, Thomas, Lord, Psalm i.
MS. *Fairfax 40, p. 1 (autogr.).
MS. *Fairfax 38, p. 115.

Blest is the man, who free from anxious strife, 439
And binds her vassal with a stronger chain.
Standen, —, 'In praise of a Country life out of Horace Ep[ode] 2'.
MS. Ballard 47, fol. 77.

Blest is the man who hears thy word 440
For lo! Eternity's at hand.
Kenton, James.
MS. *Eng. poet. e. 20, p. 136 (autogr.).

Blest is the upright and the just 441
He looks upon them as his own.
Gough, Richard, Psalm i.
MS. *Eng. poet. c. 5, fol. 53 (autogr.).

Blest is the youth, whom Cælia doth approve 442
He must be happy, whom she deigns to love.
'Cælia Loves'.
MS. Eng. poet. e. 40, fol. 131.

Blest is thy presence mighty king 443
To hope for bliss above.
Skinner, John, Psalm xv 'translated from Buchannan'.
MS. *Eng. poet. d. 22, fol. 41v (autogr.).

Blest isle from thee what wonder springs 444
Can just as well attain it.
Skinner, John, 'To the Author of a Poem entitled Corsica published at Oxford in 1794'.
MS. *Eng. poet. d. 22, two copies, fols. 46v, 62.

445 Blest Jesu, in thy truth and grace I trust
And that we perish not thy grace extend.
Williams, John, 'To the Blessed Jesus'.
MS. *Rawl. poet. 188, fol. 75 (autogr.).

446 Blest leaf, whose aromatic gales dispence
And let me taste thee unexcised by kings.
Browne, Isaac Hawkins, 'In Praise of Tobacco'. Imitation of Pope.
Pr. Dodsley's *Collection of Poems*, ii, 1748, p. 281.
MS. Top. London e. 9, p. 175.

447 Blest order which in power dost so excel
What pride by opposition.
Herbert, George, 'The Priesthood'.
Pr. *The Temple*, 1633, p. 154.
MSS. Rawl. D. 924, fol. 339, attr. to Herbert; *Tanner 307, fol. 117$^{v}$.

448 Blest pair by death not severed, whom as one
The world at last shall burn, and make it day.
On Thomas and Ursula Pecke, St. Michael at Pleas Chancel Norwich, died 1591 and 1601.
MS. Top. gen. e. 32, fol. 28$^{v}$.

449 Blest saint to whose renown, this well
Shall bathe and make thy spring more pure.
Weaver, Thomas, 'A Hymne to St. Winifrid'.
Pr. *Songs and Poems by T. W.*, 1654.
MS. *Rawl. poet. 211, fol. 4$^{v}$ (autogr.).

450 Blest spirit! what a pious cheat th' hast given
That minute when he overcame he died.
Wells, Jeremiah, 'On the Death of Mr. Robert Fell of Christ Church, Oxon', 20 Jan. 1666.
MS. Eng. poet. e. 4, p. 44.

451 Blest union! Where the fates consent to pair
May you yourselves to many mutiply.
[Roach, Richard], 'On A Great Marriage: To the Bride-Groom and Bride'.
MS. Rawl. D. 832, fol. 178 (autogr.).

452 Blest with thy favour here
And evermore rejoice.
Kenton, James.
MS. *Eng. poet. e. 20, p. 238 (autogr.).

453 Blind fortune if thou want'st a guide
Not Fortune called, but Providence.
Harvey, Martin, 'A guide to Fortune'.
MS. Rawl. poet. 147, p. 64.

454 Blind love to this hour
Or were she less charming I'd hate.
'A song the words by a Person of Quality sett to Musick By Mr. Mathew Novell'.
MS. Mus. Sch. C. 95, p. 253.

Blind to thy faults I ne'er did see 455
A heart, than glory in its pain.
'A copy of Verses'.
MS. Montagu e. 13, fol. 108.

Blind were those poets who a threefold grace 456
Puzzle arithmetic, much more my skill.
Briggs, S[amson], 'On Eumorphe his fancied Mistris'.
MSS. Rawl. poet. 116, fol. 73$^{v}$ rev.; 147, p. 272 rev., attr. to S. Briggs.

Blood in a cassock hides the crown and flies 457
Put off the clergy's coat and get their tongue.
'The Answer' to W988.
MS. Douce 357, fol. 81.

Blood-sucking woe, long boiling in my heart 458
Importune her, that first did throw thee down.
Sonnet 2 of a sequence.
MS. Add. B. 97, fol. 21$^{v}$.

Blood-thirsty Athaliah bearing sway 459
But Justice cries, Let Athaliah bleed.
'The cruell Queene'.
MS. Rawl. poet. 154, fol. 109.

Blooming innocence adieu! 460
Kiss my little friend above.
Kenton, James, 'A Funeral Ode' on Richard Kenton Cope, d. 31 Dec. 1780.
MS. *Eng. poet. e. 19, p. 235 (autogr.).

Blow gently passion in my fair one's breast 461
Ay me I sink despair my brink.
Song, music by William Caesar.
MS. Don. c. 57, fol. 70$^{v}$.

Blow high blow low 462
Blow high blow low . . . (incomplete).
MS. Percy d. 9, fol. 60$^{v}$.

Blow thy horn hunter 463
Now blow thy horn jolly hunter.
3-part song by W. Cornyshe. Transcript from B.M. Add. MS. 31922.
MS. Mus. d. 183, fol. 4.

Blowing my pipe, as custom taught, 464
For ever happy be.
Imitation of Latin verses by A. Alsop 'Reverendo viro Johanni Dolben Baronetto, extracted out of the Gentleman's Magazine, Vol. V, p. 384' [July 1735].
MS. Ballard 47, fol. 51$^{v}$.

Blown but i'th' morning, thou shalt fade ere noon 465
Anticipating life, to hasten death.
Fanshawe, Sir Richard, translator, from the Spanish, Sonnet 6 'To a Rose'.
MS. *Firth c. 1, p. 75.

466 Blows are designed to punish, mend, reprove,
Refuse when judges meanly make request.
Williams, John.
MS. *Rawl. poet. 192, fol. 158 (autogr.).

467 Blowzabella my bouncing doxie
Is Blowzabella's and Collin's case.
D'Urfey, Thomas.
MS. Mus. Sch. C. 95, p. 130.

468 Blush down my muse to see the damned pollutions
It's time to leave when flesh and bones are rotten.
MS. Don. d. 58, fol. 34.

469 Blush not, my friend, to own the love
All his flames and all thy tears.
Duke, [Richard], Horace, *Odes* II. iv.
Pr. Dryden's *Miscellany Poems*, 1684, p. 207.
MS. Rawl. poet. 222, fol. 33$^v$.

470 Blush not, ye fair, to own me but be wise
And even lend mortality a charm.
'The Ladys Skull'. Inscription in an alcove in the garden of Mr. Tyers at Denbygh, Surrey.
MS. Montagu e. 13, fol. 177$^v$.

471 Boast not blind boy that I'm thy prize
Since fate concludes their urn her breast.
Song, music by John Wilson.
Pr. *Cheerfull Ayres or Ballads*, 1660, p. 78; and *Wit and Drollery*, 1661.
MSS. Don. c. 57, fol. 77$^v$; Mus. b. 1, fol. 109$^v$.

472 Boast not of Bolinbroke's retreat,
All smiling join in chorus.
'The New Toast', June 1715.
MSS. Eng. poet. e. 87, p. 121; Rawl. poet. 155, p. 119.

473 Boast not to me that at the George
To barter freedom for a dinner!
Parsons, William, extempore verse.
MS. *Don. d. 123, p. 24 (autogr.).

474 Boast not ye English lads, ye British crew
He were a hero, were he not a priest.
Spoure, Edmund, 'A poem in praise of . . . Mr. George Walker, late Governour of London-Derry'.
MS. *Eng. poet. c. 52, fol. 50 (autogr.).

475 Boast not your charms, my fair disdainful maid
To me your favour give; 'tis due to me.
'Forma bonum fragile est. Ovid. An Epistle', 1735.
MS. Eng. misc. e. 240, p. 313.

Boast not your parts, or ought beside 476
Excellent maid is done by thee.
Bulteel, John, 'An Acrostick', on Bridget Tynte.
MS. *Rawl. poet. 159, fol. 224.

Bob Harlye South-Sea bobbing did begin 477
Merry Bob Molespret cured us of the spleen.
'An Epigram. Four notable Bobs'.
MS. Top. London e. 9, p. 23.

Bob Spring he was a seaman bold 478
Mix liquors never more.
'Bob Spring'.
MS. Firth c. 18, fol. 182.

Bobby Shaftoe's gone to sea 479
Pretty Bobby Shaftoe.
MS. Douce d. 59, fol. 51$^v$.

Bold and undaunted shall the righteous stand, 480
And on the ground, its monarchs' thrones shall cast.
'The Wisdom of Solomon', ch. v, 'Paraphras'd'.
MS. Montagu e. 13, fol. 153.

Bold Bacchus! must the muses now attend 481
By the same art to set off's drinking well.
'On a Good Scholler and a Goodfellow'. Epitaph, T3307.
MSS. Add. A. 301, fol. 94$^v$ rev., amongst poems attr. to J. S.; Rawl. D. 361, fol. 230$^v$.

Bold bee how darest thou try 482
Administer this rare restorative.
Sterrill, —, 'On a Bee lighting on his M$^{rs}$ lypp'.
MS. Ashmole 47, fol. 162$^v$.

Bold Edward Gardener to the seas he is gone 483
The Commander brave boys of the Fly sloop of war.
'A New Sea Song' [Edward Garner commanded H.M.S. *Fly* 1776–9].
MS. Firth c. 18, fol. 47.

Bold General Wolfe to his men did say 484
Be a soldier's friend, my boys and they'll fight for evermore.
'The Death of General Wolfe', 1759.
MS. Firth c. 17, fol. 52.

Bold in the cause of righteousness 485
Through Jesus my redeemer's name.
Kenton, James.
MS. *Eng. poet. e. 20, p. 375 (autogr.).

Bold Japet's son: thou to inspire thy clay 486
I still will die, that I have wrong in this.
Ch. M., Sonnett 2.
MS. Eng. misc. d. 239, fol. 6.

487 Bold Oliver came into the house like a spight
A king and a parliament, too.
Cromton, Eaththeldred, 'Song'.
MS. Rawl. poet. 214, fol. 73.

488 Bold prayer will soar above the heavens
I'm sure I grace shall have.
Tipping, William, 'Of Prayer'.
MS. *Rawl. poet. 101, fol. 60v (autogr.).

489 Bold was the bard! and wondrous was his spell!
Whose hands repair the mischiefs of their eyes?
Knollys, Fra[ncis], 'To the ingenious Artist Mrs. M[ary] B[eale (?)] upon her making the Picture of one that was dead seeme after the life. 3 Apr. 1670'.
MS. *Rawl. poet. 60, p. 176 (autogr.).

490 Boldly to turn each leaf and fix your sight
Upon a book, I swear 'twas lect'ring right.
Pestell, Thomas, couplet, 'To Courtlie Neophyte, or the new Divinitie reader'.
MS. *Malone 14, p. 36.

491 [Bones among stones] Bonys emonge stonys lys ful steyl
Qwylste the sawle wanderis were that god wylethe.
Inscription on 'one of the Savils', 28. Hen. VIII, Thornhill Church near Wakefield.
Pr. *Guilelmus Neubrigensis*, ed. Hearne, 1719, ii. 763.
MS. Rawl. D. 1164, fol. 245.

492 Bonny Jocky now with clasping and kissing
The pleasures cross fortune denied us below.
'A Scotch Song'.
MS. Rawl. poet. 196, fol. 32.

493 Bonny lad prithee lay pipe down
Ha! then 'tis she kills me outright.
[D'Urfey, Thomas], 'A Song in the Marriage Hater match'd'.
MSS. Mus. Sch. C. 95, p. 230, set by Mr. Tho: Tollett; Rawl. poet. 196, fol. 43v.

494 Bonny lass! bonny lass! will you be mine?
And thou shall have strawberries and cream.
MS. Douce d. 59, fol. 48v.

495 Born at the first to bring another forth
Dying herself renews it in her seed.
'On A Lady dying in Child-bed'.
Pr. *Wits Recreations*, 1640, Sig. Cc2.
MSS. Ashmole 38, p. 207; 47, fol. 38; Douce f. 5, fol. 34; Eng. poet. e. 14, fol. 46.

Born for millions are the kings 496
And hails the king whose birthday is its own.
[Whitehead, William], Birthday Ode, 1773.
Pr. *Poems*, 1790, ii. 113.
MS. Mus. Sch. D. 330. Music by Boyce.

Born to a triple empire I submit 497
Than all the wonders of her milder reign.
'King James the [III] on a sight of his own and his sister [Queen Anne]'s Picture'.
MS. Rawl. poet. 155, p. 41.

Born to be slaves our fathers freedom sought 498
And born to freedom for our chains we vote.
'Written extempore by a Lady'; in the hand of Lady Mary Wortley Montagu.
MS. Don. c. 56, fol. 36v.

Born to engage all hearts, and charm all eyes 499
Her mind was virtue by the graces dressed.
'On Mrs. Lyttleton. L[ondon] M[agazine] . . . by her Husband'.
MS. Eng. poet. e. 39, p. 195.

Boswell! whose love though past my dearest pride is, 500
Cotswoller's and Motteux's envied death be thine!
Parsons, William, 'Heroic Epistle from Mary Broad (one of the Convicts who made their escape from Botany Bay) to James Boswell'.
MS. *Don. d. 123, p. 201 (autogr.).

Both day and night oh Lord I sent 501
Of me regardless as they're of my woes.
Fairfax, Thomas, Lord, Psalm lxxxviii.
MS. *Fairfax 40, p. 209 (autogr.).
MS. *Fairfax 38, p. 347.

Both fresh and green, the laurel standeth sound, 502
The others like the blasted boughs that die.
Whitney, Geoffrey, 'Murus æneus, sana conscientia'.
MS. *Rawl. poet. 56, fol. 39.

Both God and man a cheerful giver love 503
Receives the wages of a churlish mind.
Williams, John, 'Of Gifts'.
MS. *Rawl. poet. 191, fol. 50 (autogr.).

Both good and evil comes to men 504
Which all men with him undergo.
MS. Rawl. poet. 26, fol. 157v.

Both good and wise, of many thousands one, 505
He chides the bad, and gives the best the prize.
Wyat, William, 'Virgil's Vir bonus'.
MS. Eng. poet. e. 4, p. 155.

506 [Both kind and fortunate the year began]
The great, the good, the just Maria's gone.
Gould, R[obert], 'On the Death of Queen Mary pub: 1695', two extracts.
MS. Eng. poet. c. 9, pp. 219, 223.

507 Both raw in thought and legs between
But hope for something better next.
Borroughs, Benjamin, of Exeter Coll. Oxf., 'An Epistle', 1735.
MS. Eng. misc. e. 240, p. 236.

508 Both *rex* and *grex* do bear each other's sound,
That *dux* bears *crux*, and *crux* not *dux* again.
On the Duke of Buckingham.
MSS. Ashmole 36, 37, fol. 62; see also R185, T1236.

509 Both shores were lost to sight. When at the close
Lay hold, and swim, but while the[y] swim despair.
Dryden, John, 'The Description of a Storm, from [Ovid, *Metamorphoses* xi] beginning Cum Mare sub Noctem'.
Pr. *Fables*, 1700 (Ceyx and Alcyone).
MS. Add. B. 105, fol. 53ᵛ.

510 Both work and strokes: both lash and labour too,
Thou grind'st for sinning: scourg'd for not repenting.
[Quarles, Francis], 'Th' afflicted Mans Complaint'.
Pr. *Emblemes*, 1635, III. iv.
MS. Rawl. poet. 90, fol. 38ᵛ.

511 Bothmar is Father Peters in disguise
Have sent a greater King than you to France.
'On the present Ministry', George I's first ministry, 1714–17.
MSS. Eng. poet. e. 87, p. 54; Firth b. 4, fol. 51; see also A1881, B620.

512 Bought by a suffering God
And to myself no more.
Kenton, James.
MS. *Eng. poet. e. 20, p. 27 (autogr.).

513 Bound with the chains of sin behold the fair
Itself's a diamond of celestial price.
Translation of Latin verses 'De Mariae Magdalae conversione'.
MS. Rawl. poet. 153, fol. 39ᵛ.

514 Bow Albion thy inglorious head in dust
Than those who freed themselves and righted James.
'Albion upbraided'.
MS. Rawl. poet. 155, p. 198; see also B517.

515 Bow down thine ear, oh Lord,
Dost help and comfort me.
Psalm lxxxvi.
MS. *Montagu e. 10, fol. 37.

Bow down thine ear, oh Lord, to my request 516
For which I firmly wait.
Williams, John, Psalm lxxxvi.
MS. *Rawl. poet. 191, fol. 54 (autogr.).

Bow England thy inglorious head in dust 517
Than those that free'd themselves and righted James.
MS. Rawl. poet. 181, fol. 60ᵛ; see also B514.

Boy fetch me my theorbo 518
So all in time may victors prove.
Translation of Latin verse on twin brothers, 'In victorum epulum melos'.
MS. Rawl. D. 1110, fol. 161.

Boys have their gimcracks, those are their joys 519
Ladies have their jewels: they are but the same.
Robinson, Robert, 'Vanitas vanitatum, omne vanitas'.
MS. *Rawl. poet. 218, p. 167 (autogr.).

Brag on old Christ Church, [do not, neither] never fret or [nor] grieve 520
That makes his sabbath less than Holiday.
On *The Marriage of the Arts* by Barten Holiday, Sunday 26 Aug. 1621.
Answered by I812.
MSS. Ashmole 36, 37, fol. 283ᵛ; Douce f. 5, fol. 10ᵛ; Eng. poet. e. 14, fol. 56ᵛ; f. 10, fol. 86ᵛ; Rawl. D. 1048, fol. 61ᵛ.

Brandy, thou cursed spirit sent from Hell, 521
Have nought their thirst t' allay, but brandy left alone.
Chatwin, John, 'A Satyr against Brandy'.
MS. *Rawl. poet. 94, p. 112 (autogr.).

Brasenose I do lament thy fate 522
Look to thy nose, for thou hast lost thy pate.
'On the death of Mr. Pate of Brasenose'.
MS. Rawl. D. 1092, fol. 267ᵛ.

Brave Amazon, though you with greater skill 523
There is no more than does at first appear.
Williams, John, 'To Mrs. Matthews of Hamstead', 24 May 1710.
MS. *Rawl. poet. 192, fol. 155 (autogr.).

Brave bold Brooke whose early death 524
And for an Admiral animate your brother.
'A coppy of Verses writ by a mad Lady of Quality on Capt. Caesar Brooke when Dying'.
MS. Eng. misc. c. 116, fol. 13ᵛ.

Brave boys upon the raging main 525
Like noble sons of England.
'The Briton's Resolution'.
MS. Firth c. 18, fol. 27.

526 **Brave Britons prepare**
**Whilst Popes are the porters of Heaven.**
Hawkins, [Philip (?)], 'A Song', endorsed 'made in the month of Feb. 1745/6'.
MS. Ballard 47, fols. 150 and 169; cf. fol. 157$^{v}$.

527 **Brave Captain Medor wears a chain of gold**
**The guard will sleep and gates fly open wide.**
Davies, Sir John, 'In Medoritem'.
Pr. amongst 'Epigrames' published with *Ouids Elegies*, tr. C. M., [*c.* 1600].
MS. *Add. B. 97, fol. 42.

528 **Brave, grave, admired peer, amongst our peers,**
**The *summum bonum* of eternal bliss.**
'Charles Howard Earle of Nottyngham: Annagrama: O Heauen cal's and Hath true Glory for me'. Inscription on book of Knights of the Garter, 1620.
MS. Bodley 69, fol. 1$^{v}$.

529 **Brave Holland leads, and with him Falkland goes**
**And charge his foes who thought him mad before.**
Waller, Edmund, 'To my Lord of Falkland', February 1639.
Pr. *Poems*, 1645, p. 138.
MSS. *Don. d. 55, fol. 35$^{v}$; Malone 13, p. 63, attr. to Waller; Rawl. poet. 147, p. 77, attr. to Mr. Waller; *Rawl. poet. 174, p. 46.

530 **Brave infant of Saguntum clear**
**Had sowed these fruits, and got the harvest in.**
Jonson, Ben., 'Ode On the death of S$^{r}$. Henry Morison to the noble S$^{r}$ Lucius Cary'.
Pr. *Underwood*, lxx.
MSS. Ashmole 36, 37, fol. 49.

531 **Brave loyal Britons all rejoice**
**At the taking of Carthagena.**
'English Courage Display'd: on Admiral Vernon's taking of Carthagena', 1741.
MS. Firth c. 18, fol. 30.

532 **Brave man of arms whose metal in the field**
**Wish to be spurred at his funeral.**
'On an Herauld'.
MS. CCC. 328, fol. 61$^{v}$.

533 **Brave Mars and mighty Pallas**
**Natt Feild, and Harry Cundy.**
Ballad on a dramatic performance (?) by Burbage, Nat Field, Henry Cundy and Jenninges (*sic* for Heming) at one of the Inns of Court.
MS. Eng. poet. c. 11, fol. 72.

**Brave Nero's favourite, my Julius** 534
**By th' lads whose privilege is to be jolly?**
J. D., translator, Horace, *Epistles* II. ii.
Pr. *Poems of Horace*, A. Brome, 2nd ed. 1671, p. 370.
MS. Rawl. D. 261, p. 93.

**Brave news and tidings here we bring** 535
**Arrive in England, which did glory bring.**
'The Glory of the Northern parts of England', Chester and Lancaster receiving the Prince of Orange.
MS. Firth d. 14, fol. 20.

**Brave news brave news we're out of fears** 536
**Lest hey boys up go we.**
'The Whiggs Cock a Whoop. A new Ballad', *temp.* George I.
MSS. Rawl. poet. 155, p. 195, initialed 'F. G.'; 207, p. 41.

**Brave news from our expedition that sailed away,** 537
**We hope that old England will flourish once more.**
'A New Song on the Taking of Martinico', February 1762.
MS. Firth c. 18, fol. 62.

**Brave Northumberland heroes I pray now attend** 538
**Long life unto Allgood, and Wood my brave boys.**
'A New Song of the gallant Behaviour of the Northumberland Militia, lying at Bridlington, on the appearance of Paul Jones'.
MS. Firth c. 18, fol. 72.

**Brave Prince! although thy fate seem yet too strange** 539
**Left thy example to be general.**
'An Elegy upon the K$^{g}$ of Swedens Death [1632]'.
MS. Malone 21, fol. 7, attr. to Henry King.

**Brave rose, alas where art thou? in the place** 540
**Which falls by night and pour it out for you.**
Herbert, George, 'Church rents or schismes'.
Pr. *The Temple*, 1633, p. 134.
MS. *Tanner 307, fol. 101$^{v}$.

**Brave scene of death! These roses were** 541
**Call this dust royal, that the guards.**
Paman, C[lement], 'On Distilled Roses'.
MS. Rawl. poet. 147, p. 46.

**Brave Young thy grief will make thee old,** 542
**A man may soon non-suit them.**
'Of my L. Chancelor [Bacon]'s retainers. Apr. 1621'.
MS. Rawl. B. 151, fol. 102$^{v}$.

543 **Bravely resolved [brave sparks] great hearts, I see some good**
**Outlives an everlasting Parliament.**
'On the Kentish rising', 1643.
MSS. Rawl. poet. 62, fol. 43$^{v}$; 65, fol. 55, attr. to Guil. Taylor A:B: promus Joann:'; 71, p. 64.

544 **Bravely resolved; you mean the world shall see**
**I'll work you sober, or my self well drunk.**
Weaver, Thomas, 'To certaine gentlemen Prisoners in Manchester, who in a Poem describ'd theyr resolutions to be drunk'.
Pr. in *Songs and Poems by T. W.*, 1654.
MS. *Rawl. poet. 211, fol. 6$^{v}$ (autogr.).

545 **Break sacred morn on our expecting isle**
**As flints are struck, before they show their fires.**
Endorsed 'Mr. [Edmund] Wallers verses uppon the meetinge of the Parlement, 1679 . . . not in his printed works'.
MS. Montagu d. 1, fol. 51.

546 **Break your silence sons of grace**
**Sing salvation to our God.**
Kenton, James.
MS. *Eng. poet. e. 20, p. 235.

547 **Breaking through shades of night the grey eyed morn**
**And bid adieu to thought, and worldly care.**
Bate, Sally, 'Morning. A Poem taken from the Eastern Language versified'. 1760.
MS. *Eng. poet. e. 28, p. 286.

548 **Breathe soft ye winds**
**My love in yonder vale asleep does lie.**
Glee by Gilbert Heathcote, 1787, from Ambrose Philips's *Pastorals.*
MS. Mus. d. 177, fol. 40$^{v}$.

549 **Brethren, by this my mind you'll know**
**Will soon fill up their proper places.**
Mander, John, 'To a Clergyman that read in too much hurry . . . 1741. Corrected and printed in the General Evening post. March 25, 1749'.
MS. Eng. misc. e. 183, fol. 57$^{v}$; see also B606.

550 **Bretton, though thou wert vexed with the rheum**
**For thee, at every word's thou speakest to spit.**
Davis, [Sir] John, of Gray's Inn, 'In Bretton'.
MS. *Rawl. poet. 212, fol. 57$^{v}$ rev.

551 **Bridewell I come, be valiant muse and strip**
**Is not the writer's but the reader's shame.**
'A satire', *temp.* James I.
MS. Eng. poet. c. 50, fol. 30.

**Bright Albion, where the queen of love** 552
**In crimson streams I'll force the red sea flow.**
[Carew, Thomas (?)], on 'the Greene Sickness of Mrs. K[atherine] N[evill]'.
See *Poems*, ed. Rhodes Dunlap, 1949, pp. 194 and 286.
MS. *Don. b. 9, fol. 7$^{v}$.

**Bright Apollo who dost shine** 553
**Go, or creep to Akemanchester.**
James, Henry, of Merton College, 'Bathonia', on the waters of Bath, *temp.* Charles II.
MS. Rawl. poet. 171, fol. 233$^{v}$.

**Bright Cynthia's power divinely great,** 554
**And I shall die with pleasure.**
Cheek, —, 'A song . . . Love a Feast for all the Senses'.
MS. Rawl. poet. 173, fol. 76$^{v}$.

**Bright Dian, queen of chaste delights** 555
**That they may numbered children tell.**
'The Dinner songe', at a wedding, continuing 'Rise, rise fayre Groome'.
MS. Ashmole 38, p. 108.

**Bright Eous, tell thy master** 556
**On earth she gazed, in heaven now shines on thee.**
W. T., on [Mrs. Antonetta Lowr:].
MS. Eng. poet. e. 14, fol. 90 rev.

**Bright goddess, whether Jove thy father be;** 557
**That fetcheth fresh life from her fruitful urn.**
Crashaw, R[ichard], 'Ex Euphormione. O Dea syderei seu tu stirps alma Tonantis etc.'.
See *Poems*, ed. L. C. Martin, 1927, pp. 392 and 457.
MS. Tanner 465, fol. 60$^{v}$; attr. to Mr. Crashaw on fol. 1*a*.

**Bright Lucifer son of the morning star,** 558
**Oh grave where is thy victory?**
'A Hymne Uppon the Resurrection'.
MSS. Add. A. 301, fol. 27$^{v}$ rev.; Rawl. D. 361, fol. 329.

**Bright Sorrell of immortal breed** 559
**The mongrel race of George.**
'Epigram to the Devil'.
MS. Firth b. 4, fol. 51.

560 **Bright soul of whom, if any country known**
**Eternity into one bed.**

[Herbert, George (?)], 'To the Queene of Bohemia', *temp.* her exile in Holland, 1621.

Pr. *Works of Herbert*, ed. F. E. Hutchinson, 1941, amongst 'Doubtful Poems', p. 211, and by H. Huth, *Inedited Poetical Miscellanies*, 1870, Sig. M7v, attr. to G[eorge (?)] H[erbert (?)].

MSS. Eng. poet. c. 50, fol. 60; Firth d. 7, fol. 173; Rawl. poet. 160, fol. 84.

561 **Bright spark shot from a brighter place,**
**And garland streams.**

Herbert, George, 'The Starre'.

Pr. *The Temple*, 1633, p. 65.

MS. *Tanner 307, fol. 50v.

562 **Bright star of beauty, in whose eyelids sit**
**Be you most worthy whilst I am most true.**

Drayton, [Michael], 'Idea 4th'.

MS. Eng. misc. e. 241, fol. 126.

563 **Bright star of majesty, oh shed on me**
**And I'll not blur it with my paraphrase.**

[Crashaw, Richard], 'Upon the birth of the Princesse Elizabeth'.

See *Poems*, ed. L. C. Martin, 1927, pp. lxx, 391, 457.

MS. Tanner 465, fol. 57v; cf. fol. 1*a*.

564 **Bright star thou art, I pity thee thy doom**
**Such stars should fall into the sea of Rome.**

'On Stella a Jesuite, commenting on St. Luke'. Translation from Latin.

MS. Rawl. poet. 246, fol. 18.

565 **Bright Venus with tears lately said to her son.**
**To shoot at fair Chloe a gold-headed dart.**

'Bella mihi video, bella parantur, ait—Ovid', 1735.

MS. Eng. misc. e. 240, p. 335.

566 **Bright virgin of the morn**
**I'll crown ye with the day.**

MS. Rawl. poet. 37, p. 87.

567 **Bright was the morning cool the air,**
**I never shall have rest.**

'A Song'.

MSS. Montagu e. 13, fol. 7; Mus. Sch. G. 460, fol. 37 rev.; Rawl. poet. 196, fol. 19v, attr. to W. Turner.

568 **Brighter than Phoebus in his fine career**
**Borrows all nature, and is nature's right.**

'Countess of Waldegrave' (d. 1807).

MS. Eng. poet. e. 28, p. 31.

**Brightest Cynthia heavenly maid** 569
**Save me from a loathed embrace.**

MS. Mus. c. 107, fol. 51.

**Brilliant are her eyes** 570
**I'd soften every part.**

MS. Eng. poet. d. 152, fol. 95.

**Bring back my comfort and return** 571
**To constancy.**

[Cotton, Charles], subscribed 'Dr. Coleman', who set the song to music.

Copied after 2 July 1651.

Pr. *Poems*, 1689, p. 370.

MS. Rawl. poet. 65, fol. 22.

**Bring, bring us more drink** 572
**Be confounded for ever i'th'dismal Abyssus.**

Chatwin, John, 'Song'.

MS. *Rawl. poet. 94, p. 73 (autogr.).

**Bring forth the pris'ner, Justice: Thy commands** 573
**Th'offended dies, to set th'offender free.**

[Quarles, Francis], 'Another [Dialogue] between Jesus, Justice, and the guilty Sinner'.

Pr. *Emblemes*, 1635, III. x.

MS. Rawl. poet. 90, fol. 100.

**Bring in the bowl, I'll toast an health** 574
**And you'll repent, when 'tis too late.**

'An Health to the tune of Ore the Hills and far away', 1714/15.

MS. Eng. poet. e. 87, p. 163; see also B579.

**Bring me a bottle brisk and true** 575*a*
**While in sheer wit our time we pass.**

Barnes, Joshua, 'Anacreon 57 v. 915'.

MS. Hearne's diaries 11, p. 99.

**Bring me a bowl with fragrant chaplets crowned.** 575*b*
**What 'tis to drink well, and as well to love.**

Chatwin, John, 'The Rapture'.

MS. *Rawl. poet. 94, p. 214 (autogr.).

**Bring me a man whose [with] animating strokes,** 576
**These worst of times, and time itself survive.**

'Advice to the Carver . . . on the execution of Lord Stafford', 29 Dec. 1680.

Pr. *A Collection of 86 Loyal Poems*, 1685, p. 97. See M. T. Osborne, *Advice-to-a-Painter Poems*, 1949, pp. 48–49.

MS. Douce 357, fol. 158; pr. bk. Firth b. 20, fol. 139.

**Bring me quoth one a trowel quickly quick** 577
**Scatter their stuff and tumble down their tools.**

'The tower of babel'.

MS. Eng. misc. b. 21, fol. 6.

578 **Bring the bowl, and cool Nants**
**And drink richer liquor.**
[d'Urfey, Thomas], 'A Punch. Catch. 3 voc. Mr. Pursell', from *The Richmond Heiress*, 1693.
F. B. Zimmerman, *Purcell*, 1963, no. 243.
MS. Mus. Sch. C. 95, p. 99.

579 **Bring the bowl I'll toast a health**
**To over the hills and far away.**
'Scotch song in . . . 1659', 1715.
MS. Rawl. poet. 155, p. 113; pr. bk. Firth b. 22. fol. 17; see also B574.

580 **Brisk brags that he writes billets up and down,**
**But I dare swear none of them write to thee.**
Walsh, William, 'Upon Briske'.
MS. Malone 9, fol. 29 (autogr.).

581 **Brisk Nell t'other day (not suspecting a crime)**
**Cork becomes us much better than lead becomes you.**
Boswell, James, 'Epigram'.
Pr. *A Collection of Original Poems by Scotch Gentlemen*, ii, 1762, p. 70.
MS. *Douce 193, two copies, fols. 32$^v$, 84 (autogr.).

582 **Britain a lovely orchard seemed to be,**
**The Gard'ner catch you, as Moss catcht his mare.**
'An Epigram on the Parliament'.
MS. Rawl. poet. 173, fol. 106$^v$, attr. to Mr. Cleveland.

583 **Britain! attend the warning voice,**
**Nor love the doom revoke.**
'Occasion'd by the late Earthquake. G[entleman's] M[agazine]'.
MS. Eng. poet. e. 39, p. 199.

584 **Britain be glad, Rome, though thy foe**
**To give to him, by whom we live in peace.**
Flower, —, 'An Ode' on the Gunpowder Plot.
MS. Tanner 306, fol. 422.

585 **Britain has rivers which regale the view**
**And nothing droops, but most ingenious art.**
[Lepipre, Gabriel (?)], 'Britain Epitomiz'd in Imitation of Milton, 1747'.
MS. Eng. poet. e. 40, fol. 84, in Lepipre's hand.

586 **Britain, how canst thou France's pride control**
**And full reform her own.**
Roach, Richard, 'France Supplanted . . . Written in the Time of War with France', i.e. before the Peace of Utrecht, 31 March 1713.
MS. Rawl. D. 832, fol. 218 (autogr.).

**Britain like carrier's horse trussed up with pack** 587
**This beast his drudge; if once he slip,—God b'ye.**
Bulteel, John, 'A Tyr'd Jade'.
MS. *Rawl. poet. 159, fol. 206$^v$.

**Britain no more her Chatham's loss deplores** 588
**The son alone the rival of his sire.**
Pitt, Thomas, 1st Baron Camelford, on the younger William Pitt, 1783 (?).
MS. Eng. lett. d. 84, fol. 144 (autogr.).

**Britain once famed through many a distant region** 589
**She loves the Stuarts and reveres the name.**
'The State of great Brittain', *temp.* George I.
MS. Rawl. poet. 155, p. 94.

**Britain! the mighty ocean's lovely bride!** 590
**This rural wreath dares be thy sacrifice.**
Cr[ashaw] R[ichard], 'A Panegyrick. Upon the birth of the Duke of Yorke'.
MS. Tanner 465, fol. 56; cf. fol. 1*a*.

**Britain with Greece and Rome contended long** 591
**For Pope has fix'd it to his native shore.**
'The Triumvirate of Poets'.
MS. Eng. misc. e. 183, fol. 69$^v$.

**Britannia mourn lament thy sinking state** 592
**Long live great James our true and lawful king.**
'A Poem', on George I.
MS. Rawl. poet. 155, p. 27.

**Britannia sees brave William shine** 593
**To George's glory William's praise.**
'Song, 1746'.
Pr. bk. Firth b. 22, fol. 48.

**Britannia wake! to glory's brightest ray** 594
**Britannia's leading star.**
'Ode to General [George Augustus] Elliott, 1784', music by Philip Hayes. Composer's autograph.
MS. Mus. d. 65, fol. 2.

**Britons awake, old England begs your aid** 595
**And James the third his own retrieved had.**
'Upon the standing Army'.
MS. Rawl. poet. 181, fol. 65$^v$.

**Britons commemorate** 596
**Daily increase!**
Allen, —, Rector of Spernall, 'To the Tune of "God Save Great George our King"', on the battle of Culloden, 16 Apr. 1746.
MS. Ballard 47, fol. 149.

**Britons in praise as you in glory rise** 597
**But live and sully twenty-ninths of May.**
'On the Returne of his Majestie King George to the British Throne'.
MS. Rawl. poet. 89, fol. 3.

598 **Britons now let us regret**
**Is James our faith's defender.**
'Britains woful Condition', *temp.* George I.
MS. Rawl. poet. 155, p. 108.

599 **Britons, once so famed in story**
**Rouse to virtue, wake to art.**
'A song for New-years day from a New's Paper'.
MS. Eng. poet. c. 5, fol. 27.

600 **Britons shake off the gloomy veil**
**From their devouring cursed Nero.**
'Copy of verses . . . in Charles the 2nd time'.
MS. Top. Oxon. b. 116, fol. 111.

601 **Broad o'er the bosom of the atmosphere**
**And with a learned friend there pass the sultry hours.**
Stott, Thomas, 'The Dog-day'.
MS. Percy c. 8, fol. 189 (autogr.).

602 **Broken in pieces, all asunder,**
**Till I reach heaven, and much more, Thee.**
Herbert, George, 'Affliction'.
Pr. *The Temple*, 1633, p. 82.
MS. *Tanner 307, fol. 62.

603 **Broker, and usurer, like the fox and cub:**
**This shall be Mammon and that Beelzebub.**
Couplet.
MS. Sancroft 53, p. 367 rev.

604 **Brother in arts and arms renowned**
**And drag truth from the deepest well.**
Gough, Richard, 'Addressed to Edward Haistwell on his election to . . . the Soc. of Antiquaries in 1768. May 2'.
MS. *Eng. poet. c. 5, fol. 142.

605 **Brother soldier do you hear of the news**
**I return them abundance of thanks.**
'The Soldiers' Complaint'.
MSS. Firth c. 17, fol. 57; c. 20, fol. 37.

606 **Brother, this comes to let you know,**
**Will soon fill up their proper places.**
'To a Clergyman that preach'd in a careless Hurry'; written before 29 Aug. 1741.
MS. Ballard 29, fol. 66; see also B549.

607 **Brothers in more than civil wars engage**
**And each his fate that he was conquered too.**
Wilmott, —, translation of 'An Epigram [by W. Alabaster] on two Brothers one a Papist the other a Protestant . . . vid. [J. Chamberlayne's] the Present State of Great Britain p. 164'.
MS. Ballard 47, fol. 48$^{v}$.

**Brothers, sisters should agree** 608
**They should love and never jar.**
Lines written on the margin of a copy of a letter from Lady Suzan Caesar to Lady Lake.
MS. Don. c. 54, fol. 1*b*.

**Brought forth in sorrow, and bred up in care** 609
**By taking this inheritance of dust.**
King, Henry, 'On two Children dying of one Disease, and buryed in one Grave'.
Pr. *Poems*, 1657, p. 60.
MSS. *Eng. poet. e. 30, fol. 31; *Malone 22, fol. 21.

**Brought on by lust to view thy face** 610
**But far more pity that one so pretty should play the whore.**
MS. Ashmole 47, fol. 74$^{v}$.

**Brought through all my tribulation** 611
**'Stablish thy dominion here.**
Kenton, James.
MS. *Eng. poet. e. 20, p. 372 (autogr.).

**Brown as a berry a perfect maid** 612
**Danced as she would the garland win.**
MS. Rawl. D. 859, fol. 97.

**Brown lies here the maker of bellows** 613
**That he that made bellows could not make breath.**
'Uppon a bellowes-maker'.
MS. Douce f. 5, two copies, fols. 10, 15; see also H783, H846, H848, H1000, H1019, H1026, H1034.

**Brows bending quaintly your round ebony arks** 614
**Mistook his Venus hither hies.**
MS. Rawl. poet. 142, fol. 26$^{v}$.

**Brunus which thinks himself a fair sweet youth** 615
**At Trolops by St. Clements Church in pawn.**
Davies, Sir John, 'In Brunum'.
Pr. amongst 'Epigrames' with *Ouids Elegies*, tr. C. M., *c.* 1600.
MSS. *Add. B. 97, fol. 45; *Rawl. poet. 212, fol. 64$^{v}$ rev.

**Brutus that all religion does despise** 616
**That if they do no good, they do no hurt.**
Walsh, William, 'On Brutus'.
MS. Malone 9, fol. 40$^{v}$ (autogr.).

**Bully do not grieve in vain** 617
**That out-scolds the Adrian wave.**
Polwhele, John, translation of Horace, *Odes* I. xxxiii.
MS. *Eng. poet. f. 16, fol. 58$^{v}$ (autogr.).

618 **Bunnings, Polings, Stemples, forks, and slider**
**Sole of the Rake Smitham and many more.**
'Rhyme on terms used' by Edward Manlove in *Liberties and Customs of Leadmines*, 1653.
MS. Ashmole 816, fol. 33$^{v}$.

619 **Burnet for ever has [hath] the Whigs forsook**
**Be the region light or dark.**
'On Burnet and Wharton'. Jacobite verses, 1715.
MSS. Eng. poet. e. 87, p. 18; Rawl. poet. 155, p. 111; 181, fol. 70$^{v}$.

620 **Burnet is Father Peters in disguise**
**That sent a better king than thee to France.**
'A Friendly Caution' to George I.
MS. Rawl. poet. 155, p. 31; see also A1881, B511.

621 **Burnet to heaven's [Burnet's to heaven] gone if Whigs go thither**
**If non-resistance be the Holy Ghost.**
'Bishop Burnett's Funeral Ticket', 1715.
MS. Rawl. poet. 155, p. 149; pr. bk. Firth b. 22, fol. 17.

622 **Burst forth my tears assist my forward grief**
**That both the shepherd kills, and his poor flocks.**
Pr. Dowland's *Songs or Ayres*, 1597, viii.
MSS. Mus. f. 7–10: f. 7, fol. 11$^{v}$.

623 **Burthen'd with care, o'erwhelm'd with flowing grief,**
**For grief let us with him together die!**
Twyman, Ant[hony], 'On the . . . Death of Mr. T. M.'
MS. Rawl. D. 360, fol. 106.

624 **Busy curious thirsty fly.**
**Will appear as short as one.**
Oldys, William, 'The fly'.
Pr. *Scarborough Miscellany*, 1732, p. 15.
MS. Eng. misc. b. 48, fol. 44.

625 **Busy inquiring heart, what wouldst thou know?**
**My God hath promis'd; he is just.**
Herbert, George, 'The Discharge'.
Pr. *The Temple*, 1633, p. 138.
MS. *Tanner 307, fol. 105.

626 **Busy old fool, unruly sun,**
**This bed thy centre is, these walls thy sphere.**
Donne, John, 'Ad solem'.
Pr. *Poems*, 1633.
MSS. *Eng. poet. e. 99, fol. 105; *f. 9, p. 70.

627 **But ah! this night, adieu the mirthful mien**
**But live the proudest feeling of her heart.**
'Lines spoken by Mr. Wroughton on Miss Farren quitting the stage', 1797.
MS. Percy d. 9, fol. 81$^{v}$.

**But all this while I fear a spice of pride;** 628
**Our Christian burial to a pagan urn.**
Oldisworth, Nicolas, 'To a Separatist'.
MS. *Don. c. 24, fol. 16$^{v}$ (autogr.).

**But am I sure he's dead? whom yet I see** 629
**Write you this epitaph: 'here lies Grayes Inn'.**
Lewis, William, 'On Dr. [Roger] Fenton of Grayes Inn', d. Jan. 1615/16.
MSS. CCC. 327, fol. 13$^{v}$, attr. to Lewis; Eng. poet. e. 97, p. 79; Rawl. poet. 117, fol. 198 rev., attr. to W. Lewis; 209, fol. 6$^{v}$.

**But are you Calax, and your gentle bride** 630
**In fire the Phoenix takes, and leaves its breath.**
Hacket, John, 'A Pastorall Epithalamine eglogue', on Sir John Hare and Elizabeth, daughter of Lord Keeper Thomas Coventry, 1620.
MSS. Malone 19, p. 67; Rawl. poet. 26, fol. 73$^{v}$, attr. to Dr. Hacket.

**But art thou come, dear Saviour: hath thy love** 631
**Will make a stall a court: a cratch a throne.**
[Hale, Sir Matthew], 'A Poem upon Christmas Day'.
MS. Rawl. poet. 90, fol. 164; see also A1242.

**But Dido, who love's hook long since had caught** 632
**Heat left her, and th' uncaged soul flew through the air.**
Fanshawe, Sir Richard, translator, 'The Loves of Dido, and Æneas', Virgil, *Æneid* iv.
MS. *Firth c. 1, fol. 1.

**But doubtless that which most, Adam and Eve** 633–4
**They hid them in the garden 'mong the trees.**
MS. *Rawl. poet. 97, fol. 7 (autogr.).

**But hark what hear I in the heavens? methinks** 635
**Had need for counters take the ocean sand.**
'A discription of Thunder'.
MS. Eng. poet. e. 14, fol. 86$^{v}$ rev.

**But he might have replied, Good wife you mock,** 636–7
**Will do it if it open lie to all.**
[Davies, John of Hereford,] reply to A526.
Pr. *Wits Bedlam*, 1617, Sig. B5.
MS. Eng. poet. f. 25, fol. 15$^{v}$.

**But here alone to sigh and moan** 638
**And put me from my pain.**
MS. Ashmole 208, fol. 249$^{v}$.

**But hold my muse! you're now too rig'rous grown.** 639
**Those necessary creatures which the pow'rs divine have sent.**
Chatwin, John, 'A Counter-counter-Satyr'.
MS. *Rawl. poet. 94, p. 43 (autogr.).

640 But I a better surety have
And save me for his sake alone.

Kenton, James.
MS. *Eng. poet. e. 20, p. 13 (autogr.).

641 But I entreat them since cares must befall
'Tis an old saying, care will kill a cat.

[Newman, Thomas], 'Of Sorrow: satyr'.
MS. Top. Oxon. f. 39, fol. 22 (autogr.).

642 But if there's nothing that can slack
And spare me for complexion.

'Dr. Hoskin on the fleas which vext him'.
MS. Lat. misc. c. 19, p. 424.

643 But if those graces we together see
Not knowing which to choose they set us free.

'The picture of Miss Kitty Gunning'.
MS. Firth b. 4, fol. 53.

644 But if you think I jest you ask my wife
If e'er she heard such gibberish in her life.

[Newman, Thomas], 'Irish speech, a distick'.
MS. Top. Oxon. f. 39, fol. 23 (autogr.).

645 But in the glorious gospel day
And oh, my Lord, may I be one.

Kenton, James.
MS. *Eng. poet. e. 20, p. 90 (autogr.).

646 But is it true, the court misliked the play,
All that which they want brain to comprehend.

King, Henry, 'To his Freinds of Christ Church upon the mislike of the Marriage of the Artes, acted at Woodstock'.
Pr. *Poems*, 1657, p. 22.
MSS. *Eng. poet. e. 30, fol. 35; *Malone 22, fol. 24$^{v}$.

647 But Jesus died my soul to save
To worship Thee above.

Kenton, James.
MS. *Eng. poet. e. 20, p. 82 (autogr.).

648 But Jesus our almighty king
And feast with Him forever there.

Kenton, James.
MS. *Eng. poet. e. 20, p. 55 (autogr.).

649 But Jesus our triumphant head
And everlasting rest.

Kenton, James.
MS. *Eng. poet. e. 20, p. 20 (autogr.).

650 But Judah's true eternal son
And gain the everlasting prize.

Kenton, James.
MS. Eng. poet. e. 20, p. 125 (autogr.).

But let her be of count'nance ne'er so fair 651
Her maids do laughing run and cry, 'oh foh there'.

'Translation from Lucretius, iv.'
MS. Eng. poet. e. 57, fol. 17$^{v}$.

But neither Median groves, whose happy soil 652
And your just praise in lasting numbers sing.

Chetwood, Knightly, translator, 'The Praises of Italy', from Virgil, *Georgics* ii.
MS. Rawl. poet. 173, fol. 24.

But now heaven comes home again, the same 653
Complete and meet the equal skies.

Beaumont, Joseph, of Peterhouse, 'Whit-Sunday'.
MS. Rawl. poet. 62, fol. 17$^{v}$.

But now, let our prayers grow a little more civil 654
And desert the dull crowned corn'd Statholder!

'The Second Part' of F785.
MS. Firth e. 6, fol. 13$^{v}$.

But of our quaffing while the cup goeth out 655
Where all's drunk all, no strife can be at all.

4 lines at the end of a verse translation of *Apocalypsis Goliæ Episcopi*.
MS. Bodl. 538, fol. 61*b*$^{v}$.

But oh look here; for I have surely found 656
As we in this age scorn to be without them.

'Imbecillitas'.
MS. Rawl. poet. 174, p. 99.

But oh the god of gods, that heaven sways, 657
Acted this tragi-comedy.

Polwhele, John, translator, 'Horace Epod. the 5th agaynst the Witch Canidia'.
MS. *Eng. poet. f. 16, fol. 60 (autogr.).

But one at once, I may not take more, 658
By one at once I may have half a score.

Williams, John.
MS. *Rawl. poet. 191, fol. 92$^{v}$ (autogr.).

But one that is a friend much more may do 659
Or with affection lay aside the name.

Williams, John.
MS. *Rawl. poet. 191, fol. 154 (autogr.).

But punishment like lightning should appear 660
To few men's hurt, but unto all men's fear.

Couplet.
MS. Rawl. poet. 117, fol. 275 rev.

But say thou very woman; why to me 661
I shall find ten as fair, and yet more true.

King, Henry, 'To his Unconstant Freind'.
Pr. *Poems*, 1657, p. 32.
MSS. *Eng. poet. e. 30, fol. 13; *Malone 22, fol. 8$^{v}$.

662 But see she comes: bright lamp o'th' sky
In veneration of her brow.
MS. Rawl. poet. 142, fol. 16.

663 But shall my soul no wealth possess,
His ancient ways, are His and my estate.
Traherne, Thomas, 'The Estate'.
MS. *Eng. poet. c. 42, fol. 9*a*ᵛ (autogr.).

664 But Sir I am compelled to take care
With them, Sir, there, they, both, may kindly greet.
Woode, Andrew, 'To the right worshipful, Peter Venables, Esq., Baron of Kinderton', 1642.
MSS. Ashmole 36, 37, fol. 272 (autogr.).

665 But soft, what white is that which I espy
All my desire, is, thou would'st keep my dust.
[Heylin, Peter], 'On his return to England', 1625.
Pr. *A full relation of his Journeys*, 1656, p. 275.
MS. Eng. misc. e. 178, p. 407.

666 But stay nature hath overwrought my art
So a revolt of hers procure it not.
MS. Rawl. poet. 116, fol. 54ᵛ.

667 But stay! What smell is this so near the graves?
And live two lives, where others live but one.
Clarke, John, on Samuel Clarke's *English Martyrologie*, 1652.
MS. Rawl. poet. 65, fol. 68.

668 But that (great president of this fair round)
Brag of the better, and the worser smother.
North, Dudley, 3rd Baron.
Pr. *A Forest of Varieties*, 1645.
MS. *North e. 41, fol. 42.

669 But that I forth advise (if any need
My constant mind, I will prepare myself.
Translation from Horace, *Epistles* I. xviii.
MS. Rawl. poet. 31, fol. 16ᵛ.

670 But that thou art my wisdom, Lord,
Since thou hast both mine eyes.
Herbert, George, 'Submission'.
Pr. *The Temple*, 1633, p. 87.
MS. *Tanner 307, fol. 66.

671 But that which most I wonder at, which most
I must become a child again.
Traherne, Thomas, 'Innocence'.
MS. *Eng. poet. c. 42, fol. 4 (autogr.).

672 But the best music far more sweet than honey
Is when a man's own purse jingles with money.
Couplet.
MS. Rawl. D. 1372, fol. 24ᵛ.

But the unceasing priesthood 673
Triumphantly we enter.
Kenton, James.
MS. *Eng. poet. e. 20, p. 96 (autogr.).

But their heads some stone bare up, their brawny sides 674
But add withal he's slothful and unjust.
MS. Rawl. poet. 172, fol. ii.

But this disdain could not yet move 675
Upon her bosom dropped his drooping head.
Locke, John, continuation of S118.
MS. Locke c. 32, fol. 21 (autogr.).

But Thou thy wrath will turn away 676
For his dear sake alone.
Kenton, James.
MS. *Eng. poet. e. 20, p. 154 (autogr.).

But t'other day my friend i'th'way 677
Of me and thee't will so be said.
Robinson, Robert.
MS. *Rawl. poet. 218, p. 92 (autogr.).

But two souls innocent on earth, and they 678
Are of ourselves propense to fail and fall.
MS. *Rawl. poet. 97, fol. 12ᵛ (autogr.).

But two souls reasonable and righteous made 679
He could have ate it then that did it break.
MS. *Rawl. poet. 97, fol. 11 (autogr.).

But we another language speak 680
And rebels to his arms receives.
Kenton, James.
MS. *Eng. poet. e. 20, p. 385 (autogr.).

But we find all altered, now, and the due 681
Without *quid dabis*? nothing can be had.
Newman, Thomas.
MS. Top. Oxon. f. 39, fol. 22 (autogr.).

But we through grace the truth receive 682
In consummate eternal bliss.
Kenton, James.
MS. *Eng. poet. e. 20, p. 293 (autogr.).

But what is it wherein Dame Nature wrought 683
To join with nature's framing God 'tis woman.
On Elizabeth Pordage, 9 November, 1687, Waltham Abbey Church.
MS. Rawl. D. 682, fol. 66.

But when alas men come to die 684–5
The stroke the very moment it does kill.
'In favour of temperance'.
MS. Rawl. D. 361, fol. 266.

686 But wherefore all this pother about fame
The author's friend, most humble servant, and...
Buckingham, [George Villiers, Duke of], on two verses from Howard's *British Princes*.
Pr. Dryden's *Miscellany Poems*, 1716, iii. 74.
MS. Eng. poet. e. 4, p. 197.

687 But why this fury? All that e'er was writ,
Houses blown up have stopped a fire's course.
'A Satyr. Ignis Ignibus extinguitur, 1682'.
MS. Firth c. 15, p. 133.

688 But will you [now to] unto peace incline
We'll have the spoil at last.
[Denham, John], 'Mr. Hampden's speech against Peace', 23 March 1643.
Pr. broadside, 1643, and in *Rump*, 1662.
MSS. Ashmole 36, 37, fol. 71; Douce 357, fol. 38v.

689 But you who whiles you would to heaven aspire
But by that monarch whom the north brought forth.
'To the king in his just arms to suppress the late rebellious practices in Scotland 1640'.
MSS. Ashmole 36, 37, fol. 101; Top. Cheshire c. 6, fol. 190.

690 Butler and baker banished Pharaoh's court
Yet Joseph left i'th'stocks, and not reliev'd.
'The Interpreter'.
MS. Rawl. poet. 154, fol. 103.

691 Buxton, the glory of the Peakish wells
So was the old name lost, and new one won.
[Lepipre, Gabriel (?)], 'writ at Buxton Wells in Derbyshire, 1747'.
MS. Eng. poet. e. 40, fol. 21, in Lepipre's hand.

692 Buy time and keep it, thou shalt surely see,
No gem so precious in this world can be.
Robinson, Robert, couplet.
MS. *Rawl. poet. 218, p. 16 (autogr.).

693 By a bank as I lay
Derry cum derry cum dan.
'Extracted from the broken plainsong' from B.M. MS. Reg. Append. 58.
MS. Mus. d. 184, fol. 25.

694 By a bold people's stubborn arms oppressed
And on an open stage unburied lie.
'Mr. C.', 'Charles the Ist pricking . . . in Virgill hapned on the ensuing lines Æneid: lib. 4. *At bello audacis populi vexatus* etc.'
MS. Eng. poet. d. 53, p. 4.

By a cool fountain's flowery side 695
To share a death like thine.
'The Bee. a Song'.
MS. Top. London e. 9, p. 154.

By a cruel brother slain 696
We behold him face to face.
Kenton, James.
MS. *Eng. poet. e. 20, p. 237 (autogr.).

By a few seeds, that sown are in the earth, 697
Man's spirit by letters' product is sustained.
Robinson, Robert.
MS. *Rawl. poet. 218, p. 98 (autogr.).

By Adam in the dust I lie 698
By Christ I have the victory.
Epitaph on Susan, wife of John Ricard, town-clerk of Ludlow, 1640.
MS. Top. gen. e. 1, p. 79.

By all that hath been said it doth appear 699
These thoughts ensuing God infused in me.
MS. *Rawl. poet. 97, fol. 67v (autogr.).

By all the gods of Hellespont and Greece 700
I love thee better, than the Welshman cheese.
Couplet.
MS. Rawl. poet. 153, fol. 20v.

By all thy glories willingly I go 701
Whilst you are fair he loves himself, not you.
Champneys, H.
MS. Malone 13, p. 99.

By an eternal and a statute-law 702
Which being banished now at death, returneth nearer.
'The Markett'.
MS. Eng. poet. e. 51, p. 49.

By Babel's brooks we sit and weep 703
Shall brain and slay your little babbs.
Harington, Sir John, Psalm cxxxvii.
MS. *Douce 361, fol. 85.

By Babylon's great rivers we 704
Thy children against stones.
Psalm cxxxvii.
MS. *Rawl. C. 113, fol. 97 (autogr.).

By birth a Greenvill, and that name 705
A while to stay, and weep for her.
On Mrs. Bridget Weeks, Bristol Cathedral, 17th cent.
MS. Rawl. D. 1090, fol. 118v.

By Caroline's command does Rysbrack engage 706
My muse wisely resolves not to hazard her ears.
'On the figures in Merlin's Cave', 1735.
MS. Eng. misc. e. 240, p. 336.

707 By Christ th' eternal word, were all things framed
We from God's love in our redeemer have.
MS. *Rawl. poet. 97, fol. 19v (autogr.).

708 By closest ties of love divine
Wrapp'd up in love's divine embrace.
Kenton, James.
MS. *Eng. poet. e. 20, p. 43 (autogr.).

709 By conscious genius rais'd above the crowd
That if we do not eat, we cannot hear!
Parsons, William, 'To a poet in love with his cook-maid'.
Pr. *Travelling Recreations*, 1807, i. 7.
MS. *Don. d. 123, p. 91 (autogr.).

710 By craft of Lucifer, and spite of hell
Which surely [ ] own heart was made.
Lines against *The Craftsman.*
MS. Rawl. D. 833, fol. 192.

711 By Danae's progeny, the Fates decreed
He conquers all who conquers Jove.
'Danae, A Cantata'.
MS. Mus. c. 3, fol. 76.

712 By drunken heat urg'd on some puny god
And will be so in spite of heav'n, by G——.
Chatwin, John, 'Tompsonius Reiteratus'.
MS. *Rawl. poet. 94, p. 16 (autogr.).

713 By England's true monarchs, great William and Mary
That usurpers and rebels may ne'r get the day.
'The Proclamation for a General Fast'.
MS. Firth e. 6, fol. 27.

714 By Euphrates' flow'ry side
With their brains and blood besmearing.
[Davison, Francis (?)], 'Psalm 137'.
Pr. Donne's *Poems*, ed. Grierson, 1912, i. 424.
MSS. Eng. misc. e. 13, fol. 10, attr. to John Donne; Rawl. poet. 61, fol. 62, attr. to Fr[ancis] Da[vison]; 117, fol. 267 rev., attr. to D. Donne; Tanner 466, fol. 17, attr. to Dr. Donne.

715 By Euphrates we captives sat lamenting
Our harps we hang'd on willow trees there growing.
Transcript with music.
MS. Mus. d. 195, fol. 17 rev.

716 By fancy looks the eye aside
By due that is not his.
Used as a copy by Wiman Ramsey, *c.* 1595.
MS. Rawl. D. 649, fol. 27.

717 By fortune not by nature I am sad
Sad, mad, and merry, is a woman's vein.
MS. Ashmole 38, p. 132.

By hands forced down, of tenderness deprived 718
With me to make such churlish physic stay.
Williams, John, 'To a Lady that said bitter things are wholsome'.
MS. *Rawl. poet. 191, fol. 86 (autogr.).

By heav'n and all its gods I swear 719
They all depend on that alone.
Oldham, John, 'A Rant to his Mistress . . . 1676'.
MS. *Rawl. poet. 123, p. 228 (autogr.).

By heaven, by earth, by sea, by all, I swear 720
But, with your healing smiles, abate my pain.
Morrice, John, 'The Protestation'.
MS. *Rawl. poet. 114, fol. 212 (autogr.).

By Heav'n! Dear Sylvia, now unkind you prove, 721
As burning-glasses through long mediums centre light.
Chatwin, John, 'To Sylvia who accus'd him of inconstancy'.
MS. *Rawl. poet. 94, p. 216 (autogr.).

By hell 'twas bravely done! what less then this? 722
Or what his father is —.
Oldham, John, 'Garnet's Ghost'.
Draft for the first 'Satyr Upon the Jesuits'.
MS. *Rawl. poet. 123, p. 244 (autogr.).

By help of saints come let our tongues relate 723
May everlasting praise repay.
'English Primer of our Ladie. 1631 . . . p. 33'.
MS. Eng. poet. e. 56, p. 56.

By his industrious providence and merit, 724
A good repute and precious memory he's gained.
Epitaph on James Greenewood in Darrington Church, 13 Oct. 1670.
MS. Top. Yorks. c. 26, two copies, fols. 129v and 131.

By Israel's paschal lamb was typified 725
And clear of hands in heaven alone have part.
MS. *Rawl. poet. 97, fol. 25v (autogr.).

By lawful mart and by unlawful stealth 726
Wherein he drowneth all that wealth of his.
Davies, Sir John, 'In Paulum'.
Pr. amongst 'Epigrames', with *Ovids Elegies*, tr. C. M. [*c.* 1600].
MSS. *Add. B. 97, fol. 46; *Rawl. poet. 212, fol. 65 rev.

By learned books a witty head 727
Makes not a blockhead wise.
Robinson, Robert.
MS. *Rawl. poet. 218, p. 69 (autogr.).

728 By lease without writing one once let a farm
Else without writing you cannot let a fart.

'Haywards Rent'.
Pr. *A Helpe to Discourse*, 1623; cf. *N. & Q.* ccvi, 1961, p. 426.
MS. Don. d. 58, fol. 34v.

729 By lip love, and by tongue pretending piety,
Man loves his neighbour, and doth serve the deity.

Robinson, Robert, couplet.
MS. *Rawl. poet. 218, p. 28 (autogr.).

730 By milk white doves as drawn of old
As Venus is by Hyde.

'On the Lady Catherine Hyde's Picture drawn by Sr. Godfrey Kneller'.
MS. Rawl. poet. 116, fol. 106.

731 By miracles exceeding power of man
Moist with one drop of thy blood, my dry soul.

Donne, John, 'Holy Sonnetts. La Corona. 5'.
Pr. *Poems*, 1633.
MS. *Eng. poet. e. 99, fol. 42v.

732 By my elder brother known
My saviour, brother, friend.

Kenton, James.
MS. *Eng. poet. e. 20, p. 323 (autogr.).

733 By nature, Lord, men worse than nothing be:
Where is that something, thou so boasts, proud man.

[Quarles, Francis], 'On Man'.
Pr. *Divine Fancies*, 1632, ii. 15.
MS. Rawl. poet. 90, fol. 66.

734 By nature meant, by want a pedant made
To give us drenches for the plague of wit.

Lampoon on Richard Blackmore.
MS. Ballard 20, fol. 47.

735 By nature prone to ill
My heart to follow thee.

Kenton, James.
MS. *Eng. poet. e. 20, p. 78 (autogr.).

736 By nature we are apt t'extenuate
Much less can now depraved wretched we!

MS. *Rawl. poet. 97, fol. 15 (autogr.).

737 By nature womankind was born to please
She drowns all pleasure but the wealth she brings.

'The Progress of Love'.
MSS. Eng. misc. e. 183, fol. 14v; Eng. poet. f. 12, p. 90.

738 By nature's course 't has been of common use
If love gets hate, then hate her, and she'll love.

'Love Cross-graind'.
MS. Rawl. poet. 173, fol. 89v.

By numbers rational (our wise clerks say) 739
Frailt' in loose prose: in verse perfection moves.

'On the praise of Verse, above prose'.
MS. Eng. poet. e. 97, two copies, pp. 1*a* and 2*a*, attr. to Randolph on p. 338.

By our first strange and fatal interview 740
Think it enough for me, t'have had thy love.

Donne, John, Elegy XVI.
First pr. *Poems*, 1635.
MSS. Eng. poet. e. 14, fol. 32v, attr. to D. Dun; *e. 99, fol. 21; *f. 9, p. 126, attr. to J. D.; Rawl. poet. 117, fol. 219v rev.

By our past joys it must not be 741
In my as much as much fixed love.

MS. Rawl. poet. 196, two copies, fols. 39v and 41.

By our pastor perplexed 742
Go to sleep, says the sermon.

'Epigram'.
MS. Eng. poet. c. 51, p. 89.

By Ovid 'mong many more wonders we're told 743
Now there's meat without grace, where was grace without meat.

Whitehead, Paul, 'On Lord Doneraile's altering his Chappel at Grove into a Kitchen'.
Pr. *Poems*, 1777, p. 172, and in *Works of Sir Charles Hanbury Williams*, ed. Horace Walpole, 1822, ii. 36.
MS. Eng. poet. d. 10, fol. 40.

By parents' care instructed to feed poultry 744
Pollux procur'd for her in heaven a place.

MS. Douce 357, fol. 143v.

By point of knife died both the twins; 745
Did end their woeful life.

Powle, Stephen, translation of Latin 'Devil's verses'.
MS. Tanner 169, fol. 145.

By rig'rous fate, though learned, pious, fair! 746
'Tis thine in heav'nly harmony to dwell!

Russell, George, translator, 'A Lamentation for . . . Mrs. K. Killigrew', d. Dec. 1583, 'by her Sister, Lady Eliz[abeth Russell]'; Latin version pr. Stow's *Survey of London*, 1633, p. 259.
MS. Ballard 37, fol. 135v (autogr.).

By sea and land etc. 747

'Philomathes', 1667, 'On the sad spectacle of the Cathedral on fire'. First words quoted with ref. to p. 63 of a 4° book. From the Greek of St. Gregory Nazianzen.
MS. Eng. th. d. 52, fol. 4.

748 By something form'd I nothing am
Then prithee tell me what am I.
'A Riddle'.
MS. Eng. poet. e. 8, fol. 16.

749 By sportive youth and busy manhood blest,
That holds a Christian worthy of his God.
On William Bryant, 1779, Eartham Church Yard, Sussex.
MS. Top. gen. e. 32, fol. 117.

750 By sudden fate, lo! Jane is mix'd with earth!
And, dying, seal'd religion with her blood.
Russell, George, translation of 'verses relating to Lady Jane Grey'.
MS. Ballard 37, fol. 135 (autogr.).

751 By swallows note, the spring we understand
How seasons change, and times do come and go.
Whitney, Geoffrey, 'In quatuor anni tempora'.
MS. *Rawl. poet. 56, fol. 31.

752 By sweet magic drawn away
Till she smile—and all is gay!
Parsons, William.
MS. *Don. d. 123, p. 35 (autogr.).

753 By the beer as brown as berry
True blue will never stain.
MS. Mus. c. 107, fol. 27.

754 By the border's side as I did pass
And through the birks and a'.
Ballad, partly in border dialect, with a tune.
MSS. Ashmole 36, 37, fol. 116.

755 By the fair hands of this fair maid
Is in plain English, honest Will.
Plaxton, William, 'An Epistle to Dr. [Thomas] Brett . . . 1732'.
MS. Add. D. 79, fol. 89 rev.

756 By the grey groat I swear and by the mass
With all my heart I love a lusty man.
'Man speaks', answered by 'Woman speaks'.
MS. Malone 19, p. 154.

757 By the odour of Thy name
While eternal ages roll.
Kenton, James.
MS. *Eng. poet. e. 20, p. 99 (autogr.).

758 By the same means that Satan misery
And person; but him thereby to exalt.
MS. *Rawl. poet. 97, fol. 3 (autogr.).

759 By the side of a glimmering fire
Stares wishfully over the pew.
'A Song'.
MS. Montagu e. 13, fol. 33*a*.

By the side of a murmuring stream, 760
Shall pleasantly glide o'er the green.
'A Song'.
MS. Montagu e. 13, fol. 27.

By the still-streams of Babylon 761
And dash 'gainst stones, their brains and blood.
Jos. Br., Psalm cxxxvii.
MS. Rawl. poet. 61, fol. 60ᵛ.

By the sweet attracting grace 762
Till I all his goodness know.
Kenton, James.
MS. *Eng. poet. e. 20, p. 361 (autogr.).

By the two rosy blushes that did move 763
I'll centre all my joys cloister my bliss.
[Jordan, Thomas], 'A Vow to His Mrs.'
Pr. *Poeticall Varieties*, 1637, p. 16.
MS. Rawl. poet. 142, fol. 16.

By the unerring Spirit's power 764
On earth below, in heaven above.
Kenton, James.
MS. *Eng. poet. e. 20, p. 386 (autogr.).

By the years of Christ comen and gone 765
Then shall these things be fully done.
Prophecy.
MS. Rawl. C. 813, fol. 149.

By this large margent did the poet mean 766
These empty folios only please the cooks.
Brome, Richard, 'Upon Aglaura printed in Folio'.
Pr. *Musarum Deliciæ*, 1655, p. 51, and *Parnassus Biceps*, 1656, p. 57.
MSS. Eng. poet. c. 53, fol. 22, attr. to R: W:; Sancroft 53, p. 26, attr. to Richd. Brome.

By this one action judge who lovest most 767
I shall outstrip you will be tardy found.
Beaumont, Thomas, 'Upon his Mrs. cominge after him to the place apoynted'.
MS. *Malone 18, p. 46 (autogr.).

By this small statue, reader, is but shown 768
Saintlike she lived and like a saint she died.
'In St. Dunstans West'.
On 'the Hon. Margaret Talbot, widow, ob. 1620', in B.M. MS. Egerton 1160, fol. 13ᵛ.
MS. Sancroft 59, p. 292 rev.

By thy looks Hecuba: Helen by thy song 769
Let thy voice speak: bid thy face hold her tongue.
Translation of Latin distich on 'a verie deformed Gentlewoman of a voice incomparably Sweete'.
Attr. to Tho. R. in Harward M.S. Eng. 626 F*, fol. 46ᵛ.
MS. Eng. poet. c. 50, fol. 98.

770 By Thy word and Spirit taught
And praise Thee in the skies.
Kenton, James.
MS. *Eng. poet. e. 20, p. 64 (autogr.).

771 By two fair eyes, both armed with bow and dart
Judge me to death as one well worthy it.
Ch. M., 'Sonnett 6'.
MS. Eng. misc. d. 239, fol. 7.

772 By Villeroy's fate learn ladies to be wise
But forty past tool's weak and cannot enter.
MS. Eng. poet. d. 152, fol. 94.

773 By virtue hid, behold the iron hard,
And win at length, the port of endless bliss.
Whitney, Geoffrey, 'Mens immota manet'.
MS. *Rawl. poet. 56, fol. 23$^{v}$.

774 By what correcting line
Nor once will I thy words forget.
Herbert, Mary (*née* Sidney), Countess of Pembroke, Psalm cxix 'B'.
MSS. *Rawl. poet. 24, p. 175; *25, fol. 118$^{v}$.

775 By what glass of resemblance may we see
How are they conjoined? As God would.
Alabaster, William, 'Sonnet 36'.
MS. *Eng. poet. e. 57, fol. 9.

By what I did hear the little bird sing 776
And we from their prickles that did so much harm.
'Dialogue between Supple and Sturdy (1688) . . . the Earls of Nottingham and Pembrook's being against the Abdication'.
MS. Eng. poet. e. 49, p. 34.

By what I saw I am undone 777
To glory in my pain.
MS. Rawl. poet. 196, fol. 42.

By what power was love confined 778
Without a rival, monarch of the breast.
Carew, Thomas, 'Of the Incommunicabilitie of Love'.
MSS. *Don. b. 9, fol. 6; Malone 13, p. 70.

By wisdom, virtue, and by beauty swayed, 779
Ye've chose a patroness wise, chaste and fair.
'On Miss Betty Tracy's being chosen Lady Patroness of the High-Borlace for the year 1737 Augst. 18th'. Acrostic.
MSS. Ballard 47, fol. 74; 50, fol. 111.

By woman and an apple all men fell 780
The bad condemn'd, the good are glorified.
'On Mans fall Restoration Reseurection And Judement'.
MS. Rawl. D. 1334, fol. 27$^{v}$ rev.

By your Honour's command an example I stand 781
Oh, save me from this that has nine.
'Upon A Cat of Nine-tails'.
MS. Eng. poet. c. 9, p. 233.

# C

ENTRIES 1–835

1 Cadmus a king, his letters spread his fame;
Wealth sets it forth, gives it a glorious name.

Robinson, Robert.
MS. *Rawl. poet. 218, p. 116 (autogr.).

2 Cadmus his fame, St. George his fame alone
In spite of Satan here he lies entombed.

Duckworth, [Richard], 'The monument of Perse Stronke who flourished 1087'.
MS. Sancroft 59, p. 237 rev.

3 Caecus awaked was told the sun appear'd,
The sun hath further far to go than I.

MS. Tanner 465, fol. 94v.

4 Caecus the pleader hath a lady wed.
By Eve's fair offering till he shall be dead.

Series of stanzas on Caecus, Olimpia his wife, Maecus her lover.
MS. Rawl. D. 1048, fol. 59v.

5 Caesar and Pompey now are met;
By a sad Pharsalian doom.

12 lines on the battle of Pharsalia in the hand of Sir Thomas Browne.
MS. Rawl. D. 108, fol. 74.

6 Caesar I'll give his due, yet won't aspire
This new-year's gift unto my country friend.

Coley, Henry. See Coley's *Almanack*, 1696, Sig. C2v.
MS. *Add. B. 8, fol. 6v (autogr.).

7 Caesar was murther'd in another age
Our iron, there's a Golden Age.

Polwhele, John, 'Horace Epode 16th to The people of Rome'.
MS. *Eng. poet. f. 16, fol. 53 (autogr.).

8 Caesar with a safe breast the sea divides
The ship to wrack its rich freight doth deny.

Southwell, Sir Robert, 'Caesar per mare innatans Commentarios Gerit: ex E[manuelis] T[esauro]'.
MS. *Eng. poet. f. 6, fol. 46 (autogr.).

9 Cain, in disgrace with heav'n, retir'd to Nod;
Which he from Eden Edenburgh did name.

'On Cain's banishment'.
MSS. Ballard 29, fol. 62v; Eng. misc. e. 147, fol. 121v; e. 183, fol. 57.

Cains having killed their Abel, laid 10
Death took her King, and left a flood.

Q[uarles], J[ohn], 'An Epitaph upon Charles King of England', acrostic.
Copied from *A Kingly Bed*, 2nd ed., 1649, p. 84.
MS. Rawl. B. 165, fol. 138.

Caldora what have you and I 11
And what preparatory had been.

'To Caldora upon two dreams'.
MS. *Don. f. 5, fol. 26.

Call it no more the king's high way the king 12
Dare wade up to the very neck in blood.

'The Kings High way'.
MS. Rawl. poet. 84, fol. 117.

Call me the fiend that knoweth all, and is right sage and wise 13
Do tremble at the whip of God, who all the world doth guide.

'Apollo being urged to tell who himself was . . . sayd'.
MS. Rawl. D. 1372, fol. 68v.

Call not the winds, nor bid the rivers stay 14
Tombs but a while, tell where our bodies are.

[Davenant, Sir William], 'An Elegie on the death of Francis late Earle of Rutland', 17 Dec. 1632.
Pr. *Madagascar*, 1638, p. 108.
MSS. Eng. poet. c. 53, fol. 5; Malone 21, fol. 5, attr. to W. Davenant.

Call ye this equity 15
Rewards to each, according as he lives.

Knollys, Fra., Psalm lviii.
MS. *Rawl. poet. 60, p. 57 (autogr.).

Call'd by the gospel's joyful sound 16
Shall with th' eternal judge sit down.

Kenton, James.
MS. *Eng. poet. e. 20, p. 34 (autogr.).

Call'd by the spirit and the word 17
Till all thy life I find.

Kenton, James.
MS. *Eng. poet. e. 20, p. 232 (autogr.).

18 Call'd by thy Spirit's gracious call
And all my glory see.
Kenton, James.
MS. *Eng. poet. e. 20, p. 272 (autogr.).

19 Call'd the Saviour's grace to know
To our eternal home.
Kenton, James.
MS. *Eng. poet. e. 20, p. 128 (autogr.).

20 Callest thyself Christian th'art oblig'd to live
Works in their wills, to their own God they pray.
'A reasoning with the world that call themselves Christian'.
MS. *Don. f. 5, fol. 10v.

21 Calling to mind mine eye went long about
I loved myself because myself loved you.
Ralegh, Sir Walter.
Pr. *The Phœnix Nest*, 1593, p. 72.
MSS. Ashmole 781, p. 138, attr. to Sr. Wa: Raleigh; Rawl. poet. 31, fol. 2; 84, fol. 58; 85, fol. 104v; 153, fol. 20.

22 Calm as the ful-orb'd moon is seen
Resolved again on marriage.
Stukeley, William.
MS. *Eng. misc. d. 450, fol. 38 (autogr.).

23 Calm shines the moonbeam on that mournful grave
And now, his Saviour's starry crown in heaven.
Maitland, Charlotte Mary (b. 1767), 'On the Death of her Brother Col. Augustus Maitland'. November 1799.
MS. Eng. poet. c. 51, p. 173.

24 Calm thy displeasure, nor in heat
Do not thy help delay.
Psalm xxxviii.
MS. *Rawl. C. 113, fol. 32.

25 Calm thy tempestuous thoughts; my mind
Of woe to taste no kind.
Da[vison], Fr[ancis].
MS. Rawl. poet. 61, fol. 41v.

26 Calm was the evening and clear was the sky
He laugh'd out with a ha ha ha ha.
[Dryden, John], song in *An Evening's Love*, IV. i.
MS. Rawl. poet. 65, fol. 33.

27 Calmly, as the morning's soft tears shed
Will lie and wait your eyelids fair uprising.
Song.
MS. Mus. b. 1, fol. 58, music by John Wilson.

28 Calms appear when storms are past
Venus comes not every day.
Vanbrugh, Sir John, 'Verses in the Pilgrim set by Mr. Finger'.
MS. Mus. Sch. C. 95, p. 95.

Calthenus had some land but had no wife 29
To chance a heavy burden [for a] light.
'Calthenus weife'.
MS. Rawl. poet. 172, fol. 2.

Calvary mount is my delight 30
Thy servant to the end.
Pr. *Epitaphs*, 1604 (see Allison and Rogers, no. 293); see also L. I. Guiney, *Recusant poets*, 1938, pp. 268 and 274; H. E. Rollins, *Old English Ballads*, 1920, p. 147.
MS. Eng. poet. b. 5, p. 115.

Calvus is pleased with none but with the best 31
For he is worst, who ever prove the best.
F[itzjames], Lew[eston], 'In [Calvum Poetam]'.
MS. Add. B. 97, fol. 17 (autogr.).

Cambridge is a merry town 32
The other with disgraces.
'A song made on both the Universities'.
MS. Rawl. poet. 26, fol. 30v.

Cambridge, though in thy praise we dare not write 33
In faith thy gowns and aprons both did well.
Oldisworth, Nicolas, 'On the Commencement at Cambridge, 1632'.
MS. *Don. c. 24, fol. 59 (autogr.).

Camella fair tripped o'er the plain, 34
I will not kiss at all.
Pr. Thomas Bateson's *Second Set of Madrigales*, 1618, xv.
MSS. Mus. f. 20–24: f. 20, fol. 35v.

Camilius strong, that did repulse the Gauls, 35
An act most rare and glass of true renown.
Whitney, Geoffrey, 'Habet et bellum suas leges'.
MS. *Rawl. poet. 56, fol. 74.

Can any man in gilded rooms attend, 36
With various healthful pleasures fill the day.
MS. Rawl. poet. 213, fol. 5.

Can any show where Plinies people dwell 37
My armour proof is incredulity.
Strode, William, 'On a dissembler'.
MSS. CCC. 328, fol. 31; Rawl. poet. 206, p. 23, attr. to Will Strode, Ch. Ch.

Can any that's not void of his reason expect 38
*Quis nisi mentis inops.*
'Quis nisi mentis inops', on the election of a burgess at Lynn, endorsed 'on Gestwick'.
MS. Tanner 306, fol. 419.

39 Can aught oh love thy mighty power o'ercome
Has wing'd to yon blue heav'n her radiant way.
'Translation of Petrarch after the death of Laura'.
MS. Eng. poet. c. 51, p. 70.

40 Can christendom's great champion sink away
Dying in war to leave peace still alive.
On Gustavus Adolphus.
Pr. *The Swedish Intelligencer*, The Third Part, 1633.
MSS. Eng. poet. f. 10, fol. 85; Rawl. poet. 199, p. 54.

41 Can christendom's great champion sink away
And see a new sun rising in the east.
'On the death of King James', 1625. The first 10 lines adapted from C40. Attr. to 'W'm Strowd' in B.M. Add. MS. 14874, fol. 48$^{v}$.
MSS. Ashmole 47, fol. 112*c*; CCC. 328, fol. 6, attr. to Poole; Douce f. 5, fol. 31$^{v}$; Eng. poet. e. 14, fol. 46$^{v}$; e. 97, p. 59; Rawl. poet. 142, fol. 21, attr. to Poole; Tanner 465, fol. 71, attr. to Dr. Goad.

42 Can he be fair, that withers with a blast
Th'art neither fair, nor strong, nor wise nor rich, nor young.
Quarles, Francis, 'Mors Tua'.
From Pentelogia, pr. with *A Feast for Worms*, 1620, Sig. N4$^{v}$.
MSS. Ashmole 38, p. 19, attr. to Mr. Francis Quarlls; Rawl. poet. 127, fol. 18.

43 Can he that loves be man
Follows him to break his neck.
Song.
MS. Mus. b. 1, fol. 14$^{v}$, music by John Wilson.

44 Can indignation so much [then such] rage infuse?
How like thy poem, neither head nor tail.
'In Answer to Strephon's Revenge written [against the] Oxford Toasts'.
MSS. Ballard 47, fol. 73; Rawl. D. 833, fol. 153.

45 Can it suffice, and for him serve the turn
For grief you've not the same felicity.
Southwell, Sir Robert, 'On the Death of Mr. Seldin the great and famous Antiquary'. 1654.
MS. *Eng. poet. f. 6, fol. 44 (autogr.).

46 Can John's earnest zeal for God
With Jesus only in my view.
Kenton, James.
MS. *Eng. poet. e. 20, p. 151 (autogr.).

Can joy be where there doth dwell 47
Where's all true joy.
Colman, Henry, 'On Joy'.
MS. *Rawl. poet. 204, fol. 30$^{v}$ (autogr.).

Can love be controll'd by advice 48
We may always find time to grow old.
'The Modest Question'.
Pr. single sheet folio, London.
MSS. Eng. poet. c. 9, p. 275, reference to setting by Russel; Eng. misc. b. 48, two copies, fols. 80, 81; Mus. e. 20, fol. 19, dated 7 Dec. 1747, 'Set by Mr. Russel'.

Can man be silent and not praises find 49
That her whole life was a communion-day.
On Lady Katherine Paston, 1628, Paston Church, Norfolk.
MS. Top. gen. e. 32, fol. 72$^{v}$.

Can man possess a greater curse 50
And not enjoy the power to taste.
J. M., 'Spoken extempore'.
MS. Eng. poet. c. 9, p. 81.

Can my unskilful pen describe the feature 51
Great is the treasure hidden in that vault.
Burton, Francis, 'Commendatorie' acrostic on 'Catherine Vaughan'.
MS. *Add. A. 267, fol. 15$^{v}$ (autogr.).

Can Sacharissa then forsake, 52
Like frighten'd rats when cat does cry.
Walsh, Octavia, 'The following Copy [C739] Burlesq'd'.
MS. *Eng. poet. e. 31, fol. 161$^{v}$ rev. (autogr.).

Can she disdain, can I persist to love, 53
To equal my desires, with like disdain.
Pr. Pilkington's *First Book of Songs*, 1605, iii.
MSS. Mus. f. 7–10: f. 10, fol. 18$^{v}$.

Can she excuse my wrongs with virtue's cloak 54
Who for thy sake did die contented.
Pr. J. Dowland's first book of *Songes or Ayres*, 1597, v.
MSS. Douce 280, fol. 67$^{v}$; Mus. f. 7–10: f. 9, fol. 7$^{v}$.

Can smooth-tongue'd eloquence or rhetoric paint 55
We trust to hail thee on th'eternal shore.
Kenton, James, 'On the Death of Mr. Abraham Harley', 1769.
MS. *Eng. poet. e. 19, p. 212 (autogr.).

Can Strephon change his constant love 56
And in its room grim winter bring.
Middleton, Lady Elizabeth.
MS. Mus. c. 16, fol. 115$^{v}$, autograph music of W. Davis.

57 **Can such perfection fade? Can virtue die**
**That every heart an epitaph shall wear.**
[Crashaw, Richard], 'On the death of the Lady Parker'.
Pr. from this MS. by L. C. Martin, *Poems of Crashaw*, 1927, p. 403; cf. pp. lxx–lxxiii, 460.
MSS. Rawl. poet. 147, p. 40; Tanner 465, fol. 72.

58 **Can that small mass of words which man can frame**
**Thy glory's great to make, but more to save.**
Reresby, Sir John, 'A Paraphrase', Psalm viii.
MS. Rawl. D. 204, fol. 93 rev. (autogr.).

59 **Can the adventures of four hours thrive**
**If not, his praise is written in the sand.**
'A prologue to the designed play of the four hour's adventure'. Reference to Sir Samuel Tuke's play, *The Adventures of Five Hours*, 1663.
MS. Rawl. poet. 84, fol. 24v rev.

60 **Can the dumb accents of a vanished breath**
**Where thy dear saviour is the corner-stone.**
Digges, Dud[ley], 'On the death of his dear Uncle Mr. Leonard Digges', 7. Apr. 1635.
MS. CCC. 309, fol. 36.

61 **Can the physician for a life engage**
**Who lengthen human race into a span?**
Southwell, Sir Robert, 'On the pittied death of Mr. Thomas Hide Commoner of Queen's Coll. Oxon'.
MS. *Eng. poet. f. 6, fol. 21 (autogr.).

62 **Can the same fountain yield a pleasant stream**
**Thou sovereign Lord, and judge of quick and dead.**
Williams, John, 1 John iii. 9, 1710.
MS. *Rawl. poet. 192, fol. 32 (autogr.).

63 **Can virtue die, and yet not find a room**
**Even then, impartial death unhous'd his spirit.**
Sancroft, William, 'On the much lamented death of Sr. [Daniel] Bowles student in Emmanuel Colledge', 22 Aug. 1639.
Verses 7 and 10 are also in F369.
MS. Sancroft 48, fol. 7v (autogr.).

64 **Can we dare doubt thou art a saint in heaven:**
**All that I wished thee thou dost now receive.**
Gough, Richard (?), 'Lines on the loss by Death of a loved Fair one'.
MS. *Eng. poet. c. 5, fol. 108, in Gough's hand.

**Can we forget that God** 65
**Whom thine own arm has made.**
Beddome, Benjamin.
MS. *Eng. misc. e. 227, fol. 49.

**Can we suppose partiality** 66
**By zealous diligence secure.**
Kenton, James.
MS. *Eng. poet. e. 20, p. 38 (autogr.).

**Can you forbid me to adore that face** 67
**Where she the blessing of her presence does bestow.**
Chatwin, John, 'To Emilia, who desir'd him not to love'.
MS. *Rawl. poet. 94, p. 6 (autogr.).

**Can you leave ranging** 68
**Your fate you know.**
Song for two voices.
MS. Mus. c. 107, fol. 1v rev.

**Can you when sullen grown, be cheerful made** 69
**With no less sport than death in masquerade.**
MS. Add. B. 8, fol. 74.

**Candour, sweet inmate of the generous breast;** 70
**Christian! anticipate the praise of God!**
Butler, Weeden, Jr., translator of Latin verses on Dr. Stephen Hales by Dr. Jortin.
MS. Top. gen. e. 32, fol. 114v.

**Canidia thy skill's great** 71
**Works not upon thy body wondrous well.**
W. A., translator, Horace, *Epode* xvii.
MS. *Rawl. poet. 104, fol. 58 (autogr.).

**Canonical black coats like birds of a feather** 72
**When from *Jure de Aleo* they became *Jure divino*.**
'The Convocation 1688'.
MSS. Eng. poet. c. 18, fol. 60; d. 53, p. 29; e. 49, p. 26; Firth e. 6, fol. 109v.

**Canst be idle? canst thou play?** 73
**Neither sin, nor saviour feels.**
Herbert, George, 'Busines'.
Pr. *The Temple*, 1633, p. 105.
MS. *Tanner 307, fol. 79v.

**Canst not thou weave bone lace** 74
**You't kiss your belly full.**
'Scotch song', without music.
MS. Mus. Sch. C. 95, p. 190.

**Canst thou be dead, we be still the same** 75
**To live for ever in thy company.**
'An Eligie on Henrye Fredericke Eldest sonn unto the King and Queen of Behemia Lately Drownd'. 1629.
MSS. Ashmole 38, p. 191; 47, fol. 74v.

76 **Canst thou dear God forgive so soon,**
**A thousand souls to give?**
Shirley, James.
Pr. from this MS., *Works*, ed. A. Dyce, 1833, vi. 502.
MS. *Rawl. poet. 88, p. 71.

77 **Can'st thou in dungeon smother up that pelf,**
**To breed the ore; But thine its tomb.**
[Tate, Nahum], 'On an old miser, hoarding up his Treasure in a Steel Chest'.
Pr. *Poems*, 1677, p. 57.
MS. Rawl. poet. 173, fol. 158^v^.

78 **Canst thou pen a sigh, or limb**
**Transplanted him into their spheres.**
Briggs, S[ampson], 'Upon the death of Thomas Knowles Chorister of Westminster Abby'.
MS. Rawl. poet. 246, fol. 25.

79 **Canst thou recover thy consumed flesh**
**Th'art not asleep, but thou art dead in sin.**
[Quarles, Francis], 'On Repentance'.
Pr. *Divine Fancies*, 1632, i. 95.
MS. Rawl. poet. 90, fol. 65^v^.

80 **Capacious goblet, stor'd with all delight,**
**And snatch one hour of real life.**
Cowley, Abraham, 'Verses upon a Punch Bowl'.
MS. Rawl. poet. 173, fol. 141.

81 **Captain Cobb in Lynn doth dwell**
**Nor to face the enemy.**
'Captain Cobb's Bravery'.
MS. Firth c. 18, fol. 32.

82 **Captain Hume is bound to sea**
**Hey the brave Scottish boys ho.**
'A proper new Ballad . . . the Granadier's rant'.
Pr. *Roxburghe Ballads*, vii. 532.
MS. Firth c. 17, fol. 19.

83 **Captain of martyrs thou didst lead the van**
**Thy name and day near the first martyr's crown.**
E. S., 'On S. Stephen'.
MS. Rawl. poet. 65, fol. 81^v^.

84 **Captive Briseis sends the lines you read:**
**Or still remain, oh, let me be restor'd.**
Percy, Thomas, Bishop of Dromore, 'Ovid's Epistles . . . 3, Briseis to Achilles'.
MS. Percy e. 6, fol. 57^v^ (autogr.).

85 **Captive brother, break thy chain,**
**A willing slave's for ever tied.**
Littleton, [George], Lord, 'The Squirrels of Hagley Park to Miss Warburton's Squirrel', with an answer, 17 May 1763.
MS. Eng. poet. e. 28, p. 59.

***Caput apri differo*** 86
**The boar's head with mustard.**
'A caroll bringyng in the bores heed'. Transcribed by Hearne from Wynkyn de Worde's *Christmasse carolles*, 1521.
Pr. *Guilelmus Neubrigensis*, ed. Hearne, 1719, iii. 745.
MS. Rawl. D. 1164, fol. 231^v^.

**Care-charming sleep the easer of all woes** 87
**And kiss him into slumbers like a bride.**
[Fletcher, John], from *Valentinian* v. ii.
MS. Don. c. 57, fol. 19^v^, with music.

**Care having got possession of my heart** 88
**And left me wretch unto my lamentation.**
Cornwallis, Will[iam].
MS. Tanner 306, fol. 236.

**Care, if by care aught can effected be,** 89
**If not, why car'st thou, since God cares for thee.**
'On Care', couplet.
MS. Rawl. poet. 90, fol. 104.

**Care not for women's tears I counsel thee** 90
**They teach their eyes as much to weep as see.**
Couplet, translation of Latin epigram.
MS. Rawl. D. 1372, fol. 33.

**Care the consuming canker of the mind** 91
**Denouncing worst to him that is his friend.**
MS. Eng. poet. e. 14, fol. 14.

**Care, thou canker of all joys** 92
**Night my boys for you and me.**
'Catch by [Wm.] Shield'.
MS. Mus. d. 177, fol. 60.

**Cares, fears, afflictions, discontent** 93
**Hasten my course to my long home.**
'Sad Complaint'.
MS. Rawl. poet. 90, fol. 101^v^.

**Carew, of youths the very prime** 94
**Devoted, oh my friend, by me!**
Gough, Richard.
MS. *Eng. poet. c. 5, fol. 186 (autogr.).

**Carus by hardy Epicurus taught** 95
**Such generous minds are form'd where blest religion reigns . . .**
Sir Richard Blackmore, *Creation*, 1712, book II, opening lines.
MS. Rawl. D. 868, fol. 16^v^.

**Cary's face is not the best; but she as useful as the rest** 96
**But he's like to recover.**
A lampoon on Court ladies *temp.* Charles II.
MS. Don. b. 8, p. 179.

97 Cast not away thy strength thy stock
Ev'n so much of thy life thou endest.
Robinson, Robert.
MS. *Rawl. poet. 218, p. 69 (autogr.).

98 Cast off, and scattered in thine ire
And make them firmly permanent.
Sandys, George, Psalm lx, 3-part setting by H. Lawes.
Pr. *A Paraphrase upon the Divine Poems*, 1638, p. 73, and H. and W. Lawes, *Choice Psalmes*, 1648.
MS. Mus. Sch. E. 451, p. 40.

99 Cast your caps and cares away
He doth owe unto his rags.
[Fletcher, John], from *Beggars Bush*, II. i.
Pr. John Wilson's *Cheerfull Ayres or Ballads*, 1660, p. 22.
MSS. Don. c. 57, fol. 75$^{v}$; Mus. b. 1, fol. 45$^{v}$, both with music by J. Wilson.

100 Castara, see that dust the sportive wind
Betray them to the sport of every breath.
[Habington, William], 'Upon Beauty. Castara'.
Pr. *Castara, The Second Part*, 1634, Sig. I2$^{v}$.
MS. Eng. poet. f. 25, fol. 19$^{v}$.

101 [Castara weep not, though her tomb appear]
Whence rivers may, we ne'er return again.
[Habington, William], fragment of poem.
Pr. *Castara, The Second Part*, 1634, p. 55.
MS. Rawl. poet. 65, fol. 90.

102 Castara whisper in some dead man's ear
Hath no abode; where dwells it but in love.
[Habington, William], 'To Castara where true happiness abides'.
Pr. *Castara, The Second Part*, 1634, p. 53.
MS. Rawl. poet. 65, fol. 90$^{v}$.

103 Castell is his own horse's groom
And stands to be Mat. Wren's basoon.
'George Castell', couplet.
MS. Gough misc. antiq. 11, fol. 82.

104 Catch me a star that's falling from the sky
And then find faith within a woman's mind.
'On Women'.
MSS. Ashmole 47, fol. 36; CCC. 328, fol. 19; Malone 21, fol. 45$^{v}$; Rawl. poet. 153, fol. 8.

105 Cato went barefoot to the judgement seat
Towards souls enlight'ned made angelical.
MS. *Don. f. 5, fol. 21.

106 Catulla's witty, fair, and young,
Her beauty's delight, but not a snare.
Ayloffe, Captain [John], 'Upon a fine whore'.
MS. Rawl. poet. 173, fol. 69.

'Cause no man will a poor man's care relieve, 107
Need and opportunity do make him thieve.
Robinson, Robert, couplet.
MS. *Rawl. poet. 218, p. 124 (autogr.).

Cease busy music none thy trouble pays 108
Money goes round.
Creswell, Robert, 'Regina Pecunia'.
MS.* Eng. poet. f. 24, fols. 66, 65$^{v}$ and 64$^{v}$ (autogr.).

Cease, cease of Cupid to complain 109
Charming raptures, matchless sweets.
[Motteux, Peter Anthony], song, with music. In *The Mad Lover*; pr. *Mercurius Musicus*, 1701.
MS. Mus. Sch. E. 397, p. 85 rev.

Cease Damon to pursue me 110
Should virtue ever miss.
'Verses given me [G. Lepipre] by . . . Mrs. Carbonell. April 21. 1748'.
MS. Eng. poet. e. 40, fol. 54.

Cease, Eliza, thy locks to despoil 111
For attraction will always be thine.
'To a Lady who drew the Pins from her Bonnet in a Thunder-storm'.
MS. Eng. poet. c. 51, p. 109.

Cease, envious bird, let not thy siren throat 112
Which is the greatest monster, he or I.
Oldisworth, Giles, lines in 'The Patterne of Pietye'.
MS. *Rawl. C. 422, fol. 43 (autogr.).

Cease fair enchantress cease to mourn 113
A less enchantress than before.
'To Signora Strada in the Character of Alcina' [1776].
MS. Percy c. 8, fol. 127.

Cease fond desire to wish me better hap: 114
That for my sake in love content none be.
MS. Rawl. poet. 85, fol. 76.

Cease, fools of birds, and four-legged cattle, 115
Up to the moon—I know not where.
Blyth, John (b. 1682), 'The Fairies', for the Lent Probation at the Merchant Taylors' School, 1700 (?).
Pr. bk. Vet. A3 c. 123, fol. 29 (autogr.).

Cease not, thou heavenly voiced glorious creature 116
And never die but so far ever languish.
MS. Don. c. 57, fol. 62, music by John Jenkins.

Cease now the talk of wonders nothing rare; 117
Give them to what they love, that troublers be.
Strode, William, 'On his majesty's Fleet'. 1635.
MS. *CCC. 325, fol. 121$^{v}$ (autogr.).
MS. Rawl. poet. 172, fol. 31.

118 Cease, oh cease this hum of grieving
When the dead hath won the field.
MS. Mus. b. 1, fol. 18v, music by John Wilson.

119 Cease pen to drop the honey azure dew
That shall from flinty heart wring signs of pity.
H. S.
MS. *Rawl. poet. 120, fol. 19v (autogr.).

120 Cease thou afflicted soul to mourn
Myself, that mine own rival am.
Carew, Thomas, 'The Amazons song'.
Pr. *Poems*, 1640.
MS. *Don. b. 9, fol. 26v.

121 Cease thy wishes gentle boy
Thou wert Cupid or his brother.
MS. Don. c. 57, fol. 47, with music.

122 Cease to lament ye rich, nor weep ye poor
Be pious, just and good, as she was here.
'Epitaph on Mrs. Pitt of Blandford'.
MS. Eng. poet. e. 40, fol. 44.

123 Cease warring thoughts, and let his brain
And drop down from the trees with broken hearts.
Song in the hand of W. Lawes, with music.
MS. Mus. Sch. B. 2, p. 36.

124 Cease we to weep, to wail; 'Tis all in vain
So may you cease to weep when Christ appears.
G[ilbert (?)], W[illiam (?)], of King's School, Sherborne, on Robert Whetcombe, 'Antientest Governour of the King's Schoole of Sherebourne', 24 Oct. 1656.
MS. Gough Dorset 35 (1), fol. 20*d*.

125 Cease your invective, nor fair woman blame
I cannot say how Eve had acted then.
'The Apology'.
MS. Percy c. 8, fol. 125.

126 Cease, zealots, cease to blame these heavenly lays
T'exalt the soul from earth, and make, of hell, a heaven.
'On Mr. Handels new Oratorio perform'd at the Theatre Royal Covent Garden . . . Daily Advertiser Mar. 31. 1743' [*The Messiah*].
MS. Eng. poet. c. 9, p. 100.

127 C[eci]l and B[u]tts have both obtained the lawn
Since graced by C[eci]l and adorned by Butts.
'On the two New Bishops Anno 1732', Bristol and Norwich.
MS. Eng. misc. e. 147, fol. 188v.

128 Celebrate this festival
Peace and her hero to depart no more.
[Tate, Nahum], 'Ode on Queen Mary's Birthday, 1689'. Music by H. Purcell.
F. B. Zimmerman, *Purcell*, 1963, no. 321.
MS. Mus. c. 28, fol. 78.

Celestial herald, thou dost draw the line 129
And who alone could ope the book, and seals.
E. S., 'On St. John the Evangelist'.
MS. Rawl. poet. 65, fol. 82.

Celestial muse that dost command the soul 130
As the goddess descends.
Cantata.
MS. Mus. c. 3, fol. 2.

Celestial muse, Urania fair, 131
Led by your author's works to seek his face.
Gough, Richard, 'On the Signs of the Zodiack . . . Aug. 16. 1754'.
MS. *Eng. poet. c. 5, fol. 31v, r (autogr.).

Celestial powers on you I invocate 132
And with a loyal [resolv'd wheale (?)] be writ.
Corrected draft.
MS. Rawl. D. 864, fol. 234v (autogr.).

Celia do you deny me still, 133
No more can I endure to freedom born.
Williams, John, 'The 2ds. [second words] are—I wait for them'.
MS. *Rawl. poet. 184, fol. 52 (autogr.).

Celia does say kisses to none she'll give 134
She knows in taking kisses she a kiss does give.
[Owen's Epigram] '25, On Caelia'.
MS. *Rawl. poet. 197, fol. 9 (autogr.).

Celia, for many a circling year 135
She spake, and hurried out of town.
'The Conversion'.
MS. *Eng. poet. d. 47, fol. 1.

Celia has a thousand charms 136
She wishes all mankind in heaven.
[Gould, Robert], song in *The Rival Sisters*, 1695.
In *Purcell*, by F. B. Zimmerman, 1963, no. 609 (10a).
MSS. Add. B. 106, fol. 52v; Mus. Sch. C. 95, p. 120, set by Purcell.

Celia hath been at cookery many a day 137
That flesh hath come from her half-raw, half-burned.
'Of Celia'.
MS. Eng. poet. e. 14, fol. 80v rev.

Celia is sick, and if that heaven die 138
Would turn to chaos for the loss of thee.
[Hyde, Humphrey], 'upon a Lady's sickness'.
In B.M. Add. MSS. 19268, fol. 18v, attr. Humphrey Hide; Add. 30982, fol. 53v, attr. Hū Hyde; Harl 6931, fol. 19, attr. Loyde.
MS. Eng. poet. c. 50, fol. 127.

139 Celia methinks so long an age is past,
To be revived by thy inflaming eyes.
Reresby, Sir John, 'To Cælia absent. Letter'.
MS. Rawl. D. 204, fol. 95v rev. (autogr.).

140 Celia retired: 'Twas time to rest;
She wakes and lo, 'twas all a dream.
'Pleasure, a Dream'.
MS. *Eng. poet. d. 47, fol. 21.

141 Celia, since blest with every grace
So well adorn'd before.
Webb, Foster, 'A Song . . . alter'd'.
MS. Eng. poet. c. 9, p. 114.

142 Celia tell me why my suit you still disdain
Then Celia don't my love refuse nor keep me still in pain.
Song, with music.
MS. Mus. Sch. C. 97, fol. 2v at end.

143 Celia that I once was blest
Love that's true is love forever.
[Dryden, John], song in *Amphitryon*, Act III.
In *Purcell*, by F. B. Zimmerman, 1963, no. 572 (9a).
MSS. Rawl. poet. 196, fol. 35v; Mus. Sch. C. 95, p. 220, set by Purcell.

144 Celia, this sullen pride forsake
The fair distribute love.
'Song by [Mr. G.]'.
MS. Firth e. 6, fol. 132v.

145 Celia whose judgement wisest men approve
Even that Celia doth vouchsafe to love.
'On Cælia's loving'.
MS. Eng. poet. e. 40, fol. 132.

146 Celia's all my joy, my treasure
So ravishing as Celia's eyes.
'Song'.
MS. Rawl. poet. 152, fol. 154v.

147 Censorio takes in hand, by sharp reproof:
The Temple-snuffers must be perfect gold.
[Quarles, Francis], 'On Censorio'.
Pr. *Divine Fancies*, 1632, ii. 50.
MS. Rawl. poet. 90, fol. 77.

148 Censure not sharply then but me advise
Her fury; though no friendship he betray.
Jonson, Ben., An Epistle to a Friend.
Pr. *Ben Jonson*, ed. Herford and Simpson, viii, 1947, p. 421.
MSS. Eng. poet. f. 9, p. 12, attr. to B. J.; Rawl. poet. 31, fol. 23v.

Certain and sure under this stone 149
To be antichristian self denial.
'An Epitaph upon Passive Obedience. Anno Ætatis 1689'.
MSS. Rawl. poet. 181, fol. 28; Willis 83, fol. 53; Wood D. 19 (2), fol. 107.

Certain it is, and past all doubt 150
And take this letter as a jest.
'An Epistle to a Jealous Husband', 1735.
MS. Eng. misc. e. 240, p. 192.

Chamberlain, loud do I call, dost hear 151
Yet here I end to treat of vanity.
Newman, Thomas, 'Of Vanitie'.
MS. *Top. Oxon. f. 39, fols. 21v, 22v (autogr.).

Change not that friend whom thou hast tried as gold, 152
Men silent often pass for men of wit.
'Good Advise'.
MS. Rawl. poet. 173, fol. 159v rev.

Change now Castalian sisters, change your song 153
Who finds one so may boast she wisely lov'd.
Moore, Thomas, 'On the equall match of youth with youth. To Cyrene'.
MS. *Rawl. poet. 3, fol. 57v (autogr.).

Change places Charles, and put on Pym's grave gown 154
We'll all be kings as well as Pym and thee.
[Autumn, 1641].
MSS. Ashmole 36, 37, fol. 73.

Change that dost make each mortal nature feel 155
Some lightening is in change though to the worse.
J. F., 'Desire of Change'.
MS. *Eng. poet. f. 17, p. 8 (autogr.).

Change thy mind since she doth change 156
She was best but yet untrue.
[Devereux, Robert, Earl of Essex].
Pr. Dowland's *Musicall Banquet*, 1610, attr. to Essex.
MSS. Rawl. poet. 85, fol. 125; 148, fol. 67.

Changed from the shape wherein I first was born 157
And since I die not leave off thine ado.
W. A., Horace, *Odes* II. xx.
MS. *Rawl. poet. 104, fol. 20v (autogr.).

Chant birds in every bush 158
Oh how thy do begin, hark, hark.
MS. Rawl. poet. 152, fol. 19.

Chant on you chirping quire 159
Yet love cures love's disease.
D[arell], Sir S[ampson], 'On the Lady Coke in the woods'.
MS. Rawl. poet. 210, fol. 55 rev.

160 **Charity's that grace which most lovely is**
**Should this I do and still want charity.**
Tipping, William, 'Of Charitie'.
MS. *Rawl. poet. 101, fol. $32^v$ (autogr.).

161 **Charles, at present having no need**
**Thanks you as much as if he did.**
Couplet, 'The King's Answer' to 'the Commons' Petition'; see I1230, J189.
MSS. Rawl. poet. 81, fol. 26; 173, fol. $116^v$, attr. to Ld. Rochester.

162 **Charles died, Fernando, and they say**
**In thine own shadow thee to catch.**
Translation of 4 lines on the brothers of Philip IV of Spain, from James Howell's *History of Lewis XIII*, 1646, p. 132.
MS. Rawl. D. 1110, fol. 119 rev.

163 **Charles doth rule, can we then fear a foe**
**We *Angli* all shall be his *Angeli*.**
MS. Douce f. 5, fol. 11.

164 **Charles in vain thou to thy friends dost call**
**For you less pitied like to them shall fall.**
'Found fixed on his Majesty's Privy Chamber Door'. Charles II, 1675 (?). Cf. R261.
MS. Rawl. D. 924, fol. 310.

165 **Charmed, or with moral or religious views**
**And your own worth immortalize your name.**
'To Miss Jenny Boys, of Deal, with the Rev. Dr. Watt's Horae Lyricae. . . L[ondon] Mag.'
MS. Eng. poet. e. 39, p. 65.

166 **Charmed with the theme no venal muse essays**
**And angels guide your flight to friendship's god.**
Whaley, John, 'To a Lady in years, Who married a Gentleman of a Suitable Age to Herself'.
Pr. *Poems*, 1732, p. 93.
MS. Rawl. poet. 222, fol. 8.

167 **Charming Chloe look with pity**
**Soon would be a silent shade.**
'A Song' published as 'True Love'.
MSS. Montagu e. 13, fol. $5^v$; Mus. c. 107, two copies, fols. $9^v$ and $49^v$, music by Maurice Greene.

168 **Charming Jenny is fair and gay**
**Thus 'tis beauty whom all decoys.**
MS. Rawl. poet. 196, fol. 26.

169 **Charming Phyllis has an air**
**I could be deceived for ever.**
MS. Rawl. poet. 196, fol. $43^v$.

**Charon, come hither, Charon** 170
**Proud of our new society.**
Upon Hobson, the Cambridge Carrier, and Charon [1631].
MSS. Don. c. 57, fol. $6^v$, with music; Firth e. 4, p. 93.

**Charon, oh Charon, hear a wretch oppressed** 171
**We'll sing such woes as ne'er came there before.**
Pr. with music by W. Lawes in Henry Lawes' *Select Ayres and Dialogues*, 1669, p. 112.
MS. Don. c. 57, fol. 4, with music by Robert Ramsey.

**Charon, oh Charon, the wafter of all souls to bliss or bane** 172
**Then come aboard and pass till then be wise.**
[Fletcher, John], song in *The Mad Lover*, IV. i.
MS. Rawl. poet. 65, fol. $32^v$.

**Charon! oh gentle Charon, let me woo thee** 173
**Who else with tears will doubtless drown the ferry.**
[Herrick, Robert, 'Charon and Phylomel, a Dialogue sung'.]
Pr. *Hesperides*, 1648; Playford's *Select Musicall Ayres and Dialogues*, 1652, ii. 18.
MSS. Don. c. 57, fol. $57^v$, music by W. Lawes; Mus. Sch. C. 95, p. 226, music by W. Lawes; Rawl. poet. 65, fol. 32.

**Charon, take Hobson's ghost, and let it pass** 174
**And he shall ride to heaven in his own wain.**
R[andolph], T[homas], on Hobson, 1631.
MS. Firth e. 4, p. 115.

**Chaste Arria pulling the unhappy sword** 175
**But that will pain me, Paetus, thou wilt make.**
Translation from Martial, *Epigrams* I. xiii.
MS. Rawl. D. 1147, fol. $89^v$.

**Chaste coyness never can alarm** 176
**A soul from loose desire refined.**
MS. Eng. poet. e. 47, p. 62.

**Chaste, pious, prudent Charles the second** 177
**Prove wretched, kinged by storks and logs.**
Wilmot, John, Earl of Rochester, 'History of Insipids'.
See J. Prinz, *Rochester, his Life and Writings* (*Palaestra* cliv), 1927, p. 129.
Pr. *Poems on Affairs of State*, 1697, i. 149; *Newest Songs against Popery and Tyranny*, 1689; *Works of . . . Rochester and Roscommon*, 1709, p. 130.
MSS. Don. b. 8, p. 527; Douce 357, fol. 103; Rawl. poet. 173, fol. 111, attr. to Ld. Rochester; Tanner 466, fol. 82; see also G538.

178 Chaste sovereign of the sable night
Presaging Duncan's death.
Gough, Richard, 'To the Moon . . . Scotland 1771'.
MS. *Eng. poet. c. 5, fol. 184 (autogr.).

179 Cheat another, or he'll cheat thee:
Thus doth this wicked world agree.
Robinson, Robert, couplet.
MS. *Rawl. poet. 218, p. 76 (autogr.).

180 Cheer up Malfido, lay thy thoughts more level,
And thou shalt find no scorpion: if no fish.
[Quarles, Francis], 'To Malfido'.
Pr. *Divine Fancies*, 1632, iv. 85.
MS. Rawl. poet. 90, fol. 75$^{v}$.

181 Cheer up my mates the winds do fairly blow
And never never be poor, no never any more.
Pr. *Choice Ayres, Songs and Dialogues*, 2nd ed., 1675, p. 2.
MS. Mus. Sch. F. 572, p. 8, music by Pelham Humphrey.

182 Cheer up small wits, now you shall crowned be
Both caustic cod, and squalid sprats devour.
'To Daphne', i.e. W. Davenant.
Pr. *Certain verses, . . . to be reprinted with Gondibert*, 1653, p. 20.
MS. CCC. 309, fol. 55$^{v}$.

183 Cheer up your hearts, bold Britons, our troops are now advancing
Whene'er 'tis o'er, you'll hear more, what they have been about, sir.
'A Song in Praise of our Forces'.
MSS. Firth c. 17 fol. 45; c. 20, fol. 25.

184 Cheronean Plutarch to thy deathless praise
Their lives have parallels, but thine has none.
Translation of 'Agathias his Epigram . . . on A statue erected by the Romans to [Plutarch's] Memory'.
Pr. Dryden's *Plutarch*.
MS. Rawl. D. 1372, fol. 47 from end.

185 Chester, that noble county palatine
To pass all counties in the way of peace.
Woode, Andrew, 'To Robert Viscount Kilmorey and Orlando Bridgeman, Vice-Chamberlains of Chester', on the agreement of 23 Dec. 1642.
See *Journal of the Chester Arch. Soc.*, N.S. XXV, 1923, p. 34.
MSS. Ashmole 36, 37, fol. 270 (autogr.).

186 Chick still and chick Torpedo calls his wife
Still chick? Then he's more capon of the twain.
James, Richard, 'Upon a slothful husband still calling his wife chick'.
MS. *James 35, p. 21 (autogr.).

Chickens in crumbs and corn delight 187
Or good or bad with men 'tis so.
Robinson, Robert.
MS. *Rawl. poet. 218, p. 37 (autogr.).

Chide not thy sprouting lip, nor kill 188
The root below cannot be dry.
Strode, William, 'On a blistered Lip'.
MS. *CCC. 325, fol. 77 (autogr.).
MS. Eng. poet. e. 14, fol. 14.

Child of the light, fair morning hour 189
The Muse's modest gift, her present to a friend.
Dyer, George, 'Ode To the Morning'.
Pr. *Poems*, 1792, p. 20.
MS. *Eng. poet. c. 21, fol. 7.

Childhood, youth, manhood, all these I have passed: 190
Now in old age death, death will come at last.
Robinson, Robert, couplet.
MS. *Rawl. poet. 218, p. 165 (autogr.).

Children and fools as English proverbs say 191
To speak what's false; but folly truth to own.
[Owen's epigram] '104, Children and Fools tell Truth'.
MS. *Rawl. poet. 197, fol. 9$^{v}$ (autogr.).

Children are pretty, and young men are witty, 192
We must begin the world again.
Robinson, Robert.
MS. *Rawl. poet. 218, p. 21 (autogr.).

Children of Cheap, hold you all still, 193
For you shall have the Bowbell rung at your will.
Couplet, Reply to C317.
MS. Sancroft 59, p. 280 rev.

Children, poor babes, we ought to love 194
Supply the world again.
Robinson, Robert.
MS. *Rawl. poet. 218, p. 55 (autogr.).

Chloe a coquette in her prime 195
Rust to a point and fix at last.
Travin, R., 'On the marriage of an old maid'.
MS. Top. Oxon. e. 172, fol. 20$^{v}$.

Chloe, a darling, favourite bitch 196
To death a destined tender.
'Cloe's Disaster'.
MS. *Eng. poet. d. 47, fol. 13.

Chloe has a melting heart 197
Indifference best wins the field.
'Song between Strephon and Cupid'.
MS. Rawl. poet. 152, fol. 177$^{v}$.

198 **Chloe, in verse by your command I write**
**But you are tired, and so am I. Farewell.**
Wilmot, John, Earl of Rochester, 'A Letter from Artemisa in the town to Chloe in the country'.
Pr. brds. (Ashmole 1094) and Rochester's *Poems*, 1691, p. 65. See Vieth, p. 378.
MSS. Don. b. 8, p. 490, attr. to the Earle of Rochester or Mr. Wolseley; North b. 24, fol. 60; Rawl. poet. 123, pp. 116 and 108 (transcript by Oldham, corrected by Rochester (?). See *Poems*, ed. V. de S. Pinto, 1953, p. 186); 152, fol. 50; 173, fols. $65^{v}$, 132; see also Y350.

199 **Chloe when crammed with hearty meals**
**And all the yeast bescatter.**
'On a Lady'.
MS. Top. London e. 9, p. 159.

200 **Chloe's the wonder of her sex**
**A boundless will to ease us.**
'Song by [Mr. G.]'.
MS. Firth e. 6, fol. 132.

201 **Chlora's false love made Chlora weep**
**Shall equal my desire.**
Pr. *Select Musicall Ayres and Dialogues*, 1652, and John Wilson's *Cheerfull Ayres or Ballads*, 1660.
MS. Mus. b. 1, fol. $122^{v}$, music by Wilson.

202 **Chloris enlarge the empire of your face**
**Of all his easy conquests in the east.**
Walsh, William, 'To Chloris. El. 11'.
MS. Malone 9, fol. 16 (autogr.).

203 **Chloris farewell I now must go**
**But make my constant meals at home.**
Pr. *Select Musicall Ayres and Dialogues*, 1652.
MS. Rawl. poet. 116, fol. $38^{v}$.

204 **Chloris forbear awhile do not o'erjoy me**
**And that's enough.**
[Bold, Henry].
Pr. *Poems*, 1664, p. 6.
MS. Rawl. poet. 65, fol. 35.

205 **Chloris, I cannot say your eyes**
**Who can express what 'tis he likes.**
Sedley, Sir Charles, 'To Chloris . . . The Entire Lover'.
Pr. *Poems on Several Occasions, by several Persons*, 1672, p. 12, and Sedley's *Miscellaneous Works*, ed. W. Ayloffe, 1702, p. 15.
MSS. Rawl. poet. 173, fol. $75^{v}$, attr. to Sir Ch. Sedley; Sancroft 53, p. 3.

**Chloris I fain would try to love again** 206
**For him that would not live to love again.**
Song, music by John Wilson.
MS. Mus. b. 1, fol. 171.

**Chloris I loved, and Sappho now I love** 207
**And though I change my mistress, keep my love.**
Walsh, William, 'Elegie'.
MS. Malone 9, fol. 54 (autogr.).

**Chloris, it is not thy disdain** 208
**This scorn one day, one day by endless love.**
Godolphin, S[idney], Song, 'To the tune of, In faith I cannot keep my father's sheep'.
MS. Malone 13, p. 83.

**Chloris, let my passion ever** 209
**Still my ashes to admire.**
'A song'.
MS. Rawl. poet. 84, fol. 42.

**Chloris, may I unhappy prove** 210
**Then may I never love thee more.**
Godolphin, Sidney, 'Cloris'.
MS. Malone 13, p. 8.

**Chloris, now thou art fled . . .** see Chloris since thou art fled. . . .

**Chloris [sat, and sitting slept] sighed and sung and wept** 211
**They weeping hid them from the sun.**
Pr. *New Ayres and Dialogues*, 1678, p. 88.
MSS. Don. c. 57, fol. $14^{v}$, with music as pr. in *New Ayres*; Eng. poet. e. 14, fol. $38^{v}$; f. 16, fol. $2^{v}$.

**Chloris since thou art fled away** 212
**Amyntas dying, welladay, welladay.**
'Upon the Queens Departure'.
Attr. to Dr. Henry Hughes in the index to H. Lawes's *Ayres and Dialogues*, iii, 1669; included in B.M. Add. MS. 28622, fol. 39, amongst poems of R. Ayton.
MSS. Ashmole 38, fol. 238; Rawl. poet. 65, fol. 36; 84, fol. 88 rev.

**Chloris the nymph loved Corilas** 213
**That she so lightly should lose Corilas.**
MS. Eng. poet. f. 16, fol. 5.

**Chloris when I those blubbered cheeks do view,** 214
**I'll crown myself with honour I'll achieve.**
Mordant, Lord, 'To Chloris weeping'.
MS. Top. Oxon. e. 202, fol. 75.

**Chloris you must no more expect** 215
**A noble love, to avarice.**
'Written on the Frame of Chloris's pocket-glass, the Glass being broken out'.
MS. Don. c. 55, fol. $3^{v}$.

216 Chloris your self you so excel
But of his voice the boy had mourned.
Waller, Edmund, 'To a lady singing a song of his composing'.
Pr. *Poems*, 1645, p. 151.
MSS. *Don. d. 55, fol. 37v; Rawl. poet. 116, fol. 42.

217 Chommodius, when he would Commodius, said
No more Ionian but Hionian were.
J. F., translator, 'Catullus on Arrius, strictly'.
MS. *Eng. poet. f. 17, p. 20 (autogr.).

218 Choose friend with eagle's eyes, though few yet good
Are counted simple; and with frumps oft crossed.
MS. Tanner 306, fol. 241.

219 Choose no atheist
I hope I'm understood.
Election advice.
Note in B.M. MS. Harl. 4931, fol. 8v: 'This paper was throwne out in Lincolnshire . . . March 23 1639'.
MSS. Ashmole 36, 37, two copies, fols. 87 and 162.

220 Christ among men lived but in mean esteem,
While he is nothing much deceived is.
MS. *Rawl. poet. 97, fol. 49v (autogr.).

221 Christ as He in Himself performed hath
As I my Saviour for example have!
MS. *Rawl. poet. 97, fol. 42v (autogr.).

222 Christ as His father had determined
And so of Christ are all the prophecies.
MS. *Rawl. poet. 97, fol. 60 (autogr.).

223 Christ as His father Him commanded, so
But after by Himself was fully done.
MS. *Rawl. poet. 97, fol. 49v (autogr.).

224 Christ asked not questions 'cause He did not know
To hear Him speak in such sublimity.
MS. *Rawl. poet. 97, fol. 45 (autogr.).

225 Christ at a Leper's house sat down to meat
No ointment smells so sweet as her good name.
'The rich perfume'.
MS. Rawl. poet. 154, fol. 112.

226 Christ bids the dumb tongue speak: it speaks. The sound
Hell hath a wilder fire, and that shall tame thee.
[Crashaw, Richard], 'Upon the tongue'.
MS. Tanner 465, fol. 35, attr. to Mr. Crashaw on fol. 1*a*.

Christ born was King of Jewry, yet He went 227
Who should support them soonest them betray.
MS. *Rawl. poet. 97, fol. 40 (autogr.).

Christ came out of the virgin's closed womb: 228
To magnify Thine holy name for ever.
MS. *Rawl. poet. 97, fol. 67 (autogr.).

Christ Church a marriage [mask, match] [did make, late] made before the King 229
*or* Christ Church prepared [presents] a marriage for the King
*or* Christ Church th' Arts' marriage showed before the King
He offered twice or thrice to go away.
On Barten Holyday's *Marriage of the Arts*, acted before James I at Woodstock, 1621. Answered by A1341.
Possibly by William Meredith, organist of New College; see *Poems . . . by Henry King*, ed. J. Hannah, 1843, p. x.
MSS. Ashmole 38, p. 31; Eng. poet. e. 14, fol. 57; f. 10, fol. 121; Malone 19, p. 106; Rawl. poet. 116, fol. 67v; 147, p. 4; 199, p. 86; 210, fol. 51; Tanner 466, fol. 67; see also T392.

Christ come from banishment doth turn aside 230
We cannot see the truth, nor yet believe.
MS. *Rawl. poet. 97, fol. 41 (autogr.).

Christ comes four churches three 231
And tree of life.
Kynder, Philip, 'The Argument' of 'The Revelation interp'ted by Philip Kynder'.
MS. Ashmole 788, fol. 77 (autogr.).

Christ conquered that huge Leviathan 232
What shall we say? but, God the more be praised.
MS. *Rawl. poet. 97, fol. 3 (autogr.).

Christ did not only miracles while here 233
Can the Jews then another Christ expect.
MS. *Rawl. poet. 97, fol. 57 (autogr.).

Christ first on earth came in humility 234
Of Him who made them, gave them life and breath.
MS. *Rawl. poet. 97, fol. 61 (autogr.).

Christ for a while leaving His parents go; 235
For even of such God's kingdom doth consist.
MS. *Rawl. poet. 97, fol. 44 (autogr.).

Christ found was in the Temple, made abode 236
In our obedience, in true holiness.
MS. *Rawl. poet. 97, fol. 46v (autogr.).

Christ found was in the Temple: when you roam 237
But doth his father's will with all His might.
MS. *Rawl. poet. 97, fol. 46 (autogr.).

238 Christ from His birth sustained grief and want
And will not man for Christ scarce spend his breath?
MS. *Rawl. poet. 97, fol. 29v (autogr.).

239 Christ from His youth unto His baptism did
A man; much less would they when he was young.
MS. *Rawl. poet. 97, fol. 49 (autogr.).

240 Christ God eternal in time's plenitude
That day thou eatest thou shalt live for aye.
MS. *Rawl. poet. 97, fol. 37 (autogr.).

241 Christ, God of Love; in his etern decree
For ever, in his peace, and joy, remaining.
MS. Rawl. poet. 66, fol. 57.

242 Christ greater favour of a heathen found
Then beware truth, and plain simplicity.
MS. *Rawl. poet. 97, fol. 62v (autogr.).

243 Christ grew, while He at Nazareth abode
In Him God's love in fulness still remains.
MS. *Rawl. poet. 97, fol. 48v (autogr.).

244 Christ hath not only born, but healed all
Who gives each penitent believer, 's sight.
MS. *Rawl. poet. 97, fol. 54 (autogr.).

245 Christ having parted the unfaithful Jews
Or else the fisher had been fishes' food.
'Upon our Saviors walking on the sea'.
MS. Rawl. poet. 116, fol. 134.

246 Christ he was poor only that thou might'st be
Freed in the world to come from poverty.
Anagram: 'Christopher Wase. Christ [he] was pore'; couplet.
MS. Rawl. poet. 117, fol. 33v.

247 Christ here with toils thirty-three years was tossed
As he His saviour for example hath!
MS. *Rawl. poet. 97, fol. 29v (autogr.).

248 Christ in the scriptures bids us praise
By signs showed, before the doom.
Forman, Simon, 'Of Antichriste . . . finis 1603, 22 Nov.'
MS. Ashmole 802, fol. 111 (autogr.).

249 Christ in the tongue and money in the heart,
For conscience sake, alas, but few are teachers.
Robinson, Robert, 'In lingua Christianus', etc., translated.
MS. *Rawl. poet. 218, p. 85 (autogr.).

250 Christ is a perfect pattern for all them
That nothing spoil her, naught her undermine.
MS. *Rawl. poet. 97, fol. 30 (autogr.).

Christ is a witness just and true 251
His statutes evermore obey.
Beddome, Benjamin.
MS. *Eng. misc. e. 227, fol. 2v.

Christ is that good chirurgion, who doth cure 252
When among them shall be my sanctuary.
MS. *Rawl. poet. 97, fol. 30 (autogr.).

Christ is the blessed root 253
And have access to God.
Beddome, Benjamin.
MS. *Eng. misc. e. 227, fol. 9v.

Christ is the life, who ever draweth breath 254
And shall continue when all time is past.
MS. *Rawl. poet. 97, fol. 37 (autogr.).

Christ is the truth, they much deceived are 255
In my unfeigned keeping His behest!
MS. *Rawl. poet. 97, fol. 36v (autogr.).

Christ no respecter of men's persons is: 256
And those who coldly pray, He will not hear.
MS. *Rawl. poet. 97, fol. 55 (autogr.).

Christ of His parents in the Temple found 257
Kept all His sayings in her memory.
MS. *Rawl. poet. 97, fol. 46 (autogr.).

Christ our redeemer be thou pleas'd 258
While everlasting ages run.
'Engl. Primer of our Lady, 1631 . . . p. 28'.
MS. Eng. poet. e. 56, p. 52.

Christ our redeemer ever blest 259
Be glory now and ever done.
Huish, Alexander, 'Christe redemptor omnium', translated 'Dec. 14, 1638'.
MS. Eng. poet. e. 56, p. 52 (autogr.).

Christ rode some seven years since to court 260
He would not give the ass for all the horses in the mews.
'Verses found in a box sealed, found at the Court, and delivered to the King', 30 September, 1621.
MSS. Malone 19, p. 145; Rawl. poet. 26, fol. 88v, apparently attr. to John Willyams of Essex Esq., once of the Middle Temple.

Christ seemed to lose patience for a space 261
Father forgive them when he was cru[c]ified.
'Upon the casting of the buyers and sellers out of the temple'.
MS. Rawl. poet. 116, fol. 124.

Christ subject to His parents was so far 262
Us from the duty which to God we owe.
MS. *Rawl. poet. 97, fol. 43v (autogr.).

263 Christ that Jews might not for another look
He is the Christ then, who doth these fulfil.
MS. *Rawl. poet. 97, fol. 57v (autogr.).

264 Christ the son of God, He was at our suit
Sealed with his blood, that I might be enlarged.
H. W., Divine Meditations 3, 'Of our Saviour's death and passion'.
MS. Tanner 466, fol. 105.

265 Christ to the cross is nailed.
Who wipes all sins away.
'Engl. Primer of our Lady, 1631 . . . p. 316'.
MS. Eng. poet. e. 56, p. 10.

266 Christ was miraculous in all His ways,
Thy faith hath made thee whole; be not afraid!
MS. *Rawl. poet. 97, fol. 51v (autogr.).

267 Christ was not only wonderful, even then
Turns to his greater grief, man's greater light.
MS. *Rawl. poet. 97, fol. 56 (autogr.).

268 Christ was the word that spake it
That I believe, and take it.
'On the words *hoc est corpus meum*'.
Pr. Donne's *Poems*, 1635; attr. to Queen Elizabeth in Fuller's *Holy State*, 1648, IV. XV, p. 135; Francis Sandford's *Genealogical History*, 1677, p. 483.
MSS. Eng. poet. b. 5, p. 5; Rawl. poet. 116, fol. 101v, attr. to Q. Eliz.; Sancroft 98, p. 149, attr. to Qu. Eliz.; see also A1473, T3371, T3378.

269 Christ was, they say, a carpenter by birth:
But a great workman: He built Heaven and Earth.
[Jordan, Thomas], 'On our Saviour, his being call'd the Carpenter'.
Pr. *Divinity and Morality*, 1660, Sig. §§5v.
MS. Rawl. poet. 90, fols. 85 and 103.

270 Christ when he did forsaken man renew
All is his justly that all freely sends.
Clifford, Henry, Earl of Cumberland, 'Saint Bartholomew'.
MS. *Rawl. poet. 95, fol. 35.

271 Christ whose redemption all doth free,
And th' holy Ghost for ever more.
'Engl. Primer of our Ladie, 1631 . . . p. 2'.
MS. Eng. poet. e. 56, p. 25.

272 Christian, Pagan, Turk or Jew?
Knaves, fools and priests i' the world do make mad work.
Robinson, Robert.
MS. *Rawl. poet. 218, p. 19 (autogr.).

Christian religion doubtless is the best, 273
But oh th' hypocrisy that's in thy breast.
Robinson, Robert.
MS. *Rawl. poet. 218, p. 70 (autogr.).

Christmas hath made an end 274
Will I be merry.
'A caroll for Candlemas'.
Pr. *New Carolls for . . . Christmas*, 1661, Sig. B2.
MS. Eng. poet. b. 5, p. 61.

Christmas is a-coming, and merry we will be 275
And all in a chorus, cry, God save the King!
Pr. bk. Firth b. 22, fol. 49.

Christmas surcharged with feasting got at last 276
In wooden monuments let every breast be.
'An epitaph on the much deplored state of Christmas whose death and obsequies were celebrated on Candlemas night'.
MS. Ashmole 47, fol. 65.

Christ['s] agony no sooner ended, His 277
Once chosen hath, He keeps eternally.
MS. *Rawl. poet. 97, fol. 58v (autogr.).

Christ's body is the real manna, whence 278
Enabled to obtain the victory.
MS. *Rawl. poet. 97, fol. 22v (autogr.).

Christ's honour must for ever be displayed 279
Of all, Christ's honour ought to be expressed.
MS. *Rawl. poet. 97, fol. 37v (autogr.).

Christ's life unto a ship we may compare 280
Before the ship could to his haven pass.
MSS. Ashmole 36, 37, fol. 145; see also C282.

Christ's life was most pure, pious, and holy 281
And those that are dumb, he makes for to speak.
H. W., 'Of our Saviour's blessed life'.
MS. Tanner 466, fol. 104.

Christ's life we may unto a ship compare 282
Before the ship could to the haven pass.
'Christ'.
MSS. CCC. 328, fol. 87; Malone 19, p. 147; see also C280.

Christ's love to man is so exceeding good 283
He rose for his justification.
MS. *Rawl. poet. 97, fol. 74 (autogr.).

Christ's meekness, love, humiliation 284
Without remorse Him often crucify!
MS. *Rawl. poet. 97, fol. 23v (autogr.).

285 Christ's most inveterate, what dost thou fear
Which God, and man, and sovereign prince confess.
Samber, Robert, 'On twelfth Day' from 'the Bellman's Verses'.
MS. *Rawl. poet. 134*b*, fol. 154v (autogr.).

286 Christ's pains do no man's heart so truly strike
We everywhere shall find our cross, our sin.
MS. *Rawl. poet. 97, fol. 36 (autogr.).

287 Christ's passion hath that power, the imitation
It drives them, whence, the devil hath his ejection.
MS. *Rawl. poet. 97, fol. 29 (autogr.).

288 Christ's passion is a book wherein is writ
To study it, therein his life to spend.
MS. *Rawl. poet. 97, fol. 29 (autogr.).

289 Christ's passion is the only succour left
With grace, fits them for glory after this.
MS. *Rawl. poet. 97, fol. 29 (autogr.).

290 Christ's passion to Himself pain and annoy,
That our redemption is the harder task.
MS. *Rawl. poet. 97, fol. 29v (autogr.).

291 Christ's resurrection puts to silence them
The prophecies, which said, it so should be.
MS. *Rawl. poet. 97, fol. 66v (autogr.).

292 Christ's rules are all infallible: men err.
And not proceed in doing His command.
MS. *Rawl. poet. 97, fol. 30 (autogr.).

293 Christ's subject to His parents to convince
Thus, to reduce man to humility.
MS. *Rawl. poet. 97, fol. 47v (autogr.).

294 Christ's sufferings plain remonstrances have been
Our Saviour should be tortured for us!
MS. *Rawl. poet. 97, fol. 65v (autogr.).

295 Christ's sufferings we should daily keep in sight,
Consisteth every Christian's chiefest good.
MS. *Rawl. poet. 97, fol. 28 (autogr.).

296 Christ's venerable passion doth present
And with Christ travel to Jerusalem.
MS. *Rawl. poet. 97, fol. 28 (autogr.).

297 Christ's witnesses were many innocents
Maketh himself to wicked men a prey.
'Mors innocentum'.
MS. *Rawl. poet. 97, fol. 40 (autogr.).

298 Christ's words, His wisdom and great works express,
From Satan's band he's set at liberty.
MS. *Rawl. poet. 97, fol. 53v (autogr.).

Chronicles and annual books of kings 299
God grant them to be his servants good men and old.
Peeris, William, 'Secretary to . . . the Vth Earle of Northumberland', 'The discent of the Lord Percies'.
MS. Dodsworth 50, fol. 119.

Churchmen have set us all at strife, 300
So greatly be perplexed.
Robinson, Robert.
MS. *Rawl. poet. 218, p. 131 (autogr.).

Churchmen of all men most do break the peace: 301
Set an edge to soldier's swords!
Robinson, Robert.
MS. *Rawl. poet. 218, p. 129 (autogr.).

Church-Warden I've been, let me see very often 302
A snug little dinner and plenty of booze.
'The Vestry Dinner' 'by Mr. Reeves'.
MS. Mus. e. 19, p. 59.

Cicely saith plain-work's altogether worn 303
That she's content to let you rip her seaming.
Ashmole, Elias, 'On Cicely the Sempstres'.
MSS. Ashmole 36, 37, fol. 224 (autogr.).

Cinna cries out, I am not worth a groat 304
And is, plague on him, what he would be thought.
'An Epigram', couplet.
MS. Eng. poet. e. 40, fol. 40.

Claps on his hand, prays he may never thrive 305
If that his gelding be not under five (fingers sc[*ilicet*]).
'The Hors-courser's Equivocation'.
MS. Sancroft 53, p. 367 rev.

Claps were the bays old stagers once did use 306
Let him say what he would, he got a clap.
Bulteel, John, 'Of Sr W[illiam] D[avenant]'.
MS. *Rawl. poet. 159, fol. 209v.

Clara had your lovely face 307
Stop my false and perjured breath.
Hammond, Anthony, 'To Clara'.
Pr. *Miscellany of Original Poems*, 1720, p. 73.
MS. Rawl. D. 360, fol. 74 (autogr.).

Clara, I do not wish thee grossly send 308
A blushing rose, that kissed thy lily hand.
'In Claram'.
MS. Don. d. 58, fol. 37.

309 Clarendon had law [some law, wit] and sense
Or France bring in another.
'The Chits', Sunderland, Godolphin and Lawrence Hyde. From 'The Game of Chess'.
Pr. as Dryden's, with date 1680, *Poems on Affairs of State*, 1697, i. 173; also pr. *The works . . . of the Earls of Rochester and Roscommon*, 1709, p. 142.
MSS. Don. b. 8, p. 645; Sancroft 53, p. 40; Wood D. 19 (2), fol. 106v.

310 Clarinda the pride of the plain
And fainting in silence expired.
MS. Montagu e. 13, fol. 35v.

311 Clarinda's lips such magic virtue show
Enough to thaw and warm a frozen heart.
Morrice, John, 'On Clarinda's Lips', 1707.
MS. *Rawl. poet. 114, fol. 116 (autogr.).

312 Clarissa's charms poor Strephon struck.
Would warm you in December.
'The Looking Glass'.
MS. Ballard 50, fol. 104v.

313 Clarus all health to fair Clarinda sends
Calls me to prayers. My life, my soul, farewell.
'An Epistle to Clarinda', 1735.
MS. Eng. misc. e. 240, p. 176.

314 Clean without fear truth doth me constrain
God grant us all grace in heart to repent.
Watertoune, Thomas, 'A complaint of various oppressions'.
MS. Ashmole 48, fol. 7.

315 Clear Ankor on whose silver-sanded shore
And thou sweet Anchor art my Helicon.
D[rayton], M[ichael], 'Ankor'.
Pr. *Idea's Mirrour*, Amour 13.
MS. Rawl. poet. 142, fol. 19v.

316 Clear is the air and the morning fair
Dead, dead, dead, ah dead.
'The Hunting of the Hare. 2d song'.
Pr. *Wit and Drollery*, 1661, p. 115.
MS. Rawl. poet. 246, fol. 10v.

317 Clerk of the Bowbell with the yellow locks
For thy late ringing thy head shall have knocks.
'Bowbell being rung somewhat late, the Prentices set up a rime against the Clerke as followeth'. Couplet. Answered by C193.
MS. Sancroft 59, p. 280 rev.

318 Cleveland was certainly to blame
So many buttered buns.
'On the Duchess of Cleveland'.
MS. Don. b. 8, 2 copies, pp. 212 and 250.

Climb at court for me that will 319
Death's to him a strange surprise.
[Marvell, Andrew], translator, Seneca, *Thyestes*, chorus ii.
Pr. *Miscellaneous Poems*, 1681.
MSS. Rawl. poet. 90, fol. 165; 196, fol. 13v.

Climb not to highness' seat too fast, 320
The horse, that gallops, soon doth fall.
Robinson, Robert.
MS. *Rawl. poet. 218, p. 2 (autogr.).

Climb oh heart climb to thy rest, 321
Dying yet complain not on her.
Pr. Pilkington's *First Book of Songs*, 1605, xiii.
MSS. Mus. f. 7–10: f. 7, fol. 20v.

Clio, behold this charming day, 322
To comfort English widows.
[Williams, Sir Charles Hanbury], 'An Ode to Hen. Fox Esq.' *c.* 1743, on the marriage of the Dowager Duchess of Manchester to Edward Hussey, later Lord Beaulieu.
Pr. *An Ode to Hen. Fox Esq.*, 1746. See S1222.
MS. Ballard 50, fol. 96.

Cloak (if I so may call thee) though thou art 323
Tell him, his wits are gone a wool gathering.
[Jordan, Thomas], 'A Poet's farewell to his thred-bare cloake'.
Pr. *Wit in a Wilderness* [1665 (?)], fol. 1, and Sir John Mennes's *Musarum Deliciae*, 1665.
MS. Rawl. poet. 65, fol. 69: 84, fol. 76 rev.

Cloaks for the senate are, they say, decreed 324
'Twill raise a tax the nation cannot bear.
'On the House of Comons', amongst 'Jacobite Satyrs'.
MS. Add. A. 301, fol. 51v rev.

Clog of my spirit prithee get thee hence 325
Which prophecy's absolved in your wish.
Cavendish, Lady Jane, 'The discoursive Ghost'.
MS. *Rawl. poet. 16, p. 26.

Clorinda with disdain rejects my love; 326*a*
Nor can I rest—but in Aurelia's arms.
'The Disconsolate Lover, an Epigram', in the hand of Dr. Philip Doddrige.
MS. Montagu d. 12, fol. 232.

Cloris . . . see Chloris . . .

Close by a crystal river's side 326*b*
Left to the mercy both of wind and tide.
'The Dreame'.
MS. *Rawl. poet. 87, p. 64.

327 **Close by a fringed bank I found**
**Farewell, oh farewell, and so died.**
Song.
MS. Mus. b. 1, fol. 114$^{v}$, music by John Wilson.

328 **Close by a stream, whose flowery bank might give**
**And arms my tortured soul to bear my pains.**
Scrope, Sir Car[r], translator, 'The Parting of Sireno and Diana'. 'F[rom] D[ryden's] Miscellany Poems', 1684, p. 173.
MS. Rawl. poet. 222, fol. 31$^{v}$.

329 **Close by this small remembrance you may find**
**These have they parted *etc.***
MS. Sancroft 59, p. 295 rev.

330 **Close in her hallowed grot, where mildy bright**
**And calm, prefer oblivion to disgrace.**
'Isis, wrote by Dr. Cooper a Physician in Berkshire', 1747–50.
MS. Ballard 29, fol. 103.

331 **Close not the grave as yet, rude hands; forbear,**
**Where faith is your supporter, and your tomb.**
King, John (?), 'An Elegie upon the death of Mistress Anne Berkley, wife to Mr. Henry King'.
See *B.Q.R.* v, 1929, p. 331, and *B.L.R.* iv, 1953, p. 238.
MS. Rawl. D. 398, fol. 172, in John King's hand.

332 **Close stools thus made by Astragon we have**
**As well to purge, as wipe the tail.**
'On [Davenant's] Gondibert'.
Pr. *Certain Verses, . . . to be reprinted with . . . Gondibert*, 1653, p. 22.
MS. CCC. 309, fol. 56.

333 **Close to the gates a spacious garden lies**
**The people one and one supplies the King.**
'The Gardens of Alcinus from Homer's Odyss. 7'.
MS. Rawl. poet. 116, fol. 98$^{v}$.

334 **Close up those wonders which make blind mine eyes**
**Of heat to die, than starve through absent beams.**
Ashmole, Elias, 'A song . . . 4 May 1649'.
MSS. Ashmole 36, 37, fol. 236$^{v}$ (autogr.).

335 **Close wrapped in Port[smouth]'s smock thy senses are**
**Secure thy nation and thyself from harms.**
Acrostic on Charles [II].
MS. Firth c. 16, p. 91.

336 **Closed in this earth's voracious womb**
**And meet his saviour in the skies.**
Webb, Foster, 'Epitaph' [on his father (?)].
MS. Eng. poet. c. 9, p. 112.

**Clothed in state, and girt with might,** 337
**In thy house where we adore.**
Herbert, Mary (*née* Sidney), Countess of Pembroke, Psalm xciii.
MS. *Rawl. poet. 24, p. 138.

**Coarcted hearts with care, sojourning long,** 338
**Ah! aim at heaven, the life of your desire.**
F. W., 'Sonnet 4. To the Christian reader'.
MS. *Rawl. C. 639, p. 12.

**Cobblers and [colliers] coopers and the rest** 339
**Old officers which still continue true.**
Ballad, new year 1641 (?). Attr. to I. Shirley in B.M. MS. Harl. 6918, fol. 28. See *R.E.S.* ix, 1933, p. 27.
MSS. Ashmole 36, 37, fol. 127; Rawl. poet. 26, fol. 139$^{v}$; 62, fol. 44$^{v}$.

**Cock a doodle doo** 340
**And didn't know what to do.**
MS. Douce d. 59, fol. 57.

**Cock Lorell [Cocklorin] would needs have the Devil his guest,** 341
**From whence it was called the Devil's arse.**
[Jonson, Ben.], song from *The Metamorphosed Gipsies.*
Pr. *Ben Jonson*, ed. Herford and Simpson, vii, 1941, p. 601.
MSS. Rawl. poet. 172, fol. 78$^{v}$; Tanner 465, fol. 85; Wood F. 34, fol. 161; see also C712.

**Cocus the centaur as I hear of late** 342
**Till shame send you down where first you begun.**
Libel on Edward Coke and his second wife Lady Hatton, *c.* 1598.
MS. Don. c. 54, fol. 6$^{v}$.

**Cocus the pleader hath a lady wed** 343
**And thou ne'er saw'st it till the game was played.**
'A Libell upon Mr. Edw. Cooke, then Attorney general and sithence Cheefe Justice of the Comon pleas [1606–1613] upon some disagreement betweene him and his wife . . .' *c.* 1598.
MS. Don. c. 54, fol. 6$^{v}$.

**Codrus hath chose Turpilia for his wife** 344
**In that he joined so well, a pair so ill.**
'In Codrum'.
MS. Rawl. poet. 212, fol. 55$^{v}$.

**Cold and raw the [north] wind doth blow** 345
**Some other should buy her barley.**
[d'Urfey, Thomas].
Pr. *New Poems*, 1690, p. 132.
MSS. Douce d. 59, fol. 52; Rawl. poet. 196, fol. 24$^{v}$.

346 Cold is that heart. Alive to friendship warm,
Who long admir'd thee as the best of men.
MS. Toynbee b. 1, fol. 181$^{v}$.

347 Cold is the senseless heart that hath not strove
Formed to enslave my heart and grace my lay.
Bampfylde, J[ohn Codrington], 'A Sonnet'.
Pr. *Poetical Works*, Routledge's British Poets, 1881, p. 6.
MS. Eng. misc. e. 241, fol. 60.

348*a* Cold winter ah! why art thou gone
That I see the same object with him.
'A Ballad'.
MS. Montagu e. 13, fol. 59.

348*b* Colin the clown comes when he'd sown his seed
Only take care the locusts hurt it not.
Walsh, William, translator, [Greek Anthology] 'p. 192'.
MS. *Malone 9, fol. 28 (autogr.).

349 Columns and laboured urns but vainly show
Or kindred tempers have a tear to lend.
Grove, William, epitaph on Lady Smith.
MSS. Don. c. 57, fol. 87; Eng. poet. c. 51, p. 50, attr. to William Grove.

350 Come again, sweet love doth now invite
Did tempt while she for triumph laughs.
Pr. John Dowland, *First Booke of Songes or Ayres*, 1597, xvii.
MSS. Don. d. 58, fol. 24$^{v}$; Douce 280, fol. 67; Mus. f. 7–10: f. 10, fol. 12$^{v}$.

351 Come Alecto lend me thy torch
Therefore, gentlemen, be merry in prose.
On Thomas Churchyard, d. 1604.
Pr. Camden's *Remaines*, 1605, p. 59.
MSS. Ashmole 38, p. 170; Don. d. 58, fol. 16; Eng. poet. e. 40, fol. 118.

352 Come all fast friends let's jointly pray
We'll drink his health that's far awaw.
'A Scotch Song on the 10th of June', the Old Pretender's birthday.
MS. Rawl. poet. 155, p. 142.

353 Come all loyal subjects I pray you draw near,
For now to our comfort the peace is proclaimed.
MS. Firth c. 18, fols. 49 and 90.

354 Come all my brave soldiers of every degree,
Here's a health to them for ever in a flowing bowl.
'The Battle of Minden', 1 August 1759.
MS. Firth c. 20, fol. 26.

355 Come all my dear delights
There's nothing sweet, save wine and wenches.
Answer to H593; see also R177.
MSS. Ashmole 36, 37, fol. 26.

Come all my gay lads that love frisking and dancing 356*a*
A few active measures will ever be best.
Gough, Richard, 'The New Pond, a Song. Enfield, 177 . . .'.
MS. *Eng. poet. c. 5, two copies, fols. 238–9 (autogr.).

Come all my people to my law give ear 356*b*
He justly fed them: Wisely guided all.
Fairfax, Thomas, Lord, Psalm lxxviii.
MS. *Fairfax 38, p. 333; see also C662.

Come all the world submit yourselves to care 357
Care chiefly stands to either make or mar.
'Madrigal for five voices'. Music by Daniel Taylor.
MS. Mus. d. 8, fol. 49$^{v}$.

Come all tricking papists, lady abbess and nuns, 358
The church that gets heirs; but I doubt she's a whore.
'Loretta and Winifred'. On James II's son, 1688.
MSS. Douce 357, fol. 152; Firth c. 16, p. 261.

Come all valiant sailors of courage stout and bold, 359
Then drink about till it's out, and drive away all sorrow.
'A New Sea Song'.
MS. Firth c. 18, fol. 114.

Come all whose dulled and earthly minds 360
Will not admit the sunbeams bright.
Hobart, John, translator, Boethius, *Consolations*, III. x; sent to Sir Nicholas Bacon 1664.
MS. Tanner 306, fol. 314$^{v}$.

Come all ye bold Britons that plough the raging main, 361
So here is a health to all jolly sailors bold.
MS. Firth c. 18, fol. 51.

Come all ye brave Britons, let no one complain 362
Can e'er be compared with the year fifty-nine.
'The Year 59'.
MS. Firth c. 18, fol. 110.

Come all ye discontented souls 363
You'll care no more than I do.
Weaver, Thomas.
Pr. *Songs and Poems*, 1654.
MS. *Rawl. poet. 211, fol. 65$^{v}$ (autogr.).

Come all ye gallant seamen, come listen unto me, 364
Likewise their dear children, who are left fatherless.
'The Polly Privateer'.
Pr. *Real Sailor Songs*, ed. J. Ashton, 1891, p. 28.
MS. Firth c. 18, fol. 77.

365 Come all ye muses and rejoice
At our Apollo's happy choice.
'On Dr. Corbett's marriage'.
Pr. *Wit Restored*, 1658, p. 132.
MSS. Eng. poet. e. 97, p. 69; Rawl. poet. 199, p. 83.

366 Come all ye nobles that are great ones
Trade like their husbands their own way.
MS. Ashmole 421, fol. 177[v].

367 Come all ye nymphs and every swain
As more divinity betrays.
'Of the Dutchesse made by Mrs. Taylor'.
MS. Rawl. poet. 172, fol. 110.

368 Come all ye pale lovers, that sigh and complain
No rival can lessen, or envy destroy.
MS. Mus. Sch. C. 95, p. 70, music by Anthony Young.

369 Come all ye sacred tuneful nine,
Nor less like them in paths of virtue shine.
S. R., 'An Acrostick, to Lady Charlotte Compton, Aug. 8. 1741'.
MS. Eng. misc. e. 183, fol. 67[v].

370 Come all ye valiant martial sons
To serve the world as just, as once did he.
Spoure, Edmund, on 'Prince Charles Leopold, Duke of Lorrain', d. 1690.
MS. *Eng. poet. c. 52, fol. 30[v] (autogr.).

371 Come all ye young lovers who wan with despair
For in spite of grave lessons, by Jove I'll be free.
'A ne[w & f]avourite Song', 18 Nov. 1747.
MS. Mus. e. 20, fol. 18.

372 Come all ye young nuns who are tired of St. Clare's
Since thanks to [offarall's (?)] I am fairly got free.
'The Nuns of St. Clare'.
MS. Eng. misc. b. 48, fol. 113.

373 Come all ye young sailors, of courage bold,
In the year ninety-two boys, unto my life's end.
'Bold Captain Avery'.
MS. Firth c. 18, fol. 127*c*; see also C375.

374 Come all you bold tars who long for glory and renown,
And victory complete crown'd the glorious day.
More, —, 'A Song in praise of Admiral Duncan'.
MS. Firth c. 18, fol. 38.

Come all you brave boys, whose courage is bold, 375
For the sword shall maintain me as long as I live.
'The Commission or Rodomontade of Captain Every, just after he run away with the ship Charles the 2nd from the Groyne and went on the Pirate Trade . . .' *c.* 1693.
MS. Add. A. 301, fol. ii[v]; see also C373.

Come all you brave sailors wherever you be, 376
Bold Britons they never will yield to the slaves.
'A New Song in Praise of Admiral Rodney's late Victory', 1780.
MS. Firth c. 18, fol. 82.

Come all you brave seamen that have a mind to enter 377
And we will sing a quellieux to those Irish dear joys.
'The Weymouth Frigate', 1695.
MS. Firth c. 18, fol. 107.

Come all you brisk young women, to Drypool side repair, 378
From jilting jades God bless our hearts wherever they do go.
'The jovial Sailor's Jollity. To the Tune of, Moss catch'd his Mare'.
Song III in *The Beau's Garland*, pr. bk. Douce PP. 161.
MS. Firth c. 18, fol. 202.

Come all you British heroes of courage stout and bold 379
With British guards to boldly fight, and drive the French away.
'On the Battle of Lincelles', 18 Aug. 1793.
MSS. Firth c. 17, fol. 62; c. 20, fol. 40.

Come all you Britons bold, 380
To Liverpool again.
'Captain Barber'.
MS. Firth c. 18, fol. 7.

Come all you farmers out of the country 381
Honour invites you to delights.
MS. Rawl. poet. 160, fol. 185.

Come all you heroes of courage stout and bold 382
And the troops that took Bellisle.
'A New Song on the Taking of Bellisle'.
Song VIII in *The Exeter Garland*, Bodl. pr. bk. 8° E. 281(3). B.S.
MS. Firth c. 18, fol. 16.

Come all you honest voters 383
And a-begging we must go.
'The Oxfordshire Voters', 2 Apr. 1753. In shorthand.
Pr. *The Oxfordshire Contest*, 1753, p. 36.
S. Mus. e. 20, fol. 24*b*.

384 Come all you jolly boys
For the landladies they are all cheats.
'The Jolly Sailor's Advice'.
MS. Firth c. 18, fol. 200.

385 Come all you jolly Britons of every degree,
The French to fight was our delight, when e'er they gave command.
'The Battle of Warburg', 31 July 1760.
MSS. Firth c. 17, fol. 53; c. 20, fol. 33.

386 Come all you jolly sailors bold
Unto the Bank of England.
'A New Song on the Capture of the Dumourier Privateer and the Spanish Galleon'.
MS. Firth c. 18, fol. 36.

387 Come all you lads and buxom lasses, young and old of each degree,
Get your little cradles ready for the jackets of true blue.
'The Sailor's Visit'.
MS. Firth c. 18, fol. 209.

388 Come all you noble bold commanders, that the raging ocean use,
Captain Eldeb, for cruel murder, on a gibbet now must die.
'Capt. Eldeb's Cruelty to his boy'.
MS. Firth c. 18, fol. 195.

389 Come all you religious whom envy doth move
When this wine they tipple they shall o'er the mountains spring.
MS. Rawl. poet. 37, p. 97.

390 Come all you valiant sailors, of courage, stout and bold,
Though he knew it was our due, 'twould help to increase his store.
'The Sailor's lamentation', 23 December 1736.
MS. Firth c. 18, fol. 112.

391 Come all you valiant seamen,
In the time of war.
'The Vice Admiral's Advice to all loyal hearted Men'.
MS. Firth c. 18, fol. 104.

392 Come all you youths that yet are free
Like Arundel and Gray.
'A Ballad to the tune of Chevy Chase or When as King Henry, 1682'.
MSS. Douce 357, fol. $95^v$; Firth c. 15, p. 124.

393 Come Amarillis come away
I will crown thee, I will crown thee, with the stars.
'Christ and his spouse'.
MS. Rawl. poet. 37, p. 28.

Come and crown your lover's wishes 394
That through them I safe may gaze.
'Verses to a girl cleaning Pewter'.
MS. Eng. misc. b. 48, fol. 99.

Come and let us live my dear 395
As shall mock the envious eye.
Crashaw, Richard, translator, Catullus, v.
MSS. Eng. poet. f. 25, fol. 13; Tanner 465, fol. $50^v$, attr. to R. Cr., and to Mr. Crashaw on fol. 1*a*.

Come and listen to my ditty. 396
Since in yours I cannot be.
MS. Montagu e. 13, fol. 61.

Come and listen to my ditty 397
Be't known that G—h's his name.
'A Good enough Ballad on a Bad [enough subject] 4 June 1753'.
Pr. *The Oxfordshire Contest*, 1753, p. 59.
MS. Mus. e. 20, fol. 25*c*$^v$.

Come and trip it as you go 398
On the light fantastic toe.
[Milton, John].
From Handel's *Il Penseroso*, with music.
MS. Mus. c. 107, fols. $42^v$, 41.

Come, attend, British boys 399
By St. George, but another convention.
'On Porto Bello, and the Convention', Admiral Vernon's victory, 16 Nov. 1739.
Pr. 1740 (Bodl. pr. bk. Firth c. 8 (14)).
MS. Eng. misc. b. 48, fol. 13.

Come away, 400
And the music shall be praise.
Herbert, George, 'Doomes Day'.
Pr. *The Temple*, 1633, p. 181.
MS. *Tanner 307, fol. $137^v$.

Come away, come away, 401
They lovingly hang altogether.
Weaver, Thomas, 'A Christmas Carol, 1647'.
Not in *Songs and Poems by T. W.*, 1654.
MS. *Rawl. poet. 211, fol. $24^v$ (autogr.).

Come away come away you lady gay 402
Appear, appear! I come, I come.
Beaumont and Fletcher, song in *The Chances*, v. iii.
MS. Don. c. 57, fol. $67^v$, with music by Robert Johnson.

Come away, come sweet love. 403
Winged with sweet hopes and heavenly fire.
Pr. Dowland's *Songs or Ayres*, 1597, xi.
MSS. Mus. f. 7–10: f. 9, fol. $5^v$.

404 Come away, Hymen doth stay,
Haste and let the rites be done.
Shirley, James, 'Paranimphi'.
Pr. from this MS., *Works*, ed. A. Dyce, 1833, vi. 501.
MS. *Rawl. poet. 88, p. 27.

405 Come, beauteous nymph, can'st thou embrace
You and I shall lie together.
'An old man courting a young girl'.
Pr. Cleveland's *Works*, 1687, p. 224.
MS. Rawl. poet. 173, fol. 84.

406 Come, bend thy studious mind to what I say
Not hope; nought hard to God, all easy be.
J. F., 'Linus, of Wisdome'.
MS. *Eng. poet. f. 17, p. 58 (autogr.).

407 Come Billy, come Susan, come Harry, come Kate
Yet still I must love her because she is new.
MS. Eng. misc. b. 48, fol. 27.

408 Come blessed bird of hers: Oh how I will
Was ever man such strange penance assigned?
Ch. M., 'Sonnett'.
MS. Eng. misc. d. 239, fol. 8ᵛ.

409 Come blessed comforter and shed
Live to my God and sing his praise.
Beddome, Benjamin, 'An Hymn'.
MS. *Eng. misc. e. 227, fol. 173.

410 Come bold British tars give an ear to my song,
And straight to Newcastle we sail'd away.
1782.
MS. Firth c. 18, fol. 130.

411 Come bonds, come death, nor do you shrink, my ears
Nor other death, than that; the fear to die.
Crashaw, Richard, 'Paul's resolution'.
MS. Tanner 465, fol. 37, attr. to Mr. Crashaw on fol. 1*a*.

412 Come brave boys
So to Lockett's to dinner.
'Tune, Let the Soldiers rejoice etc.'
MS. Mus. Sch. C. 95, p. 212; tune, p. 213.

413 Come, brave boys, we're on for marching
If I die, my soul in glory is, Love, farewell.
'The March of the Connaught Rangers'.
MS. Firth c. 17, fol. 66.

414 Come brave soldiers, come and see
That were before of victory.
Crashaw, Richard. 'In cicatrices Domini Jesu'.
MS. Tanner 465, fol. 37, attr. to Mr. Crashaw on fol. 1*a*.

Come bring the song 415
Bring forth more such fruit as glad Glovernia bears.
'A song on the Princes berthday', [Queen Anne, 1700].
MS. Mus. c. 6, fol. 41. Music by Blow.

Come, bring thy gift, if blessings were as slow, 416
And be my salvation.
Herbert, George, 'An Offering'.
Pr. *The Temple*, 1633, p. 141.
MSS. Rawl. poet. 90, fol. 143ᵛ; *Tanner 307, fol. 107.

Come, bring us out the widest bowl, 417
And quenches purgatory.
Owen, Corbett, 'The Goodfellow'.
MS. Eng. poet. e. 4, p. 158; see also C455.

Come bring us wine in plenty 418
Ne'er call, drawer what's to pay?
'Words to a Tune of Mr. Richard Loe's'.
MS. Mus. Sch. C. 95, p. 56.

Come Britons give ear 419
Twice a day to besh-t you, for me to make clean.
'On the Prince of Wales befouling himself', lampoon *c.* 1714–15.
MS. Eng. poet. e. 87, p. 20.

Come brother of the flood let's drink 420
In the valiant Salamander.
MS. Firth c. 18, fol. 86.

Come brother sailors lend an ear 421
All their want for to redress.
'On the distresses of the sloop Peggy, Capt. Harrison, bound from Fyall to New York, 1765'.
See Archibald Duncan, *The Mariners' Chronicle*, [1810], i. 229.
MS. Firth c. 18, fol. 118.

Come buy my new almanacks every one 422
Come buy my new almanacks buy.
1641.
MS. Rawl. poet. 71, p. 5.

Come Celia fix thine eyes on mine 423
Though the blind mole discern not day.
Carew, Thomas, 'To a lady not yet enjoyed by her husband'.
Pr. *Poems*, 1640.
MS. *Don. b. 9, fol. 32ᵛ; pr. bk. 27980 e. 86, opp. p. 19, attr. to Carew.

Come christian people all give ear 424
And God bless some of th' peers.
'On the burning of London Bridge and three children drowned in the Thames'.
Pr. bk. Vet. A3 e. 806.

425 Come Clio sweet, my never-idle muse
And long time lived, and died in endless bliss.
[Sabie, Francis], 'Flora's Fortune. The second parte of the fisherman's Tale'.
Pr. 1595.
MS. Douce 280, fol. 161ᵛ.

426 Come come all noble souls, who skilled in music's art
Is love and harmony.
'Glee . . . by Dr. Rogers', 3 parts.
MS. Mus. d. 177, fols. 31ᵛ with 4th part by G. Heathcote, and 45ᵛ.

427 Come, come away
Anon, anon, anon, Sir what's it you say?
Catch by John Hilton.
MS. Mus. d. 177, fol. 31.

428 Come, come blest Flora to my circling arms
Nor death nor fate our blisses shall destroy.
Chatwin, John, 'A Dialogue. Alexis and Flora'.
MS. *Rawl. poet. 94, p. 84 (autogr.).

429 Come come, cavaliers
From hell but the devil and the roundhead.
Weaver, Thomas, 'A carol for Christmas day, 1646'.
Pr. *Songs and Poems by T. W.*, 1654.
MS. *Rawl. poet. 211, fol. 20ᵛ (autogr.).

430 Come come great monarch come away
Except to dance a Tyburn jigg Couragio Couragio Couragio.
'Revolution on Revolution a Song', *c.* 1715.
MS. Rawl. poet. 155, p. 131.

431 Come, come, I faint, thy heavy stay
If living thus I live or dead I be.
Strode, William, 'Song to his mistress'.
MS. *CCC. 325, fol. 129ᵛ (autogr.).
MS. Malone 21, fol. 84ᵛ.

432 Come, come, let us drink
And jointly we will spend it.
[Brome, Alexander], 'The Careless'.
Pr. *Poems*, 1661, p. 48.
MS. Ashmole 47, fol. 135ᵛ.

433*a* Come, come, let us with joyful voice
I will so work you never shall obtain.
Herbert, Mary (*née* Sidney), Countess of Pembroke, Psalm xcv.
MS. *Rawl. poet. 24, p. 140.

433*b* Come come my blessed infant and immure thee
And seal that granted pardon with a kiss.
[Quarles, Francis], 'The holy Virgins Lament, over her blessed Infant'.
Pr. *Emblemes*, 1635, iv. 9.
MS. Rawl. poet. 90, fol. 26ᵛ.

Come, come my Orinda and now let us prove 434
So long as I'm blest in Orinda's soft arms.
Chatwin, John, 'Song'.
MS. *Rawl. poet. 94, p. 121 (autogr.).

Come come sweet love why dost thou stay 435
Let's take our pleasure while we may.
MS. Don. c. 57, fol. 39, with music.

Come, come: thy stay methinks is such a thing 436
As if along with thee all worth were gone.
Oldisworth, Nicolas, 'To his Friend beyond Sea'.
MS. *Don. c. 24, fol. 58 (autogr.).

Come, come, to th' bar, to th' bar they cry 437
It would dissolve the Parliament.
W. R., 'The Parliament Articles against a handsome wench'.
MS. Rawl. poet. 142, fol. 39.

Come, come you king of terrors, for I crave 438
Sweet hallelujahs to the ethereal King.
'A Call to Death'.
MS. Rawl. poet. 84, fol. 34.

Come, come you'd have it so; sooner than I 439
Like Phaeton to set the world on fire.
'On the received report of Prince Ruperts death to Ananias Simple . . .'.
MS. Rawl. poet. 26, fol. 147ᵛ.

Come constant hearts that so prevail 440
Free from vain sighs sad groans and tears.
Pr. John Wilson's *Cheerfull Ayres or Ballads*, 1660, p. 32, and E. P[hillips], *The Mysteries of Love and Eloquence*, 1658.
MS. Mus. b. 1, fol. 43ᵛ, with music by Wilson.

Come dear Laurinda let's retreat 441
Than scorn and a big belly too.
Chatwin, John, 'A Pastoral Dialogue. Lysidas and Laurinda'.
MS. *Rawl. poet. 94, p. 138 (autogr.).

Come do not blush, but speak your mind, 442
A woman then an angel I'll believe.
Chatwin, John, 'A Dialogue'.
MS. *Rawl. poet. 94, p. 197 (autogr.).

Come, doctor, use thy roughest art 443
That I should hope 't would almost quench my fire.
Cowley, Abraham, 'The Cure'.
Pr. *Works*, 1668, 'The Mistress', p. 69.
MS. Rawl. poet. 173, fol. 80ᵛ.

Come Dorus come let songs thy sorrows signify 444
Seen and unknown heard but without attention.
Sidney, Sir Philip, from the *Arcadia*.
MS. *e Mus. 37, fol. 34.

445 Come drawer and fill us about some wine
And our drink shall be cordial gold.
[Brome, Alexander], 'The Souldiers Resolve'.
Pr. *Poems*, 1661, p. 69, 'The Independants resolve . . . written in 1648'.
MS. Ashmole 47, fol. 153.

446 Come drawer some wine
Till the gallow-tree takes 'em from danger.
Weaver, Thomas, 'The Compounder's Song'.
Pr. *Songs and Poems by T.W.*, 1654.
MS. *Rawl. poet. 211, fol. $72^{v}$ (autogr.).

447 Come dry your eyes: He lives; 'twas but to see
More to rejoice that he now joys above.
Elegy on Brian Cave, student of the Middle Temple.
MS. Rawl. D. 400, fol. 79.

448 Come, each death-doing dog who dares venture his neck,
So at you, ye b—rs, here's give you hot stuff.
'Hot Stuff'.
Pr. Parkman, *Montcalm and Wolfe*, 1897–8, ii. 254.
MS. Firth c. 17, fol. 49.

449 Come Echo I thee summon
This is a woman truly.
MSS. Ashmole 38, p. 119; Don. d. 58, fol. $28^{v}$; Eng. poet. e. 14, fol. $73^{v}$; f. 25, fol. 65; Malone 19, p. 161.

450 Come fates I fear you not; all whom I owe
How is't I now was there, and now I fell.
Donne, John, 'Elegie'.
Pr. *Poems*, 1635.
MSS. *Eng. poet. f. 9, p. 56; Rawl. poet. 31, fol. $26^{v}$.

451 Come Favonius! spread thy wing,
Kisses sweet as those you bring.
'Wrote in an Alcove in Vaux-Hall Gardens'.
MS. Eng. poet. c. 9, p. 139.

452 Come fill it up; and fill it high,
And be throughout like those above.
'Anacreon Imitated: a Drunken Catch'.
MS. Rawl. poet. 173, fol. 61.

453 Come fill [the] up our glasses until they run o'er
Here here's to the best, I mean the best wine.
MSS. Douce 357, fol. $84^{v}$; Mus. Sch. C. 95, p. 144 (no tune).

454 Come fill up the bowl with liquor that fine is
Punch cheers the heart.
'A Song in praise of Punch. The Tune Subligny's Minuet'.
MS. Mus. Sch. C. 95, p. 254.

Come fill us up the widest bowl, 455
And quenches purgatory.
'The Good-fellow. A Song'.
MS. Eng. misc. e. 255, fol. 33; see also C417.

Come follow follow me / Good neighbours all that be 456
The sun will light us home to bed.
Amherst, Elizabeth, 'The Fairy Song alter'd for the New Year's day Merry-meeting at Sevenoakes'.
MS. *Eng. poet. e. 109, p. 17.

Come follow follow me / With mirth and merry glee 457
Jack's Cloak is better than chalk.
'Jacks Cloake'.
MSS. Mus. f. 17–19: f. 19, fol. $27^{v}$.

Come follow follow me / Ye brave nobility 458
We live in love and peace with all.
MS. Rawl. poet. 37, p. 74.

Come follow, follow me, ye jovial boys that be 459
We'll circle Cambridge round about.
MS. Eng. poet. f. 25, fol. 67.

Come follow, follow me; you fairy elves that be 460
The glow-worm lights us home to bed.
'A Song'.
Pr. E[dward] P[hillips], *Mysteries of Love and Eloquence*, 1658, p. 74. Percy's *Reliques*, 1765, iii. 207, and Ritson, *Fairy Tales*, 1831, p. 195.
MSS. Ashmole 36, 37, fol. 187; Eng. poet. e. 14, fol. $18^{v}$; Montagu e. 13, fol. $15^{v}$; Rawl. poet. 153, fol. $13^{v}$.

Come follow me fair nymphs 461
But I love killed the deer.
Pr. Thomas Bateson's *First Set of English Madrigales*, 1604, v.
MSS. Mus. f. 17–19: f. 19, fol. $23^{v}$.

Come follow me to the greenwood tree, 462
Then follow.
'Canon. Dr. W. Hayes. 1765'.
MS. Mus. d. 177, fol. $14^{v}$.

Come folly's leopard and tell me why 463
The sign of th' chequer in thy face says so.
Filer, Samuel, 'Uppon his Mistresses Black patches'. 'Recantation', T1069.
MS. Rawl. poet. 65, fol. $66^{v}$.

Come forth and let my dull soul ravished be 464
Nor write it till thy wing affords the quill.
Southwell, Sir Robert, 'An invitation to a Bee to come out of her hive'.
MS. *Eng. poet. f. 6, fol. 39 (autogr.).

465 **Come forth bright nymphs and jolly swains**
**Still keeping holiday.**
'English Song' for Oxford Act, music by Mr. Bowman.
Pr. *Songs for 1, 2 and 3 voices . . . by Henry Bowman*, 1678, p. 69.
MS. Mus. Sch. C. 145, fol. 9.

466 **Come forth, come forth most equal pair**
**Th' embraces which endeavoured you.**
Weaver, Thomas, 'Epithalamie on the marriage of the Earle of Athol and the Lady Æmilia Stanley', daughter of the seventh Earl of Derby, 5 May 1659.
MS. *Rawl. poet. 211, fol. 40 (autogr.).

467 **Come from the dungeon to the throne**
**First they are crowned; and then they bleed.**
Cartwright, William, 'The Preests Song when the slave was invested in the Royall Robes'.
In *The Royal Slave*, I. ii.
MS. Rawl. poet. 172, fol. 30.

468 **Come, gentle cousins, come with funeral blacks**
**This scene of woe is mine. Yours is to come.**
Chamber, N[ath'], on the death of his brother 'George Chamber Priest Mr in Artes [1626], of Queen's Colledg: in Cambridge'.
MS. Ashmole 38, fol. 240.

469 **Come gentle reader, gentle friend**
**The man who made soles at his will.**
'On one Cosier a Cobler'.
MS. Eng. poet. e. 40, fol. 113; see also C485.

470 **Come, gentle sleep, attend thy votary's prayer**
**Thus, without dying, oh how sweet to die!**
Wolcot, John (Peter Pindar), translation from Latin.
MS. Eng. poet. c. 51, p. 242.

471 **Come gentlemen, and hear this ditty**
**And dare presume to take a purse.**
'The Politick Squire, or the highwaymen catched in their own Play'.
MSS. Firth c. 20, fol. 91; d. 14, fol. 170.

472 **Come gentlemen come and see my fine show**
**'Tis to drink one good healt to de noble King Jemmy.**
'A New Ballad to the Tune of Dear Catholick Bro:'.
MS. Rawl. poet. 155, p. 177.

473 **Come God's eternal virgin wisdom see**
**Ill to themselves and hurt thine too.**
'An offering to God . . . for the Justification of the Divine Wisdome . . . in Francis Hoffman'.
MS. Rawl. poet. 172, fol. 91.

**Come, happy flowers! Dame Nature's pride** 474
**It there lies down and lulls itself to rest.**
Chatwin, John, 'To Sylvia. On his snatching a Posie from her'.
MS. *Rawl. poet. 94, p. 215 (autogr.).

**Come hark to our ditty, which shall not be long** 475
**So beginning with nothing, in nothing they end.**
'On Nothing'.
MS. Ballard 47, fol. 145.

**Come haste away Palaemon from thy shade** 476
**Pan keep your flocks, and guide you with his light.**
'A Pastorall Dialogue between Sylvander, and Palaemon'.
MS. *Don. e. 19, fol. 22.

**Come heavy souls oppressed with the weight** 477
**Sigh: and sigh out! groan once, and groan no more.**
Strode, [William], song from *The Floating Island.*
MS. Rawl. poet. 172, fol. 30.

**Come, help, my melting muse, come, help bewail,** 478
**With open mouth tells all what fate they have.**
Jones, Robert, of King's School Sherborne, on Robert Whetcombe, 'Antientest Governour of the King's Schoole of Sherebourne', 24 Oct. 1656.
MS. Gough Dorset 35(1), fol. 20*e*.

**Come hither all whom lust doth bind** 479
**Will think the sunbeams are not bright.**
Bacon, Sir Nicholas (1623–66), translator of Boethius, *Consolations* III. x. Sent to John Hobart 1664.
MS. Tanner 306, two copies, fols. 312v and 330v (autogr.).

**Come hither all you that have been** 480
**Chaste snow, and sunbeams are not white.**
Polwhele, John, 'Boet. L. 3. Met. X'.
MS. *Eng. poet. f. 16, fol. 31 (autogr.).

**Come hither Apollo's bouncing girl** 481
**For I never will be your . . .**
Cleveland, [John], 'Square Cappe'.
MS. Firth e. 4, p. 101.

**Come hither friends and listen unto me,** 482
**Cast up your caps and cry Vi vel a Roy.**
I. W., 'England's honour, and London's glory', proclamation of Charles II, 8 May 1660. 'The tune is Vi vel a Roy'.
MS. Firth c. 20, fol. 102.

483 Come hither good people, both aged and young
And the man ne'er the worse had his mare back again.
'The Yorkshire Tale a Ballad'.
MS. Top. Oxon. b. 170, fol. 10v.

484 Come hither my lads awhile
And sphere about his jovial cup.
'11th songe'.
MS. Ashmole 38, p. 114.

485 Come hither read my gentle friend
The man who made him soles at will.
'On a Shoemaker'.
Pr. *Wit Restor'd*, 1658, p. 64, and Camden's *Remaines*, 1637, p. 411.
MSS. Ashmole 36, 37, fol. 145; 38, p. 185; Don. d. 58, fol. 15; Douce f. 5, fol. 9; Eng. poet. e. 14, fol. 80v rev.; Malone 19, p. 41; see also C469.

486 Come hither the merriest of all the land
Where nought shall be heard but to me boy to me.
Murray, W[illiam, first Earl of Dysart], 'To the tune of Blew Capp for me'.
Pr. *Wit Restor'd*, 1658, as 'The Gallants of the Times. Supposed to be made by Mr. William Murrey of His Majesties Bed-Chamber'.
MS. Malone 13, p. 38.

487*a* Come hither to me and I'll tell you some news
He got from his parliament.
'A Court Ballad'.
MS. Top. Oxon. b. 170, fol. 17.

487*b* Come hither Topham with a hey
To Cologne or Bredagh.
'Oh Raree Shew', 1671 (?).
MS. Douce 357, fol. 56.

488 Come hither, women, leave your vanities
Yourselves like angels in eternity.
MS. Sancroft 59, p. 281 rev.

489 Come hither Xerxes with thy threatening lash
The wit and mirth lies in the deep.
Booth, [Thomas], of Corpus Christi, Cambridge, 'On the death of Mr. Ed. King of Christ Coll. in Cambr., who was drowned as he was going into Ireland'.
Not pr. in *Obsequies to the Memory of Mr. Edward King*, 1638.
MSS. Rawl. poet. 147, p. 61, attr. to Mr. Booth CCC. Cant.; Tanner 465, fol. 74, attr. to Booth of Corpus Christi; see also O565.

490 Come hither, young sinner,
And honour will bid thee good night.
'Ovid de Arte Amandi: or the marks of an amorous Theif'.
MS. Ballard 47, fol. 146.

Come holy friendship from above 491
Behold the marriage of the Lamb.
[Baynes, Sir Thomas (d. 1681)], 'An hymne of true freindship the new heaven and new earth the marriage of the Lamb'. Tune, 'Greece and Troy'.
Attr. to Sir Thomas Baynes in B.M. Add. MS. 29921, fol. 69v.
MS. Rawl. poet. 37, p. 29.

Come Holy Ghost eternal God 492
Revive, sing praises, be divine.
Traherne, Thomas, from 'Meditations, etc. for Rogation Week'.
MS. Eng. th. e. 51, fol. 30 (autogr.).

Come Holy Ghost, eternal God 493
From hence to the world's end.
'Veni Creator'.
MS. Mus. Sch. G. 632, fol. 45v; Rawl. poet. 112, fol. 28 rev.; 200, fol. 95.

Come Holy Ghost our souls inspire 494
Father, Son and Holy Spirit.
'Veni Creator Spiritus'.
Pr. John Cosin's *Collection of Private Devotions*, 1627, p. 91.
MSS. Eng. poet. e. 56, p. 75; Mus. c. 11, fol. 28, music by William Boyce; d. 12, fol. 5, music by Thomas Tallis; Rawl. poet. 200, fol. 94v.

Come holy spirit the god of might, comforter of us all 495
As it is now and so shall be henceforth for evermore.
'A prayer unto the holy ghost to be songe before the sermon'.
MS. Rawl. poet. 112, fol. 24v rev.

Come honest neighbour, said Simpkin the sot 496
To live sober and sound and to know what I see.
Williams, John.
MS. *Rawl. poet. 192, fol. 81v (autogr.).

Come, honest sexton, take thy spade 497
Farewell, my loving friends, farewell.
'The Passing Bell'.
MS. Rawl. poet. 196, fol. 51v.

Come Hymen come; Jove's daughters say 498
Of missing heaven who hath an heaven in her.
Pierce, Dr. Thomas, President of Magdalen College (1661–1672), 'An Epithalamium'.
MSS. Mus. Sch. C. 32–37: C. 32, fol. 2, music by Dr. William Childe; Wood F. 34, fol. 144, attr. to Dr. Tho. Pierce, President of Magd: Coll:

499 Come join
This is our only play.
MSS. Ashmole 36, 37, fol. 193.

500 Come join in a carol
And prove your next Christmas laughter.
Weaver, Thomas, 'A Caroll for Xtmasse day 1650'.
Not pr. in *Songs and Poems by T. W.*, 1654.
MS. *Rawl. poet. 211, fol. 34ᵛ (autogr.).

501 Come jolly shepherd, let us pipe and play
Fair fall ye, gentle shepherd, for your tale.
Bedell, William, 'The Shepherds Tale of the Powder Plot. Written by the Right Reverend . . . late Lord Bishop of Kilmore'.
Pr. 1713.
MS. Rawl. poet. 154, fol. 14.

502 Come Juno come Jove
Hang fate and be merry.
'Mercury's Banquet set by Mr. William Richardson'.
MS. Mus. Sch. C. 95, p. 140.

503 Come ladies you that would appear
Go learn of her humility.
On Rebecca Berry, 1696, Stepney Churchyard.
MSS. Rawl. D. 1334, fol. 27 rev.; Top. gen. e. 32, fol. 73ᵛ.

504 Come lads let's be merry and chant out a ditty
But I thank you my muse hath heartily dined.
Thomas, Henry, 'of University Coll. Oxon.', 'A Libell on Mr. John Lambe, Taylor, and Maior of Oxon A.D. 1659'.
MS. Tanner 466, fol. 64.

505 Come Laura come let's live and love
And decline and suddenly are ended.
Set by William Webb.
MS. Don. c. 57, fol. 26ᵛ.

506 Come lay aside your murmuring
When they had none at all.
'A Song on the present Tymes', [*c.* 1689].
MSS. Rawl. D. 361, fol. 53ᵛ; Rawl. poet. 196, fol. 30.

507 Come lay aside your sporting.
We'll kick their arse to a jelly.
'A Song'.
MS. Rawl. poet. 84, fol. 27.

Come, leave the loathed stage 508
And see his chariot triumph 'bove his wain.
Jonson, Ben., 'Ode to himself'.
Pr. in *The New Inne*, 1631.
MSS. Ashmole 38, p. 80, attr. to Ben Johnson; CCC. 328, fol. 45ᵛ, attr. to Ben. Johnson; Rawl. poet. 166, p. 83, attr. to Ben. Jhonson; 209, fol. 11, attr. to Ben. Johnson.

Come leave this savage [saucy] way 509
Since braver theme no Phoebus ever saw.
[Felltham, Owen], 'An answer to Ben Jonson's ode in dislike of his New Inn', C508.
Pr. *Resolves*, 1661, 'Lusoria', xx.
MSS. Ashmole 38, p. 71; 47, fol. 108ᵛ.

Come lend your ears and also lend your eyes 510
Precepts may command but examples draw.
Nalson, Robert, On 'Margaret Savile daughter of Jo: Savile of Methley Esq.', 16 Jan. 1683/4.
MS. Top. Cheshire c. 6, fol. 241ᵛ (autogr.).

Come Lesbia come, let's live and freely play 511
We both enjoy, when thus we kiss.
Catullus, v.
MS. *Rawl. poet. 87, p. 52.

Come, Lesbia, let us live and love 512
When they know by the number how happy we've been.
Warrick (?), translator, Catullus, v.
MS. Eng. misc. e. 241, fol. 79ᵛ.

Come, let me reason with thee Death, ere I 513
Yet with the first let me receive my sum.
Corbet, W., on the death of his brother and sister.
MS. *Rawl. poet. 210, fol. 24ᵛ.

Come let this bumper for the next make way 514
Who's sure to live and drink another day.
Catch (words only).
MS. Mus. Sch. C. 95, p. 185.

Come let us all a-maying go 515
And so we'll pass the time away.
Catch by John Hilton.
MS. Mus. d. 177, fol. 4.

Come let us leave the town 516
Thus time shall slide away.
[Settle, Elkanah], 'Set by Mr. Henry Purcell'.
From *The Fairy Queen*; F. B. Zimmerman, *Purcell*, 1963, no. 629 (4b).
MS. Mus. Sch. C. 95, p. 105.

517 Come let us sit, let's drink and sing
Let us now sing all together.
Music by John Playford, copied by P. Hayes.
Pr. *The Musical Companion*, 1673.
MS. Mus. d. 8, fol. 42.

518 Come, let's adore the king of love,
Now and for ever be.
[Austin, John].
Pr. *Devotions in the Ancient Way of Offices*, Paris, 1668, p. 226.
MS. Rawl. poet. 202, fol. 33.

519 Come let's be merry let's be airy
Shakes he'll drink off his glass.
'A Ballad'.
MS. Eng. poet. e. 8, fol. 22.

520 Come let's begin and with our lays
Struck mute may voices change for ears . . . (incomplete).
Part song on the months.
MS. Mus. c. 5, fol. 14.

521 Come let's discharge affection, once let's try
Like Eli when the ark was took, and die.
On 'Dr. Fell Deane of Christ Church'.
MS. Rawl. poet. 84, fol. 118.

522 Come, liberal souls and freely bring
And then receive th' eternal crown.
Kenton, James.
MS. *Eng. poet. e. 20, p. 284 (autogr.).

523 Come life, come death I care not
She cools my desire.
Pr. Michael East's *Third Set of Bookes*, 1610, vi.
MSS. Mus. f. 20–24: f. 20, fol. 29.

524 Come listen awhile, my concern it is great
Had not Jerry been there and stood squire for the day.
Amherst, Elizabeth, 'A Song'.
MS. *Eng. poet. e. 109, p. 83.

525 Come listen fair maidens and help me to sing
The quite contrary man.
'The Duke of Buckingham'.
MS. Rawl. poet. 26, fol. 61ᵛ.

526 Come, listen, good people, to what I shall say
To the shame and confusion of Perkin Warbeck.
'Perkin's Figary'.
On the Duke of Monmouth, Sept. 1679.
MS. Don. b. 8, p. 600.

527 Come listen, I sing to the lovers of fun
To all knights of the thimble, wherever they be.
Beresford, James, 'Upon the Advantages attending a Tailor'.
MS. Eng. poet. c. 51, p. 177.

Come listen to me, and I'll tell you some news 528
He got from his parliament.
Lord Grantham, [Henry d'Auverquerque], 'A Ballad To the Tune of Under a Green Tree'.
MS. Ballard 47, fol. 132.

Come listen ye Tories and Jacobites now 529
And whoe'er disbelieves it, is one of the plot.
Westley, —, 'On the Bishop of Rochester's Plot'. [Atterbury, 1722].
MS. Ballard 29, fol. 129.

Come live with me and be my love 530
Come live with me, and be my love.
[Marlowe, Christopher].
Pr. *Englands Helicon*, 1600.
MS. Rawl. poet. 148, fol. 96ᵛ.

Come live with me and be my love 531
Alas is wiser far than I.
Donne, John, 'The Baite'.
MSS. Ashmole 47, fol. 100ᵛ, attr. to Joh. Earles Martin. coll. ox.; Eng. poet. e. 97, p. 183, attr. to Sir H. Wotton; *e. 99, fol. 100ᵛ; *f. 9, p. 93; Rawl. poet. 84, fol. 59 rev.; 117, fol. 204 rev., attr. to Dunne.

Come Lord, my head doth burn, my heart is sick 532
Or take me up to thee!
Herbert, George, 'Home'.
Pr. *The Temple*, 1633, p. 99.
MSS. Rawl. poet. 213, fol. 57ᵛ, attr. to Herbert; *Tanner 307, fol. 75.

Come Lord thy powers exert 533
Oh gracious God of thee!
Kenton, James.
MS. *Eng. poet. e. 20, p. 263 (autogr.).

Come lovely Cloris while I am willing 534
And find out a muse to crown my song.
Pr. in *The Musical Companion*, 1673, p. 139.
MS. Mus. c. 5, fol. 9ᵛ, music by W. Lawes.

Come, lovely creature, come let's kiss, 535
But kissing live and kissing die.
Morrice, John, 'Platonic Love', 1707.
MS. *Rawl. poet. 114, fol. 136 (autogr.).

Come lovely maid and let us walk 536
Than base affected barrenness.
'To the Bride', Anne Baynton.
MS. Rawl. poet. 65, fol. 51.

Come lovely virgin, fair-eyed peace 537
In a people so blest no monarch so great.
[Cibber, Colley], Birthday Ode, 1736.
MS. Mus. d. 38. Music by Dr. Maurice Greene.

538 **Come lovers all to me and cease your mourning**
**H' has lost a thousand servants to kill one.**
Pr. with music by H. Lawes, *Select Musical Ayres and Dialogues*, 1652, i. 7; also set by W. Porter, *Madrigales and Ayres*, 1632, xvi.
MS. Don. c. 57, fol. 92, music by H. Lawes.

539 **Come lovers forth**
**Curiously wrought to set men's hearts on fire.**
Pr. Morley's *Madrigals to Five voices*, 1598, iv.
MSS. Mus. f. 16–19: f. 19, fol. 81v.

540 **Come loyal Britons let's rejoice—**
**Brave boys that will be fine work.**
'Great Britain's Glory'. Capture of Cape Breton 26 July, and Prince Ferdinand's victory, 5 August, 1758.
MS. Firth c. 18, fol. 28.

541 **Come loyal hearts, make no delay,**
**Increase of empire, with blest issue, to the King.**
Lanier, Nicholas, 'An imperfitt Oade, to his Sacred Maiesty, for the new yeare 1665', set by Mathew Lock.
MSS. Add. C. 304A, fol. 166, attr. to Nich. Lanier; Ashmole 36, 37, fol. 167, attr. Nich. Lanier.

542 **Come madam be easy**
**So charming a lady can need.**
'Cho[rus]', part of a longer work.
MS. Mus. c. 16, fol. 126, autograph music by W. Davis.

543 **Come madam, come, all rest my powers defy**
**What needst thou have more covering than a man.**
Donne, John, Elegy XIX.
Pr. *Poems*, 1669, p. 97.
MSS. Ashmole 38, p. 63, attr. to Donne; Don. b. 9, fol. 57v; Eng. poet. c. 50, fol. 42v; e. 97, p. 103, attr. to Doctor Donne; *e. 99, fol. 14*b*; *f. 9, p. 64; f. 25, fol. 17, attr. to Dr. Dunne; Rawl. poet. 160, fol. 171, attr. to J. D.; see also C546.

544 **Come merry boys, let's sing a word**
**This morrice to be danced.**
'Another Ballett at the Parliament. 1640'.
MS. Rawl. poet. 26, fol. 123v.

545 **Come mild and holy dove**
**One equal glory be.**
[Austin, John], 'Pentecost'.
Hymn xxxiv in *Devotions in the Ancient Way of Offices*, Paris, 1668, p. 398.
MS. Rawl. poet. 200, fol. 123.

**Come mistress come all rest my powers defy** 546
**What need'st thou have more covering than a man.**
Donne, John, Elegy XIX.
Pr. *Poems*, 1669, p. 97.
MSS. Rawl. poet. 117, fols. 222v and 221 rev., attr. to Dunne; 199, p. 14, attr. to Corbet; see also C543.

**Come Montaigne, come I'll love thee with my heart** 547
**Rarest of art.**
Corne, Sir William, junr., 'Upon Montaigne's Essayes'.
Pr. H. Huth, *Inedited Poetical Miscellanies*, 1870.
MS. Firth d. 7, fol. 163.

**Come muse, and leave those wings that soar** 548
**And thy sharp bays will sprout into a crown.**
M. A., 'The Invitation . . . made June 28 1683'. The first of a collection of poems presented to Archbishop Sancroft in 1689.
MS. Rawl. poet. 154, fol. 52.

**Come muses all lament the fall** 549
**In England fit to live.**
'An Elogy on the P[rin]ce', the son of George, Prince of Wales, 1717.
MS. Rawl. D. 383, fol. 116.

**Come my Alexis, come my lovely boy,** 550
**The fates are deaf, loved Damon can't return.**
Chatwin, John, 'Melibœus and Alexis bewail the untimely Death of Damon. A Pastoral'.
MS. *Rawl. poet. 94, p. 266 (autogr.).

**Come my Celia, let us prove** 551
**Those have crimes accounted been.**
[Jonson, Ben.], *The Forrest*, v.
MS. Rawl. poet. 172, fol. 2; see also C608.

**Come my Daphne come away** 552
**Till they embrace a deity.**
[Shirley, James], song in *The Cardinal*, v. iii.
MS. Rawl. poet. 65, fol. 30.

**Come my dear friend, into this bower** 553
**Enjoy what princes wish in vain.**
'A retir'd freinship to a friende'.
MS. Rawl. poet. 90, fol. 79.

**Come my Jesus haste away** 554
**And God alone to move.**
MS. Rawl. poet. 200, fol. 81.

**Come my lov'd Stella tune your lyre,** 555
**Then to Amanda's cot will speed my way.**
Bate, Sally, 'Dialogue between Stella and Hebe on the Marriage of —'.
MS. *Eng. poet. e. 28, p. 201.

556 Come, my masters, draw near
For 'tis decency here for to leave 'em.

W[ ]ley, S., 'On the knights of the Bath. . . . See Vocal. Miscel. Vol. 2, p. 166'.
On George I's reviving the Order, 18 May, 1725.
MS. Eng. poet. f. 12, p. 121.

557 Come my Oenone let us do
The faith of Paris and Oenone's love.

MS. Don. c. 57, two copies, fols. 11ᵛ and 42ᵛ, with music by Robert Ramsey.

558 Come my shadow, constant, true,
Unless I fall upon her.

King, John (1595–1638/9).
See *B.Q.R.* v, 1929, p. 239, and *B.L.R.* iv, 1953, p. 208.
MS. Rawl. D. 317, fol. 173 (autogr.).

559 Come, my Urania, and with needle fine
And in immortal lays fair Rhedecyna sings.

[Roach, Richard], 'An Ode. Presented on the Annual Feast [at the Merchant Taylors' School] of the Gentlemen Educated therein'.
MS. Rawl. D. 832, fol. 237 (autogr.).

560 Come my way, my truth, my life
Such a heart as joys in love.

Herbert, George, 'The Call'.
Pr. *The Temple*, 1633, p. 150.
MS. *Tanner 307, fol. 114ᵛ.

561 Come my white-head let our muses
Let's crave pardon of one head.

Mortershead, Thomas, 'Pirotrichus and Levitrix, or white and Red-head'.
MS. Eng. poet. e. 97, p. 123.

562 Come near lady muses and help me to sing
The clean contrary way.

'A Libell censured in starr-chamber Octob: 17, 1627', on the Duke of Buckingham.
MS. Add. C. 302, fol. 18.

563 Come noble nymphs and do not hide
That you could mean no less.

[Jonson, Ben.], from *Neptune's Triumph*.
Pr. *Select Ayres and Dialogues*, 1659, p. 14, with music by William Webb.
MSS. Ashmole, 36, 37, fol. 29; Don. c. 57, fol. 53, with music, not by Webb.

564 Come not to me for scarves, nor plumes,
To take a scrip, and shepherds gray.

Townsend, Aurelian.
MS. Malone 13, p. 75.

Come now, for a round of our true-hearted tars, 565
Come finish my boys, with the lord of the Nile.

'Hearts of Oak for ever. A Round of British Tars'.
MS. Firth c. 18, fol. 53.

Come now my sweet tormentress, now will I 566
Was my revenge henceforth 't will service be.

W. R., 'The revenge'.
MS. Rawl. poet. 199, p. 71.

Come, oh come, I brook no stay 567
But sprightful kisses strike the hours.

Cartwright, William, song in *The Ordinary*, III. iii.
MSS. Rawl. D. 1092, fol. 270ᵛ, attr. to W. Cartwright; Rawl. poet. 199, p. 16, attr. to W. C.

Come on, strike up, thou rhyming goddess 568
Rais'd from her wicker chair of state.

[Scudamour, James, *c.* 1642–1666], 'Homer's Iliads. The first Rhapsody'.
Draft of *Homer a la Mode*, pr. Oxford, 1664.
MS. Locke e. 17, p. 120.

Come on ye [you] critics find one fault who dare 569
Did ever libel yet more sharply bite.

[Sackville], Charles, Lord Buckhurst, later Earl of Dorset, satire on Edward Howard's *British Princes*, 1669. See Vieth, pp. 252, 442.
MSS. Add. B. 105, fol. 71; Don. b. 8, p. 284, attr. to Ld. Buckhurst; Douce 357, fol. 142ᵛ, attr. to B.; Eng. poet. e. 4, p. 190, attr. to Charles, Baron Buckhurst, now E. Dorsett; Rawl. D. 260, fol. 30ᵛ, attr. to Ld. Buckhurst.

Come on you searching quintessence of wit 570
But happier gardener whom my soul envies.

North, Dudley, 3rd Baron, Sonnet 7.
Pr. *A Forest of Varieties*, 1645.
MS. *North e. 41, fol. 12.

Come over the bourn Bessy 571
Come over the bourn Bessy to me.

Pr. *Harleian Misc.* x. 260; cf. *King Lear* III. vi, and W. Wager, *The Longer thou livest* (S.T.C. 24935; reprinted Tudor Facsimile Texts), Sig. Aiii.
MSS. Ashmole 176, fol. 100; Mus. d. 184, fol. 47.

Come over the woods fair and green 572
For comfort is none alone to be.

Pr. from this MS. by J. Zupitza, *Archiv*, lxxxvii, 1891, p. 433.
MS. Rawl. C. 813, fol. 58ᵛ.

573 Come painter once again assume thy skill
Damn'd gulf of lust.
Oldham, John, 'Advice to a Painter'.
See *Advice-to-a-Painter Poems 1633–1856*, M. T. Osborne, 1949, no. 23.
MS. *Rawl. poet. 123, p. 289 (autogr.).

574 Come pass about the bowl to me,
Let's tipple round, and so 'tis here.
[Brome, Alexander], 'The Royalist'.
Pr. *Poems*, 1661, p. 43, 'Written in 1646'.
MS. Ashmole 47, fol. 134.

575 Come, Pembroke lives, oh, do not fright our ears
Thy noble corpse is its own monument.
Earles of Merton [John Earle], on William Herbert, third earl of Pembroke, d. 1630.
MS. Rawl. poet. 142, fol. 35; see also D295.

576 Come Phyllis come into these bowers
Crowning thy name with lasting praise.
Copied from Thomas Ford's *Musicke of Sundrie Kindes*, 1607, vi.
MS. Mus. d. 8, fol. 16$^{v}$.

577 Come pretty nymph fain would I know
Betwixt the husband and the wife.
'A Riddle'.
MSS. Ashmole 38, p. 82; Firth d. 7, fol. 120.

578 Come prisoners come, let's have a fit
How they play taming of the shrew.
Meredith, Will[iam], 'On Will. Wise a fiddler in Oxford, who killed his wife with beatinge'.
MS. Malone 19, p. 141.

579 Come Ptolemie thou liest, or tell me why
These bunches blossom cannot look more gay.
'Upon a virgins brest'.
MS. Ballard 50, fol. 12.

580 Come push about the booze, my boys,
Yeo ho! haul away; fal de ral de ral de ra.
Male, Mr.
MS. Firth c. 18, fol. 217.

581 Come reach my sword, my rebel heart
May she (good God) like kindness have for me.
Knight, Gowin, of Merton [*sic* for Magdalen (?)] College, 'The Unwellcome to my heart'.
MS. Top. Oxon. e. 202, fol. 78.

582 Come resignation fill my drooping breast
And felt thy aid diffused to give me rest.
Leaver, Dorothy, verses in a letter, 1781.
MS. Eng. misc. d. 257, fol. 23.

583 Come Rosalinda, come and see
The envy of the human race.
'To Rosalinda'.
MS. *Eng. poet. d. 47, fol. 155.

Come rosy health, celestial maid, 584
And Harold's beauties yield to thine.
'An Ode to Health'.
MS. Eng. misc. b. 48, fol. 110.

Come rouse from your trances, 585
Hark hark to the huntsman's sweet hollo.
[Burgoyne, John], 'A Hunting Song in Maid of the Oake', 1774.
MS. Mus. e. 19, p. 46.

Come sable night . . . put on thy mourning stole, 586
Whilst all his hopes do faint and life is failing.
Pr. John Ward's *First Set of English Madrigals*, 1613, xxvii.
MSS. Mus. f. 20–24: f. 20, fol. 83$^{v}$.

Come saints and see the place 587
And God declare you sons.
Pr. *Hymns . . . of B. Beddome*, 1818, no. 602.
MS. *Eng. misc. e. 227, fol. 73.

Come see a man from whom is nothing hid, 588
Who told me all things that I ever did.
Couplet.
MS. Rawl. poet. 209, fol. 36.

Come see a petty miracle, where thought 589
More swift, more light, more vain than vanity.
'On the vanity of thought'.
MS. Eng. poet. e. 14, fol. 47.

Come shepherd swains, that wont to hear me sing, 590
Lo! now I die.
Pr. Wilbye's *Madrigals*, 1609, i.
MS. Mus. d. 8, fol. 58.

Come shepherds all both great and small 591
Swaddled up in a poor manger.
MS. Rawl. poet. 196, fol. 7.

Come shepherds deck your heads 592
So plain a dealing woman.
'The forsaken sheaperd'.
MS. Ashmole 38, p. 127.

Come shepherd's weeds become your master's mind 593
Helpless his plaint who spoils himself of bliss.
Sidney, Sir Philip, from the *Arcadia*: 'Musidorus' complaint'.
MS. *e Mus. 37, fol. 23.

Come silent night and in thy gloomy shade 594
Be but as though they had ne'er been.
Pr. J. Wilson's *Cheerfull Ayres*, 1660.
MSS. Eng. poet. c. 50, fol. 58; Mus. b. 1, fol. 31, with music by John Wilson.

595 Come sing the great Jehovah's praise
In sacred hymns rejoice.

[Sandys, George], Psalm xcv; 3-part setting [by W. Lawes].
Pr. *A Paraphrase on the Divine Poems*, 1638, p. 116, and H. and W. Lawes, *Choice Psalmes*, 1648.
MS. Mus. Sch. E. 451, p. 53.

596 Come sing to God new ditties frame
And give a true and righteous doom.

Harington, Sir John, Psalm xcvi.
MS. *Douce 361, fol. 58.

597 Come sinner come and bathe thy sin-sick soul
That didst without sin die and diedst for me.

'Christ death'.
MS. Rawl. poet. 142, fol. 80v.

598 Come sinner come with eyes that swim in tears
This is the sea that leads to th' Holy Land.

'Upon the receiving of the Sacrament'.
MS. Rawl. poet. 142, fol. 78v.

599 Come sinners seek the way
For God himself is there.

Beddome, Benjamin.
MS. *Eng. misc. e. 227, fol. 56.

600 Come sirrah Jacko
The sweet of Trinidado.

Pr. Weelkes' *Airs or Fantastic Spirits*, 1608, vi.
MSS. Mus. f. 7–10: f. 9, fol. 14.

601 Come sister Mal, let's take out wonted flight
Till death does our souls and our bodies too sever.

Chatwin, John, 'The Night Ramble, A Dialogue betwixt Malkin and Saga'.
MS. *Rawl. poet. 94, p. 25 (autogr.).

602 Come, sit thee down, young swain
I'll pipe full merrily.

Pipe, Richard, 'Eglogue the vii' of 9 'satirical eclogues', 1617.
MS. *Don. e. 22, fol. 26 (autogr.).

603 Come sit ye down by these cold streams
Your maidenhead.

'A sonnet'.
MS. CCC. 328, fol. 75.

604 Come sorrow help me to lament,
Whose absence causeth all my grief.

Pr. Thomas Bateson's *Second set of Madrigales*, 1618, xxiv.
MSS. Mus. f. 20–24: f. 20, fol. 39v.

605 Come sorrow wrap me in thy sable cloak
Then cried again she's dead and his heart brake.

MS. Don. c. 57, fol. 25v, with music.

Come stingless death! have o'er, to her's my pass 606
Faith in fruition, hope in seeing ends.

McLehan, John, 'An Epitaph on Marion McNaught'.
MS. Rawl. poet. 213, fol. 60.

Come Strephon come 607
And change their state for mine.

'Song'.
MS. Rawl. poet. 152, fol. 143v.

Come, sweet Celia, let us prove 608
These have crimes accounted been.

[Jonson, Ben.].
Pr. *The Forrest*, v.
MS. Rawl. poet. 31, fol. 7; see also C551.

Come sweet justice do not tarry 609
At the brightness of thy face.

MS. Rawl. poet. 37, p. 19.

Come sweet oblivion sad Amanda cries 610
Heaven virtue, by affliction tries.

Bate, Sally, '1766'.
MS. *Eng. poet. e. 28, p. 105.

Come sweet religion dissipate this gloom. 611
Which even Cato's daughter could not bear.

Bate, Sally, 'To Miss Arabella Bate—1767'.
MS. *Eng. poet. e. 28, p. 118.

Come, Sylvia, freely let's enjoy 612
To make none truly happy, but the wise.

Weaver, Thomas, 'A Dialogue betwixt Thirsis and Sylvia'.
Pr. *Songs and Poems by T. W.*, 1654.
MS. *Rawl. poet. 211, fol. 11 (autogr.).

Come tears if ever you'll bedew mine eyes 613
Pray gods his soul and body rest in peace.

Riv., Guil. de, 'Elegus in obitum' J. Seddon, Magdalene College, [matric. Easter 1622].
MS. Rawl. poet. 104, fol. 63 (autogr.).

Come tell me fancy whence is it those joys 614
We dream not of our losses in the shade.

Reresby, Sir John, 'A dialogue bytween a sheapard and his fancy in a pastorall straine'.
MS. Rawl. D. 204, fol. 88v rev. (autogr.).

Come thou celestial dove 615
And dwell forever there.

Kenton, James.
MS. *Eng. poet. e. 20, p. 220 (autogr.).

Come thou father of the spring 616
Sweeter than a sacrifice.

Music by John Wilson.
Pr. *Cheerfull Ayres or Ballads*, 1660, p. 80.
MS. Mus. b. 1, fol. 128.

617 Come thou God of life and peace
Fully save me by thy grace?
Kenton, James.
MS. *Eng. poet. e. 20, p. 234 (autogr.).

618 Come thou Maecenas shalt drink wine with me
For never vines strained there did fill my cup.
W. A., translator, Horace, *Odes* I. xx.
MS. *Rawl. poet. 104, fol. $7^v$ (autogr.).

619 Come to me! shall we not come Christ to gain?
Sans sinking, less Christ take us by the hand.
MS. *Rawl. poet. 97, fol. 32 (autogr.).

620 Come Tom, come Will, come Roger, come Harry
For Christmas comes but once a year.
'Another [caroll] for Christmasday to the tune of the A.B.C.'
MS. Eng. poet. b. 5, p. 63.

621 Come unto me, and I will be to Thee
In whom alone our curing doth consist.
MS. *Rawl. poet. 97, fol. $31^v$ (autogr.).

622 Come unto me, at God's call Abraham
Unto their hurt, or their confusion.
MS. *Rawl. poet. 97, fol. 33 (autogr.).

623 Come unto me, can it be burthensome
As not to come when he may saved be?
MS. *Rawl. poet. 97, fol. $32^v$ (autogr.).

624 Come unto me! doth Christ call? what then shall
Have brought mankind to all his misery.
MS. *Rawl. poet. 97, fol. 34 (autogr.).

625 Come unto me each weary wayfaring man
Ere we the land of promise, heaven, possess.
MS. *Rawl. poet. 97, fol. $32^v$ (autogr.).

626 Come unto me! for all the balm that grows
To his most glory, his folks' greatest good.
MS. *Rawl. poet. 97, fol. 35 (autogr.).

627 Come unto me! I am omnipotent,
To have Christ's and his father's company.
MS. *Rawl. poet. 97, fol. $31^v$ (autogr.).

628 Come unto me! I can not yet have done
And follow fond devices of our own?
MS. *Rawl. poet. 97, fol. 31 (autogr.).

629 Come unto me, it is the bridegroom's voice
Infected all mankind with our disease.
MS. *Rawl. poet. 97, fol. 34 (autogr.).

630 Come unto me! Jesus excepteth none
You from your graves to spread abroad my praise?
MS. *Rawl. poet. 97, fol. 32 (autogr.).

Come unto me! Lord I would come to thee 631
So by them, to be wholly ruined.
MS. *Rawl. poet. 97, fol. $34^v$ (autogr.).

Come unto me! Lord we would come, alack! 632
To come to Christ to get a stock of grace.
MS. *Rawl. poet. 97, fol. $34^v$ (autogr.).

Come unto me! Lord, where else should we flee? 633
That it is I myself, handle me, see 't.
MS. *Rawl. poet. 97, fol. 32 (autogr.).

Come unto me! methinks, Lord, this should be 634
Who lead another way do but delude.
MS. *Rawl. poet. 97, fol. $30^v$ (autogr.).

Come unto me! my way will prove the best 635
Each troubled soul sinks under his own grief.
MS. *Rawl. poet. 97, fol. 35 (autogr.).

Come unto me! Oh Lord! what can be said 636
Enable, Lord, all thine elect to come.
MS. *Rawl. poet. 97, fol. $30^v$ (autogr.).

Come unto me, the way's not beaten broad; 637
Never look back, let Sodom be forgot.
MS. *Rawl. poet. 97, fol. $34^v$ (autogr.).

Come unto me! these words although but three 638
For ever, one; distinguished in three.
MS. *Rawl. poet. 97, fol. $31^v$ (autogr.).

Come unto me, this path old Enoch trod, 639
He heals each sore, hears each oppressed one.
MS. *Rawl. poet. 97, fol. $33^v$ (autogr.).

Come unto me! this sentence is but short, 640
Them ere His coming who in darkness sat.
MS. *Rawl. poet. 97, fol. 31 (autogr.).

Come unto me! this subject seems to me 641
And ne'er fails them that to the end endure!
MS. *Rawl. poet. 97, fol. 31 (autogr.).

Come unto me! 'tis Christ himself doth call; 642
And would omit nought might procure the same.
MS. *Rawl. poet. 97, fol. 34 (autogr.).

Come unto me; 'tis Christ who calls us, can 643
Our course so for us that we never err.
MS. *Rawl. poet. 97, fol. $33^v$ (autogr.).

Come unto us holy ghost 644
Give the joys that never cease.
'English Primer of our Lady, 1631 . . . p. 477'.
MS. Eng. poet. e. 56, p. 64.

Come up my soul unto thy rest 645
That can these flowers find.
'Seeke flowers of heaven'.
MS. Eng. poet. b. 5, p. 14.

646 Come Urania, heavenly muse
Let it sing in this best choir.
Davison, Francis, 'An introduction to the Translation of the Psalmes'.
MSS. *Rawl. D. 316, fol. 124, attr. to Fra: Davidson; Rawl. poet. 61, fol. 3, attr. to Fr. Da.

647 Come viol come let me thy neck embrace
Sith love in sorrow sorrow in love sings.
MS. Don. c. 57, fol. 17, with music.

648 Come virtue, honour, wealth and pleasure
To them that have enough before.
Oldisworth, Nicolas, 'A sonnet, played by a musician at my Entertaining of Mr. Mic. Oldisworth'.
MS. *Don. c. 24, fol. 24ᵛ (autogr.).

649 Come we shepherds, who have seen
We'll burn our own best sacrifice.
Crashaw, Richard, 'A hymne of the Nativitie sung by the shepheards'.
Pr. *Steps to the Temple*, 1646.
MSS. Eng. misc. e. 241, fol. 96ᵛ, attr. to Crashaw; Tanner 465, fol. 38ᵛ, attr. to Mr. Crashaw on fol. 1*a*.

650 Come weavers, come butchers, come cobblers [come cobblers, come butchers], come all,
With hunger and cold. God-a-mercy good Scott.
'A Song or Ballad, in Parliament-tyme, 1640'.
MSS. Douce 357, fol. 21; Rawl. poet. 26, fol. 122ᵛ.

651 Come White prepare to grave that man once more
Who's been of e'ry side, but true to none.
'Advice to Mr. [Robert] White whoe Engrav'd the 7 Bishopps', 1691.
*Advice-to-a-Painter Poems*, M. T. Osborne, 1949, no. 41.
MSS. Eng. poet. d. 53, p. 93; Rawl. poet. 169, fol. 20.

652 Come with a joyful voice let's raise
In Canaan they should not rest there.
Fairfax, Thomas, Lord, Psalm xcv.
MS. *Fairfax 40, p. 233 (autogr.).
MS. *Fairfax 38, p. 362.

653 Come with me, you jolly tars
My boys you'll find him in the end.
'A New Song'.
MS. Firth c. 18, fol. 6.

Come with our voices let us war 654
May wish us of their choir.
[Jonson, Ben.].
Pr. *The Underwood*, 1640.
MSS. Don. c. 57, fol. 48ᵛ, with music, anon; Eng. poet. c. 53, fol. 2ᵛ; Mus. b. 1, fol. 81, with music by John Wilson; Mus. Sch. C. 142, Act Song, Oxford, music by John Wilson.

Come ye are deceived; he never meant the world 655
Thy gilded, cheating, beauties, foh! begone.
Wake, William, of Cambridge, 'Quid mihi cum Mundo . . . Ps. lxii. 9, Isaiah xl, 23'; see M118.
MS. Eng. misc. d. 1, fol. 36.

Come ye hither all, whose taste 656
Where is all, there all, should be.
Herbert, George, 'The Invitation'.
Pr. *The Temple*, 1633, p. 174.
MS. *Tanner 307, fol. 132ᵛ.

Come ye lovers of peace who are said to have sold 657
[And her navies in port are the terror of Spain].
'Englands Glory Being an Excellent New Ballad on the Fleet of Spithead'.
MS. Malone 41, fol. 228; see also C661.

Come ye ransomed sons of grace 658
All ye ransomed sons of grace.
Kenton, James.
MS. *Eng. poet. e. 20, p. 10 (autogr.).

Come ye swarms of thoughts and bring 659
All's provided for but I.
MS. Eng. poet. c. 50, fol. 80.

Come ye that share the Saviour's grace 660
Our way to endless life.
Kenton, James.
MS. *Eng. poet. e. 20, p. 39 (autogr.).

Come you lovers of peace, who are said to have sold 661
[And her navies in port are the terror of Spain].
'Englands Glory . . . on the Fleet at Spit-head, 1729'.
MS. Top. Oxon. b. 170, fol. 7ᵛ; see also C657.

Come you my people to my law give ear 662
He justly fed them, wisely guided all.
Fairfax, Thomas, Lord, Psalm lxxviii.
MS. *Fairfax 40, p. 176 (autogr.); see also C356*b*.

Come you that do boast 663
And Neptune's the god of good fellows.
'A Song of the Drinkers of the iron waters at Tunbridge'.
MS. Rawl. poet. 152, fol. 206.

664 Come your ways
And a fig for death or undoing.
[Brome, Alexander], 'The Commoners', with extra verse.
Pr. *Poems*, 1661, Sig. D8, 'written in 1645'; see also Sig. E1$^{v}$.
MS. Ashmole 47, fol. 134$^{v}$.

665 Comely swain why sits tho[u] so, fa la
Chose another let her go, fa la.
Song, with melody by John Playford.
Pr. *The Musical Companion*, 1673, p. 117.
MS. Mus. Sch. F. 572, p. 53.

666 Coming by chance into St. Lawrence kirk
Much more to kings, who God's vicegerents are.
'To the Rev. Dr. Beveridge, an Eucharisticon, occasioned by his . . . sermon about restitution . . . March 17, 1690'.
MS. Rawl. poet. 181, fol. 5.

667 Commend his care, although the cure do miss.
Because, he could not live, would die in peace.
MS. Rawl. poet. 66, fol. 51.

668 Commend me, for his wealth, to brewer B.
The court ne country have no power to save them.
MS. Rawl. poet. 66, fol. 59.

669 Commit thy ship unto the wind
To make a good thing of a bad.
Translation of Latin verses, 'Q. Cicero', *De mulierum levitate* [Baehrens, *Poetae Latini Minores*, iv, 1882, p. 359].
Pr. *Wits Recreations*, 1640, 168, and Charles Cotton's *Poems*, 1689, p. 296.
MSS. Eng. misc. f. 49, fol. 4; Eng. poet. c. 50, fol. 38.

670 Common births, like common things
Such may Britain ever find her kings.
[Whitehead, William], Birthday Ode, 1763.
Pr. *Poems*, 1790, ii. 79.
MS. Mus. Sch. D. 313. Music by Boyce.

671 Common opinion's a common mistake
Of things that were never done.
Williams, John, 'Of Common Opinion, and Common tradition'.
MS. *Rawl. poet. 184, fol. 93.

672 Compare we may this mortal life, a vale whose corn is woe
And Christ himself most lovingly the same again hath sealed.
'A Vew or spectacle of Vanity . . . 1584'.
Pr. *Inedited Poetical Miscellanies*, H. Huth, 1870, from commonplace book of Gabriel Harvey.
MS. Firth d. 7, fol. 54.

Compassionate reader could thy melting eye 673
In the celestial orb doth ever shine.
Beaumont, Thomas, 'An epitaph ensculpd upon the Tombe of the Much deplored Doc$^{tr.}$ Richard Wigfall, attested by his sadd ffrend T: B:'.
MS. *Malone 18, p. 97 (autogr.).

Compel the hawk to sit that is unmanned 674
He serves but those that feel sweet fancies fit.
5-part setting by Byrd, pr. *Songs of sundrie natures*, 1589, xxviii.
MSS. Mus. f. 11–15: f. 11, fol. 28.

Complain I may where so ever I go 675
Whom of all creatures I trusted most.
MS. Rawl. C. 813, fol. 46$^{v}$.

Complain we may, much is amiss 676
Glory to thee for aye. Amen.
'Totus mundus in maligno positus'.
Pr. Tottel's *Miscellany*, 2nd ed., 1557, under 'uncertain authors'.
MS. Rawl. poet. 82, fol. 1$^{v}$.

Complaints like ours in Ramah's Vale was heard 677
Once more applaud her pious monarch's choice.
Tate, Nahum, 'Elegy on Dr. Tillotson pub. 1695'. (*An Elegy on . . . John Late Archbishop of Canterbury*, 1695).
MS. Eng. poet. c. 9, p. 235.

Comus away, away, with all thy revel train, 678
On earth our universal love.
Cantata in praise of 'Masonry', by Dr. William Hayes. Performed (?) at the opening of the Radcliffe Camera, April 1749.
MS. Mus. d. 81, fol. 96.

Conceal fond man, conceal thy mighty smart 679
And never never from thy bosom stray.
MS. Rawl. poet. 116, fol. 96.

Conceit is quick, would so were sweet content 680
Eyes shall behold but spirits shall not speak.
MS. Rawl. poet. 85, fol. 103$^{v}$.

Conceive a fault, by me conceived 681
To clothe and give a name.
'Certayn verses fixed on a child laid in St. Thomas Hospitall'.
MS. Ashmole 38, p. 175*a*.

Conceive the holy ghost Christ's Church's heart, 682
The souls of men and senses will renew.
F. W., 'Sonnet 48'.
MS. *Rawl. C. 639, p. 226.

683 Conception of our Saviour was the day
The earth his corpse yet heaven his soul contains.
'On Mr. Richard Harwood', 28 March 1615, All Hallows Church, York.
MS. Dodsworth 161, fol. 33.

684 Concording graces for thy temples fit
Thou be with glorious saints matriculate.
Ashemore, John, acrostic, 'Charles [I] Stewart'.
MS. Dodsworth 61, fol. 60 (autogr. (?)).

685 Condemned on Caucasus to lie
Who begins to discover an end of his pain.
'Peleus and Thetis'.
MS. Mus. Sch. C. 113. Music by Boyce.

686 Condemned to Hope's delusive mine
And freed his soul the nearest way.
Johnson, Dr. Samuel, 'On Mr. Levet an apothecary who died suddenly aged 79'.
Pr. *Gentleman's Magazine*, August 1782; see *R.E.S.* iii, Oct. 1927, p. 472, and Boswell's *Life*, ed. G. B. Hill, revised L. F. Powell, 1934, iv. 137.
MS. Eng. misc. e. 241, fol. 95.

687 Conductors, come away.
For nothing.
'A Ballad from the English Camp in the North. 1640'.
MSS. Rawl. poet. 26, fol. 122; 71, p. 73; 117, fol. 151$^{v}$ rev.

688 Confer oh Lord
My counsel to advise me right.
Herbert, Mary (*née* Sidney), Countess of Pembroke, Psalm cxix, 'C'.
MSS. *Rawl. poet. 24, p. 175; *25, fol. 118$^{v}$.

689 Conscience thine accusation cease
Cause then to show and cease to rear.
Beddome, Benjamin.
MS. *Eng. misc. e. 227, fol. 2$^{v}$.

690 Conscious of our own case, and of your pain
We'll all turn cooks and vintners for your sake.
'Prol[ogue] etc.'
MS. Rawl. poet. 194, fol. 20$^{v}$.

691 Consecrated to the Lord
My offering here below.
Kenton, James.
MS. *Eng. poet. e. 20, 180 (autogr.).

692 Consider, dear Cloe, how time flies away;
And love me today—for tomorrow we die.
'A Song'.
MS. Eng. poet. c. 9, p. 23.

Consider fond shepherd how fleeting the pleasure. 693
But life is too little to measure our care.
From John Gay's *Acis and Galatea.*
MS. Mus. c. 107, two copies, fols. 41$^{v}$ and 54$^{v}$, music by Handel.

Consider friend Pitt, you whose cases well hit 694
She'll still be a sickly Miss F-ke.
'To a Physician, who had the care of a Female Patient in Love'.
MS. *Eng. poet. d. 47, fol. 55.

Consider the dust moving in this glass, 695
The ashes of lovers find no rest.
'B: Jo: Upon an houre glasse'.
MS. Firth e. 4, p. 51; see also D353.

Consider this ye that pass by 696
For as you are even so was I.
Lines from a gravestone.
MS. Rawl. D. 1372, fol. 57 from end.

Considering God's mercy great 697
Whose name for ever let us praise.
Subscribed 'finis quod [Henry] Spon[ar]'.
MS. Ashmole 48, fol. 66.

Considering the great goodness of god full of might 698
Therefore our lauds and praises be given to the heavenly [physician].
A poem on the 'heavenly physician'.
MS. Ashmole 48, fol. 105$^{v}$.

Considering this world and the increase of vice. 699
Believe well this for true is that hear say.
Subscribed T. S. P.
MS. Ashmole 48, fol. 45.

Contemn not gracious king our plaints and tears 700
Which death and life in instant doth effect.
Answer to O803.
MSS. Ashmole 36, 37, fol. 59; Eng. poet. c. 50, fol. 25$^{v}$; Rawl. poet. 26, fol. 20; 152, fol. 4.

Contemn the world, and be my love. 701
So thou refuse all loves for mine.
'Our Blessed Saviours love letter'. Answered by F450.
MS. Eng. poet. b. 5, p. 86.

Contemplate, when the sun declines, 702
The day of resurrection.
Cowper, William, translation from Owen, 'Sunset and Sunrise'.
Pr. Hayley, *Life and Posthumous Works*, 1803, iii. 380.
MS. Autogr. d. 21, fol. 192$^{v}$ (autogr.).

703 Contending priests, when one against
So to maintain their game.
Robinson, Robert.
MS. *Rawl. poet. 218, p. 143 (autogr.).

704 Content, the false world's best disguise,
Enjoy content, or else the world hath none.
[Philips, Katherine], 'Content, to my dearest Friend'.
Pr. *Poems*, 1664, p. 45.
MS. Rawl. poet. 90, fol. 80.

705 Content thee, greedy heart.
These seas are tears, and heaven the haven.
Herbert George, 'The Size'.
Pr. *The Temple*, 1633, p. 131.
MS. *Tanner 307, fol. 99ᵛ.

706 Content thyself with thine estate
Thy fortune to advance.
Copied by Wiman Ramsey, *c.* 1595.
MS. Rawl. D. 649, fol. 4.

707 Continual toil, and labour, is not best
But not too much, lest sloth do set her snares.
Whitney, Geoffrey, 'Interdum requiescendum'.
MS. *Rawl. poet. 56, fol. 64.

708 Contrary messengers from God?
The truth (great Lord) unto us show.
Robinson, Robert.
MS. *Rawl. poet. 218, p. 156 (autogr.).

709 Convert to tears thy ink, to sighs thy pen,
Britain's loss here buried is.
On Prince Henry's death, 1612.
MS. *Rawl. poet. 116, fol. 2.

710 [Convertiez vous] you huguenots
Short time will show you what's behind.
'Dated 5th novem. in the year of salvation 1666 in the first yeare of the restoration of the romish church in england'.
MS. Add. A. 48, fol. 13ᵛ.

711 Cony skins maids
Spanish gloves silk ribands and golden rings.
4-part song.
MSS. Mus. e. 1–5, at end.

712 Cook [Lawrick] Lorell [invited] would needs have the devil his guest
From whence it was called the devil's arse.
Jonson, Ben. from *The Metamorphos'd Gypsies*.
MSS. Eng. poet. e. 14, fol. 16, attr. to Ben Johnson; f. 10, fol. 100ᵛ, attr. to Ben. Johnson; Malone 19, p. 95, attr. to Ben Johnson; Rawl. poet. 62, fol. 32, attr. to Ben. Jonson; 160, fol. 175; see also C341.

Corinda's an exquisite creature 713
The trifling gewgaw away.
'Song'.
MS. Rawl. poet. 152, fol. 180ᵛ.

Corinna false it cannot be, 714
Return my Corinna and revive my soul.
'Corina'.
MS. Ashmole 47, fol. 71ᵛ.

Corinna in the bloom of youth 715
And age is virtue's season
'Song by Mr. G.'
MS. Firth e. 6, fol. 131.

Cornutus called his wife both whore and slut 716
For you have horns to but, if I am a whore.
Pr. *Description of Love*, 2nd ed., 1620, Sig. C6ᵛ; *Wits Recreations*, 1640, 237.
MSS. Eng. poet. c. 50, fol. 33ᵛ; f. 25, fol. 16ᵛ; Tanner 465, fol. 95.

Corruption 'tis doth bring us in (no doubt) 717
When death comes in, and smites them with his hammer.
Robinson, Robert.
MS. *Rawl. poet. 218, p. 142 (autogr.).

Corydon arise my Corydon 718
The heavens keep our love alway.
'Coridon and Philida: In an Italian verse'.
MS. Rawl. poet. 148, fol. 88ᵛ, with music.

Cosmus hath more discoursing in his head 719
As none at all can perfect passage find.
Davies, [Sir] John, 'In Cosmum'.
Pr. amongst 'Epigrames' with *Ouids Elegies*, translated by C. M., [*c.* 1600].
MSS. *Add. B. 97, fol. 42ᵛ; *Rawl. poet. 212, fol. 59 rev.

Could a painter draw a grief 720
And through the world's great frame thy mighty deeds disperse.
Earbery, Matthias, 'Repentance. Psalm xiii', sent to Charles Trimnell, Bishop of Norwich 1708–21.
MS. Tanner 306, fol. 465ᵛ (autogr.).

Could any show where Pliny's people dwell, 721
My armour proof is incredulity.
Strode, William, 'On a Dissembler'.
Pr. *Wits Recreations*, 1658, p. 99.
MS. *CCC. 325, fol. 77ᵛ (autogr.).
MS. Eng. poet. e. 97, p. 95, attr. to Will Stroad.

722 Could Bacchus then be so unkind?
Stands poor Anacreon for your memorandum.
[Roach, Richard], 'The Poet's Memorandum. On the Death of Anacreon by a Grape Stone'.
MS. Rawl. D. 832, fol. 261 (autogr.).

723 Could but our tempers move like this machine
And everlasting joy, when time shall be no more.
'For a Watch'.
MS. Montagu e. 14, fol. 36v.

724 Could but the crow in lonely silence eat
She then would have less envy, and more meat.
Traherne, Thomas (?), couplet, translating Latin epigram, *Centuries* iv. 12.
MS. Eng. th. e. 50, fol. 69, in Traherne's hand.

725 Could he die that day and was he mown
To rise the sun of glory heliotrope.
'On the death [of] Mr. John Haines who dyed on the consumption and fever on easter morning 1635. Non obiturus obit'.
MS. Ashmole 47, fol. 58.

726 Could I a tribute of my thanks express
To lie next her, to you our choir is free.
Fairfax, Thomas, Lord, 'To the Lady Cary Upon her Verses on my deare Wife'.
MS. *Fairfax 40, p. 598 (autogr.).
MS. *Fairfax 38, p. 269.

727 Could I, as Midas did of old,
I'd touch her also—to the quick.
'An Epigram'.
MS. Ballard 29, fol. 145v.

728 Could I excel as much as I esteem
Sure to have hit the right nail on the head.
'The Nail. By a school Boy'.
MS. Eng. poet. c. 51, p. 229.

729 Could I in wax thy features mould,
A living likeness stamp of thee!
Parsons, William, 'To a Lady sitting for her Picture'.
Pr. *Fidelity*, etc., 1798, p. 58, and *Travelling Recreations*, 1807.
MS. *Don. d. 123, p. 256 (autogr.).

730 Could I not think your love was true
January and your suit, is cold.
Creswell, Robert, 'Her Answer' to N581.
MS. *Eng. poet. f. 24, fol. 33v (autogr.).

731 Could I with thee in virtue vie
Even flesh that's in the grave.
'An Address To the Sheep, whose Skin, apply'd to Di St[one]hou[s]e's Bowels, sav'd her Life'.
MS. *Eng. poet. d. 47, fol. 18.

Could man his wish obtain 732
'Twill please my ghost when I am dead.
MS. Mus. Sch. C. 95, p. 199.

Could Marlborough's soul debase itself so low 733
True to the King and to the nation's trust.
'A Copy of Verses wrote on the Duke of Marlborough's Speech, Dropt amongst the 1st Regiment of foot Guards, by a Lady', *c.* 1714.
MS. Ballard 62, p. 94.

Could mourning sighs or floods of tears prevent 734
A cheerful look, and an unconquer'd eye.
Yalden, Thomas, 'Agst. Immoderate grief to a young lady weeping. An ode in imitation of Casmire'.
Pr. *Examen Poeticum*, John Dryden, 1693, p. 111.
MS. Rawl. poet. 173, fol. 156v.

Could not a wounded heart suffice 735
I loose my intellectual eyes.
'Upon a faire Gentlewoman threding of Pearle'.
MSS. Ashmole 36, 37, fol. 27.

Could not once blinding me, cruel, suffice: 736
When first I looked on thee, I lost mine eyes.
[Crashaw, Richard], 'Sampson to his Dalilah'.
Pr. *Steps to the Temple*, 1646, p. 24.
MS. Rawl. poet. 90, fol. 108.

Could our love no joy dispense 737
Then I departed am, and dead.
Beaumont, Thomas, 'Goinge from her'.
MS. *Malone 18, p. 79 (autogr.).

Could pitying verse thy griefs remove 738
When such the kind decree of heaven.
Bird, Lucy (Mrs. Levett), 'To a friend upon a Disappointment'.
MS. Eng. poet. c. 51, p. 65.

Could Sacharissa leave the town 739
Pleased with a nymph so good so wise so fair.
MS. Eng. poet. e. 31, fol. 161 rev.

Could style and fancy be on me conferred 740
Nature's great maim in this our punishment.
North, Sir Dudley (later fourth Baron), 'An elegy upon the buryall of . . . Lady An: Rich', 1638.
MS. Eng. misc. e. 262, fol. 34.

Could tears, and sighs, and prayers recall the dead 741
By virtue to console th' afflicted breast.
'To the Author of "Why shoots this sudden horror . . ." Collect. Poems'.
MS. Eng. poet. e. 39, p. 102.

742 **Could we judge here, most virtuous Madam, then Eve's nakedness is only clothed by you.**
Cartwright, William, 'To . . . the Ladie Elizabeth Powlet upon her Present to the Universitie of Oxon being the Birth, Death, Resurrection and Ascension of our Saviour wrought by her selfe in Needle-worke' [9 July 1636].
Pr. *Poems*, 1651, p. 195; *Parnassus Biceps*, 1656.
MSS. Bodl. 22, fol. 1, attr. to William Cartwright Mr. of Arts of Christ Church; Eng. poet. e. 4, p. 34; Rawl. poet. 84, fol. 90; 153, fol. 25$^{v}$.

743 **Could you but see yourself in any fit Of fury, you would ne'er return to it.**
Barksdale, Clement, 'Anger', distich.
MS. Autogr. c. 9, fol. 154 (autogr.).

744 **Could youth these early hours to study bend Mother of sorrow, sin, diseases, strife.**
'The Young Man's Plea against Women'.
MS. Rawl. poet. 173, fol. 101.

745 **Couldst thou before thy death have given what we Heaven hath the volume, earth the manual.**
F. N. G., 'Upon his Sacred maiesties incomparable Eikon Basilice', copied 1653 by J. Phillips, Woodstock.
MS. Add. B. 108, p. 319.

746 **Couldst thou, old Bluff, rise from thy massive tomb And shew thee kinder than the nearest kin.**
Gough, Richard, 'She knew not when she was well. A Fragment'.
MS. *Eng. poet. c. 5, fol. 226 (autogr.).

747 **Counsel that comes, when ill hath done her worst, Blesseth our ill, and makes our good accurst.**
Couplet.
MS. Malone 19, p. 76.

748 **Counsel which afterward is sought is like untimely showers Distilling from the duskish clouds when heat hath parched the flowers.**
Couplet.
MSS. e Mus. 63, fol. 146$^{v}$, copied three times; Rawl. D. 649, fol. 28, copied by Wiman Ramsey, *c.* 1595.

749 **Count me (Vice-Chancellor Duppa) or a traitor God were no god, if god could prove a stranger.**
Oldisworth, Nicolas, 'On his Majesty's Recovery from the Small pocks. Decemb. 1632'.
MS. *Don. c. 24, fol. 12 (autogr.).

750 **Courage courage my soul now learn to wield And is thy everlasting store.**
'A Combat Between the Soule and Sense'.
MS. Rawl. A. 176, fol. 80.

**Courage, dear Mal, and drive away despair With pride, vain glory, and hypocrisy.** 751
'A Madame, Madame, B., Beauté Sexagenaire (Ldy. Manchester)' or 'an affected Court Lady'.
Pr. *Poems on Affairs of State*, iii, 1698, p. 138.
MSS. Eng. poet. c. 18, fol. 135$^{v}$, attr. to Ld. Dorset; Rawl. poet. 173, fol. 69$^{v}$, attr. to Mr. Fleetwood Shepherd.

**Courage my dear, since last I heard from thee I'll venture through them all, to come to thee.** 752
Tipping, William, 'An Answer to a Letter from a nunn, Now in the nunnerie at Pontwoys, June 8th 1695'.
MS. *Rawl. poet. 101, fol. 68 (autogr.).

**Courage ye saints in God's own ways Nor fear to live nor fear to die.** 753
Beddome, Benjamin.
MS. *Eng. misc. e. 227, fol. 50.

**Court ladies laugh and wonder Thou sufferest loss of, in each chaste tear shed.** 754
[Fletcher, John], song, from the *Queen of Corinth*, III. i.
MS. Mus. b. 1, fol. 38, music by John Wilson.

**Court mistress money, get her love. She'll be to thee a nurse.** 755
Robinson, Robert.
MS. *Rawl. poet. 218, p. 163 (autogr.).

**Courtiers and heralds by your leave Let Bourbon or Nassau go higher.** 756
Prior, Matthew, 'An Epitaph made on [himself] before his decease'. Cf. M221.
MSS. Rawl. poet. 116, fol. 112, attr. to Matthew Prior; Top. gen. e. 32, fol. 52$^{v}$, attr. to Matthew Prior.

**Court's commender, state's maintainer. Returning the halter, contemning the wrong.** 757
'Erroris Responsio' to C758.
MSS. Ashmole 781, p. 164, attr. to Sr. Wal. Ra.; Rawl. poet. 172, fol. 13; 212, fol. 91$^{v}$.

**Court's scorn, state's disgracing Worthy to be rewarded with a halter.** 758
'The answer to the lye', G205; answered in C757.
MSS. Ashmole 781, p. 164; Rawl. poet. 172, fol. 13, attr. to Sr. Wal. R.; 212, fol. 91, 'thought to be made by R[obert Devereux, Earl of] Essex'.

**Cousin what needs this compliment 'twixt friends To do you service or your friend and rest . . .** 759
Burton, Francis.
MS. *Add. A. 267, fol. 122 (autogr.).

760 Cousin whilst you were one of London-people
Whose naked grass seems skin, whose trees seem hair.

Oldisworth, Nicolas, 'To the worshipfull, his honoured Cosin, Mris. Susan Oldisworth: upon her Removall from London to Thisselworth'.
MS. *Don. c. 24, fol. 26 (autogr.).

761 Cowards fear to die, but courage stout
Rather than live in snuff will be put out.

'Sr. W. Raleigh On the Snuffe of a Candle the night before hee dyed'.
MSS. Ashmole 1463, p. 13, attr. to Sr. W. Raleigh; Don. e. 6, fol. 16$^{v}$, attr. to Sr. Walter Rawleigh.

762 Cowley, to soothe his anxious mind
As envied as his verse.

'To a Lady, who desir'd him to write something on Cowley's wish'.
MS. Rawl. poet. 153, fol. 47.

763 Coy Celia dost thou see
Lest I take heat from thee and so revive.

[Randolph, Thomas], 'a Madrigall'.
Pr. *Poems*, 1638.
MS. Eng. poet. c. 50, fol. 109$^{v}$.

764 Crabbed satire begone why alone upon John
Who can tell us which county they plunder.

An addition to T2926.
MS. Eng. poet. c. 41, fol. 46.

765 Craddock whose venturous hand alone could dare
In both 'tis Yates that carries off applause.

Gough, Richard, 'On Joseph Craddock Esq. his tragedy of Zobeide, see Gent. Mag. 1827 p. 21' (note by J. B. Nichols).
MS. *Eng. poet. c. 5, fol. 189.

766 Crassus, his lies are not [penurious] pernicious lies
That for such lies, an action will not lie.

Davies, Sir John, 'In Crassum'.
Pr. amongst 'Epigrames' with *Ovids Elegies* . . . By C. M., [*c.* 1600].
MSS. *Add. B. 97, fol. 45; *Rawl. poet. 212, fol. 61 rev.

767 Creator, holy Ghost, descend
Beyond all time imagined.

'Engl. Primer of our Ladie. 1631. . . p. 16'.
MS. Eng. poet. e. 56, p. 39.

768 Creator Lord of every thing
To blame our sloth and negligence / When . . . (incomplete).

Huish, Alexander, translator, 'Æterne rerum Conditor'.
MS. Eng. poet. e. 56, p. 136 (autogr.).

Creator Spirit, by whose aid 769
Eternal Paraclete to thee.

Dryden, John, 'Veni Creator Spiritus—Paraphras'd'.
Pr. *Miscellany Poems*, iii, 1693, p. 307.
MS. Add. B. 105, fol. 29, attr. to John Dryden; Rawl. D. 1293, fol. 27$^{v}$, attr. to Mr. Dryden.

Credit is always chaste, for like a maid 770
Once falsely broke, it ever lives decayed.

Couplet.
MS. Rawl. poet. 117, fol. 276 rev.

*Credo* is not common unto all alike 771–2
This is as true as is the creed.

Annotated verses on heresies, 16th cent.
MS. Eng. misc. c. 93, fol. 20.

Crispinius gives, where gifts he looks for greater 773
This kindness proves him but a kind of cheater.

Couplet.
MS. Malone 19, p. 14.

Crispus if ever it could well be said 774
In satin hast the bastinado had.

Davis, [Sir] John, 'of Gray's Inn', 'In Crispum'.
MS. *Rawl. poet. 212, fol. 57$^{v}$ rev.

Crispus loves music no man more than he 775
He will admire it a whole summer's day.

Davis, [Sir] John, 'of Gray's Inn', 'In Crispum'.
MS. *Rawl. poet. 212, fol. 58 rev.

Critics, avaunt, tobacco is my theme. 776
For which we drink, eat, sleep, smoke, everything.

Browne, Isaac Hawkins, 'In praise of Tobacco'. Imitation of Young.
Pr. Dodsley's *Collection of Poems*, ii, 1748, p. 280.
MS. Top. London e. 9, p. 173.

Cross patch 777
And call your neighbours in.

MS. Douce d. 59, fol. 63.

Crowland, thy once-fam'd abbey now appears 778
Of wealthy abbots and of scepter'd kings.

Mills, the Revd. Joseph, of Cowbit, 'In 1784 . . . to Mr. Gough on a late History of Crowland . . . Printed in Gent. Mag. 1784'.
MS. Eng. poet. c. 5, fol. 249.

Crow-like young Lofty struts and Demme cries. 779
Vast is the patent, that a traitor gives.

'An Epigram on a lewd Gentleman-Commoner'.
MS. Eng. poet. f. 12, p. 70.

780 Crowned be the man with lasting praise
For Tucker!—Thou'rt the man.
[Jenyns, Soame], 'The last Resource'.
Pr. *The Cambridge Chronicle*, 13 Jan. 1776, 'on the American Madness in 1775'.
Pr. bk. Firth b. 22, fol. 63.

781 Crowned with flowers I saw fair Amarillis
Blew all her faith and sand away together.
Pr. Byrd's *Psalmes, Songs, and Sonnets*, 1611, xxii.
MSS. Mus. f. 20–24: f. 20, fol. 48.

782 Crowned with May-flowers, by night there came to me
A token with the harp and crown.
Oldisworth, Nicolas, 'His rewarding a Musician'.
MS. *Don. c. 24, fol. $40^{v}$ (autogr.).

783 Crowns hath their compass, length of days their date
But knowledge makes the king most like his Maker.
'Certayne verses wrighten by Mr. Robert Barker His Matis. Printer under his Matis. picture'. James I. See C784.
MSS. Ashmole 38, p. 39, attr. to Mr. Robert Barker; Rawl. D. 1372, fol. $2^{v}$.

784 Crowns have their compass, length of days their date
I once was high enough, but now am low.
Knap, J[ohn], parody in the conclusion of a letter to Abp. Sancroft, 13 July 1686.
MS. Tanner 306, fol. 431 (autogr.).

785 Cruel Amynta can you see
Whom much security beguiles.
[Congreve, William].
Pr. *Works*, 1710.
MS. Mus. c. 107, fol. 5.

786 Cruel Clarinda tell me why
Letting none 'scape away.
MS. Mus. b. 1, fol. $173^{v}$, music by John Wilson.

787 Cruel Myrtillo by what fault of mine
I shall be pleas'd, so I enjoy the first.
'A Copy of Verses'.
MS. Montagu e. 13, fol. $144^{v}$.

788 Cruel they were and full of envious pride
Shall by one title more increase thy fame.
Mervall, Alphonso, 'To Cloris'.
MS. *Rawl. poet. 166, p. 9 (autogr.).

789 Cuckold my friend if thou wilt me believe
His wife lets others in his saddle ride.
MS. Ashmole 48, fol. 136.

Cuckoo Cuckoo 790
So merrily sings the cuckoo.
Song (words incomplete).
MS. Mus. d. 184, fol. $66^{v}$ rev.

Cupid a boy and yet a god of might 791
For wanting wings he cannot fly away.
MS. CCC. 327, fol. $30^{v}$.

Cupid ah thy power I feel 792
At the worst 'tis but denial.
MS. Rawl. poet. 117, fol. 157 rev.

Cupid calls oh young men come 793
And reap their maidenheads.
Shirley, James, 'The Curtizane'.
Pr. with H224 as 'Cupids Call', *Poems*, 1646, p. 1.
MS. *Rawl. poet. 88, p. 54.

Cupid did hold his court upon a plain 794
What she or wisely speaks, or sweetly sings.
E[des], D[r. Richard], 'On the Lady Riche', *c.* 1596–7.
MS. Rawl. poet. 148, fol. 69.

Cupid forbear, no further mischief do 795
But may command the life y'ave helped to save.
Walsh, William, 'Elegy 23'.
MS. Malone 9, fol. 4 (autogr.).

Cupid, forbear thy childish arts 796
I cannot, will not love.
'A Defiance to Cupid'.
MS. Rawl. poet. 153, fol. $40^{v}$.

Cupid God of pleasing anguish, 797
Love [does all that's great below].
'A Song'.
MS. Montagu e. 13, fol. 15.

Cupid has placed us in this bower 798
To please my love and grace the spring.
Pr. *The Musical Companion*, 1673.
MS. Mus. d. 8, fol. 64.

Cupid hath by his sly and subtle art, 799
With women's hearts, and then they'll ne'er fly true.
'On Cupid'.
Pr. *Wits Recreations*, 1663, Ep. 120.
MS. Eng. poet. d. 152, fol. $106^{v}$; see also H1511, H1514.

Cupid if thou tell-tale prove 800
I love a god, and that's no sin.
Song, music by John Wilson.
MS. Mus. b. 1, fol. $112^{v}$.

Cupid in a bed of roses 801
Whom thy empoisoned arrows cause complain.
Pr. Thomas Bateson's *Second Set of Madrigales*, 1618, xxv–xxvi.
MSS. Mus. f. 20–24: f. 20, fol. $63^{v}$.

802 Cupid my mistress' heart assailed
To gain her heart, or there to die.
MS. Mus. b. 1, fol. 22, music by John Wilson.

803 Cupid no wonder was not clothed of old,
For love though naked seldom e'er is cold.
Couplet, pr. *Wits Recreations*, 1663, Ep. 334.
MS. Eng. poet. d. 152, fol. 106$^v$.

804 Cupid oh at length reward me
Let her crown her faithful lover.
MS. Mus. c. 107, two copies, fols. 11 and 71.

805 Cupid once a-weary grown,
Thou'lt learn more pity towards men.
'A song'. From Anacreon, 35, *Ἔρως ποτ' ἐν ῥόδοισι*.
MS. Rawl. poet. 84, fol. 27$^v$ rev.

806 Cupid once having robbed a hive.
After stolen sweets, the girls can tell.
'In Imitation of Theocritus', Idyll xix.
MS. *Eng. poet. d. 47, fol. 157.

807 Cupid once I did defy
It to a vapour thus in smoke.
Briggs, S[amson], 'Loves Duell'.
MSS. Rawl. poet. 116, fol. 67$^v$ rev.; 147, p. 252 rev., attr. to S. Briggs.

808 Cupid the slyest rogue alive
And yet how wise, how deep the wound!
'Theocritus Idyllium 19'.
Pr. *Theater of Music*, ii, 1685, and Dryden's *Sylvae*, 1685, p. 378.
MSS. Add. B. 8, fol. 12, in Henry Coley's hand; B. 105, fol. 30$^v$.

809 Cupid thou art a wanton boy
For the blind boy I'll ne'er endure.
Pr. *Cheerfull Ayres or Ballads*, 1660, p. 38.
MS. Don. c. 57, fol. 76, music by John Wilson; see also C811.

810 Cupid thou art blind indeed
Not my nature but my fate.
'To Cupid'.
MS. Ashmole 47, fol. 83.

811 Cupid thou wert a wanton boy
For the blind boy I'll ne'er endure.
Pr. *Cheerfull Ayres or Ballads*, 1660, p. 38.
MS. Mus. b. 1, fol. 101, music by John Wilson; see also C809.

812 Cupid weary on a time with walking long
Thy lover true.
Butt[erris], S[imon], 'Song the 29'.
MS. Ashmole 38, p. 123.

Cupid, why hath fair bonny Cupid 813
Diana, chaste Diana given.
Lilliat, John, 'A Dialogue betweene Venus and Cupid, in commendation of Chastetie, Italianally versed'. 18 Jan. 1598/9.
MS. Rawl. poet. 148, fol. 92$^v$ (autogr.).

Cupid with Venus once disputed 814
The richest pearl that Anna wears!
Parsons, William, 'The three Noses', 2 Feb. 1795.
MS. *Don. d. 123, p. 240 (autogr.).

Cupid's dead who would not die 815
Seeing themselves out-shined by jet.
[Habington, William], 'Upon Cupids death and buriall in Castara's Cheeke'.
Pr. *Castara*, 1634, p. 17.
MSS. Rawl. poet. 65, fol. 89$^v$; 142, fol. 16.

Curio's rich sideboard seldom sees the light; 816
For Curio dresses nothing, but himself.
'On a stingy Beau'.
MS. *Eng. poet. d. 47, fol. 22.

Curl let me advise you whatever betides 817
So pray keep the third for your own.
'Loving adv. to E. Curl on his advertis. 3d vol of Letters'.
MS. Rawl. poet. 207, p. 181.

Curl raves and is poisoned he'll tell you 818
And now he's flown up to his head.
'On E. Curll's last words'.
MS. Rawl. poet. 207, p. 181.

Curse not your fate ye hawkers shrill, 819
By pamphlet proclamations.
'Upon the king's proclamation against Hawkers', 12 June 1716 (Bodl. pr. bk. B. 8. 23 (5). Jur.).
MS. Eng. poet. e. 87, p. 54.

Curse on that sordid miser's lust of gold 820
And wonders how he could mistake the case.
'The Patriot', epigram on the 4th Duke of Newcastle.
MSS. Ballard 50, fol. 105$^v$; Eng. misc. e. 183, fol. 3.

Curse on those critics, ignorant and vain 821
But some are fools enough to take their own.
'Satyr on the Court Ladyes. 1680'.
MS. Firth c. 15, p. 78.

Cursed and fore'er curst be the day wherein 822
Than cutting off all the royal progeny.
'On the powder plot'; written *c.* 1678.
MS. Rawl. poet. 123, p. 255.

823 Cursed be the star, which did ordain
Prove that 'mongst us, and curse me too!

'Ash-Wednesday'.
Pr. *Poems on Affairs of State*, ii, 1703, p. 398.
MS. Firth e. 6, fol. 151v.

824 Cursed be the timerous fool whose feeble mind
A steady, resolute, heroic soul.

'The true-born Englishman only personal Reflections left out'.
Pr. *Collections of the Newest . . . Songs . . . against Popery*, 1689, iii. 7.
MS. Rawl. poet. 173, fol. 116v.

825 Cursed be those dull unpointed doggerel rhymes
When old Hyde was catch't with *Rem in Re . . . cetera desunt.*

[Sackville, Charles, Earl of Dorset], 'A Faithfull Catalogue of our most eminent Ninnies'.
Pr. *Works of Rochester* . . . etc., 1721, ii. 27.
MSS. Eng. poet. c. 18, fol. 44; Firth c. 15, p. 232; c. 16, p. 201.

826 Cursed be ye all, ye roving fires,
She mounts aloft to immortality.

Chatwin, John, 'A Defiance to Love'.
MS. *Rawl. poet. 94, p. 261 (autogr.).

827 Cursed with the lewdest, vilest, basest, soul
Death brings the direful reckoning for the past.

MS. Don. c. 57, fol. 85v.

828 Custom has taught the peasants to present
Pay all my thanks, yet still have all to pay.

'To his honoured Parents'.
MS. Rawl. poet. 84, fol. 118 rev.

829 Custom it is that makes us to believe
Are but the empty dreams, which in death's sleep we make.

MS. Rawl. poet. 213, fol. 49.

Custom makes some obsequious, others send 830
Though I my loose addresses do conclude.

Hooton, Henry (matric. Queen's College Oxford 1682), acrostic on Catharine Pritchett.
MS. Lat. misc. e. 38, p. 168 rev. (autogr.).

Cydonia! see each brilliant fair 831
Leaves every sense of pain behind.

Dyer, R., 'To Cydonia. An Invitation to Vaux-Hall-Gardens'. 'Daily Advertiser Augt. 4, 1743'.
MS. Eng. poet. c. 9, p. 66.

Cymon does vow, nay he doth swear 832
Why Sir—you'd never dance again.

'Spoken extempore'.
MS. Eng. poet. c. 51, p. 10.

Cynthia thy song and chanting 833
Of bodies buried in perpetual slumber.

Madrigal à 5 from 'Young', i.e. *Musica Transalpina*, ii, 1597, music by Giovanni Croce.
MSS. Mus. Sch. D. 233–6: d. 236, fol. 72*a* rev.

Cyphers to cyphers added seem to come 834
Eternity.

Dimock, Colonel Cressy, 'Æthicks'.
MS. *Firth f. 1, fol. 1 (autogr. (?)).

Cyriac, this three years day, these eyes, though clear, 835
Content, though blind, had I no other guide.

'Milton's account of his Blindness'.
First pr. by Edward Phillips, *The Life of Mr. John Milton*, 1694.
MS. Eng. poet. c. 9, p. 83.

# D

ENTRIES 1–505

1 D.P's an old woman of wonderful skill
Serves at all times to all for vexation or mirth.
Williams, John, 'Upon a skillfull old woman in distinguishing herbs'.
MS. *Rawl. poet. 191, fol. 165 (autogr.).

2 *Da* is a verb, and signifies to give;
And, when thy noun is well declin'd, 'tis swiv'd.
Morrice, John, 'An Epigram upon Davis'. Jan. 16. 1707.
MS. *Rawl. poet. 114, fol. 109 (autogr.).

3 Dacus among the poets numbered is
Yet 'mongst the poets Dacus numbered is.
Davies, Sir John, '30 In Dacum'.
Pr. amongst 'Epigrames' with *Ovids Elegies*, by C. M. [*c.* 1600].
MS. *Add. B. 97, fol. 44v; see also A1168.

4 Daddy Neptune one day
But not a bit more of the island.
Dibdin, Thomas John, 'The Island'.
MS. Mus. e. 19, p. 13.

5 Daffy down dilly is now come to town
With a yellow petticoat, and a green gown.
Couplet.
MS. Douce d. 59, fol. 48.

6 Daily disgracer of our English satire
The body's half abortive like the wit.
'Mr. Wo[l]sely to Mr. Wharton . . . A Seacond Familliar Epistle'.
Pr. *Poems on Affairs of State*, iii, 1698, p. 10.
MS. Firth c. 16, p. 234.

7 Dainty fine bird, that art encaged there
Thou livest singing, but I sing and die.
Pr. Orlando Gibbons's *First Set of Madrigals*, 1612, ix.
MSS. Mus. f. 20–24: f. 20, fol. 54v.

8 Dainty white pearl, and you fresh smiling roses,
Some relief thence desiring.
Madrigal for 6 voices subscribed 'Young', i.e. *Musica Transalpina*, ii, 1597, music by Antonio Bicci.
Another setting pr. Michael East's *Third Set of Bookes*, 1610, xviii.
MSS. Mus. Sch. D. 233–6: D. 236, fol. 96v rev.

Dale is dead, which Dale I pray you? 9*a*
When they closely met together.
'Epitaphs of Doctor Dale'.
MS. Firth d. 7, fol. 159.

Dame Briton of the grange once famed 9*b*
My self a beggar and a fool.
'A fable thought to be wrote by Mr. Prior'.
Cf. Prior's *Poems*, ed. H. B. Wright and M. K. Spears, 1959, ii. 808.
MS. Hearne's diaries 69, p. 156.

Dame French lies underneath, who knew 10
In vain to keep a man alive!
'Epitaph upon Dame French of Wigginton, in Oxfordshire'.
MS. Ballard 29, fol. 159.

Dame Law, to maintain a more flourishing state 11
And fourteen new sergeants stepped out at the call.
'On the call of serjants in 1736'.
MS. Ballard 50, fol. 106.

Dame Mary Lassells corpse are here 12
With Christ his son to reign.
'A brasse fixt in alabaster' 9 June 1615, Worksop, Notts.
MS. Top. gen. e. 1, p. 28.

Dame or lady of high price 13
Except you mend this enterprise.
Translation of French verses 'of Isabell Quene of England', wife of Edward II.
MS. Tanner 306, fol. 187v.

Dames are endued with virtues excellent 14
Such are their humours; there's grace in such.
MS. Rawl. poet. 172, fol. 9v.

Damn'd fool! to think that I so tame could be, 15
Those be her lot, nay, and ten thousand more.
Chatwin, John, 'A Satyr upon Silvia'.
MS. *Rawl. poet. 94, p. 238 (autogr.).

Damn'd tyrant can't profaner blood suffice 16
And teach thee kill-priest to revere just laws.
'Richardus Adlam. 1670. Apostrophe to Death . . . In Kingsleington church'.
MS. Eng. misc. e. 241, fol. 102.

17 Damocles once, desirous for to taste,
Who night and day, of subjects stood in fear.
Whitney, Geoffrey, 'In sortis suae contemptores'.
MS. *Rawl. poet. 56, fol. 62$^{v}$.

18 Damon a copying miss of female spite
A vast mishap'd Colossus of a Cupid.
Lampoon.
MS. Eng. misc. b. 48, fol. 50.

19 Damon a very hag espied
*Probatum est*, that love is blind.
'Illuc praevertamur . . . etc., 1735', Horace, *Satires* I. iii. 38.
MS. Eng. misc. e. 240, p. 268.

20 Damon awake; from anxious thoughts arise
Our wishes, Damon, now have gained the assent divine.
'Congratulatio, An Ode upon the Duke of Marlbouroughs return to England', 1 March, 1708/9.
MS. Rawl. poet. 169, fol. 48.

21 Damon be ruled [forbear] and don't [disturb] your [muse] self expose
And may his glory with his hours increase.
'To Damon. 1700'.
MSS. Eng. poet. e. 50, p. 134; Rawl. D. 361, two versions, fols. 201$^{v}$ and 202$^{v}$.

22 Damon, if thou wilt believe me
Much more gentle, not so kind.
'Answer' to D317.
Pr. *Poems on Affairs of State*, iii, 1698, p. 198; see *Works of Sir Charles Sedley*, V. de S. Pinto, 1928, ii. 148.
MSS. Eng. poet. c. 18, fol. 79, attr. to L. Dorset; Rawl. poet. 173, fol. 71$^{v}$, attr. to Sir Ch. Sedley.

23 Damon my beauty doth adore
But love and hate alike are blind.
'The browne Lasses complaint'.
MSS. Don. c. 57, fol. 98$^{v}$, with music; Eng. poet. c. 50, fol. 109.

24 Damon, regardless of his flocks
Protected by her charms.
'Urania; A Pastoral Song on the Arrival of the Princess of Orange', February 1689.
MS. Rawl. poet. 159, fol. 152.

25 Damon, thy faithful Flora writes these lines
Nor from your Flora longer stay.
'An Extempore Letter to my Brother—1768'.
MS. *Eng. poet. e. 28, p. 220.

Damsel, to marriage thou art no whit near 26
Would cast all strangers as t'were in a maze.
W. A., translator, Horace, *Odes* II. v.
MS. *Rawl. poet. 104, fol. 14$^{v}$ (autogr.).

Dance little baby dance up high 27
Ding a ding ding.
MS. Douce d. 59, fol. 54.

Dancing is a kind of wanton modesty 28
To hide the villainy of a loose affection.
MS. Eng. poet. f. 10, fol. 119$^{v}$.

Dancing was first a maggot bred 29
Makes women Lucifers, and men but apes.
'A Song upon Dancing'.
MS. Rawl. poet. 173, fol. 146$^{v}$.

Daphne, in scorn, not knows me. In all shows, 30
More know Jack Pudding, than Jack Pudding knows.
'The Poet is angry, being censured by One he knowes not', couplet on Sir William Davenant.
Pr. *Certain Verses . . . to be reprinted with . . . Gondibert*, 1653, p. 12.
MS. CCC. 309, fol. 53.

Daphnis a youth adorn'd with ev'ry charm 31
In the poet's deathless lays.
Webb, Foster, 'Cantata'.
MS. Eng. poet. c. 9, p. 86.

Dark in the rising surge 32
Toward its destined haven.
Proby, John, of Rochdale.
MS. Montagu d. 5, fol. 178 (autogr.).

Dark is the maze poor mortals tread; 33
Then sought a cure far worse than the disease.
Sheffield, John, 1st Duke of Buckingham, 'Third Chorus of Roman Senators'.
Pr. *The Works*, 1721, p. 141.
MS. Eng. poet. c. 41, fol. 37.

Dark was the night, and wild the storm, 34
All worthy of their name.
Percy, Dr. Thomas, 'The Hermit of Warkworth A Northumberland Ballad'.
MS. Montagu e. 14, fol. 58$^{v}$.

Dark was the time as ere new lights first dawn, 35
Compar'd to which our night would be a day.
Oldham, John, 'Satyr'. Draft for 'The Vision'. *Cf.* T3384.
MS. *Rawl. poet. 123, p. 268 (autogr.).

Darkness and light can ne'er agree 36
And in thy sacred footsteps tread.
Kenton, James.
MS. *Eng. poet. e. 20, p. 70 (autogr.).

37 Darkness which fairest nymph disarms
Though neither day nor stars appear.
Waller, Mr. [Edmund], 'The Night Piece or a Picture drawn in the dark'.
Pr. *Poems*, 3rd ed., 1668, p. 231.
MS. Rawl. poet. 173, fol. 64.

38 Daughter of Britain! in whose Gallic style
Where British thoughts in British language shine!
Parsons, William, 'To the Countess of Rosenburg'.
MS. *Don. d. 123, p. 127 (autogr.).

39 Daughter of gaiety and mirth,
And asks an abler hand.
Greaves, Mr., of Lichfield, 'To Lady Smith', Dec. 13 1779.
MS. Eng. poet. c. 51, p. 125.

40 Daughter of grief, who o'er a father's urn
Raises this tribute to the honour'd dead.
'Miss G— on her mother'.
MS. Eng. misc. e. 241, fol. 94v.

41 Daughter of Jove, relentless power
What others are to feel, and know myself a man.
Gray, Thomas, 'Hymn to Adversity'.
MS. Eng. misc. f. 79, p. 107.

42 Daughter of Paeon!—balmy power
And more than Garrick's art—by female powers attained!
Parsons, William, 'Ode on the indisposition of Mrs. Siddons 16 Apr. 1788, . . . Printed in the World'.
MS. *Don. d. 123, p. 174 (autogr.).

43 Daughter of Zion thy joy entertain
The pow'r does of [Salvation] with him bring . . .
4 lines from part of a 'Paraphrasd collection of some Prophecyes of the Old Testamt. concerning Christ'.
MS. *Rawl. C. 113, fol. 10.

44 Daughters of beauty who enraptur'd hail
Fame to virtue unallied shines the meteor of a night.
Commemoration Ode 1773, 'Dr. W. Hayes'.
MS. Mus. d. 81, fol. 52.

45 Daughters of Jove, unenvying tuneful maids,
A patron, and a theme in Walter's line.
'An Epithalamium on Sr Robt. Walter [of Sarsden, Bart. 1722] and his Lady'.
MS. Eng. poet. f. 12, p. 106.

46 David Dee, had voices three
And blew away his knee.
'On one who stood to be Collector who had a wooden legge, which [was] stolne away from him over-night. . . . Schoole Mr. of Choristers in N. Colledge'.
MS. Malone 19, p. 139.

David th'unwelcome news receives 47
And say 'Father thy Will be done'.
Kenton, James.
MS. *Eng. poet. e. 20, p. 81 (autogr.).

David's son and Israel's king. 48
Save us quite from earth to heaven.
Kenton, James.
MS. *Eng. poet. e. 20, p. 350 (autogr.).

Dawson the butler's dead although I think 49
My life for his John Dawson had been here.
Corbett, Dr. [Richard], 'On John Dawson, Butler of Christ Church', 1622.
Pr. *Certain Elegant Poems*, 1647, p. 30.
MSS. CCC. 328, fol. 30v, attr. to D. Corbet; Don. d. 58, fol. 18; Douce f. 5, fol. 3v; Eng. poet. c. 50, fol. 128; e. 14, fol. 93 rev.; e. 97, p. 170, attr. to Dr. Corbett.

Dazzled with the height of place 50
Let another mend the play.
'By [*sic* for On (?)] the moste Illustrious Prince George Duke of Buckingham'.
Pr. *Reliquiae Wottonianae*, 1651, p. 522.
MS. Rawl. poet. 166, p. 83, ascribed to James Cobbes in a Latin rendering on the opposite page; see also T2532, T2562.

Dead, as if I were 51
Free grace hath fully freed my heart.
Herbert, Mary (*née* Sidney), Countess of Pembroke, Psalm cxix, 'D'.
MSS. *Rawl. poet. 24, p. 176; *25, fol. 119.

Dead headless, heedless, matchless Raleigh lies 52
Thus right for wrong paid the desert of crime.
Epitaph on Sir Walter Ralegh.
MS. Eng. hist. c. 272, p. 51.

Dead Helmont's but a span 53
Quench not weak flax, nor break a bruised reed.
Polw[hele], Jo[hn], 'Upon Van Helmonts Ternarye of paradoxes . . . translated by Dr. [Walter] Charleton Phisitian to . . .' Charles I. '1649. 12th Aprilis'.
MS. *Eng. poet. f. 16, fols. 50–51, 48v (autogr.).

Dead! no, 'tis all mistake, he cannot die 54
He died so rich, no one can be his heir.
'On the Death of Ino. Dryden Esqr.'
MS. Rawl. poet. 153, fol. 33v.

Dead to the soft delights of love. 55
Oh take my life, or crown my love.
'Song per Mr. Somervile', endorsed 'Songs composed by Wm. Somervile Esq. Of Edstone in Com. War'.
Pr. *Occasional Poems*, 1727, p. 112.
MS. Ballard 47, fol. 11.

56 Deaf from the birth, to pleasures of the mind
Their duty 'tis their happiness to hear.
Williams, John, 'He that has Ears to hear let him hear'.
MS. *Rawl. poet. 184, fol. 118$^{v}$ (autogr.).

57 Dean Swift first in vogue
That thy heart is the stone of the mill.
'The Lass of Isleworth Mill'.
MSS. Eng. misc. e. 183, fol. 74; Eng. poet. f. 12, p. 85; Top. Oxon. e. 379, fol. 6$^{v}$.

58 Dear and so worthy both by your desert
And with sweet junkets, doth her table spread.
Alabaster, William, 'Son: 20'.
MS. *Eng. poet. e. 57, fol. 4$^{v}$.

59 Dear Astragon by what new passion led,
You may expect the happy hour of love.
Chatwin, John, 'Astragon's Complaint for the Scorn of Corinna. Astragon and Dorylas'.
MS. *Rawl. poet. 94, p. 164 (autogr.).

60 Dear authoress of the simple story!
A paltry Petrarch found in me!
Parsons, William, 'To Mrs. Inchbald'.
MS. *Don. d. 123, p. 244 (autogr.).

61 Dear Ben, this comes to let you know
Sir your slave as much as can be.
Ireland, George, of Exeter Coll., Oxf., 'An Epistle. 1735'.
MS. Eng. misc. e. 240, p. 163.

62 Dear blame my love, if wanting ways to send
Of my misfortune, and my love the sum.
Burton, Francis, 'The concluding sonnett'.
MS. *Add. A. 267, fol. 151$^{v}$ (autogr.).

63 Dear books! you are my trusty guide
God's grace, which he doth freely give.
MS. Rawl. poet. 66, fol. 22.

64 Dear Britain mine blind not with tears thine eyes
My spirit exchang'd did but to heaven pass.
G. B., epitaph on Prince Henry in 'Cestria Lugens', 1612.
MS. *Rawl. poet. 116, fol. 11$^{v}$.

65 Dear brother, thou art gone before.
Where self's put off, and God is all?
Baxter, [Richard], on Richard Vines.
Pr. Richard Vines' *Treatise of the . . . Sacrament of the Lords Supper*, 1657, and Baxter's *Poetical Fragments*, 1681, p. 121.
MSS. Rawl. C. 580, p. 315, attr. to Mr. Baxter; Rawl. poet. 58, fol. 62$^{v}$, attr. to Mr. Baxter.

Dear Burney, skill'd in Greek and Latin 66
For trust me, Charles, the burns will keep!
Parsons, William, 'To Dr. Charles Burney'.
MS. *Don. d. 123, p. 231 (autogr.).

Dear but remember it is I 67
That for thy love will live, and die.
'A Poesie, written by a gentleman in the ende of a booke'. Couplet.
MS. Add. B. 97, fol. 19.

Dear C— so late from England's northern bourn 68
Grace from her arms, a language from her tongue!
Parsons, William, 'Advice to a Gentleman'.
Pr. *Travelling Recreations*, 1807, i. 63.
MS. *Don. d. 123, p. 181 (autogr.).

Dear Charles! the goose which t'other day 69
Shall drown the memory of the goose!
Parsons, William, 'To Charles B.' 1782.
MS. *Don. d. 123, p. 67 (autogr.).

Dear child it makes me blush for shame 70
Increase in wisdom as in years you grow.
'Mamma's advice to her Daughter on her Eleventh Birthday'.
MS. *Eng. poet. d. 47, fol. 52.

Dear Chloe attend to th'advice of a friend 71
'Twould be strange [if the] clock should go ri[ght] . . . (incomplete).
'To a young lady of 18 etc. . . . 13 Sep. 175[ ]'.
MS. Mus. e. 20, fol. 14.

Dear Chloe, while the busy crowd 72
And smooth the bed of death.
Cotton, Dr. Nathaniel, 'The Fire-Side'.
Pr. Cotton's *Various Pieces*, 1791, i. 65; and Dodsley's *Collection of Poems*, iv, 1755, p. 258.
MSS. Eng. poet. c. 9, p. 233, attr. to Dr. Cotton; e. 47, p. 63, attr. to Mr. Cotton.

Dear Colin prevent my warm blushes, 73
Indeed is too mellow for me.
[Montague, Lady M. W., and Sir William Yonge], 'A Song', 'The Answer', and 'Another answer'.
Pr. Dodsley's *Collection of Poems*, vi, 1758, p. 230; cf. *D.N.B.* on Yonge.
MS. Montagu e. 13, fol. 66$^{v}$.

Dear Col'nel name the day 74
My loss quickly to repair.
Amherst, Elizabeth, 'From a Young Woman to an old Officer who courted her'.
MS. *Eng. poet. e. 109, p. 51.

75 Dear cousin when I took my pen in hand
Words being but wind may bide a greater shock.
Burton, Francis.
MS. *Add. A. 267, fol. 123v (autogr.).

76 Dear Damon never let our love decay
Hope's ne'er deluded where true love is seen.
Williams, John, 'The 3ds [i.e. 3rd words]—Never be so deluded'.
MS. *Rawl. poet. 184, fol. 52v (autogr.).

77 Dear dear soul awake awake
Loud singing Holy, Holy, Holy.
'A preparation to a joyfull resurrection'; paraphrase of *Dies irae*.
MS. Rawl. poet. 160, fol. 13.

78 Dear do not your fair beauty wrong
And flies away from aged things.
[Randolph, Thomas], 'Love's Prime'.
MS. Rawl. poet. 116, fol. 72v rev.; see also S 1370.

79 Dear Dorinda, do I love
With unfeign'd sincerity.
'Love to Dorinda'.
MS. Eng. poet. e. 40, fol. 146.

80 Dear eye that dost peruse my muse's style
When grace in virtue's key, tunes nat[ure's string].
[Southwell, Robert], 'To the Reader'.
Prefixed to *St. Peter's Complaint*, 1595 and MS. copies.
MS. Eng. poet. b. 5, p. vii.

81 Dear friend, for surely I may call him so
A grateful soul and a contented mind.
Mr. Dryden, translator, Horace, *Epistles* I. xviii, 'Si bene te novi, etc. Good Counsell'.
MS. Rawl. poet. 173, fol. 40.

82*a* Dear friend, I fain would try once more
Brains are not needful to be base.
'To Julian'.
MS. Firth c. 16, p. 97.

82*b* [Dear friend, I hear this town does so abound]
From the innocent reproach of infamy?
[Wilmot, John, Earl of] Rochester.
See Vieth, p. 369.
MS. Rawl. poet. 173, fol. 132.

83 Dear friend! I question, nor can yet decide
Congratulate th'accession of thy name.
Stanley, Thomas, 'To Edward Sherburne Esq. upon our Mutuall Freindship'.
Pr. Sherburne's *Tragedies of Seneca*, 1702; a different version in Stanley's *Poems*, 1651.
MS. Wood F. 44, fol. 242.

Dear friend, it is with trouble that I part 84
I hope to be thus happy and secure.
Williams, John, 'Mrs. Ashe parting with Coll. Townsend'.
MS. *Rawl. poet. 184, fol. 69v (autogr.).

Dear friend, since I am now at leisure, 85
Then home and sup, and thus we end the day.
'The Footman wrott by Mrs. Lowther's Footman rather Dean Swift An Epistle to my Friend Mr. W.'
Not in H. Williams' *Poems of Swift*, 1937.
MS. Ballard 50, fol. 90.

Dear friend sit down. The tale is long and sad. 86
Who fain would have you be, new, tender, quick.
Herbert, George, 'Love unknowne'.
Pr. *The Temple*, 1633, p. 121.
MS. *Tanner 307, fol. 92v.

Dear friend, when those we love are in distress 87
And 'tis the thoughtful traitor that offends his king.
'A Consolatory Epistle to Mr. Julian in his confinement'.
Note by Dr. P. Simpson: Cf. 'An Exclamation against Julian, secretary to the Muses . . . By a Person of Quality', which the B.M. Catalogue dates '1688?' and queries 'Sir R. L'Estrange' for Julian. Pr. Robert Gould's *Poems*, 1689, p. 279, and Buckingham's *Miscellaneous Works*, i, 1704, p. 20.
MSS. Ashmole, 36, 37, fol. 315; Douce 357, fol. 141v; Firth c. 16, p. 53; Rawl. poet. 173, fol. 133, attr. to the D. of Buckingham; Wood F. 34, fol. 157.

Dear friend, you cannot wonder when you hear 88
Here lies my poor but yet my loving friend.
[Dalby, Edward (?)], 'To his Friend William Talbott of Shropshire From Figtree court' (W. T. adm. to the Inner Temple Nov. 1637).
MS. Ashmole 47, fol. 127v.

Dear friends either for love or hire. 89
Or send it home to me.
[Drayton, Michael], 'The 24th' song, copied twice.
Pr. *Odes*, 1619.
MS. Ashmole 38, p. 121; see also G384.

Dear friends I do remember 90
And also pray for me.
MS. Rawl. poet. 58, fol. 65.

91 **Dear friends laments art gives me life to show**
**Man's highest pitch, to men, might pattern forth.**
Mervall, Alphonso, 'An Epitaphe the right honourable Sr. Jhon Rooper, Lord Tenham . . . in Kent deceased the 26 Feb. 1628'.
MS. Rawl. poet. 166, p. 62.

92 **Dear give me a thousand kisses**
**If you do love as well as I.**
Pr. John Wilson's *Cheerfull Ayres or Ballads*, 1660, p. 62.
MSS. Eng. poet. c. 50, fol. 81; Mus. b. 1, fol. 46, music by John Wilson.

93 **Dear God by whom in dark womb's shade**
**Did other lords than God adore.**
James, Richard, 'A consultation with myself when I was confin'd into close keeping by the Lords', 1628–30.
Pr. Hearne's *Collections*, ed. C. E. Doble, i, O.H.S. ii, 1885, p. 9.
MS. *James 35, p. 11 (autogr.), and James's printed works presented to J. Rous, 1633, 4° H. 11 Th., before title-page (autogr.).
MSS. Hearne's diaries 1, p. 138, attr. to Mr. Rich. James; Rawl. poet. 172, fol. 114, attr. to Dr. Rich. James; Wood D. 19 (2), fol. 99, attr. Mr. Ric. James.

94 **Dear heart, remember that sad hour**
**Shall bind doubly your own.**
Verses on a binding, 17th cent.
MS. Ashmole 943, at end.

95 **Dear if you change I'll never choose again**
**Ere I prove false to faith, or strange to you.**
Pr. Dowland's *Songs or Ayres*, 1597, vii.
MSS. Mus. f. 7–12: f. 7, fol. $9^v$.

96 **Dear if you wish my dying**
**And I my life's sweet treasure.**
Pr. Thomas Bateson's *First set of English Madrigales*, 1604, xxiii.
MSS. Mus. f. 20–24: f. 20, fol. $85^v$.

97 **Dear ivy-mantled ruin that dost bow**
**Of thy few viewst Miltonic Bowles . . .**
(incomplete).
Gough, Richard, on Wytham, fragment.
MS. *Eng. poet. c. 5, fol. 300 (autogr.).

98 **Dear Jack! I easily can guess**
**I'll draw a cork,—with any major!**
Parsons, William, 'To Major W.'
MS. *Don. d. 123, p. 94 (autogr.).

99 **Dear Jesus hast thou given**
**Cannot with it compare.**
Beddome, Benjamin.
MS. *Eng. misc. e. 227, fol. 12.

**Dear Keil, if bant'ring friend says true,** 100
**None else from me has such a portion.**
'Doctori Keil, e Coll. Baliol Astronomice Professori', by A. Alsop, imitated in English verse.
MS. Ballard 47, fol. 54.

**Dear knight both my kinsman and friend** 101
**And envy I never shall feel.**
Boswell, James.
MS. *Douce 193, fol. 60 (autogr.).

**Dear ladies you requested I would write** 102
**Name not worth the note of envy nor of fame.**
Wentworth, Miss, 'To Mrs. Merrow'.
MS. Eng. poet. e. 17, fol. 6.

**Dear Lesbia let us love and play,** 103
**My Lesbia and I did kiss.**
Chatwin, John, 'The 5th Epigram of Catullus imitated'.
MS. *Rawl. poet. 94, p. 191 (autogr.).

**Dear, little, pretty, favourite ore,** 104
**Though he should shut me out of heav'n.**
'On a Helf-penny, which a Lady gave to a Beggar and the Author purchased for sixpence'.
MS. Ballard 50, fol. 108.

**Dear Lord if I thy presence feel** 105
**A Hell if thou remove.**
Beddome, Benjamin.
MS. *Eng. misc. e. 227, fol. $4^v$.

**Dear loss, to tell the world I grieve, were true** 106
**Which thy frail flesh denied, and her disease.**
Corbett, Dr. [Richard], 'On the Lady Haddington who dyed of the Smalpox' [6 Dec. 1618].
Pr. *Poems*, 1647, p. 43; *Poetica Stromata*, 1648; and the last section, beg. 'O thou deformed unwomanlike disease', in *Parnassus Biceps*, 1656, p. 48.
MSS. Ashmole 47, fol. 116, attr. to Dr. Corbett; CCC. 328, fol. 53, attr. to D. Corbet; Don. d. 58, fol. 56; Eng. poet. e. 97, p. 65, attr. to Dr. Corbet; Malone 21, fol. $17^v$, attr. to Dr. Corbett; Rawl. poet. 117, fol. $18^v$, attr. to Doctor Corbet.

**Dear love continue nice and chaste** 107
**My love, your sport, your godhead end.**
Pr. Donne's *Poems*, 1635–69; cf. *Poems*, ed. Grierson, 1912, ii, pp. cxxix foll., and attributions to [Sir] J[ohn] R[oe] in B.M. MS. Lansdowne 740, fol. $94^v$ and Soc. of Antiquaries, Edinburgh, MS. Hawthornden 15.
MSS. CCC. 327, fol. $30^v$, attr. to Donne; Eng. poet. f. 9, p. 137; Rawl. poet. 31, fol. $48^v$; 117, fol. 205 rev., attr. to Dunne.

108 **Dear love, do not your beauty wrong**
**And flies away from aged things.**
'Loves Prime'.
Pr. *Wits Recreations*, 1663, Sig. Q7^v^.
MS. Eng. poet. d. 152, fol. 108.

109 **Dear love, for nothing less than thee**
**Will dream that hope again, but else would die.**
Donne, John, 'The Dream'.
Pr. *Poems*, 1633, p. 227.
MSS. CCC. 327, fol. 4^v^, attr. to Donne; *Eng. poet. e. 99, fol. 120; *f. 9, p. 66; Rawl. poet. 31, fol. 40.

110 **Dear M—t come not quite so near**
**A miser of thy words.**
'On Mr. M. a great gamester whose breath stunk'.
MS. Eng. misc. c. 292, fol. 106.

111 **Dear Madam, As my stupid rider**
**Your faithful, honest horse, old Chesnut.**
Madan, Spencer, 'An Epistle . . . from his horse . . . to Lady Charlotte Madan'.
MS. Eng. poet. c. 51, p. 265.

112 **Dear madam! dear'st of all the female train!**
**If you'll but smile, to live in banishment.**
Morrice, John, 'The distracted Loyalist. Jan. 10, 1707'.
MS. *Rawl. poet. 114, fol. 138 (autogr.).

113 **Dear Madam, some compassion show**
**Severe commands at best are cruel laws.**
Williams, John, 'To Phillis. The 2ds [i.e. 2d words] are—Madam I will obey Your Commands'.
MS. *Rawl. poet. 191, fol. 8 (autogr.).

114 **Dear Madam! think it no reproach**
**Who rode before behind.**
'Written to a Lady who married her Footman'.
MS. Eng. poet. c. 51, p. 152.

115 **Dear Major! ever since this earth**
**And soon got children like themselves!**
Parsons, William, 'The origin of Evil'.
MS. *Don. d. 123, p. 109 (autogr.).

116 **Dear Merry! did'st thou never see**
**Than him from that confounded place.**
Parsons, William, 'To Robert Merry Esq. from Leghorn . . . October 1785'.
MS. *Don. d. 123, p. 129 (autogr.).

117 **Dear Miss Ashe be not rash in your long lasting choice**
**'Twill be sad to repent when you think to rejoice.**
Williams, John, 'My first Verses to Miss Ashe'. Couplet.
MS. *Rawl. poet. 191, fol. 14 (autogr.).

**Dear Miss Betty, young and fair,** 118
**Be more esteemed for being wise.**
Williams, John, 'To Miss Betty Ashe'.
MS. *Rawl. poet. 191, fol. 105 (autogr.).

**Dear Miss, it is with trouble that I part** 119
**All seeds of virtue nourish and improve.**
Williams, John, 'To Miss Ashe upon his parting with Her'.
MS. *Rawl. poet. 184, back endpaper (autogr.).

**Dear Miss, since part we must, I hope you may** 120
**Whilst wit is pleasing, and Miss Betty's fair.**
Williams, John, 'To Miss Betty Ashe upon her going to the Bath in Aprill. 1709'.
MS. *Rawl. poet. 184, fol. 53 (autogr.).

**Dear Miss the joy of my expecting eyes,** 121
**Strive daily to attain a truly glorious mind.**
Williams, John, 'The Wellcome. To Miss Ashe July 30th 1709'.
MS. *Rawl. poet. 191, fol. 95^v^ (autogr.).

**Dear Miss, whose long possession of my heart** 122
**Her long increase, and much reward above.**
Williams, John, 'A Copy to Miss Betty Ashe in her illness'.
MS. *Rawl. poet. 184, fol. 70 (autogr.).

**Dear Miss, whose love I very much commend** 123
**A joy to which I always shall aspire.**
Williams, John, 'To Miss Ashe upon Miss Betty being gone to Bath'.
MS. *Rawl. poet. 184, fol. 54^v^ (autogr.).

**Dear Miss your tender age with caution guard.** 124
**Guard us from error and from wilful faults.**
Williams, John, 'To Miss Ashe'.
MS. *Rawl. poet. 191, fol. 2^v^ (autogr.).

**Dear Misses, now the melancholy day** 125
**Let God our friendship, guide, increase, and bless.**
Williams, John, 'Upon my being parted from Miss Ashe and Miss Betty Nov. the 12th 1709'.
MS. *Rawl. poet. 184, fol. 87^v^ (autogr.).

**Dear Mistress wheresoever you do rest** 126
**No real separation but a vow.**
MS. Eng. poet. c. 50, fol. 72^v^.

**Dear Molly say, what shall we teach** 127
**We all our lives must glory pay.**
[Ken], Thomas, [Bp. of] Bath and Wells, letter to Frances and Mary Thynne, daughters of Thomas Thynne of Longleat: dated Dec. 14th.
MS. Bodl. Add. C. 219, fol. 5 (autogr.).

128 **Dear Mother my time has been wretchedly spent**
**When such easy designs such fine touches they see.**
Percy, Thomas, nephew of the Bp. of Dromore.
MS. Percy c. 8, fol. 80 (autogr.).

129 **Dear Nan, I would not have thy counsel lost,**
**Thou'lt rhyme me back again into my wits.**
King, Henry, 'To my Sister Anne King who chid mee in verse for being angry'.
Pr. *Poems*, 1657, p. 83.
MS. *Eng. poet. e. 30, fol. 52; *Malone 22, fol. 34$^{v}$.

130 **Dear native shades and flow'ry fields**
**Nor will tomorrow any diff'rence prove.**
Walsh, Octavia.
MS. *Eng. poet. e. 31, fol. 23$^{v}$ (autogr.).

131 **Dear noble captain, who by sea and land**
**Is now at large a bedlam or a stage.**
James, Richard, 'To Captaine Jhon Smith on the edition of his owne life'.
Pr. Smith's *True Travels, Adventures, and Observations . . . 1593–1629*, 1630, Sig. A5.
MS. *James 35, p. 8 (autogr.).

132 **Dear noble friend I in the city hear**
**Nor clouds more arrows drop, yet men must die.**
James, Richard, during his imprisonment, 1629–31, 'To Mr. I[ohn] S[elden]'.
MS. *James 35, p. 9 (autogr.).

133 **Dear object of my late and early pray'r**
**And sweeter breathe their little lives away!**
Langhorne, Dr. [John], 'To a Lady. Wrapped round a Nosegay of Violets'.
MS. Montagu e. 17, fol. 46.

134 **Dear P—! didst thou never see**
**Think they may marry whom they please!**
Parsons, William, 'On Bath Fortune hunters'. 15 Dec. 1783.
MS. *Don. d. 123, p. 103 (autogr.).

135 **Dear Parsons, I've heard in old time**
**May teach me to write something better.**
Sturch, William, 'To William Parsons'. 'June 27, 1778'.
MS. Don. c. 81, fol. 17 (autogr.).

136 **Dear Parsons skill'd in every art**
**And find both appetite, and laugh.**
'Dr. [Charles] Burney's answer' to W. Parsons. 'York House, 22 Jan. 1795'.
MS. Don. d. 123, p. 231.

137 **Dear Peggy since the single state**
**And blushing throw the rest aside.**
'Advice to a Young Lady lately Married'.
MS. Eng. poet. e. 47, p. 38.

**Dear Phillis, trust me with your thoughts** 138
**Your wounds I'll do the best I can to heal.**
Williams, John, 'Damon . . . To Mr. Wilson's disconsolate sister'.
MS. *Rawl. poet. 191, fol. 8 (autogr.).

**Dear Prescot Street I'm sorry to see** 139
**A Travers a Ashurst no Gayer no Wren.**
'A Letter to Prescot Street From a Dissenting Brother'. [1714/15]. *Cf.* W2489.
MS. Rawl. poet. 155, p. 118.

**Dear prisoner, whom fate has hither sent,** 140
**Thou may'st enjoy a perfect freedom here.**
'Advice to the Gentlemen Prisoners'.
MS. Rawl. poet. 181, fol. 62.

**Dear S. in the fictitious strain** 141
**'Tis no defence from Laura's eyes!**
Parsons, William, 'To a friend'.
Pr. *Travelling Recreations*, 1807, i. 19.
MS. *Don. d. 123, p. 99 (autogr.).

**Dear Sally! This short epistle unto you I write** 142
**But mostly so by your sincere S. Bate.**
Bate, Sally, 'A Letter to Miss Sally Bradgate—1764'.
MS. *Eng. poet. e. 28, p. 101.

**Dear Sappho, tell me, why thy lyre** 143
**Thy silence 'tis which kills.**
'On Miss Tr[ollope]'s quitting her Spinnet and Singing'.
MS. *Eng. poet. d. 47, fol. 31.

**Dear Segkar, thy disease, which I before** 144
**I'm sick myself, because I am not so.**
Weaver, Thomas, 'To his deare freind Cap. Segkar, sick of a fever at Baghilt'.
Pr. *Songs and Poems*, 1654.
MS. *Rawl. poet. 211, fol. 5$^{v}$ (autogr.).

**Dear Sir, a lady cried, that's much renowned** 145
**And reign the monarch coxcomb of the little town.**
'On Mr. Grevile, at Astrop Wells, 1692/3'.
MS. Eng. poet. e. 49, p. 140.

**Dear Sir I promised poetry, 'tis true** 146
**Not spare the namesake of your faithful Spencer.**
Spencer, [John], 'March 18th 1677/8'.
MS. Rawl. poet. 123, p. 198.

**Dear Sir! if you're in mood to whistle** 147
**To your high Worship makes a bow.**
Boswell, James, 'A Poetical Epistle to Doctor Sterne Parson Yorick and Tristram Shandy', *c.* 1760–7.
MS. *Douce 193, fol. 7 (autogr.).

148 Dear Sir, I've read your papers o'er
His everlasting praise.
Kenton, James, 'Epistle to Mr. Thos. Holloway . . . [on] the Death of his Mother . . . Aug. 25. 1782'.
MS. *Eng. poet. e. 19, p. 251 (autogr.).

149 Dear Sir, this comes to let you know
Laid down his book—blow'd out the candle.
'The Spinning-Wheel. An epistolary Tale'.
MS. Ballard 29, two copies, fols. 103$^{v}$ and 128.

150 Dear skilful Betty, who dost far excel
How often, when, and where, and what you did.
Creech, Thomas (translator), Ovid, *Amores* II. viii. 'To the Chambermaid her selfe'.
MS. Rawl. poet. 173, fol. 47$^{v}$.

151 Dear Somerton once my beloved correspondent
But betwixt you and I 'tis your servant Jack How.
Howe, Jack, 'An Epistle to Somerton Secretary to the Muses', 1691.
MSS. Douce 357, fol. 144$^{v}$; Eng. poet. c. 18, fol. 114$^{v}$; e. 49, p. 113.

152 Dear Son! from Nelson learn to be
Then you'll be lov'd by God and me.
'A Father's Present of Mr. Nelson's Festivals, etc. [1704] to his Son; in which were written the following Lines'.
MS. Ballard 29, fol. 161$^{v}$.

153 Dear Steele! to whom are in blest union given
'Quit these vain joys, and seek domestic bliss'.
Parsons, William, 'To Thomas Steele Esq. with the Florence Miscellany'.
MS. *Don. d. 123, p. 127 (autogr.).

154 Dear sweet Richards William
Who will come to your chamber as long as she has shoes.
'Mrs. Mathews to Wm. Richards'.
MS. Firth c. 16, p. 227.

155 Dear Sylvia, let thy Thyrsis know
Where fortunes, not affections equal are.
Weaver, Thomas, 'A Pastoral Dialogue betwixt Thirsis and Sylvia'.
Pr. *Songs and Poems*, 1654.
MS. *Rawl. poet. 211, fol. 10 (autogr.).

156 Dear take thy ring thy broken ring again
As the sun's greater light obscures the moon.
Beaumont, Thomas, 'Of a ringe with Stones about it which beinge put upon his finger the ringe broke and stones dropt out'.
MS. *Malone 18, p. 14 (autogr.).

Dear throw that flatt'ring glass away 157
And burn perhaps as well as I.
[Reynolds, Henry], 'On my Mrs looking in her glasse'.
Pr. with music by Henry Lawes in his *Ayres and Dialogues*, iii, 1658, p. 43; ascribed to Reynolds in the index.
MS. Mus. b. 1, fol. 64, with music by John Wilson; Rawl. poet. 116, fol. 48.

Dear Thyrsis! tell thy Corydon 158
Let's hope ere long, 'twill not be so.
'A Pastorall Dialogue betweene Corridon and Thyrsis. 13 Jan. 1648'.
MS. Eng. misc. e. 255, fol. 50.

Dear Tottie, since old Father Lee 159
And mirth here end in happy marriage.
Gough, Richard, 'Addressed to Edward Forster, Esq. On Mr. Haistwell's approaching marriage'.
MS. Eng. poet. c. 5, two copies, fols. 198 (autogr.) and 199.

Dear, what need my devotions charge the air. 160
Let Orcus, rich in his dull waters, take.
J. F., 'Tibullus lib: 3 Eleg. 3'.
MS. *Eng. poet. f. 17, p. 100 (autogr.).

Dear when I think upon my first sad fall 161
To make the music of our bliss the sweeter.
'On the Losse of his Mrs. and regaining her'.
MS. Ashmole 47, fol. 42.

Dear why do you joy and take such pleasure 162
And with thy love, for my true love reward me.
Pr. Michael East's *Second set of Madrigales*, 1606, xvi.
MS. Douce 280, fol. 69$^{v}$.

Dear, why do you say you love 163
Prove true, and say you cannot love.
'On his Mistresse'.
Attr. to Sir Robert Ayton by his nephew Sir John Ayton, B.M. Add. MS. 10308, fol. 3$^{v}$.
MSS. Don. d. 58, fol. 43$^{v}$; Eng. poet. e. 14, fol. 74; Rawl. poet. 116, fol. 55.

Dear wife, let's learn to get that skill 164
To love Christ Jesus, and to loathe our sin.
Payler, George, 'Written . . . at the death of . . . Robert Payler, . . . Covent-Garden. Dec. 8th 1650'.
MS. Rawl. D. 1308, p. 177.

Dear wood born often on mine armed arm: 165
A ship to Neptune, and to Mars a shield.
Davison, Fr[ancis], 'A souldier Havinge escaped shipwrecke uppon his sheelde, dedicates it'. 'Mr. Fr. Davison gave me [Stephen Powle] these Verses as of his owne makinge: July 1609'.
MS. Tanner 169, fol. 76$^{v}$.

166 **Dearest Albina my desire**
**If twice you enter purgatory.**
James, Richard, 'To Albina'.
MS. *James 35, p. 13 (autogr.).

167 **Dearest fair one be not coy**
**Beyond the joys of Jove.**
'Song'.
MS. Rawl. poet. 152, fol. 174.

168 **Dearest heart do not forsake me**
**A love more pleasing to thy mind.**
'Song'.
MS. Ashmole 38, p. 122.

169 **Dearest: I call you so, because I spend**
**Never to ask me anything again.**
Oldisworth, Nicolas, 'For an Innes of courts man. To his Mistris'.
MS. *Don. c. 24, fol. 63 (autogr.).

170 **Dearest Mira since thou hast**
**Distilling nectar in a kiss.**
'Madrigall'.
MS. Eng. poet. c. 50, fol. 83$^{v}$.

171 **Dearest of husbands, he whose life records.**
**I live in patience, but die in desire.**
Verses on a monument to Sir George Warburton of Arley, Cheshire, d. May 18, 1676, initialed D[iana] W[arburton].
MS. Rawl. D. 682, fol. 10.

172 **Dearest of men in best of causes lost**
**Rear up their heads and hallelujahs sing.**
'An Acrostick on the Earl of Derwentwater'. James Radcliffe, lord Derwentwater, executed 24 February 1716.
MS. Rawl. poet. 181, fol. 63$^{v}$.

173 **Dearest thy tresses are not threads of gold**
**Be goddess like disposed, be good, be true.**
[Carew, Thomas], 'To his Mrs.'
Pr. *Poems* 1640.
MSS. Ashmole 47, fol. 42$^{v}$; CCC. 328, fol. 75; Don. d. 58, fol. 43; Eng. poet. c. 50, two copies, fols. 43 and 64$^{v}$; e. 14, fol. 69; e. 97, p. 120; f. 10, fol. 102; Firth e. 4, p. 119; Rawl. poet. 142, fol. 16; 160, fol. 115; see also F115.

174 **Death and an honest cobbler fell at bate**
**Honest Jack Cobbler here lies underlaid.**
'On a Cobler'.
MS. Eng. poet. e. 14, fol. 93$^{v}$ rev.; see also D177.

**Death and the [this] cobbler [man] were long at a stand** 175
**And ripped his soul from the upper leather.**
'On a Cobler'.
MSS. CCC. 309, fol. 49; Don. d. 58, fol. 16$^{v}$; Douce f. 5, fol. 11; Eng. poet. e. 14, fol. 94 rev.

**Death as a king rampant and stout** 176
**Till Christ doth raise the dead.**
[Bunyan, John], 'of Death'.
Pr. *One Thing is Needfull*, 3rd ed., p. 3.
MS. Rawl. poet. 58, fol. 2$^{v}$.

**Death at the cobbler's door oft made a stand,** 177
**Here lies Tom Cobbler underlaid.**
'Upon a Cobler at Northampton'.
MS. Rawl. D. 316, fol. 111$^{v}$; see also D174.

**Death be not proud, though some have called thee** 178
**And death shall be no more; death thou shalt die.**
Donne, John, 'Sonnett 6'.
Pr. *Poems*, 1633.
MSS. *Eng. poet. e. 99, fol. 44$^{v}$.

**Death be not proud, thy hand gave not this blow** 179
**The grave no conquest gets death hath no sting.**
[Harington, Lucy, Countess of Bedford (?)], 'Elegie on the Ladye Markham, by L: C: of B:'.
See Donne's *Poems*, ed. Grierson, 1912, ii, p. cxliv.
MS. Rawl. poet. 31, fol. 39; see also D187.

**Death came by** 180
**And killed her in the midst of a snow.**
'Old mother Slye an Oxford Huckster dying in a frosty and snowy season, Georg. Payne the witty and waggish cook of St. Albans hall made this epitaph on her'.
Pr. *Modius Salium*, 1751, p. 22.
MS. Wood E. 32 (Modius Salium), fol. 18.

**Death came into the garden and could see** 181
**Prepar'd I hope, unto these flowers to go.**
'Epitaph in the Minster Churchyard, Peterborough'.
MS. Eng. poet. c. 51, p. 233.

**Death came to thee, as bold as brief** 182
**And killed at once a miller and a thief.**
'Of a miller'. Couplet.
MS. Lat. misc. c. 19, p. 419; see also D217.

**Death, cruel Death, to please his palate** 183
**Has cropped my Lettice to make him salad.**
'Epitaph on Miss Lettice in a Country Churchyard'. Couplet.
MS. Eng. poet. c. 51, p. 4.

184 Death hath been deemed a period unto woe
Death welcome life, and lead me unto bliss.
H. S.
MS. *Rawl. poet. 120, fol. 15v (autogr.).

185 Death hath been ever harsh but now most cruel
You seld shall find the like in any place.
'In obitum Dominae Franciscae Davenport'.
MS. Ashmole 47, fol. 105.

186 Death hath drawn our golden car
Into a briny ocean fall.
[Crashaw, Richard (?)], 'An Elegie Upon the death of Mr. Wm. Carr in Eman. Coll', buried at Great St. Andrews, Cambridge, 12 November 1634.
See *Poems of Crashaw*, ed. L. C. Martin, 1957, pp. lxx–lxxiii; pr. from MS. Tanner 465, op. cit., p. 402.
MSS. Rawl. poet. 147, p. 42, attr. to Cornwallis; Tanner 465, fol. 63, attr. to Pet. Cornwallis.

187 Death I recant, and say, unsaid by me
Because the chain is broke, but no link lost.
Donne, John, 'Elegye on Mrs. Boulstred'.
MSS. *Eng. poet. e. 99, fol. 26; *f. 9, p. 119, including D179, *q.v.*

188 Death is the antecedent judgement is
A heart to judge himself whilst here he lives.
'A meditation upon Judgement'.
MS. Rawl. poet. 142, fol. 81v.

189 Death is the issue of a carnal mind,
His to support, instruct, comfort, defend.
MS. *Rawl. poet. 97, fol. 24 (autogr.).

190 Death is the last end of our mortal race:
Help us then Lord, no aid but thee we crave.
'Acrostick on Death'.
MS. Rawl. poet. 90, fol. 110v.

191 Death is the salve that healeth all annoy
A living death a never turning stream.
MS. Rawl. poet. 172, fol. 6v.

192 Death knew not how t'invite thy soul away
He took the earth we lov'd and made it heaven.
'On the Lord Herbert who died of the small pox'.
MS. Rawl. poet. 199, p. 92.

193 Death leagued with sickness to disgrace
And 'gainst their nature force them kind.
Epigram on a gentlewoman that had the small pox.
MS. CCC. 328, fol. 82v.

[Death may dissolve my body now] 194
Shall place it on his head.
Watts, Dr. Isaac, 'At the Funeral of . . . John William De La Flechere, Vicar of Madeley, Shropshire by the desire of Anna Maria Gilpin'.
Pr. *Hymns and Spiritual Songs*, 1709.
MS. Montagu c. 5, fol. 14.

Death no man spares, all men must surely die. 195
As to deserve at death a rebel's shame.
Robinson, Robert.
MS. *Rawl. poet. 218, p. 79 (autogr.).

Death of all men is the total sum, 196
And death the broom which sweeps us all away.
MS. Rawl. poet. 90, fol. 113.

Death passing by, and hearing Parsons play 197
For Parsons rests his service being done.
Rand[olph,] Th[omas], 'On Mr. Parsons Organist of Westminster Abbey', buried at Westminster 3 Aug. 1623.
Pr. Camden's *Remaines*, 1637, p. 415.
MSS. Ashmole 38, p. 184, attr. to Th. Randall; Ballard 50, fol. 196; Eng. poet. e. 40, fol. 118.

Death, put on some kind disguise 198
I'd relapse to life for joy.
'A Song'.
MS. Rawl. poet. 222, fol. 37v.

Death seems to boast a Margaret he hath got 199
Thou wast as true a friend as lives in earth.
William and Margaret Rudyerd. He d. 16 June 1626. All Hallows' Church, Leicester.
MS. Top. gen. e. 1, p. 17.

Death strikes each minute: oh that we could then 200
Mind our last minute ere death strike again.
Robinson, Robert, couplet.
MS. *Rawl. poet. 218, p. 36 (autogr.).

Death (that on human flesh doth use to feed) 201
Not since by any living creature found.
Shirley, James, 'Upon Sr. G. Ca: Ladie: Ep:'
A different version, 'Upon a Gentlewoman that died of a Fever', printed in *Poems by James Shirley*, 1646, p. 55.
MS. *Rawl. poet. 88, p. 28, attr. to J. S.

Death the last end of all is fix'd is sure 202
No matter what the means by which you fall.
'Ann wife of John Farlam', Chatham, 28 Sept. 1748.
MS. Eng. misc. c. 136, fol. 17v.

203 Death thou art proud, and cruel, oh thy power
Thou had'st prolong'd thy few but glorious days.
'An elegye on the Lord Chichester', Arthur, Lord Chichester of Belfast, d. 19 Feb. 1624/5.
MS. Ashmole 47, fol. 77.

204 Death thou was once an uncouth hideous thing.
Making our pillows either down or dust.
Herbert, George, 'Death'.
Pr. *The Temple*, 1633, p. 180.
MS. *Tanner 307, fol. 137.

205 Death thought these young ones old and gave them place
Me an imposthume killed: thee what god please.
'Upon Mr. Geo. Hulbert and his youngest Children . . . in St. Martins in the feilds . . . in the Church yard'.
MS. Ashmole 38, fol. 240.

206 Death to a just equality does bring
Of these my starving worms before 'tis day.
Fragments of a song.
MS. Mus. d. 10, fol. 92 rev., 81$^{v}$–82.

207 Death to a wrestler gave a fine fall
That tripp'd up his heels and took no hold at all.
Couplet. Pr. Camden's *Remaines*, 1637, p. 416.
MS. Rawl. D. 1372, fol. 10 from end; see also D209.

208 Death to show himself most cruel
Parts an imposthume and prevails.
Polwhele, John, 'In morbum . . . Sam. Pendarres'.
MS. *Eng. poet. f. 16, fol. 1 (autogr.).

209 Death to this wrestler gave a fine fall
That tripped up his heels, and took no hold at all.
Couplet. 'Epitaph on a famous Wrestler'.
MS. Eng. poet. e. 40, fol. 112; see also D207.

210 Death took away Colemore in the midst of frost
Leaves not a coal more for to make a fire.
'On Mr. Colemore'.
MS. Eng. poet. e. 14, fol. 86 rev.

211 Death was not by Jehovah made
And shout thy praise above.
Kenton, James.
MS. *Eng. poet. e. 20, p. 333 (autogr.).

212 Death we may chide who like an envious wind
And thus dissolve yourselves upon her urn.
Manwaring, D., on Mrs. Sarah Manwaring.
MS. Ashmole 47, fol. 87$^{v}$.

213 Death what am I a doing! do I write
A king was humble and his subjects proud.
'Englands Teares for Scotland'.
MS. Rawl. poet. 160, fol. 206.

Death, what dost? Oh hold thy blow. 214
All hope of never dying here is dead.
Cr[ashaw], R[ichard], 'An Elegie on Mr. Herris', including 'If ever pity were acquainted'.
See *Poems*, ed. L. C. Martin, 1957, p. 168.
MS. Tanner 465, fol. 67, attr. on fol. 1*a* to R. Cr.

Death who'ld not change prerogatives with thee, 215*a*
I cannot write but I will weep her one.
R[andolph], T[homas], 'An Elegy on the Lady Venetia Digby'.
Pr. *Poems*, 1638, p. 36.
MSS. Ashmole 47, fol. 59$^{v}$; Firth e. 4, p. 132, attr. to T. R.

Death why dost thou grin so this sad day 215*b*
Thou hast got the shell but heaven the kernel.
Epitaph on Silance Carnel, d. 1714 *æt* 77.
MS. Hearne's diaries 96, p. 145.

Death with his dart hath us bereft 216
Our soul shall be reposed.
Newton, Thomas, 'An Epitaph upon the worthy and Honourable Lady, the Lady Knowles [Knollys]', d. 15 Jan. 1568/9. Typed from a printed copy licensed 1568/9.
MS. Firth d. 14, fol. 157.

Death without warning was as bold as brief 217
When he kill'd two in one: a miller and a thief.
'Epitaph on a Miller'.
MS. Eng. poet. e. 40, fol. 106; see also D182.

Death's dismal parting of this pair asunder 218
Yet thou in virtue did'st them all excel.
Hall, [John], 'A funerall Elegy on [Elizabeth] wife of Dr. Henry Willkinson'.
MS. Lat. misc. c. 19, p. 116.

Death's envious hand with his impartial stroke 219
Bids all good night and rests your loving friend.
Sampson, John, on John Freind, 1672.
MS. Top. Oxon. f. 31, p. 283.

Death's first encroachments on our narrow soil 220
Thence, where he so great bondage underwent.
'To the memory of the Pious and learned Mr. Jo. Christian Sen: Fellow of Trin. Coll. November [16]71'.
MS. Rawl. poet. 127, fol. 5.

Death's uncontrolled summons unto all 221
Nor yet the wicked proud not insolent.
'A funeral Ticket stuck in the Poultry Curch'.
MS. Rawl. D. 1334, fol. 29 rev.

222 **[Deceit] disceit disceyvyth and shalbe diceyved**
**To such a defraudor yet the frawde shall ay rebounde.**

Lydgate, John, a stanza of *Fall of Princes*, Brown Robbins Index no. 674, written notes on end-papers.
Pr. bk. Auct. VII. Q.2.21.

223 **December once in frosty weather**
**That would have crept through our laws.**

Whig poem on the Jacobite rising 1715–16.
Pr. *A Collection of State Songs*, 1716, p. 116.
MS. Rawl. poet. 169, fol. 6.

224 **Decius of a gentle disposition**
**Within an hour no man so strange as he.**

Davies, [Sir] John, of Gray's Inn, 'In Decium'.
MS. *Rawl. poet. 212, fol. 57v rev.

225 **Declare thy grief wherewith thou art oppressed**
**May well be pitied but no way relieved.**

MS. Eng. poet. e. 14, fol. 26v.

226 **Declined with age, no view of rising**
**Are instruments of providence.**

'The Curate and Footman. A Tale'.
MS. *Eng. poet. d. 47, fol. 70.

227 **Declining Venus has no force o'er love.**
**The dial speaks not, but it points, Jack How.**

'Satyr', 1693.
Pr. *Poems on Affairs of State*, iii, 1704, p. 370.
MS. Eng. poet. c. 18, fol. 130v.

228 **Decreed it is for all men once to die.**
**Hope to have found, being often told the way.**

Roman, Joseph, of King's School, Sherborne, on the death of Robert Whetcombe, 'Antientest Governour of the King's Schoole of Sherebourne', 24 Oct. 1656.
MS. Gough Dorset 35 (1), fol. 20*f*.

229 **Deep are her strong foundations laid,**
**And all my words thy fame display.**

Psalm lxxxvii.
MS. *Montagu e. 10, fol. 38.

230 **Deep in a lonely vale, beneath a bower**
**Resign their fated breath.**

On George III's Queen Charlotte, 1761.
MS. Malone 41, fol. 62.

231 **Deep in earth are more precious gems**
**Rejoice with wine and minstrelsy.**

'Robbers Song'.
MS. Montagu c. 5, fol. 70v.

232 **Deep lamenting loss of treasure**
**So his faith shall live for ever.**

'Britton [Nicholas Breton] one S[ir] P[hilip] S[idney]'.
MS. Rawl. poet. 85, fol. 26v.

**Deign at my hands this crown of prayer and praise** 233
**Salvation to all that will is nigh.**

Donne, John, 'Holy Sonnetts—La Corona. 1'.
Pr. *Poems*, 1633.
MS. *Eng. poet. e. 99, fol. 41v.

**Deign, gracious God, to hear my feeble lays** 234
**For ever praise thee, and for ever love.**

'The Author . . was buried under a scaffold . . . Tower Hill . . . at the execution of Simon, Lord Frazer of Lovat', 9 April 1747.
Pr. *Gentleman's Magazine*, 1747, p. 193, subscribed R. W.
MSS. Eng. poet. e. 39, p. 113; e. 40, fol. 16.

**Deign, worthiest sir, t'accept of worthless this** 235
**Your honour, name and praise shall last th' like time.**

Cheyney, William, 'The Epistle. To the right worshipfull and worthy Gentleman Sir Gyles Allington of Horsheath hall Knight'.
MS. *Rawl. poet. 86, fol. 2v (autogr.).

**De'il take the war that hurried Willy from me** 236
**When he silly loon might have plunder'd me.**

D'Urffey, Tho[mas], 'In a Wife for any man . . . set by Mr. Cha. Powell'.
MS. Mus. Sch. C. 95, p. 113.

**Delia a hundred pounds desir'd in gold** 237
**He'll pay for's lady's pleasures, so many do.**

'In Deliam', epigram.
MS. Don. d. 58, fol. 33.

**Delia! let's walk in yonder grove:** 238
**And Delia be like Venus kind.**

'To Delia, upon Valentine's Day'.
MS. Ballard 29, fol. 128v.

**Delia we wonder and 'tis strange that you** 239
**Yet thee thy dress and her her actions blame.**

Butt[erix], S[imon], epigram.
MS. Ashmole 38, p. 138.

**Delightful pastime of my tender age!** 240
**And let me whistle sorrow from my heart.**

Boswell, James, 'Ode on Whistling'.
MS. *Douce 193, fol. 5 (autogr.).

**Delights good servants, but bad masters are** 241
**Doted on, turn diseases our soul's snare.**

North, Dudley, 3rd Baron.
MS. *North e. 41, fol. 54v.

**Delights which are in virtue found** 242
**Of sorrows are the spring.**

Copied by Wiman Ramsey, *c*. 1595.
MS. Rawl. D. 649, fol. 29.

243 Deliver me, oh God, from all my foes that be
From traps and snares and bloody hands (good Lord) deliver me.

MS. Rawl. poet. 23, p. 141, reference to setting by Dr. Bull.

244 Democritus I see and laugh: 'tis so
Heraclitus I see their mischiefs; oh I weep amain.

Robinson, Robert, 'Democritus, video, rideo, Heraclitus, eo, fleo'.
MS. *Rawl. poet. 218, p. 117 (autogr.).

245 Demure as witch's tabby cat.
Unless you have a mind to play.

Boswell, James, 'An Epistle to Miss Home'.
MS. *Douce 193, fol. 23 (autogr.).

246 Demure with formal dress, and visage sage
For she could ne'er have one to grant it to.

Walsh, William, 'Upon Mrs. Demure'.
MS. Malone 9, fol. 29$^{v}$ (autogr.).

247 Denham, come help me to laugh at old Daph,
Advis'd thee to scribble no more?

'Upon the Author', Sir William Davenant.
Pr. *Certain verses . . . to be reprinted with . . . Gondibert*, 1653, p. 14.
MS. CCC. 309, fol. 53$^{v}$.

248 Denied our gracious sovereign's sight
(No doubt) to hold her tongue.

'The following Copy was lately directed (from Oxford) to . . . the Pr. of Wales' (Frederick Louis, 1707–51).
MS. Ballard 29, fol. 137.

249 Denmark my cradle, Scotland a spouse me gave
Anna is dead, and gone, her fame shall never die.

R. B., on Queen Anne, wife of James I, d. 1619.
MS. Malone 19, p. 5.

250 Denys hath merited no slender praise
Unto her knight was this, that she died first.

Strode, William, 'On his [i.e. Sir Wm. Strode's] Lady Denys', his second wife.
MS. *CCC. 325, fol. 40 (autogr.).

251 Departed to Jesus and gone
And ever rejoice and adore.

Kenton, James, 'To the Memory of Mr. Isaac and Mrs. Anne Moore . . . 1781'.
MS. *Eng. poet. e. 19, p. 242 (autogr.).

252 Derwent, what scenes thy wandering waves behold.
And mix my briny sorrows in your urn.

Darwin, Erasmus, 'This poem not in Print'.
MS. Eng. poet. d. 10, fol. 82.

Descend from heaven thou most worthy muse 253–4
And that Pirithous still in chains must be.

W. A., translator, Horace, *Odes* III. iv.
MS. *Rawl. poet. 104, fol. 23$^{v}$ (autogr.).

Descend some angels of your warbling throng 255
Conduct this world to that above.

'A View of Paradise or a Sketch of the New Jerusalem'.
MS. Rawl. poet. 89, fol. 1.

Descend ye nine! Descend and sing 256
Yet music and love were victorious.

Pope, [Alexander], 'An Ode Compos'd for the Publick Commencement at Cambridge . . . July 19th 1730 At the Musick Act . . . Musick by Maurice Green D. Mus.' [St. Cecilia's day ode].
MS. Mus. d. 36, fol. 11.

[Descended of an ancient line] 257
And see the storm a shore.

Dryden, John, translator, 'Fates Uncertainty'. Part of Horace, *Odes* III. xxix.
Pr. *Sylvae*, 1685, addressed to Laurence Hyde, Earl of Rochester.
MS. Rawl. poet. 90, fol. 176.

Descending from above 258
And thus the genuine gospel preach.

Kenton, James.
MS. *Eng. poet. e. 20, p. 98 (autogr.).

Descent of birth is a vain good 259
Thy praise is all thine own; thy name.

R[andolph], T[homas], 'An Anagr. upon his Mris Name. Vertue alone thy blisse'.
MS. Firth e. 4, p. 120.

Desert's not ours (none dare say few) 260*a*
But th' just his praise shall ever sing.

Fairfax, Thomas, Lord, Psalm cxv.
MS. *Fairfax 38, p. 404; see also L744.

Deserted, and scorn'd the proud Marlborough sat 260*b*
For betraying the church and enslaving the land.

'The false Favorites Downfall', 1692.
MS. Eng. poet. c. 18, fol. 119$^{v}$.

Design or chance makes others wive 261
As love has me, for only you.

[Waller, Edmund], 'Att the marriage of the Dwarfes'.
Pr. *Poems*, 1645, p. 152, and *Wits Recreations*, 1640.
MS. *Don. d. 55, fol. 37$^{v}$.

262 Desire desires you grant to give me my request
Mind then my troth the rest let gain no place.
'Swerdna', i.e. Andrews.
MS. Rawl. poet. 92, fol. 7v.

263 Desire not riches, wealth is a rod
When God says ye've had your consolation.
[Jordan, Thomas], 'On Riches'.
Pr. *Divinity and Morality*, Sig. §§3v, beg. Labour not to be rich . . .
MS. Rawl. poet. 90, fol. 102.

264 Desire's the vast extent of human mind
It mounts above, and leaves poor hope behind.
Couplet.
MS. Sancroft 85, p. 282 rev.

265 Desist, fond man; nor seek to know
Nor think of what the next will bring.
Manning, —, translator, Horace, *Odes* I. ii, 'Tu ne quaesiveris etc. . . . Lead thy short life merrily, and be not over-solicitous about future Contingencies'.
MS. Rawl. poet. 173, fol. 28v.

266 Desist fond mortal to blaspheme that power
Constrain'd for ever in the dark abyss.
Chatwin, John, 'The Epilogue. Spoken to the Libertine'.
MS. *Rawl. poet. 94, p. 72 (autogr.).

267 Despair, thy name
That foster the disease and not remove.
J. F., 'Despaire'.
MS. *Eng. poet. f. 17, p. 15 (autogr.).

268 Despairing beside a clear stream
His ghost shall glide over the green.
Rowe, [Nicholas], 'Colin's Complaint a Song'.
Pr. *Poems on Several Occasions*, 1714, p. 29.
MS. Ballard 47, fols. 160 and 68v.

269 Despise not him that's fall'n to poverty
And a false friendship trusts that fails at need.
Bulteel, John.
MS. *Rawl. poet. 159, fol. 214.

270 Despised I to my God complain
And I his image gain.
Kenton, James.
MS. *Eng. poet. e. 20, p. 128 (autogr.).

271 Despoil'd of nature's boast
Conquering and to conquer go.
Kenton, James.
MS. *Eng. poet. e. 20, p. 236 (autogr.).

272 Destin'd while living to sustain
A broken heart can bleed no more.
Mrs. Wright, daughter of Samuel and Susanna Wesley, 'written [on] herself'.
MS. Top. gen. e. 32, fol. 85.

Detestable are those who when they might 273
Ill custom change, and false applause despise.
Williams, John, 'A Satyr against grand entertainments for the rich, and abuses in feasting the poor'.
MS. *Rawl. poet. 188, fol. 60 (autogr.).

Devil thou know'st we're thine 274
To see great Lucifer tonight.
Cavendish, Lady Jane, 'The Songe' of witches in a pastoral.
MS. *Rawl. poet. 16, p. 54.

Devils can change their shapes but not their natures 275
And seventy-nine prove England's Jubilee.
'A Copy of the last verses made by Dr. [Robert] Wild Author of Iter Boreale', *c.* 1679.
MSS. Douce 357, fol. 75, attr. to Dr. Wild; MS. Eng. poet. c. 11, fol. 102, attr. to Dr. Wild.

Devoid of judgement destitute of sense 276
Proud to inferiors, fawning to the great.
Bate, S[ally], 'Characters'.
MS. *Eng. poet. e. 28, p. 225.

Devoted Anna did so long frequent 277
Confirmed by an angel that descended.
R. H., On the death of Queen Anne, wife of James I, 1619.
MS. Malone 19, p. 5.

Devotion fills our mind, and we appear 278
Before this deity, with praise or prayer.
'On Giveing a Petition to the Queen of Spain at Barcelona', 1711, couplet.
MS. Rawl. D. 360, fol. 80.

Devotion is the hand by which we reach 279
And seeking day finds a perpetual night.
Co[ventry], Jo[hn].
MS. Ashmole 47, fol. 82v.

Diana Cecil that rare beauty thou dost show 280
The ill of ignorance prove better than the good.
H[erbert, Lord] Ed[ward, of Cherbury], 'To Lady Diana Cecill'.
Pr. *Occasional Verses*, 1665, p. 34.
MSS. Ashmole 36, 37, fol. 305; Rawl. poet. 147, p. 75, attr. to Ed. H.

Diana stick thy virgin waxen torch 281
With its repaired shine in this our sphere.
'To the Moone the cleare pearle of Heaven'.
MS. Rawl. poet. 142, fol. 45v.

Diana watchful o'er young Ammon's fate 282
Charles could not be restored, till George was born.
George I, b. 28 March, 1660.
MS. Rawl. poet. 153, fol. 55v.

283 **Diaphenia like the daffdowndilly,**
**Then in requite, sweet virgin love me.**
[Chettle, Henry(?)].
Pr. Pilkington's *First Book of Songs*, 1605, xvii. Subscribed H.C. in *England's Helicon*: see H. E. Rollins's ed., 1935, ii. 133.
MSS. Mus. f. 7–10: f. 9, fol. 22.

284 **Dick Ecclesiae supposed a papist**
**Lived a Machiavel, but died an atheist.**
'On A great Bishope of this kingdom', couplet.
MS. Ashmole 38, p. 199.

285 **Dick, I had wrote to thee before,**
**For giving her a satin doublet from Lester.**
[Lleuelyn, Martin], 'Newes from Oxford or . . . The Welch Dove', Royalist verses on the first siege, May–June 1645. With preface, etc. beg. 'Jack Price the feirce'.
Pr. *Men Miracles*, 1646, p. 53.
MSS. Ashmole 36, 37, fol. 83.

286 **Dick Star and his moon together did wed**
**The Star might be seen as the man in the moon.**
'On Mr. Starre and Mrs. Moon'.
MS. CCC. 328, fol. 44.

287 **Dick with his dogs in such an outrage grew**
**Nay, up thou goest quoth Dick, and th'wert my father.**
'Irati Implacabiles'.
MS. Tanner 465, fol. 94.

288 **Did Abraham in God believe**
**Whilst it is called today.**
Tipping, William.
MS. *Rawl. poet. 101, fol. 83 (autogr.).

289 **Did ancient Socrates his fame advance**
**No change of any vestiment about him.**
'On Tom. Coriatt'.
MS. Malone 19, p. 89.

290 **Did Celia's person and her mind agree**
**Enrich'd the image, but defac'd the mind.**
'On the Dutchess of Queensbury by Mr. Pope'. Answered by H28.
See *Minor Poems*, ed. Norman Ault and John Butt, 1954, p. 443.
MS. Ballard 50, fol. 49.

291 **Did he to antidate the day awake?**
**Or turn pale Niobe and ever weep.**
Southwell, Sir Robert, 'On the Death of . . . Cornish Coryster of New Coll. . . . Aug. 25 [16]55. The day they went to Winch: Election'.
MS. *Eng. poet. f. 6, fol. 26 rev. (autogr.).

**Did he who thus inscribed this wall!** 292
**That house is not a House of Lords!**
Barrington, —, 'Chichester Cathedral Vault of the Richmond Family inscribed, Domus ultima'.
MS. Eng. poet. c. 51, p. 199.

**Did I but dare to undertake the task** 293
**Nobody then shall need our names to tell.**
Burton, Francis, acrostic: 'Dorothie Stapleford' and 'Frauncis Burton'.
MS. *Add. A. 267, fol. 66v (autogr.).

**Did men but think on dang'rous ruins,** 294*a*
**And methodize away desire.**
1735.
MS. Eng. misc. e. 240, p. 132.

**Did not God abide** 294*b*
**That are thus protected.**
Fairfax, Ferdinando, 2nd Baron, Psalm cxxiv.
MS. Fairfax 38, p. 482.

**Did not my sorrow sigh'd into a verse** 295
**Without forefathers thine own pedigree.**
[Earle, John (?)], on William Herbert, Earl of Pembroke, d. 10 April, 1630.
Pr. *Parnassus Biceps*, 1656, p. 40.
MS. CCC. 328, fol. 52, attr. to G. Maine; Rawl. poet. 147, p. 151, attr. to Cl. P.; 199, p. 66; 209, fol. 10; see also C575.

**Did not the learned Glynne and Maynard** 296*a*
**Declar'd a traitor through the nation.**
Hudibrastic verse: see *D.N.B.* viii. 17, on Sir John Glynne (1603–66).
MSS. Aubrey 6, fol. 115; Rawl. poet. 152, fol. 130.

**Did sweeter sounds adorn my flowing tongue** 296*b*
**For ever blessing, and for ever blest.**
Prior, Matthew, 'Charity', paraphrase of 1 Corinthians xiii.
Pr. *Poems*, 1707.
MS. Rawl. poet. 153, fol. 70v.

**Did you call sir?—no Harry—pray keep at a distance,** 297
**Of porter he'll pour us a plenteous libation!**
Parsons, William, 'The Welsh Rabbit . . . Chichester Coffee house . . . 21 Dec. 1782'.
MS. *Don. d. 123, p. 66 (autogr.).

**Did you ever see the day** 298
**So let our heavenly angel rest.**
A[y]ton, Sir Ro[bert], 'On the Princes death unto the King'. Prince Henry, 1612.
MS. Rawl. poet. 160, fol. 29.

299 Did you hear of the news? An invisible fleet
For a Parliament's sunk, and six regiments raised.
'The Invasion'. 1688.
MSS. Eng. poet. c. 18, fol. 67; e. 49, p. 44.

300 Did you hear of the news (oh the news) howit thunders
Sing, and play, while the city was burning.
[Flatman, Thomas], 'A Song'.
Pr. *Poems*, 1682, p. 116.
MS. Rawl. poet. 84, fol. 106$^{v}$ rev.

301 Did you n'er see a white rose fully blown
Now gone for that supply will never fail.
Moore, John, of King's School Sherborne, on the death of Robert Whetcombe, 'Antientest Governour of the King's Schoole of Sherebourne', 24 Oct. 1656.
MS. Gough Dorset 35 (1), fol. 23.

302 Did you not know, about three weeks ago
And hereafter may dig for their living.
Ballad on the parliament's victory at Bradock Down, Jan. 1643, and the royalist victory following, Stratton, 16 May.
MSS. Ashmole 36, 37, fol. 2.

303 Did you not once Lucinda vow,
Springs not from wealth nor lands.
'Dialogue the words by Dryden'.
MS. Mus. c. 3, fol. 21, with music.

304 Did you not see his pedlars standing
The Scotch will ne'er come here again.
Siege of Hereford, Sept. 1645 (?).
MSS. Ashmole 36, 37, fol. 252.

305 Did you not see the Scotch man's wallet
The Scotch shall n'ere come here again.
One verse added to D304.
MSS. Ashmole 36, 37, fol. 252.

306 Dido cried mum. With silence all did wait
Their gift is nought but a design to cheat.
Rough translation of *Æneid* ii. 1–49.
MS. Rawl. C. 986, fol. 34.

307 Didst thou by begging Brutus rise so high
Do beg you for a fool when you are aged.
Epigram: 'In Brutum'.
MS. Don. d. 58, fol. 33.

308 Didst thou not find the place
Where fools with ease go in and out.
'A Dialogue betw: T[homas] C[arew] and Sr: I[ohn]: S[uckling]'.
Pr. Suckling's *Fragmenta Aurea*, 1646, p. 26.
MS. Rawl. poet. 199, p. 95.

Didst thou not once Lucenda vow 309
Than thou hast found in this.
'Dialogue'.
MS. Rawl. poet. 65, fol. 24.

Die, die, desert, poor hope go hang thy self 310
Tw'as glorious honour . . . (incomplete).
MS. Rawl. poet. 160, fol. 43$^{v}$.

Die, die, desire, and bid delight adieu 311
Curse ye desire, I die, farewell, farewell.
Headed 'A farewell to desire geven by J. T.' in B.M. MS. Harl. 3910, fol. 24$^{v}$.
MS. Eng. poet. d. 3, two copies, fols. 2 and 36; Rawl. poet. 85, fol. 49$^{v}$.

Die, die I must, and lie i'th' dust: 312
Yet God's as merciful, as just.
Robinson, Robert, couplet.
MS. *Rawl. poet. 218, p. 38 (autogr.).

Die, Jonson, cross not our religion so 313
With thee began all art, with thee it ends.
Oldisworth, Nicholas, 'A Letter to Ben Johnson', 1629.
Pr. *Wit Restor'd*, 1658, p. 79.
MS. *Don. c. 24, fol. 8 (autogr.).
MSS. Ashmole 47, fol. 107; Eng. poet. e. 97, p. 147, attr. to Nic: Oldishworth; Firth e. 4, p. 104.

Die not fond man before thy day 314
Shall conclude a happy peace.
Pr. John Ward's *First Set of English Madrigals*, 1613, xxv.
MSS. Mus. f. 20–24: f. 20, fol. 67$^{v}$.

Die sinful wretch since that thy life is nought 315
Since longer life but makes thy sins the more.
J. F., 'A flash of Remorse'.
MS. *Eng. poet. f. 17, p. 10 (autogr.).

Die we must all; or else must changed be 316
And dying here may live with thee forever and forevermore.
'A meditation upon death'.
MS. Rawl. poet. 142, fol. 82.

Die wretched Damon, die quickly to ease her 317
Never of love so true let her complain.
How, John, 'Song'. Answered by D22.
Pr. *Poems on Affairs of State*, iii, 1698, p. 197.
MS. Eng. poet. c. 18, fol. 78$^{v}$.

318 Dignified things may I your leave implore
You're downright rogues; they, only knaves and fools.
'The ten Dispensing Judges'.
Pr. as a broadside in 1688, and in *A Collection of the Newest Poems against Popery*, i, 1689, p. 8.
MSS. Firth c. 16, p. 282; Rawl. poet. 173, fol. 121ᵛ.

319 Ding Dong Dell
Little Tommy Trout.
MS. Douce d. 59, fol. 55.

320 Dingty diddledy
I do believe.
MS. Douce d. 59, fol. 48.

321 Diogenes was merry in his tub
The more we laugh the more we may.
Glee by John Playford.
Pr. *The Musical Companion*, 1667, p. 108.
MS. Mus. c. 5, fol. 2.

322 Dire faith now would you touch my wounds you stern
While you still doubt they do more grievous grow.
'Christ and Thomas'.
MS. Rawl. poet. 194, fol. 40.

323 Disanchored from a blissful shore
And grace my ruin did repair.
[Southwell, Robert], 'The prodigall Childes soul wrack'.
Pr. *Maeoniae*, 1595; see J. H. McDonald, *Robert Southwell*, Roxburghe Club, 1937, p. 104.
MS. Eng. poet. b. 5, p. 16.

324 Discord hence! the torch resign
And from this era let their course begin.
[Whitehead, William], Birthday Ode 1770.
Pr. *Poems*, 1790, ii. 101.
MS. Mus. Sch. D. 324. Music by Boyce.

Discourteous death . . . see U10.

325 Discreet? what means this word discreet?
When naked bound to th'stake.
Cowley, Abraham, 'Love Know's no Discretion'.
Pr. *Works*, 1668, 'The Mistress', p. 66.
MS. Rawl. poet. 173, fol. 79.

326 Discretion may bestow of good humour a show
Our happiness all praise, and our comforts all invite.
Williams, John, 'Of Discretion mony and good humour'.
MS. *Rawl. poet. 188, fol. 19ᵛ (autogr.).

Disdain me still that I may ever love 327
Love surfeits with rewards; his nurse is scorn.
'A Lover that would not be lov'd againe'.
Pr. *Poems of Pembroke and Ruddier*, 1660, pp. 5 and 45.
MSS. CCC. 328, fol. 78; Rawl. poet. 116, fol. 53ᵛ; 160, fol. 103ᵛ, attr. to J. D.

Disdain thou art a god for nothing less 328
'Twixt it and her such an antipathy.
'The Repulse'.
MS. Rawl. poet. 84, fol. 49 rev.

Disdain ye not ye magistrates 329
Praise God then for the same.
Forrest, William, '[That no] Degre theare is: but maye take profyte by this Booke', i.e. his History of Joseph.
MS. Eng. poet. d. 9, fol. 158 (autogr.).

Diseases oft are cured and men made sound 330
But for old age, no cure hath yet been found.
Robinson, Robert, 'Pro morbo est medicus: non est medicabilis aetas', couplet.
MS. *Rawl. poet. 218, p. 175 (autogr.).

Disengag'd from all below 331
Him, on his eternal throne.
Kenton, James.
MS. *Eng. poet. e. 20, p. 298 (autogr.).

Disgraced, undone, forlorn, made Fortune's sport, 332
Next after you by God I will be king.
'The Duke of Monmouth', 1679.
Pr. *Poems on Affairs of State*, iii, 1698, p. 165, attr. to E. R. Answered by U72.
MSS. Don. b. 8, p. 627; Douce 357, fol. 61ᵛ; Rawl. poet. 152, fol. 247; 169, fol. 22; 173, fol. 115, attr. to Ld. R-r.

Dishevell'd still like Asia's bleeding queen 333
And pity greet her with a sister's love.
Sheridan, Richard Brinsley, 'Epilogue to Semiramis spoken by Mrs. Yates'.
Pr. *Semiramis*, by George Edward Ayscough, 1776.
MS. Eng. misc. e. 241, fol. 37ᵛ.

Disputers vain your strife give o'er 334
The glory give to God alone.
Kenton, James.
MS. *Eng. poet. e. 20, p. 100 (autogr.).

Disputing for the patriarch's dust 335
I shall thy saving grace record.
Kenton, James.
MS. *Eng. poet. e. 20, p. 286 (autogr.).

336 Dissenters countenanced, churchmen cashiered,
Without thine own right hand man's help is vain.
'On the Late Toleration', 1687.
Pr. bk. Firth b. 20: 2 copies, fols. 135, 136.

337 Distracted man condemns what he desires
And making conscience bow unto his will.
MS. Rawl. poet. 66, fol. 4.

338 Distracting thoughts oft held me in suspense
For, t'have the greater fall, they're rais'd so high.
Morrice, John, 'Part of the first Book of Claudian to Rufinus, translated', 1707.
MS. *Rawl. poet. 114, fol. 114 (autogr.).

339 Distressed man, what kind of thing is love?
Nor rainy storms can quench my fiery smart.
MS. Rawl. poet. 85, fol. 90.

340 Disturb me not, my thoughts are mounting high
I'll cease to write, and practise to admire.
Q[uarles], J[ohn], 'An Elegy . . . on . . . Lord Capell . . . beheaded . . . March. 9. 1648'; copied from *A Kingly Bed*, 2nd ed., 1649, p. 85.
MS. Rawl. B. 165, fol. 138v.

341 Disturb not this [ ] but let me ha[ve]
As undisturbed as restful too as I.
'Mortui votum'.
MS. Rawl. D. 912, fol. 691v.

342*a* Divert your eyes from this seducing sight
The picture's lively, though the men be dead.
Browne, Thomas, 'verses upon . . . pictures . . . at York-House'. Really part of V42.
Pr. H. Huth, *Inedited Poeticall Miscellanies*, 1870.
MS. Firth d. 7, fol. 184.

342*b* Divide, for Christ, of year the date
Forty eight seat i'th' after noon, o'th age is Southing of the Moon.
'To find Easter Sundays; The Sunday Letter each Year; The Epact; Prime; Cycles of the Sun, and Moon, and Moon's Age'.
Pr. bk. Gough Middlesex 12, fol. 28.

343 Divide my times and race my wretched hours
Whose better hap may live to more delight.
Dier, [Sir Edward].
Pr. *The Phoenix Nest*, 1593, p. 88; *Englands Helicon*, 1600, p. 7.
MS. Rawl. poet. 85, fol. 40.

344 Divided in your sorrows I have strove
Hope for no favour, I will love no more.
'The Countess of Hartforde to Sr. George Radney'; answer to F723. *c.* Dec. 1600.
MSS. Ashmole 38, p. 34; Rawl. poet. 160, fol. 118v.

Divine each feature, every charm and grace 345
No mortal yet was ever fram'd so fair.
MS. Eng. misc. b. 48, fol. 84.

Divine Euripides, this tomb we see so fair 346
Thy praise and lasting name adorns the stone.
Catch by G. Heathcote.
MS. Mus. d. 177, fol. 35.

Divine Sir Philip, I avouch thy writ 347
I am no pickpurse of another's wit.
D[rayton], Mich[ael], couplet on 'The Admired Sr. Philip Sidneye', following parody of Sonnet 'Catalogue of the Heroicall Loves'.
MS. Douce 280, fol. 124v.

Divines dispute, where, whence and what is hell. 348
But the weary waiting suitor best can tell.
Couplet.
MS. Eng. poet. c. 50, fol. 23.

Divines there be; which do perchance appear 349
Wherein you bid us walk, preach every day.
Oldisworth, Giles (?), to Robert Tooker, rector of Streatham 1637.
MS. *Rawl. C. 422, fol. 29v, in Oldisworth's hand.

Divinest: we confess, when we did view 350
Your like again when you your self were she.
Oldisworth, Nicolas, 'To the fair Mris. Burch, at his first sight of her'.
MS. *Don. c. 24, fol. 69v (autogr.).

Divorce is death, whilst my poor widowed heart 351
As when i' the last day souls and bodies meet.
MS. Malone 16, p. 18.

Dixon and Almont with the good lords of hosts 352
To see these three pass Saint Giles in a cart.
On Mompesson, Mitchell, etc., 1621.
MS. Tanner 73, fol. 22.

Do but consider this small dust 353
Even ashes of lovers find no rest.
[Jonson, Ben.].
Pr. *Underwood*, 1640, viii.
MSS. Ashmole 36, 37, fol. 257; Eng. poet. c. 50, fol. 113; Rawl. poet. 172, fol. 74v, attr. to D. D.; see also C695.

Do but observe, (now you in full possess 354
Does the true emblem of my self appear.
Ashmole, Elias, '[Lady Helen Thornborough (?)] being in the Country June 17 1646'.
MSS. Ashmole, 36, 37, fol. 248 (autogr.).

Do congregations now upon 355
A just God takes regard.
Psalm lviii.
MS. *Rawl. C. 113, fol. 43.

356 Do gods reward deserts with even hands?
Welcome the heavens high decreed course.
H. S.
MS. *Rawl. poet. 120, fol. 16$^{v}$ (autogr.).

357 Do I behold thy feverish heart, which lies
He's more than wretched, that knows not himself.
Oldisworth, Giles. 'To his sick Sister. Mrs. Fr[ancesca] Old[isworth.]'.
MS. *Rawl. C. 422, fol. 25$^{v}$ (autogr.).

358 Do men by art and conversation win
Soon melt away before the Lord of Hosts.
Williams, John, 'The countermine'.
MS. *Rawl. poet. 188, fol. 21$^{v}$ (autogr.).

359 Do not a poor man's well meant words despise,
Oh God, the God of truth open our eyes.
Robinson, Robert.
MS. *Rawl. poet. 218, p. 103 (autogr.).

360 Do not a simple man despise
A fool in something may be wise.
Robinson, Robert, couplet.
MS. *Rawl. poet. 218, p. 43 (autogr.).

361 Do not ask me charming Phyllis
I would, I would, oh would you.
MS. Top Oxon. c. 108, p. 22.

362 Do not beguile my heart;
That I may climb and find relief.
Herbert, George, 'Complaining'.
Pr. *The Temple*, 1633, p. 137.
MS. *Tanner 307, fol. 104.

363 Do not correct me in thy wrath, oh God
Shame, and confusion shall them befall.
Gipps, Rich[ard], Psalm vi.
MS. Rawl. poet. 61, fol. 12.

364 Do not despise a fool although that he's a woe thing
But of a knave take heed; by him you'll lose, get nothing.
Robinson, Robert, couplet.
MS. *Rawl. poet. 218, p. 90 (autogr.).

365 Do not disdain, oh straight upraised pine
The giver given from gift shall never part.
Sidney, Sir Philip, from the *Arcadia*.
MS. *e Mus. 37, fol. 114.

366 Do not most fragant Earl disclaim
Am turn'd of five and forty.
[Rowe, Nicholas], Horace, *Odes* II. iv, for 'my Lord Granville inscrib'd to the Earl of Scarsdale', on Lord Scarsdales' supposed attachment to Mrs. Bracegirdle.
Pr. *Poems on Several Occasions*, 1714, p. 10.
MSS. Ballard 50, fol. 81; Montagu e. 13, fol. 94.

Do not, my Lord, a grateful song refuse 367
But all things have their time so I take my leave.
Samber, Robert, to George second Earl of Dumbarton.
MS. *Rawl. poet. 134*b*, fol. 184 (autogr.).

Do not, oh God refrain thy tongue 368
And reign throughout the world.
[Hopkins, John], Psalm lxxxiii.
MS. Rawl. poet. 112, fol. 46$^{v}$ rev.

Do not perplex thyself when thou shalt see 369
Because in him alone they put their trust.
Knollys, Fra., Psalm xxxvii.
MS. *Rawl. poet. 60, p. 43 (autogr.).

Do not rack my bleeding heart 370
And hate thy love.
Ramsay, He[nry], 'To his Mrs. feigning to conceale love'.
MS. Rawl. poet. 199, p. 1.

Do not reject those titles of your due 371
Yet duty bids me, fair entitle you.
North, Dudley, 3rd Baron.
Pr. *A Forest of Varieties*, 1645.
MS. *North e. 41, fol. 38.

Do not rumple my topknot 372
You shall not rumple my commode.
MS. Mus. Sch. C. 95, p. 126.

Do not their profane orgies hear, 373
Rich discontents a glorious hell.
[Habington, William], 'To Castara'.
Pr. *Castara*, 1634, p. 5.
MS. Rawl. poet. 65, fol. 88$^{v}$.

Do pack on my load of evils 374
Still untainted loyalty.
Bulteel, John, 'Semper Idem'.
MS. *Rawl. poet. 159, fol. 215.

Do pious marble let thy readers know 375
An ever lasting monument to thee.
[Quarles, Francis (?)], poem on the monument to 'Mr. Michael Drayton the poet'.
Pr. Aubrey, *Brief Lives*, ed. A. Clark, 1898, i. 240, from MS. Aubrey 8.
MSS. Ashmole 38, p. 184, attr. to Tho: Randall; Aubrey 8, fol. 8$^{v}$, attr. to Mr. Francis Quarles; Sancroft 59, p. 296 rev.

Do rich men plenteously relieve 376
Their work they must give o'er.
Robinson, Robert.
MS. *Rawl. poet. 218, p. 34 (autogr ).

377 Do, show thy art. But yet half way up fly.
Thou scornedst or to follow, or be followed.
Oldisworth, Nicolas, 'His Reply to Poëtrie'.
MS. *Don. c. 24, fol. 77$^{v}$ (autogr.).

378 Do this and live. 'Tis true great God then who
Thy drooping shoulders rest: do this and live.
[Quarles, Francis], 'Doe This and Live'.
Pr. *Divine Fancies*, 1632, i. 34.
MS. Rawl. poet. 90, fol. 61.

379 Do Thou oh God but rise, and in a moment's space
The mighty God of Israel, to him be praises still.
Herbert, Mary (*née* Sidney), Countess of Pembroke, Psalm lxviii, rejected version.
MS. *Rawl. poet. 25, fol. 57$^{v}$.

380 Do thy worst spiteful love
Since Tyllysweet is author of my smart.
'Mrs. B$^{a}$. Syms's Song . . . sett by Captaine Cooke'.
MS. Rawl. poet. 84, fol. 39, without music.

381 Do women want? their tongues are loud;
More then is fit to be allowed.
Robinson, Robert.
MS. *Rawl. poet. 218, p. 75 (autogr.).

382*a* Do ye oh people speak as you ought to do
They have reward, sure a just God is he.
Fairfax, Thomas, Lord, Psalm lviii.
MS. *Fairfax 40, p. 130 (autogr.).
MS. *Fairfax 38, p. 221.

382*b* Do you be charm'd by neither love, nor wine,
Beyond these bounds they will offensive prove.
Morrice, John, 'The translation of an Epigram, attributed to Virgil', Feb. 12, 1707.
MS. *Rawl. poet. 114, fol. 20 (autogr.).

383 Do you not know
Or shortly you'll dig for your living.
'A Libell Concerning a Misreport of Sr. Raeph Hoptons death', July 1643.
MSS. Douce 357, fol. 39$^{v}$; Rawl. poet. 71, p. 174.

384 Do you not see that dust, the sportive wind
To beauty's madness: for it courts but dust.
[Habington, William], 'Upon Beauty'.
Pr. *Castara, The Second Part*, 1634.
MS. Rawl. poet. 65, fol. 90$^{v}$.

385–6 Do you not wonder at the strange rare sound
A greater wonder to your ears and eyes.
MS. Mus. b. 1, fol. 85$^{v}$, with music by John Wilson.

Doctor, as you with artful skill, 387*a*
Else she's a drug, will ne'er go off.
'Advice to an Apothecary'.
MS. *Eng. poet. d. 47, fol. 24.

Doctor Ashworth's man Denton 387*b*
And lost a groat more than his fees.
Copied by Hearne from MS. in Queen's [Coll.] library 'relating to' William Denton's *Horæ Subsecivæ*, 1664.
Pr. Hearne's *Collections*, ed. C. E. Doble, ii, O.H.S. vii, 1886, p. 263.
MS. Hearne's diaries 21, p. 179.

Doctor Berefeild, he that lov'd no strife 388
To ride before, and kiss his wife behind.
MS. Tanner 465, fol. 95.; see also A107, O1006.

Dr. Latimer preaching did fairly describe 389
And God bless the commons, for biting the biters.
[Swift, Jonathan], 'A Poem, occasioned by the Bishops indeavouring to obtain an act of Parliament to divide the Livings in Ireland. By an honest Curate'.
See *Poems*, ed. H. Williams, 1937, iii. 801–5.
MS. Rawl. D. 921, fol. 139.

Doctor, my system's all my own. 390
That you yourself should live.
'Dr. Cheyne's Answer' to T84.
MS. Eng. poet. f. 12, p. 99.

Dr. Spencer 391
And built for us a brew house.
'The Fellows of Corpus Christi College have these verses running among them'.
Pr. *Modius salium*, 1751, p. 35.
MS. Wood E. 32 (Modius salium), fol. 29$^{v}$.

Dr. Story for you I am sorry 392
For all your triple crown.
'Of Dr. Story'.
MS. Lat. misc. c. 19, p. 427.

Doe is my name, and here I lie 393
My grammar tells me, *do fit di*.
'On Mr. Doe', couplet.
MS. CCC. 328, fol. 51$^{v}$.

Does not the sun call in her light, and day 394
In Heav'n might shine a constellation.
Elegy on Charles the First.
Attr. to Cleveland, *Works*, 1687.
MS. Rawl. poet. 173, fol. 104, attr. to Mr. Cleveland.

395 Does true felicity on grandeur wait
Might the rich seals of royalty adorn.
'B', 'On Sr Walter Blackett's Birthday', i.e. Sir Walter Calverley-Blackett, Bart., 18 Dec. 1707–1777, of Calverley, Co. York.
MS. Eng. poet. e. 47, p. 102.

396 Does worthy Bolingbroke now failing here
And turn'd out statesman strive to be a king!
'On the Report of Ld. Bolingbroke setting up for king of Poland', 1735.
MS. Eng. misc. e. 240, p. 155.

397 Dogs at the moon indeed in times more dark
But thou even at the sun hast dared to bark.
Couplet.
MS. Rawl. D. 833, fol. 192v.

398 Doing a filthy pleasure is, and short
Doth this decay, but is beginning ever.
[Jonson, Ben.].
Pr. *Underwood*, 1640, lxxxviii.
MS. Ashmole 38, p. 62.

399 Doll held the candle John would fain be doing
And yet Doll burnt him though the fire was out.
'Epigrame'.
MS. Ashmole 38, p. 150.

400 Doll learning *propria quae maribus* without book
Like *nomen crescentis genetivo* did look.
Couplet, pr. *Wit's Recreations*, 1640, ep. 501.
MSS. CCC. 327, fol. 5v; Malone 19, p. 14.

401 Dolorous mournful cares, ruthless tormenting
The bitter gall exceeding.
Madrigal for 5 voices, subscribed 'Young', i.e. *Musica Transalpina*, ii, 1597, music by Luca Marenzio.
MSS. Mus. Sch. D. 233–6: D. 236, fol. 72*a*v rev.

402 Donne the delight of Phœbus and each muse
But leave because I cannot as I should.
[Jonson, Ben.], 'To John Donne'. Epigram xxiii.
MS. Ashmole 47, fol. 45.

403 Don't Æsop say a time was when
His slaves oft hung to save himself.
'The Farmer, the Mastiff and the Fox: A Fable'.
MS. *Eng. poet. d. 47, fol. 66.

404 Don't think, my Delia, fortune's smile
Should ever be forgot.
'Damon's Profession of disinterested Love'.
MS. *Eng. poet. d. 47, fol. 168.

Don't you remember some time since 405
And so this tedious letter ends.
Lumby, John, 'To Mr. J. Dalton, advising him not to undertake the Care of a School'.
MS. *Eng. poet. e. 42, fol. 5.

Dorinda's sparkling wit and eyes 406
She took up with the blind and lame.
[Sackville, Charles Earl of] Dorset, 'A Satyr Or Dorsett on Dorchester', i.e. Catherine Sedley, Countess of Dorchester.
Pr. *Works of Rochester*, 1707, ii. 107.
MSS. Add. A. 301, fol. 65v rev. attr. to Dorset; Rawl. D. 361, fol. 263, attr. to Dorsett.

Doris I now recant, and see 407
And crown us for the victory they gave.
Bromley, Henry, 'To Doris, The Recantation'.
MS. *Don. e. 19, fol. 18v (autogr.).

Dorne, Norton, Rippley, and no more 408
I must pass forth to the siege of Troy.
Charnocke, Thomas.
MS. Ashmole 972, fol. 275v, copied from autograph.

Dorset no gentle nymph can find 409
For she'll have Moll no more.
'Dorsetts Lamentation for Moll Howards Absence'.
Dated 1682 in B.M. MS.Harl. 7319, fol. 103.
MS. Firth c. 16, p. 8.

Dorus tell me where is thy wonted motion 410
Thus for each change my changeless heart I fortify.
Sidney, Sir Philip, from the *Arcadia*, eclogue.
MS. *e Mus. 37, fol. 80.

Dost see how unregarded now that piece of beauty passes 411
Have certain periods set and hidden fates.
Suckling, John.
Pr. *Fragmenta Aurea*, 1646.
MS. Ashmole 788, fol. 18; see also T3087.

Dost thou bring profit? welcome every day: 412
Thus surely doth the greedy miser say.
Robinson, Robert.
MS. *Rawl. poet. 218, p. 51 (autogr.).

Dost thou desire (my friend) of wealth great store 413
Shalt make exchange of thy philosophy.
W. A., translator, Horace, *Odes* I. xxix.
MS. *Rawl. poet. 104, fol. 10 (autogr.).

414 **Dost thou desire to know the end of life**
**For future times 'tis best thou do not trust.**
W. A., translator, *Odes* I. xi.
MS. *Rawl. poet. 104, fol. 4v (autogr.).

415 **Dost thou desire to learn and know much**
**Love learning then and thou shalt soon be such.**
[Newman, Thomas (?)], couplet translating Greek.
MS. Top. Oxon. f. 39, fol. 2, in T. Newman's hand.

416 **Dost thou intend i'th' world to thrive and live?**
**But mind thou money, that comes from the bag.**
Robinson, Robert.
MS. *Rawl. poet. 218, p. 47 (autogr.).

417 **Dost thou money with thee bring?**
**Money's music for a king.**
Robinson, Robert, couplet.
MS. *Rawl. poet. 218, p. 133 (autogr.).

418 **Dost wonder winter powder did desire?**
**Cease from thy wondering: winter covets fire.**
'On Winter the Powder traitor', [executed 1606]; couplet.
MS. Tanner 465, fol. 96.

419 **Doth death come suddenly? so much the better**
**T'enjoy my soul's perpetual rest.**
'Death's advantage to a good Man'.
MS. Rawl. poet. 90, fol. 49v.

420 **Doth God forsake the man he made at first,**
**Of righteous men forlorn, or beg their bread.**
Cheyney, William, 'A motto. Deus non deseret'.
MS. *Rawl. poet. 86, fol. 5.

421 **Doth many heads the body guide?**
**Politic bodies best are governed.**
Robinson, Robert.
MS. *Rawl. poet. 218, p. 139 (autogr.).

422 **Doth no light shine? how wondrous dark's that night:**
**A medium voice unto the ear is pleasing.**
Robinson, Robert.
MS. *Rawl. poet. 218, p. 134 (autogr.).

423 **Doth William Cole lie here, henceforth be stale**
**Burned up the coal and turn'd it into ashes.**
'On Wm. Cole an Alehousekeeper at Coton neer Cambridg'.
MS. Rawl. poet. 160, fol. 157.

**Doubt not but God who sits on high** 424
**Conveys soft whispers to thine ear.**
Wheeler, Maurice (1648(?)–1727), master of the King's School, Gloucester, verses 'On the wall in the whispering place', in Gloucester Cathedral.
Pr. Browne Willis, *Survey of Cathedrals*, 1727, ii. 714.
MSS. Rawl. D. 1090, fol. 141, attr. to Maurice Wheeler; Rawl. poet. 84, fol. 34; Willis 71, p. 292, attr. to Maurice Wheeler.

**Doubt not my dear that I'll reveal** 425
**The world will find thy picture there.**
[Carew, Thomas].
MS. Rawl. poet. 65, fol. 29; see also F262, T1884.

**Doubt thou the stars are fire** 426
**But never doubt I love.**
Catch by Gilbert Heathcote, 1784, from *Hamlet* II. ii. 116.
MS. Mus. d. 177, fol. 35v.

**Doubt upon doubts, delay upon delays** 427
**Even as I wish to mine own proper soul.**
Burton, Francis, 'His Farewell to his Booke'.
MSS. *Add. A. 267, fol. 153v (autogr.).

**Doubtless the Thespian spring doth overflow** 428
**I, as the night invites me, fall asleep.**
King, Henry, 'To a Lady that sent mee a Copy of Verses at my going to Bed'.
Another version pr. *Poems*, 1657, p. 20.
MSS. *Eng. poet. e. 30, fol. 52v; *Malone 22, fol. 34.

**Down adown thus Phillis sung** 429
**Forsooth and so will I.**
Pr. Pilkington's *First Book of Songs*, 1605, xvi.
MSS. Mus. f. 7–10: f. 7, fol. 22.

**Down all ye tiptoe-standers of the trade** 430
**And make his children turn idolators.**
Southwell, Sir Robert, 'On Mr. Philip Hodgson drawing his owne Picture by a looking-glasse (a grave senators head being by)'.
MS. *Eng. poet. f. 6, fol. 19v (autogr.).

**Down by a crystal river side.** 431
**Will make Jack Frenchman rattle.**
'The Battle of Almanza'.
Pr. W. H. Logan, *A Pedlar's Pack of Ballads and Songs*, 1869, p. 82.
MS. Firth c. 17, fol. 30.

432 Down by a crystal stream
Ring him from your twining arms.
MS. Malone 19, p. 130.

433 Down by Euphrates streams we sat
And throweth them against the stones.
Knollys, Fra., Psalm cxxxvii.
MS. *Rawl. poet. 60, p. 11 (autogr.).

434 Down by the crystal streams
Have I sought thee all the day.
MS. Eng. poet. e. 14, fol. 19 (incomplete).

435 Down came grave [brave, grand] ancient sergeant [Sir John] Crooke
We will bury it and I will make an epitaph too.
Hoskins, Serjeant John, 'The Parliament Fart', 1607.
Pr. *Musarum Deliciæ*, Sir J. Mennes, 1655, p. 65.
MSS. Ashmole 36, fol. 131; CCC. 328, fol. 94v, attr. to Hoskins; Douce f. 5, fol. 28; Malone 23, p. 1b; North b. 24, fol. 28; Rawl. poet. 26, fol. 7; 117, fol. 196 rev.; 172, fol. 8; Sancroft 53, p. 53, attr. to Serjeant Hoskins; Tanner 306, two copies, fols. 254, 256, and 255; see also P470.

436 Down down discoverers who so long have plotted
Will drink and do more service for the nation.
'A Song'.
Pr. Matthew Taubman, *An Heroick Poem*, etc., 1682; and *A Collection of 180 Loyal Songs*, 1685, p. 305.
MS. Firth c. 16, p. 45.

437 Down, down, Melampus, what? your fellow bite.
Come come my curs, 'tis late, I will go in.
Sidney, Sir Philip, from the *Arcadia*.
MS. *e Mus. 37, fol. 43v.

438 Down in a dale on Dee's most holy bank
The poor are ever soon'st undone.
Pipe, Richard, 'Eglogue i' of 9 'satirical eclogues', 1617.
MS. *Don. e. 22, fol. 4v (autogr.).

439 Down in a garden my sweet rose did sport her
Be you the prick, and I will be the rose.
'A mayds Embleme'.
MS. Ashmole 47, fol. 54v.

440 Down in a garden sits my dearest dear
Be you the sun, I'll be the marigold.
'A Song'.
MS. Eng. poet. e. 14, fol. 24v.

441 Down in a vale, one morn ere Phoebus bright
A mistress like my thoughts in every thing.
'Cupids Metamorphosis'.
MS. Rawl. poet. 210, fol. 67 rev.

Down in the meadow the river running clear 442
As Moss took his mare.
MS. Rawl. B. 35, fol. 54 rev.

Down lay the shepherd swain 443
Hey nonny nonny no.
'Pastorall verses' on Sir John Selby and Mrs. Overall, copied by Aubrey, said to be 'in Musaeo Sheldoniano'.
MS. Aubrey 8, fol. 93v.

Down on the down while lovers lie together 444
The down seems down, and every stone a feather.
Couplet.
MS. Rawl. poet. 153, fol. 20.

Down sat the sheep-swain so sober and demure 445
And all for the loss of his hey nonny nonny no.
MS. CCC. 327, fol. 12v.

Down stormy passions, down: no more 446
Which cures a tempest by a calm.
King, Henry, 'To Patience'.
Pr. *Poems*, 1657, p. 12.
MSS. *Eng. poet. e. 30, fol. 38v; *Malone 22, fol. 33.

Down swelling thoughts, and do not press 447
Nothing left of me but my love.
Beaumont, Thomas, 'His dispayre'.
MS. *Malone 18, p. 4 (autogr.).

Down the bourne and through the mead 448
Sung her praise the whole day long.
Catch by Gilbert Heathcote. 7 Sept. 1784.
MS. Mus. d. 177, fol. 4v.

Down the hills . . . see U152.

Down too far usurping day 449
Hymen Hymen come away.
MS. Don. c. 57, fol. 48, with music.

Down with your oaths 450
That you have wrought your king and kingdom's overthrow.
On the execution of Charles I, 30 Jan. 1649.
MSS. Ashmole 36, 37, fol. 74.

Downberry down, hey down now am I exiled my lady fro' 451
And never to remain hey-how.
'A Rownde', transcribed from [B.M. MS.] Reg. Append. 58.
MS. Mus. d. 184, fol. 9v.

Dowries of old men gave, dowries men do 452
What David saith? the help of man is vain.
'On Woman'.
MS. Eng. poet. d. 152, fol. 104.

453 Drag him down to the abyss
Proud tyrants on earth shall be slaves here below.
'A Chorus for 2 voices', by Henry Hall.
Pr. *The Theater of Music*, ii, 1685, in 3 parts; see there 'A Dialogue betwixt Oliver Cromwell & Charon', pp. 47–51.
MS. Mus. Sch. C. 96, fol. 10.

454 Drake Howard, th'impudentest bawd in town.
I can say more, but let that pass.
'Upon my Lord Salisbury and his Sisters'.
MS. Firth e. 6, fol. 133$^v$.

455 Draw England ruin'd by what was given before
Which most, the Dutch or parliament they fear.
'New instructions to the painter', August 1667.
Pr. as a broadside, and, attr. to Denham, in *Poems on Affairs of State*, 1697, p. 41.
No. 21 in *Advice-to-a-Painter Poems*, M. T. Osborne, 1949.
MSS. Add. A. 48, fol. 10; Don. b. 8, p. 218; Don. e. 23, fol. 22$^v$, attr. to Sr. John Denham; Eng. poet. e. 4, p. 241; Rawl. poet. 84, fol. 4$^v$.

456 Draw me a lord, that hath less wit, than years
Who with the clerk will shout and say Amen.
'Directions to an Irish Paynter upon the Removall of the Ld. Roberts', [Lord Lieutenant of Ireland till April 1670.]
Not in M. T. Osborne, *Advice-to-a-Painter Poems*, 1949.
MS. Don. b. 8, p. 285.

457 Draw me first her lovely face
Fit for love, and fit for me.
Chatwin, John, 'Advice to the Painter how to draw his Mistress'.
MS. *Rawl. poet. 94, p. 136 (autogr.).

458 Draw near and see this heap of dust
He fell in his full strength and so may'st thou.
MSS. Eng. poet. e. 39, p. 76.

459 Draw near brave sparks, whose spirits scorn to light
To find the way to rest, must seek the way to leave her.
Quarles, [Francis], 'The world passeth away'.
Pr. *Emblemes*, 1635, I. ix.
MSS. Rawl. poet. 84, fol. 122$^v$, ref. to Quarles emb: 90, fol. 20; see also extract, T130.

460 Draw near you factious citizens prepare
Must in their nature needs be false to you.
'The Citty'.
MS. Rawl. poet. 71, p. 147.

Draw near you lovers that complain 461
To love and fate an equal sacrifice.
[Stanley, Thomas].
Pr. T. Stanley's *Poems*, 1647, p. 41, and with music by John Gamble in his *Ayres and Dialogues*, 1656, p. 60.
MS. Mus. b. 1, fol. 145$^v$, music by John Wilson.

Draw not too near unless you shed a tear 462
Unto a place more rare.
Pr. *Poems of Pembroke and Ruddier*, 1660, p. 116.
MS. Don. c. 57, fol. 33$^v$, with music.

Draw on sweet night best friend unto those cares 463
I then shall have best time for my complaining.
Pr. Wilbye's *Second Set*, 1609, xxxi.
MSS. Mus. Sch. D. 233–6: D. 236, fol. 102 rev.

Draw out the minutes twice as long swift night 464*a*
All will adore that she.
Song, no tune.
MS. Mus. Sch. G. 640, fol. 34 rev.

Draw, painter, draw the highly valued face, 464*b*
Dear painter, do thy best Here's gold, my boy.
Barnes, Joshua, Acrostick on Dorothea Ashfield.
MS. Hearne's diaries 11, p. 98.

Drawer with thee now even is thy wine
see T2128.

Drawn by the sweet attractive name 465*a*
And in his glory share.
Kenton, James.
MS. *Eng. poet. e. 20, p. 150 (autogr.).

[Dread Sir, the prince of light] 465*b*
Our monarch for ever and ever shall reign.
[New Year Ode, *temp.* Charles II.]
Music by Dr. John Blow, incomplete. See *M. & L.* xlvi, 1965, p. 103.
MS. Mus. c. 26, fol. 115.

Dread, sovereign and ever loving prince 466
To leave to read my verse, and read my fortune.
'Sir John Harrington to Queen Elizabeth'.
Pr. *Epigrams*, 1618, iv. 13.
MS. Rawl. poet. 31, fol. 3.

Dread sovereign, gracious queen, great prince we pay 467
Till so propitious stars are seen again.
'A speech to the King, Queene and Duke of York, att her Majesties entrance into her Court Royall at Merton Coll. Oxon. Sept. 26 1665'.
Pr. Wood's *Life and Times*, ed. Clark, ii, O.H.S. xxi, 1892, p. 59.
MS. Wood F. 34, fol. 179.

468 Dress is the female sole delight
For Fanny's brown and dusky face.
'Fanny and the Looking Glas'.
MS. *Eng. poet. d. 47, fol. 27.

469 Drink, drink all you that think
With a cup of Apollo's nectar.
'A song of sacke'.
MS. CCC. 328, fol. 41.

470 Drink drink jolly soul
Let's make no delay. Come Tom.
Song with melody.
MS. Mus. Sch. G. 610, two copies, fols. 11$^{v}$ and 24$^{v}$.

471 Drink on, drink on, drink on, till night be spent.
Who's sure to live and drink another day.
Ayres, Philip, 'Music by Mr. Henry Purcell'.
Pr. *The Second Book of the Pleasant Musical Companion*, 1686, i. 3. F. B. Zimmerman, *Purcell*, 1963, no. 248.
MS. Mus. Sch. C. 95, p. 126.

472 Drink sack be merry my boys
For better reformation.
'The newe reformation of the tymes'.
MS. Rawl. poet. 71, p. 156.

473 Drink to me only with thine eyes
Not of itself but thee.
J[onson], B[en.], 'A health to his Mris.'
Pr. *The Forrest*, ix.
MSS. Eng. poet. e. 14, fol. 21; Firth e. 4, p. 25, attr. to B. J.

474 Driven out from heaven's ethereal domes
Of that auspicious day which Britain gives to joy.
[Whitehead, William], Birthday Ode 1777.
Pr. *Poems*, 1790, ii. 127.
MS. Mus. Sch. D. 337. Music by Boyce.

475 Droop not beneath thy wants, as if forlorn,
To Abr'am's bosom, finds his way by crumbs.
[Quarles, Francis], 'To Macio'.
Pr. *Divine Fancies*, 1632, iv. 88.
MS. Rawl. poet. 90, fol. 75$^{v}$.

476 Drooping beneath denials, and despairs
To keep love's flame in her as kindle it.
Beaumont, Thomas, 'upon his unexpected winninge of his Mrs.'
MS. *Malone 18, p. 5 (autogr.).

477 Drop, drop, thy pencil, thou aspiring girl
Paint charity, and you'll paint Germain.
'To Miss Poyntz drawing the Picture of Lady Betty Germain, dress'd in a Gown Embroider'd with Gold and Pearl'.
MS. *Eng. poet. e. 28, p. 26.

Drunk as a dragon sure is he 478
I tumbled senseless on the ground.
Erskine, the Hon. Henry, 'A Parody of "Blest as the immortal Gods"'.
MS. Eng. misc. e. 241, fol. 106$^{v}$.

Drunkards, and thieves, and those that are profane 479
Deserved reproaches and disgrace attend.
Williams, John, 'To those that boast of making others fools'.
MS. *Rawl. poet. 191, fol. 123 (autogr.).

Dry those fair, those crystal eyes 480
In love with sorrow for thy sake.
King, Henry, 'Sonnet'.
Pr. *Poems*, 1657, p. 18, and *Poems of Pembroke and Ruddier*, 1660, p. 91.
MSS. Ashmole 47, fol. 44$^{v}$; *Eng. poet. e. 30, fol. 19$^{v}$; Malone 21, fol. 46; 22,* fol. 12$^{v}$; Mus. b. 1, fol. 83$^{v}$, with music by John Wilson.

Dry up thy eyes and let thy looks 481
Thy care be wrought by smart.
'Upon the death of a Deceased friend'.
MS. Rawl. poet. 58, fol. 51.

Dry up ye fountains of my endless woe 482
This only view were a full recompense.
Juxon, Rich[ard], 'To his eyes'.
MS. Rawl. poet. 62, fol. 34$^{v}$.

Dry up your tears, there's enough shed by you 483
It doth appear your funeral to us.
Philips, Katherine, 'To Mrs. Wogan on the Death of her Husband, a Good Man'.
Pr. *Poems*, 1664, p. 182.
MS. Rawl. poet. 173, fol. 155$^{v}$.

Dryden and Pope both eagles were 484
But stoop to carrion such as thee!
Parsons, William, on Sir Horace Mann and *The Florence Miscellany*.
MS. *Don. d. 123, p. 126 (autogr.).

Dryden's and Pope's superior strain 485
So eagerly renew!
Parsons, William, on Sir Horace Mann and *The Florence Miscellany*.
MS. *Don. d. 123, p. 125 (autogr.).

Duke had two words that did maintain him ever 486
Be blest again with that sweet word deliver.
'On Duke'.
MS. Don. d. 58, fol. 33$^{v}$.

Duke Lauderdail that lump of grease 487
Then our faith, freedom, and our pence.
'A Lampoone. 1674/5'.
MS. Don. b. 8, p. 515.

488 Duke William and a nobleman, heroes of England's nation,
Crying, blessed be that happy day whereon was born Duke William.

'Duke William's Frolic'.
Pr. *Real Sailor Songs*, ed. J. Ashton, 1891, p. 37.
MS. Firth c. 18, fol. 193, typed copy with MS. variants.

489 Dull and unthinking! had'st thou none but me
That dares pull down the vengeance of my hate.

Oldham, John, 'Upon a Bookseller that exposed him by printing a Piece of his grosly mangled and faulty', 1680.
MS. *Rawl. poet. 123, p. 61 (autogr.).

490–1 Dull heart how shall I into thee beat
If I forget, yet Christ, remember thou.

Alabaster, William, 'Son. 42'.
MS. *Eng. poet. e. 57, fol. 10$^{v}$.

492 Dull mortals measure by th'external hue
Outside, and inside strive to make alike.

Colman, Henry, 'On Deformitie'.
MS. *Rawl. poet. 204, fol. 24 (autogr.).

493 Dull mortals with the same prepost'rous breath
And when the parties clash, makes a divorce.

'The Ingrates'.
MS. Rawl. poet. 90, fol. 119.

494 Dull sect, why make you fond opinion
Plainly begets a metempsychosis.

MS. Eng. poet. e. 14, fol. 47$^{v}$.

495 Dull sonnet writing now runs dry
Must sentries thus your chamber clear.

Acrostics, DIMPLE BELINGHAM and KATHERINE VILLIERS.
MS. Firth c. 16, p. 91.

496 Duly you star, that o'er the falling day
And wake to bolder strains my votive lyre.

R. L., 'Sonnet'.
MS. *Eng. poet. e. 16, fol. 29.

497 Dunces in love how long shall we
Whose mouth can touch, but take not in.

MS. Rawl. poet. 117, fol. 155$^{v}$ rev.

Dunkirk is sold, Dutch, French and Dane our foes 498
A cunning trick to save his head.

'In Edoardum Comitem Clarindensem Dominum Cancellarium Angliae Tetrasticon—Paraphras'd'. 1667.
MS. Rawl. D. 260, fol. 28$^{v}$.

During North's cold and icy sway 499
As stone, to raise her monument.

Skinner, John, 'On the Duke of Portland being chose Chancellor of Oxford after Lord North', 1792.
MS. *Eng. poet. d. 22, fol. 31$^{v}$ (autogr.).

Durst ere the hellish sisters once assay 500
Laid on her neck and wafted up amain.

'Upon one who dyed of a consumption'.
MS. Don. d. 58, fol. 12.

Durst I attempt a flight so high? 501
I'd rather be in battle slain.

Morrice, John, 'The Rash Attempt'.
MS. *Rawl. poet. 114, fol. 214 (autogr.).

Dust from my earthy surface fell 502
What, you, ah cruel! will not cure.

Sedley, Sir Charles, 'To Clarissa, Upon Dirtying her Logings'.
MS. Rawl. poet. 222, fol. 28.

Dutch, Flemings, English are your only guests 503
Only the Fleming eats and drinks his fill.

Translation from Latin.
MS. Lat. misc. c. 19, p. 431.

Dwell, dwell, thou worm of conscience in her breast 504
That breaks with heaven can keep no faith with me.

'Valedictio Amori'.
MS. Rawl. poet. 84, two copies, fols. 45 rev. and 98 rev.

D'ye hear the news? says Dick to Ned; 505
But the dear drop would give him life again.

Lumby, John, 'Dialogue'.
MS. *Eng. poet. e. 42, fol. 22.

# E

ENTRIES 1–210

1 Each blest drop, on each blest limb
While it falls hence, 'tis a tear.

Crashaw, Richard, 'Upon the water, $w^{ch}$ baptiz'd Christ'.
MS. Tanner 465, fol. $34^{v}$, attr. to Mr. Crashaw on fol. 1*a*.

2–3 Each Briton join chorus with me
And Keppel in the Victory.

'Admiral Keppel Triumphant or Monsiers in the suds'.
MS. Firth c. 18, fol. 59.

4 Each country hath its custom, and 'tis strange
To see how loth bad customs are to change.

Bulteel, John, couplet.
MS. *Rawl. poet. 159, fol. $214^{v}$.

5 Each creature that the God of nature framed
By the first letters of each verse combined.

Burton, Francis, acrostic 'Edward Hutchins to Anne Woodhouse beareth true love'.
MS. *Add. A. 267, fol. $130^{v}$ (autogr.).

6*a* Each day new proofs of new despair I find
And only death I for my pardon crave.

[Constable, Henry], sonnet, pr. *Diana*, 1594, IV. vi.
MS. Ashmole 38, p. 55.

6*b* Each eye that sees thee, stays upon the sight,
Thy miracle of beauty, and thy name.

MSS. Ashmole 36, 37, fol. 30.

7 Each greedy hand doth catch and pluck the flower
From lords to lackeys and at last to all.

'A caveat for maids'.
MS. Eng. poet. e. 14, fol. $35^{v}$.

8 Each in your face this truly now do see
They read you right by heart, without the book.

Cavendish, Lady Jane, 'On an Acquaintance'.
MS. *Rawl. poet. 16, p. 17.

9 Each like begets its like: nor can we look
To catch poor souls makes daily inquisition.

MS. *Rawl. poet. 97, fol. $8^{v}$.

Each loyal Briton raise your voice, 10
And likewise to Admiral Rodney.

MS. Firth c. 18, fol. 39.

Each man can say, and no man can deny it 11
That war is sweet to those that have not tried it.

Couplet.
MS. Rawl. poet. 117, fol. 274 rev.

Each man desires to have report, 12
Preserve both night and day.

F. G.
MS. Firth d. 14, fol. 118.

Each scurvy Jack commands my cap and knee 13
And yet the king is sometime bare to me.

Burton, Francis, 'A [riddle] of a Barber'.
MS. *Add. A. 267, fol. $6^{v}$ (autogr.).

Each sweet attraction warmed with gentle fires 14
With raptures gaze, and call the graces four.

'Countess of Essex' (d. 1759).
MS. Eng. poet. e. 28, p. 28.

Each thing must have a time, 15
Enjoy my faithful friend.

MS. Ashmole 51, fol. $7^{v}$.

Each woman is a brief of womankind 16
Woman converts to man not man to her.

Sir Thomas Overbury, 'A Wife'.
Pr. 1614.
MSS. Don. c. 54, fol. 4, attr. to Sir Thomas Overbury; Eng. poet. e. 37, p. 39, attr. to Sir T. O.

Eager to join the tuneful train 17
Tries his weak voice, and strives to sing!

Parsons, William, answer to Sir Coote Molesworth, 25 Jan. 1779.
MS. *Don. d. 123, p. 46 (autogr.).

Eager to use his prattling tongue 18
Not my own merit I assure ye.

Boswell, James.
MS. *Douce 193, fol. $84^{v}$ (autogr.).

19 Earl's voice once good, now almost lost through age
He scorns the Saviour and derides his grace.
'On Salters Hall Lecturers in 1757'.
MS. Eng. poet. c. 9, p. 273.

20 Early in the dawning of a winter's morn
With a thwack.
Farquhar, George, 'In Love and a Bottle. set by Mr. Leveridge'.
MS. Mus. Sch. C. 95, p. 119.

21 Early oh Lord my fainting soul
His care and power will me sustain.
[Patrick, John], Psalm lxiii, '4 voc', music by H. Purcell.
F. B. Zimmerman, *Purcell*, 1963, no. 132 (1).
MS. Mus. c. 28, fol. 113v.

22 Early one morn old Tithon's spouse arose
That use t'attend the goddess, queen and maid.
'Of the troope of silvan virgins and light paced Huntresses of Dianna the goddesse of Hunting, whose habits and aspects were thus by authors described'.
MS. Rawl. poet. 160, fol. 109v.

23 Early one morn, on a raw windy day,
Together to lie till they die.
'A Pastoral Adventure'.
MS. Montagu e. 13, fol. 97.

24 Early one morning a jolly brisk tar
That is all I require.
'The Jolly Brisk Tar'.
MS. Mus. e. 19, p. 71.

25 Early to bed and early to rise
Will make a man healthy wealthy and wise.
Couplet attr. to Mr. Rich. Jones; cf. H120.
MS. Eng. poet. f. 24, fol. 1v.

26 Earth builds on earth castles and towers
Earth no more earth at angels blast.
'Disce mori mundo vivere disce deo'.
MS. Top. Cheshire c. 6, fol. 443v.

27 Earth-heaven-possessing gods! Why's this I pray
Shedding their brinish tears for want of me.
W. A., translator, Horace, *Epod.* 5.
MS. *Rawl. poet. 104, fol. 49v (autogr.).

28 Earth is the stage, heaven the spectator is
Only we die in earnest not in jest.
'Epitaph . . . Peterborough Cathedral'.
MS. Eng. poet. c. 51, p. 32.

29 Earth out of earth cleansed pure
Into a pure substance, ye wot what I mean.
Alchemical verses.
MS. Ashmole 972, fol. 184.

Earth praise the Lord him reverence bear. 30
And to eternity do hold.
Fairfax, Thomas, Lord, 'A Songe of Prayse'.
MS. *Fairfax 40, p. 549 (autogr.).
MS. *Fairfax 38, p. 77.

Earth receives and keeps the dust 31
Heaven the spirits of the just.
An Epitaph, couplet.
MS. Don. f. 5, fol. 24.

Earth, take my [mine] earth [body], Satan my sin I leave [my sin let Satan have] 32
My flesh my sin my goods my soul I had.
'A will'.
MSS. Ashmole 38, p. 173; Eng. poet. d. 152, fol. 18; e. 14, fol. 57; Rawl. poet. 90, fol. 103v.

Earth what art thou? a point a senseless centre 33
Sickness what art thou? Heavens churlish porter.
First verse only; complete (two verses) in B.M. MS. Sloane 2623, fol. 80.
MS. CCC. 327, fol. 24.

Earth's entertainments are like those of Jael, 34
Her left hand brings me milk; her right a nail.
[Quarles, Francis], 'On the Worlds Welcome', couplet.
Pr. *Divine Fancies*, 1632, iii. 95.
MS. Rawl. poet. 90, fol. 73.

Eating makes a glutton: 35
His roast-meat in his pipe.
'Tobaconnist'.
MS. Rawl. poet. 26, fol. 6.

Edward whose skilful hand and curious eye 36*a*
From Comus feast and Circe's charmed cup.
Gough, Richard, 'To my much esteemed Friend Mr. Edw. Forster. Sept. 14 1770'.
Pr. Nichols, *Literary Anecdotes* vi, 1812, p. 333.
MS. *Eng. poet. c. 5, fol. 182 (autogr.).

E'er since the deluge, when a spreading rheum 36*b*
Good store of trickling moisture through my eyes.
Oldisworth, Nicolas, 'On a packet of letters, drowned'.
MS. *Don. c. 24, fol. 40 (autogr.).

E'er since war ceased, and Ate fell asleep 36*c*
He wants no weapons to annoy his foes.
Subscribed 'The daughter of Henry 7° marryed the King of Scotts'.
MS. Rawl. poet. 84, fol. 116v.

Egrimund Thinne lies in this box 37
If he could speak he would deny it.
With a Latin version.
MS. Rawl. D. 947, fol. 82v rev.

38 **Either the Goddess draws her troupes of loves**
**To lead the steps of her blind son aright.**
B[eaumont (?)], J[ohn (?)], 'To the Author', Francis Beaumont, on 'Salmacis and Hermaphroditus'.
Pr. *Salmacis and Hermaphroditus*, 1602, Sig. A3.
MS. Rawl. poet. 120, fol. 93.

39 **Either the love which to ourselves we bear**
**Though nought she gives, all in ourselves we find.**
Mervall, Alphonso, 'Nature and selfe love, to Phillis'.
MS. *Rawl. poet. 166, p. 23 (autogr.).

40 **Eleven days are already past**
**Then farewell Christmas for a year.**
'A caroll for twelfe day. The tune As I went to Walsingham'.
MS. Eng. poet. b. 5, p. 66.

41 **Elisha by a Shunamite receive'd**
**Was to bestow a child upon her twice.**
'The good Shunamite'.
MS. Rawl. poet. 154, fol. 109.

42 **Eliza is the fairest queen**
**Whose looks yield joys exceeding measure.**
5-part song by Mr. E. Johnson or Mr. Philipps. Transcribed 19–20th cent.
MS. Mus. d. 183, fol. 27.

43 **Eliza, sweeter than the rose**
**The queen of beauty and of may.**
'The Sixteenth of May Eliza's Birth Day'.
MS. Eng. poet. e. 40, fol. 39.

44 **Eliza: that great maiden queen lies here**
**Subjects her good deeds, princes her imitation.**
Best, Char[les], 'On Queen Elizabeth'.
MS. Ashmole 38, p. 172.

45 **Eliza thou whose sympathetic heart**
**Where pain and sorrow cease, and ev'ry thought is joy.**
'Scriblerus', 'Sonnet. To Eliza recovering from sickness. (Nov^r^. 1788)'.
MS. Montagu e. 14, fol. 31^v^.

46 **Eliza's much my thoughts employed, how near**
**When all the soul's enlivened.**
Lepipre, Delicia or Gabriel (?), 'Writ at Matlock . . . in August. 1747. on Miss Elizabeth Stanhope only Daughter of Sir William Stanhope K.B.'
MS. Eng. poet. e. 40, fol. 22 (in the hand of G. Lepipre).

**Eliza's name (of famous memory)** 47
**Would vertue should be crowned with praises still.**
Burton, Francis, acrostic, 'Elizabeth Beaumonte'.
MS. *Add. A. 267, fol. 31 (autogr.).

**Embalm'd here lies, as 'twere with dirt** 48
**His soul bemired in earth does lie.**
Drake, Dr. Samuel, of St. John's College, Cambridge, 'Epitaph' on Richard Rawlinson.
MS. Rawl. D. 1191, three copies, fols. 66^v^, 70, and 72.

**Emblem of what my soul should be** 49
**And all my task fulfil!**
Maitland, Mrs., 'A Thought upon the Camel'.
MS. Eng. poet. c. 51, p. 278.

**Embrace a sunbeam and on it** 50*a*
**More than a Delphian deity.**
'Impossibilities'.
Pr. Camden's *Remaines*, 1637, p. 417.
MSS. Ashmole 38, p. 61; 47, fol. 75^v^, attr. to John Coventrye; Rawl. poet. 153, fol. 8.

**Embraced with charms, with food ambrosial fed,** 50*b*
**Kind heaven, avert the dark eclipse of night.**
Barnes, Joshua, extempore acrostic on Edward [Montagu, Viscount] Hinchinbrook, 1703.
MS. Hearne's diaries 11, p. 127.

**Emmanuell [College] sent my Lord Keeper [out] a teacher they say** 51
**Mason and Creswell are the vicechancellor's friends.**
'A songe of the Lord Keeper his entertainment, in Cambridge as hee went to Yorke', 1640 (Sir John Finch).
MSS. Douce 357, fol. 5^v^; Rawl. poet. 26, fol. 19.

**[Encircled by thy filial band]** 52
**Ingenious, and ingenuous Vyse.**
Seward, Miss [Anna], extract from Epistle to N. Lister, Esq.
MS. Eng. poet. c. 51, p. 64.

**Encloistered in these piles of stone** 53
**He shared his corpse, his soul, his store.**
On Henry Triget, 2nd son of Thomas Triget, d. 1631. All Saints, Harleston.
MS. Top. Cambr. c. 1, fol. 127^v^.

**Enclosed within this silent tomb** 54
**To join the rapturous song.**
'An Epitaph on Mr. Pope'.
MS. Ballard 50, fol. 195.

55 **Encouraged by thy promise Lord**
**And not that help obtain.**
Beddome, Benjamin.
MS. *Eng. misc. e. 227, fol. 77ᵛ.

56 **Endeared mother, I do well remember**
**Your very loving and obedient child.**
Burton, Francis, 'A New yeares guifte to his mother Mrs. Margaret Burton'.
MS. *Add. A. 267, fol. 35 (autogr.).

57 **Endless I am, yet ends have I sure.**
**Because I do serve both king lord and knight.**
Riddle.
MS. Rawl. poet. 217, fol. 76.

58 **Endure chastisements, Roman, thou must needs**
**Are worse, our children worst of all will be.**
W. A., translator, Horace, *Odes* III. vi.
MS. *Rawl. poet. 104, fol. 25ᵛ (autogr.).

59 **Enflamed with love and led by blind desires**
**He'll love no longer and she'll fear no more.**
Dorset, E[arl] of, translator of 6 lines beg. '*Captus amore procul*'.
MS. Firth c. 16, p. 135; see also I 1680.

60 **Enfolded here in silent dust doth lie**
**Souls once enthroned true Hallelujahs sing.**
[Jenkins, John], 'Epitaph on my Lord North', [Dudley, 1582–1666].
In John Watson's collection, B.M. Add. MS. 18220, 'Communicatur a D°. Jo. Jenkins Musicæ facile Magistro Authore'.
MS. Rawl. D. 260, fol. 34ᵛ.

61 **England adieu thy most unworthy son**
**Conceals perhaps his faith; he will not thee.**
[Heylin, Peter], verses in an account of a journey into France, 1625.
Pr. *A Full Relation of two Journeys*, 1656, p. 3.
MS. Eng. misc. e. 178, p. 4.

62 **England and France unhappily at wars**
**This child and angel was the prince of Wales.**
'Upon the abortive birth and death of the young Prince' [12 May 1629].
MSS. Eng. poet. f. 10, fol. 118; Rawl. poet. 26, fol. 11ᵛ.

63 **England beware for the people are come**
**Sure none but the devil himself will come after.**
'The Hanover Crew', 1714.
MS. Rawl. poet. 155, p. 112.

64 **England, farewell, th' affections that I bear**
**Where furies reign, there needs must be a hell.**
Q[uarles], J[ohn], 'The Authors Farwell to England'.
Copied from *A Kingly Bed*, 2nd ed., 1649, p. 103.
MS. Rawl. B. 165, fol. 144ᵛ.

**England, I cast thee off: thou shalt not be** 65*a*
**Rarely performed, at once to preach and sing.**
Oldisworth, Nicolas, 'To the Witts of Oxford, Cambridge, and London . . . written about the yeare 1630'.
MS. *Don. c. 24, fol. 35 (autogr.).

**[England] Ingland ys ryght good I wene, hyt ys lond best** 65*b*
**He wanne the signorye were they nevere so proute.**
Robert of Gloucester's Chronicle of England, copied *c.* 1700. Brown-Robbins Index, no. 727.
MS. Rawl. poet. 13.

**England men say of late is bankrupt grown** 66
**Faith one good Steward would put all in order.**
Harington, Sir John.
Cf. *Letters and Epigrams*, ed. N. M. McClure, 1930, Epigr. 375.
MSS. Ashmole 781, p. 134, attr. to Sr. Jo: Harrington; CCC. 327, fol. 24, attr. to Sr. Jo. Harrington; Eng. poet. f. 10, fol. 97; Malone 23, p. 121; Rawl. poet. 212, fol. 87ᵛ; Sancroft 53, two copies, pp. 47 and 57, both attr. to Sr. Jo. Harrington.

**England, Netherland the heavens and the arts** 67
**All soldiers the grief, the world his good name.**
'Uppon Sr. Phillip Sidney A man of rare vertues'.
Pr. *Ortho-epia Gallica*, J. Eliot, 1593, p. 163, and Camden's *Remaines*, 1605, p. 54.
MSS. Ashmole 38, p. 178; Aubrey 6, fol. 83; Douce f. 5, fol. 15; Rawl. D. 859, fol. 89; Rawl. poet. 153, fol. 9; 172, fol. 15ᵛ.

**England of late of glorious state** 68
**Why St. Johns Abigail and Harley.**
'A Song [Peace of Utrecht] 1713'.
MS. Eng. poet. c. 9, p. 227; pr. bk. Firth b. 21, fol. 134.

**England, once Europe's envy now her scorn** 69
**But God alone can cure.**
'Upon these civil distractions. 1644'.
MSS. Rawl. poet. 71, p. 168, subscribed F.; 153, fol. 15, attr. to Fuller; Top. Cheshire c. 6, fol. 521.

**England, Scotland, Ireland are three** 70
**Of the tried protestant my king.**
Polwhele, John, 'Febr. 1659 [/60] When the Renowned Generall Monke had out-witted Lamberts Army . . . The Presbiterians began to comply with Cavaleers In recallinge the kinge'.
MS. *Eng. poet. f. 16, fol. 64 (autogr.).

71 England, thy proper native thee betrays
Dost thine own misery still more increase.
'Merlin's Prophecy . . . Englished'.
MS. Douce 357, fol. 12v.

72 England with the sea compassed about
Till Bayards green with blood do over run.
Prophecy in Ashmole's hand.
MS. Ashmole 1835, fol. 29.

73 England's a perfect world, has Indies too
And gives her a black bag, for a green gown.
'New Castle Colemines'.
Pr. as 4° pamphlet, 1651, *Upon the Coalpits of Newcastle-upon-Tyne*.
MSS. Locke e. 17, p. 86; Rawl. poet. 65, fol. 56; 246, fol. 31, attr. to Winwood.

74 Enjoy [this] thy bondage, make thy prison know
Stout Felton England's ransom here doth lie.
Townley, Zouch, 'To Felton in the tower', 1628.
Pr. *Wit Restored*, 1658, p. 56.
MSS. CCC. 328, fol. 51; Eng. poet. e. 14, fol. 14v, attr. to Mr. T.; e. 97, p. 91, attr. to Zouch Tounly; Malone 21, fol. 4, attr. to Mr. Tounly of Christ Ch.; 23, p. 205; Rawl. poet. 26, fol. 34; 142, fol. 42v; 199, p. 62.

75 Enjoy thy calm repose (blest soul) whilst we
Fills more a prophet's than a poet's strain.
'On a younge man dyeing of a consumption'.
MS. CCC. 328, fol. 59v.

76 Enjoy'd I but a mean estate,
And never wish for more.
Robinson, Robert.
MS. *Rawl. poet. 218, p. 32 (autogr.).

77 Enough, all-pow'rful nymph, the day is thine:
My ancient liberty, and ease my pain.
Morrice, John, 'The languishing Lover's Request . . . 15th Oct. 1704'.
MS. *Rawl. poet. 114, fol. 91 (autogr.).

78 Enough, blest stars! My happy fate
And you have all you ask.
'An Excuse made by a Gentleman, who was passionately in love with a young Lady, that charg'd him with Plagiary'.
MS. Ballard 29, fol. 168v.

79 Enough God's love can never be extolled
In all respects, the former doth surpass.
MS. *Rawl. poet. 97, fol. 5.

Enough hath Jove of cruel storm 80
Thou being our guide.
Fanshawe, Sir Richard, translator, 'to Augustus Caesar', Horace, *Odes* I. ii.
MS. *Firth c. 1, p. 33; see also E84.

Enough my muse of earthly things, 81
That he will still require some waters to his blood.
[Cowley, Abraham], 'Christs Passion'.
Pr. with Dr. Henry Savile's *Oratio coram regina Elizabetha*, Oxford, 1658, p. 32; translation from the Greek ode by Thomas Masters of New College.
MS. Rawl. poet. 90, fol. 91.

Enough of actors. Let them play the player 82
To grace a Stuart brow, she plants on thine.
Churchill, Charles, 'The Candidate'.
MS. *Eng. poet. d. 113, p. 205.

Enough of enmity ye jarring sons. 83
And harmony and peace forever reign.
Kenton, James, 'On the Death of William Augustus Duke of Cumberland'.
MS. *Eng. poet. e. 19, p. 196 (autogr.).

Enough of hail and cruel snow 84
Thou being our guide.
F[anshawe], Sir R[ichard], translator, Horace, *Odes* I. ii. Published in *Poems of Horace*, A. Brome etc., 1666 and 1671, p. 4.
MS. Rawl. D. 261, p. 2; see also E80.

Enough of life, my soul has tried 85
And dead to ev'ry charm beside.
Lumby, John, 'Poem'.
MS. *Eng. poet. e. 42, fol. 46.

Enough of rural sports and fancied swains 86
And by thy mercy let the bard be bless'd.
'Natale Christi'.
MS. Top. London e. 9, p. 123.

Enraged death why dost thou strike the best 87
Purchased freehold of life for lease of breath.
On Dr. Bartholomew Warner, d. Jan. 1618/19.
Pr. bk. Wood 460, after *Threnodia in obitum E. Lewkenor*, 1606.

Enter not into judgement with thy servant oh Lord. 88
My merits plead thy vengeance not my cause . . . (incomplete).
[Dialogue between Jesus, the sinner, and Justice].
MS. Eng. poet. b. 5, p. ii.

89 Enter of welcome sure beneath this shade
And herds loud-lowing in the dale beneath.
'Inscription for an Arbour'.
MS. Eng. poet. e. 47, p. 91.

90 Enter oh see this tomb Sirs do not fear
A speedy resurrection from thy grave.
'Verses upon bottles of Wine laid in sand made Tombe fashion'.
MS. Don. e. 6, fol. 16.

91 Enter Tim Crampe of the noble stamp
Until he hath got him a scar.
'Upon Tim: Crampe the tailor's sonne who ever would boast that he had bine in warre'.
MS. Malone 19, p. 8.

92 Entirely beloved and most in my mind
But only you to love I take God to witness.
MS. Rawl. C. 318, fol. 52.

93 Entombed here lies sweet smiling Nan
Who, laid by her, can be so cold.
'Epitaph on N[anc]y J-gs'.
MS. Eng. poet. e. 40, fol. 5.

94 Entombed with kings though Gay's cold ashes lie
In life be loved in death be mourned by Pope.
'To Mr. Pope'.
MS. Eng. poet. e. 47, p. 83.

95 Entombed within this earth a heaven lies
So now it shines in a more brighter sphere.
'An Epitaph'.
MS. Ashmole 47, fol. 34v.

96 Entreaty shall not serve, nor violence
And then inspire someone to write like me.
[Sackville, Charles, Earl of Dorset], 'Epilogue to Every Man in his Humour'.
Pr. *A Collection of Poems on Several Occasions by several Persons*, 1672, p. 29.
MS. Sancroft 53, p. 6.

97 Envy is a sorriness of another man's weal
And a gladness of his sorrow and unheal.
Couplet.
MS. Gough Norfolk 43, fol. 28v.

98 Envy is bad, yet in one thing 'tis good
That it destroys an envious heart and blood.
Walsh, William, couplet, translation from [Greek Anthology], 'p. 168'.
MS. Malone 9, fol. 27v (autogr.).

99 Envy pine; my Cælia's beauty
Like to her; a heaven on earth.
MSS. Ashmole 36, 37, fol. 30v.

Epilogues we know, if well fitted may 100
Preserve the credit, of so rash a man.
Killigrew, Sir William, 'Epelogue' to 'The Siege of Urbin'.
Pr. 1666.
MS. Rawl. poet. 29, fol. 70v.

Erasmus you in folly's praise have writ 101
That very folly does commend your wit.
Translation of Owen's Epigram 'on Erasmus Book of Manners', couplet.
MS. *Rawl. poet. 197, fol. 10 (autogr.).

Ere Adam sinned, him all things strove to please, 102
Brought these our first deceived parents in!
MS. *Rawl. poet. 97, fol. 8 (autogr.).

Ere biting prologue or epilogue did begin 103
I'll boast t'was I, Jo. Heynes reformed the age!
'Epilogue at the last New Play . . . [16]95'.
MS. Rawl. poet. 172, fol. 167.

Ere bright Aurora streaked with rose the east 104
And all dissolved in day the golden phantoms fled.
[Stubbes, George], 'The Laurell and the Olive' [on the Peace of Utrecht].
Pr. 1710.
MS. Eng. poet. c. 19.

Ere I go hence and be no more 105
Nourish in's breast, a tree of life.
Herrick, Robert, 'My daughter's Dowrye'.
Not printed amongst his poems, 1648.
MSS. Ashmole 38, p. 94, attr. to Mr. Hericke; Eng. poet. c. 50, fol. 91v.

Ere Phosphor could redeem his head 106–8
And thus days metaphor was ended.
Dillingham, G., 'The Stoop or Perigæum'.
'Curas sic fefellit G. D[illingham]', name completed by Wood.
MS. Tanner 306, fol. 382.

Ere sorrow taught any tears to flow
For William's lost at sea. 109
[Knight, Thomas], 'Song . . . Turnpike Gate'.
MS. Percy d. 9, fol. 18.

Eret en short months have run their swift career 110–11
Be ever hers, who transiently was thine.
Seward, Anna, 'On Hannah . . . Robinson of Lichfield . . . d. Feb. 17 . . . Feb. 18th 1785'.
Pr. *Poetical Works*, ed. Sir W. Scott, 1810, ii. 181.
MS. Eng. poet. c. 51, p. 74.

112 Ere yet the flowery tribes appear
Unseen amid the secret glade!
Parsons, William, 'To Miss M. M. Jesser', 29 Nov. 1778.
MS. *Don. d. 123, p. 37 (autogr.).

113 Ere you pass this threshold stay
Should Jove descend, they could no more.
Cary, Tho:, 'To the Kinge att his entrance to Saxham'.
Pr. T. Carew's *Poems*, 1640.
MS. Eng. poet. c. 53, fol. 7.

114*a* Erewhile (dear consort) I was leas'd to thee
T'will then be fellow saints for evermore.
Reynolds, Dr. Edward, of Brainceton, acrostic, Elizabeth Wilkinson; on her death.
MS. Lat. misc. c. 19, p. 86.

114*b* Erewhile invaded by a barbarous foe
And critics do your worst, we'll do our best.
'Prologue. For the opening the new Theatre at Madras, 1785'.
MS. Eng. poet. d. 10, fol. 21.

115 Error and lust, guides of adulterous men,
The husband wears the horn as doth the moon.
'On the Stewes'.
MSS. Malone 19, p. 71; Rawl. poet. 212, fol. 117^v^, attr. to Mr. R. A.

116 Error hath always most words
That to thee I am ever kind.
W. C.
MS. Rawl. poet. 214, fol. 74.

117 Erst in the morn of time to heaven arose
And her eyes lighten, goddess, like thy own.
Darwin, Dr. Erasmus, 'A Gentleman desires Miss Seward to characterize the Frequenters of the Litchfield Assembly. He begins with her character'.
MS. Eng. poet. d. 47, fol. 86.

118 Escape; by all the gods he never shall
'Till we no more can add, and thou no more canst bear.
'An Invitation of Mr. Dreyden to his New Provostship By a Fresh Man of the Colledg of Dublin'.
MS. Don. e. 23, fol. 82.

119 Escuriall of the sea; which art (now grown
Whilst Charles his ship is placed by Charles his wain.
Fanshawe, Sir Richard, 'On his Majesties Great Ship lying almost finisht at Wollage 1637', English and Latin.
Pr. R. Fanshawe's *Il Pastor Fido*, 1647, p. 240.
MSS. *Firth c. 1, p. 100; Jones 56, fol. 13; Wood F. 34, fol. 142^v^.

Essex and Warwick, God you save and bless 120
Deeds may advance your worths, above all words.
Pestell, Thomas, 'To the Earles of Essex and Warwick going by the Lo: Say, and Earle of Hartford to the Parliament, 1615'.
MS. *Malone 14, p. 29.

Essex bird hath flown her cage 121
A car may enter on every side.
'Upon Sr. Robert Carre, Viscount Rochester, Earle of Somerset: who marryed the Ld. of Essex's wife'.
MS. Rawl. poet. 26, fol. 17^v^.

Essex prays, Southampton plays; 122
They brought in Lord Pembroke for his lechery.
MS. Rawl. poet. 26, fol. 2.

Essex thy death's revenged; Lo here I lie 123
To say we two died of the same disease.
'On Sr. Walter Rawleigh'.
MS. Eng. poet. e. 14, fol. 95^v^ rev.

Eternal Deity 124
All Thine unexhausted love.
Kenton, James.
MS. *Eng. poet. e. 20, p. 96 (autogr.).

Eternal Father sovereign Lord 125
To gain our seats in paradise.
Kenton, James.
MS. *Eng. poet. e. 20, p. 83 (autogr.).

Eternal Father! Whose almighty hand 126
And grant a speedy pardon for th'eternal Jesu's sake.
Chatwin, John, 'The Contemplation'.
MS. *Rawl. poet. 94, p. 1 (autogr.).

Eternal first begotten word 127
Of Thy dear self in Heaven.
Kenton, James.
MS. *Eng. poet. e. 20, p. 102 (autogr.).

Eternal glorious majesty 128
To make true love abound at last.
Huish, Alexander, 'Æterna cæli gloria', translated 11 May 1637.
MS. Eng. poet. e. 56, p. 71 (autogr.).

Eternal God, from whom 129
And in dark nooks my dark condition shun.
J. F., 'The 88 Psalme'.
MS. *Eng. poet. f. 17, p. 55 (autogr.).

Eternal joy will best befit 130
For him that lived and died for thee.
Colman, Henry, 'On His Birth-day'.
MS. *Rawl. poet. 204, fol. 30 (autogr.).

131 Eternal judge who reigns on high
Me to the realms of peace and joy.
Kenton, James.
MS. *Eng. poet. e. 20, p. 337 (autogr.).

132 Eternal lord, thy ear incline
My endless aid and comfort giver.
Herbert, Mary (*née* Sidney), Countess of Pembroke, Psalm lxxxvi.
MS. *Rawl. poet. 24, p. 127.

133 Eternal love! what 'tis to love thee well
None, not himself who feels it, none can tell.
Crashaw, Richard, 'In amorem divinum (Hermannus Hugo)'.
MS. Tanner 465, fol. 37$^{v}$, attr. to Mr. Crashaw, fol. 1*a*.

134 Eternal mover whose diffused glory
And thou wilt know thy marked flock in dust.
Wotton, Sr. Henry, 'A Hymne made . . . In the unquiet nights of his late Sicknes'.
Pr. *Reliquiae*, 1651, p. 529.
MSS. Eng. poet. c. 50, fol. 53, attr. to Sr. Henry Wootton; Rawl. poet. 160, fol. 85, attr. to Sr. Henry Wotton; Tanner 466, fol. 4$^{v}$, attr. to H. Wotton.

135 Eternal Reason, Glorious Majesty
But t'imitate, enjoy, and study thee.
[Philips, Katherine], 'A Prayer'.
Pr. *Poems*, 1667, p. 68.
MS. Rawl. poet. 65, fol. 20$^{v}$.

136 Eternal rock of ages
My friend, my God, and saviour.
Kenton, James.
MS. *Eng. poet. e. 20, p. 261 (autogr.).

137 Eternal shades screen in the cheerful light,
Themselves exposed to every raging wind.
Chatwin, John, 'On the 30th of January', anniversary of Charles I's execution.
MS. *Rawl. poet. 94, p. 227 (autogr.).

138 Eternity that ever lasts
Whene'er I do amiss.
Tipping, William, 'O Eternitie'.
MS. *Rawl. poet. 101, fol. 64 (autogr.).

139 Eternity the womb of things created
That under compass of this life do level.
Alabaster, William, 'So[nnet] 9. The Eternety'.
MS. *Eng. poet. e. 57, fol. 2$^{v}$.

140 Euridice, my fair my fair Euridice
Helpless, undone Euridice from hell.
Flatman, Thomas, 'A Dialogue. Orpheus and Euridice . . . Sept. 15. 1663. Set by Mr. Wm. Gregory'.
MS. *Firth d. 7, fol. 26.

Europe gives Lincoln's happy shape due praise, 141
She stoutly once refused her husband's bed.
'Countess of Lincoln', 'Dead' [d. 1760].
MS. Eng. poet. e. 28, p. 28.

Eve like a nightingale was placed to sing 142
He hath beheld even me a servile maid.
Pr. *Parthenia Sacra*, ed. I. Fletcher, 1633, p. 148.
MS. Eng. poet. b. 5, p. 106.

Eve once deceived, 'twas not long ere she 143
Enfeebled so that we can do no other.
MS. *Rawl. poet. 97, fol. 11 (autogr.).

Eve was bewitched to be deluded so, 144
He missed of apples and a godship Sir.
Chatwin, John, 'Paradise lost'.
MS. *Rawl. poet. 94, p. 169 (autogr.).

Even as a flower, or like unto the grass, 145
As none hath seen, nor any heart can guess.
Whitney, Geoffrey, 'Super est quod supra est'. An enlargement of a couplet, A669.
MS. *Rawl. poet. 56, fol. 125$^{v}$.

Even as chameleons vary with their object, 146
So princes' manners do transform the subject.
Couplet.
MS. Rawl. poet. 117, fol. 273 rev.

Even as Diana did her nymphs excel 147
Excelling theirs, the maids thereat repine.
Burton, Francis, acrostic, 'Elisabeth Morison that most praise worthy virgin Francis Burton wisheth all welfare and increase of grace'.
MS. *Add. A. 267, fol. 16$^{v}$ (autogr.).

Even as the dove which Noah forth let fly 148
There springs some good where ill was all abounding.
Burton, Francis, 'A New yeares guifte presented to his mother. A.D. 1612'.
MS. *Add. A. 267, fol. 34 (autogr.).

Even as the poor petitioner that waits 149
For making verse again.
Burton, Francis.
MS. *Add. A. 267, fol. 90 (autogr.).

Even as the sledge hardens with strokes the steel 150
So the more beaten, still the less we feel.
Couplet.
MS. Rawl. poet. 117, fol. 273 rev.

151 **Even as the waves of brainless buttered fish**
**Ground with a quinsill, tipped with marble praise.**
[Hoskins, John], 'Cabalisticall Verse, which by transposition of words, syllables, and letters made excellent sence, otherwise none in laudem Coriatti'.
Pr. *Coryats Crudities*, 1611, Sig. e5.
MS. Malone 19, p. 137.

152 **Even as there are three blue beans in a blue bladder,**
**In England Universities three.**
'On Dr. Corbett of Christ Church in Oxford: who would Prove that there were 3 Universityes in England. According to Stoe'.
MS. Firth e. 4, p. 98.

153 **Even as you see two lovers in a night**
**Doings the fruit of doing well: farewell.**
R[obert] Herrick, 'Farewell to Poetry'.
MS. Rawl. poet. 160, fol. 46$^{v}$; see also I198.

154 **Even before kings (by thee as Gods commended)**
**Thy work begun shalt leave unended never.**
Herbert, Mary (*née* Sidney), Countess of Pembroke, Psalm cxxxviii.
MS. *Rawl. poet. 24, p. 205.

155 **Even now the miserable few**
**Of my intended wing.**
P. O., 'On the Catalans', incomplete, 1710 (?).
MS. Firth b. 4, fol. 15 (autogr.).

156 **Even so a strong power and a sovereign purse**
**The bridges again may come over the rivers.**
Creswell, Robert, 'To my Ld. Willam. Chandos on his Theme The Rivers overflow the Bridges'.
On the death of George Brydges Baron Chandos in Feb. 1654/5 his brother William succeeded to the title but his widow, Jane, daughter of Earl Rivers, inherited the lands.
MS. *Eng. poet. f. 24, fol. 9 (autogr.).

157 **Even so dead Hector thrice was triumphed on**
**So vile a Price ne'er ransomed such a prince.**
Corbett, Richard, on Daniel Price's Anniversary sermon on the death of Prince Henry, published 1614. Answered by S900.
MSS. Don. c. 54, fol. 29, attr. to Doctor Corbett; d. 58, fol. 4, attr. to Dr. Corbett; Malone 19, p. 101, attr. to R. Corbet; Rawl. poet. 209, p. 8.

**Even so the greatest Alexander by** 158
**Like Turpin, or the law, unquestioned kill.**
S[trode], W[illiam], 'On the Death of Mr. Francis Lancaster', killed in a duel by Knevett.
MS. Eng. poet. e. 97, p. 115.

**Even such is time which [that, who] takes in [on] trust** 159
**The lord shall raise me up I trust.**
Ralegh, Sir Walter, epitaph on himself.
Pr. Richard Brathwayte, *Remains after Death*, 1618; Ralegh's *Prerogative of Parliaments*, 1628, etc.; see *Poems*, ed. A. M. C. Latham, 1951, pp. 152–3.
MSS. Ashmole 230, fol. 343$^{v}$, attr. to Sr. Walter Rawleigh by R. Napier, 1618–19; 1463, p. 13, attr. to Sir Walter Raleigh; Don. c. 54, two copies, fols. 3$^{v}$ and 11, attr. to Sr. W. Rawleighe; Eng. hist. c. 272, p. 50, attr. to Sr. Walter Raleigh; Eng. poet. c. 50, fol. 31$^{v}$, attr. to Rawleigh; Rawl. C. 986, fol. 15; Rawl. D. 383, fol. 140, attr. to Sr. Walter Rawleigh; 859, fol. 85$^{v}$, initialled W. R.; 1334, fol. 29 rev.; Rawl. poet. 26, fol. 4, three copies, fol. v, attr. to John Cooke; fol. 2$^{v}$, attr. to Sr. Walter Raleigh; and 69$^{v}$, attr. to W. Raleigh; 208, fol. 3; Tanner 82, fol. 244, 'found in Sr. Walter Raleighs Bible'; 299, fol. 28$^{v}$, attr. to Sr. Walter Rauleigh.

**Even temper not presuming** 160
**Lest it should conceal the same.**
'An Acrostick' on Emma Cornwall.
MS. Montagu e. 13, fol. 163$^{v}$.

**Evening, as slow thy placid shades descend** 161
**Should smile like you and perish as they smile.**
Bowles, [Wm. Lisle], of Trinity College Oxford (1788), 'To Evening'.
Pr. *Sonnets*, 1791.
MS. Eng. misc. e. 241, fol. 118$^{v}$.

**Ever bear this in mind** 162*a*
**For in time of wealth every man seemeth friendly.**
Verses used as a copy by Wiman Ramsey, *c.* 1595.
MS. Rawl. D. 649, fol. 30.

**Ever six is the best chance of the dice** 162*b*
**And I shall help thereto amen.**
Prophesy.
MS. Hearne's diaries 104, p. 105.

**Ever washing! never clean!** 163
**Both my marksman and my rest.**
'Non-proficiencie' and 'The Reflexion'.
MS. *Eng. poet. e. 51, p. 36.

164 Evermore idleness
Doth wavering minds address.
'Variam semper dant otia mentem'.
MS. Rawl. D. 986, fol. 109$^{v}$.

165 Every creature has his time of breeding
Then to the earth again his time of speeding.
Robinson, Robert.
MS. *Rawl. poet. 218, p. 11 (autogr.).

166 Every fool would be thought a wise man,
And show himself such as well as he can.
Robinson, Robert, couplet.
MS. *Rawl. poet. 218, p. 110 (autogr.).

167 Every hour a pleasure dies
Lives today and mocks tomorrow.
Catch by Gilbert Heathcote, 1785.
MS. Mus. d. 177, fol. 35$^{v}$.

168 Every man is expected his duty to do
Success to the army and navy again.
'The Army and Navy'.
MS. Firth c. 18, fol. 181*c*.

169 Every man looks on his friend,
But if these fail, there's an end.
Robinson, Robert.
MS. *Rawl. poet. 218, p. 71 (autogr.).

170 Every man seeks out, to have
In place above their brother.
Robinson, Robert, 'Avaritia et Ambitio nunquam satiantur'.
MS. *Rawl. poet. 218, p. 62 (autogr.).

171 Every man thinks he still may live,
There is no remedy.
Robinson, Robert.
MS. *Rawl. poet. 218, p. 66 (autogr.).

172 Every man would have command,
And at height he fears to fall.
Robinson, Robert.
MS. *Rawl. poet. 218, p. 91 (autogr.).

173 Every man would rule (forsooth)
For justice men must fight.
Robinson, Robert, 'Pares in imperio raro concordant: / ubi omnes regnant, nullus imperat'.
MS. *Rawl. poet. 218, p. 3 (autogr.).

174 Every man would rule, we see,
To peace the ready way.
Robinson, Robert.
MS. *Rawl. poet. 218, p. 105 (autogr.).

175 Every thing is judged first by his contrary
So can there be no brown, without purple.
MS. e Mus. 63, inside front cover.

Every true wife hath an indented heart 176
Which only god doth write and angels see.
'The way of harts'.
MS. Eng. poet. c. 50, fol. 33$^{v}$.

Exact must be the art whose fancy can 177
Now lost in silence, since we do rise armed.
'Edward Seymor: Anagr. we doe rise armed'.
MS. Rawl. poet. 84, fol. 28.

Exalted creature, nature's best design 178
A form all lovely, and a soul divine.
[Lepipre, Gabriel (?)], 'given to the Charming Mrs. Carbonnel at Hampstead, 27 June 1748'.
MS. Eng. poet. e. 40, fol. 53, in G. Lepipre's hand.

Exalted freedom! long thy favouring smile 179
Him, in whose worth thy Guildford lives restored.
Prowett, J[ohn], of New College, at the installation of the Duke of Portland Chancellor of Oxford University, 1792.
MS. Top. Oxon. d. 163, fol. 289$^{v}$.

Exalted mind, that guidest thy beauteous sphere 180
Thyself to us, thou should'st be still a wonder.
[Herbert, Lord Edward of Cherbury], 'To hir mynde'.
MS. Rawl. poet. 31, fol. 16.

Exceeding cold in frost and snow 181*a*
Me almost think it summer.
Jacket, J., 'a poor man of Folkstone', 'One swallow does not make a Summer'.
MS. Eng. misc. e. 241, fol. 86$^{v}$.

[Excellent Brutus, of all human race] 181*b*
Pleased with the strength and beauty of the ravisher.
[Cowley, Abraham], 'Brutus', adapted.
Pr. *Works*, 1668, 'Pindarique Odes', p. 33.
MS. Rawl. poet. 213, fol. 49$^{v}$.

Excellent mistress brighter [fairer] than the moon 182
As I'm an honest man, I love you most dearly.
Pr. *Wits Recreations*, 1641, Sig. V1$^{v}$.
MSS. Don. c. 57, fol. 20$^{v}$, with music; Eng. poet. d. 152, fol. 107; e. 97, p. 165; Rawl. poet. 142, fol. 39$^{v}$; 153, fol. 28$^{v}$.

Except the Lord do build the house 183
Quells their undaunted breast.
Psalm cxxvii.
MS. *Rawl. C. 113, fol. 93.

Except the Lord had helped us 184
That seek us to invade.
MS. Rawl. poet. 23, fol. 104, reference to setting by Nathaniel Giles.

185 Except the Lord himself will deign
But eagle-like his fame shall mount.
Jos: Br:, Psalm cxxvii.
MS. Rawl. poet. 61, fol. 55v.

186 Except the lord the house do make
Against his foes which bear him grudge.
Whittingham, William, Psalm cxxvii.
MS. Rawl. poet. 112, fol. 33.

187*a* Except the Lord the house doth build
He descries his enemy.
Fairfax, Ferdinando, 2nd Baron, Psalm cxxvii.
MS. Fairfax 38, p. 484.

187*b* Except the Lord the house doth shield
'Fore the tribunal pleads his cause.
Fairfax, Thomas, Lord, Psalm cxxvii.
MS. *Fairfax 40, p. 335 (autogr.).
MS. *Fairfax 38, p. 430.

188 Except the Lord to build the house
In strife they fear no wrong.
Psalm cxxvii.
MS. *Rawl. C. 113, fol. 92 (autogr.).

189 Except your house Jehovah build
And are dismayed with no alarms.
Harington, Sir John, Psalm cxxvii.
MS. *Douce 361, fol. 81.

190 Excess of bathing, wine, and lust
Our bodies quickly turn to dust.
James, Richard, translator, 'Greek, epigr. on excesse', couplet.
MS. *James 35, p. 17 (autogr.).

191 Excessive grief is tongue-tied, blubbered eyes
How ever natured, nurtured, down we must.
'An Elegy'.
MS. CCC. 328, fol. 64.

192 Excuse me Elyott if here I name thee
Much from the purpose, few did notice take.
'Upon the naminge of the Duke of Buckingham in the Remonstran[c]e in the Parliament, 1628'.
Pr. *Poems and Songs relating to Buckingham*, Percy Society Publications, xxix (5), 1850, p. 24.
MSS. Malone 23, p. 110; Tanner 465, fol. 100v.

193 Excuse me Sir, thus freely to impart
And join the dismal howl to wail him dead.
T. R., 'Verses on the Death of William Bali . . . in The East Indies . . . addressed to Richard Wyatt Esq. Aug. 21st 1785'.
MS. Montagu e. 17, fol. 48.

Excuse my saucy pen that thus hath brought 194
Burn it 'twas destined for your sacrifice.
[Dalby, Edward (?)], 'Anagrams upon the Names of Mr. Henry and Mr. Robert Stapylton, Brothers', 'The Proem'.
MS. Ashmole 47, fol. 121v.

Exeter his birth great tidings can rehearse 195
This chest his rest his silent grave his bed.
S[adleir], G[eorge], on the death of Sir Thomas Bodley, 1613.
Pr. bk. Wood 460, after *Threnodia in obitum E. Lewkenor*, 1606 (autogr.).

Exhausted, dead, exhal'd to air 196
Who gives both light and life to me.
Mervall, Alphonso, 'To Cloris of her Tulipps'.
MS. *Rawl. poet. 166, p. 7 (autogr.).

Exhausted wit, yes, Parsons, you 197
And animate your ev'ry vein.
Temple, R. G.
MS. Don. c. 81, fol. 139 (autogr.).

Exit Burbadg. 198
'On Mr. Richard Burbadg the famous Tragedian'.
MSS. Ashmole 38, p. 190; Rawl. D. 1372, fol. 9v from end.

Expect but fear not death, death cannot kill 199
Which once gone cannot recall but redeem.
'On Death'.
MS. Rawl. D. 1334, fol. 27v rev.

Expect not fluent verses now, for why 200
T'will be no change, we now are turned to dust.
'On the dry summer', [1635 (?)].
MS. Rawl. poet. 199, p. 39.

Expect who can the Dutch fleet should come out 201
As London is so royal York shall be.
Bradshaw, John (d. 1682), 'Some thoughts upon the Dutch Navies demurr'.
MS. Tanner 306, fol. 432.

Expend the bloody rose, or lily white, 202
Producing all, imparting more than needs.
F. W., 'Sonnet. 59'.
MS. *Rawl. C. 639, p. 196.

Experience out of observation says, 203
The righteous man, to punish sinful folly.
'Of Tasting'.
MS. Rawl. poet. 90, fol. 54v.

Explain oh Lord, the way to me 204
Oh let thy justice aid my will.
Herbert, Mary (*née* Sidney), Countess of Pembroke, Psalm cxix 'E'.
MSS. *Rawl. poet. 24, p. 177; *25, fol. 120.

205 **Exposed to wrath defiled with sin**
**To realms of everlasting day.**
Beddome, Benjamin, Hymn.
MS. *Eng. misc. e. 227, fol. 50$^{v}$.

206 **Express with joyful noise on earth all you**
**From me's mercy nor ear when I do pray.**
Fairfax, Thomas, Lord, Psalm lxvi.
MS. *Fairfax 40, p. 45 (autogr.).
MS. *Fairfax 38, p. 230.

207 **Extol the Lord his praises sing**
**And you that do in Salem dwell.**
Fairfax, Thomas, Lord, Psalm cxxxv.
MS. *Fairfax 40, p. 347 (autogr.).
MS. *Fairfax 38, p. 437.

**Eye-flattering fortune look thou ne'er so fair** 208
**Ever after a calm look I for a storm.**
More, Sir Thomas, verses written in the tower, copied from Roper's *Life of More*.
MS. CCC. 318, fol. 126.

**Eyes gaze no more, as yet you may** 209
**That all that sorrow 's for her sake.**
MSS. Ashmole 38, p. 144; Mus. Sch. F. 575, p. 8, with melody and lute accompaniment.

**Eyes weep your last these eyes must weep their last** 210
**Weep weep in tears persever.**
'On the death of a frend'.
MS. Ashmole 38, p. 183.

# F

ENTRIES 1–810

1 **Fabius would oft the eager youth delay**
**And thus to him the vanquished Pæni bowed.**
Hammond, Samuel, schoolboy's translation of Ennius, 'Unus homo nobis cunctando'.
MS. Rawl. D. 174, fol. 77ᵛ (autogr.).

2 **Fain I would, if I could**
**And make that too your own.**
'Songe'.
MS. Rawl. poet. 62, fol. 43.

3 **Fain thou wouldst know whom I would choose,**
**By not at all, or over doing.**
'On the Choice of a Mistrisse'.
MS. Firth c. 15, p. 334.

4 **Fain would I: but I dare not**
**Nor of my ruin rue not.**
Subscribed 'W. R.' [Walter Ralegh] at a later time. More probably by Sir Edward Dyer: see *Poems of Ralegh*, ed. A. M. C. Latham, 1951, p. 172.
MS. Rawl. poet. 85, fol. 43ᵛ.

5 **Fain would I Chloris (whom my heart adores)**
**The night departs, yet still my woes abide.**
Set by John Wilson.
Pr. *Select Musicall Ayres and Dialogues*, 1652, i. 23, and John Wilson's *Cheerfull Ayres or Ballads*, 1660, p. 60.
MS. Mus. b. 1, fol. 65, with Wilson's music.

6 **Fain would I great Atrides sing,**
**Heroes farewell, let love alone inspire.**
Skinner, John, 'Translation from Anacreon', Ode 1.
MS. *Eng. poet. d. 22, fol. 27ᵛ.

7 **Fain would I have a plot of ground**
**By my example, love, and die.**
Sh[irley], J[ames], 'Cardia's Garden'.
See *R.E.S.* ix, 1933, p. 24.
MS. Ashmole 38, p. 39.

8 **Fain would I have a pretty thing**
**That my good lady wisheth.**
'To the tune of lustye gallaunt'.
Pr. Clement Robinson's *A Handful oj Pleasant Delights*, 1584. Cf. *British Bibliographer*, ii, 1812, p. 617.
MS. Rawl. poet. 108, fol. 44.

**Fain would I kiss those lips** 9
**Doth heavenly nectar suck.**
MS. Rawl. poet. 85, fol. 12.

**Fain would I like the sky-lark sing** 10
**Not God to hear but we are slow to pray.**
MS. Rawl. C. 17, fol. 23ᵛ rev.

**Fain would I love, but that I fear** 11
**Love neither fair, black, brown, but all.**
Sedley, Sir Charles (?), 'The Resolve' and 'The Reply'.
Attributed to Sedley in Jane Barker's *Poetical Recreations*, 1722, ii; see Sedley's *Poetical Works*, ed. V. de S. Pinto, 1928, i, p. xvi, and ii, p. vi.
MS. Rawl. poet. 222, fol. 38.

**Fain would I sing but fury makes me fret** 12
**I rest revenged of whom I am abused.**
[de Vere, Edward], Earl of Oxford.
Pr. by P. Bliss from this MS., *Fasti* i. 177.
MS. Tanner 306, fol. 115ᵛ.

**Fain would I well deserve assisted by** 13
**And such my crown as are the fruits I bear.**
Williams, John, 'The vain desire of Fame and fear of reproach now or after death'.
MS. *Rawl. poet. 188, fol. 81 (autogr.).

**Fain would my grateful pen some thanks express** 14
**To deck the lamb's refulgent diadem.**
[Dalby, Edward (?)] 'One's ffarewell at his departure from Oxford', [to Dr. Robert Pincke (?)].
MS. Ashmole 47, fol. 126ᵛ.

**Fain would my soul do honour to thy hearse** 15
**In husband's, children's, country's deep lament.**
Williams, Thomas, of the Inner Temple, introductory verses to J. Rosse's 'Teares upon the death of . . . Sir William Sackvile', son of Thomas Sackville, Lord Buckhurst, 1592.
MS. Douce 277, fol. 2.

**Fain would we say you're welcome but we know** 16
**You'll lead us off by your assisting hands.**
'Mr. Moore's revells nere Eastgate in Oxon. 1636'. A masque.
MS. Ashmole 47, fol. 122ᵛ.

17 Faintly brayed the battle's roar
To worse than death and deepest night.
Penrose, [Thomas], 'The Field of Battle'.
Pr. *Poems*, 1781, p. 77.
MS. Montagu e. 14, fol. 22.

18 Fair Alaraph that placed art so near
Some blessed answer that may bring me rest.
Ashmole, Elias.
MSS. Ashmole 36, 37, fol. 221$^{v}$ (autogr.).

19 Fair Amoret is gone astray
She is the thing that she despises.
[Congreve, William], 'A Hue and Cry after fair Amoret (Lord Fitzhardings daughter) 1696'.
Pr. Tonson's *Miscellany*, v, 1704, p. 353.
MS. Eng. poet. e. 50, p. 75 attr. to E. of Dorset.

20 Fair and foolish, little and loud
Pale and peevish, red and bad.
'On the sundry sorts of weomen', couplet.
MSS. Ashmole 47, fol. 41$^{v}$; Malone 19, p. 44; see also F23.

21 Fair, and no more! Hath mother nature tried
'Tis not my crime, it is but my unhappiness.
'The Tulip'.
MS. Eng. poet. e. 51, p. 56.

22 Fair and scornful do thy worst,
I can laugh until thou burst.
MSS. Ashmole 36, 37, fol. 28$^{v}$.

23 Fair and wanton; black and proud;
Long and lazy; little and loud.
'The English proverb, as I remember', couplet.
MS. Sancroft 53, p. 58; cf. F20.

24 Fair Arcabella, to whose eyes
That you would me your martyr call.
MSS. Eng. poet. d. 152, fol. 108$^{v}$, attr. to Sir Hamond L'Strange; Rawl. poet. 65, fol. 23$^{v}$, subscribed 'Ignot'; 116, fol. 41$^{v}$; 147, p. 167, attr. to George Lord Digby.

25 Fair as lilies was her face
But her coldness hath undone me.
19th–20th cent. transcript of song by Dowland.
MS. Mus. d. 194, p. 6.

26 Fair as the dawning light! auspicious guest!
A grateful tribute of perpetual praise.
'On Chearfulness'.
MS. *Eng. poet. d. 47, fol. 127.

Fair Babylonian walls were built with brick by fairest Queen 27
With new-found wall of wood.
Vian, Tho[mas], verses in commendation of William Wodwall's 'Actes of Queene Elisabeth'.
MS. Eng. hist. e. 198, fol. 3.

Fair Beatrice tucked [used to tuck] her coats up somewhat [so] high 28
And yet between them both a man was born.
[Taylor, John].
Pr. *Taylors Water-works*, 1614, Sig. D2$^{v}$.
MSS. Ashmole 47, fol. 42; CCC. 327, fol. 27; Eng. poet. e. 14, fol. 46$^{v}$; see also A1230, B102, M411.

Fair beauty void of pride and wanton guile 29
Pure innocence that beams an endless smile.
'Mr. Ford e Coll: Reg:' [Oxford], couplet.
MS. Wood F. 34, fol. 172$^{v}$.

Fair boy alas why fliest thou me 30
And thou shalt need no shade but I.
[Rainolds, Henry], 'The blacke mayd to the fayre boy'.
Pr. H. King's *Poems*, 1657, p. 6.
MSS. Ashmole 47, fol. 48$^{v}$; Malone 21, fol. 63; Rawl. poet. 199, p. 4; see also F288, S1145, W2373.

Fair but why fair let petty pendlings go 31
That is thy due, my bankrupt muse were broken.
'To his fayre Mistress'.
MS. Firth d. 7, fol. 188.

Fair by inheritance, whom born we see 32
That few for thee to conquer will remain.
[Constable, Henry], 'A Calculation uppon the birth of the Ladye Rich [formerly Penelope Devereux]'s Daughter, borne Anno 1588, and on a friday'.
Pr. *Diana*, 1592, Sig. D3.
MS. Ashmole 38, p. 52.

Fair cases for foul carcases 'tis folly much to prize, 33
From death he best preserves his name, whose life is truly wise.
Williams, John, 'upon Tombs'.
MS. *Rawl. poet. 191, fol. 102 (autogr.).

Fair Chloe my breast so alarms 34
For the joy she might give and the joy she might find.
Glanvill, John, 'Set by Mr. Henry Purcell'.
Pr. *Banquet of Musick*, vi, 1692, and Glanvill's *Poems*, 1725, p. 96.
F. B. Zimmerman, *Purcell*, 1963, no. 486.
MS. Mus. Sch. C. 95, p. 64.

35 **Fair Chloris [sitting] standing by the fire**
**Repentant ashes left behind.**
[Philipott, Thomas], 'On a spark falling into a Gentlewoman's brest'.
Pr. *Poems*, 1646.
MSS. Eng. misc. e. 13, fol. 19; Rawl. poet. 199, p. 93; Tanner 465, fol. 42$^{v}$, attr. to Dr. Corbett.

36 **Fair copy of my Celia's face**
**Only because you are her coin.**
[Carew, Thomas] 'Of one like his Celia . . . Song'.
Pr. *Poems*, 1640.
MSS. *Don. b. 9, fol. 3; Eng. poet. e. 37, p. 79, attr. to T. C.; Firth d. 7, fol. 125, attr. to Tho. Carew; Malone 16, p. 34, attr. to T. C.

37 **Fair creature, thou prodigious beauteous one**
**As this your lover brought upon Sorbiere.**
'To a Lady who made Dr. S[prat] Passionately in Love with her. Written about the year 1674'.
MS. Don. c. 55, fol. 13.

38 **Fair Cynthia, by thy silver beam**
**Wishing for thy return.**
'Song'.
MS. Percy d. 9, fol. 15.

39 **Fair Cytherea sitting by a brook**
**He blushed and ran away, oh fool too froward.**
MS. Mus. b. 1, fol. 60$^{v}$, music by John Wilson.

40 **Fair dame conceive my words as they were meant,**
**To mend the same (behold) my faith I vow.**
Swerdna, i.e. Andrews, 'To a Gentlewoman that was offended because hir Servaunt saied, that it was his unfortunate hape to thinke to well of her'.
MS. *Rawl. poet. 92, fol. 21.

41 **Fair Dorinda**
**May they ever smile on thee.**
Song with music.
MS. Mus. c. 107, fols. 10$^{v}$ and 11.

42 **Fair Doris break thy glass, it hath perplext**
**I die a martyr, you an heretic.**
[Carew, Thomas].
Pr. *Poems*, 1640.
MS. Top. Oxon. e. 380, fol. 199$^{v}$; see also L578.

43 **Fair Eve a maid of honour**
**No scorching fire of anger nor nipping frosts of fear.**
MS. Rawl. poet. 37, p. 22.

**Fair eyes that courteously deign** 44
**And it embalms as it away doth waste.**
Codrington, Robert, 'on the Death of Henry O'Bryan Earle of Thomond', 1639.
MS. *Rawl. poet. 96, fol. 22$^{v}$ (autogr.).

**Fair fairer than the fairest** 45
**It is my lovely maistress.**
Subscribed 'Britton' [Nicholas Breton].
Pr. *Complete Works*, ed. A. B. Grosart, 1879, 'Daffodils and Primroses', 9.
MS. Rawl. poet. 85, fol. 25.

**Fair [fall] fare their muses [that] which in well chimed verse** 46
**That will not say Amen.**
Shirley, James, 'On the prince's birth', Charles II, 29 May 1630.
Pr. *Poems*, 1646, p. 28.
MSS. CCC. 328, fol. 96; Malone 21, fol. 50$^{v}$; *Rawl. poet. 88, p. 40.

**Fair fellow servant, may your gentle ear** 47
**Had not the muse redeemed them from the flame.**
Waller, Edmund, 'To Mrs. Braughton'.
Pr. *Poems*, 1645, p. 126.
MSS. *Don. d. 55, fol. 34; *Rawl. poet. 174, p. 37.

**Fair France, the arrow, dole gave them the Bow** 48
**Who shall the string which they deserve bestow?**
Couplet, translating Latin couplet headed 'In Arcum et Sagittam, 2 Converts'.
MS. Rawl. poet. 84, fol. 45$^{v}$ rev.

**Fair, fruitful blossom; from thy sacred skill** 49
**Art now translated to a better place.**
Oldisworth, Giles, 'Enneacharisticon' on his sister Francesca, acrostic.
MS. *Rawl. C. 422, fol. 25$^{v}$ (autogr.).

**Fair give me leave to call you cruel** 50
**Not plaints, nor yet deserts.**
North, Dudley, 3rd Baron.
Pr. in *A Forest of Varieties*, 1645.
MS. *North e. 41, fol. 49.

**Fair great and good, since seeing you, we see** 51
**And though I burn my library, be learned.**
Donne, John, 'To the Countesse of Salisbury. Aug: 1614'.
Pr. *Poems*, 1633.
MS. *Eng. poet. e. 99, fol. 40.

**Fair hair, oh tell me why** 52
**Or like the flattering mind.**
Mervall, Alphonso, 'To Cloris on a lock of her hayre'.
MS. *Rawl. poet. 166, p. 38 (autogr.).

53 **Fair half-blind boy born of a half-blind mother**
**The queen of beauty, thou the god of love.**
Latin epigram 'Paralell'd in English'.
Pr. *Wits Recreations*, 1640, no. 458.
MS. Eng. poet. f. 25, fol. 16$^v$; see also A179, A324, H142, T2227.

54 **Fair hand that canst on virgin paper write**
**So far the scissors go beyond the pen.**
Waller, [Edmund], 'To my Lady Isabella Thinn cutting trees in paper'.
Pr. in *Poems*, 1668, with the title 'Of a tree cut in paper'. See *Poems of Edmund Waller*, ed. G. Thorn-Drury, ii, pp. 68, 211.
MSS. Ashmole 1819, between nos. 22/23; Locke e. 17, p. 80, attr. to Waller, with lines not pr. in 1668; Rawl. poet. 84, fol. 113$^v$; 116, fol. 64, attr. to Waler.

55 **Fair Hebe, when dame Flora meets**
**Slow crawling age forbids such ware.**
Pr. Tho: Bateson's *First Set of English Madrigales*, 1604, xxiv.
MSS. Mus. f. 20–24: f. 20, fol. 88$^v$.

56 **Fair, I received thy letter, but dost hear**
**As tedious as marriage. Fair, Adieu.**
P[aman], Cl[ement], 'The departure. To Stella'.
MS. Rawl. poet. 147, p. 117.

57 **Fair in a morn, oh fair morn, was never morn so fair,**
**No shepherd no, work out the week and Sunday shall be holyday.**
Subscribed 'Britton' [Nicholas Breton].
Pr. *Englands Helicon*, 1600, 1614; see H. E. Rollins's edition, 1935, ii. 110.
MS. Rawl. poet. 85, fol. 1$^v$.

58 **Fair Iphigenia (as the poets tell)**
**In purchasing of husbands do the same.**
'To a great Fortune who married a great Fool'.
MS. Percy c. 8, fol. 127.

59 **Fair Iris and her swain**
**Tomorrow will restore.**
Dryden, John, [from *Amphitryon*], music by 'Mr. Hen. Purcell'.
F. B. Zimmerman, *Purcell*, 1963, no. 572 (11a).
MS. Mus. Sch. C. 95, p. 224.

**Fair Iris I love** . . . see F459.
**Fair is my love** . . . see A 772.

60 **Fair is the rose, yet fades with heat or cold.**
**Breathing delight today, but none tomorrow.**
Pr. Orlando Gibbons, *First set of Madrigals*, 1612, xvi.
MSS. Mus. f. 11–15: f. 11, fol. 31$^v$.

**Fair ladies all glad ye, here comes Doctor Paddie** 61
**So farewell bawdy Doctors.**
'Of London Phisicions'.
MS. Firth d. 7, fol. 109.

**Fair ladies are man's representatives** 62
**They choose new members to perform their laws.**
E[dwards], T[homas], 'The Womans Parliament'.
MS. Rawl. poet. 65, fol. 62.

**Fair ladies! I am come naked truth to unfold** 63
**Will pray for your health, and increase of finances.**
'Oedipus; Or the Interpreter: . . . By the Revd. Mr. Potters, Rect$^r$. of Eltham, in Kent. Aged 70, or more'.
MS. Ballard 29, fol. 103$^v$.

**Fair ladies sometimes will frolic and sport** 64
**Let love the director appear.**
Williams, John, 'Some love Politicks'.
MS. *Rawl. poet. 191, fol. 92 (autogr.).

**Fair ladies that to love captived are** 65
**And in each gentle heart desire of honour breeds.**
Pr. Gibbons, *First set of Madrigals*, 1612, x–xi.
MSS. Mus. f. 11–15: f. 11, fol. 29$^v$.

**Fair lady cast those diamonds away** 66
**Fitter for you, and yours more fit for me.**
'To a Lady richly adorn'd with Jewells, beinge more beautifull'.
MSS. Ashmole 36, 37, fol. 30$^v$; see also F71.

**Fair lady I pray thee** 67
**Without hurt of lineage how may this be, tell me that.**
'A question and the answer'.
MS. Gough Norfolk 43, fol. 51.

**Fair lady, what's your face to me**
Shirley, James.
See L32.

**Fair lady when you see the grace** 68
**When you so much the shadow love.**
R[andolph], T[homas], 'On his Mistresse admiring herselfe in a lookinglasse'.
Pr. *Poems*, 1638, p. 92.
MS. Firth e. 4, p. 82.

**Fair Lais strives to be the mirror of our age** 69
**Should be annoyed with such a beastly neighbour.**
'In Laidem'.
MSS. Don. d. 58, fol. 31; Eng. poet. e. 14, fol. 70$^v$.

**Fair Lydia, most soft delight,** 70
**One touch of thine restores my breath.**
Manning, —, 'An Amorous Lyrick out of Cornelius Gallus'.
MS. Rawl. poet. 173, fol. 56$^v$.

71 Fair madam cast [these] those diamonds away
Fitter for you, and those more fit for me.
'To his Mrs.'
Pr. H. Huth, *Inedited Poetical Miscellanies*, 1870.
MSS. Ashmole 47, fol. 37; Malone 21, fol. 46; see also F66.

72 Fair Madam: since the world begun
Behold, three suns at once appear.
Oldisworth, Nicolas, 'To a Lady, on her walking abroad'.
MS. *Don. c. 24, fol. 25v (autogr.).

73 Fair mistress I would gladly know,
What would you more, here's t'one for t'other.
'On a mayden head'.
MS. Ashmole 38, p. 151.

74 Fair moralist accept my humble lays,
All must submit to his most powerful nod.
'The Ladies Answer, on the Prospect of her Friends Recovery from . . . Illness'.
MS. *Eng. poet. e. 28, p. 57.

75 Fair mounted phebus brightly casting forth
Then suffer not fair son my heart to perish.
MS. Rawl. B. 88, fol. 31v (autogr.).

76 Fair natures by oft changing often do good turns
A fool before the fire for want of turning burns.
North, Dudley, 3rd Baron, couplet.
MS. *North e. 41, fol. 54v.

77 Fair nymph, I do congratulate
Eternally and him obey.
Song with melody.
MS. Mus. Sch. G. 610, fol. 8v.

78 Fair one I have received your gift and take
Must choose a pair of stones of larger size.
'To a gentlewoman who sent a payre of olive stones ffor a present'.
MS. Ashmole 47, fol. 127.

79 Fair one, you did on me bestow
Must ever your (sweet) creature live.
King, Henry, 'Sonnet: The Pink'.
Pr. *Poems*, 1657, p. 21.
MSS. *Eng. poet. e. 30, fol. 53v, title added by H. King; *Malone 22, fol. 33v.

80 Fair ones why flock you hither? what have we
You'll wash a blackamore without a trope.
Prologue to 'Mr. Moores revells nere Eastgate in Oxon. 1636 . . . the third night being private for Gentlewomen'.
MS. Ashmole 47, fol. 126.

Fair Philip William Henalde's child and youngest daughter dear 81
Queens College she, Dame Palace Schools, that did her fame resound.
'The Epitaph of Queene Philippe Wife of Edward III'.
Pr. Keepe's *Monumenta Westmonasteriensia*, 1682, p. 307.
MS. Willis 71, p. 68.

Fair Philoclea being chastely bred 82
Why that's not lost (quoth she) is given you.
'On Philoclea'.
MSS. Don. d. 58, fol. 32; Eng. poet. e. 14, fol. 69v.

Fair piece of angel gold, which art yet hot 83
Supposed to be some pretty cherubin.
Jefferies, John, 'Upon the death of the only sonne of Mr. Dr. [William] Sancroft Mr. [1628–37] of Emmanuel College in Cambridge'.
MSS. Rawl. poet. 147, p. 50; Rawl. poet. 160, fol. 41, 'Obitum filii domini Rich: Anderson Militis'; Tanner 465, fol. 73v, attr. to Jo. Jefferies.

Fair pledges of a fruitful tree 84
Into the grave.
Herrick, Robert, 'To Blossoms'.
Pr. *Hesperides*, 1648.
MS. Eng. misc. e. 241, fol. 60v, attr. to Robert Herrick; pr. bk. 27980 e. 86, opp. p. 3, attr. to Herrick.

Fair politician 'tis in vain 85
And as you cease to love, forbid my dream.
'To Celia attempting to make him dream of Marriage'.
MS. Rawl. poet. 87, p. 46.

Fair princess let me not complain 86
With beauty wit and treasure.
'A Song' and 'The Answer'.
MS. Montagu e. 13, fol. 17.

Fair Quelot with Jenyn her wedded fere 87
She jerked her bum and sweetly slept till day.
Translation from Rabelais.
MS. Rawl. poet. 120, fol. 29.

Fair rocks goodly rivers sweet trees when shall I see peace? 88
To the hells I do go (Echo) go.
Sidney, Sir Philip, from the *Arcadia*. 'Disputacon' with an echo in hexameters.
MS. *e Mus. 37, fol. 92v.

89 **Fair, seek not to be feared most lovely be loved by thy servants.**
**For true it is that they fear many whom many fear.**
Sidney, Sir Philip, translation from Seneca, *Oedipus*, 705–6.
Pr. *Arcadia*, 1598, p. 477.
MS. *e Mus. 37, fol. 246.

90 **Fair shadow stay, may I forever see**
**My thoughts, and in your scorn, your beauty dies.**
Godolphin, S[idney], originally written as if part of the preceding poem, C210.
MS. Malone 13, p. 8.

91 **Fair shepherdess thy faithful swain**
**No date but death shall terminate my love.**
Burton, Francis, acrostic on his own name.
MS. *Add. A. 267, fol. 142$^{v}$ (autogr.).

92 **Fair shepherds queen,**
**Whose only joy is Phyllis.**
'Pastrolett . . . A 5. Voc. Tho. Ravenscroft'.
MSS. Mus. f. 11–15: f. 11, fol. 40$^{v}$.

93 **Fair soul, which wast not only [so] as all souls be,**
**Behindhand yet hath spoke, and spoke his last.**
Donne, John, 'Obsequies on the L[d] Harrington brother to the Count. of Bedford'.
Pr. *Poems*, 1633.
MSS. Eng. poet. e. 14, fol. 43; *e. 99, fol. 138$^{v}$.

94 **Fair spotless scarf, once by my goddess born,**
**Contented in the office of my love.**
North, Dudley, 3rd Baron.
Pr. in *A Forest of Varieties*, 1645.
MS. *North e. 41, fol. 18$^{v}$.

95 **Fair sweet cruel why dost thou fly me**
**Tarry then, oh tarry then, and take me with you.**
Copied from Thomas Ford's *Musicke of Sundrie Kindes*, 1607, vii.
MS. Mus. d. 8, fol. 17$^{v}$.

96 **Fair sweet I cannot court thy sprightly eyes**
**Hark in thine ear, zounds I can [—] thee soundly.**
'To his M[rs].'
MS. Rawl. poet. 199, p. 9; see also F104.

97 **Fair Sylvia does my soul inspire**
**But mine will constant prove.**
'A Song by Mr. John Baptist Grano'.
MS. Mus. Sch. B. 8*, fol. 23.

98 **Fair that you may truly know**
**Wonder is shorter lived than love.**
Waller, Edmund, 'To Amorett'.
Pr. *Poems*, 1645, p. 53.
MSS. *Don. d. 55, fol. 3$^{v}$; Eng. poet. c. 50, fol. 123$^{v}$.

**Fair torch of heaven, day's dearest light** 99
**Love and jealousy are one.**
Sheppard, Samuel, 'Epithalamium' in 'The Faerie King', book V, canto 5.
MS. Rawl. poet. 28, fol. 62.

**Fair Valentine since once your welcome hand** 100
**A weak edge turn meeting a softer touch.**
Strode, William, 'To a Valentine'.
MSS. CCC. 328, fol. 85, attr. by W. Fulman to Str.; Eng. poet. e. 97, p. 104, attr. to William Stroad.

**Fair Venus they say** 101
**He'll at least leave a score in the place on't.**
'Cupid turn'd Tinker'.
MS. Rawl. poet. 153, fol. 37.

**Fair virtue, should I follow thee** 102
**His holy life, design and art.**
'The World Against Virtue . . . H. Stonecastle's Univ. Spect[r]. No. 139 Jun. 5. 1731'.
MS. Eng. poet. f. 13, fol. 194.

**Fair virtue was from heaven sent** 103
**And is, though in misfortunes, great.**
'On Virtue'.
MS. Eng. poet. e. 47, p. 24.

**Fair wench I cannot court thy [your] sprightly [spritlike] eyes** 104
**Hark in the ear wench I can love thee soundly.**
'A wooer'.
MSS. Eng. poet. e. 14, fol. 75$^{v}$; e. 97, p. 93; Malone 21, fol. 51$^{v}$; see also F96.

**Fairer than the rosy east** 105
**Heaven it is to have her love.**
Mervall, Alphonso, 'To Cloris'.
MS. *Rawl. poet. 166, p. 15 (autogr.).

**Fairer than Venus, or the morning star** 106
**Dainty sweet lady, in my faith you are.**
'To his Mistris'.
MS. Rawl. poet. 153, fol. 20.

**Fairest Clarinda, she whom truth calls fair,** 107
**First picked the lock and then she stole my heart.**
'On Clarinda, begging a lock of her Lovers haire'.
Pr. *Wits Recreations*, 1663, Sig. Q3$^{v}$.
MS. Eng. poet. d. 152, fol. 108.

**Fairest isle all isles excelling** 108
**Those shall be renowned for love.**
[Dryden, John], song of Venus in *King Arthur*.
MS. Rawl. poet. 196, fol. 36$^{v}$.

**Fairest Jenny thou mun love me** 109
**'Tis too cold to lie alone.**
MS. Rawl. poet. 196, fol. 38$^{v}$.

110 Fairest, my praise will stain you, yet my quill
Your courtesy assures, you'll pardon me.
Atkins, F., 'To his Mrs. The courting period of a spanish breath'.
MS. Rawl. poet. 142, fol. 45.

111 Fairest of years blest be thy happy time
Then ope fair heaven and let me into thee.
Bredwell, St[ephen], 'A Passion of Joy or Sonnet on St. Valentines day'.
MS. Add. A. 267, fol. 143v.

112 Fairest piece of well form'd earth
To all the wonders I shall sing.
Waller, Edmund, 'Palamede to Zelinde. Ariana: Lib: 6:' [by Des Marets].
Pr. *Poems*, 1645, p. 170.
MS. *Don. d. 55, fol. 41.

113 Fairest Theina let me know
Lest my desire should fatal prove.
MS. Mus. b. 1, fol. 131v, music by John Wilson.

114 Fairest though you are wise
And take me for your pain.
'A song'.
MS. Rawl. poet. 84, fol. 42v.

115 Fairest, thy tresses are not hairs [threads] of gold
Be goddess-like in all; be good, be true.
[Carew, Thomas], 'On his Mrs Features'.
Pr. *Wits Recreations*, 1641, Sig. V1, with variation from the version pr. in *Poems*, 1640.
MSS. Ashmole 38, p. 154; CCC. 328, fol. 22, attr. to Beamont; see also D173.

116 [Faith and truth] Fath and trath then, I bleeve in ten parishes rouand
Ef I can't wi' ma vistes, I will wi ma tongue.
'A Cornish Dialogue . . . From a MS. Copy communicated by the Revd Charles Lethbridge A. B. St. Stephens Oct. 30th 1790'.
MS. Gough Cornwall 2, fol. 37.

117 Faith gentlemen I do not blame your wit
With your dull advocate, or ignorant.
On G. Ruggle's *Ignoramus*, acted March and May, 1615, before James I, satire on lawyers. 'Unto the Comedians of Cambridge . . . John a Stile student of the Comon lawes wisheth a sounder ingent, and a more reverent opinion of their betters'.
MSS. Don. c. 54, fol. 26; Firth d. 7, fol. 106; Malone 19, p. 125; Rawl. poet. 26, fol. 31v; 153, fol. 10; Tanner 465, fol. 79.

Faith is a loving grace and very bold 118
There 's no such mother 'mongst them all as this.
Tipping, William, 'Of Faith. The Triumph of Faith'.
MS. *Rawl. poet. 101, fol. 38v (autogr.).

Faith is the hand stretched out 119
How happy should I be.
Beddome, Benjamin.
MS. *Eng. misc. e. 227, fol. 8v.

Faith! Moll, I think it mighty odd 120
You'll break your glass for spite!
Parsons, William.
MS. *Don. d. 123, p. 7 (autogr.).

Faith 'tis an active grace, 121
With all his glitt'ring store.
Beddome, Benjamin.
MS. *Eng. misc. e. 227, fol. 8.

Faith wench I love but I cannot sue 122
I'll freely spend my thrice decocted blood.
'A Plaine Sutor'.
MS. Douce f. 5, fol. 19.

Faith without works is dead will do none good 123
True penitent he is.
Tipping, William, 'Of Repentance, The Necessetie thereof and of Good works'.
MS. *Rawl. poet. 101, fol. 57 (autogr.).

Faith, you're mistaken, I'll not love 124
This makes the beggar trample o'er the king.
[Brome, Alexander], 'The wary woer'.
Pr. *Poems*, 1661, p. 5.
MS. Ashmole 47, fol. 136v.

Faithful Alexis pardon me 125
Another to subdue.
'The Willow Garland Presented to Alexis on Amintas Leaving him'.
MS. Montagu e. 13, fol. 129v.

Faithful and true word 126
What a mystery divine.
Kenton, James.
MS. *Eng. poet. e. 20, p. 393 (autogr.).

Faithful friend at last adieu 127
Blest, and forever blest.
Kenton, James. 'On the Death of Mr. Robert Lloyd of Mitcham in Surrey', 1760.
MS. *Eng. poet. e. 19, p. 185 (autogr.).

Faithful souls, with exultation 128
Adoration on his throne.
Kenton, James, 'to Dr. Bradshaw. 22. v. 1772'.
MS. *Eng. poet. e. 20, p. 398 (autogr.).

129 Faithful to the grace bestowed
And rest with thee in Heaven.
Kenton, James.
MS. *Eng. poet. e. 20, p. 133 (autogr.).

130 Faithless, and fond mortality!
Thus much, he's dead and weep the rest.
Cr[ashaw], R[ichard], 'Ad exequias in obitum desideratissimi M[ri] [Michael] Chambers Coll: Reginal. Socii', Sept. 1633.
MS. Tanner 465, fol. 64.

131 Fallen is thy grandeur, Berry! Where are now
And time shall triumph o'er thine utter ruin.
Boyce, G., 'On the Ruins of Berry Pomeroy Castle near Totness Devonshire'.
MS. Montagu c. 5, fol. 62 (autogr.).

132 False Britons false and faithless are you grown
But from it keep us Lord I ever pray.
'On [the Thanksgiving Jan. 20th 1714/15'], anniversary of the beginning of Charles I's trial.
MS. Rawl. poet. 155, p. 148.

133 False glozing pleasures, casks of happiness,
Then miseries are here.
Herbert, George, 'Doteage'.
Pr. *The Temple*, 1633, p. 161.
MSS. Rawl. poet. 90, fol. 146; *Tanner 307, fol. 123.

134–5 False man whose best religion hath but been
He died for treason, I for martyrdom.
R[andolph], T[homas], 'A Wronged Mistresse to a False seruant'.
Pr. *Palaestra*, no. 148, 1925, p. 253, from this manuscript.
MS. Firth e. 4, p. 42.

136 False on his [my] deanery? false? nay more I'll lay
Should raise itself by ballads more than merit.
Satire on Dr. Richard Corbett; see his *Poems*, ed. J. A. W. Bennett and H. R. Trevor-Roper, 1955, p. xxii.
MSS. Ashmole 36, 37, fol. 155; Don. d. 58, fol. 42; Malone 19, p. 30; Rawl. D. 1048, fol. 53.

137 False world thou liest, thou canst not lend
Can these bring cordial peace, false world thou liest.
[Quarles, Francis], 'The Worlds deceite'.
Pr. *Emblemes*, 1635, II. v.
MS. Rawl. poet. 90, fol. 21[v].

138 Falsehood disguised under religion's veil
As mists are scattered by Appollo's ray.
MS. Eng. poet. d. 152, fol. 4.

Falsehood's jewell, 139
That soon did end him.
On Robert Cecil, Earl of Salisbury, 1612.
MS. Tanner 299, fol. 11[v].

Fame, register of time, 140
And ripe in worth, though green in years did die.
Drummond, [William], 'Scotch Nobleman'.
MS. Top. gen. e. 32, fol. 72[v].

Fame than which mischief none hath swifter course 141
With fictions fraught, as well as with the right.
Mervall, Alphonso, 'A description of fame out of Virgil. 4 Æneid'.
MS. *Rawl. poet. 166, p. 63 (autogr.).

Famed stream by whose restrictive force were taught 142
Great is the running and from weakness too.
'On a prating young Lady of the Hot well at Bristol'.
MS. Rawl. poet. 207, p. 171.

Fancy the Indies treasured 143
As sauce to taste the loss of it.
H. P. [Henry Proby (?)], 'On the death of that virtuous young Gentlewom M[rs] Mary Bainbrigge'.
MS. Rawl. poet. 62, fol. 24[v].

Fancy thou grand inquisitor of all, 144
For in kind dreams our greatest pleasure lies.
Chatwin, John, 'Fancy'.
MS. *Rawl. poet. 94, p. 144 (autogr.).

Fanline adieu since thou wilt part 145
And yet at home due tribute pay.
'The answere to Cloris'.
MS. Rawl. poet. 116, fol. 39.

Far above all the wounds of earthly things 146
Too dear none can celestial glories prize.
Williams, John, 'To Miss Ashe . . . The 2[ds] [i.e. second words] make Dear Miss Ashe let us in Love Imitate the blest above'.
MS. *Rawl. poet. 191, fol. 8[v] (autogr.).

Far exiled from our native land 147
Thy bloody self outdone in cruelty.
Burton, [John, C.C.C. Oxford], Psalm cxxxvii.
MS. Eng. misc. e. 241, fol. 110.

Far from our pleasant native Palestine, 148
And fill thy glutted channels with their scatter'd brains and gore.
Oldham, John, 'Paraphrase on the 137 Psalm. Pindarique'.
MS. *Rawl. poet. 123, p. 21 (autogr.).

149 Far from the lover and the friend removed
To joys eternal and the throne of God.
Gough, Richard.
MS. *Eng. poet. c. 5, fol. 151 (autogr.).

150 Far from the noisy follies of the great
Their short inestimable hours away.
MS. Eng. poet. e. 47, p. 47.

151 Far from the noisy town direct my feet.
Shall gently under arches glide.
Percy, Thomas, nephew to the Bp. of Dromore, 'Ode to Retirement . . . about Nov. 1776'.
MS. Percy c. 8, two copies. fols. 47 (autogr.) and 92.

152 Far in a lonely vale where poplars spread
The guardian angel to your flocks and you.
Samber, Robert, 'Cassandra. A Pastoral Eclogue On the death of the Duchess of Chandos', 1735.
MS. *Rawl. poet. 11, fol. 22 (autogr.).

153 Far in the distant east Sol sheds his ray
And charming the prospect in view.
'A Hunting Song', copy early 19th cent.
MS. Mus. e. 19, p. 42.

154 Far off no matter whether east or west,
I know it duty, and I feel it fame.
Churchill, Charles, 'Gotham', in three books.
MS. *Eng. poet. d. 113, pp. 165–204, 232–54.

155 Farewell? Ah! Lord!
Let both be pleased with mutual delight.
'Loath to depart'.
MS. *Eng. poet. e. 51, p. 33.

156 Farewell all future hopes that guide the course
Beauty, love, youth and graces all besides.
Answered by B372.
MS. Don. c. 57, fol. 50v, with music.

157 Farewell base world I bid thee quite adieu
I'm hasting in a better world to dwell.
Corbet, W., 'A ffarewell to the World'.
MS. *Rawl. poet. 210, fol. 40v (autogr.).

158 Farewell conscience since thou art grown
[hoe ters (*sic*)] runs tickling down my thighs . . . (incomplete).
MS. Wood F. 34, fol. 171v.

159 Farewell, dear Miss, again I'm forced to leave
And I'll endeavour still for you to live.
Williams, John, 'The Parting. To Miss Ashe. Thursday Augst. 4th 1709'.
MS. *Rawl. poet. 191, fol. 96 (autogr.).

Farewell (dear saint) go tell the better world 160
Our English Israel had a Samuel.
'Carmen Funebre sacratum memoriæ Domini Samuelis West'.
MS. Rawl. poet. 84, fol. 99 rev.

Farewell, dear sister, you shall heaven enjoy 161
Dead by that fatal stroke, I can no more.
Russell, George, translator, 'Lamentation for the death of Mrs. K. Killigrew, [d. Dec. 1583] by her Sister Eliz:' [Russell].
Original Latin pr. Stowe's *Survey of London*, 1633, p. 259.
MS. Ballard 37, fol. 135v.

Farewell Elyzian isle, thou curious coy 162
By me for love the other charity.
Brathwaite, Richard, 'The Author's farewell to the Elyzian Isle'.
MS. Eng. poet. c. 25, fol. 62.

Farewell England's gracious queen 163
The lord of hosts us send.
On the death of Queen Elizabeth and accession of James I.
MS. Top. Cheshire c. 6, fol. 568.

Farewell example, living rule farewell; 164
Fair memory, no judgment, and blest heaven.
Strode, William, 'An Epitaph on Sr John Walter, Lord cheife Baron', d. Nov. 1630.
MS. *CCC. 325, fol. 98 (autogr.).
MSS. Eng. poet. e. 97, p. 61; Rawl. poet. 84, fol. 65v rev.

Farewell fair Armida my joy, and my grief 165
You'd say with a sigh, Ah 'twas given by me.
MS. Rawl. poet. 65, fol. 36v.

Farewell fair saint may not the seas [and] nor wind 166
Whilst both contribute to your own undoing.
[Cary, Thomas], 'On his Mrs going to sea'.
Pr. *Il Pastor Fido*, Sir R. Fanshawe, 1648, p. 254, attr. to Mr. T. C. of his Majesties Bed-Chamber; and H. Lawes's *Ayres and Dialogues*, 1653, i. 10, attr. to Mr. Thomas Cary, son of the Earl of Monmouth.
MSS. Ashmole 47, fol. 111; Eng. poet. c. 53, fol. 9v, attr. to Sir K. D.; Firth e. 4, p. 101; Malone 21, fol. 48; Rawl. poet. 116, fol. 47v, attr. to W. Murry; 160, fol. 112v.

Farewell false friends, farewell ill wine, 167
Nothing so ill as what I leave behind.
'The Farewell'.
MS. Rawl. poet. 81, fol. 35v.

168 Farewell false love, thou oracle of lies
Dead is the root whence all these fancies grew.
[Ralegh, Sir Walter (?)].
See *Poems*, ed. A. M. C. Latham, 1951, p. 98.
MS. Rawl. poet. 85, fol. 48.

169 Farewell, farewell, farewell,
So many years.
'A mournfull Dittie . . . Elizabeth's losse, . . . with a welcome for King James'.
MS. Firth d. 14, fol. 114.

170 Farewell, farewell, illustrious friend!
Thy loss an amputation seems.
'Elegy on the death of Sir Joshua Reynolds', 1792.
MS. Malone 30, fol. 113.

171 Farewell fields of Fontenay
Farewell fields of Fontenay.
Doubtfully attributed to Sir John Moore [translation] 'From the Abbé Chaulieu'.
MS. Eng. misc. e. 241, fol. 108$^{v}$.

172 Farewell fond love, under whose childish whip
The hollow eccho will reply, 'Twas I.
King, Henry, 'Splendidis longum valedico nugis'.
Pr. *Poems*, 1657, p. 4.
MSS. *Eng. poet. e. 30, fol. 22; *Malone 22, fol. 13$^{v}$; Rawl. D. 692, fol. 111$^{v}$.

173 Farewell good heart though place us part
And both like place above.
'R[obert] M[ills] farwell to his freend J[ohn] F[inet]'.
MS. Rawl. poet. 85, two copies, fols. 36$^{v}$ and 54$^{v}$.

174 Farewell great prince; though late we'll now be just
That goodness we have wronged, we now adore.
'Verses upon the death of K. James', 7 Sept. 1701.
MS. Smith 23, p. 119.

175 Farewell illustrious maid: heavens know I part
And 'twill o'erwhelm them in their own despair.
'To his M^rs^ Goinge beyond Seas', completed on fol. 10, ending 'I beare thy losse that thou art deifide'.
MS. Eng. poet. c. 53, fol. 10$^{v}$.

176 Farewell ingrateful traitor farewell my perjured swain
But dying is a pleasure, when loving a pain.
[Dryden, John], song in *The Spanish Friar*, act v.
MS. Rawl. poet. 196, fol. 2$^{v}$.

Farewell Lorinda 'tis in vain 177
That it should at your altar bleed.
'The Resolute Lover'.
MS. Rawl. poet. 87, p. 68.

Farewell my dear! but all the gods to know 178
And from so sweet a murtherer bless my death.
Chatwin, John, 'The Departure'.
MS. *Rawl. poet. 94, p. 83 (autogr.).

Farewell, my dear Danby, my pimp and my cheat 179
From a popish successor for ever set free.
'The King's Farewell to Danby with his speedy Recantation, and the Authour's paraphrase thereupon', Dec. 1678.
MSS. Don. b. 8, p. 590; Rawl. A. 188, fol. 91$^{v}$.

Farewell, my dear Miss Ashe, and ever be 180
Let heaven direct and all our friendship bless.
Williams, John, 'The Farewell. To Miss Ashe, 1709'.
MS. *Rawl. 184, fol. 38$^{v}$ (autogr.).

Farewell, my dearest dear! 181
Greater than any queen on earth.
Morrice, John, 'Her Epitaph. Jan. 16, 1707'.
MS. *Rawl. poet. 114, fol. 174 (autogr.).

Farewell, my dearest Nancy 182
None has my heart but she.
'Nancy of Bristol'.
MS. Firth c. 18, fol. 155.

Farewell my false Olinda I bid the world and thee adieu 183
To glory in my ruin more.
MS. Mus. Sch. G. 640, fol. 36 rev., no tune.

Farewell my friend, my much loved friend farewell, 184
Think of thy lover, and thy absent friend.
'On the Absence of a Friend, by a Lady—1766'.
MS. Eng. poet. e. 28, p. 112.

Farewell my friends the tide attendeth no man 185
That shed thy blood for my redemption.
Tomb at Northleach.
MSS. Willis 83, fol. 54$^{v}$; Wood C. 11, fol. 40$^{v}$.

Farewell my little book, now take thy stage 186
I'll send thee out next year, much better clad.
Coley, Henry, 'The valediction to my Almanack 1694'.
MS. *Add. B. 8, fol. 72 (autogr.).

Farewell my lovely bird 187
Would I were with her there.
Tipping, William, 'My last farewell to my deere Bird'.
MS. *Rawl. poet. 101, fol. 16 (autogr.).

188 Farewell my lovely bird farewell
It will rejoice my heart.
Tipping, William, 'My Farewell to my deere Bird . . . this was putt on her Brest in her Coffin'.
MS. *Rawl. poet. 101, fol. 15ᵛ (autogr.).

189 Farewell my worn out friend
We shall meet to part no more.
Kenton, James, 'On the Death of Mr Isaac Waldron . . . 1782, Bristol', dated 1 Sept. 1782.
MS. *Eng. poet. e. 19, p. 257 (autogr.).

190 Farewell now my lady gay
I take my leave against my will.
MS. Rawl. C. 813, fol. 52ᵛ.

191 Farewell oh sun Arcadia's chiefest light
Farewell direction, farewell all affection.
Sidney, Sir Philip, from the *Arcadia*.
MS. *e. Mus. 37, fol. 192ᵛ.

192 Farewell old bully of these impious times
None but the reverend Kennet can display.
'Lord Whiggloves Elegy', on the Marquess of Wharton, d. 12 April 1715.
MS. Rawl. poet. 155, p. 129.

193 Farewell old year, for thou canst ne'er return
Farewell old England. Thou hast lost thy glory.
Tory lament 'On the old year, 1714'.
MS. Eng. poet. e. 87, p. 161; pr. bk. Firth b. 22, fol. 19.

194 Farewell poor world, I must be gone
In leaving thee, my Lord I meet.
'The Pilgrims farewell to the world. Heb. XIII. 14'.
MS. Rawl. C. 580, fol. 15ᵛ.

195 Farewell proud city; of unequall'd fame
And in my breast, a bridegroom's joy renew.
Scott, Thomas, Dissenting Minister of Ipswich, 'Verses . . . when leaving London'.
MS. Eng. poet. c. 9, p. 60.

196 Farewell rewards and fairies
Were lost; if it were addle.
[Corbett, Richard], 'The Fairies Farewell, or God have mercye will'.
Pr. *Poems*, 1648, p. 91.
MSS. Malone 19, p. 84; Rawl. D. 398, fol. 186.

197 Farewell stout iron side, not all thy art
[Ho (?)] these and him hath death knocked in the head.
'On a Smith'.
MS. CCC. 328, fol. 60.

Farewell sweet vale! No more thy shades can be 198
But trust in providence and God adore.
'From Mrs. Fonnereau to her Husband on leaving Thornhaugh'.
MS. Eng. poet. e. 28, p. 340.

Farewell the flowers, that paint the mossy green 199
And nature seems again both blithe and gay.
Percy, Thomas, nephew to the Bp. of Dromore, 'On Winter'.
MS. Percy c. 8, fol. 91.

Farewell the glory of those former days, 200
Such I once saw, but such must see no more.
Ashmole, Elias, 'Good night 9th July 1646', on the death of his mother.
MSS. Ashmole 36, 37, fol. 250 (autogr.).

Farewell the parliament with hey with hey 201
With hey troni noni noni no. no.
'London's farewell to the Parliamt: To the Tune of the Begger laid him down to sleepe'.
MS. Rawl. poet. 71, p. 32.

Farewell the seat where hospitality 202
Lest happiness distract thee once again.
Strode, William, 'Shiptons Distraction'.
MS. *CCC. 325, fol. 118ᵛ (autogr.).

Farewell the thing, time past so known so dear 203
Hereafter shall smell of the lamp not thee.
'Mr. Herrick His farewell to Sacke'.
MS. Rawl. poet. 160, fol. 165; see also F210.

Farewell Thomas I wend my way 204
His soul thus take into his hand.
Headed 'T. A.'.
MS. North c. 80, fol. 12ᵛ.

Farewell thou brightest soul farewell thou all 205
And no truth tell.
MS. Rawl. B. 35, fol. 46ᵛ rev.

Farewell thou lovely babe adieu 206
Since loved her more than they.
Tipping, William, 'An Elloge On a Lovly Childe of Mr. Chirches'.
MS. *Rawl. poet. 101, fol. 86 (autogr.).

Farewell thou man of men! our fruitless tears 207
Not single Vaulx but physic's self is dead.
N. D., 'Upone the death of that Noble Phisition and his ever honourde Freind Mr. James Vaulxe'.
MS. Rawl. poet. 206, p. 17.

Farewell thou mighty prince of bass 208
Here lies the bass and wharf at rest.
Stukeley, William, 'On Jo: Wharf who playd on the Bass Viol . . . Written on his graveston in Boston churchyard'.
MS. *Eng. misc. e. 386, fol. 7.

209 Farewell thou mortal stage
On the dry land.
Williams, Richard, of Queen's College, Cambridge, 'A Farewell to a chamber known by the name of Taylors Inne'.
MS. Rawl. poet. 147, p. 15.

210 Farewell thou thing, time past so true and dear,
Shall smell hereafter of the lamp not thee.
[Herrick, Robert], 'A farewell to Sacke'.
Pr. *Hesperides*, 1648.
MSS. Eng. poet. c. 53, fol. 14; Firth e. 4, p. 18, attr. to Mr. Hearick; see also F203.

211 Farewell to all the glittering pleasures here below,
I'll hate her, and forget that once I loved.
Chatwin, John, 'The Farewell'.
MS. *Rawl. poet. 94, p. 181 (autogr.).

212 Farewell to blind ambition now,
Of Charnock, Keys, and King.
'The Penitent Traitors', executed 18 March 1695/6.
MS. Firth d. 14, fol. 35.

213 Farewell to Europe, and at once farewell
She cannot starve, if there was only Clive.
Churchill, Charles, 'The Farewell'.
MS. *Eng. poet. d. 113, p. 256.

214 Farewell vain world, I've known enough of thee
And look at home, enough there's to be done.
'Epitaph'.
MS. Top. Yorks. c. 2, fol. 4.

215 Farewell wit and wisdom farewell game and glee
And a muirne till I dee for my true lieue and a las.
4 lines in the margin.
Pr. bk. C. 8. 31(12) Linc., Sig. C1.

216 Farewell ye gilded follies, pleasing troubles
I'll never look for't but in heaven again.
[Wotton, Sir Henry (?)], 'Valediction'.
Pr. *Compleat Angler*, 1653, p. 243, 'some say . . . by Dr. D.'; 1661, '. . . by Sir H. Wotton'; also in *Recreation for Ingenious Head-pieces*, 1663, at end.
MSS. Ashmole 38, p. 1*a*, attr. to Doctor Donn; CCC. 328, fol. 20, attr. to Dr. Donne; Don. e. 6, fol. 7, attr. to Sir Kellam Digbye; Eng. poet. e. 57, fol. 15$^{v}$; Rawl. B. 144, fol. 68; Rawl. D. 260, fol. 38, attr. to Sr. Kenelm Digby; Rawl. poet. 90, fol. 1; 153, fol. 16, attr. to Dr. Donne; 153, fol. 45$^{v}$; 172, fol. 106; Tanner 465, fol. 59.

Farewell ye gilded follies, ye pleasing troubles 217
Inherited, not purchased, nor our own.
'Some Verses of S. Kenelme Digby, upon the vanity of earthly things; though a little altered from what they were'. See F216.
MS. Rawl. poet. 213, fol. 59 rev.

Farewell ye hills and vallies 218
To spend away with you.
'The Country [ ]', song, incomplete.
MS. Mus. e. 20, fol. 8.

Farewell ye Naiads, who your tresses lave 219
Be mine like him to conquer and to die.
Howard, [Middleton (?), matric. Wadham 1767], 'The Conquest of Quebec'. Prize verses, 1768, Oxford.
MS. Top. Oxon. c. 216, fol. 19.

Farewell ye shades of dear Lismore 220
Thy glories I shall then adore.
MS. Percy b. 1, fol. 140.

Farthing unconstant proved yet no disgrace 221
(Venus !) that you should lose your brazen face.
'An Extemporary on Mr. Farthing', couplet.
MS. Add. A. 301, fol. 60$^{v}$.

Farts stifled in the guts make many die 222
As great a power as you, to kill or save.
James, Richard, 'Nicarctius his epigram on fartes'.
MS. *James 35, p. 18 (autogr.).

Fast by the banks of Cam was Colin bred: 223
As various hour advised, in different habit dressed.
'Colin's mistakes at Wimpole. In Spencers style'.
MS. Rawl. poet. 172, fol. 160.

Fast ran the sun from fiery east to west 224
My tongue must plain for aye; my heart must bleed.
'A passion'.
MS. Rawl. poet. 85, fol. 92.

Fat — from breakfast now pretty well rested 225
Whom the church and religion have chose, to defend them.
[Whaley, John], 'A Tale'.
Pr. *Poems*, 1732, p. 114.
MS. Rawl. poet. 222, fol. 15$^{v}$.

Fat paunches make lean pates, and dainty [grosser] bits 226
Make rich the ribs but bankrupt quite the wits.
Couplet.
MSS. Rawl. D. 954, fol. 44$^{v}$; Rawl. poet. 117, fol. 276 rev.

227 Fat soil full spring, sweet olive, grape of bliss
A sack of dust, a mass of flesh and blood.
[Southwell, Robert], 'Of Christs bloudy sweat', 4 verses.
See J. H. McDonald, *The Poems . . . of Southwell*, Roxburghe Club, 1937, pp. 103, 45, 160.
MS. Eng. poet. b. 5, p. 81.

228*a* Fatal aspect that hast an influence.
Sure Adam sinned not, in that spotless face.
[Herbert, Lord Edward of Cherbury], 'To Hir Face'.
Pr. *Occasional Verses*, 1665.
MS. Rawl. poet. 31, fol. 15v.

228*b* Fate guides us: unto fates yield we
The first prescribeth the last day.
Tr. from Seneca, *Oedipus*. Quoted from G. Sandys' *Relation of a Journey*, [1615, p. 57].
MS. Rawl. poet. 117, fol. 260 rev.

229 Fates caused him die by night with this intent
Each saint it seems this saint desired to have.
Freind, Nathaniel, translator, 'In obitum Joh. Friend. Joh. Fayrer'. 1672.
MS. Top. Oxon. f. 31, p. 279 (autogr.).

230 Father and king of powers, both high and low
Oh praise the lord my soul praise ye the Lord.
Bacon, Francis, Psalm civ.
Pr. Bacon's *Translation of Certaine Psalmes*, 1625.
MS. Eng. poet. c. 50, fol. 55v.

231 Father and son and Holy Ghost you shall beseech with faithful heart
The wicked man in that day hid to Christ shall be on the side left.
Keigwin, John, translator, 'The History of the passion, Death, and resurrection of our Lord and Saviour Jesus Christ written in Cornish . . . some centuries past interpreted in the English Tongue in the year 1682'. Two copies.
MSS. Gough Cornwall 3 and 4.

232 Father behold a guilty wretch
Eternally shall live.
Kenton, James.
MS. *Eng. poet. e. 20, p. 120 (autogr.).

233 Father, creator of what is
And ever more shall be.
King. Mr. — of Farnham, 'The Lord's Prayer Versified'.
MS. Montagu e. 13, fol. 168v.

Father divine, thy piercing eye 234
Thy suppliant to confess.
Orton, The Revd. —, Hymn.
MS. Eng. misc. e. 227, fol. 47v.

Father of all, in every age 235
All nature's incense rise.
Pope, Alexander, 'The Universal Prayer'.
See *Minor Poems*, ed. N. Ault and J. Butt, 1954, p. 145.
MS. Eng. poet. c. 9, p. 1.

Father of all that live, and move, 236
To sing thy high, eternal praise.
Kenton, James.
MS. *Eng. poet. e. 20, p. 389 (autogr.).

Father of heaven, and Him by whom 237
As sin is nothing, let it nowhere be.
Donne, John, 'The Letanye'.
Pr. *Poems*, 1633.
MS. *Eng. poet. e. 99, fol. 48v.

[Father of heaven] ffader of heven yblessed þu be 238
For att thys tyme borne ys he.
'Alleluya Alleluya deo patri sit gloria Salvator mundi dominus'.
MS. Ashmole 189, fol. 107.

Father of light and life! thou good supreme! 239
Sacred, substantial, never-fading bliss.
Thomson, James, lines from 'Winter' on his memorial in Richmond Church, Surrey, 1748.
MS. Top. gen. e. 32, fol. 83v.

Father of light that shines above 240
Both now and still whilst ages run.
'Engl. Primer of our Lady. 1631'.
MS. Eng. poet. e. 56, p. 48.

Father of men thy care we bless 241
To join the family above.
Orton, The Revd. —, Hymn.
MS. Eng. misc. e. 227, fol. 48.

Father of mercies bow thine ear 242
And feel thy new creating power.
Beddome, Benjamin.
Pr. *Hymns . . . of B. Beddome*, 1818, no. 700.
MS. *Eng. misc. e. 227, fol. 174v.

Father of mercies God of grace 243
And wash our num'rous sins away.
Beddome, Benjamin.
MS. *Eng. misc. e. 227, fol. 11v.

244 Father of Totty, man of fancy fine
Oh happy man who calls this life his lot.
Gough, Richard, 'To Edward Forster Esq. 1773 or 1774'.
MS. *Eng. poet. c. 5, fol. 195 (autogr.).

245 Father, part of his double interest
Is all but love, oh let that last will stand.
Donne, John, 'Sonnett 12'.
Pr. *Poems*, 1633.
MS. *Eng. poet. e. 99, fol. 46.

246 [Father] Fader that art in heaven blisse,
Oac fro evil thu syld us all. Amen.
Version of the Lord's prayer quoted by Hearne in 'Specimen drawn up . . . towards an Epitome of *English* History', from Camden's *Remaines*, 1657, p. 24.
MS. Rawl. D. 1171, fol. 11.

247 *Fatis agimur, cedite fatis!*
What have you against this to say?
Pope, Alexander, lines in a letter to Henry Cromwell, 12 Oct. 1710.
Pr. Curll's *Miscellanea*, 1727, i. 45.
MS. Rawl. letters 90, fol. 33 (autogr.).

248 Faulty that somebody no fault might find
That I would have 'em all in love with me.
Williams, John, on 'Love is blind'.
MS. *Rawl. poet. 191, fol. 99 (autogr.).

249 Faustina grateful for the applause she gains
And every night returns them claps for claps!
Parsons, William, 'Epigram on an Opera Singer in Paris'.
MS. *Don. d. 123, p. 117 (autogr.).

250 Faustinus, Sextus, Sylla, Ponticus
Which straight did part them ere they did some evil.
Davies, Sir John, 'In multos'.
Pr. amongst 'Epigrammes' with *Ovids Elegies* by C. M. [*c.* 1600].
MS. *Add. B. 97, fol. 41v.

251 Faustus is free and hath the world at will
But falls into a whorehouse by the way.
Davis, [Sir] John, of Grayes Inn, 'In faustum'.
MS. *Rawl. poet. 212, fol. 62 rev.; see also F810.

252 Faustus nor lord nor knight nor wise nor old
That shortly he will quite forget to go.
Davis, [Sir] John, 'In faustum'.
Pr. amongst 'Epigrames' with *Ovids Elegies* by C. M. [*c.* 1600].
MSS. *Add. B. 97, fol. 42; *Rawl. poet. 212, fol. 63v rev.

Faustus stabbed Flora and [but] would you know why 253
To give him the lie till he stabbed her again.
'On faustus and flora'.
MSS. CCC. 328, fol. 88; Don. d. 58, fol. 36v; Eng. poet. e. 14, fol. 80v rev.; f. 25, fol. 13.

Favonius having thawed sharp winter's ice 254
Her sex's envy, our delight.
Fanshawe, Sir Richard, translator, 'To Sextius. Ode [III]. 4', Horace.
MS. *Firth c. 1, p. 37.

Favoured of heaven her awful voice exclaimed 255
And distant ages kindle at thy bier.
Maurice, T[homas], 'An Elegiac Poem sacred to the memory . . . of Sir William Jones', (1746–94).
MS. Eng. poet. c. 51, p. 235*a*.

Favourites of beauty, to these sorrowing lines 256
He whom alone she favoured slumbers here.
R. L., 'Epitaph. 1781' on Myra's Sparrow.
MS. *Eng. poet. e. 16, fol. 14.

Favours are writ in dust, but stripes we feel 257*a*
Depraved nature stamps in lasting steel.
Couplet.
MS. Rawl. poet. 117, fol. 164 rev.

Fear, affection, and doubts what may ensue 257*b*
Are cause that stories seldom can be true.
Couplet.
MS. Mus. f. 22, fol. 2.

Fear ere thou sin, thyself though none else nigh, 258
That 's not enough that to excess extends.
[Stanley, Thomas], translator, 'The Advice'.
Pr. *History of Philosophy*, 1655, p. 24, from Ausonius.
MS. Rawl. poet. 90, fol. 104v.

Fear God ye sons of men 259
To his rich mercy fly.
Beddome, Benjamin.
MS. *Eng. misc. e. 227, fol. 59v.

Fear no more the scorching sun, 260
Consign to thee and come to dust.
'A Dirge in Cymbeline of Shakespear's', music by William Boyce, for performance at Covent Garden, 1746; copied in his hand.
MS. Mus. c. 35.

Fear not a ranter's threats in the least part, 261
His lion's throat had but a poor cow's heart.
Robinson, Robert, couplet.
MS. *Rawl. poet. 218, p. 66 (autogr.).

262 **Fear not dear love that I'll reveal**
**The world will find thy picture there.**
[Carew, Thomas].
Pr. *Poems*, 1640, and with music by H. Lawes in his *Second Book of Ayres and Dialogues*, 1655, p. 39.
MSS. Don. c. 57, fol. 26, with music by H. Lawes; Douce f. 5, fol. $33^v$, attr. to the Earle of Dorset; Eng. poet. c. 50, fol. $76^v$; e. 14, fol. 12; f. 10, fol. $117^v$; Malone 16, p. 12; Mus. Sch. B. 2, p. 37, in the hand of W. Lawes, with fragment of music; see also D425, T1884.

263 **Fear not my dear a flame can never die,**
**My love removed and to thy soul assign'd.**
Sedley, Sir Charles, 'Constancy'.
Pr. as Sedley's, 17th cent. See *Works*, ed. V. de S. Pinto, 1928.
MSS. Rawl. poet. 116, fol. $96^v$; 173, fol. $74^v$, attr. to Sr. Ch. Sedley.

264 **Fear not the guilt, if you can pay for it well**
**But want of money is a deadly sin.**
MS. Sancroft 58, p. 158.

265 **Fear not the worst, but trust in God,**
**Th'other gives peace and rest.**
Robinson, Robert.
MS. *Rawl. poet. 218, p. 144 (autogr.).

266 **Fear not ye sailors when black storms arise**
**More dangerous lightenings flash from Bilby's eyes.**
Couplet.
MS. Eng. misc. b. 48, fol. 83.

267 **Fear of an after-clap makes many store**
**Happy for me thou hast afflicted me.**
Colman, Henry, 'On Affliction'.
MS. *Rawl. poet. 204, fol. $38^v$ (autogr.).

268 **Fear then unbreasts all wit,**
**That in my mind did sit.**
Couplet translating 'Tum pavor sapientiam omnem mihi ex animo expectorat . . . Ennius apud Cicero, Tusc. Disp. 4. 8. 19'.
MS. Rawl. D. 986, fol. 108.

269 **Fearless follow, thou sad soul**
**All comfort still attending thee.**
MS. Mus. b. 1, fol. $36^v$, music by John Wilson.

270 **Fears of my purpose friend adieu**
**The bonds are sealed 'twixt heaven and me.**
MS. Malone 16, p. 22.

271 **Feeble like me, with such grey locks as these**
**I kiss the hand stained in my Hector's gore.**
'From Homer's Iliads By Mr. T. B. Priam's Speech to Achilles'.
MS. Rawl. poet. 222, fol. 3.

**Feed on my sheep my charge my comfort feed** 272
**Your wool is rich no tongue can tell my gain.**
Sidney, Sir Philip, from the *Arcadia*. Answered by L115.
MS. *e Mus. 37, fol. 72.

**Fell slaughter ceased, and hushed the din of arms,** 273
**For canst thou doubt that these will charm thee more?**
Parsons, William, 'Sonnet to Capt. W. 1783'.
MS. *Don. d. 123, p. 90 (autogr.).

**Fell'd by death's surer hatchet, here lies Spong** 274
**Whose pales and gates were for eternity.**
On John Spong, carpenter, 1736, Ockham Churchyard.
MS. Top. gen. e. 32, fol. $73^v$.

**Fellow of thy father's light** 275
**All that we do sing or say.**
'Primer Engl. and latin of K. Hen. 8. 1546. The hymne for Prime'.
MS. Eng. poet. e. 56, p. 68.

**Felton, awake, and cheer thyself from sorrow,** 276
**T'obtain forgiveness for the bloody crime.**
'1628. Felton's dreame Aug. 22nd being the night before the murder' [of the Duke of Buckingham].
MS. Tanner 465, fol. 102.

**Females in finery delight** 277
**And wives do thus confound.**
'On Female Extravagance'.
MS. *Eng. poet. d. 47, fol. 167.

**Few and evil are our days** 278
**To a better place above.**
Kenton, James.
MS. *Eng. poet. e. 20, p. 209 (autogr.).

**Few be the days that feeble man must breathe** 279
**Accounted pure, before such purity.**
Flatman, Thomas, 'Job. Set by Mr. Wm. Howes'.
MS. *Firth d. 7, fol. 23.

**Few things we guess at, which we see,** 280
**With us it is dark night.**
Robinson, Robert.
MS. *Rawl. poet. 218, p. 1 (autogr.).

**Fie away what mean you by this** 281
**God's body man you kill me.**
MS. Don. c. 54, fol. $25^v$.

282 Fie bretheren scholars, fie for shame
And so my breth'ren dear Adieu.
Bastard, Thomas, 'Libell cal'd Martin marre prelates bastarde'.
See Wood, *Athenae Oxonienses*, ed. Bliss, ii, 1815, 228.
MSS. CCC. 327, fol. 17v; Gough. misc. antiq. 11, fol. 81, attr. to Tho. Bastard fell. of N. Coll.; Rawl. poet. 212, fol. 123v, attr. to Bastarde.

283 Fie false scout do you grow mad
Those that know not, whither else to go.
Cavendish, Jane, 'On a false reporte of your Lordship's landinge'.
MS. *Rawl. poet. 16, p. 8.

284 Fie fie I pray you be content
Though now 'tis done I am content.
'A French translation'.
MS. Rawl. poet. 172, fol. 3v.

285 Fie, fie, let marriage life
Marry, marry to rejoice.
Cavendish, Lady Jane, 'A Songe sunge by an Angell' in 'The Concealed Fancies'.
MS. *Rawl. poet. 16, p. 150.

286 Fie fie Mongmory Fie etc.,
They say to praise you is not fit.
'A new song', doggrel verses naming amongst others William Pulteney son of the Earl of Bath.
MS. Eng. misc. b. 48, fol. 87.

287 Fie, fie upon't! What not to send
I sing, but break off in the middle.
'An Epistle from Exon to a Friend at Greenwich', 1735. Answered by P420.
MS. Eng. misc. e. 240, p. 324.

288 Fie lovely boy why fliest thou me
And thou shalt need no other shade than I.
Rainolds, Henry.
MS. Rawl. poet. 116, fol. 48; see also F30, S1145, S1385, W2373.

289 Fie, Miss, what faces wry you make,
And beauty's blameless wash.
[Roach, Richard], 'To a young ladie, making Faces at her Spring Broth'.
MS. Rawl. D. 832, fol. 179 (autogr.).

290 Fie! nay! prithee John do not quarrel, man!
Who cares for you.
Catch, pr. H. Playford, *Wit and Mirth*, 1682. Possibly by Blow: cf. F. B. Zimmerman, *Purcell*, 1963, no. D100.
MS. Mus. Sch. C. 95, p. 118.

Fie on religious jealousies 291
Why set they us by th'ears.
Robinson, Robert.
MS. *Rawl. poet. 218, p. 11 (autogr.).

Fie, Rome's abus'd: can any be thought able 292
To move her suit by a collateral saint.
[Quarles, Francis], 'On Merits'.
Pr. *Divine Fancies*, 1632, i. 29.
MS. Rawl. poet. 90, fol. 60.

Fie, scholars, fie! have [ye] you such [hungry] thirsty souls 293
Cut did the deed, but Longtail bears the blame.
Stone, Benjamin, 'On Samburne, Sheriff of Oxford'.
Cf. *Philological Quarterly*, xxxiv, 1955, p. 448.
MSS. CCC. 328, fol. 5v; Douce f. 5, fol. 17; Malone 19, p. 62, attr. to Ben. Stone; 21, fol. 62; Rawl. poet. 117, fol. 190v rev.; 199, p. 42, attr. to Ben Stone; see also O1310.

Fie Susan fie woot never leave the trade 294
By lodging and relieving of the poor.
MS. Eng. poet. e. 14, fol. 64v.

Fie that I so for thy sake 295
I'll do so, and with thee change.
MS. CCC. 327, fol. 25v.

Fie that men should so complain 296
'Tis but their art to prove you.
'A Song'.
Pr. *Poems of Pembroke and Ruddier*, 1660.
MS. CCC. 328, fol. 41.

Fie—what a life is this 297
I needs must be content.
'Mr. Rob. Jones 2d. booke For tableture and pricke song', 1601, vii.
MS. Douce 280, fol. 68.

Fierce cruel wars have wasted all the land. 298
What resteth, but a wilderness to see?
MS. Rawl. poet. 66, fol. 34.

Fierce lions roaring for their prey: and then 299
Had I but only Daniel's lion there.
[Quarles, Francis], 'On Daniel in the Den'.
Pr. *Divine Fancies*, 1632, i. 32.
MS. Rawl. poet. 90, fol. 60.

[Fifteen] years truly I practised this science 300
God giveth him this science for his succour.
Charnock, Thomas, copied by Ashmole from autograph.
MS. Ashmole 972, fol. 275v.

301 Fight on brave soldiers for the cause
The clean contrary way.
Brome, Alexander.
Pr. *Songs and other Poems*, 1661, p. 136.
MSS. Eng. misc. e. 13, fol. 21$^{v}$, attr. to Mr. Nichols; Rawl. poet. 26, fol. 146$^{v}$; 62, fol. 52; 153, fol. 23.

302 Fill all the glasses fill 'em high
The pleasures of life free from anguish and . . . (incomplete).
Song by John Eccles.
MS. Mus. d. 177, fol. 69$^{v}$.

303 Fill me a bowl of sack, and I'll carouse
You may prognosticate the fruit divine.
'On Sir Robert Shirley's son', Seymour, b. 23 Jan. 1646/7.
MS. Eng. poet. e. 4, p. 66.

304 Fill me some wine
That I am fallen in love and 'tis with you.
MS. Rawl. poet. 37, p. 114.

305 Fill the bowl with easy wine,
To the gods belong tomorrow.
Cowley, [Abraham], 'The Epicure'.
Pr. *Works*, 1668, 'Miscellanies', p. 36.
MS. Rawl. poet. 173, fol. 140$^{v}$.

306 Filled with love's divinest essence
Of my everlasting friend.
Kenton, James.
MS. *Eng. poet. e. 20, p. 219 (autogr.).

307 Fimus is coached, and for his greater grace
And that a cart would serve to carry dung.
'In Fimum'.
MS. Malone 19, p. 12.

308 Find me out an end in a ring
Then teach a woman constancy.
'A Charge upon the Ladies from a Newspaper'.
MS. Eng. poet. c. 5, fol. 29.

309 Findest thou no comfort in this fickle earth:
Sure, heavens reward sufficient to requite the same.
[Quarles, Francis], 'On Fido'.
Pr. *Divine Fancies*, 1632, ii. 64.
MS. Rawl. poet. 90, fol. 50.

310 Finding [these] those beams which I must ever love
A blinded mole or else a burned fly.
Sidney, Sir Philip.
Pr. *Arcadia*, 1598, p. 481.
MSS. *e Mus. 37, fol. 239$^{v}$; Rawl. poet. 85, fol. 12, attr. to Nowell.

Fine Madam Would-bee, wherefore should you fear 311
Of the not borne, yet buried, here 's the tomb.
'Ben Johnson on the fine Lady Would-Bee'.
*Epigrammes* lxii.
MSS. Don. e. 6, fol. 22$^{v}$, attr. to Ben Johnson; Rawl. poet. 26, fol. 1$^{v}$.

Fine Mistress Phippes, a proper friend of mine 312
Was asked; fair lady is this house to let?
MS. Tanner 465, fol. 94.

Fine, young, folly though you were 313
And your clothes that set you out.
[Habington, William], 'To his Mistrisse', song in *The Queen of Arragon*, 1640, act IV.
Pr. *Sportive Wit*, 1656, p. 58.
MSS. Rawl. poet. 84, fol. 66; 142, fol. 46.

Finger of God's right hand 314
Us, work no hurtful things.
'Engl. Primer of Our Lady. 1631. p. 327'.
MS. *Eng. poet. e. 56, p. 19.

Finish me one task more, for critic muse, 315
Thou only to be his, he to be thine is fit.
'A Postscript', Wolseley to Wharton.
Pr. *Poems on Affairs of State*, iii, 1698, p. 15.
MS. Firth c. 16, p. 238.

Fire, fire, fire fire; the bells all backward ring, 316
The silks that haughty Naples brags . . . (incomplete).
[Owen, Corbet], 'Of the intolerable Heat in the latter End of May and the beginning of June 1665', pindaric ode written at Oxford.
Pr. *A New Collection of Poems and Songs*, John Bulteel, 1674, p. 121, attr. to Owen.
MS. CCC. 309, fol. 73.

Fire fire, lo here [how] I burn in such desire 317
Oh, drown both me and my desire.
[Campion, Thomas], 'songe'.
Pr. Campion's *Third Booke of Ayres* (n.d.), xx, and with music by Nicholas Lanier in H. Lawes's *Select Ayres and Dialogues*, 1669.
MSS. Ashmole 38, p. 120; Don. c. 57, fol. 31$^{v}$, with music by Lanier; Mus. Sch. D. 247, fol. 55$a^{v}$, with music by Lanier; Rawl. poet. 65, fol. 34$^{v}$.

Fire, thunder, threat'nings, and a trembling-mount 318
And may your joys, in those rich gifts increase.
Crane, R[alph], 'A Summary and true Distinction betweene the Lawe and the Gospel'.
MS. Rawl. poet. 61, fol. 97 (autogr.).

319 Fire, water, and women are man's ruin
And great thy wisdom Vander Bruin.
[Prior, Matthew], 'A Dutch Proverb'.
Pr. *Poems*, 1709.
MS. Rawl. poet. 152, fol. 129$^v$.

320 Firm as th'eternal pillars stand
Long as eternity shall last.
Kenton, James.
MS. *Eng. poet. e. 20, p. 327 (autogr.).

First a cobweb shirt . . . see W1527.

321 First an ensign by all good men 'curst,
Raised by his whoredom and his sister's lust.
'This Distick in Satyr found o're the D[uke] of M[arlborough's] Door'.
MS. Rawl. D. 361, fol. 345$^v$.

322 First bespoke the captain of the ship
And most of our merry men drowned.
'The Gallant Frigate in Distress'.
MS. Firth c. 18, fol. 115.

323 First born of chaos, who so fair didst come
From thence took first their wish, thither at last must flow.
[Cowley, Abraham], 'Hymn to Light'.
Pr. *Works*, 1668, 'Verses . . . on several occasions', p. 35.
MS. Rawl. poet. 213, fol. 5$^v$ (in margin).

324 First by St. Johns they ransacked Mrs. Betty
As 'tis established by Dame Nature's laws.
Langford, [Emanuel], of Christ Church, Oxford, 'The Epilogue' to the Music Speech, 1683.
MS. Top. Oxon. e. 280, p. 674 rev.

325 First draw an arrant fop from top to toe
Hath made them woeful ministers of state.
[Villiers, George, Duke of Buckingham], 'Advice to a Paynter, to draw the Delineaments of a Statesman, and his Underlings', on the Earl of Arlington, 11 Sept. 1674 (?).
Pr. *Miscellaneous Works*, ii, 1705, p. 80. *Advice-to-a-Painter Poems 1633–1836*, M. T. Osborne, 1949, no. 20.
MS. Don. b. 8, fol. 482.

326 First enters prologue-speaker with a grace
We'll neither want Calphurnia, nor my lord.
'Some Account of the Play acted at the Rt. Honourable the Lord Guilford's Gallery at Epsom', 11 June 1715.
MS. North b. 24, fol. 70.

327 First for your kind epistle we
And with you well, and so God b'w'ye.
'Answer to Mr. B[orroug]h's Epistle', B507.
MS. Eng. misc. e. 240, p. 273.

First he the strong Nemean lion slew 328
In that one act than all the twelve before.
[Wither, George], 'The 12 Labours of Hercules'.
Pr. with *Faire-Virtue*, 1622.
MS. Eng. poet. e. 97, p. 134.

First here's a pocket baroscope 329
As the lady's charms the author do.
'Dr. Vincent's Experiments'.
MS. Rawl. D. 214, fol. 80$^v$.

First I would have her richly sped 330
For pleasure, but are naught for food.
'A wish'd mistresse described'.
MS. Eng. poet. f. 25, fol. 11$^v$.

First in our cups the sovereign queen of toasts, 331
Well drest, well bred, well featur'd, and well born.
Amhurst, Mr. [Nicholas], 'Upon Mrs. Tyrrell'.
MS. Montagu e. 13, fol. 87.

First is my note and Blenheim is my name; 332
With union blest, and all those glories crowned.
'Bells at St. Helen's Church in Worcester', the inscription on seven bells, 1706–19.
MS. Top. Oxon. c. 326, fol. 60$^v$.

First learn to move with fantastic air 333
For this is an infallible receipt.
MS. Add. B. 105, fol. 96.

First let me ask my self, why I would try 334
Meant for my grief for him with joy for those.
Sr. H. G., on the death of Prince Henry, 1612 (?).
MS. Eng. poet. e. 37, p. 49.

First love, the same I here the first do call 335
For had I say more: I myself had blust.
Newman, Thomas, 'of the passion of love'.
MS. Top. Oxon. f. 39, fol. 20 (autogr.).

First take thy calling thankfully 336
Both laud and praise the Deity.
Couplet, used as a copy by Wiman Ramsey, *c.* 1595.
MS. Rawl. D. 649, fol. 31.

First then the love of God appears from hence 337
God's Love declared in our Redeemer is.
MS. *Rawl. poet. 97, fol. 4$^v$ (autogr.).

First to the gods thy humble homage pay: 338
Immortal, incorruptible, divine.
Rowe, N[icholas], translator, 'Moral Precepts; Collected from the Golden verses of Pythagoras'.
Pr. in full in *The Life of Pythagoras* by Dacier, translated, 1707, p. 151.
MS. Ballard 47, fol. 35.

339 First we did fast and then we prayed for peace,
And then the Irish learned the Scottish pranks.
4 lines, 1642.
MSS. Ashmole 36, 37, fol. $159^v$.

340 First when thou nature all things brought to pass
For to serve their turn both night and day.
Complaint of a crab-tree. Dated 1558.
MS. Ashmole 48, fol. $102^v$.

341 First worship God, he that forgets to pray
Starves in his grave, being wretched, when he's dead.
[Randolph, Thomas], 'Necessary Observations'.
Pr. *Poems*, 1638, p. 42.
MSS. Mus. Sch. G. 632, fol. $1^v$; Rawl. poet. 90, fol. 111; 170, fol. 75; see also S1078.

342 Fitly to th' lamb these lambs they consecrate
In heaven a triumph find, on earth, a tomb.
Creswell, Robert, 'On St. Innocents Day'.
MS. *Eng. poet. f. 24, fol. $6^v$ (autogr.).

343 Fitter a match hath never been
The flesh is married to the skin.
[Strode, William], 'Upon a Butcher marryinge a tanners daughter'.
MS. Eng. poet. c. 50, fol. $130^v$; see A130.

344 Five and five and fifty-five
And make a young man mad.
MS. Rawl. poet. 153, fol. 46.

345 Five brethren born at once
The other had but half a one.
Riddle, 'A Rose'.
MS. Rawl. poet. 148, fol. 3.

346 Five grievous sins to God on high
These be the sins we crying call.
Huish, Alexander, 'The [five] crying sins', Oct. 25. 1637.
MS. Eng. poet. e. 56, p. 128 (autogr.).

347 Five hundred pounds!—too small a boon
It would not buy the paper.
'An Epigram . . . the Duchess Dowager of Marlborough had offer'd £500 to the Poet who should best . . . Honour . . . the late Duke . . . From the Old Whig, Sept. 16, 1736'.
MSS. Ballard 29, fol. $110^v$; Eng. poet. c. 9, p. 77.

348 Five thousand in a week in one poor city:
But rather wonder there are men to die.
[Quarles, Francis], 'On the sight of a Plague Bill'.
*Divine Fancies*, 1634, ii. 76.
MS. Rawl. poet. 90, fol. $69^v$.

Five vowels joined together make a name 349
In heaven or earth, none greater than the same.
'Ie[h]oua', couplet.
MSS. Rawl. D. 954, fol. 40; Rawl. poet. 209, fol. $35^v$.

Flatterers confound human state, they make 350
In robe or royalty, if deeds be naught.
James, Richard, 'On flatterers of greatnesse'.
MS. *James 35, p. 18 (autogr.).

Flattering words, and artful sighs 351
Lead hand in hand our festal pow'rs.
'Song 1765'. Answered by T232.
MS. *Eng. poet. e. 28, p. 77.

Flavia, the least and slightest toy 352
To every other breast a flame.
Atterbury, Francis, 'The Fan'.
MS. Eng. misc. f. 79, p. 53.

Flea-bitten synod! an assembly brewed 353
Is clergy-lay, party-per-pale compounded.
Cleveland, J[ohn], 'On the Synod', the Westminster Assembly, 1643. Cf. L119.
MS. Tanner 465, fol. 91.

Fled is my love, for ever gone 354
To her thou shalt go tomorrow.
D'Urfey, Thomas, song 'in the 3 Dukes of Dunstable', set by H. Purcell.
F. B. Zimmerman, *Purcell*, 1963, no. 571 (3).
MS. Mus. Sch. C. 95, p. 206.

Fled is the auburn hue from Bromia's hair, 355–6
Which friendly nature has, unasked, allowed her?
'On an Old Lady, who powder'd her Grey Locks'.
MS. Eng. poet. c. 9, p. 23.

Fleeting fame flieth, increaseth, lieth, 357
I just reward purchas'd for world's disdains.
F. W., 'Sonnett 8. heavenly glory'.
MS. *Rawl. C. 639, p. 29.

Fleshly delights and covetous desires 358*a*
Unapt to entertain the Deity.
MS. *Rawl. poet. 97, fol. 21 (autogr.).

[Fleshly] fflesly lustes and festes 358*b*
Haue almost lost thys londe.
In the hand of T. Urmston, Chaplain of Lyme, Cheshire, *c.* 1477–89. Brown-Robbins Index 811.
MS. Bodl. 123, fol. $6^v$.

Fletcher thy muse at once improved and marred 359
Despairing stand, their sport is at the best.
Waller, Edmund, sonnet on Fletcher.
Pr. Beaumont and Fletcher, *Comedies and Tragedies*, folio, 1647, and Waller's *Poems*, 1664.
MS. Sancroft 29, p. 63.

360 **Flight is but the preparative. The sight**
**Sees and enjoys the holy one.**
Traherne, Thomas, 'The Vision'.
MS. *Eng. poet. c. 42, fol. 5 (autogr.).

361 **Float miser in thy sea of gold, yet thou**
**Than ebbing wealth slides from your company.**
Polwhele, John, 'Boet[hius], L. 3. m. 3'.
MS. *Eng. poet. f. 16, fol. 27v (autogr.).

362 **Flora a nymph of high desert**
**But study her and be complete.**
MS. North b. 24, fol. 157.

363 **Flora fair nymph, whilst silly lambs are feeding**
**And die I shall, except you quench the anguish.**
Pr. John Ward's *First Set of English Madrigals*, 1613, xv.
MSS. Mus. f. 20–24: f. 20, fol. 10v.

364 **Flora goddess ever blooming**
**Bless'd by love and crowned with flowers.**
'Rural Beauty or Vauxhall Gardens'.
MS. Montagu e. 13, fol. 71.

365 **Flora in her grove she lied**
**Strephon thou art fled from me.**
'Floras lamentable passion'.
Pr. *Roxburghe Ballads*, vi, ed. J. Woodfall Ebsworth, 1889, p. 98.
MS. Firth c. 20, fol. 69.

366 **Flora she did sore lament**
**And cast all grief away . . . (incomplete).**
MS. Firth c. 20, fol. 69.

367 **Flora will keep her vaulting house no more**
**She is preserved by the thing she loathes.**
Davis, [Sir] John, of Grayes Inn, 'In floram'.
MS. *Rawl. poet. 212, fol. 57v rev.

368 **Flourish ye hillocks set with fragrant flowers.**
**Sounding my sorrows tuned in notes of anguish.**
Pr. John Wilbye's *Second Set of Madrigales*, 1609, ii.
MSS. Mus. f. 17–19: f. 19, fol. 12v.

369 **Flow forth, my tears, and with your floods assuage**
**Death was his usher to eternity.**
Sancroft, William (?), 'On the much lamented death of Mr. Martin Peirce, Mayer of Cambridge, who died 28 April 1636'.
MS. Sancroft 48, fol. 4, in Sancroft's hand.

370 **Flow oh my tears and cease not**
**To swell so high that I may drown me in you.**
Pr. Wilbye's *First set of Madrigals*, 1598, iv.
MS. Mus. d. 8, fol. 57.

**Flow on thou spring-tide of my tears and rise** 371
**The next unto the best e'er came in it.**
Ryder, Henry, 'To the Kinge et spes et ratio studiorum in caesare tantum' [Charles I, 1639].
MSS. Ashmole 47, fol. 101v, subscribed 'your majesties humblest subject, Henry Ryder'; Malone 21, fol. 91v.

**Fly envious time till thou run out thy race** 372
**When death and chance, and thou oh time shall be no more.**
[Milton, John], 'Upon a Clocke case or Dyall'.
Pr. *Poems*, 1645, p. 19.
MSS. Ashmole 36, 37, fol. 22.

**Fly fame, report that all the world may know** 373
**But Raleigh's name shall live eternally.**
'Upon Sr. Walter Raleighe'.
MS. Rawl. poet. 26, fol. 70.

**Fly fly ye winged Cupids fly** 374
**If she'll but pity I'll for ever love.**
Song with music.
MS. Mus. Sch. E. 397, p. 111 rev.

**Fly from Olinda young and fair** 375
**He like a god is every where.**
Answered by A802.
MSS. Rawl. poet. 152, fol. 47; 196, fol. 11v; Top. Oxon. c. 108, p. 67.

**Fly from the world, oh Bessy! to me** 376
**And a kiss be our passport to heaven!**
Moore, [Thomas], 'Song'. Answered in O777.
MS. Percy d. 9, fol. 51.

**Fly hence pale care no more remember** 377
**His soul to glad you in perfumes.**
Herrick, Rob[ert], 'A Charroll presented to Dr. Williams Bp. of Lincolne as a Newyears guift'.
Pr. *Poetical Works*, ed. L. C. Martin, 1956, p. 413, from this MS.
MSS. Ashmole 36, 37, fol. 298.

**Fly hence shadows that do keep** 378
**Watchful sorrows charm'd in sleep . . . (incomplete).**
[Ford, John], song from *The Lovers Melancholy*, v. i. Pr. John Wilson's *Cheerfull Ayres or Ballads*, 1660, p. 88.
MS. Mus. b. 1, fol. 99, music by John Wilson.

**Fly hence ye gentle muses all** 379
**With damned dullness.**
'On the Ball at Court'.
MS. Firth c. 16, p. 129.

380 Fly, Madam fly! from the infection run
With his cold hand does stop your ling'ring breath.

Chatwin, John, 'Advice to a young Lady going to marry with a very old Gent'.
MS. *Rawl. poet. 94, p. 277 (autogr.).

381 Fly merry muse unto that merry town
A general vice, that merits public blame.

Davies, Sir John, 'Ad Musam'.
Pr. amongst Epigrames, with *Ouids Elegies*, tr. C. M., [*c.* 1600].
MSS. *Add. B. 97, fol. 41; *Rawl. poet. 212. fol. 66v rev.

382 Fly misty fogs, black clouds that dark the skies
Ev'n so Lord Jesus come, Amen, Amen.

'Tho. Narien', i.e. Tanner, John, 'A Sober Whisper, concerning the Evil of Things present, and the Good of Things to come, 1665,' Fifth Monarchy poem.
See pr. bk. Bliss B. 394, 1665.
MS. Don. e. 23, fol. 1.

383 Fly, oh fly sad sigh and bear
Fear my fate would kill thee too.

Cartwright, [William], 'Absence'.
Pr. *Poems*, 1651, p. 258.
MS. Eng. misc. e. 241, fol. 25.

384 Fly oh fly thou lazy groan
And death unto her constant lover.

MS. Eng. poet. c. 50, fol. 116.

385 Fly paper kiss those hands
To her even so would I.

'To his Paper'.
MSS. Ashmole 47, fol. 47v; Douce f. 5, fol. 20.

386 Fly pleasure as a serpent which doth lie,
Earth's short contentment and th'eternal lose.

MS. *Don. f. 5, fol. 16v.

387 Fly ravished soul
And tender kisses, bowing down his head.

'A. 5. Voc., Martin Peerson'.
MSS. Mus. f. 11–15: f. 11, fol. 55v.

388 Fly soul as banished from my body's presence
Her only wink would fetch me home again.

MS. Rawl. poet. 120, fol. 9v.

389 Fly swift ye hours
Still court my ruin and embrace my chain.

Song.
F. B. Zimmerman, *Purcell*, 1963, no. 369.
MS. Mus. Sch. C. 61, p. 63 rev., music by H. Purcell.

Fly swift ye hours, ye sluggish minutes fly 390
And the famed Penshurst to our Windsor yield.

Duke, [Richard], 'To Cælia', 'F[rom] D[ryden's] Mis[cellany] Poems', 1684, p. 260.
MS. Rawl. poet. 222, fol. 35.

Fly swiftest winds to Strephon fly 391
The first-born softness of her soul.

Catch by Gilbert Heathcote, 1785.
MS. Mus. d. 177, fol. 17v.

Fly the falsehood of the fiend 392
And I shall help thee.

'Upon a Crucifixe in St. Alban's Church'.
MSS. Gough Herts. 3, fol. 75v; Rawl. poet. 26, fol. 1v.

Fly to my mistress yellow footed bee 393
Toll forth my death, and to my funeral come.

MS. Ashmole 38, p. 152.

Foe unto none, but to the foes of god 394
This prince of Britain god doth here dispose.

On Prince Henry's death, 1612.
MS. Rawl. poet. 116, fol. 2.

Foggers and flattering foisters 395
That are of the same nation.

'[John] Lilliat, Minister; his Prophesie. Octob. 2. 1599'.
MS. Rawl. poet. 148, fol. 109 (autogr.).

Foh! by my soul thou art a beastly word 396
Thou'rt gone; egad, thou stinkst too strong to last.

'A Satyr . . . Written by an Irishman'.
MS. Eng. poet. f. 13, fol. 16.

Follow a shadow it still flies you 397
Still the shadows of us men.

[Jonson, Ben.], 'Women mens shadowes'.
Pr. *The Forest*, vii.
MSS. Eng. poet. e. 14, fol. 75v; Rawl. D. 954, fol. 44; Rawl. poet. 209, fol. 34.

Follow me, my jovial boys 398
Ho! boy, fill a quart of sherry.

Catch by Ed. Nelham.
MS. Mus. d. 177, fol. 18.

Follow me sweet love of souls delight 399
Oh have thine own if thou wilt not do mine.

Pr. Michael East's *Second set of Madrigales*, 1606, v.
MS. Douce 280, fol. 70.

Folly and meanness only does inspire 400
And may we both His praises ever sing.

Williams, John, 'Goodness more to be desire'd than Praise'.
MS. *Rawl. poet. 191, fol. 97 (autogr.).

401 Folly in any I despise
And if she's wise she'll hold her peace.
Webb, Foster, 'Sit Doctissima Conjux'.
MS. Eng. poet. c. 9, p. 114.

402 Fond, feverish boy, why madly feed
To wish thou ne'er hadst enter'd there.
Homer, Philip Bracebridge, 'Reason's expostulation with Love'.
MS. *Add. C. 282, p. 50.

403 Fond flattering world thou ne'er shalt boast
With thine oh happy shore.
Walsh, Octavia.
Pr. *Poems upon Divine and Moral Subjects* by Dr. Patrick . . . and other . . . hands, 1719, p. 102.
MS. *Eng. poet. e. 31, fol. 164 rev. (autogr.).

404 Fond, hapless man, lost in thy vain desire,
If it but lodge, will quench, my flame.
King, John.
Pr. in *Poems of Henry King*, ed. Laurence Mason, 1914, p. 178. MS. reproduced *B.Q.R.* v, March 1929; cf. *B.L.R.* iv, 1953, p. 208.
MS. Rawl. D. 317, fol. 161 (autogr.).

405 Fond idle man! who toil'st in vain
And to almighty gain a drudging slave is made.
Chatwin, John, 'Humane Folly'.
MS. *Rawl. poet. 94, p. 21 (autogr.).

406 Fond idolizing eyes attempt no more
But tempt such lightning pointed looks no more.
MSS. Ashmole 36, 37, fol. 191.

407 Fond love farewell, I've something else to do
And ever vain, fantastic love I've sung this victory.
'The Retreive. Ode Pindarique'.
MS. *Don. c. 55, fol. 8 (autogr.).

408 Fond love is blind, blind therefore lovers be,
With those sharp arrows, she stole from thy quiver.
Pr. Thomas Bateson's *Second Set of Madrigales*, 1618, xxviii–xxix.
MSS. Mus. f. 20–24: f. 20, fol. 65$^{v}$.

409 Fond love, what dost thou mean.
The fault lies not in her, but you.
'Another' [Antiplatonick].
Pr. *Cleveland's Works*, 1687, p. 324.
MS. Rawl. poet. 173, fol. 83$^{v}$, attr. to Mr. Cleveland.

410 Fond love why dost thou dally
And thou of all cruelty go quit and clear.
MS. Ashmole 38, pp. 121 and 122.

Fond lunatic forbear. Why do'st thou sue 411
Doth in effect but cuckold his own bed.
King, Henry, 'Loves Harvest'.
Pr. *Poems*, 1657, p. 14.
MS. *Eng. poet. e. 30, fol. 57$^{v}$, corrected by H. King; *Malone 22, fol. 36.

Fond man, that canst believe her blood 412
Shed all the blood, felt all the smart.
[Carew, Thomas], 'A Lover upon his Mrs being lett Blood'.
Pr. *Poems*, 1640.
MSS. Eng. poet. e. 14, fol. 64; Mus. b. 1, fol. 73$^{v}$, music by John Wilson; Rawl. poet. 84, fol. 86$^{v}$.

Fond man that durst intrude thy rudest hand 413
And leave my substance, the second part to play.
'A Speech of a Weaver, once deputie Maior of Holt; in answer of a Libell against their authority'.
MSS. Ashmole 36, 37, fol. 48.

Fond man, why dost thou now adore 414
Thou shalt like it too be but reprobate.
Weaver, Thomas, 'To his Rivall Kissing a glove, which he had gotten from Sylvia'.
Pr. *Songs and Poems*, 1654.
MS. *Rawl. poet. 211, fol. 2$^{v}$ (autogr.).

Fond man, why vainly curious didst thou toil 415
Too fair a hanging for so mean a room.
Higham, E., 'On a gentle womans picture'.
MS. CCC. 328, fol. 27.

Fond men, that do so highly prize 416
You please the sense, and not the brain.
Pr. Thomas Tomkins *Songs*, 1622, iv.
MSS. Mus. f. 17–19: f. 19, fol. 5*b*$^{v}$.

Fond parents of their children fools do make 417
Not fond, nor harshly, but in manners sweet.
Robinson, Robert.
MS. *Rawl. poet. 218, p. 112 (autogr.).

Fond syllogism in vain 418
Thrice holy, holy, holy Trinity.
Beaumont, Jos[eph], 'Trinity Sunday'.
MS. Rawl. poet. 62, fol. 16.

Fond woman which wouldst have thy husband die, 419
Do London's mayor, or Germans the Pope's pride.
Donne, John, 'Elegye'.
Pr. *Poems*, 1633.
MSS. *Eng. poet. e. 99, fol. 15; *f. 9, p. 14; Rawl. poet. 117, fol. 186$^{v}$ rev., attr. to Mr. Donne.

420 Fond world farewell
Of slander and disgrace.
MS. Rawl. poet. 37, p. 115.

421 Fondness of man to love a she
Shipwracks his love on every shore.
Pr. Wilson's *Cheerfull Ayres or Ballads*, 1660, p. 110.
MS. Mus. b. 1, fol. 96$^{v}$, music by John Wilson.

422 Fool! Dost thou think that thou resemblest youth
That thou resemblest more the swan, than crow.
Hammond, Anthony, 'Martial Imitated', 'Oct. 1714'.
MS. *Rawl. poet. 129, fol. 1 (autogr.).

423 Fooled man be wise, consider and awake
Such magic power have eyes a conquest when they've won.
'A Religious Poem'.
MS. Rawl. poet. 19, fol. 17.

424 Foolish lover go and seek
For these flames extinguish thine.
[Stanley, Thomas].
Pr. Stanley's *Poems*, 1647, p. 20, and with music by John Gamble in his *Ayres and Dialogues*, 1656, p. 14.
MS. Mus. b. 1, fol. 140, music by John Wilson.

425 Fools and silly knaves knave-wise,
Lest knaves and fools do you surprise.
Robinson, Robert.
MS. *Rawl. poet. 218, p. 65 (autogr.).

426 Fools as they're fools, are scarce 'mongst men included
Wisemen, as men, in faith may be deluded.
Robinson, Robert, couplet.
MS. *Rawl. poet. 218, p. 135 (autogr.).

427 Fools at the other house to try the priest
You that can make your kings, can make your lords.
Address to the House of Commons in reference to the impeachment of Sacheverell, December 1709.
MS. Eng. poet. c. 41, fol. 23$^{v}$.

428 Fools from good rules learn only to transgress,
The best advice imprudently apply.
Williams, John, 'Of Rules'.
MS. *Rawl. poet. 191, fol. 15$^{v}$ (autogr.).

429 Fools most for empty short lived pleasures wed,
And not once fear or of their danger think.
Williams, John, 'Upon Marriage'.
MS. *Rawl. poet. 188, fol. 85 (autogr.).

Fools must be meddling in matters of state 430
The apartment for swiving in the verge of White-hall.
'Satyr on the Ladys of Honor. 1686'.
MSS. Eng. poet. c. 18, fol. 33$^{v}$; e. 49, p. 14; Firth c. 15, p. 209; c. 16, p. 115.

Fools who have money left them store, 431
So cheat them of it all.
Robinson, Robert.
MS. *Rawl. poet. 218, p. 170 (autogr.).

Fools will be fools, knaves will be knaves, 432
Are all, are all laid in the ground.
Robinson, Robert.
MS. *Rawl. poet. 218, p. 62 (autogr.).

For a poor living good men take great pains 433
Then come in knaves, that fetch away their gains.
Robinson, Robert, couplet.
MS. *Rawl. poet. 218, p. 90 (autogr.).

For ages past has Rome her pardons sold, 434
The pious doctor's laughed at for his pains!
Parsons, William, 'The Compounder for Adultery'.
MS. *Don. d. 123, p. 75 (autogr.).

For ages past, since Angelo the bold 435
For when you paint the face, you draw the life and soul.
'Upon his Painter Mr. Rob$^{t}$ Knapton'.
MS. Rawl. poet. 152, fol. 191.

For an apple of gold 436
As a dish of our coffee or tea.
'Strange news from St. James's . . . 1714'.
MSS. Eng. misc. c. 116, fol. 9$^{v}$; Eng. poet. c. 41, fol. 35; e. 87, p. 1; Rawl. poet. 81, fol. 47; 155, p. 73; 169, fol. 42; 181, fol. 52; pr. bk. Firth b. 22, fol. 17.

For banish'd J[ame]s prepare the bowl 43
And Western back as good ones carry.
'The British Toast for the 10th of J[une] 1715'.
MSS. Eng. misc. c. 116, fol. 8; Eng. poet. e. 87, p. 128.

For Christ his spouse, his cause, and at Christ tide 438
Within Christ temple, Christ's true lover died.
Couplet 'Uppon Tho: Beckett . . .' translating Latin printed in Camden's *Remaines*, 1605, p. 36.
MS. Ashmole 38, p. 175*a*.

For ever blessed be the Lord 439
Into the ways of peace and truth.
'The Song of Zacharias called Benedictus. Luk: 1. 68 ad 80'.
MS. Eng. poet. e. 51, p. 176.

440 For ever dear, for ever dreaded prince
To leave to read my verse and read my fortune.
[Harington, Sir John] 'To the Prince' [*sic*, for Queen Elizabeth].
Pr. Harington's *Letters and Epigrams*, ed. N. E. McClure, 1930, p. 258.
MS. Ashmole 47, fol. 21, attr. to R. Corbet; see also D466.

441 For ever fortune wilt thou prove.
Make but the dear Amanda mine.
Thomson, James, 'Song'.
Pr. without ascription in *The Hive*, 1732, iv. 1.
MS. Montagu e. 14, fol. 28.

442 For ever Lord are we cast off?
Of those contemn thy name.
Psalm lxxiv.
MS. *Rawl. C. 113, fol. 53.

443 For ever may the man be blest
And Christ shall come to judge us all.
On 'Rev. Philip Moore, 1783, Kirk-Braddan Church Isle of Man . . . [pr. Weedon] Butler's memoires of Bp. Hilderley [1799]'.
MS. Top. gen. e. 32, fol. 111.

444 For every hour that thou wilt spare me now
One that loves me.
Donne, John.
Pr. *Poems*, 1633.
MSS. *Eng. poet. e. 99, fol. 106$^v$; *f. 9, p. 74.

445 For every prince, that hit my fancy
Take pity on a gartered sinner.
'A Paraphrase of the D. of Bucks. Latin Epitaph' [John Sheffield].
MS. Ballard 50, fol. 193.

446 For fair Palmeria Blagden breathed his sighs
A duchess I—no—every inch a queen!
Parsons, William, 'Epigram on the approaching marriage of Miss Palmer with Lord Inchiquin'.
MS. *Don. d. 123, p. 206 (autogr.).

447 For fluent speech no birds with me compare
But though you speak most I write more than you.
[Owen's Epigrams]. '198. Crow' and 'Goose', translated.
MS. *Rawl. poet 197, fol. 9$^v$ (autogr.).

448 For giving me desire,
As light in flame, and heat in fire.
Traherne, Thomas, 'Desire'.
MS. *Eng. poet. c. 42, fol. 14$^v$ (autogr.).

For Gloucester's death (which sadly we deplore) 449
And to preserve the man destroy'd the boy.
'On the Death of the Duke of Gloucester. 1700'.
MSS. Eng. poet. e. 50, p. 148; Rawl. D. 361, fol. 55$^v$.

For God and man with wavering tongue 450
For thee all loves left, thou art mine.
'The Answer' to C701.
MS. Eng. poet. b. 5, p. 88.

For god I know did man create 451
From which you can not flee.
MS. *Rawl. poet. 100, fol. 1 (autogr.).

For God's sake come away and hand 452
Then joy in my companions; total sum.
Cavendish, Lady Jane, 'Passions invitation'.
MS. *Rawl. poet. 16, p. 15.

For god'sake hold your tongue, and let me love, 453
A pattern of your love.
Donne, John, 'The Canonization'.
Pr. *Poems*, 1633.
MSS. Eng. poet. c. 9, p. 6, attr. to Dr. Donne; *e. 99, fol. 107; *f. 9, p. 87; Rawl. poet. 117, fol. 203$^v$ rev., attr. to Dunne.

For health of body cover from cold thy head 454
To all indifferent richest dietary.
[Lydgate, John], 'Dietarium Salutis'.
Brown-Robbins Index, 824.
MS. Lat. th. d. 15, fol. 132.

For health, on air and exercise depend, 455
God never made his work for man to mend.
Dryd[en, John], couplet quoted in a note-book belonging to John Abbot of St. John's Coll. Oxford, matr. 1671.
MS. Rawl. D. 954, fol. 19.

For high prized ware no money's to spare: 456
Because it is basely wrought.
Robinson, Robert.
MS. *Rawl. poet. 218, p. 73 (autogr.).

For I have twigging wings can fly 457
Thou'lt see in banishment.
Polwhele, John, translator 'Boet[hius] L. 4 met. 1'.
MS. *Eng. poet. f. 16, fol. 33$^v$ (autogr.).

For if I did none other deed 458
Up into heaven to receive his mede.
Prophecy.
MS. Rawl. C. 813, fol. 145.

459 For Iris I sigh, and hourly die
So easy to part, and so easily joined.
Dryden, John, song from *Amphitryon*, set by 'Hen: Purcell'.
F. B. Zimmerman, *Purcell*, 1963, no. 572 (10b).
MS. Mus. Sch. C. 95, p. 222.

460 For Jesus sake in whose name I humbly crave
Move not this stone, nor disturb this grave.
Couplet 'In Hampstead Church Yard'.
MS. Eng. poet. e. 40, fol. 15.

461 For justice I'll appeal your father's care
But cry both mercy, and crave pardon here.
Pestell, Thomas, 'To the truly noble and gracious . . . the Lo: Visc: Mandevile', i.e. Edward Montagu (1602–71), Earl of Manchester 1642.
MS. *Malone 14, p. 46.

462 For love's sake kiss me, once again
Or wish our death.
[Jonson, Ben.], 'On Begging A kiss of his Mistress'.
Pr. *The Underwood*, ii. 7.
MS. Ashmole 38, p. 84.

463 For mankind Christ such great things suff'red hath
By the same word made man again anew.
MS. *Rawl. poet. 97, fol. 20$^{v}$ (autogr.).

464 For many unsuccessful years
What she for years denied.
Yalden, Thomas, 'Advise to a Lover, or, the way to win a woman'.
MS. Rawl. poet. 173, fol. 68$^{v}$.

465 For money and to please the flesh,
Wedlock's a sorry trade.
Robinson, Robert.
MS. *Rawl. poet. 218, p. 177 (autogr.).

466 For mountains, bridges, rivers, churches fair,
Women and wool, England is past compare.
Couplet translating hexameter.
MS. Lat. misc. c. 19, p. 425.

467 For my love sleeps now in his watery grave
We'll teach them to love and their cockles to kiss.
MS. Mus. Sch. C. 95, p. 255, no music.

468 For naughty boys and girls, 'tis fit,
They taste the rod, to teach them wit.
Robinson, Robert, couplet.
MS. *Rawl. poet. 218, p. 140 (autogr.).

For nimble wings have I 469
Whom wretches so much fear.
Bacon, Sir Nicholas (1623–1666), translation of Boethius, *Consolations*, IV. i, 1664.
MS. Tanner 306, fol. 340 (autogr.).

For no offence of mine my parents me 470
I will cares oblivion find.
James, Richard, 'Greeke epigram on wine'.
MS. *James 35, p. 19 (autogr.).

For one true generous silkworm, there are found 471
With covetous worldlings doth the world abound.
Robinson, Robert.
MS. *Rawl. poet. 218, p. 42 (autogr.).

For pity's sake banish the worms away 472
I will forget a tomb, and s[er]ve a shrine.
MS. Rawl. poet. 117, fol. 165 rev.

For present time a merry mind 473
Hates to respect what is behind.
Couplet, [translating Horace, *Odes* II. xvi. 25].
MS. Rawl. D. 986, fol. 110.

For shame Leuconoe leave thy oft know 474
That universe of joys were yet behind.
[le] N[eve], P[eter] (?), 'A paraphrase upon Horace', *Odes* I. xi, in P. le Neve's hand, initialed P. N.
MS. Eng. poet. d. 152, fol. 9$^{v}$.

For shame man wilt thou never leave this sorrow 475
To shorten the way as we gang along.
'Infortunatus', Ch. M., 'Ecgloga. Amor constans', between 'Dickye' and 'Bonnybootes'.
MS. Eng. misc. d. 239, fol. 2.

For shame thou everlasting wooer, 476
With the nice caution of a sword between.
Cleveland, John, 'The Antiplatonick'.
Pr. *Clievelandi Vindiciæ*, 1677, p. 14.
MSS. Add. B. 109, fol. 99; Rawl. poet. 116, fol. 62, attr. to Cleavland; 147, p. 94, attr. to Cleveland; 173, fol. 82, attr. to Mr. Cleveland.

For shame you doting fools, for shame be wise 477
Of your own ruin, and your sovereign's doom.
'On the Bishops', referring to Sacheverell, 1710.
MS. Rawl. poet. 169, fol. 12.

For standing Ubstft we kind nature thank, 478
. . . (incomplete).
Wilmot, John Earl of Rochester, 'Actus primus . . . etc. The Scene a Bed-chamber'.
See Vieth, p. 437.
MS. Add. B. 106, fol. 44$^{v}$.

479 For that I know thine humble eyes
Thou mayst live many a merry day.
Burton, Francis, [letter with a looking glass].
MS. *Add. A. 267, fol. 59ᵛ (autogr.).

480 For the few hours of life allotted me,
I'll thank for this, and go away content.
Cowley, Abraham, 'A short Prayer', from 'Essays, in Verse and Prose, 1. Of Liberty', pr. *Works*, 1668.
MSS. Rawl. poet. 90, fol. 90ᵛ; 173, fol. 168ᵛ; 213, fol. 5.

481 For the good cheer
Thus do I end my rhyme.
[Sheale, Richard], [A minstrel's farewell to a kind host]. In l. 4 'my name is Sheale'.
Pr. the *British Bibliographer*, Brydges and Haslewood, iv, 1814, p. 105.
MS. Ashmole 48, fol. 98ᵛ.

482 For the king's royal voyage and new expedition
Blazes awhile, goes out, and is no more.
'Momus Ridens; Or Comicall Reports on the Weekeley Reports' [8], 1690–1.
MS. Eng. poet. d. 53, p. 126.

483 For the Lord's goodness render thanks
For ever doth afford.
Psalm cxviii.
MS. *Rawl. C. 113, fol. 81.

484 For the miracles done
From the headpiece of William and Mary.
'Ballad of J (?)', written in 1691.
MS. Rawl. poet. 181, fol. 2.

485 For the promise of the Lord
The temples of our God.
Kenton, James.
MS. *Eng. poet. e. 20, p. 105 (autogr.).

486 For the year of Christ's incarnation
And as well for do as they have hitherto done.
'A mery prognostication', 1544. 19th-cent. copy from a 16th-cent. printed book.
MS. Eng. poet. e. 97, p. 197.

487 For thee all the hardships of life I could bear
And the friend of her heart to partake of it too.
'Nancy—a song'.
MS. Eng. misc. e. 241, fol. 101.

488 For thee, dear youth! my sorrows daily flow,
But mercy's deeper stream involves the immortal mind.
Maitland, Penelope, *née* Madan, 'Upon the untimely death of William Maitland . . . 1782'.
MS. Eng. poet. c. 51, p. 152.

For thee, sweet maiden of the Leame 489
Fierce winter's surly blast can never chill the soul.
Homer, Philip Bracebridge, 'A Summer Walk, written during the hard Frost, Janʳʸ. 1789: addressed to Miss S. Wheler'.
MS. *Add. C. 282, p. 8.

For thee, the muse's friend, a muse sincere 490
And add one vot'ry to sedition's train!
Percy, Thomas, nephew of the Bp. of Dromore, to R. B. Sheridan, 1782.
MS. Percy c. 8, fol. 83 (autogr.).

For them, that leave no monument 491
To say his tomb were rich, not he.
Shirley, James, 'Upon a Parson', with an 'Epitaph inscribed in a smale peice of Marble'.
Pr. from this MS., *Works*, ed. A. Dyce, 1833, vi. 501.
MS. *Rawl. poet. 88, p. 35.

For this additional declaration 492
By the next synod of the nation.
'The Dissenters Thanksgiving for the late Declaration' [1688].
Pr. *A Collection of the Newest . . . Poems . . . against Popery*, 1689, iii. 31.
MS. Firth c. 16, p. 264.

For this poor life we struggle and strive, 493
As if 'twere but a fable.
Robinson, Robert.
MS. *Rawl. poet. 218, p. 133 (autogr.).

For thy name's sake save me oh God 494
My enemies' defeat.
Psalm liv.
MS. *Rawl. C. 113, fol. 40ᵛ.

For to begin a work as yet unknown 495
To guide us right in truth even as it was.
'A newe worke Intittiled The offeringe of wisdom', verse prologue, 23 April 1609.
MS. Ashmole 1496, fol. 48.

For to love Charles our royal king 496
Like rogues that fight against our king.
'A song'.
MS. Rawl. poet. 152, fol. 20.

For treason taken ere the birth, doth come 497
Abortive, and her womb is made her tomb.
Couplet.
MS. Rawl. poet. 117, fol. 275 rev.

498 For two and twenty years long care
James the peaceful and the just.
Epitaph on James I.
Pr. Camden's *Remaines*, 1637, p. 399; attr. to G. M. in B.M. Add. MS. 30982, fol. 59v.
MS. Ashmole 38, fol. 186.

499 For virtue rarest
These ever marry, to be ever blest.
'The Lilly'.
MS. Rawl. poet. 84, fol. 116.

500 For wealth and place, why do we vainly strive?
Oh grief! he leaves his place and wealth behind him.
Robinson, Robert.
MS. *Rawl. poet. 218, p. 29 (autogr.).

501 For what do I unto Apollo sue
Contented always that on harp I play.
W. A., translator, Horace, *Odes* I. xxxi.
MS. *Rawl. poet. 104, fol. 10v (autogr.).

502 For what's the favour or the love of men
A thing long getting, and soon lost again.
Newman, Thomas, 'a distick'.
MS. Top. Oxon. f. 39, fol. 23 (autogr.).

503 For who can longer hold? when every press
Each drop of ink like aquafortis gnaw . . .
Oldham, John, 'Satyr'.
Drafts of prologue to the 'Satires upon the Jesuits', pr. *Compositions . . . of John Oldham*, ed. E. Thompson, 1770, i. 1.
MS. *Rawl. poet. 123, two drafts, pp. 174 and 177 (autogr.).

504 For why good lord thou hast me saved and kept
That I might amend whilst I have time and space.
MS. Ashmole 59, fol. 134v.

505 For wisdom and wealth, with other gifts more
From stately seat cast down to dust.
MS. Gough Norfolk 43, fol. 39v.

506 For wisdom, courage, valour every way;
Of the battle; as Deborah prophesied.
H. W., 'Sacred Epigram [8], Of Deborah a prophetesse and Judge of Israell'.
MS. Tanner 466, fol. 100.

507 For wondrous rare I late heard told
But thee to please, thee to admire.
North, Dudley, 3rd Baron.
Pr. *A Forest of Varieties*, 1645.
MS. *North e. 41, fol. 21.

For your good looks and for your claret 508
The spirits which your sack hath lent.
Strode, William, 'Thankes for a welcome'.
Pr. *Wits Recreations*, 1658, p. 104.
MS. *CCC. 325, fol. 84v (autogr.).
MSS. Eng. poet. e. 97, p. 108, attr. to W. S.; Rawl. poet. 142, fol. 43, attr. to W. Stroud.

For your rich roman ore, so well refined 509
Till you're both cloyed with full felicities.
'To Mr. T. B. in answer to a very kind and ingenious Epistle I Received from him in Latine Verse'.
MS. *Don. c. 55, fol. 21 (autogr.).

Forbear fond heart! while thou hast time retire 510
*Gratis* enjoy, what purchace must buy here.
Ashmole, Elias, '15 April 1649 10 A.M.'
MSS. Ashmole 36, 37, fol. 236v (autogr.).

Forbear fond swain I cannot love 511
Our selves as blameless as our sheep.
Pr. *Select Musicall Ayres and Dialogues*, 1653, ii. 5.
MSS. Don. c. 57, fol. 65v, with music by William Caesar; Rawl. poet. 65, fol. 27v.

Forbear, forbear all tears, he is not dead, 512
Blest hallelujahs to the heavenly king.
Fisher, William, of King's School, Sherborne, on the death of Robert Whetcombe, 'Antientest Governour of the King's Schoole of Sherebourne', 24 Oct. 1656.
MS. Gough Dorset 35 (1), fol. 23.

Forbear, forbear, unthinking wretch how long 513
Though oaths pass smoothly they at last will choke.
Williams, John, 'To a young Gentleman addicted to swear'.
MS. *Rawl. poet. 192, fol. 179 (autogr.).

Forbear my friend so rash a vow 514
You'll alter soon your love.
M[adan], M[artin], 1725–90, 'By a Gentleman who knew the Lady' of T313.
MS. Eng. poet. c. 51, p. 31.

Forbear my friend this fruitless zeal 515
Then I will weep no more.
'To a friend'.
MS. *Eng. poet. e. 28, p. 338.

Forbear my headstrong heliotropian thoughts 516
Suitors for grace, to her the most divine.
North, Dudley, 3rd Baron.
Pr. *A Forest of Varieties*, 1645.
MS. *North e. 41, fol. 23.

517 Forbear rash friend, and add not to thine own
In this life's sea; a way-mark unto thee.
'On Weymark an usurer': addressed to the author of S1112.
MS. Ashmole 38, p. 205.

518 Forbear thou crocodile, to mourn
Adieu to all thy joy.
Hulse, Thomas, 'Advice to the Widow'.
MS. *Rawl. poet. 152, fol. 77ᵛ (autogr.).

519 Forbear thou fair one and no more engage
That for your sake poor Tony fled and died.
'On Mrs. Kilmanseck's reading Cleopatra', [tr. from French by R. Loveday, 1687. Baroness Kielmannsegge, afterwards Countess of Darlington].
MSS. Rawl. poet. 155, p. 26; 207, p. 38.

520 Forbear thy grave advice, and let me love
Nor, by a cure, my fancied bliss destroy.
Webb, Foster, 'Paraphras'd from Dr. Donne', 1741.
MS. Eng. poet. c. 9, p. 6.

521 Forbear to boast your palaces, ye great
A murderess sure should for forgiveness pr[ay].
Warton, Joseph, 'On Miss Acton's Closet'.
MS. Don. c. 75, fol. 15 (autogr.).

522 Forbear to wonder how this comes to pass
Repent this fact that used his help to kill.
'On a Physitian'.
MS. CCC. 328, fol. 61ᵛ.

523 Forbear ye slanderers for pity
Each noon and eke each night.
'Excuse for the Prince's going to the play when the great fire hapned in the City 1715', Jacobite lampoon.
MSS. Eng. poet. e. 87, p. 113; Rawl. poet. 155, p. 106.

524 Forbear you cruel nymph forbear
Was, oh! my charming Betty Wade.
'On a Soldier's Dying for Love of a Servant Maid. 1720'.
MS. Eng. poet. e. 40, fol. 12.

525 Forbear your stoic rules, go read
Some court rich vices or a grave.
'An Epicures Speech'.
MS. Rawl. poet. 65, fol. 87ᵛ.

526 Forced from home and all its pleasures
Though theirs they have enrolld me . . . (incomplete).
'The Neg[r]o's complaint', on English slave-owners, *c.* 1790–1800.
MS. North e. 34, fol. 10ᵛ.

'Fore Caiaphas our Saviour silent stood 527
When time, and this world's troubles all are past.
MS. *Rawl. poet. 97, fol. 60ᵛ (autogr.).

Forgive blest shade the tributary tear 528
And trace thy journey to the realms of day.
'Epitaph in the Church Yard at Brading . . . Isle of Wight'.
MS. Percy d. 9, fol. 37.

Forgive him, no, damn me if I do 529
There scarce had now been left a man to bleed.
'Against Duelling . . . By Mr. H. C. of Kings Colledge'.
MS. Rawl. poet. 222, fol. 4ᵛ.

Forgive me blessed saint! that I 530
They may no greater ills than in their body find.
Chatwin, John, 'A Counter-Satyr to the Foregoing against Sobriety'.
MS. *Rawl. poet. 94, p. 40 (autogr.).

Forgive me Celia if I prove 531
Then devil take despair.
Song 'to the 6th Tune', i.e. tune on fol. 15.
MS. Mus. Sch. G. 636, fol. 11ᵛ.

Forgive me, if your looks I thought 532
Divinely blest if you prove true, undone if you forsake me.
MS. Rawl. poet. 196, fol. 2.

Forgive me, oh my God, my soul forgive 533
Thee love indeed, and ever trust thy care.
'A Prayer upon my having indiscreetly reported words spoke[n] by another . . .' *c.* 1711.
MS. Rawl. poet. 170, fol. 82 (autogr.).

Forgive me therefore if you sometimes see 534
Not to be angry with a man that's blind.
Williams, John, 'Love is blind'.
MS. *Rawl. poet. 191, fol. 158 (autogr.).

Forgive the infant muse whose artless lays 535
Beauty though much admired, must yield to these.
'Verses address'd to a Married Lady'.
MS. Eng. poet. e. 47, p. 67.

Forgive the muse, who in unhallowed strains 536
And glad all Heav'n with millions thou hast sav'd.
Prior, Matthew, 'To Dr. Sherlock, on His Practical Discourse Concerning Death'.
See Prior's *Literary Works*, ed. H. Bunker Wright and M. K. Spears, 1959, ii. 857.
Pr. *The Medley*, 7 May 1715.
MS. Eng. poet. e. 39, p. 24.

537 Forgive the muse, who in unpolished strains
And fly with transport to a bridegroom's arms.

'An Epistle from a Young Lady to a Revd Divine' endorsed '. . . to . . . Mr. Hall 1743 By Miss Jenny Best'.

MS. Ballard 47, fol. 60.

538 Forgive us oh ye new immortal pair
A better fate will make the sacred current dry.

'On the Ld. Derwentwater [and Lord Kenmure] who [were] beheaded on st. matthias day Feb. 25 17[15/]16'.

MSS. Rawl. poet. 181, fol. 78v; 207, p. 80.

539 Formed long ago, yet made today
And none would ever wish to keep.

Riddle.

MS. Eng. poet. c. 51, p. 130.

540 Forming, by degrees to bliss, mankind
And new perfections, new delights bestow.

'The Goodness of God to Man'.

MS. Eng. poet. e. 39, p. 215.

541 Forrest hath changed a weary life *for rest*
A weary life for rest in Abraham's lap.

'On one Forrest'.

MS. Don. d. 58, fol. 16.

542 Forsaken first and now forgotten quite
And love to change . . .

A fragment, crossed out.

MS. Rawl. poet. 85, fol. 83v.

543 Forsaken Strephon in a lonesome glade,
Refreshed, like slave from racks, to greater pain.

[Villiers, George], D[uke] of Buckingh[am], 'The lost Mistress a Complaint agst. the Countess etc.'

Pr. *Works*, 3rd ed., 1715, i. 147.

MS. Rawl. poet. 173, fol. 70.

544 Forth from my sad and darksome [the dark and dismal] cell
Will fire the bush at his back.

'A new Tom of Bedlam'.

Pr. *Prince d'Amour*, 1660, p. 170; J. Playford's *Choice Songs and Ayres*, 1673, p. 66. See Percy's *Reliques*, ed. H. B. Wheatley, 1876, ii. 344, and Ritson, *Select Collection of Songs*, ed. T. Park, 1813, ii. 162. Cf. *Poetical Works of Basse*, ed. R. W. Bond, 1893, p. 133.

MSS. Malone 19, p. 65; Mus. Sch. C. 96, fol. 3, with melody as pr. by Playford; see also L49.

545 Forth from the den, where the mad merry men
And there's an end of my medley.

MS. Rawl. poet. 26, fol. 154v.

Forth in a morning a morning of May 546
And I'll row it in my apron fine.

'My Apron Deary'.

MS. Eng. poet. e. 8, fol. 6v.

Forth walking to receive the breathing air 547
And not your persons or your virtues woo.

James, Richard, 'On Altesa a Noble commelye Ladye'.

MS. *James 35, p. 19 (autogr.).

Fortunate isles no more your vines adore 548
And soon expect some dreadful thunder stroke.

'Of the Scudamore Crab or Red-strake Cider'.

MS. *Don. f. 5, fol. 36.

Fortune contended [contending] whether she should yield 549
That Day should lose the field and Field the day.

'On Feild and Day standing for the Procteorshippe'.

Pr. *A Crew of Kind London Gossips*, 1663, p. 100.

MSS. CCC. 328, fol. 80v; Eng. poet. c. 50, fol. 132v; Firth e. 4, p. 103.

Fortune does blush at the bold minds of those 550
Who, what is long in gaining, rashly lose.

Couplet.

MS. Add. B. 8, fol. 75v.

Fortune had never raised thee but to show 551
That nothing is so strange but she can do.

Walsh, William, couplet 'out of the Greek [Anthology, p.] 163'.

MS. Malone 9, fol. 27 (autogr.).

Fortune had once a darling she did store 552
They'll rather die there rich; than live here poor.

Southwell, Sir Robert, 'A Storme'.

MS. *Eng. poet. f. 6, fol. 34 rev. (autogr.).

Fortune is blind, and oft we know, 553
And keeps from them of worthy parts.

Robinson, Robert.

MS. *Rawl. poet. 218, p. 120 (autogr.).

Fortune made up of toys and impudence, 554
Rather than follow such a dull, blind whore.

Vill[i]ers, Geo[rge], D[uke] of Buck[ingham]. Adapted from Horace, *Odes* III. xxix. 49–56.

Pr. *Works*, 3rd ed. 1715, i. 139.

MS. Rawl. poet. 173, fol. 34.

Fortune nature love long have contended about me 555
But most wretched I am now love awakes my desire.

Sidney, Sir Philip, 'elegiall verses' from the *Arcadia*.

MS. *e Mus. 37, fol. 45.

556 Fortune proud in her dexterous returns
To see man fall, and rise in the same hour.
Polwhele, John, translator, 'Boet[hius] L. 2. m. 1'.
MS. *Eng. poet. f. 16, fol. 20v (autogr.).

557 Fortune [that blind supposed Goddess is]
You make the fault, and call your saint unkind.
Quarles, [Francis], 4 lines from the 9th 'Pious Meditation' printed with *A Feast for Wormes*, 1620, Sig. M3v.
MS. Sancroft 59, p. 162.

558 Fortune's a false inconstant fickle jade
Riches they have and would be quality.
'Epilogue, by the Sham Marquiss in [Susan Centlivre's] the Gamester'.
MS. *Rawl. poet. 197, fol. 13 (autogr.).

559 Fortune's darling king's content
And yet (alas) here lies but one.
Epigram on the Duke of Buckingham. 1628.
MS. Malone 23, p. 143.

560 Fortune's so blind she law and reason hates
Because that shows her power unbounded best.
Walsh, William, 'out of the Greeke [Anthology, p.] 163'.
MS. Malone 9, fol. 27v (autogr.).

561 [Forty] or black appear certain
. . . or this rose be red.
'Thomas Charnock his pose Upon the White and Red Rose'. 1572.
MS. Ashmole 972, fol. 191v.

562 Forward, Janus, turn thine eyes
By whom all nature smiles, and beauteous order reigns.
[Whitehead, William], New Year Ode 1770.
Pr. *Poems*, 1790, ii. 99.
MS. Mus. Sch. D. 323. Music by Boyce.

563 Foul envy thou
Thy actions end in blood.
Lilliat, John, 'A Description of Envy, or the Image of Envy'.
MS. Rawl. poet. 148, fol. 112 (autogr.).

564 Foul fall him brought the second match to pass
He knew not what he did, not what it was.
Translation of Latin epigram.
MS. Rawl. D. 1372, fol. 33.

565 Foul grief and death this year have played their parts
The birth to my discomfort and sad breath.
North, D[udley], L[ord], 'On . . . Lady Rich', 1638.
Pr. *A Forest of Varieties*, 1645, p. 79.
MS. Eng. misc. e. 262, fol. 32v.

Foul I am, and cannot tell 566
Least by his blood in vain w'have purged been.
Colman, Henry, 'On the Lords Supper'.
MS. *Rawl. poet. 204, fol. 32v (autogr.).

Foul vanities, to you; 567
For evermore adieu.
Lilliat, John, couplet translating 'Splendidis longum valedico nugis'.
MS. Rawl. poet. 148, fol. 1 (autogr.).

Founded upon the hills of holiness 568
Of my fresh fountains every spring.
Herbert, Mary (*née* Sidney), Countess of Pembroke, Psalm lxxxvii.
MSS. *Rawl. poet. 24, p. 128; *25, fol. 82v.

Fountain of all our happiness 569
Thy brightest glories show.
Kenton, James.
MS. *Eng. poet. e. 20, p. 168 (autogr.).

Fountain of endless life divine 570
And shall forever last.
Kenton, James.
MS. *Eng. poet. e. 20, p. 13 (autogr.).

Fountain of holiness 571
To worlds of endless day.
Beddome, Benjamin.
MS. *Eng. misc. e. 227, fol. 53v.

Fountain of light and life divine 572
Outshine the orbs of yonder skies.
Kenton, James.
MS. *Eng. poet. e. 20, p. 212 (autogr.).

Fountain of light unsetting sun 573
A heaven prepared for me.
Beddome, Benjamin.
MS. *Eng. misc. e. 227, fol. 11.

Fountain of pity, now with pity flow 574
Where light of life with living men I see.
Herbert, Mary (*née* Sidney), Countess of Pembroke, Psalm lvi.
MSS. *Rawl. poet. 24, p. 79; *25, fol. 47.

Fountain of Wotton, clear as glass 575
And yield them like relief.
Gough, Richard. 'Gratitudini sacrum, [1763] Printed [Nichols] Lit. Anecdotes vi 336 . . . Imitation of Horace Carm. III 13'.
MS. *Eng. poet. c. 5, fol. 102 (autogr.).

Four brothers and a sister such I had 576
They were most his, so saved amongst the few.
Cavendish, Lady Jane. 'On my deare Brothers and Sisters'.
MS. *Rawl. poet. 16, p. 31.

577 Four Chief Justices late we had
Upstart Sir Nicholas Hyde.
'Uppon 5 Cheyff Iustices of the Kings bench', Sir Ed. Coke, Sir Henry Montagu, Sir James Ley, Sir Ranulph Crew, Sir Nicholas Hyde, 1613—5 Feb. 1626/7.
MS. Ashmole 38, p. 87.

578 Four clerks of Oxford, doctors two and two
As Rawleigh from his voyage and no more.
Corbett, Richard, 'Iter Boreale'.
Pr. *Poems*, 1647, p. 120.
MSS. Ashmole 47, fol. 8, attr. to Dr. Corbet; Eng. poet. c. 50, fol. 47, attr. to Docter Corbet; e. 14, fol. 2, attr. to Dr. Corbett; e. 97, p. 14, attr. to Dr. Corbett; Rawl. poet. 172, fol. 143, attr. to Dr. Corbet; 206, p. 1, attr. to Ri. Corbet; Wood D. 19 (2), fol. 72, attr. to Rich. Corbet.

579 Four evils there are that chiefly trouble a house;
When children cry for hunger, wanting bread.
MS. Rawl. D. 954, fol. 43.

580 Four harnessed steeds came up in pompous state.
Her monkey has. Let men then have their apes.
'On the honourable Mr. Spencer Cowper and his Man in a Chariot', 1735.
MS. Eng. misc. e. 240, p. 259.

581 Four impudent cits, stockjobbers I mean,
This once she would pardon, 'cause 'twas midsummer moon.
'On the Banks Men'.
On the visit of Sir Gilbert Heathcote etc., representing the Bank, to Queen Anne on the dismissal of Sunderland, June 1710.
MSS. Eng. poet. e. 87, p. 130; Rawl. poet. 81, fol. 45; pr. bk. Firth b. 21, fol. 73$^{v}$.

582 Four months i'th' cold, four months i'th' heat.
Into three parts the year's divided.
Robinson, Robert.
MS. *Rawl. poet. 218, p. 73 (autogr.).

583 Four rivers watered paradise of old
Job, David, and wise Salomon can tell.
Gray, —, 'To the Right Hon:ble Sr John Rivers . . . on his bounty to the Schole of Tunbridge in divers excellent bookes'.
MS. Rawl. poet. 246, fol. 35.

584 Four sapskulls met in deep debate
They all decamped, but oh! their beds.
Cf. W946.
MS. Don. c. 57, fol. 89.

585 Four squires o'th' body and brothers are we,
He keeps both the hands warm, cleanly and fine.
Robinson, Robert.
MS. *Rawl. poet. 218, p. 47 (autogr.).

Four teeth of late thou hadst, both black and shaking 586
Now from the tooth ache, thou dost live secure.
Martial, *Epigrams* I. xix. Pr. Davison's *Poetical Rhapsody*, 1608.
MS. Don. d. 58, fol. 38.

Four teeth she had, she coughed, and spit out twain, 587
The third cough has nought left to work upon.
Martial, *Epigrams* I. xix.
MS. Rawl. D. 1147, fol. 89.

Four teeth thou hadst, that ranked in goodly state 588
Th' hast left the third cough now no business there.
Cr[ashaw], R[ichard], Martial, *Epigrams* I. xix.
MS. Tanner 465, fol. 96.

Four things in drinking breed one discontent 589
Fly dice, fly women, but fly drinking most.
'Of Drunkardes'.
MS. Malone 19, p. 48.

Four tongues like trumpets Rome do sound thy fame 590
Thy height of strength, is backward love of place.
'Roma', Protestant rhyme.
MS. Rawl. D. 317, fol. 76.

Frail are a lover's hopes 591
That does his heart insnare.
[Mr. Northman, translator], song from *Camilla*, by M. A. Bononcini.
Cf. A. Nicoll, *History of English Drama, 1660–1900*, ii, 3rd ed. 1955, p. 274.
MS. Mus. c. 107, fol. 67.

Frail beauty, boast not of that face 592
Love me, and live to all eternity.
T[atham], J[ohn].
Copied from *Ostella*, 1650, p. 76.
Pr. bk. 27980 e. 86, p. 26.

Frail glass, thou bearest my name, as well as I. 593
And no man knows, in which it first shall die.
Ruddyard, Benjamin, couplet 'In a Window in Lambhith-House Gallerie', with Latin translation by Sancroft.
MS. Sancroft 48, fol. 23$^{v}$.

Frail nature's dissolution, and the hour 594
And reign with him through all eternity.
Kenton, James, 'An Essay on Death'.
MS. *Eng. poet. e. 19, p. 1 (autogr.).

595 France totters under these three royal names
For William fate reserves both name, and thing.
Translation of libel fixed on 'the King of France's Statue in the Place of Victory', for which the libellers were tried 8 August 1689.
MS. Sancroft 53, p. 308 rev.

596 Francisca dead! strange not, to think this voice
The common course, and wish ourselves the joy.
Oldisworth, Giles or Robert, 'Verses once upon Mrs. Margery Apjohn's death', adapted for the death of Francesca Oldisworth.
MS. *Rawl. C. 422, fol. 29, in the hand of Giles Oldisworth.

597 Frankly pour oh Lord on me
Striving them to understand.
Herbert, Mary (*née* Sidney), Countess of Pembroke, Psalm cxix 'F'.
MS. *Rawl. poet. 24, p. 178; *25, fol. 120.

598 Franklyn's beauty does surprise
She's safe from writing and from talking.
'On the Maids of Honor'.
MS. Firth e. 6, fol. 106.

599 Free from ambition, free from care
And join with me, to welcome you.
Bate, Sally, 'The Wish . . . written in 1764'.
MS. *Eng. poet. e. 28, p. 285.

600 Free grace alone elected some to bliss
Let God's sole glory all our motion guide.
[Arrowsmith, Dr. John], translation of Latin poem: *Gratia sola Dei certos elegit* . . . 'Syn[odus] Dordresis', 1620.
See Arrowsmith's *Armilla Catechetica*, 1659, p. 175.
MS. Rawl. D. 1372, fol. 56 from end.

601 Freed from his keepers, thus with broken reins,
Before his ample chest the frothy waters fly.
'The similitude of an Horse from Homers Iliads'.
MS. Eng. poet. c. 9, p. 51.

602 Free'd from th'oppressive power
A rest of endless love.
Kenton, James.
MS. *Eng. poet. e. 20, p. 85 (autogr.).

603 Freedom with virtue takes her seat,
To kites and meaner birds he leaves the mangled prey.
[Cowley, Abraham], 'Upon Liberty'.
Pr. *Works*, 1668, 'Discourses by way of Essays in Verse and Prose', p. 88.
MSS. Rawl. poet. 90, fol. 92v; 213, fol. 47v.

French valets in spite of all clamour inherit 604
But a Frenchman's a slave ready made.
'Quære Peregrinum'.
MS. Percy c. 8, fol. 26.

French wine makes meagre and thin 605
A health to King Portugal John.
Samber, Robert, 'The old woman cloathed in gray'.
MS. Rawl. poet. 11, fol. 33 (autogr.).

Fret not dear Tom that you have lost the race 606
Above he domineers, and rules below.
Plaxton, Mr., 'A Satyre on the Yorkshire Elections, In a letter from Jemmy Singleton to his Friend Tom Pullen about the Races', 1708.
MS. Eng. poet. c. 18, fol. 194v.

Fret not thyself for wicked men 607
Because in God they trust.
Psalm xxxvii.
MS. Rawl. poet. 170, fol. 42 (autogr.).

Fret not thyself, if thou do see 608
Because on him their trust is laid.
Sidney, Sir Philip, Psalm xxxvii.
MSS. *Rawl. poet. 24, p. 50; *25, fol. 29v.

Fret not thyself nor envious be 609
Who their trust on him place.
Psalm xxxvii.
MS. *Rawl. C. 113, fol. 30v.

Fret not thyself nor yet envious be 610
Save from the wicked those that in him trust.
Fairfax, Thomas, Lord, Psalm xxxvii.
MS. *Fairfax 40, p. 79 (autogr.).
MS. *Fairfax 38, p. 179.

Fret not thyself when thou shalt see 611
In him they put their trust.
Psalm xxxvii.
MS. *Montagu e. 10, fol. 56v.

Fret on fond Cupid curse thy feeble blow 612
I'll laugh and bid him shoot them o'er again.
MS. Rawl. poet. 65, fol. 26v, subscribed 'Jer. Savill', composer of setting.

[Frewen] Fruyn and Pottir glorious and divine 613
That all thy sons may prove like thee their father.
'A libell uppon the Doctors of Oxon 1627'.
MS. Douce f. 5, fol. 12v.

Friend I salute thee in the Lord 614
Of their malignity.
Bunyan, John. 'Prison-Meditations Directed to the heart of Suffering Saints and Reigning Sinners', 1665.
Printed as a broad-sheet.
MS. Rawl. poet. 58, fol. 25.

615 **Friend if you will now show your skill**
**And then what man can mend her.**
'To chuse a wife'.
MS. Eng. poet. e. 14, fol. 48v.

616 **Friend, let not care, how to increase thy store,**
**And whether rich or poor, I leave to fate.**
Mervall, Alphonso, 'A satir. To his freind Parthenus': 'agst Covetousness' added later.
MS. *Rawl. poet. 166, p. 68 (autogr.).

617 **Friend of the moss-grown spires and crumbling arch,**
**Deep from thy eyes profane her gothic charms!**
'An Epistle from Thomas Hearn, Antiquary, to [Thomas Warton] the Author of *The Companion to the Oxford Guide* etc.' 1760.
MS. Top. Oxon. c. 296, fol. 39.

618 **Friend since Metellus days thou dost rehearse**
**And cheer my heart with singing songs of love.**
W. A., translator, Horace, *Odes* II. i.
MS. *Rawl. poet. 104, fol. 13 (autogr.).

619 **Friend, sister, partner of that gentle heart,**
**To teach that prudence which itself admires.**
Langhorne, Dr. [John], 'Precepts of Conjugal Happiness; Address'd to a Lady on her Marriage'.
MS. Montagu e. 14, fol. 52.

620 **Friend sit not here, unless thou be**
**Do not these sacred shadows haunt.**
'To the new Peripatetique Colledge Errant of Novellists, Rumourists, Buzzists . . . in Graye's Inne Walkes', dated May, 1628.
MS. Rawl. poet. 166, p. 89.

621 **Friend: think not time, or wind, or place**
**Take water, and come back again.**
Oldisworth, Nicolas. 'To his Friend beyond Sea . . . Written 1629 to Mr. Richard Bacon'.
MS. *Don. c. 24, fol. 9 (autogr.).

622 **Friend, thou hast stained the cheek of priase to see**
**A Parian quarry, and forever live.**
Wood, H., 'To the much honoured and most accomplisht Mr. Howell on the 2d part of his Grove' [1650].
MS. Rawl. poet. 142, fol. 49 (autogr.).

623 **Friend to the poor! for sure, oh king**
**And hail our monarch's natal day.**
[Whitehead, William], Birthday Ode, 1767.
Pr. *Poems*, 1790, ii. 90.
MS. Mus. Sch. D. 319. Music by Boyce.

**Friends give me leave I cannot but lament** 624
**Tears blurs my paper I can write no more.**
Hooper, J[ohn], 'A poem uppon the deaths of my Father and Brother who dyed in the yeare 1665'. Cf. F625.
MS. *Rawl. poet. 208, fols. 4, 3v and 5 (autogr.).

**Friends give me leave in this poor ragged verse** 625
**Tears blur my paper I can write no more.**
'A poem of Mr. Gosnalls who made it uppon the death of Mrs. Sarah Hanes'.
MS. Rawl. poet. 208, fol. 5.

**Friends like to leaves that on the trees do grow,** 626
**But he more happy, that no friend doth need.**
'Friends'.
MS. Rawl. poet. 90, fol. 54v.

**Friends mutually should strive to show** 627
**Who wont delight to please his friend.**
MS. Eng. poet. e. 47, p. 77.

**Friends partly fools, but chiefly knaves, who stand** 628
**Turn to your duty, *ergo*, hang yourselves.**
'Amend Your Lives'.
MS. Rawl. poet. 181, fol. 17.

**Friends, soldiers, women in their prime** 629
**Friends soldiers women are not thought upon.**
Epigram.
MSS. Ashmole 38, p. 14; Eng. poet. f. 10, fol. 114v.

**Friendship is less apparent when too nigh,** 630
**That their love then seems but self-love to be.**
Fleming, Robert.
MS. Rawl. poet. 213, fol. 65 (autogr.).

**Friendship is love, from all its dross refined** 631
**To aid our joys, and dissipate our woes.**
'On friendship, to Miss Arabella Bate'.
MS. *Eng. poet. e. 28, p. 64.

**Friendship like kingdoms have more surely stood** 632
**Now sigh his elegy and the Kingdom's next.**
Paman, Clem[ent], 'On the death of Mr. Hervy'.
MS. Rawl. D. 945, fol. 38.

**Friendship on earth we may as easily find,** 633
**He that has many pays for it in the end.**
'On Freindship'.
Pr. *Poems of Pembroke and Ruddier*, 1660, p. 48.
MSS. Ashmole 36, 37, fol. 124, attr. to Dr. Donne; 781, p. 162; Rawl. poet. 117, fol. 270 rev.

634 Friendship, peculiar boon of heaven
Shall aid our happiness above.

Johnson, Dr. Samuel, 'Friendship an ode'. First pr. *Gentleman's Magazine*, July 1743; see *Poems*, ed. Nichol Smith and McAdam, 1941, p. 99.
MS. Eng. poet. c. 51, p. 5.

635 Friendship, so much by sots professed
To bubble one another.

'On Fashionable Friendship'.
MS. *Eng. poet. d. 47, fol. 161.

636 Friendship's become at best an empty name,
To love your neighbour and in God to trust.

Bate, Sally, 'To Miss Arabella Bate . . . 1767'.
MS. *Eng. poet. e. 28, p. 130.

637 Frogs make, they say, a savoury mess
Let none but Frenchmen eat 'em.

'Quære Peregrinum'.
MS. Percy c. 8, fol. 25v.

638 From a dissimilynge [*sic*] friend unjust
I cannot imagine a more dangerous evil.

Note at end: 'finis ye autor unsertayn'.
MS. Ashmole 48, fol. 98.

639 From a dozen of peers made all at a start
And from the French harpies preserve us once more.

'A New Litany', Dec., 1711.
MS. Firth c. 3, fol. 1.

640 From a Dunstable dean beneath a degree
And a wife who's already provided a mitre.

'The new Litany to be Sung in three parts', on Dean Herbert Ashly or Astley, of Norwich 1670–1681, his father-in-law John Hobart, and his wife Barbara.
MS. Tanner 95, fol. 120v.

641 From a gipsy in the morning
And whilst he is mortal we'll not think him so.

Jonson, Ben., 'prayer for King James, a Caracter of his humours'.
From the Masque *The Gipsies Metamorphos'd*.
MS. Eng. poet. f. 16, fol. 9.

642 From a religion that put the devil i' th' stocks
Who have contrived all our sorrows, *quaesumus te*.

'The True Englishmans Litany', two parts *c*. 1685 (?).
MS. Don. e. 23, fol. 56v.

643 From a sensual, proud atheistical life,
From making our heirs to be Morris and Clayton.

'A Litany', on George Villiers, second Duke of Buckingham.
MS. Eng. misc. d. 295, fol. 7.

From a servant of Diana, as faithful as the best 644
And at her foot go.

See *D.N.B.* on Robert Cecil, at end.
MS. Don. c. 54, fol. 7v.

From a small acorn, see! the oak arise 645
And by the expanded acorn rules the main.

'De minimus maxima', Latin verses by L. Duncombe of Merton College, 'Translated by another Hand'.
MS. Eng. misc. e. 183, fol. 77v.

From a tall precipice on the sea-side, 646
Stands most exposed to th' shock of sudden fate.

[Tate, Nahum], 'The Prospect'.
Pr. *Poems*, 1677, p. 24.
MSS. Rawl. poet. 90, fol. 116; 173, fol. 156.

From age to age the Lord was our refuge 647
And bring the same to well succeeding end.

Harington, Sir John, Psalm xc.
MS. *Douce 361, fol. 54v.

From all implacable tormentors 648
No traitor like Jack Presbyter.

'A Grace out of Hudibras', Jacobite imitation; the opening months of the reign of George I.
MS. Eng. poet. e. 87, p. iii.

From all the mischiefs I shall mention here, 649
The rightful heir, and we will ask no more.

'Litany for the year 1715'. Jacobite verse.
MSS. Eng. poet. e. 87, p. 105; Rawl. poet. 155, p. 98.

From all the women we have whored 650
And never see Breda again.
*Quaesimus* [*te Audire nos Domine.*]

'A Litany for the Holy time of Lent', satirically subscribed 'Obediah Walker', 1688.
MS. Douce 357, fol. 154v.

From an impudent town that was always unjust 651
Is both our duty and our gain to pray.

'A New Litany', 1689.
MS. Firth e. 6, fol. 57v.

From an old inquisition and new declaration 652
For ever good heaven deliver me.

'A Short Littany . . .' [1688].
Pr. *Poems on Affairs of State*, 1689, iv. no. 25.
MS. Firth c. 16, p. 286.

From an old king of Bashan I challenge my birth, 653
Which with ease you may do, since the same is half told.

Hulse, R[alph (?)], 'Ænigma'.
MS. Eng. misc. e. 183, fol. 80v.

654 From ancient stock she did descend
Her soul in heaven enjoys eternal life.
Lincoln cathedral: inscription, 1612, copied 'from Bp. Saundersons MS in 1641'.
Pr. Browne Willis's *Cathedrals*, 1742, iii. 25.
MS. Willis 71, fol. 208$^v$.

655 From authors seldom understood
And manage her rebelling clay.
Hammond, Anthony, 'A Letter to a Freind'.
MS. *Rawl. poet. 129, fol. 19.

656 From barren highlands in the frozen north
Deem that their honour others count their shame.
'The Scotchmans Character out of Edwd. Wards Works'.
MS. Eng. misc. c. 116, fol. 3.

657 From beauty's queen, and Bacchus ever young
The gout an offspring maimed and crippled sprung.
'An Epigram on the Gout', couplet.
MS. Eng. poet. c. 9, p. 107.

658 From bitter bottom of my stiff strained heart
And all that him adore of Jacob's stock.
Lilliat, John. 'Davids Dumpe'.
MS. Rawl. poet. 148, fol. 108 (autogr.).

659 From Campden in county of Gloucester we're told,
Consider the kingdom, 'tis cut after kind.
'London Evening Post Dec$^r$ 8th 1784', on fox-hunting.
MS. Ballard 47, fol. 138.

660 From Carrick, where the noble Ormond met
He'll write as bad. God bless my Lord Lieutenant.
Weaver, Thomas, 'A relation of an Entertainment to a Country-gentlemans house in Ireland'.
Pr. *Songs and Poems*, 1654.
MS. *Rawl. poet. 211, fol. 30$^v$ (autogr.).

661 From Citheron the warlike boy is fled
And must dissolve by fire.
Pr. Byrd's *Songs of sundrie natures*, 1589, xix–xxi.
MSS. Mus. f. 11–15: f. 15, fol. 18$^v$.

662 From city unto city having fled
And set me free from sin and sequestration!
Wake, William, of Cambridge, Psalm cxliii. 9.
MS. Eng. misc. d. 1, fol. 36.

663 From clime to clime with restless toil we roam
And (Daphne like) transforming, fool us in th' embrace.
'Disappointed'.
MS. Rawl. poet. 90, fol. 119$^v$.

From conscience the second, and prerogative pother 664
From all men, that mean it, when they cry, vive le roy.
'A new Letany', *c.* 1680.
MS. Don. b. 8, p. 656.

From death our saviour eke hath raised them 665
To that Elijah did at Zarephath.
MS. *Rawl. poet. 97, fol. 51$^v$ (autogr.).

From deep gulfs of misfortune 666
He gently will untie.
Da[vison], Fr[ancis], Psalm cxxx.
MSS. *Rawl. poet. 61, fol. 57$^v$; 117, fol. 256$^v$.

From depth of grief 667
Forgetting follies, faults forgiving.
Herbert, Mary (*née* Sidney), Countess of Pembroke, Psalm cxxx.
MSS. *Rawl. poet. 24, p. 197; 25, fol. 131$^v$.

From depth of sin, oh lord to thee 668
To hear me day and night.
Byrd's 3-part setting of Psalm cxxx.
Pr. *Songs of sundrie natures*, 1589, vi.
MSS. Mus. f. 11–15: f. 11, fol. 5$^v$.

From dreary shades [wastes] and winding cells 669
Shall run to meet me at my birth.
'A Riddle on a Sir-Reverence'.
MSS. Eng. poet. e. 40, fol. 135; Eng. misc. e. 241, fol. 121$^v$.

From Dunkirk in France, in the month of September, 670
And drink a health to great George our King.
'Thurot's Defeat'.
MS. Firth c. 18, fol. 100.

From earth we came, here live a while, 671
In bliss eternally.
Robinson, Robert.
MS. *Rawl. poet. 218, p. 173 (autogr.).

From earth we have our mortal bodies, death: 672
On earth peace, love to men perpetually.
MS. *Rawl. poet. 97, fol. 18$^v$ (autogr.).

From earthly mould through the womb's door, 673
Through that to earth we're hurled.
Robinson, Robert.
MS. *Rawl. poet. 218, p. 40 (autogr.).

From easing females of their pain 674
The first such knight as e'er was seen.
'The Midnight Knight', Sir David Hamilton.
MS. Eng. poet. e. 50, p. 15.

From Egypt Christ to His own country came 675
To save all nations, that believe, repent.
MS. *Rawl. poet. 97, fol. 41$^v$ (autogr.).

676 From Eleanor, my friend, these lines pray read
And in such wishes make me blest.
Peart, Eleanor, 'To Miss Arabella Bate. Dec. 19, 1768'.
MS. *Eng. poet. e. 28, p. 308 (autogr.).

677 From England, Scotland, Wales and Ireland
Obedience, till the rest conform to it.
Weaver, Thomas, 'The Isle of Man'.
Pr. *Songs and Poems*, 1654.
MS. *Rawl. poet. 211, fol. 26$^{v}$ (autogr.).

678 From England when with favouring gale
Proclaim all's well.
'In the Heartford Bridge [by William Pearce] . . . composed by Mr. Shield' [1792].
MS. Mus. e. 19, p. 49.

679 From England's happy and unequal state
Guilt shuns the light; foxes the lion's paw.
Harvy, John, 'One the Princes goeinge to Spayne', 1623.
MS. Malone 19, p. 35.

680 From evils of every kind, I perceive
For a lock that is open to all.
C[owper], M[aria] F. C., 'The Locke Chapel'.
See *The Madan Family*, F. Madan, 1933, p. 112.
MS. Eng. poet. c. 51, p. 39.

681 From exile Christ returned to Nazareth
And such is Christ, therefore best fits His state.
MS. *Rawl. poet. 97, fol. 41$^{v}$ (autogr.).

682 From famed Augusta, pride of Albion's isle
I will be ever dear Zaretta thine.
'Epistle to Zaretta'.
MS. Rawl. poet. 195, fol. 157$^{v}$.

683*a* From famed Barbados on the Western main
And fall on fiercely like a starved dragoon.
'For makeing a sack Possett'.
MS. Firth c. 16, p. 138.

683*b* From fame's desire, from love's delight retired
For she less secret and as senseless is.
MS. Douce 280, fol. 69.

684 From famous St. Peter's, we are lately advised
Cried Zounds 'tis an earthquake, come let us drink on.
'Momus Ridens, or Comicall Remarks on the Publick Reports. 4', 1690–1.
MS. Eng. poet. d. 53, p. 114.

685 From farthest west, to where the Ganges flows
Fools only place blind fortune in the skies.
Juvenal, *Satires*, II. x.
MS. Douce 201, fol. 96.

From Father Hopkins whose vines did inspire him 686
Either ten to one the prices will fall.
'Bays his Blind Side', on Dryden.
MS. Firth c. 16, two copies, pp. 96, 101.

From flesh to fish, from flap to fan 687
From fast to loose, from man to man.
'Dr. Haydock of his wife that before was a butchers wife', Epigram.
MS. CCC. 327, fol. 32$^{v}$.

From fleshly lust, from thirst of gold 688*a*
So great are their temptations.
Robinson, Robert.
MS. *Rawl. poet. 218, p. 135 (autogr.).

From Foxhole coppice roused, Great Britain's king I fled 688*b*
But what, in Kiddington Pond he overtook me dead.
Couplet at Ditchley on stag killed by James I, 24 Aug. 1608.
MS. Hearne's diaries 67, p. 28.

From Foxhole driven what could I do being lame I fell 688*c*
Before the king and Prince near Rozamond her well.
Couplet at Ditchley on stag killed by James I, 25 Aug. 1610.
MS. Hearne's diaries 67, p. 29.

From going to Bath with little money in my purse 689
Good Mercury defend me.
Weaver, Thomas, 'A Letanie upon occasion of a Journey to Bath'.
Pr. *Songs and Poems*, 1654.
MS. *Rawl. poet. 211, fol. 67$^{v}$ (autogr.).

From grave lessons and restraint 690
If he's false I'll be so too.
'A Song'.
MS. Montagu e. 13, fol. 55.

From grave seasons and restrain 691
I must not durst not cannot fly.
Verse written in music book.
MS. Mus. Sch. F. 576, fol. 37$^{v}$.

From grinding care, and thrift secure 692
Complete is my felicity.
Stukeley, William, 'The Druid', 19 Oct. 1758.
MSS. *Eng. misc. d. 450, fol. 32 (autogr.); d. 454, fol. 1 (autogr.).

693 **From happy climes where virtue never dies**
**And call one injured James from exile home.**
[Meston, William], 'Cato's Ghost', Jacobite verses on Addison's play.
Pr. Meston's *Decadem alteram*, 1738.
MSS. Eng. misc. c. 116, fol. 10v; Eng. poet. e. 87, p. 116; Rawl. D. 383, fol. 106; Rawl. poet. 155, p. 34.

694 **From harmony from heavenly harmony**
**And music shall untune the sky.**
'Song for St. Cecilia's Day by Mr. [John] Dryden composed by G: F: Handel', dated at end 10 May 1749.
MS. Mus. d. 58.

695 **From heaven no doubt, we are descended all:**
**For why? who may not god his father call?**
Oldisworth, Nicolas, 'On Nobility', couplet.
MS. *Don. c. 24, fol. 57v (autogr.).

696 **From heaven the father views his son below**
**Who signs the pardon and his wounds are seals.**
Pr. *Parthenia Sacra*, ed. I. Fletcher, 1633, p. 100.
MS. Eng. poet. b. 5, p. 105.

697 **From hell and judgement Judas saved mankind,**
**It's fit Iscariot should be canonized.**
'Englished' from Latin verse on 'Mr. Porter'.
MS. Rawl. poet. 181, fol. 9.

698 **From hell's dread monarch sent I envoy come**
**Distant as good was ever from this soul.**
Oldham, John, 'Garnet's Ghost', draft for the first 'Satyr Upon the Jesuits'.
MS. *Rawl. poet. 123, p. 246 (autogr.).

699 **From high Olympus and the realms above**
**The queen of love is queen of beauty crowned.**
'Masq of Paris and the 3 Goddessess . . . words . . . set for the prize for Music'.
MS. Top. Oxon. c. 108, p. 2.

700 **From horror huge of dark despair and deep**
**Can cleanse thee from thy sins and set thee free.**
Harington, Sir John, Psalm cxxx.
MS. *Douce 361, fol. 82.

701 **From hunger or cold who lives more free**
**And tumble in the grass or in the haycock.**
[Brome, Richard], 'The Soldier's Songe'. From *A Jovial Crew, or The Merry Beggars*, act I.
MSS. Rawl. poet. 142, fol. 45v; 153, fol. 24.

702 **From hunting whores and haunting play,**
**To all the ports she has designed.**
'Sir George Etheredge to the Earl of Middleton Greeting'.
MS. Firth c. 16, p. 172 and incomplete on p. 86.

**From immoderate fines and defamations** 703
**And from all that to this paper will not say Amen.**
'A New Littany in the year 1684'.
MS. Rawl. poet. 159, fol. 101.

**From Isis's banks which, near the poet's seats** 704
**Flow backwards must the streams, and I'll forget to love.**
Jones, J. of Balliol, 'On Nancy Brickenden's going to Newnham by Water'.
Pr. *The Oxford Sausage*, 1764, p. 109.
MSS. Ballard 50, fol. 99, attr. to Mr. Jones; Eng. poet. f. 12, p. 101, attr. to J. Jones of Balliol College; Top. Oxon. e. 379, fol. 8.

**From Jesse's stem a branch shall shoot, of grace** 705
**The leopard with the kid in peace shall lie . . . (incomplete).**
Isaiah xi, from 'A Paraphras'd collection of some Prophecyes of the old Testamt. concerning Christ'.
MS. *Rawl. C. 113, fol. 5v (autogr.).

**From Jesuitical polls who proudly expose** 706
**For ever good Lord deliver me.**
'A New Littany'.
Pr. *A Collection of the Newest Poems against Popery*, 1689, iii. 8.
MS. Firth c. 16, p. 254.

**From Julia's whiter hand a snow ball came** 707
**Neither with snow nor ice but equal love.**
MS. Rawl. poet. 116, fol. 92.

**From Katherine's dock was launched a pink** 708
**And make her fit for any port.**
Lampoon on Frances Howard, Countess of Somerset, 26 Dec. 1613.
MSS. Ashmole 38, two copies, pp. 135 and 136; Firth d. 7, fol. 151; Malone 19, p. 94; Rawl. D. 1048, fol. 64v; Rawl. poet. 26, fol. 18; 160, fol. 163.

**From Kings, that would sell us, to pay their old scores** 709
**When all are as false, as the saving of Flanders.**
'A new Letany', 1680.
Pr. *Poems on Affairs of State*, iii, 1704, p. 205.
MS. Don. b. 8, p. 650.

**From lasting and unclouded day** 710
**Nor shall Cornelia shed a tear.**
Phillips, Mrs. [Katherine], song in *Pompey*, act III.
MS. Rawl. poet. 196, fol. 19.

**From London to Scotland** 711
**King George's youngest son.**
'A New Song. By Mr. Rann, one of his Majesty's Foresters at Windsor'.
MS. Firth c. 20, fol. 47.

712 From Mahomet and paganism
Than usquebath or aquavite.
Pr. *Merry Drollery*, 1670, i. 174.
MSS. Ashmole 36, 37, fol. 46$^{v}$.

713 From me dear Charles inspir'd with ale
The cart would drive and I be hang'd.
'A Letter from W: Tunstal in the Marshalsea To Charles Woogan in Newgate'. Answered by Y253.
[Sir Charles Wogan was captured at Preston 14 Nov. 1715 and escaped from Newgate 4 May 1716].
MS. Rawl. poet. 155, p. 221.

714 From measuring devotion with beads or with sand
From a representative monster thats all over rump.
'The second part of the loyall subjects Litany' [1680].
Pr. as a broadside (pr. bk. Godw. Pamph. 2204/38).
MS. Douce 357, fol. 92.

715 From my devotions yonder am I come
You come both the entertainer and the guest.
[Cartwright, William], 'The Prologue to the K. & Q.', from *The Royal Slave*.
MS. Rawl. poet. 172, fol. 25$^{v}$.

716 From my pleasant hermitage
Which (as I've heard) was my birth day.
Ashmole, Elias, verse letter, 23 May 1648. See W2433.
MSS. Ashmole 36, 37, fol. 231$^{v}$ (autogr.).

717 From my sad cradle to my subtle chest
And after comes the judgment of the just.
Inscription at Long Ashton to Joseph Crossman, d. 20th Jan. 1671.
MS. Rawl. D. 1090, fol. 170.

718 From night, and night alone, black fate descends,
Just mild in temper, and in council wise.
'Terribiles visu formæ. Virgil'. 1734.
MS. Eng. misc. e. 240, p. 97.

719 From noise, from crowds, from all th' ill judging world
The judge of all the earth will do what's right.
Lumby, John, 'A Serious Fit'.
MS. *Eng. poet. e. 42, fol. 50.

720 From noise of scarefires rest ye free
My masters all, good day to you.
Herrick, Robert, 'The Belman'.
Pr. *Hesperides*, 1648.
Pr. bk. 27980 e. 86, before p. 57.

From Nottingham ale, and Halifax law 721
Oh Devil, I say take Musgrave and Clargis.
'The Devil Tavern Clubb'.
MS. Eng. poet. c. 18, fol. 96$^{v}$.

From Oberon and fairy land 722
And wind out laughing, ho ho, ho.
MS. Malone 19, p. 93.

From one that languisheth in discontent 723
Rest you in much content, I in despair.
'S$^{r}$ George Radney to the Countess of Hartford', December 1600; cf. D344.
Cf. G.E.C., s.v. Hertford.
MSS. Ashmole 38, p. 32; 781, p. 158, copied between 16 June 1626–8 Oct. 1639; Rawl. poet. 160, fol. 117$^{v}$.

From out the depth of misery, I cry 724
Sing praise to Thee.
Jos. Br., Psalm cxlii.
MS. Rawl. poet. 61, fol. 64.

From outward cares, and noise retir'd 725
On the bright sun, and never die.
Bromley, Henry, 'The wish'.
MS. *Don. e. 19, fol. 10 (autogr.).

From Oxford to — did my horse jog, 726
Neither master, nor horse, would be able to move.
'On a Horse and his Master alternately lean and fat'.
MS. Ballard 47, fol. 43$^{v}$.

From Paphos isle, so famed of old 727
Where Cupid is captain and Venus the queen.
'Cupids Recruiting Serjeant'.
MS. Mus. e. 19, p. 33.

From pastoral scenes and rural love 728
You'll always love your fireside.
Endorsed 'The Fireside. A song by Mr. [Henry] P[ercy] in his own Handwriting'.
MS. Percy c. 8, fol. 1 (autogr.).

From peaceful vales where murm'ring waters flow 729
And hug his memory in the arms of death.
'The slighted Lover'.
MS. Rawl. poet. 152, fol. 166.

From pensioner papist and dragoons 730
That would bring us all to pay Peter pence.
'A new Litany'.
MS. Rawl. poet. 172, fol. 80.

From Persia's throne to earth's remotest ends 731
And, whom so much you mimic, ah forgive!
Shenstone, William, 'Flattery, or the fatal Exotick, a Satirical Rhapsody'.
MS. Montagu d. 1, fol. 194 (autogr.).

732 **From Pindus' top where rules the god of day,**
**But angels join Cecilia's song.**
'Ode on Music', autograph of the composer Philip Hayes, dated Sept. 3, 1783.
MS. Mus. d. 69.

733 **From poor folk's bellies, poor folk's backs,**
**Whilst a poor creature all things lacks.**
Robinson, Robert.
MS. *Rawl. poet. 218, p. 101 (autogr.).

734 **From pure, and upper regions come**
**But sinking shall the happy port attain.**
Bromley, Henry, 'The Voyage'.
MS. *Don. e. 19, fol. 13$^v$ (autogr.).

735 **From R. to H. distant two**
**God send thee good fortune.**
Prophecy.
MS. Rawl. C. 813, fol. 155.

736 **From Rome's infallibility take one grain**
**And 'tis the true catholic cordial posset.**
'To make a Caudle for a Sick Jesuit'.
Pr. *The Muses Farewell to Popery and Slavery*, 2nd ed., 1690, p. 213.
MSS. Don. e. 23, fol. 61; Firth c. 16, p. 136.

737 **From rural cot the lines I write to you**
**To make it Heaven nought I want but you.**
'An Epistle from a Gentleman in the Country to a Young Lady in Town'.
MS. *Eng. poet. d. 47, fol. 120.

738 **From sable regions of eternal night**
**It shrinks it back into eternal night.**
'The Prophetic Speech of the Earl of Desmond's Ghost, to the Lord Pore [John, Baron Le Power] . . . Aug. 25, 1688'.
Pr. *Poems on Affairs of State*, iii, 1698, p. 202; see also G.E.C. iv, 1916, p. 257.
MS. Firth e. 6, fol. 79.

739 **From Salamis that glorious isle I come**
**And bring you news and noble verses home.**
Verses from Plutarch's Life of Solon, not North's translation, nor 'Dryden's'.
MS. Rawl. D. 1372, fol. 28 from end.

740 **From scenes of blood and lowering skies**
**And angels hymn th' eternal reign of peace.**
'Annual Address', to Sylvanus Urban, 1781. *Gentleman's Magazine*.
MS. Eng. poet. c. 5, fol. 247.

741 **From scenes of death, and deep distress.**
**Beneath a Brunswic's reign.**
[Whitehead, William], Birthday Ode, 1772.
Pr. *Poems*, 1790, ii. 109.
MS. Mus. Sch. D. 328. Music by Boyce.

**From scenes of ruin and of blood** 742
**Which Britain's wealth and fame destroy'd.**
Duncombe, J. (?), '1777. To Sylvanus Urban Gent. From [back] of Title'. *Gentleman's Magazine*.
MS. Eng. poet. c. 5, fol. 244.

**From school, mature in books and knowledge,** 743
**And sick of pleasures scarce enjoy'd.**
Warton, Thomas (1728–90).
Pr. as 'The progress of discontent' in *The Student*, Oxford, 1750, i. 235.
MS. Don. c. 75, fol. 62 (autogr.).

**From Scotland some let letters fully tell** 744
**I will not have one papist on my side.**
Rhymed newsletter sent to Daniel Fleming, 10 Oct. [1681].
MS. Don. c. 38, fol. 290.

**From scourging rebellion and baffling proud France** 745
**To his glory your voices and instruments raise.**
'From Hogg's Collection of Whig Songs'.
Pr. James Hogg, *The Jacobite Relics of Scotland*, ii, 1821, p. 465.
MS. Mus. e. 20, fol. 11.

**From shamming of popish plots and treason** 746
**Having just slipped the halter there.**
'Jeffries's Appeal to Pluto: on the late Votes of Attainder', endorsed '1689'.
MS. Rawl. poet. 159, fol. 62.

**From silent shades and from the Elysian groves** 747
**In her thoughts is as great as a king.**
'Bess of Bedlam'.
Pr. *Choice Ayres and Songs*, iv, 1683, p. 45. F. B. Zimmerman, *Purcell*, 1963, no. 370.
MSS. Eng. poet. c. 6, fol. 97; Mus. Sch. C. 96, fol. 4$^v$, melody by H. Purcell.

**From six mishaps good god thou me defend** 748
**For where they live there is but woe and strife.**
MS. Rawl. poet. 172, fol. 38.

**From smutty small coal kindling angry flame;** 749
**Strephon the wild, the bold, the witty, and the gay.**
Roach, Richard, 'To Mr. T. Briton: Alias the True Briton: On the famous Panegyric, in his Paper, upon the Bp. of R[ocheste]r'.
*The True Briton*, vii, 24 June 1723.
MS. Rawl. D. 832, fol. 258 (autogr.).

**From sounds celestial sounds arose** 750
**And to the stars exalt her name.**
'Song on St. Cecilia's Day', composer's draft (?).
MS. Mus. c. 6, fol. 53.

751 **From such a fate whose excellence**
**Heaven bless my sovereign and all his senses.**
[Drummond, William (?)], 'The five senses'.
Pr. first in *Works of William Drummond*, 1711, 'Poems', p. 55; see *Poems of Drummond*, ed. Kastner, ii, Scottish Text Soc. N.S. iv, 1913, p. 296.
MSS. Eng. poet. c. 50, fol. 25; e. 37, p. 72; Malone 23, p. 28; Rawl. poet. 26, fol. 72, dated 1623; 117, fol. 23$^{v}$; 160, fol. 14$^{v}$; Tanner 465, fol. 97.

752 **From suffering clean escap'd away**
**Where all is harmony and love.**
Kenton, James, 'Epitaph . . . for Mrs. Elizabeth Honalt', 1788.
MS. *Eng. poet. e. 19, p. 338 (autogr.).

753 **From sweet bewitching tricks of love**
**The blind eat many a fly.**
'The Caution [. . .] recd. from Atchem 12 April 174[ ]' (damaged).
Pr. Ritson's *Select Collection of English Songs*, 1783, i. 104.
MS. Mus. e. 20, fol. 13; pr. bk. 27980 e. 86, after table of contents.

754*a* **From the beginning we have evidence**
**From earthly things to thoughts far more sublime.**
MS. *Rawl. poet. 97, fol. 51$^{v}$ (autogr.).

754*b* **[From the beseiged Ardea all in haste]**
**And wastes huge stones with little water drops.**
[Shakespeare, William], extract from *Lucrece*, ll. 958–9.
MS. Rawl. D. 954, fol. 41$^{v}$.

755 **From the blest region [regions] of [the] eternal day**
**Britain shall be his throne for time to come.**
'The Lord Lucas His ghost'.
Pr. *A Third Collection of songs against Popery*, 1689, p. 22, etc., as 'The Earl of Essex's Ghost, 1687'.
MSS. Add. A. 48, fol. 45; Don. b. 8, p. 554; e. 23, fol. 44; Rawl. D. 924, fol. 315.

756 **From the blest regions, the ethereal plains,**
**You in these rejoins, will rejoin your friend.**
Bate, Sally, 'From Lady Tavistock (After her Death) To [her sister-in-law], the Duchess of Marlborough, 1768'.
MS. *Eng. poet. e. 28, p. 301.

757 **From the brat of a king by a queen of the stage**
**For ever kind Heaven deliver me.**
'A Littany for the Lady Mary Ratcliff'.
MS. Firth c. 16, p. 245.

758 **From the bright orient to the west**
**The Lamb alone shall be my kind.**
Tune, 'Poore Robins dreame'.
MS. Rawl. poet. 37, p. 58.

**From the cold caverns of the north** 759
**And we as willing slaves obey!**
Parsons, William, 'To [Miss Catherine Clarke] on her wishing for a heavy fall of snow to prevent Lady Clarke from leaving Bath'.
MS. *Don. d. 123, p. 224 (autogr.).

**From the contagious breathing of the rude** 760
**You are the voice I but your echo am.**
'A Mixt Elegie in allusion to Ladies Verses'.
MS. Eng. poet. e. 97, p. 159.

**From the dark caverns of the earth I come** 761
**That Oxford did for treason lose his head.**
'The Apparition Or Gregg's Ghost to the Earl of Oxford'.
Pr. 1715. Wm. Gregg, clerk in Harley's office, executed for treason, 1708.
MS. Rawl. poet. 155, p. 64.

**From the dark Stygian banks I come** 762
**Th' Assyrians palace to his urn.**
[Ayloffe, John], 'Mervill's Ghost'.
Ascribed to Jo. Ayloffe in *Poems on Affairs of State*, 1697, p. 160; cf. *D.N.B.*
MS. Don. b. 8, p. 572.

**From the deep caves of hell below** 763
**And heavens eclipsed face did shroud.**
MS. Rawl. poet. 213, fol. 48$^{v}$.

**From the deep dungeon of the infernal cave** 764
**And use a language I can live and hear.**
'A song by S:W:'; cf. F765.
MS. Rawl. poet. 84, fol. 107$^{v}$ rev.

**From the deep entrails of a gloomy cave** 765
**For 'tis a language all the world would hear.**
'T. ff$^{s}$: A$^{r}$: perswadeing Cæ[lia] to sigh on'; cf. F764.
MS. Rawl. poet. 84, fol. 107 rev.

**From the Dutch coast when you set sail,** 766
**'Tis the advice of Dr. Lower.**
'Dr. Lowers advice . . . to K. W[illiam]', on the Marquis of Carmarthen, 1690.
MSS. Eng. poet. c. 18, fol. 95$^{v}$; e. 49, p. 92; Firth d. 13, fol. 71; Rawl. poet. 159, fol. 127; 169, fol. 14.

**From the fair Lavinian shore** 767
**For here it is to be sold.**
[Davenant, Robert].
Pr. *The Mysteries of Love and Eloquence*, E[dward] P[hillips], 1658; *Prince d'Amour*, 1660, p. 177; and *The Musical Companion*, 1673.
MSS. Mus. d. 8, two copies, fols. 27$^{v}$–29$^{v}$, glee by John Wilson re-written by Philip Hayes; Rawl. poet. 65, fol. 23.

768 From the goblin and the spectre
And while he's mortal, we'll not think him so.
'Ben Johnson to King James', in *The Masque of Gypsies*.
MS. Ashmole 47, fol. 90.

769 From the hag, and hungry goblin
Me thinks it is no journey.
'Blesse thy faire eyes from the foule feind', indexed as 'Tom o' Bedlam's Song to K. James'.
MS. Tanner 465, fol. 86$^{v}$.

770 From the honoured dead I bring
And for your dead friend shed a tear.
MS. Mus. b. 1, fol. 43, music by John Wilson.

771 From the lawless dominion of mitre and crown
From the King of France, and the French King.
'The Antiphone to the late protestant petition', 1680.
MS. Don. b. 8, p. 696.

772 From the man whom I love, though my heart I disguise
He will sure take a hint from the picture I draw.
'Song. The Picture of a Frenchman'.
MS. Eng. poet. e. 39, p. 217.

773 From the saint to the sinner, from the prince to the clown
This silver and gold is sweeter than honey.
Robinson, Robert.
MS. *Rawl. poet. 218, p. 66 (autogr.).

774 From the same stock the human race
True worth alone has praise.
Skinner, John, translator, 'The 6th Section of the Verses of Boethius, [*Consolations*], Book 3'.
MS. *Eng. poet. d. 22, fol. 99.

775 From the Stygian abyss
But no art can soften hell.
S[hirley], J[ames], 'Orpheus'.
Pr. from this MS., *Works*, ed. A. Dyce, 1833, vi. 499.
MS. *Rawl. poet. 88, p. 21.

776 From the womb of the earth
What a whimsical creature am I.
'A Riddle'.
MSS. Eng. poet. e. 8, fol. 15; Montagu e. 13, fol. 155; Rawl. D. 833, fol. 196.

777 From thee Eliza I must go
And thine the latest sigh.
Burns, Robert, 'The Ayrshire Plowman'.
Pr. *Poems*, 1787, p. 332.
MS. Montagu e. 14, fol. 11.

From thee I nothing hear; yet I can tell 778
No more breath, than would sigh thee to thy grave.
Oldisworth, Nicolas, 'For a Lover. To his absent Mistris'.
MS. *Don. c. 24, fol. 71$^{v}$ (autogr.).

From them that rise against me Lord defend 779
Who art my strength thy goodness Lord I'll sing.
Fairfax, Thomas, Lord, Psalm lix.
MS. *Fairfax 40, p. 131 (autogr.).
MS. *Fairfax 38, p. 222.

From these few lines, this lesson let me learn 780
I need not wish, or fear to die.
Bate, Sally, 'A Soliloquy . . . upon seeing some Verses on a Tombstone in Metheringham Church Yard in Lincolnshire, 1767'.
MS. *Eng. poet. e. 28, p. 117.

From this blest minute I'll begin to date 781
And (though a younger son) make me his heir.
Ashmole, Elias, 'To my worthily honour'd William Backhouse Esqr. Upon his adopting of me to be his Son. . . 13 May 1653'.
See C. H. Josten in *Ambix*, iv, Dec. 1949, pp. 17, 21.
MSS. Ashmole 36, 37, fol. 241$^{v}$ (autogr.).

From this one crime what various woe 782
Where all but fools, are in disguise.
'On Drunkeness'.
MS. Engl. poet. e. 28, p. 360.

From this small token take the letter G 783
And then 'tis love, and that I send to thee.
Couplet, 'On sending a paire of Gloves'.
MS. Rawl. D. 954, fol. 40; see also I764, I766, I964.

From twelve years old to thirty we do find 784
And daily for increase of wisdom, pray.
MS. *Rawl. poet. 97, fol. 48$^{v}$ (autogr.).

From unnatural rebellion, that devilish curse, 785
And from swearing to be true to W[illiam] and M[ar]y.
'The Litany . . . till Ireland be reduc'd'. Second part, B654.
MS. Firth e. 6, fol. 12.

From verdant fields my birth I claim 786
Ambition, such thy gains at last.
Amherst, Elizabeth, 'A riddle'.
MS. *Eng. poet. e. 109, p. 56.

From versifying I'm resolved to rest 787
On whom I have all my affections stayed.
W. A., translator, Horace, *Epodes* ii.
MS. *Rawl. poet. 104, fol. 53 (autogr.).

788 From villany dressed in a doublet of zeal
From the plagues that are kept for a rebel in store.
'A new Litanie'.
Pr. R. Fletcher's *Ex Otio Negotium*, 1656, and hence Cleveland's *Poems*, 1659.
MSS. Jones 56, fol. 173; Rawl. poet. 246, fol. 14$^v$.

789 From Virgil's tomb, and Baia's coast
A subject for a Virgil lyre!
Parsons, William, 'Verses to Miss Clarke at Bath'.
MS. *Don. d. 123, p. 223 (autogr.).

790 From whence first was this fury hurled
And raging as the northern wind.
[Carew, Thomas], 'First Chorus of Jealousie'.
Pr. *Poems of Pembroke and Ruddier*, 1660, p. 69.
MS. Malone 13, p. 67; see also F792.

791 From whence proceeds this great surprise?
And from your eyes receive my doom.
'Spoken to Pulcheria', 1735.
MS. Eng. misc. e. 240, p. 316.

792 From whence was first this fury hurled?
And raging as the northern wind.
Carew, Thomas, 'A Chorus of jealousie'.
MS. *Don. b. 9, fol. 4; see also F790.

793 From witty men and mad
Bedlam's the best of universities.
MS. Mus. f. 19, fol. 83$^v$.

794 From York to London [town] we [are] come
Amen Amen Amen.
'London's defiance to Rome . . . Procession and solemn burning of the Pope at Temple Barr 17 Nov. 1679 as it was then printed'.
MSS. Ashmole 36, 37, fol. 325; Don. b. 8, p. 609.

795 Frown whilst you'll frown, since you your smiles deny
We'll kindly sleep in an eternal kiss.
'A Frown To my incomparable Philista'.
MS. Add. B. 106, fol. 27$^v$.

796 Frugality is no philosophy
A spawn of lust, in sack and Johnson sod.
Chapman, Ge[orge], 'Epicures frugallitie'.
Pr. from this MS., *Poems*, ed. P. B. Bartlett, 1941, p. 373.
MS. Ashmole 38, p. 10.

Full as a bee, with thyme, and red 797
He'll do no doubt, this yarn is spun.
Herrick, Robert, 'King Oberons Pallace'.
MSS. Ashmole 38, two copies, pp. 101, 105; Firth e. 4, p. 52, attr. to Mr. Hearick; Rawl. poet. 160, fol. 167, attr. to R. Herick.

Full easy we in others find a spot 798
When what we should be, we ourselves are not.
Robinson, Robert, couplet.
MS. *Rawl. poet. 218, p. 143 (autogr.).

Full fathom five thy father lies 799
Ding dong bell.
[Shakespeare, William], song from *The Tempest*.
Pr. J. Wilson's *Cheerfull Ayres*, 1660, p. 6 (air by Johnson).
MSS. Mus. c. 5, fol. 10, three-part song by John Wilson; Mus. d. 184, fol. 64, two of Wilson's parts, copied 19th–20th cent.

Full forty times over I strived to win 800
If you once but approach they can ne'er hold it out.
At end, 'Rich: Bawdybrowne'.
MSS. Ashmole 36, 37, fol. 188.

Full forty years, I think, are now expir'd, 801
But fate has sheath'd it in eternal shade.
'Damon complains to Delia of the Infirmities of his Age'.
MS. *Eng. poet. d. 47, fol. 96.

Full fourscore years and six it was before 802
Thou may'st with fearless valour meet thy fate.
Fry, Charles, of King's School, Sherborne, on the death of Robert Whetcombe, 'Antientest Governour of the King's School of Sherebourne', 24 Oct. 1656.
MS. Gough Dorset 35 (1), fol. 21.

Full hard it is all minds content to have 803
And specially in matters hard and grave.
Verses found in North's Plutarch, Life of Solon (folio 1603, p. 95).
MS. Rawl. D. 1372, fol. 26$^v$ from end.

Full low on ground then did I lie 804
Both hand and feet.
Ollivier, Isaack, 'To his freind S. B.', i.e. Samson Briggs (?).
MS. Rawl. poet. 210, fol. 67$^v$.

Full of my God, and victory, I come 805
Virgin's and angel's lives agree.
Paman, Cl[ement], verse dialogue, 'Jud[ges] XI 34'—end.
MS. Tanner 466, fol. 28$^v$.

806 Full of rebellion, I would die,
To hide my dust, then thee to hold.
Herbert, George, 'Nature'.
Pr. *The Temple*, 1633, p. 37.
MS. *Tanner 307, fol. 28ᵛ.

807*a* Full often times ev'n from my youth
That you may get your corn together.
Harington, Sir John, Psalm cxxix.
MS. *Douce 361, fol. 81ᵛ.

807*b* Full paunches have lean pates, and dainty bits
Make rich the ribs, but bankèrupt the wits.
Couplet.
MS. Rawl. poet. 117, fol. 156 rev.

Full sixteen hours and eke a half! 808
This moment send me word by Ned.
Lumby, John, 'To Mr. Goodenough then out of order with a Pain in his left Ear'.
MS. *Eng. poet. e. 42, fol. 86.

Further example seek thou none 809
Thou canst but see the dust of man.
G. B., 'Epitaph 13' in 'Cestria Lugens', on Prince Henry, 1612.
MS. *Rawl. poet. 116, fol. 8.

Fuscus is free and hath the world at will 810
But falls into the whorehouse by the way.
Davies, Sir John, 'In Fuscum'.
Pr. amongst 'Epigrames' with *Ovids Elegies*, tr. C. M., [*c.* 1600].
MS. *Add. B. 97, fol. 45ᵛ; see also F251.

# G

ENTRIES 1–608

1 Gaily I lived as ease and nature taught
Should think on me who never thought on him.
'Regnier's Epitaph'.
French version written by F. Douce in *Oeuvres*, Mathurin Rengier, 1616, pr. bk. Douce R. 84.
MS. Eng. misc. e. 241, fol. 101v.

2 'Gainst harmless science is defiance,
Where troops of soldiers are.
Robinson, Robert.
MS. *Rawl. poet. 218, p. 130 (autogr.).

3 Galbus hath been this summer in Freezeland
We part as wisely as we came together.
Davies, Sir John, 'In Gallum'.
Pr. amongst 'Epigrames' with *Ovids Elegies*, tr. C. M., [*c*. 1600].
MS. *Add. B. 97, fol. 43v.

4*a* Galla will pawn her maidenhead on this
To join unto it deserves her maiden head.
MS. Eng. poet. e. 14, fol. 66v.

4*b* [Gallants come list awhile a story I will tell]
And made a way with speed right through the enemy.
'The Valiant Commander with his resolute Lady 1644'.
Pr. *Roxburghe Ballads*, ed. J. Woodfall Ebsworth, vi, 1889, p. 282.
MS. Firth c. 17, fol. 84.

5 Gallants I'd know before you do depart
That you love sport which makes you damn his play.
Epilogue to 'The Lover's Stratagem'.
MS. Rawl. poet. 18, p. 55.

6 Gargaphy did yield a valley
Where with my pen I wish to rest.
MS. Rawl. poet. 120, fol. 60v.

7 Garret some called him, but that was too high
To heaven, where grocers there are many more.
'In St. Saviours Southwarke'.
MS. Sancroft 59, p. 294 rev.

Gate open to the good, and shut out none, 8
For one poor point is all from Martin gone.
Translated from Latin.
MS. Rawl. poet. 209, fol. 34v.

Gather [those] your rose buds while you may 9
Time still succeeds the former.
[Herrick, Robert].
Pr. Playford's *Select Musicall Ayres and Dialogues*, 1653, iii. 26.
MSS. Don. c. 57, fol. 72v, with music by W. Lawes; Mus. Sch. E. 451, p. 335, 3-part setting by W. Lawes; Rawl. poet. 65, fol. 30, subscribed H. Laws.

Gathering to the sacred sign 10
Triumphant through thy love.
Kenton, James.
MS. *Eng. poet. e. 20, p. 121 (autogr.).

Gay, kind, and airy, 11
I'm of all mock love a despiser.
Williams, John, 'Miss Ashe being taught to sing'.
MS. *Rawl. poet. 184, fol. 38 (autogr.).

Gay, kind, and airy, 12
All care to please us is over.
Williams, John, 'An answer made by me, to gay, kind, and airy'.
MS. *Rawl. poet. 184, fol. 74 (autogr.).

Gay Myra toast of all the town 13
Enchanting sound dwelt on her tongue.
'To the 8th Tune', i.e. tune on fol. 17v.
MS. Mus. Sch. G. 636, fol. 13v.

Gaze not for comets, nor expect a star, 14
Pay poll-money for our heads once every year.
Spinedge, Anthony (1651(?)–1694), 'On the execrable Murther of that Glorious Martyr Charles. I. of blessed memory'. Addressed to Sancroft as Dean of St. Paul's (1664–78).
MS. Tanner 306, fol. 102.

15 Gaze not on swans in [on] whose soft [fair, white] breast
Sunk in their sockets and decayed.
Pr. in H. Lawes's *Ayres and Dialogues*, 1653, i. 15.
MSS. Don. c. 57, fol. 81, with music by Henry Lawes; Eng. poet. d. 152, fol. 107$^{v}$, attr. to Dr. [Richard] Love; Lat. misc. c. 19, p. 422, headed 'Doctor Loves verses upon his daughter Grace Love'; Rawl. poet. 116, fol. 37$^{v}$; 147, p. 93, attr. to 'Henry Noel, son to the Ld. Viscount Cambden'.

16 [Gehazi] Gehesy Lot's housewife and Argus's eyes
With bishop that turneth and burneth up all.
'Tenne faultes in cheese', riddling rhyme.
MS. Rawl. D. 273, p. 275.

Geif patient eire . . . see Give patient ear, G90.

17 Gella if thou dost love thy self take heed
Thy canker-eaten gums and rotten teeth.
Davies, Sir John, 'In gellam'.
Pr. amongst 'Epigrames', with *Ovids Elegies*, tr. C. M., [*c.* 1600.]
MSS. *Add. B. 97, fol. 42; *Rawl. poet. 212, fol. 59$^{v}$ rev.

18 Gella of late is grown a puritan
Unless she jape, she will not kiss a man.
Davies, Sir John, 'In Gellam'.
MS. *Rawl. poet. 212, fol. 57$^{v}$ rev.

19 Gemellus fain would Maronilla wed
What is it then? She coughs. Oh, that's the matter.
Sancroft, William, translator [Martial], *Epigrams* I. x.
MS. Sancroft 48, fol. 26 (autogr.).

20 Gemellus Maronilla courts and prays,
What's that which takes him then? a killing cold.
[Martial] *Epigrams* I. x.
MS. Rawl. D. 1147, fol. 89$^{v}$.

21 General George that valiant knight fa la
Cried rump etc.
'Song'. Subscribed 'W. C. Scripsit'.
MS. Rawl. poet. 214, fol. 74$^{v}$.

22 Genius, and beauty, side by side
The least of either guest.
Birch, [George, of Remenham, Berks.], 'On hearing of two distinguished Guests at Ld. B[e]ssb[orou]gh's Table', in a pr. copy of *Love Elegies*, 2nd ed. 1777.
Pr. bk. 280 l. 98, before 'Advertisment'.

Genius and innocence were walking 23
Let's take Myrtilla for our home.
'Dr. S.'
MS. Don. c. 81, fol. 182.

Genius of Chadwell's spring 24
To the worlds lords the cool draught gave / Nor the . . . (incomplete).
Gough, Richard, 'Nov. 13. 1776'.
MS. *Eng. poet. c. 5, fol. 220 (autogr.).

Genius of this blissful place 25
I oft would wish to woo thy stay.
Setting signed by the composer, 'Phil. Hayes May 1 1786'.
MS. Mus. d. 64, fol. 2.

Genteel is my Damon, engaging his air 26
Since the picture I've drawn is exactly the man.
'Verses said to be written by Queen Charlotte in 1765'.
MSS. Add. B. 83, fol. 5, 'Transcribed [by Bulkeley Bandinel] from a MS. note by Mr. Charles Godwyn of Balliol . . . Godw. 516'; Eng. poet. d. 47, fol. 48.

Gentility and sweetness here combine 27
Then think how truly Ancaster is blest.
'Duchess of Ancaster' (d. 1793).
MS. Eng. poet. e. 28, p. 30.

Gentle breezes, silent glades 28
Appeasing love each tender breast invades.
'Reset . . . by Mr. [John Baptist] Grano'.
MS. Mus. Sch. B. 8*, fol. 24.

Gentle eyes, your tears distil, 29
A woman wept into a stone.
Shirley, James, 'Uppon the Ladye Ryvers who dyed with greife. Epitaph'.
Pr. from this MS., *Works*, ed. A. Dyce, 1833, vi. 500.
MS. *Rawl. poet. 88, p. 25.

Gentle love hath no dissension 30
In his new Jerusalem.
'The second part to the same tune [True blew] concerning Love who will bring all things into tune'.
MS. Rawl. poet. 37, p. 91.

Gentle love this hour befriend me 31
Take my soul into thy eyes.
MS. Eng. poet. e. 8, fol. 29$^{v}$.

Gentle lyre begin the strain 32
O'er thy foes and self victorious.
Harte, [Walter], 'Pinders Ode Set by Mr. Boyce', 1740/1.
MSS. Mus. Sch. C. 111, 112.

33 Gentle reader, see in me
For every cup of water given.
Warton, Thomas, the younger, 'Inscription'.
Pr. *Poems*, 1791, p. 114.
MS. Don. c. 75, fol. 92.

34 Gentle shepherds saw you not
My harm wrought by thy too much pride.
Ballad.
MSS. Ashmole 36, 37, fol. 28v.

35 Gentlemen of England,
It is a mile long or very near.
On the restoration of St. Paul's Cathedral, *c.* 1620–3.
MSS. Douce 357, fol. 2; Tanner 306, fols. 259, 260, 259v.

36 Gentles and lords, your most obedient
Choose for your regent—Doctor Willis.
Jessop, William, 'To the Lords and Commons of Ireland, on the [intention of choosing the Prince unlimited Regent. 1789]'.
MS. Percy b. 1, fol. 62v (autogr.).

37 Gentlewomen do surfeit
But all's our disease.
MS. Eng. poet. c. 50, fol. 35.

38 Gently oh gently without fright
And make night clear.
MS. Mus. b. 1, fol. 23, music by John Wilson.

39 Gently touch the warbling lyre
And indulgent whispers sound.
'Seignor Geminianii the words by A. Bradley', endorsed 'Mr. Bradley's Song at Opera'.
MS. Ballard 47, fol. 159.

40 George as he walked along, Brittania eyed
Glory of Albion, honour of her coast.
Gough, Richard, 'To the King'. 1750.
MS. *Eng. poet. c. 5, fol. 31 (autogr.).

41 George in this piece, something like thee I spy
And love of friendship it is his I'll swear.
'T. R. upon his deade ffreinds picture'.
See *Palaestra*, cxlviii, 1925, p. 249: Thomas Randolph on George Hatton, d. *c.* 1630 (?).
MS. Firth e. 4, p. 109.

42 G[eorge] values himself on his lacks of rupees,
Vast lacks of good breeding discernment and wit.
Parsons, William, 'On [George —] taking too much consequence on him, his fortune being made in the East Indies'.
Pr. *Travelling Recreations*, 1807, ii. 192.
MS. *Don. d. 123, p. 171 (autogr.).

Geron whose mouldy memory corrects 43
And happiest accident of all his life.
Davies, Sir John, 'In Gerontem'.
Pr. amongst 'Epigrames', with *Ovids Elegies*, tr. C. M., [*c.* 1600].
MS. *Add. B. 97, fol. 43.

Get hence foul grief the canker of the mind 44
And never ended.
Sidney, Sir Philip, from the *Arcadia*.
MS. *e Mus. 37, fol. 129v.

Get money and keep it: 'twill be thy best friend: 45
They'll count thee a fool; thou shalt be no more.
Robinson, Robert.
MS. *Rawl. poet. 218, p. 95 (autogr.).

Get money, get money, go on, live ever: 46
Oh you idolators, you all must die.
Robinson, Robert.
MS. *Rawl. poet. 218, p. 70 (autogr.).

Get money, get money (oh 'tis a brave sport) 47
Alas, you shall not hold it.
Robinson, Robert.
MS. *Rawl. poet. 218, p. 164 (autogr.).

Get wisdom first be sure, and then be bold: 48
Wild thoughts unseason'd: oh they'll never hold.
Robinson, Robert.
MS. *Rawl. poet. 218, p. 52 (autogr.).

Geta, from wool and weaving first began 49
He swelled to be a lord and then he burst.
'In Getam'.
Pr. *A Help to Discourse*, 1623; cf. *N. & Q.* 206, p. 426.
MS. Don. d. 58, fol. 34v.

Getting of money is the way to thrive, 50
And mirth sometimes doth help to keep alive.
Robinson, Robert.
MS. *Rawl. poet. 218, p. 126 (autogr.).

Ghosts of every occupation 51
Knaves and fools of every class.
'In Dr. Faustus or the NegroMancer . .. 13 Sept. 1751', with music.
MS. Mus. e. 20, fol. 21v.

Giles Jolt as sleeping in his cart he lay 52*a*
If not, Ods boddikins I've found a cart.
'The Carter turn'd Logician. An Epigram'.
MS. Eng. misc. e. 219, fol. 8.

Gil's history appears to be 52*b*
Whose fathers were Gil's skeletons.
Green, Mathew, 'An Epigram on Mr. Echard's and Bp. Burnet's Histories'.
Pr. Dodsley's *Collection of Poems*, 1748, i. 60.
MS. Eng. misc. f. 79, p. 110.

53 Gipsies and physic sell me fear
Which scorned lightnings weaker dart.
I. A., 'A Song'.
MS. Rawl. poet. 199, p. 65.

54 Give a child his own will,
And make him fit for nothing but ill.
Robinson, Robert.
MS. *Rawl. poet. 218, p. 175 (autogr.).

55 Give a child his own will, till he grows man,
No doubt you may rule him then, if you can.
Robinson, Robert, couplet.
MS. *Rawl. poet. 218, p. 159 (autogr.).

56 Give Caesar what is Caesar's due
For it can only mean—a f-t!
Parsons, William.
Paraphrase of Latin epigram on the Pope's arms.
MS. *Don. d. 123, p. 138 (autogr.).

57 Give Celia, but to me alone
Since judge who will, the odds are mine.
'To Celia'.
Pr. *Poems on Affairs of State*, iii, 1698, p. 208.
MS. Eng. poet. c. 18, fol. 79v.

58 Give ear beloved Londoners
Will rise and do so too.
'Reasons given by divers Members of both Houses why they would have noe peace nor accomodation'.
Pr. by L. Lichfield, Oxford (?), March 1643: see F. Madan, *Oxford Books*, ii. 1912, p. 234.
MS. Rawl. poet. 71, p. 125.

59 Give ear those ears that long to know my grief,
And I may boast *gagné l'amour perdu*.
Andrews, —.
MS. *Rawl. poet. 92, fol. 18.

60 Give ear ye people who the world inhabit
Thus fools in honour hath with beasts like end.
Fairfax, Thomas, Lord, Psalm xlix.
MS. *Fairfax 40, p. 109 (autogr.).
MS. *Fairfax 38, p. 209.

61 Give ear you British hearts of gold,
And die for Rodney's glory.
'Rodney's Glory'.
MS. Firth c. 18, fol. 79.

62 Give ear young man; take heed of hasty wiving:
Make many one, to feed upon a crust.
Robinson, Robert.
MS. *Rawl. poet. 218, p. 87 (autogr.).

63 Give every one, their due; and not exact thine own,
Let not thy wife, be nosegay of the town.
MS. Rawl. poet. 66, fol. 46.

Give father power, son wisdom, spirit goodness, 64
By god by persons three, and so are right.
F. W., 'Sonnet: 37'.
MS. *Rawl. C. 639, p. 187.

Give glory to the Lord ye sons of might 65–66
Thy people bless and praise thee they'll endeavour.
Fairfax, Thomas, Lord, Psalm xxix.
MS. *Fairfax 40, p. 59 (autogr.).
MS. *Fairfax 38, p. 166.

Give laud unto the lord from heaven that is so high: 67
And him obey.
[Pullain, John], Psalm cxlviii.
MS. Rawl. poet. 112, fol. 29 rev.

Give leave to praise you though you are 68
And so as prisoner, you are kept I swear.
Cavendish, Lady Jane, 'On an Honourable Lady'.
MS. *Rawl. poet. 16, p. 28.

Give list'ning ear my people to my laws 69
And governed them in war and peace discreetly.
Harington, Sir John, Psalm lxxviii.
MS. *Douce 361, fol. 46v.

Give Lord true judgment to the king from high 70
Let earth his glory fill his name extol Amen.
Fairfax, Thomas, Lord, Psalm lxxii.
MS. *Fairfax 40, p. 161 (autogr.).
MS. *Fairfax 38, p. 243.

Give me a generous friend, ye powers above, 71
Let him be just, or be no friend of mine.
'Nil ego contulerim jucundo sanus amico—Hor.' [*Satires* I. v. 44] 1735.
MS. Eng. misc. e. 240, p. 266.

Give me a girl (if one I needs must meet) 72
Is to enjoy their ashes or their fire.
Cartwright, William, 'On Women'.
Pr. *Comedies . . . with other Poems*, 1651, p. 218.
MSS. Don. e. 6, fol. 17v, attr. to Wm. Cartwright ex æde Xti Oxon; Eng. misc. e. 241, fol. 24v, attr. to Cartwright.

Give me a kiss from those sweet lips of thine, 73
Pierce with your eyes my heart, or pluck it out.
'An incomparable kisse'.
Pr. *Wits Recreations*, 1663, Sig. Q5.
MS. Eng. poet. d. 152, fol. 106.

Give me a kiss, I'll make that odd one even, 74
You will for pity give me some again.
'A Loving Bargaine'.
Pr. *Wits Recreations*, 1663, Sig. Q4v.
MS. Eng. poet. d. 152, fol. 106.

75 Give me a man that something knows
That man shall purchase ten.
Williams, John, 'Moreover . . . much Study is a weariness to the flesh', etc.
MS. *Rawl. poet. 192, fol. 81 (autogr.).

76 Give me great God what thou see'st good for me
Who leaves to God to choose, as well as give.
'The Resignation'.
MS. Rawl. poet. 90, fol. 41$^{v}$.

77 Give me, kind Heav'n to spend my days
And make the gloomy desert smile.
'A Song', 1735.
MS. Eng. misc. e. 240, p. 234.

78 Give me my scallop shell of quiet
To tread those blest paths which before I writ.
Ralegh, Sir Walter, 'Verses Made the night before hee was beheaded'.
MSS. Ashmole 38, p. 59, attr. to Sir W. Ralegh; Eng. hist. c. 272, fol. 49, attr. to Sr Walter Raleigh; Rawl. poet. 160, fol. 57, attr. to Sir Walter Raleigh.

79 Give me one kiss; faith lovers do
Then give me kisses without number.
Quarles, Fr[ancis], 'Cupids table of Multiplicacon'.
Pr. from this MS., *Works*, ed. Grosart, 1880, i, p. lxxiii.
MSS. Ashmole 36, 37, fol. 280$^{v}$.

80 Give me that golden age again
The buttery and pantry will fly open to all.
'The second part to the same tune [as G403] concerning hospitality'.
MS. Rawl. poet. 37, p. 73.

81 Give me that man, whose frowning brow is death.
I such an one, as can kill men with breath.
'A Judge. Captaine', couplet.
Pr. *Wits Recreations*, 1640, no. 7, *beg.* Were I to choose.
MS. Rawl. poet. 153, fol. 27$^{v}$.

82 'Give me the paper' cried the rabble rout
No lawyers, monks, nor foxes share thy spoil.
Gough, Richard, 'Ode to Edward Haistwell Esq. Aug. 17 1768'.
MS. *Eng. poet. c. 5, fol. 149.

83 Give me the world and all her wealth
For who alas, can speak so that lives here?
Bulteel, John, 'Health'.
MS. *Rawl. poet. 159, fol. 212.

84 Give me thy love, I ask no more,
Pure, bright, sublime, angelical.
'The Request'.
MS. *Don. f. 5, fol. 4$^{v}$.

Give me, ye gods! some pleasant safe retreat, 85
Ye powers divine I beg no greater bliss!
Chatwin, John, 'His Wish'.
MS. *Rawl. poet. 94, p. 122 (autogr.).

Give not thy gifts to aged men 86
And women change their mind.
MS. Rawl. poet. 85, fol. 83$^{v}$.

Give not thy mind to read such things 87
That wisdom do contain.
4 lines used as a copy by Wiman Ramsey, *c.* 1595.
MS. Rawl. D. 649, fol. 8.

Give o'er foolish heart and make haste to despair 88
Though they still are unkind I will ever adore.
Pr. with music by Alphonso Marsh in *Choice Ayres, Songs and Dialogues*, 2nd ed., 1675, p. 28.
MS. Mus. Sch. F. 572, p. 94, without music.

Give o'er ye poor players depend not on wit 89
Shall turn all my Burdoux to Champaine and Nants.
'Julians fairwell to the famelys of the Coquets'.
MS. Firth c. 16, p. 161.

Give patient ear to something I mun say 90
Crake not again no farther nor the creed.
James I, 'Ane admonition to [Sandirs, i.e. Alexander Montgomerie] the maister poete to leave of greit crakking'.
MS. *Bodl. 165, fol. 47 (autogr.).

Give peace in these our days oh lord 91
And shine in every place.
G[ridal(?)], E[dmund(?)], 'Da pacem Domine'.
MS. Rawl. poet. 112, fol. 24$^{v}$ rev.

Give place to plaints, you that in pleasure sway 92
Doth now in heaven, with angels sing his part.
Lilliat, John, 'Funebre carmen in obitum Mag: Tho: Lewkner. July 12, 1596'.
MS. Rawl. poet. 148, fol. 63$^{v}$ (autogr.).

Give praise unto Gods holy name, 93
Fair children to embrace.
Psalm cxiii.
MS. *Rawl. C. 113, fol. 79.

Give praises to the Lord, oh praise his name, 94
And joyfully to see her long-lived progeny.
Br., Jos., Psalm cxiii.
MS. Rawl. poet. 61, fol. 51.

Give praises unto god the lord 95
Praise ye the lord therefore.
[Norton, Thomas], Psalm cv.
MS. Rawl. poet. 112, fol. 41 rev.

96 Give room for Don Andreas doth approach
Who is't would work that can live so by begging.
'On Don Andreas'.
MS. Don. d. 58, fol. 32.

97 Give thanks and praise to God, for good is he;
In mercy great his kindnesses to know.
Fleming, Robert, 'The cvii Psalm paraphrased in Hexameters'.
Pr. *The Mirrour of Divine Love*, 1691, 'Poems', p. 61.
MS. Rawl. poet. 213, fol. 45 (autogr.).

98 Give thanks to God for good is He.
Because his mercies ever flow.
Fairfax, Thomas, Lord, Psalm cxviii.
MS. *Fairfax 40, p. 305 (autogr.).
MS. *Fairfax 38, p. 409.

99 Give thanks to God for he is good
His mercies will impart.
Psalm cvii.
MS. *Rawl. C. 113, fol. 74$^{v}$.

100 Give thanks unto our gracious God
Men say for evermore.
Psalm cvi.
MS. *Rawl. C. 113, fol. 73.

101 Give thanks unto the lord our god for gracious is he
For certainly he shall perceive the kindness of the lord.
[Kethe, William], Psalm cvii.
MS. Rawl. poet. 112, fol. 39 rev.

102 Give to the Lord, ye mighty men,
With everlasting peace.
Psalm xxix.
MS. Montagu e. 10, fol. 49.

103 Give to the lord ye potentates ye rulers of the world:
The lord will bless his chosen folk, with everlasting peace.
[Sternhold, Thomas (?)], Psalm xxix.
MS. Rawl. poet. 112, fol. 63$^{v}$ rev.

104 Give what thou hast whilst it is thine
When life is past.
MS. Mus. f. 19, fol. 2.

105 Give women leave to pelt it now and then:
Who would not rather be above than under?
Robinson, Robert, 'In excuse of womens peevishness'.
MS. *Rawl. poet. 218, p. 37 (autogr.).

106 Give young men leave to get, before they pay:
Which young men cannot do so well as they.
Robinson, Robert.
MS. *Rawl. poet. 218, p. 137 (autogr.).

Gladly the call of friendship I obey 107
Not only both must love but both obey.
'A Nuptial Card'.
MS. Eng. poet. e. 47, p. 45.

Glide gently waves, and as along you pass, 108
I'd melt in tears and make a crystal flood.
Chatwin, John, 'On a young Lady bathing in the River'.
MS. *Rawl. poet. 94, p. 276 (autogr.).

Glide soft ye silver floods 109
Sad Willy's pipe shall bid his friend farewell.
Browne, William, of Tavistock.
Pr. *Brittannia's Pastorals*, 1625, Book 2 (Sig. M3).
MS. Eng. misc. e. 241, fol. 45$^{v}$.

Glorious and powerful God, we understand 110
Be praised in eternity.
MS. Rawl. poet. 23, p. 139, reference to setting by Orlando Gibbons.

Glorious saint, and late the sun of all chast music fire 111
Thy praise: 'Tis psalm, or unexpressible.
'D: Mariæ Cecill virgineæ manes gloriæ adoranti proximus admiratur I: A:'.
MS. Rawl. poet. 199, p. 69.

Glory and empire to the Lord 112
And bless with peaceful days.
Psalm xxix.
MS. *Rawl. C. 113, fol. 26.

Glory and thanks to Thee be given 113
Enter that rest above.
Kenton, James.
MS. *Eng. poet. e. 20, p. 226 (autogr.).

Glory be, to God on high! 114
And with united praise, united glories blest.
Milbourne, Dr. [Luke], 'The Churches Hymn after the Eucharist'.
MS. Rawl. D. 1293, fol. 48$^{v}$.

Glory to the God of grace 115
Let me now my friend embrace.
Kenton, James, 'On the Death of Mr. Richard Clark', 1786.
MS. *Eng. poet. e. 19, p. 264 (autogr.).

Glory to thine almighty grace 116
And let me die that bliss to know.
Kenton, James.
MS. *Eng. poet. e. 20, p. 189 (autogr.).

117 *Go–add* this verse to [unto] Goad's hearse
'Twas death's goad drove him thither.

'Upon Doctor [Thomas] Goad'.
In B.M. Add. MS. 22603, 'Dr. Wren on Dr. Goad' [Matthew Wren (?)].
MSS. Don. d. 58, fol. 17; Douce f. 5, fol. 9, attr. to Mr. Wren.

118 Go and catch a falling star
False ere I come: to two or three.

Donne, John, 'Song'.
Pr. *Poems*, 1633, p. 196.
MSS. Eng. poet. e. 37, p. 58, attr. to J. D.; *Eng. poet. e. 99, fol. 103v; Rawl. poet. 117, fol. 217 rev., attr. to Mr. Dunne; see also G136.

119 Go and choose what sport you will
Oh I dare not lest I die.

MS. Don. c. 57, fol. 38, with music.

120 Go and count her better hours
Fair sun, that governs thee and me.

[Strode, William], 'On a watch borrowed of [sent home to] his Mrs.'
MSS. Ashmole 47, fol. 37; Eng. poet. c. 50, fol. 133v; e. 14, fol. 49; Firth d. 7, fol. 182; Mus. b. 1, fol. 57, with music by John Wilson; Rawl. poet. 206, p. 66.

121 Go and perfume the east, th' whole kingdom where
Drugs may turn physic yet 'tis hazardous.

Paman, Clement, 'The Patches made into a black Crosse'.
MS. Rawl. poet. 147, pp. 58, 125.

122 Go and seek some other love
And there double damn'd for me.

MS. Mus. b. 1, fol. 164v, with music by John Wilson.

123 Go and speak truth; It is thy office now,
Though here a while thou triumph on his tomb.

Roe, Sir Thomas, 'To the living memory of the late and last Sr John Harington'.
Pr. *The Churches Lamentation for John Lord Harington*, Richard Stock, 1614, Sig. H8.
MS. CCC. 318, fol. 203.

124 Go: and with this parting kiss
Know virtue taught thee, not thy self.

Herrick, Robert, 'his charge to his wife'.
Pr. *Hesperides*, 1648, p. 201, *beg*. Go hence.
MSS. Ashmole 38, p. 93, attr. to Mr. Hericke; Eng. poet. c. 50, fol. 92v; Rawl. poet. 160, fol. 47v, attr. to R. Herrick.

Go Anna nature said to Oxford go 125
One is but that's the least to make a poet.

Lines in praise of 'Anna'.
MS. Eng. misc. b. 48, fol. 26.

Go, April, go, capricious thing, 126
Choose any other day than this.

Dyer, George, 'Invocation to May'.
Pr. *Poetics*, 1812, i. 39, *beg*. 'Let April'.
MS. *Eng. poet. c. 21, fol. 28.

Go ask thy wench, if any were 127
Chance kill her; for the pox cannot.

Paman, Clement, 'The Inquisitive'.
MS. Rawl. poet. 147, p. 51.

Go bashful muse. Thy message is to one 128
Accept thou what I can not what I would.

Hooper, John, 'A Newyeares gift. To my Mother. Mrs. Mary Hooper'.
MS. *Rawl. poet. 208, fol. 3 (autogr.).

Go bastards go to Cambridge schools 129
And their skill Ignoramus.

'A generall verdict . . . Ignoramus'.
Pr. H. Huth, *Inedited Poetical Miscellanies*, 1870.
MS. Firth d. 7, fol. 84.

Go bid the courtier that he be not proud 130
And then be sure no evil can betide thee.

'Pasquils Mad-cappe. His Mess: breviter'.
MS. Douce 280, fol. 122v.

Go bid the needle its dear north forsake 131
Then shall I cease, thee, thee alone to love.

'Cowley to his Mistress'.
Pr. *Works*, 1668, 'The Mistress', p. 56.
MS. Eng. poet. e. 40, fol. 100.

Go bleeding heart, before thou die 132
Enjoys her sweetness, thou disdain.

Song for 3 voices by W. Lawes.
MSS. Mus. Sch. B. 2, p. 36, in the hand of W. Lawes, incomplete; E. 451, p. 219, incomplete.

Go blessed soul, the muses wait on thee 133
But lived until the world's last burning fit.

P[roby], H[enry], 'An Elegy on the death of Rob. Meadows student of Em[manuel College, Cambridge]'.
MS. Rawl. poet. 246, fol. 18v.

Go book upon thy verses feet t'enshrine 134
Confess on earth's no pleasure without Paine.

Beaumont, Thomas, 'To his valentine Mrs Payne sendinge her Donns verses'.
MS. *Malone 18, p. 48 (autogr.).

135 Go burn your perrukes, ladies, tear your locks.
The will to good, to truth th' enquiring mind.

Owen, Corbett, 'To Chloris upon her Haire'.
MS. Eng. misc. e. 255, fol. 29.

136 Go catch a falling star
False ere I come to two or three.

Donne, John.
MS. *Eng. poet. f. 9, p. 44; see also G118.

137 Go count those atoms which attend the sun
What they in many I enjoy in one.

Earbery, Matthias, 'The Vanity of Numbers in War . . . Psalm 3d', sent to Charles Trimnell, whilst Bishop of Norwich, 1708–21.
MS. Tanner 306, fol. 455 (autogr.).

138 Go crystal tears like to the morning showers
Both from a spotless heart and patient eyes.

Music by Dowland, pr. *Songs or Ayres*, 1597, ix.
MSS. Mus. f. 7–10: f. 7, fol. 10.

139 Go despicable virtue go
Henceforth my only business shall be how to live.

'Vertue', presented by M. A. to Archbishop Sancroft, 1689.
MS. Rawl. poet. 154, fol. 84v.

140 Go die thou old decrepit year,
A day a year, an age to come.

Oldham, John (?), 'The Epicure. Wrote the last day of the year 1675', subscribed 'Philomusus'.
MS. *Rawl. poet. 123, p. 236 (in Oldham's hand).

141 Go echo of the mind
And tell them how to die.

'An aunswere to the lie', G205.
MSS. Rawl. poet. 172, fol. 13, attr. to 'Lo: of Essex'; 212, fol. 90, 'by an unknowne author'.

142 Go empty joys
In heaven's high court of parliament.

'Ode upon the Lord Strafford and Answer', 1640.
MSS. Don. c. 57, fol. 30v, with music; Douce 357, fol. 12; Rawl. poet. 26, fol. 126v, 'by, or upon the Earle of Strafford'; 117, fol. 152v rev., attr. to 'My lord of Straford'; Tanner 465, fol. 61, 'said to be made by Th. Earle of Strafford': index, fol. 1*a*, 'verses of the E.' corrected to 'verses for the E.'.

Go, fair example of untainted youth, 143
'Tis all a father, all a friend can give.

Pope, Alexander, 'In Memory of Robert, second son; and Mary eldest Daughter of William, Lord Digby', Sherborne Church, 1726, 1729.
Pr. *Minor Poems*, ed. N. Ault and J. Butt, 1954, p. 313.
MSS. Ballard 50, fol. 185; Top. gen. e. 32, fol. 2; Top. Oxon. c. 108, p. 46.

Go fasten pillars in the ocean sea 144
As to find one so of the same sex.

MS. Eng. poet. c. 50, fol. 34.

Go, fetch your brother (said the Egyptian lord) 145
The brother's Jesus: and the suitor's we.

[Quarles, Francis], 'On Joseph's speach to his Brethren'.
Pr. *Divine Fancies*, 1632, i. 38.
MS. Rawl. poet. 90, fol. 61v.

Go [find] vind the vicar of Taunton Dean 146
Tom sing heydledom deydledom cudden.

D'Urfey, Thomas, 'The Somersetshire Cl[ ] . . . words to a Comical Country Tune', 13 Sep. 1751.
MS. Mus. e. 20, fol. 22, attr. to Dursey.

Go flattering hope, by whose uncertain fire 147
To doubt, as to despair.

MS. Rawl. A. 176, fol. 79.

Go Flora said th' impatient queen 148
How much to thee we owe, queen of connubial love!

[Whitehad, William], Birthday Ode, 1762.
Pr. *Poems*, 1790, ii. 74.
MS. Mus. Sch. D. 311. Music by Boyce.

Go forth my lines; Jehovah great 149
And therein be you bold.

Robinson, Robert.
MS. *Rawl. poet. 218, back of fly-leaf (autogr.).

Go forward trifler mend thine easy pace 150
Thou graspest at an everlasting crown.

Bromley, Henry, 'Against Procrastination'.
MS. *Don. e. 19, fol. 6 (autogr.).

Go, gentle Oriana, go 151
Whether we e'er shall meet again below?

Flatman, Thomas, 'To Oriana weeping at parting . . . Decemb. ult. 1664. set by Mr. Roger Hill'.
MS. *Firth d. 7, fol. 41.

152 Go, get thee back to heaven, thou sacred fire
Those which put all their confidence in night.
Oldisworth, Nicolas, 'His Farewell to Poëtrie'. Answered by S1228.
MS. *Don. c. 24, fol. 77 (autogr.).

153 Go glittering type of constancy well tried
A woman who three days has known her mind.
Grove, William, '. . . to Miss Cotton upon his giving her Sixpence for which she offered to stay from the Amusements of Lichfield Races'.
MS. Eng. poet. c. 51, p. 20.

154 Go glorious soul: we now do think of thee
While thou art compassed with a glorious crown.
Culverwell, N[athaniel], 'On the death of Mr Holden Inceptor in Arts of Eman. Coll. Cant.' Probably William Holden, buried at St. Andrew's, Cambridge, 13 April 1642.
MSS. Rawl. poet. 147, p. 37, attr. to Culverwell; Tanner 465, fol. 66, attr. to N. Culverwell.

155 Go happy book and let my Candia see
And in true lovers' parts remember me.
Beaumont, Thomas, 'To his M[rs] sendinge her the Arcadia'.
MS. *Malone 18, p. 67 (autogr.).

156 Go happy gloves, and kiss those hands whose touch
From your joint happiness receive relief.
'To the same Gentlewoman after Hir Husband Had Taken her away, sent with a payre of gloves:' See J180.
MS. Rawl. poet. 84, fol. 95[v] rev.

157 Go happy heart for thou shalt lie
Pleased with hearts of men not kine.
Fletcher, John, Song from *The Mad Lover*, III. iv.
MSS. Don. c. 57, fol. 63[v], with music by John Wilson; Mus. b. 1, fol. 27[v], with music by John Wilson.

158 Go happy insect! flit thy way
Take thou a parting kiss!
Maitland, Penelope, 'Upon . . . a Butterfly' (1774–9).
MS. Eng. poet. c. 51, p. 180*i*.

159 Go happy paper by command
Even thought to her is gross and dull.
Strode, William, 'A Letter impos'd'.
MS. *CCC. 325, fol. 88[v] (autogr.).
MSS. Ashmole 47, fol. 115, attr. to W. Str.; CCC. 328, fol. 84; Rawl. poet. 84, fol. 87.

Go, happy spirit, claim thy rest 160
Embrace thee and my friend.
Kenton, James, 'On the Death of Mrs. Catherine Badcock, 1781'.
MS. *Eng. poet. e. 19, p. 238.

Go hence . . . see G124.

Go hunt the whiter ermine and present 161
Give what is oftener heard of than received.
'Will Davenants Newyears-guift to Endimion Porters wife'.
Pr. John Eliot's *Poems*, 1658, attr. to Davenant.
MS. Rawl. poet. 117, fol. 165 rev.

Go into bodies; there be your view 162
'Tis your own rule no victory no reward.
Gough, Richard, 'Heaven to hum[an] Souls'.
MS. *Eng. poet. c. 5, fol. 87 (autogr.).

Go Joseph gentle: deprived thy coat, 163
To every true Christian's castigation.
Forrest, William, 'An Excusation: to voyde Indygnation. 1569. die vero Aprilis 11'.
MS. Eng. poet. d. 9, fol. 157 (autogr.).

Go keep that hand 164
For Hymens band.
Strode, William, 'Poses—For Braceletts'.
MS. *CCC. 325, fol. 79 (autogr.).

Go, let the fatted calf be killed 165
But quite has left his women and his swine.
[Cowley, Abraham], 'Upon the Heart's Return'.
Pr. *Works*, 1668, 'The Mistress', p. 37.
MS. Rawl. poet. 90, fol. 122.

Go little bill and do me recommend 166
And her to love *sans variance*.
Endorsed 'For the Revd. Mr. Percy'.
MS. Eng. misc. d. 244, fol. 84.

Go little book, and be thou read by those 167
Than such gross wrongs from those dull F— endure.
Moore, Thomas, 'The Author to his Booke'.
MS. *Rawl. poet. 3, fol. 56 (autogr.).

Go little book and kindly say 168
Warble adieu and fall away.
James, Richard, 'The dedication of a sermon to Mr. Selden'.
Pr. before *An Apologeticall Essay . . . a Sermon at St. Maries in Oxford*, [1632].
MS. *James 35, p. 8 (autogr.).

169 Go little gloves salute my Valentine
Weep; this in mourning water, that in blood.
'To his refused Valentine (Palinode)'.
Pr. H. Huth, *Inedited Poetical Miscellanies*, 1870, Sig. Q1.
MS. Firth d. 7, fol. 187.

170 Go little quhair now unto Wealdhamtun
Tell him thus earnest prayeth R[ichard] G[ough].
Gough, Richard, 'To Edward Foster Esq.', 'Printed in [Nichol's] *Literary Anecdotes* vol. 6, p. 332'.
MS. *Eng. poet. c. 5, fol. 91 (autogr.).

171 Go little winged archer and convey
And left her burning in her chast desire.
Words attr. to I. C. in *The Second Book of Ayres and Dialogues* by Henry Lawes, 1655.
MS. Don. c. 57, fol. 73, different setting from that pr. by H. L.

172 Go lock unto the fairest she
The only blessing on the earth shalt gain.
Beaumont, Thomas, 'of A lock he gave his mistris'.
MS. *Malone 18, p. 6 (autogr.).

173 Go, love, thy banners round the world display,
And learn to mend their now imperfect joys by mine.
'The Enjoyment'.
MS. Add. B. 105, fol. 75.

174 Go lovely girl and live in ease,
He'd live obscure, and die forgot.
J. F., 'The Silent Farewell', 17 Feb. 1754.
MS. Eng. poet. c. 9, p. 269.

175 Go lovely rose
That are so wondrous sweet, and fair.
Waller, Edmund, 'Songe'.
Pr. *Poems*, 1645, p. 89.
MSS. *Don. d. 55, fol. 24; *Rawl. poet. 174, p. 76.

176 Go (lovely soul) go, go; 'tis too great wrong
That through thy flames, thy clay became thine urn.
Oldisworth, Giles, 'Verses upon [Mr. Giles Overbury's] course at Borton on the Hill'. [G. O. d. 1637.]
MS. *Rawl. C. 422, fol. 15 (autogr.).

177 Go mighty prince and those great nations see
To shine in peace or war, and be again admired.
Garth, Sir Samuel, 'to . . . the Duke of Marlborough; On his going into Germany Nov. 30: 1712'.
Pr. Garth's *Works*, 1769, p. 103. See G190.
MSS. Eng. poet. c. 9, p. 229; e. 87, p. 153, attr. to Dr. Garth.

Go muse and to my Laura tell 178
Still purer joys than sleep can feign.
H. H., of Balliol Coll: Ox: 1777, 'A Song. To miss Martin'.
MS. Eng. misc. e. 241, fol. 68.

Go my disdain and with a constant brow 179
And let her know I am and will be free.
'To his proude M[ris]'.
MS. Ashmole 38, p. 4.

Go not without me for he only stands 180
I can not versify without a staff.
'Written on a stafe'.
MS. Eng. poet. e. 14, fol. 47.

Go now, with some daring drug 181
Hark hither, reader.
Crashaw, Richard, 'Upon Lessius his Hygeiasticon', 15 lines only, followed by a note in Sancroft's hand 'the Rest I suppose printed in Lessius': see H235.
MS. Tanner 465, fol. 60[v], attr. to Mr. Crashaw on fol. 1*a*.

Go on brave man; get what you can. 182
Within the grave be rotting.
Robinson, Robert.
MS. *Rawl. poet. 218, p. 67 (autogr.).

Go on, brave soldier! Venus is thy guide! 183
Europe in safety may defy the French.
'London Mag. Novr: 1743', on Col. Mentzel, etc.
MS. Eng. poet. c. 9, p. 118.

Go on (great Prætor) let your justice sway 184
Heaven crown your days with everlasting peace.
6 lines, translating 6 Latin lines, to be substituted for the ending of an existing piece so that the whole might be addressed to Sir John Frederick, Lord Mayor of London, on St. Matthew's Day at Christ's Hospital, 1662.
MS. Rawl. D. 1401, two copies, fols. 124[v] and (incomplete) 120.

Go on thou wicked man 185
The cureless fall of the unjust.
J. F., 'Psalme 36'.
MS. *Eng. poet. f. 17, p. 136 (autogr.).

Go out of this place thou right ugly beast 186
But they dare not fear of me alone.
'Of An assault Agaynst a snayle. The woman speaketh with [harty (?)] corage', and 'The snayle speakethe'.
MS. Ashmole 378, fol. 11[v].

187 Go passions to the cruel fair
Of blasted hopes and slack delays.
From Thomas Ford's *Musick of Sundrie Kindes*, 1607, v.
MS. Mus. d. 8, fol. 15$^{v}$.

188 Go patter to lubbers and swabs, do ye see,
Will look out a good berth for poor Jack!
Dibdin, [Charles], 'Poor Jack'.
MS. Montagu e. 14, fol. 57.

189 Go perjured man, and if [when] thou e'er [shalt] return
May blow my ashes up, and strike thee blind.
[Herrick, Robert], 'A forsaken Ladye that dyde for Love'.
Pr. *Hesperides*, 1648, p. 53, and with music by John Blow in Playford's *Choice Ayres and Songs*, iv, 1683, p. 78.
MSS. Ashmole 38, two copies, pp. 4 and 179; Don. c. 57, fol. 11, with music by Robert Ramsey; Eng. poet. c. 50, two copies, fols. 39 and 113; f. 25, fol. 19$^{v}$; Mus. b. 1, fol. 45, with music by John Wilson; c. 26, fol. 134, with music by Blow; Mus. Sch. C. 12–16, with music by Blow: C. 12, p. 84; C. 95, p. 116, with music by Blow: C. 96, fol. 5$^{v}$, with music by Blow: Rawl. poet. 196, fol. 15; Tanner 465, fol. 60, subscribed Mr. Rob. Ramsy.

190 Go, petty prince, that boggy nation see,
And in some nasty ditch the wretch expired.
Answer to G177.
MSS. Eng. poet. e. 87, p. 154; Rawl. poet. 181, fol. 64.

191 Go, pitiable fair! The grave cries speed,
'Tis the severer punishment to live.
Evans, W., 'After Miss Blandy's Sentence'.
MS. North d. 6, fol. 73.

192 Go preach the everlasting word
Triumphant o'er sin, earth and hell.
Kenton, James.
MS. *Eng. poet. e. 20, p. 361 (autogr.).

193 Go prop and basis to thy king and peers
Flourish in honour as thou dost in years.
Anagram: 'Joannes Greenvilius, *I basis i columen*', etc., translated, couplet [on John Grenville, Earl of Bath, 1628–1701].
MS. Rawl. D. 1110, fol. 156.

194 Go restless ghost! tell that proud fair
And I shall rest contented.
'A Song'.
Pr. *Academy of Complements*, 1650, p. 135.
MSS. Eng. misc. e. 13, fol. 18$^{v}$; Mus. b. 1, fol. 95$^{v}$, music by John Wilson.

Go restless thoughts fly from your master's breast 195
And speak her praises, and forget your wrong.
Pr. John Wilson's *Cheerfull Ayres or Ballads*, 1660, p. 70.
MS. Mus. b. 1, fol. 46$^{v}$, music by Wilson.

Go, rose! my Chloe's bosom grace: 196
You die with envy, I with love.
[Gay, John], 'The Rose'.
Pr. Walsh, *A Cantata and four English Songs*, by Maurice Greene.
MSS. Ballard 29, fol. 138; Eng. poet. e. 40, fol. 33; Mus. c. 107, fols. 7 and 48$^{v}$, music by Greene.

Go rose my gardens gayest pride 197
Maintains a verdure through the year.
Bate, Sally, 'The Rose to Celia, 1768'.
MS. *Eng. poet. e. 28, p. 166.

Go silly wench, mayest thou ever be 198
That he may ne'er obtain thy maidenhead.
'A Farewell to his home-spunne Mistresse Sarah Jud'.
MS. Firth e. 4, p. 94.

Go sinner and before the Lord 199
But his must be the power.
Beddome, Benjamin.
MS. *Eng. misc. e. 227, fol. 57$^{v}$.

Go, smiling souls, your new-built cages break: 200
Milk all the way.
Crashaw, Richard, 'To the infant Martyrs'.
MS. Tanner 465, fol. 33, attr. to Mr. Crashaw on fol. 1*a*.

Go soft thou gentle whispering wind 201
Or else quite extinguish mine.
[Carew, Thomas], 'On a Sigh'.
MS. Ashmole 47, fol. 36$^{v}$; see also G215, G233.

Go sons; whom I to exile must confine. 202
In that your luckless birth forth coming slew her.
Ch. M., Sonnett 1.
MS. Eng. misc. d. 239, fol. 6.

Go sordid earth and hope [think] not to bewitch 203
I might perchance get riches and be poor.
Randolph, Thomas, 'Of the inestimable content he enjoyes in the muses'.
Pr. *Poems*, 1638, p. 1.
MSS. CCC. 328, fol. 9, attr. to Randolph; Eng. poet. c. 50, fol. 65, attr. to T. R.; e. 97, p. 3, attr. to Tho. Randolph; Firth e. 4, p. 122, attr. to T. R.; Rawl. poet. 209, fol. 23$^{v}$, attr. to Tho. Randolph.

204 **Go, sots, home to your gammons, go and boast**
**A medicine may be found, to cure your spleen.**
'The Banish't Preists farewell to the House of Commons', March 1672/3.
MS. Don. b. 8, p. 450.

205 **Go soul the body's guest**
**No stab the soul can kill.**
Ralegh, Sir Walter, 'The Lie'.
Pr. Davison, *A Poetical Rapsodie*, 2nd ed., 1608, etc.; see A. M. C. Latham, *Poems of Sir Walter Ralegh*, 1951. Answered in G141, S1134.
MSS. Ashmole 51, fol. 6; Douce f. 5, fol. 11, attr. to Sr. Walter Rawleighe; Eng. poet. d. 3, fol. 2v; Firth d. 7, fol. 146, attr. to Doctor Latworth; e. 4, p. 3, attr. to Sir Walter Rawley; Rawl. poet. 172, fol. 12v, attr. to Dr. Latworthe; Rawl. poet. 212, fol. 88, headed 'W. R. farewell made by D. Lat' and including answering verses, 'Fly soule the bodies guide'; Tanner 306, fol. 188.

206 **Go, spend thy days where fame and honour move**
**God send me still grace to live without you.**
MS. Don. d. 58, fol. 25v.

207 **Go suffering friend from pain at length released,**
**Whose tears inscribed thy monumental stone.**
Kenton, James, 'Epitaph' on John Peter Harley, 1772.
MS. *Eng. poet. e. 19, p. 227 (autogr.).

208 **Go take away Celia, I freely consent,**
**I'll always pay what is so justly due.**
Williams, John.
MS. *Rawl. poet. 191, fol. 9 (autogr.).

209 **Go take that monstrous bowl from hence**
**Immortal nectar's only in your kiss.**
Owen, Corbett, 'The Answer', with a postscript, to C417, C455.
MSS. Eng. misc. e. 255, fol. 34, attr. to C. Owen; Eng. poet. e. 4, p. 159, attr. to Corbett Owen.

210 **Go tell't the easy citizens, whose wide**
**As well as preach men out of every sense.**
Proby, H[enry], 'On the Report of Sr George Lisle his death', 1648.
MS. Rawl. poet. 62, fol. 19.

211 **Go, the rich chariot instantly prepare;**
**And life, alas, allows but one ill winters day.**
[Cowley, Abraham]. Pr. *Works*, 1668, 'Pindarique Odes', p. 23, 'The Muse', stanza 1.
MS. Rawl. poet. 213, fol. 50.

**Go then blest paper which salutes the hands** 212
**That give you freedom, yet keep me in bonds.**
'To a paper sent to his Mrs', couplet.
MS. Ashmole 47, fol. 34v.

**Go then; enjoy the joys; yet, do not go;** 213
**First, I must imitate, then follow thee.**
Oldisworth, Giles, 'Verses first made on Mr. Gyles Overbury', d. 1637.
MS. *Rawl. C. 422, fol. 17 (autogr.).

**Go then, vain fool, some cheaper mistress seek,** 214
**May suit some sorry wench, they'll ne'er suit me.**
Williams, John, 'The answer' to 'The unconcerned'.
MS. *Rawl. poet. 191, fol. 9 (autogr.).

**Go thou gentle whispering [whistling] wind** 215
**Or else quite extinguish mine.**
Carew, Thomas, 'A Prayer to the winde. Song'.
Pr. *Poems*, 1640.
MSS. *Don. b. 9, fol. 20v; MS. Don. c. 57, fol. 72, with music by H. Lawes; d. 58, fol. 23v; Eng. poet. c. 50, two copies, fols. 115v and 127; e. 37, p. 78; Firth e. 4, p. 116, attr. to T. R.; Malone 16, p. 11; Rawl. poet. 209, fol. 5; see also G201, G233.

**Go thou my muse, and on this happy day.** 216
**And think that pleasure which can ne'er be writ.**
'On [the Birthday of Pulcheria, July 20]' 1735.
MS. Eng. misc. e. 240, p. 210.

**Go thou, that vainly do'st my eyes invite** 217
**When fierce winds rock them on the foaming wave.**
King, Henry, 'Sonnet'.
Pr. *Poems*, 1657, p. 11.
MSS. *Eng. poet. e. 30, fol. 42; *Malone 22, fol. 32; Mus. b. 1, fol. 111, music by John Wilson.

**Go thy ways and turn no more** 218*a*
**And I poor wretch, alas am left alone.**
MS. Mus. b. 1, fol. 27, music by John Wilson.

**Go thy ways since you will go** 218*b*
**Oh I dare not lest I die.**
MS. Don. c. 57, fol. 38, with music.

**Go to the dull churchyard and see** 219
**His shin-bone, or his cranion.**
'An Emblem of Mortality'.
MS. Rawl. poet. 213, fol. 52v.

**Go to thy native skies (oh! happy shade!)** 220
**For us to live, for us to die like thee.**
'On the Rev. David Netto', D.D.
MS. Percy c. 8, fol. 131.

221 Go to ye sons of Antichrist, confess,
Attends your fall and waits your overthrow.
On the accident at Blackfriars, 26 Oct. 1623. See S. R. Gardiner, *Prince Charles and the Spanish Marriage*, 1869, ii. 435.
MSS. Ashmole 36, 37, fol. 109 (autogr.).

222 Go treacherous hopes by whose uncertain fire
And such a task to live.
Song 'out of the Spanish Decameron'.
MS. Rawl. poet. 116, fol. 93.

223 Go trustless hope that every way
For fates the willing lead, th' unwilling draw.
J. F., 'Of Hope'.
MS. *Eng. poet. f. 17, p. 7 (autogr.).

224 Go tuneful bird, that pleased the woods so long
For heaven alone is worthy such a lay.
Glee by Gilbert Heathcote, 1784.
MS. Mus. d. 177, fol. 28$^v$.

225 Go turn away your cruel eyes
Poor women but for fashion.
'Per Captaine Cooke Mrs. Barbara Syms'.
MS. Rawl. poet. 84, fol. 123.

226 Go wailing verse, fly to thy mother care,
I'll live with thee, for care lives in thy brest.
Cornwallis, Will[iam], 'Another' [on Care].
MS. Tanner 306, fol. 236.

227 Go weather-beaten thoughts, with storms of tears
And she repent that all this never moved her.
Pr. John Wilson's *Cheerfull Ayres or Ballads*, 1660, p. 67.
MS. Mus. b. 1, fol. 47$^v$, music by Wilson.

228 Go when I bid thee Muse, and wish my friend
As thou demean'st thy self, will value thee.
B[rome], A[lexander], translator, Horace, *Epistles* I. viii.
Pr. *Poems of Horace*, A. Brome etc., 2nd ed. 1671, p. 329.
MS. Rawl. C. 261, p. 47.

229 Go wise man, go sometimes 'mongst fools
That yet not know of it.
Robinson, Robert.
MS. *Rawl. poet. 218, p. 108 (autogr.).

230 Go worthy patrons go on
Go home and look after your wives.
'An Encomium upon a Parliament', 1699.
Pr. bk. Firth b. 21, fol. 46.

Go! Yarrow flower thou shalt be blest 231
The charm of beauty is possessing.
[Hamilton, William of Bangour], 'The Flower of Yarrow. To Lady Mary Montgomery', one of the twenty children of Alexander Montgomerie, 9th Earl of Eglintoun.
Pr. *Poems*, 1748.
MS. Montagu e. 14, fol. 29.

Go ye tame gallants, ye that have the name 232
I'll yield and give to Wisbich cock the day.
[Wild, Robert], 'Upon a Cockfighting'.
MS. Malone 21, fol. 76$^v$; see also G235.

Go you gentle whistling wind 233
Or else quite extinguish mine.
[Carew, Thomas], 'On a sigh'.
Pr. *Poems*, 1640; the version of the MS. agrees with that in *Poems of Shakespeare*, 1640.
MS. CCC. 328, fol. 19; see also G201, G215.

Go you may call it madness, folly, 234
Monarchs are too poor to buy.
Rogers, Samuel.
MS. Percy d. 9, fol. 80.

Go you [tame] young gallants you that have the name 235
I yield and give to Wisbech cock the day.
Wild, Robert, 'A Terrible, true, troublesome, Tragicall, rellation, of a Wisbech duell . . . 17 June, 1637'.
Pr. *Iter Boreale*, 1668, p. 56, and *Wit and Drollery*, 1661, p. 110.
MSS. Rawl. poet. 142, fol. 14$^v$, attr. to Randolph; Don. d. 58, fol. 54; Eng. poet. c. 53, fol. 8, attr. to T. R.; Tanner 465, fol. 88, attr. to R. Wild; Top. Cheshire c. 6, fol. 520; see also G232.

God and man, though in this amphitheatre 236
No border unto thee, but to our eyes.
Alabaster, William, 'Son: 31. Omnia propter Christum facta'.
MS. *Eng. poet. e. 57, fol. 8.

God and my right shall after all prevail 237
God and my right must surely now prevail.
'Under King James III's Picture standing on the Sea-shore. Dieu et mon Droit'. Cf. T2963.
MSS. Rawl. poet. 81, fol. 48; 155, p. 180; 207, p. 39.

238 God and the soldier men alike adore
God is forgotten, and the soldier slighted.

[Quarles, Francis], 'Of God and the Soldier'.
Pr. *Divine Fancies*, 1632, i. 39; see *N. & Q.*, May 1952.
MS. Rawl. poet. 90, fol. 42; see also O1271, and W91 in MS. Rawl. poet. 153, fol. 21.

239 God and the world are masters opposite
Cannot receive in heavenly delectation.

MS. *Rawl. poet. 97, fol. $21^v$ (autogr.).

240 God bless King James our joy
Thus must come buy it.

MSS. Don. c. 54, fol. $60^v$; Rawl. D. 398, fol. 192.

241 God bless me, and my husband Davy Dee,
And nobody else Lord I beseech thee.

'A Woeman comming to Church began her prayers after this manner', and 'The Clearke['s] reply'.
MS. Malone 19, p. 139.

242 God bless our gracious sovereign Ann
On t'other side the main.

[Maynwaring, Arthur], 'The History of the Fall of the Conformity Bill, 1703'.
See *Life and posthumous works of A. Maynwaring*, by J. Oldmixon, 1715, p. 40. Attr. to R. Wisdom, B.M. Add. MS. 7122, fol. 6.
MSS. Locke c. 32, fol. 44, attr. to Rob. Wisedom; Rawl. D. 360, fol. 62; Rawl. poet. 169, fol. 29; pr. bk. Firth b. 21, fol. 51.

243 God bless our gracious sovereign Anne
No other guarantee.

'To the Tune of Chevy Chase. The Managers'. 1713.
Pr. bk. Firth b. 21, fol. 133.

244 God bless our young prince and endow him with grace
And send him instructors no worse than the last.

On the quarrel among the governors of the Prince of Wales, 1752.
MS. Eng. misc. b. 48, fol. 89; pr. bk. Firth b. 22, fol. 54.

245 God bless Queen Ann, and send her when she dies
To reign in Heaven where all the angels flies.

Ashe, Betty, couplet.
MS. Rawl. poet. 191, fol. $105^v$.

God bless the King, God bless our faiths defender 246
God bless us all. Thats quite another thing.

Byrom, Dr. John, of Manchester, 'Epigram . . . 1745'.
Pr. in *D.N.B. s.v.* Byrom.
MS. Eng. poet. c. 18, fol. 202.

God bless the king, the queen, god bless 247
And then the kingdom shall be safe.

'Ben: Jonson's grace', cf. O1289, T854.
MS. Rawl. poet. 160, fol. $175^v$.

God bless the wean! meschanter fa' me 248
And brag the name o't.

'A Poet's Welcome to his Bastard-Wean. by Rob. Burns . . . communicated to [Francis Douce] by Captain Grose, who had [it] from Burns himself'.
Pr. bk. Douce B. 426, MS. p. 11 at end.

God freely gives, as freely we receive: 249
It is not, do: but, ask, and thou shalt have.

[Quarles, Francis], 'On Gods Bounty'.
Pr. *Divine Fancies*, 1632, iii. 73.
MS. Rawl. poet. 90, fol. 72.

God from his heavenly throne 250
When he from them departs.

'Engl. Primer of our Ladie. 1631 . . . p. 324'.
MS. *Eng. poet. e. 56, p. 16.

God from whose work mankind did spring 251
[Reigning whilst times and ages last].

'Engl. Primer of our Ladie. 1631 . . . p. 10'.
MS. Eng. poet. e. 56, p. 33.

God gave Satan leave that he should take 252
T' increase his misery he left his wife.

[Owen's Epigram], '199. The Miseries of Job'.
MS. *Rawl. poet. 197, fol. $9^v$ (autogr.).

God gives not kings the style of gods in vain 253
Resembling right the mighty king divine.

King James I (?), 'The Argument of the booke. Sonnet', *Basilikon Doron*, 1603.
Pr. in King James's *Works*, 1616, p. 137; see MS. Eng. poet. c. 11, fol. 66.
MSS. Douce 97, p. ix; Eng. poet. c. 11, fol. 67; Rawl. C. 744, fol. 36.

God gives us strength, and keeps us sound 254
Above the reach of harms.

Herbert, Mary (*née* Sidney), Countess of Pembroke, Psalm xlvi.
MS. *Rawl. poet. 24, p. 67; 117, fol. $255^v$ rev.

255 God grant us grace
Gives us a perfect rise.
Robinson, Robert, 'Grace / race / ace'.
MS. *Rawl. poet. 218, p. 67 (autogr.).

256 God hath our bodies framed so fit, so fair
Want we a finger: in our work we linger.
Robinson, Robert.
MS. *Rawl. poet. 218, p. 128 (autogr.).

257 God hie thee me to save
Lord make no long delay.
Herbert, Mary (*née* Sidney), Countess of Pembroke, Psalm lxx.
MS. *Rawl. poet. 24, p. 99.

258 God I extol that high hath raised
Shall yield thanks all my days.
Psalm xxx.
MS. *Rawl. C. 113, fol. 26.

259 God in displeasure brought us low,
Our adversaries slain.
Psalm lx.
MS. *Rawl. C. 113, fol. 44.

260 God in Eden's garden's shade
Cuckolds are of women's making.
'Uppon a Cuckold'.
MSS. Ashmole 47, fol. 97v; Douce f. 5, fol. 30v; Rawl. D. 1092, fol. 268v, attr. to Tho. Randolph.

261 God, in the world's first age, seeing sin abound
And know the messenger of peace is near.
Mervall, Alphonso, 'To Mr Noe his Maiestyes Attorny generalle' [1631–4].
MS. *Rawl. poet. 166, p. 64 (autogr.).

262 God is in all his servants needs at hand
What will he do for them that overcome?
MS. *Rawl. poet. 97, fol. 25 (autogr.).

263 God is made man, and being man doth deign
No sin made sin, that sin be made no sin.
Clifford, Henry, Earl of Cumberland, 'New Years Day'.
MS. *Rawl. poet. 95, fol. 32v.

264 God is my gift, himself he freely gave me
God's gift am I, and none but he shall have me.
[Newman, Thomas (?)], distich.
MS. Top. Oxon. f. 39, fol. 14, in Newman's hand.

265 God is my health and saving strength;
Wait on the Lord, I say.
Psalm xxvii.
MS. *Montagu e. 10, fol. 18.

God is our refuge and our hope, 266
On him our hope depends.
Psalm xlvi.
MS. *Montagu e. 10, fol. 66v.

God is our refuge, present help 267
Jacob's God on our side.
Psalm xlvi.
MS. *Rawl. C. 113, fol. 36v.

God is the fountain whence 268
My swift revolving days.
Beddome, Benjamin, Psalm xxiii.
MS. *Eng. misc. e. 227, fol. 84.

God is the object of my hope 269
And my eternal home.
Beddome, Benjamin.
MS. *Eng. misc. e. 227, fol. 8v.

God is the potter, we the pots, dear brother 270
'Tis sin that breaks us one against another.
[Jordan, Thomas], couplet. 'The Comparison of Pott and Potter'.
Pr. *Divinity and Morality*, 1660, Sig. §§5v.
MS. Rawl. poet. 90, fol. 103.

God longed for man's love, and down was sent 271
But why we should not, or how we should none are.
Alabaster, William, 'Sonnet 28. Veni mittere ignem'.
MS. *Eng. poet. e. 57, fol. 7.

God loves not man, because that man is good: 272
Makes but a syllogism of his own confusion.
[Quarles, Francis], 'On Mans Goodnesse and Gods Love'.
Pr. *Divine Fancies*, 1632, i. 44.
MS. Rawl. poet. 90, fol. 62.

God made a building rare on earth 273
Which makes the owners rue.
Verses added at the end of 'The Pilgrimage of Man'.
MS. Laud misc. 740, fol. 129.

God made men pure; 'gainst God man sins 274
Christ doth to life restore.
Robinson, Robert.
MS. *Rawl. poet. 218, p. 121 (autogr.).

God many blessings on us doth dispense; 275
Not worthy are of the sweet joys to come.
MS. *Rawl. poet. 97, fol. 33 (autogr.).

God mongst th' assemblies sets his throne 276
God's King though your power cease.
Fairfax, Thomas, Lord, Psalm lxxxii.
MS. *Fairfax 40, p. 194 (autogr.).
MS. *Fairfax 38, p. 82.

277 God moves in a mysterious way
And He can make it plain.
Cowper, William, 'God inscrutable'.
*Olney Hymns*, III. xv.
MS. Eng. poet. c. 51, p. 192.

278 God my defence, my rock, my worthy arm,
Doth, hath and will preserve my soul from harm.
[Daniel, Richard], 'alt[erum anagramma]' on Lady Whitmore.
MS. Rawl. poet. 97, fol. 77^v (autogr.).

279 God of everlasting power
With that ecstatic gaze.
Kenton, James.
MS. *Eng. poet. e. 20, p. 338 (autogr.).

280 God of love and truth and power
What is holiness above.
Kenton, James.
MS. *Eng. poet. e. 20, p. 276 (autogr.).

281 God of love thy grace bestow
Filled with all thy grace and love.
Kenton, James.
MS. *Eng. poet. e. 20, p. 226 (autogr.).

282 God of my health, whose tender care
Who stamped his image there.
Lewis, John, Hymn I.
MS. Eng. th. f. 9, p. 267.

283 God of my life for ever blest
Since the great saviour's mine.
Beddome, Benjamin.
MS. *Eng. misc. e. 227, fol. 31^v.

284 God of revenge, revenging God appear,
And what they mean, their own malicious will.
Herbert, Mary (*née* Sidney), Countess of Pembroke, Psalm xciv.
MS. *Rawl. poet. 24, p. 138.

285 God of slaughter, quit the scene
To save the land of liberty and laws.
[Whitehead, William], New Year Ode, 1762.
Pr. *Poems*, 1774, ii. 276.
MS. Mus. Sch. D. 310. Music by W. Boyce.

286 God of sleep for whom I languish
Let Strephon know 'twas all a dream.
MS. Top. Oxon. e. 379, fol. 14^v.

287 God of the patriarchal race
But fulness of delight obtain.
Kenton, James.
MS. *Eng. poet. e. 20, p. 117 (autogr.).

God of universal grace 288
For ever to endure.
Kenton, James.
MS. *Eng. poet. e. 20, p. 392 (autogr.).

God of universal nature 289
Fixt immoveably to stand.
Kenton, James.
MS. *Eng. poet. e. 20, p. 160 (autogr.).

God of winds, when thou art grown 290
Fitter for thy churlish war.
Part-song.
MS. Mus. c. 5, fol. 12^v.

God, oh our god, we praise thy name: 291
Confounded let me never be.
Oldisworth, Nicolas, 'At the Command of his reverend diocesan Godfry Goodman, bishop of Glocester [1625–1640] A translation of Te deum laudamus after the tune of the 100 Psalme'.
MS. *Don. c. 24, fol. 75^v (autogr.).

God on us thy mercy show 292
All lands his force shall fear.
Herbert, Mary (*née* Sidney), Countess of Pembroke, Psalme lxvii.
MSS. Rawl. poet. *24, p. 93; *25, fol. 56^v.

God prosper long from being lost 293
Nor rivals break the chain.
Sheppard, Elizabeth, 'a somewhat in shape of a ballad', 1738.
MS. Top. Oxon. d. 287, fol. 46 (autogr.).

God prosper long our gracious king. 294
Descend from F[oo]l to F[ool].
'An Ode for the New-Year' after 1730.
MSS. Eng. poet. f. 12, p. 114, satirically attr. to Colley Cibber; Top. Oxon. b. 170, fol. 13^v.

God prosper long our gracious queen 295
In all the world may cease.
'On the Battle of Audenard', 1708.
Pr. bk. Firth b. 21, fol. 66.

God prosper long our gracious Will 296
And so God save the prince.
'K[ing] W[illiam's] Triumph . . . an Excellent new Ballad of all his glorious Atchievements since his Landing', 1690.
MSS. Eng. poet. c. 18, fol. 173^v; e. 50, p. 43.

God prosper long our noble king 297
Than they infringe thy laws.
Amherst, Elizabeth, 'A pious old Song in praise of Chastity'.
MS. *Eng. poet. e. 109, p. 95.

298 God prosper long our noble king,
With all their royal progeny.
T. S., 'The English-mans Valour, or The Hampshire-Friggets fight with six Spanish Ships in Cales-Road'.
MS. Firth c. 18, fol. 50.

299 God prosper long our noble king
Till they are at Hanover.
'A Ballad on the Christening 1718'.
Pr. bk. Firth b. 22, fol. 20.

300 God prosper long our noble king
Which God grant may be soon.
'The Belgick Bore, or Chivy Chace Revived'.
Pr. black-letter broadside, 1695.
MSS. Rawl. poet. 169, two copies, fols. 3, 4$^{v}$; 207, p. 10.

301 God prosper long our noble king
And all the people laugh.
'An excellent new and long Historical Ballad upon the Times. 1755'.
Pr. bk. Firth b. 22, fol. 55.

302 God prosper long our noble king
To birth and merit cease.
'Parody on Chevy-Chace' 1766.
Pr. bk. Firth b. 22, fol. 66.

303 God prosper long the varsity
In Bagley-Wood may cease.
Robinson, [Thomas], Fellow of Merton College, Oxford, 'A full and true Account of a Robbery Not committed at Bagley-Wood . . . Novr. 4, 1728. In humble imitation of Chevey Chase'.
MS. Ballard 29, fol. 59.

304 God reigns in glorious majesty above,
To deck thy holy house, the place of thine abode.
Knollys, Fra., Psalm xciii.
MS. *Rawl. poet. 60, p. 31 (autogr.).

God rest you . . . see Sit you . . .

305 God save great George our king
Huzza Huzza.
'God save the King Sung at the Theatres Royal'.
MS. Mus. e. 19, p. 73.

306 God save great Marlborough's Duke
Though the bells must not ring, we will huzza.
'A new Song' in shorthand.
Pr. in *The Oxfordshire Contest*, 1753, p. 48.
MS. Mus. e. 20, fol. 25*c*.

307 God save me for thy holy name,
On them my heart's desire.
[Hopkins, John], Psalm liv.
MS. Rawl. poet. 112, fol. 55$^{v}$ rev.

God save us all, and well to speed 308
From goo[d] company must turn his back.
Six lines on the value of money written early 16th cent. on a printed indulgence for the ransom of prisoners, dated 1515, *S.T.C.* 15472.
Pr. bk. Arch. A. b. 8(10).

God seeing man in that deplored estate 309
From him divert can God's affection.
MS. *Rawl. poet. 97, fol. 15$^{v}$ (autogr.).

God send us peace, 310
And never cease.
Robinson, Robert.
MS. *Rawl. poet. 218, p. 112 (autogr.).

God shield me from those friends I trust: and be 311
My firm defence from such, as trust not thee.
[Quarles, Francis], 'On Friendes', couplet.
Pr. *Divine Fancies*, 1632, iii. 12.
MS. Rawl. poet. 90, fol. 71$^{v}$.

God spake these words, and said, I am thy God 312
Nor covet what is his (by right, or labour).
[Jordan, Thomas], 'The Ten Comandem$^{ts}$ in ten lines'.
Pr. *Divinity and Morality*, Sig. §§§6$^{v}$.
MS. Rawl. poet. 90, fol. 84$^{v}$.

God stands between the prince, the peer, the judge, 313
For thou shalt take the heathen to thy possession.
Harington, Sir John, Psalm lxxxii.
MS. *Douce 361, fol. 50.

God takes the good, too good on earth to stay 314
And leaves the bad too bad to take away.
'Epitaph . . . Peterborough Cathedral'.
MS. Eng. poet. c. 51, p. 32.

God that schope both sea and sonde 315
To Elizabeth of England our Queen.
'Kinge Richards feilde . . . Bosworth feild fought Aug. 22. A.D. 1485, between R.3. and H.7'.
MS. Tanner 306, fol. 164.

God the beginner is of every thing 316
Of all good thing God the beginner is.
MS. *Rawl. poet. 97, fol. 2 (autogr.).

God to th'upright in heart's a sure reward 317
To draw near god and trust is best to do.
Fairfax, Thomas, Lord, Psalm lxxiii.
MS. *Fairfax 40, p. 163 (autogr.).
MS. *Fairfax 38, p. 245.

God was in love with man, and sued then 318
How must we love him, that so loves his creature?
Alabaster, William, 'Son: 30. Incarnatio divini amoris argumentum'.
MS. *Eng. poet. e. 57, fol. 7$^{v}$.

319 God was made lower than the angels, that
But man alone was not so soon restored.
MS. *Rawl. poet. 97, fol. 17v (autogr.).

320 God which art most merciful,
According, to the multitude, of thy compassions seen.
Byrd's 3-part setting of Psalm li.
Pr. *Songs of sundrie natures*, 1589.
MSS. Mus. f. 11–15: f. 11, fol. 3v.

321 God who all the world doth hold
In thy courts in heavenly pleasure.
Psalm xxiii.
MS. Rawl. poet. 117, fol. 267 rev.

322 God who is infinitely good and wise,
But kills it young, that it may ne'er be old.
Williams, John, 'To a Parent guilty of false Indulgence'.
MS. *Rawl. poet. 184, fol. 5 (autogr.).

323 God, who of naught at all, this all did fashion
Thy house is still graced with sanctification.
Jos. Br., Psalm xciii, 'To St. Bernards Hymne of Cur Mundus militat'.
MS. Rawl. poet. 61, fol. 47v.

324 God who rebuked heathen kings for his
So the Lord His doth in all ages keep.
MS. *Rawl. poet. 97, fol. 26 (autogr.).

325 God who th'universe doth hold
In thy courts with heavenly pleasure.
Davison, Francis, Psalm xxiii.
MSS. Rawl. D. 316, fol. 127v; *Rawl. poet. 61, fol. 16v.

326 God works [by miracles] wonders now and then
Here lies a lawyer an honest man.
[Harington, Sir John], 'On a Lawyer'.
Pr. *Alcilia*, 1613, amongst 'Epigrammes by Sir I. H. and others'; and in *Wits Recreations*, 1640, no. 47.
MSS. CCC. 328, fol. 20v; Don. d. 58, fol. 19v; Eng. poet. f. 10, fol. 101v; Sancroft 53, p. 44; Tanner 465, fol. 62; see also H995*b*, H1020.

327 God would no longer spare this treasure lent,
When Christ her mortal shall immortalize.
Aylett, Robert, LL.D. of Trinity Hall, 'Charissimæ suæ Iudithæ filiæ Johannis Gaell de Hadleigh gen.', 11 Dec. 1623.
MS. Rawl. D. 317, fol. 178.

328 Goddess blest with sprightly mien
Owned the force of comic song.
Boswell, James, 'Ode to Comedy'.
MS. *Douce 193, fol. 64 (autogr.).

Goddess of discord who persuading power 329
Shall equal Stopfords Christian life by S[cott].
Gough, Richard, 'On the Presbyterian Minister at Enfield 1773 Jan. 4'.
MS. *Eng. poet. c. 5, fol. 219 (autogr.).

Goddess of ease leave Lethe's brink 330
And find a pleasing end in thee.
[Percy, Thomas, nephew of the Bishop of Dromore (?)], 'Ode to Idleness'.
MS. Percy c. 8, fol. 24, in T. Percy's hand.

Goddess of golden dreams! whose magic power, 331
And give me, more than fortune can bestow!
'Fancy—An Elegy'.
MS. Montagu e. 14, fol. 30.

Goddess of shades, and huntress who at will 332
Shall awe the world, and conquer nations bold.
Hearne, Thomas (?), translation of Brute's address to Diana from Geoffry of Monmouth, I. vii; quoted by Hearne in his manuscript 'Epitome . . . of English History'.
MS. Rawl. D. 1171, fol. 13v, in Hearne's hand.

Goddess! thou whose potent sway 333
May we sit, secure from piles.
Parsons, William.
MS. *Don. d. 123, p. 19 (autogr.).

God's boundless bounty there we shall behold 334
Who joyed above in all eternity.
F. W., 'Sonnet 40'.
MS. *Rawl. C. 639, p. 198.

God's foot, God's blood God's heart, God's 'oonds 335
They have stolen away all my Male-go-toones.
Weston, Dr., couplet.
MS. Malone 19, p. 1.

Gods have their flying Mercury, and we 336
The jarring world in bonds of amity.
Morrice, John, 'Upon Letters . . . Jan. 30. 1707'.
MS. *Rawl. poet. 114, fol. 124 (autogr.).

Gods, how it rains! how sad the sun appears! 337
Cuckolds to Heaven go. God save the king.
'On the Sun's shining in a rainy Day'.
MS. Top. Oxon. b. 170, fol. 21.

Gods! How you promised, how you spoke, 338
In memory of your faithful injured lover, I.
Chatwin, John, 'Forsaken'.
MS. *Rawl. poet. 94, p. 14 (autogr.).

God's infinite immenseness doth confound 339
Or more and thus through th' whole expanse of heaven.
MS. *Don. f. 5, fol. 20v.

340 God's is the praise of every thing. Th' least good
Redound may to His glory: their hearts grief.
MS. *Rawl. poet. 97, fol. 4 (autogr.).

341 God's law was broken, 's justice was offended,
The woman's seed hath broke the serpent's head.
MS. *Rawl. poet. 97, fol. 69ᵛ (autogr.).

342 God's life! we're undone, a pox of your son
Turn which way, we will, we're undone.
'A summ of a Discourse, that past betweene H[is] M[ajesty] and R[oyal] H[ighness] 5° Junij. 1678'.
MSS. Don. b. 8, p. 577; Douce 357, fol. 76.

343 God's love to man did put His power in action
More plain are, and perspicuous made to all.
MS. *Rawl. poet. 97, fol. 68ᵛ (autogr.).

344 God's love to man is of so large extension
Of great Jehovah's mercy, love, and might.
MS. *Rawl. poet. 97, fol. 2ᵛ (autogr.).

345 God's love to man is the prime spring from whence
The virtue of Christ's passion, and God's love.
MS. *Rawl. poet. 97, fol. 68 (autogr.).

346 God's love to man (it is most manifest)
Himself in this one action did unite.
MS. *Rawl. poet. 97, fol. 71ᵛ (autogr.).

347 God's love to man was of such virtue, that
The Lord doth thence good to His Church derive.
MS. *Rawl. poet. 97, fol. 69 (autogr.).

348 God's love's unutterable He ordained
So woman's eke remade, a help for man.
MS. *Rawl. poet. 97, fol. 73ᵛ (autogr.).

349 God's mercy towards us is so great, that 'twould
That might not die to live, shall live to die.
Oldisworth, Giles or Robert.
MS. *Rawl. C. 422, fol. 28ᵛ, in the hand of Giles Oldisworth.

350 God's mighty works in her appear
And let her see his face, Amen.
MS. Eng. poet. b. 5, p. 69.

351 God's only good; the devil's wholly bad:
God gives true joy; the devil makes men mad.
Robinson, Robert, couplet.
MS. *Rawl. poet. 218, p. 164 (autogr.).

352 God's power in making man is eminent:
To God, for our wellbeing then much moe.
MS. *Rawl. poet. 97, fol. 18 (autogr.).

Gods! What a form was there, how ev'ry part 353
So bravely they beyond excess would love.
Chatwin, John, 'On Lisonia's Rising'.
MS. *Rawl. poet. 94, p. 27 (autogr.).

Gods! What a night was that! How soft the bed! 354
I'll perish thus, and nobly die with love.
Chatwin, John, 'Out of Petronius Arbiter'.
MS. *Rawl. poet. 94, p. 220 (autogr.).

Gods! who'd e'er tempt the stormy main 355
To bless his offspring's future days.
Whaley, John, 'Verses wrote in the Summer House', in which Steele wrote his *Conscious Lovers*.
Pr. *Poems*, 1732, p. 101.
MS. Rawl. poet. 222, fol. 14.

God's will revealed was opposite unto 356
But in thy favour is eternal pleasure!
MS. *Rawl. poet. 97, fol. 70ᵛ (autogr.).

God's wonderful in all his works: His Name 357
The Lord works miracles by contraries.
MS. *Rawl. poet. 97, fol. 19 (autogr.).

God's word's his work: so soon as he hath said, 358
Man's work must make his word good; else 'tis vain.
Robinson, Robert.
MS. *Rawl. poet. 218, p. 52 (autogr.).

God's works are admirable all; nor can 359
The Gospel preached heard, and did obey.
MS. *Rawl. poet. 97, fol. 53 (autogr.).

Going to bed 360
To bed for good and all.
'Bed-Time'.
MS. Eng. poet. e. 51, p. 55.

Gold father of flatterers son of grief and care 361*a*
Who have thee not have grief, who have thee fear.
Walsh, William, couplet.
MS. Malone 9, fol. 27 (autogr.).

Gold is a cordial and that is the reason 361*b*
You misers lives so long in season.
Couplet.
MS. Rawl. poet. 5, fol. iii.

Gold is restorative. How can I than 362
If I should separate what so is knit.
S[trode], W[illiam], 'Letter . . . to Sir Tho: Ferrers'.
MS. Eng. poet. e. 97, p. 135.

363 Gold like a flattering glass does all deceive
Who look in often, and the cheat believe.
Williams, John.
MS. *Rawl. poet. 184, fol. 53 (autogr.).

364 Gold rules within, and reigns without these doors
He votes for interest, and she f-ks for coin.
'Writ over the House of Commons Door. 1700 . . . Mountague and Lady Orkney'.
Pr. Anthony Hammond's *Miscellany*, 1720, p. 131.
MS. Eng. poet. e. 50, p. 133.

365 Gold weighs down laws, the saxons used of old
That sold for gold which should by law be given.
MS. Rawl. poet. 206, p. 33.

366 Gold's worth we by the touchstone find.
Gold is the touchstone of the mind.
'On Gold', couplet.
MS. Rawl. poet. 90, fol. 104.

367 Gone are my happy days all lost for she
Then her reproachful eyes will strike me dead.
MS. Rawl. poet. 196, fol. 29v.

368 Good and bad fruit springs up in every ground:
Virtue and vice in every man is found.
Robinson, Robert, couplet.
MS. *Rawl. poet. 218, p. 25 (autogr.).

369 Good and good do well agree:
They've heavenly joy, or hellish strife.
Robinson, Robert.
MS. *Rawl. poet. 218, p. 171 (autogr.).

370 Good arguments without coin will not stick
To pay and not to say's best rhetoric.
Couplet.
MS. Rawl. poet. 153, fol. 28.

371 Good arts and good parts where's want of good hearts
Are the devil's gilded, but poisonous darts.
Robinson, Robert, couplet.
MS. *Rawl. poet. 218, p. 16 (autogr.).

372 Good audience hearken to me in this case
Is to know where I shall have a new.
Wallys, J[ohn].
MS. Ashmole 48, fol. 78v.

373 Good bearer of thy cross, etc.
'Philomathes', 1667. From Prudentius; *incipit* quoted with ref. to '4° paper book p. 50'.
MS. Eng. th. d. 52, fol. 117.

374 Good cheer with small beer (the case is most clear)
It comforts the stomach, and helps to digest.
Robinson, Robert.
MS. *Rawl. poet. 218, p. 69 (autogr.).

Good creatures we are, which serve in men's need 375
Yet oft do they force us to give that we have not.
Riddle.
MS. Rawl. poet. 217, fol. 78v.

Good Daniel's sifting, in God's church about, 376
And to all such preachers, and use well the sieve.
'A new ballad Intituled, Daniels siftyng in these our dayes . . . 1572'.
MS. Firth d. 14, fol. 106.

Good day Mirtello. And to you no less. 377
We'll bless his face, then back to country pleasure.
'A pastoral on' [the birth of Charles II].
MS. Eng. poet. e. 14, fol. 48.

Good deeds ill placed, which we on all men heap 378
He that hath many pays for't in the end.
'In Amicitiam'.
MS. Don. d. 58, fol. 39v.

Good doctor, brother of the string, 379
And bear in friendship's fane the biggest bell away.
[Roach, Richard], 'Æson: or The Golden Branch. Epistle to Dr. B-r'.
MS. Rawl. D. 832, fol. 165 (autogr.).

Good ever due destroyed with present ill 380
Beyond her life that made you err in vain.
'An Aunswere to I760, 'in the faver of the Duke of Norfolk', 1569.
MS. Gough Norfolk 43, fol. 53v.

Good faith I never was but once so mad 381
Or I'll be as indifferent as she.
'The Humourist'.
Pr. bk. Vet. A3 e. 40, fly-leaf.

Good fellows matter not, nor bush nor sign 382
That when the sign is down can't find the house.
Dated, '1674/5'.
MS. Add. B. 8, fol. 6.

Good fellows must go learn to dance 383
For we must merry be.
Song for four voices by William Parson.
MS. Mus. e. 1–5: e. 1, fol. 72v.

Good folk [folks] for gold [love] or [else for] hire 384
Or send it home to me.
[Drayton, Michael], 'The Crier'.
Pr. Drayton's *Poems*, 1619; *Wits Recreations*, 1663, Sig. R1; and *Songs for 1, 2, and 3 voices*, H. Bowman, 1678, p. 63.
MSS. Don. b. 9, fol. 18; Eng. poet. c. 53, fol. 1v; d. 152, fol. 107v; e. 14, fol. 20; e. 97, p. 163, attr. to Ben. Jonson; Eng. poet. f. 9, p. 8; Malone 21, fol. 66; Mus. Sch. C. 145, fol. 2, set as Oxford Act Song by Henry Bowman; see also D89.

385 **Good friend, for Jesus' sake, forbear**
**And curst be he that moves my bones.**
'On [Shakespeare's] Grave-Stone', Stratford on Avon.
Pr. 'Some Account of the Life', *Works* of S., ed. N. Rowe, 1709, i, p. xxxvii.
MSS. Eng. poet. e. 40, fol. 165; Tanner 89, fol. 262ᵛ; Top. gen. e. 32, fol. 52ᵛ; see also R38.

386 **Good God; how dull a thing am I, to make**
**Advanced above earth, sin, dark night and sleep.**
[Ingelo, Nathaniel], 'A Holy Morning Song'.
Pr. as Ingelo's in *Miscellanea Sacra*, 2nd ed., 1732.
MS. Rawl. poet. 90, fol. 134.

387 **Good god unlock thy magazines**
**With many sacrificed beast.**
Carew, Thomas, Psalm li.
MSS. Ashmole 38, p. 98*b*; *Don. b. 9, fol. 8.

388 **Good God, what weather's here: these souls of our**
**She may arrive where's neither clouds nor showers.**
[Quarles, Francis], 'On These Showres'.
Pr. *Divine Fancies*, 1632, iii. 43.
MS. Rawl. poet. 90, fol. 54.

389–90 **Good Halifax and pious Wharton cry**
**First stops her mouth, and then deflowers the dame.**
'The Church in no Danger'.
Copied by Hearne 18 Dec. 1705.
Pr. Hearne's *Collections*, ed. C. E. Doble, i, O.H.S. ii, 1885, p. 132. Dated 1705 in B.M. MS. Lansdowne 852.
MSS. Hearne's diaries 6, p. 191; Rawl. poet. 81, fol. 42ᵛ; see also G396.

391 **Good humoured, noted for an early wit**
**With bright esteem, and glorious lustre shine.**
Williams, John, 'To Miss Betty (Ashe)'.
MS. *Rawl. poet. 191, fol. 105 (autogr.).

392 **Good Jerome, your sermon I've read, and I vow**
**That you, Reverend Sir, are to preach.**
'Epigram. Take heed how ye hear'.
MS. Eng. poet. c. 51, p. 89.

393 **Good lessons are better for vices confusion,**
**Then queries and questions, that work dis-affection.**
Robinson, Robert.
MS. *Rawl. poet. 218, p. 58 (autogr.).

394 **Good Lord how vain are men, whose very lives**
**Informed with true wisdom, that's with thee.**
'A Meditation Occasioned by the death of that worthy Knight Sr. Samson Darell'. 1635.
MS. Rawl. poet. 210, fol. 64 rev.

**Good Madam Fowler do not trouble me** 395
**Against her self conceived an epigram.**
B., F., 'Epigram'.
Attr. to 'F. Beo', B.M. MS. Egerton 2026, fol. 67.
MSS. Eng. poet. e. 37, p. 29, attr. to F. B.; f. 9, p. 136; Rawl. poet. 31, fol. 48.

**Good Marlborough, and pious Wharton cry,** 396
**First stop the mouths, and then deflower the dame.**
'The Church out of Danger'.
MS. Eng. poet. e. 87, p. 72; see also G389.

**Good men desire, that wars may cease;** 397
**Wars, or not wars, t'increase.**
Robinson, Robert.
MS. *Rawl. poet. 218, p. 35 (autogr.).

**Good Mr. Church-Warden,** 398
**Is St. Bridget, and Bride again.**
[Roach, Richard], 'To the Church-Warden of St. B[ride]'s on the Bells not Ringing the First of August' [Proclamation of George I, 1714].
MS. Rawl. D. 832, fol. 175 (autogr.).

**Good Mr. Gill I doubt not your skill** 399
**And send me my hair back again.**
'Mr. Vaughan to Mr. Gill his Periwig maker or the Revd. Mr. Vaughan at Eddingal by Tamworth to Mr. Gill at Litchfield'.
MS. Ballard 47, fol. 47.

**Good morning to your chastest loves, the day** 400
**Each night a Cupid, and be youthful yet.**
'On the Union' of Humphrey Rogers and Anne Baynton.
MS. Rawl. poet. 65, fol. 50.

**Good morrow gentle mistress I may say** 401
**To see the saint whom I so much adore.**
Burton, Francis.
MS. *Add. A. 267, fol. 76 (autogr.).

**Good morrow unto her, who in the night** 402
**But none so full of faith, and flame as mine.**
Shirley, James.
Pr. *Poems*, 1646, p. 3.
MS. *Rawl. poet. 88, p. 57.

**Good neighbour Will I prithee be plain** 403
**Drink liberal cups of innocent love.**
'A dialogue between Will and Tom, Tune, The drainers are up'.
MS. Rawl. poet. 37, p. 71.

**Good news in arrived** 404
**Wherever he goes.**
'The Soldiers Praise of Duke William', William Augustus, Duke of Cumberland, 1721–65.
MSS. Firth c. 17, fol. 46; c. 20, fol. 48.

405 Good or bad you must take it as 'tis
For I can't make it otherwiz.

Couplet, 'My Cousin Mary Wagstaffe made upon some of her verses . . . for which they call'd her wiz' copied by John Williams.
MS. Rawl. poet. 191, fol. 105[v].

406 Good people all compose this scrape
In summer with the other.

'On the Bangorian controversy'.
Pr. bk. Firth b. 22, fol. 17.

407 Good people draw near
Let no married man praise his wife.

'The Husband deceived in a Wife'.
MS. Mus. e. 19, p. 84.

408 Good people draw near
Level coil with a prince and a player.

MS. Don. b. 8, p. 184.

409 Good people, I pray ye come hither
We never shall see any Moor.

'Jan. 3. 1691'.
MS. Firth d. 13, fol. 74.

410 Good people, I pray you, give ear unto me
We've witnesses ready to swear it all out.

'A new Narrative of the popish plot . . . To the tune of Packingtons pound'. *c.* 1678.
MS. Rawl. poet. 169, fol. 24.

411 Good people let me beg attention
Let's pray to God our King to bless-a.

'The Secret Expedition'.
MS. Firth c. 18, fol. 91.

412 Good people what will you of all be bereft
Why should we, why should we be kept in the dark?

[Ward, Edward], 'A Song', 1696.
Pr. *Poems on Affairs of State*, ii, 1703, p. 264; Ward's *Miscellaneous Writings*, iii, 2nd ed. 1712, p. 326; and Tom Brown's *Works*, 1730, iv, 'Supplement', p. 278. Also found in MS. of verse by Henry Hall, Brotherton Collection, University of Leeds.
MSS. Rawl. D. 361, fol. 211[v]; 383, fol. 55.

413 Good proverbs show the wisdom of a nation
We charge our blunders on ill luck, or fortune.

Roach, Richard, verse and answer.
MS. Rawl. D. 833, fol. 136[v] rev. (autogr.).

414 Good Robert King, we humbly pray,
That all they've said are lies.

'The Country-Mens Petition' to Sir Robert Walpole, 1732.
MS. Ballard 50, fol. 109[v].

Good Sace for Church of England's carse 415
Cause he more money craves.

MS. Rawl. poet. 196, fol. 30.

Good sir he that dwells everywhere; 416
No where can we say, that he dwelleth there.

Couplet, translating Martial, *Epigrams* VII. lxxiii. 6.
MS. Rawl. D. 986, fol. 109[v].

Good sir to you, for your kind letter 417
Sir your true servant Thomas Weaver.

Weaver, Thomas, 'From Llangiby Castle in Monmouthshire, To Sir Evan Lloyd in London'.
Pr. *Songs and Poems*, 1654.
MS. *Rawl. poet. 211, fol. 69[v] (autogr.).

Good Sirs, forbear, whoe'er strives to beguile 418
To guard my breast from flames, give hers new heat.

Weaver, Thomas, 'To his freindes who sought to comfort him after the fayre Sylvia's departure'.
Pr. *Songs and Poems*, 1654.
MS. *Rawl. poet. 211, fol. 2 (autogr.).

Good time go tell the truth 419
Upon my soul is true.

MS. Ashmole 51, fol. 6[v].

Good we must love, and most hate ill. 420
Who doth not fling away the shell.

Donne, John.
Pr. *Poems*, 1633.
MSS. *Eng. poet. e. 99, fol. 117[v]; *f. 9, p. 102.

Good wench, deny, my love is cloyed 421
Unless joys grieve, before enjoyed.

MS. Rawl. D. 431, fol. 138[v] rev.

Good words as words, indeed are truly civil, 422
But oh take heed: good words oft tend to evil.

Robinson, Robert, couplet.
MS. *Rawl. poet. 218, p. 133 (autogr.).

Good works are necessary to be done 423
Love will the longest last none can deny.

Tipping, William, 'Of Good Works Absolutely Necessarie'.
MS. *Rawl. poet. 101, fol. 58[v] (autogr.).

Good works can merit nought, they say, yet sure 424
To see them prosper, Heaven's reward will find.

Wingfield, Edward, of King's School, Sherborne, on the death of Robert Whetcombe, 'Antientest Governour of the King's Schoole of Shereborne. 24. Oct. 1656'.
MS. Gough Dorset 35 (1), fol. 21.

425 Good worthy captain if I were so fraught
And love could work like their black murmuring art.
James, Richard, 'Ad Capitaneum Davidem Gilbertum Scotum. cum una navigaremus in Dwina flumine', 1618.
MS. *James 13, fol. 237 (autogr.).

426 Goodness by nature as trial teacheth
Then god by giving god, must work the same.
F. W., 'Sonnet 42'.
MS. *Rawl. C. 639, p. 202.

427 Gormando for gluttony famed through the town
Prithee step, and bring hither the rest of my fish.
Whaley, John, 'The Glutton; a Tale'.
Pr. *Poems*, 1732, p. 114.
MS. Rawl. poet. 222, fol. 15$^{v}$.

428 Gospel and physic gifts bless'd Luke reveals
More that, in teaching how to die a saint.
'Upon St. Luke the Evangelist', epigram.
MS. Top. London e. 9, p. 2.

429 Gout! I conjure thee by the powerful names
Their herring trade is brought unto its last.
[Wild, Robert], 'An Essay upon the late Victory obtained by his Royall Highnesse the Duke of Yorke against the Dutch upon June 3rd 1665. By the Author of Iter Boreale'.
Pr. in *Iter Boreale with large Additions*, 1668, p. 64.
MSS. Don. b. 8, p. 434; Eng. poet. c. 11, fol. 99.

430 Grace said in form, which sceptics must agree
Who lives to reason, and who dies a man.
Churchill, Charles, 'The Conference'.
MS. *Eng. poet. d. 113, p. 102.

431 Grachus his house hath chimneys round about
Makes all the smoke in's house go through his nose.
MS. Eng. poet. c. 50, fol. 34.

432 Gracious creator and our guide
Who reign always one God alone.
Huish, Alexander, 'Rerum creator optime', translated 5 May 1637.
MS. Eng. poet. e. 56, p. 70 (autogr.).

433 Gracious God most omnipotent
(Incomplete. Refrain:) *quem ventre puella baiulavit, etc.*
MS. Eng. poet. b. 5, p. 54.

434 Grafted upon the Christian stock
In all my intercourse below.
Kenton, James.
MS. *Eng. poet. e. 20, p. 193 (autogr.).

Grains of wheat shall be sown in the sea 435
Our joy into sorrow turned shall be.
'Thomas of Canterbury', prophecy.
MS. Rawl. C. 813, fol. 157.

Grammar's that art doth teach to speak and write 436
And t'know Thee and our selves that art of arts.
Cheyney, William, 'Liberall Artes'.
MS. *Rawl. poet. 86, fol. 26.

Grand Lewis let pride be abated 437
And take them *l'épee a la main.*
'On the battle of Audenard 1708'.
Pr. bk. Firth b. 21, fol. 67*a*.

Grant liberty of conscience; do: 438
And subject to least change.
Robinson, Robert.
MS. *Rawl. poet. 218, p. 149 (autogr.).

Grant me, Gods, a little seat, 439
When I ask a little more.
'A Little Wish . . . from the Old Whig' 15 Jan. 1735/6.
Pr. Dodsley's *Collection of Poems*, iv, 1755, p. 250.
MS. Eng. poet. c. 9, p. 73.

Grant me indulgent Heaven a rural seat, 440
From silent life I'd steal into my grave.
'The Choyce'.
MS. Rawl. poet. 90, fol. 120$^{v}$.

Grant me, ye fates, a calm retreat 441
Hangs down its head, and gently dies away.
Stukeley, William, 'The Druid'. 16 Apr. 1759.
Partly pr. by S. Piggott, *William Stukeley*, 1950, p. 178.
MS. Eng. misc. e. 138, fol. 48 (autogr.).

Grant mercy heavenly king 442
On all this earth below.
Harington, Sir John, Psalm lvii.
MS. *Douce 361, fol. 33$^{v}$.

Grant mercy Lord and grace 443
Shall laud and fear his name.
Harington, Sir John, Psalm lxvii.
MS. *Douce 361, fol. 39.

Grant mighty power that I may find 444
And more I'll ne'er require.
'The Lover's Supplication'.
MS. Eng. poet. e. 40, fol. 32.

Grant, oh my God, that I much profit may 445
Bless every help, and grant the wisht for end.
Williams, John, 'A prayer before Sermon. Copy'd'.
MS. *Rawl. poet. 192, fol. 31$^{v}$ (autogr.).

446 **Grateful Britons grace the day**
**Long and happy live the king.**
[Cibber, Colley], 'Ode compos'd for the New Year 1736/7 and perform'd at Court on that Day'; professional copy annotated by the composer, Dr. Maurice Greene.
MS. Mus. d. 37.

447 **Grateful's to me, the fire, the wound, the chain,**
**That burns, that binds, that hurts I must desire.**
'On Prince Charles when adressing himselfe to the Infanta', translation from Latin.
MS. Rawl. poet. 84, fol. 45.

448 **Grave Cicero whose sage edicts**
**Came both to's brewer and his baker.**
H. S.
MS. *Rawl. poet. 120, fol. 8ᵛ (autogr.).

449 **Grave deep in thy remembrance, lord,**
**In the deeds thy words command.**
Herbert, Mary (*née* Sidney), Countess of Pembroke, Psalm cxix, 'G.'
MSS. *Rawl. poet. 24, p. 179; *25, fol. 120ᵛ.

450 **Grave father, to thy much lamented hearse**
**Next! 'tis my hope at all saints we shall greet.**
On Dr. Bartholomew Warner, d. Jan. 1618/19.
Pr. bk. Wood 460, after *Threnodia in obitum E. Lewkenor*, 1606.

451 **Grave fathers in council, whose weighty command**
**To raise a monument that's worthy me.**
'Queen Elizabeth's Ghost', on 'an Equestrian Statue of William 3rd'.
MS. Eng. poet. e. 45, fol. 16.

452 **Grave friend I have received your gift but know**
**And be let in some though you come but late.**
[Dalby, Edward (?)], 'To his freind Edward Dawson Porter of new colledge in Oxford'.
MS. Ashmole 47, fol. 129.

453 **Graves are lodgings to the blest,**
**In this hope they here reside.**
'Old Church of Banbury. Gentleman's Magazine March 1799'.
MS. Top. gen. e. 32, fol. 118ᵛ.

454 **Great Aaron's son, one of the Levite's train**
**A faithful Abra'm lived, and made an end.**
On Wm. Savage, 1619, Rottingdean Churchyard. *Gentleman's Magazine*, 1798.
MS. Top. gen. e. 32, fol. 116ᵛ.

455 **Great and good if she deride me**
**'Tis but oh unconstant man.**
MS. CCC. 327, fol. 26.

**Great Apollo, gods divine** 456
**Graces three and muses nine.**
Cole, R., of King's College, Cambridge, 'On the death of Queene Anne'. 1 Mar. 1618/19.
MS. Eng. poet. e. 14, fol. 100 rev.

**Great are the joys this day expects, so fair** 457
**Yields us examples high as Heaven above.**
[Hodnett, Will], 'An Epithalamie written on the names and nuptialls of . . . George Mountagu and . . . Elizabeth Irby'.
MS. Rawl. poet. 116, fol. 74ᵛ.

**Great artist, why would'st thou leave us so soon** 458
**Exchanged it for eternity.**
Reynoldes, Lance., 'On the Mirrour of Art and learning, Nicholas Culpeper gent.'
MS. Ashmole 423, fol. 204 (autogr.).

**Great bard and prophet of our British isle,** 459
**And wear the bays before your brain turns addle.**
MS. Montagu e. 13, fol. 128.

**Great Britain rejoice** 460
**Who's nicknam'd our master.**
Lampoon on George I.
MS. Rawl. D. 383, fol. 129.

**Great Britain's defender** 461
**Their plunder surrender.**
'The Whim', addressed to the Old Pretender.
MS. Rawl. poet. 155, p. 115.

**Great Britain's genius in a pensive mood** 462
**Shall be the paradise of God, and earth's great empress owned.**
Roach, Richard, 'Palladium Britannicum. On the Projection of a Temple of Praise'.
MS. Rawl. D. 832, fol. 233 (autogr.).

**Great Buckingham** 463
**Will bear him quite away.**
MS. Eng. poet. c. 50, fol. 27.

**Great Buckingham's buried under a stone** 464
**Th' avaricious actor of things unjust.**
'Epitaph' [on the Duke of Buckingham].
MS. Malone 23, p. 143.

**Great by my birth; more by my match; by son than both the other:** 465
**King Henry's daughter; Henry's wife; and valiant Henry's mother.**
Powle, Sir Stephen, couplet, translation of Latin epitaph on the Empress Maud, d. 1167. See Matthew Paris, *Chronica Majora*, Rolls Ser. XLIV, ii, 1866, p. 324.
MS. Tanner 168, fol. vi (autogr.).

466 Great captain Medont wears a chain of gold
The guard will stoop and gates fly open wide.
Davies, [Sir] John, of Gray's Inn, 'In Medontem'.
MS. *Rawl. poet. 212, fol. 62v rev.

467 Great Charles and James two brethren dear
How soon they'll pick his crown.
R. W., 'Epigram . . . translated Bard-like from Latin upon the Treasonable Conspiracy A.D. 1683'. Sent to Archbishop Sancroft.
MS. Tanner 306, fol. 404.

468 Great Charles, who full of mercy [didst] would'st command
Till the stroke's struck, which they can ne'er survive.
[Savile, Henry], 'To the king', following S1099, 1673.
Pr. *Poems on Affairs of State*, 1689, i. 14. See Margoliouth, *Poems of Marvell*, 1927, i. 322.
MSS. Don. b. 8, p. 466; Douce 357, fol. 110; Rawl. poet. 81, fol. 3; Tanner 395, fol. 76; Top. Yorks. c. 26, fol. 123.

469 Great child, who gazest on the world new-shown
Now, Simeon, how thy song accords with me!
Corbet, Richard, on the birth of Charles II, 29 May 1630, 'for Dr. Leonard Hutton (being blind)'.
Latin version by W. Strode pr. *Britanniae Natalis*, 1630.
MSS. CCC. 315*b*, fol. 350, attr. to Corbet; 325, fol. 24v, in the hand of W. Strode.

470 Great copy of this solemn day
And highest still, though ne'er so low debased.
Llewellin, M[artin], 'Caroll. Sung to his Ma[jest]y on Christmas day. 1645'.
Pr. *Poems*, 1646, p. 145.
MS. Tanner 466, fol. 33.

471 Great councils when together met,
Yet quite neglect the poor.
Robinson, Robert.
MS. *Rawl. poet. 218, p. 119 (autogr.).

472 Great crowns are coined by steel and stamped by might
Good with ten thousand losses no right of blood.
'Summum jus'.
MS. Rawl. poet. 155, p. 118.

473 Great cures done at Lemington
In finer lights than B. Satchwell.
Satchwell, Ben, Shoemaker, 'Eulogy of S. T. Pratt Esq.'
MS. Montagu c. 5, fol. 64v (autogr.).

Great dame Voluntas sits and bears chief sway 474
None's truly noble, be he ne'er so rich.
Cheyney, William, 'Moral Vertues. The proeme'.
MS. *Rawl. poet. 86, fol. 11v.

Great David's root and son 475
Wrapped in love's ecstatic gaze.
Kenton, James.
MS. *Eng. poet. e. 20, p. 67 (autogr.).

Great favourites seldom their resentments hide 476
Revenge shows not their anger, but their pride.
Couplet.
MS. Add. B. 8, fol. 74.

Great fire, great frost, great plague, great dearth, we see 477
Will the great porter died this year, in May.
Chamber, N[ath.], 'on Wm. Evans the great Porter', 1636.
MS. Ashmole 38, p. 196.

Great fool is he who dares a woman trust 478
Grant me thy grace, I ne'er from thee depart.
Tipping, William, ['To trust in God alone']. Title from B.M. MS. Harley 6645, fol. 268.
MS. *Rawl. poet. 101, fol. 81v (autogr.).

Great George, escap'd the narrow seas of storms 479
Returns with pleasure to his guts again.
'On George 2nd coming to Engd. after having been in a Storm 1736–7'.
MS. Firth c. 16, p. 307.

Great gifts he sent, but under his gifts, 480
Can the cunning fisher look.
Translation of Latin epigram in note on 'Encouragment' by Traherne.
MS. Eng. poet. c. 42, fol. 37v.

Great God! arise! and thine own cause defend! 481
And fix us firmly on a sure foundation.
'An Early Adresse For St. Peters Day June 29 1688'.
Pr. bk. Firth b. 20, fol. 132.

Great God! at whose all-powerful call 482
And earthly harvests rise no more.
'An Autumnal Hymn. G[entleman's] Mag.'
MS. Eng. poet. e. 39, p. 155.

Great God by whose almighty word alone, 483
I'll pluck a quill from off a seraph's wing.
Chatwin, John, 'An Hymn to God in the Morning'.
MS. *Rawl. poet. 94, p. 270 (autogr.).

Great God how dreadful is thy wrath 484
And set me on thy throne.
Beddome, Benjamin.
MS. *Eng. misc. e. 227, fol. 58v.

485 Great God, I dare not to approach thy throne,
And not by Satan's snares be cheated any more.
Spoure, Edmund, No. 2 of 'Three Petitionary Penitentiall Anthems'.
MS. *Eng. poet. c. 52, fol. $41^v$ (autogr.).

486 Great God! Inspire and heal the cripple-motion
Doth sanctify the gift, my gift enrich.
'Invocation' to 'Divine Poems'.
MS. *Eng. poet. e. 51, p. 1.

487 Great God may I become a child
In Jesus all complete.
Beddome, Benjamin.
MS. *Eng. misc. e. 227, fol. $3^v$.

488 Great God my actions all declare
Come Lord and set me free.
Beddome, Benjamin.
MS. *Eng. misc. e. 227, fol. $29^v$.

489 Great God my inmost soul
Where'er I am thou Lord art there.
Beddome, Benjamin.
MS. *Eng. misc. e. 227, fol. $84^v$.

490 Great God, no sooner born, but we begin
Confound our language, and our building too.
[Quarles, Francis], 'On Babels Building'.
Pr. *Divine Fancies*, 1632, i. 73.
MS. Rawl. poet. 90, fol. $64^v$.

491 Great god of wine
'Twill drive away all sorrow.
'A Song'.
MS. Rawl. poet. 84, fol. 109 rev.

492 Great God stretch out thy conquering arm
But all thy just commands obey.
Beddome, Benjamin.
MS. *Eng. misc. e. 227, fol. 50.

493 Great God stretch out thy conquering hand
That change must come from thee.
Beddome, Benjamin.
MS. *Eng. misc. e. 227, fol. 58.

494 Great God that art all eye! Who first gave sight
Up to thy throne of grace . . . [incomplete: 'The rest is lost'.]
Pestell, Thomas, 'On that noble gentleman Mr. H. Hast[ings]: losing his eye'.
Dated 1634 in a manuscript described in *History of Leicestershire*, J. Nichols, III. ii, 1804, p. 929. Pr. Pestell's *Sermons and Devotions*, 1659, p. 5.
MS. *Malone 14, p. 3.

Great God though I my sins conceal 495
His grace doth more abound.
Beddome, Benjamin.
MS. *Eng. misc. e. 227, fol. 11.

Great God thy penetrating eye 496
And ev'ry lust subdue.
Beddome, Benjamin.
MS. *Eng. misc. e. 227, fol. $71^v$.

Great God to thee I'll make 497
For ever so, for, who can tell.
Beddome, Benjamin, hymn '. . . to a sermon on' Jonah xxx. 9.
Pr. *Hymns of B. Beddome*, 1818, no. 478.
MS. *Eng. misc. e. 227, fol. $44^v$.

Great God, to thee, what gratitude I owe, 498
New heart, new spirit, and new life be mine.
'Verses on the Entrance of a New Year'.
MS. Eng. poet. e. 47, p. 27.

Great God to what a glorious height 499
Safe to conduct my spirit home.
Watts, Isaac, 'Upon Angels'.
MS. Rawl. D. 868, fol. $35^v$.

Great God, whence my salvation comes alone, 500
And two, whom God made one, death again two has made.
Psalm lxxxviii.
MS. Rawl. poet. 90, fol. $160^v$.

Great, good and just could I but rate 501
And write thy epitaph in blood and wounds.
Graham, James, Marquis of Montrose, 'Epitaph on King Charles I'.
Pr. *Reliquiæ Sacræ Carolinæ*, 1650, p. 355.
MSS. Add. B. 83, fol. 13, attr. to Montrose; Rawl. B. 473, fol. $183^v$, attr. to Montrose; Rawl. C. 986, fol. 15, attr. to the Marquis Montross; Rawl. D. 108, fol. 109, attr. to the Lord Montross; Rawl. poet. 173, fol. $105^v$, attr. to the E. of Montrose; Top. gen. e. 32, fol. 73, attr. to Montrose; see also T2188.

Great, good, chief shepherd: Do'st thou send us out, 502
Is the best life of immortality.
Woode, Andrew, 10 lines on his calling.
MSS. Ashmole 36, 37, fol. 274 (autogr.).

Great guardian of my feeble frame, 503
Her song of love and praise.
Shepperd, Mrs., of Holborn, 'Hymn . . . on her return to England, after a dangerous Voyage'.
MS. Eng. poet. c. 9, p. 67.

504 Great heart, who taught thee so to die
We died; thou only livedst that day.

'On Sir Walter Raleigh'.
Pr. *Wits Recreations*, 1641, Sig. S1; Shirley's *Life* of Raleigh, 1677, p. 239.
MSS. Eng. hist. c. 272, p. 51, attr. to Captaine Kinge; Eng. poet. e. 14, fol. 98$^{v}$ rev.; Rawl. D. 954, fol. 35; Rawl. poet. 26, fol. 69$^{v}$; 209, fol. 10; Tanner 306, fol. 251.

505 Great is desire that leadeth to the death,
And she may know the truth that dwells in me.

Andrews, —.
MS. *Rawl. poet. 92, fol. 8.

506 Great is the lord and with great praise,
Our guider shall he be.

[Hopkins, John], Psalm xlviii.
MS. Rawl. poet. 112, fol. 58 rev.

507 Great is the Lord, and with great praise
He still shall be our guide.

Psalm xlviii.
MS. *Montagu e. 10, fol. 67$^{v}$.

508 Great is thy name oh Yaniewicz!
Faster destroy than thou couldst build!

Parsons, William, 'To [Miss Browne] requesting a Ticket for the benefit Concert of Mr. Yaniewicz'.
MS. *Don. d. 123, p. 227 (autogr.).

509 Great Jehovah deigns
Free from change, or ending.

Davison, Francis, Psalm xxiii.
MSS. Rawl. D. 316, fol. 128, attr. to Fra. Davidson; *Rawl. poet. 61, fols. 17$^{v}$ and 31, attr. to Fra. Da.

510 Great Jehovah, Jacob's keeper,
In thy house, to blaze thy praise.

Br., Jos., Psalm xxiii.
MS. Rawl. poet. 61, fol. 15.

511 Great Jove, look down on us poor whigs,
Or have no God at all.

'The Whigs Prayer', 1735.
MSS. Eng. misc. e. 240, p. 150; Rawl. poet. 155, p. 11.

512 Great Julius was a cuckold, and may I
His desires, may catch a fall.

B[onham (?)], T[homas (?)], 'Song'.
MS. Rawl. poet. 147, p. 132.

513 Great Jupiter, being at a solemn feast
Their tongues yield idle breath; their noses smoke.

'In Tobaconistas'.
MSS. Ashmole 38, p. 86; Rawl. poet. 160, fol. 159.

Great King of Gods, whose gracious hand hath led 514
His living flesh to thy celestial state.

MS. Rawl. poet. 23, p. 168; reference to setting by Orlando Gibbons.

Great learned clerks, such fancies they 515
Unmad the man again.

Robinson, Robert.
MS. *Rawl. poet. 218, p. 163 (autogr.).

Great learned witty Ben: be pleased to light 516
In vulgar praise, had never bound thy . . . (incomplete).

'An Invective wrighten by Mr. G[eorge] Chapman against Mr. Ben: Johnson'; at end, 'More then this never came to my hands, but lost in his sickenes'.
Pr. from this MS., *Poems*, ed. P. B. Bartlett, 1941, p. 374.
MS. Ashmole 38, p. 16.

Great length of days the Lord on earth me gave 517
Eternal joy in heaven I hope to have.

'An Epitaph upon Thomas Hix in blubery Church'. [Bloomsbury (?)]. Couplet.
MS. Rawl. D. 1334, fol. 28$^{v}$ rev.

Great Lord, let clemencies allay thy rage 518
Glory next life, in this my consolation.

J. F., Psalm xxxviii.
MS. *Eng. poet. f. 17, p. 44 (autogr.).

Great M[ ]e of arts! sprung from Minervae's brain 519
Th'wouldst cure the body, soul and mind of man.

Boun, Abraham, 'To Doctor [Thomas] Brown[e] on his Learned Treatise of Common errours'.
MS. Rawl. poet. 152, fol. 215.

Great magistrates whom kings and realms do choose 520
There is a god that judgement doth regard.

Harington, Sir John, Psalm lviii.
MS. *Douce 361, fol. 34$^{v}$.

Great maker of man's earthly realm 521
Reigning whilst times and ages last.

'Engl. Primer of our Ladie. 1631 . . . p. 7'.
MS. Eng. poet. e. 56, p. 30.

Great maker of the heavens wide 522
Reigning whilst times and ages last.

'Engl. Primer of our Ladie. 1631. p. 6'.
MS. Eng. poet. e. 56, p. 29.

523 Great master of still life, I said in Greek
But to the statue's silence breathes his own.
Robinson, Northon, 'On a Busto of Pythagoras in Trin. Coll. Library, Camb.', *Whitehall Evening Post*, 13 Dec. 1737.
MS. Eng. misc. e. 183, fol. 74.

524 Great master of thy church below
What thou hast promised to give.
Kenton, James.
MS. *Eng. poet. e. 20, p. 42 (autogr.).

525 Great masters with your jargon arts embroil
You teach the art without its pompous toil.
Bradbury, Mr.
MS. Rawl. D. 347, fol. 2ᵛ.

526 Great minister, whose generous soul disdains
Prevented wars are more than battles won.
Whaley, John, 'An Epistle to the Right Honourable Sr. Robert Walpole'.
Pr. *Poems*, 1732, p. 83.
MS. Rawl. poet. 222, fol. 8ᵛ.

527 Great moderator of the starry sky,
From thence my consummation shall appear.
King, John.
See *B.Q.R.* v, 1929, p. 327, and *B.L.R.* iv, 1953, p. 208.
MS. Rawl. D. 317, fol. 147 (autogr.).

528 Great monarch, hasten to thy native shore
And willing nations own their rightful king.
'England's address to her Lawfull Prince'.
MS. Rawl. poet. 181, fol. 72ᵛ.

529 Great monarch of the world whence power springs
Yet though I perish bless the church and state.
'Majesty in Misery, An imploration of the King of Kings, wrote by his Majesty King Charles the 1st during his Captivity in Carisbrook Castle 1648'.
Pr. H. Walpole's *Catalogue of Royal and Noble Authors*, ed. T. Park, 1806, i. 144; N. Thompson's *Collection of Loyal Poems*, 1685, p. 218.
MS. Rawl. poet. 116, fol. 90ᵛ.

530 Great monarch of the world whose people do
May give him praise the lord of host is he.
Fairfax, Thomas, Lord, Psalm xxiv.
MS. *Fairfax 40, p. 50 (autogr.).
MS. *Fairfax 38, p. 158.

531 Great Nassau, from his cradle to his grave
And which it self as well as earth admired.
'On King William 3d', 1702.
MS. Add. B. 105, fol. 35ᵛ.

Great ones die, so must thou, and so must I, 532
Death visits all spares none, doth none pass by.
Robinson, Robert, couplet.
MS. *Rawl. poet. 218, p. 166 (autogr.).

Great ones take heed; do not poor men oppress: 533
To faction, theft, rebellion, needs doth run.
Robinson, Robert.
MS. *Rawl. poet. 218, p. 152 (autogr.).

Great pain and poverty its known 534
She will you rail to death.
Tipping, William.
MS. *Rawl. poet. 101, fol. 102ᵛ (autogr.).

Great Pan that wont to chase the fair 535
Unites to deck the Andrews name.
Gough, Richard, 'To Joseph Andrews, Esq., of Shaw Place'.
MS. *Eng. poet. c. 5, fol. 92 (autogr.).

Great Panomphæo Moses erst did say 536
And live in paradise.
Inscription at Rochester, copied 2 July 1663.
MS. Top. gen. e. 1, p. 57.

Great persons think it needless to excuse 537
Of all they suffer whom the great neglect.
Williams, John.
MS. *Rawl. poet. 191, fol. 102 (autogr.).

Great, pious, prudent, Charles the second 538
Is wretched king'd by stocks or logs.
[Wilmot, John Earl of Rochester], 'The Chronicle'.
Pr. *Works of Rochester*, 1709, p. 130, and *A second Collection of Songs against Popery and Tyranny*, 1689, p. 9.
MS. Rawl. D. 924, fol. 316; see also C177.

Great potent duke, whom fortune raised so high 539
For want of letters, here I am to end.
'An Acrostic', on George Villiers Duke of Buckingham after his death, August 1628.
MS. Tanner 465, fol. 102ᵛ.

Great prince! and so much greater as more wise 540
To woods and groves what once the painter sings.
'To the King, By Sr. John Denham'.
Pr. as *Directions to a Painter*, etc., 1667, envoy; see M. T. Osborne, *Advice-to-a-Painter Poems*, 1949, no. 10.
MSS. Don. e. 23, fol. 22; Rawl. poet. 123, p. 105.

Great prince if word a tomb to thee could frame 541
Here for a time his body doth repose.
G. B., on Prince Henry's death, 1612.
MS. *Rawl. poet. 116, fol. 2ᵛ.

542a Great queen of Europe, where thy offspring wears
And with your Thuscan muse exalt the fight.
Waller, Edmund, 'To the Queene Mother upon her Landinge', 19 Oct. 1638.
Pr. *Poems*, 1645, p. 113.
MSS. *Don. d. 55, fol. 33$^v$; Malone 13, p. 20; *Rawl. poet. 174, p. 8.

542b [Great queen of shades bring here thy flowers]
And virgins kissed it as they bled.
Palmer, Francis, of Christ Church, 'Upon the death of [William] Cartwright, and his poems'.
Pr. Cartwright's *Poems*, 1651, Sig. **5$^v$.
MS. Eng. misc. f. 49, fol. 52$^v$ rev.

543 Great saviour to my mournful prayer give ear,
But to thy servant favour show.
'Psalm CXLIII 7 Penetential Psalm'.
MS. Rawl. poet. 90, fol. 158.

544 Great school of virtuous wisdom, mighty love,
And use with wisdom his unenvied bounty.
Gough, Richard, 'To Love (A Fragment) Translation from Euripides'.
MS. *Eng. poet. c. 5, fol. 136 (autogr.).

545 Great shepherd of thine Israel
When from our bondage we're made free.
Fairfax, Thomas, Lord, Psalm lxxx.
MS. *Fairfax 40, p. 188 (autogr.); see also T2254*a*.

546 Great sir, beloved of God and man, admit
And, like a Jove, fighting in clouds and thunder.
[Wild, Robert], 'To the king . . . Licensed. June 16. 1665'.
Pr. *Iter Boreale With large Additions*, 1668.
MS. Don. b. 8, p. 436.

547 Great sir; forgive my duty. 'Tis a sin
Read Overburyes wife, and that is she.
'A Panegyre in memory of the Lady Theophila Cooke'.
MS. Rawl. poet. 246, fol. 40.

548 Great sir, Septimius understands how vast
A stouter, better man you ne'er did see.
B[rome], A[lexander], translator, Horace, *Epistles* I. ix.
Pr. *Poems of Horace*, A. Brome etc., 2nd ed., 1671, p. 330.
MS. Rawl. D. 261, p. 48.

549a Great sir, we are hither come
As some years since I did the church.
'Dr. Mill . . . addressed himself to the Duke [of Marlborough]'.
Pr. Hearne's *Collections*, ed. C. E. Doble, i, O.H.S. ii, 1885, p. 219.
MS. Hearne's diaries 9, p. 99.

Great sir, whene'er your gracious voice we hear 549b
Like Joseph's sheaves, pay reverence and bow.
'A Penegyrique humbly addresst to the Kings most Excellent Matie. On His . . . meeting his two Houses of Parliament. 4 and 5 Febr. 1672/3 by R. Wilde', at end, 'Iter Boreale'.
Printed as a broadsheet.
MS. Don. b. 8, p. 380.

Great sir whose sufferings we may deplore 550
That piles of rebels make, a glorious king.
'Ad Regem Vectæ Incarceratum', endorsed 'Verses upon his Matie in the Isle of Wight', 1648–9.
MS. Tanner 306, fol. 274.

Great sir, your land self-conquered was, and poor 551
Subscrib'd, the father of his native land.
Wase, Christopher, 'To the Kings Majesty'. See T114.
MS. Eng. poet. e. 4, p. 62.

Great son of God, but born the son of man 552
Is both, and yet not God, by man consumed.
Langewoorth, —, 'To God the Sonne'.
MS. Rawl. poet. 148, fol. 105.

Great sorrows yea death's pangs do compass me 553
Not only I, but both and yet but one.
'On his sicke Love'.
MS. Ashmole 47, fol. 56$^v$.

Great sovereign disposer of all 554
The essence of heavenly love.
Kenton, James, 'A Versification of the Anthem composed by Dr. Boyce', funeral of George II, 'The souls of the righteous are in the hands of God'.
MS. *Eng. poet. e. 19, p. 179 (autogr.).

Great Strafford, worthy of that name, though all 555
Our nations glory and our nations hate.
Denham, [Sir] J[ohn], 'A Elegie on the Earle of Strafford'.
Pr. in a revised version, *Poems*, 1668, p. 65; see *Works*, ed. T. H. Banks, 1928, p. 153.
MSS. Ashmole 36, 37, two copies, fols. 33$^v$ and 214; Douce 357, fol. 8; Locke e. 17, p. 81; Rawl. poet. 26, fol. 127$^v$; 147, p. 76, attr. to J. Denham.

Great thanks we give our god most high 556
He lifteth up though laid in dust.
Harington, Sir John, Psalm lxxv.
MS. *Douce 361, fol. 45.

557 Great thou! who mak'st it crime almost to dare to praise;
And still tread round the endless circle of eternity.
Oldham, John, 'Upon the Works of Ben. Jonson, reprinted', written 1677/8, two drafts.
MS. *Rawl. poet. 123, pp. 32 and 224 (autogr.).

558*a* Great Tite that hath done so much for the nation
Expose 'em all about in hanged up frames.
'The Salutation', satire on William III's reception of Oates, 1689.
MSS. Ashmole 36, 37, fol. 323.

558*b* Great Tom of Lincoln though the deepest bell
The plot goeth on *cum priveligio*.
'Febr. 1678/9'.
MS. Wood D. 19(2), fol. 101.

559 Great Tybaulte being joyous for to couch
Said then my Mallet may knock down my home.
H. S., 'Translated out of Rableys ex pag. 572'.
MS. *Rawl. poet. 120, fol. 29 (autogr.).

560 Great Verulam is very lame
Is turn'd franciscan martyr.
'Sir Francis Bacon Lord Chancellor of England deposed', 1 May 1621.
Pr. *Ballads from Manuscripts*, ed. F. J. Furnivall and W. R. Morfill, ii, 1873, p. 277.
MSS. Douce f. 5, fol. 37$^{v}$; Eng. poet. c. 50, fol. 32$^{v}$; f. 10, fol. 96; Malone 23, p. 23; Rawl. poet. 117, fol. 22$^{v}$.

561 Great was the star that Beathlem bred
By whom we all are blessed.
Forman, Simon.
MS. Ashmole 195, fol. 73$^{v}$ (autogr.).

562 Great was the thought, his statue to conceive
That his own statue to his strains must move.
'On viewing Mr. Handel's statue in Vaux-Hall-Gardens', subscribed 'X' in the *Daily Advertiser*, 17 Aug. 1743.
MS. Eng. poet. c. 9, p. 104.

563 Great wealth comes in to many a churlish boor
He must or starve, or beg from door to door.
Robinson, Robert.
MS. *Rawl. poet. 218, p. 72 (autogr.).

564 Great wealth rich men's felicity
Full safe are in their station.
Robinson, Robert.
MS. *Rawl. poet. 218, p. 19 (autogr.).

Great were thy wrongs, thy Parliament still as great, 565
Took off thy head, because themselves would headless be.
'On the Pious Martyr K. Charles I'.
MS. Rawl. poet. 173, fol. 104.

Great W[illia]m concern'd to leave his galled boobies 566
That he swore the next year he would make them a dozen.
'Upon the Nine Chitts . . . 1697'.
Found in MS. of verses by Henry Hall in the Brotherton Collection, University of Leeds.
MSS. Eng. poet. e. 50, p. 86; Rawl. poet. 181, fol. 10.

Great words, small tittle? promise much; do little? 567
Too much goodmen thus abuse.
Robinson, Robert.
MS. *Rawl. poet. 218, p. 129 (autogr.).

Great world's architect, how excellent 568
Advanced most high above the starry frame.
Fleming, Robert, 'The VIII Psalm paraphrased, In Heroicks'.
Pr. *The Mirrour of Divine Love*, 1691, 'Poems', p. 59.
MS. Rawl. poet. 213, fol. 42 (autogr.).

Greatest 'mongst women's sons, God's messenger 569
The good, remission had, bad chastisement.
Clifford, Henry, Earl of Cumberland, 'Saint John Baptist'.
MS. *Rawl. poet. 95, fol. 34$^{v}$.

Greatest of beings, source of life, 570
A grateful tribute pays to thee.
Dyer, George, 'Ode to the Deity'.
Pr. *Poems*, 1792, p. 39.
MS. *Eng. poet. c. 21, fol. 43.

Greatness and goodness herein well agree 571
For my relief that you will both express.
Dimoke, Col. Cressy, dedication of poem to William Russell, Earl of Bedford (1641: cr. Duke, 1694).
MS. Firth f. 1, fol. iii (autogr. (?)).

Greatness is goodness: thus men cry: 572
Goodness is greatness in God's eye.
Robinson, Robert, couplet.
MS. *Rawl. poet. 218, p. 98 (autogr.).

Greece likeneth man to an inverted tree 573
Doth spring afresh in the Elysian field.
Marsham, Mr. J., 'On Mr. Wm. Blagrave fellow of St. Johns Oxon'.
MS. Eng. poet. e. 14, fol. 96$^{v}$ rev.

574 Greedy, envious, malicious, proud, unstable
Who list to know her, 'tis the Lady Lake.
On Lady Lake in the Tower, 1619–20.
MS. Malone 23, fol. 5.

575 Greedy lover pause awhile
Thou wouldst burn though not for me.
Pr. John Wilson's *Cheerfull Ayres or Ballads*, 1660, p. 50.
MS. Mus. b. 1, fol. 92v, music by John Wilson.

576 Greedy worms, needy worms rich and poor;
Needy worms, greedy worms all the world o'er.
Robinson, Robert, couplet.
MS. *Rawl. poet. 218, p. 28 (autogr.).

577 Greeke, guineys,[1] heresy, and beer
Came to England all in a year.
Couplet.
MS. Malone 19, p. 139.

578 Greene being askd the quantity of ô
Was that he said all 'oh's were too too common.
MS. Malone 19, p. 98.

579 Green flowering age of your manly countenance
In my body it will not abide.
MS. Rawl. C. 813, fol. 53v.

580 Green groweth the holly
Blow never so nigh.
Transcript of 3-part song by 'The King H. VIII', from B.M. Add. MS. 31922, fol. 37v.
MS. Mus. d. 198, fol. 4.

581 Green were the fields where my forefathers dwelt—oh
*Boie yudh ma Vorneen Erin go Brah.*
'The Exiled Irishman's Lamentation', song written before the Rebellion of 1798.
MS. North e. 34, two copies, fols. 15v and 17v.

582 Gregg in the train of modest Themis seen!
And shine a Hardwicke—and a Sedley too!
Parsons, William, 'Sonnet to a Friend on the Northern Circuit'.
Pr. *Travelling Recreations*, 1807, ii. 107.
MS. *Don. d. 123, p. 171 (autogr.).

583 Grey hairs do usher in old age,
'Scape death, do what we can.
Robinson, Robert.
MS. *Rawl. poet. 218, p. 146 (autogr.).

584 Grief keep within, and scorn to show
Pine, fret, swell, burst, consume, and die.
Polwhele, John.
MS. *Eng. poet. f. 16, fol. 5 (autogr.).

[1] guinea-cock, turkey. *O.E.D.*

Grief knows no measured bounds, how then can I 585
Until the limbeck of my tears be dry.
MS. Rawl. poet. 142, fol. 11.

Grief, love and gratitude devote this stone 586
Bowed her sweet head, and sunk into the grave.
Grove, [William (?)], of Lichfield, 'Epitaph . . . on his wife'.
MS. Eng. poet. c. 51, p. 13.

Grief makes a poet, I which ne'er made verse 587
I have my wish, my verse is pitiful.
'On the death of a friend'.
MS. CCC. 328, fol. 63v.

Grief sadness sounds what shall she take 588*a*
Mixed, he is landed safe, and then she'll live.
Cavendish, Jane, 'Passions delate'.
MS. *Rawl. poet. 16, p. 7.

Grief's passion child, this night had died 588*b*
Until good news it self, joy doth proclaim.
Cavendish, Jane, 'The revive'.
MS. *Rawl. poet. 16, p. 8.

Grief's prodigals where are you, unthrifts where, 589
The poor and blank remainder left behind.
Halswell, Henry, 'Upon Mr. William Hopton'.
Pr. by H. Huth, *Inedited Poetical Miscellanies*, 1870. Hopton was a retainer at Wilton.
MSS. Firth d. 7, fol. 178; Malone 21, fol. 12v.

Grieve, mighty power, grieve, thy house is down, 590–1
As easie as the Q— her self can sh-te.
'The Garden qualis-qualis est sub Finem Anni 1688 composita'.
MS. Firth e. 6, fol. 125.

Grieve not for me, my friends, that I am dead 592
Delightful when awaked, then e'er before.
Spoure, Edmund, 'An Acrostick Epitaph on Mrs. Grace Rodd'.
MS. *Eng. poet. c. 52, fol. 30v (autogr.).

Grieve not great poet in thy blest retreat 593
By flames to perish, then to choak in T-d.
'Upon unluckily taking . . . a . . . Poem called Prince Arthur . . .'.
MS. Percy c. 8, fol. 128v.

Grieved with my pain, but much more with my sin 594
Suffer sweet Jesu my sins to gain remission.
MS. Mus. Sch. D. 247, fol. 55*b*, with music.

595 Griffin, bustard, turkey, capon,
It was a swopping swopping mallard.
'All-Souls Mallard . . . An Ode Printed 1752', sung at All Soul's College, Oxford, on 14 January.
Pr. Hearne's *Collections*, ed. C. E. Doble, ii, O.H.S. vii, 1886, p. 111.
MSS. Ballard 47, fol. 116; Hearne's diaries 17, p. 46; Rawl. C. 867, fol. 59.

596 Grim death perceiving, he had far outran
The elder youths mistook him for a man.
'On an ingenious Youth', couplet.
Pr. *Recreation for Ingenious Head-peeces*, 1663, Epitaph 19.
MS. Sancroft 53, p. 44.

597 Gross ignorance (to truth the opposite)
Rates wisdom's lore, led by uncertain chance.
MS. Rawl. poet. 172, fol. 83$^{v}$.

598*a* Gross sin is like a shower which ere we can get in
On Sodom strikes, and strikes to th' pit of hell.
[Quarles, Francis], 'On severall Sinnes'.
Pr. *Divine Fancies*, 1632, iii. 42.
MSS. Rawl. poet. 90, fol. 53$^{v}$; 213, fol. 54.

598*b* Grounded advice on danger seldom trips
Revenge in tears doth ever wash his hands.
Added to T1611.
MS. Ashmole 781, p. 131.

599 Grow plump, lean death; his holiness a feast
And rugged touch of Pluto's multitude.
Crashaw, Richard, 'Upon the gunpowder treason'.
MS. Tanner 465, fol. 54, attr. to Mr. Crashaw on fol. 1*a*.

600 Grown slaves by bribery and venerable gold
And learn distinguished virtue to reward.
'On Mr. [John] Whaley of Pembr. Hall elect Master of Peterhouse', 1733.
MS. Rawl. poet. 207, p. 174.

601 Groyne, come of age, his state sold out of hand
For his whore; Groyne doth still occupy his land.
[Jonson, Ben.], 'In Groyne', couplet.
*Epigrammes* cxvii.
MS. Don. e. 6, fol. 23$^{v}$.

Grudge not in youth with painfulness 602
Use reverence, mixed with humbleness.
Verses used as a copy by Wiman Ramsey, *c.* 1595.
MS. Rawl. D. 649, fol. 32.

Grudge not to see the wicked men 603
In him do put their trust.
[Whittingham, William], Psalm xxxvii.
MS. Rawl. poet. 112, fol. 61$^{v}$ rev.

Guard well your hearts postillion post-boy groom, 604
His guide, his shield, his curry comb for life.
'Duchess of Chandois . . . Dead' (d. 1759).
MS. Eng. poet. e. 28, p. 30.

Guardian angels now protect me 605
Oh may she ever be sincere.
'The Forsaken Nymph'.
Engraved, with arrangement for flute, 18th cent.
MSS. Mus. c. 107, fol. 50; Mus. e. 19, p. 37; Mus. Sch. B. 8,* fol. 26.

Guess, gentle ladies, if you can 606
And tickling, when you take it.
'An Enigma. A Pinch of Snuff'.
MS. *Eng. poet. d. 47, fol. 114.

Gurney, Hampton, Cradock, Newton last 607
Such love assures a life that dies no more.
Inscription in Bristol Cathedral to Sir Henry Newton of Burscourt, Glos', Bart., 1599.
Pr. Browne Willis, *Cathedrals*, 1742, ii. 769.
MSS. Rawl. D. 1090, fol. 121; Willis 71, p. 318.

Gustavus, in the bed of honour died 608
Whilst victory lay weeping by his side.
Couplet on Gustavus Adolphus, 1632.
MS. Rawl. poet. 160, fol. 38$^{v}$.

# H

ENTRIES 1–1606

1 **Ha! for orders designed**
**And waits for the orders of Chloe.**
Canton, John, 'On the Author of [T2812], pub: in the Gent: Mag.'
MS. Eng. poet. c. 9, p. 88.

2 **Ha, let me see; is t[his tha]t Traytrous [ ]**
**Rodom[ontade] Champion for the Par . . .**
Taylor, John, 'Cacafogo. George Wither Wrung in the Withers'.
Part of an autograph copy from which the printed copy, 10 Feb. 1644/5 (?) was set up. See F. Madan, *Oxford Books*, ii, 1912, no. 1726.
MS. Add. C. 209, fol. 8 (autogr.).

3 **Ha! the king dead and are we yet alive?**
**There's no man living need to fear his way.**
Bulteel, John, 'Upon the beheading of . . . King Charles'.
MS. *Rawl. poet. 159, fol. 225. (autogr.)

4 **Ha! what's this that I see**
**In Christ Church school are hung, a sad *memento mori*.**
'A Dialogue in the Shades', Tweedledum [Dr. Philip Hayes] and Tweedledee [G. Monro], 1780.
MS. Top. Oxon. e. 48, fol. 21$^{v}$.

5 **Ha! whaur ye gaun ye blastet fairlie!**
**An even devotion!**
Burns, Robert, 'On seeing a Louse on a Lady's bonnet at Church'.
MS. Add. A. 111 (autogr.).

6 **Habits and form! as fire and water; these**
**Must teach you how to mind 'em when and why.**
Oldisworth, Giles or Robert, 'A meane in following the Fashions'.
MS. Rawl. C. 422, fol. 10, in the hand of Giles Oldisworth.

7 **Had all the latin all the grecian quire**
**Firm till time's glass hath run out all its sands.**
'To Mr. George Sandys on his paraphrase on the sacred hymns'.
MS. Ashmole 47, fol. 113.

**Had Delia but her charms resigned** 8
**To curse your wedding day.**
'To Delia inviting her deceived Lover to her Wedding'.
MS. *Eng. poet. d. 47, fol. 80.

**Had Dorothea lived, when mortals made** 9
**Then for a pardon that he dares admire.**
Waller, Edmund, 'Att Penshurst'.
Pr. *Poems*, 1645, p. 40.
MSS. *Don. d. 55, fol. 11$^{v}$; *Rawl. poet. 174, p. 32.

**Had fates indulged this pair alternate breath,** 10
**His brother's own date run, he might live his.**
'Ad Lucanum et Tullum', translation from Martial, *Epigrams* I. xxxvi.
MS. Rawl. D. 1147, fol. 90.

**Had he no more bowels of mercy but** 11
**He put the fiddle in a fearful case.**
'On a vicar that zealously at a Maypole strooke at a fiddle and broke two of the strings'.
MS. Rawl. poet. 199, p. 80.

**Had I a pen made of a golden quill,** 12
**He sits in's peerage with Christ, and his spouse.**
G. P., 'An humble Oblation to the . . . memory of his . . . Freind Sr. Gervas Clifton, Knt. and Barronet', 1587–28 June 1666.
MSS. Ashmole 36, 37, fol. 205.

**Had I a voice like to a dying swan** 13
**Write out at length in my sweet saviour's blood.**
Briggs, S[ampson], 'A Groane'.
MSS. Rawl. poet. 147, p. 240 rev. attr. to S. Briggs; 210, fol. 60$^{v}$.

**Had I been never born, I had not lived.** 14
**'Till mortal put on immortality.**
MS. Rawl. poet. 66, fol. 56.

**Had I but known some years ago** 15
**Or never courted, or enjoyed their love.**
Flatman, Thomas, 'Song. 1671. Set by Rog. Hill'.
MSS. *Firth d. 7, fol. 50; Rawl. poet. 173, fol. 101$^{v}$, attr. to Mr. Flatman.

16 Had I but world enough and time
Go back, nor stand, we'll make him run.
[Marvell, Andrew], ['To his Coy Mistress'].
Pr. *Miscellaneous Poems*, 1681.
MS. Don. b. 8, p. 283.

17 Had I least hope complaints could reach our loss
And she to our souls' joy might still have lived.
North, D[udley], L[ord], 'An Elegy . . . Lady Rich', 1638.
Pr. *A Forest of Varieties*, 1645, p. 77.
MS. Eng. misc. e. 262, fol. 31v.

18 Had I my choice of women, I'd have one
Am no patron of singularity.
Morrice, John, 'What wife he would have'. Owen, *Epigrames* II. 145.
MS. *Rawl. poet. 114, fol. 165 (autogr.).

19 Had I with Plato's eloquence been filled
And in the temple we anoint you his.
Savage, R., 'To his most Sacred Majesty' James II.
MS. Rawl. poet. 181, fol. 64v.

20 Had I your richer genius, or could strain
A downy chin may have a full summed brain.
'To the trulie noble Sir Thomas Salusbury Baronett upon . . . his Poems'.
Not pr. in *The History of Joseph*, 1636.
MS. Eng. poet. c. 53, fol. 4.

21 Had not Egerton's dam to posterity blind
Nor could Hell e'er have littered so precious an evil.
Warrick, Mr. T. of Cornwall (?).
MS. Eng. misc. e. 241, fol. 72.

22 Had not our fearful parents certain been
Which our seduced parents did sustain.
MS. *Rawl. poet. 97, fol. 7v (autogr.).

23 Had not the Lord been on our side
Did heaven and earth prepare.
Psalm cxxiv.
MS. *Rawl. C. 113, fol. 91.

24 Had not the Lord may Israel say
Who made th' earth and heaven's vast frame.
Fairfax, Thomas, Lord, Psalm cxxiv.
MS. *Fairfax 40, p. 331 (autogr.).
MS. *Fairfax 38, p. 427.

25 Had not this man been rich he might have been
Had no desire to purchase in reversion.
'Upon him that had kept the comandements'.
MS. Rawl. poet. 116, fol. 127v.

Had parts and merit gained the chair 26
Do this, and then the chair's thine own.
'To Mr. [William] Bromley standing for Speaker 1705'. Tory verses on the election of John Smith, 24 Oct. 1705.
Pr. from Hearne's copy, 1 Nov. 1705, in his *Collections*, ed. C. E. Doble, i, O.H.S. ii, 1885, p. 62.
MSS. Eng. poet. e. 87, p. 71; Hearne's diaries 5, p. 1.

Had Phyllis neither charms nor graces 27
From storms and tempests ever free.
Flatman, [Thomas], 'The Unchangable Lover. a Song'.
Pr. *Poems*, 1674, p. 56.
MS. Rawl. poet. 173, fol. 78v.

Had Pope a person equal to his mind 28
Deformed the body, but enriched the brain.
'The Answer' to D290.
In B.M. MS. Burney 523, fol. 121, headed 'Lady Kitty's Answer'.
MS. Ballard 50, fol. 49.

Had she a glass and feared the fire 29
But what is bred by their own cruelty despair.
[Herbert, William, Earl of] Pembroke, 'When my Carliles Chamber was on fire'.
MS. Rawl. poet. 116, fol. 49v.

Had sweet-tongued Ovid knighthood for his merit, 30
More lasting than brass marble, porphyry.
Murford, Michael, 'To his ingenious friend Mr. William Lilly, on his Works'.
MS. Ashmole 423, fol. 141 (autogr.).

Had these excluded virgins been so wise 31
To knock but were not known nor did not enter.
'Upon the 5 wise and foolish virgins'.
MS. Rawl. poet. 116, fol. 131v.

Had thy spouse, Dr. Douglas, been ta'en from thy side 32
Thou with truth mightst have said, 'Thou art bone of my bone'.
Mansel, Dr. [William Lort], 'On Doctor Douglas'.
MS. Eng. poet. c. 51, p. 86.

Had we for terms of law four terms of war 33
Th'one takes good angels th'other takes cracked crowns.
'An Epigram'.
MS. Rawl. poet. 160, fol. 182v.

Had women wit, methinks they should not boast 34
I'm sure we thrust them from us all we can.
'An Epigram'.
MSS. CCC. 327, fol. 28; Rawl. poet. 160, fol. 183.

35 Hadst thou as other knights and sirs of worth
What th'life of man is worth by valuing thine.
'On the death of Sr. Thomas Overburye poysen'd in the tower', Sept. 1613.
MSS. Ashmole 47, fol. 112*a*; Firth d. 7, fol. 138, attr. to Beamond; Rawl. poet. 117, fol. 261$^{v}$ rev.

36 Hadst thou not caused Uriah's death
It's hard to pick that bone.
Tipping, William, 'King David'.
MS. *Rawl. poet. 101, fol. 111$^{v}$ (autogr.).

37 Haggy winter hide thy face
In innocent harmonious lays.
Percy, Thomas, nephew of the Bp. of Dromore, aged 7: 'On the Month Feb$^{y}$. 1776'.
MS. Percy c. 8, fol. 43.

38 Hail aged tree; Jove keep thee from all harms
In Rome of old the sacred cornel tree.
Philips, Katherine, 'Upon the Hollow Tree unto which his Mtie. escaped'.
Not amongst her printed poems.
Pr. bk. Firth b. 20, fol. 140.

39 Hail all ye princes, hail bright shining gems!
Whom you, as all, must honour, love, revere.
[Samber, Robert], 'On the Royal Family' [of George II] from 'the Bellman's Verses'.
MS. Rawl. poet. 134*b*, fol. 155 (autogr.).

40 Hail bishop Valentine whose day this is
Till which hour we thy day enlarge oh Valentine.
Donne, John, 'Epithalamium at the mariage of the Palsgrave and Lady Elizabeth on St. Valentines Day', 1613.
Pr. *Poems*, 1633, p. 118.
MSS. Eng. poet. e. 37, p. 63, attr. to J. D.; *e. 99, fol. 130$^{v}$; *f. 9, p. 128; Rawl. poet. 117, fol. 216$^{v}$ rev., attr. to D. Donne; 142, fol. 23; 160, fol. 29$^{v}$, attr. to J. Dunne.

41 Hail blessed solitariness
To her prepared eternity.
'Ode of an Happy Life'.
MS. Eng. poet. e. 97, p. 158.

42 Hail blest projected pearl of union!
Your gains immense and your returns secure.
[Roach, Richard], 'On the Union of the Two East-India Companies', 1702, ratified 1708.
MS. Rawl. D. 832, fol. 185 (autogr.).

Hail bright Cecilia hail fill every heart 43
Great patroness of harmony.
[Brady, Nicholas], 'St. Cecilia's song', 1692. Music by Henry Purcell.
F. B. Zimmermann, *Purcell*, 1963, no. 328.
MSS. Mus. b. 10, p. 1; c. 26, fol. 21.

Hail brightest nymph! who headst with youthful grace 44
Those who live merrily must still be young.
Wadsworth, Dr. Thomas, 'The Virtues of Coffee addrest to Health, . . . 1702'.
MS. Montagu c. 5, fol. 2$^{v}$ (autogr. (?)).

Hail day of wonders! now we may 45
Then in thy rising we shall bear a part.
'On Easter Day'.
MSS. Add. A. 301, fol. 21$^{v}$ rev.; Rawl. D. 361, fol. 331$^{v}$.

Hail flowery mead, soft purling rill 46
How much his cruel fate I now deplore.
'Catch. Dr. [W.] Hayes'.
MS. Mus. d. 177, fol. 61$^{v}$.

Hail, genial goddess! bloomy spring 47
And suns eternal rise.
Ferrar, Miss Martha, 'Ode to the Spring'.
Pr. Dodsley's *Collection of Poems*, v, 1758, p. 311.
MSS. Eng. poet. c. 6, fol. 100, attr. to Miss Martha Farrer of Huntingdon; e. 18, p. 28.

Hail, gentle love and soft desire 48
And make the cruel tyrant bleed.
'Song'.
MSS. Firth e. 6, fol. 124, attr. to Col. Cutts; Rawl. poet. 196, fol. 32.

Hail glorious James be not as yet dismayed 49
Our king and church, and none our peace destroy.
'A Character of K. G[eorge I]'.
MS. Rawl. poet. 181, fol. 71$^{v}$.

Hail glorious planet ruler of my state 50*a*
Which uncontrolled doth sure too true appear.
Moore, Thomas, 'Strephon to Urania'.
MS. *Rawl. poet. 3, fol. 47*a* (autogr.).

[Hail God of verse! pardon that I thus take in vain] 50*b*
And ruled and fought and vanquished by the conduct of a muse.
Oldham, John, drafts of 'The Praise of Homer', pr. *Poems*, 1770, ii. 50.
MS. *Rawl. poet. 123, pp. 88, 92, 258 (autogr.).

51 **Hail goddess virtue! Who sitt'st crown'd above**
**With gods themselves a vast eternity.**
Chatwin, John, 'A Fragment imitated'.
MS. *Rawl. poet. 94, p. 11 (autogr.).

52 **Hail graceful morning of eternal day**
**Should have a morning that for ever lasteth.**
Alabaster, William, 'Sonnet 4 to the blessed Virgine'.
MS. *Eng. poet. e. 57, fol. 1v.

53 **Hail gray eyed morn, strike off that maiden blush**
**To crown their board with babes, their bed with peace.**
'A Prothalamium at the marriage of his deare Freind Mr. John Rendall and Mtis. Katherine Knight'.
MS. Rawl. poet. 210, fol. 60 rev.

54–55 **Hail! Hail! Auspicious day**
**No subject so blest, no monarch so great.**
[Cibber, Colley], New Year Ode, 1756.
MS. Mus. Sch. D. 300, music by Boyce.

56 **Hail hail, my Stella hail the rising morn;**
**Let's go, and pay the tribute on her bier.**
Bate, Sally, 'Hebe and Stella, a Tragic Pastoral'.
MS. *Eng. poet. e. 28, p. 88.

57 **Hail, hail, thou most auspicious day**
**The wise and valiant with the good and fair.**
'An ode on the King [William III]'s Birth Day' (1690–4).
Pr. bk. Vet. A3 c. 123, fol. 5.

58*a* **Hail! happy Albion, thou art strangely blest,**
**Thou hast the evil, but thou wantest the touch.**
On the day of Thanksgiving, 20 Jan. 1714/15.
Pr. as a broadsheet.
MSS. Eng. poet. e. 87, p. 77; Rawl. D. 383, fol. 110; Rawl. poet. 155, p. 147; 181, fol. 75.

58*b* **Hail happy bride! for thou art truly blest**
**With fellow angels you enjoy it now.**
From *Mist's Journal*, 26 Dec. 1724, 'On the Death of Mrs. Bowes . . . extempore . . . by the Rt. Hon. Lady M[ary] W[ortley] M[ontagu]'.
MS. Hearne's diaries 106, p. 23.

59 **Hail happy Britain! Freedom's blest retreat!**
**And what thou art, America shall be.**
'Address to Britain'.
MS. Eng. poet. c. 51, p. 4.

**Hail happy Britain hail** 60
**She gives the word and Heaven the blow.**
'Duett. Jer: Clarke from his own copy in an old Book of his', on Queen Anne.
MS. Mus. d. 8, fol. 71.

**Hail happy day! in which to sinful man** 61
**Good will to men on earth, be peace and joy.**
'Ode on Christmas Day'.
MS. Rawl. poet. 153, fol. 38.

**Hail happy genius of this ancient pile!** 62
**In raising him the wisdom of my king.**
Jonson, Ben., 'Ld. Bacons Birthday'.
'Pr. [*The*] *Underwoods*, [1640, li] p. 222'.
MS. Aubrey 6, fol. 69.

**Hail happy isle, to whom the wind** 63
**In this Lord long, in this line ever.**
Weaver, Thomas, 'To the Isle of Man, upon occasion of my Ld. Byron's Landing there Septem: 27 1648'.
Pr. *Songs and Poems*, 1654.
MS. *Rawl. poet. 211, fol. 25v (autogr.).

**Hail, happy light! propitious morn!** 64
**His glory through the universe.**
Morrice, John, 'An Hymn, wrot upon Christmas-day in the morning 1707'.
MS. *Rawl. poet. 114, fol. 130 (autogr.).

**Hail happy men! Who by your martial toil** 65
**Ruin on land, and battle on the seas.**
Endorsed 'to the Hoble. Sr. Charles Wager and Sr. John Norris present Membrs. for the Town of Portsmoth These present', 1722 or 1727.
MS. Rawl. poet. 169, fol. 46.

**Hail happy monarch! thou art strangely great,** 66
**Must serve their masters, though they damn their souls.**
MS. Rawl. poet. 81, fol. 34; see also H70.

**Hail happy pair permit an humble swain** 67
**But know not their felicity.**
'A song upon Mr. Spelman's weading', subscribed 'Will Davis August the 3rd [16]97'. Composer's autograph.
MS. Mus. c. 16, fol. 126v.

**Hail happy people, blessed age!** 68
**And this would be a golden age.**
'On the Golden Age', *c.* 1760.
Pr. bk. Firth b. 22, fol. 62.

**Hail happy Scot! who well provided came** 69
**And in their bed we may the union see.**
'On the D[uke] of Roxborough's Marriage with the Marchioness of Hallifax on New Years Day 1707–8'.
MS. Eng. poet. e. 87, p. 84.

70 **Hail happy William thou art strangely great**
**Must serve their master though they damn their souls.**

Bold, Michael, 'Panegyrick on King William', 1697.
Pr. *Poems on Affairs of State*, ii, 1703, p. 401. Also found in MS. of verses by Henry Hall, Brotherton Collection, University of Leeds.
MSS. Hearne's diaries 11, p. 102, attr. to Mr. Michael Bold; Rawl. poet. 169, fol. 9; see also H66.

71 **Hail, holy mother of the christian band**
**In spite of all the blows your foes can give.**

Colman, Henry, 'To the Church'.
MS. *Rawl. poet. 204, fol. 33ᵛ (autogr.).

72 **Hail holy sacrament**
**That tears may thence gush out with them to blend.**

'Upon the blessed Sacrament'.
MS. Eng. poet. b. 5, p. 2.

73 **Hail holy thing!**
**God sits and rules in his imperial majesty alone.**

'On the Bible A Pindarique Ode'.
MS. Don. b. 8, p. 478.

74 **Hail holy tide**
**Of faith of hope of love.**

[Howell, James], 'A hymn for Christmas Day'.
Pr. *Epistolæ Ho-Elianæ*, 1645, vi. 13.
MS. Eng. poet. b. 5, p. 4.

75 **Hail Janus who shut'st out the sliding year**
**Soft as his smiles great as his majesty.**

Stukeley, William, 'To the King'.
MS. *Eng. misc. e. 386, fol. 7ᵛ.

76 **Hail, learning's Pantheon! Hail, the sacred ark,**
**As the best blood of man's employed on generation.**

Cowley, Abraham, 'Pindarique Ode. The Book Humbly presenting it selfe to the Universite Librarie at Oxford'. Written in the copy of *Poems . . . and . . . Davideis*, presented by Cowley to the Bodleian, 1656.
Pr. bk. C. 2. 21. Art., before title-page (autogr.).

77 **Hail lovely daughters of the vernal year!**
**Why love to bloom unseen and unadmired.**

'To the violets at Cumner'.
MS. Eng. misc. e. 241, fol. 100ᵛ.

**Hail lovely pair! be ye for ever blest,** 78
**May so conjoined into Elizium fly.**

Chatwin, John, 'Epithalamium on the Nuptials of . . . William Cole, Esq., and Emm. daughter to . . . Major Warner'.
MS. *Rawl. poet. 94, p. 86 (autogr.).

**Hail lovely power! Whose bosom heaves the sigh,** 79
**Beneath thy feet no hapless insect dies . . . (incomplete).**

MS. Eng. poet. e. 18, p. 30.

**Hail Mary full of grace.** 80
**One God in persons three.**

'Ave Maria gracia plena'.
MS. Eng. poet. b. 5, p. 74.

**Hail Mary, mother of thy father** 81
**With thousands better anes praise thy name.**

'Ave Maria: or a Hymne in memorie of our Saviours blessed virgin mother'.
MS. Eng. poet. c. 50, fol. 53ᵛ.

**Hail mighty bard! Whose eloquence was such** 82
**Whilst he for ever in my thoughts shall still survive.**

Chatwin, John, 'An Elegy on . . . Mr. John Burroughs, Rector of Stonesby in the County of Leicester'.
MS. *Rawl. poet. 94, p. 102 (autogr.).

**Hail mighty Charles, joy of our life and eyes;** 83
**But what secures from faction and from Rome.**

'To the King', epilogue to P8.
MS. Don. b. 8, p. 595.

**Hail mighty Cynthia! Whose triumphant light** 84
**And he like a bold vig'rous youth performs.**

Chatwin, John, 'To the Night'.
MS. *Rawl. poet. 94, p. 11 (autogr.).

**Hail mighty James! a king without a crown** 85
**He's his priest's cully, and his people's scorn.**

'The Wish', 1692.
MSS. Eng. poet. c. 18, fol. 129; e. 49, p. 139.

**Hail mighty prince,** 86
**To carry on the royal fruitful line.**

Roach, Richard, 'A Welcome to his Royal Highness Frederick, Prince of Wales', December 1728.
MS. Rawl. D. 832, fol. 246 (autogr.).

**Hail mirth inspiring nymph! to thee** 87
**And commerce ev'ry day and hour increase.**

Greaves, —, of Lichfield, 'Ode to Commerce'.
MS. Eng. poet. c. 51, p. 163.

88 Hail! more refulgent than the morning star,
To live in thy embrace, or at thy feet expire.

Dyer, George, 'Ode to Liberty . . . on a Public Anniversary'.
Pr. *Poems*, 1792, p. 32.
MS. *Eng. poet. c. 21, fol. 53.

89 Hail my dear mistress whom I honour more
An epitaph without a stone.

Creswell, Robert, 'Love within Book'.
MS. *Eng. poet. f. 24, fols. 20ᵛ, 21ᵛ (autogr.).

90 Hail mystic powers of heavenly love
Thro' time to all eternity.

Kenton, James.
MS. *Eng. poet. e. 20, p. 180 (autogr.).

91 Hail, old patrician trees, so great and good!
And noble fires beget.

[Cowley, Abraham].
Pr. *Works*, 1668, 'Essays in Prose and Verse', p. 93.
MS. Rawl. poet. 213, fol. 4.

92 Hail, patriot youth! lost in life's bloom
Who Britain loves, shall drop a tear.

'On Edmund late Duke of Buckingham . . . Extempore', 1735.
MS. Eng. poet. c. 9, p. 263.

93 Hail Phoebus, hail! thy radiant beams forebode
And with new spirit fired away he writes.

Gough, Richard, 'To the Sun shining on New-Year's day', 1751.
MS. *Eng. poet. c. 5, fol. 32ᵛ (autogr.).

94 Hail potent King! through whose capacious soul
Thy days prove peaceful, and thy Lydia kind.

'The Address of all his Majesty's Most thirsty Subjects in Merriment Assembled to His most Potant Majesty Robert King of Messopots Humbly Presented by Henry Earl of Banbury'.
MS. Eng. poet. e. 45, fol. 3.

95 Hail reverend shades! whose monuments decay,
Since heavenly brains can scarcely keep their station.

Chatwin, John, 'Viewing the Ruines of the Monuments in Knaptoft Church'.
MS. *Rawl. poet. 94, p. 229 (autogr.).

96 Hail sacred architect
Where Herbert's Angel's flown away before.

Polwhele, John, 'On Mr. Herberts devine poeme the church. Jo. Polw. post mortem authori mestus posuit'.
MS. *Eng. poet. f. 16, fol. 11 (autogr.).

Hail sacred art! thou gift of heaven designed 97
And Fust and Coster's names for ever live.

'A Poem on the art of Printing'.
MS. Montagu e. 13, fol. 158.

Hail sacred Nymph! Whose bright victorious eyes 98
So long as you would be my kind, bright, guiding star.

Chatwin, John, 'To Aurelia'.
MS. *Rawl. poet. 94, p. 91 (autogr.).

Hail sacred oak! whose happy shade 99
Will add eternal vigour to the poet's fire.

Chatwin, John, 'On the Royall Oke'.
MS. *Rawl. poet. 94, p. 173 (autogr.).

Hail sacred pair! tell by what wondrous charms 100
He stones and trees, she ministers of state.

'Orpheus and Margarita . . . the famous Italian songsters [songstress] gon from Greber Her Mr.', on Jacob Greber and Marguerite de l'Épine, sent to Dr. Charlett by Wm. Bishop, July 1703.
MS. Ballard 31, fol. 26; see also H132.

Hail sacred princes who vouchsafe to make 101
Bless you the fountain of our future kings.

Newton, —, 'Spoken in Trin[ity] Coll[ege]', May 1683, to the Duke and Duchess of York and Princess Anne.
MS. Add. B. 106, fol. 33.

Hail! sacred Salem, placed on high! 102
The happy plains surround.

'Hymn on Heaven. Collect Poems'.
MS. Eng. poet. e. 39, p. 90.

Hail, sacred source of learning bright 103
Till fame itself shall cease thy fame to raise.

Gough, Richard, 'On Homer. Nov. 15, 1750'.
MS. *Eng. poet. c. 5, fol. 35 (autogr.).

Hail, sacred tree! whose trembling leaves declare 104
The scorpion's sting with its own oil is cured.

'The Birch-Tree'.
MSS. Eng. poet. f. 12, p. 79; Top. Oxon. e. 379, fol. 5ᵛ.

Hail serviceable utensil! first made 105
But now to mortals as a blessing sent.

Chatwin, John, 'Made in the Tunn on a Chamber-pot'.
MS. *Rawl. poet. 94, p. 116 (autogr.).

Hail shameless model of a cursed whore 106
That once did know thee in the state of grace.

'On A Whore'.
MS. Ashmole 38, p. 36.

107 **Hail sister springs**
**A worthier object our Lord's feet.**
Crashaw, Richard, 'The Weeper'.
Pr. *Steps to the Temple*, 1646.
MSS. Eng. misc. e. 241, fol. 20ᵛ, attr. to Crashaw; Rawl. poet. 142, fol. 29; Tanner 465, fol. 28, attr. to Mr. Crashaw on fol. 1*a*.

108 **Hail sister to your snowy breast**
**Hath no such rags of Babel in't.**
'Sanctified Courtship'.
Pr. *Cleaveland Revived*, 1668, p. 108.
MSS. Ashmole 36, 37, fol. 204.

109 **Hail! Source of sympathy refined**
**Where nought but virtue's sure!**
'Ode to Sensibility'.
MS. Percy c. 8, fol. 141.

110 **Hail spotless flame! connubial love, designed**
**And bless the influence of connubial love.**
'Mr. M[erric]k', 'On Marriage'.
MS. Eng. poet. e. 39, p. 166.

111 **Hail star of the sea most radiant**
**One God and persons three.**
'The Howers of the B. Virgin ad usum Sarum. Eng. and Lat. The hymne at Evensong'.
MS. Eng. poet. e. 56, p. 84.

112 **Hail sweetest innocents, ye martyrs' flowers**
**In Rama when her children Rachel mourned.**
Samber, Robert, 'On the Holy Innocents', from 'the Bellman's Verses'.
MS. *Rawl. poet. 134*b*, fol. 154 (autogr.).

113 **Hail sweetest season of the year**
**Only for repose and shade . . . (incomplete).**
P. O., 'La Primavera'.
MS. Firth b. 4, fol. 15ᵛ (autogr.).

114 **Hail the great day of learning and of power**
**The spirit of comfort on my heart may flow.**
Creswell, Robert, 'On Whit Sunday, May 25. 1658 Grey[s] Inne'.
MS. *Eng. poet. f. 24, fol. 60ᵛ (autogr.).

115 **Hail those Religious etc.**
'Philomathes', 1667, translation of Latin hymn, incipit only, 'On the Prospect of the University' of Oxford; 'see page 64 of the quarto-paper book'.
MS. Eng. th. d. 52, fol. 3.

116 **Hail thou first sacrifice in martyr's roll**
**Th'eternal crown that on thy head shall sit.**
Clifford, Henry, Earl of Cumberland, 'Saint Stephen's'.
MS. *Rawl. poet. 95, fol. 32.

**Hail thou my native soil! thou blessed plot** 117
**By winning this, tho' all the rest were lost.**
Browne, William of Tavistock, extract from *Britannia's Pastorals*, II. iii.
MS. Eng. misc. e. 241, fol. 46.

**Hail thriving nation let us wish you joy** 118
**In his auspicious mild and gentle reign.**
'Brittains lasting bliss in the happy Revolution', on George I.
MS. Rawl. poet. 155, p. 226.

**Hail to the bride! may ev'ry night** 119
**But may you ever ever love.**
Chatwin, John, 'An Epithalamium To the Nuptials of Mr. G. R. and Madame E. J.'
MS. *Rawl. poet. 94, p. 146 (autogr.).

**Hail to the lusty bridegroom and the bride** 120–1
**That nat'ral motion last we strongest find.**
Creswell, Robert, 'Epithalamium on the due joyning together in Concord of Mr. Rich: Jones gent. of the Middle Temple and Mrs. Eliz. Wats daughter to Dr. Wats. Sept. 1655'.
MS. *Eng. poet. f. 24, fol. 15ᵛ (autogr.).

**Hail to the man, so sings the Hebrew bard** 122
**The king who bends to Heav'n must Heav'n itself approve.**
[Whitehead, William], Birthday ode, 1766.
Pr. *Poems*, 1790, ii. 85.
MS. Mus. Sch. D. 318. Music by Boyce.

**Hail to the myrtle shade** 123
**But sets with eternal spring.**
[Lee, Nathaniel], a song in *Theodosius*, II. ii, set by H. Purcell.
MS. Rawl. poet. 196, fol. 15ᵛ.

**Hail to the new-born King** 124
**'Tis all Thou knowst I have to give.**
Kenton, James.
MS. *Eng. poet. e. 20, p. 356 (autogr.).

**Hail to the new born year, what boon from Heaven** 125
**When the next comes I'll hail it thus again.**
'Epistle of Mr. Loyd to his wife. Newyears Day 1762'.
MS. Eng. poet. e. 47, p. 115.

**Hail to the new gigantic Mars of years,** 126
**That unto wisdom we apply our hearts.**
[Townley, James], 'The New Century . . . Jan. 1. 1801', but in his privately printed collection, 1785.
MS. Top. Oxon. c. 296, fol. 43.

127 **Hail to the rosy morn, whose ray**
**On the sweet prospect smiles of long succeeding years.**
[Whitehead, William], Birthday Ode, 1765. Pr. *Poems*, 1790, ii. 83.
MS. Mus. Sch. D. 316. Music by Boyce.

128 **Hail to the twilight hour,**
**Be the hour of the flowing, soul!**
MS. Don. d. 95, fol. 309.

129 **Hail to the witty genius of our shores,**
**So spake the goddess parting from my sight.**
'To Sr. Rogr. L'Estrange, Occasion'd by the perusal of his Mythology'.
MS. Rawl. poet. 91, fol. 5.

130 **Hail! to thy parents' wishes born,**
**And higher place above.**
'On the Birthday of a Child of a Year Old . . . Collect. Poems'.
MS. Eng. poet. e. 39, p. 60.

131 **Hail tricking monarch! more successful far**
**Led her himself unto the royal bed.**
'The Brittish Embassadress Speech to the french king'. Louis XIV and the Duchess of Shrewsbury, 1712.
MSS. Eng. misc. c. 116, fol. 2; Rawl. C. 986, fol. 23; Rawl. D. 383, two copies, fols. 67 and 112; Tanner 306, fol. 475; pr. bks. Firth b. 21, fol. 113; Fol. θ 665, fol. 218.

132 **Hail tuneful pair, say by what wondrous charms,**
**To her Shrub Hedges and tall Nottingham.**
'Transcrib'd'. *temp.* French wars, 1702, on Marguerite de L'Épine.
MS. Montagu e. 13, fol. 104v; see also H100.

133 **Hail! undaunted Hibernian, true offspring of light**
**But stand firm by each other or conquer or die.**
'The Virtuous Warriors' 'Tune Roslin [Corke (?)]', [1798 (?)].
MS. North e. 34, fol. 11.

134 **Hail venerable age! in Jesus blest**
**And share in that eternal bliss that never more shall end.**
Kenton, James, 'An Epitaph . . . for Mr. John Harley senr., 1754'.
MS. *Eng. poet. e. 19, p. 135 (autogr.).

135 **Hail venerable names in sacred writ**
**And rank me with thy saints in endless bliss.**
Kenton, James.
MS. *Eng. poet. e. 20, p. 72 (autogr.).

**Hail vice! Thy glorious empire all proclaim** 136
**Schisms attempts and Colliers heresy.**
'A congratulatory Poem to Vice on the success of the Play house in Oxon'.
MS. Rawl. D. 697, fol. 2.

**Hail, whom the diamonds proclaim their king** 137
**Her lip, severely guarded by her eyes.**
Fanshawe, Sir Richard, 'On a faire Rubie, sett in a Ring with manie Diamonds about it'.
MS. *Firth c. 1, p. 87.

**Hail you that are the martyr flowers,** 138
**And th' holy Ghost for evermore.**
'Upon the feast of the Holy Innocents . . . Engl. Primer of or. Ladie. 1631 . . . p. 3'.
MS. Eng. poet. e. 56, p. 26.

**Hail youthful Faunus! prosper now your sheep** 139
**And never crave the help of any deity.**
Chatwin, John, 'A Description of Winter. Sylvanus and Faunus'.
MS. *Rawl. poet. 94, p. 162 (autogr.).

**Hale be that hand which wrote your last to me.** 140
**T'observe that boy in one so old as me.**
Palmer, Ralph, lines addressed to Dr. Charlett, 10 Dec. 1728.
MS. Ballard 33, fol. 94 (autogr.).

**Half beautiful! Imperfect piece of clay:** 141
**That makes you not so fair as this doth foul.**
Strode, William, 'On a Faire Crooked Gentlewoman, Proude and Disembling'.
MS. *CCC. 325, fol. 101v (autogr.).

**Half blinded boy, son to an one eyed mother** 142
**The queen of beauty thou the god of love.**
'Of a Lady with one eye which brought forth a Child with one'.
MS. Rawl. poet. 116, fol. 54; see also A179, A324, F53, T2227.

**Half Herod's kingdom offers to a miss** 143
**For malice with a woman to compare.**
Tipping, William, 'Of Herod the Greate Prodigall foole of A Kinge'.
MS. *Rawl. poet. 101, fol. 74 (autogr.).

**Halfpence and farthings** 144
**Say the bells of St. John's.**
MS. Douce d. 59, fol. 58.

**Hallelujah to our king** 145
**Hallelujah to our king.**
Septuagesima hymn, 'Alleluia dulcia carmen', translated.
MSS. Eng. th. d. 52, fol. 114, attr. to 'Philomathes', 1667, reference to '4° paper book p. 92'; Rawl. poet. 72, fol. 61*a*v (autogr.).

146 Handsome clothing, wholesome diet.
Who needs more, to live at quiet.
Robinson, Robert, couplet.
MS. *Rawl. poet. 218, p. 135 (autogr.).

147 Handy pandy Jacky dandy
And pleas'd away went hop, hop, hop.
MS. Douce d. 59, fol. 50$^{v}$.

148 Hang the poor lover and his pedigree.
I lost my beauty ere I got this wit.
'The old Bawds advice'.
MS. Add. B. 8, fols. 11, 10, 8 rev.

149 Hang this whining way of wooing
To your wishes but her own.
[Southerne, Thomas], song in *The Wives Excuse*, act. V, set by H. Purcell.
MS. Rawl. poet. 196, fol. 40$^{v}$.

150 Hang up Mars.
Brome, Alexander, 'A Mock Song', see C664.

151 Hans Carvel, impotent and old
You've thrust your finger G-d knows where.
Prior, Matthew, 'Hans Carvel. De la Fountain Imitated'.
Pr. *Poems on several occasions*, 1709.
MS. Eng. poet. c. 41, fol. 12.

152 Happily housed [these] those Lares are,
*Sic siti lætantur Lares.*
'On the motto of the D[uches]s of B[uckingham]'s House in the Park', rebuilt by the Duke, 1703.
Pr. *A New Collection of Poems relating to State Affairs*, 1705, p. 566. cf. H 1116.
MSS. Eng. poet. e. 87, p. 89; Smith 23, p. 131.

153 Happy Acrisius [was] when first a child
Was to a statue metamorphosed.
Briggs, S[amson], 'Danäe'.
MSS. Rawl. poet. 116, fol. 71 rev.; 147, p. 265 rev., attr. to S. Briggs.

154 Happy and blest is he
Shall wander to their utter overthrow.
Knollys, Fra., Psalm i.
MS. *Rawl. poet. 60, p. 8 (autogr.).

155 Happy and only happy is that swain
Is what was done a many days ago.
Walsh, Octavia, 'True Happiness'.
MS. *Eng. poet. e. 31, fol. 151 rev. (autogr.).

156 Happy are the foul that are so honoured
But nought can well express you but a [heart].
'To his Mris'.
MS. Eng. poet. e. 14, fol. 76.

Happy are they [that] who wisely do forsee 157
The injured monarch, your own lawful king.
'The Result of the Lords of the Treasury. March 1697'.
MSS. Eng. poet. e. 50, p. 87; Rawl. poet. 169, fol. 13.

Happy are you, whom Quantock over-looks 158
For tho' the world be burned, this never will be Brent.
[Diaper, William], 'Brent. A Poem to Thomas Palmer Esqr.'
Pr. from this manuscript, *Complete Works of Diaper*, ed. D. Broughton, 1952. In Curll's *Miscellany*, 1727, i. 120.
MS. Rawl. poet. 157 (autogr.).

Happy beneath this cooling shade 159
No matter what she is tomorrow.
MS. Eng. misc. e. 241, fol. 125.

Happy candidate for bliss 160
And bear him to his Saviour God.
'Mrs. [Judith] Madan [*née* Cowper] on her grandson James Maitland, Oct. 2nd 1769'.
MS. Eng. poet. c. 51, p. 44.

Happy completely happy's he 161
And sin with punishment rewards.
Psalm i.
MS. Rawl. poet. 170, fol. 43 (autogr.).

Happy dear departing spirit 162
Quickly all our souls receive.
Kenton, James, 'On the death of Mrs. Ann Phipps of Mitcham in Surry', 1758.
MS. *Eng. poet. e. 19, p. 138 (autogr.).

Happy foundations, where well order'd schools 163
Their parents honour and, their country's love.
Samber, Robert, 'On the Charity Schools' from 'the Bellman's Verses'.
MS. *Rawl. poet. 134*b*, fol. 157 (autogr.).

Happy grave [thou] which dost enshrine 164
Clothe it so neatly as its own.
'Epitaph' on Mary Prideaux. A conclusion to S803.
In B.M. MSS. Harl, 6917, fol. 72 and Sloane 1446, fol. 62, attr. to G. Morley. Pr. Sir J. Mennes and J. Smith, *Musarum Deliciae*, 1656, p. 91.
MSS. CCC. 328, fol. 57; Rawl. poet. 142, fol. 44$^{v}$, attr. to Stroud.

Happy great Prince! and so much happier thou, 165
And mid'st a glorious heap of burning C-ts expire.
Oldham, [John], 'Sardanapalus. Ode. 1683'.
MS. Firth c. 15, p. 155.

166 Happy he! Happy again
A peaceful old man may I die.
Sancroft, William (?), 'Laus et Votum Vitæ beatæ. Lips. cent. 1. Epist. 8'. (Lipsius, 1586, pp. 13–14).
MS. Sancroft 48, fol. 27$^{v}$ in Sancroft's hand.

167 Happy his state above the fate of kings,
That could but truly know the cause of things.
Couplet.
MS. Rawl. poet. 209, fol. 36.

168 {Happy I love and {haste to enjoy her
{Hopeless {ne'r must
Oh the {pleasures that {blest lovers {steal.
{torments {poor {feel.
Northman, Mr., duet from *Camilla* by M. A. Bononcini.
MS. Mus. c. 107, fols. 69$^{v}$ and 71.

169 Happy hours all hours excelling
Griefs when told soon disappear.
'A Song . . . the Pleasures of Solitude'.
Pr. *c.* 1735.
MSS. Eng. poet. e. 40, fol. 51, dated 1742; Malone 22, fol. 46; Montagu e. 13, fol. 21$^{v}$.

170 Happy is a country life,
Age is no pain, nor youth no snare.
'The Country Life'.
MS. Rawl. poet. 90, fol. 166.

171 Happy is a country life
And I with you will choose to live.
Stukeley, William, 'On A Country life . . . The two first Stanzas are wrote by another hand' (fol. 5).
MS. *Eng. misc. e. 386, fol. 4$^{v}$.

172 Happy is he
And with a little doth not want.
MS. Rawl. poet. 66, fol. 4.

173 Happy is he and most secure
And with an easy sigh resign his breath.
Flatman, Thomas, 'The Happy Man . . . Decemb. 27 1664'.
Pr. *Poems*, 1674, p. 50, *beg.* Peaceful is he . . .
MS. *Firth d. 7, fol. 40; see also P99.

174 Happy is he that from all business clear
At the kalends, put all out again.
[Jonson, Ben.], 'An Ode in Horace in prayse of a Countrye lyfe, translated'. *Epode* ii. Pr. *The Underwood*, lxxxv.
MS. Rawl. poet. 31, fol. 28.

175 Happy is he, that in a quiet life
That there he rules as king, that wears a crown.
MS. Rawl. poet. 66, fol. 70.

Happy is he that standeth free, 176
And pleadings at the bar.
Fragment.
MS. Ashmole 51, fol. 6.

Happy is he who from his cradle's blind, 177
Where he does one compact idea find.
Chatwin, John, 'Against the Senses'.
MS. *Rawl. poet. 94, p. 169 (autogr.).

Happy is the man that knows 178
'Tis lost ever by the sight.
Polwhele, John, translator, 'Boet[hius] L. 3. met. 12'.
MS. *Eng. poet. f. 16, fol. 32 (autogr.).

Happy is the man that takes delight 179
Kind and always coming.
Song, no tune.
MS. Mus. Sch. C. 95, pp. 183, 185.

Happy me! oh happy sheep 180
Warm into the arms of death.
Crashaw, Richard, Psalm xxiii.
Pr. *Steps to the Temple*, 1646, p. 25.
MSS. Eng. misc. e. 241, fol. 97; Tanner 465, fol. 31, attr. to Mr. Crashaw, fol. 1*a*; Tanner 466, fol. 18$^{v}$, attr. to R. Crashaw.

Happy sons of Israel 181
Trophies to his glory raise.
Catch by W. Lawes.
Pr. *Choice Psalmes*, 1648, Thorough-Bass part Sig. Oo2.
MS. Mus. Sch. E. 451, p. 1.

Happy that man who first could raise 182
That God that still is loving, still the same.
'Easter Day. 1703'.
MS. *Don. f. 5, fol. 45.

Happy the bard (though few such bards we find) 183
Be your hearts honest, as your cause is good.
Churchill, Charles, 'Independance'.
MS. *Eng. poet. d. 113, p. 273.

Happy the house, the goods whereof excel, 184
When th'owners godly, and those gotten well.
Couplet, translated from Latin.
MS. Rawl. poet. 209, fol. 33.

Happy the man that all his days hath spent 185
This man hath lived though that travailed more.
R[andolph], T[homas], 'De Sene Veronesi ex Claudiano', [*Carm. min.* xx].
Pr. *Poems*, 1638.
MS. Eng. poet. c. 50, fol. 103.

186 Happy the man that doth not walk
Shall by his hand be overthrown.
Carew, Thomas, Psalm i of 'Eight Psalmes Translated'.
Pr. from this MS., *Poems*, ed. R. Dunlap, 1949, p. 135.
MS. Ashmole 38, p. 98*a*.

187 Happy the man who fears the lord
And from himself a numerous race.
Fairfax, Thomas, Lord, Psalm cxxviii.
MS. *Fairfax 40, p. 337 (autogr.).
MS. *Fairfax 38, p. 431.

188 Happy the man, who free from care,
Tell where I lie.
Pope, Alexander, 'Ode on Solitude . . . written when I was not Twelve years old', copied in a letter to Henry Cromwell, 11 July 1709.
Pr. Curll's *Miscellanea*, 1727, i. 16.
MS. Rawl. letters 90, fol. 14 (autogr.).

189 Happy the man, who free from crowds and courts
I'd beg of heav'n Almeria for a wife.
[Ireland, George, of Exeter College, Oxford (?)], translating Horace, *Epode* ii, 1735.
MS. Eng. misc. e. 240, p. 329.

190 Happy the man, who his whole time doth bound
The voyage, life is longest made at home.
Cowley, Abraham, translator, 'Claudian's Old man of Verona . . . The Health and Security of a Country Life'. *Carm. min.* xx.
Pr. *Works*, 1668, 'Essays in Verse and Prose', p. 135.
MS. Rawl. poet. 173, fol. 55$^{v}$.

191 Happy's the man who in some private shade
'Twas for the object of your contemplation made.
Chatwin, John, 'Solitude'.
MS. *Rawl. poet. 94, p. 235 (autogr.).

192 Happy the man who knows how to retreat
To make them silence know, and Thee.
Bromley, Henry (?), 'Silence'.
MS. *Don. e. 19, fol. 34.

193 Happy the man! Who nescious of restraint
To the dark bottom of the vast abyss.
'Liberty a Poem In Imitation of Philips's Splendid Shilling'.
MS. Rawl. poet. 195, fol. 155.

194 Happy the man whom bounteous gods allow
Than lamb and kid, lettuce and olives here.
Cowley, Abraham, translator, Horace, *Epode*, ii, 'In praise of a Country Life . . . Beatus ille qui procul, etc.'
Pr. *Works*, 1668, 'Essays in Verse and Prose', p. 107.
MS. Rawl. poet. 173, fol. 35.

Happy the world in that blest age 195
You are poor, he flings the door at you.
'Parents antient and modern'.
MS. Montagu e. 13, fol. 72$^{v}$.

Happy those islands where no sullen sky 196
She can win back the treasure she has lost.
'A Poem Panegyricall on . . . the Duke of Albemarle With Remarks on his voyage to Jamaica 1687'.
MS. Rawl. poet. 127, fol. 40.

Happy thou makest my days with true delights 197
Not to torment men but to give them bliss.
Knight, Gowin, 'M.A., fellow of Merton Coll. Oxon.', 'The Anti-thiefe in opposition to Cowley's thiefe'.
MS. Top. Oxon. e. 202, fol. 77.

Happy thou wert poor glove if thou didst know 198
That thou so sweet an hand, so oft dost kiss.
'Delivered in a glove'.
MS. Rawl. poet. 212, fol. 56.

Happy, thrice happy are those rural swains 199
Which does confound the wise, amaze the fools.
Morrice, John, 'The Countrey Life. March 13, 1707'.
MS. *Rawl. poet. 114, fol. 151 (autogr.).

Happy, thrice happy is the man who stands 200
And peace which God to Israel will give.
Knollys, Fra., Psalm cxxviii.
MS. *Rawl. poet. 60, p. 77 (autogr.).

Happy, thrice, happy man whose constant heart 201
Shall be o'erthrown.
Clifford, Henry, Earl of Cumberland, Psalm i.
MS. *Rawl. poet. 95, fol. 2.

Happy were he could finish forth his fate 202
Where harmless robin dwells with gentle thrush.
Essex, Robert Devereux, Earl of, 'Certaine verses', Ireland, 1598 (?).
Pr. *Biographia Britannica*.
MSS. Ashmole 781, p. 83, attr. to the Earl of Essex; Malone 19, p. 77; Rawl. C. 744, fol. 29$^{v}$, attr. to the Earle of Essex; Tanner 76, fol. 92$^{v}$, attr. to Robertus Comes Essexiæ.

Happy were man, if sin had never been; 203
Sighs shall cause tears; those tears shall make me blind.
'A Penitentiall wch. [Abp. Sancroft] found with other Papers concerning the Earl of Essex's Crimes, and Arraignmt. in a MS. of that time'.
MS. Tanner 76, fol. 89.

204 Happy while with sportive pleasure
When it ceases to be gay.
Song with music.
MS. Mus. c. 107, fol. 6.

205 Hard fate! (alas) by two I'm overcome,
And find no footing for my restless love.
Chatwin, John, 'The Divided Heart'.
MS. *Rawl. poet. 94, p. 179 (autogr.).

206 Hard fate to face, but yet a glorious fate
'Tis cowardly to live, but yet 'tis sweet.
MS. Add. B. 8, fol. 47.

207 Hard heart canst read, hath not a shower of tears
His mother's womb be re-ent'red cloth'd in clay.
'On the death of Mr. Atherton Bruch of Brasenose colledge', matric. 1615.
MS. Ashmole 47, fol. 105v.

208 Hard hearted fair if thou wilt not consent
And only pray that thou wilt fancy me.
Sonnet.
MSS. Eng. poet. c. 50, fol. 36; e. 97, p. 216.

209 Hard hearted foolish maids, whose high swollen pride
May a base dildo cure your languishment.
W. T., 'A neglected Lover angry with the female sexe'.
MS. Eng. poet. e. 14, fol. 69v.

210 Hard is the fate of him who loves
Inspiring something all-divine.
Thomson, James, 'Song'. Heading: 'Copy 8th Sept. 1801. Dromore House'.
MS. Eng. poet. d. 10, fol. 74.

211–12 Hard is the task for me, a rustic swain
Freedom and valour hold their ancient state!
Parsons, William, 'To a Scotch Lady . . .' 1784.
MS. *Don. d. 123, p. 107 (autogr.).

213 Hard stools are caused by costive claret
And when it's over f- again.
'Another Motto for a House of Office'.
MS. Add. A. 301, fol. 81v rev.

214 Hardly can a wench say nay
Her mind is but a masking.
Translation of Latin couplet.
MS. Tanner 306, fol. 185v rev.

215 Hardness assuming from toucht air alone
Under the sea a twig, above a stone.
'Corall. Ovid. Met. lib: 4', couplet.
Pr. Sandy's *Relation of a Journey*, 1615, p. 236.
MS. Don. e. 6, fol. 26v.

Hark! away! 'tis the merry ton'd horn 216
[No mortals on earth are so jolly as we.]
Hunting song.
MS. Ballard 47, fol. 4.

Hark Celia hark but lay thou close thine ear 217
And light their loves at ours.
MS. Mus. b. 1, fol. 135v, music by John Wilson.

Hark! from afar the solemn bell 218
In happier realms to dwell.
'Scriblerus', 'The Death-Bell. Written at Warminster Augt. 1788'.
MS. Montagu e. 14, fol. 21.

Hark! hark! alas! alas! what's this I hear? 219
In sum of all he was great, just, and good.
'On the Death of his Royal Highness Prince George of Denmark, 1708. Being the first I ever made'.
MS. *Rawl. poet. 197, fol. 1v (autogr.).

Hark hark, and hear 220
Then blessings will be our rich pay.
Cavendish, Lady Jane, song in 'The Concealed Fancies'.
MS. *Rawl. poet. 16, p. 141.

Hark hark brave boys have you heard the report 221
This high elevation betokens a fall.
'A New Song Warbled out of the Oracular Oven of Tho: Baker after the Duke of Marlborough's Entry through . . . London', 4 August 1714.
MS. Rawl. poet. 155, p. 176.

Hark, hark, death knocks us up with importunity 222
But all dance after him, that hear his melody.
Translation of Latin verse beg. *Heus Heus mors*.
MS. Eng. poet. c. 25, fol. 39.

Hark! hark! from ev'ry tongue loud accents rise 223
And rule where kings have learn'd to reign.
Installation Ode for Lord Westmorland, Chancellor of Oxford University, 1759.
MSS. Mus. d. 116–17, music by William Hayes.

Hark hark how in every grove 224
For age will snow upon your heart.
Shirley, James, 'Curtisan'.
Pr. *Poems*, 1646, p. 1.
MSS. Eng. poet. c. 50, fol. 110; *Rawl. poet. 88, p. 56, attr. to J. S.

Hark hark how swift the moments fly 225
The hopes of an eternal state.
Wheeler, Mr. M[aurice], 'A meditation upon death To the Tune of the Chimes at the Cathedral in Gloucester'.
MS. Willis 43, fol. 74.

226 Hark hark? nay there are three; 'tis not these rocks
Of triple hammers smite a double round.
Ashmole, Elias, 'Upon hearing three Coockoes singe together', 26 May.
MSS. Ashmole 36, 37, fol. 231 (autogr.).

227 Hark, hark, the huntsman sounds his horn
We'll follow in chorus with sprightly ton.
'Hunting song'.
MS. Ballard 47, fol. 3ᵛ.

228 Hark hark! the huntsman winds his horn
That warms the heart, unmasks the soul.
'A Song for a Hare Feast'.
MS. Ballard 47, fol. 148.

229 Hark hark the lark at heaven gate sings
My lady sweet arise.
[Shakespeare, William], song from *Cymbeline* II. iii.
MSS. Don. c. 57, fol. 40ᵛ, with music, possibly by Robert Johnson; Sancroft 53, p. 43, attr. to W. Sh. (reference to folio 1664).

230 Hark hark! the spheres enticing notes!
Clear up, and boast both His and your ascent.
Llewellin, M[artin], 'Caroll sung to his Majestie on Christmas Day 1644'.
From *Men-miracles*, 1656, p. 106 [1646, p. 143].
MS. Tanner 466, fol. 32.

231 Hark hark what uncouth noise is this
Their money's their defence.
Tipping, William.
MS. *Rawl. poet. 101, fol. 112ᵛ (autogr.).

232 Hark: hear you not a cheerful noise
And sing (through but a bass) in this sweet quire.
A[ustin], W[illiam], 2nd of two hymns for Christmas-day.
Pr. *Certain . . . Meditations*, 1635, p. 53.
MS. Rawl. poet. 61, fol. 80.

233 Hark, hear you not, a heavenly harmony
In heaven lives Oriana.
Pr. Thomas Bateson's *First Set*, 1604, xxii.
MSS. Mus. f. 20–24: f. 20, fol. 45ᵛ.

234 Hark! heard ye not yon foot-step dread
Again for freedom fights, again for freedom dies.
Mason, [William], 'A chorus in . . . Charactacus', pr. 1777.
MS. Eng. misc. e. 241, fol. 58ᵛ.

235 Hark hither, reader: wouldst thou see
Hark hither and thy self be he.
Crashaw, R[ichard], Pemb[roke College, Cambridge], 'To the reader on Lessius Hygiasticon'.
Pr. Leonardus Lessius, *Hygiasticon*, 1634, Sig. ¶9. See also G181.
MS. Eng. misc. e. 13, fol. 23.

Hark how chimes the passing bell 236
Sad bell-wether to the rest.
Shirley, James, 'The Passing Bell'.
A shorter version pr. *Poems*, 1646, p. 66.
MS. *Rawl. poet. 88, p. 64, attr. to J. S.

Hark how I had designed to meet the news 237
To tell what follows is a sad relation.
Bulteel, John, 'Upon the fatal Decree against Croke'.
MS. *Rawl. poet. 159, fol. 210ᵛ (autogr).

Hark how my Celia with the choice 238
Are all turned into stones again.
[Carew, Thomas], 'Upon Celia singing in the vault at Yorkehouse'.
Pr. *Poems*, 1640.
MSS. Ashmole 36, 37, fol. 52ᵛ; CCC. 328, fol. 84ᵛ; Don. c. 57, fol. 47ᵛ, with music by H. Lawes; Firth d. 7, fol. 124, attr. to Tho. Carew; e. 4, p. 114; Rawl. poet. 199, p. 1, attr. to Tho. Carew.

Hark, how the birds do sing, 239
To turn his double pains to double praise.
Herbert, George, 'Mans Medly'.
Pr. *The Temple*, 1633, p. 123.
MS. *Tanner 307, fol. 94.

Hark how the cries in every street 240
Of famous London town.
'To the tune of Christ Bells'.
MS. Rawl. poet. 196, fol. 50.

Hark how the drums and trumpets sound, 241
And all her fears may vanish.
'King George's Welcome to London from Hampton Court. In *The Provok'd Wife's Garland*', Song III (pr. bk. Douce PP 183(13)).
MS. Firth c. 20, fol. 53.

Hark! how the thundering cannons roar 242
In heavenly glory shall forever live.
1759, capture of Quebec.
Pr. bk. Firth b. 22, fol. 59.

Hark! how these sweet and clear reports inform 243
Music's best strains will die, if you should close.
Ashmole, Elias, 'To Maddam de G[ray (?)] Upon her playing on The Lute'.
MSS. Ashmole 36, 37, fol. 237ᵛ (autogr.).

Hark how they sound the roman drums 244
No doubt he will give them their right.
'The Academicall Army of the Epidemicall Arminians'; with postscript initialed E:O. A:*Π*. T:M:K.
MS. Eng. poet. e. 97, p. 127.

245 Hark, in proud Granada's city
Every wish he now possessed.
Percy, Thomas, Bp. of Dromore, translator, 'The Moorish Bull Feast'.
MS. Percy c. 7, fol. 46 (autogr.).

246 Hark, in what soft and moving strains
And make it tender as her song.
'Song To a Lady by Mr. W.'
MS. Firth e. 6, fol. 137.

247 Hark Israel and what I say give heed to understand:
Nor any other thing that to thy neighbour proper is.
'Audi Israell', the ten commandments.
MS. Rawl. poet. 112, fol. 26 rev.

248 Hark, Lucinda! to the wooing.
To December change her May.
'Ariette'.
MS. Eng. misc. e. 183, fol. 70$^{v}$.

249 Hark, my gay friend, that solemn toll
Let it, my God, be happy too.
'The Unknown World—Verses occasion'd by hearing a Pass-Bell By the Rev. Mr. St-n'.
MS. Eng. poet. e. 39, p. 134.

250 Hark, news o' envy; thou shalt hear described
No poison's half so bad as Julia.
'Dr. Dun: his Julia supposd to be his Mrs. Mother'.
Pr. amongst 'Dubia', *The Elegies and the Songs and Sonnets*, ed. H. Gardner, 1965, p. 100.
MS. Eng. poet. c. 14, fol. 36.

251 Hark! now the drums beat up again,
Over the hills and far away.
'The Recruiting Officer: or, The Merry Volunteers'.
MS. Firth c. 17, fol. 24.

252 Hark! Or does the muse's ear
And hail with us our monarch's natal day.
[Whitehead, William], Birthday Ode, 1774.
Pr. *Poems*, 1790, ii. 117.
MS. Mus. Sch. D. 332. Music by Boyce.

253 Hark plaintful ghosts, infernal furies hark
Death wrapt in flesh to living grave assigned.
Sidney, Sir Philip, from the *Arcadia*.
MS. *e Mus. 37, fol. 103$^{v}$.

254 Hark! she's call'd the parting hour is come
Sweet angels come and sing the rest.
Crashaw, Richard, 'A Hymne of the Assumption'.
MSS. Rawl. poet. 199, p. 97; Tanner 465, fol. 40$^{v}$, attr. to Crashaw.

Hark the cock crowed 255
And take it all night for your quarters.
'The Country Farmer set by Mr. Clerke'.
MS. Mus. Sch. C. 95, p. 115.

Hark! through the hollow vale what noise resounds 256
Spared thee in mercy and thy sons preserved.
Weston, Charles, 'On Occasion of the Earthquakes at Lisbon Nov. 1755 etc. 1756'.
MS. Lat. misc. e. 53, p. 18 (autogr.).

Hark! 'Tis a kingdom groans. Her heartstrings crack 257
Sleep folded in three dying nations' arms.
Paman, Robert, senior, 'To the memory of Mr. Wm. Holgate' 1672 (?).
MSS. Rawl. poet. 62, fol. 12, attr. to Paman (pater); Tanner 306, fol. 408, attr. to Rob. Paman Senr. by W. Sancroft.

Hark! 'tis the merry bells that ring 258
To part no more my love and me!
Robinson, Mrs. [Mary], 'Stanzas'.
MS. Percy d. 9, fol. 16$^{v}$.

Hark! 'Tis the nuptial day of heaven and earth; 259
The word will dwell among and in us too.
Cartwright, W[illiam], 'On the Nativitie. For the Kings Music'.
Pr. *Comedies . . . with other Poems*, 1651, p. 313.
MS. Tanner 466, fol. 32$^{v}$.

Hark to the ruins of a man 260
To have the power and yet to spare to kill.
MS. Mus. b. 1, fol. 40$^{v}$, music by John Wilson.

Hark! 'Twas the trump of death that blew 261
That begs for mercy not for life.
MSS. Ashmole 781, p. 135, attr. to W. Strachie; Eng. poet. e. 57, fol. 13.

Hark with what loud applause the Britons place 262
The giddy youth huzza'd the old men cried.
'Brittains Lunacy', 1714–15.
MS. Rawl. poet. 155, p. 98.

Hark ye virgins that so prize 263
They are withered so must you.
Cf. H265.
MS. Eng. poet. c. 50, fol. 39$^{v}$.

Hark you, hark you Dr. T[eniso]n 264
To make the mob fierce mad and blind.
'On the Thanksgiving day to be on Aug. 23 next: being a Feast on a Fast of the Church To the A[rch]B[ishop]'.
MS. Rawl. poet. 181, fol. 54.

265 Hark you ladies that despise
He can raise, and set on fire.
[Fletcher, John], from *Valentinian*, 1647, II. iv. Cf. H263.
MS. Eng. poet. c. 50, fol. 39.

266 Harmonious nymph! to thee I fly.
Is more obdure than rocks, or adamantine clay.
Chatwin, John, 'The Eccho'.
MS. *Rawl. poet. 94, p. 58 (autogr.).

267 Harmonious strings, your charms prepare
The praise of their victorious king.
Prior, Matthew, 'Song to the king after the Takeing of Namur' 1695.
Pr. *Poems on Affairs of State*, iii, 1698, p. 277.
MS. Eng. poet. c. 18, fol. 157.

268 Harry come parry, when will you marry?
And stay with the bride all night.
MS. Douce d. 59, fol. 49v.

269 Harsh maid suppose not this clear spring
They that changed her can alter you.
Attr. to Mr. Reynolds, B.M. MS. Harl. 6917, fol. 73v.
MS. Mus. b. 1, fol. 72v, music by John Wilson.

270 Harshly I strike the lyre and sorrowing lead
And die a lesson to succeeding times.
Howard, Henry, Earl of Suffolk and Berkshire, 'On the Installation of the Earl of Westmoreland Chancellor of the University of Oxford July 3. 1759'.
MS. Lat. misc. e. 53, p. 35.

271 Has Delia lost an eye? Shed not a tear:
But dreaded death before from too great blaze.
'On Delia's Loss of an Eye'.
MS. *Eng. poet. d. 47, fol. 119.

272*a* Has heaven once more espoused Britannia's cause?
And by his mercies point us for his own.
'Britains Review L[ondon] Mag. 1746'.
MS. Eng. poet. e. 39, p. 42.

272*b* Hast thou a longing gadding vein
More safely live at home.
Translation of Latin couplet.
MS. Rawl. poet. 117, fol. 156v rev.

273 Hast thou at last that mother church too quitted
And have no hope of heaven but his word.
'A New Address to Mr. Bayes on his Late Conversion to the Church of Rome (viz. Dr. Parker [Bishop 1686–8] of Oxford)'.
Pr. *The Muses Farewell to Popery & Slavery*, 2nd ed., 1690, p. 174.
MS. Don. e. 23, fol. 63.

Hast thou been dead [lost] a month and can I be 274
I'll come a pilgrim to weep o'er thy tomb.
'An Elegye on Mr. Thomas Washington's death', in Spain, 1623.
MSS. Ashmole 47, fol. 61; Eng. poet. c. 50, fol. 44; e. 14, fol. 92v rev.; f. 10, fol. 114v; Rawl. poet. 26, fol. 75v; 160, fol. 55v, attr. to Lewis.

Hast thou beheld, when from the goal they start 275
Such is the love of fame, an honourable thirst.
Stukeley, William, 'Cursus'.
MS. *Eng. misc. d. 450, fol. 36 (autogr.).

Hast thou forsaken all thy sins but one. 276–7
Believe it, Partio, thou'ast forsaken none.
[Quarles, Francis], 'On Partio', couplet.
Pr. *Divine Fancies*, 1632, ii. 58.
MS. Rawl. poet. 90, fol. 68v.

Hast thou money? friends stand by thee; 278
And with scorn turn up their snout.
Robinson, Robert.
MS. *Rawl. poet. 218, p. 150 (autogr.).

Hast thou not heard my soul the trumpets sound 279
They perish'd all, and mankind is no more.
Boswell, James, 'Jeremiah, iv. 19–26, Paraphrased'.
MS. *Douce 193, fol. 103v (autogr.).

Hast thou not seen of hounds a pack 280
Insisting on an apple-pudding.
Lumby, John, 'To Mr. J. G. Novr. 4. 1730'.
MS. *Eng. poet. e. 42, fol. 87.

Hast thou observed how the curious hand 281
And lighter: 'Tis but lighter by the dross.
[Quarles, Francis], 'On the refineing of Gold'.
Pr. *Divine Fancies*, 1632, ii. 7.
MS. Rawl. poet. 90, fol. 65v.

Hast thou, Oh Lord, then cast us quite away? 282
For thy forbearance serves but to increase their pride.
Knollys, Fra., Psalm lxxiv.
MS. *Rawl. poet. 60, p. 84 (autogr.).

Hast thou store of money by? 283
His hands are numb'd, and hard as steel.
Robinson, Robert.
MS. *Rawl. poet. 218, p. 153 (autogr.).

Haste away thou tardy lover 284
You shall find a welcome here.
'Song'.
MS. Montagu e. 14, fol. 35.

285 Haste beauteous eve to close the eye of day
And seems to whisper to the listening trees.
'On Evening: the second Attempt of a Young Lady not yet fourteen years of Age'.
MS. Eng. poet. e. 47, p. 69.

286 Haste haste oh Lord and help make haste to save
Haste haste oh Lord my need of it doth press.
Fairfax, Thomas, Lord, Psalm lxx.
MS. *Fairfax 40, p. 157 (autogr.).
MS. *Fairfax 38, p. 240.

287 Haste night into thy center, are thy wings
No rival shall him of his death deprive.
'A Gentleman before hee kild himselfe'.
Attr. in B.M. MS. Sloane 1792, fol. 20$^v$, to Mr. Henrie Arscall.
MSS. Ashmole 47, fol. 91$^v$; CCC. 328, fol. 22$^v$; Malone 21, fol. 47.

288 Haste shepherds, haste and come away
And join in chorus with my amorous lay.
Song.
MS. Rawl. poet. 116, fol. 113$^v$.

289 Haste sovereign mistress of my soul
No more distressful times I see . . . (incomplete).
Gough, Richard.
MS. *Eng. poet. c. 5, fol. 192$^v$ (autogr.).

290 Haste thee oh God to rescue me oppress'd
Oh stay not long, for I am sore dismayed.
Jos. Br., Psalm lxx.
MS. Rawl. poet. 61, fol. 41.

291 Haste thee to have me, Lord
Oh Lord, make no delay.
Psalm lxx.
MS. *Montagu e. 10, fol. 20.

292 Haste ye long desired hours
Shall tune to melody the lyre.
Glee by Gilbert Heathcote.
MS. Mus. d. 177, fol. 36$^v$.

293 Haste ye nymphs, make haste away
For this is Pan's high holiday.
'Dialogue between Nymphs and Swaines'.
MS. Rawl. poet. 246, fol. 39$^v$; see also H296.

294 Haste ye soft gales to my relief
Tell her for her alone I die.
Catch by Dr. [W.] Hayes.
MS. Mus. d. 177, fol. 62.

295 Haste you beauteous nymphs of shades
Till unto her I make my way.
'A Song'.
MS. Montagu e. 13, fol. 53.

Haste you nymphs, make haste away 296
For this is love's high holiday.
'A Dialogue'.
Pr. with music by William Lawes in *Select Ayres and Dialogues*, 1669, p. 108.
MS. Mus. b. 1, fol. 76, with music by John Wilson; see also H293.

Haste, young eyed May, and gently pour 297
This fairest daughter of the year.
Farmer, Richard, whilst a scholar of Emmanuel College, [1754–9].
MS. Eng. poet. c. 6, fol. 27.

Hasten (great prince) unto the British isles 298
As desolate a place as he designed.
P[hilips], Mrs. K[atherine], 'Upon the Numerous accesse of the English Gentry to his Matie. in Flanders'. 1660.
Pr. *Poems by the Incomparable Mrs. K. P.*, 1664, p. 3.
MS. Tanner 306, fol. 367.

Hath aged winter fledg'd with feathered rain 299
Let each eye water't with a courteous tear.
Crashaw, Richard. 'An Elegie on the death of Mr. Stanninow fellow of Queens Colledge Camb.'
MSS. Rawl. poet. 147, p. 69; Tanner 465, fol. 63$^v$, attr. to Mr. Crashaw on fol. *1a*.

Hath any man, the glorious hearses seen 300
That is so sure on earth to find his hell.
Mervall, Alphonso, 'The Picture'.
MS. *Rawl. poet. 166, p. 28 (autogr.).

Hath Christmas furr'd your chimneys 301
When I have rubbed and raked it.
Strode, William, 'Song'.
MS. *CCC. 325, fol. 68 (autogr.).
MS. Rawl. poet. 199, p. 45, headed 'Pidgeons songe'.

Hath Cupid ne'er an arrow left 302
Thy wings; be wise and soon return.
'On his Mistresse'.
MS. Malone 21, fol. 50.

Hath David Christ to come foretold? 303
The new ones shall inspire.
'The Rev. Mr. S. Westley Junr. on Mr. I. Watts a Dissenting Minister altering the Psalme to apply (quoth he) to the Christian State 1730'.
MS. Eng. poet. c. 51, p. 26.

[Hath heaven withdrawn the talent] 304
Pose thee too hard, he will instruct thee too.
[Quarles, Francis], last lines of 'In Adversity', *Iob Militant*, 1624.
MS. Rawl. poet. 127, fol. 17$^v$.

305 Hath only anger an omnipotence
That thou hadst none.
Crashaw, Richard, 'Upon the Asse that carried our Saviour'.
MS. Tanner 465, fol. 33v, attr. to Mr. Crashaw on fol. 1*a*.

306 Hats are for use; [and ornament but] I'd know the reason why
Men put their heads there, where their tails should be.
'Steeple crown'd hatts'.
MSS. Don. d. 58, fol. 38v; Douce 357, fol. 3.

307 Have a care of thy money, while money is by thee
This is the course of the public weal.
Robinson, Robert.
MS. *Rawl. poet. 218, p. 150 (autogr.).

308 Have as oft by thy will sorrow and sighing
As thou hadst in thy sin lust and liking.
Couplet.
MS. Lat. liturg. e. 17, fol. 53.

309 Have communion with few
Speak evil of none.
MS. Rawl. D. 947, fol. 80v rev.

310 Have I a corner in your memory
Will beautify the soul that thinks thereon.
Strode, William, 'An Answer to a frinde' at Cambridge.
MS. *CCC. 325, fol. 96 (autogr.).

311 Have I for this employ'd so well
As Hoadly Clark and Whiston.
'Dr. Tindall's speeach; upon reading Ben's Sermon'. 1710.
Pr. bk. Firth b. 21, fol. 76.

312 Have I found her,
Chain me to thee with that hair.
Pr. Tho: Bateson's *Second Set of Madrigales*, 1618, xiii.
MSS. Mus. f. 20–24: f. 20, fol. 30v.

313 Have I my fingers? and have I my eyes?
I've often said beside 'em.
'A Shorter and Truer Advertisement', subscribed 'Flamingo'; see M504 on Mary Toft.
Pr. bk. Gough Surrey 15.

314 Have I no place within my charmer's breast?
And live as if ambitious of her favour.
Boswell, James, 'An imitation of Lysander's celebrated Soliloquy. Agis Act 4'.
MS. *Douce 193, fol. 73 (autogr.).

Have I renounc'd my faith or basely sold 315
At once to wish the devil and her farewell.
Corbett, Richard, 'On Mrs. Mallet'.
Pr. *Poems*, 1647, p. 26.
MSS. Ashmole 47, fol. 69v, attr. to Dr. Corbett; CCC. 328, fol. 12, attr. to Corb; Eng. poet. e. 14, fol. 25, attr. to Dr. Co.; Malone 21, fol. 48v, attr. to Dr. Corbett; Rawl. poet. 117, fol. 16; 199, p. 30, attr. to R. Corbet.

Have mercy Lord of thine abundant grace 316
The calves of lips on altar of our hearts.
Harington, Sir John, Psalm li.
MS. *Douce 361, fol. 30v.

Have mercy lord on me I pray, for man would me devour: 317
That I before thee may ascend, with such as live in light.
[Hopkins, John], Psalm lvi.
MS. Rawl. poet. 112, fol. 55 rev.

Have mercy on me lord after thy great abounding grace: 318
Thou shalt accept, and calves they shall upon thine altar lay.
[Norton, Thomas], Psalm li.
MS. Rawl. poet. 112, fol. 56 rev.

Have mercy on me, oh my God, 319
My tongue shall sing to thee.
Psalm li.
MS. *Montagu e. 10, fol. 69.

Have mercy on us Lord 320
Of Him shall stand in fear.
[Hopkins, John], Psalm lxvii.
MSS. Rawl. poet. 23, p. 172, reference to setting by Dr. Giles; 112, fol. 52v rev.

Have mind of bliss that never blyn 321
To help a man to heavenly bliss.
'Sensus interni . . . Ex MS. . . . c. temp. Henry V' (similar to B.M. MS. Harl. 1706, fol. 207v), copied by Alexander Huish.
MS. Eng. poet. e. 56, p. 118.

Have others other choice 322
That in thy laws I may thy scholar be.
Herbert, Mary (*née* Sidney), Countess of Pembroke, Psalm cxix, 'H'.
MSS. *Rawl. poet. 24, p. 180; *25, fol. 121.

323 Have pity on us all good lairds
And every one gives licks and wipes.
Smith, Thomas, B.A., of Christ Church, 'Lowe's Lamentation . . . made as 'twas reported by one Thomas Smith . . . of Christ Church' on events at Christ Church 21 January 1660/1.
See Wood *Life and Times*, ed. A. Clark, i, O.H.S. xix, 1891, p. 358.
MS. Tanner 306, fol. 373.

324 Have ye not heard ye princes great
I never heard thing make such moan.
[Philosophy and Experience].
MS. Rawl. poet. 121, fol. 78.

325 Have ye not seen
Upon which these inscriptions I did find.
Wake, William, of Cambridge.
See M118.
MS. Eng. misc. d. 1, fol. 34$^v$.

326 Have you beheld a swaddled infant lie,
Gold buying food, food buying gold to spill.
'Upon burning of a Barne wherein was hid much wealth'.
MSS. Ashmole 36, 37, fol. 251.

327 Have you heard of a lord of noble descent?
Now the Lord send's heaven at our ending.
'Ballade on the Lord Mordaunt', [Charles, 3rd Earl of Peterborough] 1680.
MS. Don. b. 8, p. 681.

328 Have you not heard of a pious fray
To St. Andrew's we will go.
'The Church Scuffle: or, News from St. Andrew's'.
MS. Firth c. 20, fol. 96.

329 Have you now read, my Lord, pray do not speak
And so as witty, I shall ever live.
Cavendish, Lady Jane, to the Earl of Newcastle, on 'The Concealed Fancies'.
MS. *Rawl. poet. 16, p. 157.

330 Have you observed, one, whom the times of old,
Let me not live, this is my Decian.
'Ad Decianum'. Martial, *Epigrams* I. xxxix.
MS. Rawl. D. 1147, fol. 90.

331 Have you seen a blackheaded maggot
Oh so black, oh so rough, oh so sour is she.
Parody of H334.
MS. Eng. poet. f. 25, fol. 64$^v$.

332 Have you seen battledore play?
But in your arms.
MSS. Mus. Sch. C. 95, p. 176 with music by 'Mr. [Ralph] Courtiville'; Rawl. poet. 196, fol. 9.

Have you seen fairies dance the ring? or clowns 333
I stand still faster than most men do go.
Oldisworth, Nicolas, 'On my loosing my way'.
MS. *Don. c. 24, fol. 25 (autogr.).

Have you seen the white lily grow 334
Oh so sweet, oh so soft, oh so sweet, so sweet is she.
[Jonson, Ben.], *The Underwood*, 4, 'See the Chariot at hand . . .', verse 3.
MSS. Don. d. 58, fol. 26$^v$, with 2 additional stanzas; Eng. poet. f. 25, fol. 64$^v$; Rawl. poet. 116, fol. 50$^v$; 199, p. 74.

Have you the colic heavens? or stand you still 335
The reason is my ink my brain is dry.
W. R., 'On the great drought. 1635'.
MS. Rawl. poet. 199, p. 77.

Having been tenant long to a rich lord 336
Who straight your suit is granted, said, and died.
Herbert, George, 'Redemption'.
Pr. *The Temple*, 1633, p. 31.
MS. *Tanner 307, fol. 24$^v$.

Having no wealth to show my gratitude 337
Nature, as name to honour your brave mind.
Colman, Henry, 'Anacrostica Dedicatoria', to William Rokeby; acrostic on the poet's own name.
MS. *Rawl. poet. 204, fol. v$^v$ (autogr.).

Having thanked me so much for the news in my last 338
For I'll leave 'em of age fit to govern themselves.
'A Conference, Between K[ing] W[illiam] and the E[arl] of Sund[er]land. In a Letter to a Friend. June 1700'.
MS. Eng. poet. e. 50, p. 142.

Having to do [a late] of late 'mongst all the laws 339
I missed my suit and she missed her desire.
'In uxorem causidici'.
MSS. Don. d. 58, fol. 31; Eng. poet. e. 14, fol. 11.

Hawks hounds and horses, servants, pride and stealth 340
Are oft times found devour their master's wealth.
Couplet translating Latin distich.
MSS. Rawl. D. 954, fol. 42$^v$; Rawl. poet. 209, fol. 32$^v$.

He and she can ne'er agree 341
If when one's high, the other bends.
Robinson, Robert.
MS. *Rawl. poet. 218, p. 172 (autogr.).

342 He at the tavern on a day
For shaking off the devil's bones.
'On Fown's of Peter house loosing his money and credit at one blow'. [William Fownes, Fellow of Peterhouse, 1687].
MS. Rawl. D. 214, fol. 81.

343 He beareth vermin the piles of Sir reverence
An ill-favoured knave pendant by a line.
'[George Canning's] armes blased'; cf. T3127.
MS. Tanner 306, fol. 239.

344 He blessed is, who neither loosely treads,
The way they go, shall be their way to perish.
Sidney, Sir Philip, Psalm i.
MSS. *Rawl. poet. 24, p. 1; *25, fol. 1.

345 He blessed is, who with wise temper can
Oh so, oh be it so.
Sidney, Sir Philip, Psalm xli.
MSS. *Rawl. poet. 24, p. 58; *25, fol. 34v.

346 He both in age and fame exceeds
That reckons not, by years, but deeds.
Couplet.
MS. Rawl. poet. 66, fol. 51.

347 He butchered? ah no more away forbear
As when the trump shall his last summons blow.
On Charles I, 1649 (?).
MS. Rawl. poet. 152, fol. 245.

348 He came; saw; cured! Could Caesar's self do more;
On earth with grace, in Heaven with glory crowned.
N. S., 'A Cordiall return of thanks unto Dr. [Thomas] Brown[e] for the despaired off Cure of Mrs. E. S.'
MS. Rawl. D. 391, fol. 33.

349 He comes he comes the hero comes
Royal royal royal [ ].
MS. Mus. e. 20, fol. 16v.

350 He comes whose brow though for a crown so fit
Since kings are God's and ours of kings the best.
Philips, Mrs. [Katherine], 'On the Coronation'.
Not pr. in *Poems* 1667.
MS. Locke e. 17, p. 94.

351–2 He could have picked no fitter time to die,
Great Britain is the centre of his love.
Oldisworth, Nicolas, 'On Alexander Bainham Esquier, who was killed at the Siege of Mastrich. 1632'.
MS. *Don. c. 24, fol. 39v (autogr.).

He died and gave all to his Megge 353
For he had no issue but one in his leg.
'Upon a rich churle that made his wife Megge his Heyre', couplet.
MS. e Mus. 227, fol. 10.

He dipped not his hand in any blood 354
Since [ ] no longer is alive.
MS. Rawl. poet. 66, fol. 3.

He doeth much, but little doth dispute 355*a*
His mind is active, though his tongue be mute.
Couplet.
MS. Rawl. poet. 66, fol. 4.

He easily will dispense 355*b*
With greatest sins, who hath of small no sense.
Couplet.
MS. Rawl. poet. 117, fol. 164v rev.

He falls the matchless master of the heart 356
It mourns that Richardson was born to die.
Hawksworth, Dr., 'On Mr. [Samuel] Richardson', d. 1761.
MS. Eng. poet. c. 51, p. 185.

He fears for to approach your sight 357
His heart lies prostrate doth you greet.
Burton, Francis.
MS. *Add. A. 267, fol. 81 (autogr.).

He first deceas'd: she for a little tried 358
To live without him; liked it not, and died.
Couplet.
Pr. *Wits Recreations*, 1641, Epitaph 17; and *Reliquiae Wottonianae*, 1685, p. 359 'Upon the death of Sir Albert Morton's wife'.
MSS. Don. e. 6, two copies, fols. 16 and 17; Rawl. D. 947, fol. 80 rev., headed 'on Sir Henry Woottons Lady'; Rawl. poet. 84, fol. 46; Sancroft 53, p. 44; see also H1241, S366.

He in a vial the sun's atoms takes 359
Asks he, that toils to find a woman chaste.
'Femina nulla bona est', G. de Cespades, 'Gerardo the unf[ortunate] Span. [translated Leonard Digges, 1622] p. 140'.
MS. Sancroft 53, p. 39.

He is a cook, and a cold one too, 360
And a cuckold long ago.
'On a Coockold'.
MS. Malone 19, p. 100.

He is a fool, and ever shall, 361
Who takes a window, for a wall.
'One wrote his name in a window' and 'Replye'.
MS. Malone 19, p. 103.

362 He is a knave, a knave indeed,
Doth out the Devil's work.
Robinson, Robert.
MS. *Rawl. poet. 218, p. 105 (autogr.).

363 He is neither rich happy nor wise.
That is a bondman to his own avarice.
Couplet.
MS. Gough Norfolk 43, fol. 46.

364 He is no good swain
That stayeth his journey for a shower of rain.
Couplet.
MS. Gough Norfolk 43, fol 28.

365 He is not here, if you would see
Death he fear'd not, and so ended.
On Jerome Keyt Esq., B.C.L. of St. John's College, Oxford, 1631. Woodstock.
Pr. Hearne's *Collections*, ed. C. E. Doble, iii, O.H.S. xiii, 1889, p. 231.
MSS. Hearne's diaries 31, p. 23; Top. Oxon. a. 29, fol. 197ᵛ.

366 He is not rich, that's rich in goods; nor he
But the poor-man wants least, since both do want.
Morrice, John, 'De divite et paupere. 25 Jan., 1707'.
MS. *Rawl. poet. 114, fol. 120 (autogr.).

367 He is now dead,
No such disgraces.
On Robert Cecil, Earl of Salisbury, 1612.
MS. Tanner 299, fol. 11ᵛ.

368 He is so covetous, so base, and vild
He will not spend, no not to get a child.
Couplet.
MS. Rawl. poet. 117, fol. 271 rev.

369 He is stark mad who ever says
But after one such love, can love no more.
Donne, John, 'Song'.
MSS. Eng. poet. e. 14, fol. 40, attr. to D. Dun; *e. 99, fol. 101ᵛ; *f. 9, p. 42; Rawl. poet. 117, fol. 205ᵛ rev.

370 He killed her not say some, he only stayed
Her from all marrying; Ah that kills a maid.
Couplet 'On Jephthas Daughter'.
MS. Eng. poet. d. 152, fol. 103ᵛ.

371 He let make an axe for the nones
Thereon were twenty pound of steel.
'When Ric[hard] I Conquered Cyprus (saith Rob[ert] of Gloster):'
From Francis Sandford's *Genealogical History of the Kings of England*, 1677, p. 76.
MS. Sancroft 98, p. 143.

He lies entombed, within that temple there 372*a*
Our sympathizing souls, and body have.
'In the Chamber window which stands in view of her husbands tombe'.
Pr. bk. Wood 460, after *Threnodia in obitum E. Lewkenor*, 1606.

He like the gods appears 372*b*
Would die a good old man.
'Translated out of Lipsius In Epist. 8'.
MS. Rawl. poet. 62, fol. 41ᵛ.

He like the Phoenix ashes dead doth rise 373
In glory now enthroned above the skies.
On the tomb of George Fineux, d. 1653, in St. Paul's Church, Canterbury.
MS. Rawl. D. 376, fol. 220.

He lives, he lives, the glorious patriot lives 374
A guide and glory to posterity.
'On a Mr. Addison's Recovery of a fitt of sickness before that of which he dyed', 1719.
MS. Rawl. poet. 152, fol. 181.

He loved and loved and loved again 375
To live is all she hath to do.
Elys, Edmund, 'upon Occasion of one's Asking me whether I would never have done with my Friendships etc. 1686'.
MSS. Autogr. d. 21, fol. 236 (autogr.).

He needs no bows, no warlike force 376
I shall be melted all to love.
'In imitation of Horace', *Odes* I. xxii.
MS. Top. London e. 9, p. 29.

He nine ways looks, and needs must learned be 377
That all the muses at one view can see.
'On a blinkeing Poett', couplet.
MS. Rawl. poet. 84, fol. 106 rev.

He now is sick, and he must die; 378
Against it is no remedy.
Robinson, Robert.
MS. *Rawl. poet. 218, p. 105 (autogr.).

He of all men is least wise, 379
That thinks he's most, in his own eyes.
Robinson, Robert, couplet.
MS. *Rawl. poet. 218, p. 113 (autogr.).

He, oh! pray father come 380
Would it were my dear.
'In the Novelty set by Mr. John Eccles'.
MS. Mus. Sch. C. 95, p. 61.

He, on whose birth the lyric queen 381
Oh goddess! is thy gift alone.
Atterbury, Francis, Horace, *Odes* IV. iii.
MS. Eng. misc. f. 79, p. 54.

382 He quenched the fires ere it to burn began
So he may say I came, I saw, I wan.
Couplet.
MS. Rawl. poet. 117, fol. 274 rev.

383 He seeks for ours as we do seek for his.
Causing its being and its measure.
Traherne, Thomas, 'Recovery'.
MS. *Eng. poet. c. 42, fol. 12v (autogr.).

384 He that a bad wife follows to the grave
For who can weep indeed to lose a shrew?
MS. Rawl. poet. 209, fol. 44.

385 He that a christian or a saint would be
From George's court as from a plague must flee.
Couplet, 'Exeat Aula qui vult esse pius. Hor: Imitated'.
MS. Rawl. poet. 155, p. 111.

386 He that a fertile field will sow
And leave, for those which real are.
Bacon, Sir Nicholas, translation of Boethius, *Consolations* III. i. Sent to John Hobart 1664.
MS. Tanner 306, fol. 327 (autogr.).

387 He that a lady's water will distil
May take't for *aqua mirabilis* if he will.
Couplet.
MS. Rawl. poet. 209, fol. 43v.

388 He, that a man ingenious is,
And he to that a debtor.
Robinson, Robert.
MS. *Rawl. poet. 218, p. 130 (autogr.).

389 He that accord by might would altered see
He in a cord by weight should haltered be.
Couplet.
MS. Rawl. poet. 117, two copies, fols. 271 rev. and 269 rev.

390 He that adheres to God shall safe
With gifts of saving grace.
Psalm xci.
MS. *Rawl. C. 113, fol. 66.

391 He that an apple chooseth by the skin
And a french core in th' other.
'In feminam'.
MSS. Don. d. 58, fol. 37v; Rawl. poet. 117, fol. 272 rev.

392 He that buildeth his house all of sallows
Is well worthy to be hanged on the gallows.
Couplet.
MS. Gough Norfolk 43, fol. 19v.

393 He that buys land buys stones
He that buys good ale buys nothing else.
MS. Malone 19, p. 148.

He that by chance doth fall upon the plain 394
His ghost went down to Pluto king of hell.
MS. Rawl. poet. 209, fol. 47.

He that called souls an harmony 395
To woo the steel when the diamond's by.
Paman, C[lement], 'The Diamond'.
MS. Rawl. poet. 147, p. 57.

He that can [read] spell a sigh, or read [spell] a tear 396
By blessing them once more against their will.
'On the Duke of Buckingham'.
Pr. *Recreation for Ingenious Head-peeces*, 1663, Epitaph 186 (short form).
MSS. Eng. poet. e. 97, p. 60; Rawl. poet. 26, fol. 37v, attr. to Dr. Lewis; Sancroft 53, p. 46.

He that considereth the poor 397
World without end. Amen.
Psalm xli.
MS. *Montagu e. 10, fol. 62.

He that could load his cannon pike advance 398
Of lordly death, the frightful standard bears.
G. B. 'Epitaph 10' on Prince Henry, 1612, in 'Cestria Lugens'.
MS. *Rawl. poet. 116, fol. 7v.

He that descended man to be 399
The glorious triumphs of our king.
'Out of John Amner's set of bookes [*Sacred Hymns*] . . . 1615', xvii.
MSS. Mus. f. 21–24: f. 20, fol. 6v.

He that desires, to pass the surging seas, 400
That as they should, they might your virtues touch.
Whitney, Geoffrey, 'In prayse of the right vertuous Gentlewoman Mris. Elyzabeth Parrott'.
In *A Choice of Emblemes*, 1586, sig. O2, the Earl of Leicester's name is substituted.
MS. *Rawl. poet. 56, fol. 67.

He that did ever scorn love's might 401
That wound all hearts, but murther mine.
MS. Ashmole 38, p. 144.

He that did tip stone jugs about the brim 402
Met with a black pot, and that pot tipped him.
'Epitaph or a Gold-smith', couplet.
MS. Eng. poet. e. 40, fol. 117.

He that died so oft in sport 403
Died at last no colour for't.
'Uppon a Dyer', couplet.
Pr. Camden's *Remaines*, 1637, p. 410.
MSS. Ashmole 38, p. 184; Eng. poet. e. 40, fol. 106.

404 He that doth ask Saint James doth say shall speed
Oh that King James would answer so my need.

'In Jacobum' [James I], couplet.
Translated from Owen, i. 170.
Pr. *A Helpe to Discourse*, 1623; cf. *N. & Q.* ccvi, 1961, p. 426.
MSS. CCC. 327, fol. 32$^{v}$; Rawl. poet. 209, fol. 33$^{v}$.

405 He that doth drink whole draughts in Venus' cup
Once being old he scarce therein can sup.

Couplet.
MS. Rawl. poet. 117, fol. 273 rev.

406 He that doth in the secret place
See most assuredly.

Psalm xci.
MS. *Montagu e. 10, fol. 43$^{v}$.

407 He that doth know the ways of good,
The wisest amongst men.

Robinson, Robert.
MS. *Rawl. poet. 218, p. 137 (autogr.).

408 He that doth love unlov'd again
Hath better store of love then brain.

Couplet, 'Of love'.
MS. Don. d. 58, fol. 42$^{v}$.

409 He that doth seek all men to please,
There's no pleasing every man.

Robinson, Robert.
MS. *Rawl. poet. 218, p. 51 (autogr.).

410 He that drinks is immortal and ne'er can decay
How can he turn to dust that still moistens his clay.

Pr. *The Second Book of the Pleasant Musical Companion*, 1686; cf. F. B. Zimmerman, *Purcell*, 1963, no. 254.
MS. Rawl. poet. 196, fol. 11.

411 He that enough has, is not poor.
Although he have too much in store.

Robinson, Robert.
MS. *Rawl. poet. 218, p. 43 (autogr.).

412 He that first falls (for one of us must die)
And death makes room, when life is grown too strait.

MS. Rawl. poet. 209, fol. 37$^{v}$.

413 He that for wealth doth seas and land explore,
Danger, and for thy friend, or country die.

Manning, —, translator, Horace, *Odes* IV. ix. 45–52.
MS. Rawl. poet. 173, fol. 35.

414 He that from his first planting always grew
Have pow'r to blow me from thy blessed shore.

Beaumont, Thomas, 'upon his return after A revolt'.
MS. *Malone 18, p. 63 (autogr.).

He that had told me this and said he dreamed 415
Whose tomb should be another new Escurial.

Holland, Hugh (?), [on the death of Prince Henry, 1612]; after these verses are 6 lines of Latin verse, *Crudeli crudaque Patri*, etc., of which the first 4 are printed with the ascription 'Hugo Hollandus' under an engraving which accompanied Chapman's poem on the occasion; see pr. bk. 4° P 35. Th.
MS. Eng. poet. e. 37, p. 52.

He that had youth and friends and so much wit 416
Wit's a disease, consumes men in few years.

'On Mr. Fran: Beaumont'.
MS. Eng. poet. e. 14, fol. 93$^{v}$ rev.

He that has much to wish or choose 417
A woman's mercy and her mind.

Subscribed 'M. N.'
MS. Rawl. poet. 196, fol. 24.

He that has no learning, 418
His learning may put out his eyes.

Robinson, Robert.
MS. *Rawl. poet. 218, p. 49 (autogr.).

He that has not a purse in suit to spend, 419
So many bad debtors bad times do send.

Robinson, Robert.
MS. *Rawl. poet. 218, p. 174 (autogr.).

He that hath eternal being 420
Us till death forsaking never.

Herbert, Mary (*née* Sidney), Countess of Pembroke, Psalm xlviii.
MSS. *Rawl. poet. 24, p. 69; *25, fol. 40$^{v}$.

He that hath eyes now wake and weep 421
Rake in their graves to prove them men.

'Epitaph on King James' I.
Pr. Camdens *Remaines*, 1637, p. 398.
Attr. to George Morley in B.M. MSS. Harl. 6917–18.
MS. Ashmole 38, p. 186; see also A1016.

He, that hath gotten by the sword, 422
His hold's but weak and vain.

Robinson, Robert, 'Qui per gladium acquisivit, per gladium (necesse est) teneret'.
MS. *Rawl. poet. 218, p. 21 (autogr.).

He, that hath once (alas) his conscience sold, 423
But when death comes, the right touch they'll not hold.

Robinson, Robert.
MS. *Rawl. poet. 218, p. 4 (autogr.).

He that hath penned his doleful passions here 424
That I must love her though I die for it.

Burton, Francis.
MS. *Add. A. 267, fol. 67 (autogr.).

425 He that hath thought
Would not do a sin.
MS. Tanner 407, fol. 36$^{v}$.

426 He that hears crying ravens, and them feeds,
What e'er we ask, seek, knock for, or do want?
Cheyney, William, 'A Motto. The proeme to the motto. Psalme 147. 9'.
MS. *Rawl. poet. 86, fol. 4$^{v}$.

427 He that his joys would heap
Heavenly joys on earth are bitter-sweet.
'Some few lines concerning the moderating of spiritual joy'.
MS. Rawl. poet. 213, fol. 58$^{v}$ rev.

428 He that his mirth hath lost,
His pleasures are full fain'd.
Dyer, Sir Edward.
Pr. *Poems of Pembroke and Ruddier*, 1660, p. 29.
MSS. Ashmole 781, p. 140, attr. to Sr. Ed. Dyer; Tanner 306, fol. 173, attr. to Dier; Rawl. poet. 85, fol. 109, attr. to E. Dier.

429 He that in Belgia fought for England's Queen;
Him cankered Cecill slew, but not disease.
'Of Robert [Devereux] Earl of Essex'.
MS. Firth d. 7, fol. 158.

430 He that in drinking taketh pleasure
His wits be surely out of measure.
Couplet.
MS. Tanner 306, fol. 289.

431*a* He that in itching no scratching will forbear
He must suffer the smart that will follow there.
Couplet.
MS. Gough Norfolk 43, fol. 28.

431*b* He that in youth no virtue will use
In age all honour with him refuse.
Couplet.
MS. Laud misc. 299, end leaf.

432 He that intends to drink a health in hell
But fire and fume and coals is all their cheer.
'On tobacco'.
MS. Eng. poet. f. 10, fol. 86$^{v}$.

433 He that is fond does need no other charms,
All that will hug may have her in their arms.
Williams, John, 'Love-Characters'.
MS. *Rawl. poet. 184, fol. 94 (autogr.).

434 He that is in distress
From all evil. Amen.
'The pater noster or our Father'.
MS. Eng. poet. b. 5, p. 3.

He, that is not a knave, must live like a slave, 435
No greater advancement he's like for to have.
Robinson, Robert.
MS. *Rawl. poet. 218, p. 105 (autogr.).

He that is out of case, and in decay 436
And take us out, or keep us better in't.
Bulteel, John, 'The Cruell Effects of poverty'.
MS. *Rawl. poet. 159, fol. 206$^{v}$.

He, that is proud and with an empty purse, 437
Would surely were it full, be ten times worse.
Robinson, Robert, couplet.
MS. Rawl. poet. 218, p. 66 (autogr.).

He that is sworn a true liege man to love 438
Who to you wish better felicity.
H. S., 'A letter written to his halfe-displeased frinde K. H.'
MS. *Rawl. poet. 120, fol. 24$^{v}$ (autogr.).

He that is the great profound sapience 439
From all affliction.
'Patris Sapientia', 'English Primer of our Lady 1631'.
MS. Eng. poet. e. 56, p. 7.

He, that is weary, let him sit 440
Until the grave increase our cold.
Herbert, George, 'Imployment'.
Pr. *The Temple*, 1633, p. 70.
MS. *Tanner 307, fol. 54.

He that is wise will covet gold 441
Then gold or goods or other see.
MS. Ashmole 236, fol. 151.

He that is wisely neat 442
Laughing at winds and seas.
Polwhele, John, 'Boet[hius]', *Consolations* II. iv, 'quisquis volet'.
MS. *Eng. poet. f. 16, fol. 22 (autogr.).

He that lieth under this stone, 443*a*
That his name was Martyne Expence.
'At Cleworth near New Windsor, on a Brass Plate, fixed in a Grave-Stone, is this Inscription in Capitals'.
Pr. by Hearne, *Guilelmus Neubrigensis*, 1719, ii. 766.
MSS. Ballard 38, fol. 111; Hearne's diaries 66, p. 21; Rawl. D. 1164, fol. 246$^{v}$.

He that lives by others' breath 443*b*
Dieth also by their death.
Couplet.
MS. Rawl. poet. 117, fol. 165$^{v}$ rev.

444 He that loves a rosy cheek
That love to her I cast away.

Carew, Thomas, 'An invective against his Mris'.
Pr. *Poems*, 1640. In Walter Porter's *Madrigales and Ayres*, 1632, iii (the first two verses only).
MSS. Ashmole 38, p. 7, attr. to Mr. Th. Carew; Firth d. 7, fol. 123, attr. to Tho. Carew; Malone 16, p. 29, attr. to C; Rawl. poet. 65, fol. 22v.

445 He that of nothing made all things
That first devised the leather bottell.

['Song of the bottel'].
Pr. *New Academy of Complements*, 1713.
MS. Eng. poet. b. 5, p. 129.

446 He that owns with his heart, and helps with his hand,
Whose healths I now drink, and whose friendship I own.

'The Welch Health', against Occasional Conformity.
Headed 'Oxford Health' in B.M. MS. Egerton 924, fol. 31v.
MS. Eng. poet. e. 87, p. 56.

447 He that pursues truth with a profound wit
Learned conjectures are considerate.

Polwhele, John, 'Boet[hius] L. 3 met. xi'.
MS. *Eng. poet. f. 16, fol. 31v (autogr.).

448 He that reads a book rashly at random doth run
He goes on his errant and leaves it undone.

Couplet, 1579 (?).
MS. Rawl. D. 273, p. 110.

449 He that relieves his brother in distress
It is not lent, Glorioso, 'Tis but lost.

[Quarles, Francis], 'On Glorioso'.
Pr. *Divine Fancies*, 1632, iv. 79.
MS. Rawl. poet. 90, fol. 75.

450*a* He that resolves in all to serve the court
Makes virtue a pretence, religion sport.

Couplet.
MS. Hearne's diaries 11, p. 107.

450*b* He that seems a man precise,
But doth practise nothing less.

Robinson, Robert.
MS. *Rawl. poet. 218, p. 7 (autogr.).

451 He that shall shed, with a presumptuous hand
Believe't, shall plead thy pardon, not thy guilt.

[Quarles, Francis], 'The Sinners Refuge'.
Pr. *Divine Fancies*, 1632, i. 90.
MS. Rawl. poet. 90, fol. 51.

He that so builds his house, doth build as he 452
As if his house his sepulchre should be.

'De depopulante Domino'.
MS. Lat. misc. c. 19, p. 427.

He that so many soles had made of late 453
Being bare themselves to look for dead men shoes.

'On a shoomaker'.
MS. CCC. 328, fol. 60v.

He, that speaks with the power, his tongue need not spare, 454
He may think what he will, but speak, if he dare.

Robinson, Robert.
MS. *Rawl. poet. 218, p. 18 (autogr.).

He, that the first and last point of eternity 455
God's so transcendent 'bove poor mortal man.

Robinson, Robert, 'Vera est inscrutabilis Divinitas'.
MS. *Rawl. poet. 218, p. 136 (autogr.).

He that the sturdy Normans ruled and over English reigned 456
And twenty-three degrees had past, even at that time he died.

Translation of Latin epitaph on William the Conqueror.
MS. Rawl. D. 859, fol. 89.

He that thy praises into one sum will gather 457
Need say no more but this th'art like thy father.

Couplet on Ferdinando Lord Fairfax (1584–1648).
MS. Top. Yorks c. 26, fol. 175v.

He that to gain great riches does offend 458
God's just commands, consider and obey.

Williams, John, 'He that makes hast to be rich shall not be Innocent'.
MS. *Rawl. poet. 191, fol. 128v (autogr.).

He that trusts before he try, 459
May repent before he die.

Couplet, with Latin.
MSS. Rawl. D. 954, fol. 17v; Rawl. poet. 209, fol. 36.

He that unburied lies wants not a hearse 460
For unto him a tomb's the universe.

'Lucian (*sic*). Caelo tegitur, qui non habet urnam', couplet.
Lucan, *Pharsalia* vii. 819.
MS. Ashmole 38, p. 162.

He that wants faith, and apprehends a grief 461
H'as a true grief, and the best faith of all.

[Quarles, Francis], 'On Faith'.
Pr. *Divine Fancies*, 1632, iii. 97.
MSS. Rawl. poet. 90, fol. 52v; 117, fol. 170v rev.

462 He, that wants heat, to digest well his meat,
Will fall from his seat, no more he must eat.

Robinson, Robert, couplet.
MS. *Rawl. poet. 218, p. 47 (autogr.).

463 He that when he lusts dare swear
Complain in earnest but be heard in jest.

MS. Eng. poet. c. 50, fol. 118.

464 He that whilst we stood off did press us so close
Or we have been shamefully blind.

Williams, John.
MS. *Rawl. poet. 184, fol. 74 (autogr.).

465 He that will cast his eye upon a seat
To sing eternal hymns, great God to thee.

Spoure, Edmund, 'A Poem on Trebartha House'.
MS. *Eng. poet. c. 52, fol. 18 (autogr.).

466*a* He that will court a lass [wench] that is coy
Mad girls love wild men.

MSS. Ashmole 36, 37, fol. 185; Rawl. poet. 142, fol. 45v; Eng. poet. e. 14, fol. 69v.

466*b* He that will fish for a Lancashire lad
Or an apple with a red side.

Pr. Hearne's *Collections*, ed. C. E. Doble, iii, O.H.S. xiii, 1889, p. 156.
MS. Hearne's diaries 29, p. 106.

467 He that will learn to drink a health in hell
But fire and smoke: and stink as we do here.

'On dispraise of Tabacco'.
MS. Rawl. poet. 153, fol. 21v.

468 He that will measure
Of ribands a great nest.

'The sayinges or proverbes of King Salomon . . .' copied by Douce 'from one of Mr. Hebers very curious 4to volumes of black letter tracts' [*S.T.C.* 22899 or 22900].
MS. Douce 309, fol. 16v.

469 He that will not when he may
When he will he shall have nay.

Couplet, 'A Maxim prov'd fatally true in 1747', modernization of Robert Henryson, *Robene and Makyne*, 91–92.
MSS. Eng. poet. e. 40, fol. 19; Rawl. poet. 153, fol. 50.

470 He that will please our most religious age
Next venture, Posture-Mall shall be his muse.

MS. Add. B. 8, fol. 1v rev.

He that will powerful be, 471
Shows imbecility.

Bacon, Sir Nicholas, 1623–1666, translation of Boethius, *Consolations* III. v. Sent to John Hobart 1664.
MS. Tanner 306, fols. 312 and 328v, two versions (autogr.).

He that will sow a fruitful field 472
Clears darkened minds with heavenly light.

Polwhele, John, 'Boet[hius] L. 3. met. 1'.
MS. *Eng. poet. f. 16, fol. 26 (autogr.).

He that will teach us, as he ought, 473
Humility he taught, not pride of life.

Robinson, Robert.
MS. *Rawl. poet. 218, p. 165 (autogr.).

He that will thrive in court must oft become 474
Both blind, and deaf, and dumb.

Couplet, from Davison's *Poeticall Rapsodie*, 1621, p. 259.
MS. Sancroft 53, p. 367 rev.

He that will thrive in state, he must neglect 475
The trodden paths, that truth and right respect.

[Jonson, Ben.], couplet from *Sejanus*, act III.
MS. Don. e. 6, fol. 17v.

He that will wisely place 476
The fury of the skies.

Bacon, Sir Nicholas, 1623–1666, translation of Boethius, *Consolations* II. iv. Sent to John Hobart 1664.
MS. Tanner 306, fol. 320 (autogr.).

He that will write an elegy for thee 477
He must be dead first: Let't alone for me.

Corbett, Richard, 'Upon the most famous Dr: Donne once Deane of Paules'.
MS. CCC. 325, fol. 50, attr. to R. Norv.; Eng. poet. e. 14, fol. 87v rev.; see also H492.

He that with frowns is not dejected, 478
Only waiting for translation.

Dyneley, Johan., 'Upon the . . . death of the Palsgrave's eldest sonne, who was drowned. Decemb. 1628'.
MS. Rawl. poet. 26, fol. 13v.

He that with praise will ease another's smart 479
A lion's paws might make as happy cures.

Williams, John, 'To a Rough Lady'.
MS. *Rawl. poet. 191, fol. 106 (autogr.).

He that with quietness is not content 480
Must sometime lie and sometime say sooth.

Rhymed aphorisms.
MS. Gough Norfolk 43, fol. 19v.

481 He that with wonder does behold
Here dead death entombed lies.
Owen, C[orbet], 'On Christ's Resurrection'.
MS. Locke c. 41, fol. 1643 (autogr.).

482 He that within the secret place of god most high doth dwell
The goodness of my saving health I will declare to him.
[Hopkins, John], Psalm xci.
MS. Rawl. poet. 112, fol. 44 rev.

483 He that without grace sitteth down to his meat
Sitteth down like an ox and riseth like an ass.
Distich, 'Sir John Herses grace, by Retforde and nere Knathe and Gaynsboroughe'. [Sir John Hercy knighted 1546/7].
MS. Gough Norfolk 43, fol. $50^v$.

484 He that would a courtier be
Would rather heat than quench desire.
MS. Rawl. poet. 26, fol. 155.

485 He that would catch and catching hold
Or which humour liked her best.
MS. Mus. b. 1, fol. $64^v$, music by John Wilson.

486 He that would die once well, must often try:
The Gospel comes, and begs us leave to play.
[Quarles, Francis], 'On Dyeing'.
Pr. *Divine Fancies*, 1632, iv. 64.
MS. Rawl. poet. 90, fol. $74^v$.

487 He that would do what Pyndar did before
Yellow throughout save th' head's white to behold.
W. A., translator, Horace, *Odes* IV. ii.
MS. *Rawl. poet. 104, fol. 38 (autogr.).

488 He that would know how minutes steal away,
Proclaims our lives short span in their swift speed.
'On a Clock', with Latin distich.
MSS. Rawl. D. 954, fol. $41^v$; Rawl. poet. 209, fol. $34^v$.

489 He, that would learn, how to fight for his life
All the day he consults with a stinking-close-stoole.
'The Statesmans Academy erected in the Tower of London . . . where at present inhabitt foure of the best Masters of their tyme in Europe'. February 1676/7.
'D. Bucks, Salisbury, Shaftesbury, Wharton', B.M. MS. Harl. 6914, fol. 23.
MS. Don. b. 8, p. 582.

490 He that would live in peace and rest
Must hear and see and say the best.
Couplet, 'A good Maxim'.
MS. Eng. poet. e. 40, fol. 32.

He that would my mistress know 491
In my bed or in her tomb.
MS. Ashmole 38, p. 49.

He that would write an epitaph for thee 492
He must be dead first; Let't alone for me.
Corbett, Richard, 'An Epitaph on Dr. Donne, Dean of St. Pauls'.
Pr. Donne's *Poems*, 1633, and Corbet's *Poems*, 1647, p. 25.
MSS. Ashmole 36, 37, fol. 60; 38, p. 194, attr. to Rich. Oxon.; CCC. 328, fol. 94; Rawl. poet. 26, fol. $70^v$, attr. to Dr. Corbett, Bishop of Oxford; see also H477.

He that's imprisoned in this narrow room 493
Whose virtue must outlive his epitaph.
'Barkeley his Epitaph'.
On Sir Robert Berkeley, 1616, tablet in Canterbury Cathedral. Pr. *Parnassus Biceps*, 1656, p. 95.
MSS. Eng. poet. e. 14, fol. 99 rev.; Rawl. C. 233, fol. 86 rev.; Rawl. poet. 160, fol. 53; 206, p. 65.

He to that passion vainly does pretend 494
Who can resign his mistress to his friend.
Couplet.
MS. Rawl. poet. 209, fol. 38.

He was a preacher who for all his pains 495
All this and more due to his memory.
'To the memory of the pious and laborious minister of Christ N. N. Batchlour of Divinity, and late Rector of this Church'.
MS. Wood D. 19(2), fol. 95.

He was and is see then where lies the odds 496
The life yet of his line shall never out.
'On Spencer, by H. H.' [Query by Dr. Percy Simpson, Hugh Holland].
MS. Malone 16, p. 37.

He was as fresh as is the rose in May, 497
More durable than brass or Niob's womb.
G. B., 'Epitaph. 23', on Prince Henry in 'Cestria Lugens', 1612.
MS. *Rawl. poet. 116, fol. 11.

He who commits any notorious evil 498
Nor are they mad at Christ, more than he is.
MS. *Rawl. poet. 97, fol. 59 (autogr.).

He, who of Speldherst is the Rector 499
You know for whom without a note.
K[earsley] or Keerly, James, verses on the general election, 1754.
MS. Eng. poet. c. 41, fol. 58 (autogr.).

He who resigns his love though for his king 500
He casts off love, a greater power than it.
MS. *Add. B. 8, fol. 74 (autogr.).

501 He who the grateful field would sow,
Thy mind will soon the truest good perceive.
Translation of Boethius, *Consolations* III. i.
MS. Rawl. D 1095, fol. 127v.

502 He who while living was our ornament
Where joyfully he evermore remains.
Herbert Pye, verses on John Freind, d. 1672.
MS. Top. Oxon. f. 31, p. 299.

503 He who with learning and his wit
Was fain to take his death upon't; 'twas so.
'On Treasurer Buckhurst', 1st Earl of Dorset, d. 1608.
MSS. CCC. 328, fol. 97; Douce f. 5, fol. 11.

504 He, who wou'd act, must think: For thought will find
And the shot soul in ev'ry start ascend.
'The actor's Epitome'.
MS. Eng. poet. d. 10, fol. 78.

505 He whom the muses have forbid to die
For whose fam'd name all Britain's isles want room.
Parry, J.
MS. Top. Cheshire c. 6, fol. 590v.

506 He whose advent'rous keel ploughs the rough seas
That value wit and arts below their crimes.
King, Henry, 'Epigram: Qui Pelago credit magno se fænore tollit, Petron[ius] Arbit[er, *Saturæ*, lxxxiii. 10]'.
MSS. *Eng. poet. e. 30, fol. 54v; *Malone 22, fol. 31v.

507 He whose iniquities are purged away,
If any to rejoice have cause, sure you much more.
Psalm xxxii.
MS. Rawl. poet. 90, fol. 152.

508 He whose profaner verse of late
Hold your immortal whips 'twas I.
'Selecta quædam Martialis Epigrammata Anglice Castrata. Ep: [x. v]. In maledicam Poetam'.
MS. Malone 16, p. 68.

509 He whose sad carcass in this place you see
Thrust out his soul by keeping of it in.
'On one that dyed by stopping his owne breath'.
MS. CCC. 328, fol. 43v.

He'll, etc., see with Hell.

510 Health from the lover of the country, me;
The horse doth with the horseman run away.
Cowley, Abraham, translator, Horace, *Epistles* I. x. 'To Fuscus Aristius'.
Pr. *Works*, 1668, 'Essays in Verse and Prose', p. 111.
MS. Rawl. poet. 173, fol. 39.

Health is a jewel; what this jewel cost 511
As oft as this is found, or lost in you.
Oldisworth, Giles, 'Verses once to Mr. Busby while he lay sicke'.
MS. *Rawl. C. 422, fol. 24 (autogr.).

Health, may the gods unto thee never grant, 512
And end at once my letter, and my life.
Walsh, William, 'Fausta to Constantin'.
MS. *Malone 9, fol. 40v (autogr.).

Health sends Leander to his absent love 513
Soon at your feet its writer hopes to sigh.
Grainger, James, translator, Ovid, *Epistles* xviii, copied by Thomas Percy.
MS. Percy e. 8, fol. 11v.

Health to dear Colin. Hobinolkin prays 514
To fill up the rhyme, that you will be n[ou]ght.
'Another' [letter from J[oshua] J[ones] to S.B].
MS. Rawl. poet. 147, p. 32.

Health to good Colin. Every gentle mind 515
Where many a nun had lived or many a learned cowl.
'A letter from J[oshua] J[ones] to S.B.' 'From Mells in Somersetshire'.
MS. Rawl. poet. 147, p. 28.

Health to great Gloster, from a man unknown 516
How low how mean and full as poor as I . . . *cetera desunt.*
Churchill, Charles, 'Dedication to The Bishop of Gloster'. [William Warburton].
MS. *Eng. poet. d. 113, p. 293.

Health to her Collatine Lucretia sends 517
And die the spotless wife I could not live.
Walsh, William, 'Lucretia to Collatine'.
MS. *Malone 9, fol. 22v (autogr.).

Health to his best belov'd her lover sends 518
And leave no traces of themselves behind.
Scott, Thomas, of Ipswich, 'An Epistle . . . to his Wife'.
MS. Eng. poet. c. 9, p. 239.

Health to the bard in Leasowe's happy groves 519
Shenstone, be fancy, fame and fortune thine.
'Verses received by the Post, from a Lady unknown, 1761, written by Mrs. Thomas [*née* Elizabeth Amherst]'.
MS. *Eng. poet. e. 109, p. 60.

Health, which herself must want, if he denies; 520
Imagine too, those pearly drops you see.
Percy, Thomas, Bp. of Dromore, translator, 'Ovid's Epistles . . . iv. Phædra to Hippolitus'.
MS. Percy e. 6, fol. 69v (autogr.).

521 Hear . . . [page torn]
To 'mind thee of thy maker's love and fear.
Prologue to a collection of metrical versions of the Prophets and the Psalms.
MS. *Rawl. C. 113, fol. 1 (autogr.).

522 Hear all ye nations
Nor take away.
Skinner, John, Psalm xlix.
MS. *Eng. poet. d. 22, fol. 133.

523 Hear, all ye people, reason's wise decrees
Yea, curs'd be all, that would reform the times.
'The Free-Thinker's Catechism'.
MS. Ballard 29, two copies, fols. 157v and 167.

524 Hear, all you friends to knighthood
Whereon you build your glory.
'Upon Sir Wm Morgan's loosing his Riband'.
[Sir William Morgan of Tredegar, knighted 1725, among George I's first knights of the Bath when he revived the order].
MS. Ballard 50, fol. 100.

525 Hear and believe, the Gentile and the Jew
Which fills their mouths with words, hearts with desire.
Clifford, Henry, Earl of Cumberland, 'Whit Sunday'.
MS. *Rawl. poet. 95, fol. 34v.

526*a* Hear and indulge me, father Jove
And die a good old fellow of a college.
Lumby, John, 'To Mr. J. G., Trifle by Way of Exercise for a Young Gentleman at Oxford'.
MS. *Eng. poet. e. 42, fol. 42.

526*b* Hear and regard once more, I do relate
For ever, ever, thrice for ever more.
'Of the Certainty of Death and Judgm't'.
MS. Bankes 20/3.

527 Hear, beauteous mischief, cautious fair
A temper cheerful, soft and gay.
Lumby, John, 'To Sylvia'.
MS. *Eng. poet. e. 42, fol. 78.

528 Hear hear ye sullen powers below
For hell's broke up and ghosts have holy day.
[Dryden, John, and Lee, Nathaniel], 'The Mask in Oedipus. By Mr. Henery Purcell'.
F. B. Zimmerman, *Purcell*, 1963, no. 583 (1b).
MS. Mus. c. 27, fol. 37.

529 Hear heaven on this propitious day
Who loves, from other cares are free.
[Lepipre, Gabriel (?)], 'presented to the Widow Carbonnel. 11 March 1747/8'.
MS. Eng. poet. e. 40, fol. 50, in G. Lepipre's hand.

Hear Lord my prayer [t']accept withal 530
And prosper whilst Jehovah reigns.
Fairfax, Thomas, Lord, Psalm cii.
MS. *Fairfax 40, p. 246 (autogr.).
MS. *Fairfax 38, p. 372.

[Hear me dull prostitute worse than my wife] 531
With her ten devils could have equall'd him.
[Shadwell, Thomas], 'Satyre against Dryden's Achitophel. p. 14': 4 lines from *Satyr to his Muse by the author of Absalom and Achitophel*, 1682.
MS. Sancroft 53, p. 59.

Hear me, my muse, and all thy aid impart 532
And I shall cheerful walk my midnight rounds.
Samber, Robert, 'The Prologue' to 'The Bellman's Verses'.
MS. *Rawl. poet. 134*b*, fol. 153 (autogr.).

Hear me (oh God) 533
Beneath thy cross.
[Jonson, Ben.], anthem.
*The Underwood* i. 2.
MS. Rawl. poet. 23, p. 158, reference to setting by William Crosse.

Hear me oh hear me when I call 534
I dwell laid up in safest nest.
Sidney, Sir Philip, Psalm iv.
MSS. *Rawl. poet. 24, p. 3; *25, fol. 2v.

Hear me oh Lord 535
And please yourselves with lies.
[Patrick, John, Psalm iv], '3 voc', music by H. Purcell.
Pr. *A Century of Select Psalms*, 1684.
F. B. Zimmerman, *Purcell*, 1963, no. 133.
MS. Mus. c. 28, fol. 120v.

Hear me you nymphs and airy swains 536
To lonely wilds I'll wander.
'A Song'.
MS. Montagu e. 13, fol. 43v.

Hear my entreaty lord, the suit I send 537
Thy servant should thee find.
Herbert, Mary (*née* Sidney), Countess of Pembroke, Psalm cxliii.
MS. *Rawl. poet. 24, p. 211.

Hear now my prayer, oh gracious Lord 538
Shall ever stand secure.
Psalm cii.
MS. *Montagu e. 10, fol. 77v.

Hear now oh lord my request for it is full due time 539
And let thine ears aye be prest unto this prayer mine.
MS. Rawl. poet. 112, fol. 76 rev.

540 Hear now you rebels saith the lord
I see it was for me.
MS. Rawl. poet. 58, fol. ii.

541 Hear this all people of the world
Like to beasts perish quite.
Psalm xlix.
MS. *Rawl. C. 113, fol. 38.

542 Hear this ye Christians of our day
Where thirst insatiate ever dwells.
Kenton, James.
MS. *Eng. poet. e. 20, p. 141 (autogr.).

543 Hear thou great herdman, that doth Jacob feed:
So we shall safely dwell, all darkness vanished.
Herbert, Mary (*née* Sidney), Countess of Pembroke, 'Qui Regis Israel. Psalm lxxx'.
MS. *Rawl. poet. 24, p. 120.

544 Hear us great Rugwith
Fight and record your selves in Druid's songs.
'In Bonduca', music by H. Purcell.
See F. B. Zimmerman, *Purcell*, 1963, no. 574 (11b).
MS. Mus. c. 28, fol. 64.

545 Hear ye hardened rebels hear
And all thy goodness see.
Kenton, James.
MS. *Eng. poet. e. 20, p. 37 (autogr.).

Hear ye ladies that despise . . . see H265.

546 Heardst thou the hounds hunting the fearful hare
Avaunt you curs, no further follow me.
'Upon the sight and hearinge of Sir Edward Lewys dogs'; written at end, 'Anagram. Hit not on us. John Sutton'.
MS. Don. c. 54, fol. 2ᵛ.

547 Hearken, oh God! unto a wretch's cries,
Before I fall into the silent grave.
King, Henry, 'A Pœnitentiall Hymne'.
Pr. *Poems*, 1657, p. 139.
MSS. *Eng. poet. e. 30, fol. 5; *Malone 22, fol. 27; Rawl. poet. 23, p. 41, reference to setting by John Wilson.

548 Hearken speeches of many kind thing, of great fearfulness and wondering
Well a way shall men say all the most, as step-children that were forlorn.
'Prophecia Johannis herimit'.
MS. Rawl. C. 813, fol. 148.

549*a* Hearken (ye nations) oh come see and hear,
To keep this day ever holy to the Lord.
Anthem.
MS. Rawl. poet. 23, p. 175, reference to setting by E. Hooper.

Heart take thine ease 549*b*
Say better: there an end.
Holland, Phil., verses at end of Camden's *Britannia*, 1600, owned by Rawlinson.
MS. Hearne's diaries 59, p. 174.

Hearts of oak who wish to try 550
Can British tars wish more?
'A New Sea Song'.
Pr. J. Ashton, *Real Sailor Songs*, 1891, p. 85.
MS. Firth c. 18, fol. 56.

Heathens Lord spoil thy heritage, 551
Every succeeding age.
Psalm lxxix.
MS. *Rawl. C. 113, fol. 57ᵛ.

Heaven bless king James our joy 552
Thus must you buy it.
'The Duke of Bucks. kindred . . . 1622'.
MSS. Douce 357, fol. 16; Rawl. poet. 160, fol. 178ᵛ; Tanner 306, fol. 257.

Heaven hath endowed your beauty with such grace 553
First die ere fancy's well built fortress leave.
Mervall, Alphonso, 'Anagrammes on his mʳˢ Name F. F.': 1, fortis, fac, Sterne', 2, 'Rest, force faints', 3, 'Rest set for fanci', 4, 'fanci's forttres'. [Query, 'Frances Forsitte' or 'Fostteir'].
MS. *Rawl. poet. 166, p. 5.

Heaven hath my soul in happiest joy and bliss 554
And as I am so think to be.
Verses on the tomb of George Tompson, 'qui obijt: 28. Novemb. 1603', Herefordshire (?).
MS. Rawl. D. 697, fol. 74.

Heaven is a place also a state 555
Unto eternity.
[Bunyan, John], 'of Heaven', from 'One Thing is Needful'.
MS. Rawl. poet. 58, fol. 10ᵛ.

Heaven is Hampton Court, here's but a cell 556
Our she professor of divinity.
'Epitaph . . . on Elizabeth Hampton', a presbyterian laundress who lived in Holywell.
See Wood's *Athenae*, ed. Bliss, iv, 1820, cols. 226 and 606. Pr. Hearne's *Collections*, ed. C. E. Doble, ii, O.H.S. vii, 1886, p. 140.
MSS. Hearne's diaries 17, p. 196; Rawl. C. 867, fol. 54.

Heaven is the place of happiness and hell 557
That Heavens too high for them that fly too low.
'On Heaven and Hell'.
MS. Rawl. D. 1334, fol. 27ᵛ rev.

558 **Heaven is the thing my lad, you ought to prize**
**Do this, then wed, and jerk the copyhold.**
Spoure, Edmund, 'An Acrostick on M[r] Henry Bond, a yong Student in the Law'.
MS. *Eng. poet. c. 52, fol. 4 (autogr.).

559 **Heaven knows for what great crying sin of mine**
**But a *sub-poena* or a messenger.**
Oldham, John, 'A Satyr upon the Town and Times', fragment.
MS. *Rawl. poet. 123, p. 222 (autogr.).

560 **Heaven's a place, some say, where angels dwell,**
**My purse wants angels, therefore call it hell.**
Couplet written by Thomas Hamond in a music book.
MS. Mus. f. 19, fol. 83[v].

**Heavens bless King James . . .** see H552.

561 **Heavens bless this treaty and prepare**
**Else knaves and fools will quite undo us.**
'Upon the treaty' [of Uxbridge, 1645], subscribed 'F'.
MS. Rawl. poet. 71, p. 79.

562 **Heavens decreed before the world begun**
**I wish my arms a cloister for thy sake.**
'On a gentlewoman that would Marry'.
MS. Rawl. poet. 209, fol. 21[v].

563 **Heavens dire flame sits on thy curled tresses**
**If Christ in th' end pour not his wrath on thee.**
Fairfax, Thomas, Lord, translator, 'A Carracter of the Romish church by Francisco Petrarca, Laura can: 106. Fiamma dal ciel su tue treccie pioua'.
MS. *Fairfax 40, p. 604 (autogr.).
MS. *Fairfax 38, p. 305.

564 **Heaven's hand is sure, though it the stroke defer**
**The face of France doth full of change appear.**
Coley, Henry.
Pr. *Almanack*, 1695, Sig. B1.
MS. *Add. B. 8, fol. 75[v] (autogr.).

565 **Heavens just consider what you've done**
**And for your favours basely did discard ye.**
'On [King George I]' . . . 1714/15, 'this was writ on his discharging the Duke of Ormond'.
MS. Eng. misc. c. 116, fol. 2[v].

566 **Heaven's pledge! Batavia's wonder! such a birth**
**Shap'd like a man; but god-like all the rest.**
Sancroft, William (?), translator, 'Depositum Coeli, under Grotius's Picture'.
MS. Sancroft 48, fol. 31[v], in Sancroft's hand.

**Heavens! Saturnalize whole years? make all** 567
**Restor'd again entire meat's chivalry.**
E[dwards], T[homas], 'On perpetuall Gluttons'.
MS. Rawl. poet. 65, fol. 60[v].

**Heavens we thank you, that you thund'red so,** 568
**For us like their's, and some not thank them for 't.**
Bold, H[enry], e Coll. Novo [Oxford], 'On the Thunder at the Coronation. April 23. 1661'.
MS. Eng. poet. e. 4, p. 151.

**Hebe though decked with all the charms of spring,** 569–70
**And praise, and pleasure, shall to age secure.**
'On Miss Sally Bate. 1767'.
MS. *Eng. poet. e. 28, p. 126.

**Heir of thy father's goods, and his good parts** 571
**That has them. Light through every chink is spied.**
Stonehouse, Walter, 'To John Tradescant the younger, surviving', copy for printer of *Museum Tradescantianum*, 1656.
MS. Ashmole 826, fol. 34.

**Helen hath left the court, but who knows why** 572
**No no, old mother midwife hath more skill.**
MS. Don. d. 58, fol. 34.

**Hell bred despair choke all my hopes at first** 573
**Though fortune frown she may hereafter smile.**
H. S.
MS. *Rawl. poet. 120, fol. 19 (autogr.).

**He'll naught disburse** 574
**He makes a halter of the thread of life.**
Southwell, Sir Robert, [On a miser].
MS. *Eng. poet. f. 6, fol. 53 (autogr.).

**Hell take thy brother death unto thee** 575
**For ever can preserve his name.**
Boteler, George, 'Upon Richard Washington of University College'.
MS. Malone 13, fol. 28.

**Hell's porter and a bawd on time being met** 576
**She said the firing of her touch-hole killed her.**
Burghe, Nicholas, 'On that famous (Infamous) whore Grace Coocke'; author's name in code.
MS. Ashmole 38, p. 37.

**Help! Help! Oh help divinity of love** 577
**And for ever constant prove.**
[Hughes, Dr. Henry].
Ascribed to Hughes in the index to Henry Lawes' *Second Book of Ayres*, 1655.
MS. Rawl. poet. 65, fol. 25[v].

578 Help help oh Lord high time it is to call
And will the good men's forces reinforce.
Harington, Sir John, Psalm xii.
MS. *Douce 361, fol. 7.

579 Help, Lord, for good and godly men
So highly is extoll'd.
[Sternhold, Thomas], Psalm xii.
MSS. Rawl. D. 886, fol. 11, verse 8 set for 5 bells; Rawl. poet. 112, fol. 68 rev.

580 Help, Lord, for good and godly men
With power are dignified.
Psalm xii.
MS. *Rawl. C. 113, fol. 16.

581 Help Lord, for good men cease, no more
And highest honours gain.
Psalm xii.
MS. *Montagu e. 10, fol. 3.

582 Help Lord, now dying piety cries
Virtue's deject, vice only countenanced.
J. F., Psalm xii.
MS. *Eng. poet. f. 17, p. 150 (autogr.).

583 Help me furies, ye that dwell
Of devil killer in these days.
'A description of a late memorable fight betwixt a mann and a hogg'.
MS. Don. d. 58, fol. 59v.

584 Help me nature help me heart
If he [be] false I'll be so too.
Verse written in music book.
MS. Mus. Sch. F. 576, fol. 39v.

585 Help me wonder here's a book
And the world shall make one cinder.
MS. Eng. poet. c. 50, fol. 110v.

586 Help me ye british muses to rehearse,
Ap Curd ap Milk, ap Cow, ap Grass, ap Earth.
'Upon Welch Cheese'.
MS. Ashmole 47, fol. 133v.

587 Help mistress help the flames of my desire
For nothing else will put it out I know.
MS. Eng. poet. c. 50, fol. 117v.

588 Help oh help kind Abraham and send
All fine spun pleasures end in endless woes.
MS. Don. c. 57, fol. 2, music by Robert Ramsey.

589 Hen[ce ]te names which virgin state doth mint
In such gifts only liberty's increas'd.
[Johnston, Nathaniel], 'William Lister. Mii will releast'.
MS. Eng. poet. c. 25, fol. 32v (autogr.).

Hence all my grief and sorrow 590
And perfectly redeem.
Kenton, James.
MS. *Eng. poet. e. 20, p. 175 (autogr.).

Hence all those glorious outsides which within 591
He is purely constant both in name and mind.
[Dalby, Edward (?)], anagram on 'Henricus Stapylton / H'is purely constant'.
MS. Ashmole 47, fol. 122.

Hence all ye dark intrigues! ye base designs! 592
But flat denial wants both wit and grace.
Cromwell, Edward, 'Dec. 25. 1715. The nativity of our Lord. Luke 2. 10'.
MS. *Rawl. poet. 165, fol. 30 (autogr.).

Hence all you vain delights, 593
There's nothing dainty sweet, save melancholy.
[Fletcher, John], from the *Nice Valor*, III. i.
Pr. *A Description of the King and Queen of Fayries*, 1635; *Wit Restor'd*, 1658, p. 65.
MSS. Ashmole 36, 37, fol. 26; Eng. poet. c. 50, fol. 130; e. 14, fol. 84 rev.; Firth e. 4, p. 72; Malone 21, fol. 80; Mus. Sch. F. 575, fol. 7v, with lute accompaniment; Rawl. D. 1092, fol. 273, attr. to W. Strode; Rawl. poet. 84, two copies, fols. 40 rev. and 66 rev., both including extra stanza from F172 by Henry King; 153, fol. 13.

Hence childish boy too long have I 594
And you will lo[ve].
MS. Mus. b. 1, fol. 120v, music by John Wilson.

Hence common eyes! spare your ambitious tears 595
He shall receive their fate too, die unknown.
'On the death of Sr. Charles Lucas and Sr. George Lisle', August 1648.
MSS. Ashmole 36, 37, fol. 168; Eng. poet. e. 4, p. 35, attr. to Thomas Winnard [Fellow of St. John's College, Oxford (?)].

Hence Cupid with your cheating toys 596
And is not much transported, but still pleas'd.
Philips, Katherine, 'Against Love'.
Pr. *Poems*, 1667, p. 143.
MSS. Rawl. poet. 65, fol. 10v; 173, fol. 100v, attr. to Mrs. Phillips.

Hence dull mortality, and sordid rules 597
From all the pains and cares of human life as free.
Chatwin, John, 'The Libertine'.
MS. *Rawl. poet. 94, p. 67 (autogr.).

598 **Hence each perfidious look and clouded face,**
**Joined by a sacred and immortal love.**
Chatwin, John, 'An Epithalamium to the Heroick Prince, George (of Denmark), and his illustrious Princess, the Lady Ann' [1683].
MS. *Rawl. poet. 94, p. 63 (autogr.).

599 **Hence, every gloomy care away!**
**That makes thee ever mine?**
'Verses written before Marriage'.
MS. Percy d. 9, fol. 26v.

600 **Hence fear, hence sorrow**
**Would do his merit too much wrong.**
Sancroft, William, translator, Horace, *Odes* I. xxvi, 'freely and paraphrastically'.
MS. Sancroft 48, fols. 24, 23v (autogr.).

601 **Hence, hence unhallowed tongues and move not here**
**A temple sacred unto modesty.**
Weaver, Thomas, 'The three incomparable Ladyes at Llangiby Castle'.
Pr. *Songs and Poems*, 1654.
MS. *Rawl. poet. 211, fol. 21v (autogr.).

602 **Hence, hence ye curst infernal train**
**I chase the gloomy shades away.**
[Hughes, John], 'In the Amalasont Queen of the Goths etc. set by Mr. Daniel Purcell'.
MS. Mus. Sch. C. 95, p. 114.

603 **Hence hence ye furies which inspire**
**And things none else can parallel.**
Fairfax, Thomas, Lord, 'Hymnes. The Soveraine God'.
MS. *Fairfax 40, p. 510 (autogr.).
MS. *Fairfax 38, p. 45.

604 **[Hence loathed melancholy]**
**On the light fantastic toe . . . (incomplete).**
[Milton, John], extract from *L'Allegro*.
MS. Mus. c. 107, fols. 42v, 41, music by Handel.

605 **Hence stars, too dim of light,**
**Long live faire Oriana.**
Pr. *Triumphs of Oriana*, 1601, i; and Michel East's *Second set of Madrigales*, 1606, xxi.
MSS. Mus. f. 16–19: f. 19, fol. 79v.

606 **Hence superstition fly away,**
**Who rules us with a golden rod.**
Bate, Sally, 'On Superstition'.
MS. *Eng. poet. e. 28, p. 169.

**Hence then despair my hopes why should it bury** 607
**Than Chessnut that begot thee or Brid-la-dore his sire.**
Fairfax, Thomas, Lord, 'Upon the Horse which his Majestie Rode upon att his Coronation 1660'.
MS. *Fairfax 40, p. 612 (autogr.).
MS. *Fairfax 38, p. 274.

**Hence those dull metaphors that call't a hellish plot** 608
**King, prince and nobles at one fatal blow.**
'On Gunpowder Plot'.
MS. Rawl. poet. 65, fol. 62.

**[Hence vain deluding joys]** 609
**Her mansion in this fleshly nook.**
[Milton, John,] extract from *Il Penseroso* in a literary collection called 'A Summer Week's Conference' (after 1712).
MS. Rawl. D. 868, fol. 13v.

**Hence vain intruder haste away** 610
**Nor on her purer altars lay . . . (incomplete).**
Carew, Thomas, 'To his Rivall'.
Pr. *Poems*, 1640.
MS. *Don. b. 9, fol. 23v.

**Hence with this wedlock chain and smart** 611
**And never live a married man.**
Pr. Wilson's *Cheerfull Ayres or Ballads*, 1660, p. 116.
MS. Mus. b. 1, fol. 65v, music by John Wilson.

**Hence ye profane: I hate ye all:** 612
**Much will be missing still, and much will be amiss.**
[Cowley, Abraham], 'An Ode of Horace', *Odes* III. i.
Pr. *Works*, 1668, 'Essays in Prose and Verse', p. 125.
MSS. Rawl. poet. 90, fol. 89; 173, fol. 32v.

**Hence ye profane with all your sparks of wit!** 613
**I'll nobly die a martyr to almighty love.**
Chatwin, John.
MS. *Rawl. poet. 94, p. 233 (autogr.).

**Hence, ye ungodly! fly! presumptuous train!** 614
**And all my acts a comment on thy text.**
'The Church, A Religious Satire. G. Mag.', by 'Philargyrus' of Oxon. 18 Sept.
MSS. Eng. poet. e. 39, p. 151; Top. Oxon. c. 220, p. 26.

**Hence you complaining thoughts away,** 615
**And afterwards for ever blest.**
'The Thanksgiving', presented by M. A. to Abp. Sancroft, 1689.
MS. Rawl. poet. 154, fol. 90v.

616 Henceforth be every tender tear suppress
And in the eleventh winter died a man.
Smart, Christopher, 'On the death of Master Newbury'.
MS. Top. gen. e. 32, fol. 82$^{v}$.

617*a* Henceforth farewell to woman kind
Men ne'er were fools till they thought women fair.
MS. Mus. b. 1, fol. 148$^{v}$, music by John Wilson.

617*b* [Henceforth I'll never credit those that say]
For one two lines, than thy four hundred score.
A. R., on *Hygiasticon* by L. Lessius, 1634, where it is printed.
MS. Eng. misc. e. 13, fol. 22$^{v}$.

618 Henry Ward also entombed is here
The trees being dead, the fruits do spring again.
Epitaph, Shenstone Church, near Lichfield.
MS. Rawl. D. 377, fol. 68.

619 Her anger soon does end and soon begin,
Like fire that's quickly out, and quickly in.
Williams, John, 'Upon Miss Betty (Ashe)', couplet.
MS. *Rawl. poet. 191, fol. 105 (autogr.).

620 Her being was in him alone
And she not being he was none.
Couplet. See H1216.
MSS. Don. e. 6, fol. 28, attr. to Sir Phillip Sidney; Rawl. D. 954, fol. 26.

621 Her brow is virtue's court where she alone
Oh would that I a constellation were.
Atkins, F.
MS. Rawl. poet. 142, fol. 43$^{v}$.

622 Her comely woe, her beautiful distress
'Tis God that fights, and will her wrongs redress.
Potenger, John, 'In Ecclesiam periclitantem'.
MS. *Eng. poet. d. 16, p. xxii (autogr.).

623 Her eyes diffuse around each pleasing ray
And softly sooth the anxious soul to rest.
Okeden, William, lines dated 27 June 1759.
MS. Eng. poet. d. 10, fol. 26.

624 Her eyes do please me; but god knows
Nothing more grieves me than her nose.
Couplet.
MS. Eng. poet. f. 16, fol. 3.

625 Her eyes flood licks his feet's fair stain;
This flood, thus stained, fairer streams.
Crashaw, [Richard], 'Upon Mary Magdalene'.
MS. Tanner 465, fol. 34, attr. to Mr. Crashaw on fol. 1*a*.

Her eyes victorious as great Marlborough's arms 626
Good nature weeps: behold a mourning bride.
'Countess of Pembroke' (d. 1794).
MS. Eng. poet. e. 28, p. 29.

Her face, her tongue, her wit, 627
Mine eyes, mine ear, my heart.
[Ralegh, Sir Walter (?)], 'To his Mrs.'
See *Poems of . . . Ralegh*, ed. A. M. C. Latham, 1951, p. 159.
MS. CCC. 328, fol. 74$^{v}$; see also Y461.

Her faithless guest the Thracian Phyllis chides 628
Th'occasion he, the stroke herself supplied.
Percy, Thomas, Bp. of Dromore, translator, 'Ovid's Epistles . . . ii Phyllis to Demophoon'.
MS. Percy e. 6, fol. 41 (autogr.).

Her food is grain, her beak doth not offend 629
No gall this creature hath nor no bad end.
Couplet 'On the Dove', from Latin distich.
MS. Rawl. D. 954, fol. 42; Rawl. poet. 209, fol. 34$^{v}$.

Her for a mistress I would fain enjoy 630
Hang her, she's good for nothing but a wife.
'A mistress', from Ausonius, Epigram 78, *Qualis velit habere amicam.*
Pr. *Parnassus Biceps*, 1656, p. 64, and *Wit Restor'd*, 1658, p. 124.
MSS. CCC. 328, fol. 80$^{v}$; Don. d. 58, fol. 44*b*; Eng. poet. e. 14, fol. 75$^{v}$; f. 25, fol. 18; Firth d. 7, fol. 180; Rawl. poet. 199, p. 11; see also S367, T1531.

Her generous male his nobler female twines 631
By sympathetic virtues of her own.
On Hugh and Jane Watts, 1656, St. Mary's, Leicester.
MS. Top. gen. e. 1, p. 11.

Her hair but thin in all they are but three 632
So large a mark as whoso shoots may hit.
'On the praise of a gentlewoman'.
MS. Eng. poet. e. 14, fol. 73.

Her hair cheeks and teeth my sweet Emily buys 633
What a pity it is that no person sells eyes!
Couplet, 'From Martial' [*Epigrams* XII. xxiii].
MS. Eng. misc. e. 241, fol. 99.

Her hair, her person, and her arm 634
The blame be laid on them not me.
'Thirty Perfections, Love, impart, To Her Who shou'd possess my Heart', (translation from Latin).
MS. Eng. poet. e. 45, fol. 25.

635 Her hair, the net of golden wire
Then break one hair, to gain her liberty.
Pr. Thomas Bateson's *Second Set of Madrigales*, 1618, xxvii.
MSS. Mus. f. 20–24: f. 20, fol. 64$^{v}$.

636 Her hairs are Cupids, which when she spreads,
When Venus means to make it holiday.
Shirley, James; in the *Poems*, 1646, incorporated in a 'Dialogue', beginning 'I prithee, tell me, what prodigious fate'.
MS. *Rawl. poet. 88, p. 18.

637 Her heart a sphere where all good thoughts did move
T'embalm her virtues in the hearts of men.
[Epitaph].
MS. Sancroft 59, p. 282 rev.

638 Her high-toss'd airs each self-known beauty speak,
She looks to conquer, but she talks to save.
'From a Window at Sandy Lane', epigram.
MS. Eng. misc. b. 48, fol. 82.

639 Her husband present, Lesbia rails at me
While her continual railing says—I love.
'*Lesbia me* . . . imitated from Catullus [lxxxiii], 1735'.
MS. Eng. misc. e. 240, p. 156.

640 Her last adieu still vibrates on my ear,
Love-darting eyes! and mirth inspiring smile!
Parsons, William, 'To Miss B-d on her quitting Margate', Sept. 1794.
MS. *Don. d. 123, p. 215 (autogr.).

641–2 Her life was such, as well may be denied
To end the strife, she went to him that gave her.
[Epitaph].
MS. Sancroft 59, p. 285 rev.

643 Her loved a thing was fingel fangel
Yet spite her nose must mingel mangel.
MS. Rawl. poet. 120, fol. 28$^{v}$.

644 Her soul is gone to God who at first gave it
Till (it to raise) her saviour shall appear.
On Mrs. Elizabeth Searle, d. 23 Oct. 1674, buried in Acton church.
MS. Rawl. D. 896, fol. 31$^{v}$.

545 Her to invite the great God sent his star
But like the sun, doth only set to rise.
'K. Iam's on Q. Anne's death'. 1618.
MS. Rawl. poet. 153, fol. 8$^{v}$; see also T1631, T3410.

646 Her trials o'er her sufferings past
On Him eternally shall gaze.
Kenton, James, 'An Epitaph for Mrs. Ann Hill of Deptford . . . 1786'.
MS. *Eng. poet e. 19, p. 273 (autogr.).

Her viol de gambo is her best content 647
For twixt her legs she holds her instrument.
Couplet.
MS. Rawl. poet. 117, fol. 273 rev.

Her, who beneath this stone consuming lies 648
Of such a month; and as she said she did.
Wither, G[eorge], 'Upon a Gentlewoman, that had for told the tyme of her death'.
Pr. *Faire-Virtue*, 1622, Sig. O6$^{v}$.
MS. Ashmole 38, p. 167.

Her words forbid, then thousand charms invite, 649*a*
And mind that most that gives me most delight.
Williams, John, 'Of a Refusing Lady or One of an Unpleasant Conversation'.
MS. *Rawl. poet. 191, fol. 6$^{v}$ (autogr.).

Heralds at arms do three perfections quote 649*b*
Thrice happy he that in his arms it weareth.
[Constable, Henry], sonnet, pr. *Diana*, 1594, I. x.
MS. Ashmole 38, p. 54.

Here a happy day hath end 650
No man certain of a day.
'Upon Mtis. Dorothy Day', epitaph.
MS. Ashmole 38, p. 173.

Here a musician lies, whose well-tuned tongue 651
Death was the *habeas corpus*, heaven the bail.
Polw[hele], Jo[hn], 'On Sr Jo: Elliott who died a prisoner in the Tower of London: 1631', 27 Nov. 1632.
See *Traditions and Recollections*, R. Polwhele, 1826, i. 14.
MS. *Eng. poet. f. 16, fol. 12 (autogr.).

Here a sheer hulk lies poor Tom Bowling 652
His soul is gone aloft.
'Tom Bowling', copy *c.* 1802.
MS. Mus. e. 19, p. 7*b*.

Here Abbot's virtues, great example, lies 653
To Heav'n, than that he staid so long below.
'Epitaph'.
MS. Eng. poet. e. 39, p. 65.

Here all may see, how vain's the life of man 654
Whom Christ will bail soon have his liberty.
Ford, J., of King's School, Sherborne, on the death of Robert Whetcombe, 'Antientest Governour of the King's Schoole of Sherebourne', 24 Oct. 1656.
MS. Gough Dorset 35(1), fol. 20*f*.

Here are some conceits grown old reader 'tis true 655
*Nil dictum est quod non dictum prius.*
MS. Eng. poet. f. 10, fol. 86$^{v}$.

656 Here are two geese come to the town gentle brother
Do you pluck the one, and I will pluck the other.

Couplet, 'One Lawyer letter to another'.
MS. Lat. misc. c. 19, p. 427.

657 Here awful solitude her seat has placed
And cheerful listen to his strains of wit.

Boswell, James, fragment on Boswell and Murray.
MS. *Douce 193, fol. 59v, r (autogr.).

658 Here Bad-Cocke lies, a cock too bad by kind
Under his head to play with under ground.

'The Cacademons Epitaph'.
MS. Ashmole 38, p. 176.

659 Here beginneth a little proper jest
Ones to be gossip like send or that you hence wend.

Copied from an undated book printed by W. de Worde.
MS. Eng. poet. e. 97, p. 207.

660 Here Bishop Parker lies, whose last words were,
Was this all God Almighty made me for?

Couplet, epitaph on Bp. Samuel Parker, d. 20 March 1688.
MS. Don. c. 55, fol. 18.

661 Here biting Aretine lies buried
His sense was this quoth he I know him not.

'Aretine's Epitaph'.
MS. Rawl. poet. 160, fol. 182v.

662 Here born here Bishop buried here
Who changed this life for happy state.

Nicholas Bullingham, Bp. of Worcester. d. 18 Apr. 1576. Inscription in the Cathedral.
MS. Top. gen. e. 1, p. 92.

663 Here Bowen lies of high renown
And every lamp extinct with Bowen.

'Epitaph on James Bowen late under-Porter at Merton College . . . from Oxford Journal 25 Oct. 1775'.
MS. Top. Oxon. a. 29, fol. 73.

664–5 Here Brawn the *quondam* beggar lies
He had been still alive.

'On Brawn the Cornish Beggar'.
MS. Lat. misc. c. 19, p. 421.

666 Here (by the world's ill custom) lies asleep
That one spark shall flash it to his soul.

Felltham, Ow[en], 'Epitaph on Sr. John Done Kt.', d. 1629.
MS. Ashmole 47, fol. 83v.

Here by this pillar interred doth lie 667
With them the immortal God shall see.

MS. Rawl. poet. 81, fol. 28v.

Here Caelia for thy sake I part 668
Not in the quarry, but the flight.

Waller, Edmund, 'Upon the mutable faire'.
Pr. *Poems*, 1645, p. 119.
MSS. *Don. d. 55, fol. 17v; *Rawl. poet. 174, p. 69.

Here Campuzano doth lie 669
But his goods had St. Anthony.

MS. Wood D. 19(2), fol. 109v.

Here chested in this tomb and closed in this clay 670
His deeds deserve his noble fame may live in everlasting name.

On Sir Thomas Cokayn, Kt., Ashbourne Church.
MS. Ashmole 854, fol. 44v.

Here Churchill lies. Ah! sacred name! 671*a*
So Britannia grace his earth!

'Faithfull not ffortunate, . . . Mens tua, non vaga Sors, . . . imitated by way of epitaph' on the Duke of Marlborough, 1722.
MS. Eng. poet. e. 45, fol. 36.

Here comes my faithless Rover 671*b*
Of mankind all the world round.

'A Song'.
MS. Montagu e. 13, fol. 45.

Here, Damon, feel my pulse, and let me know, 672
Oh! tell me quickly, tell the cure!

Hammond, Anthony, 'The Disease. Printed', [in *Miscellany of Original Poems*, 1720, p. 103].
MS. Rawl. D. 360, fol. 73 (autogr.).

Here Day and night conspire a cunning flight. 673
My life to yours, Day comes again to-morrow.

'On Mr. Day, who was oblig'd to abscond for a Debt'.
Pr. *The Cambridge Chronicle*, 5 Aug. 1780.
MS. Eng. misc. e. 183, fol. 54v.

Here did my joys begin, increase, and grow 674
Which lost, their memory is made my woe.

'In her bedd Chamber'.
Pr. bk. Wood 460, after *Threnodia in obitum E. Lewkenor*, 1606.

Here died my life, my light, and living heart 675
Unfeigned mine, shall weep unfeignedly.

'In the Chamber where hee dyed'.
Pr. bk. Wood 460, after *Threnodia in obitum E. Lewkenor*, 1606.

676 Here do I lie stretch'd out both hand and feet
My self a tomb stone to my self shall be.
'Mr. [Benjamin] Stones Epitaph on himselfe'.
MS. Douce f. 5, fol. 17$^v$.

677 Here do repose but in lamented waste
Obtained a tomb within our broken hearts.
MSS. Ashmole 38, p. 171, attr. to N. H.; Don. b. 9, fol. 34$^v$.

678 Here doth lie by cock and pye
Of Sir John Foulles.
'On John Hodgson Alias John of powles or cogging John'. Died 1615.
MS. Ashmole 38, p. 199.

679 Here dwells Dr. Ryves [Balliol] the New College Master
That brake the University's head, and gave the schools a plaster.
Couplet, 'Of one that tooke away some of the Universitye landes and afterwards dressed up the schooles' [George Ryves, Warden of New College, d. 1613]. 'Replye', I826.
Pr. *Modius Salium*, 1751, p. 20.
MSS. Malone 19, p. 51; Tanner 466, fol. 66$^v$; Wood E. 32 (*Modius Salium*), fol. 14$^v$; see also H796, H858, H1004.

680 Here ends notwithstanding her specious pretences
She was too bad a daughter and too good a wife.
'An Epitaph', on Queen Mary, 1694.
MS. Add. A. 301, fol. 50$^v$ rev.; see also H770, H880.

681 Here fast asleep, full six foot deep
And first that found the way.
'On the Lord of Kilwicke'.
MS. Don. d. 58, fol. 16$^v$; see also H1101, H1117.

682 Here for a while we creep about,
Till death comes in and life goes out.
Robinson, Robert, couplet.
MS. *Rawl. poet. 218, p. 24 (autogr.).

683 Here Francis Charters lies. Be civil
The rest God knows, perhaps the Devil.
Pope, Alexander, epitaph on Mirandula 'Apply'd to Col. Chartres', couplet.
Pr. *Miscellanies*, iii, 1732.
MS. Eng. misc. f. 79, p. 77.

684 Here friend is little Daniel's tomb
Was his wife happy in her tears.
Busk, Sir W[adsworth], on Daniel Tear, 1787, Kirk Santon, Isle of Man. *Gentleman's Magazine*, Jan. 1799.
MS. Top. gen. e. 32, fol. 118.

Here gallants find their arms, and so 'tis meet; 685
But where they find their arms, they loose their feet.
'On Parnassus Chamber, where Coats of Arms are painted'.
MS. Eng. poet. e. 4, p. 186.

Here [Gibbons] Cobbons lies, who must in heaven commence, 686
But what he lost was late in Worwick found.
'An Epitaph on Orlando Cobbons [Gibbons] Organist of his Majesties chappel, who deceas'd in Canterbury', 1625.
MSS. Ashmole 36, 37, fol. 144$^v$.

Here God by outward signs 687
Possess the substance too.
Beddome, Benjamin, 'On Baptism'.
MS. *Eng. misc. e. 227, fol. 79.

Here gross deformities in shape, we find 688
The inside's crooked, though the outside's straight.
Antithetical couplets, on Æsop and Sir Roger L'Estrange.
MS. Don. c. 55, fol. 25.

Here have I lingered out two tedious hours 689
As if the ripened project were complete.
'A Friend [ ] the Court', dialogue on Count Gondomar; and on Ralegh still in the Tower, Autumn 1618.
MS. Rawl. poet. 172, fol. 115 (autogr.).

Here heedless headless matchless Raleigh lies 690
Thus right for wrong, paid the desert of crime.
'Epitaph upon Sr Wa: Raleigh'.
MS. Ashmole 781, p. 151.

Here, here, my pale Licoris, 691
But in love's richest ground.
Killigrew, H[enry].
MS. Malone 13, p. 71.

Here, here she lies! Oh! could I once more view 692
And glad all heaven with thy creator's praise.
'A Thought over the Grave of a beloved Child. By the Father. Collectn. Poems'.
MS. Eng. poet. e. 39, p. 96.

Here here's the king's health 693
Confusion to them who set it up again Huzza Huzza Huzza.
'An Health' to 'King James III'.
MS. Rawl. poet. 155, p. 112.

Here Hermes, says Jove, who with nectar was mellow 694
You, Hermes, shall fetch him to make us sport here.
Garrick, David, 'Jupiter and Mercury, a Fable', on Goldsmith.
Pr. bk. Vet. A5 d. 569 (added at end).

695 Here Hobbinoll lies, our shepherd while'er
In spite of his tar-box, he died of the scab.
Ralegh, Sir Walter, 'Upon Sr Robert Cecill, Earle of Salisbury and Ld. Treasurer'.
Pr. F. Osborne, *Historical Memoires on the Raigne of Queen Elizabeth, and King James*, 1658.
Also ascr. to Ralegh by John Shirley, *Life*, 1677, p. 179.
MS. Rawl. poet. 26, fol. 78; see also H822, H908.

696 Here Hobson lies amongst his many betters
And supreme wagoner, next Charles his wain.
'Hobson the Carrier'.
MSS. CCC. 309, fol. 48; Eng. poet. f. 10, fol. 101$^{v}$; see also H823, H882.

697 Here Hobson lies, who did most truly prove,
Only remains this superscription.
[Milton, John] 'Hobson the Carrier'.
Pr. *Banquet of Jests*, 1640; Milton's *Poems*, 1645.
MSS. CCC. 309, fol. 48, introducing H696; Malone 21, fol. 69$^{v}$.

698 Here I am until I die,
When I am dead no more am I.
Robinson, Robert, 'Stultus', couplet.
MS. *Rawl. poet. 218, p. 107 (autogr.).

699 Here I do intend, God willing to declare
To feed so grossly: they are nothing Creese (*sic*).
Forman, Simon, 'What Chaos is'.
MSS. Ashmole 802, fol. 8 (autogr.), and 240, fol. 33 (autogr.).

700 Here I do lie alone
My work which ne'er shall end.
Fleming, Robert, 'An imaginary Landskopp. 1680'.
Pr. *The Mirrour of Divine Love*, 1691, 'Poems', p. 45.
MS. Rawl. poet. 213, fol. 64 rev. (autogr.).

701 Here I live until I die
Then though dead, yet still live I.
Robinson, Robert, 'Sapiens', couplet.
MS. Rawl. poet. 218, p. 107 (autogr.).

702 Here I was born, and being born did cry,
So all men breathing, all as well as I.
Robinson, Robert.
MS. *Rawl. poet. 218, p. 11 (autogr.).

703 Here idleness and poverty combine
And fast because you want whereon to dine.
'Inscription for a franciscan convent'.
MS. Eng. misc. e. 241, fol. 27$^{v}$.

Here in a distant land I roam 704
On Thy eternal love.
Kenton, James.
MS. *Eng. poet. e. 20, p. 86 (autogr.).

Here in a hollow trunk 705
To stir 'em is not best.
'On Dulcinea [Don Quixote's] Lady'.
MS. Rawl. D. 1372, fol. 10$^{v}$ from end.

Here in death's closet (reader) know 706
Of watery pearls from each kind eye.
[Crashaw, Richard], 'An Epitaph'.
Pr. from this MS., *Poems*, ed. L. C. Martin, 2nd ed. 1957, p. 405.
MSS. Rawl. poet. 147, p. 38; Tanner 465, fol. 73.

Here in my silent grave I lie 707
And then we'll meet again.
'Epitaph in Bray Church Yard, near Maidenhead'.
MS. Eng. poet. e. 40, fol. 141.

Here in one horrid ruin lies 708
And mix with them among the dead.
'Contemplating the Period of Human Glory among the Tombs in Westminster Abbey written by a Gentlewoman 1736'.
MS. Ballard 47, fol. 70.

Here in these beauteous moral numbers see 709*a*
Raised by his pen, 'twould be depress'd by mine.
Lumby, John, 'To Miss — with Pope's Works'.
MS. *Eng. poet. e. 42, fol. 91$^{v}$.

Here in this inn of travailers doth lie 709*b*
Till a redeemer come to set it free.
Memorial to Sir John Mandeville, described in J. Shrimpton's history of St. Alban's.
MS. Gough Herts. 3, fol. 74.

Here in this narrow room is hurl'd 710
A life so wet, a death so dry.
'On Oliver Cromwell'.
MS. Rawl. poet. 84, fol. 58 rev.

Here is a new song. 711
To us I am sure.
'The Crafty Scotch Pedler; or, the Downfal of Trading'.
MS. Firth d. 14, fol. 16.

Here is Death's chair of state. Our governor 712
Save the Protector, some cry Long live Death.
Creswell, Robert, 'Epicedium Proctectoris Oliveri Cromwell Sept. 3 1658', translation.
MS. *Eng. poet. f. 24, fol. 7 (autogr.).

713 Here is Elderton lying in dust
For who knew him standing all his life long.
Of 'Thomas Elderton a druncken ballatt maker . . . was made this'.
Pr. Camden's *Remaines*, 1605, p. 56.
MSS. Ashmole 38, p. 187; Eng. poet. e. 40, fol. 188.

714*a* Here is Francis de Verulane, Lord Chancellor, God save him.
*Franciscus superbus non sic cogitavit.*
'An Epitaph upon Sir Francis Bacon'.
MS. Firth d. 7, fol. 154.

714*b* Here is Joseph and his brethren: he in state
Which would stream out, might they not spoil the paint.
'Thomas Browne's verses upon . . . pictures . . . at York House, 2'. Really part of V42.
Pr. H. Huth, *Inedited Poetical Miscellanies*, 1870.
MS. Firth d. 7, fol. 113; see also H722.

715 Here is one dead under this marble stone
Which when she lived lay under moe then one.
Couplet on Penelope Lady Rich.
MSS. Douce f. 5, fol. 9; Hearne's diaries 30, p. 212.

716 Here is one flower whose splendour and whose breath
Surely her muse beyond her sphere should rise.
'Annagram Henry foulis I floure shyn'. Acrostic.
Pr. Wood's *Life and Times*, ed. A. Clark, ii, O.H.S. xxi, 1892, p. 179.
MS. Wood F. 34, fol. 184.

717 Here is paper, pen and ink
His favour, heart and soul may steal.
Strode, William, 'With Pen, Inke and paper these to a distressed etc.'
MS. *CCC. 325, fol. 63 (autogr.).

718 Here is the rarity of the whole fair
A pox take the May'r.
Song, 'Second part of Bartholomew Fair. Dr. Blow'.
MS. Mus. Sch. C. 95, pp. 145, 153.

719 Here is the spring where water flows:
When god by death thee calls.
'Of the incomparable treasure of the holy scriptures with a prayer', *c.* 1580 (?); see pp. 110, 64 of MS.
MS. Rawl. D. 273, p. 136.

Here James Wallace urn doth lie 720
Was brought down to death, then all's done.
'Epitaph in St. Giles's Church Yard Oxford'.
MS. Top. Oxon. b. 116, fol. 105ᵛ.

Here joined you see white snow, and purple fire 721
Where still the cure is equal to the pain?
Oldisworth, Nicolas, 'On the picture of Beauty'.
MS. *Don. c. 24, fol. 51ᵛ (autogr.).

Here Joseph and his brethren: he in state 722
Which would stream down: would they not hurt the paint.
'Buckinghams gallery. 2d picture'. Really part of V42.
MS. Rawl. poet. 142, fol. 25ᵛ; see also H714*b*.

Here Kath'rine lies, deriv'd of noble kind, 723
To her, the muses' friend, and saint of heaven.
Russell, George, translator, 'Another epitaph' on Katherine Killigrew, d. Dec. 1583. Latin by William Chark, pr. Stow's *Survey of London*, 1633, p. 260.
MS. Ballard 37, fol. 136ᵛ (autogr.).

Here kind he lies who troubled with a wife 724
Will make his brother Peter keep her out.
'On one troubled with a curst wife'.
MS. Eng. poet. e. 14, fol. 57.

Here let me, careless and unthoughtful lying 725–6
How prettily they talk.
MS. Add. B. 105, fol. 97ᵛ.

Here lie I Martin Eltinbrode 727
And ye were Martin Eltinbrode.
'A Scotch Epitaph'. 'Edinburgh Church-yard'.
MSS. Rawl. D. 377, fol. 142; Top. gen. e. 32, fol. 58.

Here lie in the ignoble grave 728
Did switch and snatch this member hence.
'On Phillipp Earle of Pembroke and Montgomery', d. 1650.
MS. Wood D. 19(2), fol. 116.

Here lie the consecrated bones 729
The Dutchman's *templum pacis.*
'Upon Clarendon house built by the Lord Chancellor Hyde 1665'.
MSS. Ashmole 36, 37, fol. 117; 1463, p. 2; see also H971.

730 Here lie the relics of a martyred knight
So to cut H[ollan]d's head from England's shoulders.

'An Epitaph on Sir John Fenwick', executed 28 Jan. 1696/7.
Found amongst MS. verse by Henry Hall in the Brotherton Collection, University of Leeds.
MS. Rawl. C. 986, fol. 15.

731 Here lies a blossom of the world's great tree
His mournful parents prays to have as much.

'In All Saints Church [Canterbury] In the Chancell', epitaph on 'Tho: Sheldon Dyed 1700 Aged 2 years'.
MS. Rawl. D. 376, fol. 215[v].

732 Here lies a bond under this tomb
Sealed and delivered god knows to whom.

'On Mr. Bond a usurer', couplet.
MS. CCC. 328, fol. 15[v].

733 Here lies a chandler dead, I need not tell it
He could make many weeks, but not one day.

'On a Chandler'.
MS. CCC. 328, fol. 61; see also H766.

734 Here lies a Church from error full as free
Sometimes on earth not visibly may be.

'On the death of Mrs. Elizabeth Church'.
MS. Ashmole 47, fol. 40[v].

735 Here lies a corpse, which living has a spirit
They lived beloved and died bewailed of all.

'Johannes Blagrave, totus Mathematicus, cum matre sepultus'. 1611.
MS. Top. Oxon. b. 116, fol. 129[v].

736 Here lies a courtier, soldier, handsome, good.
Shall ever swell the cheeks of glorious fame.

On William Basset, Blore Church, Staffs.
MS. Ashmole 853, fol. 43.

737 Here lies a creature of indulgent fate
By his preposterous translation.

'Epitaph on Lory Hide, 1687'.
Pr. *Poems on Affairs of State*, iii, 1698, p. 303.
MS. Firth c. 15, p. 229, attr. to Mr. Dryden.

738 Here lies a dogged fellow, who hath run
Brought to his grave with a great cry may be.

'An epitaph on a Hunter'.
MS. CCC. 328, fol. 59.

739 Here lies a fair wife in earth foul and dirty
Who drew at fifteen and went out at thirty.

'On a faire wife', couplet.
MS. Don. d. 58, fol. 16[v].

Here lies a fool. You are deceived 740
Such fool, such knave, there no where lies.

'An Epitaph made on Tom Mayo' carpenter, d. 1657 (?).
See *Wood, Life and Times*, ed. A. Clark, iv, O.H.S., xxx, 1895, pp. 53, 63, 205.
MSS. Ashmole 36, 37, fol. 215.

Here lies a gallant gentleman of note 741
Who living could never change a groat.

'Epitaph on a Spendthrift', couplet.
Pr. Camden's *Remaines*, 1623, p. 349.
MS. Eng. poet. e. 40, fol. 114; see also H752.

Here lies a gem a jewel rare 742
For filling of six pots she counted eleven.

'One Mr. John Powell that kept an all house att Lancaster', epitaph on his daughter with a line 'the boyes added'.
MS. Ashmole 38, two copies, p. 182.

Here lies a gem (in worth esteem'd no worse) 743
Yet living still in paradise doth dwell.

'Epitaphium'.
Pr. bk. Wood 460, after *Threnodia in obitum E. Lewkenor*, 1606.

Here lies a gracious graceless peer 744
Was that he let him live so long.

'Epitaph' [on the Duke of Buckingham], 1628.
MS. Malone 23, p. 144.

Here lies a head that often ached 745
With higher spirits may he dwell!

'The following Epitaph was found in the Scrutoir of the Rev. Mr. Gouldsby of Bristol after his Decease'.
MS. Eng. poet. e. 39, p. 223.

Here lies a judge will lie no more 746
All this is Lord chief Justice Scrogg.

'A Poem on Ld. Cheife Justice Scrogg. 1679'.
MS. Eng. poet. d. 53, p. 19.

Here lies a knight, a king, a saint 747
Of knight St. George, and of King Henry.

'On Sir Henry St. George, Knight, Garter Principal King of Englishmen . . . from a MS. in the Office of Arms, London'.
MSS. Ballard 29, fol. 60; Eng. misc. e. 183, fol. 18.

Here lies a knight, who now is dead 748*a*
Have turned their red ones into blue.

'Upon Sir James Baker's death'.
MS. Hearne's diaries 113, p. 30.

Here lies a knight, whom men called Walter Gore 748*b*
Death payd his debts . . . (incomplete).

'Epitaph on a poore knight'.
MS. Add. B. 97, fol. 40.

749 Here lies a lass cut off in early bloom
Think of blest state and immortality.

On Mary Snowdon, wife of Thomas Snowdon. West Hatton Churchyard, Lincolnshire.
MS. Eng. poet. c. 51, p. 291.

750 Here lies a lawyer, who till his time of dying
Within this grave, where let him lie for me.

'On A lawyer'.
MS. Ashmole 38, p. 203; Firth d. 7, fol. 171, headed 'On Mr. J. H. . . . of Lincolne's Inn'.

751 Here lies a maid, for heaven by her pure life
In heaven your Margarite is richly set.

MS. Sancroft 59, p. 293 rev.

752 Here lies a man, a gentleman of note
Who all his life time ne'er could change a groat.

'On A beggerly Gentellman'.
MS. Ashmole 38, p. 181; see also H741.

753 Here lies a man, like hive without honey
His honest life will never be forgotten.

'Upon a poor honest man'.
MS. Ashmole 38, p. 173.

754 Here lies a man of reckoning, often seen
Soon you shall have a fresh one at the tap.

'On a tapster'.
MS. CCC. 328, fol. 60.

755 Here lies a man (oh foul unhappy lot)
Thy love to liquor would have saved his skull.

'On Mr. Denne of All S: kill'd with a Jugge'. Henry Denne (?), B.A. Feb. 1562/3, Fellow of All Souls in 1564.
MS. CCC. 328, fol. 43; Eng. poet. e. 14, fol. 78 rev.

756 Here lies a man that when a was born he cried
Told three-score years and ten felt sick and died.

'On one Borne and cryed', couplet.
MS. Eng. poet. e. 14, fol. 88 rev.; see also H1011, H1038.

757 Here lies a man, who all he got
Who all his life did never live.

Chatwin, John, 'An Epitaph on a Miser'.
MS. *Rawl. poet. 94, p. 99 (autogr.).

758 Here lies a man whom death of life beguil'd
Lived long a cozening knave and died a child.

Delicar, Robert, epitaph 'on an old miser'.
MS. Add. B. 97, fol. 40.

759 Here lies a multitude, let none infer
And I shall smile at mine own funeral.

Paynter, Rich[ard], 'On the pious memory of the famous Speed'.
MS. Rawl. poet. 65, fol. 48.

Here lies a parent's hopes and fears 760
Thou'lt say he's best that's soon'st at home.

Duppa, [Brian], 'An Epitaph on a Child'.
MS. Malone 21, fol. 6v; see also H964.

Here lies a peer, beneath this place 761*a*
That shot him. I will say no more.

'An Epitaph on the Duke of Grafton, kild att the Seige of Corke', 1690.
MSS. Add. A 301, fol. 49v rev.; Firth c. 15, p. 330; Rawl. D. 361, fol. 46.

Here lies a piece of Christ, a star in dust, 761*b*
Be used in heaven, when Christ shall feast the just.

On the wife of Robert Nation, Silton, Dorset.
MS. Hearne's diaries 84, p. 58.

Here lies a proof, that wit can never be 762
The world admires and the muses praise.

'Epitaph on Mrs. Afra Behn the Poetess. 1689'. Westminster Abbey.
MSS. Eng. poet. e. 40, fol. 38; Top. gen. e. 32, fol. 13.

Here lies a rose, a budding rose 763
And blooms a rose in heaven.

'Epitaph on a little Girle nam'd Rose. June 14 1747/8'.
MS. Eng. poet. e. 40, fol. 126.

Here lies a shrew, was troubled with her head. 764
Nor she her head, as she did heretofore.

Robinson, Robert, 'An Epitaph upon a shrewe, who allwayes complayned of her head'.
MS. *Rawl. poet. 218, p. 31 (autogr.).

Here lies a sportsman, jolly, kind and free. 765
In hopes to find a joyful resurrection.

'Epitaph'.
MS. Eng. poet. c. 51, p. 32.

Here lies a tallow chandler I need not tell it 766
He that made many wicks, could not make one day.

'On a chandler'.
MS. Douce f. 5, fol. 18v; see also H733.

Here lies a thief nay there thou liest 767
He is no thief that doth rob AntiChrist.

'An Epitaph on one that rob'd the Pope', 'Sr. Oratio Palausen', 'Pallavicini'.
MSS. Eng. poet. e. 14, fol. 89 rev.; Malone 19, p. 137; Tanner 465, fol. 62.

Here lies a treasure in this pit 768
The grave his corpse, Stukelye his shame.

Epitaph on Sir Walter Ralegh.
MS. Eng. hist. c. 272, p. 51; see also H1013.

769 Here lies a woman [there's] no man can deny it
You'll gently tread, for if she wake she'll talk.
'On an unquiet wife'.
Pr. Camden's *Remaines*, 1637, p. 414.
MSS. Ashmole 38, p. 177; CCC. 309, fol. 49$^{v}$; 328, two copies, fols. 43$^{v}$ and 58; Eng. poet. f. 10, fol. 89; Firth d. 7, fol. 171.

770 Here lies, after all her specious pretences
She was too bad a daughter, and too good a wife.
'On the death of Q. Mary. Decr. 1694. By a Jesuit. English'd by Dryden'.
MS. Eng. poet. f. 13, fol. 74$^{v}$; see also H680, H880.

771 Here lies Alderman Taylor of Coleman street
Item I give all to my son Freak.
MS. Tanner 89, fol. 264$^{v}$.

772 Here lies Ambrose Pudsey of Barford Esquire
He was nobleman-like, for he never spake truth.
'An Epitaph'.
MS. Don. b. 8, p. 368.

773 Here lies [an] ane author wha had made
But chanc'd to die while he was living.
Ramsay, Allan, 'On Ane Author who staw the maist feck of his Performances an Epigram'.
MS. Eng. poet. e. 8, fol. 21$^{v}$.

774 Here lies an honest cobbler whom curst [just, hard, malignant, sad] fate
But honest Tom Cobler here is underlaid.
'On a Cobler'.
Pr. *Wits Recreations*, 1641, Epitaph 127; *Wit Restor'd*, 1658, p. 78.
MSS. Ashmole 38, two copies, pp. 166 and 199; CCC. 309, fol. 49; 328, fol. 43; Rawl. D. 1092, fol. 268; Tanner 465, fol. 65; see also H825.

775*a* Here lies an honest man, reader, if thou seek more
To die an honest man than full of praise.
Epitaph on John Ford, Goring Church Yard, 1718.
MS. Hearne's diaries 107, p. 16.

775*b* Here lies an horse beneath this stone
Oh, may you trip, but never tumble.
'An Epitaph on a Stumbling Horse'.
Pr. *Poems on Affairs of State*, ii, 1703, p. 195.
MS. Rawl. poet. 173, fol. 142$^{v}$.

776 Here lies an old woman
She was there before seven.
Holland, T., 'An Epitaph on Old Mother Allen', with Latin version.
MS. Eng. poet. f. 13, fol. 1.

Here lies Andrew Kirkawdey 777
I give him leave.
'Andrew Kirkawdey Churchyard near Queens Ferry on this side the River Tay in Scotland'.
MS. Top. gen. e. 32, fol. 53.

Here lies at last ten in the hundred. 778
'Tis a hundred to ten he's scarce gone to heaven.
'Upon the usurer'.
MS. Rawl. poet. 209, fol. 33.

Here lies beauty in the dirt 779
Pull out your p. and piss upon her.
'Epitaph'.
MS. e Mus. 227, fol. 10.

Here lies Ben Johnson that was once one 780
And now being dead is nothing.
'Mr Ben Iohnson and Mr. Wm. Shakespeare Being Merrye at a Tavern'.
Pr. by J. O. Halliwell-Phillipps in Introduction to *A Midsummer Nights Dream*, 1845, and *Life of Shakespeare*, 1848.
MS. Ashmole 38, p. 181.

Here lies bonny bumpin Jillian 781
And eat the bacon with the bean.
MS. Add. B. 8, fol. 73.

Here lies both flesh and fish—that's meat for no man 782
Appeared above she had an ugly face.
'On the death of Nell Herring'.
MS. CCC. 328, fol. 34.

Here lies Bounce a maker of bellows 783
He that made bellows could not make breath.
'Uppon a bellows Maker'.
MS. Ashmole 38, p. 172; see also B613, H846, H848, H1000, H1019, H1026, H1034.

Here lies buried Mr. Prinn 784
Some times out and sometimes in.
'An epitaph of Mr. [William] Prinn' [1600–69].
MS. Top. Cheshire c. 6, fol. 415$^{v}$.

Here lies [buried] puried under these stones 785
He went to Cott by a fery mischance.
Pr. *Wits Recreations*, 1640, Epitaph 97, 'On a Welshman'.
MS Rawl. poet 153, fol. 28$^{v}$.

Here lyes Chares the first, the great 786
The honest man the honest man the righteous king.
MS. Rawl. D. 317, fol. 171*.

787 Here lies consumed consumptive Whettum;
If folks will die, in God's name let'em.

'Designed for Mr. Whettum a hippish fellow of Ex[eter] Coll:', couplet. [John Whetcome (?), d. 1640].
MS. Eng. misc. e. 241, fol. 101ᵛ.

788 Here lies craft Jone deny it who can
Whilst one leg stood still the other was running.

'On Jone Trueman who had a runninge issue in her leg'.
MS. Eng. poet. e. 14, fol. 89 rev.

789 Here lies Dame French: alas! how fall'n to dust,
She liv'd forgiving, and she died forgiv'n.

'Epitaph upon Dame French of Wigginton, in Oxfordshire'.
MS. Ballard 29, fol. 159.

790 Here lies Dame French; whose fame to raise
Some live, and yet deserve to die.

'Epitaph upon Dame French of Wigginton, in Oxfordshire'.
MS. Ballard 29, fol. 159.

791 Here lies Dick Ecclesie that liv'd a papist
And wanting grace died an Atheist.

'On Archbishop Richard Bancroft', couplet, 1610.
MS. Don. d. 58, fol. 18; see also H793.

792 Here lies Dick Freeman
That could not hear nor see man.

Couplet, 'Uppon on that was blind and Deafe'.
Pr. Camden's *Remaines*, 1637, p. 412, and *Wits Recreations*, 1640, Sig. Aa5ᵛ.
MSS. Ashmole 38, p. 177; Eng. poet. e. 40, fol. 113.

793 Here lies Dick of Canterburie, suspected a papist
Who lived a Machiavillan, and died an atheist.

'Of Richard Bankroft', Abp. of Canterbury, couplet.
Pr. H. Huth, *Inedited Poetical Miscellanies*, 1870.
MS. Firth d. 7, fol. 160; see also H791.

794 Here lies Dicke Pinnire, oh [most] cruel death
He made better dust; than thou canst make of him.

[Bastard, Thomas], 'Uppon a pinner'.
Pr. Bastard's *Chrestoleros*, 1598, iv. 28, 'Epitaph Richardi Pinner', and *Wits Recreations*, 1641, Sig. P7.
MSS. Ashmole 38, p. 170; Eng. poet. e. 14, fol. 80ᵛ rev.; Malone 19, p. 43.

Here lies doctor [Hall] Holland doctor of the chair 795
Whom Mors took napping as Mosse took his mare.

Couplet, 'On Doctor [Hall or] Holland doctor of the chaire'.
MSS. Don. d. 58, fol. 17ᵛ; Eng. poet. e. 14, fol. 77ᵛ rev.; Malone 19, p. 41.

Here lies doctor [Ryves] Balliol College master 796
That brake the university's head and gave the schools a plaster.

Couplet 'On a Dr. who tooke the university lands and plastered the schooles'.
MSS. Don. d. 58, fol. 19ᵛ; Eng. poet. e. 14, fol. 81ᵛ rev.; see also H679, H858, H1004.

Here lies Dr. Sergeant within these cloisters, 797*a*
Whom if the last trump don't waken then cry oysters.

Couplet on Dr. Thomas Sergeant, fellow of All Souls, d. 23 Oct. 1708.
Pr. Hearne's *Collections*, ed. C. E. Doble, ii, O.H.S. vii, 1886, p. 142.
MS. Hearne's diaries 17, p. 203.

Here lies Dr. Tyndall who interest *ut fertur* 797*b*
Pray for his soul who ne'er prayed for't himself.

On Matthew Tindal, copied 23 Feb. 1706.
Pr. Hearne's *Collections*, ed. C. E. Doble, i, O.H.S. ii, 1885, p. 193.
MS. Hearne's diaries 8, p. 192.

Here lies (dry eyes, read not this epitaph!) 797*c*
Here lies great Britain's stay, great Jacob's staff.

Taken from 'Dr. Holdsw.'s Note-books', Dr. Richard Holdsworth, 1590–1649 (?).
Pr. Joshuah Sylvester, *Panaretus*, 1614, Sig. X3, 'Lachrymae Lachrimarum' on Prince Henry.
MS. Sancroft 98, p. 192; see also p. 217.

Here lies Dumbelowe 798
His heart had never broken.

MS. Eng. poet. f. 9, p. 1.

Here lies Du Val, reader, if male thou art 799
Du Vall the ladies' joy Du Vall the ladies' grief.

'An Epitaph. By Buttler'.
MS. Rawl. poet. 152, fol. 130.

Here lies entombed a walking thing 800
That blind whore doth she knows not what.

Howell, [James], 'Epitaph on himselfe while in the fleet 1646'.
MS. Rawl. D. 1372, fol. 17 from end.

801 Here lies entombed a wondrous wight,
Both its own sepulchre, and body.

Roach, Richard, translator, 'The Gordain knot: . . . From an Enigmatic Inscription . . . in the Senator Volta's House near Bolognia in Italy . . . Render'd Ludicrously . . .', with notes.
Pr. *The Postman*, Feb. 10–12, 1729.
MS. Rawl. D. 832, fol. 280 (autogr.).

802 Here lies entombed more men then Greece admired
Wild fruits hang long, the purer timely fall.

Epitaph on William Hyckes, d. 1652, in Shipton-upon-Stour Church, Worcester.
MSS. Ballard 29, fol. 59^v^; Eng. misc. e. 183, fol. 49^v^.

803 Here lies entombed old Sir Harry
He doth lie, and she doth kneel.

Epitaph on a knight.
MS. Ashmole 38, p. 197; see also H1073, H1099.

804 Here lies entomb'd Sir Anthony Ramme
And then gave all to the blacksmith's daughter.

'Uppon a Gentleman that buried his wife and his daughter, gave all his goodes to a Blacke Smithes daughtr. whom he loved'.
MS. Malone 19, p. 56.

805 Here lies entombed within these bricks
Pull out your bables and piss upon her.

'Upon a whore'.
MS. Ashmole 38, p. 173.

806 Here lies entombed within this compassed stone
Doth now with deadly staunch infest the rose.

[Monogram] F. L. or L. F., 'Epitaphiam . . . Rosamund'.
Pr. bk. Malone 354, Sig. H3^v^.

807*a* Here lies father Sparges
Who died to save charges.

'Epitaphium', couplet.
Pr. Camden's *Remaines*, 1605, p. 57.
MSS. Ashmole 36, 37, fol. 142; 38, p. 172; Eng. poet. e. 40, fol. 107; f. 6, fol. 53.

807*b* Here lies for Adam's first offence
Time shall throw a dart at death.

On Samuel Okey, 1706–11, Dissenters' Burial Place, near the City of London.
MS. Hearne's diaries 46, p. 61.

808 Here lies Franke Morley the son of a bearward
Three crooked apostles, and six arrant whores.

'On Francis Morley . . . a notorius Liare; who would needs challeng kindred of the Lord Morley'.
Pr. Camden's *Remaines*, 1637, p. 410.
MS. Ashmole 38, p. 185; see also H871.

Here lies George Monke 809
Be writ on his grave.

'An Epitaph on the Lord Generall Monke', 1670.
MS. Don. b. 8, p. 189.

Here lies great Mary, England's queen 810
And fly, with Christ, to Heaven away.

Spoure, Edmund, 'An Epitaph in Memorie of . . . Queen Mary . . . 28 Decr. 1694'.
MS. *Eng. poet. c. 52, fol. 40 (autogr.).

Here lies great Otho underneath this marble 811
I cannot tell: I leave it to examine.

'An Epitaph on Otho Nicolson'.
MS. Malone 19, p. 147.

Here lies Gregorie Crumwell who loved a bum well 812
Half to his bastard and half to his whore.

'On Gregorie Crumwell'.
MS. Eng. poet. e. 14, fol. 88 rev.

Here lies Gressham under ground 813
Drink was his life, drink was his end.

MS. Firth d. 7, fol. 157; see also H1002, H1008.

Here lies he that once was poor 814
A wife, a witch, a poisoner and a whore.

A satire on Robert Carr, Earl of Somerset.
MSS. Malone 23, p. 7; Rawl. poet. 26, fol. 18.

He[re] lies he underneath this stone 815
There's none that knows, nor none that cares.

'Epitaph on a Usurer'.
MS. Eng. poet. e. 40, fol. 108.

Here lies he who by learning and his wit 816
Was fain to take his death upon't 'twas so.

'On the L. Treasurer Buckhurst, who died at the Counsell Table swearing falsely against Sr. J. Luson' [1608].
MS. Eng. poet. e. 14, fol. 96 rev.

Here lies he who had a horn who when he blew it 817
Called many a cuckold to dinner and great men knew it.

Couplet.
MS. Eng. poet. f. 10, fol. 103^v^.

Here lies her dust whom second love 818
Live in the love of her posterity.

On Margaret Clarke, d. 1618, in Sevenoaks Church.
MSS. Rawl. D. 682, fol. 54; Top. gen. e. 1, p. 45.

Here lies his frailty, his fair soul above 819
Only to write 'tis Inglethorp lies here.

Inscription on — Inglethorp, Worcester Cathedral, copied 1664.
MS. Top. gen. e. 1, p. 99.

820 Here lies his grace that lived bad
And dying wanted what he had.
'In Rich: Archiepisc'. i.e. Archbishop Richard Bancroft.
MS. Don. d. 58, fol. 18; see also H1014.

821 Here lies his grace very deep in the dirt
Who rose by the smock and fell by the shirt.
'His Epitaph when Dead' [The Duke of Marlborough].
MS. Rawl. poet. 155, p. 162.

822 Here lies Hobinall, our shepherd while here
In spite of his tarbox, he died of the scab.
Ralegh, Sir Walter, 'Upon Sir R[obert] C[ecil] Lord Treasurer'.
MSS. Eng. poet. e. 14, fol. 79 rev.; Tanner 299, fol. 12$^{v}$, attr. to Sr. Walter Ralegh by Sancroft, who refers to Francis Osborne's *Memoirs*, [1658] and J. Shirley's *Life* [1677]; see also H695, H908.

823 Here lies Hobson amongst his [many] betters
And supreme waggoner next Charles his wain.
'Upon Thomas Hobson, the Carryer of Cambridge'.
MSS. Rawl. poet. 26, fol. 64$^{v}$; 117, fol. 175 rev.; see also H696, H882.

824 Here lies honest Harry
Of pipes and tobacco to relish his drink.
'A catch . . . Mr. James Hart'.
MS. Mus. Sch. C. 95, p. 94.

825 Here lies honest John Cobler, whom curs'd fate
Honest John Cobler here lies underlaid.
'On a cobler'.
MS. CCC. 328, fol. 61; see also H774.

826 Here lies Hugh Thornton quiet and safe
But chaffing of wax was all his trade.
'On one Thornton A sealer in Chancerye'.
MS. Ashmole 38, p. 208.

827 Here lies I, no wonder I'm dead
For a broad-wheel'd waggon went over my head.
'Epitaph in Bedwell Church Yard, Hertfordshire', couplet.
MS. Eng. poet. c. 51, p. 241.

828 Here lies in gold, and not in brass,
Now dead a golden calf.
'Of Sir Christopher Hatton'.
MS. Firth d. 7, fol. 154.

829 Here lies, in the fair flower of his youth,
As well thy ruin, as the end of me.
'On Master Kitchen'.
MSS. CCC. 309, fol. 49$^{v}$; Rawl. D. 1092, fol. 268$^{v}$.

Here lies inhumed a noble English dame, 830
Must pluck a quill, from some good angel's wing.
W[harton], G[eorge], 'To Perpetuate the Sacred Memorie of Mrs. Anne Squib Aug. 29 1656'.
MS. Ashmole 423, fol. 279 (autogr.).

Here lies interred a massy lump 831
Surpassed Christendom, and Kent.
'On An Old fatt Bawde'.
MS. Ashmole 38, p. 203.

Here lies interred, for worms meat [to eat] 832
That stunk while he lived and died of the pox.
'On S$^{r}$ Robert Siscell late Earl of Salisburye this invictive Epitaph was wrighten by an unknown person'; d. May 1612.
MSS. Ashmole 38, p. 182; Rawl. poet. 155, p. 70; see also H1016.

Here lies interred the pious and the just 833
Did over dust triumphantly control.
Epitaph on Thomas Dod the younger, 24 March 1685, Gamlinghay.
MS. Top. Cambr. c. 1, fol. 112.

Here lies interred what death hath left behind 834
For only she can sound great Morgan's name.
On the tomb Sir Thomas Morgan in 'Sommerton Church'.
MS. Tanner 89, fol. 233.

Here lies interred within this cave 835
They need not fear but Charles will soon unlock.
'On Charls the Porter of Lincons Inn'.
MS. Eng. poet. e. 14, fol. 11.

Here lies interr'd within this ground 836
So God be thanked was his life.
'On Sir W. S.'
MS. Wood D. 19(2), fol. 110$^{v}$.

Here lies Jack careless 837
And died in the street.
'Upon a spendthrifte'.
MS. Don. d. 58, fol. 19$^{v}$.

Here lies Jack Gill 838
And hearts very sad, which he ne'er used to do.
'An epitaph on Jack Gill the Gamester'.
MS. Don. e. 24, p. 10.

Here lies Jack Presbyter, void of all pity, 839
Therfore in great haste, he's gone thither to see.
'Epitaph . . . They went in July. 1647 and are no yet return'd'.
MS. Mus. f. 23, fol. 109$^{v}$.

840 Here lies James Cabone buried in the year
It is all one.
'My Ld. Oxford found this Epitaph wrote in a Blank Leaf at the end of' Dugdale's *History of St. Paul's Cathedral.*
MS. Ballard 19, fol. 218[v]; see also H841–2.

841 Here lies James Cadone under this stone
But if you chance, to forget him, All's one.
MS. Don. b. 8, p. 494; see also H840, H842.

842 Here lies James Gazall all alone
Anything or nothing it's all one.
MS. Wood D. 19(2), fol. 110; see also H840–1.

843 Here lies Jane, and Susan, and Ellenor Higgs
And here lies honest William, who whim'd all their gigs.
'Epitaph on William Higgs, and his three Wives'. Couplet.
MS. Eng. poet. e. 40, fol. 5.

844 Her lies Joan of Arc, the which
Whether saint, witch, man, maid, or, whore.
'Joan of Arc'.
Pr. *Monthly Review*, March 1792.
MSS. Rawl. poet. 66, fol. 50; Top. gen. e. 32, fol. 86[v].

845 Here lies John Baker enrolled in mould
That undid the barber and starved up the lice.
'Uppon on that was balde'.
Pr. Camden's *Remaines*, 1637, p. 412.
MSS. Ashmole 38, p. 177; Eng. poet. e. 40, fol. 116; see also H855, H881, H1003.

846 Here lies John Broker a maker of bellows
He that made bellows could not make breath.
'On Jo: Broker a Bellows maker of Oxon'.
MS. Eng. poet. e. 14, fol. 93[v] rev.; see also B613, H783, H848, H1000, H1019, H1026, H1034.

847 Here lies John Button, heavens and poles!
Are graves become but Button-holes?
Couplet, 'An Epitaph on John Button'.
MS. Rawl. D. 377, fol. 142.

848 Here lies John Cooker [Cruken] [a] maker of bellows
He that made bellows could not make breath.
'On John Cooker'.
Pr. Camden's *Remaines*, 1605, 'Poems', etc., p. 56.
MSS. Eng. poet. e. 14, fol. 88 rev.; Rawl. D. 1372, fol. 9 from end, attr. to J. Hoskins; see also B613, H783, H846, H1000, H1019, H1026, H1034.

Here lies John Death the very same 849
That went away with a cousin of his name.
'Upon on John death', couplet.
Pr. Camden's *Remaines*, 1637, p. 412.
MSS. Ashmole 38, p. 177; Eng. poet. e. 40, fol. 110.

Here lies John Dodd, 850*a*
Being Whitson Monday.
'In St. Paules was this', 1515.
Pr. Camden's *Remaines*, 1637, p. 407.
MSS. Ashmole 38, p. 195; Eng. poet. e. 40, fol. 107.

Here lies John Dryden who had enemies three 850*b*
He had nicked both devil and the Collier.
'Epitaph upon Mr. John Dryden'.
Pr. Hearne's *Collections*, ed. C. E. Doble, ii, O.H.S. vii, 1886, p. 34.
MS. Hearne's diaries 16, p. 34.

Here lies John Flin 851
Spurned at this earth, and flew to heaven.
'Mr. John Flin a Painter at Galway in Scotland', d. 19 Sept. 1747, on himself, written during his sickness.
MS. Eng. poet. e. 40, fol. 16.

Here lies John Flower under this stone 852
In the year of our lord god 1567 being Whitson Monday.
'In St. Margetts at Westminster Uppon on John Flower', 23 May 1567.
MS. Ashmole 38, p. 181.

Here lies John Gregorie buried 853
Amongst the rest a Gregorie.
On John Gregorie a Perriwike maker, 1544–1622. St. Clements Church yard.
MS. Ashmole 38, p. 195.

Here lyes John Hall the [university] capper 854
Live by the bell when you die by the rope.
'On John Hall of Cambridge', with answer, I53; also answered by J118.
MSS. Eng. poet. e. 14, fol. 89 rev.; MS. e Mus. 227, fol. 10; Rawl. poet. 147, p. 7; 210, fol. 50.

Here lies John Hobson enwrapped in mould 855
To tear up his hair and grub up his lice.
'On John Hobson'.
MS. Eng. poet. e. 14, two copies, fols. 86[v] rev., 88 rev.; see also H845, H881, H1003.

Here lies John Hodgson 856*a*
The clergy's fool, and the devil's godson.
Couplet on [John Hodgson], d. 1615.
MS. Ashmole 38, p. 199.

856*b* Here lies John Hough
And that's enough.
Inscription in Cheshire on a royalist, *æt.* 95.
MS. Hearne's diaries 83, p. 121.

857 Here lies John Hubberton
Hey for brave John Hubberton.
'In the North Cuntry this'.
Pr. Camden's *Remaines*, 1637, p. 408.
MSS. Ashmole 38, p. 184; Eng. poet. e. 40, fol. 112; Rawl. D. 1372, fol. 9$^v$ from end.

858 Here lies John Jeggons Bennet College Master
Who broke the schollars' heads and gave the schools a plaster.
Couplet 'On Dr. Jegons who bestowed the mulcts of the Schollars in playstering the Scholes' [Master of CCC. Cambridge, 1590–1603].
MSS. Rawl. poet. 147, p. 7; 210, fol. 50; see also H679, H796, H1004.

859 Here lies John Owen, who always had this trick
Though he could not make a poem he could make a distick.
'One Mr. John Owen the Poett', d. 1622. Couplet.
MS. Ashmole 38, p. 205.

860*a* Here lies John Pricket King Alfred's butler
As great a rogue as was Ben Cutler.
Epitaph for the Butler of University College Oxford. He d. 1725.
MS. Hearne's diaries 107, p. 129.

860*b* Here lies John Tree, both branch and root
Returned to earth again.
'An Epitaph designed for one John Tree'.
MS. Ballard 29, fol. 79.

861 Here lies Johnny Cole
With his crimes undigested, poor sinner!
'John Cole . . . Gentleman's Magazine 1792'.
MS. Top. gen. e. 32, fol. 86.

862 Here lies Judge Owen that never took bribe
Here lies Judge Richardson, that never denied.
'Upon Judge Owen [d. 1598 (?)] and Judge Richardson [d. Feb. 1634/5] bothe buried In Westminster neare on a nother'.
MS. Ashmole 38, p. 181.

863 Here lies Judge Richardson locked in a chest
Oh no quoth St Peter, you come to jeer.
Translation of Latin epitaph on Sir Thomas Richardson, d. 4 Feb. 1634/5.
MS. Ashmole 48, fol. 133$^v$; see also H874.

Here lies Julius Mazarine 864
Translating is but cobbling work you know.
R. W., translator, 'Julii Mazarini Epitaphium'.
MS. Ashmole 826, fol. 45$^v$.

Here lies King Charles the last of Spain 865
Nay, not so much as made his will.
Charles II, d. 1 Nov. 1700.
MS. Tanner 89, fol. 261$^v$; see also H955.

Here lies lechery, treachery, pride; 866
He swore Gods wounds, and then he died.
'An Epitaph', couplet on the Duke of Buckingham, 1628.
MS. Tanner 465, fol. 102$^v$.

Here lies little Robin who justly was reckoned 867
Great pity the pox should couzen the halter.
'On the late L. Treas. Sr R[obert] C[ecil]', d. 24 May, 1612. Translation from Latin.
MSS. Eng. poet. e. 14, fol. 95$^v$ rev.; Malone 23, p. 4.

Here lies Lorenza, my dear brother, 868
And then the news, is no sad hearing.
Earles, [John (?)] 'An Epitaph on the Living Sr. Lorenza Carew' [Ktd. 1634].
MS. Malone 13, p. 29.

Here lies Lucrece in name, Thais in life 869
The same Pope's daughter, lemman, and his own son's wife.
Translation of Latin by Pontanus, pr. Flacius, *Pia quaedam vetustissima poemata*, 1552, 392.
MS. Rawl. D. 1372, fol. 69$^v$.

Here lies Lucretia in name, indeed yet more. 870
Pope Alexander's daughter his and his brother's whore.
Fairfax, Thomas, Lord, translator, 'Pontanus writes this epitaph on Lucretia daughter of Alexander 6'. Latin pr. Flacius, *Pia quaedam vetustissima poemata*, 1552, 392.
MS. *Fairfax 40, p. 606 (autogr.).

Here lies M. F. the son of a bear-ward 871
Three crooked Apostles, and six arrant whores.
'Epitaph on M. F.'
MS. Eng. poet. e. 40, fol. 113; see also H808.

Here lies Moore and no more but he 872
More and no more how can that be.
Couplet, 'On one Moore'.
MS. Eng. poet. e. 14, fol. 96 rev.; see also H891.

873*a* Here lies Mother Davies
To such sots as Cary and Troheer.
'Epitaph on Mrs. Davies Mother in Law to Will Sherwin the Beadle'.
Pr. Hearne's *Collections*, ed. C. E. Doble, ii, O.H.S. vii, 1886, p. 69.
MS. Hearne's diaries 16, p. 35.

873*b* Here lies my body in corruption's bed,
Then welcome death, step to eternity.
Verses from a tomb stone.
MS. Top Yorks. c. 26, fol. 135$^{v}$ rev.

874 Here lies my Lord Richardson locked in a chest
No quoth he Peter I came but to jeer.
'An Epigram on my Lord Richardson', [Sir Thomas Richardson, d. Feb. 1634/5].
MSS. Ashmole 38, two copies, pp. 182 and 198; Rawl. poet. 152, fol. 22; see also H863.

875 Here lies my lord's grace at six and at seven
Since all the world knows it was never his seeking.
'On the death of Arch. Bpp. Bancroft'. 1610.
MS. Ashmole 1463, p. 13.

876 Here lies my wife under the grass
Which she never was in her life-time, alas!
'Epitaph—on a Scold'.
MS. Eng. poet. c. 51, p. 241.

877 Here lies N. a man of fame
The first of his house the last of his name.
'Epitaph on N . . a Mushroom'.
MS. Eng. poet. e. 40, fol. 114; see also H1032.

878 Here lies nature's jewel, on which sh' had wrought
Heaven that long had long'd for't stole't away.
Lynnett, William, 'An epitaph on the Lady' [Theophila Coke, 1643].
MS. Eng. misc. e. 13, fol. 21 (autogr.).

879 Here lies Ned Hyde
The world had ne'er miss'd her.
'Epitaph on the youngest Sonne of the Earle of Clarendon'.
MS. Don. b. 8, p. 182.

880 Here lies, notwithstanding all [her] specious pretences,
She was too bad a daughter, and too good a wife.
Queen Mary II.
MSS. Rawl. poet. 81, fol. 35, headed 'On the Princess of Marocco'; 181, fol. 15; see also H680, H770.

Here lies old Dobson, yea clad in mould, 881
That grubb'd up the hair, to sarve up the lice.
MS. Malone 19, p. 20; see also H855, H1003.

Here lies old Hobson among his betters 882
And supreme waggoner, next to Charles wain.
'Upon Hobson the Carrier'.
Pr. *Wit Restor'd*, 1658, p. 83.
MS. Tanner 465, fol. 73; see also H696, H823.

Here lies old Magdaline, sister to Harry 883
Certain you'll never find her like again.
Spoure, Edmund, 'in Memorie of M[rs] Magdaline Spoure'.
MS. *Eng. poet. c. 52, fol. 6$^{v}$ (autogr.).

Here lies old Owen that lately did die 884
Did not you know him, no more did I.
Couplet on the Butler of Christ Church.
MS. Eng. poet. e. 14, fol. 95 rev.; see also H894, H1040.

Here lies one, as all men must 885
But only gives her a dry Bob.
'The Epitaph of Robert King of Mesopott'.
MS. Eng. poet. e. 45, fol. 9$^{v}$.

Here lies one blown out of breath 886
Who lived a merry life and died a merry death.
'On Merideth Organist of New College. 1637', couplet.
Pr. *Modius Salium*, 1751, p. 16.
MS. Wood E. 32 (Modius Salium), fol. 10$^{v}$.

Here lies one dead under this marble stone 887
When thou nam'st stone she'll rise again I fear.
'An epitaph on a whore'.
MS. Ashmole 47, fol. 101$^{v}$.

Here lies one dead under this marble stone 888
Who when she lived lay under more than one.
Couplet, 'On the Ladye Riche'.
Pr. *Wits Recreations*, 1663, Epitaph 15.
MSS. Don. d. 58, fol. 15$^{v}$; Eng. poet. d. 152, fol. 104$^{v}$; see also H898, H944, H1042.

Here lies one deny it who can 889
That lived an old woman and died a Newman.
'Upon An. Newman'.
MS. Eng. poet. f. 25, fol. 10; see also H911.

Here lies one enclosed under this brick 890
To pull out your p. and piss upon her.
'Epitaph'.
MS. CCC. 327, fol. 5$^{v}$.

Here lies one More and no more but he, 891
More and no more how may this be.
Couplet, 'Epi: on one More'.
MS. Eng. poet. f. 10, fol. 94; see also H872.

892 Here lies one now not worth despising
Who living stunk in the face of men.
'Upon Sr. Thomas Overburie who dyed in the Tower', 1613.
MS. Malone 23, p. 6.

893 Here lies one proper and well shapen
Whose name was William Glascapon.
'The replye of Mr [Henry] Andertowne on Glascock that made' H895. Couplet.
MS. Malone 19, p. 55*b*.

894 Here lies one that lately did die
Did not you know him? neither did I.
'On a stranger'. Couplet.
MS. Don. d. 58, fol. 17v; see also H884, H1040.

895 Here lies one, the more the pity
His name was Henry Andercitty.
William Glascock 'Uppon one Mr Andertowne', with a note 'because Towne would not stand in the verse'. Couplet.
For Andertowne's retort, see H893.
MS. Malone 19, p. 53.

896 Here lies one whom Heavens forbade
When we had all great cause to fear.
'Dr. Pryn's als. St Pryn's verses on the Ld Strafford', 1641.
MS. Douce 357, fol. 11v.

897 Here lies our dearest child who's gone from we
But him can ne'er go back again to we.
'In x x x x x x x x'.
MS. Rawl. D. 316, fol. 110v.

898 Here lies Penelope [or] the Lady Rich
Her that in life was not content with two.
'Uppon the lady Rich'.
MSS. CCC. 328, fol. 43; Douce f. 5, fol. 9; Hearne's diaries 30, p. 212; Malone 23, p. 5; see also H888, H944, H1042.

899 Here lies poor Frank Upton
He'd been heartily welcome to Jahn Toms.
Leach, Thomas Cary, Fellow of Exeter College, Oxford, 'on old Frank Upton senior Fellow of Ex: Coll:' d. 1778.
MS. Eng. misc. e. 241, fol. 125v.

900 Here lies poor Gill, and well he played his part;
He clinch'd the joke, confessed, and died a papist.
Woodcock, Thomas, 'Attorney in Bromsgrove', 'An Epitaph upon Gilbert Herne'.
MS. Ballard 47, fol. 59.

Here lies poor Johnson! Readers have a care. 901
Will tell you how he wrote and talk'd and cough'd and spit.
Jenyns, Soame, 'Epitaph on Dr. Johnson'.
MS. Eng. poet. c. 51, two copies, pp. 21 and 59.

Here lies pure and precious dust, 902
To this dumb stone did give.
T[raherne], T[homas], 'In Obitum viri optimi I[ohn] C[holmeley] Eirenarchae', died 30 Jan. 1660.
MS. Lat. misc. f. 45, p. 211 (autogr.).

Here lies Randolph Peter 903
For if he chance to wake, be sure he'll eat you.
'Epitaph on Peter Randolph of Oriel Col[ege] a great Eater'.
MS. Eng. poet. e. 40, fol. 166.

Here lies religion's friend, profaneness' scorn 904
Yet still survives the just's memorial.
On Edward Eardley, 1656, Audeley Church, Staffs.
MS. Ashmole 853, fol. 32v.

Here lies rich Hewett, a gentleman of note 905
He was wise, because rich, and now you know all.
'On Rich. Hewett . . . in the Old Cathedral Church of St. Paul'.
Pr. Camden's *Remaines*, 1637, p. 411
MSS. Ashmole 38, p. 169; Eng. poet. e. 40, fol. 115.

Here lies Richard a [Green] Preen 906
And he that will die after him may.
Pr. Camden's *Remaines*, 1605, p. 58.
MSS. Ashmole 38, p. 170, dated 20 March 1589; Eng. poet. e. 14, fol. 88 rev., dated 22 May 1599; see also H1044.

Here lies Richard Hobbs 907
On whose soul Jesu have mercy amen.
'In St. Martins In the feilds' epitaph, 19 Feb. 1561.
Pr. Camden's *Remaines*, 1637, p. 412.
MSS. Ashmole 38, p. 175*b*; Eng. poet. e. 40, fol. 110.

Here lies Robert our shepherd whilom 908
In spite of the Tarbox he died of the scab.
Ralegh, Sir Walter, incomplete epigram on Sir Robert Cecil, given to Aubrey by 'Sir Thomas Malett . . . who knew Sr. W. Raleigh'.
MS. Aubrey 6, fol. 78v; see also H695, H822.

Here lies S. H. for estate an esquire 909
Who want neither fire meat drink cunt or clothes.
'An epitaph on Mr. Sam. Hinde on old usurer'.
MS. Eng. poet. d. 152, fol. 11v.

910 Here lies Salisbury that little great commander
Yet say Lord have mercy on Beeston and Cope.
On Robert [Cecil], Earl of Salisbury, d. 1612.
MS. Malone 23, p. 65.

911 Here lies she deny it that can
That lived an old woman and died a new man.
'On an old woman named Newman'.
MS. Eng. poet. f. 10, fol. 95; see also H889.

912 Here lies she that was Not born, Not begot,
For, whilst thou readest this, thou readest Not.
'An Epitaph by vicount S. Alban: ut fertur. The party's name was Not'.
MS. Rawl. B. 151, fol. 103.

913 Here lies she, who if ever bad
It was for want of that she had.
'Epi: on Grace a maid's name'.
MS. Eng. poet. f. 10, fol. 94ᵛ.

914 Here lies she whom death befriended
Sees whom you wrong and whom you right.
'Epitaph', on Lady Arabella Stuart, 1615, following Epicedium, T3290.
MS. Ashmole 781, p. 148.

915*a* Here lies Simon clad in clay
Who while he lived cried tip away.
On Simon Miller, bookseller on Ludgate Hill. Couplet.
Pr. Hearne's *Collections*, ed. C. E. Doble, ii, O.H.S. vii, 1886, p. 27.
MS. Hearne's diaries 15, p. 42.

915*b* Here lies Sir Henry Franckland knight
That man should be entombed in dust.
MS. Don. d. 58, fol. 18ᵛ.

916 Here lies Sir John Shipsquire an ell under ground
For he had no issue but one in his leg.
'On Sʳ John Shipsquire'.
MS. Firth e. 4, p. 110; see also H917.

917 Here lies Sir John Skinner lowly (?) in ground
For he had no issue but one in his leg.
'On Sʳ Jo: Skinner'.
MS. Eng. poet. e. 14, fol. 93 rev.; see also H916.

918 Here lies Sir John Spencer an ell under ground
And goods are committed into the Lord's hands.
'On Sr. John Spencer', 1610.
MS. Eng. poet. e. 14, fol. 95 rev.; see also H919.

919 Here lies Sir John Spencer like Dives in ground
Are in a mad keeping yet in the Lord's hands.
'Upon Sir John Spencer', 1610.
MS. Rawl. poet. 160, fol. 182ᵛ; see also H918.

Here lies Sir John Spencer six foot underground 920
He played the unthrift and gave all away.
'On Sr. John Spencer', 1610.
MS. Ashmole 38, p. 186.

Here lies Sir Richard Salkeld the knight 921
For as they are now, so mun we be.
'Over a Tombe in Wetherelle Church by Corby' (Sir R. Salkeld knighted 1487).
MS. Rawl. D. 692, fol. 4ᵛ.

Here lies Sir Steven Some with his head full low 922
To whom death came and told him before god you shall go.
Couplet, 'on Sʳ Steven Some that used this woord; before god you shall goe'.
MSS. Ashmole 38, p. 186; Eng. poet. e. 14, fol. 94 rev.; Rawl. poet. 26, fol. 163.

Here lies ten in the hundred 923
But his soul is damned.
'On an Usurer'.
Pr. Camden's *Remaines*, 1637, p. 403.
MSS. Eng. poet. e. 14, fol. 95ᵛ rev.; e. 40, fol. 108; Rawl. D. 1372, fol. 9 from end.

Here lies that eminently learned man 924
When they with crowns in happiness do meet.
Cromwell, Edward, epitaph on Joseph Lambert, schoolmaster at Beverley, dated 'Jan. 21. 1716–17'.
MS. *Rawl. poet. 165, fol. 39 (autogr.).

Here lies that prize and knowing head 925
And therefore I do write his epitaph.
MS. Top. Oxon. c. 108, p. 7.

Here lies the beard, the wart and all 926
Beggared all should be by Habell.
G. C., 'On Habel Tash a Contentious Soliciter Having A Great beard and A wart on his nose and affected the word, Rationall'.
MS. Ashmole 38, p. 180.

Here lies the best and worst of fate 927
The great man's volume, all time's story.
Shirley, James, epitaph on the Duke of Buckingham. 1628.
Pr. *Poems*, 1646, p. 62.
MSS. Malone 23, p. 195; *Rawl. poet. 88, p. 59, attr. to J. S.

Here lies the best of wives, of mothers, and of friends 928
That made its benefactor thus to bleed.
Epitaph at Cheam on Eliza Dutton 'who was murdered the 13th of July 1687 by her neighbour indeavering to make peace between him and his wife aged 53 years'.
MS. Rawl. C. 800, fol. 78ᵛ.

929 Here lies the body of a soul as good
(Reader) and the rest from fame.
Pierce, Dr. Thomas, on Margaret Palmer, 5 May 1671: Carlton, Northants.
Pr. *The History and Antiquities of Northamptonshire*, John Bridge and P. Whalley, 1791, ii. 295.
MS. Willis 71, p. 122.

930 Here lies the body of Col. Don Francisco
Of all the descendants of Adam.
'An Epitaph on Colonel Charteris'.
MS. Eng. misc. f. 79, p. 59.

931 Here lies the body of Daniel Saul
Spittle-fields weaver, and that's all.
'On Daniel Saul, St. Dunstan's Ch[h]. yard, Stepney'. Couplet.
MS. Top. gen. e. 32, fol. 53.

932 Here lies the body of honest John Dye,
Oh does he so, let him lie, let him lie.
Couplet.
MS. Add. B. 8, fol. 70.

933 Here lies the body of John Noakes
Who lived and died like other folks!
'Epitaph', couplet.
MS. Eng. poet. c. 51, p. 241.

934 Here lies the body of Mary Sexton
Not like the woman, who lies under the next stone.
'On Mary Sexton', in Bideford Churchyard.
MS. Eng. poet. c. 51, p. 45.

935 Here lies the body of my Lord Protector
There's no man alive can say but he's dead.
'Upon the Protector Oliver Cromwell'.
MS. Rawl. poet. 26, fol. 163[v].

936 Here lies the body of old Joan Pegg
For whilst one leg stood still, the other kept running.
'An Epitaph gave me by Miss Molly Clarke'.
MS. Eng. poet. e. 40, fol. 160.

937*a* Here lies the body of the brave Cleander,
They most deserve to live, who die for love.
Barnes, Joshuah, 'Cleander's Epitaph'.
MS. Hearne's diaries 11, p. 138.

937*b* Here lies the bones of him that was of late
The warden lives, though death hath took the porter.
Wither, George, 'On the porter of a prison'.
Pr. 'A Miscelany of Epigrams' in *Faire-Virtue*, 1622, Sig. O5.
MS. Ashmole 38, p. 179.

Here lies the bookworm John Selden 938
That the lawyers pray for it.
Paman, Clem[ent], 'Epitaph' on John Selden, d. 30 Nov. 1654.
MS. Rawl. D. 945, fol. 2[v].

Here lies the bride [brief] of badness vice's nurse 939
Worse than all these here lies the lady Lake.
'Encomium' on Lady Lake, widow of Sir Thomas; buried 25 February 1642/3; but the verses were probably made 1619–20; cf. G574.
MSS. Ashmole 36, 37, fol. 70; Malone 23, p. 5; see also H966, H1054, H1161.

Here lies the cobbler that dwelt in the Strand 940
The soul was rent from the upper leather.
'An Epitaph on a cobler'.
MS. CCC. 328, fol. 43.

Here lies the collier John of Nashes, 941
And being dead he is no more.
'On a Collier'.
Pr. Camden's *Remaines*, 1637, Sig. Fff4[v].
MSS. Ballard 50, fol. 196; Eng. poet. e. 40, fol. 114.

Here lies the corpse of Dolbin John 942
To make rebellion thrive and grow.
'Epitaph'.
MS. Rawl. poet. 197, fol. 7[v].

Here lies the corpse of William Prin, 943
Death takes the remnant of his lugs.
D. 24 Oct. 1669.
Pr. Wood's *Athenae*, ed. Bliss, 1817, iii. 876.
MSS. Ashmole 36, 37, two copies, fols. 10[v] and 117; 1463, p. 2; Don. b. 8, p. 565.

Here lies the Countess of Devon or the Lady Rich 944
Who in her life was not content with two.
'On the Countess of Devon', Penelope, d. 7 July 1607.
MS. Ashmole 38, p. 169; see also H888, H898, H1042.

Here lies the dust of him, who never bowed 945
Be wise like him take neither oath nor wife.
On Wm. Nicholson, 6 March 1726.
MS. Eng. misc. d. 295, fol. 13.

Here lies the Earl of Suffolk's fool 946
To laugh at by and by.
'Dicky—Berkeley Churchyard'. 1728.
See Swift's *Poems*, ed. H. Williams, 1958, iii. 1131.
MS. Top. gen. e. 32, fol. 71, attr. to Swift.

947 Here lies the earth of him whom fame
Their rendered errors, is now broke.
Clerke, R., 'One Mr. George Clerke havinge bine both Souldier and Courtier'.
MS. Rawl. poet. 206, p. 56.

948 Here lies the famous learned Doctor Bidgood
To some he would, to others, he ne'er did good.
Spoure, Edmund, 'An Epitaph on Doctor Bidgood', couplet.
MS. *Eng. poet. c. 52, fol. 10v (autogr.).

949 Here lies the fellow if report be true
Where never Serjant yet durst shew his face.
By R. J.
MSS. Ashmole 36, 37, fol. 33.

950 Here lies the great. False marble, where?
Nothing but small and sordid dust lies there.
Couplet.
MS. Rawl. poet. 213, fol. 49v.

951 Here lies the great, the loyal, wise Dundee
Thou brave, thou noble, thou divine, Dundee!
'Epitaph on . . . Viscount Dundee', 1689.
MS. Firth e. 6, fol. 63.

952 Here lies the hair, the flesh and eke the bones
Of Rexom clerk, poor Daniel Jones.
Couplet.
MS. Tanner 89, fol. 264v; see also H1122.

953 Here lies the horse that died but
Should make him go that made him lame.
'On a Horse'.
MS. Firth e. 4, p. 110.

954 Here lies the Lady Marie in earthly press
That died thirty yeares before she was Countess.
'Of Ladie Marie Rogers', couplet.
MS. Firth d. 7, fol. 160; see also H1027.

955 Here lies the last King Charles of Spain,
Nay, not so much as made his will.
'An Epitaph on the late King of Spain'.
MS. Rawl. poet. 173, fol. 126v; see also H865.

956 Here lies (the Lord have mercy upon her)
And died a maid, more's the pity.
'Uppon on of the Mayds of Honor to Queen Elizabeth'.
Pr. Camden's *Remaines*, 1623, p. 349. Pr. from this MS., *Life*, etc., of J. Hoskyns, L. B. Osborn, 1937, p. 170.
MSS. Ashmole 38, p. 181, attr. to Sergt. Hosking; Eng. poet. e. 14, fol. 93v rev.; see also H1029.

Here lies the man so long forgot by death 957
Where not is death, if air be such a knife?
Strode, William, epigram 'On the Old man that died by chang of Ayre'.
Cf. Wood's *Annals*, ed. Gutch, ii, 1796, p. 348, on the death of Will. Knight from this cause, 1622.
MS. *CCC. 325, fol. 124 (autogr.).

Here lies the man, that madly slain 958
One life to loose another to live.
Epitaph.
Pr. Camden's *Remaines*, 1605, p. 58.
MSS. Ashmole 38, p. 175*a*; Eng. poet. e. 14, fol. 93v rev.; e. 40, fol. 119; Rawl. D. 1372, fol. 9v from end.

Here lies the man who in his life 959
Pray for his soul's health gentle brother.
'Uppon A Contentious Companion'.
Pr. Camden's *Remaines*, 1623, p. 57.
MSS. Ashmole 38, p. 170; Eng. poet. e. 40, fol. 111.

Here lies the man, whom generous nature blessed 960
Must leave this world, and settle in the skies.
'Epitaph on William Bunbury who died at Hadleigh in Suffolk September 12 1748'.
MS. Eng. poet. e. 40, fol. 70.

Here lies the man whose horse did gain 961
You or your horse rather to read it.
Epitaph.
Pr. Camden's *Remaines*, 1605, p. 58. Cf. *Life*, etc., of John Hoskyns, L. B. Osborn, 1937, pp. 189, 284.
MSS. Ashmole 38, p. 170; Eng. poet. e. 40, fol. 119; Rawl. D. 1372, fol. 9v from end.

Here lies the mistress of the gods, 962
She will for ever youthful anthems sing.
Chatwin, John, 'On Celia'.
MS. *Rawl. poet. 94, p. 213 (autogr.).

Here lies the nag that bore the bag 963
In hopes to get another.
'The Epitaph'; see A849.
MS. Tanner 306, fol. 409.

Here lies the parents' hopes and fears 964
Thou'lt say he's blest that's soonest home.
'On a childs death'.
MSS. Ashmole 47, fol. 38v; CCC. 328, fol. 49v, attr. to Dr. [Brian] Duppa; see also H760.

965 Here lies the picture of pure honesty
Here lies, that friend whom young and old bemoan.

'On Mr. Edwards A Dearly Beloved Schoole Master'.
Pr. from this MS., *Cephalus and Procris*, by Thomas Edwards, ed. W. E. Buckley, Roxburghe Club, 1882, p. 76.
MS. Ashmole 38, p. 176.

966 Here lies the prize of badness, vice's nurse,
Worse than all these here lies my lady Wake.

'On the Lady Wake', rather, Lady Lake (wife of Sir Thomas).
MSS. Ashmole 36, 37, fol. 145v; see also H939, H1054, H1161.

967 Here lies the pulverized pearl
And angels food his cheer.

'An Epitaph in Lesslie Church Yard on an Old Servant in the Earl of Rothes's Family'.
MS. Eng. poet. e. 40, fol. 152.

968 Here lies the relicts of a martyred earl
To join three nations, and its head together.

'An Epitaph on James Earl of Derwentwater', executed 24 Feb. 1716.
MS. Rawl. poet. 181, fol. 64.

969 Here lies the ruined cabinet
Angels can only speak the rest.

On the grave-stone of William Hyckes at Shipton-upon-Stour, d. 1652.
Pr. *Ex otio negotium*, R. Fletcher, 1656.
MSS. Ballard 29, fol. 59v; Eng. misc. e. 183, fol. 49v.

970 Here lies the ruined mansion of that soul
Time saw not, nor consumed a goodlier frame.

'On the Lady Pellam of Buck'shire deseased Anno 1612'. See G. Lipscomb, *History and Antiquities of . . . Buckingham*, 1847, iii. 525.
MS. Ashmole 38, p. 183.

971 Here lies the sacred bones
The Dutchman's *templum pacis*.

[Marvell, Andrew], 'Upon [Clarendon's] House', *c.* 1665.
Pr. *Directions to a Painter*, 1667 (Gough MS. London 14).
MSS. Don. e. 23, fol. 29; Rawl. poet. 26, fol. 163v; see also H729.

972 Here lies the shame of the mitre
Could not and died.

'On the Bishop of Oxford', Samuel Parker, appointed 1686.
MS. Firth c. 16, p. 259.

Here lies the soldier that never drew his sword 973
Here lies the courtier that never kept his word.

'On Sir Robert Dudley Earle "of Warwicke" and Leicester', d. 1588.
Pr. *The Complete Peerage* as Jonson's. Not printed amongst his poems.
MS. Ashmole 38, p. 181.

Here lies the wife and daughter to a knight and a[n] esquire 974
Pray thou for foul Gillam that had the good p.

'On a gentellwoman In Lancastshire whose name Ile conceale'.
MS. Ashmole 38, p. 185.

Here lies the woman 975
Who refused no man.

Couplet, 'Epitaph on Miss Frydisweed Shawford of Windsor'.
MS. Eng. poet. e. 40, fol. 127.

Here lies the woman which did feign 976
Before is now detected.

Lines on Pope Joan copied in a music book.
MS. Mus. f. 19, fol. 53.

Here lies the worthy knight 977
And died alas therefore.

'Epitaphium'.
MS. Rawl. poet. 120, fol. 36*a*.

Here lies the worthy warrior 978
Whom earth, and heaven hates.

'The Earle of Leicesters Epitaph'; Robert Dudley, d. 1588; note in Peter le Neve's hand, MS. Don. b. 8, 'printed in [*Miscellanies Historical and Philological*, 1703]'.
MSS. Don. b. 8, p. 107; Wood D. 19(2), fol. 110v.

Here lies thrown for the worms to eat 979
Who stank while he lived and died of the pox.

'On the Death of Sir Robert Cecill Earl of Salisbury etc. on whome the black Cloud of detraction fell upon all hee said or did'.
Pr. Francis Osborne's *Historical Memoires on . . . King James*, 1658, p. 87.
MS. Ashmole 1463, p. 13.

Here lies thy urn, oh what a little blow 980
How much thou'st wronged thy maker, how mankind.

Hemmings, W[illiam], 'A Contemplation over the Duke [of Buckingham]'s grave', 1628.
MS. Malone 23, p. 130.

981 Here lies to make worms meat
Like to a dying lamp stunk and went out.
'Rober: Cæcilius comes Sarisburiensis', 1612.
MS. Eng. poet. f. 10, fol. 97.

982 Here lies [Tom] Thom Dashe that notable railer
That in his life ne'er paid shoemaker nor tailor.
'Epitaph on a Spendthrift'.
MS. Eng. poet. e. 40, fol. 114.

983 Here lies Tom Nick's body
Whether fools souls goes to heaven or hell.
'Upon A foole'.
Pr. Camden's *Remaines*, 1605, p. 56.
MS. Ashmole 38, p. 170; see also H1056.

984 Here lies unpitied both by church and state
And unforgiving, unforgiven died.
Chesterfield [the Earl of], 'An Epitaph on Q. Caroline', 1737.
Pr. bk. Firth b. 22, fol. 37.

985 Here lies Veale, whom death hath lately taken
That Veale, and bacon should no better agree.
'On Thomas Veale who died of a surfett of Bacon'.
MS. Ashmole 38, p. 204.

986 Here lies where hard marble may well be a mourner
All the bells in Allhallowes thy worth will proclaim.
Pancroft, Thomas, 'Epitaph on George Blagrave Clarke of Allhallows Church in Derby', 165–.
MS. Ashmole 1463, p. 2.

987 Here lies Will, and there lies his brother
Sampson slew one, and Dallila the other.
'Upon two Oxford fellow-Commoners Brothers', couplet.
MS. Rawl. poet. 26, fol. 163$^{v}$.

988 Here lies William Emerson
Who lived and died an honest man.
Couplet, in the church of 'St. Mary Overy' or 'St. Mary Saviours'.
MSS. Ashmole 38, p. 180; Eng. poet. e. 40, fol. 111.

989 Here lies wise and valiant dust
Speechless still, and never cry.
Cleveland, [John](?) 'On the Earl of Strafford'.
Pr. *Character of a London Diurnal and Poems*, 1647. Included in MS. 'Golden Remains' of C. Paman.
MSS. Don. e. 6, fol. 29$^{v}$, attr. to Cleaveland; Eng. poet. c. 50, fol. 122; e. 97, p. 193; Rawl. D. 1099, fol. 190 rev.; Rawl. poet. 71, p. 146; see also H1090.

Here lies wise, chaste, hospitable, humble 990
Here lies her body but her soul's below.
'An Epitaph on the Dutches of Newcastle' [Margaret, 2nd wife of the first Duke, d. 15 Dec. 1673].
MSS. Ashmole 36, 37, fol. 186$^{v}$; 1463, fol. 62$^{v}$.

Here lies within a cabinet of stone 991
And now enjoys it with the saints in heaven.
Wither, Ge[orge], 'An Epitaph on A Child Sonn unto Sr. W. H. Knight'.
Pr. 'A Miscelany of Epigrams' in *Faire Virtue*, 1622, Sig. O6$^{v}$.
MS. Ashmole 38, p. 167.

Here lies within this holy place 992
As once he did his conscience.
'Epitaph on the Wheasel', [Dr. Wm. Sherlock, Dean of St. Paul's, d. 19 June 1707].
MSS. Eng. poet. e. 87, p. 72; Rawl. poet. 81, fol. 44$^{v}$.

Here lies within this maestful monument 993
Henry sans peer, great Britain's lost delight.
G. B. (?), 'On Prince Henry's death'.
MS. *Rawl. poet. 116, fol. 3.

Here lies wrapped up in mould for worms to smell at 994
Whose good deeds in his lifetime none remembers.
Endorsed, 'Epitaph on ABC' i.e. Abp. of Canterbury, Tillotson, 1694.
MS. Rawl. poet. 181, fol. 18.

Here lieth a church warden 995*a*
Who died in good fame.
'In Wrexham church', on Joseph Cratchley.
MS. Hearne's diaries 102, p. 145.

Here lieth a lawyer, and an honest man 995*b*
God doth work miracles now and than.
MS. Malone 19, p. 151; see also G326, H1020.

Here lieth an honest man 996
To be an honest man than live many days.
'An Epitaph'.
MS. Ashmole 781, p. 156.

Here lieth Andrew Gray 997
For he was wont them for to stone.
MS. Wood D. 19(2), fol. 109$^{v}$.

Here lieth bald John Hussillo 998
And wenches to dance very trim.
MS. Wood D. 19(2), fol. 110.

Here lieth Bellandrando 999
And that which he had not he gave away.
MS. Wood D. 19(2), fol. 109$^{v}$.

1000 Here lieth Bounce a maker of bellows
He that made bellows could not make breath.

'Upon a bellows maker'.

MS. Ashmole 38, p. 172; see also B613, H783, H846, H848, H1019, H1026, H1034.

1001 Here lieth buried Sir Henry Wallope
After whose soul the devil did gallop.

Couplet.

MS. Ashmole 38, p. 203.

1002 Here lieth C. under ground
Drink was his life, and drink was his end.

'Epitaph on a hard Drinker'.

MS. Eng. poet. e. 40, fol. 118; see also H813, H1008.

1003 Here lieth Dick Dobson y-wrapped in mould
That grubbed up the hair, to starve up the lice.

'qd. D.', i.e. Sir John Davies, 'An other Epitaph: of one who died with the Maple buttons'.

MS. Rawl. poet. 148, fol. 4v; see also H855, H881.

1004 Here lieth Doctor Jiggins of Bennet college master
That broke the university's head and gave the schools a plaster.

Couplet, on J. Jegons of C.C.C. Cambridge.

MS. Rawl. poet. 117, fol. 271 rev.; see also H679, H796, H858.

1005 Here lieth entombed John Bonner by name,
Evil's his kinsman and so I do end.

'The Epitaph of John Bonner', 1618, 'in the chancel of Mickleton Church in Gloucestershire', given by the Hon. B. L. Calvert to Hearne.

Pr. Hearne's *Guilelmus Neubrigensis*, 1719, ii. 764.

MSS. Hearne's diaries 66, p. 3; Rawl. D. 1164, fol. 245v.

1006 Here lieth for all that please to see
As any could be found in all our country.

Inscription on Robert Smith, 1596, 'Engraven upon a Brasse in Brancaster Church [in Norfolk]'.

Pr. Hearne's *Guilelmus Neubrigensis*, 1719, ii. 764.

MSS. Rawl. D. 1164, fol. 245v; Rawl. poet. 26, fol. 161.

1007 Here lieth graven under this stone
And nineteen children they had in feere.

Epitaph on Thomas Knowles, grocer and alderman.

MS. Sancroft 59, p. 282 rev.

Here lieth Gresham underground 1008
Drink was his life, and drunk his end.

'On Gresham a drunkard'.

MS. Malone 19, p. 150; see also H813, H1002.

Here lieth he 1009
Which with himself could never agree.

Couplet, 'Epitaph on a fretful man'.

MS. Eng. poet. e. 40, fol. 108.

Here lieth he, who liveth not 1010
For killing of a handsome Scot.

Couplet.

MS. Rawl. poet. 31, fol. 37.

Here lieth he who was born and cried, 1011
Told threescore years, fell sick and died.

'On one that lived ingloriously', couplet.

Pr. Camden's *Remaines*, 1605, p. 58.

Cf. *Life*, etc., of J. Hoskyns, L. B. Osborn, 1937, p. 171.

MSS. Eng. poet. e. 14, fol. 95 rev.; e. 40, fol. 115; see also H756, H1038.

Here lieth hid under this stone 1012
God did her call from house to heaven.

On Jane Calthorpe, 1550. St. Martin at the Plain's Chancel, Norwich.

MS. Top. gen. e. 32, fol. 29.

Here lieth hidden in this pit 1013
The grave his corpse, Stukley his shame.

'On Sir Walter Rawleigh', copied by Aubrey from among 'the papers of . . . Tho. Tyndale Esq. obit 167–, ætat 85'.

MS. Aubrey 6, fol. 79; see also H768.

Here lieth his grace, and if his race be bad 1014
It is for want of that which whilst he lived he had.

'On Richard Bankroft' Abp. of Canterbury.

Pr. H. Huth, *Inedited Poetical Miscellanies*, 1870.

MS. Firth d. 7, fol. 160; see also H820.

Here lieth interred in mouldy bed of clay 1015
Henceforth in joy: princess regent always.

'Epitaph found in St. Worbars church in Chester'.

MS. Dodsworth 61, fol. 65.

Here lieth interred worm's meat; 1016
That stank alive, and died of the pox.

On Robert Cecil Earl of Salisbury, 1612.

Pr. Francis Osborne's *Historical Memoires on . . . King James*, 1658, p. 87.

MS. Tanner 299, fol. 12; see also H832.

1017 Here lieth John,
And yet died young.

Inscription on the tomb of John Young, d. Nov. 19th 1688 aged 100, in the church-yard at Headington.
Pr. Hearne's *Guilelmus Neubrigensis*, 1719, ii. 763.
MS. Rawl. D. 1164, fol. 244v.

1018 Here lieth John Bently
For Godsake tread on him gently.

Couplet.
MS. Wood D. 19(2), fol. 109.

1019 Here lieth John Cruker a maker of bellows
He that made bellows could not make breath.

'An Epitaph writ several years since by Mr. John Hoskins on a Bellows Maker at Oxford'.
MS. Eng. poet. e. 40, fol. 106; see also B613, H783, H846, H848, H1000, H1026, H1034.

1020 Here lieth John Doulton deny it who can
That was a lawyer and an honest man.

'On a Lawyer', couplet.
MS. Rawl. poet. 172, fol. 15v; see also G326, H995.

1021 Here lieth Jo[hn] Loddington
Who was burnt with a whore at Abbington.

MS. Wood D. 19(2), fol. 109v.

1022 Here lieth John Owen
Or he lies in his throat.

'Epitaph'.
MS. Rawl. poet. 172, fol. 15v.

1023 Here lieth John Swan of Lumbard street
That was bearded to the belly, and bellied to the feet.

Couplet.
MS. Rawl. poet. 117, fol. 271 rev.

1024 Here lieth John the chandler,
Yet he could not make days.

'Epitaph'.
MS. Rawl. poet. 172, fol. 15v.

1025 Here lieth Katherine Prettyman
Now lives and ever shall.

Subscribed 'Aug. the 11 1594'.
MS. Rawl. poet. 117, fol. 158 rev.

1026 Here lieth Kitt Craker, the King of good fellows
He that made bellows, could not make breath.

'qd. D[avies]', [Sir John], 'An Epitaph'.
MS. Rawl. poet. 148, fol. 4v; see also B613, H783, H846, H848, H1000, H1019, H1034.

Here lieth lady Maria in earthly press 1027
That died thirty days before she was a countess.

Couplet.
MS. Wood D. 19(2), fol. 109v; see also H954.

Here lieth Lightborne dead in a ditch 1028
As down with your hose and shit in his face.

'An Epitaph upon Lightborne a sergeant A very knave'.
MS. Rawl. poet. 160, fol. 163v.

Here lieth (Lord have mercy upon her) 1029
And yet died a maid the more was the pity.

'Epitaph'.
MSS. Rawl. poet. 117, fol. 179 rev.; 172, fol. 15v; see also H956.

Here lieth Menalcas as dead as a log 1030
Without either book candle or bell.

'Upon Menalcas a wicked fellow'.
Pr. Camden's *Remaines*, 1605, p. 51.
MSS. Ashmole 38, p. 177, Eng. poet. e. 40, fol. 120.

Here lieth Mr. Dillaman 1031
And therefore he lieth here in poverty.

MS. Wood D. 19(2), fol. 109.

Here lieth N. a man of fame 1032
The first of his house and last of his name.

Pr. Camden's *Remaines*, 1605, p. 59.
MS. Ashmole 38, p. 176; see also H877.

Here lieth now dead, that late was quick 1033
Upon her soul say god have mercy.

'In St. Bartholomews hospitall in Smithfilde this', on Ann Westwicke, 1556.
MS. Ashmole 38, p. 202.

Here lieth old [Coker] Croker the mender of bellows. 1034
For he that made wind could never make breath.

'Epitaph'.
MSS. Rawl. poet. 172, fol. 15v; Wood D. 19(2), fol. 109; see also B613, H783, H846, H848, H1000, H1019, H1026.

Here lieth old Cromwell 1035
But half to his bastards and half to his whore.

MS. Wood D. 19(2), fol. 109.

Here lieth old father Lock's body at rest 1036
For, he carefully locked it up all in his heart.

Robinson, Robert.
MS. *Rawl. poet. 218, p. 59 (autogr.).

Here lieth old Henery 1037
Which was surnamed Abingdon.

'Epitaph'.
MS. Rawl. poet. 172, fol. 15v.

1038 Here lieth one was born and cried
Told ninety years, fell sick and died.
'Upon an old man noted for nothing butt his Age', couplet.
MS. Ashmole 38, p. 172; see also H756, H1011.

1039 Here lieth one who vexed with a wife
Would cause his brother Peter to lock her out.
'On the death of Andrew'.
MS. Eng. poet. f. 10, fol. 94v.

1040 Here lieth Owen, that of late did die
You did not know him, no more did I.
Couplet.
MSS. Firth e. 4, p. 13; Rawl. poet. 172, fol. 15; see also H884, H894.

1041 Here lieth Palavaseen of Babram
Who is now in the bosom of Abram.
Couplet on Sir Horatio Palavicino, d. 1600. Answered by S925.
MS. Malone 19, p. 148.

1042 Here lieth Penelope or my Lady Rich
Which in her life was not content with two.
'Epitaph, Laydie Rich'.
MS. Rawl. poet. 172, fol. 15v, see also H888, H898, H944.

1043 Here lieth Rascobell
To make a man to bleed.
MS. Wood D. 19(2), fol. 109.

1044 Here lieth Richard A Preene
And he that will die after him, may.
'Epitaph'.
MS. Eng. poet. e. 40, fol. 111; see also H906.

1045 Here lieth Rich[ard] Saywell
Who never spent daywell.
Couplet.
MS. Wood. D. 19(2), fol. 109v.

1046 Here lieth Robbin Crooktback, unjustly reckoned
A Crooktback great in state is England's curse.
On Robert Cecil, Earl of Salisbury, 1612.
MS. Tanner 299, fol. 13.

1047 Here lieth she, she lieth here
Alas fell sick and died.
'Upon A love sicke maide'.
MS. Ashmole 38, p. 174.

1048 Here lieth she who brooking ill the light,
Whilst nature long stood doubting, she consumed.
Pagitt, Thomas, 'Epitaph' on Elizabeth Pagitt, sister of the poet.
MSS. Ashmole 36, 37, fol. 175.

Here lieth Sir John Spenser an ell deep in ground 1049
That after a Spencer there should come a Spender.
'Epitaph upon Sir John Spencer', d. 3 March 1609/10.
MS. Ashmole 781, p. 152.

Here lieth Sir John Spencer an ell under ground 1050
For since that he died we had four eggs a penny.
Epitaph on Sir John Spencer, 3 March 1609/10.
MS. Rawl. poet. 117, fol. 179 rev.

Here lieth Sir Thomas Cokain made knight at tourney 1051
Live here in everlasting fame.
Sir Thomas Cokain, Kt., [d. 1592], Ashbourne, Derbyshire.
MS. Ashmole 854, fol. 44v.

Here lieth the body of Perkin a Leigh 1052
In Pariis.
Monumental verses, 1620, to Perkin Leigh and his son Sir Piers, Macclesfield.
MS. Top. Cheshire c. 9, fol. 80v.

Here lieth the body of Will Fauntleroye Esquier slain 1053
For ever in Heaven with saints there to remain.
'Epitaphium. An. 1607 13 Martii'.
MS. Add. B. 97, fol. 24v.

Here lieth the brief of badness, vice's nurse 1054
Worse then all these, lieth here the Lady [Lake].
'Of the Lady Lake'.
MS. Smith 17, p. 113; see also H939, H966, H1161.

Here lieth Thomas Peirce whom no man taught 1055
Until he rise again no more to die.
'Berkely Cemitery On a Tomb', no date.
MS. Rawl. D. 1090, fol. 225.

Here lieth Tom Nick's body 1056
Whether fool's souls go to heaven or hell.
'An epitaph'.
MS. Eng. misc. e. 240, fol. 34; see also H983.

Here lieth W. Wise with his little kitty 1057
I prethee Will do put a tune to 't too.
MS. Malone 19, p. 142.

Here lieth Watt Lightfoote, that many a race run, 1058
Death so hath benumbed him, he can run no longer.
Robinson, Robert, 'An Epitaph upon a race runner'.
MS. *Rawl. poet. 218, p. 26 (autogr.).

1059 Here lieth Willyam Sydney, Thomasine and Isabell
Pray all we in heaven that they may have a place.
'Th' epitaphie' on William Sydney, d. 6 July 1449.
MS. Ashmole 836, fol. 105.

1060 Here lieth willing Wills
With his head full of windmills.
'Epitaph on the Whimsical Doctor Wills. he died at Vienna 1630. or there abouts'. Couplet.
MS. Eng. poet. e. 40, fol. 109.

1061 Here lived and died an useless thing,
A peevish, stiff, pedantic clown.
'On an Old Fellow of a College', *Whitehall Evening Post*, 12 Jan. 1737–8.
MS. Eng. misc. e. 183, fol. 71$^{v}$.

1062 Here lives a man whose age is fifty-four
Then kill'd his wife and now he keeps a whore.
'A true History, 1738'.
MS. Firth c. 16, p. 308.

1063 Here lives a peer raised by indulgent fate
True to his God, and faithful to his trust.
'An Elogy', answer to T1177.
Pr. *Poems on Affairs of State*, iii, 1698, p. 304.
MSS. Firth c. 15, p. 230; c. 16, p. 135.

1064 Here lives the tiny Foot. Each creature knows him
Since here's analogy 'twixt *rem* and *vocem*.
'Epigram, On the little Foot, written over his Door'. 1735.
MS. Eng. misc. e. 240, p. 259.

1065 Here low in dust the vain Hortensio lies
And on his tomb all of Hortensio lives.
'On seeing the Monument of Hortensio'.
MS. Eng. poet. d. 47, fol. 8$^{v}$.

1066 Here man who first, should heavenly things attain,
Their gain is loss, and seek their souls to sterve.
Whitney, Geoffrey, 'Nemo potest duobus dominis servire'.
MS. *Rawl. poet. 56, fol. 124.

1067 Here meet the dust of Caesar, Alexander,
Till fame sounds consort to the trump of doom.
Roach, Richard, 'An Epitaph. On John Duke of Marlborough etc.', English and Latin.
MS. Rawl. D. 832, fol. 168 (autogr.).

1068 Here Milossa surrend'red up his ghost
A place most fit for such a damned crew.
'On a drunkard'.
MS. Eng. poet. e. 14, fol. 93 rev.

Here Mrs. Ashe's Townsend lies 1069
But death her hopes did in the birth destroy.
Williams, John, 'The Epitaph on Miss Ashe's Thrush apply'd to Collonel Townsend who died about the same time'.
MS. *Rawl. poet. 184, fol. 91 (autogr.).

Here must we rest; and where else should we rest? 1070
Since this wherein I lie, my grave's become.
[Austin, William], 'a serious and a curious night-Meditation'.
MS. Lat. misc. f. 45, p. 209, in the hand of Philip Traherne; see also H1132.

Here Myra lies within this massy tomb, 1071
And hungry worms riot on her charms.
'On Myra's Tomb, who died on her Wedding Day'.
MS. *Eng. poet. d. 47, fol. 6$^{v}$.

Here neighbour here's to thee, 1072
For the red-lettered tory, and roundheaded whig.
'A Catch, To the Tune now the Tyrant hath stol'n etc.'.
MS. Eng. poet. d. 53, p. 1.

Here old Sir Henry Lee doth lie 1073
He doth lie; and she doth kneel.
Randale, T., 'On Sir Hen: Leigh nere Salisburie and his Concubine pictured kneeling beside his tomb'.
MS. Top. Cheshire c. 6, fol. 415$^{v}$; see also H803, H1099.

Here Oldfield lies, enrolled be her name. 1074
In pleasure sweetly lost ten thousand ways.
'An Epitaph on . . . Mrs. Anne Oldfield, Decd. Oct. 23 1730'.
MS. Eng. poet. e. 40, fol. 36.

Here on a river rides the silver swan 1075
The pictures lively, though the men be dead.
Browne, Thomas, 'verses upon severall pictures in the gallerie at York-House'. Really part of V42.
Pr. by H. Huth, *Inedited Poetical Miscellanies*, 1870.
MSS. Firth d. 7, fol. 183, attr. to Thomas Browne; Rawl. poet. 142, fol. 25$^{v}$.

Here on earth (which but a stage is) 1076
Then comes death, and pays their wages.
Robinson, Robert.
MS. *Rawl. poet. 218, p. 22 (autogr.).

1077 Here once my princess when she first did meet
So rare a gem should not be set in lead.

'On the print of a Lady's foot carved on Kings Coll. Chappell leads where [be]fore shee had fallen'.

Pr. *Wit and Drollery*, 1661, p. 134.

MSS. Rawl. poet. 116, fol. 42ᵛ; 147, p. 1, attr. to Geo. Goad; 210, fol. 49, attr. to Geo. Goad.

1078 Here or elsewhere (all's one to you or me)
Not how you live, but how you spend your days.

Acrostic on Henry Marten, 1680, with prefatory verse *beg.* 'Who in Berkshire was well known'.

MS. Top. Oxon. b. 116, fol. 100ᵛ.

1079 Here, or not many feet from hence,
Ask who they were, and thou hast done.

Corbett, Richard, 'Certaine true Words Spoken concerning one Benet Corbet [his mother] after her death', 2 Oct. 1634.

MS. CCC. 315*b*, fol. 351ᵛ, attr. to Ri. Norv.; 325, fol. 26ᵛ, attr. to Ri: Norv:

1080 Here our well-founded friendships first commence,
Good faith and love and loyalty be ours.

'To the Gentlemen educated at Abingdon School'.

MS. Eng. misc. e. 183, fol. 57.

1081 Here over I'm come I'd as good gone to Rome
Not care of a farthing who's undone.

'K. George [I]'s just Complaint'.

MSS. Rawl. poet. 155, p. 116; 207, p. 21.

1082 Here Plautus' old unpolish'd scenes impart
And lose the critic in the father's smile.

Hammond, James.

MS. Rawl. poet. 129, fol. 1ᵛ.

1083 Here poor worms we creep and crawl.
Thus it has been, is, will be so.

Robinson, Robert.

MS. *Rawl. poet. 218, p. 35 (autogr.).

1084 Here reading how fond Adam was betrayed
Adam had never fallen, or Milton wrote.

Prior, Matthew, 'To my Lady Dursley on her reading Milton's Paradise Lost'.

Pr. Dryden's *Miscellany*, iv, 1694, p. 110.

MSS. Add. B. 105, fol. 82; Rawl. poet. 153, fol. 70ᵛ.

1085 Here reigns Queen Sarah and K[ing] John
Here lives P[rince] G[eorge] and P[rincess] Anne.

'Another Satyr o'er St. Jam's Gate', on the Duke and Duchess of Marlborough, couplet.

MS. Rawl. D. 361, fol. 345ᵛ.

Here rest I Henry Franckland knight 1086
Too long I stood, too soon I fell.

'Sir Henry Franckland upon himself'.

MS. Don. d. 58, fol. 18ᵛ.

Here rests her mortal frame; her spirit flies 1087
She wags her tail and barks at the great bear.

'Epitaph on a Lady's Lapdog'.

MS. Eng. misc. e. 241, fol. 95ᵛ.

Here rests his dust who came to find 1088
Holy holy holy prince of peace.

James, Richard, 'A funerall meditation on Richard Windsore a gentle condiciond man whoe found his death where he sought peace'.

MS. *James 35, p. 7 (autogr.).

Here rests the just and pious Jane 1089
Enforced her husband these to write.

On Jane Tyrrel, 1638, by her husband, Southry Church in the Fens. Copied by E. Ashmole, 1658.

MS. Ashmole 784, fol. 18ᵛ.

Here rests wise and valiant dust 1090
Speechless still and never cry.

[Cleveland, John( ?)], 'Epitaph on the Earle of Strafford Beheaded on tower Hill, May 12, 1641'.

MSS. Douce 357, fol. 11ᵛ; Rawl. poet. 26, fol. 131ᵛ; see also H989.

Here Robbin roosteth in his last nest 1091
And now the worms this Robbin eat.

On Robert Cecil, Earl of Salisbury, 1612.

MS. Tanner 299, fol. 13.

Here Samuel of Oxon lies under this stone 1092
But his tongue, and his horns both, are put in the grave.

'Epit. in Sam: [Parker] Episc: Oxon: Hac Calieni Raptor etc. Englished', 1688.

MS. Don. c. 55, fol. 18.

Here Sarum lies of late as wise 1093
For Marlborough and his Duchess.

On the death of Bp. Burnet, 1715.

Pr. from Hearne's 'Remarks and Observations', 11 April 1715, *Collections* v, O.H.S. xlii, 1901 p. 44.

MSS. Ballard 50, fol. 176; Eng. poet. e. 87, p. 10; f. 12, p. 94; Hearne's diaries 53, p. 117*e*; Rawl. D. 169, fol. 21; Rawl. poet. 155, p. 148; pr. bk. Firth b. 22, fol. 17.

1094 Here several ways Lot, and great Abram go;
And Lot talks with them both on either side.

Cowley, A[braham], 'The separation of Lott, and Abram in picture' 'David p. 89'.
Pr. *Poems . . . and Davideis*, 1656, p. 89.
MS. Tanner 466, fol. 15.

1095 Here she lies and lies not
And yet a woman.

Epitaph on a woman whose name was Not.
Pr. bk. Douce P 690, *An Antidote against. Melancholy*, 1661, stuck on to the back cover.

1096 Here she lies in, who held a strife
He by the font she by the grave.

Paman, Clement, 'Epitaph on Mrs. Warnar who died in Child-birth'.
MS. Rawl. poet. 147, p. 159.

1097 Here she lies, whose spotless fame
The grave is but a cabinet.

'In the temple church in London. For Mrs. Anne Littleton'.
MS. Sancroft 59, p. 291 rev.

1098 Here silken twine, there locks you see
Now tell me which the softer be.

Strode, William, Posy for 'An Earestring', couplet.
MS. *CCC. 325, fol. 79$^v$ (autogr.).
MS. Eng. poet. c. 50, fol. 130$^v$.

1099 Here Sir H. L. is lying
He lies down and she do's kneel.

'Upon Sir H. L. who had a fair Monumt. for himself, his own statue in marble lying at length; and his Mistresse kneeling by him'.
MS. Don. e. 6, fol. 23; see also H803, H1073.

1100 Here sits a nymph in nature's shady grace
This stone once walked and Jennings was its name.

'On a Lady at Bath'.
MS. Eng. misc. e. 241, fol. 63$^v$.

1101 Here six [feet] foot deep
And first that found the way.

'An Epitaph upon one who dyed in the Act of Venery'.
MSS. Add. B. 8, fol. 71$^v$ 'upon the Lord Lamport'; Ashmole 38, p. 183; Douce f. 5, fol. 9; Eng. poet. e. 14, fol. 94$^v$ rev.; Hearne's diaries 30, p. 212; Malone 19, p. 94; Top. Oxon. e. 202, fol. 104, headed 'On my Lord of Dunsmore'; see also H681, H1117.

Here sleeps a brother, wake him not; 1102
So it never had been known.

'An Epitaph. 1649'.
MS. Mus. f. 5, fol. 95$^v$.

Here sleeps beneath in dust (oh sad to see 1103
Do make her dust to blush, for so would she.

Budd, —, 'Epitaph' on Mistress Anna Budd, 1665; see S1187.
MS. Rawl. poet. 65, fol. 93$^v$.

Here sleeps thirteen, together in one tomb 1104
Took pet, and withered.

'On Mr. Thomas Randolphe'.
MS. Ashmole 38, p. 208.

Here slumber free among the dead 1105
It rapt her to her native skies.

'Epitaph on Mrs. Hole. Collect. Poems'.
MS. Eng. poet. e. 39, p. 72.

Here sooner or later all mortals I trow 1106
Their burdens lay down, both the high and the low.

Amherst, Elizabeth, 'Inscriptions intended for Newbold, 1771, Over the Grotto Door. *Necessitas non habet legem*', couplet.
MS. *Eng. poet. e. 109, p. 64.

Here Spinola lies hid, enough is said, 1107
Spain had on earth ta'en fewer places far.

Copied by Abednego Seller from James Howell's *History of Lewis XIII*, 1646, p. 95.
MS. Rawl. D. 1110, fol. 119$^v$ rev.

Here stands a thing usurps the British throne 1108
None but his whore e'er found him flesh and blood.

'On K. G[eorge]'s Statute Sett up in the Royal Exchange'. Marked 'R. C.'
MS. Eng. misc. c. 116, fol. 7.

Here — stay, tears, until these obsequies 1109
And keep it fair until the day of doom.

Kindar, Philip (1597– ), 'Upon the death of the Lord Hastings . . . printed amongst other Elegies', in *Elegies* collected . . . by R. B[rome], 1649, p. 37.
MS. Ashmole 788, fol. 148$^v$ (autogr.).

Here (strangers) lies proud Sam of Oxon 1110
With everlasting infamy.

'Epitaphium', Samuel Parker, Bp. of Oxford, d. 1688.
MS. Firth c. 16, p. 249.

Here such a creature breeds whose ugly sight 1111
The scorn of men and gods eternal curse.

'The Presbyterian unmasked'.
MS. North b. 1, fol. 245.

1112 Here take my picture, though I bid farewell
To feed on that which to disused tastes seems tough.
Donne, John, 'Elegye' v.
MSS. *Eng. poet. e. 99, fol. 18$^{v}$; *f. 9, p. 80; Rawl. poet. 117, fol. 219 rev., copied as continuation of Elegy **xvi**; 160, fol. 113, attr. to J. D.

1113 Here take this Warcop: spread it up and down
With horns instead of bays the hero crowned.
'To Capt. Warcop'.
MS. Firth c. 16, p. 69.

1114 Here, take your staff (brave Palmer) carry far,
I am your priest, will clerk be too; Amen.
Dalt[on (?)], I., S.T.P., 'To the Oliver Palmer, of Bedford, shared, 'twixt Earth and Heaven'. 20 May 1657.
MS. Rawl. D. 886, fol. 6.

1115 Here Tantalus, as poets do divine,
And dares not touch, his store, when he doth need.
Whitney, Geoffrey, 'Avaritia'.
MS. *Rawl. poet. 56, fol. 44$^{v}$.

1116 Here the poor Lares housed are
Then might the merry Lares sing.
'On the Lares fixt on the Duke of Buckingham's House in St. James's Park'. Cf. H152.
MS. Rawl. poet. 116, fol. 111.

1117 Here three foot deep in his last sleep
And first that found that way.
'Æpita.'.
MSS. Eng. poet. f. 10, fol. 116$^{v}$; Hearne's diaries 12, p. 92, answer attr. to Charles II and the Earl of Rochester; see also H681, H1101.

1118 Here thrown by time old Parkyns laid
As soon as he gets up again.
'Sir Thomas Parkyns 1741'.
MS. Top. gen. e. 32, fol. 15$^{v}$.

1119 Here to a period is the scrivener come
A dash alone of his pen ruined many.
'An Epitaph on a scrivener'.
MS. CCC. 328, fol. 58.

1120 Here two rich ravished spirits kiss and twine
Who has outdone, and quite undone the rest.
Pestell, Thomas, 'on the Interlinearie pöeme bigott twixt Sir H. Goo[dyere] and Dr. Donne'.
MS. *Malone 14, p. 28.

Here under lies Prince Henry wrapped in lead 1121
In his young brother Charles new life they have.
G. B., 'Epitaph 31', on Prince Henry in 'Cestria Lugens', 1612.
MS. *Rawl. poet. 116, fol. 13$^{v}$.

Here under lieth amongst these stones 1122
Of Rixam Clark old Daniel Jones.
Pr. Hearne's *Guilelmus Neubrigensis*, 1719, ii. 763.
MS. Rawl. D. 1164, fol. 245; see also H952.

Here under Pie, lies Furioso tamed 1123
All hence depart till further news, we bring ho.
'An Epitaph', with changes rung upon it.
MS. Rawl. D. 832, fol. 155.

Here under this stake lies Strephon interred 1124*a*
Then he had survived, and drove his stake into her.
'On Mr. . . . A Hopefull young Gentleman who upon the Disdain of his Mistress slew himself, and was buryed in the Highway with a Stake drove through him. Epitaph'.
MS. Don. c. 55, fol. 20$^{v}$.

Here under was buried Robert Barnes by name 1124*b*
How godly he departed the twentieth on November.
Epitaph on Robert Barnes, St. Michael's, Cornhill.
Pr. Hearne's *Collections*, ed. C. E. Doble, i, O.H.S. ii, 1885, p. 278.
MS. Hearne's diaries, 11, p. 175.

Here underneath grim Oxford lies 1125
Or had an honest thought.
'An Epitaph design'd for the E. of Oxford'. [Robert Harley].
MS. Rawl. poet. 155, p. 65.

Here underneath lies Osteler Will 1126
How much! I cannot tell, can you?
'An Epitaph on a Tomb-Stone at Edmonton', Latin and English.
MS. Eng. poet. e. 40, fol. 1.

Here underneath lies Phillip Sidney, Knight 1127
Which oft he termed a diamond set in brass.
B. W. [Whetsone, Bernard (?)], 'Of Sidney, the Epitaph'.
MS. Malone 6, fol. 52$^{v}$.

Here underneath this stone doth lie 1128
Who spared no cost for clothes or diet.
'On J[ames], E[arl] of C[arlisle]', d. 1636.
MS. Ashmole 38, fol. 240.

Here underneath this stone doth lie . . . see also Wouldst thou hear . . .

1129 **Here uninterred, suspends, though not to save Contend, to reach his body to his soul.**

'Jo. Feltons Epitaph'.

In B.M. Add. MS. 15226, fol. 28, attr. to H[enry] Ch[olmley]. Pr. *Wit Restor'd*, 1658, p. 56; *A New Collection of Poems relating to State Affairs* 1705, p. 162, absurdly attr. to 'the . . . Duke of Buckingham'.

MSS. Ashmole 38, p. 20, attr. to D. Donn; 47, fol. 48; CCC. 328, two copies, fols. 11$^{v}$ and 62; Eng. poet. c. 53, fol. 9; e. 14, fol. 12$^{v}$; Malone 21, fol. 4$^{v}$; 23, p. 210; Rawl. poet. 84, fol. 114; 147, p. 40; 160, fol. 53; 199, p. 56; Tanner 465, fol. 71$^{v}$.

1130 **Here we all the same danger run The thread when cut both same scissors feel.**

Fairfax, Thomas, Lord, 'Of Impartial Fate'.

MS. *Fairfax 40, p. 601 (autogr.); see also I1392*b*.

1131 **Here we do live, strange things we spy: Christ our whole man at last will save.**

Robinson, Robert.

MS. *Rawl. poet. 218, p. 157 (autogr.).

1132 **Here we must rest: and where else should we rest? *Sepulcrum enim domus mea est.***

Austin, William, 'Sepulcrum domus mea est, meditatio 5' in 'Divers devout and zealous meditations upon our Saviour's Passion'.

Pr. *Certain . . . Meditations*, 1635, p. 289.

MSS. Rawl. D. 301, fol. 20, attr. to W.A., fol. 1; Rawl. poet. 61, fol. 25, attr. to W. Austen; see also H1070.

1133 **Here where by all, all saints invoked are, He that believes himself, doth never lie.**

Donne, John, 'A letter to the lady Carey, and Mrs. Essex Riche from Amyens'.

MSS. *Eng. poet. e. 99, fol. 38$^{v}$; *f. 9, p. 77.

1134 **Here where fair fancy, sad neglected maid She sees, with transport sees, a Jesser's name.**

Parsons, William, 'To Miss M. M. Jesser'.

MS. *Don. d. 123, p. 33 (autogr.).

1135 **Here, where our Lord once laid his head, Now the grave lies buried.**

Crashaw, Richard, 'On our Saviours Sepulcher', couplet.

Pr. *Steps to the Temple*, 1646.

MS. Tanner 465, fol. 37$^{v}$, attr. to Mr. Crashaw, fol. 1*a*.

**Here Whitefoord reclines, and deny it who can, Yet content if the table he set in a roar.** 1136

[Goldsmith, Oliver], 'Postscript to the Retaliation, Epitaph on Mr. Whitefoord'. An incomplete note reads 'Mr. W was so notorious a punster, that Goldsmith . . .'.

Pr. bk. Vet. A5 d. 569, added at end.

**Here William lies; a name by Britons loved And love young Watkin for his father's sake.** 1137

'Memoriæ W. W. W. Baronetti' [Sir Watkin Williams-Wynn, 3rd Baronet, 1749].

MS. Eng. poet. c. 51, p. 58.

**Here Withers rest, thou bravest, gentlest mind, The last true Briton lies beneath this stone.** 1138

Pope, [Alexander], 'General Withers Epitaph'.

Pr. Pope's *Minor Poems*, ed. N. Ault and J. Butt, 1954, p. 320.

MSS. Add. D. 79, fol. 88$^{v}$ rev.; Rawl. poet. 207, p. 154; Top. Oxon. c. 108, p. 45, attr. to Mr. Pope.

**Here without law condemned Strafford lies So in an age his death revenged may be.** 1139

'On the E. of Strafford', 1641.

MS. Rawl. poet. 246, fol. 24$^{v}$.

**Here worthy of a better chest Too good a stone to be engraved.** 1140

'On Mr. Ben Stone of New College'.

MSS. CCC. 328, fol. 62$^{v}$; Eng. poet. e. 14, fol. 77 rev.; Malone 19, p. 61, attr. to R[ichard] Zouch; Rawl. poet. 199, p. 57; Tanner 466, fol. 66$^{v}$.

**Here youthful innocence of humble birth Each modest virtue that becomes thy state.** 1141

On Frances Kent, 1777, Eartham Church Yard, Essex.

MS. Top. gen. e. 32, fol. 117.

**Here's a health . . .** see also **Here's an health . . .**

**Here's a health to great George heavens bless him A minute of midnight is worth a whole . . . (incomplete).** 1142

Samber, Robert.

MS. Rawl. poet. 11, fol. 33$^{v}$ (autogr.).

**Here's a health to great William, I'm sure then no harm can betide here.** 1143

Spoure, Edmund, 'A Health to our King [William III] in Flanders'.

MS. *Eng. poet. c. 52, fols. 54$^{v}$, 58–60 (autogr.).

1144 Here's a health to honest John Bull
To be happy as long as he's good.
'Honest John Bull'.
MS. Mus. e. 19, p. 53.

1145 Here's a health to jolly Baccus
And thou'rt a boon companion hi ho.
Song, no tune.
MS. Mus. Sch. C. 95, p. 177.

1146 Here's a health to the doctor
Is a whig and an ass.
'Dr. Sacheverel's Health'. 1710.
MS. Rawl. D. 383, fol. 63.

1147 Here's a health to the king about let it pass
And he's but a fop who asks which king I mean.
'A Health to the King in Dialogue'. Jacobite song.
MSS. Firth d. 13, fol. 40; Mus. Sch. C. 95, p. 205, with a tune, cf. F. B. Zimmerman, *Purcell*, 1963, no. D. 571/9; Rawl. poet. 181, fol. 78$^{v}$.

1148 Here's a health to the king the crown does belong to
But we'll drink a health (boys) a health to all true hearts.
'The Health'.
MS. Firth e. 6, fol. 62; see also H1150*a*.

1149 Here's a health to the king to the king that prevails,
They'll over a bottle compose new thanksgivings.
'A true Swearing Parsons Health'.
MS. Firth d. 13, fol. 41.

1150*a* Here's a health to the king whom the crown does belong to,
And then 'twill be better for me and for you, boys.
'The Loyal Bumper: or, England's Comfort'.
MS. Firth d. 14, fol. 68; see also H1148.

1150*b* Here's a health to the queen and a prosperous reign
But he's a false boother that wont pledge the same.
'A Ketch'.
Pr. Hearne's *Collections*, ed. C. E. Doble, iii, O.H.S. xiii, 1889, p. 375.
MS. Hearne's diaries 36, p. 84*c*.

1151 Here's a mad shaver, and a cutting lad,
Here yet are left his equal at a hair.
'An Epitaph on a barbour'.
MS. CCC. 328, fol. 52.

1152*a* Here's a mad world, mad world indeed:
Young prodigal sons do spend it.
Robinson, Robert.
MS. *Rawl. poet. 218, p. 172 (autogr.).

Here's a sweet place whose ravishing delight 1152*b*
That it might tempt a more judicious hand.
'Buckingham's gallery, 3rd picture'. Really part of V42.
MS. Rawl. poet. 142, fol. 25$^{v}$.

Here's a worm peeping: 1153
Death spares none, nor great nor small.
Robinson, Robert, 'Homo vermis'.
MS. *Rawl. poet. 218, p. 5 (autogr.).

Here's an health to the knight 1154
And your cart did always go wrong Sir.
'The Reply' to W287.
Pr. *Poems on Affairs of State*, iv, 1707, p. 5.
MS. Eng. poet. e. 87, p. 51.

Here's an health to the tackers, brave boys, 1155
Will be surely a rogue on occasion.
'A Song on the Tack 1705'. Tory rhyme before the General Election.
MSS. Eng. poet. e. 87, p. 94; Tanner 306, fol. 476, satirically ascribed to H[oratio] Walpole Tacker.

Here's artificial beauty to the life 1156
Enjoys this glorious tulip called fools coat.
C[ater], G[erard], 'On a painted Lady'.
MS. Add. A. 301, two copies, fols. 59$^{v}$ rev., attr. to G. C., and 14$^{v}$ rev.

Here's health to our good landlady 1157*a*
We hope they are but few.
Amherst, Elizabeth, 'Healths for the New Year's day. To the tune of the Jovial Beggar'.
MS. *Eng. poet. e. 109, p. 19.

Here's Monmouth the witty 1157*b*
And yourself for a great politician.
Rochester, [John Wilmot, Earl of], extempore, to Charles II.
Pr. Hearne's *Collections*, ed. C. E. Doble, i, O.H.S. ii, 1885, p. 308.
MS. Hearne's diaries 12, p. 93.

Here's no more news than virtue; I may as well 1158
At court; though from court were the better stile.
Donne, John, 'From Court'.
Pr. *Poems*, 1633.
MSS. *Don. c. 54, fol. 8, copied April 1624; *Eng. poet. e. 99, fol. 33$^{v}$; *f. 9, p. 50.

Here's old Johnny Anderson lying in dust 1159*a*
For we all know old Johnny lied all his life long.
'Epitaph'.
MS. Eng. poet. c. 51, p. 12.

1159b Here's something rare
And here he lies in dust.
On Richard Akerman, d. 7 Oct. 1717, at Elsfield, Oxford.
MS. Hearne's Diaries 103, p. 13.

1160 Here's that will challenge all the fair
Come here's your dainty pig and pork.
Pr. *The Musical Companion*, 1673; cf. F. B. Zimmerman, *Purcell*, 1963, no. 253.
MS. Mus. Sch. C. 95, p. 143.

1161 Here's the breast of badness; vice's nurse
Worse then all this, here lies the lady Lake.
'Upon Infamous Ladie Lake'.
MS. Firth d. 7, fol. 153; see also H939, H966, H1054.

1162 Here's to be let, the steward hath swore
Kept it shut many years, but paid for't at last.
'At the House of Commons Doore. 26º Januar. 1679/80'.
MS. Don. b. 8, p. 644.

1163 Here's to Neæra Heaven designed
And pity me as I love her.
Song by J. Bishop.
MS. Mus. c. 26, fol. 142.

1164 Here's your pure love; thus must true lovers woo
Scarce worth a fart and so I owe you noth.
'Crepitus ingenii Or A Poem made on a voluntary escape from a Lover; . . . having recd. a finall Answer from the Mrs. of Charles Stenit in the County of Devon Esq.'
MS. Add. A. 301, fol. 85ᵛ rev.

1165 Hermes flew down from heaven with hue and cry
With Mira sweet, who likewise stole my heart.
MS. Eng. poet. c. 50, fol. 83.

1166 Hermes (for thy sweet art being taught
My epitaph.
Fanshawe, Sir Richard, translator, 'To Mercurie. Ode ii' Horace, *Odes* III. ii.
MS. *Firth c. 1, p. 51.

1167 Heroes of old, whose temples laurels bound
The traitor still will blast the warrior's name.
Title added by Hearne, 'Upon the Prince of Orange'.
MS. Smith 23, p. 116.

Heroic [Sirs] you glorious nine or ten 1168
That when they have their due, you may have yours.
[Jordan, Thomas], 'The Players Petition' [on the closing of the theatres, Sept. 1642].
Pr. *The Royal Arbor of Loyal Poesie*, [*c.* 1664], p. 78.
MSS. Ashmole 47, fol. 132; Rawl. poet. 71, p. 164.

He's a stately thing 1169
From whom the king of kings protect us all.
MS. Locke c. 32, fol. 7.

He's blessed that walks not after ill men's way 1170
Shall perish utterly and come to naught.
Jos: Br:, Psalm i.
MS. Rawl. poet. 61, fol. 7.

He's blessed that wicked counsel nev'r obeys. 1171
But knows all good men's ways, and them rewards.
Gipps, Richard, Psalm i.
MS. Rawl. poet. 61, fol. 7ᵛ.

He's dead! Heaven shut the cloisters of mine eyes 1172
What earth and men admire, what heaven doth prize.
[Pool, Matthew, 1624–79], 'On the Death of Lawr: Leigh of Eman: Coll.' [Cambridge, matr. 1645].
In B.M. Add. MS. 18220, fol. 32, headed 'sic [flevit (?)] reliqua pars tui Matthaeus Pool, 1647', and at end 'Communicatur ab Authore 1647'.
MS. Rawl. D. 260, fol. 31ᵛ.

He's dead. Oh what harsh music's there 1173
The music of his name yet soundeth shrill.
Crashaw, Richard, 'Upon the Death of a Friend'.
MSS. Rawl. poet. 147, p. 37; Tanner 465, fol. 65, attr. to Mr. Crashaw on fol. 1*a*.

He's for the earth no more; he's gone, he's dead, 1174
Join arms: join, death death will have the field.
Robinson, Robert.
MS. *Rawl. poet. 218, p. 8 (autogr.).

He's gone the bright way that his honour directs him 1175
For he looks like a god and he moves as commanding.
'By a Lady when her Lover went with King Wm. to the Battle of the Boyne'.
MS. Eng. poet. c. 9, p. 245.

1176a He's gone! the glory of the British stage
Since my dear friend's at rest with heaven's great king.
'An Elegy on the Death of Mr. Robert Wilks', 27 Sept. 1732.
MS. Rawl. poet. 222, fol. 26.

1176b He's o'er the seas and far away
We'll drink his health that's far away.
'A Scotch Health to K. J.'
Pr. Hearne's *Collections*, ed. C. E. Doble, iii, O.H.S. xiii, 1889, p. 222.
MS. Hearne's diaries 30, p. 208.

1177 He's safe from death secur'd from harms
And daily scandals grow.
Milbourne, [Luke], part of Psalm xci.
Pr. *The Psalms...in English Metre*, 1698, p. 198.
MS. Rawl. D. 868, fol. 27$^{v}$.

1178 He's the most richest who coveteth no more
And the least storer hath the greatest store.
Bulteel, John, couplet.
MS. *Rawl. poet. 159, fol. 212$^{v}$.

1179 Hey day! a challenge and to write!
Be secret and be more than woman.
'To a Lady . . . Weekly miscell. 1779'.
MS. Eng. misc. e. 241, fol. 72$^{v}$.

1180 Hey ding a ding I heard a bird sing
The Parliament soldiers are gone to the king.
MS. Douce d. 59, fol. 64.

1181 Hey ding a ding, what shall I sing?
Pray mamma give me some dinner.
MS. Douce d. 59, fol. 63$^{v}$.

1182 Hey down a down derry
Until I am weary.
Catch by J. Hilton.
MS. Mus. d. 177, fol. 7.

1183 Hey! Hey! ye monkeys what a rout's here
Which will the raptures of your praise insp[ire].
Salt[i]er, Nathaniel (b. 1681 or 1679), 'Æneas', verses written at the Merchant Taylors' School for the Election, 1699.
Pr. bk. Vet. A3 c. 123, fol. 13 (autogr.).

1184 Hey ho! Care, I prethee be gone from me
To drive old care away.
MS. Rawl. poet. 84, fol. 123.

1185 Hey ho to the green-wood now let us go
Sing heave and ho.
Catch, with music.
MS. Mus. c. 107, fol. 47$^{v}$.

Hey [Jonny Waaf (?)] darst hear the decree 1186
Halston, Halston, Timothy, Halston, Timothy, Tim.
Verses to the tune of Lillibulero; against Timothy Hall, 1688 (?).
MS. Smith 27, p. 56.

Hey the bonny Jocky 1187
Call the royal J—y come.
MS. Rawl. poet. 181, fol. 87.

Heywood who did in epigrams excel 1188
Or as a schoolboy putteth down his hose.
Davies, Sir John, 'In Haywooddum'.
Pr. amongst 'Epigrames' with *Ovids Elegies*, tr C. M. [*c.* 1600].
MSS. *Add. B. 97, fol. 44$^{v}$; Rawl. poet. 148, fol. 3$^{v}$ attr. to D[avies]; *212, fol. 64 rev.

Hibernia lay languishing, wasted with care 1189
When freedom's bright star shall arise.
'Hibernia in Woe. Tune . . . county of Leitrim', on the eve of the Rebellion of 1798.
MS. North e. 34, fol. 13.

Hibernia's sons, with hearts elate, 1190
For us they cant keep under.
'Honest Pat. Tune—Girl I left behind'. Song on the Irish situation, *c.* 1796–7.
MS. North e. 34, fol. 3$^{v}$.

*Hic* Catharine *jacet*, *jacet* Ursula, Barbara, *tres hæ* 1191
And friar Andrew, whom these three did bear.
On Catherine Carr, Countess of Essex; Barbara Villiers, Duchess of Cleveland.
MS. Firth d. 7, fol. 157.

*Hic jacet ille qui centies et mille* 1192
So Gentleman *vale*.
Macaronic epitaph.
Pr. Camden's *Remaines*, 1637, p. 409.
MS. Rawl. D. 1372, fol. 9$^{v}$ from end.

*Hic jacet* Tom Shorthose 1193
*Sine* cloak *sine* shirt, *sine* breeches.
'The simplicitye of the Poett [of a Latin distich on Sir John Woodcock, 1405] being noted thes verses was adjoynde uppon Tom Shorthose'. St. Alban's Church, Woodstreet.
Pr. Camden's *Remaines*, 1623, p. 330.
MSS. Ashmole 38, p. 176; CCC. 309, fol. 49; Rawl. poet. 117, fol. 158 rev.

Hiccory, diccory, dock 1194
Hiccory diccory dock.
MS. Douce d. 59, fol. 65$^{v}$.

1195 Hide in some gloomy dungeon my loathed face
In grains of dust dissolve me, I'll endure.
'Guiltie Conscience'.
MS. Rawl. poet. 206, p. 28.

1196 Hide not thy love and mine shall be
If our sparks die, his fire will out.
MS. Eng. poet. c. 50, fol. 78.

1197 High and exalted is thy throne
Is good as well as just.
Beddome, Benjamin, Hymn.
Pr. *Hymns . . of B. Beddome*, 1818, no. 402.
MS. *Eng. misc. e. 227, fol. 54.

1198 High and mighty wilt thou be
Will melt mighty power in tears.
Polwhele, John, 'Boeth. L. 3. met. 5'.
MS. *Eng. poet. f. 16, fol. 48v (autogr.); earlier drafts on fol. 28.

1199 High holt of woods, or haye enclosed with woods
Greeting and fair observance so it ends.
James, Richard, 'Iter Lancastrense Richardi Jamesii'.
Ed. by Thomas Corser for the Chetham Society, vol. vii, 1845.
MS. James 40, p. 1 (autogr.).

1200 [High in the heavens] Heigh in the hevynns figure circulare
And eke thair saulis unto the bliss of hevin.
King James I of Scotland. Transcription of three verses of the Kings Quair, by John Price for Bp. Percy.
MS. Don. c. 56, fol. 121v.

1201 High in thought, good for nought;
And well doth merit.
Robinson, Robert.
MS. *Rawl. poet. 218, p. 48 (autogr.).

1202 High in thought will not be taught,
No pressure in a flight is wrought.
Robinson, Robert.
MS. *Rawl. poet. 218, p. 47 (autogr.).

1203 High Jove whom living she did truly honour
They are but poor which do profess the same.
Pr. bk. Wood 460, *Threnodia in obitum E. Lewkenor*, 1606, Sig. A2v.

1204 High mounted on an ant Nanus the tall
Thus did I fall, and thus fell Phaëthon.
Cr[ashaw], R[ichard].
MS. Tanner 465, fol. 95v.

1205 High o'er mankind triumphant from her chains
Till man immortal grew beneath his hand.
Fellowes, H. A. W., 'Vidimus evectam regno super omnia Roman Æquantem imperio sceptra vetusta novo'.
MS. Don. c. 81, fol. 149.

High on a rock, where not a shrub 1206–7
Kissed her sweet babe and died.
'A Ballad'.
MS. Percy d. 9, fol. 75v.

High-throned in power the everlasting fear, 1208
Involve in plagues the universal world.
'The Plague of Marseilles—Collec. Poems'.
MS. Eng. poet. e. 39, p. 123.

Higher than all the kings of earth 1209
A follower of the Prince of Peace.
Kenton, James.
MS. *Eng. poet. e. 20, p. 324 (autogr.).

Him do I term a puritan whose grace 1210
He held God made the nose for man to speak.
Carpenter, Rich[ard], 'A Puritan'.
MSS. Ashmole 36, 37, fol. 173v.

Him I dare happy call whose end I see, 1211
And if unsure, there is of fear less need.
'Advice'.
MS. Rawl. poet. 90, fol. 105.

Him who loves always one, why should you call 1212
More constant then the man loves always all.
Couplet, extract from I 360.
MS. Rawl. poet. 213, front cover.

Himself the scavenger, his house the cart, 1213
He's but the mimic of a vast rich man.
'The Character of a Banker'.
MS. Rawl. poet. 173, fol. 151.

Hirus doth pray his tenants all may die 1214
For if all die he gaineth all their states.
Davi[e]s, [Sir] John, of Gray's inn, 'In Hirum'.
MS. *Rawl. poet. 212, fol. 63 rev.

His absence makes me think I am 1215
The winter of a summer's colder year.
Cavendish, Lady Jane. 'A Songe', in a pastoral.
MS. *Rawl. poet. 16, p. 66 (*sic*, for 67).

His being was in her alone 1216
That tombs the two is justly one.
[Sidney, Sir Philip], eight-line epitaph on Argalus and Parthenia.
Pr. *Works of Sidney*, ed. A. Feuillerat, i, 1912, p. 557. Also Pr. *Parthenia Sacra*, ed. I. Fletcher, 1633, p. 158.
Pr. bk. Douce D 238(3), sig. A6.

His birth was prophesied and foretold; 1217
In pulling down the house on every limb.
H. W., 'Sacred Epigrams', 10, 'Of Sampsons birth, life, and death'.
MS. Tanner 466, fol. 100v.

1218 His breeches if you tear or needs must wear
And then go both abroad to take the air.

Williams, John, 'Who should wear the breeches?'.
MS. *Rawl. poet. 184, fol. 93 (autogr.).

1219 His country's atlas, terror to his foes
Here for a time his body doth repose.

[G. B. (?)], couplet, with poems on Prince Henry, 1612.
MS. *Rawl. poet. 116, fol. 2$^{v}$.

1220*a* His country's hope, when now the blooming heir
Or of the moral, or the martial seed.

Warton, Thomas (1728–90), 'Newmarket. A Satire . . . Nov. circiter 1750'.
Pr. *Newmarket, a satire*, 1751.
MS. Don. c. 75, fol. 66 (autogr.).

1220*b* His crime was for being a felon in verse
Yet the last was an impudent thing.

On Cibber's *Non-Juror*, 1717/18.
MS. Hearne's diaries 65, p. 140.

1221 His eminence the second's here interred
We may pray God to keep us from the third.

Fairfax, Thomas, Lord, translator, 'Epitaph', couplet translated from French, 'Sur le mort du Cardinal Mazarin', 1661.
MS. *Fairfax 40, p. 603 (autogr.).
MS. *Fairfax 38, p. 289.

1222 His friends' delight the glory and the pride
Brother, and son of Walter, that's enough.

On Arthur Moyle, Esq., 1681, in East Twyford Church.
MS. Rawl. D. 896, fol. 120.

1223 His golden locks time hath to silver turnd
To be your beadsman now, that was your knight.

Pr. G. Peele's *Polyhymnia*, 1590, Sig. B4$^{v}$; and Dowland's *Songs or Ayres*, 1597, xviii; see *Life and Minor Works of Peele*, D. H. Horne, 1952, p. 165.
MSS. Mus. f. 7–10: f. 8, fol. 10$^{v}$, music by Dowland; see also M716.

1224 His hairs, and sins, no man can equal call
For as his sins increase, his hairs do fall.

[Donne, John], Pr. *Poems*, 1633.
'Off an ould vitious man', couplet.
MS. Rawl. poet. 31, fol. 22.

1225 His heavenly part up to the heaven is gone
His earth in earth here lies under this stone.

Couplet.
MS. Add. B. 97, fol. 47.

His holiness has three great friends 1226
It rules both church and state.

[College, Stephen], 'The Pope's three Friends'. [James Duke of York, the Duchess of Portsmouth, and Lord Chief Justice Scroggs].
MS. Rawl. poet. 159, fol. 157.

His horse must needs be skewbald, as is he, 1227
Wise Satan's self in such a shape did walk.

[Pestell, Thomas], 'A village Villane Baylife describ'd in riding positure'.
MS. *Malone 14, p. 38.

His labour's lost that hither comes and seeks 1228–9
For here you see that this weeks days are ended.

'On Mr. Weekes'.
MSS. Ashmole 38, p. 151; Rawl. poet. 117, fol. 174$^{v}$ rev.; see also U44.

His life pure white, years green, his manners grey 1230
Browne was his name, black was his fatal day.

'Upon one Browne'. Couplet.
MSS. Ashmole 36, 37, fol. 176$^{v}$; 47, fol. 31.

His Majesty's affairs must needs now thrive 1231
A fox, the Devil, and the hog.

'Mense Febr. Anno domini 1672/3'.
MS. Don. b. 8, p. 429.

His mind doth firm remain, 1232
Tears are distilled in vain.

Couplet translating 'Mens immota manet, lacrymae volvuntur inanes'. [Virgil, *Æneid* IV. 449].
MS. Rawl. D. 986, fol. 108.

His name by me be magnified 1233
To praise and thank thee now and ever.

Harington, Sir John, Psalm xxx.
MS. *Douce 361, fol. 16$^{v}$.

His right eye Aeon wants, and Leonel 1234
So thou a Cupid, she's a Venus made.

'On Leonella and Aeon, each blind of an Eye'.
MS. Top. London e. 9, p. 15.

His Royal highness says 'tis cold 1235
And then he swears 'tis summer.

Sheridan, Richard Brinsley, impromptu epigram on the Prince of Wales.
MS. Eng. letters d. 103, p. 142 rev.

His sacred name with reverence profound 1236
Exalt thy kingdom, and thy glory raise.

Waller, Edmund, 'Some Reflections upon the Several Petitions in the Lord's Prayer'.
Pr. *Divine Poems*, 1685, p. 33.
MS. Rawl. poet. 173, fols. 185$^{v}$, 186$^{v}$.

1237 His soul grew up so fast within
And so was hatched into a cherubin.
MS. Rawl. poet. 66, fol. 40.

1238 His soul so much was sensible of fear
Advanced the cursed traitors and his crew.
'Upon our saiver Last prayer in the garden'.
MS. Rawl. poet. 116, fol. 143.

1239 His still fair speaking tongue doth scorn to hide
Fair think, fair say, fair do, *in's gylte no gall.*
Cheyney, William, 'An Anagramme, Gyles Allington'.
MS. *Rawl. poet. 86, fol. 3v.

1240 His vagabond desires no limit found
For lust is endless. pleasure hath no bound.
Couplet.
MS. Rawl. poet. 117, fol. 275 rev.

1241 His wife deceased he after lived and tried
To live without her, liked it not, and died.
'On a Gentleman dying soon after his wife'.
MS. Eng. poet. e. 97, p. 153; see also H358, S366.

1242 Historians write, when Bourdeaux reigned,
And then it will be their turn to win.
'The Wager'.
MS. Ballard 47, fol. 37.

1243 Hither from farthest east to west
Instead of silver pence?
'A New Ballad On the Jews getting Liberty to purchase Land in England'.
See Act of Parliament, 10 Geo. I c. 4, and C. Roth, *History of the Jews in England*, 1941, p. 214.
MS. Eng. poet. f. 12, p. 82.

1244 Hither, Hymen, speed your way,
Let toil and care be gone.
'Masque in the Tempest', in the hand of William Boyce.
MS. Mus. d. 14, fol. 2.

1245 Hither we come into this world of woe
We fall to what we are and end the day.
[Fletcher, John].
Pr. W. Porter's *Madrigales and Ayres*, 1632, and Henry Lawes' *Second Book of Ayres and Dialogues*, 1655, p. 33.
MSS. Don. c. 57, fol. 32, with music by H. Lawes; Mus. b. 1, fol. 16, music by John Wilson.

1246 Hither you active flames that cold despise
Ever enjoy, might they ne'er thaw again.
E[dwards], T[homas], 'On the generall Cold'.
MS. Rawl. poet. 65, fol. 65.

Ho! all that would their drowth, or thirst allay, 1247
Labour to be nor satisfied, nor fed?
'Isaiah 55 chapter', incomplete, from a 'Paraphras'd collection of some Prophecyes of the Old Testament concerning Christ'.
MS. *Rawl. C. 113, fol. 9v (autogr.).

Ho, behold, each sinful wight, 1248
If preparation you bring hither.
Colman, Henry, 'The Invitation'.
MS. *Rawl. poet. 204, fol. 32 (autogr.).

Ho brother Teague dost hear de decree 1249
Lero, Lero, Lilli Burlero, etc.
[Wharton, Thomas, 1st Marquis, Lilliburlero, with tune. 1688.
F. B. Zimmerman, *Purcell*, 1963, no. 646].
See Macaulay's *History*, ed. 1849, ii. 428, and *D.N.B.* under Wharton.
MS. Mus. Sch. C. 95, p. 200.

Ho Eccho thee I summon 1250
If not beloved she cares not.
'A dialogue betweene Echo and an other concerning a Woman. by Doctor [William] Barlowe'.
MS. Don. c. 54, fol. 25.

Ho! God be here: Is Christ my Lord at leisure? 1251–2
Ten thousands may themselves likewise impart.
Alabaster, William, 'A new yeares guift to my Saviour'.
Pr. Malone, *Plays and Poems of Shakespeare*, 1821, ii. 262.
MSS. CCC. 309, fol. 9v, attr. to William Alabaster; Tanner 465, fol. 40, attr. to Alabaster; 466, fol. 27v, attr. to Dr. Alabaster.

Ho, ho, John a dogs what news? see A1318, W631.

Ho jolly shepherd [Thyrsis] whither in such haste? 1253
Pan's cornet's blown, and the great sheepshear kept.
Randolph, Thomas, 'An Eglogue'.
Pr. *Poems*, 1638, p. 93.
MSS. Ashmole 38, p. 66, attr. to Mr. Tho. Randall; Firth e. 4, p. 66, attr. to T. R.

Ho, little animal, what news below 1254
Get money, boys, and girls, eat, drink, farewell.
[Roach, Richard], 'A Dialogue between the Dragon on Bow Steeple and the Grashopper on the Exchange', see note on fol. 231v.
MS. Rawl. D. 8 2, fol. 229 (autogr.).

1255 Ho! stop thou spindle shanks with scout-like haste
As Haman was exalted 'bove the Jews.
Skinner, John, 'Eclogue 2', Trinity College, Oxford.
MS. *Top. Oxon. e. 41, p. 143.

1256*a* Ho the broom the bonny bonny broom
To milk my daddy's ewes.
Catch transcribed from B.M. Add. MS. 11608 (1640–60).
MS. Mus. d. 184, fol. 45ᵛ.

1256*b* Hoar headed time full slowly creeps
He bringeth forth to light.
Lines in Rawlinson's copy of Camden's *Britannia*, 1600.
MS. Hearne's diaries 59, p. 174.

1257 Hobbs his religion, Hyde his morals gave
To God, and man a most ingrateful knave.
'Over the privy Stayres att Whitehall found written with a black-lead pen. C. R. IIus', couplet.
MS. Don. b. 8, p. 183.

1258 Hodge had a goodly wain well built and strong
And his tight wain, was drawn by lazy Jades.
MS. Rawl. poet. 66, fol. 59.

1259 Hodge held a farm, and smiled content
The case will alter too beyond the grave.
'Insulted Poverty or the Case is alterd', *c.* 1749.
MS. Eng. misc. e. 219, fol. 4.

1260 Hoist sail my muse let the vast ocean be
Whitlocks the priest or else justice of peace.
'On my Lord [Bulstrode] Whitlock's Embassy into Sweadland', [1654]; 'by Mr. John Blagrave', crossed out.
MS. Rawl. poet. 65, fol. 58ᵛ.

1261 Hold cruel love oh hold I yield
And borrow not my brain.
MSS. Don. c. 57, fol. 46ᵛ, with music; Mus. Sch. F. 575, fol. 5ᵛ, with melody and lute accompaniment.

1262 Hold, fair Lucretia hold, that harmless breast
Make a full wound; this only bleeds within.
'Turning to the Picture of Lucretia'.
MS. Rawl. poet. 87, p. 39.

1263 Hold fast thy sword and sceptre Charles
And raising civil wars.
1667 (?).
Pr. *Poems on Affairs of State*, iii, 1704, p. 189.
MSS. Douce 357, fol. 103, attr. to Sr. William Jones; Eng. poet. d. 152, fol. 58.

Hold, heedless man, what wilful haste dost make? 1264
That I come fully fitted when I die.
[Corbet, W.], 'A Check to' verses with motto *Nemo fœlix ante obitum*.
MS. *Rawl. poet. 210, fol. 26.

Hold, hold, quaff no more 1265
For an act and two red-coats will rout all the ranters.
J[ordan], T[homas], 'The mock song to Stay shut the Gate etc.' by A. Brome.
Pr. *Songs and other Poems*, by A. Brome, 1661, pp. 49, 51.
MS. Ashmole 47, fols. 137ᵛ and 138ᵛ, attr. to T. J.; see also H1272.

Hold, hoops and hinges, burst not I beseech 1266
I may fare better next, or ne'er know more.
'Upon a Christmas day Dinner in the Compter in Woodstreete'.
MSS. Ashmole 36, 37, fol. 297.

Hold Madam Modena, you come too late, 1267
The Queen's water's broke, and washed 'em all away.
'On the Deponents. 1688', on the birth of the son of James II.
MS. Firth c. 15, p. 308.

Hold not thy peace, God of my praise 1268
To save from those pursued.
Psalm cix.
MS. *Rawl. C. 113, fol. 76ᵛ.

Hold off, presumptuous eyes, she is divine 1269
Can shew a vermin like our country louse.
W. B., 'On the Picture of Mother Louse'.
MS. Eng. poet. e. 4, p. 162.

Hold out brave Charles and thou shalt win the field 1270
It may by angels be restored again.
'Uppon his majestie coming to Holmby', Charles I, 16 Feb. 1647.
MS. Malone 21, fol. 34ᵛ.

Hold, passenger, here's shrouded in this hearse 1271
Embalms the story of great Pend'rell's name.
'In the Church Yard of St. Giles in the Fields Middlesex, Richard Penderell, d. 8th Feb. 1671'.
MS. Ballard 50, fol. 186ᵛ; see also S1216.

Hold quaff no more 1272
For an act and two [red] coats can rout all your ranters.
[Jordan, Thomas].
Pr. Jordan's *Claraphil and Clarinda*, [1650], Sig. D6ᵛ; reply to A. Brome's 'Stay shut the gate'.
MSS. Rawl. poet. 26, fol. 152ᵛ; 147, p. 137; see also H1265.

1273 Holiness on the head
Come people; Aaron's dressed.
Herbert, George, 'Aaron'.
Pr. *The Temple*, 1633, p. 168.
MS. *Tanner 307, fol. 128.

1274 Holy fasting was required
Both threat'ned and inflicted.
Bibbee, John, 'Wensday Ap. 16. 90 . . . Joell I 14. Sanctify a fast'.
MS. Ballard 47, fol. 42.

1275 Holy, holy, holy Lord unnamed
Holy, holy, holy Lord unnamed.
Alabaster, William, 'Son: 17'.
MS. *Eng. poet. e. 57, fol. 4.

1276 Holy Marie most pure of virgins all
Where thou dwellest with him world without end.
'Howres of the B. Virgin ad usum Sarum. The 1: 2: and 3: lesson for Mattins'.
MS. Eng. poet. e. 56, p. 89.

1277 Holy Mary the Lord save ye
When ever death calls us away.
South, John, translator, 'A Hymn of the Ave Maria', from Portuguese.
Prepared for publication in *The Christian Doctrine*, 1686.
MS. Rawl. C. 527, p. 171.

1278 Homer of moly and nepenthe sings
All our brave gallants in the town to allure.
Davies, [Sir] John, 'Of Tobacco'.
Pr. amongst 'Epigrames' with *Ovids Elegies*, translated by C. M. [*c.* 1600].
MSS. *Add. B. 97, fol. 46v; *Rawl. poet. 212, fol. 58v rev.

1279 Homer, seemed living brass, not destitute
Like Syren warbling soft Pierian airs.
Dyer, George, translator, 'Homer's Statue', for 'the fifth section of the Greek Anthologia published by Henry Stephens'.
Pr. *Poems*, 1801, p. 53.
MS. *Eng. poet. c. 21, fol. 48.

1280 Honest consort if my love
As to the centre so, adieu.
[Dalby, Edward (?)], 'To his much respected freind mr ffrancis witwicke in Staffordshire'. [F. Wightwick, Stafford, adm. to the Inner Temple Nov. 1634].
MS. Ashmole 47, fol. 128.

Honestly done however, though the stuff 1281
And may these prayers of mine not be in vain.
Wild, Robert, 'My Second and last Paper to Mr. Wanley'.
From *The Ingenious Contention*, 1668.
MS. Eng. poet. c. 25, fols. 64, 64v, 66 (fol. 65 should come before fol. 64).

Honesty is like a stock of money, laid to sleep, 1282
Which ne'er so little broke, will never keep.
Couplet.
MS. Malone 19, p. 48.

Honey moon spend money soon: 1283
All's gone by noon.
Robinson, Robert, couplet.
MS. *Rawl. poet. 218, p. 176 (autogr.).

Honour, and wealth, wit, beauty, strength, and power 1284
He cannot be in any other place.
Spoure, Edmund, 'Epitaph in Memorie of Henry Spoure'. 1688.
MS. *Eng. poet. c. 52, fol. 6v (autogr.).

Honour, and wealth, wit, beauty, strength and power 1285
Eternal rest at last, to such men will be given.
Spoure, Edmund, 'An Acrostick on Henry Spoure'.
MS. *Eng. poet. c. 52, fol. 26v (autogr.).

Honour, thou sacred name . . . see W679.

Honour thou spongy idol of man's mind, 1286
That though you would, you cannot leave your cares.
'A Copy of Verses'.
MS. Montagu e. 13, fol. 130v.

Honour, worth, greatness, or what parts soe'er 1287
Though earth in earth, his soul in heaven doth dwell.
'In the Dukes Comendation', 1628.
MSS. Ashmole 38, p. 14, attr. to Jo. Heape; Dodsworth 79, fol. 158; Malone 23, p. 138.

Honour your God, your king, your parents, friend 1288
Even all who practice it unto their heavenly king.
Spoure, Edmund, 'Acrostick on Henry Spoure'.
MS. *Eng. poet. c. 52, fol. 26v (autogr.).

Honour's idea! of admired delight 1289
'Mongst bypast ages 'tis not to be found.
'Anacrostick' on Henry Foulis, 1638–69.
Pr. Wood's *Life and Times*, ed. A. Clark, ii, O.H.S. xxi, 1892, p. 179.
MS. Wood F. 34, fol. 170.

1290 Hope checked by fear is like a wintry sun
Till winter broods perpetual o'er the soul.
A[shwell], A[nna].
MS. Eng. poet. c. 51, p. 116.

1291 Hope is a grace oft-times so feeble is
And never hope in vain.
Tipping, William, 'Of Hope'.
MS. *Rawl. poet. 101, fol. 59$^v$ (autogr.).

1292 Hope, of all ills that men endure,
To which all soon return that travel out.
'Of Hope'.
MS. Rawl. poet. 90, fol. 57$^v$.

1293 Hope of my heart, oh wherefore do the words
On him whose life depends upon your pleasure.
Pr. John Ward's *First Set of English Madrigals*, 1613, xvii.
MSS. Mus. f. 20–24: f. 20, fol. 12$^v$.

1294 Hope, whose weak being ruined is
The god of nature in the field of grace.
'On Hope: By way of Question and Answer', A. Cowley and R. Crashaw.
Pr. Cowley's *The Mistress*, and in *Steps to the Temple*, 1646.
MS. Rawl. poet. 90, fol. 108$^v$.

Hopeless I languish . . . see I240.

Hopeless I love see H 168.

1295 Hopes farewell adieu to all pleasure
For him who when living she would ne'er believe.
MS. Rawl. poet. 196, fol. 6.

1296 Hoping acceptance else I had not dared
My sincere love is subject of my song.
Corrected draft.
MS. Rawl. D. 864, fol. 235$^v$ (autogr.).

1297 Horace in poor estate, might sing
Grac'd by an August, would be June.
[Pestell, Thomas], 'To [Carolus et Maria], Mart[ial *Epigrams* VIII. lv. 5] Sint Maecenates . . .'.
MS. *Malone 14, p. 28.

1298 Horror horror the pen of fate dipped in its deepest gall
Thus the Almighty spake: he spake and called me Truth.
[Mason, William], 'Ode from Elfrida'.
Words pr. *Elfrida*, 1752, p. 42.
MS. Mus. d. 68, fol. 2,
set by Phil. Hayes; partly in his hand. Dated August 10 1780.

1299 Hoskins the lawyer is merrily sad:
And Chute the carver, foolishly wise.
'Of 4 clapt up in the Tower', June 1614.
MS. Rawl. poet. 26, fol. 2.

Hot livered Gallus, could not long forbear 1300
That to the mare I should straight married be.
'Omnia venalia Roma'.
MS. Ashmole 38, p. 87.

Hot love the proverb said is quickly cold 1301
And truth doth fear the more shall quench the fire.
'In fuscum'.
MS. Don. d. 58, fol. 32$^v$.

How all the creatures upon earth do keep 1302
The body being almost angelical.
Polwhele, John, 'Boet[hius *Consolations*] v. v.'
MS. *Eng. poet. f. 16, fol. 42 (autogr.).

How am I changed? how are my senses bound 1303
In pleasures change? since I must live forsaken.
MSS. Ashmole 36, 37, fol. 245.

How amiable Lord of hosts 1304
And on that [trust (?)] depends . . . (incomplete).
Psalm lxxxiv.
MS. *Rawl. C. 113, fol. 60.

How animals differ in their forms, 1305
That thy soul may be than thy body higher.
Bacon, Sir Nicholas, translation of Boethius, *Consolations* v. v, 1664.
MS. Tanner 306, fol. 345$^v$ (autogr.).

How anxious is the pensive parents' thought! 1306
Go cater where ye list.
'The Magpie and her brood: a fable . . . from the French of Bonaventure de Perriers Addressed to Miss Hotham' . . . probably by Horace Walpole.
MS. Eng. poet. c. 6, fol. 107.

How apt are men to number out our days 1307
And bless the nations now ordained to live.
Cromwell, Edward, from a series of poems on 25 Dec. 1715.
MS. *Rawl. poet. 165, fol. 30$^v$ (autogr.).

How aptly do the mighty prospects rise! 1308
And gained her freedom from the hands of death.
Powell, Sir Herbert, 'A New Epilogue to Cato, spoken at Abergavenny, Oct. 17, 1720'.
MS. Eng. poet. f. 13, fol. 60.

How are men cozened still with shows of good! 1309
The bawd's best mark is the grave friar's hood.
Couplet.
MS. Sancroft 58, p. 158.

How are my foes increased oh God my Lord 1310
Thy comfortable blessings and thy love.
Harington, Sir John, Psalm iii.
MS. *Douce 361, fol. 1$^v$.

1311 How are the gentiles all on fire,
And cast their cords from our free hands.
[Sandys, George], Psalm ii.
Pr. *A Paraphrase upon the Divine Poems*, 1638, Psalms, p. 2, and H. and W. Lawes, *Choice Psalmes*, 1648.
MS. Mus. Sch. E. 451, p. 26 set for 3 parts by H. Lawes.

1312 How are the mighty fallen! Scene of woe!
Due to our gratitude, great Holmes, and you.
Hitchcock, Mr. [Thomas] of St. John's College, 'On the Death of the Rev. Dr. Wm. Holmes . . . President of St. John Baptist's College, Oxon', [d. 1748].
MS. Eng. poet. e. 39, p. 177.

1313 How are thy servants blest, oh Lord
Shall join my soul to thee.
'A Poem composed by Mr. Addison after his Travels', from *Spectator*, 489, 20 Sept. 1712.
MS. Rawl. D. 868, fol. 44.

1314 How art thou thralled, oh poor despised creature
Oh let me die lamenting.
Pr. Orlando Gibbons' *First Set of Madrigals*, 1612, vii–viii.
MSS. Mus. f. 20–24: f. 20, fol. 55.

1315 How? at the other bar to try a priest?
They that can make their kings can make their lords.
'Said to be dropt in the House of Commons, about the time of Dr. Sache[v]rell's Tryal'.
MS. Rawl. poet. 173, fol. 2.

1316*a* How base hath sin made man to fear the thing
All is but oh when they shall come to die.
L. M. (?), 'In Mortis timorem'.
Pr. bk. Wood 460, *Threnodia in obitum E. Lewkenor*, 1606, Sig. A2$^v$.

1316*b* [How blessed is he, who leads a country life]
God never made his work for man to mend.
Dryden, John, extract from 'Epistle to John Driden', pr. *Fables*, 1700.
MS. Eng. poet. c. 9, p. 17.

1316*c* How blest a life, how short its date
The victim of too fierce a flame.
'From the Reading Mercury, Feb. 6. 1724–5'. On Mrs. Bowes.
MS. Hearne's diaries 106, p. 107.

1317 How blest and happy is the life
Forever modest, ever true.
Song from play 'Avarice Outwitted', 1731.
MS. Rawl. poet. 15, fol. 28$^v$.

How blest art thou canst love the country Wroth 1318
Thou mayst think life, a thing but lent.
[Jonson, Ben.], 'To Sir Robert Wroth in prayse of a Countrye lyfe'.
Pr. *The Forrest*, iii.
MS. Rawl. poet. 31, fol. 34.

How blest is the man 1319
Of glory and peace.
Kenton, James, Psalm xciv.
MS. *Eng. poet. e. 20, p. 314 (autogr.).

How blest is the man 1320
And be happy forever with God.
Kenton, James.
MS. *Eng. poet. e. 20, p. 49 (autogr.).

How blest the man 1321
Till ages are no more.
Skinner, John, Psalm xli.
MS. *Eng. poet. d. 22, fol. 139.

How blest the man who with a heart sincere 1322
Dispersed and scattered by the wind.
Skinner, John, [paraphrase of Psalm cxii (?)].
MS. *Eng. poet. d. 22, fol. 127.

How blindly and how monstrously they mix 1323
In Babel's libraries, which rather blind.
'Physicians'.
MS. *Don. f. 5, fol. 39$^v$.

How bold a work attempts that pen 1324
Than he who stole celestial fire.
Waller, Edmund, 'To Mr. George Sands on his Translation on some parte of the Bible'.
Pr. Sandys' *Paraphrase upon the Divine Poems*, 1638, and Waller's *Poems*, 1645, p. 156.
MSS. *Don. d. 55, fol. 38$^v$; Eng. poet. e. 39, p. 28, attr. to Mr. Waller.

How bold is G[eorge] to venture o'er 1325
And leave you to the axe, your fate, Quite brain-sick.
'On King George [I]'s Accession to the Throne', 1714.
MSS. Rawl. C. 986, fol. 20; Rawl. poet. 155, p. 4.

How bordering are life's confines upon death! 1326
And yet no end unto their woe . . .
'Reflections occasioned by the death of Mr. Nathaniel Sheff drowned June 17th [16]76'.
MS. Rawl. poet. 172, fols. 89, 90.

1327 How bravely this centurion did appear
He had not found such faith in Israel.
'Upon the centurion'.
MS. Rawl. poet. 116, fol. 128v.

1328 How bright this negro rose from th' holy fount!
And th' Holy Dove o'er swarthy towers doth hover.
Sancroft, William, 'In Æthiopem baptizatum. Acts viii. Out of Mr. Crashaw's Latin' [*Epigrammata Sacra*, 1634].
MS. Sancroft 48, fol. 12 (autogr.).

1329 How brim-full of nothing's the life of a beau
Such, such is the life of a beau.
'The Life of a Beau sung by Mrs. Clive'.
MS. Eng. poet. c. 9, p. 31.

1330 How came dear Duck, thy artless muse
Nor envy W[a]lp[o]le's fainter star.
'To Stephen Duck, on his Poem to Dr. [George] Clark on a good Conscience', 31 Oct. 1734.
MS. Eng. misc. e. 240, p. 75.

1331 How came the streaks of red, here where pure white
For senseless things an everlasting vein.
'On a Scratch on a Ladys Arme'.
MS. Rawl. poet. 84, fol. 82 rev.

1332 How can an aged silly foolish ass
Till the frozen age be pleasant unto youth.
'Inequaletie in marriage'.
MS. Eng. poet. c. 50, fol. 33.

1333 How can dull idiots think that providence
Rouse up from your dull zealous lethargy.
MS. Add. B. 8, fol. 70v.

1334 How can I but envy my papers hap
And think me blest in their great slavery.
MSS. Ashmole 36, 37, fol. 213v rev.

1335 How can I undertake to draw
The town, or him that gives the painter fees.
Williams, John, 'Painting by Direction without sight'.
MS. *Rawl. poet. 191, fol. 117 (autogr.).

1336 How can I want the lord my shepherd seems
Him in his house for ever I'll serve there.
Fairfax, Thomas, Lord, Psalm xxiii.
MS. *Fairfax 40, p. 49 (autogr.).
MS. *Fairfax 38, p. 157.

How can my mournful muse now sing of death? 1337
To be with Christ, my soul doth most admire.
Taylor, J[ohn], of G[rays] I[nn], 'Dum terram aspicio, Cælum cupio; vel cupio dissolui. A Christmas charoll. . . December 25, [16]85', addressed to 'Madam Warner the best of Wifes'.
MS. Rawl. poet. 170, fol. 37.

How can that grief be fettered in a verse 1338
And all our hearts are suited to the bier.
Darell, Sr. Sams[on], on the death of Lady Darell.
MS. Rawl. poet. 210, fol. 56 rev.

How can the emblem of mortality 1339
Armd with our strong affection scorned to break.
Strode, William, 'On a Glasse falling on the Stones without breaking'.
MS. *CCC. 325, fol. 93 (autogr.).

How can the feeble fort but yield at last 1340
Women poor souls I see are born to bear.
Subscribed 'Mrs. M. R.'
MS. Rawl. poet. 85, fol. 114.

How can the muse to Anna be ingrate 1341
Who innocent; but courts you in lampoon.
Roach, Richard, 'The Innocent Lampoon: or the Devote turn'd Lover', 1702. Proof-copy with autogr. corrections and additions.
MS. Rawl. D. 832, fol. 285.

How can you lovely Nancy, thus cruelly slight 1342
Since I'm constant as your sex, be not fickle as ours.
'Strephons Complaint'.
MS. Montagu e. 13, fol. 69.

How capricious were nature and art to poor Nell 1343
She was painting her cheeks at the time her nose fell.
Prior, [Matthew], couplet, 'A Critical Moment'.
Pr. *Poems on Several Occasions*, 1718.
MS. Rawl. poet. 152, fol. 122v.

How changed the scene! where smiling sat 1344
Will ask no questions—but will eat.
Sadleir, H. Vernon, 'Lines written at the House of Doctor Warton in the Absence of the Family in the Isle of Wight'. In a letter to Joseph Warton, 4 Aug. 1791.
MS. Don. c. 75, fol. 54 (autogr.).

How charming's my Sylvia? Sweet her looks as the morn 1345
What Waller, what Dryden, what Pope could ne'er do.
'Sylvia's Picture drawn by Damon'.
MS. *Eng. poet. d. 47, fol. 49.

1346 How comes it (great Mæcenas) that there's not
'S like Crispin's volumes, I will not add a line.
B[rome], A[lexander], translator, Horace, *Satires* I. i.
Pr. *Poems of Horace*, 2nd ed., 1671, p. 187.
MS. Rawl. D. 261, p. 18.

1347 How comes it I have sight enough to find
So many charms in you, if love is blind?
Williams, John, couplet, 'Love is Blind'.
MS. *Rawl. poet. 191, fol. 98v (autogr.).

1348 How comes it I have sight enough to find
How many things in you deserve to please.
Williams, John, 'To a Lady saying Love is Blind'.
MS. *Rawl. poet. 191, fol. 98v (autogr.).

1349 How comes it that our gentry
Are consumed in pimps punks and players.
MS. Eng. poet. d. 152, fol. 99.

1350 How comes the welcome news of Christ his birth
Who will not his sufficient grace despise.
Cromwell, Edward, one of a series of poems on 25 Dec. 1715.
MS. *Rawl. poet. 165, fol. 31 (autogr.).

1351 How comes the world so sad? for whom doth death
It may regain by transmigration.
Stutvile, George, 'The Genius of the stage Deploring the death of Ben Johnson'.
Pr. *Ben Jonson*, ed. Herford and Simpson, xi, 1952, p. 486, from this MS.
MS. Ashmole 38, p. 97.

1352 How cool and temperate am I grown
I must enjoy my self a while.
MS. Rawl. poet. 65, fol. 35v.

1353 How could I triumph in my bliss
Oh that I might do so with thee.
MS. Eng. poet. f. 10, fol. 121v.

1354 How could my error merit thy disdain
That I love thee and thou lov'st not again.
Mervall, Alphonso, 'Cur faciem tuam abscondis, et arbitraris me Inimicum tuum. Ioab. 13°'.
MS. *Rawl. poet. 166, p. 79 (autogr.).

1355 How could vile sycophants contrive
Though spoke in his own praise.
'On Dr. Bentley applying to himself these following Lines:—Sunt et mihi Carmina; me quoque dicunt, Vatem pastores: sed non ego credulus illis. Virgil'.
MS. Ballard 50, fol. 111.

How! Cut it down? Nay lord, wilt thou not spare 1356
And to repair all, without cutting down.
'Humble Expostulation'.
MS. Eng. poet. e. 51, p. 30.

How dares the author pass into the press 1357
His name being king, he thinks himself a king.
On Humphrey King's *Halfe-penny worth of Wit*, 1613; transcribed from R. Heber's copy.
MS. Douce 190, fol. 9.

How distant sinners are from thee 1358
And bid the worst of sinners live.
Kenton, James, Psalm cxix.
MS. *Eng. poet. e. 20, p. 311 (autogr.).

How do base minds watch for their fall that show 1359
To honest artists, or to meat and drink.
Williams, John, 'A Vindication of those who thro' infirmity cannot always avoid offences', etc.
MS. *Rawl. poet. 188, fols. 80, 79v (autogr.).

How do I thank thee death, and bless thy power 1360
And what my birthright claimed, my death hath paid.
[Corbett, Richard], 'On the death of the Ladie Arabella' [Stuart], d. 27 Sept. 1615.
Pr. *Poetica Stromata*, 1648.
MSS. Eng. poet. c. 50, fol. 133v; e. 14, fol. 99v rev.; Rawl. poet. 160, fol. 15v; see also H1432.

How do my chariot wheels run back 1361
There let me ever, ever live.
Bromley, Henry, 'Heb. 12. 1. Let us run with Patience the race set before us'.
MS. *Don. e. 19, fol. 14v (autogr.).

How do we mock our hopes that call (in strife 1362
Setting to this 'twill rise to th'other world.
Beaumont, Thomas, 'On Mans fraylty an Elegie Occasiond by sickness'.
MS. *Malone 18, p. 85 (autogr.).

How does man start [up] death at every stride 1363
And let her live for she preserved me.
M[asters], T[homas], of New College, 'εωτηριον from the danger of the water'.
MS. Ashmole 47, fol. 23.

How does the sovereign power of love 1364
None so damning as this passion.
'A Poem on the various effects and operations of Love In imitation of Mr. Burtons upon Melancholy'..
MS. Rawl. poet. 152, fol. 38.

1365 **How dost spin my time away**
**Its cover off, grant it a crown.**
Colman, Henry, 'On the Spirit, adulterated by the flesh. My soule cleaveth to the dust, Quicken thou me. Psalm: 119 v. 25'.
MS. *Rawl. poet. 204, fol. 9 (autogr.).

1366 **How doth my heart revolt**
**Oh may I cleave to thee.**
Beddome, Benjamin.
MS. *Eng. misc. e. 227, fol. 7.

1367 **How doth the city solitary**
**Against us very wroth.**
Fleming, Robert, 'The Lamentations of Jeremiah in Meter written A°. 1677 at Ormistoun in Scotland'. Subscribed 'written 1677 in the 26 year of my age'.
MS. Rawl. poet. 213, fol. 74ᵛ rev. (autogr.).

1368 **How doth the day confederate with the night**
**Of flowers spring, and give the birds a voice.**
Beaumont, Thomas, 'To her beinge absent'.
MS. *Malone 18, p. 80 (autogr.).

1369 **How dull and cheerless are my days**
**The helpless and the blind.**
Perkins, Henry, 'The Blind Man's Complaint', 1734.
MS. Eng. poet. e. 40, fol. 80.

1370 **How dull and how insensible a beast**
**Learn to write well, or not to write at all.**
[Sheffield, John, Duke of Buckingham], 'An Essay upon Satyre'.
Pr. *Works*, 1729, i. 111; not in *Works*, 1721.
MSS. Don. b. 8, p. 634; Rawl. poet. 81, fol. 29.

1371 **How dull's my muse! she's loth sure to rehearse**
**Our too suspicious coins. Write her name.**
Lynnett, William (?), 'An elegy on the lady [Theophila] Cook, [1643]'. At end 'Deflevit [ ]', page torn.
MS. Eng. misc. e. 13, fol. 26, in Lynnett's hand.

1372 **How durst this dog doomed to eternal night**
**Descended to congratulate the sun.**
'Upon Satans temting our Savior in the deseort'.
MS. Rawl. poet. 116, fol. 122.

1373 **How durst thus factious pharisees condemn**
**To [cudgell (?)] on the Sabbath for a straw.**
'Upon the desipels plucking the eares of corne on the sabaoth'.
MS. Rawl. poet. 116, fol. 135ᵛ.

1374 **How easily doth nature teach the soul**
**That ev'ry one might reign like God alone.**
Traherne, Thomas, 'Ease'.
MS. *Eng. poet. c. 42, fol. 8ᵛ (autogr.).

**How easily with more legs than his own** 1375
**Let nothing deter a noble design.**
Williams, John, 'A Song in a Coach'.
MS. *Rawl. poet. 192, fol. 183ᵛ (autogr.).

**How easy is our God, and liberal, who** 1376
**Counts it as done, what we have will to do.**
'Gods acceptance of our Will'.
MS. Rawl. poet. 90, fol. 77.

**How easy our minutes whilst our conscience is clear,** 1377
**And who should protect him but the powers of Heaven.**
MS. Firth d. 13, fol. 39.

**How excellent thy name oh Lord** 1378
**Shall crowd to own thy righteous sway.**
[Jennens, Charles], 'Saul', by G. F. Handel, full score bought for the Musical Society in Oxford by Dr. Thomas Bever, 1771.
MS. Mus. b. 13.

**How excellent thy name oh Lord** 1379
**Through all the earth declare.**
Psalm viii.
MS. *Rawl. C. 113, fol. 13ᵛ.

**How fain would we forget this fatal war!** 1380
**And England's tears the Heliconian spring.**
'An Elegie upon the death of Sr. Charles Rich slaine at the Isle of Ree', [1627].
MS. Rawl. poet. 160, fol. 53ᵛ.

**How far are they deceiv'd, who hope in vain** 1381
**Before your pity, I would choose your hate.**
[Etherege, Sir George] 'Epelia (a Deserted Lover) to Bajaset, which may serve as a Caveat to Women'.
See *Roxburghe Ballads*, iv, 1883, p. 574, and D. M. Vieth, *Attribution in Restoration Poetry*, 1963, p. 465.
MS. Rawl. poet. 173, fol. 66ᵛ, attr. to Ld. Ro:

**How far do some for knowledge seek? how near** 1382
**Completed find the helps in them begun.**
Williams, John, 'Are there not twelve hours in the Day? John xi. 9'.
MS. *Rawl. poet. 192, fol. 7 (autogr.).

**How fares my pupil now? upon my life** 1383
**So ho my roaring muse? Pupil farewell.**
'This fancy was vented Septemb. 9th 1633 at three a clock in the morning, when I was waiting the appearance of a comet reported to have bene seene some nights before'.
MS. Wood D. 19(2), fol. 95ᵛ.

1384 How fast my griefs come on, how thick a shoal
Than now doth live in all thy sex besides.
Gill, Alex[ander], 'An Eligie uppon the death of Mris Penelope Nowell Daughter to the Lo: Vicount Camden'.
MS. Ashmole 36, p. 188.

1385 How firm the managed war-horse keeps his ground.
And when to stop; and when to charge the foes.
'The docility of a Horse'.
MS. Eng. poet. c. 9, p. 51.

1386 How firm the union of the saints
And own him as your Lord.
Beddome, Benjamin.
MS. *Eng. misc. e. 227, fol. 5.

1387 How fit our well-ranked feasts do follow!
All-mischief comes after All-Hallow.
[Crashaw, Richard], couplet, 'In conjurationem sulphuream'.
MS. Tanner 465, fol. 37$^{v}$, attr. to Mr. Crashaw on fol. *1a*.

1388 How fitly poets unto time apply
On earth must labour to live righteously.
Colman, Henry, 'On Time'.
MS. *Rawl. poet. 204, fol. 23 (autogr.).

1389 How foolish 'tis to languish
Which does so quickly cloy.
'Song'.
MS. Rawl. poet. 152, two copies, fols. 165$^{v}$ and 179.

1390 How frail is man, how short his time!
A hundred years is old.
Robinson, Robert, 'Vita brevis, vita levis'.
MS. *Rawl. poet. 218, p. 136 (autogr.).

1391 How frail is man's estate whose confines lie
And London's chair with strictest justice swayed.
Shute, James, 'Upon the Death of his much Honoured Friend Sr Thomas Rawlinson late Lord Major of London' [d. 11 Nov. 1708].
MS. Rawl. D. 863, fol. 110.

1392 How fresh, oh Lord, how sweet and clean
Forfeit their paradise by their pride.
Herbert, George, 'The Flowre'.
Pr. *The Temple*, 1633, p. 160.
MS. *Tanner 307, fol. 121$^{v}$.

1393 How glad was I when they said so
Grant Zion peace, Lord thou dwells there.
Fairfax, Thomas, Lord, Psalm cxxii.
MS. *Fairfax 40, p. 329 (autogr.).
MS. *Fairfax 38, p. 425.

How glorious, happy, and how blest, 1394
And both death and fate defy.
Chatwin, John, 'In imitation of another Ode of Anacreon's', xxxvi.
MS. *Rawl. poet. 94, p. 81 (autogr.).

How glows my heart, when I behold your lines, 1395
And Swift's ill-natur'd muse, be proud to praise.
'Lines Address'd to Miss E. Peart by — . . . 1765'.
MS. Eng. poet. e. 28, p. 70.

How goes the time? Thy Xenophon in hand 1396
Phœnix (of logic) springing from its flame.
Skinner, John, 'Eclogue 3', Trinity College, Oxford.
MS. *Top. Oxon. e. 41, p. 299.

How good a God thou art, how great and free 1397
Perpetual praise to thee, th'Almighty king.
Colman, Henry, 'On God's mercie'.
MS. *Rawl. poet. 204, fol. 2 (autogr.).

How good, and how beseeming well 1398
Men may for ever blessed live.
Herbert, Mary (*née* Sidney), Countess of Pembroke, Psalm cxxxiii.
MS. *Rawl. poet. 24, p. 200.

How good how sweet a thing it is 1399
Descends on Zion, blessings drop.
Fairfax, Thomas, Lord, Psalm cxxxiii.
MS. *Fairfax 40, p. 346 (autogr.).
MS. *Fairfax 38, p. 436.

How great delight [breed] from those sweet lips I find [taste] 1400*a*
And grant her kissing words, or speaking kisses.
Pr. Thomas Tomkins' *Songs of 3, 4, 5 and 6 parts*, 1622, v.
MSS. Mus. f. 17–19: f. 19, fol. 8$^{v}$; Rawl. poet. 199, p. 5, words only.

[How great's the love of God unto his creature] 1400*b*
His death a winter's night without a morrow.
[Quarles, Francis], extract from *A Feast for Wormes*, 1626, Med. 1.
MS. Sancroft 29, p. 63.

How gross are th'odours and perfumes below 1401
To fit for Eden's aromatic gales.
MS. *Don. f. 5, fol. 23$^{v}$.

How happily my life I led 1402
In the joy of an humble state.
Copy *c.* 1802, with a tune.
MS. Mus. e. 19, p. 4.

1403 How happy are they that ne'er are deceived
For which money is offered in vain?
Williams, John, 'A Song to be Sung when it may be supposed a loose woman is not far off, either sitting in a Publick place for walking, or in private company'.
MS. *Rawl. poet. 191, fol. 35 (autogr.).

1404 How happy art thou and I
Hath made me now thus wise.
MSS. Rawl. poet. 65, fol. 35; 116, fol. 60ᵛ.

1405 How happy I! to whom propitious heaven
'Tis mutual love true happiness bestows.
'O festus dies hominum!' 1735.
MS. Eng. misc. e. 240, p. 314.

1406 How happy in that temple to reside
With safe delights, by care nor fear oppress.
MS. Malone 13, p. 93.

1407 How happy is he born or taught,
And having nothing yet hath all.
Wotton, Sir Henry, 'The character of the happy life'.
Pr. in Overbury's *Wife*, 'fift impression', 1614; *Reliquiae Wottonianæ*, 1651, p. 522. Cf. *The Library*, 5th ser., x, 1955, p. 270.
MSS. Ashmole 47, fol. 29ᵛ; Don. c. 57, fol. 51ᵛ, with music; Malone 13, p. 11, attr. to Sr. H. Wotton; Malone 19, p. 146, attr. to Sr. Hen. Wootton; Rawl. D. 1048, fol. 58, attr. to Sr. Henr. Wotton; Rawl. poet. 26, fol. 1ᵛ, attr. to Sr. Henry Wootton; 31, fol. 5; 66, fol. 55, attr. to Sr. Henry Wotton; 208, fol. 1; 212, fol. 150 rev.

1408 How happy is he in these times
I dare conclude as I began.
'My happy Man'.
MS. Dodsworth 79, fol. 166.

1409 How happy is our British Isle to bear
For he with all he wished for had been blest.
Dryden, Charles, verses addressed to John Dryden's Corinna, i.e. Mrs. Thomas.
Pr. Curll's *Miscellanea*, 1727, i. 154.
MS. Rawl. letters 90, fol. 56 (autogr.).

1410 How happy is the harmless country maid,
Love of all cares, the sweetest and the best.
MS. Montagu e. 13, fol. 77.

1411 How happy is the patient soul.
And show thyself to me.
Kenton, James, Psalm xl.
MS. *Eng. poet. e. 20, p. 328 (autogr.).

How happy sleeps this prince within his chest 1412
Men's general love to him, and his to men.
G. B., 'Epitaph 15' on Prince Henry in 'Cestria Lugens', 1612.
MS. *Rawl. poet. 116, fol. 8ᵛ.

How happy they who still secure 1413
And live as I would wish to die.
Kenton, James.
MS. *Eng. poet. e. 20, p. 6 (autogr.).

How happy was the state of man 1414
Then let me live to him, or let me live no more.
Earbery, Matthias, 'The Sicke Mans Prayre Psalme 6', sent to Bp. Charles Trimnell, Bp. of Norwich 1708–21.
MSS. Tanner 306, fol. 457 (autogr.); Rawl. D. 842, two copies, fols. 83 (autogr.) and 94.

How happy were good English faces 1415
And the soldiers henceforth do their duty.
'The Womans Complaint to Venus. 1698/9'.
MSS. Eng. poet. e. 50, p. 119; Rawl. poet. 159, fol. 32.

How happy were the shepherds living 1416
Unto the starry firmament.
MS. Ashmole 38, p. 127.

How happy's that lover who after long years 1417
Let the sun rise in state for tomorrow's the day.
MS. Rawl. poet. 196, fol. 22.

How happy's that prisoner who conquers his fate 1418
For man's the world's epitome.
Printed, with the title 'The Royal Captive, or the Worlds Epitome', in *Wit and Drollery*, 1661, p. 148.
MS. Rawl. B. 35, fol. 41 rev.

How happy's the husband whose wife has been tried 1419
As whene'er it is so, if it don't I'll be hanged.
Congreve, William, song in Dryden's *Love Triumphant*, 1694, v.i.
MS. Rawl. poet. 196, fol. 44ᵛ.

How happy's the life 1420
At sight of them I do ween.
Part-song, music incomplete.
MS. Mus. c. 5, fol. 8.

How haps it that the spring so long does stay? 1421
We should no beauty lack in any place.
Oldisworth, Nicolas, 'To his Friend beyond Sea, March 26. 1633'.
MS *Don. c. 24, fol. 69 (autogr.).

1422 How hard is the case, with a limb of the curse,
Where Cupid admits of two strings to his bow.
Roach, Richard, 'The Platonic's Reply to the Ladie's Banter'.
MS. Rawl. D. 832, fol. 251 (autogr.).

1423 How hard on women is the marriage state
That peace more pleasure can bestow than love.
MS. Eng. poet. e. 47, p. 70.

1424 How hard the human heart, and blind
Into thy paradise.
Kenton, James.
MS. *Eng. poet. e. 20, p. 325 (autogr.).

1425 How hard, ye gods, was Dido's fate
The second flying, Dido dies.
'An Epigram on Dido', 1735.
MS. Eng. misc. e. 240, p. 225.

1426 How hard's the fate
Love's race-horse should quite round be shod.
Roach, Richard, 'The Formal Widow. On a Lady Mourning in State'.
MS. Rawl. D. 832, fol. 226 (autogr.).

1427 How has Saint Clodius, on Ashwednesday's morn
A generous heart has worn a sterner mien.
Samber, Robert.
MS. *Rawl. poet. 134*b*, fol. 176 (autogr.).

1428 How hath my passion made me Cupid's scoff!
Puzzle me so, I am resolved on neither.
[Villiers], G[eorge] D[uke of] Buckingham, 'On the humour in Mr. [Edward] Howards Play, where Mr. Kinaston diputes his staying in, or going out . . . In Imitation of the Earle of Orrery'.
MS. Eng. poet. e. 4, p. 198.

1429 How have I praised thy cheeks, where roses blow!
And when I praise thee next, shall praise thy hand.
'To a Lady who deceived the Author by Painting her Face'.
MS. *Eng. poet. d. 47, fol. 146.

1430 How have we lost ourselves, what hath destroyed
Or not regard the person where't does dwell.
Beaumont, Thomas, 'Of his Mrs. Jealousie'.
MS. *Malone 18, p. 16 (autogr.).

1431 How! How! who is here?
That I left, that I lost.
Robert and Margaret Byrkes of Doncaster, Yorks., 1597.
MSS. Top. gen. e. 32, fol. 34$^{v}$; Willis 83, fol. 75$^{v}$, copied 'out of the genera Atlas'.

How I do thank thee death and bless thy power 1432
And what my birth right claimed; my death hath paid.
[Corbett, Richard], 'On the Ladye Arbella' [Stuart; d. in the Tower, 25 Sept. 1615].
MS. Ashmole 38, p. 168; see also H1360.

How ill doth he deserve a lover's name 1433
Shall like a hallow'd lamp for ever burn.
C[arew], T[homas], 'Eternity of love protested'.
Pr. *Poems*, 1640.
MSS. CCC. 328, fol. 22$^{v}$; Eng. poet. e. 37, p. 76, attr. to T.C.; Rawl. poet. 116, fol. 66$^{v}$ rev.

How ill doth he deserve the name of man 1434
In what in beasts doth detestation breed.
Colman, Henry, 'On Drunckenesse'.
MS. *Rawl. poet. 204, fol. 17 (autogr.).

How is a jewel of the brightest ray 1435
Their lease of honour's justly forfeited.
Beaumont, Thomas, 'Of conferring honors'.
MS. *Malone 18, p. 91 (autogr.).

How is my sun whose beams are shining bright 1436
Nor mazed head think nor faltering tongue recite.
Sidney, Sir Philip, from the *Arcadia*, pr. 1593.
MS. *e Mus. 37, fol. 104.

How is the anxious soul of man 1437
Of earth without a cross, has earth without a rest.
[Quarles, Francis], 'All's vanitye'.
Pr. *Emblemes*, 1635, I. vi.
MS. Rawl. poet. 90, fol. 19.

How is the jealous wretch involved in woes 1438
Unequal consorts and unequal friends.
Herbert, Basil, 'The moral Reflexion' on the history of 'A Specifick for the Cholick'.
MS. Rawl. poet. 134*a*, fol. 109, attr. to Basil Herbert on fol. 45.

How is't nine tailors make a man up? when 1439
I'll mak't as short as thou hast made my gown.
Williams, Richard, 'On a London Tayler who spoyld a Commencement gowne in the making'.
MS. Rawl. poet. 147, p. 17.

How joyful and how glad a thing 1440
In health and unity.
'An Antheme for the Garter'.
MS. Rawl. poet. 23, p. 178.

1441 How just is then the tribute of our eyes
And bathe with tears of joy each Bishop's hearse.

'Upon the Sickness of the Archbp. of Canterbury [Sancroft] Feb: 14. 1688'.
MSS. Eng. poet. c. 18, fol. 63; e. 49, p. 30; Firth e. 6, fol. 72$^{v}$.

1442 How kind has nature unto Bluster been,
And—kinder still—gave legs to run away.

'Epigram'.
MS. Eng. poet. c. 51, p. 308.

1443 How liberty of conscience that's a change
*Jure divino* whip and spur again.

'Dr. Wild's Ghost on his Matye.'s Declaration for Liberty of Conscience' [1687].
Pr. *Poems on Affairs of State*, ii, 1703, p. 166.
MSS. Don. e. 23, two copies, fols. 65 and 67; Firth c. 3, fol. 13; c. 16, p. 159; pr. bk. Firth b. 20, fol. 137.

1444 How life, and death in thee
Them both.

Crashaw, Richard, 'In Sepulcrum Domini'.
MS. Tanner 465, fol. 37$^{v}$, attr. to Mr. Crashaw on fol. 1*a*.

1445–6 How like an angel came I down!
When I was born.

Traherne, Thomas, 'Wonder'.
MS. *Eng. poet. c. 42, fol. 2 (autogr.).

1447 How like this paper (sweet) whilst it was white
How my heart thrives, that keeps you company.

Beaumont, Thomas, 'To his Mrs. beinge absent'.
MS. *Malone 18, p. 12 (autogr.).

1448 How lily-white soe'er my hand
As Tewkesberry mustard-ball.

Lines supposed to be addressed to Pope by Nicholas Lechmere after the publication of the Ballad 'Duke upon Duke', pr. 1720; see also T2235.
MS. Ballard 47, fol. 7.

1449 How little cause we have for mirth
So that my after may be crowned.

Colman, Henry, 'On Mourninge'.
MS. *Rawl. poet. 204, fol. 31 (autogr.).

1450 How little do the landsmen know
And the royal family.

Pr. as 'The Sailor's Resolution', *The Choice Spirit's Chaplet*, G. A. Stevens, 1771.
MS. Firth c. 18, fol. 215.

How long at balls has each ill starr'd Ashburnham 1451
And fills at once his belly, and his arms!

Parsons, William, 'Epigram on the Bishop's daughters . . . at Chichester'.
MS. *Don. d. 123, p. 87 (autogr.).

How long dear Lord and bridegroom dost thou stay 1452
Amen. So let it be.

'A Dialogue. Representing the Holy Violence of Faith and Love, as wrestling and prevailing with God'.
MS. Rawl. poet. 200, fol. 116.

How long (fair soul) wilt thou adjourn my joys 1453
The next fit time I dally will with thee.

Beaumont, Thomas, 'urging A quick Answer from his Mistris'.
MS. *Malone 18, p. 33 (autogr.).

How long great poet, shall thy sacred lays 1454
A nobler change, than he himself can tell.

Addison, Joseph, 'To Mr. John Dryden' dated from 'Mag. Coll. Oxon [June] 2. 1693'.
Pr. Dryden's *Examen Poeticum*, 1693, p. 247.
MS. Add. B. 105, fol. 27$^{v}$.

How long has our vile gazeteer mistook 1455
You're King of Spain, as Anna's Queen of France.

'On Queen Anne's sending assistance to the Arch Duke'.
Pr. bk. Firth b. 21, fol. 61$^{v}$; see also B8.

How long inglorious, strenuous youths you stand, 1456
Who can superior to all others rise.

Courtenay, J[ohn], 'Tyrtaeus's Elegies, No. 2'.
MS. Malone 41, fol. 51$^{v}$.

How long might this poor wretch have missed his ends 1457
That bore their master eight and thirty year.

'Upon the bedrid mann att the poole probatica. John chap. 5'.
MS. Rawl. poet. 116, fol. 125.

How long (oh Lord) shall I forgotten be 1458
Songs ditty.

Sidney, Sir Philip, Psalm xiii.
MSS. *Rawl. poet. 24, fol. 15; *25, fol. 9.

How long oh Lord wilt thou forget 1459
And bid me then depart in peace.

Kenton, James.
MS. *Eng. poet. e. 20, p. 110 (autogr.).

1460 How long oh Lord wilt thou persever
Will make my deepest sorrows sing.
J. F., Psalm xiii.
MS. *Eng. poet. f. 17, p. 157 (autogr.).

1461 How long shall we wait this horrible funeral?
He loved not his king, nor himself, nor his wife.
'Rithmes made in a Belcony by one who Impatiently Expected the shews att the E[arl] of E[ssex] his Funeral', 1646.
MS. Douce 357, fol. 12^v^.

1462 How long (vain hope!) dost thou my joys suspend?
By scorning hope, ne'er to rely on thee.
King, Henry, 'The Forlorne Hope'.
Pr. *Poems*, 1657, p. 15.
MSS. *Eng. poet. e. 30, fol. 56^v^; *Malone 22, fol. 36^v^.

1463 How long wilt thou forget me Lord,
And granted my wishing.
[Sternhold, Thomas], Psalm xiii.
MS. Rawl. poet. 112, fol. 68 rev.

1464 How long wilt thou forget me, Lord?
The name of God most high.
Psalm xiii.
MS. *Montagu e. 10, fol. 3^v^.

1465 How long ye bards! Shall your great patron mourn?
With him oh! may my love and constant zeal supply.
Gildon, Charles, 'A letter to Mr. Congreve occasioned by the Death of the Countess Dowager of Manchester etc.'
MS. Rawl. poet. 99, fol. 2.

1466 How loudly do these vaunting sons of Mars
While Heaven shook above, and the earth crack below.
Harris, Samuel, 1682–1733, 'Caesar', lines written at the Merchant Taylors' School [for the Election June 1699 (?)].
Pr. bk. Vet. A3 c. 123, fol. 39 (autogr.).

1467 How lovely does this coyness seem!
Who her disdain itself can love.
Owen, Corbett, 'Disdaine'.
MS. Eng. misc. e. 255, fol. 35.

1468 How lovely is thy dwelling
Whose confidence is built on thee.
Herbert, Mary (*née* Sidney), Countess of Pembroke, Psalm lxxxiv.
MSS. *Rawl. poet. 24, p. 125; *25, fol. 79^v^.

1469 How many are beneath thee in degree
Some beg, some rent, most labour with their hands . . . (incomplete).
MS. *Don. f. 5, fol. 11^v^.

How many days in one whole year there be 1470
Most true, yet most it for a wonder take.
'The Cathedral in Salisbury . . . Heylin [*Micrososmus*, 1621, p. 244] English'd'.
MSS. Add. B. 8, fol. 50; Eng. poet. f. 13, fol. 46^v^.

How many give a farewell to their soul 1471
We neither pass the guard, nor stand; but fall.
Southwell, Sir Robert.
MS. *Eng. poet. f. 6, fol. 12 (autogr.).

How many miles is it to Babylon 1472
Yes, and back again.
MS. Douce d. 59, fol. 50^v^.

How many of thy captives (love) complain 1473
If so, be merciful and punish me.
Randolph, Thomas, 'Complaint to Cupid that he never made him inamored'.
Pr. *Poems*, 1638, p. 15.
MSS. CCC. 328, fol. 23, attr. to Randolphe; Eng. poet. c. 50, fol. 98^v^; e. 97, p. 85, attr. to Randall.

How many paltry foolish painted things 1474
Still to survive in my immortal song.
[Drayton, Michael], 'Idea 6th'.
Pr. *Poems*, 1619.
MS. Eng. misc. e. 241, fol. 126.

How may I live, since that my life is gone 1475
All honour, might and majesty / Be given to Christ our King. Amen.
[Southwell, Robert], 'Our Blessed Ladies complaint when she had lost her sonne'.
See J. MacDonald, *Poems and Prose Writings of R. Southwell*, Roxburghe Club, 1937, p. 54.
MS. Eng. poet. b. 5, p. 84.

How merrily we live that shepherds be 1476
We have no envy which sweet mirth confounds.
Pr. Michael East's *Second Set of Madrigales*, 1606, iv.
MSS. Douce 280, fol. 70; Mus. d. 177, fol. 49^v^.

How much, egregious Moore, are we 1477
Or who shall print his works?
Pope, Mr. [Alexander], 'To the Ingenious Mr. Moore, Author of the Celebrated Worm-Powder . . . [1716] . . . printed for E. Curll, on a single Half-Sheet, price 2d'.
Printed copy, MS. Ballard 47, fol. 117.
MS. Eng. misc. e. 183, fol. 61^v^.

How much esteemed the mathematics are 1478
Since here you cannot carp are silent too.
MS. Rawl. poet. 194, fol. 31.

1479 How much the more the miser man
Doth over him oppress.
4 lines used as a copy by Wiman Ramsey, *c.* 1595.
MS. Rawl. D. 649, fol. 9.

1480 How much the stronger, hopes on life rely,
So much the weaker is my faith to die.
[Quarles, Francis], 'On Faith and Hope'. Couplet.
Pr. *Divine Fancies*, 1632, iv. 13.
MS. Rawl. poet. 90, fol. 73$^{v}$.

1481 How nobly did the city Dublin join,
Great Nassau's glory, and the Boyne shall last.
'On K. Will: 3d's Statue At Dublin'.
MS. Add. B. 105, fol. 33.

1482 How now my masters married priests,
May wish such Tyborne fare.
Knell, Thomas, 'An answer to a Papisticall Byll cast in the streetes of Northampton, and brought before the Judges at the last Syses. 1570'.
MS. Firth d. 14, fol. 134.

1483 How now pretty Phillis, what no queen of May.
Ten to one, but a hatter will throttle his charms.
'The Answer to' A58.
MS. Don. c. 55, fol. 18$^{v}$.

1484 How now shepherd what means that
Love a new love every day.
Pr. *Cantus, Songs and Fancies*, Aberdeen, 1662, Sig. H2; and by F. W. Sternfeld from Skene manuscript, in *Elizabethan and Jacobean Studies presented to F. P. Wilson*, 1960, p. 154.
MSS. Eng. poet. f. 16, fol. 3$^{v}$; Mus. d. 184, fol. 40, words only, from B.M. Add. MS. 29481.

1485 How now? turn'd soldier? Leave th'Athenian gown
Of poisoned darts; or Hell-spit bullets hot.
Cheyney, William, 'A compleate armour'.
MS. *Rawl. poet. 86, fol. 19.

1486 How now? What's here? What noise is this? What news?
That we may know and live like those above.
Roach, 'Richard, On the Postman Remounted'.
Cf. *Oedipus or the Postman remounted*, 21–24 Feb. 1729.
MS. Rawl. D. 833, fols. 154, 155, 154$^{v}$ (autogr.)

1487 How oft Clarinda swore by mighty Jove,
She in the wind should write or rapid seas.
'On Clarinda's falshood imitated from Catullus' [lxx], 1735.
MS. Eng. misc. e. 240, p. 156.

How oft have I with impious haste 1488
An home above to share.
Kenton, James.
MS. *Eng. poet. e. 20, p. 129 (autogr.).

How oft Lucinda have I strove, 1489
She frowned, then flung away, and would not hear me speak.
Chatwin, John, 'The Denial'.
MS. *Rawl. poet. 94, p. 46 (autogr.).

How oft my feet with willing mind 1490
Nor more with anxious thoughts opprest.
Gough, Richard, 'The Search after true Happiness'.
MS. *Eng. poet. c. 5, fol. 35$^{v}$ (autogr.).

How oft, my soul hast thou sighed for an hour 1491
My body eats the bread the flesh my faith.
'Communion on Christmas day'.
MS. Rawl. poet. 246, fol. 34$^{v}$.

How oft the wretch who, still deluded, strays 1492
And finds short comfort to her troubled breast.
Homer, Philip Bracebridge, 'on Love'.
MS. *Add. C. 282, p. 7.

How oft when thou, dear dearest music playest 1493
Give them your fingers me your lips to kiss.
[Shakespeare, William, sonnet cxxviii].
MS. Rawl. poet. 152, fol. 34.

How often, in our selves, we see reflections 1494*a*
At morn we leave our graves again, and rise.
Oldisworth, Nicolas, 'On Mortals'.
MS. *Don. c. 24, fol. 27$^{v}$ (autogr.).

How our good king doth papists hate 1494*b*
But bear the little ones in mind.
'Satyr' on Charles II.
MS. Douce 357, fol 108.

How perished is the joy that's past, 1495
Is, in its absence, pain.
'Joyes Past'.
MS. Rawl. poet. 90, fol. 161$^{v}$.

How pleasant a sailor's life passes, 1496
Goes through the world brave boys.
'A Song'.
MS. Montagu e. 13, fol. 32.

How pleasant a soldier's life passes 1497
Go thorough the world, dear joy.
Amherst, Elizabeth, 'supposed to be sent from her Brother who was then in Ireland but written by herself'.
MS. *Eng. poet. e. 109, p. 54.

1498 How pleasant is it, to behold on shore,
And freely grants her favours to the wise.
Somervile, William, 'A Receipt to be happy' 1733, endorsed 'printed'.
Not in *Poems*, etc., 1727, or 1779.
MSS. Ballard 47, fol. 19, attr. to Wm. Somervile; 50, fol. 111, attr. to Wm. Somervile.

1499 How pleasant is the mansions where
Is in the Lord his God that man is blest.
Fairfax, Thomas, Lord, Psalm lxxxiv.
MS. *Fairfax 40, p. 199 (autogr.).
MS. *Fairfax 38, p. 188.

1500 How pleasant is thy dwelling place
To trust all times in thee.
[Hopkins, John], Psalm lxxxiv.
MS. Rawl. poet. 112, fol. 46 rev.

1501 How! Poetry and painting both in one,
Shin'st with a double and unsullied light.
Chatwin, John, 'To the Pious Memory of Mrs. Ann Killigrew. A Pindarique'.
MS. *Rawl. poet. 94, p. 149 (autogr.).

1502 How poor our best returns
Interpretation's thine!
Maitland, Penelope, [*née* Madan, d. 1805], 'Address'd to God'.
MS. Eng. poet. c. 51, p. 4.

1503 How prodigious is my fate
That I fear 'twill break my heart.
MS. Rawl. poet. 65, fol. 28$^{v}$.

How, providence, and yet . . . see W653.

1504 How quick a flying rumour is contrived
To be so common, for with all she lies.
Bulteel, John, 'Against busy tongs'.
MS. *Rawl. poet. 159, fol. 212.

1505 How richly is thy work rewarded! See!
Thou mak'st Gustavus live, Gustavus thee.
Jones, St[ephen], of St. John's College, Cambridge, couplet, to John Russell, author of *The two famous pitcht Battles of Lypsick and Lutzen*, 1634.
MS. Sancroft 53, p. 44.

1506 How rigid are the laws of fate
Though fame and honour speak them ne'er so loud.
'On Death'.
MS. Rawl. poet. 90, fol. 165.

How sacred and how innocent 1507
But chose to spend my life.
P[hilips], K[atherine], 'O[rinda]', 'A Country Life'.
Pr. *Poems*, 1664, p. 177.
MSS. Rawl. poet. 65, fol. 14$^{v}$, attr. to K. P. O.; 90, fol. 3.

How sad's that life when cruel fate 1508
Waste all its hours 'twixt love and hate?
Ashmole, Elias, couplet, 27 Apr. 1655.
MSS. Ashmole 36, 37, fol. 233$^{v}$ (autogr.).

How Salmacis, with weak enfeebling streams 1509
To weaken it and make his wishes good.
Addison, Joseph, 'The Story of Salmacis from the fourth Book of Ovid's Metamorphoses'.
Pr. Dryden's *Miscellany*, iv, 1694, p. 139.
MS. Add. B. 105, fol. 59.

How shall his days end that made weeks? or he 1510
Is an extinguisher of all his light.
'On a Chandler'.
MS. CCC. 328, fol. 61.

How shall I do to be revenged on love? 1511
With women's hearts and then they'll ne'er fly true.
'On Women'.
MS. Malone 21, fol. 45; see also C799, H1514, W 681.

How shall I then describe my love, 1512
From whence she springs, but happiest he, that grafts in such a stock.
Copied from Thomas Ford's *Musicke of Sundrie Kindes*, 1607, no. x.
MS. Mus. d. 8, fol. 20$^{v}$.

How shall the muse, the muse of late so gay 1513
The rose content, if not the diamond fame.
Miss E. S. T., 'Sonnett. To T. E. T. on his birthday 4 Janry. 1789'.
MS. Montagu e. 14, fol. 37.

How shall we be revenged on love 1514
With women's hearts and then they'll ne'er fly true.
'Of Love'.
MS. Ashmole 47, fol. 36$^{v}$; see also C799, H1511. W 681.

How shall we (Sir) your glorious fame display? 1515
Will pay our debt unto the utmost penny.
Barton, Jo., translation of Latin verses 'Senatoribus Londinensibus' recited at Christ's Hospital, St. Matthew's Day 1660 (?).
MS. Rawl. D. 1041, fol. 123$^{v}$.

1516 How short a time of breath was lent
The tidings to King James he bears.
[Andrewes, Frank or Francis], on the birth of the first child of Charles I and Henrietta Maria, 13 May 1629. Attr. to Andrewes in B.M. MS. Harl. 4955, fol. 189.
MSS. Don. c. 57, fol. 37ᵛ, with music; Rawl. poet. 26, fol. 9.

1517 How short of heaven, must human prayers advance
But whence can conquest come without the fight?
'On a Certaine Solemn Occasion a Fable'. [a day of prayer during inaction against Spain, 1739–40 (?)].
MS. Eng. misc. b. 48, fol. 11.

1518 How should I praise thee Lord, how should my rhymes
Make one place everywhere.
Herbert, George, 'The Temper'.
Pr. *The Temple*, 1633, p. 46.
MS. *Tanner 307, fol. 36.

1519 How should I praise these sugared plenties
So says the fox, and so sing I.
MS. Mus. b. 1, fol. 17ᵛ, music by John Wilson.

1520 How simply fond are those that tempt their lives
When men not half enough keep women under.
Bulteel, John, 'Fondnes'.
MS. *Rawl. poet. 159, fol. 213ᵛ.

1521 How Sir Godfry is killed, how his corpse they do hide
The truth [of my story if any one doubt] etc.
'A New Ballade of the Popish Plott'.
MS. Firth c. 16, p. 75.

1522 How sleep the brave who sink to rest,
To dwell a weeping hermit there.
Collins, [William], 'Epitaph written in the year 1745'.
Pr. Dodsley's *Collection of Poems*, 2nd ed. 1748, p. 330.
MS. Montagu e. 14, two copies, fols. 43ᵛ and 57ᵛ.

1523 How slippery is youth's path how hardly can
Is as a martyr though he shed no blood.
Briggs, S[amson], 'Castitas martyrium sine sanguine'.
MSS. Rawl. poet. 147, p. 241 rev., attr. to S. Briggs; 210, fol. 60 rev.

1524 How small joy have those who love truly and well
Take my word, you shall never prerogative lose.
Song.
MS. Don. c. 55, fol. 6.

How smoothly the minutes, dear Celadon, flow 1525
Give love to the nymph, or ease to the swain.
'The Complaining Shepherd'.
MS. Top. London e. 9, p. 162.

How soon a year is come about, 1526
And in few years our life's run out.
Robinson, Robert, couplet.
MS. *Rawl. poet. 218, p. 132 (autogr.).

How soon a year is come about, 1527
And so man's life is done.
Robinson, Robert.
MS. *Rawl. poet. 218, p. 146 (autogr.).

How soon doth man decay? 1528
That all these dyings may be life in death.
Herbert, George, 'Mortification'.
Pr. *The Temple*, 1633, p. 90.
MS. *Tanner 307, fol. 68.

How sore am I laden with sin and wickedness; 1529
[When thou shalt come at the later day].
'Howers of the B. Virgin, Engl. and Lat. ad usum Sarum. Fowerth Lesson for the Dirige'.
MS. Eng. poet. e. 56, p. 100.

How stands the fund? Five pounds in hand 1530
Give me, I beg one plateful more.
Hobhouse, Sir Benjamin, or Smith, W.
MS. Don. c. 81, fol. 146, in the hand of Sir B. Hobhouse.

How surely God loves wondrous well 1531
In Sion's gate.
Clifford, Henry, Earl of Cumberland, Psalm lxxiii.
MS. *Rawl. poet. 95, fol. 17.

How sweet a thing 1532
Of peace, wealth, issue, joy, eternity.
J. F., Psalm cxxxiii.
MS. *Eng. poet. f. 17, p. 73 (autogr.).

How sweet are the pleasures 1533
Thyself to my heart!
Kenton, James, 'Psalm xlii. A Parody on the Song "How sweet in the woodland"'.
MS. *Eng. poet. e. 20, p. 394 (autogr.).

How sweet are these verdurous bowers 1534
Ere summoned as angel, to shine.
Jessop, William, 'Written in 1784 on a visit to Castlerichard . . . near Lismore'.
MS. Percy b. 1, fol. 118 (autogr.).

How sweet the memory of his grace is? 1535
No candidate for that has put up one request.
'On the Death of his Grace', John, Duke of Montagu, d. 1749.
MS. Eng. misc. e. 219, fol. 9ᵛ.

1536 How sweet those words drop from those honey lips
Which while she speak they still each other kiss.
MS. Rawl. D. 954, fol. 28.

1537 How sweet to see my structure's rising frame
Eternal, in the heavens, let mercy grant.
Jessop, William, 'Written in 1774, upon building my house at Lismore'.
MS. Percy b. 1, fol. 118$^v$ (autogr.).

1538 How sweetly doth my master sound? My master
Should all my life employ and busy me.
Herbert, George, 'The Odour. 2 Cor: 2'.
Pr. *The Temple*, 1633, p. 169.
MS. *Tanner 307, fol. 128$^v$.

1539 How sweetly that harmonious music strikes mine ear,
Dissolve to flesh in teary-water.
Colman, Henry, 'On Praier'.
MS. *Rawl. poet. 204, fol. 14$^v$ (autogr.).

1540 How swift flies time on silken wings
Where joys eternal move.
'A young Lady's reflections on her Birthday . . . N.B. The Lady died in her Sixteenth Year'.
MS. Eng. poet. e. 47, p. 149.

1541 How to respect my friends I partly know
A rush for him that cares a straw for me.
[Newman, Thomas].
MS. Top. Oxon. f. 39, fol. 23 (autogr.).

1542 How transient's bliss! of what duration's pain
And the most cheerful heart may deepest bleed.
Maitland, Penelope (1759–1846), 'A Fragment', *c.* 1774–9.
MS. Eng. poet. c. 51, p. 180*b*.

1543 How unaffected Lord am I
And turn the heart of stone to flesh.
Beddome, Benjamin.
MS. *Eng. misc. e. 227, fol. 3.

1544 How unhappy a lover am I
For the souls to meet closer above.
'Song in two parts for Dryden's Conq: of Gran: 2 part', in Act IV.
MS. Rawl. poet. 65, fol. 38.

1545 How vain a thing is man, who toys delight
As if its entertainments were surprising all, and new.
[Tate, Nahum], 'The Round'.
Pr. *Poems*, 1677, p. 104.
MS. Rawl. poet. 90, fol. 118.

How vain a thing is man, whose noblest part, 1546
Shall never need another law.
P[hilips], K[atherine], 'O[rinda]', 'The Soul'.
Pr. *Poems*, 1664, p. 222.
MSS. Rawl. poet. 65, fol. 9, attr. to K. P. O.; Rawl. poet. 173, fol. 184$^v$, attr. to Mrs. Phillips.

How vain are all the joys of man 1547
Would ravish the remaining senses.
Yonge, Sir William (d. 1755), 'On the Loss of an Eye by the Blow of a Tennis-Ball'.
Pr. by John Nichols in *A Select Collection of Miscellany Poems*, 1780, p. 258.
MSS. Eng. poet. f. 12, p. 84, attr. to Sir William Yonge; Top. Oxon. e. 379, fol. 6.

How vain are my pursuits 1548
And welcome heavenly joys.
Beddome, Benjamin.
MS. *Eng. misc. e. 227, fol. 46.

How vain is art to palliate real grief 1549
To thy redeemer, and immortal God.
'The following Lines were written Extempore on the Death of a much Regretted Infant 1761'.
MS. *Eng. poet. e. 28, p. 11.

How vain is man! how anxious his designs! 1550
And with their dirty drabs, sport all the rest away.
'The 1st satire of Persius' translated.
MSS. Ballard 50, fol. 79; Rawl. poet. 172, fol. 169.

How vain is man! how flutt'ring are his joys! 1551
Or never hope to meet with happy days.
'Select Reflections on the Uncertainty of all Sublunary Enjoyments'.
MS. Eng. poet. c. 9, p. 218.

How vain is youth, how ripe to be undone 1552
Pray hold your tongue, he scorns to learn of you.
'A Præmonition to young Heires'.
MS. Rawl. poet. 173, fol. 145.

How vainly do you argue when you say 1553
As you are frank so let your love be free.
Beaumont, Thomas, 'soone consentinge makes not les the esteem'.
MS. *Malone 18, p. 31 (autogr.).

How various is the matter of delight 1554
Satan showed Christ before the eternal light.
MS. *Don. f. 5, fol. 17.

1555 How vile are the sordid intrigues of the town
A curse of this Mounsier what luck have I.
Song from d'Urfey's *The Marriage Hater Match'd*, 1692; music by Purcell.
F. B. Zimmerman, *Purcell*, 1963, no. 602(2).
MS. Mus. Sch. C. 95, p. 218.

1556 How weak a star doth rule mankind
Shall die, as infants go to sleep.
P[hilips], K[atherine], 'O[rinda]', 'Death'.
Pr. *Poems*, 1664, p. 232.
MSS. Rawl. poet. 65, fol. 11, attr. to K. P. O.; 173, fol. 152v.

1557 How well doth this harmonious meeting prove
For he once a year is reputed to laugh.
[Act song] by John Blundevile.
Words pr. *New Court Songs*, 1672.
MS. Mus. Sch. C. 44, fol. 181v.

1558 How well her name an army doth present,
In whom the Lord of hosts did pitch his tent.
Herbert, George, 'Ana{Mary / Army}gram'.
Couplet.
Pr. *The Temple*, 1633, p. 69.
MSS. Rawl. poet. 90, fol. 138; *Tanner 307, fol. 44v.

1559 How well the hour-glass emblems forth frail man
How is he lost that heavenly joys doth taste?
Jones, H[enry], of King's School Sherborne, on the death of Robert Whetcombe, 'Antientest Governour of the King's School of Sherebourne', 24 Oct. 1656.
MS. Gough Dorset 35(1), fol. 20*d*.

1560 How were good folks of ancient days deceived!
How Gods above will like our Gods below.
Prologue to 'A Burletta of Errors founded on the fable of Jupiter and Alcmena', 18th cent.
MS. Eng. poet. c. 11, fol. 26.

1561 How will ye then when fame's immortal blast
Exclaim with fondness—did we weep for this?
'Address'd to Lord and Lady Spencer'.
MS. Eng. poet. c. 51, p. 6.

1562 How willing Dulcia am I
None but yourself your self can dignify.
Beaumont, Thomas, 'of his mrs. poetry'.
MS. *Malone 18, p. 10 (autogr.).

1563 How wise and safe are those that only trust
Establish a sure peace on Israel's lot.
J. F., Psalm cxxv.
MS. *Eng. poet. f. 17, p. 124 (autogr.).

How wise, how good, how fair art thou, my dear. 1564
I'll hug that thing, that thing, I'll vow, is thine.
Oldisworth, Nicolas, 'A lover's fancie'.
MS. *Don. c. 24, fol. 53 (autogr.).

How wisely nature did agree 1565
These seeing eyes these weeping tears.
Marvell, Andrew, 'Eyes and teares'.
Pr. *Poems*, 1681.
MS. Tanner 306, fol. 388, attr. to Mr. Marvil.

How wretched is a lay-man's life, 1566
Of women, wit and wine.
Verses supposedly addressed to Bp. Sprat by a Westminster boy. Sent to Dr. John Fitzwilliam by Ja. Wilcom, 12. Feb. 1694/5.
MS. Rawl. D. 1251, fol. 275.

How wretched is he born or taught 1567
Laid by false feigned and common breath.
Song, with music. Parody of H1407.
MS. Don. c. 57, fol. 51v.

How wretched is the state we all are in 1568
Oh have in mind the last and bitter day.
Song with music for voice and theorbo; additional bass part, fol. 98.
MS. Don. c. 57, fol. 97v.

How wretched is thy state, how full of woe, 1569
Some will cry, take, as fast as thou criedst, give.
'To the Covetous man'.
MS. Rawl. poet. 173, fol. 159v.

How wretchedly he rules 1570
That's served by cowards, and advised by fools!
Couplet.
MS. Sancroft 85, p. 282 rev.

Howe'er averse to flesh and blood 1571
And thus to heaven his servant lead.
Kenton, James.
MS. *Eng. poet. e. 20, p. 158 (autogr.).

Howe'er he lived judge not 1572
Did crown him in his latter deeds.
'A covetous rich man' John Comb 'being dead, and making the poore his heiers [Mr. Wm. Shak-spear] after wrights this for his Epitaph'. See W2117.
Pr. Halliwell, *Introduction to Midsummer Nights Dream*, 1841, p. 90, and *Life of Shakespeare*, 1848, p. 241.
MS. Ashmole 38, p. 180; see also T148, W2117.

Howe'er it happeneth for to fall 1573
As near as the ninth degree.
'Tho: Ryver [Rymer (?)] his prophesie. 300 yeares sithense', of James I.
MS. Eng. poet. c. 50, fol. 26v.

1574 However former ages this, we know
I'll covet for no wealth, wish for no more.
Colman, Henry, 'On Poverty'.
MS. *Rawl. poet. 204, fol. 37$^{v}$ (autogr.).

1575 However it be yet god is good,
His wonders will I tell.
[Sternhold, Thomas], Psalm lxxiii.
MS. Rawl. poet. 112, fol. 50 rev.

1576 However that some have boasted,
That our rightful prince may reign.
'The Covenant Or, No King but the Old King's Son'.
MS. Firth c. 20, fol. 120.

1577 Howl howl my sadder muse and weep a strain
And dance about the same a fairy ring.
Hemminge, William, elegy on Thomas Randolph's finger 'cut of by a Riotous Gentleman'.
MS. Ashmole 38, p. 26.

1578 Howl not you ghosts and furies whilst I sing
When thou buildst Thebes and cast it down again.
Herrick, Robert, song with music by Robert Ramsey.
Pr. from this MS., *Works of Herrick*, ed. L. C. Martin, 1956, p. 421.
MS. Don. c. 57, fol. 53$^{v}$.

1579*a* [How's this? A book for temperance? That first page]
Learn to make meaner, yet far better cheer.
J. Jackson, on L. Lessius' *Hygiasticon*, 1634.
MS. Eng. misc. e. 13, fol. 22$^{v}$.

1579*b* Howsoe'er the world doth deem thee
Still in God's own Israell.
Da[vison], Fr[ancis], Psalm cxxviii.
MS. Rawl. poet. 61, fol. 56$^{v}$.

1580 Howsoe'er they be, thus do they seem to me,
They be and seem not, seem what least they be.
'On Woman', couplet.
From *Wits Recreations*, 1663, Ep. 501.
MS. Eng. poet. d. 152, fol. 104.

1581 Hugh should have gone to Oxford th'other day;
But turned at Tiburn, and so lost his way.
[Peacham, Henry], couplet.
Pr. *Thalia's Banquet*, 1620, Epigram 36.
MS. Sancroft 53, p. 368 rev.

Hum to your witty worships, or rather 1582
This synod of war ended in a diet.
Scrivener, Matthew, [of Catherine Hall], 'Batracho-myo-machia, A Publique Commencement at Cambridge. July 1 and 2 1650'.
MSS. Rawl. poet. 246, fol. 37, attr. to Scrivener; Sancroft 53, p. 35, attr. to Matthew Scrivener.

Humanity the field of miseries 1583
And still it soareth, [gaze] no more my mind.
Alabaster, William, 'Son: 26. Exaltatio humanae Naturae'.
Pr. by B. Dobell, *Athenaeum*, No. 3974, 26 Dec. 1903.
MS. *Eng. poet. e. 57, fol. 7.

Humble thy soul, confess thy sins and grieve 1584
Deny thy self, amend thy life, believe.
Couplet.
MS. Rawl. poet. 66, fol. 61.

Humbly in the flesh appearing 1585
Sharers of his joys above.
Kenton, James.
MS. *Eng. poet. e. 20, p. 124 (autogr.).

Humility loves humility: 1586
She would have none so proud as she.
Robinson, Robert.
MS. *Rawl. poet. 218, p. 161 (autogr.).

Humility's a vine whose root though earth 1587
Only to heaven, and thee may fructify.
Colman, Henry, 'On Humilitie'.
MS. *Rawl. poet. 204, fol. 26$^{v}$ (autogr.).

Humility's the garment Christ did wear: 1588
Else how can they Christ's doctrine truly teach.
Robinson, Robert.
MS. *Rawl. poet. 218, p. 82 (autogr.).

Hunger is sharp, the sated stomach dull 1589
He should do penance, when the sin was his.
Carew, Thomas, 'The Epilogue to the same Play'.
See *Poems*, ed. R. Dunlap, 1949, pp. 127 and 271.
MS. *Don. b. 9, fol. 32.

Hurt by her husband's sword but not his will 1590
Though one survive yet she hath slain them both.
'Margaret Rawlyns, wife of Tho. Rawlyns, d. 28 Jan. 1645', formerly in St. Peter le Bayley Church, Oxford.
MSS. Hearne's diaries 102, p. 131; Top. Oxon. c. 299, fol. 198$^{v}$.

1591 Husband and wife could ne'er so fitly join
Who in their lives and deaths did so agree.
'On the . . . Epitaph' on Francis and Mary Huntrods, in the Churchyard at Whitby.
MS. Ballard 29, fol. 81.

1592 Husband, I would not have thee to conceive
That made both thee and me.
Oldisworth, Nicolas, 'An Ode'.
MS. *Don. c. 24, fol. 17 (autogr.).

1593 Husband, thou dull insipid miscreant,
Confound's soul, body, credit, and estate.
[Oldham, John (?)], 'against Marriage'.
See Rochester's *Poems*, ed. V. De Sola Pinto, 1953, p. xlvii.
MS. Rawl. poet. 173, fol. 94, attr. to Ld. Rochester.

1594 Hush a bye baby be still with thy daddy
So pray, my dear baby, lie still.
MS. Douce d. 59, fol. 63.

1595 Hush! and the dismal tidings shall be told
May they partake the mercies of the omnipotent.
'On the Death of the Lord Russell, capite truncatus July 21mo. 1683. Pindarique Ode'.
MS. Don. c. 55, fol. 16$^v$.

1596 Hush, hush, the god of love here sleeping lies!
His useless shafts lie scatter'd on the ground.
'Love asleep', catch by Samuel Long.
MS. Mus. d. 177, fol. 5$^v$.

1597 Hush, ye pretty warbling quire
Too faint your gales to cool my love.
Gay, John, song from *Acis and Galatea.*
MS. Mus. c. 107, fol. 63$^v$, music by Handel.

1598 Hushed be each ruder breath, and clam'rous tongue
And all is sense, and harmony divine.
Jephson, Robert, lines sent to Malone by J. P. Kemble, 19 July 1788.
Pr. in *Roman Portraits*, 1794, pp. 194–8, 202.
MS. Malone 26, fol. 143.

Hushed was the storm, the fleet was moved 1599
And calmed the tempests of her breast.
'A Ballad'.
MS. Percy d. 9, fol. 73$^v$.

Hydrus the horse courser that cunning mate 1600
If that his gelding be not under five.
'On a Horse Courser'.
MSS. CCC. 328, fol. 39; Eng. poet. e. 14, fol. 91 rev.

Hylas a child, and dead how should it come? 1601
Surely his thread of life was but a thrum.
Couplet.
MS. Malone 19, p. 14.

Hylas oh Hylas why sit we mute 1602
The oak now resembles which lightning has blasted.
Waller, Edmund, 'Chloris and Hylas'.
Pr. *Poems*, 1645, p. 157.
MS. *Don. d. 55, fol. 38$^v$.

Hymen, god of pure desire, 1603
His poor petitioner must die a maid.
'The Lady's Choice of an Husband'.
MS. Eng. poet. f. 12, p. 54.

Hymen, great, mysterious power 1604
And records the happy pair.
'A Petition to Hymen'.
MS. *Eng. poet. d. 47, fol. 167$^v$.

Hymen is summoned to unite a pair 1605
What I have said may prove a prophesy.
Ivory, Abraham, 'Epithilamium. In Celebration of the happie Nuptiall of the much honoured Master Hine and his late endeared Consort'.
MS. Rawl. poet. 208, fols. 2$^v$, 3$^v$.

Hymen the chaste [united (?)] hath his peace 1606
To make the match with like accord.
Darcie, Ab[raham], translation from Latin verses on the marriage of Sir Gervase Cutler and Lady Magdalen Egerton at Ashridge, 12 Sept. 1633.
MS. Top. Yorks c. 26, fol. 140.

# I

ENTRIES 1–1929

1 I A. B. do truly swear
If God won't help me, I'll help my self.
'The Complying Priests Oath'.
MSS. Firth d. 13, fol. 47; Rawl. poet. 207, p. 20.

2 I, Achil here am laid to rest,
Entombed had not lain.
[Price, E. (?)], 'The Epigrame insculped one the grave of Achilles'.
MS. Douce 290, fol. 96$^{v}$ (autogr. (?)).

3 I admire, dear friend, how it does come to pass,
The old plain way, ye gods, let me be poor.
[Cowley, Abraham, translator], 'A Copy of Verses to a Friende', translation of Horace, *Satires* I. i.
Pr. *Works*, 1668, 'Essays in Verse and Prose', p. 128.
MSS. Rawl. poet. 90, fol. 85$^{v}$; Rawl. poet. 173, fol. 36, attr. to Mr. Cowley.

4 I admire you should write to me for a cloak
If you'll let me have the cloak.
'Drollery on the Cloak'.
MS. Tanner 465, fol. 84$^{v}$.

5 I all things see with various beauties crowned,
Where you are not I can no longer stay.
Williams, John, 'Upon Miss Ashe. She at Tunbridge, I at Whitton'.
MS. *Rawl. poet. 191, fol. 106 (autogr.).

6 I am a bonny scot sir
We shall nose you all.
[Jordan, Thomas], 'The New Medley', series of 7 songs, 'Scotch, Dutch, ffrench, Spanish, Welch, Irish, English'.
Pr. *An Antidote against Melancholy*, 1661, p. 59; *Merry Drollery*, pt. i, 1670, p. 127; for attribution see note by Thorn-Drury, Bodl. pr. bk. Thorn-Drury d. 29, p. 252.
MSS. Ashmole 36, 37, fol. 157; Rawl. poet. 26, fol. 156; 37, p. 109.

I am a brisk young lively lass, 7
My mother was so before me.
'A Song. To the Tune of the Hemp-Dressers'. Endorsed 'Ballad made on the late Countess of Coventry'.
MS. Ballard 47, fol. 140.

I am a child that's daily fed 8
Nor other God but thee.
Attr. to Sir Thomas Baynes, B.M. Add. MS. 29921, fol. 75$^{v}$.
MS. Rawl. poet. 37, p. 3.

I am a cripple, lame and blind 9
Here I shall rest for ever more.
'An Hymne'.
MS. Rawl. poet. 37, p. 50.

I am a faithful deputy 10
Unlock Heaven gates as soon as these.
Strode, [William], 'Upon the Register of a Bible'.
MS. Rawl. D. 1092, fol. 270$^{v}$; see also I43, I47.

I am a jolly bowler, and of the William club 11
And a bowling we will go.
'The Bowling Ballad'.
MS. Top. Oxon. b. 170, fol. 3.

I am a jolly huntsman 12
And a hunting [we will go].
MS. Ballard 47, fol. 5.

I am a jolly sailor bold, lately come from cruising, 13
I'll live a sober honest life, and go no more a cruising.
'I'll go no more a cruising'.
Pr. Ashton, *Real Sailor Songs*, 1891, p. 62.
MS. Firth c. 18, fol. 148.

I am a jolly soldier, 14
Be destin'd to the cord.
'Bunker's Hill, or the Soldier's Lamentation'.
MS. Firth c. 17, fol. 59.

I am a lover, and 'tis true. 15
When you and I do part asunder.
Dialogue.
MS. CCC. 327, fol. 11$^{v}$.

16 I am a lusty lively lad
To purchase many kisses.
Sedley, Sir Charles, 'The Extravagant'.
MS. Rawl. poet. 222, fol. 28.

17 I am a poor and harmless maid,
Then may I have as wise as you.
MSS. Ashmole 36, 37, fol. 190$^{v}$.

18 I am a senseless thing with a hey
Leaves the body in a lurch.
'Another base Songe' on Charles II, *c.* 1678.
Pr. in *Poems on Affairs of State*, iii, 1704, p. 70.
MS. Don. b. 8, p. 567.

19 I am a stranger and a pilgrim here
Holy longings to be gone.
'The Christian Pilgrim'.
MS. Rawl. poet. 90, fol. 43.

20 I am a widow, wedded to distress,
Till Heaven adorns me with a second sun?
Q[uarles], J[ohn], 'England sonnents of her beloved king', copied from *A Kingly Bed*, 2nd ed., 1649, p. 95.
MS. Rawl. B. 165, fol. 141$^{v}$.

21 I am amazed to see theology's
Will weep for him when all our eyes are dry.
'An Elegie upon the death of Mr Ambrose Fisher divine, M[r] of Arts of Trinity College in Cambridge', 1617.
MS. Rawl. poet. 160, fol. 10$^{v}$.

22 I am an Englishman and naked I stand here
Musing in my mind what garment I shall wear.
'Dr. Bourd painted for an English-man A poor fellow . . . with these Rhimes', couplet.
MS. Rawl. D. 1372, fol. 3 from end.

23 I am arrested by the sting of death
That now or next day sin will have his due.
'Stipendia peccati Mors', on a marble table, Rochester, copied 2 July 1663.
MS. Top. gen. e. 1, p. 57.

24 I am assured that thou my little book
But love sincerely and do simply show it.
Burton, Francis, 'To his Booke'.
MS. *Add. A. 267, fol. 34$^{v}$ (autogr.).

25 I am at once both tender and tough.
Many my father's claim, and scorn their own.
Williams, John, 'A Riddle. It is one Betty Wise a crazy ravenous old woman'.
MS. *Rawl. poet. 193, fol. 81$^{v}$ (autogr.).

26 I am athirst, what shall I say?
But drink away.
Canon, late 18th cent.
MS. Mus. d. 177, fol. 8$^{v}$.

I am born to die, I know, 27
I'll do nothing else but play.
'The Young Epicurean upon Death'.
MS. Rawl. poet. 173, fol. 145$^{v}$.

I am come to borrow . . . see I116.

I am confessed unto the priest 28
My venial sins soon put away.
'The Papists teach that sins venial are done away and purged by Prayer'. Anglican satire.
MS. Rawl. D. 1372, fol. 14 from end.

I am confirm'd in my belief 29
Then never mind us more.
[Felltham, Owen], 'Upon a breach of Promise'.
Pr. *Resolves*, 1661, 'Lusoria', p. 28.
MSS. Mus. b. 1, fol. 145, music by John Wilson; Rawl. D. 737, fol. 17 rev.

I am convinced, and will henceforth no more 30
And help to force the library door.
Roberts, George, of Merton College, Oxford, 'A Poem on a Black Night'.
MSS. Eng. misc. e. 255, fol. 30; Eng. poet. e. 4, p. 163.

I am much like a hoop, and always am found 31
In miry roads and barren ground.
William, John, 'The letter O'.
MS. *Rawl. poet. 191, fol. 101 (autogr).

I am no captive, I, I find 32
No bondage, nor no thraldom is.
Weaver, Thomas, 'His song beeing a Prisoner'.
Pr. *Songs and Poems*, 1654.
MS. *Rawl. poet. 211, fol. 14$^{v}$ (autogr.).

I am no quaker that I cannot swear 33
But farewell London farewell corporations.
'What a Non-Conformist Can Swear and what he Cannot'.
MS. Lat. misc. c. 19, p. 273.

I am old Davenant, with my fustian quill, 34
Oh gentle knight, thou writest to them that shite.
[John Denham], 'The Author [Davenant] upon himself'.
Pr. amongst *Certain verses . . . to be reprinted with . . . Gondibert*, 1653, p. 9. Cf. *T.L.S.* 1 Sept. 1966, p. 788.
MS. CCC. 309, fol. 52.

I am *Past on*, of life, I've had my fill 35
All that pass off this stage of misery.
'Some anagrammatical conceits of S[r] William Paston being dead'.
MS. Rawl. poet. 152, fol. 195.

36 I am poor 'tis not my fault my father and my mother
Did ill not getting me before my eldest brother.
Couplet, 'upon a younger brother'.
MS. Rawl. poet. 152, fol. 23.

37 I am proud of my tail, and ashamed of my feet,
But many are pleased with what sticks to my coat.
Williams, John, 'A Peacock'.
MS. *Rawl. poet. 191, fol. 101 (autogr.).

38 I am so full of love
I'm wholly swallowed up.
MS. Rawl. poet. 37, p. 83.

39 I am so much in love
And love is all in all.
'A frollick'.
MS. Rawl. poet. 214, fol. 74.

40 I am Sunday most honourable
Whose I serve above all other.
'The daies of the weeke moralized . . . Howers of the B. Virgine. Engl. and lat. ad usum Sarum before Mattins, after the Kalendar'.
MS. Eng. poet. e. 56, p. 85.

41 I am swift yet it never is seen how I move,
In vain both call after me when I am gone.
Williams, John, [riddle], 'it is Time'.
MS. *Rawl. poet. 191, fol. 102 (autogr.).

42 I am that Dido, passenger behold!
Who prais'd the God for robberies and lust.
Mr. Ogilby, translator from Latin, *Illa ego sum Dido*.
MS. Rawl. poet. 109, fol. 26$^{v}$.

43 I am that faithful deputy
Himself to heaven in a string.
[Strode, William], 'A register for a bible'.
MS. Eng. poet. c. 50, fol. 127$^{v}$; see also I10, I47.

44 I am that Saviour that vouchsafed to die
Happy in death, than you in happiness.
Colman, Henry, acrostic and telestich spellings, 'Iesus of Nazareth, King of the Iewes'.
MS. *Rawl. poet. 204, fol. 39$^{v}$ (autogr.).

45 I am the bell of Jesus, and Edward is our king:
Sir Thomas Heywood first caused me to ring.
Couplet, inscription on a bell at Lichfield, destroyed 26 July 1653.
Pr. by Hearne in notes to *Guilelmus Neubrigensis*, 1719, ii. 790.
MS. Rawl. D. 1164, fol. 259.

I am the D[uke] of Norfolk and will be well attended 46
And here is good fellow to thee.
MS. Rawl. B. 35, fol. 48 rev.

I am the faithful deputy 47
Himself to Heaven in a string.
Strode, William, 'A Register for a Bible', corrected.
MS. *CCC. 325, fol. 79 (autogr.).
MS. Eng. poet. e. 97, p. 140; see also I10, I43.

I am the man (I would all wist) 48
Hath, having naught, all his desire.
'Omnia habeo Nequicquam habeo'.
MS. Eng. poet. e. 97, p. 94.

I am the noblest lady on the earth 49
If they'll accept it captains of her guard.
'A Riddle . . . True Religion'.
MS. *Rawl. poet. 197, fol. 14 (autogr.).

I am two fools, I know 50
Who are a little wise, the best fools be.
Donne, John, 'Song'.
Pr. *Poems*, 1633.
MSS. *Eng. poet. e. 99, fol. 108; *f. 9, p. 67.

I am unable yonder beggar cries 51
To stand or go, if he say true he lies.
[Donne, John], 'On a cripple'.
Pr. *Poems*, 1633.
MSS. Ashmole 47, fol. 97$^{v}$; *Eng. poet. f. 9, p. 47; Sancroft 53, p. 58; see also I85, I92, N320, T444.

I am very much concerned to find 52
And love King George of Kings the best.
'The Speech of his Grace the Duke of Marl[boroug]h . . . to the first regiment of foot-guards. June 2. 1715'. Tory satire.
MS. Eng. poet. e. 87, p. 145.

I am yet alive and shall still I hope 53
Live by the bell when you die by the rope.
'Ans.' to H854.
MS. e Mus. 227, fol. 10.

I anagrammatize, *he meanes no il*, 54
I do baptize him Phoenix of our times.
G. de Riv., 'Joannes Helme anag. He meanes no Il'.
MS. Rawl. poet. 104, fol. 62 (autogr.).

I and my love for kisses played 55
Take your own kisses, and I'll take mine again.
MS. Rawl. poet. 31, fol. 2$^{v}$; see also M793.

I, and the world, are neither friends nor foes 56
The milky way seems plain, to faith and love.
MS. Rawl. poet. 66, fol. 5.

57 I, Apollo's kind aid don't require
So potent the charms of Miss R—d . . . (incomplete).
Motteux, Peter, Junr., 'Miss R—d, A Burlesque Song'.
MS. Eng. poet. c. 9, p. 143.

58 I appeal (oh God) to thee
Who my countenance sets right.
[Davison, Francis], Psalm xliii.
MS. Rawl. poet. 61, fol. 35v.

59 I ask not love, but I ask reason why
That dares not swear, There is no love in lust.
'In prayse of true love'.
MS. Rawl. poet. 153, fol. 14v.

60 I ask not wit, nor beauty do I crave
Give me a mind to suit my slavish state.
'The Wish of Miss Morton Daughter to Ld: L—M'.
Attr. to Mrs. Pen. Moreton in B.M. Add. MS. 28101, fol. 49.
MS. Eng. poet. e. 40, fol. 6.

61 I ask ten thousand pardons for my crime
Of him who does remain your slave, Trueboy.
Hulse, Thomas, 'Mr. Trueboy's Answer'.
MS. *Rawl. poet. 152, fol. 85v (autogr.).

62 I asked of Heaven a partner for my bed
Adieu! All gracious Heaven! receive my breath!
[Birch, George, of Remenham, Berks.], 'Elegy 8th, Dissolution', added to *Love Elegies*, 2nd ed., 1777.
MS. Eng. poet. d. 48, MS. p. 1.

63 I asked of time, for whom these temples rose
I reck not whose, he said, they now are mine!
'Sonnet on a pile of Ruins'.
MS. Eng. poet. c. 51, p. 162.

64 I asked philosophy how I should
Content thy self thou get'st not me.
Rhyme on Alchemy.
MS. Rawl. D. 1217, fol. 13.

65 I at my window sit and see
But cherish Autumn in her stead.
MS. Eng. poet. c. 41, fol. 19.

66 I attempt from love's sickness to fly in vain
And love those that hate.
Howard, Robert, 'In the Opera of the Indian Queen . . . set by Mr. Henry Purcell'.
F. B. Zimmerman, *Purcell*, 1963, no. 630(17h).
MS. Mus. Sch. C. 95, p. 132.

67 I baptized am into thy holy fire
I feast upon eternity.
MS. Rawl. poet. 200, fol. 82v.

I beggar take thee beggar 68
And God be thy speed.
Mock marriage vow.
MSS. Ashmole 36, 37, fol. 115v.

I bend my wits and beat my weary brain 69
That feigning might have greater grace procured.
MS. Rawl. poet. 152, fol. 34v.

I bless the Lord my strength, from him 70
The Lord their God obey.
Psalm cxliv.
MS. *Rawl. C. 113, fol. 100v (autogr.).

I bless thee, Lord, because I grow 71
And such beginnings touch their end.
Herbert, George, 'Paradise'.
Pr. *The Temple*, 1633, p. 125.
MSS. Rawl. poet. 90, fol. 136; *Tanner 307, fol. 95v.

I bow my neck oh Lord and do submit 72
Although a king is still an arrant slave.
Bromley, Henry, 'Liberty'.
MS. *Don. e. 19, fol. 16 (autogr.).

I burn, and cruel you in vain 73
Till you burn as well as I.
Carew, Thomas, 'To his Mistress, hee burning in Love'.
Pr. *Poems*, 1640.
MS. *Don. b. 9, fol. 22v.

I burn, I burn, oh, oh, my hearth-burn'd heart 74
And so thy self for want of sust'nance, perish.
MS. Eng. poet. f. 25, fol. 21.

I burn my brain consumes to ashes 75
Which I poor I endure.
d'Urfey, Thomas, 'In Don Quixote set by Mr. John Eccles'.
MS. Mus. Sch. C. 95, p. 136.

I call and cry and make continual moan 76
By Moyses and with Arons careful hand.
Harington, Sir John, Psalm lxxvii.
MS. *Douce 361, fol. 46.

I call and cry to thee (oh Lord) give ear unto my plaint 77
Forget my wickedness (oh Lord) I beseech Thee.
MS. Rawl. poet. 23, p. 13, reference to setting by T. Tallis.

I call no muse, no fury to inspire 78
Courting his virtuous age though[t] him three-score.
'On Gil: Drake' of Wadham, d. 1629.
MS. CCC. 328, fol. 62v.

79 I called to God in greatest straits
As fast to fight they ready made them.
Harington, Sir John, Psalm cxx.
MS. *Douce 361, fol. 79.

80 I came from England into France
Who men say did the same.
[Goodwyn, Thomas].
Pr. *Parnassus Biceps*, 1656, p. 24; Corbet's *Poems*, 1672, p. 129.
See *Parnassus Biceps*, ed. Thorn-Drury, 1927, p. 171.
MSS. Ashmole 36, 37, fol. 44$^{v}$; Eng. poet. c. 50, fol. 113$^{v}$; Rawl. D. 398, fol. 188$^{v}$; Rawl. poet. 62, fol. 29$^{v}$, attr. to Dr. Corbett; see also I418, I572.

81 I came unto a Puritan to woo her
I'll come (quoth she) be't but to keep your oath.
'The woeing of a Puritan'.
MSS. Douce f. 5, fol. 22; Rawl. poet. 199, p. 47.

82 I can be wanton and if I will
I will be still and cry how no more.
MS. Ashmole 176, fol. 98$^{v}$.

83 I can love both fair and brown,
You shall be true to them who're false to you.
Donne, John, 'Song'.
Pr. *Poems*, 1633.
MSS. *Eng. poet. e. 99, fol. 106; *f. 9, p. 48.

84 I can love half an hour when I'm at leisure
He that loves half a day loves beyond measure.
Couplet from 'The Man-hater', *Wit and Drollery*, 1661, p. 193.
MS. Rawl. B. 35, fol. 53 rev.

85 I can neither go nor stand, the cripple cries
What doth he then? If he say true, he lies.
[Donne, John], 'In Claudipedem'.
MS. Don. d. 58, fol. 37$^{v}$; see also I51, I92, N320, T444.

86 I can no longer hold, my body grows
Whole volumes in the twinkling of an eye.
Shirley, James.
Pr. *Poems*, 1646, p. 15.
MS. *Rawl. poet. 88, p. 10; see also I93.

87 I cannot bend the bow, wherein to shoot I sue,
This shaft, must have a notch, whereat my lady laughed.
'To the Lady Bendbow'.
MSS. CCC. 327, fol. 27$^{v}$, attr. to Rawly; Eng. poet. e. 14, fol. 85 rev.; Malone 19, p. 44; Rawl. poet. 26, fol. 2, attr. to Sr. Walter Raleigh.

I cannot boast, I am the happy swain 88
Thus generates thy flame a muse in me.
Pipe, Richard, 'Introduction' to 9 'satirical eclogues' composed 1617.
MS. *Don. e. 22, fol. 3 (autogr.).

I cannot do, as do I would; 89
To a new course I then would fall.
Robinson, Robert.
MS. *Rawl. poet. 218, p. 90 (autogr.).

I cannot forget these unworthy blades yet 90
And give us some sack for the poet.
'The Nine unworthies of Dorsetshire', *temp.* civil wars. Cf. O343.
MS. Rawl. poet. 84, fol. 19$^{v}$ rev.

I cannot fulminate or tonitruate words 91
Admits no caprioles of nonsence here.
[Randolph, Thomas], 'To his Bombasted Frind', James Shirley.
Printed in Shirley's *Grateful Servant*, 1630; Randolph's *Poems*, 1640, p. 131.
MS. Rawl. poet. 142, fol. 16.

I cannot go, sit, stand, the cripple cries 92
What doth he then? if he say true he lies.
[Donne, John], 'On a cripple'.
MSS. CCC. 328, fol. 26$^{v}$; Tanner 465, fol. 95; see also I51, I85, N320, T444.

I cannot longer hold, my body grows 93
Whole volumes in the twinkling of an eye.
[Shirley, James], 'one that Lov'd a great Mrs and durst not discover it'.
Pr. *Poems*, 1646, p. 15.
MS. Eng. poet. c. 50, fol. 110; see also I86.

I cannot ope mine eyes 94
Then by a sun-beam I will climb to thee.
Herbert, George, 'Mattens'.
Pr. *The Temple*, 1633, p. 54.
MS. *Tanner 307, fol. 42.

I cannot pray you in a studied style 95
Nor speak words distant from my heart a mile.
Couplet.
MS. Rawl. poet. 153, fol. 28$^{v}$.

I cannot say I in your service starve. 96
But or discard, or ne'er long, niggards are.
North, Dudley, 3rd Baron.
Pr. *A Forest of Varieties*, 1645.
MS. *North e. 41, fol. 22.

I cannot say that here Prince Henry sleeps 97
To parents kingdoms signed from above.
G. B., on Prince Henry's death, 1612.
MS. *Rawl. poet. 116, fol. 2.

98 I cannot send you back my heart
Perhaps may from your net.
Cavendish, Lady Jane, 'An answeare to my Lady Alice Edgertons Songe Of I prethy send mee back my heart'.
MS. *Rawl. poet. 16, p. 16.

99 I cannot sigh nor sing nor speak nor woo
And go unto some wholesome nut-brown whore.
'Incerti authoris'.
MS. Add. B. 97, fol. 19.

100 I cannot skill of these thy ways
I cannot skill of these my ways.
Herbert George, 'Justice'.
Pr. *The Temple*, 1633, p. 88.
MS. *Tanner 307, fol. 66ᵛ.

101 I cannot speak, nor look, nor nothing say,
For if you will not come I'll make a hermit's vow.
Cavendish, Lady Jane.
MS. *Rawl. poet. 16, p. 41.

102 I cannot think on wretched Cleopatra
There is no doubt but you are cony-catcht.
E. H., 'On a Wife wearing the breeches'.
MS. Rawl. poet. 65, fol. 86.

103 I can't, Celinda, say I love,
Of those bare things, called men.
'Virtuous Affection preferrable to Carnal Love. by an Ingenious Lady. to Celinda'.
MS. Rawl. poet. 173, fol. 100.

104 I can't conceive why in decline of life
The only one he had not done't before.
'Upon Sr. Rob: Walpole's Marriage with Miss Skirret 1738'.
MS. Firth c. 16, p. 308.

105 I can't forbear, oh trifling vicious age
And have all loyal virtuous men your friend.
'Admonition' [1744 (?)].
Pr. bk. Firth b. 22, fol. 44.

106 I can't imagine why you men incline
Or with a dash of wine.
Roach, Richard.
Draft of verses printed in *Oedipus or the Postman Remounted*, 21–24 Feb. 1729.
MS. Rawl. D. 833, fol. 188 (autogr.).

107 I carried late my head on high
And so must you, do what you can.
MS. Don. c. 54, fol. 46*b*ᵛ.

I chanced [my] sweet Lesbia's voice to hear, 108
Or make her dumb or strike me blind.
Randolph, Thomas, 'On a deformed Gentelwoman with a Sweet voyce'.
Pr. *Poems*, 1638, p. 110. 'A French woman attending the Queen' in B.M. MS. Sloane 1446, fol. 63ᵛ.
MSS. Ashmole 38, p. 21, attr. to Mr. Th: Randell; CCC. 328, fol. 77; MS. Eng. poet. c. 50, fol. 97ᵛ; e. 97, p. 26, attr. to Tho. Randolph; Firth e. 4, p. 57, attr. to T. R.; Malone 21, fol. 64ᵛ, attr. to Dr. Lewis; Rawl. poet. 142, fol. 19, attr. to T. R.; see also S1382.

I charge thee muse, with speedy wing to flee 109
As I repair to courteous readers' hands. / Heare Muse thy charge?
Price, E., 'The Translator to his muse', related to W1263 or more probably to T856.
MS. *Douce 290, fol. 1 (autogr.).

I charge ye oh daughters of Jerusalem 110
And this is my friend oh daughter oh daughters of Jerusalem. Hallelujah.
'An Anthem'.
MS. Rawl. poet. 196, fol. 31ᵛ.

I Charles your King will be so kind 111
Shall never ask no more.
'His Majestyes Answer' to I708.
MS. Ballard 47, fol. 9ᵛ.

I come, I come, the messenger of death 112
Into annihilation shall be hurled.
'On the death of the Learned Mr Selden' [1654].
MS. Rawl. poet. 84, fol. 117.

I come my future fate to seek 113
Live unbelov'd, and unlamented die.
'A dialogue Between K- and Head'.
Pr. *A Collection of the Newest . . . Poems . . . against Popery*, 1689, i. 17.
MSS. Firth c. 16, p. 253; Rawl. poet. 159, fol. 180.

I come, my masters, to complain 114
That beasts are men and men are cattle.
Goodwin, J[ohn], 'Beasts', lines written for the Lent Probation, 1700 (?), Merchant Taylors' School.
Pr. bk. Vet. A3 c. 123, fol. 27 (autogr.).

I come ten thousand thanks to pay 115
In only saying that he pleases you!
'1686. Incip. A Satyr To a Lady of quality who commanded mee to Read Boileau'.
MS. Rawl. poet. 159, fol. 60.

116 I come to borrow [and] you'll grant my demand Sir
By bringing th'exchequer in office again.
[Jonson, Ben.], 'The Lord Treasurer [Sir Henry Montagu]'s fortune', from *The Gypsies Metamorphosed*, 1621.
MSS. Rawl. poet. 172, fol. 78; Tanner 306, fol. 252$^{v}$, endorsed 1621.

117 I come to tell thee Joan,
I left the child a crying, G[ossip] Joan.
'Gossip Joan 2 Pt.' John Jowling sent the copy to Thomas Rawlins with a note '. . . Gossip Joan . . . I am inform'd was compos'd by Dean Swift'; not in *Swift's Poems*, ed. H. Williams, 1937.
MS. Ballard 47, fol. 130.

118 I could endure your eye although it shot
That men may kiss their hearts away.
Shirley, James, 'Songe'.
Not pr. in *Poems*, 1646. Pr. from the Rawlinson MS., *Works*, ed. A. Dyce, 1833, vi. 499.
MSS. Ashmole 38, p. 120; *Rawl. poet. 88, p. 20, attr. to J. S.

119 I could have once sung down a summer's sun;
Untun'd's my soul for poetry or rhyme.
Lines on the title-page of 'Lusus Seniles'.
MS. *Eng. poet. d. 47, fol. iv.

120 I could love thee till I die
These are the only sweets of love.
'The Platonick Lady'.
MS. Add. A. 301, fol. x, attr. to Lord Rochester; Rawl. D. 361, fol. 336$^{v}$.

121 I cried to God, he heard my voice
Moses and Aron chose.
Psalm lxxvii.
MS. *Rawl. C. 113, fol. 54$^{v}$.

122 I cried to God with sighs and groans
Thy bounty then will we relate.
Fairfax, Thomas, Lord, Psalm cxlii.
MS. *Fairfax 40, p. 366 (autogr.).
MS. *Fairfax 38, p. 447.

123 I cry and lift my voice to thee
But let me 'scape them all.
Harington, Sir John, Psalm cxli.
MS. *Douce 361, fol. 87.

124 I dare not curse, for 'twas a sacred place
Death bids me to despair, disdain to die.
'Lovers teares'.
MS. Eng. poet. f. 25, fol. 13$^{v}$.

I dare not pass these sorrows to the press 125
You are the priests that must them consecrate.
G. B., 'To the honorable Sonnes of Apollo and Pallas and to no other', in 'Cestria Lugens', on Prince Henry, 1612.
MS. *Rawl. poet. 116, fol. 4$^{v}$.

I dare not question her descent 126
United in her cheek.
'Upon his M$^{rs}$.'
MS. Ashmole 47, fol. 41$^{v}$.

I desire you all in the lord's behalf 127
To pray for the soul of poor John Calfe.
Couplet 'Uppon on Medcalfe'. Answered by O312.
Pr. Camden's *Remaines*, 1623, p. 326.
MS. Ashmole 38, p. 187; see also A913.

I did awhile attend my god's good pleasure 128
Make Lord no long delay.
Harington, Sir John, Psalm xl.
MS. *Douce 361, fol. 24.

I did but crave that I might kiss 129
Not I, I'll vow, not I.
Flatman, Thomas, 'Song. Aug. 1666'.
Pr. *Poems*, 1674, p. 70.
MSS. *Firth d. 7, fol. 39, with a note, 'Set by Mr. Sylvanus Taylour'; Rawl. D. 260, fol. 27*b*$^{v}$.

I did in heart rejoice 130
So much always as lieth in me.
[Kethe, William], Psalm cxxii.
MS. Rawl. poet. 112, fol. 33$^{v}$ rev.

I did intend in rhyme heroic 131
All quickly will return to forty-eight.
'The Converts'.
Pr. *Collection of the Newest . . . Poems . . . against Popery*, 1689, i.2.
MS. Firth c. 16, p. 297.

I did not flatter thee alive, and now 132
But run to pay their tears upon thy hearse.
'An Apologie, in memorie of the most illustrious Prince George Duke of Buckingham', 1628.
MS. Malone 23, p. 123.

I did unto Apollo go 133
Suppose 'twas but a scholar's dream.
'Verses to the Queene passing thorough Oxon . . . to meete the king at Woodstock comming from Scotland'. September 1617.
Cf. *Poems of Corbett*, ed. J. A. W. Bennett and H. R. Trevor-Roper, 1955, p. 174, for ascription to Corbett.
MS. Rawl. D. 1048, fol. 66.

134 I die whenas I do not see
For seeing of her cruelty.
Headed 'Song. Jo: Richards' in B.M. Add. MS. 30982, fol. 36.
MS. Eng. poet. e. 97, p. 164.

135 I do believe in God, Lord of creation:
Sins' pardon, soul and body's resurrection.
[Jordan, Thomas], 'The Material Substance of our Creed Contracted in twelve lines'.
Pr. *Divinity and Morality*, Sig. §§§6v.
MS. Rawl. poet. 90, fol. 85.

136 I do but name thee Pembrooke and I find
Both which are asked to have thee understood.
[Jonson, Ben.], 'To William Earle Pembrooke', *Epigrammes* cii.
MS. Ashmole 47, fol. 44v.

137 I do confess great God my sins are great
I may be thine, and saved by thy death.
Cavendish, Lady Jane, 'To Heaven or a confession to God'.
MS. *Rawl. poet. 16, p. 36.

138 I do confess I love thee
I am paid for all my grief.
MS. Mus. b. 1, fol. 22v, music by John Wilson.

139 I do confess my flea-blown muse doth swell
Your ever-verdured praise, eternal worth.
Vaux, Francis, of Queen's College, Oxford (matr. 1655), 'These few lines are subscribed by him, who professes himself to be your most devoted servant'.
MS. Wood F. 34, fol. 173 (autogr.).

140 I do confess, oh God, my wand'ring fires
My sins with night, but winds to purge my breast.
'Confession. W[illiam] Cartwright. poems [1651] p. 320'.
MS. Tanner 466, fol. 4.

141 I do confess that thou art fair
Content to think thou mayest love, but not me.
MS. Mus. b. 1, fol. 165v, music by John Wilson.

142 I do confess thee smooth and fair
Has brought thee to be loved by none.
MS. Eng. misc. e. 241, fol. 123.

143 I do desire to live
A gallant man for fame.
Cavendish, Lady Jane, 'A Songe'.
MS. *Rawl. poet. 16, p. 21.

144 I do love, only but thee,
For any service done to thee.
Burton, Francis.
MS. *Add. A. 267, three copies, fols. 126v, 128, 150 (autogr.).

I do not flatter when I praise to mend 145
To cure is more than to contest.
Williams, John, 'To Praise is not to flatter'.
MS. *Rawl. poet. 191, fol. 3v (autogr.).

I do not think you can so guilty be 146
Your face would wear no patches but a cloud.
MS. Rawl. poet. 26, fol. 155v.

I do presume, my dear, once more to write 147
My self, your captivated love, Nan Hide.
Hulse, Thomas, 'A letter From an old Cook-maid in England to George Blunderbuss, A Trooper in Flanders'.
MS. *Rawl. poet. 152, fol. 71 (autogr.).

I don't well understand at what you laugh, 148
Till you can smell it out you should not smile.
Williams, John, 'To a Lady that laught at me for saying something backwards'.
MS. *Rawl. poet. 184, fol. 41 (autogr.).

I dote, I dote, yet am a [fool] sot to show't 149
And that is the short and the long on't.
Pr. *Wit Restor'd*, 1658, p. 165, as 'The drunken Lover. J. D. Delight'.
MSS. Ashmole 36, 37, fol. 146; Locke e. 17, p. 73; Rawl. poet. 84, fol. 57v rev.; 214, fol. 69 rev.

I dread alas to plead my woful case 150
And for thy sake doth loath this life of mine.
Andrews, —.
MS. *Rawl. poet. 92, fol. 14.

I dream't that buried in my [fellow] native clay 151
That is thy rotting place, and this is mine.
'Pulvis et umbra sumus . . . A Nobleman's Dream', 1735.
MSS. Eng. misc. e. 240, p. 282; Eng. poet. c. 9, p. 237; f. 13, fol. 74; Rawl. D. 842, fol. 103.

I envy no man's rest 152
Thou art unto my heart the ever welcome guest.
MS. Mus. b. 1, fol. 29, music by John Wilson.

I envy not those graves, that take up room 153
Shall dignify all places where it's thrown.
Lines from the tomb of Francis Osborn, 7th son of Sir John Osborn, at Nether Worton, Oxon., d. 4 Feb. 1658.
MS. CCC. 309, fol. 121v.

I envy not thy mortal triumphs death: 154
Thus strive to canonize thy memory.
King, Henry, 'An Elegy upon . . . Lady An: Rich.'
Pr. *Poems*, 1657, p. 84.
MSS. Eng. misc. e. 262, fol. 37v, attr. to Dr. Hen. King; *Eng. poet. e. 30, fol. 83v.

155 **I even I will always**
**Who him their trust esteem.**
Sidney, Sir Philip, Psalm xxxiv.
MSS. *Rawl. poet. 24, p. 45; *25, fol. 26.

156 **I every day, early and late,**
**On those the fruits of my deceased love.**
[Corbet, W.], 'On my Deceased second Self'.
MS. *Rawl. poet. 210, fol. 27v.

157 **I fear no rubs nor dangers I can meet**
**Have bent my heart's desires to all eternity.**
Knollys, Fra., Psalm cxix, 'Nun'.
MS. *Rawl. poet. 60, p. 7 (autogr.).

158 **I fear not fortune's wheel, nor envy's tooth.**
**By doing right, and bearing wrong, and speaking sooth.**
MS. Rawl. poet. 66, fol. 40.

159 **I feed a flame within that so torments me**
**Nor lower can I fall mounting no higher.**
[Dryden, John], song from *The Maiden-Queen*, 1668, p. 46 (Act IV, sc. ii).
MS. Rawl. poet. 65, fol. 29v.

160 **I feel oh Lord thy mercy lift me up**
**Gaining by Christ, a sempiternal crown.**
Lilliat, John, 'A Christians Triumphe'.
MS. Rawl. poet. 148, fol. 102 (autogr.).

161 **I felt my heart, and found a chillness cool**
**The rock, that can't be melted, may be cleft.**
'Gods love, and Power. Song . . . M[artin] Llewellin poëm. [*Men-Miracles with other Poems*, 1656] p. 112'.
MS. Tanner 466, fol. 6v.

162 **I felt my heart and found a flame**
**But by the ruins of her nest.**
MS. Mus. b. 1, fol. 136v, music by John Wilson.

163 **I find by this hand, you have the command**
**Being a true one by blood and office too.**
[Jonson, Ben.], 'The Lord Duke [of Lennox]'s fortune'. From *The Gypsies Metamorphosed*, 1621.
MSS. Rawl. poet. 172, fol. 78; Tanner 306, fol. 252, endorsed 1621.

164 **I find that God is good to Jacob's race**
**In Salem's gate still singing loud they praise.**
Harington, Sir John, Psalm lxxiii.
MS. *Douce 361, fol. 43.

165 **I first was dead, now this glad vantage have**
**Beyond sea, far beyond my sea of wit.**
Pestell, Thomas, 'A second Elegie on' Elizabeth, Countess of Huntingdon.
MS. *Malone 14, p. 8.

**I fix mine eye on thine and there** 166
**Being in thine own heart from all malice free.**
Donne, John, 'The Picture'.
Pr. *Poems*, 1633.
MSS. *Eng. poet. f. 9, p. 34, attr. to J. D.; Rawl. poet. 31, fol. 39*b*.

**I flag, frail man: how gladly would I keep** 167
**My tears prove *aqua-vitae* for her sake.**
Oldisworth, Giles, 'once upon Mrs Margery [Apjohn]'; recited with reference to the death of [his sister-in-law] Mrs. Brumfield, in 'The Pattern of Piety'.
MS. *Rawl. C. 422, fol. 18 (autogr.).

**I gave to hope a watch of mine: but he** 168
**I did expect a ring.**
Herbert, George, 'Hope'.
Pr. *The Temple*, 1633, p. 114.
MS. *Tanner 307, fol. 86v.

**I gently took my horse** 169
**I am, and am not dead.**
Oldisworth, Giles (?), 'The Provision', 'The Discoverye', 'The Expence', 'The Newes', verses found in the pocket of one supposed to be [Paul Viscount Bayning, d. 11 June 1638] in 'The Patterne of Pietye'.
MS. *Rawl. C. 422, fol. 35, in the hand of Giles Oldisworth.

**I give not (though I love them well) the lilies** 170
**The wholesomest herb, under the firmament.**
Mabbe, J[ames], of Magdalen College Oxford, 'To Sr G. T. K.'
MS. Add. B. 97, fol. 56v.

**I go dear saint away snatched from thy arms** 171
**And thus united be by death's divorce.**
[Stanley, Thomas], song.
Pr. Stanley's *Poems*, 1647, p. 32, and with music by J. Gamble in his *Ayres and Dialogues*, 1656, p. 61.
MS. Mus. b. 1, fol. 172v, music by John Wilson.

**I grant, my bark, oars, men, too slow, weak, pale,** 172
**End, meanly ended, better is, than undone.**
Lane, John, 'Lectori acrosticum', on his continuation of *The Squiers Tale*.
Pr. Chaucer Soc., ser. 2, xxiii, 1888, p. 13.
MS. Douce 170, fol. 4v (autogr.).

**I grieve and dare not show my discontent** 173
**Or die and so forget what love e'er meant.**
'Eliza Regina upon mounsurs departure'.
MSS. Ashmole 781, p. 142; Tanner 76, fol. 94.

**I had a little hen, the prettiest ever seen** 174
**And sat by the fire and told many a fine tale.**
MS. Douce d. 59, fol. 51.

175 I had a little hobby horse
Without a new coat.
MS. Douce d. 59, fol. 59.

176 I had a little husband
To blow his dirty nose.
MS. Douce d. 59, fol. 49.

177 I had a mother which to speak was such
And now sweet Saint, thy happy soul's at rest.
Cavendish, Lady Jane, 'On my deare mother the Countess of Newcastle', d. 17 Apr. 1643.
MS. *Rawl. poet. 16, p. 31.

178 [I] had [a] soul but prized it not
[D]ear Lord what have I done.
MS. Mus. Sch. G. 632, fol. 63.

179 I had a vision yesternight,
Who would not die up[on] the spot?
[Cleveland, John], 'The Seate of Love, or the Senses Festivall'.
Pr. *Poems*, 1651, p. [1].
MS. Tanner 306, fol. 424.

180 I had and have a purpose to be kind
Hissing in holes till they truth-bitten die.
Townsend, Aurelian, 'Elegy on the death of the King of Sweden sent to T: Carewe'. 1632.
MSS. Don. b. 9, fol. 28 (incomplete); Rawl. poet. 209, fol. 18v.

181 I had my failings be the truth confessed
He'll prove our friend, who lived and died for all.
'Epitaph designed for its Author'.
MS. Top. gen. e. 32, fol. 59.

182 I had rather break my neck in climbing up an oak
Than once prick my finger in stooping for a thistle.
Couplet.
MS. Rawl. poet. 148, fol. 4v.

183 I had resolved at last to put an end
Those whom to further follies she'd bewitch.
'To Iris'.
MS. Montagu e. 13, fol. 131v.

184 I had to poets an alarum given
Sith printers, may not preach, yet they will pray.
Lane, John, 'The Muse [of *The Squiers Tale*] to the fowre winds'.
Pr. Chaucer Soc., ser. 2, xxiii, 1888, ed. F. J. Furnivall, p. 7.
MS. Ashmole 53, fol. ii.

I hate a lie [and] yet late a lie did run 185
Ten thousand times, then had the lie been true.
'Upon the death of Sir G. Goring and the Earl of Kensington Falsely rumored', at the siege of Breda, 1637.
Pr. *Wits Recreations*, 1640, no. 135.
MSS. Firth e. 4, p. 6; Rawl. D. 398, fol. 228v; Rawl. poet. 160, fol. 23.

I hate fruition, now 'tis past 186
But fresh, and always but begun.
Oldham, John, 'A Fragment of Petronius paraphras'd'.
Pr. Oldham's *Compositions in Prose and Verse*, 1770, iii. 1.
MSS. Rawl. D. 1480, fol. 204, attr. to Oldham; Rawl. poet. 173, fol. 56, attr. to Mr. Oldham.

I hate that drum's discordant sound 187
To fill the catalogue of human woes.
Scott, Mr. [John of Amwell], 'an ode'.
MS. Eng. misc. e. 241, fol. 83.

I hate the noise of greatness, and a name 188
And let the restless monarch distant countries trace.
Chatwin, John, 'A Moderate Estate and a true Friend is to be prefer'd before pomp and Grandeur'.
MS. *Rawl. poet. 94, p. 175 (autogr.).

I have a cure, to be oft absent thence 189
It will, I doubt, be call'd non-residence.
Barksdale, Clement, 'Residence', distich.
MS. Autogr. c. 9, fol. 154 (autogr.).

I have a mistress suiteth so 190
All-hallowed good, she bears in chief.
Ashmole, Elias, 'To Laureola', Lady Mainwaring, 1649.
MSS. Ashmole 36, 37, fol. 235 (autogr.).

I have a silent sorrow here 191
Unpardoned, love, by thee.
Sheridan, Richard Brinsley, 'in the play of the Stranger'.
MS. Eng. poet. c. 51, p. 60.

I have a suit, Crispinus, pray deny not 192
(If put thereto) she has not lost her hair.
'In Crispinum'.
MS. Don. d. 58, fol. 32v.

I have been a foster long and many a day 193
Yet have I been a foster.
Song by Dr. Cooper, transcribed from B.M. Add. MS. 31922.
MS. Mus. d. 183, fol. 8.

194 I have been captived very long
A true repenting heart.
'The Author's relation of his owne Captivitie under sinn in particular as followeth'.
MS. *Rawl. poet. 100, fol. 41 (autogr.).

195 I have been troubled heretofore
But *veritas odium parit.*
Endorsed 'George Blagrave Christmas Caroll about the late tymes' [i.e. the Commonwealth].
MS. Eng. poet. c. 25, fol. 60.

196 I have been young, but now am old,
Oh Jesus fit me for thy fold.
Robinson, Robert.
MS. *Rawl. poet. 218, p. 82 (autogr.).

197 I have before loved often I allow,
And for each year thou hast a thousand pound.
Walsh, William, 'Upon his being in Love wth: an old Woman [Greek Anthology], El: 24'.
MS. Malone 9, fol. 32 (autogr.).

198 I have beheld two lovers in a night
Doing's the fruit of doing well, farewell.
'Mr. Robert Hericke his farwell unto Poetrie'.
Not printed in *Hesperides*, 1648. Pr. from this MS., *Works*, ed. L. C. Martin, 1956, p. 410.
MS. Ashmole 38, p. 106; see also E153.

199 I have considered it, and find,
The man, who once against thee fought.
Herbert, George, 'The Reprisall'.
Pr. *The Temple*, 1633, p. 28.
MS. *Tanner 307, fol. 22v.

200 I have done one braver thing
Which is, to keep that hid.
Donne, John.
Pr. *Poems*, 1633.
MSS. *Eng. poet. e. 99, fol. 124v; *f. 9, p. 107.

201 I have encumbered in this present life
The saints great rest come Lord Jesus come.
Initialed N.C.
MS. Ashmole 38, p. 185.

202 I have entreated and I have complained
Tears cannot pierce her heart nor sighs her ears.
[Davison, Walter].
Pr. John Ward's *First Set of Madrigals*, 1613, xxvi.
MSS. Mus. f. 20–24: f. 20, fol. 82v.

I have lost my milch cow 203
And our purses they are empty.
B[rackley], E[lizabeth], 'The Songe' in a pastoral.
MS. *Rawl. poet. 16, p. 61.

I have lost my mistress, horse and wife, 204
I am sorry for my horse.
'On Losses'.
MS. *Eng. poet. d. 47, fol. 30.

I have loved very much and very long 205
In Cupid's court I should non-suited be.
Creswell, Robert, 'Love and poverty'.
MS. *Eng. poet. f. 24, fol. 23 (autogr.).

I have no feet and yet can walk, (with crutches) 206
To read I need not any light (being blind).
Williams, John.
MS. *Rawl. poet. 191, fol. 101 (autogr.).

I have no hands and yet I trace 207
Will be yourself to know.
B[urton], J., 'The Looking glass—a Riddle'.
MS. Top. Oxon. e. 172, fol. 76v.

I have no humour to adore the face 208
Contains what's good in women and his own.
Shirley, James, 'To a Gentleman that Magnified his Mrs. the prayse of a Mr.'
Cf. *Poems*, 1646, p. 67, 'Friendship'.
MSS. Eng. poet. c. 50, fol. 108v; *Rawl. poet. 88, p. 17.

I have no pleasure in you saith the Lord, 209
Their devout worship to his Holy name.
'Malachy I. chaptr. 10 vers:'.
MS. *Rawl. C. 113, fol. 10v (autogr.).

I have no vein in verse but if I could 210
Whilst other muses writes mine only cries.
Sinewes, [Richard Senhouse (?)], 'Epitaph on Prince Henery', 1612.
Attr. in B.M. Add. MS. 15226, fol. 4, to 'Dr. Synowes, Col. S. J.'
MSS. Ashmole 781, p. 163, attr. to Sinewes; CCC. 327, fol. 15; 328, fol. 28; Douce f. 5, fol. 4.

I have now received thy sacrament so find 211
Thy father landed safe, hath sent for thee.
Cavendish, Lady Jane.
MS. *Rawl. poet. 16, p. 41.

I have oft wondered, why thou didst elect 212
Can mend that night piece: that is, make her worse.
King, Henry, 'Con mala Muger el remedio Mucha Terra por el medio'.
Pr. *Poems*, 1657, p. 35.
MS. *Eng. poet. e. 30, fol. 15v; *Malone 22, fol. 10; see also I369.

213 **I have often admir'd what should be the cause,**
**In spite of the devil and the word abdicate.**
'Pandora's Box or the Mischievous Effects of the word Abdicate'.
MS. Firth d. 13, fol. 78.

214 **I have read of bull fights,**
**Ye follow't as the devil were in ye.**
'The Baiting of the Tyger'.
MS. Firth d. 14, fol. 11.

215 **I have received dear father what you sent**
**Well may you think you shall not plough the shore.**
'Upon a Paire of Bandstrings sent from my father for a Token'.
MS. Rawl. poet. 194, fol. 30.

216 **I have seen many great anes, and sat in great ha's**
**[Oh charming's the blink o' my ain fire-side].**
Hamilton, Mrs., 'My Ain Fire Side'.
MS. Percy d. 9, fol. 68.

217 **I have seen the rose-bud blow**
**Till crowned with endless joys above!**
C[owper], Mary Frances Cecilia, 'On viewing her sleeping Infant C[harles] C[owper]. 1767'.
MS. Eng. poet. c. 51, p. 278.

218 **I have seen thee far, I have seen thee near**
**But union in perfection.**
Tune, 'Winter and could weather'. Answered by L90.
MS. Rawl. poet. 37, p. 36.

219 **I have the golden and green lyen truly**
**In me lieth hidden the secrets of philosophy.**
Translation from Dutch in *Rosarium Philosophorum*, 1550.
MS. Ashmole 1459, p. 465.

220 **I have this while a prisoner close**
**Art-masters to control.**
'The wanderers Lament, Preface . . . A song for this sad time . . . 1667'.
MS. Rawl. poet. 170, fol. 48.

221 **I have too long endured her guilty scorn,**
**That down love's current drives me fast away.**
Oldham, John, Ovid, *Amores* III. xi, 'Upon an underserving and ungratefull Mistress, whom he cou'd not forbear to love, paraphrastically translated'.
MS. Rawl. poet. 173, fol. 50$^{v}$.

**I hear Brerinda's tender soul** 222
**May his soul prove a seraphim.**
MS. *Don. f. 5, fol. 31.

**I hear that you of late are grown** 223
**But when the glass was out the cant was done.**
Knapp, Francis, of Magdalen College, Oxford, 'An Epistle to Mr. B.'
Pr. *Fourth Part of Miscellany Poems*, 1694, p. 266.
MS. Add. B. 105, fol. 2.

**I hear the whistling ploughman, all day long,** 224
**T'one's at God's finding: t'other, at his own.**
[Quarles, Francis], 'On the Ploughman'.
Pr. *Divine Fancies*, 1632, i. 77.
MS. Rawl. poet. 90, fol. 64$^{v}$.

**I heard a noise and wished for a sight** 225
**Blest be the thing that brought the shadow thither.**
Pr. Thomas Bateson's *Second Set of Madrigales*, 1618, xviii.
MSS. Rawl. poet. 85, fol. 45$^{v}$; 148, fol. 67$^{v}$.

**I heard lately to a lady** 226
**And grant good will I n'ill quoth she.**
MS. Ashmole 48, fol. 18$^{v}$, two copies, one subscribed F. G., the other Christopher Curtis.

**I heard men say tell her anon** 227
**But oh no man could keep it for t'was thine.**
MS. Rawl. poet. 116, fol. 52$^{v}$.

**I [heard] heer'd much take of Oxford Town** 228
**An moather an zister Joan.**
'A Country-Man's ramble to Oxford'. 1735.
MS. Eng. misc. e. 240, p. 142.

**I heard of one is lately gone** 229
**The purse hath lost his master.**
'A oyes'.
MS. Douce 357, fol. 9$^{v}$.

**I heard the virgins sigh. I saw the sleek** 230
**Thus even by rivals to be deified.**
Carew, Thomas, 'on Carlisles daughter', the Lady Ann Hay.
Pr. *Poems*, 1640.
MSS. Rawl. poet. 142, fol. 43, attr. to Th. Carew; Rawl. poet. 209, fol. 3$^{v}$, attr. to T. C.

231 I hold as faith
Makes Christians worse than Turks.
Equivocal verses on Protestant and Papist.
Pr. *Wits Recreations*, 1640, and *Parnassus Biceps*, 1656.
MSS. Ashmole 38, p. 116; Dodsworth 144, fol. 98[v]; Douce 357, fol. 129; Eng. poet. e. 97, p. 181; f. 10, fol. 95[v]; Hearne's diaries 35, p. 171; Malone 21, fol. 78; Rawl. D. 859, two copies, fols. 119, 139[v], the second dated 1636; 1092, fol. 268[v], attr. to Dr. Strode of Christ Church; Rawl. poet. 26, fol. 105; 153, fol. 28[v]; Tanner 465, fol. 61; see also W102.

232 I honestly confess this text too true
May friendly kind reproof be ever near.
Amherst, Elizabeth, 'To a Gentleman who convinced me I had too much vanity'.
MS. *Eng. poet. e. 109, p. 32.

233 I hope at this time 'tis no news
She strives to eat it with her eye.
'On Fairford windowes'.
Cf. *Poems of Corbett*, ed. J. A. W. Bennett and H. R. Trevor-Roper, p. 157, for ascription to Jerameel Terrent.
MS. Eng. poet. e. 97, p. 33, attr. to Dr. Corbett; not pr. among his poems.

234 I hope bright nymph that you'll excuse
If that's perform'd a pox on fame.
MS. Top. Oxon. c. 108, p. 9 (autogr.).

I hope by this time . . . see I233.

235 I hope conceived that fortune had done frowning
The worst is past, I shall be hang'd tomorrow.
H. S.
MS. *Rawl. poet. 120, fol. 10[v] (autogr.).

236 I hope gentlemen you'll thank me for making English of 'em
Can write such lines as Humphrey Hody.
Aylworth [or Aldworth, Henry], of Christ Church, verses in *Terrae filius* speech, 10 July 1693.
Mentioned by Wood, see *Life and Times*, ed. A. Clark, iii, O.H.S. xxvi, 1894, p. 427.
MS. Rawl. D. 912, fol. 159.

237 I hope these feeble efforts you'll excuse
And long preserve you member of this town.
Bate, Sally, 'on her Uncle Mr. Aufreres being Chosen Member of Parliament for Stamford' [21 Jan. 1765].
MS. *Eng. poet. e. 28, p. 58.

I hope this morning lecture's to your mind 238
To furnish scandal for th'ensuing year.
Smith, —, of University College, 'The Epilogue', Oxford Act, 8 July 1693.
MSS. Eng. poet. f. 13, fol. 63; Top. Oxon. c. 326, two copies, fols. 52[v] and 55; e. 280, p. 668 rev., attr. to Smith of University College.

I hope you are not come to sit 239
And Bacchus guide his men.
Olivier, Is[aack], 'Second-course Verses at Recent-time at Eaton'.
MS. Rawl. poet. 246, fol. 3.

I hopeless languish out my days 240
Confirm's the conquest of her eyes.
Etheredge, Sir Geo[rge], 'Voiture's Urania. Love more prevalent than Reason'.
Pr. *A Collection of Poems written on Several Occasions, by Several Persons*, 1672, beg. Hopeless I . . . .
MS. Rawl. poet. 173, fol. 62.

I humbly entreat you for charity's sake 241
I'll sing t'ee from evening till day all abroad.
'A song made for a child of [4] by Mr. Richard Brown'.
MS. Mus. Sch. C. 95, p. 60.

I, I have sinned against the Lord 242
And save me by thy richest grace.
Kenton, James.
MS. *Eng. poet. e. 20, p. 250 (autogr.).

I in a dusky'sh evening very late 243*a*
Me with her eyes and now as easily with her name.
'The Valentine'.
MS. Don. c. 55, fol. 1.

I in assemblies praise will sing 243*b*
Th' are only wise his statutes heed.
Fairfax, Thomas, Lord, Psalm cxi.
MS. *Fairfax 38, p. 399; see also I1450.

I intend with true report to praise 244
God keep it so still with the same property.
'The Stanleys antiquytyes in englyshe meeter'.
MS. Rawl. poet. 143, fol. 12.

I invocate no nymph, no grace, no muse 245
And ev'ry leaf may celebrate thy praise.
Colman, Henry, 'The Invocation [to] Divine Meditations'.
MS. *Rawl. poet. 204, fol. 1 (autogr.).

I Joan in haste 246
Or else pure need.
'On A whore purposing to turne honest'.
MS. Ashmole 38, p. 156.

247 I joy, dear mother, when I view
And none but thee.
Herbert, George, 'The British Church'.
Pr. *The Temple*, 1633, p. 102.
MS. *Tanner 307, fol. 76v.

248 I joy in grief and do detest all joys
And from our burning breath, the trees do bend.
Sidney, Sir Philip, from the *Arcadia*.
MS. *e Mus. 37, fol. 185v.

249 I joy in that, wherin all should rejoyce
Though lily white, doth bear most sway in me.
Lilliat, John, anagram on his name. 'That John, signifyeth: gracia Dei'.
MS. Rawl. poet. 148, fol. 2 (autogr.).

250 I joyed to hear so godly motion
And for God's house this prayer I make.
Harington, Sir John, Psalm cxxii.
MS. *Douce 361, fol. 79v.

251 I judge by your motto, if rightly I ween
And wide let your deeds like your sealing-wax spread.
'To Lt. Col. R. V[yse 1746–1825] keeper of a great seal'.
MS. Eng. poet. c. 51, p. 188.

252 I judge not as I love, I hate, or fear,
But sentence on the truth of what I hear.
Couplet translated from Latin.
MS. Rawl. poet. 209, fol. 35v.

253 I judge the muse of lewd desire
Break down the timber, and dig up the stone.
Watts, Isaac, ['Burning several Poems of Ovid, Martial, Oldham, Dryden, etc. 1708'].
Pr. *Horæ Lyricæ*.
MS. Rawl. D. 868, fol. 63.

254 I just received I own
Your [ ] L[ords] and C[ommons]
Incomplete.
MS. Firth b. 4, fol. 48.

255 I keep my horse, I keep my whore
[Deliver] your purse Sir.
'Thee High Lawyer's song in the playe called the Widdowe' [ascr. to Jonson, Fletcher and Middleton, by the printers, 1652.]
In Dodsley's *Old Plays*, 1780, xii. 271.
MS. Ashmole 38, p. 127.

256 I know a poor servant, yet true I dare say it
To give his attendance without any strife.
Riddle.
MS. Rawl. poet. 217, fol. 76v.

I know as well as you, she is not fair 257
'Tis because she is she, and I am I.
'Doctor Donn verses'.
Pr. *Wit Restor'd*, 1658, p. 109.
MS. Ashmole 38, p. 62.

I know brother tar, those French durst not stand us 258
We'll cover our descent with huzzas and down drinking.
'A catch upon a victory at sea set by Dr. John Blow'.
MS. Mus. Sch. C. 95, p. 55.

I know I am a mortal man, 259
We've time for thinking after death.
Walsh, William, translator, [Greek Anthology] '486'.
MS. Malone 9, fol. 31v (autogr.).

I know it is my sin which locks thine ears; 260
His blood's sweet current much more loud to be.
Herbert, George, 'Lock and Key'.
Pr. *The Temple*, 1633, p. 57.
MSS. Rawl. poet. 90, fol. 135v; *Tanner 307, fol. 44v.

I know it should be so; the church which he 261
With thankful odes bribe heaven to a reprieve.
P[aman], C[lement], 'The E. of Strafford's recovery to G[odfrey] R[hodes].'
MS. Rawl. poet. 246, fol. 19.

I know many sisters twins born of one mother 262
Are slain by their lovers, a pitiful case.
Riddle.
MS. Rawl. poet. 217, fol. 77v.

I know no fitter subject for your view 263
Prove good to you, and perfect as this wife.
King, Henry, 'To a Freind upon Overburies Wife given to hir'.
Pr. *Poems*, 1657, p. 7.
MSS. *Eng. poet. e. 30, fol. 36; *Malone 22, fol. 23v.

I know no paint of poetry 264
Might be its own evangelist.
Strode, William, 'On Faireford windores'.
MS. *CCC. 325, fol. 58v (autogr.).
MSS. Eng. poet. e. 97, p. 32, attr. to W. Stroad; Malone 21, fol. 1, attr. to W. Stroud.

I know not how it fares with other men 265
And I (poor I) have lost a noble friend.
Bulteel, John, 'An Elegy upon the much-bewayled Sr Peircy Smith Knight' (knighted Jan. 1629/30).
MS. *Rawl. poet. 159, fol. 222.

266 I know not how our Oxford wits do date
'Tis said in Oxford, that Bred-a is lost.
On Christ Church losing the proctorship, [1625], 'Ch. Ch. called Bread eaters'.
MS. Eng. poet. e. 14, fol. 60.

267 I know not how to go about to state
Smile on thy wretched patient, say amen.
'The Distressed Patient'.
MS. Eng. poet. e. 51, p. 11.

268 I know not, reader, with what eyes
Tears trickled fast from mine!
Russell, George, translator, 'verses relating to Lady Jane Grey'.
MS. Ballard 37, fol. 135 (autogr.).

269 I know not, to whose hands may fall.
Before my body turned to dust.
MS. Rawl. poet. 66, fol. 20.

270 I know not what affliction means,
Than all the tinsel glories of a crown.
'Affliction', presented by M. A. to Archbishop Sancroft, 1689.
MS. Rawl. poet. 154, fol. 87$^{v}$.

271 I know some parks where is no deer
Wherwith, their master make good cheer.
Riddle.
MS. Rawl. poet. 217, fol. 72$^{v}$.

272 I know that my redeemer lives
To the fair dawn of life's eternal day.
'A Paraphrase upon part of . . . Job' xix.
MS. Don. c. 57, fol. 74$^{v}$, with music by Henry Lawes; Rawl. poet. 84, fol. 111$^{v}$.

273 I know the thing that's most uncommon.
Alas! She's deaf, and does not hear.
[Pope, Alexander], 'The Lady with one fault'.
See *Minor Poems*, ed. Norman Ault and John Butt, 1954, p. 250.
MS. Ballard 50, fol. 102$^{v}$.

274 I know the ways of learning both the head
To climb to Thee.
Herbert, George, 'The Pearle. Math. 13'.
Pr. *The Temple*, 1633, p. 81.
MS. *Tanner 307, fol. 61.

275 I know we're parted, yet I plainly find
Your next sweet stroke will call't to life again.
Ashmole, Elias, 'To Maddam de G[ray (?)] in the Country', 1649.
MSS. Ashmole 36, 37, fol. 238$^{v}$ (autogr.).

276*a* I know we're resolved each shall see
For than shall think the sea is condensed me.
Cavendish, Lady Jane, 'The Songe' in a pastoral.
MS. *Rawl. poet. 16, p. 69.

I know your heart cannot so guilty be 276*b*
Your face will wear no patches but a cloud.
[John Suckling (?)] 'To the Lady Desmonde'.
Pr. as 'Of another Author', Dudley North's *Forest of Varieties*, 1645, p. 75.
MS. Malone 13, p. 101, attr. to P. Apsley.

I labour to resist in vain 277
When we both love and are belov'd again.
'A Song'.
MS. Montagu e. 13, fol. 58.

I late used to resort unto the brook 278
To ease my present grief.
'A Prisoners Complaint'.
MS. Rawl. poet. 90, fol. 56.

I laugh to see, how vain men be, 279*a*
Perplexed am, would live, yet wish to die.
Robinson, Robert, 'Democritus and Heraclitus'.
MS. *Rawl. poet. 218, p. 1 (autogr.).

[I leave mortality, and things below] 279*b*
And mount herself, like him, to eternity in fire.
Cowley, A[braham] 'Raptus Eliæ 2 Reg. 2' [from 'The Extasie'].
Pr. *Poems and Davideis*, 1656, 'Pindarique Odes', p. 42.
MS. Tanner 466, fol. 28.

I left this irksome world with all my heart 280
Least worse then death, should happen to my part.
Couplet.
MS. Ashmole 38, p. 180.

I lift mine eyes to Sion hill from whence I do attend 281
God will thy things bring about.
[Whittingham, William], Psalm cxxi.
MS. Rawl. poet. 112, fol. 33$^{v}$ rev.

I lift mine heart to thee 282
From all their pain and grief.
[Sternhold, Thomas], Psalm xxv.
MSS. Rawl. D. 886, fol. 11$^{v}$, verse 6 set for 5 bells; Rawl. poet. 112, fol. 64$^{v}$ rev.

I lift my eyes to thee oh lord, 283
Our mourning they deride.
Psalm cxxiii.
MS. *Rawl. C. 113, fol. 91.

I lift my eyes unto the hills 284
Shall his protection have.
Psalm cxxi.
MS. *Rawl. C. 113, fol. 90.

285 I lift my longing eyes
Of him in all extremes.
Harington, Sir John, Psalm cxxi.
MS. *Douce 361, fol. 79.

286 I, like a jewel, tost by sea, and land,
Am bought by him, that wears me on his hand.
Couplet, 'On the death of Margaret etc.'
MS. Sancroft 59, p. 280 rev.

287 I like not tears in tune, nor do I prize
We floating islands living Hebrides.
Cleveland, John, 'Upon the death of Mr. King drownd in the Irish Seas', 1637.
Pr. *Obsequies to the memory of Mr. Edward King*, 1638, Sig. G2, and Cleveland's *Poems*, 1651, p. 10.
MS. Rawl. poet. 142, fol. 12.

288 I like not wars nor strife t'increase:
That righteousness may never cease.
Robinson, Robert.
MS. *Rawl. poet. 218, p. 64 (autogr.).

289 I like the warbling of the winged quire.
Want no content, only thy company.
'Amico suo Roberto T.' subscribed 'Tuissimus. W. C[orbet]'.
MS. *Rawl. poet. 210, fol. 9.

290 I list not paint upon my tomb my fame
Suffice it Britain lost, death got the game.
G. B., 'Epitaph 16' on Prince Henry in 'Cestria Lugens', 1612.
MS. *Rawl. poet. 116, fol. 9.

291 I live a life that draweth to an end
I hope for one, which may for ever last.
E[edes], D[r. Richard] of Christ Church, 'A Ditie Divine'.
MS. Rawl. poet. 148, fol. 70.

292 I lived in darkness (such th'all seeing fate)
To life and virtue and eternal day.
'On a Lady that was blind long before she died'.
MS. Top. gen. e. 32, fol. 2v.

293 I loathe that I did love
So shall you turn to dust.
Vaux, [Thomas], Lord.
Pr. Tottel's *Miscellany*, 1557, Sig. x iii.
MSS. Ashmole 48, fol. 23v; Mus. d. 184, fol. 11v, with music transcribed from B.M. Add. MS. 4900.

294 I long have thought my youthful friend
Than ever did th'adviser.
Burns, Robert, 'Epistle to a Young Friend'.
Pr. *Poems*, 1787, p. 252.
MS. Montagu e. 14, fol. 13v.

I long observed disquiet in your face 295
The people's freedom and the tyrant's doom.
'Verses fix'd upon K. J[ames] II's statue in the Privy Garden on [22 Apr. 1715] during the great Eclypse'.
MS. Rawl. poet. 155, p. 180.

I long to see my saviour Christ 296
Upon a cross alone.
Tipping, William.
MS. *Rawl. poet. 101, fol. 2v (autogr.).

I long to sing the siege of Troy 297
'Tis dumb to all but love, love, love.
Berkenhead, John, translator, Anacreon, xxiii.
Pr. H. Lawes, *Ayres and Dialogues*, 1653.
MSS. Mus. Sch. C. 71, fol. 81, with music by H. Lawes; Rawl. poet. 147, p. 156, attr. to John Berkenhead.

I long to talk with some old lover's ghost 298
If she whom I love, should love me.
Donne, John, 'Loves Deytye'.
Pr. *Poems*, 1633.
MSS. *Eng. poet. e. 99, fol. 125; *f. 9, p. 47.

I look on him to be an ass, and no man 299
Before that they into this place are sent.
Tipping, William.
MS. *Rawl. poet. 101, fol. 75v (autogr.).

I loose my time: whose fault is it I pray 300
On nature lay, for day itself does break.
Creswell, Robert, 'Inconstancy. Epigr.'
MS. *Eng. poet. f. 24, fol. 1v (autogr.).

I lost my heart the other day 301
Then do thy worst love her in spite of me.
MS. Mus. b. 1, fol. 125v, music by John Wilson.

I love a lass [a bonny lass, alas] but cannot show it. 302
Bring back my life or else my hearse.
Pr. *Select Musicall Ayres and Dialogues*, 1652, i. 24, and John Wilson's *Cheerfull Ayres or Ballads*, 1660, p. 46.
MSS. Don. c. 57, fol. 76v, music by Wilson; Mus. b. 1, fol. 114, music by Wilson; Rawl. poet. 65, fol. 29; 116, fol. 37v.

I love a woman for that thing alone, only good 303
In which the devil the tempting apple gave her.
'By an Anonimus'. Refers to P304.
MS. Rawl. poet. 84, fol. 121.

I love and am not lov'd again: 304
Who lives your martyr without name.
[King, John]. See *B.Q.R.* v, 1929, p. 329 and *B.L.R.* iv, 1953, p. 208.
MS. Rawl. D. 398, fol. 160 (autogr.).

305 I love (and have some cause to love) the earth,
Possessed of heaven, heaven unpossessed of thee.
[Quarles, Francis], 'The Soules Love'. *Emblemes*, 1635, v. vi.
MS. Rawl. poet. 90, fol. 27v.

306 I love but dare not show it because why
It speaks to all but takes not me.
MS. Rawl. poet. 65, fol. 34.

307 I love her that denies not she invites
That in a breath can answer no and yea.
'The Lovers choise . . . Auson[ius] Epig[ram lvi]'.
MSS. CCC. 327, fol. 33*b*; Eng. poet. f. 25, fol. 16v.

308 I love, I dote, I rave with pain.
For breaking my poor heart.
[Otway, Thomas], 'The Complaint a Song a New Scotch Tune'.
Pr. *Poems*, 1712, ii. 392.
MS. Rawl. poet. 222, fol. 4.

309 I love so sore I would fain discern
For love without steadfastness nothing avails.
MS. Rawl. C. 813, fol. 61.

310 I love the face where sits
To tempt, nor man have died.
MS. Eng. poet. c. 50, fol. 74v.

311 I love the fat I love the fair
All that is woman and will do.
MS. Wood F. 34, fol. 186.

312 I love the Lord because my voice
Wherefore the Lord praise ye.
[Norton, Thomas], Psalm cxvi.
MS. Rawl. poet. 112, fol. 37v rev.

313 I love the Lord, he doth the voice
Within thy holy court.
Psalm cxvi.
MS. *Rawl. C. 113, fol. 80v.

314 I love the world, as clients love the laws
To lose a world of grief, t'enjoy a world of bliss.
Quarles, Francis, 'Fraus Mundi'.
From Pentelogia, with *A Feast for Worms*, 1620, Sig. O1v.
MSS. Ashmole 38, p. 19, attr. to Mr. Francis Quarlls; Rawl. poet. 127, fol. 8v.

315 I love thee, mournful sober-suited night
May reach, though lost on earth the ear of Heav'n.
Smith, Charlotte, 'To Night. A Sonnett'.
MS. Montagu e. 14, fol. 18.

I love thee not, nor yet the cause I wot. 316
This only I do know, I love thee not.
'Ad Sabidum'. Martial, *Epigrams* I. xxxii.
MS. Rawl. D. 1147, fol. 89v.

I love: 'tis true. But does it follow thence 317
Because I've lost my heart, I've lost my sense?
'An Epigram', couplet, 1735.
MS. Eng. misc. e. 240, p. 155.

I love unloved I wot not what love may be 318
Till thou come there as I love best.
MS. Rawl. C. 813, fol. 45.

I love what love most true 319
I will obey.
'A Song'.
MS. Rawl. poet. 152, fol. 19.

I love with all my heart 320
Resolve to live and die.
Equivocal verses, Whig and Tory, 1714/15.
MSS. Ballard 29, fastened to fol. 162; Eng. misc. c. 116, fol. 2v, marked R. C.; e. 219, fol. 13v; Eng. poet. e. 87, p. 14; Firth d. 13, fol. 82; Rawl. poet. 155, p. 73; pr. bk. Firth b. 22, fol. 14.

I love you whom the world calls enemies 321
Implore and think it God-like so to do.
M. A., 'Enemies . . . Mar. 18. 1683', presented to Abp. Sancroft, 1689.
MS. Rawl. poet. 154, fol. 53v.

I loved a lass as well as you 322
You'd for an acre have a score.
'To Mark Antony'.
MS. Percy c. 8, fol. 127.

I loved her well and what could I do more 323
She proved unkind and woe is me therefore.
Couplet.
MS. Rawl. poet. 116, fol. 53v.

I loved no king in forty-one 324
A trimming moderator.
[Ward, Edward], 'The Religious or the Trimming Parson'. At end 'vicar of Bray'.
Pr. E. Ward's *Miscellaneous Works*, iii, 2nd ed., 1712, p. 321.
MS. Rawl. D. 383, fol. 115.

I loved thee once I love no more 325
A begging at a beggar's door.
[Ayton, Sir Robert]. Found amongst his collected poems, B.M. MSS. Add. 10308 and 28622.
Pr. *Prince d'Amour*, 1660. Answered by T2273.
MS. Rawl. poet. 116, fol. 46v.

326 I loved you lady long ago.
And come another time.
[Price, E. (?)], 'A hastie lover asked his mistres, if the hope he had to wynn her, shuld prevaile', with 'The Answer'.
MS. *Douce 290, fol. 90 (autogr.).

327 I made a posy, while the day ran by:
It be as short, as yours.
Herbert, George, 'Life'.
Pr. *The Temple*, 1633, p. 87.
MS. *Tanner 307, fol. 65v.

328 I made choice of a wife with judgment sound
And what's my meed for all, but scorn and hate!
'Terentius in Adelphis'.
MS. Don. d. 58, fol. 53.

329 I magnify the Lord
And gave it for our creed.
'The Song . . . calld the Magnificat. Luk: I. 46 ad 56'.
MS. *Eng. poet. e. 51, p. 175.

330 I make me to be called Janyuere
That we may come into his bliss amen.
'Howe every month prayseth it selfe of sum good property'.
MS. Ashmole 378, fol. 1.

331 I many graves made but enjoyed none
Out of the grave I shall come forth again.
'An Epitaph on a Sexton'.
MS. CCC. 328, fol. 58.

332 I Margery in haste
Or some other extraordinary need.
'Margery's Vow to father Thorogood'.
MS. Eng. misc. c. 116, fol. 6, marked R. C.

333 I marriage would forswear
Than gold that wants a man.
'The Mayd'.
From 'Yet other 12 wonders of the world', subscribed John Davys, F. Davison's *Poetical Rhapsody*, 2nd ed., 1608.
MS. Rawl. poet. 84, fol. 44.

334 I marvel much, at spiteful spider's gins
Blame Anacharsis then, and blame not me.
Lilliat, John, 'The Spiders Web. or Anacharsis sayinge of Solons written lawes'.
MS. Rawl. poet. 148, fol. 96 (autogr.).

335 I marvel not earth's fairest ornament
Were made to govern, be admired and seen.
North, Dudley, 3rd Baron.
Pr. *A Forest of Varieties*, 1645.
MS. *North e. 41, fol. 16v.

I Mary Pawson; lie below sleeping 336
Then Mary Pawson; for ever more blessed.
'In St. Giles att Creepell gate for the Clarkes Wyfe . . . dyed 1599'.
MS. Ashmole 38, p. 195.

I may forget to eat to drink to sleep 337
By longer looking on her quiet grave.
'Upon the countesse of Rutland's death'. 1612.
Pr. Overbury's *Wife* with Characters, 1622, Sig. C5v, without ascription.
MSS. Douce f. 5, fol. 35; Eng. poet. e. 37, p. 35, attr. to F. B.; *Eng. poet. f. 9, p. 139, attr. to J. D.; Rawl. poet. 117, fol. 185v rev.; 160, fol. 20v, attr. to Fran. Beaumont.

I mean not sad treason or scandal to sing 338
The lordling to dress, or take off his wound . . . (incomplete).
'The Duel between Mr. Poultney and Ld. Hervey', 1731.
MS. Top. Oxon. b. 170, fol. 17v.

I mean to sing [tell you] of England's sad fate 339
The roundheads can pray for themselves I know.
Pr. *Rump Songs*, 1662, Sig. D4.
MSS. Ashmole 36, 37, fol. 91; Rawl. poet. 26, fol. 142v.

I meant to write no more, for yet the blood 340
Who makes him happy: that makes all us so.
'On his Matis. Recovery from the smale Pox' [Dec. 1632].
MS. Ashmole 38, p. 72.

I mercy will and judgment sing oh lord god unto thee: 341
That I may from god's city cut the wicked workers hand.
[Norton, Thomas], Psalm ci.
MS. Rawl. poet. 112, fol. 42 rev.

I might persuade she were not dead and cry 342
Still to their figures, subjects reverence pay.
Felltham, Owen, 'An Elegie on the honourable and excellent Mris M. Coventry'.
Not included in 'Lusoria'.
MSS. Ashmole 36, 37, fol. 172.

I muse what sickness struck him dead 343
Too good this stone to be engraved.
'On Ben. Stone's death who tooke a griefe at his fathers unkindnesse'.
MSS. Douce f. 5, fol. 18; Malone 19, two copies, pp. 53 and 61.

344 I muse who first it was who sought to vex
They'll find out the philosopher's rare stone.
'A learned woman'.
MSS. Ashmole 36, 37, fol. 142; Eng. poet. e. 14, fol. 72.

345 I muse why Venus hath such fiery holes
I think that Vulcan once there blowed his coals.
Couplet, 'In venerem et vulcanum'.
MS. Eng. poet. e. 14, fol. 10.

346 I musing sat till gentle sleep
One rose, at least without a thorn.
Corrected draft.
MS. DD. Wykeham-Musgrave c. 49 (4° double sheet, no date).

347 I must be gone love, I must be gone away,
And if you leave me, love, my heart will break with pain.
'The Seaman's Departure', in *The Jolly Sailor's Garland*, pr. bk. Douce PP. 183, p. 2.
MS. Firth c. 18, fol. 163.

348 I must confess my fortunes are declined
But neither my deservings; nor my mind.
Couplet.
MS. Eng. poet. f. 10, fol. 106$^{v}$.

349 I must confess that I was somewhat warm,
And teeth are useless, where there's nought to eat.
S[ ]an, T., 'Mr. C-y's Apology'.
MS. Eng. poet. c. 9, p. 103.

350 I must confess't a task too great
As th'titular angels of our ways.
Fairfax, Thomas, Lord, 'Of Patience and Temperance'.
MS. *Fairfax 40, p. 579 (autogr.).
MS. *Fairfax 38, p. 259.

351 I must express my joy a part; for I
To praise past kings, but think the present best.
Cary, Sir Lucius [Lord Falkland], 'To the Kinge' on his recovery from smallpox, [Dec. 1632].
MS. Ashmole 38, p. 74.

352–3 I must have sixpence before I be willing
That engine wins the town without more billing.
MS. Rawl. B. 35, fol. 42 rev.

354 I need no trophies to adorn my hearse
That first gives horns and then cuts off his head?
'The L. of Castle Haven [Mervyn, 2nd Earl, executed 1631] on himselfe and his Lady'.
MSS. CCC. 327, fol. 32$^{v}$; 328, fol. 58; Eng. poet. e. 14, fol. 87$^{v}$ rev.

I ne'er was drest in forms. Nor can I bend 355
Which will in death seal the bold counterpart.
King, Henry, 'A Letter'.
Pr. *Poems*, 1657, p. 61.
MSS. *Eng. poet. e. 30, fol. 32; *Malone 22, fol. 21$^{v}$.

I never learned in wisdom's schools 356
Which all those schools did not afford.
Robinson, Robert.
MS. Rawl. poet. 218, p. 160 (autogr.).

I never saw a face till now that could my passion move 357
Yet die for want of heat.
Subscribed 'M[ary] N.'
MS. Rawl. poet. 196, fol. 18.

I never saw in all my life muckle golden treasure 358
And ever, as in duty bound say blessing on the donor.
Samber, Robert.
MS. Rawl. poet. 11, fol. 33$^{v}$ (autogr.).

I never washed that I could tell 359
Sing Pegaseian melody.
'The Prologue of Perseus'.
Pr. H. Huth, *Inedited Poetical Miscellanies*, 1870, Sig. Z8$^{v}$, from the fly-leaf of Persius, ed. John Bond, 1614.
MS. Firth d. 7, fol. 59.

I never yet could see that face, 360
Since that by every spark is set on fire.
Cowley, [Abraham], 'The Generall Lover'.
Pr. *Works*, 1668, 'The Mistress', p. 63.
MS. Rawl. poet. 173, fol. 79$^{v}$; see also H1212.

I none despise for being poor 361
And from all sin my soul protect.
Williams, John.
MS. *Rawl. poet. 184, fol. 89$^{v}$ (autogr.).

I nothing ask but due 362
The presence of thy face.
Harington, Sir John, Psalm xvii.
MS. *Douce 361, fol. 9.

I now confess I am in love 363
I would not court her and despair.
[Adapted by Mr. Freman (?)], on Osella; cf., W1154.
Pr. *Merry Drollery*, 1661, p. 1.
MS. Rawl. B. 35, fol. 38$^{v}$ rev.

I now have an ambition 364
Thus fell John Duke of Marlbro'.
'John Duke of Marborough' 1712.
Pr. bk. Firth b. 21, fol. 115.

365 I now should close with claw-back epigrams
But I want oiled tongue and supple hams.
Cheyney, William, couplet.
MS. *Rawl. poet. 86, fol. 32ᵛ.

366 I now think love is rather deaf than blind
And all these through her eyes have stopped her ears.
[Jonson, Ben.].
*The Underwood*, ix.
MS. Eng. poet. c. 50, fol. 118.

367 I oft have heard of Lydford Law
Unless by some Tymn Warrant.
[Browne, William of Tavistock], 'Lydford Law'.
Pr. J. Phillips, *Sportive Wit*, 1656, Sig. Bb1; *Worthies of Devon*, John Prince, 1701.
MS. Rawl. poet. 84, fol. 54 rev.

368 I oft have read, and sometimes did admire
To carp at science: but sweet arts t'adore.
F. T., 'On the Musick of the Sphers and his Freind Mr. Wm. Lilly'.
MS. Ashmole 423, fol. 135.

369 I oft have wondered why thou didst elect
Can mend thy night piece, that is: make it worse.
[King, Henry], 'One having married an Ill favored woman his frind wrights thus to hym'.
Pr. *Poems*, 1657, p. 35.
MSS. Ashmole 38, p. 3; Rawl. poet. 117, fol. 176ᵛ rev.; see also I212.

370 I often have admired dear friend, why we
The bold young pilot sails, to be a man.
'A Letter From One in the University to his Friend in the Country'.
MS. Rawl. poet. 222, fol. 3ᵛ.

371 I on the house of David and those who
As bitterly as one bewaileth his first born.
Zechariah '12 chaptr. 10. vers.'
MS. *Rawl. C. 113, fol. 10ᵛ (autogr.).

372 I once could sport with maids though now I'm broke
That I may the sharper upon Chloe lie.
W. A., translator, Horace, *Odes* III. xxvi.
MS. *Rawl. poet. 104, fol. 34 (autogr.).

373 I once had money and a friend,
And found a foe in change.
MS. Rawl. poet. 172, fol. 12.

374 I once saw Phoebus in his mid-day shine
And live deep rivers softly glide.
'A Song'.
MS. Rawl. poet. 84, fol. 26 rev.

I once the flower of flowers, the star 375
But cruel ways to glorify.
Paman, C[lement], 'The Distill'd Rose'.
MS. Rawl. poet. 147, p. 45.

I once was sick the doctor said that I 376
There 's none so bold as me, George Blunderbuss.
Hulse, Thomas, 'Blunderbuss's Receipt against Cowardice. Probatum est'.
MS. *Rawl. poet. 152, fol. 69 (autogr.).

I ought to love the Lord, my strength 377
Confirmed to his race.
Psalm xviii.
MS. *Rawl. C. 113, fol. 18ᵛ.

I owe oh Lord this desperate lift 378
On th'active study of my thankfulness.
J. F., Psalm xxx.
MS. *Eng. poet. f. 17, p. 161 (autogr.).

I own a good and prudent wife 379
Complete in every pleasure.
Williams, John, 'To [My Cousin William Lowndes] that asked me why I did not marry'.
MS. *Rawl. poet. 188, fol. 20 (autogr.).

I own Squire Shift of humour nice 380
Do take yourself away.
Boswell, James, 'Epigram'.
MS. *Douce 193, two copies, fols. 27, 32 (autogr.).

I paid no money for this judgement place 381
And am no richer son o'the law, judge you.
'The Carrecter of an honest Iudge'.
MS. Ashmole 38, p. 46.

I paint so ill, my piece had need to be 382
My love or feign'd, or painted should appear.
Cr[ashaw], R[ichard], 'With a picture sent to a freind'.
MS. Tanner 465, fol. 95ᵛ.

I pass all my hours in a shady old grove 383
The pleasures the pleasures of love.
Song.
Pr. *Choice Ayres, Songs and Dialogues*, 2nd ed., 1675, p. 11, music by Pelham Humphrey. In B.M. MS. Harl. 3991, fol. 155, headed '1st Song in the Masque. 1670'.
MSS. Mus. Sch. F. 572, p. 89, attr. to Charles II, [music by P. Humphrey]; G. 637, fol. 1, [music by P. Humphrey]; Rawl. poet. 84, fol. 21 rev.

I pass my dull hours in sorrow alone 384
Which hurried the charming delusion away.
'Song'.
MS. Rawl. poet. 152, fol. 160ᵛ.

385 I pass the mountains, hills, and meadows green
But god revealed, the joys he hath prepared.
F. W., 'Sonnett 2'.
MS. *Rawl. C. 639, fol. 6v, numbered [p.] 7 on recto.

386 I passed by a sow when the waters were high
She was as well as ever she was.
'A sow of iron' (riddle).
MS. Rawl. D. 986, inside front cover.

387 I passing spied a passing flower to eye
Like flower, ice, snake, are hurtful in the end.
Mills, Rob[ert], 'To a feygned faythless and ungratefull frende'.
MS. Rawl. poet. 85, fol. 83.

388 I plead my ruin, love me not,
So be my honesty your due.
Initials of author deleted.
In B.M. MS. Harley 6057, fol. 23v, subscribed Tho: Cro.
MS. Malone 16, p. 25.

389 I plucked this morn these beauteous flowers
So my odour be as sweet.
Glee by Dr. [William] Hayes.
MS. Mus. d. 177, fol. 63v.

390 I praise the Thracian mothers who do mourn
Which perish in a funeral.
James, Richard, translator, 'Archias ep. uppon humane life'.
MS. *James 35, p. 16 (autogr.).

I pray thee . . . see also I prithee . . .

391 I pray thee leave love me no more
I cannot live without thee.
[Drayton, Michael], 'Sonett'.
Pr. *Odes with other Lyrick poesies*, 1619.
MS. Eng. poet. c. 50, fol. 35; see also I405.

392 I pray thee lute when I am gone
To play upon her instrument.
'Written upon a lute the gentlewoman being absent who was the owner'.
MS. Don. d. 58, fol. 36; see also I407, L446.

393 I pray thee say Canoby of the knighthood
But ye shall love as ye were brothers.
Prophecy.
MS. Rawl. C. 813, fol. 134.

394 I pray thee spare me gentle boy
That did invite: but seek another place.
[Suckling, Sir John].
Pr. *Fragmenta Aurea*, 1646, p. 25, 'Song'.
MSS. Ashmole 36, 37, fol. 135.

I pray thee sweet to me be kind 395
How fair how sweet, how kind you are.
Pr. with music by H. Lawes in *Select Ayres and Dialogues*, 1669.
MS. Eng. poet. c. 50, fol. 76v; see also I409.

I pray you honest master B. 396
Set aught thereof aside.
Gough, Richard, 'Oct. 8. 70. Put in the box for St. Ja[mes's] Chr[onicle] Oct. 23 1770'.
MS. *Eng. poet. c. 5, fol. 208v (autogr.).

I pray you save, poor Irish knave 397
Poor John will still prove true And so Adieu.
Pr. *Wit Restor'd*, 1658, p. 110.
MS. Rawl. poet. 142, fol. 41v; see also N457.

I press not to the quire, nor dare I greet 398
Than all the flourishing wreaths by laureats worn.
Carew, Tho., 'To my Friend Mr. Georg. Sandys'.
Pr. Sandys' *Paraphrase of the Divine Poems*, 1638, and Carew's *Poems*, 1640.
Pr. bk. 27980 e. 86, opposite p. 88.

I presuppose it seemeth strange sweet friend 399
To work thy welfare if in him it rest.
Burton, Francis.
MS. *Add. A. 267, fol. 52 (autogr.).

I prithee . . . see also I pray thee . . .

I prithee cease to chide my harmless love, 400
Than the calm joys of inoffensive love.
Hawkins, Sir John, 'Sonnet, imitated from Dr. Donne' with 'improvements since by the author'.
MS. Eng. poet. c. 9, p. 8.

I prithee Clora why so coy 401
One flaming sacrifice to love.
'A Dialogue'.
MS. Mus. b. 1, fol. 78, music by John Wilson.

I prithee don't fly me 402
That'll not sometimes be mellow.
[Brome, Alexander, 'The Leveller'].
Pr. with some variation in *Songs and Other Poems*, 1661, p. 72, and *Sportive Wit*, 1656, Sig. Bb8v.
MS. Rawl. B. 35, fol. 49 rev.

I prithee fool not speak no more 403
Than witch take you for me.
Cavendish, Lady Jane, a song in 'The Concealed Fancies'.
MS. *Rawl. poet. 16. p. 110.

404 I prithee Jack didst never stay
Th' Elizian world dissolves at once away.
'On Love. A Simile in imitation of Mr. Prior'.
MS. Rawl. poet. 152, fol. 142$^{v}$.

405 I prithee leave love me no more
But in heaven to be tormented.
[Drayton, Michael], 'A sonnet'.
Pr. *Poems*, 1619.
MSS. CCC. 328, fol. 76; Don. c. 57, fol. 49$^{v}$, with music; d. 58, fol. 28; see also I391.

406 I prithee leave me love: go place desire
To court Urania; she's a love divine.
Jordan, Tho[mas], 'A gentle-man in love with Twentye Mistresses'.
MS. Ashmole 38, p. 83.

407 I prithee lute when I am gone
To play upon her instrument.
MS. CCC. 327, fol. 21; see also I392, L446.

408 I prithee send me back my heart
As much as she hath mine.
[Suckling, Sir John].
Pr. *The Last Remains*, 1659.
MS. Rawl. poet. 65, fol. 33$^{v}$.

409 I prithee sweet to me be kind
How good how sweet how fair you are.
Song, music by William Lawes.
Pr. with music by Henry Lawes in his *Select Ayres and Dialogues*, 1669, p. 19.
MS. Don. c. 57, fol. 52; see also I395.

410 I prithee sweetheart yield to my desire
Farewell and be hanged that terse goodbye.
'A Song', crossed out.
MS. Ashmole 788, fol. 208$^{v}$.

I prithee tell me, what prodigious fate . . .
see H636.

411 I prithee turn that face away
Wish thee less fair or else more kind.
King, Henry, 'Sonnet'.
Pr. *Poems*, 1657, p. 18; *Select Ayres and Dialogues*, 1659, p. 19; and *Wits Recreations*, 1641.
MSS. Don. c. 57, fol. 59$^{v}$, with music by John Wilson; Eng. poet. d. 152, fol. 107; *Eng. poet. e. 30, fol. 21; *Malone 22, fol. 13; Mus. b. 1, fol. 84$^{v}$, with music by John Wilson.

412 I promised when I left you last, 'tis true
To make your shoes according to your feet.
B[rome], A[lexander], translator, Horace, *Epistles* I. vii.
Pr. *Poems of Horace*, A. Brome etc., 2nd ed., 1671, p. 318.
MS. Rawl. D. 261, p. 39.

I raise my soul on high lord up to thee 413
Out of all troubles let thine Israel come.
Fairfax, Thomas, Lord, Psalm xxv.
MS. *Fairfax 40, p. 52 (autogr.); see also M903*b*.

I raised a little airy bower 414
It still will rankle there.
'The Parterre'.
MS. Eng. poet. c. 51, p. 251*b*.

I read how that the marble stone 415
To live in such a lasting bliss.
Headed 'To the tune of lusty gallant', subscribed 'Olyver Currant—John Gyldynge'.
MS. Ashmole 48, fol. 112.

I recommend me to you with heart and mind 416
And to him I pray you be kind.
MS. Rawl. C. 813, fol. 2.

I rise at eleven, I dine about two 417
And in bed I lay yawning 'till eleven again.
[Sackville, Charles, Lord Buckhurst (?)], 'The Debauch'.
See D. M. Vieth, *Attribution in Restoration Poetry*, 1963, pp. 169, 411.
MS. Rawl. poet. 152, fol. 89$^{v}$.

I rode from England into France 418
Of whom men thought the same.
Goodwin, Thomas, 'A Journey into France'.
MSS. Eng. poet. e. 97, p. 109, attr. to 'Dr. Corbet', corrected to 'Thomas Goodwin'; Malone 21, fol. 66$^{v}$, attr. to Dr. Corbett; see also I80, I572.

I rose of late to view the morning's pride: 419
And make it fairer for the show next day.
Charnick, —, 'Upon a fayre morning spoyld by a sudden showre'.
MS. Tanner 306, fol. 426.

I said and swore that I would never love 420
Who would not die to live in love of thee.
MSS. Rawl. poet. 85, fol. 93; 172, fol. 7.

I said, I will look to my ways, 421
From hence, and be no more.
Psalm xxxix.
MS. *Montagu e. 10, fol. 60.

I said I will look to my ways 422
Before to dust I fall.
Psalm xxxix.
MS. *Rawl. C. 113, fol. 32$^{v}$.

I said I will look to my ways, 423
And shall be seen no more.
[Hopkins, John], Psalm xxxix.
MS. Rawl. poet. 112, fol. 60 rev.

424 **I said I would take special care**
**Till time my strength restore me.**
Harington, Sir John, Psalm xxxix.
MS. *Douce 361, fol. 23$^{v}$.

425 **I said the thing for which I woe**
**And take it for his hire.**
Granger, —.
MS. Malone 13, p. 58.

426 **I said to my heart, between sleeping and waking**
**Would one think Mistress Howard ne'er thought it was she.**
Peterborough, [Charles Mordaunt, 3rd] Earl of, 'Upon Miss Howard'.
Pr. Pope and Swift, *Miscellanies, The Last Volume*, 1727, p. 166.
MS. Add. B. 105, fol. 104.

427 **I saw a pack of prick-eared knaves**
**And alas poor member of parliament.**
'A Ballad on Chusing of Burgess of Parliament'.
MS. Firth c. 16, p. 46.

428 **I saw a peacock, with a fiery tail.**
**I saw the man that saw that dreadful sight.**
MSS. Don. e. 6, fol. 38; Eng. poet. c. 6, fol. 16, 'juvenile transcript' by Richard Gough, with an extra verse.

**I saw a vision . . .** see I179.

429 **I saw a wonder, wondrous was the sight**
**Either a woman or a woman's thing.**
'Ænigma in Acum'.
MS. Rawl. poet. 212, fol. 101$^{v}$.

430 **I saw fair [Celia] Cloris walk alone**
**To deck her freez'd into a gem.**
Strode, William, 'Song'.
Pr. Walter Porter's *Madrigales and Ayres*, 1632, xxv; *Wits Recreations*, 1640, no. 180; *Parnassus Biceps*, 1656, p. 77; with music by C. Simpson and H. Lawes in *The Musical Companion*, 1673, pp. 49 and 121, and with music by H. Purcell in *The Theater of Music*, iii, 1686.
MS. *CCC. 325, fol. 64 (autogr.).
MSS. Ashmole 38, p. 9; CCC. 328, fol. 16, attr. to Str.; Don. c. 57, fol. 60$^{v}$, with music by John Hilton; Douce f. 5, fol. 3$^{v}$, attr. to Strode; Eng. misc. f. 49, fol. 1$^{v}$ rev.; Eng. poet. c. 50, fol. 34$^{v}$; e. 97, p. 30, attr. to William Strode; f. 10, fol. 89, 'On Mrs. Anion (?)'; f. 25, fol. 10, 'Mrs. Corbet'; Firth e. 4, p. 116, attr. to T. R.; Lat. misc. c. 19, p. 421, 'on Mrsse. Corbett'; f. 45, p. 201, with Latin version, in the hand of Thomas Traherne; Malone 16, p. 16; Rawl. poet. 116, fol. 42$^{v}$; 117, fol. 163 rev., attr. to Munsey; 153, fol. 8$^{v}$, attr. to W. St.; 160, fol. 113, Dr. Corbets wife; 199, p. 3, attr. to W. S.; Tanner 465, fol. 42$^{v}$, attr. to Dr. Corbett; see also A1542.

**I saw fair Sylvia, loved her, told her so** 431
**I'll give my answer, Sir I love not you.**
Weaver, Thomas, 'An Epigramme'. Not in *Songs and Poems*, 1654.
MS. *Rawl. poet. 211, fol. 4 (autogr.).

**I saw the lass whom dear I loved** 432
**To show she well approved him.**
MS. Rawl. poet. 196, fol. 1.

**I saw the virtues sitting hand in hand** 433
**At the next session-day.**
Herbert, George, 'Humility'.
Pr. *The Temple*, 1633, p. 61.
MS. *Tanner 307, fol. 47$^{v}$.

**I saw thy plume and straight guessed by the feather** 434
**That both the land and thou wouldst fly together.**
'Unthrift', couplet.
MS. Eng. poet. c. 50, fol. 33.

**I scarce believe my love to be so pure** 435
**No winter shall abate this spring's increase.**
Donne, John, 'Springe'.
Pr. *Poems*, 1633.
MSS. CCC. 327, fol. 29$^{v}$, attr. by Fulman to Donne, ref. to editions of 1649–50; *Eng. poet. e. 99, fol. 118; *f. 9, p. 68.

**I see ambitious times catch dangerous falls** 436
**To serve the Lord and to respect no more.**
'Vanitye'.
MS. Ashmole 47, fol. 49$^{v}$.

**I see my hopes must wither in the bud** 437
**I know my dream was true and yet I love.**
[Breton, Nicholas (?)]; see *Poems*, ed. J. Robertson, 1952, p. LV.
Pr. bk. Tanner 221, MS. fol. 2.

**I see no homage to Saint Thomas paid** 438
**Argues our honest, pious, thankful sense.**
Cromwell, Edward, 'Dec. 21. 1715. S. Thomas the Apostle'.
MS. *Rawl. poet. 165, fol. 29$^{v}$ (autogr.).

**I see not my self, yet help others to see,** 439
**And know more of their motions than they know of me.**
Williams, John, 'A man holding a candle near a glass', couplet.
MS. *Rawl. poet. 191, fol. 101$^{v}$ (autogr.).

440 I see not, my self, yet help others to see,
Which no man can do, unassisted by me.
Williams, John, 'Light', couplet.
MS. *Rawl. poet. 191, fol. 101$^{v}$ (autogr.).

441 I see not what your force can do to pen
Will end and so would I with satisfaction.
Bradshaw, John, 'On the first Squadron', 1664–5 (?).
MS. Tanner 306, fol. 432$^{v}$.

442 I see that wreath, which doth the wearer arm
A relic famed by all posterity.
King, Henry, 'To my Dead Friend Ben: Johnson'.
Pr. *Jonsonus Virbius*, 1638, and King's *Poems*, 1657, p. 92.
MS. *Eng. poet. e. 30, fol. 76.

443 [I see you are] ICUR good Mounsieur Carre
Hath broke your back.
Libel on Somerset, 1613 or later.
MSS. Don. c. 54, fol. 22$^{v}$; Douce f. 5, fol. 34$^{v}$; Eng. poet. e. 14, fol. 49, attr. to Sir Walter Raleigh; Firth d. 7, fol. 152; Rawl. D. 1048, fol. 64$^{v}$; Rawl. poet. 160, fol. 162$^{v}$; Sancroft 53, two copies, pp. 48 and 58.

444 [I see you be] ICUB, YY for me.
The subject of a bleeding heart.
'A Whim, sent to pretty Miss Eliza Clarke' with answer.
MS. Eng. poet. e. 40, fol. 149.

445 I seek, but cannot find
Unanswer'd, and forgot!
Proby, John, of Rochdale.
MS. Montagu d. 5, fol. 176 (autogr.).

446 I seem to pen her praise
Dame fortune is her maid.
MS. Rawl. poet. 172, fol. 3.

447 I serve sweet Flora brighter than Cinthia's light
Yet will I serve although I die therefore.
'Montanus the Shephearde [Anthony Munday (?)] his love to Flore'.
See *Englands Helicon*, ed. Rollins, 1935, i. 107.
MS. Douce 280, fol. 45$^{v}$.

448 I serve under doctor Hall—*miserere mei*
*Cum multis aliis*: besides sheep and beasts.
'Dr. Hall's Curat's Petition to the Kinge'.
MSS. Ashmole 781, p. 118; Rawl. poet. 26, fol. 2$^{v}$, subscribed Mannynge.

449 I shepherd I ploughman I horseman light
With bough with plough with mighty hand.
Translation from Latin.
MSS. Rawl. poet. 112, fol. 73 rev.; 213, fol. 1.

I should prepare a dish to entertain 450
But I, alas, have scarce so much as salt.
Oldisworth, Giles.
MS. *Rawl. C. 422, fol. 33 (autogr.).

I should write some thing in the author's praise 451
Draw but this curtain this rare piece will show it.
T. S., 'The praise of the author shadowed with his curtaine'.
MS. Rawl. poet. 152, fol. 24.

I sigh as sure to wear the fruit 452
If the pleasure for the measure of my treasure go.
Pr. Pilkington's *First Book of Songs*, 1605, xv.
MSS. Mus. f. 7–10: f. 9, fol. 21.

I sigh I languish 453
My inmost soul she knows too well.
'The Languishing Lover', with music.
MS. Mus. c. 107, fol. 8$^{v}$.

I sighed, and I pined 454
Fate dotes on a fool in the cradle.
D'Urfey, Thomas, 'A song in the 3 dukes of Dunstable . . . Set by Mr. Henry Purcell'.
F. B. Zimmerman, *Purcell*, 1963, no. 571(1).
MS. Mus. Sch. C. 95, p. 202.

I sing a woeful ditty 455
How the bullets would whistle, and the canons would roar.
'A Songe', on the slitting of John Coventry's nose by Monmouth, etc. Nov. 1670.
Pr. *Poems on Affairs of State*, iii, 1704, p. 68.
MSS. Don. b. 8, p. 210; Douce 357, fol. 110$^{v}$; Eng. poet. d. 49, p. 247, attr. to Andrew Marvell; Rawl. D. 922, fol. 196; Top. Oxon. e. 202, fol. 83.

I sing a wondrous work of god 456
And turn it to your comfort and his glory now and aye.
King James I, 'The battell of Lepante'.
Pr. *Poeticall Exercises*, 1591, Sig. G3.
MS. *Bodl. 165, fol. 1 (autogr.).

I sing dire battles and that sacred wight, 457
Left the departed chanters God to praise.
Oldham, John, 'The Desk. Canto 1'; Boileau's *Le Lutrin*.
MS. *Rawl. poet. 123, p. 70 (autogr.); other drafts pp. 66, 71, 74, 76, 77; see also I465.

I sing her worth, and praises high 458
Of whom a poet cannot lie.
'Idea: Off Sir Edw. Harbert'. [Lord Herbert of Cherbury].
Pr. *Verses*, 1665.
MS. Rawl. poet. 31, fol. 14.

459 I sing impiety beyond a name:
Lest it break forth, and burn thy sooty cell.

[Crashaw, Richard], 'On the Gunpowder Treason'.

Cf. *Poems*, ed. L. C. Martin, 2nd ed., 1957, pp. lxiii–lxx.

MS. Tanner 465, fol. 52ᵛ.

460 I sing no harm good sooth to any wight
But his kind wife gave me the very sign.

'Dunnes tale of a citizen and his wife'.

Pr. amongst 'Dubia', *The Elegies and the Songs and Sonnets*, ed. H. Gardner, 1965, p. 101.

MS. Rawl. poet. 117, fol. 223 rev.

461 I sing not of Angellica the fair
That in my want thou wilt supply me still.

Barnfield, Richard, 'Lady Pecunia or the praise of money', written in cipher.

MS. Ashmole 1153, fol. 119.

462 I sing of a duel in Epsom befell
Thy Clinias, oh Sydney, was ne'er so well match'd.

[Brown, Thomas], 'The Epsom-Duel', d'Urfey and Bell.

MS. Firth e. 6, fol. 92.

463 I sing of a meeting, has happen'd of late,
Yet he cares not a fig for his Prerogative.

'An excellent new Ballad 24 June 1719', on the meeting of the Whig lords at Devonshire house to discuss the Peerage Bill.

MSS. Rawl. D. 400, fol. 93; Tanner 306, fol. 479; pr. bk. Firth b. 22, fol. 20.

464 I sing of a sanctified lecher
Such doings can never endure.

'A Song on Parson Whyle'. Endorsed 'Song made on Humphry Whyle late of Welsborn Hastang by Charles Shuckburgh Esq. who wrote a Tragedy styled Antiochus'.

MS. Ballard 47, fol. 136.

465 I sing of battles and that sacred wight
Till supper lulls himself and cares to rest.

Oldham, John, 'The Desk. An Heroique Poem. First Canto', 1678. Boileau's 'Le Lutrin'.

MS. *Rawl. poet. 123, p. 124 (autogr.); see also I457.

466 I sing of Christ: oh endless argument
To show when he descended for our sin.

Alabaster, William, 'Son: 22. A preface to the Incarnatione'.

Pr. by B. Dobell, *Athenaeum*, No. 3974, 26 Dec. 1903.

MS. *Eng. poet. e. 57, fol. 5.

I sing of horrid tumults; 467
And so farewell my masters.

'Gout Raptures', on the civil wars and the restoration. Addressed to [Aubrey de Vere] Earl of Oxford [d. 1703].

MS. Ballard 50, fol. 55.

I sing of no heretic, turk, or of tartar 468
Than thus to be tossed in a blanket and drubbed.

'Fumbumbus: Or the North-Country Mayor. A Ballad: To the Tune of Packington's Pound', 1697.

See Chappell, *Old English Popular Music*, ed. H. F. Wooldridge, 1893, i. 260. In B.M. MS. Harl. 7319, fol. 277, attr. to Wosely.

MS. Rawl. poet. 159, fol. 112.

I sing of pious arms and of a man 469
Adores the sepulchre, and pays his vow.

T[albot], Sir G[ilbert], 'Godfry of Bullion, or Hierusalem rescued'.

MSS. Rawl. poet. 1 and 4, both attr. to Sir G. T.; 4, attr. to Sir G. T.

I sing the famous city 470
[And impeached for misdemeanours].

'A Ballad on Worcester Bells', on Bp. William Lloyd.
In B.M. MS. Lansd. 852, fol. 31, dated 1610.

MS. Rawl. D. 400, fol. 92.

I sing the fortunes of a luckless pair 471
That thou wilt turn half maid with reading it.

Beaumont, Francis, 'The Author to the Reader'. Prelude to 'Salmacis and Hermaphroditus'.

MS. Rawl. poet. 120, fol. 94ᵛ.

I sing the graces of a generous mind, 472
In which alone his sword the brave man draws.

Gough, Richard, 'On Generosity . . . Aug. 6. 1754'.

MS. *Eng. poet. c. 5, fol. 41 (autogr.).

I sing the happy and the glorious flight 473
Only to wives themselves, for to correct.

'An Elegy on . . . Sir Francis Inglefeild' May 1665.

MS. Don. b. 8, p. 347.

I sing the man, arm'd with celestial might 474
The hero's last great act, and how it fell.

Wilkins, C[harles], of Corpus Christi College, Oxford, 'Samson Agonistes', 1766.

MS. Eng. poet. e. 3 (autogr.).

475 I sing the man that raised a shirtless band
And orphans' curses all your steps attend.
'The King of Hearts'.
In B.M. MS. Harl. 1315, fol. 169, headed 'The King of Hearts. Ld. Delamere'; and in B.M. MS. Harl. 7317, fol. 102, dated 1689.
MSS. Firth d. 13, fol. 95; e. 6, fol. 35.

476 I sing the man who Judah's sceptre bore
Well-chosen and well-furnisht for the chase.
Cowley, Abr[aham], 'Davideis. 1692'.
MSS. Rawl. poet. 12, fol. 3, attr. to Abr. Cowley; Tanner 466, fol. 14$^v$, extracts, attr. to A. Cowley.

477 I sing the nation, who by God's command
Jews own one God—one universal Lord.
'The Jewiad. An Epic Poem . . . begun a little before passing the Jew Act' [1753].
MS. Douce 201, fol. 34.

478 I sing the natives of the boundless main
Preserve th'immortal sire, and aid the godlike son.
Diaper, William, 'Oppian's Halieuticks Or Of Fishes and Fishing in Five Books Part 1st containing the Natural History of Fishes in two Books . . . from the Greek Original'.
Pr. at Oxford, 1722, with a second part by John Jones of Balliol.
MS. Rawl. poet. 124, fol. 1 (autogr.).

479 I sing the praise of a worthy wight
Which nobody can deny.
'A Lampoon on the Duke of Bucks'.
MS. Top. Oxon. e. 202, fol. 118.

480 I sing the praise of heroes brave
'Tis very strange 'tween you and I.
'A Hymn to the Victory in Scotland'.
On the doubtful victory at Glenshiel. Published 25 June 1719.
MS. Eng. misc. c. 116, fol. 10.

481 I sing the story of a scoundrel lass,
To meet the prince she had so often top't.
'The Lady of Pleasure or The Life of Nelly . . . 1686'.
Attributed to Etherege in *Miscellaneous Works* of the Duke of Buckingham, 1704, i. 34.
MS. Firth c. 15, p. 254.

482 I sing the strange adventure and sad fate
I'th new militia when a turd is trump.
'Atkins alias A stink'.
MS. Rawl. poet. 71, p. 140.

I sing the war happened 'twixt templars and friars 483
There's an end of a Canterbury Tale.
'The Canterbury Tayle . . . Battle betwixt Prince Francis Kt. of the Golden Chaine and the High and Lowsy states of the Whitefryers Anno 1691'.
MS. Eng. poet. d. 53, p. 164.

I sing thy sad disaster (fatal king 484
That breath I could not: much less cry or call.
[Hubert, Sir Francis], 'The life and death of King Edward II', pr. 1628 and 1629.
MSS. Hearne's diaries 86, p. 128, extracts; Rawl. poet. 98, fol. 1; 170, fol. 79, fragment.

I sleep secure as having lost the breath 485
To gain the life which never suffereth death.
On 'Will Symons', Brookland, Kent, d. 3 Oct. 1650.
MS. Top. gen. e. 1, p. 47.

I slept, when Venus entered; to my bed 486
His lessons I retained and mine forgot.
[Cowper, William], translator, 'By Moschus'.
Pr. *Life and Posthumous Works*, ed. Hayley, 1803, ii. 191.
MS. Autogr. d. 21, fol. 191 (autogr.).

I sometime was a pilgrim king 487
I bid you study for the same.
Burton, Francis, 'A Riddle of a Swarme of Bees'.
MS. *Add. A. 267, fol. 5 (autogr.).

I sometimes wonder why 488
Rule all at thy command.
'A hymn of our Lords ascension'.
MS. Rawl. poet. 58, fol. 38.

I soon thy call shall hear 489
Is there before the throne of love.
Kenton, James.
MS. *Eng. poet. e. 20, p. 51 (autogr.).

I speak to good men; the profaner care 490
This high discourse well treasur'd in thy breast.
J. F., 'Orpheus the Thracian, of God'.
MS. *Eng. poet. f. 17, p. 53 (autogr.).

I speak to such if any such there be 491
My punishment shall shortly then surprise you.
[Sir Walter Ralegh's] 'Caveat to secure Courtiers'.
MSS. Ashmole 36, 37, fol. 14.

I spied king Oberon and his beauteous queen. 492
And out he picks the corn, which serves for rolls . . . (incomplete).
MSS. Ashmole 36, 37, fol. 47.

493 I startle at your welcome voice like one
Or, else mistrusts himself, that finds a gem!
Oldisworth, Giles, verses in his romance 'The Pattern of Piety'.
MS. *Rawl. C. 422, fol. 33 (autogr.).

494 I still must ask thee where doth stray
To thee she'd live and multiply.
Answer to Carew, A1754.
MS. Ashmole 38, p. 137.

495 I stood aghast, my hair on end,
My jaw-tied tongue no speech would lend.
'Obstupui, steteruntque comæ, et vox faucibus haesit', *Æneid* ii. 774.
MS. Rawl. D. 986, fol. 108.

496 I stood and see my mistress dance
So nimbly, with a marble heart.
Shirley, James.
Pr. *Poems*, 1646, p. 17.
MS. *Rawl. poet. 88, p. 60.

497 I struck the board, and cried no more
And I replied, My Lord.
Herbert, George, 'The Collar'.
Pr. *The Temple*, 1633, p. 147.
MS. *Tanner 307, fol. 111$^{v}$.

498 I struggle not against thy galling chain
High heap the load, and lift the scourge of pain.
Skinner, John, 'To Adversity'.
MS. *Eng. poet. d. 22, fol. 102.

499 I swear, but that thou'rt fortunate as bold,
Collier must be admir'd, must be obey'd.
'To his much esteem'd Friend, the Reverend and most Ingenious Mr. Jeremy Collier, upon his Censure of the English Stage', 1698.
MS. Rawl. poet. 91, fol. 9.

500 I swear by Athens owls and my own raven
If my wife's parsley bed I thought could breed 'em.
MS. Add. B. 8, fol. 88v.

501 I swear by muskadel
Mine answered thy black black black.
[Cavendish, William Duke of Newcastle], song in *The Variety*, IV. i.
Pr. Wilson's *Cheerfull Ayres or Ballads*, 1660, p. 108.
MS. Don. c. 57, fol. 79, music by John Wilson.

502 I swear to thee I will be gone
Or make make us a perfect *gemini*.
MS. Mus. b. 1, fol. 174, music by John Wilson.

I tell thee, Dick, where I have been, 503
And I for them be shent.
Savile, H[enry], 'The Chequer Inn . . . 1674', 'tune, I tell thee Dick'.
MS. Firth c. 15, p. 17; see also I1124.

I tell thee, Dick where I have been, 504
With Bridget, and with Nell.
[Suckling, Sir John], 'A Ballad upon a Wedding'.
Pr. *Poems*, 1646.
MS. Eng. misc. c. 292, fol. 108; see also I1123.

I tell thee fellow [fool] whoe'er thou be 505
And venture for a crown.
'Sir John Sucklinges Answeare' to I506.
Pr. *Wit and Drollery*, 1656, p. 46.
MSS. Ashmole 36, 37, two copies, fols. 54, attr. to Sir John Sucklinge, 130$^{v}$;
Tanner 465, fol. 90, attr. to Sir John Suckling.

I tell thee Jack [John] thou'st given the king 506
By carding and by dice.
[Mennes, Sir John (?)], 'Upon Sir John Sucklings hundred horse', 1639. Answered in I505.
Pr. *Wit and Drollery*, 1656, p. 44. Cf. *R.E.S.*, N.S. vii, 1956, p. 27.
MSS. Ashmole 36, 37, two copies, fols. 53$^{v}$, 130; Eng. poet. c. 53, fol. 22$^{v}$; Tanner 465, fol. 89$^{v}$.

I tell with equal truth and grief 507
And let her prison be my arms.
'The Thief'.
MS. Montagu e. 13, fol. 88$^{v}$.

I tell you a wonder, deny it if you can 508
Here lies a tailor, and an honest man.
Couplet, 'Upon a Tailour'.
MS. Malone 19, p. 41.

I tell you all both great and small 509
Of the proud pope of Rome.
'Upon the Death of Queen Elizabeth', ballad, 1603.
MSS. Ashmole 36, 37, fol. 296.

I tell you how the rose did first grow red 510
They flourish only in your livery.
'A lover to his Mrs.'
MS. CCC. 328, fol. 14; see also I1138, I1141.

I thank the lord with gratulation 511
And bring my soul to high salvation.
MS. Lat. th. d. 15, fol. 120.

512 **I thank you for your comic pains**
**Be ever coop'd in systematic bounds? . . . (incomplete).**

Roach, Richard, 'The Authers Answer to a Letter of Reflexions on his Book . . . The Great Crisis' [1725].
MS. Rawl. D. 832, fol. 163 (autogr.).

513 **I thank you kind friend, for what you have sent.**
**No Milton I am, but humble G. D.**

Dyer, George, 'To a Lady who presented me with some Flowers . . . in Winter' marked 'to omit'.
MS. *Eng. poet. c. 21, fol. 64.

514 **I thank you kindly, my good master!**
**You've flogged me with a rod of laurel!**

Parsons, William, reply to verse letter from Dr. Charles Burney.
MS. *Don. d. 123, p. 234 (autogr.).

515 **I that alone have stood such shake of foes**
**'Twas all the world that Rochell overcame.**

'Rochels Apologie', 1628.
MS. Rawl. poet. 206, p. 55.

516 **I that have robb'd so oft, am now bid stand**
**His mercy is beyond severity.**

'Upon Mr. Clavell of Brasen Nose Oxford'.
MS. Don. d. 58, fol. 13v; see I519, O197.

517*a* **I that my country did betray**
**Expect my spotted soul amongst the just.**

'On the Duke of Buckingham', 1628.
MSS. Ashmole 38, p. 14, attr. to Jo. Heape; Eng. poet. e. 14, fol. 13; Malone 23, p. 196; Rawl. poet. 26, fol. 78; Tanner 465, fol. 103.

517*b* **[I that my slender oaten pipe]**
**And up the hill me past.**

[Phaer, Thomas] 'The tale of the distruction of Troy', from *Æneid* II.
MS. Douce 280, fol. 144v.

518 **I that of late entitled thee sweet friend**
**Thy presence in the day and bed at night.**

Burton, Francis.
MS. *Add. A. 267, fol. 55v (autogr.).

519 **I that so oft have robbed, am now bid stand,**
**His mercy far exceeds severity.**

'Clavell to King James I', John Clavell, condemned 30 Jan. 1625/6.
Pr. *Soddered Citizen*, Malone Soc., 1936, p. xiv.
MSS. Add. A. 301, fol. xii, attr. to Mr. Clavell; Douce f. 5, fol. 16, with 'Answeare'; Eng. poet. c. 50, fol. 24v; e. 14, fol. 81v rev., with 'answer'; f. 10, fol. 92v; Rawl. poet. 84, fol. 73v rev., with 'The answer'; see also I516, O197.

**I that sometimes shined like the orient sun** 520
**He both in vice and virtue did excel.**

[Rogers, Thomas], 'Leicesters Ghost'.
Printed in 1641. An autograph fair copy is in B.M. Add. MS. 12132, fol. 3.
MS. Tanner 306, fol. 193.

**I that was once a careless epicure** 521
**Bestoweth all things, to the world's great wonder.**

W. A., translator, Horace, *Odes* I. xxxiv.
MS. *Rawl. poet. 104, fol. 11v (autogr.).

**I that was once an humble log** 522
**Got in my box and went to rest.**

'A true and full account of a late conference between the wonderfull speaking head fa: G[aude]n'.
'Father Gauden' in B.M. Add. MS. 29497, fol. 36.
MSS. Douce 357, fol. 126v; Firth c. 16, p. 139.

**I that was wont upon my oaten reed** 523
**Not fearing Momus bite, or Pasquill's brand.**

Sheppard, Samuel, Proem to 'The Faerie King'.
MS. Rawl. poet. 28, fol. 4v.

**I thee observed and in this sight** 524
**Be stabbed for giving me the lie.**

'On his Mris'.
MS. CCC. 328, fol. 81.

**I think I shall never despair** 525
**One hundred thirty and four.**

'The French Kings Cordiall', on Louis XIV's support of the Old Pretender.
Pr. *Poems on Affairs of State*, iv, 1707, p. 109.
MSS. Tanner 306, fol. 481; Top. Oxon. c. 108, p. 75.

**I think none mean that are with virtue blest** 526
**Which always fill, eternally invite.**

Williams, John, 'I am a Companion of all them that fear Thee and keep Thy Commandments. Ps. 119th v. 65'.
MS. *Rawl. poet. 191, fol. 156 (autogr.).

**I think old Elia that you** 527
**There's nothing for it to knock out.**

Martial, *Epigrams* I. xix.
MS. *Eng. poet. e. 28, p. 321.

**I think on thy good turns; and always will;** 528
**Their author's prating, makes them perish quite.**

Martial, *Epigrams* V. liii, 'In Posthumum'.
MS. Ashmole 38, p. 117.

529 I thirst for thirstiness, and weep for tears
That those whose rest's not here, their rest's behind.
'The Zealous Pennitant'.
MS. Rawl. poet. 90, fol. 42.

530 I thought before cold death had seized my sight
And make us render up our souls with ease.
Walsh, William, 'Guilford Dudley to Queen Jane'.
MS. Malone 9, fol. 35 (autogr.).

531 I thought I had entirely left the stage,
Which I confess, and all the rest approve.
Williams, John, epilogue to 'Love Restored'.
MS. *Rawl. poet. 184, fol. 51 (autogr.).

532 I thought I loved exceedingly before
Rather than turn, will burn, and will his martyr die.
'The Captivity. Ode Pindarique'.
MS. *Don. c. 55, fol. 4 (autogr.).

533 I thought my all was given before
Thy hand-maid's pleas'd, completely happy still.
Carey, Mary, 'Written . . . at the Death of my 4th son, and 5th Child Peregrine Payler . . . Grove Street, May 12th 1652'.
MS. Rawl. D. 1308, p. 179.

534–5 I thought that those damned rogues had done their worst
And think them not worthy of a halter.
'On the Late Plot'.
MS. Rawl. poet. 123, p. 255.

536 I thought to sent [*sic*]
But prithee what reason have you.
'To the Earl of Oxford upon his excessive Mirth at the proclaiming of King George [I, 1714]'.
MS. Rawl. poet. 152, fol. 211.

537 I threat'ned to observe the strict decree
Christ keepeth now, who cannot fail or fall.
Herbert, George, 'The holdfast'.
Pr. *The Temple*, 1633, p. 137.
MS. *Tanner 307, fol. 104.

538 I [took] teuk her by the hand so smail
We are as kind as you.
Dialect verses.
MS. Rawl. A. 176, fol. 79.

539–40 I took the wall one thrust me proudly by
The wall's the subjects', but the way's the king's.
'In superbum', epigram.
Pr. *A Helpe to Discourse*, 1623; cf. *N. & Q.* 206, 1961, p. 426.
MSS. CCC. 327, fol. 33; Don. d. 58, fol. 34v; Eng. poet. e. 14, fol. 76; see also I704.

I took to husband, my daughter's son 541
All which one marriage did lawfully grant.
MS. Rawl. poet. 66, fol. 53.

I travelled on seeing the hill where lay 542
And but a chair.
Herbert, George, 'The Pilgrimage'.
Pr. *The Temple*, 1633, p. 135.
MS. *Tanner 307, fol. 103.

I tried if books would cure my love but found 543
There where they work not well.
Cowley, [Abraham], 'The incurable'.
Pr. *Works*, 1668, 'The Mistress', p. 73.
MSS. Rawl. poet. 84, fol. 35v rev., attr. to Cowley; 173, fol. 81, attr. to Mr. Cowley.

I trumpet have the sole command of war 544
Our instruments are stopt our songs at rest.
On musical instruments, Trumpet, Horn, Organ, Pipe, Lute, Harp.
MS. Eng. poet. c. 50, fol. 125.

I trust in god how dare ye then, 545
Shows forth his pleasant face.
[Sternhold, Thomas], Psalm xi.
MS. Rawl. poet. 112, fol. 68v rev.

I trust in thee oh Lord, my life 546
And sing praise to his name.
Psalm vii.
MS. *Rawl. C. 113, fol. 13.

I.T.'s such a liar there's none can lie faster 547
Except 'tis his maid and she'll lie with her master.
Couplet.
MS. Eng. misc. e. 241, fol. 100.

I undertook a task too high for one 548
A pitch more fit for eagles than a fly.
Corbet, W.
MS. *Rawl. poet. 210, fol. 2v.

I upon whom thou laughd'st when I was born 549
And please my hearers if at all I please.
W. A., translator, Horace, *Odes* IV. iii.
MS. *Rawl. poet. 104, fol. 38v (autogr.).

I Urbicus to whom the city Rome 550
Till Nestor's age may not come near his end.
Paraphrase, Martial, *Epigrams* VII. xcvi.
MS. Rawl. poet. 194, fol. 41.

I used to sell divers wares 551
Receive us lord to thee.
Pernelly, J., haberdasher.
MS. Eng. poet. c. 3, fol. 8.

I visit poor, see how they live, 552
Alas, they're almost dead.
Robinson, Robert.
MS. *Rawl. poet. 218, p. 61 (autogr.).

553 I waddle like a duck,
And am all over muck.
Ashe, Betty, 'I have made a truer verse upon myself than Mr. Williams made', couplet 'in a letter from Bath'.
MS. Rawl. poet. 191, fol. 105^v^.

554 I waited long, and sought the lord,
With me no time delay.
[Hopkins, John], Psalm xl.
MS. Rawl. poet. 112, fol. 60 rev.

555 I waited long and sought the Lord,
Make thou no long delay.
Psalm xl.
MS. *Montagu e. 10, fol. 61.

556 I walked forth a while ago
And now I care for neither.
MS. Rawl. poet. 117, fol. 21.

557 I want no riches, nor I have no store
Oh Lord be thou my guide and lead me to it.
Cotten, Andrew.
MSS. Ashmole 36, 37, fol. 35^v^.

558 I want not the shoe-maker's peg
Peg, stop me from running all out.
Homer, Philip Bracebridge, 'To Miss Peggy Huish: aetatis ix'.
MS. *Add. C. 282, p. 56.

559 I warn the warrior not to broach
Till thou to Athens shalt approach.
Translation of an oracle received by Ægeus, translated from the Greek found in Plutarch's Life of Theseus. Not North's translation nor 'Dryden's'.
MS. Rawl. D. 1372, fol. 24 from end.

560 I was a walking I cannot tell when
Narcissus come [kiss us and love us beside].
Part of a song printed in *Sportive Wit*, 1656, Sig. C7.
MS. Rawl. B. 35, fol. 42^v^ rev.

561 I was foretold your rebel sex
Only deposed kings can know.
Carew, Thomas, 'A disposition from Love'.
Pr. *Poems*, 1640.
MS. *Don. b. 9, fol. 2.

562 I was four times at a fine lady's house,
And when freedom I sought with bars I still met.
Williams, John.
MS. *Rawl. poet. 184, fol. 92^v^ (autogr.).

563 I was love's pris'ner once, till I did find
For she shall nothing have that is in you.
Beaumont, Thomas, 'To her when he knew her falce'.
MS. *Malone 18, p. 60 (autogr.).

I was not born to caper dance nor sing 564
Hark in your ear Z— I will — you soundly.
MS. Rawl. B. 35, fol. 42 rev.

I was not born to Helicon nor dare 565
'Tis to pen anthems for an angels' quire.
'Tho: Randolph to Ben: Johnson his adopted father'.
Pr. *Poems*, 1638, p. 22.
MSS. CCC. 328, fol. 76, attr. to Tho. Randolph; Firth e. 4, p. 26, attr. to T. Randolph.

I was right glad when as they said 566
Pursue thy wealth's increase.
Psalm cxxii.
MS. *Rawl. C. 113, fol. 90^v^.

I was the first that let christendom see 567
I cried I die, and die I did.
'Uppon Dr. Fletcher Bp.' Richard Fletcher, Bishop of London, father of the dramatist, died 15 June 1596.
MS. Rawl. poet. 172, fol. 15.

I was the first, that with an oaten quill 568
And leave my memory, with thee my friend.
Jefferies, Matthew (Master of the Choristers at Wells), to John Lane on his continuation of *The Squiers Tale*, 1616.
Pr. Chaucer Society, ser. 2, xxiii, 1888, ed. F. J. Furnivall, p. 7.
MS. Douce 170, fol. iv^v^.

I was told by a lady and in her own house 569
For women will talk of what runs in their head.
'Mr. Foxes Reply to Mrs. Montague'.
MS. Eng. poet. c. 51, p. 75.

I was white, I was brown, I was black 570
Makes fair water look like sack.
Williams, John, 'A Riddle'.
MS. *Rawl. poet. 184, fol. 91^v^ (autogr.).

I well know noble Lollius you detest 571
Better than riches, a contented mind.
Polwhele, John, translator, 'Horace . . . Lollius', *Epistles* I. xviii.
MS. *Eng. poet. f. 16, fol. 54^v^ (autogr.).

I went from England into France 572
Who most thought did the same.
[Goodwyn, Thomas], 'Journey into France' [1618].
MSS. Malone 23, p. 61; Rawl. poet. 26, fol. 58, attr. to R. Goodwin; 199, p. 25, attr. to R. Corbet; see also I80, I418.

I went to Maidenhead alone 573
Our hopes, as he please, fulfil.
MS. Rawl. poet. 66, fols. 38, 39, 40, rectos only.

574 I, who admire your selves, admire to see
As meet I should (great God) I give to thee.
Oldisworth, Giles, verses to his twin brother Robin and his sister in 'The Pattern of Piety'.
MS. *Rawl. C. 422, fol. 5 (autogr.).

575 I who did erst in lofty strains aspire
And vents his indignation on the walls.
King, William, 'The Rape of the Peach', after 1717.
MS. Tanner 456*a*, fol. 71.

576 I who did verse with florid study write,
He who is fallen, did never firmly stand.
Bacon, Sir Nicholas (1623–66), translation of Boethius, *Consolations* I. i, 1664.
MS. Tanner 306, fol. 348 (autogr.).

577 I who did write heroic lofty strain
He that is fallen, let him rise if he can.
Polwhele, Jo[hn], 'Boethius de Consolatione Philo[sophiae] translated 1649', I. i.
MS. *Eng. poet. f. 16, fol. 15 (autogr.).

578 I who erstwhile the world's sweet air did breathe
Have rattling fetters bolts and gyves and chains.
MS. Don. c. 57, fol. 55, with music.

579 I who once with rebel pride
Let them now their safety know!
Parsons, William, 'Anacreontic'.
MS. *Don. d. 123, p. 119 (autogr.).

580 I will confess
Thee and thine altars empty.
[Herrick, Robert], 'An Hymne to Love'. Copied from *Wits Recreations*, 1663, Sig. S4$^{v}$ (?). Pr. *Hesperides*, 1648.
MS. Eng. poet. d. 152, fol. 108$^{v}$.

581 I will devote my grateful mind
The Lord be ever blest.
Psalm lxxxix.
MS. *Rawl. C. 113, fol. 63.

582 I will devote my heart entire
Soon brings their greatness down.
Psalm ix.
MS. *Rawl. C. 113, fol. 14.

583 I will [embrace] enjoy thee now my Celia [dearest] come
Should make men atheists and not women whores.
Carew, Thomas, 'A Rapture'.
Pr. *Poems*, 1640.
MSS. Ashmole 36, 37, fol. 197; 38, p. 68, attr. to Mr. Carye; CCC. 328, fol. 72$^{v}$; Eng. poet. c. 50, fol. 69, attr. to T. C.; c. 53, fol. 16; e. 97, p. 187, attr. to Tho: Cary; Firth d. 7, fol. 127, attr. to Tho: Carew; e. 4, p. 117.

I will extol the Lord my king 584
That to his fear incline . . . (incomplete).
Psalm cxlv.
MS. *Rawl. C. 113, fol. 101.

I will give laud and honour both, 585
Nothing shall them confound.
[Sternhold, Thomas], Psalm xxxiv.
MS. Rawl. poet. 112, fol. 62$^{v}$ rev.

I will give thanks unto the Lord 586
That put their trust in him.
Psalm xxxiv.
MS. *Montagu e. 10, fol. 53.

I will not burden fate with cruelty 587
Be my good angel, and conduct me thither.
'A Funerall elegye on the vertuous gentelwoman M$^{rs}$ R. L:'
MS. Rawl. poet. 117, fol. 188 rev.

I will not covet to aspire 588
Peace to the earth, and glory to its king.
Bromley, Henry, 'The Muse'.
MS. *Don. e. 19, fol. 4 (autogr.).

I will not have you, now love one, 589
But to thee condescend.
[Price, E. (?)], 4 'statutes' for lovers.
MS. Douce 290, fol. 92 (autogr. (?)).

I will not love one minute more, I swear 590
All, all for thee, what wilt thou love me yet?
'Capt. Tyrell, of M$^{rs}$ Winchcombe'. Answered by L861.
Pr. John Suckling's *Last Remaines*, 1659.
MS. Rawl. poet. 147, p. 158.

I will not paint to purchase praise 591
Ever to reign in his kingdom.
At end, 'Amen quod spaude' [Spalding (?)].
MS. Ashmole 48, fol. 5.

I will not seek to excuse the faults of any 592
But my ambitious raging mind approves.
Translation of Ovid, *Amores* II. iv.
MS. Don. d. 58, fol. 45$^{v}$.

I will not trust thy tempting graces 593
Than wealth or beauty could before.
[Stanley, Thomas], subscribed 'Ger Savill', (Jeremy Savile) who set the poem to music.
Pr. *Poems*, 1651.
MS. Rawl. poet. 65, fol. 22.

I will not weep, for 'twere as great a sin 594
The world must still admire, scarce imitate.
King, Henry, 'On S$^{r}$ Walter Raleigh'.
Pr. *Poems*, 1657, p. 97.
MSS. CCC. 328, fol. 63; *Eng. poet. e. 30, fol. 25; *Malone 22, fol. 16; Rawl. D. 954, fol. 35; Rawl. poet. 209, fol. 9$^{v}$.

595 I will praise thee with my whole heart
Thy creature not forsake.
Psalm cxxxviii.
MS. *Rawl. C. 113, fol. 97v.

596 I will sing you a song
And he shall be whipped tomorrow.
MS. Douce d. 59, fol. 63v.

597 I will sing you a song and a squabble quite new
So love made the quarrel and love put an end to 't.
'A Song'.
MS. Eng. misc. e. 241, fol. 82.

598 I will to my beloved sing
No help doth thence appear.
'Isaiah's Vineyard . . . Chap. 5 per totum'.
MS. *Eng. poet. e. 51, p. 140.

599 I wish I could just now conjure
Stock-like with me amazed stand.
Beale, Charles, 'To Mris Mary Cradock this prest.' 25 July 1651.
MS. Rawl. letters 104, fol. 133 (autogr.).

600 I wish my masters all a happy year
And peace and plenteousness go in hand in hand.
Samber, Robert, 'On New-years Day' from 'the Bellman's Verses'.
MS. *Rawl. poet. 134*b*, fol. 154v (autogr.).

601 I wish my self in yours I then might find
How many then might wish to live like me!
Williams, John, 'To Miss Betty [Lowndes] upon her saying to me—I wish I was in Your Case'.
MS. *Rawl. poet. 184, fol. 54v (autogr.).

602 I wish no more thou shouldst love me
My bliss if thou shouldst love again.
Pr. with music by Warner, *Select Musicall Ayres and Dialogues*, 1653, i. 3.
MSS. Don. c. 57, fol. 28, with music [by Warner]; Rawl. poet. 116, fol. 39v.

603 I wish not to salute a fairer Miss
Would all the day thus pleasantly employ.
Williams, John, 'Stand up and kiss me'.
MS. *Rawl. poet. 191, fol. 95 (autogr.).

604 I wish our English soldiers good success
Christ's emperor's church, and rule of Judah's king.
'A wish and noe wish' during the civil war, 1642.
MSS. Ashmole 36, 37, fol. 176.

I wish they'd not such trouble take, but leave alone our service; 605
A seaman true don't fear the cat will ever scratch his hulk, sir.
'The Cat'.
Pr. Marryat's *Life and Letters*, 1872, ii. 244.
MS. Firth c. 18, fol. 190.

I wish thy lot, now bad, still worse, my friend! 606
For when at worst, they say, things always mend.
[Cowper, William], translator, from Owen, 'To a friend in distress', couplet.
Pr. *Life and Posthumous Works*, ed. Hayley, 1803, ii. 378.
MS. Autogr. d. 21, fol. 191v (autogr.).

I wish to her that made these lines appear, 607
One happy match, many a happy year.
Williams, John, 'To my Cousin Betty Lownds, now Duncombe, before her wedding, written with O. V. diluted'. Couplet.
MS. *Rawl. poet. 184, fol. 52v (autogr.).

I with my voice to God did cry 608
And didst them safely keep.
Psalm lxxvii.
MS. *Montagu e. 10, fol. 27.

I with my voice to god do cry 609
Thou didst them safely guide.
[Hopkins, John], Psalm lxxvii.
MS. Rawl. poet. 112, fol. 49 rev.

I with you in woods could ever rest 610
And from a desert, banish solitude.
[Lepipre, Gabriel (?)], 'On Miss Valentina Malyn of Crutched Friars June the 4 1748'.
MS. Eng. poet. e. 40, fol. 47 (in Lepipre's hand).

I wonder at those people that do think 611
It shall not stick with them as a disease.
Cavendish, Lady Jane, 'The cautious man, or wits wonder'.
MS. *Rawl. poet. 16, p. 27.

I wonder Britons should complain 612*a*
Whose sole delight is kissing.
'Grant and Rule' on George I.
MSS. Rawl. poet. 155, p. 50, ascribed to I. W.; 207, p. 23.

I wonder, brother, when the time 612*b*
Or fame doth spread her wing.
Barnes, Joshuah, 'A Dialogue between two young Black-Birds, at Sir John Cotton's Baronett, Stratton, Bedfordshire, Aug. 13 1700'.
MS. Hearne's diaries 11, p. 140.

613 I wonder, by my troth, what thou, and I
Love so alike, that none do slacken, none can die.
Donne, John.
Pr. *Poems*, 1633.
MSS. Eng. poet. e. 99, fol. 203$^{v}$; *f. 9, p. 100.

614 I wonder how he lived thus long! to find
Which over bloom, ere we expect the seed!
Oldisworth, Giles, 'once upon my L[ord] Stafford', d. 1637, aged 16.
MS. *Rawl. C. 422, fol. 36 (autogr.).

615 I wonder men themselves should think
And made him spin her smocks.
'Song'.
MS. Locke e. 17, p. 77.

616 I wonder much that all this parliament
Subscribe your patent, ne'er to be disputed.
North, Dudley, 3rd Baron, Sonnet 6.
Pr. *A Forest of Varieties*, 1645.
MS. *North e. 41, fol. 11$^{v}$.

617 I wonder our forefathers durst their lives
City or country; they all love the sport.
'Upon mariage'.
MS. Don. d. 58, fol. 52.

618 I wonder what should madam Lesbia mean
He at one game keeps her; she him at all.
Ran[dolph], Tho[mas], 'In Lesbiam'.
Pr. *Poems*, 1638.
MS. Eng. poet. c. 50, fol. 102$^{v}$.

619 I wonder why dame Nature thus
To beauty leaves the field.
[Brome, Alexander], 'Beauties force'.
Pr. *Poems*, 1661, p. 26, 'An Ode of Anacreon paraphrased'.
MS. Ashmole 47, fol. 157.

620 I wonder why you nothing crave
Give you me nothing back again.
'Nothinge'.
MS. Rawl. poet. 26, fol. 3.

621 I wonder, wonder who first invented ships to swim
For when their money is gone and spent, we will boldly sail for more.
MS. Firth c. 18, fol. 216.

622 I won't, by heaven; and yet I will;
If I attempt to do as they do.
'J[ohn] L[umby] to R. P.'
MS. *Eng. poet. e. 42, fol. 90.

I worship thee, oh hidden Deity 623
I may be blessed, when I see thy face.
Huish, Alexander, 'An hymne of Thomas Aquinas to the holy Eucharist', translated 2 Dec. 1634.
MS *Eng. poet. e. 56, p. 63 (autogr.).

I would be married but I'd have no wife 624
I would be married to a single life.
Cr[ashaw], R[ichard], 'Marriage', couplet.
MSS. Eng. poet. f. 25, fol. 13; Tanner 465, fol. 95, attr. to R. Cr.

I would be rich, and yet to raise my purse 625
Not cheat, for wealth so got the gods will curse.
Couplet translating verses from Plutarch's Life of Solon: not the same as that in North or 'Dryden'.
MS. Rawl. D. 1372, fol. 27 from end.

I would have mercy too but cannot ask, 626
And God, the hearing of my cause I crave.
Colman, Henry, 'The unregenerate sinners plea'.
MS. *Rawl. poet. 204, fol. 12 (autogr.).

I would have my mistress be 627
Fie on her 'tis some courtesan.
'Ausonius', *Epigram* lxxviii, with 'responsio ad ausonium'.
MS. Eng. poet. c. 50, fol. 129.

I would I were a million good 628
So to him would I faster.
'The Milion speakes'.
MS. Rawl. poet. 148, inside front cover.

I would it were not as it is. 629
Must be content to pine and die.
Subscribed 'Mr Dier' [Sir Edward Dyer].
Pr. from this MS., *At the Court of Queen Elizabeth*, R. M. Sargent, 1935, p. 180.
MS. Rawl. poet. 85, fol. 6.

I would love's language tell but so 630
And this each one, will whispering speak.
Cavendish, Lady Jane, 'A Songe'.
MS. *Rawl. poet. 16, p. 24.

I would no man were angry but all women pleased 631
I would that of discord make peace and unity.
Wallys, J[ohn].
MS. Ashmole 48, fol. 90$^{v}$.

632 I would not have you, Strephon, choose a [maid] mate
Is a genteel sufficiency, and love.
Pomfret, [John], 'To his Friend inclined to Marry'.
Pr. *Poems*, 1699.
MS. Eng. misc. e. 183, fol. 9, attr. to the Rev. Mr. Pomfrett; Rawl. poet. 152, fol. 220.

633 I would not in my love too soon prevail
An easy conquest makes the purchase stale.
King, Henry, 'Epigram from Petronius', *Saturæ* xv. 9. Couplet.
MSS. Eng. poet. c. 9, p. 116, copied from *Gentleman's Magazine*, v. 380; *e. 30, fol. 55; *Malone 22, fol. 31v.

634 I would not praise a man nor on his merits dwell
Let him engage in unremitting fight.
Courtenay, J[ohn], translator, 'Tyrtaeus's Elegies No. 1'.
MS. Malone 41, fol. 51.

635 I would one question ask of you.
Which on him fixed their mind.
MS. *Rawl. poet. 100, fol. 15v.

636 I would to God these eyes of mine
The heart that would but dares not.
MS. Ashmole 38, p. 113.

637 I yield fair enemy nor know
Though got by beauty kept by love.
[Stanley, Thomas].
Pr. T. Stanley's *Poems*, 1647, p. 28, and with music by J. Gamble in his *Ayres and Dialogues*, 1656, p. 59.
MS. Mus. b. 1, fol. 160v, music by John Wilson.

638 I your memory's recorder
Unlock Heaven gate more sure then these.
Strode, William, 'Register for a Bible'.
MS. *CCC. 325, fol. 79 (autogr.).
MS. Eng. poet. c. 50, fol. 127v; e. 97, p. 140.

639 I your servant who have set you free
To live for peace, and die for liberty.
'To Charles nowe great alone King of glorious Brittaine. The bold pious petition of Free-bound Felton'. 1628.
MS. Rawl. poet. 26, fol. 33.

I'd, I'll, see as Id, Ill.

640 Ianthe the lovely, the joy of her swain,
That they still might be kind, and still might be true.
'Ianthe and Iphis'.
In B.M. MS. Sloane 4455, fol. 1v, amongst works of John King D.D., Rector of Chelsea [1694–1732].
MS. *Eng. poet. d. 47, fol. 163.

Ic'rus and Phaethon by a painter wrought 641
This to be burnt, the other to be drowned.
Walsh, William, translator, [Greek Anthology] '211'.
MS. Malone 9, fol. 29 (autogr.).

I'd have it known to everyone 642
Unto my God to go.
Tipping, William, 'The Præface . . . On my deere—who was the delight of mine eyes'.
MS. *Rawl. poet. 101, fol. 9 (autogr.).

I'd praise thy valour but Mars 'gins to frown 643
Angels tune requiems to his blessed soul.
'On Sr Walter Waller', [knighted 1622 (?)].
MS. Eng. poet. e. 14, fol. 96 rev.

I'd rather have a loving fool 644
Much rather would I know.
Robinson, Robert.
MS. *Rawl. poet. 218, p. 9 (autogr.).

I'd sing of beauty, but my muse 645
One there is—Almeria's she.
I[reland, George, of Exeter Coll., Oxford], 3 Oct. 1734.
MS. Eng. misc. e. 240, p. 43.

Idlest of men that on old Camus' banks 646
To friendship give what you to skill deny.
Gough, Richard, 'To Michael Tyson Esq.'
Pr. Nichols' *Literary Anecdotes*, vi. 335.
MS. *Eng. poet. c. 5, fol. 170 (autogr.).

Idolatry, with whoredom at the height 647
That, after thousands fallen the plague was stayed.
'The Atonement'.
MS. Rawl. poet. 154, fol. 104.

If a C- were a man of war 648
The Devil the Pope or the French.
'Debauch Fancy per Jos: Haynes on the Sea Presse'.
MS. Eng. poet. d. 53, p. 50.

If abdicate James 649
And they have for their money their jest.
'A New Ballad . . . by Cooling and [Fleetwood] Shephard', 1690.
MSS. Eng. poet. c. 18, fol. 69, attr. to Cooling and Shepherd; e. 49, p. 51, attr. to Cooling and Shephard.

If Adam's fall which man confusion brought 650
Must not too much on earthly things reflect.
MS. *Rawl. poet. 97, fol. 21.

If adverse fortune bring to pass 651
The state that chance hath him assign'd.
MS. Rawl. D. 431, fol. 99.

652 If all be true that I do think
Or any other reason why.
[Aldrich, Henry], catch set by Purcell.
Pr. *The Banquet of Musick*, iii, 1689; see in F. B. Zimmerman, *Purcell*, 1963, no. 255.
MS. Rawl. poet. 196, fol. 12ᵛ.

653 If all that I lov'd was her face
Though hopeless it ever can please.
Hammond, Mr., 'On Miss Dashwood'.
MS. Eng. poet. e. 40, fol. 23.

654 If all that love and man hath sworn
For his vow is not an oath.
MS. Mus. b. 1, fol. 15, music by John Wilson.

655 If all the acts of thund'ring Jove
If love were not the cause again.
Polwhele, John, translator, Boethius, *Consolations* IV. vi.
MS. *Eng. poet. f. 16, fol. 37 (autogr.).

656 [If] Gif all the floudis amangis thaime walle concluid
Ye floodis thou deepe quhilk warr youre deuties baith.
King James I.
MS. *Bodl. 165, fol. 51 (autogr.).

657 If all the gods would now agree
Madam your chamber fool to be.
[Edwards, Thomas (?)].
Pr. Appendix to *Cephalus and Procris. Narcissus*, ed. W. E. Buckley, Roxburghe Club, 1882, p. 72.
MS. Tanner 306, fol. 175.

658 If all the miracles that Christ hath done
The universal blind world went astray.
MS. *Rawl. poet. 97, fol. 52ᵛ.

659 If all the stars ye could define
How far adversity doth reach.
Fleming, Robert, 'An Adumbration of Eternity' translating Latin.
Pr. *The Mirrour of Divine Love*, 1691, 'Poems', p. 37.
MS. Rawl. poet. 213, fol. 57 rev. (autogr.).

660 If all the world, and love were young
To live with thee, and be thy love.
[Ralegh, Sir Walter]. Answer to C530.
Pr. *England's Helicon*, 1600.
MS. Rawl. poet. 148, fol. 96ᵛ.

661 If all the world were but a ring,
England the diamond should bring.
Couplet.
MS. Sancroft 100, p. 4.

If all the world were men 662
What should we do for oysters.
MSS. Ashmole 36, 37, fol. 48ᵛ.

If all these virtues which school critics call 663
Your turn comes next we must have Charles the Great.
'To my deare and greate Master Prince Charles' [later Charles I].
MS. Dodsworth 79, fol. 165.

If an injured monarch may his cause explore 664
Which Heaven approved of by a cheerful voice.
'Dialogue Between King James and King Wᵐ.'
MS. Rawl. D. 261, fol. 195; see also I853, I1045.

If any ask what these mixed streamers show 665
Of our friend's loss, the white his innocence.
E. L., of King's School Sherborne, on the death of Robert Whetcombe, 'Antientest Governour of the King's Schoole of Sherebourne', 24 Oct. 1656. On fol. 37 is a Latin poem subscribed Edwardus Locetus.
MS. Gough Dorset 35(1), fol. 25.

If any ask, who here doth lie, 666
The devil long since had had the dish.
'Epitaph on Sʳ Walter Pye Atturney of the Wards, who dyed on Christmas day'.
Pr. *Life [etc.] of J. Hoskyns*, L. B. Osborn, 1937, p. 214.
MSS. Don. b. 8, two copies, pp. 212 and 368; Tanner 465, fol. 62.

If any ask why Tarquine meant to marry 667
The priest must after all the people go.
On Bp. Richard Fletcher, Feb. 1594–5.
MSS. Add. B. 97, fol. 20ᵛ; CCC. 327, fol. 29ᵛ; Tanner 306, two copies, fols. 189 and 190.

If any be distressed, and fain would gather 668
With one consent of heart, and voice say—Amen.
'Uppon the Lords prayer'.
MS. Eng. poet. e. 57, fol. 12; see also I671.

If any be who thinks no ghosts survive 669
Fill barrels, feel Ixion's dreadful strain.
J. F., translator, 'Buchanan's Epitaph on Calvin'.
MS. *Eng. poet. f. 17, p. 59 (autogr.).

If any body politic 670
The next fair wind he must away.
[Brome, Alexander], 'A Mountebanke'.
Pr. *Poems*, 1661, p. 134.
MS. Rawl. poet. 62, fol. 46.

671 If any in distress desire to gather
With one consent of heart and voice say Amen.
'On the Lords prayer'.
MS. Eng. poet. f. 10, fol. 84v; see also I668.

672 If any justly weep, then surely we
Of tedious care without cessation.
Strangewaies, Giles, of King's School Sherborne, on the death of Robert Whetcombe, 'Antientest Governour of the King's Schoole of Sherebourne', 24 Oct. 1656.
MS. Gough Dorset 35(1), fol. 22.

673 If any man or woman, in earth or in Heaven
Yet I am a knight though.
Endorsed 'A Huy and Cry after a lost Ganymed'.
MS. Tanner 306, fol. 413.

674 If any, many men; think otherwise;
With my place, then, allowed on his right hand.
[Wood, Andrew (?)]; cf. J73.
MSS. Ashmole 36, 37, fol. 294.

675 If any miss the H, that's wanting here,
Let him but search her bones, he'll find it there.
Couplet, 'Anagram Elisabeth Crab, A Careless Tibb'.
MSS. Ashmole 38, p. 151; Rawl. poet. 117, fol. 268 rev.

676 If any pleasure unto man befall
Oh thus, ye gods, reward my piety.
J. F., translator, 'Out of Catullus', lxxvi.
MS. *Eng. poet. f. 17, p. 39 (autogr.).

677 If any think this day's solemnity
'Tis cheaper to condemn us than to pay.
Strode, William, 'A Prologue crownd with Flowres. On the Florists Feast at Norwich'.
MS. *CCC. 325, fol. 125 (autogr.).

678 If any traveller shall ask
A player and a puritan.
'On a player'.
MS. Don. d. 58, fol. 16.

679 If anyone henceforth shall be so bold
And not permit her bed near thine to stand.
W. A., translator, Horace, *Epodes* iii.
MS. *Rawl. poet. 104, fol. 48v (autogr.).

680 If anyone will string his instrument
Or curious nice psalms: yet love gentle singers.
Cheyney, William, 'To Any One'.
MS. *Rawl. poet. 86, fol. 2.

681 If anything a woman doth alone
If she dissemble she thinks 'tis not done.
MS. Rawl poet. 206, p. 29.

If Aphra's worth were needful to be shown 682
And what thou canst not comprehend admire.
'The Female Laureat. 1684', Aphra Behn.
Pr. *Poems on Affairs of State*, ii, 1703, p. 146.
MS. Rawl. poet. 159, fol. 116.

If art by wishing could obtained be, 683
But else have cause to curse thy power and name.
North, Dudley, 3rd Baron, Sonnet 5.
Pr. *A Forest of Varieties*, 1645.
MS. *North e. 41, fol. 11.

If art were proper in a mourning dress 684
The Egyptian queen had not so brave a tomb.
May, T[homas], 'An Elegie uppon the Ladye Digby', d. 1st May 1633.
MS. Ashmole 38, p. 192.

If, as 685
The works of light affect not secrecy.
Oldisworth, Nicolas, 'On the transparencie of Mr. Tooker's house at Strettam'.
MS. *Don. c. 24, fol. 64v (autogr.).

If as a flower doth spread and die, 686
To my poor reed.
Herbert, George, 'Imployment'.
Pr. *The Temple*, 1633, p. 49.
MS. *Tanner 307, fol. 37v.

If as logicians do believe 687
Untie the knot they tied before.
'A Rationale on Swearing'.
MS. Eng. poet. d. 53, p. 74.

If, as of law, there were four terms of war 688
One gets old angels, th' other gets cracked crowns.
[Wroth, Sir Thomas], 'Upon the Lawyer and the souldier'.
Pr. *The Abortive of an Idle Houre*, 1620, p. 17.
MS. Rawl. poet. 26, fol. 93; see also I755, I871.

If as the winds and waters here below 689
They purge the air without, within the breast.
Herbert, George, 'The Storme'.
Pr. *The Temple*, 1633, p. 125.
MS. *Tanner 307, fol. 95.

If at moon changing thou the gods dost pray 690
Touching the sacred altar not obscene.
W. A., translator, Horace, *Odes* III. xxiii.
MS. *Rawl. poet. 104, fol. 32v (autogr.).

If aught distracts thee God's not yet thy all 691
Will rise victorious and disturbance cease.
MS. *Don. f. 5, fol. 16.

692 If aught may hope of comic lays
Commend e'en authors bad as me.
'The Farce of the Bellows, etc. . . . by An Englishman'.
MS. Douce 249.

693 If aught of oaten stop, or pastoral song
And hymn thy fav'rite name!
Collins, [William], 'Ode to the Evening', published 1746, and in Dodsley's *Collection of Poems*, i, 2nd ed., 1748, p. 331.
MS. Eng. misc. f. 79, p. 111.

694 If Balam's ass his master once did chide
As 'twas that Balam's ass did silence break.
'Upon the Asse Carriing Christ'.
MS. Rawl. poet. 194, fol. 39.

695 If beauty, youth, or innocence were dear,
Pious as parent's fears, unfeign'd as mine.
'On two young Persons', brother and sister, buried at Plymouth, 1735, by their brother.
MS. Eng. misc. e. 240, p. 261.

696 If bitters, or if bitter sweets are best
No bitters named when sweets will do as well.
Williams, John, 'Another', 'that bitter things are wholesome'.
MS. *Rawl. poet. 191, fol. 45v (autogr.).

697 If bleeding hearts, dejected souls [bleeding souls, dejected hearts], find grace
New life to those that only wish to live.
'To the most high and mighty . . . Chancellor of Heaven, and Judge of earth The . . . Petitions of the Commons of Englande', 1623–4, cf. I937.
*The Commons Petition*, 1642, reprinted in *Fugitive Tracts . . . in Verse*, [ed. Henry Huth], 1875, 2nd ser., xv.
MSS. Ashmole 36, 37, fol. 303v; Eng. poet. c. 50, fol. 8v; f. 10, fol. 108; Malone 19, p. 15; 23, pp. 34, 11–12, 37–44, 13–14; Rawl. D. 398, fol. 223; Rawl. poet. 160, fol. 16v; Top. Cheshire c. 7, fol. 4.

698 If blest with gospel liberty
By duty to my prince.
Kenton, James.
MS. *Eng. poet. e. 20, p. 382 (autogr.).

699 If books be fairest pictures of the mind
Who deigns to grace those arts, which honour you.
[Creswell, Robert], 'To the Lord Viscount Falkland, upon the receipt of a book from his Lordship'.
MS. Rawl. poet. 246, fol. 26.

If both my eyes do full of water stand 700
Or chosen states-men, who . . . (incomplete).
Oldisworth, Nicolas, 'A satyre. On occasion of Mr. — his departure out of England'.
MS. *Don. c. 24, fol. 65 (autogr.).

If both the Indies were my own 701
And be friends with the parliament once again.
'The Conditional Recantation: . . . Dialogue between the Arch. of St. Patrick and the late King'. 1689/90.
MSS. Firth e. 6, fol. 119v; Rawl. poet. 159, fol. 57*c*; 173, fol. 125v, attr. to the E. of Dorset.

If breath were made for every man to buy 702
The poor man could not live; rich would not die.
'Epigram', couplet.
MS. Don. e. 6, fol. 17.

If but a harmless spark of love 703
I'll never fight, but rather yield.
'A Lad and a lasse talking togeather'.
MS. CCC. 328, fol. 90.

If by the owners we esteem of things, 704
The wall's the subject's but the way's the king's.
Couplet.
MS. Rawl. poet. 209, fol. 36v; see also I539–40.

If care may cause men cry why do I not complain 705
Woe worth the time that I to love my self did first apply.
[Howard, Henry, Earl of Surrey.]
Pr. Tottel's Miscellany, 1557, and with music, *Cantus, Songs and Fancies*, Aberdeen, 1662, Sig. A1.
MS. Ashmole 176, fol. 97.

If chance some pensive stranger hither led 706
Her woes are buried and her heart is still.
Bowles, [William Lisle]. 'Written at a Convent'.
Pr. *Sonnets*, 1791.
MS. Eng. misc. e. 241, fol. 119.

If charity, zeal, friendship, virtue's dye 707
Equal she fell, but shall not equal rise.
Inscription in Gloucester Cathedral to Mary, wife of Richard Parsons, D.C.L., d. 26 Oct. 1690.
MSS. Rawl. D. 1090, fol. 128; Willis 71, p. 259.

If Charles thou [wilt] wouldst but be [grow] so kind 708
We'll ask no more.
'The humble Petition of the house of Commons', 1642. Answered by I111.
Pr. *Rump Songs*, 1662, Sig. C1.
MSS. Ashmole 36, 37, fol. 96; Ballard 47, fol. 9; Malone 21, fol. 30v.

709 If chastity commends a wife
Who here does lie till doomis-day.
On Marion Gray, Haddington Churchyard.
MS. Top. gen. e. 32, fol. 45^v^.

710 If Chester boast her (flesh and blood) chief men:
Oh spare Manchester chief of statesmen long.
Pestell, Thomas, 'Epigram on the . . . Bp. of Winchester (deceased) [James Montagu, d. 1618] and [Edward Montagu, 1602–71] The Earle of Manchester (living)'.
MS. *Malone 14, p. 46.

711 If children young and little babes
With everlasting sorrow.
Tipping, William.
MS. *Rawl. poet. 101, fol. 87 (autogr.).

712 If Ch[rist] Church lads were sad they spent their breath
Bred-ah is lost, your bargain you maintain.
Strode, William, 'An Answere made to Maudlins Rimes, and their Factions, concerning the Proctors', dated 1625 by Fulman, answer to W2362.
MS. *CCC. 325, fol. 75*a* (autogr.).

713 If constancy a virtue be
Give me give me give me give me Dorinda's love.
Pr. *The Banquet of Music*, v, 1690, p. 14.
MS. Rawl. poet. 196, fol. 30.

714 If cudgel or stick
If our's were mute the wonder would be greater.
Question and Answer.
MS. Percy c. 8, fol. 132^v^.

715 If Cupid e'er my heart doth steal
For that those charms I'd ne'er resist.
Davenant, Charles, 'A Song'.
MS. Rawl. poet. 84, fol. 22^v^.

716 If David's troubles sojourn in my breast,
How soon we sin, and yet how late repent.
'The Surrender'.
MS. Rawl. poet. 90, fol. 97^v^.

717 If daws and dolts were dolven deep
Farewell good fool my rhyme is done.
Churchyard, Tho[mas], 'A thondring answer . . . [to] the . . . peticion of . . . William Somer . . .'.
MS. Rawl. poet. 172, fol. 38.

718 If, dear Licinius, thou wouldst fain
When thou perceiv'st them swollen with over-prosperous gales.
Sancroft, William, translator, Horace, *Odes* II. x.
MS. Sancroft 48, fol. 30^v^ (autogr.).

If, dearest Dismal, you for once can dine 719
Then order Squash to call a hackney chair.
'Toland's Invitation to Dismal, [the Earl of Nottingham] to dine with the Calves Head club, . . . 29 Jan.'
In B.M. Add. MS. 37683, fol. 2, dated Jan. 1711/2.
MS. Eng. poet. e. 87, p. 164.

If death be but a change (which all confess) 720
To him who shines with Christ like gold thrice tried.
On Henry Austen, servant to James Earl of Carlisle; he died 1638. From Waltham Abbey Church.
MS. Rawl. D. 682, fol. 65^v^.

If death be but a servant sent to call 721
One perch of Heaven's worth the whole globe of clay.
Reynolds, Dr. Edward, of Brainceton, on Jeremy Whitaker.
MS. Lat. misc. c. 19, p. 83.

If death be nought, but when the breath departs, 722
Death's but a fart, and so a fart for death.
'On Death'.
MS. Add. B. 105, fol. 6^v^; see also 1886.

If death will come, sure there will be an end 723
In a moment death may free me.
'Death: the miserable Mans Friend'.
MS. Rawl. poet. 90, fol. 45^v^.

If death would come and show his face 724
Unto a mind prepared.
'A song of Death'.
Pr. 1631 (in Roxburghe collection); and by Douglas Gray, 'Two Songs of Death', *Neuphilologische Mitteilungen*, lxiv, 1963, pp. 67–71.
MS. Eng. poet. b. 5, p. 22.

If deepest learning with a zealous love 725
Rome's foe, truth's champion, and the Rhemists' terror.
'For Dr. Fulke [d. 1589] after a plaine inscription on the North wall of the Chancell in Dinnington, are these verses'.
MS. Sancroft 59, p. 239 rev.

If devout Pawlet Mary 726
She'll be banished the sight of the king.
'A New Ballad. Truth needs no Vindication. 1686'.
MS. Firth c. 15, p. 223.

If drops of dew which from the heavens do fall 727
Awake I lie rejoicing thou art mine.
Tipping, William, 'Contemplation On Eternitie'.
MS. *Rawl. poet. 101, fol. 63^v^ (autogr.).

728 If dullness gross beyond compare
Would — be the chief of men?
Sent to Dr. Rawlinson, 1746; on George II and the Young Pretender (?).
MS. Rawl. poet. 195, fol. 165.

729 If dumb too long, the drooping muse hath stay'd
No chance could sever, nor the grave divide.
Tickell, Thomas, 'To the Right Honourable the Earl of Warwick', on the death of Addison, 1719.
Pr. *Works of Addison*, 1721, vol. i, p. xvii.
MS. Rawl. poet. 153, fols. $51^{r, v}$ and 60.

730 If duty without compliment might stand
Other may higher fly, none stoop so low.
[Lawrence, Thomas], 'An Address To her Highness the Dutchesse of Yorke In the Librarie St. John's College Oxon', endorsed 'Sept. 1663'.
See Wood, *Life and Times*, ed. A. Clark, i, O.H.S., xix, 1891, p. 498, 29 Sept. 1663.
MS. Tanner 306, fol. 366.

731 If dying piety deserve a tear
And be my progress, and my end like thine.
'On the Death of the Rev. Mr. Jos. Collett, late Minister of the Gospel. G[entleman's] Mag.'
MS. Eng. poet. e. 39, p. 110.

732 If early thus, by Joseph's worth inspired
Let Joseph shine in every step you take.
'On a Youth's commending the History of Joseph'.
MS. Ballard 29, fol. 160.

733 If e'er my words your approbation gained
Must to the day's transactions add the night's.
Gough, Richard, translator, 'The Cento Nuptialis of Ausonius. Sept. 23, 1768'.
MS. *Eng. poet. c. 5, fol. 154 (autogr.).

734 If e'er thy Emma's name was dear
And in that pleasing hope thy Emma dies content.
Shaw, Cuthbert, 'Lines from a Monody To the memory of a young lady [who died 1768] By an afflicted Husband'.
MS. Percy d. 9, fol. 22.

735 If e'er you leave us in a lasting peace
Shall crown your heads, and we shall sing your praise.
'Post-Script' to R153.
MS. Don. e. 23, fol. 36.

If eighty-eight be past then thrive 736
A Spaniard protestant to be.
'A prophesye found in St. Benedict's Abby in Norfolke'.
Pr. *Mercurius Politicus*, 1643, p. 12.
MSS. Ashmole 47, fol. 40; 423, fol. 265; Eng. poet. c. 50, fol. $7^v$; Rawl. D. 398, fol. 162; 1092, fol. 23; Rawl. poet. 26, fol. $15^v$; 117, fol. 169 rev.

If either lotteries or lots 737
Virginia gets no more of me.
'De Scoto-Britannis'.
MS. Rawl. poet. 26, fol. 1.

If error, ignorance, and conceit grown grey 738
But miracles must Sophonisba save.
MS. Rawl. poet. 207, p. 158.

If Eva had considered ere she ate 739
We do not read he did at all dissent.
MS. *Rawl. poet. 97, fol. 11 (autogr.).

If ever any angels die, 740
The like of him, his platform brake.
Oldisworth, Nicolas, epitaph 'on litle Tho. Bacon'.
MS. *Don. c. 24, fol. 31 (autogr.).

If ever, foolish Paul, thou hadst been told 741
Thou answerest straight; Paul's folly stood i' th' light.
Baker, E[dward], Clarensis (matr. 1580, M.A. 1587), 'Upon Mr Paul Thompson; for clippinge gold' 1615.
MS. Rawl. poet. 26, fol. 1.

If ever I (oh michtie goddis) have done you service treu 742
I hope to gett this ladie full of bliss.
King James I, incomplete masque, for a betrothal (?).
MS. *Bod. 165, fol. 60 (autogr.).

If ever I with thee (oh harp) did play 743
Heavens grant that ever I may thee possess.
W. A., translator, Horace, *Odes* I. xxxii.
MS. *Rawl. poet. 104, fol. $10^v$ (autogr.).

If ever in the April of my days 744
My prayer hear: sweet Jesu intercede.
King James I, 'Votum. A Vow or Wish for the felicity and fertility of the owners of this house', August, 1621.
See Nichols' *Progresses*, 1828, iv. 710. Pr. from Rawl. poet. 26, James Craigie, *Poems of James VI*, S.T.S. 26, p. 177.
MSS. Rawl. poet. 26, fol. 4, 'by the Kinge . . . August 1621'; Tanner 306, two copies, fols. 246, attr. to the King, and 253, endorsed 1621.

If ever pity were acquainted . . . see D214.

745 If ever temple stood upon no ground
Wherein such deep and learned secrets lurk.
E. S., 'To the reader in praise of the worthy authors most worthy worke'.
MS. Rawl. poet. 152, fol. 24.

746 If ever thou Barine oft forsworn
And so do wives their husbands lest thou catch them.
W. A., translator, Horace, *Odes* II. viii.
MS. *Rawl. poet. 104, fol. 15ᵛ (autogr.).

747 If every man might worship God,
'Mongst men we rare should find.
Robinson, Robert.
MS. *Rawl. poet. 218, p. 134 (autogr.).

748 If every wight, by common right
Shall come too when I die.
'A pittiful complainte of a silly poore horse, lately . . . imprisoned for papistry'. Subscribed 'Jacke Nicholls amblinge nagge'.
MS. Rawl. poet. 212, fol. 102.

749 If evil your impieties befall,
But never penetrate into the deed.
[Stanley, Thomas, translator], 'On Wicked Persons'.
Pr. *History of Philosophy*, 1655, p. 56, attributed to Solon.
MS. Rawl. poet. 90, two copies, fols. 60ᵛ and 105.

750 If eyes in tears still steept
Blunt chance t'hard patience will succumb.
J. F., translator, 'An Ode of Casimire' [IV. xiii].
MS. *Eng. poet. f. 17, p. 82 (autogr.).

751 If eyes rejoice to see the streams of light
Such mysteries to tell you both despair.
F. W., Sonnet 34.
MS. *Rawl. C. 639, p. 177.

752 If faith alone can save us, and good works do not merit
That faith alone, should save a soul, that wanteth charity.
MS. Douce 357, fol. 2ᵛ.

753 If fate be not, then what can be foreseen?
If ill, 'tis ours, if good, the act of heaven.
'Mr. Dryden's Verses'.
MS. Don. b. 8, p. 499.

754 If for a grace, or if for some mislike
Your golou's perfumed; your lips and cheeks are painted.
'On a gentelwoman tha[t] pain[t]ed her face'.
MS. Eng. poet. e. 14, fol. 81ᵛ rev.

If for four terms four terms there were in war 755
The one whole angels take the others cracked crowns.
'The disparitie of souldiers and lawiers'.
MS. Eng. poet. f. 10, fol. 89ᵛ; see also I688, I871.

If for me the fates ordain her 756
Haste and bring me to the fair.
'Song'.
MS. Eng. poet. e. 40, fol. 32.

If for the asking my wish I might have 757
On condition to take away the other two.
Translation of *Dominici Baudi Epistolæ*, Amsterdam, 1662, p. 33, 'Iambics In tres Juris perversores'.
MS. Sancroft 53, p. 59.

If for the slow delay of sleep, I've sight 758
And these sad torments shall exalt my joy.
Southwell, Sir Robert, 'Thursday night not sleeping till 4 a clock . . . [16]57'.
MS. *Eng. poet. f. 6, fol. 9 (autogr.).

If for to speed thou think it a pain 759
If that which thou mayst not thou travail to get.
MS. Gough Norfolk 43, fol. 46.

If former good, cold answer present ill 760
To England's joy betide what may of me.
'Verses sett forthe in the faver of the Duke of Norffolk his causes', 1569. Answered by G380.
MS. Gough Norfolk 43, fol. 53ᵛ.

If fortune wraps you warm 761
There you may lie and rot.
[Catch].
MS. Mus. Sch. C. 95, p. 234.

If found among thieves, an unfortunate stranger 762
Ten thousand to one, you're transported for life.
M[adan], M[artin], 1725–90, 'To the Author of' W1867.
MS. Eng. poet. c. 21, p. 187.

If friendship suit not with society 763
Nor is it meet to marry Sue to Franck.
Burton, Francis, Acrostic, {Francis Burton / Susan Bredwell.
MS. *Add. A. 267, fol. 146ᵛ (autogr.).

If from glove you take [away] the letter G 764
Then glove is love, and love I send to thee.
'On a paire of gloves', couplet.
MSS. Don. d. 58, fol. 42ᵛ; Eng. poet. e. 14, fol. 84 rev., with 'reply', 'If from this clout . . .'; see also F783, I766, I964.

765 If from our earthly friends detained
In joy and everlasting bliss.
Kenton, James.
MS. *Eng. poet. e. 20, p. 291 (autogr.).

766 If from the glove, you take the letter G
Then glove is love and so I send it thee.
'On a paire of gloves'.
MS. Eng. poet. f. 10, fol. 94, with answer; see also F783, I764, I964.

767 If from the lustre of the sun
And flying from her, met her.
'The Indifferent, wrote to a Man in Love'.
MS. *Eng. poet. d. 47, fol. 158.

768 If from the realms of never-fading joy
And England sanctify her Oxford's choice.
Lemaistre, [John Gustavus], Queen's College, Oxford. 'The triumph of Virtue', on the Duke of Portland as Chancellor of Oxford University, 1792.
MS. Top. Oxon. d. 163, fol. 269.

769*a* If from the Stygian lake a writ may come
Speak I? sith chief the worm of conscience claims . . . (incomplete).
'The Rich Glutton, to his five brothers, of the paynes of Hell', translation of 'Jac[obus] Biderman[us, S.J., *Heroum Epistolae*] L[ib]. 1. epist. 3'.
MS. Rawl. poet. 170, fol. 24.

769*b* If from the touch of that blood-born hoof
Of hideous grief, and heart-blood-sucking woe.
Sonnet. 'Canto 1' of sequence.
MS. Add. B. 97, fol. 21.

770 If garden's pride enamelled all with flowers
But all [inculme (?)], no joy can other stay.
F. W., 'Sonnet. 30. the joy of the soul in contemplation of God's essence'.
MS. *Rawl. C. 639, p. 154.

771 If Gella's beauty be examined
Than a sweet, filthy, fine, illfavoured whore.
Davies, [Sir] John, 'In Gellam'.
Pr. amongst 'Epigrames', with *Ovids Elegies*, translated C. M., [*c.* 1600].
MSS. *Add. B. 97, fol. 44; *Rawl. poet. 212, fol. 61$^{v}$ rev.

772 If genius, learning, warm thy breast
And full of days, like Abraham expir'd.
'On The Revd. Phanuel Bacon', d. 1783.
MS. Top. Oxon. a. 29, fol. 153.

If gentleness could tame the fates or wit 773
And says our sins are greater then our wits.
Corbett, [Richard], 'On Mr. Henrie Boling his death'.
Pr. *Certain Elegant Poems*, 1647, and *Wits Recreations*, 1640, no. 97. See Poems, ed. J. A. W. Bennett and H. R. Trevor-Roper, 1955, p. 145.
MSS. Douce f. 5, fol. 34$^{v}$, attr. to Dr. Corbett; Eng. poet. e. 14, fol. 97$^{v}$ rev., attr. to Dr. Corbett.

If glory be with praise, a blazing fame 774
Then print their fame in his and angel's heart.
F. W., 'Sonnet. 7. Whie the joyes of heaven are Called Glorie'.
MS. *Rawl. C. 639, p. 26.

If God as verses say a spirit be 775
And union with it in our spirit find.
Traherne, Thomas, 'Si Deus est Animus sit pura Mente Colendus', 'The Second Century', 84.
MS. Eng. th. e. 50, fol. 42$^{v}$ (autogr.).

If God be pleased when man doth cease from [forsakes his] sin 776
Then Dick pleased all by going to his grave.
'On the Tapster Dicke', epigram.
MSS. CCC. 327, fol. 22$^{v}$; Don. d. 58, fol. 16$^{v}$; see also I790, I797.

If God determined to destroy 777
And with salvation bless.
Kenton, James.
MS. *Eng. poet. e. 20, p. 112 (autogr.).

If Gods can live on air 778
Here is delicious fare.
Couplet on Buckingham house, rebuilt by the Duke of Buckingham, 1703.
MS. Smith 23, p. 131.

If God's hand be laid on thee 779
For thee if thou wilt trust in him.
Pr. bk. Tanner 221, MS. fol. 1$^{v}$.

If golden titles gild an earthen pot, 780
That it's less earth for that it follows not.
Translation of Latin.
MSS. Rawl. D. 954, fol. 40; Rawl. poet. 209, fol. 35$^{v}$.

If good men's graces in heaven with them abide, 781
The Duke is gone, the clean contrary way.
On the Duke of Buckingham, 1628.
MS. Tanner 465, fol. 104.

782 If great men wrong me, I will spare my self
If good like gods, the naught are so like devils.
[Roe, Sir John], '[Epistle] to Ben: Johnson'. Dated 9 November 1603, in B.M. MS. Lansdowne 740, fol. 102$^{v}$. Pr. *Poems of Donne*, 1635, p. 207. See *Ben Jonson*, Herford and Simpson, xi, 1952, p. 371.
MS. Rawl. poet. 31, fol. 25.

783 If grecians stout did right extol
The which before him went.
'Thomas Ellis in praise of Frobisher'. At end, 'finis qd. S. fo[rman]'.
Pr. from this MS., *Ballads from MSS.*, ed. F. J. Furnivall and W. R. Morfill, ii, 1873, p. 282.
MS. Ashmole 208, fol. 262.

784 If Hammon in his study hath such care
To hang up all old filthy things; let's wife beware.
[Donne, John]. Pr. *Poems*, 1633.
MS. Malone 19, p. 79, attr. to J. Deane; see also 1845.

785 If hands not work as well as heads contrive,
They'd want their food, they'd want their daily bread.
Robinson, Robert.
MS. *Rawl. poet. 218, p. 107 (autogr.).

786 If haughty cedars have their Libano
To view his god, and have his heart's desire.
F. W., 'Sonnet: 18. That there is a place ordained for the sowle to see god'.
MS. *Rawl. C. 639, p. 80.

787 If hearty wishes might avail dear friend
Joy in our loves and thereto well agree.
Burton, Francis.
MS. *Add. A. 267, fol. 137$^{v}$ (autogr.).

788 If heaven admit of treason, pride, and lust,
By treason likely his own end doth make.
On the Duke of Buckingham, 1628.
MS. Tanner 465, fol. 103.

789 If heaven be heaven because there angels dwell
My purse have none pray therefore call it hell.
'On an empty purse'.
MS. Eng. poet. f. 10, fol. 86$^{v}$; see 1795.

790 If heaven be pleased, when sinner leave to sin
Then all is pleased, for Graunt, is in his grave.
'Uppon H. Graunt'; in one version 'Mr. Calvin'; another, 'Burnet'.
MSS. Ashmole 38, p. 170; CCC. 328, fol. 43$^{v}$; Firth d. 7, fol. 153; Rawl. poet. 26, fol. 164, attr. to Benj. Johnson 'upon . . . Calvin'; 155, p. 105, 'on Burnet'; Sancroft 53, p. 59; see also 1776, 1797.

If Heaven indulgent to my earnest prayer 791
Whene'er I pleas'd to say a stupid thing.
Parsons, William, burlesque.
MS. *Don. d. 123, p. 16 (autogr.).

If heaven the grateful liberty should give 792
All men would wish to live and die like me.
Pomfret, John, 'The Choice of the pleasures of a Country Life'.
Pr. *Poems*, 1699.
MSS. Rawl. poet. 109, fol. 22, attr. to [John] Pomfret; 172, fol. 120; 173, fol. 170$^{v}$.

If Heaven will hear my ardent prayer 793
For he alone, to bliss can point the way.
Bate, S[ally], 'To a Child (of four Years of Age) On her Birth Day . . . 1764'.
MS. *Eng. poet. e. 28, p. 74.

If heaven's all conquering Monarch had not been 794
Who by thy word alone both heaven and earth didst frame.
Knollys, Fra., Psalm cxxiv.
MS. *Rawl. poet. 60, p. 30 (autogr.).

If heaven's called the place, where angels dwell 795
My purse wants angels, pray then call it hell.
MS. Rawl. poet. 153, fol. 28; see also 1789.

If Heaven's inheritors on earth be tried 796
Thou only left'st them to thine own to go.
On the tomb of 'Elizabeth Francklyn d. July 31 1622'.
MS. Top. Oxon. c. 299, fol. 293.

If heavens rejoice when men forsake their sins 797
Let's all rejoice, Warram Layton's laid in grave.
MS. Rawl. poet. 152, fol. 213; see also 1776, 1790.

If her disdain in you least change can move 798
Except self love seek private end.
Pr. *Donne's Poems*, 1635–69, and *Poems . . . of Pembroke and Ruddier*, 1660. Answered by T2778.
MSS. Eng. poet. f. 9, p. 133, attr. to Earle of Pembroke; Rawl. poet. 31, fol. 30, attr. to P.; 116, fol. 50, attr. to Pemb.; Rawl. poet. 117, fol. 199$^{v}$ rev., attr. to Sir H. Wootton; 147, p. 81, attr. to P., altered to Sr. H. W.

If Hercules' tall stature might be guess'd 799
If but to kiss your toe it should aspire.
Strode, William, 'One a good Leg and Foot'.
Pr. *Wit Restor'd*, 1658, p. 90.
MS. *CCC. 325, fol. 71 (autogr.).
MSS. CCC. 328, fol. 84; Eng. poet. c. 53, fol. 3$^{v}$; Eng. poet. e. 97, p. 133, attr. to William Stroad; Malone 21, fol. 49$^{v}$, attr. to Strode.

800 If here Christ His protect from injury
Which in all times God doth on His confer.
MS. *Rawl. poet. 97, fol. 25 (autogr.).

801 If here on earth God's gifts great lustre give
And in thy truth conduct me by thy spirit.
MS. *Rawl. poet. 97, fol. 27 (autogr.).

802 If here you come, no gin, no rum,
Will cheer your heart as well.
'On a Sign-Post, since the Act against Spirituous Liquors', [*c.* 1729].
MS. Ballard 47, fol. 43.

803 If hidden grief may grieve the mind,
Then all these pleasures bides in me.
Andrews, —.
MS. *Rawl. poet. 92, fol. $8^{v}$.

804 If home-bred knowledge, or yet foreign skill
The poor man's prop; and eke thy country's fame.
'Uppon S$^{r}$ Wm Herbert of Swansey', [W. H. 'of Wales', Knight Bachelor, 1576 (?)].
MS. Ashmole 38, p. 176.

805 If honour or if gratitude should move
A fond a faithful, and a generous fool.
'Transcrib'd'.
MS. Montagu e. 13, fol. 91.

806 If honour to an ancient name be due
Lest her own captive else should her subdue.
[Philips, Katherine], 'On the Welch Language'.
Pr. *Poems*, 1667, p. 131.
MS. Rawl. poet. 65, fol. 19.

807 If [hvde] Hide had taken counsel of his name
Then Hide, like Lucifer, came tumbling down.
MS. Rawl. poet. 66, fol. 32.

808 If I all gospel mysteries knew
Nay God himself for God is love.
Beddome, Benjamin.
MS. *Eng. misc. e. 227, fol. 9.

809 If I am doomed the marriage chain to wear
Or keep me happy in a single life.
'The Maiden's Prayer'.
MS. Eng. poet. e. 28, p. 15.

810 If I am God as all agree
With joys that never shall have end.
[Baynes, Sir Thomas]; for the authorship see B.M. Add. MS. 29921, fol. $76^{v}$.
MS. Rawl. poet. 37, p. 85.

811 If I be bold
The anchor is my hold.
Answered by Y202*a*.
MS. Rawl. poet. 66, fol. $31^{v}$.

If I can judge a sick man by his fit 812
What ever his country be he is a Jew.
'The answere' to B520.
MS. Rawl. D. 1048, fol. $61^{v}$.

If I could ever write a lasting verse 813
Ever to be repaired or forgot.
[Philips, Katherine], 'In Memory of T. P. who died at Acton Aged 12 and ½ 23 Mar. 60'.
Pr. *Poems*, 1664, p. 75, on 'T. P. . . . 24 May'.
MSS. Rawl. poet. 65, fol. $17^{v}$, 'of F. P.'; 90, fol. $164^{v}$, 'upon a dear friend'.

If I could find a man whom I durst hate 814
Without remorse, and like K[ing] W[illia]m die.
'Of the Abjuration'.
MS. Rawl. poet. 81, fol. 44.

If I could make grim death withhold 815
That you live longer much than we.
Hammond, Anthony, 'An Anacreontique. To the Covetouse'.
MS. Rawl. D. 360, fol. $81^{v}$ (autogr.).

If I could think how these my thoughts to leave 816*a*
Thought reason sense time you and I maintain.
Sidney, Sir Philip.
Pr. *Arcadia*, 1598, p. 480.
MSS. *e Mus. 37, fol. 239; Rawl. poet. 85, fol. $11^{v}$.

[If I could write with a poetic fire] 816*b*
Modest, not bashful; humble, yet no slave . . . (incomplete).
Shadwell, Thomas; extract from 'On the songs of Signor Pietro Reggio'.
Pr. *Songs set by . . . Reggio*, 1680.
MS. Sancroft 53, p. 40.

If I did think these changes came 817
Sin and inconstancy are their own hell.
Creswell, Robert, 'Inconstancy (Song)'.
MS. *Eng. poet. f. 24, fol. 8 (autogr.).

If I die be this my will 818
If not dead I love thee dying.
Pr. John Wilson's *Cheerfull Ayres or Ballads*, 1660, p. 48.
MS. Mus. b. 1, fol. $31^{v}$, music by Wilson.

If I durst but I dare not for dread of displeasure 819
Take ever a drop of this hope and it avoids desperation.
MS. Ashmole 48, fol. $103^{v}$.

If I freely may discover 820
Nor her peevishness annoy me.
[Jonson, Ben.], song in *Poetaster* II. ii.
MSS. CCC. 327, fol. 23; Don. d. 58, fol. 29; Eng. poet. e. 14, fol. 21; Rawl. poet. 117, fol. $32^{v}$; see also O526.

821 If I go first, then I and V make 4.
If I go first, the difference is shown, to be 4.
Williams, John, 'A Riddle. The letters I and V'.
MS. *Rawl. poet. 193, fol. 81$^{v}$ (autogr.).

822 If I had wit for to endite
Shall no man know her name for me.
Transcript of 3-part song from B.M. Add. MS. 31922, fol. 34$^{v}$.
MS. Mus. d. 183, fol. 3.

823 If I in women would take my delight
I'm thrown from God, eternity and heaven.
MS. Mus. b. 1, fol. 151$^{v}$, music by John Wilson.

824 If I Jesus would put on
That waits me in the skies.
Kenton, James.
MS. *Eng. poet. e. 20, p. 313 (autogr.).

825 If I knew that god would forgive sin
I would it not commit.
Horace, 'oderunt peccare boni [virtutis amore]'.
MS. Rawl. D. 273, p. 156.

826 If I knew thee, that wrote this in a bravery
But jerk thee for thy knavery.
'The Replye' to H679.
MSS. Don. d. 58, fol. 19$^{v}$; Malone 19, p. 51, attr. to Dr. Rives.

827 If I live to be a man as I find I grow up
[Without kibes or cut fingers or any decay].
'The Young Man's Wish'. Cf. 1828.
MS. Eng. poet. d. 152, fol. 17$^{v}$.

828 If I live to grow old, As I find I bow down
With a gentle decay.
'The Old Man's Wish'.
Pr. *A Collection of 180 Loyal Songs*, 1685, p. 234. Attr. to Dr. [Walter] Pope in B.M. Add. MS. 29921, fol. 118.
MSS. Eng. misc. f. 79, p. 60; Lat. misc. e. 19, fol. 1, attr. to Dr. Pope; Rawl. poet. 173, fol. 172$^{v}$; 196, fol. 20; Rawl. Q. d. 13, fol. 61.

829 If I might make a wife to my own mind
And next to me, my friend her love should know.
Williams, John, 'The 2$^{ds}$ [i.e. the second words] make—I will be there at five this night or next'.
MS. *Rawl. poet. 191, fol. 7$^{v}$ (autogr.).

830 If I must tell you what I love
Still moving horror not affection.
Pr. John Wilson's *Cheerfull Ayres or Ballads*, 1660, p. 122.
MS. Mus. b. 1, fol. 123$^{v}$, music by Wilson.

If I seek to enjoy the fruits of my pain 831
It fits heavenly powers to be mild of condition.
Pr. Thomas Bateson's *Second set of Madrigales*, 1618, iv.
MSS. Mus. f. 17–19: f. 19, fol. 13$^{v}$.

If I should now learn so to woo 832
When death doth ease them, of much trouble.
Against marriage 'By me Thomas Hamond'. (cf. MS. Mus. f. 7, fol. 3, where 'By me . . .' etc. refers to the copying only).
MS. Mus. f. 8, fol. 2, in Hamond's hand.

If I the precious grace have known 833
And can I wish for more success?
Kenton, James.
MS. *Eng. poet. e. 20, p. 203 (autogr.).

If I the universe could gain 834
Jesus, who loved my soul so well.
Kenton, James.
MS. *Eng. poet. e. 20, p. 192 (autogr.).

If I think I see charms yet I know I am free 835
The days I live thus I am daily but dying.
Williams, John, 'The unconcerned. The 2$^{ds}$ [i.e. second words] are—I must ca-pi-tu-late with-in ten days'.
MS. *Rawl. poet. 191, fol. 8$^{v}$ (autogr.).

If I thy Spirit's voice have heard 836
And show Thyself th' Almighty Lord.
Kenton, James.
MS. *Eng. poet. e. 20, p. 18 (autogr.).

If I were a wanton lover 837
Light, inconstant, give me age.
[Wilson, Arthur], song in 'The Inconstant Lady', III. iv.
For ascription see *S.C. of W. MSS.*
MS. Rawl. poet. 9, fol. 27$^{v}$.

If I were great I should be more vicious 838
Unless he think it. His opinion's all.
MS. CCC. 327, fol. 27$^{v}$.

If I were out of date as I find I fall down 839
The one to hold stirrup, the other the bridle . . . (incomplete).
Ballad on the Pope, 'It is sung in England to the tune of the old mans wish'. The stub of a page bearing numbers of verses 5–9 remain. Cf. 1828.
MS. Rawl. D. 1372, fol. 56$^{v}$ from end.

If I were Thou and Thou wert I 840
So high a flight, and grows profane.
'S. Augustini Votum Deo . . . J[ames] Howell. Fam[iliar] lett[ers]. vol. 2 p. 69', 21 March, 1639; reference to 3rd ed., 1650.
MS. Tanner 466, fol. 7.

841 If idle travellers ask, who lies here
Mix England's shame, and there's his epitaph.
'Epitaph on the Duke of Buckingham', 1628.
MSS. Don. b. 8, two copies, pp. 212 and 368; Eng. poet. c. 50, fol. 26; e. 14, fol. 15; Malone 23, p. 207, attr. to Zouch Towneley; Rawl. poet. 26, fol. 34; 153, fol. 10.

842 If idleness possess thy brain
I can thee show, to pass the time.
Headed 'But'; preface to rhymed riddles.
MS. Rawl. poet. 217, fol. 72.

843 If in a picture (Piso) you should see
And never leave till they have read men dead.
[Dillon, Wentworth], Earl of Roscommon, 'Horace of the Art of Poetry'.
MSS. Rawl. poet. 109, fol. 2; 152, fol. 233.

844 If in distress [oh] Lord thou'lt [thou wilt] give me aid
But Jacob's God's the tower to whom we flee.
Fairfax, Thomas, Lord, Psalm xlvi.
MS. *Fairfax 40, p. 104 (autogr.).
MS. *Fairfax 38, p. 206.

845 If in his study Haman [he] hath so much care
To hang all old strange things, let's wife beware.
Donne, John, 'The Antiquary'.
Pr. *Poems*, 1633.
MSS. Eng. poet. e. 40, fol. 46; *f. 9, p. 36; see also I784.

846 If in one day the Lorrainers must yield
What will a year produce if this be true?
Translation of Latin distich on the victories of Louis XIV, 1672.
MSS. Ashmole 36, 37, fol. 105v.

847 If in that breast so good so pure
But feel it cannot last me long.
Moore, Sir John, 'L'amour timide'.
MS. Eng. misc. e. 241, fol. 108.

848 If in the great tremendous day
All those who only speak for thee.
Kenton, James.
MS. *Eng. poet. e. 120, p. 186 (autogr.).

849 If in the vulgar road
And live by not-my-hazard so.
J. F., 'An Ode of Casimire', [IV. x].
MS. *Eng. poet. f. 17, p. 28 (autogr.).

850 If in these lawns and woods thus formed
When thus we quit the field.
'The late Earl of Carlisle's [Charles Howard, d. 1738] advice to his son . . . written a few Hours before his Death'.
MS. Ballard 50, fol. 92.

If in this glass of humours you do find 851
By others melancholy, not your own.
King, Henry, 'To [a] Lady upon Mr. Burtons Melancholy'.
Pr. *Poems*, 1657, p. 4
MSS. *Eng. poet. e. 30, fol. 51v; *Malone 22, fol. 23.

If Indies' fleet rich fraught, consumed with flame 852
Behold this Howard he hath wrought the same.
'In praise of the Lord Admirall's picture', translated from Latin.
MS. Don. c. 54, fol. 20.

If injured monarchs may their cause explore 853
For subjects are the surest guard of kings.
'A Conference between K. James and K. William at the River Boyne the day before the Battle', 1690.
MS. Eng. poet. c. 18, fol. 89, attr. to Charles Blount; d. 53, p. 33; e. 39, p. 208, attr. to Dr. [William (?)] Barrowby; e. 49, p. 82, attr. to Charles Blount; Rawl. D. 833, fol. 68; see also I664, I1045.

If it be so a fable, or a story 854
Hence no man is delivered but with paying.
'That the Bath is like Purgatory'.
MS. Rawl. poet. 117, fol. 191 rev.

If it be such a grace to hold one's peace 855
And that they should her anti-echoes be.
Creswell, Robert, 'Silence. Song . . . Theocritus in Syrinx'.
MS. *Eng. poet. f. 24, fol. 19 (autogr.).

If it be true, as Welshmen say 856
I die by resurrection.
Madan, Martin (1725–90), 'Enigma'.
MS. Eng. poet. 51, two copies, pp. 138 and 142.

If it be true that every little star 857
Will yet as much demur upon our glory.
From *Divi Britannici*: . . . *Lives of* . . . *Kings*, by Sir Winston Churchill, 1675, p. 53. Quoted by Hearne in 'Epitome of English History'.
MS. Rawl. D. 1171, fol. 13.

If it may pleasing be in poesie 858
Ourselves against that season to prepare.
'Introductio. Invocatio. Admonitio', to 372 religious meditations.
MS. *Rawl. poet. 97, fol. 1 (autogr.).

If it were not for the martin and the swallow 859
We should have honey as cheap as tallow.
Couplet.
MS. Malone 19, p. 150.

860 If it were true that James were spurious born
Let's fetch the wise one and kick out the fool.
'Of two Ills choose the least', on 'James III' and George I.
MS. Rawl. poet. 155, p. 173.

861 If it's true as you say, that I've injured a letter
And that I may be never mistaken for U.
Garrick, David, answer to a pamphlet by Dr. Hill, 1759.
Pr. *Poetical Works*, 1785, p. 490.
MS. Eng. poet. c. 51, p. 296.

862 If John marries Mary, and Mary alone
It can't be a match, 'tis a bundle of matches.
'Impromptu'.
MS. Eng. poet. c. 51, p. 286.

863 If joined to make up virtue's glorious tale
Take off my fill of life, and wait, not wish to die.
Hamilton, William, 'The Wish'.
Pr. *Poems on Several Occasions*, Glasgow, 1748, p. 108.
MS. Eng. poet. e. 47, p. 18.

864 If joy and peace do their blest souls adorn
The fruit of mercy now thy soul doth know.
'The verses on Jane Conyngsbie', Felbrigge Church.
MS. Top. Norf. c. 1, fol. 57v.

865 If judgment treads not on the heels of wit
But still his steps will be exorbitant.
MS. Rawl. poet. 117, fol. 274 rev.

866 If Jupiter from heaven should pour down gold
For golden showers I would hold up my smock.
MS. CCC. 327, fol. 22.

867 If King Manesses sunk in depth of sin
Cancel my debts, sweet Jesu say Amen.
'q[uo]d D: Such.' [Zouch (?)].
MS. Rawl. poet. 148, fol. 68.

868 If kings anointed crowned and installed
Each pack of rogues [a] parliament be termed.
E. P., 'Charles the 2d. after he was crowned King of Scotland, was proclaimed Traytor . . . by the Rump-Parliament'.
MS. Rawl. poet. 26, fol. 163.

869 If late acquaintance with the saints above
Shut all your books, ye need not study more.
'Obsequies of the Lady Elizabeth Darell'.
MS. Rawl. poet. 210, fol. 59v rev.

870 If late advices have not tired you quite
They'd still have all the fears that war can know.
'Advice to A Painter', dated by Wood 10 Nov. 1679.
Not in *Advice-to-a-Painter Poems*, M. T. Osborne, 1949.
MS. Wood F. 34, fol. 167.

If law four terms, so if for war 871
One gets flying angels the other cracked crowns.
'Uppon Lawyers'.
MS. Rawl. poet. 117, fol. 268 rev.; see also 1688, 1755.

If liberty of conscience e'er was good 872
So kindness gains, where arguments do fail.
'Written on Grays Inn Bog House'.
MS. Firth c. 16, p. 170.

If little men were patient, 873
All the world would be equal.
MS. Malone 19, p. 151.

If little things are little prized 874
The wise believe so rarely.
Williams, John, 'In defense of little things'.
MS. *Rawl. poet. 191, fol. 8 (autogr.).

If love deserves your hate, then hate me still 875
And love to pity at the length will move you.
'To a flintye mistris'.
MS. Douce f. 5, fol. 20v.

If love his arrows shoot so fast 876
Be no god, or be more mild.
Shirley, James, 'One that Lov'd two Mistresses at once'.
Pr. *Poems*, 1646, p. 19.
MS. *Rawl. poet. 88, p. 33.

If love is blind, it is what all should be 877
And love and merit rather than a throne.
Williams, John, on 'Love is blind'.
MS. *Rawl. poet. 191, fol. 99v (autogr.).

If love loves truth then women do not love 878
To have fair women false than none at all.
MS. Eng. poet. e. 14, fol. 10v.

If love now reigned as it hath been 879
All ways whereby they might it reach.
Transcript of 3-part song, from B.M. Add. MS. 31922, fol. 49, attr. to 'The Kynge H. viii'.
MS. Mus. d. 198, fol. 5v.

If love were all lost for lack of liberty 880
You shall not find me contrary for this is no lie.
'finis q[uo]d J[ohn] W[allis]', in praise of women.
MS. Ashmole 48, fol. 85.

If love's a sweet passion why does it torment 881
And our eyes tell each other what neither dare name.
[Settle, Elkanah, song from *The Fairy Queen*, music by Purcell]. F. B. Zimmerman, *Purcell*, 1963, no. 629(17bc).
Arranged 'For the Flute', and 'for the violin'.
MS. Mus. Sch. C. 95, p. 219.

1882 If lower orbs of this huge theatre
Though definite: then best to see god's face.
F. W., 'Sonnet 23. The greatnes of the emporiall heaven and Causes therof'.
MS. *Rawl. C. 639, p. 121.

1883 If madness be in lechery [poetry]
A lecher, drunkard and a poet too?
Translated from Latin.
MSS. Rawl. poet. 117, fol. 270v rev.; 246, fol. 15v.

1884 If Mary be the marigold
She's neither good for dog nor me.
MSS. Eng. poet. e. 14, fol. 58v; Rawl. poet. 147, p. 88; 210, fol. 45.

1885 If men and times were now
Who worthy come, who not, to be wise Pallas guests.
[Jonson, Ben.], 'Ode'. First ascribed to Jonson by W. D. Briggs in *The Athenaeum*, 13 June 1914. See *Ben Jonson*, Herford and Simpson, viii, 1947, p. 419.
MS. Rawl. poet. 31, fol. 8v.

1886 If men do die as oft as breath departs,
Death's but a fart, and so a fart for death.
'On Death, Compar'd to a Fart'.
MS. Rawl. poet. 173, fol. 152; see also 1722.

1887 If mercy doth forever last
The loving kindness of the Lord.
Kenton, James.
MS. *Eng. poet. e. 20, p. 218 (autogr.).

1888 If mighty Troy, with gates of steel and brass,
But love them best, that learn and write the truth.
Whitney, Geoffrey, 'Scripta manent'.
MS. *Rawl. poet. 56, fol. 85v.

1889 If mine eyes can speak to do hearty arrant
Hope we do live yet.
Sidney, Sir Philip, from the *Arcadia*, 'Cleophila's sapphicks'.
MS. *e Mus. 37, fol. 45v.

1890 If mortal plaints may pierce immortal ears
Nor yet a stain to thy posterity.
Mervall, Alphonso, 'πρὸς τὸν πατέρα'.
MS. *Rawl. poet. 166, p. 66 (autogr.).

1891 If mourning micht amend my hard unhappy case
For true and honest constant love this patient here does lie.
King James I.
MS. *Bodl. 165, fol. 46 (autogr.).

1892 If much store of golden wealth
Lay our softer ladies down.
James, Richard, 'Anacreon's follie'.
MS. *James 35, p. 14 (autogr.).

If murthers we with murthers will compare and justly scan 1893
The Jews care not, their magistrates, do let them sleep therein.
'A description of the massacres and murthers of late committed in many places of England Ireland and Wales', *temp.* Q. Elizabeth.
MS. Rawl. C. 849, fol. 395v.

If music, dancing, poetry and painting 1894
And the next mask shall be to hide their blushes.
J[ordan], T[homas], 'Cupid his Coronation . . . A Mask . . . 1654'.
MS. Rawl. B. 165, fol. 107.

If my Coelestia be content to love, 1895
May you to me, my love to you confirm.
North, Dudley, 3rd Baron.
Pr. *A Forest of Varieties*, 1645.
MS. *North e. 41, fol. 22v.

If my complaints could passions move, 1896
I was more true to love tha[n] love to me.
Pr. Dowland's *Songs or Ayres*, 1597, iv.
MSS. Mus. f. 7–10: f. 10, fol. 8v.

If my friend's poem in proper season 1897
What fills your heads with air gives your tails wind.
[Cater], Gerard, 'Gerards Appollogy'.
MS. Add. A. 301, fol. 82v rev.

If my lady bid begin 1898
Hope makes me hardy so does she.
Pr. J. Wilson's *Cheerfull Ayres or Ballads*, 1660, p. 73; words in *Academy of Complements*, 1650, p. 218.
MS. Mus. b. 1, fol. 61v, music by John Wilson.

If my verses could get me a lady like you. 1899
Now consent to my joy, all these witnesses here.
Williams, John, 'To a Lady that said she thought I was best at making love-verses'.
MS. *Rawl. poet. 191, fol. 92v (autogr.).

If Narcissus foolish boy 1900
To make me only rich, you only fair.
Pr. *The Loyal Garland*, fourth ed., 1671, sig. C6.
MS. Eng. poet. c. 50, fol. 77v.

If noble Atticus makes plenteous feasts 1901
Pleasure's a toil, when constantly pursued.
Congreve, William, 'The Eleventh Satyr of Juvenall'.
Pr. Dryden's *The Satires of Juvenalis*, 1693.
MS. Rawl. poet. 152, fol. 109.

If nothing else but a jilt or a whore 1902
Are framing a Rose-Alley greeting.
'The 8th Stanza to Advice to the Beaws'.
MS. Rawl. poet. 159, fol. 143.

903 If nought but love-charms power have
Read this reply and take it not in scorn.
Corbet, D[r. Richard], 'Replye to the Answere', B378; cf. L18.
Pr. from this MS. by Gilchrist in Corbett's *Poems*, 1807, p. 234.
MS. Ashmole 38, p. 65.

904 If now, as chance our wandering footsteps guide
On Heaven and Delia then securely rest.
By R. L., 1781.
MS. *Eng. poet. e. 16, fol. 27.

905 If of thy foe, thou dost a gift receive
Although awhile, a truce with them thou make.
Whitney, Geoffrey, 'Inimicorum dona, infausta'.
MS. *Rawl. poet. 56, fol. 19$^{v}$.

906 If one should ask me why that I
Could learn a tailor from a thief to sever.
'On a tailor'.
MS. Malone 19, p. 10.

907 If once that loathed and infamous reproach
Like goods at outcries, prized, at second hand.
'An Ould Maid'.
MS. Rawl. poet. 206, p. 32.

908 If only sight suffice
Before that it be spun.
MS. Ashmole 1113, fol. 129.

909 If others only would approve
The rest o'th world obey.
'Song. Upon Miss A. J.'
MS. Eng. poet. e. 8, fol. 12.

910 If Oxford be the kingdom's eye
The kingdom's eye-brow needs must be.
Oldisworth, Nicolas, 'On Shottover'.
MS. *Don. c. 24, fol. 16 (autogr.).

911 If pagan papists tell us they brought in
If, when they took the pair, they'd ta'en the seven.
'On Stealing the Candelsticks in Westminster Abbey', endorsed '1689/90', against the Bishops.
MS. Rawl. poet. 159, two copies, fols. 106, 131.

912 If papist, Jew, or infidel
To do what he omitted.
'A Ballad, . . . fix'd on the Ld. Dorset's Door at the Cock Pitt 1689'.
MSS. Eng. poet. c. 18, fol. 70; e. 49, p. 54.

913 If passenger, you stop, and wish to know
Ever find mercy at th' eternal throne.
On Math. Smyth, 1786, Wells [Norfolk] Chancel.
Pr. *Gentleman's Magazine*, 1800.
MS. Top. gen. e. 32, fol. 128$^{v}$.

If perchance it should come to pass 914
Who hath a constant gut a wavering sprite.
'A puritan catechised'.
MS. Rawl. poet. 172, fol. 12; see also 1929–30, S108.

If Phillis' death might force Amintas wail 915
His life (ay me) for which I sue in vain.
'Captaine Brownes Ditie', with music.
MS. Rawl. poet. 148, fol. 84$^{v}$.

If placing of some emblems here 916
Were ne'er so sweet as his.
Tipping, William, 'None But Christ'.
MS. *Rawl. poet. 101, fol. 4*a* (autogr.).

If plaints laments or sorrow 917
And of delight bereave thee.
Set for 6 voices by Robert Ramsey, 'Bachelor of Musicke. A°. 1615'.
MSS. Mus. f. 20–24: f. 23, fol. 98$^{v}$.

If Plato lived and saw these heaven-bred lines, 918
They both o'ercome, would yield to thee the bays.
On Sir John Davies. Verses in Latin and English by 'a late Poet', in Dugdale's hand.
MS. Ballard 14, fol. 10.

If pleasure follow when we think upon 919
Gods, they reward my goodness, and I ask no more.
Catullus lxxvi, 'or the honest, but unfortunate Lover's Petition to be freed from that Passion'.
MS. Rawl. poet. 173, fol. 53, attr. to Mr. Dryden.

If plenty wealth should give 920
And himself poor believes.
Bacon, Sir Nicholas, 1623–66, translation of Boethius, *Consolations* II. ii. Sent to John Hobart, 1664.
MS. Tanner 306, fol. 319 (autogr.).

If poets, ere they clothed their infant thought, 921
And humbly bring the verse which you inspire.
Prior, Mathew, 'To the Reverend Father in God Francis [Turner], Lord Bishop of Ely etc.'
See *Works*, ed. H. Bunker Wright and Monroe K. Spears, 1959, ii. 822.
MS. Rawl. D. 739, fol. 86.

If poets' spirits, wits, words, verse all divine, 922
Accounted now for matter both profane.
F. W., 'That the joyes of heaven are a convenient argument for poetrie'.
MS. *Rawl. C. 639, p. 5.

923 If poisonous minerals, and if that tree
I think it mercy, if thou wilt forget.
Donne, John, 'Sonnett 5'.
Pr. *Poems*, 1633.
MS. *Eng. poet. e. 99, fol. $44^{v}$.

924 If poor might live amongst the rich
Nor peace, nor truth, nor love is found.
Robinson, Robert.
MS. *Rawl. poet. 218, p. 109 (autogr.).

925 If prayer could make a poor man to be fat
To pray, not do, thou takest God's name in vain.
Robinson, Robert.
MS. *Rawl. poet. 218, p. 6 (autogr.).

926 If prayers, and tears had charms to turn
And save themselves, the poor remains of lost mortality.
'On the death of the Honourable Mr. Cornwallis. A Pindarick Ode', endorsed 'Mr. $Jo^{n}$ Cornwallis'.
MS. Ballard 50, fol. 51.

927 If pride and nonsense are prevailing charms
When farts from Molly's arse might do as well.
MS. Rawl. poet. 194, fol. 170.

928 If profit here, or pleasure thou hast got,
To lose good time 'bout toys that 'long'd not to thee.
Cheyney, William, 'A postscript to any reader'.
MS. *Rawl. poet. 86, fol. $32^{v}$.

929–30 If [Purisbye] Puritan it [should] come to pass
Having a constant gut, a wavering sprite.
'A Puritan and Papist'.
MSS. Ashmole 36, 37, fol. $96^{v}$; Rawl. poet. 31, fol. 10; see also 1914, S108.

931 If, reader, 'twas thy happy chance to know
Who feels a grief will never paint it well.
Jessop, William, 'Epitaph' on Richard Musgrave, d. 1785 (?).
MS. Percy b. 1, fol. 40 (autogr.).

932 If reason steals one moment yet, from grief,
And learn that they are left, and Heaven is kind.
'To her Grace the Duchess of Ancaster on the Death of Lady Mary Bertie', [1 April 1767; daughter of the third Duke].
MS. *Eng. poet. e. 28, p. 102.

933 If right and law may broken be
A crown, and be a king.
MS. Rawl. D. 431, fol. $85^{v}$.

934 If right be racked and over-run
The grief is great much hurt may hap.
Pr. Tottel's *Miscellany*, 1557, Sig. Qii.
MS. Ashmole 45(1), fol. 32.

If Rome can pardon sins, as Romans hold 935
To gull 'em of their souls and money too.
'On Romes Pardons'.
Pr. *Rome Rhym'd to Death*, 1683, p. 21; *A Second Collection of Songs against Popery*, 1689, p. 18, 'by the E. of R.'; *Works of Rochester etc.*, 1739. Cf. Vieth, p. 474 and Quarles, *Divine Fancies*, 1632, iii. 86.
MSS. Add. B. 106, fol. $33^{v}$, attr. to Roch.; Don. e. 23, fol. $29^{v}$; Rawl. poet. 152, fol. $115^{v}$; 173, fol. $123^{v}$; Sancroft 53, p. 69, attr. to E. of Rochr. by Sancroft; Smith 27, p. 7.

If royal madam, we could aught address 936
You only madam, can the loss retrieve.
Twyman, Antony, 'To her Royal Highness the Princess [Anne] upon the Loss of the Duke of Glocester', July 1700, aged 11.
MS. Rawl. D. 174, fol. 73 (autogr.).

If saints in heaven, can either see or hear, 937
Then give it to his hands that can relieve us.
Prologue to 1697.
MSS. Ashmole 36, 37, fol. 303; Eng. poet. c. 50, fol. 8; f. 10, fol. 107; Malone 23, p. 32, dated 1619, 1621, and 'ultimo Martii 1623'; Rawl. D. 398, fol. 222; Rawl. poet. 160, fol. 16; Top. Cheshire c. 7, fol. 3.

If Salem's king so blessed Abraham 938
To the world's end Christ is with His also.
MS. *Rawl. poet. 97, fol. $22^{v}$ (autogr.).

If scholars in their master's praises share 939
None but Apollo sure did them instil.
T. S., 'To the author my ingenuous friend'.
MS. Rawl. poet. 152, fol. 23.

If Scrip could imagine how hard 'twas to write 940
And both took our leaves of our br[other] and friend.
Sheppard, Elizabeth, [on a visit to Oxford, *c.* 1738].
MS. Top. Oxon. d. 287, fol. $50^{v}$ (autogr.).

If seeing's believing, and if love is blind, 941
No wonder lovers are to doubts inclined.
Williams, John, couplet on 'Love is blind'.
MS. *Rawl. poet. 191, fol. 99 (autogr.).

If self-conceited wisdom do bewray 942
I never knew conceit more poor than thine.
'Ep[igram] 1', against 'Welby'.
MSS. Ashmole 36, 37, fol. 26.

943 If sense I had, mine own estate to know
Whose children made them moan.

Whitney, Geoffrey, 'In fæcunditatem, sibi ipsi damnosam'.
MS. *Rawl. poet. 56, fol. 108$^{v}$.

944 If sentiments devoid of art,
Your presence here, will real pleasure give.

Bate, Sally, 'To Miss Eliza Affleck Extempore . . . 1768'.
MS. *Eng. poet. e. 28, p. 230.

945 If shadows [are] be a [the] picture's excellence
The black mark would I hit but not the white.

[Poole, Walton (?)], 'On A Gentlewoman [Beatrice Brydges, Mrs. Henry Poole (?)] that thought hur selfe not fayre because hur . . . heare and eyes weare blacke'.
Pr. *Wits Interpreter*, 1655; *Parnassus Biceps*, 1656, p. 75; *Poems of Pembroke and Ruddier*, 1660, p. 61. See E. K. Chambers, *Poems of Donne*, 1896, ii. 279; and E. Wolf II, *P.M.L.A.* lxiii, 1948, p. 831. Attr. to W. P. or Walton Poole in B.M. Add. MS. 11811, fol. 33$^{v}$; MSS. Harl. 6931, fol. 8$^{v}$; and Lansdowne 777, fol. 71.
MSS. Ashmole 38, p. 30; 47, fol. 35; CCC. 328, fol. 87$^{v}$; Douce f. 5, fol. 36, 'on Mris Poale my lord shandowes sister'; Eng. poet. c. 50, fol. 37$^{v}$; e. 14, fol. 82 rev.; e. 97, p. 113, 'To Mrs. Poole the Ld. of Shandois Sister'; f. 10, fol. 91, attr. to Bi. Ox. Rich. Corbett; f. 16, fol. 5$^{v}$, attr. to Dr. Donne; f. 25, fol. 12, attr. to Dr. Dun; Rawl. poet. 117, fol. 175$^{v}$ rev.; 142, fol. 27; 199, p. 12.

946 If she be coy, and scorn my noble fire
And make a mistress of my own desire.

MS. Rawl. poet. 213, front cover.

947 If she be fair, I fear the rest
That can love all, but will love none.

'A resolution not to marrye'.
MS. Ashmole 38, p. 153.

948 If she can ask what lack 'ee gentleman
But there's the top of all her commendation.

'On a shopp keppers mayde'.
MS. Ashmole 38, p. 115.

949 If she must needs deny, weep not but die
Will blow my tears away, or work my death.

'A perplexed lover'.
Attr. to Thomas Carew in B.M. Add. MS. 22118, fol. 40$^{v}$.
MS. Eng. poet. f. 25, fol. 13$^{v}$.

950 If she of cold and frozen ice be made
Kindles a fire, itself yet void of heat.

MS. Malone 16, p. 17.

If short and sweet is what you best approve, 951
And that I'm short is what you can't but see.

Williams, John, 'Short and Sweet'.
MS. *Rawl. poet. 191, fol. 43 (autogr.).

If sighs nor vows from that proud mind 952
And what a fool in youth was I!

Parsons, William, 'The Lovers Consolation. from Malherbe'.
Pr. *Fidelity* etc., 1798, p. 47, and in *Travelling Recreations*.
MS. *Don. d. 123, p. 261 (autogr.).

If sin be captive, grace must find release 953
Heaven claims the right, and bears the prize away.

[Southwell, Robert], 'Of the assumption of our Blessed Lady'.
See J. H. MacDonald, *Poems and Prose . . . of Southwell*, Roxburghe Club, 1937, pp. 21, 45.
MS. Eng. poet. b. 5, p. 83.

If so, awake dull soul, think not to be 954
New quickening to thy dead, that it may live.

'God looks not at what we were, but what we are'.
MS. *Rawl. poet. 200, fol. 97.

If so he died then I am much in doubt 955
How so much breath ta'en in could drive breath out.

Couplet 'On one that died w$^{th}$ Tobacco'.
MS. Eng. poet. e. 14, fol. 94 rev.

If solid sense by learning well-matured 956
And he dies greatest, who in Him dies best.

'On Lord Paget', Henry, Lord Paget, 1743 (?).
MS. Ballard 29, fol. 167$^{v}$.

If some deny that painters art 957
And nature cannot such another.

D[arell], Sir S[amson], 'On her Picture', i.e. Lady Coke's.
MS. Rawl. poet. 210, fol. 55$^{v}$.

If spite be pleased, when [as] that her object's dead 958
And strike the first two blind the other dumb.

'On Sir Walter Ralegh's Death'.
Pr. *Wits Recreations*, 1640.
MSS. Ashmole 781, p. 151; Sancroft 53, p. 46; Tanner 306, fol. 251.

If standers-by do more than gamesters see, 959
To any one that has but half an eye.

Williams, John, 'Upon Standers by see more than Gamesters'.
MS. *Rawl. poet. 184, fol. 42 (autogr.).

960 If Sylla's ghost made bloody Cat'line start
Send Doctor Burnet to me or I die.

'Mrs. Nelly's complaint an Elegy', on Mall Knight.
Attr. to Etherege in *Miscellaneous Works of the Duke of Buckingham*, 1704, i. 29; cf. Etherege's *Poems*, ed. J. Thorpe, 1963, p. 139.
MSS. Douce 357, fol. 145v; Firth c. 15, p. 129; c. 16, p. 13.

961 If tears could aught prevail, I'll weep amain
Shall in the spangled ceiling ever shine.

Wilkinson, Henry, 'A Funerall Elegy upon . . . Mary Lady Dowager Countesse of Warwick . . . d. Aprill 12, 1678'.
MS. Lat. misc. c. 19, p. 372 (autogr.).

962 If than your sense no bigger were your belly
'Twould cost you less in waistcoats, let me tell ye.

Whitchurch, Tom, couplet, 'celebrated Epigram on Mr Selston of Christ Ch: 1777'.
MS. Eng. misc. e. 241, fol. 100v.

963 If that bright honour have one minute's stain
An hundred years scant can it cleanse again.

Couplet.
MS. Rawl. poet. 117, fol. 274 rev.

964 If that fame's trumpet shall not speak thy wrath
A trumpet's sound make ye to live again.

'An epitaph on a Trumpeter'.
MS. CCC. 328, fol. 58v.

965 If that from glove you take the letter G
Then glove is love and that I send to thee.

'A letter of one that sent a paire of gloves'.
MS. Douce f. 5, fol. 16v; see also F783, I764, I766.

966 If that I have not all thy love
Be one and one another's all.

[Donne, John]. Pr. *Poems*, 1633.
MSS. Eng. poet. c. 50, fol. 43v; Rawl. poet. 117, fol. 199 rev.; see also I1074.

967 If that I must in order tell
This man is fit for quire or cell.

A satire on monks.
MS. Ashmole 48, fol. 135v.

968 If that in virtue thou take any pain
The pleasure abateth and the evil tarrieth still.

MS. Gough Norfolk 43, fol. 46.

969 If that man's most happy, whose life is most free
But if blest you'ld continue, continue as we.

'The Batchelor's Life'.
MS. Eng. misc. e. 183, fol. 66v.

If that my love prove false to me, 970
To pity him, and pray for her.

Beaumont, Thomas, 'Of his truth in her lightnes'.
MS. *Malone 18, p. 18 (autogr.).

If that one moment short suspense can be 971
More true a people or more just a queen.

'On the Death of her Majesty Queen Caroline', 1737.
MS. *Eng. poet. e. 28, p. 13.

If that our enemies resolve to fight 972
And may continue thus, to all eternity.

Spoure, Edmund, 'The Loyall Man's wish if we Engage with the French in a mean battle'.
MS. *Eng. poet. c. 52, fols. 60v, 56 (autogr.).

If that our prince do ask a subsidy 973
I wot not what, with their peddling french.

Ashmole's copy 'Out of an old Poem Intituled The hye way to the Spyttell hous. Compyled by John [*sic* for Robert] Copland Printer', printed [1536 (?)], *S.T.C.* 5732.
MSS. Ashmole 36, 37, fol. 290.

If that the cynics' strict commands displease 974
Which ne'er complete but may disguise the man.

Throckmorton, Job, academic exercise, 1660–4.
[Paraphrase of F. Dedekind, *Grobianus and Grobiana*, c. 1].
MS. Locke b. 7, fol. 148 (autogr.).

If that the head a serpent be, 975
In ways corrupt do go.

Robinson, Robert.
MS. *Rawl. poet. 218, p. 41 (autogr.).

If that the persevering man be blest 976
Being in hope next fight to get the field.

Wake, William of Cambridge, Psalm lv. 6; see M118.
MS. Eng. misc. d. 1, fol. 36.

If that the sick may groan 977
Though tears of blood he weep.

[Southwell, Robert], 'A song called St. Peter's afflicted mind'.
Pr. *Mæoniae*, 1595.
MS. Eng. poet. b. 5, p. 17.

If that the world and love were young 978
Thy coral clasps and amber studs . . . (incomplete).

Copied by R. Gough as 'The Nymph's Reply' to 'The Passionate Shepherd'.
MS. Eng. poet. c. 5, fol. 30; see I660.

979 If that thou yield thy self or serve
As if thou didst serve no man.
Translation of Latin couplet.
MS. Tanner 306, fol. 185v rev.

980 If that your judgement doth approve of we,
You health shall be our word today.
Cavendish, Lady Jane, Prologue to 'The Concealed Fancies', addressed to the Earl of Newcastle.
MS. *Rawl. poet. 16, p. 88.

981 If the deep sighs, of an afflicted breast
But as new showers increase the rising flood.
[Drayton, Michael].
Pr. John Ward's *First Set of English Madrigals*, 1613, xxiii–xxiv.
MS. Mus. f. 20–24: f. 20, fol. 79v.

982 If the king to my bank and me will be hearty
Pray put up your trumpery, good Foley Paul.
Hammond, Antony, 'A Dialogue: The Speaker [Paul Foley] to Harry Guy who was Sent to Him with a Message from my Lord Sunderland', endorsed 1697.
MS. Rawl. D. 174, fol. 103 (autogr.).
MS. *Rawl. poet. 129, fol. 8.

983 If the last scene, and closing up of breath
The Roman Empire, and her honour saved.
'An Elegy uppon the death of Adam (*sic*) Earle of Papenheim': Lützen, 1632.
MS. Rawl. poet. 166, p. 59.

984 If the Lord, our God, and guide
He 'tis keeps them in subjection.
Jos: Br:, Psalm cxxiv.
MS. Rawl. poet. 61, fol. 54.

985 If the power of art can draw
Nature then will yield to thee.
[Wilson, Arthur], song in 'The Inconstant Lady', II. iv.
For ascription see *S. C. of W. MSS.*
MS. Rawl. poet. 9, fol. 17v.

986 If the quick spirit, Delia, in your eye
They furnish motives strong for present love.
'To Delia'.
MS. Eng. poet. c. 9, p. 105.

987 If the remembrance of what e'er was dear
Bestow it on the dust that sleepeth here.
'An Epitaph on a Grave Stone in Windsor Castle on Mrss. Isabella Denham of Windsor . . . d. Nov. 25, 1748 . . . aet. 23'.
MS. Eng. poet. e. 40, fol. 138.

If the stock of our bliss is in stranger's hands vested 988
The warmth from the smiles of wife, children, and friends.
'Wife Children, and Friends'.
MS. Eng. poet. c. 51, p. 301.

If the way to recover our first estate 989
Will warm our frozen north and make it day.
'Reliqua desiderantur'.
MS. *Don. f. 5, fol. 19.

If then as poets say love a fire be 990
Alas! how cold is all your fire to me.
[Owen's Epigram], '26. To Caelia', couplet.
MS. *Rawl. poet. 197, fol. 9 (autogr.).

If then from nothing nothing ever came 991
Could bid, from nothing, all these wonders rise.
'Ex Nihilo nihil gignetur . . . Gentleman's Magazine'.
MS. Eng. poet. e. 39, p. 68.

If then God's glory and the good of man 992
Prefers the work of our redemption.
MS. *Rawl. poet. 97, fol. 3v (autogr.).

If there be any in this multitude 993
Ovid our master was; his art our scale.
[Heywood, Thomas, translator], Ovid, *De arte amandi*. Differs from the printed *The Art of Love*, *S.T.C.* 18935*a*.
MSS. *Rawl. poet. 198, corrected draft, licensed by Geo. Cottington, 8 June 1623 (see W. W. Greg, *Licensers for the Press*, O.B.S., 1962, p. 25); 216, fol. 2 (incomplete).

If there be any one that takes in dudgeon 994
Yet all what I have said pray leave undone.
Bennett, Thomas, academic verse exercise, 1660–4. [Translation from F. Dedekind, *Grobianus et Grobiana*, c. 1].
MS. Locke b. 7, fol. 134 (autogr.).

If there be haply any man who dares 995
There's still one beauty in the world that's yours.
Holland, Ab[raham], 'sonne to Philemon Holland the great Translator . . . To Mrs. E. F. in defence of the white blemish which lately grew in the sight of her ey'.
Pr. *Parnassus Biceps*, 1656, p. 16.
MSS. Ashmole 36, 37, fol. 152 (autogr.).

If there be man (ye gods) I ought to hate 996
Let him not love this life, that loves not me.
'The Curse for one I hate'.
MS. Rawl. poet. 90, fol. 90v.

997 If they who are to virtuous laws inclined
Eternal hymns to their creator's praise.
Sidney, William, 'A Funeral Poem. To The Memory of Mr. Thomas Sowlter. June 29 1725 . . . in his Advanc'd Age', 57.
MS. Rawl. poet. 154, fol. 123 (autogr.).

998 If this be a happy parliament
But if he should give Derrick the slip.
MS. Rawl. poet. 26, fol. 147.

999 If this book's truth, grace, order may in any wise
As having done my duty in my room.
Guillim, John, 'Conclusion', to the *Display of Heraldry*, pr. 1610.
MS. Rawl. B. 20, fol. 35.

1000 If this I did not ev'ry moment see,
Was all my whole felicity.
Traherne, Thomas, 'The Apprehension'.
MS. *Eng. poet. c. 42, fol. 8 (autogr.).

1001 If this pale rose offend your sight,
And 'tis like Heav'n to bless.
Somervile, William, 'Presenting to a Lady a White Rose and a Red on the Tenth of June'.
Pr. *Poems*, 1727, p. 65.
MS. Ballard 47, fol. 25.

1002 If this true sorrow counted be with fatal cypress bows
For I a witness to my tears abhor and eke detest.
Translation of Henry King's Latin lines on the death of Dr. John Spenser of Corpus Christi College, Oxford, d. 1614.
MS. Rawl. D. 912, fol. 305$^{v}$.

1003 If those are good, God only will approve
Who wicked are of them I'll say no more.
Tipping, William, 'Contemplation On the state and Condition of wicked men'.
MS. *Rawl. poet. 101, fol. 65 (autogr.).

1004 If thou (a guest) on a join'd stool canst sup,
Thy clients bobb'd, out at the back door glide.
F[anshaw], Sir R[ichard], translator, Horace, *Epistles* I. v.
Pr. *Poems of Horace*, A. Brome, etc., 2nd ed., 1671, p. 313.
MS. Rawl. D. 261, p. 34.

1005 If thou a long and healthful age require,
Put bounds unto thy gluttonous desire.
Couplet.
MS. Rawl. D. 954, fol. 45.

1006 If thou art with me oh my God
A little heaven below.
Beddome, Benjamin.
MS. *Eng. misc. e. 227, fol. 4.

If thou ask who lieth here 1007
Yet dissolved in this mould.
[G. B (?)], on Prince Henry's death, 1612.
MS. *Rawl. poet. 116, fol. 3.

If thou be tempted and ready to fall 1008
Deceive thee it will, be thou sure at length.
MS. Gough Norfolk 43, fol. 51.

If thou beest, for to be found 1009
May thy epicedium sing.
'On in Prison writt for his frend'.
MS. Eng. poet. e. 14, fol. 71$^{v}$.

If thou beest poor then labour first and thrive, 1010
Bring on such charge as throws them out of door.
Robinson, Robert.
MS. *Rawl. poet. 218, p. 132 (autogr.).

If thou believest I love thee, thou art lost 1011
Let him take all, for he deserves thee best.
'Mr. Ed. M. to Mrs. F. M.'
MS. Ashmole 38, p. 136.

If thou by chance shalt hope to have 1012
Find, in a wintery tide.
'Of fained frynds'.
MS. Rawl. poet. 108, fol. 16.

If thou canst brook poor stools a homely room 1013
Of your malicious prying parish spies.
Joynes, J., 'To S: B: an Invitation to a Cupp of Ale Hor. Epist.' I. v.
MS. Ashmole 788, fol. 152, attr. to Joynes on fol. 1$^{v}$.

If thou demand whose is this monument 1014
And with the golden lilies crowned of France.
[G. B. (?)], on Prince Henry's death, 1612.
MS. *Rawl. poet. 116, fol. 2$^{v}$.

If thou dost find a house to thy mind 1015
My labour is not lost.
MS. Rawl. poet. 66, fol. 32$^{v}$.

If thou dost want a horse, thou buy'st a score; 1016
Out of mere want thou wilt sell all at last.
Sed[ley], Sir Ch[arles], 'To Stertorius. a Greedy Buyer'.
MS. Rawl. poet. 173, fol. 58.

If thou goest first dear wife just grief and cries 1017
Concealed until the resurrection.
Jea (or Jay), Sir Thomas, 'On the Lady Jea going sicke into the bath'.
MSS. CCC. 328, fol. 33$^{v}$, attr. to S. Tho. Jea; Rawl. poet. 206, p. 22, attr. to Sir Tho. Jay.

1018 If thou money hast to spend,
Friends alas are very scant.

Robinson, Robert.
MS. *Rawl. poet. 218, p. 36 (autogr.).

1019 If thou our king set forth in colours fit
How far doth nature art her page surpass.

Ashemore, John, translation of Latin verses to the painter of a portrait of Charles I.
MS. Dodsworth 61, fol. 60 (autogr. (?)).

1020 If thou serve a monk a woman, and a child
Of thanks for thy pains thou shalt clean be beguiled.

Couplet, translation of Latin.
MS. Tanner 306, fol. 185v rev.

1021 If thou shoulds't strike a blow for ev'ry slip
And in condition, better far, than we.

[Quarles, Francis], 'To God'.
Pr. *Divine Fancies*, 1632, iv. 76.
MS. Rawl. poet. 90, fol. 75.

1022 If thou the God I seek
My everlasting home I gain.

Kenton, James.
MS. *Eng. poet. e. 20, p. 54 (autogr.).

1023 If thou the laws dost love
But turned by love to the cause which its life gave.

Bacon, Sir Nicholas (1623–1666), translation of Boethius, *Consolations* IV. vi. 1664.
MS. Tanner 306, fol. 342 (autogr.).

1024 If thou wilt counsel take, this I advise
That runs, and as it runs, for ever will run.

Horace, *Epistles* I. ii. 41–43.
MS. Rawl. poet. 213, fol. 3v.

1025 [If thou wilt know how to choose a shrew]
What a pox carries she below.

A verse from 'Advice to Bachelours', *Merry Drollery*, 1661, p. 22.
MS. Rawl. B. 35, fol. 57 rev.

1026 If thou wouldst learn, not knowing how to pray
At all times wi' their own mouths, not by saints.

[Quarles, Francis], 'A form of Prayer'.
Pr. *Divine Fancies*, 1632, ii. 32.
MS. Rawl. poet. 90, fol. 51v.

1027 If thou wouldst live in peace always
That ill will be his end.

Tipping, William, 'The Pathway to peace And saftie'.
MS. *Rawl. poet. 101, fol. 79 (autogr.).

1028 If through the spirit of thy grace
Secure in him alone I stand.

Kenton, James.
MS. *Eng. poet. e. 20, p. 200 (autogr.).

If thy house be fair, thy table delicate 1029
And if thou be patient, thou shalt be glad for ever.

Translation of Latin verses: 'Si tibi pulcra domus, si splendida mensa quid inde . . .'.
MS. Gough Norfolk 43, fol. 40v.

If thy mistress be too coy 1030
But fly and they'll follow thee as fast again.

Song with music.
MS. Don. c. 57, fol. 29.

If titles change th' intention of the fact 1031
Then justice weighs the actor, not the act.

Couplet.
MS. Add. B. 8, fol. 75v.

If to a woman's head a painter would 1032
Doth please; this, ten times over will delight.

J[onson], B[en.], translator of Horace's *Ars poetica.*
See *Ben Jonson*, Herford and Simpson, viii, 1947, p. 299.
MSS. Don. e. 6, fol. 18v, extracts; Rawl. D. 261, p. 104, attr. to B. J.

If to be just religious wise and free 1033
Whom as she bred her kindly doth inter.

On William Bence, Aldborough Church, Norfolk, 1606.
MS. Top. Norf. c. 1, fol. 5.

If to be rich, and to be learned 1034
God bless the King, and this new corporation.

'In Praise of the Choice Company of Philosophers and Witts, who meete on Wednesdaies weekely at Gresham Colledge', 1661–2.
MSS. Ashmole 36, 37, two copies, fols. 310 and 313; Firth c. 20, fol. 11, attr. to Mr. W. G.; Tanner 466, fol. 78, attr. to H[enry] Stubbe.

If to be sprung from virtuous noble blood 1035
Unto eternity the world inherit.

Darcie, Abraham (?), 'To the worthily honoured Knight Sir Gervase Cutler'.
MS. Top. Yorks c. 26, fol. 140v.

If to hear a droll song it is your intention 1036
As nobody is injured when nobody's named.

MS. Don. c. 57, fol. 85.

If to love sweetness in alluring eyes 1037
As hopeless to enjoy as to remove.

MS. CCC. 327, fol. 7v.

1038 If to maintain the use? I must
Here, and in Heaven an angel too.
Shirley, James, 'Uppon M: E: S. Epit.'
Pr. from this MS., *Works*, ed. A. Dyce, 1833, vi. 501.
MS. *Rawl. poet. 88, p. 30.

1039 If to my mind great lord I had a state
Aloud, and haply it may last as long.
'Benn Johnson's Newyears gift To my lord Treasurer', 1628–32.
*The Underwood*, lxxvii.
MS. Eng. poet. c. 50, fol. 58.

1040 If to your God sincerely you confide
Till time shall be no more.
Skinner, John, Psalm xci.
MS. *Eng. poet. d. 22, fol. 149.

1041 If tooth-picks of the lentick
Be wanting, of a quill then make a tooth-pick.
Couplet, translation from Martial.
Pr. G. Sandys's *Relation of a Journey*, 1615, p. 12.
MS. Don. e. 6, fol. 25v.

1042 If treasures piled as heaps to sand
Believing themselves poor.
Polwhele, John, 'Boet[hius', *Consolations*], II. ii.
MS. *Eng. poet. f. 16, fol. 21 (autogr.).

1043*a* If true love might true love's reward obtain
None loves like him (that is) none fair like me.
[Constable, Henry], sonnet, pr. *Diana*, 1592, Sig. B4v.
MS. Ashmole 38, p. 55.

1043*b* If 'twere so poor a thing, to say,
What was the doing on't, I pray?
Couplet.
MS. Sancroft 85, p. 300 rev.

1044 If Valentinus lived a single man
Learns of the wren and titmouse to live chaste.
'Upon St. Valentines daye. a Probleme'.
MS. Rawl. poet. 212, fol. 150v rev.

1045 If vanquished monarchs may their cause explore,
Which heaven approved by the people's voice.
'Dialogue between K. J. and K. Wm.'
MS. Rawl. poet. 173, fol. 125; see also I664, I853.

1046 If virtue ever must be laid aside
To bravely triumph or as bravely fall.
Hammond, Samuel, school translation of Ennius, 'Nam si violandum est jus'.
MS. Rawl. D. 174, fol. 78 (autogr.).

If virtue, honour, truth, and fame. 1047
Renew the letters with his tears.
[Randolph, Thomas (?)], 'Verses upon the death of Mr. Harrison, Vice Mr. of Trin: Coll:', 1555–1631.
See *Palaestra*, no. 148, 1925, p. 255.
MS. Firth e. 4, p. 111.

If we could see below 1048
As if grief were not foul, nor virtue winning.
Herbert, George, 'The foile'.
Pr. *The Temple*, 1633, p. 170.
MS. *Tanner 307, fol. 129v.

If we desire true Christians for to be 1049
And so displays the blessed deity.
MS. Don. e. 19, fol. 168v rev.

If wealth could keep a man alive 1050
Ne'er blush at the name of a drinker.
[Brome, Alexander], 'Content', ['out of Anacreon', xxiii].
Pr. *Poems*, 1661, p. 67.
MS. Ashmole 47, fol. 158v.

If (weeping love) enquirers seek to know 1051
Though her each atom was an angel's tongue.
'Epitaph on a young Lady unknown'.
MS. Eng. poet. e. 40, fol. 40.

If Wharton's soul is gone to heaven 1052
For M[arlborough] and his Duchess.
'On the late Lord Wharton in 1715'.
MS. Eng. misc. c. 116, fol. 7, marked 'R. C.'

If when I die to hell's eternal shade 1053
Shall heaven enjoy amidst hell's misery.
[Fowler, William (?)], song.
Printed amongst 'Poems of Doubtful Authenticity', *Works of William Fowler*, i, *S.T.S.*, N.S. vi, 1914, p. 390. See note in *S.T.S.* Ser. 3, xiii, p. 31.
MSS. Don. c. 57, fol. 44v, with music; Mus. Sch. F. 575, p. 9, with melody and lute accompaniment.

If when the sun at noon displays 1054
Both light and darkness, night and day.
Carew, Tho[mas], 'Songe'.
Pr. *Poems*, 1640.
MS. Ashmole 38, p. 151.

If when you're loved, you cannot love again 1055
Why do but say so, I am out of pain.
Couplet.
MS. Rawl. poet. 153, fol. 28v.

If while I sojourn here below 1056
Give all the praise alone to him.
Kenton, James.
MS. *Eng. poet. e. 20, p. 35 (autogr.)

1057a If winter fortune nip thy summer friends
Will take [thy] part, when all the world's again' thee.

[Quarles, Francis], 'in Slander', from *Job Militant*, 1624.
MS. Rawl. poet. 127, fol. 17$^{v}$.

1057b If wisdom, wealth, honour, or honesty
Sir William Gee had all these pleas yet died.

Epitaph at York, 1611.
MS. Eng. misc. e. 147, fol. 99$^{v}$.

1058 If wishing for the mystic joys of love
And for such forced iniquity we're damn'd.

Chatterton, Thomas.
MS. *Eng. poet. e. 6, fol. 1$^{v}$ at end (autogr.).

1059 If wit may be the child of chance and rise
Fair though she hath not one black patch about her.

'On the returne of King Charles 2d'.
MS. Rawl. poet. 84, fol. 10.

1060 If wit might warn thee to forsee
Nor to what stay by hap she fly.

MS. Ashmole 1447, part ix, p. 3.

1061 If wit or critic blame the tender swain
Are large and wide, Tydcomb and I assure ye.

Pope, Alexander, to Henry Cromwell on his writing 'Drury' for 'Drury Lane' in verse; letter, 25 April 1708.
Pr. by Curll, *Miscellanea*, 1727, i. 5.
MS. Rawl. letters 90, fol. 7$^{v}$ (autogr.).

1062 If wit or honesty could save
And mend your own by True's behaviour.

[Prior, Matthew], 'Epitaph on her Late Majesty [Queen Anne]'s Dog True'.
Pr. *Gentleman's Journal*, Oct. 1693, p. 326; cf. *Poems*, ed. H. B. Wright and M. K. Spears, 1959, i. 124.
MS. Eng. poet. e. 87, p. 39.

1063 If witches on with Satan and with hell
By faith awake it till the curse retire.

MS. *Don. f. 5, fol. 16$^{v}$.

1064 If with my tears it may not lawful be
Weep Britons weep this loss exceeds all other.

G. B., 'Epitaph 18', on Prince Henry in 'Cestria Lugens', 1612.
MS. *Rawl. poet. 116, fol. 9$^{v}$.

1065 If with no pity our fond acts be eyed
Yet be thou pleased our follies to restrain.

Mervall, Alphonso, Psalm lxviii.
MS. *Rawl. poet. 166, p. 74 (autogr.).

1066 If with the outward comforts blest
A faithful steward of my God.

Kenton, James.
MS. *Eng. poet. e. 20, p. 32 (autogr.).

If women can be courteous when they list 1067
But jades, and drabs together all were sold.

MS. Rawl. poet. 117, fol. 196$^{v}$ rev.

If women could be fair and yet not fond 1068
To play with fools, oh! what a fool was I.

de Vere, Edward, Earl of Oxford.
MSS. Add. B. 83, fol. 28, attr. to the Earl of Oxford; Rawl. poet. 85, fol. 16, attr. to Earll of Oxenforde; 172, fol. 6$^{v}$.

If women were as little as they're good, 1069
A peascod-shell would make them gown and hood.

Couplet.
MSS. Rawl. D. 954, fol. 41; Rawl. poet. 209, fol. 35.

If words are wind, which (guilt with eloquence) 1070
That the world's firmest glory, it is wind.

Fanshawe, Sir Richard, translator, Sonnet 18, 'The Praise of the Winde', from the Spanish.
MS. *Firth c. 1, p. 82.

If words will relieve thee, when need makes thee crave: 1071
Small help from the hands, but to help thee to th' grave.

Robinson, Robert.
MS. *Rawl. poet. 218, p. 8 (autogr.).

If work of wit, of life is purest act, 1072
Live evermore, no death, or harm annoying.

F. W., 'Sonnet: 10. of the joys of heaven'.
MS. *Rawl. C. 639, p. 37.

If yet a choice more worthy, cause more new 1073
Our mutual choice and our unhoped divorce.

'Sir Philip Sidney to the Lady Penelope Rich'; cf. M211.
MS. Eng. poet. f. 9, p. 224.

If yet I have not all your love, 1074
Be one, and one another's all.

Donne, John.
Pr. *Poems*, 1633.
MSS. *Eng. poet. e. 99, fol. 208$^{v}$; *f. 9, p. 110; see also I966.

If yet we further duly think upon 1075
And follow Christ in the regeneration.

MS. *Rawl. poet. 97, fol. 18$^{v}$ (autogr.).

If you do love as well as I 1076
If you do love, as well as I.

MS. Mus. b. 1, fol. 51$^{v}$, music by John Wilson.

If you do not fear 1077
. . . (unfinished draft).

Gough, Richard 'An Invitation', *c.* 1763.
MS. *Eng. poet. c. 5, fol. 103 (autogr.).

1078 If you either were angry or sorry
That men in Bath go naked not ashamed.
'To the Maior of the Bath'.
MS. Rawl. poet. 117, fol. 191 rev.

1079 If you for Saxton seek, behold his grave
His soul at rest in heaven, attends God's will.
Epitaph on Christopher Saxton.
MS. Wood D. 13, p. 203.

1080 If you had changed your flower which smelt so well,
And of that flower I pray you to allow.
'Swerdna' [Andrews], 'To A Gentelwoman that refused to change flower with a Gentelman'.
MS. *Rawl. poet. 92, fol. 21.

1081 If you on earth that live did know
To everlasting light.
Annotated: 'Richard Roper lived 70 years and dyed 1578'.
MS. Rawl. poet. 117, fol. 157$^{v}$ rev.

1082 If you remember lady the other day
You chaste and virtuous are, she was a whore.
'In Commendation of His Mris'.
MS. Ashmole 37, p. 143.

1083 If [you to I] as [I to you] am true
[I over you] must lie, and [I in you].
'To his Mrs', riddling couplet, letters and numbers for words.
MS. Rawl. poet. 153, fol. 21.

1084 If you upon my youthful lays
Malignant critic! you be d—d!
Parsons, William, 'On the Florence Miscellany'.
MS. *Don. d. 123, p. 126 (autogr.).

1085 If you will love know such to be
Your heart would live in me as mine in you.
Pr. Playford's *Select Ayres and Dialogues*, 1669, with music by Alph. Marsh.
MS. Don. c. 57, fol. 32, with music, not Marsh's.

1086 If you would hold your husband long
You must first learn to hold your tongue.
'Epigram', couplet.
MS. Eng. poet. c. 51, p. 164.

1087 If you would rise my honour boys
And be good rogues in grace.
Samber, Robert.
MS. Rawl. poet. 11, fol. 33$^{v}$ (autogr.).

If you your Blouzelind design for me 1088
B'assur'd your stile and Gay's are better known.
Amherst, Elizabeth, 'To a young lady who wrote a part of one of Gay's pastorals and sent it to me as her own'.
MS. *Eng. poet. e. 109, p. 29.

If you're deceived, it is not by a cheat 1089
Disturbed by swords, like Damocles in's feast.
[Wilmot, John, Earl of] Rochester, 'An Heroicall Epistle in answer to Ephelia'.
See Vieth, p. 468.
MSS. Don. b. 8, p. 602, attr. to Rochester; Rawl. poet. 173, fol. 67$^{v}$, attr. to Ld. Ro.

If youth itself may drop into the grave 1090
They the sooner are at rest.
'On the Death of Children'.
MS. Rawl. poet. 90, fol. 42$^{v}$.

If youth, religion, virtue and the rest 1091
By thy sad friend . . . (incomplete).
MS. Sancroft 59, p. 280 rev.

If't hap you see a maid weep for her woe 1092
The world is flinty and will lend her none.
MSS. Don. d. 58, fol. 6$^{v}$; Eng. poet. c. 50, fol. 133$^{v}$.

Ilium deplores, but still old Priam's glad 1093
The greatest cedars have the greatest fall.
Satire, *temp.* Spanish match.
MS. Eng. poet. c. 50, fol. 12$^{v}$.

*Note*: Ill, I'll in one alphabetical series.

Ill boding screech-owls guide thee ill 1094
Europe, from thee.
Fanshawe, Sir Richard, translator, Horace, *Odes* III. xxvii.
MS. *Firth c. 1, p. 56.

Ill busied man, why shouldst thou take such care 1095
Are but as tears shed for thy funeral.
King, Henry, 'Mans Misery'.
Pr. *Poems*, 1657, p. 138.
MSS. Ashmole 47, fol. 38; CCC. 328, fol. 75$^{v}$; Eng. poet. c. 50, fol. 128$^{v}$; e. 14, fol. 46; *e. 30, fol. 39; Malone 16, p. 12, attr. to H. K. (monogram); 21, fol. 2$^{v}$, attr. to John King; *22, fol. 14$^{v}$; Rawl. poet. 84, fol. 41; 199, p. 94, attr. to Dr. I. K.; see also A912.

I'll cut it down, I'll down with't, by this hand; 1096
How could it water make, when it had the stone?
'A Pump stopt with stones'.
MS. CCC. 309, fol. 49$^{v}$.

1097 I'll drink a health to the king,
By virtue of the protestation.
'An explanation of the Protestation', May 1641.
MSS. Ashmole 36, 37, fol. 92.

1098 Ill fortune presses hard, and love severe,
I suffer hunger, love I cannot bear.
Couplet, 'On a Poor Lover'.
MS. Eng. poet. c. 9, p. 87.

1099 I'll gaze no more on her bewitching face
I surfeit with excess of joy and die.
Carew, Thomas, 'On his Soules Mistris'.
Pr. Carew's *Poems*, 1640, Sig. G4[v]; *Wits Recreations*, 1640.
MSS. Ashmole 38, p. 4, attr. to I. M.; *Don. b. 9, fol. 2[v]; c. 57, fol. 21, with music; Malone 21, fol. 86[v]; Rawl. poet. 117, two copies, fols. 163[v] rev. and 172 rev.

1100 I'll give you an account of one sight more
No pity had he for the poor mare's arse.
Tipping, William, 'Out of my vision of hell'.
MS. *Rawl. poet. 101, fol. 73[v] (autogr.).

1101 I'll go! 'cause you command me I'll not stay
Which none but lovers or the damn'd do know.
[Chatwin, John], 'To Sylvia who commanded Him to see Her no more'.
MS. *Rawl. poet. 94, p. 196 (autogr.).

1102 I'll go no more to Maldon fair
The worst is worth a million.
MS. Eng. poet. f. 25, fol. 66[v].

1103 I'll go no more to the old exchange
And several sorts of sizes.
Cf. 'I'll go no more to the New-Exchange', pr. *Wit and Drollery*, 1661, p. 167.
MS. Rawl. B. 35, fol. 44 rev.

1104 I'll have a new test, which neither shall own
And France is encumbered by politic Paul.
'A New Nothing', 1692.
MSS. Eng. poet. c. 18, fol. 127[v]; e. 49, p. 126.

1105 I'll hurry . . . thee hence
As nature does in mine.
[Crowne, John], 'A Song in the Comedy . . . Justice Buisy or the Gentleman Quack. Set by Mr. John Eccles'.
MS. Mus. Sch. C. 95, p. 135.

1106 I'll love good wine
And those that love their king.
MS. Rawl. poet. 65, fol. 28, reference to setting by Dr. Coleman.

I'll love, nay I'm resolved to love, 1107
Whilst in our breasts we harbour still the foe.
[Chatwin, John], 'An Imitation of an Ode of Anacreon's', xi.
MS. *Rawl. poet. 94, p. 76 (autogr.).

Ill men whose mischievous and deadly breath 1108
Peace here and crown of joy hereafter find.
Williams, John, 'Be wise as Serpents and harmless as Doves'.
MS. *Rawl. poet. 191, fol. 117[v] (autogr.).

I'll mount the sky and pull down all the lights 1109
The wisest man, the bravest patriot.
Morrice, John, 'A Rant'.
MS. *Rawl. poet. 114, fol. 174[v] (autogr.).

I'll mount to yon blue *cælum* 1110
And scare you with eclipses.
D'Urfey, Thomas, [from *The Three Dukes of Dunstable*, 1688], 'set by Mr. Henry Purcell'.
F. B. Zimmerman, *Purcell*, 1963, no. 571(5).
MS. Mus. Sch. C. 95, p. 206.

Ill natur'd Patch! by thee is shown 1111
Shows better how you fought and loved.
MS. Eng. poet. e. 45, fol. 28.

I'll neither judge the soul, nor yet commend 1112
Jonas from out the whale, thee from the well.
'On one drown'd in a well himselfe'.
MS. Eng. poet. e. 14, fol. 24.

I'll not believe't, if fate would be so cross 1113
So great a loss, will choose not to believe.
[Randolph, Thomas], 'Upon the Rumor of the King of Swedens deathe reported in November and December 1632'.
Pr. *Poems*, 1638.
MS. Rawl. poet. 26, fol. 57.

I'll not dissemble, 'tis a thing I scorn, 1114
Whilst others choose for gold give me content.
Williams, John, 'A vindication of the noble choice'.
MS. *Rawl. poet. 191, fol. 50[v] (autogr.).

I'll not with dreaming poets sit upon 1115
So you by water thither did aspire.
Ingel[o], N[athaniel], 'On the Death of Henrietta [daughter of Charles I] who died suddently after her coming out of the Bath' [in the Seine, 30 June 1670].
MS. Rawl. poet. 172, fol. 112.

I'll observe my dubious wages 1116
'Mong men enjoy a being.
J. F., Psalm xxxix.
MS. *Eng. poet. f. 17, p. 111 (autogr.).

1117 I'll please my self (though none else) with my skill
Which fair mark if I miss, I'll burn my quill.
Cheyney, William, couplet.
MS. *Rawl. poet. 86, fol. 32ᵛ.

1118 I'll rhyme no more, by Phoebus' soul, not I,
By Phoebus' soul not I. Muse get 'ee gone.
[Weaver, Thomas], 'Poetrie abjur'd occasion'd by the misconstruction of some Ladies'.
Not pr. in *Songs and Poems*, 1654.
MS. *Rawl. poet. 211, fol. 22ᵛ (autogr.).

1119 I'll sail upon the dog star
Let all the nation judge it.
D'Urfey, Thomas, 'set by Mr. Hen. Purcell' [from *The Three Dukes of Dunstable*, 1688].
F. B. Zimmerman, *Purcell*, 1963, no. 571(5).
MS. Mus. Sch. C. 95, p. 208.

1120 I'll say that I'm a bastard born
A man or woman now.
Tipping, William.
MS. *Rawl. poet. 101, fol. 82 (autogr.).

1121 I'll sing you the praise (if you'll lend but an ear)
Then broke all their swords, and cried *Vive le Roy*.
'Jo[hn] Haines's Ballad upon the disbanding the Royall Regiment'.
MS. Rawl. poet. 173, fol. 139.

1122 I'll tell thee dear love what thou shalt do
But to mark when, and where the dark eclipses be.
Donne, John, 'The Booke'.
Pr. *Poems*, 1633.
MS. Eng. poet. *f. 9, p. 93; see also I1125.

1123 I'll tell thee Dick where I have been
With Bridget and with Nell.
[Suckling, Sir John], 'A wedding'.
Pr. *Fragmenta Aurea*, 1646, p. 37.
*Cf. Poems of Lovelace*, ed. C. H. Wilkinson, 1930, p. xxiii.
MSS. Ashmole 36, 37, two copies, fols. 51ᵛ and 292; Ballard 29, fol. 144, attr. to Sir J. Sucklin; Rawl. poet. 37, p. 105; see also I504.

1124 I'll tell thee, Dick, where I have been
And I for them be shent.
'The Checquer Inne'. 1675.
Pr. *Poems on Affairs of State*, 1704, iii. 57; Marvell's *Works*, ed. E. Thompson, 1776, i, p. xli; cf. *Poems*, ed. H. M. Margoliouth, 1953, p. 312.
MSS. Don. b. 8, p. 526; *Eng. poet. d. 49, p. 258, attr. to Andrew Marvell; see also I503.

I'll tell thee now (dear love) what thou shalt do 1125
But to mark when, and where the dark eclipses be.
Donne, John, 'Valediction of the Booke'.
Pr. *Poems*, 1633.
MS. *Eng. poet. e. 99, fol. 116; see also I1122.

I'll tell thee Sawny what I have seen 1126
Aw my soul mon 'tis twa pence too dear.
F. G., 'A Scotch ballad' on George I.
MS. Rawl. poet. 155, p. 197.

I'll tell thee what's the cure of jealousy 1127
Prithee, why then a cuckold not to be.
Cavendish, Lady Jane, 'The Cure'.
MS. *Rawl. poet. 16, p. 6.

I'll tell you a story a story so merry 1128
He could ne'er make amends but by this cavalcade.
'A Ballad on the Funeral of John Duke of Marlborough', 9 Aug. 1722.
MSS. Ballard 50, fol. 87, attr. to Sam Westley; Eng. misc. c. 292, fol. 107; Eng. poet. c. 41, two copies, fols. 52 and 55; Top. Oxon. b. 170, fol. 2.

I'll tell you a story, a story so merry 1129
That such like dark lanthorns may come unto light, derry down etc.
Samber, Robert, 'To the tune of king John and the Abbot of Canterbury. An excellent new ballet', 30 June 1730.
MS. *Rawl. poet. 134*b*, fol. 75 (autogr.).

I'll tell you a story, a story that true is, 1130
What it was for to tell a great king what he meant.
'A Dialogue between the K[in]g [George I] and the B[isho]p of R[ochester]', Francis Atterbury.
MSS. Eng. poet. f. 12, p. 100, attr. to S. W-y; Top. Oxon. b. 170, fol. 20.

I'll tell you a story and no tittle enlarge 1131
For he's out of their debt if he owed them a shame.
'An Excellent New Ballad to a true old Tune', lampoon on George I and the Duchess of Munster (later of Kendal).
MS. Rawl. D. 383, fol. 142.

I'll tell you a story, I've heard it is true 1132
For the doctor not devil provide a new head.
[Bacon, Phanuel], 'The S[pread] b[ur]y King Catcher or The Stage Robb'd', satire on the Earl of Oxford. For 'Spreadbury' see the preface to *The Oxford Sausage*, 1764.
MS. Eng. poet. e. 45, fol. 63 (autogr.).

1133 I'll tell you a story, though 'tis but a queer one,
'Tis plain from what's past that the church is in danger.

'Ballad made by Mr. [Philip (?)] Hawkins on Justice Bush of Cirencester To the Tune of the Abbot of Canterbury'; cf. fol. 157v.
MS. Ballard 47, fol. 167.

1134 I'll tell you a tale for a groat
The whole Highland army was routed.

'The Gazette of Jan. 23. 1745/6'.
Pr. bk. Firth b. 22, fol. 46.

1135 I'll tell you a tale it's as strange as 'tis true
How easy the hyp may get up in the head.

'The Doctor and Alderman of Oxford, over Head and Ears in the Hyp'.
MS. Top. Oxon. b. 116, fol. 122v.

1136 I'll tell you a tale there never was truer
And then they converted it to a dish clout.

'The Mum Brewers Feast', on George I.
MS. Rawl. poet. 155, p. 99.

1137 I'll tell you a wonder, deny it if you can
Here lies a tailor, lived and died an honest man.

'Upon one Mr. Taylor'.
MSS. Ashmole 38, p. 169; Douce f. 5, fol. 9v.

1138 I'll tell you how at first the rose grew red
They only flourish in your livery.

Pr. *Wits Recreations*, 1640, no. 267; *Parnassus Biceps*, 1656, p. 75; *Wit Restor'd*, 1658, p. 64.
MSS. Ashmole 38, p. 4; 47, fol. 52v; Don. c. 57, fol. 30, with music; Eng. poet. c. 50, fol. 126; e. 14, fol. 68; f. 25, fol. 15v; Rawl. D. 1092, fol. 272; Rawl. poet. 84, fol. 87 rev.; 116, fol. 38; 206, p. 71; see also I510, I1141.

1139 I'll tell you of another sun
Can melt and harden cross desire.

Strode, William (?), 'A Moderating Answere to A1754 and I1140
Pr. *Wit Restor'd*, 1658, p. 116.
MS. *CCC. 325, fol. 100, in Strode's hand.

1140 I'll tell you true, whereon doth light
Nor him nor him, where one should sleep.

Strode, William, 'Answere or Mock-song', to A1754.
Pr. *Wit Restor'd*, 1658, p. 115.
MS. *CCC. 325, fol. 101 (autogr.).
MS. Eng. poet. f. 25, fol. 63.

I'll tell you whence the rose grew red 1141
And only flourish in your livery.

'On his Mrs'.
MSS. Ashmole 47, fol. 37v; Don. d. 58, fol. 44*a*v; Rawl. poet. 153, fol. 9; see also I510, I1138.

Ill thrives that hapless family that shows 1142
Obeying husbands, or commanding wives.

[Quarles, Francis], Epigram.
From *Hadassa*, 1621, end of meditation 3.
Pr. *Wits Recreations*, 1640, Sig. F6.
MSS. Ashmole 38, two copies, pp. 25 and 37; Eng. poet. d. 152, fol. 103v; Rawl. poet. 153, fol. 28.

I'll trust thee lord who 'as preserved me 1143
I shall arrive to joy for ever more.

Fairfax, Thomas, Lord, Psalm xvi.
MS. *Fairfax 40, p. 29 (autogr.).
MS. *Fairfax 38, p. 142.

I'll try to advise 1144
Among all his Majesty's bitches.

J. W., 'On Mrs. Kilmansecks 26000° Purchase'.
MS. Rawl. poet. 155, p. 28.

I'll use no far-fetch'd motives to persuade 1145
To th' height of immaterialities.

Ashmole, Elias, 'To my vallued Freind Mr. Noah Bridges. upon his Vulgar Arithmatique', first published 1653.
MSS. Ashmole 36, 37, fol. 242 (autogr.).

I'll vow I think I loved you well 1146
Because I suffered all your charms and I myself live still.

'The Repulse. Ode Pindarique'.
MS. Don. c. 55, fol. 2.

I'll walk the mornings with an oaken stick, 1147
In sense and education truly so.

Epigram, 1735.
MS. Eng. misc. e. 240, p. 300.

I'll weary her with prayers till I obtain 1148
Leave from her lips to call you back again.

Couplet.
MS. Rawl. poet. 209, fol. 37v.

Illustrious bard! whose pleasing style 1149
Friend Hare, you shall succeed him.

Coney, Thomas, D.D., 'On Mr. [Thomas] Hare's Translation of the Odes etc. of Horace' [published 1737].
MS. Ballard 47, fol. 34.

Illustrious character 1150
Number me among the blest.

Kenton, James.
MS. *Eng. poet. e. 20, p. 52 (autogr.).

1151 Illustrious D[uke] and princess great, regard
Such matchless glories in your younger years.
Poem to John Egerton, 2nd Earl of Bridgwater.
MS. Top. Yorks. c. 26, fol. 139ᵛ.

1152 Illustrious prince and princess be not sad
On earth a queen and now in heaven the same.
On Queene Anne's death, 1618, addressed to Prince Charles and Princess Elizabeth.
MSS. Don. d. 58, fol. 15; Malone 19, p. 5.

1153 Illustrious Sir! Although the public weal
Your most obsequious and devoted servant.
Ford, William, Junior, 'London, July 19th 1731'.
MS. Rawl. poet. 172, fol. 127.

1154 Illustrious Sir, you are this nation's care
To give you aid, then to your throne advance.
'An Acrostick on J. S.', James Stuart, the Old Pretender.
MS. Rawl. poet. 181, fol. 78.

1155 Illustrious steed, who should the zodiac grace
But both enjoy that liberty you gave.
'On S[orrel]l', 1702.
Pr. *Poems on Affairs of State*, ii, 1703, p. 323.
Attr. to B. Higgons B.M. Add. MS. 40060, fol. 10ᵛ.
MSS. Rawl. C. 986, fol. 15ᵛ; Smith 23, p. 121.

1156 I'm a hole which though sometimes too strait at the first
Till they made it a law I should be well stitched.
Riddle.
MS. Eng. poet. e. 8, fol. 29.

1157 I'm a strange composition as e'er was in nature,
For those who first guess me, shall have me for guessing.
Amherst, Elizabeth, 'a prize riddle on herself when 24', 1740.
MS. *Eng. poet. e. 109, p. 4.

1158 I'm an old man, must therefore die
To all, all ages death is nigh.
Robinson, Robert.
MS. *Rawl. poet. 218, p. 87 (autogr.).

1159 I'm an old man; my life away is flying:
Do what I can, my flesh my flesh is dying.
Robinson, Robert, 'Of An old man', couplet.
MS. *Rawl. poet. 218, p. 104 (autogr.).

1160 I'm apt now to think
His bed should to Bridges be common.
'An Addition to "Wonder not Nelly"'.
MS. Eng. poet. d. 152, fol. 6.

I'm born a Jew yet mean no harm 1161
Nor of male nor female gender.
'Riddle' (Jews Harp).
MS. Rawl. D. 833, fol. 170.

I'm born of English flesh and blood; 1162
And as things change, so I will too.
'The Modern Fanatical Reformer: or, the Religious State-Tinker'.
MS. Firth d. 14, fol. 66.

I'm but a worm: my lines are plain 1163
Poor worms, alas, have no high strain.
Robinson, Robert, couplet.
MS. *Rawl. poet. 218, p. 44 (autogr.).

I'm glad your liking suits so well with me, 1164
In short agree to this my short address.
Williams, John, 'To a Young Lady that was for nothing but what was short'.
MS. *Rawl. poet. 191, fol. 43ᵛ (autogr.).

I'm got out from the world; and now I reign 1165
Not for a world turn to the world again.
Barksdale, Clement, saying of 'Ebsworth of [Exeter (?)]', distich.
MS. Autogr. c. 9, fol. 154 (autogr.).

I'm hard and soft; I'm black and white; 1166
And through my slit my water's black.
'Riddle'.
MS. Rawl. D. 833, fol. 170.

I'm in Italy and Spain, but never am found 1167
In England, the place where beauties abound.
Williams, John, 'A Riddle', couplet, 'The Letter I'.
MS. *Rawl. poet. 191, fol. 101 (autogr.).

I'm made of different parts, as all agree 1168
Unless time makes me drop from what I love.
'A Riddle on a Lady's Patch; given me by Miss L. Weyland 14th January 1748/9'.
MS. Eng. poet. e. 40, fol. 103.

I'm often clad in silver vest 1169
At night they cannot do without me.
'Riddle'.
MS. Eng. poet. c. 51, p. 22.

I'm often drawn to make a stop 1170
And peace, and joy, at once an entrance find.
'Religion a Simile by the Revd. Mr. Charles Rich'.
MS. Ballard 50, fol. 91.

I'm short and you are sweet, and short and sweet 1171
Be short and sweet and only say content.
Williams, John, on 'Short and Sweet'.
MS. *Rawl. poet. 191, fol. 43ᵛ (autogr.).

1172 I'm sometimes seen; though never but in part
Safe from destruction and destroying care.
Williams, John, 'A Riddle' and 'The Explication'.
MS. *Rawl. poet. 191, fol. 150 (autogr.).

1173 I'm thinking now the ceremony's over
And every maiden like Tarpeia die.
Extract from an Epilogue spoken at the Theatre at Dublin ['by Mrs. Knap. May 13. 1724'].
Pr., brds., Dublin, and the *Worcester Post or Western Journal*, 17–24 July 1724; reference to Wood's halfpence.
MS. Ballard 47, fol. 33.

1174 I'm very much concerned to find
And love king George of kings the best.
'His G. the D. of Marlborough's Speech Which was verily and truly spoken to the first Regimt. of Foot Guards. June 2nd [17]15'.
MS. Rawl. poet. 155, p. 161.

1175 I'm vext to see my muse so angry grown
The Devil and be the damning of us all.
MS. Top. Oxon. e. 280, p. 678 rev.

1176 Image of hellish humour, ignorance
So he his sons, both sire and brother hight.
MS. Rawl. poet. 172, fol. 83.

1177 Image of her, which I love, more than she
Mad with much heart, than idiot with none.
Donne, John.
Pr. *Poems*, 1633.
MSS. *Eng. poet. e. 99, fol. 104$^{v}$; *f. 9, p. 113.

1178 Imagine god in heaven in royal throne
Therefore the joys of heaven we kingdoms call.
F. W., 'Sonnet 11'.
MS. *Rawl C. 639, p. 43.

1179 Imagine madam ere these lines you read,
Till death shall part us in the silent grave.
'Verses Addressed to My Mother when Miss Richardson by —'.
MS. *Eng. poet. e. 28, p. 36.

1180 Immensity cloistered in thy dear womb
With this kind mother, who partakes thy woe.
Donne, John, 'Holy Sonnetts. La Corona 3'.
Pr. *Poems*, 1633.
MS. *Eng. poet. e. 99, fol. 42.

1181 Immensive, immortal, immutable,
When saints their souls with sin gods ocean steer.
F. W., 'Sonnet 41'.
MS. *Rawl. C. 639, p. 200.

Immodest death that would not once confer 1182
Was fain perforce to take a deadly blow.
'Thomas Earle of Dorset Lo: Treasurer', d. 19 April 1608.
MSS. Ashmole 781, p. 136; CCC. 328, fol. 97; Don. d. 58, fol. 18; Douce f. 5, fol. 11; Eng. poet. e. 14, fol. 95$^{v}$ rev.; e. 97, p. 94.

Immortal bard! for whom each muse has wove 1183
And join the patriot's to the poet's praise.
Whaley, John, 'An Epistle to Mr. Pope, From a Young Gentleman at Rome. May 7, 1730'.
Pr. *Poems*, 1732, p. 77; attr. to George, Lord Lyttelton, by W. P. Courtney, *Dodsley's Collection of Poetry*, 1910, pp. 17–18.
MS. Rawl. poet. 222, fol. 7.

Immortal gods, I crave no pelf 1184
Great men sin, and I eat root.
'Apemantus's Grace'.
MS. Eng. poet. c. 9, p. 31.

Immortal harmony explore 1185
Still may her realms enjoy the calm of peace.
Ode to the Genius of Britain, music exercise of Thomas Sanders Dupuis, 25 June 1790.
MS. Mus. Sch. Ex. d. 43.

Immortal harmony! thy heavenly strain 1186
O'ercome the captiv'd sense and shake th' astonished soul.
Pye, Henry James, 'Ode to Harmony'. Music by Philip Hayes; composer's autograph, 13 Dec. 1783. With a printed copy of the words, p. ii.
MS. Mus. d. 67.

Immortal heat, oh let thy greater flame 1187
And praise him, who did make and mend our eyes.
Herbert, George, '[Love] 2'.
Pr. *The Temple*, 1633, p. 46.
MS. *Tanner 307, fol. 35$^{v}$.

Immortal love author of this great frame 1188
Doth warm our hands, and make them write of love.
Herbert, George, 'Love 1'.
Pr. *The Temple*, 1633, p. 45.
MS. *Tanner 307, fol. 35.

Immortal lovers smile 1189
And take no further care.
MS. Mus. Sch. C, 95. p. 181.

1190 Immortal man of glory! whose brave hand
The prize of patriot to a British son.
'On Leiutenant Felton who kild the Duke', 1628.
MSS. Douce 357, fol. 17; Malone 23, p. 207; Rawl. poet. 84, fol. 74 rev.

1191 Immortal man of glory, whose stout hand
No matter what thy body here endure.
Acrostic and anagram, 'John Felton: No Fellony'. 1628.
MS. Eng. poet. e. 14, fol. 12ᵛ.

1192 Immortal queen, great arbitress of time,
That it may burgeon to eternity.
Howell, James, 'Historiæ Sacrum', prefixed to *Life . . . of Lewis XIII.*
Copied from ed. 1646 by Abednego Seller.
MS. Rawl. D. 1110, fol. 97ᵛ.

1193 Immortals say! whose vigorous minds have wrought
And medicine flourish in Britannia's isle.
'The College', canto I and notes for canto II. Satire, 1796, printed 1797.
MS. Top. London d. 3, fol. 1 (autogr.).

1194 Impartial death! the good, the bad, the brave,
Is to be ready at a moment's call.
'On Death', 1735.
MS. Eng. misc. e. 240, p. 170.

1195 Impatient Paris, urged by lustful fire,
Big with delight, and piped o'er all the plain.
Chatwin, John, 'the 27th Idyllium of Theocritus. A Dialogue between a Nymph and a Shepherd'.
MS. *Rawl. poet. 94, p. 245 (autogr.).

1196 Impatient with desire, at last
By our own folly she's unkind.
Granville, George, Baron Lansdown of Biddeford, 'Song'.
Pr. Dryden's *Miscellany*, iv, 1694, p. 276.
MS. Add. B. 105, fol. 79.

1197 Imperial Jove once in a golden shower
That precious limb where by two one are made.
'Of one that sent a payer of gloves to his Mris.'
MS. CCC. 328, fol. 79ᵛ.

1198 Imperial prince king of the seas and isles,
Advice to draw Madam L'Edificatresse.
'To the King', 'envoy' to N67.
Pr. 1667. See M. T. Osborne, *Advice-to-a-Painter Poems*, 1949, p. 28.
MSS. Don. b. 8, p. 245, attr. to Sir John Denham; e. 23, fol. 15, attr. to Sir John Denham; Rawl. poet. 123, p. 105.

Imperious Caesar dead and turn'd to clay 1199*a*
Should patch a wall to expel the water's flaw.
MS. Rawl. poet. 117, fol. 164 rev.

Important trusts committed to the care 1199*b*
And proves him worthy of superior place.
Howard, W., 'Poem . . . to Colonel Samuel Robinson Chamberlain of the . . . City of London and Receiver of His Majesty Revenue arising from Wi[n]dow Lights'.
MS. Rawl. poet. 154, fol. 143*b*.

Impressed with a sense of my sin 1200
I health and salvation receive.
Kenton, James.
MS. *Eng. poet. e. 20, p. 53 (autogr.).

Improving thus the silent lapse of time 1201
Thine life immortal, thine eternal day.
'To the Author of [T2698] by his Father'.
MS. Montagu e. 13, fol. 168.

Impudence and modesty 1202*a*
Th' other small profit brings.
Robinson, Robert, 'Impudentia et modestia contraria'.
MS. *Rawl. poet. 218, p. 86 (autogr.).

In a black cloud 1202*b*
Where passions reign.
Polwhele, John, translator, Boethius, *Consolations* I. vii.
MS. *Eng. poet. f. 16, fol. 19ᵛ (autogr.).

In a certain place appointed for pleasure 1203
That my time will be past or I shall begin.
At end, 'finis qd. John Walles'.
MS. Ashmole 48, fol. 81.

In a cobweb shirt most thin 1204
To leave fair water in the pot.
'The Fayrie kings diet and apparrell'.
Pr. more fully in *A Description of the King and Queene of Fayries*, by R. S., 1635.
MS. Rawl. poet. 142, fol. 45.

In a comely closet when the time was 1205
For the love of women is not to trust on.
Subscribed 'from Publilius Syrus . . . Amare et sapere vix deo conceditur' 'q.T.S.P.'
MS. Ashmole 48, fol. 42ᵛ.

In a dark cave whose hellish station 1206
Was it not for thy often resurrection.
'On a C.'
MS. Eng. poet. d. 152, fol. 9.

In a dark silent shady grove 1207
The prosecution of *Et Cætera*.
'A Wanton Song'.
Pr. *Poems on Affairs of State*, ii, 1703, p. 271.
MS. Rawl. poet. 173, fol. 81ᵛ.

1208 In a dish came fish
For he gave me no beer.
[Shadwell, Thomas], 'On a fish sent by the Archbp. of Canterb. to a Minister' . . .
Pr. *Modius Salium*, 1751, p. 12; cf. *Ben Jonson*, ed. Herford and Simpson, viii, 1947, p. 424.
MSS. Firth d. 7, fol. 167; Wood E. 32 (*Modius Salium*), fol. 8.

1209 In a famous street near Whetstone's park
Or 'tis forty to one but they them get a fall.
'On severall Women about Town', *temp.* Charles II.
MSS. Douce 357, fol. 57v; Firth c. 16, p. 30.

1210 In a field thraftless three dice volant
A bible dormant with a devil corvant.
'The parsons armes legges and all that good is', answer to H343.
MS. Tanner 306, fol. 239v.

1211 In a forest as I went
My name was knowyn no ulk a syde.
'Of a fowle that wantyd his fethers'.
MS. Lat. misc. e. 85, fol. 79.

1212 In a goodly night as in my bed I lay
For when I awoke there was but I alone.
MS. Rawl. C. 813, fol. 47.

1213 In a green arbour's pleasing shade we sat
Than all his gilded trifles and his glitt'ring store.
Chatwin, John, 'Eating cheries with her'.
MS. *Rawl. poet. 94, p. 134 (autogr.).

1214 In a grove most rich of shade
That therewith his heart was broken.
Sidneye, Sr. P[hilip].
Pr. *Englands Helicon*, 1600, p. 145.
MS. Rawl. poet. 85, fol. 34v.

1215 In a large frame made by the limner's art
I carry all these eight with me away.
Bulteel, John, '[ ] Picture'.
MS. *Rawl. poet. 159, fol. 227v.

1216 In a large plain that stretched it self so wide
Th' enraged idea vanished from my thought.
'A Dream at noon'.
MS. Top. Oxon. e. 202, fol. 115.

1217 In a long journey to an unknown clime
And more to tears than sleep inclines my eyes.
'I sate down under his shadow (whome I loved) with great Delight'. *Song of Songs*, ii. 3.
MS. Rawl. D. 1095, fol. 148v rev.

1218 In a maiden time professed
And this was all the Cupid then.
MS. Mus. b. 1, fol. 21, music by John Wilson.

In a melancholy study 1219
Aye aye 'tis thither, thither to I go.
[Wild, Robert].
Pr. *Iter Boreale with . . . other Poems*, 1668, p. 51.
MS. Eng. misc. e. 13, fol. 3v; see also A960.

In a pleasant arbour very quaint and quadrente 1220
For to exalt virtue and put down vice quite.
Subscribed 'finis quoth herry sponar'; composed during the reign of Mary and Philip.
MS. Ashmole 48, fol. 57v.

In a pleasant morning 1221
I'll give thee kisses three.
'A plesante New sonnge called the carmans Whistle: to the tune of o Neighbor Roberte'.
MS. Rawl. poet. 185, fol. 21.

In a poor simple girl 'tis a bold flight 1222
Oh all-sufficient God we shall be full of Thee.
'Heaven', presented by M. A. to Archbishop Sancroft, 1689.
MS. Rawl. poet. 154, two copies, fols. 75 and 96.

In a season all oppressed 1223
Oh no no sweet love I may not.
Printed John Wilson's *Cheerfull Ayres or Ballads*, 1660, p. 36.
MSS. Don. c. 57, fol. 73, music by Wilson; Rawl. poet. 84, fol. 28 rev.

In a true piece of wit all things must be 1224
All creatures dwelt, all creatures that had life.
MS. Rawl. poet. 213, fol. 65v.

In a vale with flowrets spangled 1225
Flowers smile nor fear, thy frosty bosom's blasting.
Pr. John Wilson's *Cheerfull Ayres or Ballads*, 1660, p. 146.
MS. Mus. b. 1, fol. 100v, music by Wilson.

In acting lust we're merry mad; 1226
To sport again we are full glad.
Robinson, Robert.
MS. *Rawl. poet. 218, p. 74 (autogr.).

In Adam's falling by earth's fruit, we must 1227
Should be a Christian's daily meditation.
MS. *Rawl. poet. 97, fol. 22 (autogr.).

In Adriatic seas great Neptune viewed 1228
Venice was built by gods, but Rome by men.
Translation of Latin, *Siderat Hadriacis Venetan Neptunus* [Sannazarius, *Epigrams* I. xxxv].
MS. Top. Oxon. c. 108, p. 23.

1229 In Æsop's time a wretched man we find
He without hairs, and thou without a crown.
'A Fable, reflecting on K. William's struggle . . . 'twixt the Whigs and Tories'.
Pr. Sir Charles Sedley's *Works*, 1776, i. 5.
MS. Rawl. poet. 173, fol. 1.

1230 In all humility we crave
Thanks them as much as if they did.
'The Commons petition' and the King's 'Answer'. Verse 5 of J189, 1642, applied to Charles II.
Pr. *Works of Rochester, Roscommon, etc.*, 1721.
MSS. Ballard 47, fol. 102; Don. b. 8, p. 605; Firth c. 15, p. 16, attr. to E. Rochester; Rawl. poet. 81, fol. 26; Rawl. poet. 173, fol. 116v, attr. to Ld. Rochester.

1231 In all kindness thou (Oh Lord,)
Gold, and silver dross you be.
Herbert, Mary (*née* Sidney,) Countess of Pembroke, Psalm cxix, 'I'.
MSS. *Rawl. poet. 24, p. 180; *25, fol. 121v.

1232 In all man's life he hath no blessed time
Or fool or child so with man aye it fares.
H. S., 'Fragmentum'.
MS. *Rawl. poet. 120, fol. 32*a* (autogr.).

1233 In all our prayers, th' Almighty does regard
To buy his wares by weight, and not by measure.
[Quarles, Francis], 'On Prayer'.
Pr. *Divine Fancies*, 1632, ii. 63.
MS. Rawl. poet. 90, fol. 69v.

1234 In all the ages, since the world began,
Past expectation, of so fair a shape.
MSS. Ashmole 36, 37, fol. 30.

1235 In all the earth no bird than I more white
Though less I speak than thou, yet more I'll write.
'The Controvercy betweene the Crow and the Goose', couplet, from Latin.
MSS. Rawl. D. 954, fol. 42; Rawl. poet. 209, fol. 32v.

1236 In all the legal offerings great regard
In that of glory, they are more divine.
MS. *Rawl. poet. 97, fol. 27 (autogr.).

1237 In amaze
Lofty poet! touch the sky.
Pope, Alexander, 'To Quinbus Flestrin the Man Mountain. A Lilliputian Ode', 1727.
See *Minor Poems*, ed. N. Ault and J. Butt, 1954, p. 266.
MS. Eng. misc. f. 79, p. 96.

In an arbour of honour set full quadrant 1238
When she finds the best let her say it is that.
Wallys, John.
MS. Ashmole 48, fol. 83.

In an armchair reclined at my ease by the fire 1239
He is more to be valued than lacks of rupees.
Parsons, William, 'To Mrs. F. in answer to an Enigma'.
MS. *Don. d. 123, p. 26 (autogr.).

In an erst unused song, 1240*a*
Whom the lord with love affecteth.
Herbert, Mary (*née* Sidney), Countess of Pembroke, Psalm cxlix.
MS. *Rawl. poet. 24, p. 219.

In ancient Greece when Sappho sung 1240*b*
Such as the heavenly sisters sing.
Felton, Henry, of St. Edmund's Hall and Queen's College, on 'a Ladies making a copy of verses'.
Pr. Hearne's *Collections*, ed. C. E. Doble, ii, O.H.S. vii, 1886, p. 58.
MS. Hearne's diaries 15, p. 210.

In ancient times, (as poets sing) 1241*a*
And wedlock's grown a Smithfield-bargain.
'Wedlock'.
MS. Ballard 29, fol. 138v.

[In ancient times, ere Moses wonders wrought] 1241*b*
Nor feel their leaping life's returning tide.
Blackmore, Sir Richard, extract from *Job*, 1700.
MS. Rawl. D. 868, fol. 56.

In ancient times, some hundred winters past, 1242
And boldly prints and publishes her shame.
[Graves, Richard], 'The Heroines or Modern Memoires', referring to *Peregrine Pickle*, 1751.
Attr. to Graves in Dodsley's *Collection of Poems*, iv, 1755, p. 334.
MS. Ballard 37, fol. 28.

In ancient times the friends surviving gave 1243
We find both a good woman, and a wife . . . (incomplete).
MS. Sancroft 59, p. 281 rev.

In ancient times, their heads were crowned with bays 1244
A braver bridegroom and a fairer bride.
Howes, John, chaplain to the dowager Countess of Banbury, Rector of Abingdon, 'An Epithal[am]ium uppon . . . Walter Littleton Esq. and Lady Anna-Maria [Knollys] Daughter of . . . Anne Countesse Dowager of Banbury'; [between March 1673/4 and March 1679/80].
MS. Eng. poet. d. 53, p. 169.

1245 In answer to your kind request
May God both now and ever bless.
Brett, Dr. Thomas (1667–1744), 'The Doctors Answer' [to William Paxton] 1732.
MS. Add. D. 79, fol. 89 rev.

1246 In azure robes is hope depictured fair
That gold's the surest friend we find below.
'On Seeing a Picture of Hope'.
MS. Eng. poet. e. 40, fol. 127.

1247 In beauty or wit
Who have tasted, and robbed the whole tree.
'Upon the Learned Mary Wortly Montague by Dr. Swift'. 'Mr. Pope', crossed out.
MS. Ballard 50, fol. 102ᵛ.

1248 In bed he bathes in fancy's flood
The restless lover lives.
[Price, E. (?)]. Title cut by binder.
MS. *Douce 290, fol. 91, in Price's hand.

1249 In bed I lay forecasting how to live
My stint is past and I must needs begone.
[Throckmorton, Thomas], 'The Life and Death of Sir Nicholas Throckmorton Transcribed Anno Domini 1693'. Douce's note: 'very inaccurately printed [from a different source] in Peck's life of Milton', q.v. (Douce P Subt. 95 *ad. fin.*)
MS. Douce 86.

1250 In bloody town of Newbery
If custard turn manslayer.
'A Ballad on the most Renowned Shuff of Newbery to the Tune of Chevy Chase'.
See R. L'Estrange, *Intelligencer*, 30 May 1664.
MSS. Rawl. D. 316, fol. 65 rev.; Wood F. 34, fol. 182, dated by Wood 1664.

1251 In bond of love we all are tied;
Few for men's deeds are better.
Robinson, Robert.
MS. *Rawl. poet. 218, p. 173 (autogr.).

1252 [In books a guide] In bocas an guyde I rede and fynde
And then I will say nothing.
On the evil qualities of women.
MS. Ashmole 48, fol. 99ᵛ.

1253 In Britain shall be a mitred king
The earth shall swallow thy blood.
Prophecy, partly in rhyme.
MS. Rawl. C. 813, fol. 114.

1254 In but a part of the sixth day the man
Christ in a garden was betrayed for sin.
MS. *Rawl. poet. 97, fol. 17ᵛ (autogr.).

In calm content I lived, a simple maid 1255
And bade her live in softer fetters chained!
Parsons, William, translator, 'From the Asolani of Bembo'.
Pr. *Travelling Recreations*, 1807, i. 198.
MS. *Don. d. 123, p. 267 (autogr.).

In came the herring, the king of the sea 1256
All hands go to sleep, I'll go to smoke.
'The Fishes Lamentation'.
MS. Firth c. 18, fol. 167*c*.

In Canaan, that country opulent, 1257
And so, here an end of this history.
Forrest, William, 'the Hystory of . . . Joseph'.
MS. Eng. poet. d. 9, fol. 7ᵛ (autogr.).

In [Celia's] Caelia's face a question did arise 1258
Weeping or smiling pearls to Caelia's face.
Carew, Thomas, 'Lipps and eyes'.
Pr. *Poems*, 1640; *Wits Recreations*, 1640, 179.
MSS. Eng. poet. c. 50, fol. 71, attr. to T. C.; e. 37, p. 75, attr. to Tho. Carew; f. 25, fol. 15ᵛ; Rawl. poet. 153, fol. 14ᵛ.

In Charles the second's merry days 1259
I'll drink my gallon a day sir.
'Parody on the Song of *The Vicar of Bray*' (note by Philip Bliss, fol. 1).
In B.M. Add. MS. 5832, fol. 146, 'By Thomas Dampier D.D.'
MSS. Add. A. 368, fol. 19; Mus. e. 19, p. 66, with tune.

In chests his thousands Heathcotte keeps; 1260
To some too much, to none enough hast given.
'Epigram. Martial XII. 10. imitated', 1735.
MS. Eng. misc. e. 240, p. 260.

In Christ increase my knowledge (Lord) that thence 1261
Doth all the knowledge of the world exceed.
MS. *Rawl. poet. 97, fol. 27ᵛ (autogr.).

In Christ our life is hid 1262–3
His matchless glories tell.
Beddome, Benjamin.
MS. *Eng. misc. e. 227, fol. 9ᵛ.

In christian hope this body's mould'ring dust 1264
Nor sin nor death shall e'er disturb me more.
Inscription on Anne Willing's tomb at St. Michael's Bristol, 'composed by herself and designed for her Tomb'.
MS. Rawl. D. 1090, fol. 189.

In city and in country town, 1265
High or low, they all are gone.
Robinson, Robert.
MS. *Rawl. poet. 218, p. 50 (autogr.).

1266 In city town and village God you bless
As well the greater, as such as seemen less.
[Caradocke, Edward (?)], lines appended to his poem to Queen Elizabeth, M243.
MS. Rawl. poet. 182, fol. 38.

1267 In close of day, in night betimes
Not out too late at night.
Robinson, Robert.
MS. *Rawl. poet. 218, p. 168 (autogr.).

1268 In colours some delight
All glory to our king.
[Baynes, Sir Thomas], 'The Phylosiphers stone'. Tune: 'Loraines martch'.
For the authorship see B.M. Add. MS. 29921, fol. 78.
MS. Rawl. poet. 37, p. 101.

1269 In confident hope
Eternally with him to live.
Kenton, James.
MS. *Eng. poet. e. 20, p. 122 (autogr.).

1270 In country quarters still confined
I only wake to think on thee.
'A Song'.
MSS. Eng. misc. c. 292, fol. 116v; Montagu e. 13, fol. 29v.

1271 In court and country, ploughman, peer
I could his faith to her commend.
Burton, Francis, 'a sixthe [riddle] of Linnen cloth'.
MS. *Add. A. 267, fol. 6v (autogr.).

1272 In court men longest live, and keep their ranks
By taking injuries, and giving thanks.
Da[niel, Samuel], couplet.
MS. Rawl. poet. 117, fol. 275 rev., attr. to Da[niell].

1273 In Crete when Dedalus first began
Madam your wings then would I clip.
MSS. Mus. d. 184, fol. 19, with a tune, transcribed from B.M. Add. MS. 7578; Rawl. poet. 112, fol. 18 rev.; Tanner 306, fol. 186.

1274*a* In crooked ways and straight paths men do wade:
Of straight and crooked lines men's hearts are made.
Robinson, Robert, couplet.
MS. *Rawl. poet. 218, p. 67 (autogr.).

1274*b* In crystal towers, and turrets richly set
Use you your goods, to live and die with fame.
Whitney, Geoffrey, 'Animus non res'.
MS. *Rawl. poet. 56, fol. 116v.

In cutting off my days I said 1275
Of zeal pay thanks till I expire.
Fairfax, Thomas, Lord, '[Songs of the old and New Testament:] Hezekiah's song. Isaiah 38'.
MS. *Fairfax 40, p. 422 (autogr.).
MS. *Fairfax 38, p. 91.

In dangers great Jehovah grant thee grace 1276
Oh heavenly king, when on thy name we call.
Harington, Sir John, Psalm xx.
MS. *Douce 361, fol. 11v.

In darkest gloom of night 1277
Be thou my parent, guardian, friend.
Skinner, John, 'Part of the 27th Psalm'. 1792.
MS. *Eng. poet. d. 22, two copies, fols. 42 and 122.

In darkest shades I live, and blackest night 1278*a*
And I may live to see the day.
'A Song'.
MS. Malone 13, p. 100.

[In days of old there lived of mighty fame] 1278*b*
The loss of reason, and conclude in rage.
Dryden, John. Extract 'On a Jealouse Lover', from *Palamon and Arcite*. Pr. *Fables*, 1700.
MS. Add. B. 105, fol. 57v.

In days of yore as stories go 1279
Still gives at balls away.
'The Rise and Progress of the English Garter'.
MS. Rawl. poet. 155, p. 198.

In days of yore, by fasting, watching, prayer 1280
Thus modishly are said to watch and pray.
'The Ladies Weekly Preparation. Watch and pray'.
MS. Eng. poet. c. 9, p. 105.

In days of yore, ere luxury was found 1281
Quaffed their brown bowls in gothic bower or hall.
Amherst, Elizabeth, 'Inscriptions intended for Newbold. 1771. . . Over the door of the Gothic banquetting house'.
MS. *Eng. poet. e. 109, p. 63.

In days of yore ere luxury was found 1282
She only with the wise and virtuous dwells.
Amherst, Elizabeth, 'Content and comfort' (title from the Index, p. v).
MS. *Eng. poet. e. 109, p. 85.

1283 In days of yore for ever past
Once knew among her earlier swains . . . (incomplete).
Gough, Richard, 'A Fragment on Wedded Love'.
MS. *Eng. poet. c. 5, fol. 135 (autogr.).

1284 In days of yore in Casses isle
As by their neighbours they were told.
'The Fox and the Ape A Fable'.
MS. Percy c. 8, fol. 158.

1285 In days when birds and beasts did prate
And for the next be hanged.
'The Fable of the Lurcher and the Marrow Puddings', 1712.
Pr. bk. Firth b. 21, fol. 123.

1286 In days when fables first were wrote
Though none can e'er in all excel.
Whaley, John, 'The Linx and the Mole; a Fable'.
Pr. *Poems*, 1732, p. 119.
MS. Rawl. poet. 222, fol. 16v.

1287 In deep distress, I cried to God
Into their inmost caves retire.
Dyer, George.
MS. *Eng. poet. c. 21, fol. 73v.

1288 In dismal horrors of ensuing night
To cast me off because my breast was warm.
'The mad despaire'.
MS. *Rawl. poet. 87, p. 51.

1289 In dogg'rel rhymes we seldom use
Else swear our age wants wit as well as light.
'The Practical Quaker Or the New Lights 1687/8'.
Pr. *Poems on Affairs of State*, I. 1703, ii. 243.
MS. Eng. poet. c. 18, fol. 54v.

1290*a* In doleful shape appeared old Leland's ghost
Hearne, thou hast gained immortal worth and praise.
Edwards, Stephen, 'To . . . Thomas Hearne, . . . in praise of [his] Leland', 12 Nov. 1712.
Pr. Hearne's *Collections*, ed. C. E. Doble, iii, O.H.S. xiii, 1889, p. 483.
MS. Hearne's diaries 40, p. 64*b* (autogr.).

1290*b* In doubt I lived
What faith I lived, or died in.
Epitaph on 'Tho. Middleton The Hog Man's Son'.
MS. Ballard 50, fol. 193.

In early days ere prologues did begin 1291
If satire did not grin and growl and guard the coast.
Shere, Sir Henry, 'The Strowlers Prologue at Cambridge'. 1694.
MSS. Eng. poet. c. 18, fol. 156; e. 50, p. 1, attr. to Sr. H[enry] Sheers; Locke c. 32, fol. 34, attr. to Sir H. Sheers.

In early Greece were art's proud triumphs seen, 1292
Extols th'Athenian spirit of thy choice!
Parsons, William, 'To Sir William Young Bart. on his marriage with Miss Talbot'.
MS. *Don. d. 123, p. 212 (autogr.).

In Egyptian bondage, I 1293
Speak, and say, Behold! tis I!
Kenton, James.
MS. *Eng. poet. e. 20, p. 392 (autogr.).

In eighteen years retiredness records 1294
As well to show His mercy, as His wrath.
MS. *Rawl. poet. 97, fol. 48v (autogr.).

In eighty-eight Spain sent a vast armado 1295
And Namur all your day-light overcast.
'Epigram', 1695.
MS. Rawl. D. 361, fol. 221v.

In elder time [times] an [the] ancient custom was 1296
Lost being mass cross, faith, they find damnation.
[Fitzsimon, Henry, S. J. (?)] 'Of Othes'.
First pr. *The Justification and Exposition of the Divine Sacrifice of the Masse*, Douay, 1611; see L. I. Guiney, *Recusant Poets*, 1938, p. 324; pr. Sir John Harington's *Epigrams*, 1633, iv. 9.
MSS. Add. B. 97, fol. 39, attr. to Ben Jonson; Ashmole 36, 37, two copies, fols. 117v and 126; 1463, p. 2; Douce f. fol. 34; Malone 19, p. 51; Rawl. poet. 31, fol. 3; see also I1426.

In emblems oft have been express'd 1297
And in the other may you find the same.
Amherst, Elizabeth, 'On [Miss Monk] going to see Fireworks at Ollantigh in Kent'.
MS. *Eng. poet. e. 109, p. 12.

In England London is the chiefest town 1298
The second place York claimeth as its own.
Couplet, translation from Latin.
MS. Lat. misc. c. 19, p. 431.

In England, we religions have so many, 1299
In truth they're nothing, could the truth be found.
Robinson, Robert.
MS. *Rawl. poet. 218, p. 55 (autogr.).

1300 In envy's face discern I this
'Tis the sin peculiar to the devil.
Fairfax, Thomas, Lord, 'Of Envy'.
MS. *Fairfax 40, p. 572 (autogr.).
MS. *Fairfax 38, p. 264.

1301 In every age, in every land,
Sleep in trunk-linings, soar on kites!
Parsons, William, 'Written to a lady at Bath'.
MS. *Don. d. 123, p. 140 (autogr.).

1302 In every empire, kingdom, country, state
Within their hearts, that it renewed with pain.
F. W., 'Sonnet 13', of the joys of heaven.
MS. *Rawl. C. 639, p. 59.

1303 In every faith, in every sect,
By strife in war they're still opprest.
Robinson, Robert.
MS. *Rawl. poet. 218, p. 129 (autogr.).

1304 In every heart thy form does passion move,
Saved the bright nymph, and what he saved enjoyed.
'Epigram'.
MS. Top. Oxon. c. 108, p. 15.

1305 In every house in every place, as every one can tell
An enemy I to nobody am, let nobody go to the devil.
'Of Nobody'.
MS. Eng. poet. e. 14, fol. 21.

1306 In evil hour and with unhallowed voice
Such as the wise and good might wish to share.
Crowe, William, of New College, Public Orator, verses for the installation of the Duke of Portland as Chancellor of Oxford University, 4 July 1793. Suppressed.
MSS. Add. A. 272, fol. 50; Top. Oxon. c. 236, fol. 15.

1307 In extremes bold counsels are the best
And by th'event condemned, or justified.
MS. Sancroft 85, p. 281 rev.

1308 In extremity and when
Swelling with too stiff a gale.
Translation of the last verse of Horace, *Odes* II. x. in a letter 'to Sir Edward Cooke Upon his fall'.
MS. Jones 56, fol. 123.

1309 In fairest gardens springs up many a weed,
And tares and cockle grow amongst good seed.
Robinson, Robert, couplet.
MS. *Rawl. poet. 218, p. 81 (autogr.).

In faith good Histor long is your delay 1310
To speak with her while freely speak we may.
Sidney, Sir Philip, from the *Arcadia*.
MS. *e Mus. 37, fol. 144ᵛ.

In faith I love thee but I cannot sue 1311
I'll freely spend my thrice decocted blood.
'To his Mrs.'
MS. Rawl. poet. 199, p. 9.

In faith I never was but once so mad 1312
Or I'll be as indifferent as she.
Flatman, Thomas, 'Song Set by Mr. Wm. Gregory. Apr. 29. 1664'.
MS. *Firth d. 7, fol. 24.

In famous year of eighty-eight 1313
He had swung for petty larceny.
Collier, Jeremy. 'The copy of verses transcrib'd from his own Original Manuscript'.
MS. Eng. hist. d. 220, fol. 131.

In Feverere upon a night 1314
Full well had they known the son of a Bray.
Gough, Richard, 'A Tale. 1755', about Woodman and Spede.
MS. *Eng. poet. c. 5, fol. 79 (autogr.).

In field of broom unseen 1315
I'll watch and give thee mine.
'Polwarth Thorn'.
MS. Eng. poet. e. 8, fol. 5.

In fields of blood, and feats of arms 1316
Lie in the bed of honour!
Parsons, William, verses 'on seeing Miss Honoria Gubbins at . . . Bath'.
Pr. *Travelling Recreations*, 1807, ii. 129.
MS. *Don. d. 123, p. 235 (autogr.).

In flames of grief, not love, I write to thee 1317
Thou canst no more declare my raging will.
Moore, Thomas, 'Hercules to Deianira', answer to Ovid's epistle.
MS. *Rawl. poet. 3, fol. 54 (autogr.).

In flowered meads as late I walked in May 1318
Where peace is perpetual blest is that city.
Mills, Rob[ert], 'A songe in the praise of peace by the same author R. M.'
MS. Rawl. poet. 85, fol. 82.

In friendship nothing feigned or false should be, 1319
Who would be sought to, can his friend forsake.
'Of Friendship'.
MS. Rawl. poet. 90, fol. 131.

In fruitful field, amid the goodly crop, 1320
And weigh the bad, no better than the weeds.
Whitney, Geoffrey, 'Sic discerne'.
MS. *Rawl. poet. 56, fol. 40

1321 In fruitless expectation to remain
And tasted, makes their muse herself exceed.
North, Dudley, 3rd Baron.
Pr. *A Forest of Varieties*, 1645.
MS. *North e. 41, fol. 30.

1322 In full flowing bowls while the liquor does smile
Had all been our own and the Havanna too.
'To the Tune of the Miller of Mansfield'.
Opposition ballad, *c.* 1740.
MS. Eng. poet. c. 41, fol. 63.

1323 In getting much we get more care
Is to preserve their health.
'Wealth and Povertie'.
MS. Rawl. poet. 172, fol. 7.

1324 In giving charity or food
And to your self that you do none.
'Question and Answer'.
MS. Percy c. 8, fol. 132v.

1325 In gloomy darkness where eternal night
Despair must part the fray and end my life.
MSS. Ashmole 36, 37, fol. 201.

1326 In god our strength our heart rejoices
Yea honey should from stones have stilled.
Harington, Sir John, Psalm lxxxi.
MS. *Douce 361, fol. 49v.

1327 In god the lord be glad and light,
His truth doth still remain.
[Hopkins, John], Psalm c.
MS. Rawl. poet. 112, fol. 42v rev.

1328 In God the Lord I put my trust,
The brightness of his face.
Psalm xi.
MS. *Montagu e. 10, fol. 2v.

1329 In God's own name his servants preach
Complaining to their Lord.
Beddome, Benjamin.
MS. *Eng. misc. e. 227, fol. 46v.

1330 In God's word we most sweet coherence find
Who, that the soul immortal is, decline.
MS. *Rawl. poet. 97, fol. 52v (autogr.).

1331 In good faith I am no saint,
Was subject unto love.
MS. Rawl. poet. 108, fol. 16v.

1332 In good king Charles's golden days,
I will be the Vicar of Bray, Sir.
'Vicar of Bray'.
MSS. Eng. poet. f. 12, p. 131; Top. Oxon. b. 170, fol. 14v.

In good king George's peaceful days 1333
To use wit in one's anger.
'A Ballad. 1723. Lechmere and Cadogan'.
Pr. bk. Firth b. 22, fol. 26.

In good truth old Nick 1334
The parson thy self and brother.
'At the Election at Warwick when Sir W[illiam] Keyte and Mr. Delves stood May 1722'.
MS. Ballard 47, fol. 44.

In grave apparel gravity we find; 1335
Lightness of garments lightness shows of mind.
Robinson, Robert, couplet.
MS. *Rawl. poet. 218, p. 165 (autogr.).

In great humility and poverty 1336
He still alike with th'Holy Ghost was fraught.
MS. *Rawl. poet. 97, fol. 42 (autogr.).

In great St. Hellens here lies Sir John 1337
But by his own faith, and so do the Turkes.
On Sir John Spencer.
MS. Eng. poet. e. 14, fol. 95 rev.

In greatest storms, and depth of winter weather 1338
And drive them from their dwellings, from their lives.
Robinson, Robert.
MS. *Rawl. poet. 218, p. 162 (autogr.).

In Greece seven famous wise men once was found 1339
Or Rome's imperious, unjust usurpation.
'Englands Worthys. The VII Clergy Champions'. 1688.
Pr. bk. Firth b. 20, fol. 132.

In Greenwich 'tis, where beauties wondrous fair, 1340
Stop here, my muse, with an, *etcaetera*.
MS. Eng. poet. c. 41, fols. 68v, 67r, v, 68r.

In grey-haired Celia's withered arms 1341
*Te deum* sing in quiet.
'On the Fr[ench] king and Madam Maintenon', 1692.
Pr. *Poems on Affairs of State*, iii, 1698, p. 103.
MSS. Eng. poet. c. 18, fol. 125, attr. to Ld. Dorset; Rawl. poet. 173, fol. 61v, attr. to Mr. Dryden.

In grief and troubles which afflict me sore, 1342
From those that hold us in such scorn?
Knollys, Fra., Psalm cxxiii.
MS. *Rawl. poet. 60, p. 63 (autogr.).

In guilty night and hid in false disguise 1343
Thou and thy sons shall be with me beneath.
'The Witch of Endor'.
MSS. Don. c. 57, fol. 8v, music by Robert Ramsey; Rawl. C. 580, fol. 21v.

1344 In harmony was that enchanting power
And faith their gains would make one think they do.
'On harmony', 1735.
MS. Eng. misc. e. 240, p. 314.

1345 In hasty minds the froth is apt to rise,
Begins in season, and concludes with praise.
Williams, John, 'Another' to Mrs. Matthews.
MS. *Rawl. poet. 192, fol. 157 (autogr.).

1346 In hasty wedlock are many miscarriages,
Lust doth breed beggars more, than love makes marriages.
Robinson, Robert, couplet.
MS. *Rawl. poet. 218, p. 31 (autogr.).

1347 In head and face, is Aries' place
And do the rest no wrong.
Lilliat, John, 'How the 12 signes governe in Mans bodie', translation from Antonius Mizaldus, *Zodiaci Liber Secundus*, 1553, Sig. D1.
MS. Rawl. poet. 148, fol. 111 (autogr.).

1348 In health and wealth and money store,
The wretched wordling saith.
Robinson, Robert.
MS. *Rawl. poet. 218, p. 85 (autogr.).

1349 In health for wealth we're at continual strife
When sick we'd live, yet weary are of life.
Robinson, Robert, 'litigosa vita est mors terribilis'. Couplet.
MS. *Rawl. poet. 218, p. 3 (autogr.).

1350 In heaven bright maid, that bliss receive
Thou goodness art below.
'Ode to Humanity'.
MS. Eng. poet. e. 47, p. 44.

1351 In Heaven is order, and in earth below
'Twixt prince and people, husband and the wife.
Robinson, Robert.
MS. *Rawl. poet. 218, p. 155 (autogr.).

1352 In heaven life's free from intermission
We live to die and die to live for ever.
MS. Rawl. poet. 89, fol. $5^v$.

1353 In heaven or in hell is
Here it lieth in the grave.
Epitaph on John Ellis.
MS. Wood D. 19(2), fol. 109.

In Heaven when bright Apollo tuned the spheres 1354
If both to him and you we wish the quire of Heaven.
Strode, William, 'A Song at the Musicke Lecture in the Act'.
See Wood, *Annals*, 1626, and 'Lectures', Heather's Music Lecture, in *History and Antiquities of the University of Oxford*, ed. J. Gutch, II. ii, 1796.
MS. *CCC. 325, fol. $89^v$ (autogr.).

In hell damned soul, fire, smoke and stench appear 1355
Then this is hell, for these four things are here.
Couplet.
MS. Rawl. D. 1372, fol. 16 from end.

In hell of late [did grow] there fell [there grew] a [some] great disorder 1356
If hell were pleased to bring his clerk unto him.
'On [Sir Antony] Ben Recorder of London and his Clarke', 1618.
MSS. Ashmole 38, p. 190; Don. d. 58, fol. $17^v$; Douce f. 5, fol. $10^v$; Eng. poet. e. 14, fol. 94 rev.; f. 10, fol. 93; Malone 19, p. 58; Rawl. poet. 152, fol. 16.

In hemp was his faith, and in Tyburn his hope 1357*a*
He lived by the gallows, and he died by a rope.
'An Epitaph on Jack Ketch', couplet.
MS. Eng. poet. e. 40, fol. 2.

In Henly knap to hunt me King James Prince Henry found me 1357*b*
Cornebury Parke river to end their hunting drowned me.
Couplet on a stag at Ditchley, killed by James I, 22 August 1610.
MS. Hearne's diaries 67, p. 29.

In her fair cheek two pits do lie 1358
For if thou let me live I die.
[Carew, Thomas].
Pr. *Poems*, 1640.
MS. Rawl. poet. 142, fol. $15^v$; see also I1655.

In her fair face ten thousand graces play 1359
With fair Clarinda I my verse will crown.
'Es quam petis', 25 Oct. 1734.
MS. Eng. misc. e. 240, p. 72.

In her the spirit of contradiction lies 1360
Shall have the time to know her taste the rue.
Beaumont, Thomas, 'To A Lady that in scorne sent Another A posie wherin was Time, hartseas, and rue'.
MS. *Malone 18, p. 75 (autogr.).

In his own house a fool is wiser far 1361
Then in another's the most wise men are.
Bulteel, John, couplet.
MS. *Rawl. poet. 159, fol. $214^v$.

1362 In histories of old to read
To bring us to the bliss.
A ballad of the murder of Lewes and Edmond West by John [Lord Darcy 1558] and George, sons of Lord Darcy of Aston.
MS. Ashmole 48, fol. 31.

1363 In hoary state now winter reigns
But an old lover is a jest.
'Winter, A Ballad'.
MS. Eng. poet. e. 8, fol. 10v.

1364 In holies all oh laud the Lord most holy
Oh praise the Lord all things that breathe.
Harington, Sir John, Psalm cl.
MS. *Douce 361, fol. 92v.

1365 In honour to thy memory, bless'd shade
And yearly celebrate Saint Martin's day.
Fenny Stratford Chapel, inscription, *c.* 1730.
MS. Top. Oxon. b. 116, fol. 120.

1366 In hope of speedy resurrection,
Condemned and sentenced thus she died.
'An Epitaph on Passive Obedience Executed . . . By . . . Warrant from 6 or 7 Bpps', 1688. Cf. B365.
MS. Add. A. 301, fol. xvv; see also I1368, I1370.

1367 In hope the shipman hoisteth sail
To every troubled mind.
'Hope'.
MS. Rawl. poet. 172, fol. 6v.

1368 In hopes of a sudden resurrection
Was antichristian-self-denial.
'An Epitaph upon Passive Obedience', 1688.
MS. Rawl. poet. 173, fol. 126v; see also I1366, I1370.

1369 In hopes of getting more some spend
And time for no man will attend.
Williams, John, 'Deceits in trade, and hindrances of thriving'.
MS. *Rawl. poet. 193, fol. 63v (autogr.).

1370 In hopes of sudden resurrection
Was antichristian self denial.
'An Epitaph on Passive Obedience Executed 1688'.
Pr. *Poems on Affairs of State*, iii, 1698, p. 75.
MSS. Eng. poet. c. 18, fol. 59; Firth e. 6, fol. 24; d. 13, fol. 48; Smith 27, p. 55; see also I1366, I1368.

1371 In human state, while Christ was here beneath
Than those who are alive and hate His word.
MS. *Rawl. poet. 97, fol. 56v (autogr.).

In humble prayer I always find 1372
Lord can I trust in him and die.
Beddome, Benjamin.
MS. *Eng. misc. e. 227, fol. 82.

In Huz a land which near the sun's uprise 1373
'Tis he who arms against a mortal bears . . . (incomplete).
'A Paraphrase upon Job', ending vi. 4.
MS. Rawl. B. 14, fol. 54.

In jeopardy the brave Cornwallis mark! 1374
The best of operas, in these worst of times.
'The Comfort of Taste. 23 Nov. 1781. Public Advertiser'.
Pr. bk. Firth b. 22, fol. 69.

In jeopardy we live, our warfare is 1375
Not thine but others' blame might then appear.
Cromwell, Edward, 'Be not overcome of Evil, but overcome Evil with good'.
MS. *Rawl. poet. 165, fol. 34 (autogr.).

In Jewry god is known 1376
Of thee they stand in awe.
Harington, Sir John, Psalm lxxvi.
MS. *Douce 361, fol. 45v.

In Judah is God known, his name 1377
Great princes overthrows.
Psalm lxxvi.
MS. *Rawl. C. 113, fol. 54.

In Judah's god in Israel his name's known 1378
Bring you your presents, thankful hearts return.
Fairfax, Thomas, Lord, Psalm lxxvi.
MS. *Fairfax 40, p. 171 (autogr.).
MS. *Fairfax 38, p. 250.

In June when insects flushed with sun 1379
With which mankind make such ado.
'The Fly and the Snufftaker. A Fable'.
MS. Eng. poet. d. 152, fol. 26v.

In L—d street not far from B—n lane 1380
Though the wise know, they but mere nothings are.
'On a Sempstress making mouths at a Gentleman'.
MS. Top. London e. 9, p. 21.

In life is pleasure and in life is pain 1381
When life's no more, no more of them remain.
Robinson, Robert, couplet.
MS. *Rawl. poet. 218, p. 11 (autogr.).

In life remember death 1382
In all thy works remember . . . (incomplete).
Used as a copy by Wiman Ramsey, *c.* 1595.
MS. Rawl. D. 649, fol. 10.

1383 In life upright, and therefore rightly good
One Sun remained, the truest sun declined,
Ford, John, 'Anagramma ex Camdeno. Carolus Bluntus', from 'The Earle of Devonshire deceased'.
Pr. *Fames Memorial*, 1606, at end.
Pr. bk. Malone 238, at end, licensed fair copy.

1384 In life with what surprising turns we meet,
Or truth believe, when justice is unjust.
'Epigram. On one Mrs. Justice convicted of shop-lifting'.
MS. Eng. poet. c. 9, p. 97.

1385 In life's unactive wane your shades forsake,
Wounded and maimed to your old nest.
'Disswasion of an Aged Friend from Leaving his Retirement'.
MS. Rawl. poet. 90, fol. 121$^v$.

1386 In limpid streams a thousand forms we spy,
The bright, ecstatic sense at once is lost.
'A Simile for the Ladies'.
MS. Ballard 50, fol. 113.

1387 In lingering love misliking grows
God send all lingerers happy chance.
'Of lingeringe love'.
Pr. John Lyly, *Works*, ed. R. W. Bond, 1902, iii. 463 (doubtful attribution).
MS. Rawl. poet. 148, fol. 62$^v$.

1388 In loftier lays, let loftier poets sing,
And reap the fruit of virtuous toil above.
M[erric]k, Mr., 'On Virtue, Letter to a Friend'.
MS. Eng. poet. e. 39, p. 160.

1389 In [Lombardy's] Lumbardy's land great Modena's duchess
Perhaps in Count Dago's and make her a mother.
Satire on James II's having no heir; from an imperfect copy.
MS. Douce 357, fol. 149$^v$.

1390 In love I spend my doleful days,
And all to please thy wanton will.
Andrews, —.
MS. *Rawl. poet. 92, fol. 12$^v$.

1391 In love thou livedst loved as my life dear spouse
Least with these lines should perish thy due praise.
Burton, Francis, 'An Epitaph'.
MS. *Add. A. 267, fol. 30$^v$ (autogr.).

1392*a* In love's name, you are charged hereby.
And leave the world without a soul.
Shirley, James, 'Loves Hue and Crye'.
Pr. *Poems*, 1646, p. 7.
MS. *Rawl. poet. 88, p. 23.

In lower stations all like dangers run 1392*b*
The thread (when cut) they both same scissors feel.
Fairfax, Thomas, Lord, 'Of Impartial Fate'.
MS. *Fairfax 38, p. 265; see also H1130.

In Ludgate here a complete year 1393
They ever laid us here.
'Mr. Wm. Hemminges being In prison In Ludgate wrights thus'.
MS. Ashmole 38, p. 39.

In [Lybia] Libia land as stories tell was bred and born 1394
Nay then quoth she if you love me come trim my train again.
MS. Rawl. poet. 85, fol. 4$^v$.

In making bodies love could not express 1395
God made man greater while He made him less.
Traherne, Thomas, 'Poem upon Moderation . . . som part of the verses are these'.
MS. Eng. th. e. 50, fol. 50$^v$ (autogr.).

In Manlius' reign, oh vessel sprung with me 1396
And drive the night stars from the day-light skies.
W. A., translator, Horace, *Odes* III. xxi.
MS. *Rawl. poet. 104, fol. 31$^v$ (autogr.).

In marriage may be matched full well, 1397
The middle, and the last vowel.
'Stellae, monostichon', Latin, translated into an English couplet.
MSS. Ashmole 36, 37, fol. 153$^v$.

In Matthew's gospel Christ doth show 1398
And bring them to Jerusalem.
Forman, Simon, 'Howe the Jews shallbe called'.
MS. Ashmole 802, fol. 103 (autogr.).

In meats and drink, and in thy dress 1399
And little brings too less.
Robinson, Robert, 'Strive not to exceed'.
MS. *Rawl. poet. 218, p. 86 (autogr.).

In meditation where I sat 1400
Sith thou hast bought me so dear.
MS. Eng. poet. b. 5, p. 12.

In Mercury of London, it lately appears 1401
Than thus to be balked by the men of the feather.
Lines following 'Advertisement in the City Mercury. Feb. 1693'.
MS. Eng. poet. e. 50, p. 69.

In mercy, Lord, shower down thy grace, 1402
And all the world shall him adore.
Psalm lxvii.
MS. *Rawl. C. 113, fol. 47$^v$.

1403 **In metre so sweet**
**We must all take our turn to wear flannel.**
'Crambo in Praise of Flannel'.
Dated 1771 in B.M. Add. MS. 28102, fol. 213.
MS. Eng. poet. c. 51, p. 193.

1404 **In Milford Lane near to St. Clement's Steeple**
**A commonwealth their government shall be.**
Savile, Henry, 'A Duel between two Monsters'.
Pr. *Poems on Affairs of State*, 1703, i. 201.
MS. Eng. poet. c. 18, fol. 21.

1405 **In mind I laboured whilst my life did last**
**Took me away, then all my work was done.**
Freind, John, 'English verses. of . . . John Emmott who d. 30 Sept. 1671'. Acrostic.
MS. Top. Oxon. f. 31, p. 308.

1406 **In mirth be wise, in trouble patience use**
**In dangers meek, and no man's aid refuse.**
Couplet.
MS. Rawl. poet. 172, fol. 11.

1407 **In mischief why oh mighty man**
**Thy saints do all commend.**
Psalm lii.
MS. *Rawl. C. 113, fol. 39ᵛ.

1408 **In morn of May sometime be glad**
**But what where art thou, oh so ho.**
MS. Rawl. poet. 65, fol. 34ᵛ.

1409 **In my conceit Sir John you were to blame**
**To make your quiet good-wife, a mad-dame.**
'A Cuntry Farmer knighted', couplet.
Pr. *Wits Recreations*, 1640, sig. F4.
MSS. Ashmole 38, p. 148; CCC. 328, fol. 43ᵛ; Don. c. 54, fol. 2; Douce f. 5, fol. 18ᵛ; Eng. poet. d. 152, fol. 103ᵛ.

1410 **In my dark cell, low prostrate on the ground**
**And your racked soul be calmly hushed to peace.**
Madan, Judith (*née* Cowper), 'Abelard to Eloisa, answer to Eloisa to Abelard by Mr. Pope'.
In B.M. Add. MS. 28101, fol. 150, attr. to Mrs. Judith Madan, 1720.
MSS. Eng. poet. e. 40, fol. 88, attr. to Col. Madden's Lady. late Miss Cooper; Montagu e. 13, fol. 82ᵛ, attr. to Mrs. Madden, alias Julia Cowper; Top. London e. 9, p. 146.

1411 **In my distress unto the Lord I cried**
**They (prompted on by fury) threaten war.**
Fairfax, Thomas, Lord, Psalm cxx.
MS. *Fairfax 40, p. 326 (autogr.).
MS. *Fairfax 38, p. 423.

**In my heart is there nothing of remembrance** 1412
**To truth that sowneth and so I conclude.**
MS. Rawl. poet. 36, fol. 5ᵛ.

**In my love's world, the great world I descry,** 1413
**Save only harvest which I never saw.**
Ch. M., Sonnett 14.
MS. Eng. misc. d. 239, fol. 9.

**In my master's work employed** 1414
**To the Paradise above.**
Kenton, James.
MS. *Eng. poet. e. 20, p. 186 (autogr.).

**In my minority I thought mankind** 1415
**Then drown'd in tears most pensively I sat . . .** (incomplete).
Hulse, Thomas, 'Surgit post Nubila Phoebus'.
MS. *Rawl. poet. 152, fol. 90 (autogr.).

**In my perplexity shall I** 1416
**And guide my wand'ring footsteps right.**
Kenton, James.
MS. *Eng. poet. e. 20, p. 132 (autogr.).

**In native innocence arrayed** 1417
**May tend to lift us up to heaven.**
Kenton, James.
MS. *Eng. poet. e. 20, p. 354 (autogr.).

**In nature strange, a monster bred I am** 1418
**My name, thou art an other Oedipus.**
'Riddle'.
MS. Rawl. poet. 217, fol. 78ᵛ.

**In nature's pieces still I see** 1419
**You Gods teach her some more humanity.**
[Carew, Thomas], 'A device. Mrs. X'.
Pr. *Poems*, 1640.
MS. Rawl. poet. 160, fol. 106.

**In [Nineveh] Nenevie old Toby dwelt** 1420
**With mirth and joy that was not small.**
[Ballad of Tobias], licensed 14 Dec. 1624.
Pr. *Roxburghe Ballads*, ii, ed. W. Chappell, 1872, p. 621; and see note in H. E. Rollins, *Old English Ballads*, 1920, p. 219.
MS. Eng. poet. b. 5, p. 39.

**In nonage of a winter's day** 1421
**So winter took his former seat.**
Munsey, W., 'On a gentlewoman going a frost-biting'.
MS. Rawl. poet. 210, fol. 53.

**In nothing base or mean dare to confide** 1422
**But crowned with joy in peace and plenty sleep.**
'Rules for the Conduct of Humane Life under 5 Heads'.
MS. Rawl. poet. 102, fol. 1.

1423 In old Procruste's bed, confin'd to grave?
So we must e'en think of plain truth, or new.
Roach, Richard, incomplete copy of 'Reflections' on Roach's own book, *The Great Crisis*, pr. 1725, issued 1727.
MS. Rawl. D. 832, fol. 160 (autogr.).

1424 In old times an old prophecy found in a bog
For Talbott's a dog and Terconell's an ass.
'A Prophesie'.
MS. Firth c. 16, p. 145; see also T1760.

1425 In old times past in Bethany
Was man's salvation wrought.
MS. Eng. poet. b. 5, p. 92.

1426 In older times an ancient custom was
Mass, cross, faith, troth then comes damnation.
[Harington, Sir John.] 'of swearinge'.
MS. Ashmole 47, fol. 47; see also I1296.

1427 In open shops flies often blow that flesh
Like road-ways lie between your lips and laps.
MS. Sancroft 53, p. 368 rev.

1428 In other conflicts numbers may prevail
Not knowing which to choose they set us free.
On Lady Coventry, the Duchess of Hamilton, and Miss Kitty Gunning, daughters of John Gunning. *c.* 1752.
MS. Firth b. 4, fol. 52$^{v}$.

1429 In others, faults we spy, and them we blame,
Which in our selves we see not, though the same.
Robinson, Robert, couplet.
MS. *R wl. poet. 218, p. 174 (autogr.).

1430 In our Father's house above
Oh Jesus quickly come.
Kenton, James.
MS. *Eng. poet. e. 20, p. 181 (autogr.).

1431 In our forefathers' stupid days, the name
Our modern misses are full nine and forty.
'The modern Miss'.
MS. Eng. misc. e. 219, fol. 8$^{v}$.

1432 In our great Jesus was all wisdom's store
Jesus would not have let his friends live so.
Pr. *Jesus præfigured*, John Abbot, 1623 (see Allison and Rogers, 1).
MS. Eng. poet. b. 5, p. 97.

1433 In our yard in frost and snow
Was the charming London life.
'A Mock Song' (no tune).
MS. Mus. Sch. G. 636, fol. 93$^{v}$ rev.

1434 In outward means the God I seek
And tell me Thou art love.
Kenton, James.
MS. *Eng. poet. e. 20, p. 136 (autogr.).

In paper case 1435
Pray think of yours in time.
[Gough, Richard (?)], 'On the Death of a beloved Dormouse [*c.* 1747] . . . publisht in a News-paper'.
MS. *Eng. poet. c. 5, fol. 32, in R. Gough's hand.

In paradise of late a dame began 1436
Desire had slept and I had laid at ease.
'Commendations of his mistris'.
MS. Rawl. poet. 172, fol. 3.

In Paul's churchyard in London 1437
[Frights worse than an inquisition].
Triplett, Thomas, ballad on Dr. Alexander Gill the younger, of St. Paul's School.
MSS. Aubrey 8, fol. 52, attr. to Thomas Triplett; Rawl. poet. 84, fol. 52 rev.

In peascod time when hound to horn 1438
Do rise through want of sleep.
[Churchyard, Thomas].
Headed 'The Sheepheards slumber' in *England's Helicon*, 1600, Sig. Z3.
Pr. *Churchyardes Chance*, 1580, p. 13.
MS. Rawl. poet. 85, fol. 51.

In Phillis I commend what calls for praise 1439
For the same words say different things to them.
Williams, John, to Phyllis, draft.
MS. *Rawl. poet. 191, fol. 3 (autogr.).

In pious times ere buggering did begin 1440
Be it their next care to look after me.
'Jenny Cromwells Complaint against Sodomy', 1692.
MSS. Eng. poet. c. 18, fol. 132; e. 49, p. 130.

In pious times ere priestcraft did begin 1441
Crowds mourned their error and obeyed their lord.
Dryden, John, 'Absolon and Achitophel a Poem', pr. Nov. 1681.
MSS. Add. B. 8, fol. 67, dated 1682; Rawl. poet. 12, fol. 70, attr. to Mr. John Dryden, dated 1693.

In pity to thy pains pleuritic 1442
And screw you up a pinch-note higher.
Lumby, John, 'To J. G.'
MS. *Eng. poet. e. 42, fol. 53.

In place where godly men do comen ever 1443
Fools become wise and the wise wiser.
Couplet.
MS. Gough Norfolk 43, fol. 45.

1444 In points of faith some undetermined jars
And yet both mourned, because both won the day.
Heylin, Peter, translator of 'Verses on [John] Reynolds and [William] his Brother' by W. Alabaster.
Pr. *Cosmography*, 1652, p. 257.
MSS. Eng. poet. f. 13, fol. 46$^v$; Tanner 306, fol. 139$^v$.

1445 In praise (through Christ) of grace and mercy free
And then shall hear, come thou for ever blest.
Memorial lines in Acton church, subscribed 'Philip Skippon', on Mrs. Mary Skippon, d. 24 Jan. 1655 (?).
MS. Rawl. D. 896, fols. 30 and 31$^v$.

1446 In pride of youth and heat of flesh and blood
The time then fits to think of thy offences.
MS. e Mus. 227, fol. 4$^v$.

1447 In prime of summer when as all in a fiery fury
Such many days oh such many noons Jove grant to befall me.
Mills, Robert, 'Ovids Corinna Amorum i. [v] translated Para: into Englishe Hex'.
MS. Rawl. poet. 85, fol. 81.

1448 In prime of youth when love was young
I'll say no more because I loved her.
'Tho: Say:', (composer) amongst 'Dyttyes to the Lute and Violl de Gambo'. A different version of O1118.
MS. Douce 280, fol. 68.

1449 In prosperous state let not thy mind soar high
But all as exiles must the world forget.
W. A., translator, Horace, *Odes* II. iii.
MS. *Rawl. poet. 104, fol. 14 (autogr.).

1450 In public Lord thy praise I'll sing
They only wise his statutes heed.
Fairfax, Thomas, Lord, Psalm cxi.
MS. *Fairfax 40, p. 289 (autogr.); see also I243*b*.

1451 In pursuit of his heifer once wandered a swain
Can you see a white heifer I've looked for all day?
Parsons, William, translator, 'The Clown who had lost his heifer from Fontaine'.
MS. *Don. d. 123, p. 61 (autogr.).

1452 In quest of Adriatic stores
For which the wife is sold.
'Quære Peregrinum'.
MS. Percy c. 8, fol. 25.

1453 In reading of the sacred writ, beware
Thou climb no stile, when as a gap stands fair.
Couplet, 'On the readinge of the scripture'.
MS. Rawl. poet. 117, fol. 171$^v$ rev.

In reading these my Lord you'll see I've got 1454
When I your favour and your person see.
Satire on prison life.
MS. Malone 23, p. 58.

In restless state he lives that loves 1455
And nox (that Phæbus rays doth dim) . . . wight (incomplete).
[Price, E. (?)], 'The Description of a lover'.
MS. Douce 290, fol. 89, in Price's hand.

In rhyme again? 'Tis but short warning, 1456
And so I wish you all good night.
Lumby, John, 'to R. P.'
MS. *Eng. poet. e. 42, fol. 89.

In riches titles, honours, see her soar 1457
Her pastry lasting, as a chancery suit.
'Countess of Hardwicke', 'Dead' (d. 1761).
MS. *Eng. poet. e. 28, p. 31.

In rosy morn I saw Aurora red 1458
Far speedier execution than the sun.
Fairfax, Thomas, Lord, 'Shortness of Life'.
MS. *Fairfax 40, p. 594 (autogr.).
MS. *Fairfax 38, p. 261.

[In rural strains we first our music try] 1459
And gives the swelling tones a manly grace.
Philips, Ambrose, lines from *Pastorals*, 1710, v, p. 19.
Pr. by Curll, *Miscellanea*, 1727, i. 47.
MS. Rawl. letters 90, fol. 34.

In sable weeds, the beaux and belles appear; 1460
Had Sorrell stumbled thirteen years ago.
'An answer to the Mock Mourner'.
Pr. *Poems on Affairs of State*, ii, 1703, p. 320. *Cf.* Y35. Attr. to B. Higgons, B.M. first-line-index.
MSS. Mus. Sch. C. 81, fol. 24; Rawl. D. 361, fol. 55; Rawl. poet. 169, fol. 9$^v$; 173, fol. 129; Smith 23, p. 107.

In sad and ashy weeds 1461
Let me condole his woe.
'On the death of Prince Henry', 1612.
Pr. *The Crowne Garland of Golden Roses*, 1631. Attr. to Anne Howard, Lodge's *Illustrations of British History*, 1791.
MSS. Don. d. 58, fol. 21$^v$; Rawl. poet. 160, fol. 26.

[In Saint Bede's books] In Saynt Bedes bokes writen er stories olde 1462
The fled out of Wales away tille Ireland.
Robert Mannyng of Brunne, the opening lines of Peter Langtoft's Chronicle, as printed by Hearne, 1725.
MS. Ballard 62, p. 131.

1463 In Salem dwelt a glorious king
And all his joys above the stars admire.
Traherne, Thomas, 'The Third Century', 69.
MS. Eng. th. e. 50, fol. 60 (autogr.).

1464 In Saturn's reign, at nature's early birth
And anxious cares, a never-ending train.
P[enrose, John, of Exeter Coll., Oxford (?)], translation of Hesiod, Sep. 1734.
MS. Eng. misc. e. 240, pp. 30, 35, and 40 (autogr.).

1465 In Saturn's reign, at nature's early birth
Rather than fail, the dagger does the deed.
Dryden, John, 'The Sixt Satyr of Juvenal'.
Pr. *Examen Poeticum*, 1693.
MS. Rawl. poet. 152, fol. 91.

1466 In scripture, Sir, 'tis said, we must
I took a deal of pains, to make it.
L[epipre (?)], Miss, 'Verses by Miss L. to Cornet F. on his falling down an Breacking his Nose. Sent him with a Clay Nose'. 2 Jan. 1747/8.
MS. Eng. poet. e. 40, fol. 51.

1467 In search of wisdom far from wit I fly
And, wed with wisdom, lead a happy life.
Philips, Ambrose.
Pr. *The Guardian*, 22 Aug. 1713, and *Pastorals*, etc. 1748, p. 108.
MSS. Eng. poet. c. 9, p. 55; Rawl. poet. 116, fol. 119v.

1468 In seasons mild
But little art despise.
'The Landskip. Lond. Mag.'
MS. Eng. poet. e. 39, p. 149.

1469 In seed we're sown in living ground,
That sitteth on the throne.
Robinson, Robert.
MS. *Rawl. poet. 218, p. 152 (autogr.).

1470 In seeing you, Sir, I have seen the court
Him I would honour, more than all the great.
Oldisworth, Nicolas, 'For a discontented Scholar of Oxford, 1632, these . . . verses were written while the King was at Woodstock. To Mic. Oldisworth, Esquier'.
MS. *Don. c. 24, fol. 51 (autogr.).

1471 In seeking to obtain delights we lose 'em
Dalila's lap leads not to Abraham's bosom.
[Jordan, Thomas], couplet, 'On Vaine Delights'.
Pr. *Divinity and Morality*, Sig. §§§6.
MS. Rawl. poet. 90, fol. 84v.

In seemly sort I like to love 1472
Kiss then (sweet shepherd) and no more.
Lilliat, John, 'The Sepperdisse her Replie', to S1404.
MS. Rawl. poet. 148, fol. 100v (autogr.).

In several ground, from several seeds, 1473
Their fruits the same, when men they're grown.
Robinson, Robert.
MS. *Rawl. poet. 218, p. 87 (autogr.).

In Sheldon's edifice the assembled crowd 1474
Cried out, that Maudlin's Dome repeated—Dad . . . [the rest crossed out and illegible].
Oxford, 26 October 1734.
MS. Eng. misc. e. 240, p. 73.

In sight of kings who gods are named 1475
Respect the work of thine own hands.
Harington, Sir John, Psalm cxxxviii.
MS. *Douce 361, fol. 85v.

In sign of doomsday the whole earth shall sweat 1476
Rivers of fire and brimstone flowing from heaven.
'Sybilla Erythræa's prophecy' acrostic 'Jesus Christ Sone of God the Saviour', Latin and English.
MS. Top. Cheshire c. 6, fol. 397.

In silence thus! Ah! why my friend retire 1477
More if you please: and swear I'll keep awake.
Skinner, John, 'Eclogue 1', Trinity College, Oxford.
MS. *Top. Oxon. e. 41, p. 111.

In Sion sing a hymn 1478
Such store of grain for joy they sing.
Harington, Sir John, Psalm lxv.
MS. *Douce 361, fol. 37v.

In six days numberless variety 1479
Which nothing else but sin can propagate.
MS. *Rawl. poet. 97, fol. 8v (autogr.).

In sixteen hundred seventy-eight 1480
England for all that needs not care a louse.
Mock prophecy, 1678.
Pr. Wood's *Life and Times*, ed. A. Clark, ii, O.H.S. xxi, 1892, p. 436.
MSS. Ashmole 1835, two copies, fols. 112 and 113, attr. to Richard Cox, 'a Cl[erk] in the 6 Clarks office'; Rawl. A. 188, fol. 92; Wood F. 34, fol. 169, attr. to 'our Oxonian Banterer . . .' [page torn].

In sleep I saw a pretty sight 1481
Alas I am undone.
Song with melody.
MS. Mus. Sch. G. 610, fol. 7.

1482 **In Smithfield dwells the brok'red knave whom I above did name.**

Abbott, Thomas, of East Smithfield, scrivener, one line cited in indictment for libel, 1606.
MS. Ch. Lond. and Middx. 461.

1483–4 **In softer accents or more tuneful lays**
**That him, his brother only did excel.**

M[anningha(?)]m, S. 'An Elegy on the Death of Mr. Dan. Purcell'.
MS. Mus. d. 226, p. iv.

1485 **In some vile hamlet let me live forgot,**
**But to trudge four, and miss you is the devil.**

'The Uneasy Visitor, a Paraphrase', Martial, *Epigrams* II. v.
MS. Rawl. poet. 173, fol. 53v.

1486 **In sonnets and in roundelays**
**The praises of so great a king.**

'An Hymne'. Tune: 'I'le love my owne true love or none'.
MS. Rawl. poet. 37, p. 44.

1487 **In sounds of joy your tuneful voices raise**
**And sing *Te Deum*, when the three are damned.**

'The Thanksgiving'.
In B.M. MS. Lansd. 852, fol. 29v, dated Feb. 1709/10. Pr. Hearne's *Collections*, ed. C. E. Doble, ii, O.H.S. vii, 1886, p. 352.
MSS. Eng. poet. e. 87, p. 28, dated 1708; Hearne's diaries 23, p. 186, March 1709/10; pr. bk. Firth b. 21, fol. 73, with reference to 'Blenheim'.

1488 **In Southampton City a damsel pretty**
**God bless Sir Charles [Napier] and the Baltic fleet.**

'The Baltic Lovers', an extract, verse and prose.
MS. Firth c. 18, fol. 135*c*.

1489 **In speechless silence do not hold oh god thy tongue always:**
**To save him from the man that would condemn his soul to die.**

[Norton, Thomas], Psalm cix.
MS. Rawl. poet. 112, fol. 39 rev.

1490 **In spite of the French, and their bold privateering**
**Then rumour's a rogue and the news-letter lies.**

'Momus Ridens, Or, Comicall Remarks on the weekely Reports No. 11', 1690/1.
MS. Eng. poet. d. 53, p. 134.

1491 **In state and glory bright**
**Be praised in endless ages.**

Harington, Sir John, Psalm xciii.
MS. *Douce 361, fol. 56v.

**In storms, when clouds the moon do hide,** 1492
**Shunning the knaves, and fools I scorn.**

Otway, Thomas, adapted from Horace, *Odes* II. xvi.
MS. Rawl. poet. 173, fol. 32.

**In such large compass now do turrets stand** 1493
**But their decaying temples to repair.**

W. A., translator, Horace, *Odes* II. xv.
MS. *Rawl. poet. 104, fol. 18v (autogr.).

**In summer heat and mid time of the day** 1494
**Jove send me more such afternoons as this.**

'Corinne concubitus', translating Ovid, *Amores* I. v.
MS. Don. d. 58, fol. 46*b*.

**In summer time extremity of heat doth fire us,** 1495
**In winter season tedious cold doth tire us.**

Robinson, Robert, couplet.
MS. *Rawl. poet. 218, p. 122 (autogr.).

**In summer time to Medley** 1496
**Falero, lero, loo.**

Wither, George, copied by Hearne from *A Description of Love*, 1620.
Pr. notes to *Guilelmus Neubrigensis*, 1719, ii. 756.
MS. Rawl. D. 1164, fol. 240.

**In summer time when leaves grow green** 1497
**Under the greenwood tree.**

Song with a tune.
MSS. Ashmole 36, 37, fol. 294v.

**In summer's cool shade, how delightful to sit!** 1498
**Is summer, is winter, is autumn, is spring.**

Arnold, Dr. [Samuel (?)], 'The Comforts of the Seasons . . . sung by the Gent. of his Majesty's Chapel Royal at their annual Feast. 7th Aug. 1783'.
MS. Eng. poet. e. 39, p. 224.

**In summer's heat, and winter's cold** 1499
**And I my water gruel!**

Spencer, H.
MS. Montagu d. 5, fol. 236.

**In sunny beams the sky doth show her sweet** 1500
**Or be no more, sea, sky, earth, muse nor mountains.**

Breton, Nicholas (?), 'A passionate Sonnett made by the kinge of Scots . . . geaven me by Mr. Britton who had beene . . . in Scotland with the kinges Majesty: but I rather thinke they weare made by him', note by Sir Stephen Powle.
Pr. by Grosart, *Chertsey Worthy's Library, Breton*, i. [24].
MS. Tanner 169, fol. 43.

1501 In sure and certain hope to rise
The cross exchanged for the crown.
'Epitaph on Susanna Burnel', d. March 1756.
MS. Top. Yorks. c. 2, fol. $3^v$.

1502 In Sussex late since eighty-eight
Your prince should match with Spaine-a.
'A Song', *temp.* Spanish match.
MS. Rawl. poet. 160, fol. $181^v$.

1503 In T—d's frame love's country seat we view
'Twas not the bard who sang that gained the prize.
Gough, Richard (?).
MS. *Eng. poet. c. 5, fol. 71, in Gough's hand.

1504 In tabernacle thine, oh Lord, who shall remain?
Who thus proceeds for aye in sacred mount shall reign.
Sidney, Sir Philip, Psalm xv.
MSS. *Rawl. poet. 24, p. 16; *25, fol. 10.

1505 In tadpole's brain there moves a maggot
And bid him go seek out his fellows.
'Burlesque on Mr. Pickard' of Oxford.
MS. Eng. poet. e. 4, p. 203.

1506 In tender youth we're put to learn in schools
And some as fools they came, so fools they part.
Robinson, Robert.
MS. *Rawl. poet. 218, p. 78 (autogr.).

1507 In that blest season of the circling year
And rustic tale alternate they relate . . . (incomplete).
MS. Percy c. 8, fol. 79.

1508 In that blithe season when on every spray
The muse may charm a pang, or check a rising sigh.
Dyer, George, 'Visions'.
Pr. *Poems*, 1801, p. lxx.
MS. *Eng. poet. c. 21, fol. 33.

1509 In that day of deliverance
That have thereon been slain.
'Saints Incouragement', Isaiah xxvi.
MS. Eng. poet. e. 51, p. 148.

1510 In that fair form there surely must preside
Where envy hisses, malice bites no more.
Baker, H[enry (?)], 'To the . . . Countess of Macclesfield'.
MS. Montagu c. 5, fol. 9 (autogr.).

1511 In that famed land for fish and pipes renowned
Noordwyk in sand appears . . . (incomplete).
Skinner, John, 'A scrap . . . the remainder lost—1789'.
MS. *Eng. poet. d. 22, fol. 23 (autogr.).

In that our parents both offended, we 1512
Was set on with a triple enemy.
MS. *Rawl. poet. 97, fol. 12 (autogr.).

In that, that Nazareth is sanctified 1513
In heavenly glory cannot have a place.
MS. *Rawl. poet. 97, fol. $41^v$ (autogr.).

In the . . . see also I'th'

In the Adriatick gulf when Neptune saw 1514
That placed by men you yield this by a deity.
[Johnston, Nathaniel], translation from the Latin of Sannazarius, *Epigrams* I. xxxv.
MS. Eng. poet. c. 25, fol. 75 (autogr.).

In the Armenian rocks where flight 1515
Hath bounds and cannot out of order go.
Bacon, Sir Nicholas, 1623–1666, translation of Boethius, *Consolations* v. i. 1664.
MS. Tanner 306, fol. 344 (autogr.).

In the barn the tenant cock 1516
All the jocund dawn of day.
Cunningham, J[ohn], of Edinburgh, 'Stanzas on the Morning. Public Ledger 1761'.
MS. Eng. poet. e. 39, p. 218.

In the chill icy phang of distant north 1517
And we may 'joy a golden age again.
MS. Don. c. 75, fol. 103.

In the coolness of the day 1518
And breath your air.
Beaumont, Jos[eph of Peterhouse], 'Jesus inter ubera Mariæ. Cant. 6. 2'.
MS. Rawl. poet. 62, fol. 18.

In the council of state 1519
Though the other be gone in a trice.
'On Chooseing the Motto', for George I.
MS. Rawl. poet. 155, p. 16.

In the creation first God's love was shown 1520
Which in the presence of Christ Jesus is.
MS. *Rawl. poet. 97, fol. $72^v$ (autogr.).

In the dark I met with Marget 1521
Therefore I'll ha' none but Betty.
MS. Wood F. 34, fol. 175.

In the dark morning fates would have thee die 1522
Oh earth! we shall not yet take leave of thee.
[Freind, Nathaniel (?), translator], on the death of John Freind, 1672, from Latin.
MS. Top. Oxon. f. 31, p. 290, in the hand of Nathaniel Freind.

In the day of adversity 1523
To thee our humble prayer.
Psalm xx.
MS. *Rawl. C. 113, fol. $20^v$.

1524 **In the fields of Lincolns-Inne**
**Lusty shepherd ne'er so tired.**
[Sedley, Sir Charles (?)]; see V. de Sola Pinto, *Works of Sedley*, 1928, i, p. xxvii, and Vieth, *Attribution in Restoration Poetry*, 1963, p. 404.
MSS. Don. b. 8, p. 586, attr. to Sr. Charles Sidley; Eng. poet. d. 152, fol. 79.

1525 **In the first ruder age, when love was wild**
**Itself for its own proper object melt.**
Carew, [Thomas], 'Love's Force'.
First pr. *Poems*, 1642.
Pr. bk. 27980 e. 86, opp. p. 13.

1526 **In thc full tidc of mclody and mirth**
**Recall the loved the absent and the dead.**
'To the Memory of James Webbe'.
MS. Montagu c. 5, fol. 69.

1527 **In the hill of thy holiness**
**To guide us hath decreed.**
Psalm xlviii.
MS. *Rawl. C. 113, fol. 37v.

1528 **In the isle of great Britain long since famous grown**
**For we shall never have such liberty, to swive.**
[Wilmot, John, Earl of Rochester], 'a base Copy' on Charles II.
See Vieth, p. xiii. Pr. *Works* of Rochester, 1707; *Poems on Affairs of State*, 1697, p. 181.
MSS. Don. b. 8, p. 585; Rawl. D. 924, fol. 310v, attr. to Rochester; Rawl. poet. 173, fol. 113v, attr. to Ld. Roch.

1529 **In the merry month of May**
**Was crowned the lady of the May.**
Breton, Nicholas, Song.
Pr. *Englands Helicon*, 1600, p. 27; Michael East's *Madrigals*, 1604, nos. ii–iii; and, set by John Wilson, in *Select Musicall Ayres and Dialogues*, 1653, iii. 27.
MSS. Don. c. 57, fol. 77, music by Wilson; Mus. b. 1, fol. 135, music by Wilson; d. 8, fol. 3v, music by Este; Rawl. poet. 85, fol. 3, attr. to Britton.

1530 **In the midst of his age his enemies he will confound**
**As under the heavens he shall be.**
'Theis Verses were translated out of verie old Brittish Bookes'. Ashmole's note.
MS. Ashmole 1835, fol. 29v.

**In the mild close of a hot summer's day** 1531
**Magnificent and tall without, but dead men's bones within.**
Flatman, Thomas, 'The Retirement . . . 1665' 17. Aug.
MSS. *Firth d. 7, fol. 43; Rawl. D. 260, fol. 29v (incomplete).

**In the militia I am bred** 1532
**That can both hop and fly!**
Garrick, David, 'The Character and Skeleton of Master Stephen . . . Sept. 1769 . . . first publisht in the 2d Edit. of [Thomas] Davies' Dramatic Miscellanies, 1785, iii [p. 572]'.
MS. Eng. poet. c. 6, fol. 80.

**In the month of February** 1533
**Birds do couple, build and sing.**
MS. Douce d. 59, fol. 49v.

**In the month of June I lying sole alone** 1534
**But for an exercise, and none other thing.**
Cavendish, George, 'divers Elegiacall Poems upon sundry persons'.
Pr. *Cavendish's Life of Wolsey*, ed. S. W. Singer, 1825, ii. 3.
MS. Dugdale 28, fol. 228v.

**In the name of God, Amen. I Thomas Moore** 1535
**Twenty pounds, to be paid into the hands etc.**
'A Will in Meeter'.
A copy made from this for P. le Neve is in B.M. Add. MS. 27407, endorsed by le Neve 'Moor of St. Germain's Norff'.
MS. Don. b. 8, p. 351.

**In the name of God the king of kings** 1536
**In hope the same she will fullfil.**
'Mr. Edw. Ward's Will writ by himself, author of the London Spy. 1736'.
MS. Eng. misc. c. 116, fol. 14.

**In the name of the Trinity** 1537
**Say amen amen for charity.**
'Written at the bottome of Ripley's Scrowle between the King and the Pilgrim', MS. 'penes Tho. Henshawer'.
MS. Ashmole 972, fol. 246.

**In the nonage of a winter's day** 1538
**And winter to its former seat.**
'Lavinia'.
Pr. *Poems: Written by W. Shakespear. Gent.*, 1640.
MSS. Firth e. 4, p. 106, attr. to W[illiam] Munsey; Rawl. poet. 84, fol. 116 rev.; 116, fol. 37.

1539 In the pleasant month of May
To act love's solid joys.

'Words to a Tune of Mr. Barretts'.
MS. Mus. Sch. C. 95, p. 57.

1540 In the pure fountain of thy blood
On thine exalted head.

Beddome, Benjamin.
MS. *Eng. misc. e. 227, fol. 56.

1541 In the pure times of pious Charles the second
For now we fast (God knows) throughout the year.

MS. Eng. misc. e. 143, fol. 214.

1542 In the register I search
None can vie with Carbonnel.

[Lepipre, Gabriel], 'extempore Verses in Imitation of Milton, on a certain Beautiful Widow Lady . . . 1747' [Sarah Carbonnel, *née* Weyland].
MS. Eng. poet. e. 40, fol. 30 (autogr.).

1543 In the reign of king Canute and he was a Dane
Though the ancient possessors and owners be dead.

'Lines from the Front of Castle Hall at Mirfield', copied by J. Watson.
MS. Top. Yorks. c. 2, fol. 3.

1544 In the revolving circle of the year
Her bard himself appear at last.

[Roach, Richard], 'To the Lady C—d On Her Birth-day in the Month of June'.
MS. Rawl. D. 832, fol. 24 (autogr.).

1545 In the substraction of my years
And like a flower cropped in my prime.

[Sandys, George], 'Esay 38', set for 3 voices by W. Lawes.
Pr. *Paraphrase upon the Divine Poems*, 1637, sig. Ccc 4, and H. and W. Lawes, *Choice Psalmes*, 1648.
MS. Mus. Sch. E. 451, p. 65.

1546 In the thirty-sixth year, and the third day of December
All his life after, for the heresies he had kept.

Account of the abjuration, etc., of Bp. Pecock, 1458, from 'MS. History of England', transcribed by Dan. Waterland for John Lewis, 1725.
MS. Rawl. D. 376, fol. 81.

1547 In the time of Arthur an adventure betid
In the time of Arthur.

Copied by Francis Douce from MS. Douce 324: Romance of Gawain and Galavon. Printed by J. Pinkerton from this copy.
MS. Douce 309, fol. 1.

In the time of the renewing of my suspires 1548
Then to behold her eternal bliss.

Parker, Sir Henry, Lord Morley, translator of Petrarch's *Triumphs*, from the edition printed by John Cawood, London, 1565 (?).
MSS. Montagu e. 2, p. 1; e. 3, fol. 7.

In the time of the rump (as all Urope knows) 1549
Two noses so fatal as these two have been.

'A paralel between two Noses', Oliver Cromwell and William III.
MS. Rawl. poet. 169, fol. 8.

In the wracks of Walsingam 1550
Walsingam oh farewell.

MS. Rawl. poet. 219, fol. 16.

In the written revelation 1551
Claim the universe for thine.

Kenton, James.
MS. *Eng. poet. e. 20, p. 16 (autogr.).

In the year fifteen and fifty a great eagle stoutly shall range 1552
With E. all men supposed to have been dead.

Prophecy, 1554.
MS. Rawl. C. 813, fol. 154.

In the year of our lord god fifteen-eighty-one 1553
What time a maiden shall wear a crown.

Prophecy, 1554.
MS. Rawl. C. 813, fol. 153v.

In thee I trust, preserve me Lord, 1554
With pleasures at thy right hand placed . . . (incomplete).

Psalm xvi.
MS. *Rawl. C. 113, fol. 17.

In thee my Lord I trust on thee I wait 1555
Doth shame and foil the men that meant me harm.

Harington, Sir John, Psalm lxxi.
MS. *Douce 361, fol. 42.

In thee, oh Lord, I put my trust 1556
Your hearts with strength supply.

Psalm xxxi.
MS. *Montagu e. 10, fol. 50.

In these deep solitudes and awful cells 1557
He best can paint 'em, who shall feel 'em most.

Pope, Alexander, 'Eloisa to Abelard', with French translation.
MS. Buchanan c. 3, fol. 45.

In these delightful pleasant groves 1558
Revels in the cheerful spring.

[Shadwell, Thomas], from the *Libertine*: music by Purcell, 1692 (?). F. B. Zimmerman, *Purcell*, 1963, no. 600(1d).
MS. Mus. d. 3, fol. 5.

1559a [In these gay thoughts the loves and graces shine]
The willing heart, and only holds it long.
Pope, Alexander, [extract from 'Epistle to Miss Blount with the works of Voiture'].
See *Minor Poems*, ed. N. Ault and J. Butt, 1954, pp. 64–65.
MS. Eng. poet. c. 47, p. 106.

1559b In these more dull, as more censorious days.
Till Britain boasts, she has her Catos too.
'To a Gentleman, on his acting Cato', 1734.
MS. Eng. misc. e. 240, p. 121.

1560 In these three wills, the diff'rence is but small.
Or none at all: wilful, willfool, willfall.
Pestell, Thomas, 'On the willfull man'.
MS. *Malone 14, p. 42.

1561 In [Thessaly] Thesaly, there asses fine are kept
Let scholars burn their books and go to play.
Pr. John Lyly, *Works*, ed. R. W. Bond, 1902, iii. 498 (doubtful attribution).
MS. Rawl. poet. 148, fol. 86v.

1562 In this blind age whoe'er doth speak or write
And 'stead of loving turn idolater.
Beaumont, Thomas, 'To his Mrs. beinge jealous'.
MS. *Malone 18, p. 37 (autogr.).

1563 In this chill morning of a wintry spring
Than when with health's purpureal grace they grow.
Seward, Anna, 'Sonnett'. 1771.
MS. Pigott d. 12, fol. 11v (autogr.).

1564 In this cool hour, while reason sways the soul,
Cordial and true; in all thy dealings just.
Homer, Philip Bracebridge, 'Character of Laura' i.e. Miss June Wheler.
MS. *Add. C. 282, p. 3.

1565 In this fair town
With immoderate fame.
'On the Old Black Drumer att the Crown'.
MS. Eng. poet. e. 17, fol. 5.

1566 In this history following
Let God have all the praise.
'A Christians ABC, which he compiled in English meter, for the instruction of his Children . . . Wherein is conteyned, the Argumentes of the new Testament'; date at end, 1596.
MS. Rawl. poet. 217, fol. 2.

1567 In this judicious piece, the work of years
Be mine the task, thy footsteps to pursue.
'On Reading the Rev. Mr. [Henry] Grove's System of Moral Philosophy, [1749,] L[ondon] M[agazine]'.
MS. Eng. poet. e. 39, p. 196.

In this learned age we all are preachers grown, 1568
We preach down others faults, yet keep our own.
Robinson, Robert, couplet.
MS. *Rawl. poet. 218, p. 66 (autogr.).

In this lone spot where ocean bounds the scene 1569
The sage's olive and the poet's bay!
Parsons, William, 'Sonnet to Dr. S.' 3 Sept. 1779.
Pr. *Travelling Recreations*, 1807, i. 23.
MS. *Don. d. 123, p. 56 (autogr.).

In this marble buried lies 1570
Am the next designed to die.
Jordan, Thomas, 'The Epitaph' on Fidelia.
MS. Ashmole 38, p. 194.

In this marble casket lies 1571
But showed, and put it up again.
'On a child'.
Pr. Camden's *Remaines*, 1614, p. 382; *Recreation for Ingenious Head-pieces*, 1663, Epitaph 88.
MS. Sancroft 53, p. 45; see also W2690.

In this mixture of tongues, like the jargon of Babel 1572
At dinner or after, you're sure of an ear.
MS. Don. c. 81, fol. 160.

In this, my solitude 1573
Vowed whilst a soul thy servants limbs shall sway.
J. F., Psalm xli.
MS. *Eng. poet. f. 17, p. 114 (autogr.).

In this present reign, the war to maintain, 1574
Wretched brewers.
'The Bountifull Brewers who pays the King's Taxes out of the Poor Mens Purses'.
MS. Firth d. 14, fol. 38.

In this probationary state 1575
Lord let us then, depart in peace.
Kenton, James.
MS. *Eng. poet. e. 20, p. 389 (autogr.).

In this refined and crotchet age 1576
Or may a wiser fill thy place.
'Rasper', 'To a certain Justice of Peace remarkable for *Hawkin* about a soporific History of Musick', from *The Morning Post*, 8 May 1779. [Sir John Hawkins, *History of . . . Music*, 1776].
MS. Montagu c. 5, fol. 18.

In this small character is sent 1577
Bequeathed it as my legacy.
King, Henry, 'Upon a Braid of Haire in a Heart sent by Mrs. E. H.'
Pr. *Poems*, 1657, p. 9.
MSS. *Eng. poet. e. 30, fol. 38; *Malone 22, fol. 23v.

1578 In this vain world there is many a crooked street
And poor men mun die.
'Epitaph in Well-winn C[hurch] yard'.
MS. Eng. poet. c. 51, p. 57.

1579 In this wicked world, oh Christ whiles I live
We may worthily sing praises to thee our dear.
MS. Gough Norfolk 43, fol. 40v.

1580 In this world's weary pilgrimage we see
That I may live a hermit anywhere.
MS. Wood F. 34, fol. 187.

1581 In those bright mansions to the gods above
The brightest heaven of Pelham's high-exalted praise.
Emily, C[harles], scholar [1753] of Trinity College, Cambridge.
MS. Eng. poet. c. 6, fol. 26.

1582 In those cold climates where the sun appears
A cruel tyrant and her name is death.
MS. Rawl. poet. 65, fol. 46v.

1583 In those dark ages, when the world was blind,
So like to him, that 'tis his harp new strung.
Mayne, Jasper, 'Upon Sir John Denhams Translation of the Psalms'.
MS. Eng. poet. e. 4, p. 1.

1584 In thought I paint misfortune's child
And rise superior o'er a shatter'd world.
Skinner, John, 'Composed on the Sea Coast of North Wales'.
MS. *Eng. poet. d. 22, fol. 100.

1585 In time of libelling and squabbling
Their other virtues are entirely lost.
'The Republican Procession or The tumultous Cavalcade' [The Duke of Marlborough's entry into London, 4 Aug. 1714].
MS. Rawl. poet. 155, p. 199.

1586 In time, take time, whilst time last,
For time's no time, when time's past.
'Maxim', couplet.
MS. Eng. poet. e. 40, fol. 142.

1587 In time to come a falcon driv'n out shall be
Ye shall fearless spread on every side.
Verse conclusion to prophecy.
MS. Rawl. C. 813, fol. 106.

1588 In times like these, when widows, orphans weep
Glow at a smile, and sicken at a frown!
Parsons, William, 'To a Friend in Love, during the riots . . . 1795'.
MS. *Don. d. 123, p. 259*c* (autogr.).

In times of quicker wit's day-break 1589
Himself of love and service true debars.
[Roach, Richard], 'Quatrilla. A Fable'.
MS. Rawl. D. 832, fol. 274 (autogr.).

In times when princes cancelled natures law 1590
Stands still recorded in the book of fame.
'Tarquin and Tullia', *c.* 1688.
Pr. *Poems on Affairs of State*, iii, 1703, p. 319.
MSS. Eng. poet. c. 18, fol. 166; d. 53, p. 76; Firth e. 6, fol. 51; Rawl. poet. 169, three copies, fols. 38, 39, 40.

In title, Rich, in virtue all excelling 1591
Had death had eyes he had not been so cruel.
North, D[udley] L[or]d, 'Epitaph . . .' on Lady Anne Rich, 1638.
Pr. *A Forest of Varieties*, 1645, p. 79.
MS. Eng. misc. e. 262, fol. 33v.

In Tonson's shop, at Shakespear's Head 1592
The other nothing but a dress.
Whaley, John, 'The Two Books; A Tale'.
Pr. *Poems*, 1732, p. 124.
MS. Rawl. poet. 222, fol. 18.

In troth friend Harry when you hum 1593
Or we entirely deaf.
'To an Intolerable Singer'.
MS. Percy c. 8, fol. 129v.

In trouble and adversity 1594
On thee when we do cry.
[Sternhold, Thomas], Psalm xx.
MS. Rawl. poet. 112, fol. 66 rev.

In trouble and in thrall 1595
By them that would have strife.
[Sternhold, Thomas], Psalm cxx.
MS. Rawl. poet. 112, fol. 33v rev.

In trouble to the Lord I call 1596
That doth salvation bring.
[Fleming, Robert], 'Jonah ch: 2. Jonahs prayer out of the fishes body'.
MS. Rawl. poet. 213, fol. 76v rev. (autogr.).

In troubles I called to the Lord 1597
For bloodshed doth increase.
Psalm cxx.
MS. *Rawl. C. 113, fol. 90.

In true good epigrams two virtues meet 1598
For 'tis their glory to be short and sweet.
'On Epigrams', couplet.
MS. Eng. poet. c. 9, p. 107.

In Trumpington nigh Cambridge town 1599
And wear Acteon's head.
Burton, Francis, 'One of oulde Chawcers tales put into better Englishe'.
MS. *Add. A. 267, fol. 12 (autogr.).

1600 In trying times he stood the mighty shock
His nobler soul the best translation made.
T. C., cantilenus, on Bishop Hough; 'composed by a Gentleman in Oxford, June 4th 1743'.
MS. Ballard 50, fol. 191v.

1601 In two large columns on thy motley page
Wander like him accursed through the land.
Montagu, Ldy M[ary] W[ortley, and Hervey, John, Baron], 'To the Imitator of . . . Horace', *Satires* II. i [Pope].
See Pope's *Works*, ed. Norman Ault and John Butt, iv, *Imitations of Horace*, 1939, p. xvii.
MS. Eng. misc. c. 399, fol. 76.

1602 In vain alas! My Posthumus we try
With richest wines, and broach his eloquent champagne.
Translation from Horace, *Odes* II. xiv.
MS. Top. London e. 9, p. 25.

1603 In vain are stately structures made,
Nor yet to plead against him in the judgement place.
Knollys, Fra., Psalm cxxvii.
MS. *Rawl. poet. 60, p. 13 (autogr.).

1604 In vain Argyll, with god-like virtue stood
He wakes, sees England sleep, and straight he dies.
'On . . . the Duke of Argyll, London Mag: Oct. 1743'.
MS. Eng. poet. c. 9, p. 106.

1605 In vain at happiness you aim
And what is thought a crime we cannot want.
Walsh, William, 'Happiness'.
MS. Malone 9, fol. 60v (autogr.).

1606 In vain dear Celinda I lately have strove
Or his stomach is gone, and he cares not to eat.
'Capt. Bucklye's Song to Coll: Dittons Daughter'.
MS. Add. A. 301, fol. 64v rev.

1607 In vain doth men contend against the stars
For what he seeks to make his wisdom mars.
Couplet.
MS. Rawl. poet. 117, fol. 275 rev.

1608 In vain, egregious Dennis, have you left us,
By Swift and Pope we've what your inward man was.
'An Epigram written under the Picture of the late Critic Mr. Dennis', 1735.
MS. Eng. misc. e. 240, p. 134.

In vain, fair sorceress, thy eyes speak charms, 1609
And judge thee, witch, in thy own flames to burn.
[Habington, William], 'To a wanton woman'.
Pr. *Castara*, 1635, p. 9.
MS. Eng. poet. d. 152, fol. 20.

In vain for aid to your old friends you call 1610
Thank Hyde, your whoring, and the church of Rome.
'About 9 at night . . . 26 Nov. 1675 . . . found put over the Doore of the Kings new Bed-chamber . . . C. 2us R.'
MS. Don. b. 8, p. 539.

In vain, great enterprises well begun, 1611
And their aspiring rashness undermines.
Williams, John.
MS. *Rawl. poet. 191, fol. 102 (autogr.).

In vain I seek to charm a heart 1612
She chills my hope and slights my prayers.
'A song upon a Ground' by W. Davis. 'The words by a Person of Quality'.
MS. Mus. c. 16, fol. 122v composer's autograph.

In vain in vain brisk god of love 1613
That never went astray.
MS. Rawl. poet. 196, fol. 30v.

In vain is the physician sent 1614
And Christ my Saviour be.
Beddome, Benjamin.
MS. *Eng. misc. e. 227, fol. 175v.

In vain it is to seek for help from far 1615
With Baalim, nor yet with Beliall.
MS. *Rawl. poet. 97, fol. 36 (autogr.).

In vain like Scipio you from toils remove 1616
And share that immortality you give.
Brinsden, Charles, of Balliol College, Oxford, 'Sep. 19'.
MS. Top. Oxon. c. 220, p. 30.

In vain, lovely creature! you show me your art 1617
Makes others seem trifling at best.
Boswell, James, 'Epigram To a young Lady'.
Pr. *A Collection of Original Poems by Scotch Gentlemen*, ii, 1762, p. 80.
MS. *Douce 193, fol. 38v (autogr.).

In vain men came to see Tharvleot run 1618
But never any saw him ride between.
Oldisworth, Nicolas 'On a Race'.
MS. *Don. c. 24, fol. 49v (autogr.).

1619 In vain mine eyes you labour to amend
To this strange death I vainly yield my life.
Sidney, Sir Philip, from the *Arcadia*.
MS. *e Mus. 37, fol. 50v; pr. bk. 27980 e. 86, p. viii.

1620 In vain my eyes you strive to recompense
And only raise a fond desire.
'A Copy of Verses'.
MS. Montagu e. 13, fol. 130.

1621 In vain my voice in vain thou dost impart
Freely enjoys what e'er in heaven is.
N. D., elegy on the death of a lady whose name was Honour.
Pr. bk. Wood 460, after *Threnodia in obitum E. Lewkenor*, 1606.

1622 In vain Philander at my feet
Which I before possest?
Hawkins, Sir John, 'Song . . . set . . . by Mr. Boyce . . . 1741', with copies of Boyce's letters, 6 and 13 Nov. 1741.
MS. Eng. poet. c. 9, p. 2.

1623 In vain, poor sable son of woe,
The last will do't alive.
'Verses occasion'd by a Dial being put up in one of the Inns of Court, supported by a Slave in a kneeling posture—White Hall Evening Post March 7th 1737/8'.
MS. Ballard 47, fol. 37v.

1624 In vain the angry billows roar
And soon beneath its weight will sink.
Walsh, Octavia, 'In imitation of Horace'.
MS. *Eng. poet. e. 31, fol. 143 rev. (autogr.).

1625 In vain the Bourbon and Plantagenet
The devil's nature has the devil's fate.
'On the Two Sisters', Queen Mary, Princess Anne.
In B.M. MS. Harl. 7317, fol. 108v, dated 1690.
MSS. Firth e. 6, fol. 3; Rawl. D. 1251, fol. 96.

1626 In vain the doubtful labyrinth I trace,
May you ne'er feel the sorrows felt by me.
'To Damon, by a Lady. 1768'.
MS. *Eng. poet. e. 28, p. 209.

1627 In vain the dusky night retires
A near approach to Thee.
'Hymn 5. Collect. Poems'.
MS. Eng. poet. e. 39, p. 89.

1628 In vain the fulsome errors of the age,
Thou yet hast stock enough thy self to trade.
'Satyr on both Whigs and Toryes. 1683'.
MSS. Firth c. 15, p. 142; c. 16, p. 17.

In vain the harassed people strive 1629
Yet let us not at home be nick't.
'Upon Neal's projecting new Taxes'.
Thomas Neale, master of the mint, organized a lottery-loan for £1,000,000 in 1694. Pr. *Poems on Affairs of State*, ii, 1703, p. 223.
MS. Rawl. poet. 173, fol. 128v.

In vain the Macedon death's triumphs spurned 1630
A prince as much, as he bewailed and mourned.
G. B., 'Epitaph 11' on Prince Henry in 'Cestria Lugens', 1612.
MS. Rawl. poet. 116, fol. 7v.

In vain those painted beauties think to reign 1631
To choose to which of all you'll be a slave.
Walsh, William, 'Elegie on Chloe'.
MS. Malone 9, fol. 61 (autogr.).

In vain thou dost that man advise 1632
Good counsel he will but despise.
Robinson, Robert.
MS. *Rawl. poet. 218, p. 115 (autogr.).

In vain we lift the suppliant eye 1633
There's glory in the end.
Beddome, Benjamin.
MS. *Eng. misc. e. 227, fol. 77v.

In vain we strive to cure our grief by art 1634
Lord, and th' annointed ointment of our bliss.
Colman, Henry, 'On the Names Jesus, Christ, Emanuel', with acrostics on the names.
MS. *Rawl. poet. 204, fol. 20v (autogr.).

In vain we strive to fathom H—y's mind 1635
He loves them both too well to trust them in the light.
Epigram.
MS. Top. Oxon. c. 108, p. 15.

In vain we toil and labour here 1636
And favour to his servants show.
Kenton, James.
MS. *Eng. poet. e. 20, p. 101 (autogr.).

In vain we try when once we love, 1637
We tell it with our eyes.
'Love not to be conceal'd'. 1735.
MS. Eng. misc. e. 240, p. 170.

In vain with plaintive voice, and weeping eyes 1638
Which can't be greater, till she meets you there.
'On the Death of Mrs. Fountayne, Lady of . . . the Dean of York . . . G[entleman's] M[agazine]'.
MS. Eng. poet. e. 39, p. 203.

1639 In vain you give to those that cannot take
As did th' old gran'am when she kissed her cow.
Roach, Richard, 'On Two Ladies, one kissing her little Dog, the other her Cat'.
MS. Rawl. D. 832, fol. 254 (autogr.).

1640 In we come, and out we go:
Whether they be or high, or low.
Robinson, Robert.
MS. *Rawl. poet. 218, p. 49 (autogr.).

1641 In Westminster four wonders seen, the like were never heard,
A speaker of the commons house, that ne'er before wore gown.
'Michaelmas Terme, 1672', on Anthony Ashley Cooper, Earl of Shaftesbury; Bp. Nathaniel Crewe; Sir Robert Atkins; and Edward Seymour, afterwards Bart.
MS. Eng. poet. e. 4, p. 167.

1642 In what esteem did the Gods hold
Than her false echo in the ear.
Carew, Thomas, 'The Second Chorus of Female Honour betrayd'.
Pr. *Poems*, 1640.
MSS. *Don. b. 9, fol. 5; Malone 13, p. 68.

1643 In what part of the world Claudius fights now
In sacrifice for your desired return.
B[rome], A[lexander], translator, Horace, *Epistles* I. iii.
Pr. *Poems of Horace*, A. Brome etc., 2nd ed., 1671, p. 310.
MS. Rawl. D. 261, p. 31.

1644 In what soft language shall my thoughts set free
Grasp thee through death, and be for ever thine.
Rowe, Elizabeth (*née* Singer), 'On the Death of a Husband by Mrs. Rowe'.
Thomas Rowe died 13 May 1715. Pope appended Mrs. Rowe's elegy to 'Eloisa and Abelard', 2nd ed., 1720. Also pr. Mrs. Rowe's *Poetical Works*, 1820, p. 91.
MSS. Eng. poet. e. 28, p. 39; e. 47, p. 85.

1645 In what thing more should we excel
My rock: In him's no breach of trust.
Fairfax, Thomas, Lord, Psalm xcii.
MS. *Fairfax 40, p. 225 (autogr.).
MS. *Fairfax 38, p. 357.

1646 In what torn ship soever I embark
And to scape stormy days; I choose an everlasting night.
Donne, John, 'A Hymne to Christ'.
Pr. *Poems*, 1633.
MSS. *Eng. poet. f. 9, p. 6, 'when he went with the Lo: Doncaster'; Rawl. poet. 160, fol. 51, attr. to J. D.

In whatsoever character 1647
They feel least cold and pain who plunge at once into it.
Fleming, Robert.
MS. Rawl. poet. 213, fol. 49 rev. (autogr.).

In 'wildering terror, hopeless of repose, 1648
Beam on his name the lustre of her own.
[Holmes Robert], 'Ode for the installation of the Duke of Portland [as Chancellor of Oxford University] 1793. Dr. P. Hayes', partly in the composer's hand.
MS. Mus. d. 64, fol. 63.

In woeful plaints my sad muse renders 1649
At the gasping poets under the hill.
'Mr. [Edward] Waples [of St. John's] verses In obitum Reginæ Matris, in Oxford book: Burlesq'.
The original pr. *Epicedia Universitatis Oxoniensis in obitum . . . Henriettæ Mariæ*, 1669.
MS. Eng. poet. e. 4, p. 199.

In wonted walks since wonted fancies change 1650
Infected minds infect each thing they see.
Sidney, Sir Philip, from the *Arcadia*; pr. 1598, p. 479.
MS. *e Mus. 37, fol. 238v.

In worst afflictions 'twill give us rest 1651
To think, what God allots for us is best.
Barksdale, Clement, 'Resignation', no. 5 of 10 distichs.
MS. Autogr. c. 9, fol. 154 (autogr.).

In writing happy in an Humble mind, 1652
Much more in her than can be said by me.
Williams, John, 'Upon Miss Betty's desiring me to make a Complement upon my Lady Humble'.
MS. *Rawl. poet. 191, fol. 105 (autogr.).

In written books I find it 1653
To make the water vary.
[Fable concerning the Church under Henry VIII, Queen Mary and Queen Elizabeth].
MS. Gough Norfolk 43, fol. 40.

In yonder tomb the old Avaro lies 1654
Down dropped his bags, and mortgages of land.
'On seeing the Tomb of a Miser'.
MS. *Eng. poet. d. 47, fol. 6v.

In your [fair] cheeks two pits do lie 1655
Being dead can live and living die.
[Carew, Thomas], 'To his Mrs.'
Pr. *Poems*, 1640.
MSS. CCC. 328, fol. 13; Rawl. poet. 116, fol. 56v; see also I1358.

1656 In your letter to me you desire to know
Adieu, 'tis as true news as ever was writ.
'Letter found in Dover Road, 1700'. Answered by S612.
MS. Eng. poet. e. 50, p. 138.

1657 In your stern beauty I can see
When ice itself heats other's hands.
Strode, William, 'Song', 'Loves Ætna'.
MS. *CCC. 325, fol. 74 (autogr.).
MSS. Eng. poet. c. 50, fol. 128; e. 97, p. 142, attr. to W. Stroade.

1658 In youthful hearts bare virtues wont to prove
But a weak shield against the darts of love.
Endorsed 'Animadversiones ex Amore Seraiphico 1659' [Robert Boyle: *Some motives and incentives to the love of God*], couplet.
MS. Tanner 88, fol. 138.

1659 In youth's gay hour, in beauty's loveliest bloom
She saw her native shore, bless'd God and died.
Madan, Spencer (Bp. of Peterborough, (?) or 1758–1836), 'Epitaph on Miss Susan Proby'.
MS. Eng. poet. c. 51, p. 182.

1660 In youth's gay morn of life, profusely blest!
And gilds thy way to life's remotest stage!
Parsons, William, 'To the Hon. C. Molesworth . . . 24 Jan. 1779'.
MS. *Don. d. 123, p. 45 (autogr.).

1661 In Zion Lord shall praise attend thee there
Vale's stored with flocks and corn for joy do sing.
Fairfax, Thomas, Lord, Psalm lxv.
MS. *Fairfax 40, p. 143 (autogr.).
MS. *Fairfax 38, p. 229.

1662 Incline bright Phoebus fairest of the nine,
No art can e'er discharge the native stain.
'Transcrib'd'.
MS. Montagu e. 13, fol. 128v.

1663 Incline Lord to thy suppliant's prayer,
Are sentenced by thy frown.
Psalm lxxxvi.
MS. *Rawl. C. 113, fol. 61v.

1664 Incline oh Lord thine ear unto my moan
But God shall be my trust at all assays.
Harington, Sir John, Psalm lv.
MS. *Douce 361, fol. 32v.

1665 Incline oh Lord thine ear unto my prayer
May blush to see thee send good health and hap.
Harington, Sir John, Psalm lxxxvi.
MS. *Douce 361, fol. 52.

Incline thine ears unto my words, 1666
Defend him from all ill.
[Sternhold, Thomas], Psalm v.
MS. Rawl. poet. 112, fol. 70v rev.

Inconstancy, the greatest of sins 1667
Like the same body in another place.
Herbert, Edward, of Cherbury, Lord.
Pr. from this MS. amongst doubtful poems, *Poems of Lord Herbert*, ed. G. C. Moore Smith, 1923, p. 119.
MS. Rawl. poet. 31, fol. 36, attr. to Sir Edw. Harbert, i.e. before 7 May 1629.

Indeed good Sir you're much mistaken 1668
What spirits pray possess you men?
Amherst, Elizabeth, 'Verses to be sent to Mr. Adams on his having read a french Author who supposes that the fallen Angels abide in brute beasts, etc.'
MS. *Eng. poet. e. 109, p. 77.

Indeed our triumphs great have usual been 1669
They'll hardly 'scape so well as we 'scaped here.
'Upon the returne of the English from the Ile of Rhez'. 1628.
MS. Don. d. 58, fol. 50v.

Indeed this world is so unjust 1670
Men cannot one another trust.
Note by Ebsworth, 'This is of date 6 June 1685'.
Pr. *Roxburghe Ballads*, vi, ed. J. W. Ebsworth, 1889, p. 354.
MS. Firth c. 20, fol. 65.

Indians report that whereso'ere they roam 1671
Not british pay would make a Scotchman fight.
Vansittart, Dr. Robert, of All Souls, 'Epigram'.
MS. Eng. poet. c. 51, p. 57.

Indiff'rent beauty, though thy killing eyes 1672
In such fair sins I'll choose to spend my time.
MS. Mus. b. 1, fol. 176, music by John Wilson.

Indulgent God, whose bounteous care 1673
Oh aid my soul to soar.
'An Evening Hymn'.
MS. Eng. poet. e. 47, p. 26.

Indulgent Heaven has placed my lot 1674
To one who calls but cannot stay.
'A little ode . . . the Author whereof is unknown'.
MS. Rawl. D. 868, fol. 31v.

Indulgent nature on all things bestows 1675
And bears a like antipathy to trees.
'On a Bursar cutting down a Row of Trees before the College Gate': Trinity College, Oxford (?).
MS. *Eng. poet. d. 47, fol. 11.

1676 Industrious, unfatigued in faction's cause
Abhorr'd by Heav'n is hurried now to hell.
'The Lord Wharton's Character'.
Pr. [31 Dec. 1711] as 'The Character of a Certain Whigg', MS. Rawl. poet. 207, p. 57.
MSS. Eng. poet. e. 87, p. 83; Rawl. poet. 155, p. 102; 181, fol. 67.

1677 Industrious virtue, mistress of the wise
Charms and subdues ev'n the austerest heart.
North, Dudley, 3rd Baron.
Pr. *A Forest of Varieties*, 1645.
MS. *North e. 41, fol. 24.

1678 Inexorably righteous Lord
Then take us home to Heaven.
Kenton, James.
MS. *Eng. poet. e. 20, p. 258 (autogr.).

1679 Infernal screech owl! Partner of the night!
That waked a lover in the height of joy.
Chatwin, John, 'The Owl'.
MS. *Rawl. poet. 94, p. 201 (autogr.).

1680 Inflamed by love and led by blind desires
He loves no longer, and she'll fear no more.
Sackville, Charles, Earl of Dorset, translator from Latin, 'The Maiden conjugates'.
MSS. Add. A. 301, fol. ix$^{v}$, attr. to Ld. Dorsett; Rawl. D. 361, fol. 263, attr. to the Earle of Dorsett; see also E59.

1681 Inflamed by zeal and spurred by ardent love
Britons rejoice, now dawns the joyful day.
J. W., 'On Mrs. Dean'.
MS. Rawl. poet. 155, p. 31.

1682 Ingenious men their books do always blot,
Those that disown, their faults more plainly show.
Williams, John, 'Upon a blotted book'.
MS. *Rawl. poet. 191, fol. 41$^{v}$ (autogr.).

1683 Ingenious N-w-n! who profess
The boys may flog, as well as stare!
Parsons, William, 'Epigram on seeing a Clergyman', etc.
MS. *Don. d. 123, p. 113 (autogr.).

1684 Ingenious wits shall flourish grow and thrive
If after wine to th' coffee house they slive.
Couplet, translation from Latin.
MS. Ashmole 1763, fol. 37.

1685 Ingenious youth to whom high heaven
Shall charm the eye, and warm the heart.
Parsons, William, 'To a friend . . . painting Storms and sea views'.
MS. *Don. d. 123, p. 32 (autogr.).

Ingram hath left a monument; but where? 1686
Which gave his house the best foundation.
Strode, William, 'On Mr. Ingram a Preist that built a house for his Rectory and kept it well'.
MS. *CCC. 325, fol. 118 (autogr.).

Inhabitants of heavenly land, 1687
The bliss on you he lays.
Herbert, Mary (*née* Sidney), Countess of Pembroke, Psalm cxlviii.
MS. *Rawl. poet. 24, p. 218.

Injurious Adam, in thy self accurst 1688
Thy fall's compulsion, nothing else compelling.
Langewoorth, Dr., 'Adam his fall'.
MS. Rawl. poet. 148, fol. 105$^{v}$.

Injurious time, father of ugly vice 1689
Where with the Gods humanity can bless.
North, Dudley, 3rd Baron.
Pr. *A Forest of Varieties*, 1645.
MS. *North e. 41, fol. 25.

*Inprimis* he was married late 1690
You'll soon dissolve the parliament.
'Upon a Gentleman that was committed for his wives beauty to Prison'.
MS. Rawl. poet. 71, p. 52.

Inspire me truth whilst I the praises sing 1691
Has had the luck to bring it back again.
Satire on women at court, *temp.* Charles II.
MS. Douce 357, fol. 92$^{v}$.

Inspired with high and mighty ale 1692
That is your servant to command.
Shadwell, Thomas, 'A letter . . . to Mr. Wicherley'. Answered in T207.
Pr. *Poems on Affairs of State*, iii, 1698, p. 39.
MS. Eng. poet. c. 18, fol. 9.

Instead of disticks and tetrasticks 1693
William Johnson *hic mentitur.*
'Ben Johnson upon his Brother William'.
MS. Rawl. poet. 26, fol. 162$^{v}$.

Instead of men's drink 1694
A pretty toying she.
Cavendish, Lady Jane, song in 'The Concealed Fancies'.
MS. *Rawl. poet. 116, p. 138.

Instead of news, when news falls short, 1695
Some wholsome meditation.
Robinson, Robert.
MS. *Rawl. poet. 218, p. 72 (autogr.).

Instead of prose, or something better 1696
And loud pronounced that all was good.
Lumby, John, 'To J. G.'
MS. *Eng. poet. e. 42, fol. 75.

1697 Insulting Gaul, and her blind pupil Spain,
Return, and triumph in your country's peace.
'On the March of the Duke of Cumberland towards the Rebels', 1744–5.
MS. Eng. misc. e. 219, fol. 10.

1698 Insulting rival, do not boast
But sign that she was mad.
Cutts, Col. John, 'Song'.
MS. Firth e. 6, fol. 72.

1699 Intelligence was brought (the court being sat)
Unless as a liar he were kin to a poet.
'The Additions' to A1360.
MSS. Douce 357, fol. 140v; Locke e. 17, p. 158.

1700 Interred beneath this marble stone
And so they lived and so they died.
[Prior, Matthew], 'An Epitaph Senece'.
Pr. Prior's *Poems on Several Occasions*, 1718, p. 281.
MSS. Rawl. poet. 152, fol. 121, attr. to Dr. Hulse; 153, fol. 68v.

1701 Interred here George Heyward is
From us to god did go.
'On Mr. Georg. Heyward [Mayor 1570] father to Sr. Rowland Heyward Lo: Maior of London'. 1597.
MS. Ashmole 38, p. 181.

1702 Interred here lies a hundred years and four
By nature good, the age's wonder died.
'Epitaph . . . Ellsmere, Shropshire, on William Parks, Gentleman's Magazine June 1751' [ii. 276].
MS. Eng. poet. c. 9, p. 218.

1703 Into an ass blows ne'er can change a lion,
All men might quickly find the harmless name.
Williams, John, 'Against Compulsion'.
MS. *Rawl. poet. 184, fol. 51v (autogr.).

1704 Into Hierusalem our saviour rides
Then Christ himself appears to arm their faith.
Verses on the passion, late 16th cent.
MS. Eng. poet. c. 11, fol. 70.

1705 Into the deep, and darksome cell
Gain better life by dying.
'A hymne concerning a graine of wheate . . .' Tune, 'Winter and cold weather'.
MS. Rawl. poet. 37, p. 7.

1706 Into the forty-eight
And the devil take you all.
Verses on the Scottish invasion, 1648.
MS. Wood F. 34, fol. 174.

Into the spring, whose copious flowings be 1707
'Tis sacred though but from this votaress.
Weaver, Thomas, 'On Mrs. F. P. discover'd at her devotion in Holy-Well'.
Pr. *Songs and Poems*, 1654.
MS. *Rawl. poet. 211, fol. 5 (autogr.).

Into this world as strangers to an inn 1708
But only broke his fast, and went his way.
'On a Child'.
Pr. *Wits Recreations*, 1640, Sig. Aa7.
In B.M. Add. MS. 15227, fol. 76, 'In filium Secretarii Winwood'.
MSS. Ashmole 38, p. 198; Sancroft 53, p. 45; Tanner 465, fol. 71v.

Into thy hands, thy sacred blessed hands 1709
I then may live with thee world without end.
Huish, Alexander, 'In manus tuas . . . [translated] Apr. 28, 1635'.
MS. Eng. poet. e. 56, p. 129 (autogr.).

Into thy hands, thy sacred hands 1710
I then may live world without end.
Huish, Alexander, 'In manus tuas . . .'.
MS. Eng. poet. e. 56, p. 129 (autogr.).

Into thy harbour sailing 1711
Naked leaving all behind thee.
MS. Rawl. poet. 37, p. 97.

Into what parts is holy friendship fled! 1712
To hear so ready, and to grant so free!
Williams, John, 'St. James' v. 16–18.
MS. *Rawl. poet. 184, fol. 102 (autogr.).

Intolerable wracks! 1713
Crammed in the quivers of my destiny.
Flatman, Thomas, 'Thoughts: the Answere to' T2456. 'May 18, 1659'.
MS. *Firth d. 7, fol. 16.

Intruder bold, whose impious tongue 1714
This breast had never learnt to sigh.
Homer, Philip Bracebridge, 'Love's answer to Reason'.
MS. *Add. C. 282, p. 53.

Invaluable time though thousands slight 1715
Because I don't consider, they prevail.
Williams, John, 'Of Time'.
MS. *Rawl. poet. 191, fol. 10 (autogr.).

*Io* to Buckingham great admiral, the man 1716
So rules and checks the foaming steeds he keeps.
'On Lord Villers Duke of Buckingham who being Master of his Ma:ties horse was created admirall of the Seas'; translated from Latin verses.
MS. Douce f. 5, fol. 36v.

1717 *Io victoria* round my temples bind
Mine and the charming Leonora's name Victoria.
Song, with music.
MS. Mus. Sch. C. 97, fol. 18 at end.

1718 Is Cook then dead? Pray write upon his stone,
He lived by brandy, and by water died.
I[reland, George of Exeter College, Oxford], 'An Epitaph on a Gentleman's being kill'd by the Bristol Waters', 1734.
MS. Eng. misc. e. 240, p. 59.

1719 Is death so cunning now, that all her blow
As mine will hide the truth 'cause others feign.
Strode, William, 'On the death of the young Baronet Sir John Portman, dying of an Impostume in the head Wadham Coll. Dyed Dec. 10 1624'. Details given by W. Fulman.
MS. *CCC. 325, fol. 80$^{v}$ (autogr.).
MSS. CCC. 328, fol. 54$^{v}$, attr. to Strode; Don. d. 58, fol. 12$^{v}$.

1720 Is death so great a gamester that he throws
Shall send his peaceful dove to fetch thee forth.
[Browne, William], 'Elegy on his Wives Death'.
Pr. Browne's *Poems*, ed. Gordon Goodwin, 1894, ii. 266.
MS. Don. e. 6, fol. 5$^{v}$, attr. to Dr. Donne; Eng. poet. e. 14, fol. 36$^{v}$, attr. to Dr. Dun; Malone 21, fol. 83.

1721 Is Doctor Warner dead? for him that bell?
And taking help away leave help behind.
On the death of Dr. Bartholomew Warner, Jan. 1618/19.
Pr. bk. Wood 460, after *Threnodia in obitum E. Lewkenor*, 1606.

1722 Is Dolbin gone! Is then bold Dolbin dead!
Ere death the halter's body does possess.
'An Elegy on the unlamented Death of John Dolbin Esqr'. Note at end: 'Prd. Monday after Whitsuntide by Croom 1710'.
MS. Rawl. poet. 197, fol. 6.

1723 [Is fasting then the thing that God requires?]
What sinks no deeper than the skin or clothes . . .
Quarles, [Francis], extract from 'Meditatio nona' of *A Feast for Wormes*, 1620, Sig. H2.
MS. Sancroft 59, p. 162.

1724 Is fornication deemed a sin?
Gods! Is it not a heaven.
'To Miss —', translated from Latin.
MSS. Eng. misc. e. 183, fol. 13$^{v}$; Eng. poet. f. 12, p. 170.

Is Fullwood gone? then woe is me! 1725
Love understood, preserved alive.
[Cater], Gerard, 'A Pindarick Poem in Memoire of Dr. Wm. Fullwood a Phisitian in Huntington'.
MS. Add. A. 301, fol. xiv.

Is grief by reason nourished in my breast 1726
Of blessed ones, till we all meet again.
North, John, 'An Elegy . . . on Lady Rich Aug. 24, 1638'.
MS. Eng. misc. e. 262, fol. 34$^{v}$.

Is happiness your point in view 1727
Plant virtue, and content's the fruit.
'Content true Happiness or the Means to Attain it'.
MS. Eng. poet. e. 47, p. 35.

Is he dead no opinion aims far wide 1728
Xerxes though conquering never won more hearts.
'Epita: on K. James', 1625.
MS. Eng. poet. f. 10, fol. 92.

Is he you thus commend called Campion? 1729
His *mendacia sunt opes et aurum*.
Lilliat, John, on Edmund Campion.
MS. Rawl. poet. 148, fol. 83$^{v}$ (autogr.).

Is heaven turned bankrupt? Do the Gods conspire 1730
Unless it chance to quicken from his hearse.
'On the death of Mr. Ben Love student of Christ Church in Oxford', 27 April 1649.
MS. Eng. poet. e. 4, p. 47.

Is H[unte]r dead, and nothing in the sky 1731
As it does justice to the glorious dead.
Lumby, John, 'An Elegy on the Death of Mr. [John] Hunter of Queen's College, Oxford, 1728. In a letter to Mr. Wardale'.
MS. *Eng. poet. e. 42, fol. 36.

Is it birth puffs up thy mind? 1732
To draw fair fools to this foul ill.
'To a proud Lady'. Copied from *Wits Recreations*, 1663, Sig. T5$^{v}$ (?).
MS. Eng. poet. d. 152, fol. 107.

Is it likely to confine 1733
Why fix your more inconstant man.
Amherst, Elizabeth, 'To a Lady who thought of reforming a very fickle Gentleman'.
MS. *Eng. poet. e. 109, p. 27.

Is it not strange, that every fool should find 1734
Till heaven appear, content thy self with contemplation.
'The Streight Way'.
MS. *Eng. poet. e. 51, p. 53.

1735*a* Is it not strange ye powers that mortals should
Without the least regret or anxious fear.

[Walsh, Octavia (?)] 'An enquiry into the cause of the miserys of mankind an Essay'.
MS. Eng. poet. e. 31, fol. 158 rev., in the hand of Octavia Walsh.

1735*b* Is John departed, and is Lilburn gone
For if they meet they will fall out.

'Epitaph upon John Lilburn, said to have been made by Judge Jenkins'.
Pr. Hearne's *Collections*, ed. C. E. Doble, ii, O.H.S. vii, 1886, p. 138.
MS. Hearne's diaries 17, p. 188.

1736 Is love a boy? what means he then to strike,
Power of my life, let here thy grace be shown.

4-part setting by Byrd, pr. *Songs of sundrie natures*, 1589, xv–xvi.
MSS. Mus. f. 11–15: f. 11, fol. 14v.

1737 Is love on fire? and are my words so cold
Where now you view your face to view my heart.

MS. Eng. poet. e. 97, p. 157.

1738 Is love that conquers all o'ercome? must he
Live always like your selves in Love and Grace.

Randolph, Thomas, 'Upon Dr. Rich. Love and Mrs. Grace Godman his wife'.
Love, Master of Corpus, Cambridge, married 23 January 1634. See G. C. Moore Smith, Warton Lecture on Randolph, 1927, pp. 30, 43.
MS. Rawl. poet. 26, fol. 148, attr. to Randall.

1739 Is Moeris then the man that must possess
He first uncovered your house then covered you.

Mervall, Alphonso, 'To Lycoris'.
MS. *Rawl. poet. 166, p. 27 (autogr.).

1740 Is Monmouth gone, England lament thy fate
As shall obscure and dazzle popish James.

'Terras Astræa reliquit. A Poem on the Duke of Monmouth's leaving England . . . 1683?'
Pr. bk. Firth b. 20, fol. 138.

1741 Is murther no sin? Or a sin so cheap
What water shall wash this, when this hath washed thee.

[Crashaw, Richard], 'On Pilate washing his hands'.
MS. Tanner 465, fol. 39v, attr. to Mr. Crashaw on fol. 1*a*.

Is nature's course dissolved, does time's glass stand, 1742
Of this fair land, Lord, let me see't at least.

[Quarles, Francis], 'The unhappy Mans Complaint'.
Pr. *Emblemes*, 1635, v. vii.
MS. Rawl. poet. 90, fol. 29v.

Is not Christ's church a glorious [fruitful] vine 1743
Since Goodwin's sent for to a heavenly feast.

'Upon Dr. [William] Goodwin Deane of Christ Church In Oxforde', d. 11 June 1620.
MSS. Ashmole 38, p. 171; Eng. poet. e. 14, fol. 80 rev.

Is not he well skilled in philosophy 1744
But that here lies a worthy graduate under.

'On the death of Mr. John Clarke Coll. Univ. Oxon'.
MS. Malone 21, fol. 26v.

Is not the law yet satisfied? then take 1745
His dearest life, God dies that man may live.

Clifford, Henry, Earl of Cumberland, 'Good Friday'.
MS. *Rawl. poet. 95, fol. 33v.

Is not this (great God!) the cell 1746
But to thy sacred name give all the glory!

Oldisworth, Giles, 'A Hymne to God', thanksgiving for his election to a scholarship at Westminster.
MS. *Rawl. C. 422, two copies, fols. 31v and 39v with 46v (autogr.).

Is our vane from the east 1747
And have raised 'em a trophy of bays.

[Roach, Richard], 'The Recantation. On St. Brides Bells Ringing on King Georges Coronation A° 1727'.
MS. Rawl. D. 832, fol. 172 (autogr.).

Is righteous Lot from sinful Sodom gone, 1748
We owe a death and once we needs must die.

'A dialogue of the [execution of Edmund Campion, 1581] betweene Catholic and Consolation'.
MS. Rawl. D. 111, fol. 97v.

Is Ruffus picture here? most true where's he? 1749
He's in his chair what doth he? that you see.

Translation of Ausonius, epigram ix, on Rufus the Rhetorician, 'Rhetoris haec statua est'. Couplet.
MS. Rawl. D. 1372, fol. 63v.

1750 **Is she not wondrous fair? but oh, I see
That now it freezeth, now again it burns.**
'A Lovers passion'.
Pr. *Cupids Master-Piece*, Sig. B3.
MSS. Ashmole 38, p. 155; 47, fol. 38; Douce f. 5, fol. 20ᵛ; Eng. poet. e. 97, p. 187, attr. to Dr. [William (?)] Lewes; Malone 16, p. 20; Rawl. poet. 84, fol. 93ᵛ rev.; 153, fol. 15; see also W50.

1751 **Is the bright sun so very blind
Excite their wonder and demand their fear.**
Earbery, Matthias, 'Friendship. [Psalm] XII', sent to Bp. Charles Trimnell, Bp. of Norwich 1708–21.
MS. Tanner 306, fol. 464ᵛ (autogr.).

1752 **Is the renewed heart
And give the praise to thee.**
Beddome, Benjamin.
MS. *Eng. misc. e. 227, fol. 7.

1753 **Is the sea richer for a drop of rain?
King James not dead, he was in Charles alive.**
Shirley, James, 'Upon the Death of Kinge James', 27 March 1625.
Recast in *Poems*, 1646.
MS. *Rawl. poet. 88, p. 46.

1754 **Is then religion still to be oppressed
While he triumphant wears an injured monarch's crown.**
'On the Thanksgiving Jan. 20th 1714–15'.
MS. Rawl. poet. 155, p. 24.

1755 **Is then thy thread already spun?
Indulgently he blasts the fruit; before he kills the tree.**
Walsh, William, 'Upon the death of Mrs. K. W.'
MS. Malone 9, fol. 59ᵛ (autogr.).

1756 **Is there a charm ye powers above
And triumphs o'er mankind.**
Song with music.
MS. Mus. c. 107, fol. 61ᵛ.

1757 **Is there a chastity in love begun
Where softer kisses are the only darts.**
Cartwright, [William], 'On Gentlewomens silkehoods'.
MS. Malone 21, fol. 75ᵛ; see also I1759.

1758 **Is there a God? why do the commons fool?
Like Strafford by one Pym must stand or fall.**
Preliminary to W91.
MSS. Eng. poet. e. 97, p. 194; Rawl. poet. 71, p. 94.

**Is there a sanctity in love begun
Where softer kisses are the only darts.** 1759
[Cartwright, William], 'Upon a Gentlewomans silke hoode'.
Pr. *Poems*, 1651, p. 232.
MSS. Ashmole 36, 37, fol. 171; Rawl. poet. 199, p. 48; see also I1757.

**Is there any one can find
And I'll show thee the man that all can please.** 1760
'No man canne please all'.
MS. Rawl. poet. 153, fol. 22.

**Is there no God? Let's put it to a vote:
So they could make an act there were no hell.** 1761
Satire on Pym, etc.: in B.M. Add. MS. 18044, fol. 101, 'On the Long Parliament'.
MSS. Rawl. D. 317, fol. 209; Rawl. poet. 153, fol. 21.

**Is there oh Cupid in thy reign
When he's tried, which state's the best.** 1762
Parsons, William, 'The complaint to Cupid'.
MS. Don. c. 81, fol. 8.

**Is there substantial bliss below
There vanities are vain no more.** 1763
Kenton, James.
MS. *Eng. poet. e. 20, p. 44 (autogr.).

**Is there that one amongst the wiser few
I, to my native tongue, translate thy fame.** 1764
Amherst, Elizabeth, 'Design'd as a preface for "Reflexions on Ridicule" by the Abbé de Belgarde', written *æt.* 16.
MS. *Eng. poet. e. 109, p. 36.

**Is this a time to thank when thousands mourn
And all usurpers meet deserved fate.** 1765
'On the Thanksgiving 7th June 1716'.
MS. Rawl. poet. 155, p. 253.

**Is this Britannia, this that once blest state,
Which will resettle Albion's monarchy and laws.** 1766
'Queen Anne's Ghost' (written in 1715).
MSS. Rawl. poet. 181, fol. 77; Rawl. poet. 207, p. 78.

**Is this old Cheney in his modern pride?
Quack, pedant, poet, pedlar all in one.** 1767
'On seeing Dr. Cheney's Picture'.
MS. Eng. misc. e. 183, fol. 77.

**Is this the *bon ton* with the men of Almack's
And his room is as good as his com-pa-ny.** 1768
'Mr. G.' and 'Dr. B.' [Burney (?)].
MS. Eng. misc. e. 241, fol. 15.

1769 Is this the hair that hath confined
Till so at last thou find her out.
'The Haire'.
MS. Eng. poet. c. 53, fol. 2.

1770 Is this the seat our conqueror hath given
For outward Eden lost find paradise within.
'The Fall of Angels, and Man In Innocence. By Mr. [John] Dryden . . . 'Tis printed'. [1677, etc.].
MS. Rawl. C. 146, fol. 103.

1771 Is this thy bravery, man? Is this thy pride?
That draws, like a strong net, the mighty sea upon them all.
Cowley, A[braham], 'The Plagues of Egypt'. From *Poems and Davideis*, 1656, 'Pindarique Odes', p. 54.
MSS. Rawl. poet. 213, fols. 48 rev., 213, extracts; Tanner 466, fol. 8.

1772*a* Is this your load stone Ben that must attract
The loathed stage; for thou hast made it such.
Gill, Alexander, the younger, 'Upon Ben Jonsons Magnettick Ladye. [1632] Parturient Montes Nascetur . . .'.
Pr. Wood's *Athenae*, ed. Bliss, ii. 598, and iii. 44.
MSS. Ashmole 38, p. 15, attr. to Alexander Gill; CCC. 309, fol. 67.

1772*b* [Is this your temp'rate diet? Here's no mean]
Temperance I fear will make thy work long liv'd.
Gunning, [Peter], on *Hygiasticon*, Leonardus Lessius, 1634.
MS. Eng. misc. e. 13, fol. 22$^{v}$.

1773 Is thy Charles dead? no help from all thy prayers
His brothers age of man, and his own too.
Wright, Abraham, 'Upon the death of our late most gratious soveraigne K: Charles . . . Mar. 8. 84/5. Transl. by A. W. from the Oxford Verses' of R. Wright of Magdalen, pr. *Pietas Universitatis . . . in obitum . . . regis*, Sig. F1.
MS. Eng. misc. e. 82, fol. 39 (autogr.).

1774 Is thy house fair, thy table full of plate?
We cannot call them truly good I say.
F[itzjames], L[eweston], translator, 'Transit cito gloria mundi . . . In as manie lynes thus in english'. The Latin 'Out of [Mrs. Grimstons Miscellanea]'.
MS. Add. B. 97, fol. 48 (autogr.).

1775 Is thy poor bark becalmed and forced to stay
But when the wind blows fair contract her sail.
R[andolph], T[homas], 'De moderatione animae in utraque fortuna'.
MS. Eng. poet. c. 50, fol. 105.

Is time so priceless, or one wasted hour 1776
'Tis as ill to distrust good, as to sin.
'Elegie'.
MS. Rawl. poet. 31, fol. 41$^{v}$.

Is Wolly's wife now dead and gone 1777
A thousand thanks then thou shalt have.
'A Jacobite Scott in Satyr on Englands unparralelld Losse', death of Q. Mary, 1694.
MSS. Add. A. 301, fol. 66$^{v}$ rev.; Rawl. D. 361, fol. 263.

Isca, whose fruitful streams make flowers rise, 1778
And all his pensive music went.
Chatwin, John, 'Ad Fluvium Iscam. Paraphrastically translated out of Mr. Vaughan's poems' [*Olor Iscanus*, 1646].
MS. *Rawl. poet. 94, p. 183 (autogr.).

Israel by fiery serpents stung 1779
The prince of glory dies.
Beddome, Benjamin.
MS. *Eng. misc. e. 227, fol. 12$^{v}$.

Israel has lost her ornament 1780
And Israel's worthy's rolled in dust.
Fairfax, Thomas, Lord, '[Songs of the old and New Testament:] David's Lamentation for Saule and Jonathan. 2. Sam: 1'.
MS. *Fairfax 40, p. 418 (autogr.).
MS. *Fairfax 38, p. 89.

Israel's sweet singer of Mount-Syon; 1781
Of sins committed, received free remission.
H. W., 'Of little David and great Goliah', no. 12 of 'Sacred Epigrams' sent to John Rhodes, fellow of Trinity College, Cambridge, 1618–48.
MS. Tanner 466, fol. 101.

Issue of best Father thou 1782
Heavenly seed it may produce.
J. F., translator, 'Buchanan's Morning Hymn to Christ'.
MS. *Eng. poet. f. 17, p. 81 (autogr.).

Is't for a grace or is't for some dislike 1783
Your gloves perfumed, your lips and cheeks be painted.
[Harington, Sir John].
Pr. *Epigrams*, 1618, iii. 3.
MSS. Rawl. poet. 31, fol. 4; 116, fol. 53.

Is't not a pretty humour (think ye, fie!) 1784–5
Are only meat and drink for other's laughter.
Bulteel, John, 'On a puling Madam'.
MS. *Rawl. poet. 159, fol. 209$^{v}$.

1786 Is't possible you can deny
More prized, or more hardly won.
North, Dudley, 3rd Baron.
Pr. *A Forest of Varieties*, 1645.
MS. *North. e. 41, fol. 37.

1787 Is't true? or do vain tales feared mortals cheat
Like dreams that fill our heads with causeless fear.
J. F., translator 'The Chorus of the III Act of Seneca's Troas'.
MS. *Eng. poet. f. 17, p. 1 (autogr.).

1788 Is't true that souls their bodies do survive?
Fantastic notions, idle frightful dreams.
Glanvill, [John], based on Seneca, *Troades* 371–408 'The Atheist's foolish Fancy of the Soul's Mortality'.
Pr. *Poems*, 1725, p. 250.
MS. Rawl. poet. 173, fol. 56^v^.

1789 It being proved that fighting Will ne'er fought
How to turn those ears again into nose.
'In Daphnen Causidicum', on Sir William Davenant.
Pr. *Certain Verses to be reprinted with . . . Gondibert*, 1653, p. 12.
MS. CCC. 309, two copies, fols. 53 and 59.

1790 It being provident not trusting to his heir
Went to his tomb alive, and so died there.
Couplet, 'Uppon a Candell goinge out in a snuffe'.
MS. Rawl. poet. 117, fol. 271 rev.

1791 It can be counted but a human feat
Take, and enjoy, each one a crown of bliss.
[Corbet, W.], 'Create in me a clean Heart, O Lord . . . P[salm] 51'.
MS. *Rawl. poet. 210, fol. 34.

1792 It cannot be, where is that mighty joy.
But keep a standing majesty in me.
Herbert, George, 'The Temper'.
Pr. *The Temple*, 1633, p. 47.
MS. *Tanner 307, fol. 36^v^.

1793 It cannot move thy friend firm Ben, that he
The ghost of thine slain name, would rather sleep.
Townley, Zouch, 'to Mr. Ben Johnson against Mr. Alexander Gills verses wrighten by him against . . . the Magnettick Ladye'.
See I1772*a*. Pr. Wood's *Athenae*, ed. Bliss, ii. 600, from MS. Ashmole 38.
MSS. Ashmole 38, p. 58, attr. to Mr. Souch Townlye; CCC. 309, fol. 68^v^; Rawl. poet. 147, p. 104, attr. to Townly.

[It chanced me one day . . .] 1794
Sith now I am but weeds and wasteful grass.
Spenser, Edmund, 'The Ruines of Time', verse 6, quoted in J. Shrimpton's History of St. Albans.
MS. Gough Herts. 3, fol. 56.

It chanced of late a shepherd swain 1795
And laughed, the pleasing sight to see.
'Cupid's Pastime'.
Pr. F. Davison's *Poetical Rapsody*, 1602; in Dryden's *Fourth Part of Miscellany Poems*, 1694, p. 282, attr. to Sidney Godolphin.
MS. Add. B. 105, fol. 79^v^, attr. to Sidney Godolphin.

It chanced that in the temple I 1796
None but her self can quench the same.
Weaver, Thomas, 'On Mrs. Pen: Tr. discover'd in the church at her devotion'.
Not pr. in *Songs and Poems*, 1654.
MS. *Rawl. poet. 211, fol. 11^v^ (autogr.).

It cost this woeful widow many a tear 1797
To apprehend must rend our life asunder.
'Upon the widow of naine'.
MS. Rawl. poet. 116, fol. 130.

It fell on a day when good people say 1798
And his last shall be from a cart.
Satire on Cromwell.
MS. Rawl. poet. 26, fol. 153.

It grieves me for to see: how honour's flood 1799
Ebbs into air; when men are great, not good.
Couplet, translating *Quidquid excelusm est cadat*.
MS. Eng. poet. f. 10, fol. 106^v^.

It grieves me that I thus due thanks retain 1800
Who nothing pays, pays all if what he can.
Stroad, William, 'Letter. To Sir John Ferrers'.
MS. Eng. poet. e. 97, p. 135.

It had not rained, and so the earth was dry 1801
Am troubled, 'cause I want fountain's supply.
Pr. *Parthenia Sacra*, ed. I. Fletcher, 1633, p. 220.
MS. Eng. poet. b. 5, p. 106.

It happened in the twilight of the day 1802
Starts from the couch, and bids the dame draw near.
'Sir Edmund berry Godfreyes gost'.
Pr. *Poems on Affairs of State*, i, 1703, p. 94.
MS. Add. A. 48, fol. 49^v^.

1803 It has been fabled (and it may be so,)
And at one stroke, their husband's lives destroy.
Popple, William, 'Juvenal Englished. against Women'. *Satires* II. vi.
MS. Douce 201, fol. 55.

1804 It has grieved me long that almost every song
Has been the good Laird of Craigubble.
Boswell, James, 'Song to the Lord Kenmore 1762'.
MS. *Douce 193, fol. 61 (autogr.).

1805 It is a common use to entertain
So backed with troops of followers, as he.
[Quarles, Francis], 'On a Dead man'.
Pr. *Divine Fancies*, 1632, ii. 85.
MSS. Don. d. 58, fol. 13; Rawl. poet. 90, fol. 70$^v$; 117, fol. 171 rev.

1806 It is a golden view, the sunny glow
And we will say he earns his supper well.
Seward, Anna, 'Landscape . . . copied by Miss Fleming of Lichfield . . . Feb. 1800'.
Pr. *Poetical Works*, ed. Sir W. Scott, 1810, iii. 332.
MS. Eng. poet. c. 51, p. 68.

1807 It is a good and pleasant thing
In him, my rock and trust.
Psalm xcii.
MS. *Montagu e. 10, fol. 44$^v$.

1808 It is a grace that teaches to deprave not
By selling lands; and to grow rich, by giving.
[Quarles, Francis], 'On the three Christian Graces'.
Pr. *Divine Fancies*, 1632, i. 13.
MS. Rawl. poet. 90, fol. 59$^v$.

1809 It is a joy of grievance past to prate
And now by sin my soul would overthrow.
Burton, Francis.
MS. *Add. A. 267, fol. 81 (autogr.).

1810 It is a kind of pleasing thing,
For love of this became a wife.
'In mentulam'.
MS. CCC. 328, fol. 90$^v$.

1811 It is a punishment to love
Whose hearts whose minds whose wills are not our own.
[Cowley, Abraham], Song in *Loves Riddle*, IV. i; pr. with music by William Webb, *New Ayres and Dialogues*, 1678, p. 65.
MS. Don. c. 57, fol. 40, music by W. Webb.

It is a question [made *or* now] in heraldry 1812
He my Lord F., and she my Lady Letcher.
'In Londinensem Episcopum iampridem Dominae et scortae nuptias 1595. Feb. 20'. [Richard Fletcher].
MSS. Add. B. 97, fol. 20$^v$; CCC. 327, fol. 29$^v$; Rawl. poet. 212, fol. 100$^v$; Tanner 306, two copies, fols. 188$^v$ and 189.

It is a statute in deep wisdom's lore 1813
I consecrate my idle hours to thee.
[Beaumont, Francis], 'To the true Patroness of all Poetrye Caliope'.
Pr. *Poems*, 1640, Sig. A3.
MS. Rawl. poet. 120, fol. 92.

It is a sweet and pleasant thing 1814
For no defects in thee there are.
Harington, Sir John, Psalm xcii.
MS. *Douce 361, fol. 56.

It is a thief that oft before his face 1815
Steals men away, and lays a beast in's place.
[Quarles, Francis], 'On drunkenness', couplet.
Pr. *Divine Fancies*, 1632, iii. 36.
MSS. Don. d. 58, fol. 38$^v$; Rawl. poet. 90, fol. 76$^v$; 117, fol. 171 rev.

It is a thing both good and meet 1816
In him there is none ill.
[Hopkins, John], Psalm xcii.
MS. Rawl. poet. 112, fol. 43$^v$ rev.

It is a thing more easy far, 1817
Sins though we them discern.
Robinson, Robert.
MS. *Rawl. poet. 218, p. 40 (autogr.).

It is agreed by all, that vice is taught 1818
That I should not embark, I think, intends.
'Seneca de otio et secessu'.
MS. Rawl. poet. 103, fol. 32*b*.

It is an easy matter to contend, 1819
The difficulty is to make an end.
Williams, John, couplet.
MS. *Rawl. poet. 191, fol. 101 (autogr.).

It is an error ev'n as foul to call 1820
Our sins too great for pardon, as too small.
[Quarles, Francis], 'On our sinnes', couplet.
Pr. *Divine Fancies*, 1632, ii. 96.
MS. Rawl. poet. 90, fol. 50$^v$.

It is asserted by the learned Lower 1821
Into lay blockheads makes the whelps cry ba.
'The Dogs turn'd into Sheep'.
Pr. bk. Firth b. 21, fol. 70$^v$.

1822 It is but just that the licentious should,
Who any part unfaithfully dispose.
Williams, John, 'Upon Poets are always poor'.
MS. *Rawl. poet. 184, fol. 111 (autogr.).

1823 It is confessed that great Britannia's stage
Bold to assert his injur'd country's cause.
'The Scenes'.
MS. Top. London e. 9, p. 93.

1824 It is enough my gracious Lord
All that Thy goodness waits to give.
Kenton, James.
MS. *Eng. poet. e. 20, p. 195 (autogr.).

1825 It is enough! The conflict's o'er
Embrace him on th' eternal shore.
Kenton, James, 'On [John Peter Harley] 1772'.
MS. *Eng. poet. e. 19, p. 220 (autogr.).

1826 It is expected that this epilogue now
None are exposed who in the least are pretty.
Allestree, [James], 'Epilogue' [Music Act, Oxford], 12 July 1679.
MS. Rawl. D. 1481, fol. 58.

1827 It is fond love that thinks to win
But what comes near a rape.
MS. Rawl. B. 35, fol. 57$^{v}$ rev.

1828 It is good to be merry
There God make all merry.
'A Songe'.
Copied from last leaf of *Nice Wanton*, pr. John King, London, 1560.
MS. Eng. poet. e. 97, p. 277.

1829 It is impossible; your judgements err
And in a moment wrap eternity.
Beaumont, Thomas, 'On the month after his Mariage'.
MS. *Malone 18, p. 90 (autogr.).

1830 It is long since I wrote, my reasons were good,
One thousand, seven hundred, sixty and eight.
Sutton, Lord George, 'To Miss Eleanor Peart', 3 April 1768.
MS. Eng. poet. e. 28, p. 176.

1831 It is love that doth us fill
Where peace and love, now reigns, triumphant in our veins.
Headed '[Numitar (?)] tune W. R.'
MS. Rawl. poet. 37, p. 45.

1832 It is mad world grown
And wear it on their faces.
MS. Eng. poet. e. 14, fol. 40$^{v}$.

It is man's chiefest duty to make known 1833
Of God's great works the brief compendium.
MS. *Rawl. poet. 97, fol. 2 (autogr.).

It is most just, that wicked plots and hate 1834
By her ill-doing wholly were undone.
MS. *Rawl. poet. 97, fol. 12$^{v}$.

It is most just to throw that on the ground 1835
Which would throw thee if that thou keep the round.
'Innotus quaedam extempore in Herbert poem:', couplet.
MS. Don. e. 6, fol. 16$^{v}$.

It is most true, that God to Israel, 1836
To sing his works, while breath shall give me space.
Herbert, Mary (*née* Sidney), Countess of Pembroke, Psalm lxxiii.
MSS. *Rawl. poet. 24, p. 104; *25, fol. 65.

It is no hearse-hypocrisy makes me 1837
Shalt thus be good, although thou beest not true.
P[aman], Cl[ement], 'On the 1st report of Mr. Ed. Kinges drowning'.
Marginal note 'To J. H.'
MS. Rawl. poet. 147, p. 146.

It is no marvel Adam innocent 1838
All that shall counsel 'gainst the Lord's command.
MS. *Rawl. poet. 97, fol. 9$^{v}$ (autogr.).

It is no tale, the hermit is belied, 1839
And call it truth, a tale's an infidel.
'In discommendation of the Author' i.e. Humphrey King; transcribed from *An Halfe-penny worth of Wit*, 1613, R. Heber's copy.
MS. Douce 190, fol. 9.

It is no wonder for a man to die, 1840
But to be born, there, there's a wonder high.
Robinson, Robert, couplet.
MS. *Rawl. poet. 218, p. 11 (autogr.).

It is not a full fortnight, since 1841
I'th' sale of *Rex Platonicus*.
Corbet, Dr. [Richard], 'The Oxford-Ballad'. March 1614/15. Answered by A2.
MS. Tanner 465, fol. 75; see also I1844, I1853.

It is not, Cælia, in our power 1842
To live, because w' are sure to die?
Etheredge, Sir Geo[rge], 'To a Lady, who ask'd him how long he wou'd love her'.
Not pr. in Etheredge's Works.
MS. Rawl. poet. 173, fol. 74.

1843 It is not crying serves our turn,
Death will not spare our breath.
Robinson, Robert.
MS. *Rawl. poet. 218, p. 177 (autogr.).

1844 It is not full a fortnight since
I'th sale of *Rex platonicus*.
[Corbett, Richard], 'Of the K[ing's] enterteynment at Cambridge', March 1614/15. Answered by A2.
MS. Don. c. 54, fol. 23v; see also I1841, I1853.

1845 It is not good from help and the delight
And do to all that is hereafter lead.
Williams, John, 'Upon A Wife, and a companion'.
MS. *Rawl. poet. 192, fol. 185 (autogr.).

1846 It is not I that die, I do but leave the inn
Lament you when I loose not when I win.
'Sir Phillip Sydney of himselfe', couplet.
MSS. Ashmole 47, fol. 40v, attr. to Sr. Phillip Sydney; 781, p. 150, attr. to Sr. Philip Sidney.

1847 It is not long since I could see
Unless I'm cur'd by you.
'A Sonnet'.
MS. Rawl. poet. 160, fol. 107v.

1848 It is not strange a shepherd reigns in Rome
How wolves should keep the flock secure from ill.
'On the Pope'.
MS. Eng. poet. e. 87, p. 108.

1849 It is not that I love you less
The vow I made to love you too.
[Waller, Edmund], 'The Selfe Banished'.
Pr. *Poems*, 1645, p. 83.
MSS. *Don. d. 55, fol. 27v; *Rawl. poet. 174, p. 60.

1850 It is not true as men do say
In his great virtues live he shall.
G. B., 'Epitaph 8' on Prince Henry in 'Cestria Lugens', 1612.
MS. *Rawl. poet. 116, fol. 7.

1851 It is not Virgil's silly gnat
To manifest my old good will.
Lilliat, John, 'Certayne verses sent with a Butterflie, which was framed in Networke'.
MS. Rawl. poet. 148, fol. 4 (autogr.).

1852 It is not wealth to have at will
Let us rejoice therefore at that.
MS. Gough Norfolk, 43, fol. 48v.

It is not yet [full, fully] a fortnight since 1853
The sale of *Rex Platonicus*.
Corbet, R[ichard], 'a grave poeme . . . stild liber novus de adventu regis ad Cantabrigiam faithfully done into English with some liberall advantages', March 1614/15. Answered by A2.
Pr. *Certain Elegant Poems*, 1647, p. 58; *Poetica Stromata*, 1648, p. 29.
MSS. Ashmole 36, 37, fol. 258; Douce f. 5, fol. 22v; Firth d. 7, fol. 60; Malone 19, p. 112; Rawl. D. 929, fol. 55 rev.; Rawl. poet. 26, fol. 26v; 152, fol. 200; 199, p. 18, attr. to R. Corbet; 209, fol. 16; Top. Oxon. e. 344, fol. 137; pr. bk. Gough Cambridge 98, at end; see also I1841, I1844.

It is received, that sleep's the elder brother: 1854
I'm sure that death does sweep away the land.
[Quarles, Francis], 'On Sleep and Death'.
Pr. *Divine Fancies*, 1632, iv. 77.
MS. Rawl. poet. 90, fol. 75.

It is Sir, a confess'd intrusion here, 1855
Who firm'd his name on such a pyramid.
King, Henry, 'To my honourd friend Mr. George Sandys'.
Pr. Sandys' *Paraphrase upon the Divine Poems*, 1638, and King's *Poems*, 1657, p. 118.
MS. *Eng. poet. e. 30, fol. 78.

It is the guise 1856
And leave their own unspied.
Lilliat, John.
MS. Rawl. poet. 148, fol. 110 (autogr.).

It is thou that we should love 1857
Without end to govern alone.
'Tua Jesu dilectio . . . Primer of Hen. 8. Eng. and Lat. 1536, fol. 147'.
MS. Eng. poet. e. 56, p. 110.

It is to fall when thou it find 1858
With a wicked woman woe might she be.
'The Prophesies of Merling'.
MS. Ashmole 1835, fol. 45v.

It is uncertain when a certain preacher 1859
Did ever read there was a certain woman.
Answered by T211.
MS. Rawl. poet. 206, p. 61.

It makes me to muse, to hear of the news 1860
And cloak us with silver and gold.
Satire on the first Duke of Buckingham.
MS. Malone 23, p. 104.

1861 It may perhaps presage th' old Britain's good
Let Cambria's thanks to Cimbria never rest.
On Anne of Denmark, translated from Latin.
MS. Wood D. 13, two copies, pp. 190 and 198.

1862 It moves my wonder to behold how few
And rapture crown the night, as reason rules the day!
Parsons, William, 'The Division of Time A Rhapsody', 18 March 1782.
Pr. *Travelling Recreations*, 1807, i. 3.
MS. *Don. d. 123, p. 63 (autogr.).

1863 It must be so—alas, 'tis so!
And makes us blessings to ourselves and man.
'Prudella . . . The Batchelors Soliloquy, in the manner of Cato's Speech'.
MS. Montagu e. 13, fol. 77v.

1864 It must be so, I now will prove
When war begins within, and rages there.
'An Ode translated from Anacreon', xiii.
MS. Eng. poet. f. 12, p. 72.

1865 It must be so, my shepherd ne'er shall prove
By heaven's most kind decree.
'Corydon and Miranda, A Pastoral Interlude', with music.
MS. Mus. c. 3, fol. 44.

1866 It never was, nor will be so,
That nothing knows more than another.
Robinson, Robert, 'Hee's a foole indeed, that knows nothing more then another'.
MS. *Rawl. poet. 218 p. 36 (autogr.).

1867 It never was, or ever shall be known
The motions of God's Spirit not obey.
MS. *Rawl. poet. 97, fol. 23 (autogr.).

1868 It nods, it struts, it gives itself applause
Bad is the head, but ten times worse the heart.
'On the Czarowitz a young Jackanapes'.
MS. Rawl. poet. 172, fol. 141.

1869 It plainly appears, the tongue has no ears,
He, that has all the talk, no man else hears.
Robinson, Robert, couplet.
MS. *Rawl. poet. 218, p. 94 (autogr.).

1870 It pleased the sunshine of my gracious king
Expects those drops, or my poor plants must die.
Quarles, Francis, [Dedication].
Pr. from this MS., *Works*, ed. Grosart, Chertsey Worthies Library, 1881, vol. i, p. lxxiii.
MSS. Ashmole 36, 37, fol. 22v.

1871 It seems that nature when she first did fancy
Vouchsafe me to be your familiar.
'On the praise of a blacke wench'.
MS. Eng. poet. e. 14, fol. 86 rev.

It was a bishop said it (and there may 1872
Diana or Minerva makes the feast.
Creswell, Robert, 'Of Hunting and study', from Synesius, *De insomniis*, 'p. 150'.
MS. *Eng. poet. f. 24, fol. 41v (autogr.).

It was a dismal and a fatal night 1873
Where grief and misery can be joined with verse.
[Cowley, Abraham], 'on the death of Mr. William Hervey', 16 May 1642.
Pr. *Works*, 1668, 'Miscellanies', p. 16.
MSS. Malone 21, fol. 24; Tanner 306, fol. 268, attr. to Mr. Cooley.

It was a glorious and a cheerful day 1874
At that late hour when he should bring his trophies home.
'Death', presented by M. A. to Abp. Sancroft, 1689.
MS. Rawl. poet. 154, fol. 56v.

It was a maid of Islington 1875
A member of great joy.
'A pretie dittie to the tune off ladie Jane'.
MS. Rawl. poet. 185, fol. 5v.

It was a time when silly bees could speak 1876
'Twas not tobacco stupefied my brain.
'The Apologue of the Bee'.
Note by W. Sancroft, MS. Tanner 76, 'Henry Cuff made the following verses, his Lord and Master the Earl of Essex being then in some disgrace'. 3 verses pr. John Dowland's *Third Book of Aires*, 1603, xviii.
MSS. Ashmole 781, p. 132, attr. to Essex; Douce 280, fol. 123, attr. to R. D. E. Essex; Eng. misc. c. 93, fol. 21v, attr. to the Erle of Essex; Rawl. C. 744, fol. 63, attr. to the Earle of Essex; Rawl. poet. 148, fol. 87, incomplete, attr. to Mr. John Lilly; 172, fol. 13, attr. to Lord Essex; Tanner 76, fol. 93, attr. to Henry Cuff; 306, fol. 249, attr. to Rob. Devereux Earl of Essex; see also T1764.

It was a winter's evening, and fast came down the snow 1877
Then cast her eyes to heaven, bowed her head and died.
'A Winter-Piece (Elegant Extracts)'.
MS. Montagu e. 14, fol. 28.

It was an old saying of Sir John Kettel's 1878
By that same token, the mustard pot hangs by.
MS. Rawl. poet. 85, fol. 50v.

1879 It was at evening, and in April mild
I came a partial judge to praise the screen.
Fletcher, G[iles], 'Nisus amore piu pueri etc. 'tis Encolpus in Petronius. I had it of Mr. Blois'.
See *Works of G. and P. Fletcher*, ed. F. S. Boas, i, 1908, pp. vii, 89, 279.
MS. Tanner 465, fol. 42.

1880 It was at the battle of Dettingen
That we were at Dettingen.
'The Rose of Dettingen'.
MS. Firth c. 7, fol. 39.

1881–2 It was by providence (for chance goes less)
His fortune and the world both run on wheels.
Creswell, Robert, Satire on Cromwell's accident, 29 Sept. 1654.
MS. *Eng. poet. f. 24, fol. 2 (autogr.).

1883 It was in the summer time, all in the month of May
The ship it was their coffin, and the sea it was their grave.
'The Coast of Barbary'.
MS. Firth c. 18, fol. 129.

1884 It was my chance lately abroad to be
High artists in this art so musical.
Allen, Edmund, of Wootton, 'To the much admired Bedfordian Company of Ringers; Especially to Mr. Oliver Palmer, Chiefe of that Musicall Society'. 1655.
MS. Rawl. D. 886, fol. 6[v].

1885 It was my fortune once to go
It's very seldom both prove true.
'A New Song Written by a Sailor'.
Pr. *The Little Carpenter's Garland* (B.M. 11621. c. 4(8)).
MS. Firth c. 18, fol. 156.

1886 It was on the twenty-first of July brave Martin and his fleet,
We'll fight like lions bold when our enemies we meet.
'A New Song Called the Gallant Monmouth's Glory'.
MS. Firth c. 18, fol. 65.

1887 It was that gracious season of the year
Relieve fair huntress my afflicted case.
North, Dudley, 3rd Baron.
Pr. *A Forest of Varieties*, 1645.
MS. *North e. 41, fol. 23[v].

It was that month in which the righteous maid 1888
And bad her tongue that it so bluntly told.
'Prosopopæia or Mother Hubberds tale made by Ed. Spencer and dedicated to the right honorable the Lady Compton and Mount Eagle'. Copied by John Ramsey of Peterhouse (admitted 1601).
MS. Douce 280, fol. 22.

It was that time, when the world's glorious lamp 1889
Of all mankind, stopped their envenomed breath.
Leigh, Edward.
MS. Rawl. poet. 116, fol. 57[v].

It was the merry month of February 1890
And never makes my tender belly swell.
'[Thomas] Nashes Dildo'.
The first 17 lines only pr. in Grosart's *Works of T. Nashe*, 1881, i, p. lx.
MS. Rawl. poet. 216, fol. 97.

It was the time that every bird and beast 1891
I shall be glad to have this dream prove true.
Oldisworth, Nicolas, 'To his cosin Michael Oldisworth, Febr. 15. 1631'.
MS. *Don. c. 24, fol. 29[v] (autogr.).

It was the time when chimneys all agree 1892
Like thorns and briars or this accursed frame.
Molle, Henry, 'Twilight'.
MSS. Rawl. poet. 147, attr. to Henry Molle; 210, fol. 47[v], attr. to Henry Molle.

It was unkind, Pulcheria, cruel fair, 1893
To have blessed the slaves, your conquering charms had made.
'On Pulcheria leaving the Town'.
MS. Eng. misc. e. 240, p. 315.

It was when christians kneel, and did entreat 1894
Charles in thine heart, and Devereux thine arm.
'On Sir Robert Shirleys son', Seymour, b. 23 Jan. 1646/7.
MS. Eng. poet. e. 4, p. 72.

It was when the dark mantle of the night 1895
I felt my belly wet, and slept again.
MSS. Ashmole 36, 37, fol. 281.

It was when the seas were roaring 1896
She bowed her head and died.
[Gay, John], 'A Song' from *The What D'Ye Call It*.
MS. Montagu e. 13, fol. 22; see also T3416.

It was, when traitors in the text did pass 1897
The danger, and survive its martyrdom.
Weaver, Thomas, 'On Mrs. Maurice of Llanbeder's wound which she receav'd by a Round-head'.
Pr. *Songs and Poems*, 1654.
MS. *Rawl. poet. 211, fols. 18, 19[v] (autogr.).

1898 I'th' coffee-house, just now, among the rabble,
Caesar will reign in every honest heart.
Durfey, Thomas, 'Prologue to the king, Nov. 81', endorsed 'Mr. Tho. Durfey's Prologue to Sir Barnaby Whig: Spoken by Mr. Goodman when the King was there Nov. 1681'.
MS. Rawl. poet. 159, fol. 21.

1899 I'th' face will smile ye,
Simple and just, such you may trust.
Robinson, Robert.
MS. *Rawl. poet. 218, p. 3 (autogr.).

1900 I'th' isle which did in July last declare
Of their good fate, or wearied with their bad.
Weaver, Thomas, 'The Battaile of Anglesey Sep. 27. 1648 and the desperate adventure of some Cavaliers after the defeat'.
MS. *Rawl. poet. 211, fol. 28 (autogr.).

1901 I'th' morning Germans drink pure wine
Wine from the but at supper-time.
Translation from Italian.
MS. Sancroft 98, p. 135.

1902 It's a pity Martilla ye should be a wife
Yet marriage at best is hum drum and hum drum.
Song, 3 verses in dispraise of marriage.
MS. Eng. poet. c. 11, fol. 47; see also T2821.

1903 It's a thing that you frequently make with your bum
And he that can't guess is not worthy my name.
MS. Eng. poet. e. 8, fol. 29.

1904 It's God alone I will believe
No better to love thee.
Tipping, William, 'Only my deere Hess'.
MS. *Rawl. poet. 101, fol. 92 (autogr.).

1905*a* It's good to be afflicted, David saith,
That rod deserves a kiss that makes us better.
'A Meditation on Psalm the CXIX. Verse 71'.
MS. Rawl. poet. 90, fol. 127.

1905*b* It's held more triumph to subdue one passion
Then to triumph over a bellick nation.
Couplet.
MS. Rawl. poet. 117, fol. 168v rev.

1906 It's of a London maiden
To gain my maiden-head.
'Fanny's song'.
MS. Eng. poet. d. 152, fol. 123.

1907 It's pity things should lie so long obscure
And find a loving pastor for his sheep.
Cromwell, Edward, 'The Recollection' dated at end 11 Nov. 1715.
MS. *Rawl. poet. 165, fol. 27 (autogr.).

It's true that my affections lately bent 1908
Or may you still at least seem so to me.
North, Dudley, 3rd Baron.
Pr. *A Forest of Varieties*, 1645.
MS. *North. e. 41, fol. 33.

It's true, that pride will have a fall 1909
That pride may have no fall.
MS. Rawl. poet. 217, fol. 83.

It's true the two immortal syllables remain; 1910
It's all the conquered world could give.
Fleming, Robert.
MS. Rawl. poet. 213, fol. 49v rev. (autogr.).

It's true, 'tis nowadays too great a fault 1911
To have too much pepper, and too little salt.
Couplet.
MS. Rawl. poet. 117, fol. 171v rev.

Its voyage o'er, with prosperous gales 1912
Know, that coins, seals, and men are dust.
'Verses to Sylvanus Urban from back of Title to [Gent. Mag.] Vol. [lv] for 1785 part 1'.
MS. Eng. poet. c. 5, fol. 250.

I've finished now a work that mouldering age, 1913
If ever truth was known, shall live in fame.
Woodman, John.
Pr. bk. Gough Middlesex 12, at end (autogr.).

I've given my painter instructions to draw 1914
I'm a captain of foot and a justice of peace.
'A Lampoone on the Gentry in Kent. Anno. 1691'.
MS. Eng. poet. d. 53, p. 5.

I've heard, my friend, and heard it said by you, 1915
So did he live, and so deserved to die.
Oldham, John, translator, Ovid, *Amores* II. x, 'To a Friend, acquainting him he was in Love with more than one at one time'.
MS. Rawl. poet. 173, fol. 49.

I've heard the muses were still soft and kind 1916
Blast, great Apollo, with perpetual shame.
'Advice to Apollo. 1678', on the satirists.
MS. Rawl. poet. 159, fol. 100.

I've liv'd in pleasure: thus to live is gain; 1917
And early make virtue your choice.
'A Principle of Infidelity' and 'Reason's Answer'.
MS. *Eng. poet. d. 47, fol. 148.

[I've] Ise often for my Jeney strove 1918
[Joined to none but only thee].
MS. Rawl. poet. 196, fol. 3.

1919 I've often heard my Synthya say
And so prove just to me.
'A song. Words by Cap: Sute'.
MS. Mus. c. 16, fol. 121, autograph music by W. Davis.

1920 I've read of islands floating and removed
Of all your greatness whatsoe'er you are.
Corbett, [Richard], 'On the Spanish Match', 1623.
Pr. *Poems*, 1647, p. 43.
MSS. Ashmole 47, fol. 83ᵛ, attr. to Dr. Corbet; Malone 19, p. 27, attr. to Dr. Corbett; Rawl. D. 1048, fol. 51ᵛ, attr. to Dr. Corbet.

1921 I've rivalled mighty Antony in love,
If I by fate compelled am forced to do the same.
'The Farewel or Clarus to his Mistresses'. 1735.
MS. Eng. misc. e. 240, p. 140.

1922 I've seen men learned, rich and in place full high,
Even so must all: if all, sure thou and I.
Robinson, Robert.
MS. *Rawl. poet. 218, p. 33 (autogr.).

1923 I've seen men learned, rich, honoured, yet they die;
Then poor unlearned, unworthy, sure must I.
Robinson, Robert, couplet.
MS. *Rawl. poet. 218, p. 33 (autogr.).

I've seen the lily of the morning 1924
Lifts her from pain's most thorny bed.
'Song'.
MS. Percy d. 9, fol. 14ᵛ.

I've shouldered you all the world over, 1925
May I hold you as firm as a rock,
'The Soldier to his Rifle'.
MS. Firth c. 17, fol. 73.

I've sighed an absent age away 1926
For much more misery.
Duet by Robert King; pr. *A Second Booke of Songs* [1695 (?)], p. 4.
MS. Mus. Sch. C. 97, at end, fol. 12 rev.

I've slept upon't and faith! I find 1927
Ladies and gentlemen, good night.
Lumby, John, 'To J. G. Ap. 15. 1730'.
MS. *Eng. poet. e. 42, fol. 13.

I've sought for wisdom all the world about, 1928
In throng of fools I'm never like to find her.
Robinson, Robert.
MS. *Rawl. poet. 218, p. 46 (autogr.).

I've thought the fair Clarissa cries 1929
To raise you something like a whale.
[Bacon, Dr. Phanuel], 'A Play at Similes'.
Pr. *Oxford Sausage*, 1764 (shorter version).
MS. Eng. poet. e. 45, fols. 50–52, 51ᵛ (autogr.).

# J

ENTRIES 1–191

1 J. Parry his daughter Blanch of Newcourt born,
With maiden queen a maid did end my life.
'On the Monument of Mrs. Blanch Parry Maid of Honour to Q. Elizabeth, at Bacton Church, Herefordshire'.
MS. Ballard 29, fol. 74.

2 Jack Bluster a comical, jolly, old boy
Your pipes I'd advise you to carry along.
Boswell, James, 'Epigram'.
Pr. *A Collection of Original Poems by Scotch Gentlemen*, ii, 1762, p. 83.
MS. *Douce 193, fol. 38ᵛ (autogr.).

3 Jack Careles lately ran a race (they say)
Hath got the stakes, and with them's run away.
Robinson, Robert, couplet.
MS. *Rawl. poet. 218, p. 59 (autogr.).

4 Jack Sprat
They licked the platter clean.
MS. Douce d. 59, fol. 48ᵛ.

5 Jack Sprat, had a cat
And that was too dear.
MS. Douce d. 59, fol. 55.

6 Jack swore to Kate he never more would woo her
And stiff withstanding made the friendly peace.
'On the Word Notwithstanding'.
MS. Top. London e. 9, p. 35.

7 Jack thou'rt a toper
Though watchmen cry Past two a clock.
[Powell, George (?)] from *Bonduca*, catch by Purcell.
F. B. Zimmerman, *Purcell*, 1963, no. 574(10).
MSS. Mus. c. 107, fol. 50ᵛ; Mus. Sch. C. 95, p. 95.

8 Jack's wondrous sick and thinks he shall go mad
A groat will pay thy loss when wit's at dearest.
'On Jacke'.
MSS. Don. d. 58, fol. 33ᵛ; Tanner 465, fol. 95.

9 Jacky come give me thy fiddle
My fiddle and I have had.
MS. Douce d. 59, fol. 58.

Jacob and Esau were two twins entwined 10
When the two twins do meet in love.
'An himne on Jacob and Esau'.
MS. Rawl. poet. 37, p. 55.

Jacob by contract looks to Laban's flock 11
'Twas easy to distinguish now their own.
'The Contract'.
MS. Rawl. poet. 154, fol. 102*b*.

James Brindley lies amongst these rocks 12
Water sent him to the ground.
'Humorous Epitaph for Mr. James Brindley late Engineer to the Duke of Bridgewater etc. *Chester Courant*, 1772'.
MS. Top. Yorks. c. 2, fol. 4.

James to obtain his seat of endless bliss 13
The servants envy for the master's love.
Clifford, Henry, Earl of Cumberland, 'Saint James'.
MS. *Rawl. poet. 95, fol. 35.

James' words we daily see, Phillip was known 14
Who by the way salvation gladly found.
Clifford, Henry, Earl of Cumberland, 'Phillip and Jacob'.
MS. *Rawl. poet. 95, fol. 34.

Jan whilst abroad at tables thou dost fret. 15
And doubt not but they'll point on thee as fast.
Mervall, Alphonso, 'To Telamius the Elder. Epigram': 'to J. W.' added later.
MS. *Rawl. poet. 166, p. 62 (autogr.).

Janus did ever to thy wond'ring eyes 16
And governs but to bless.
New Year Ode, [1705], on the Battle of Blenheim [August 1704] with music [by Eccles].
MS. Mus. Sch. C. 135.

Janus is old: his Pica is no less 17
But each for Pica doth a feather make.
Mervall, Alphonso, 'To Janus Telamius and his wyfe Pica'.
MS. *Rawl. poet. 166, p. 62 (autogr.).

18 Jealous Malchom believes his wife will do it
He surely would be saved by belief.
'Epigrams'.
MS. Rawl. poet. 172, fol. 7v.

19 Jeer your benefactress, that's but just
How e'er take jeer for jeer from Marey More.
More, Mary, answer to M51.
MS. Rawl. D. 912, fol. 197.

20 Jegon, joggs on, would fain be rich
And make it stoop to prelacy.
'A waggish schollar made these verses, on Doctor Jeggon, of Bennet Colledge in Cambridge', Master 1590–1603. Answered in K76.
MS. Rawl. poet. 66, fol. 64.

*Note*. Jehova, Jehovah, in one alphabetical series.

21 Jehovah calls us to repent
And let us stray no more.
Beddome, Benjamin.
MS. *Eng. misc. e. 227, fol. 72v.

22 Jehova comes to reign
His holiness make known.
Herbert, Mary (*née* Sidney), Countess of Pembroke, Psalm xcvii.
MS. *Rawl. poet. 24, p. 142.

23 Jehovah for his people cares
But ever love thine own.
Kenton, James.
MS. *Eng. poet. e. 20, p. 118 (autogr.).

24 Jehovah god of gods himself hath spoken
I shall both show and send him sure salvation.
Harington, Sir John, Psalm l.
MS. *Douce 361, fol. 30.

25 Jehovah, Lord of Heav'n and earth,
And silently adore.
'An Hymn to God the Creator . . . G[entleman's] Mag.'
MS. Eng. poet. e. 39, p. 147.

26 Jehova now is king
And give him thanks for he is holy.
Harington, Sir John, Psalm xcvii.
MS. *Douce 361, fol. 58v.

27 Jehova praise; Jehova's holy fame
What he (to whom be praise) hath said, and willed.
Herbert, Mary (*née* Sidney), Countess of Pembroke, Psalm cv.
MS. *Rawl. poet. 24, p. 153.

Jehovah preserve and restore to his throne 28
To give Caesar his due and to thee what is thine.
'The Prayer', for 'James III'.
Pr. *A Collection of Loyal Songs, Poems, etc.*, 1750, p. 34.
MS. Rawl. poet. 155, p. 175.

Jehovah reigns he reigns on high 29
All thou approvest may we do.
Beddome, Benjamin.
MS. *Eng. misc. e. 227, fol. 10v.

Jehova reigns our monarch great 30
T'adore his hill for he is holy.
Harington, Sir John, Psalm xcix.
MS. *Douce 361, fol. 59v.

Jehovah thou almighty name, 31
My strength and confidence and boast.
Kenton, James.
MS. *Eng. poet. e. 20, p. 271 (autogr.).

Jenkin that jealous lived without deserts 32
How should her parts be known, she not a —.
'Opinio major veritate'.
MS. Sancroft 465, fol. 94.

Jenkin, why man? Why Jenkin? fie for shame 33
And end our talking in some other place.
'Jokey: Jenken', pastoral dialogue alluding to the expulsion of Jenken [T. Bastard] from [New College]. See J. L. Sanderson, *The Library*, 5th ser., xvii. 146.
MS. Add. B. 97, fol. 5.

Jenny gin you can love 34
All the love you pretend is only to my undoing.
D'Urfey, [Thomas], 'A Dialogue' [from *The Three Dukes of Dunstable*].
F. B. Zimmerman, *Purcell*, 1963, no. 571 (7).
MSS. Eng. poet. d. 152, fol. 83v; Mus. Sch. C. 95, p. 210, attr. to D'Urfey, music by H. Purcell.

Jenny Man you must know made boast of the favour 35
When at parting she turned him her breech for to kiss.
'On Jenny Man's being saluted by K[ing] G[eorge I]'.
MS. Rawl. poet. 155, p. 80.

[Jenny] Jeney my blithest maid 36
Jeney alone's the lass that I adore.
MS. Rawl. poet. 196, fol. 27v.

Jerusalem is all infected over 37
Rebuild her walls, and love thy Syon still.
'The true Israelite's prayer for Syons Prosperity'.
MS. Rawl. poet. 71, p. 145.

38 **Jerusalem Jerusalem how oft have I called thee**
**In safety thou'lt keep me.**

Tipping, William, 'None but Christ. Our Saviour Lamenting over Jerusalem'.
MS. *Rawl. poet. 101, fol. 115 (autogr.).

39 **Jerusalem, that place divine**
**And sing their praise for evermore.**

'Engl. Primer of our Lady. 1631. p. 39'.
MS. Eng. poet. e. 56, p. 61.

40 **[Jerusalem] Hierusalem the vision true of peace**
**When shall I joy, assist, praise saints among.**

F. W.,'Sonnet 14. Whie the joyes of heaven are Called Heirusalem'.
MS. *Rawl. C. 639, p. 61.

41 **Jerusalem's curse shall never light on me**
**For here a stone upon a stone shall be.**

'On the death of one stone'.
Pr. *Wits Recreations*, 1640, Epitaph 42.
MSS. Eng. poet. e. 14, fol. 85ᵛ rev.; e. 97, p. 153, attr. to Stone; Rawl. D. 398, fol. 193.

42 **Jesu dost ask why thanks and praise be thine**
**As thou hast made so thou dost comfort mine.**

Anagram: 'Gervasius Cutler miles: Jesu cur grates [Illius mel (?)]' from a page of notes on Sir Gervase Cutler.
MS. Top. Yorks c. 26, fol. 137.

43 **Jesu, great governor of all**
**And, prostrate, worship round thy throne.**

Kenton, James.
MS. *Eng. poet. e. 20, p. 365 (autogr.).

44 **Jesu is in my heart, his sacred name**
**And to my whole is Jesu.**

Herbert, George, 'Jesue'.
Pr. *The Temple*, 1633, p. 105.
MSS. Rawl. poet. 90, fol. 140; *Tanner 307, fol. 79.

45 **Jesu more brighter then the sun**
**[Without end to govern alone].**

'Jesu sole serenior . . . Primer of Hen. 8 Engl. and Lat. 1536 fol. 149ᵛ'.
MS. Eng. poet. e. 56, p. 113.

46 **Jesu, no more! It is full tide**
**That stains in torrents of its own?**

[Crashaw, Richard], 'Upon our Saviours wounds'.
MS. Tanner 465, fol. 34, attr. to Mr. Crashaw on fol. 1*a*.

47 **Jesu our prayers with mildness hear**
**Whilst time lasts, and when time is done.**

'Engl. Primer of our Ladie. 1631 . . . p. 37'.
MS. Eng. poet. e. 56, p. 59.

**Jesu saw people come him till** 48–49
**That pleaseth meekly our Lord Jesu.**

'Octo benedictiones Domini nostri Jesu Christi . . . Ex MS . . . c. temp. Henry V'.
In B.M. MS. Harl. 1706, fol. 208ᵛ.
MS. Eng. poet. e. 56, p. 119.

**Jesu, the handle of the world's great ball** 50
**Yea let Christ hold us sure, or else we shall.**

Alabaster, William, 'Son: 34'.
MS. *Eng. poet. e. 57, fol. 8ᵛ.

**Jesu the most highest benignity** 51
**[Without end to govern alone].**

'Jesu summa benignitas . . . Primer of Hen. 8 Engl. and lat. 1536. fol. 148'.
MS. Eng. poet. e. 56, p. 111.

**Jesu, thy love within me is so main,** 52
**Since my heart holds not Thee, hold thou my heart.**

'A divine Sonnet . . . in Dr. [John] Boys's Postill on the Circumcision made by a friend of his an accurate poët'.
Pr. Boys's *An Exposition of al the Principal Scriptures used in our English Liturgie*, 1610, p. 137.
MS. Tanner 466, fol. 27.

**Jesus, a king most marvellous** 53
**Without end to govern alone.**

'Jesu rex admirabilis . . . Primer of Hen. 8 Engl. and Lat. 1536 . . . fol. 145'.
MS. Eng. poet. e. 56, p. 108.

**Jesus a little company** 54
**Enter, and never leave us more.**

Kenton, James.
MS. *Eng. poet. e. 20, p. 202*a* (autogr.).

**Jesus! and shall it ever be?** 55
**That Saviour not ashamed of me.**

'Hymn'.
MS. Eng. poet. c. 51, p. 56.

**Jesus before his final supper ended** 56
**To lodge the saviour of the world within them.**

'Uppon our saviours last supper'.
MS. Rawl. poet. 116, fol. 141.

**Jesus being betrayed by his friend** 57
**That so it must be? then His servants fled.**

MS. *Rawl. poet. 97, fol. 59ᵛ (autogr.).

**Jesus but twelve years old, yet posing them** 58
**A nullifidian of his impudence.**

MS. *Rawl. poet. 97, fol. 45ᵛ (autogr.).

59 Jesus Christ both god and man
Save they servant Jernegan.
Couplet 'Uppon An Auntient Knight Sr Jernegan Buried Cross Legd att Somerlye In Suffolke'.
Pr. Camden's *Remaines* 1605, 'Epitaphes', p. 47.
MSS. Ashmole 38, p. 177; Eng. poet. e. 40, fol. 120.

60 Jesus comes in great compassion
Crowned with everlasting love.
Kenton, James.
MS. *Eng. poet. e. 20, p. 85 (autogr.).

61 Jesus descended from above
And his disciples are.
Kenton, James.
MS. *Eng. poet. e. 20, p. 173 (autogr.).

62 Jesus descending to the grave
Triumphant to the upper skies.
Kenton, James.
MS. *Eng. poet. e. 20, p. 247 (autogr.).

63 Jesus forsakes his native skies
And seek to feel its vital power.
Beddome, Benjamin.
MS. *Eng. misc. e. 227, fol. 10v.

64 Jesus, friend of sinners, come
Glory be to God on high.
Kenton, James.
MS. *Eng. poet. e. 20, p. 374 (autogr.).

65 Jesus, God's eternal son
He hath bought for you and me.
Kenton, James.
MS. *Eng. poet. e. 20, p. 302 (autogr.).

66 Jesus his love hath shown
Of loving thee alone.
Kenton, James.
MS. *Eng. poet. e. 20, p. 36 (autogr.).

67 Jesus I trust in thee alone
My troubles into Heaven.
Kenton, James.
MS. *Eng. poet. e. 20, p. 278 (autogr.).

68 Jesus if thou my husband art
And I to thee so dear.
Beddome, Benjamin.
MS. *Eng. misc. e. 227, fol. 56v.

69 Jesus in peace himself doth rule
[Without end to govern alone].
'Jesu in pace imperat . . . Primer of Hen. 8 Engl. and Lat. 1536 . . . fol. 151'.
MS. Eng. poet. e. 56, p. 114.

Jesus is born: Peace, such high words forbear 70
His far weigheth down: Jesus is born.
Alabaster, William, Sonnet.
MS. CCC. 309, fol. 9.

Jesus, kindly condescend 71
Save, and claim me for thine own.
Kenton, James.
MS. *Eng. poet. e. 20, p. 333 (autogr.).

Jesus, Lord, avenge thine own 72
Save me by thy mighty love.
Kenton, James.
MS. *Eng. poet. e. 20, p. 224 (autogr.).

Jesus my Lord; If I should give my vote; 73
A sounder voice to thee th'incarnate word.
'Andreas Wood, Presbiter', on genufluxion.
MSS. Ashmole 36, 37, fol. 294.

Jesus my loving spouse 74
Sweet Christ my heart's with thee.
MS. Rawl. poet. 200, fol. 113.

Jesus oh let thy wondrous name 75
And every grace revive.
Beddome, Benjamin.
MS. *Eng. misc. e. 227, fol. 5.

Jesus our only hope 76
And worship give to David's son.
Kenton, James.
MS. *Eng. poet. e. 20, p. 106 (autogr.).

Jesus our Saviour and our King 77
Great Prince of Peace and King of Love.
MS. Mus. Sch. F. 605*, p. vii.

Jesus, Saviour, gracious Lord 78
Go in peace and sin no more.
Kenton, James.
MS. *Eng. poet. e. 20, p. 227 (autogr.).

Jesus, Son of Man and God 79
Thy Spirit cries Amen.
Kenton, James.
MS. *Eng. poet. e. 20, p. 333 (autogr.).

Jesus, the covert safe prepare 80
In everlasting day.
Kenton, James.
MS. *Eng. poet. e. 20, p. 280 (autogr.).

Jesus the eternal Lord 81
Fullness of the life divine.
Kenton, James.
MS. *Eng. poet. e. 20, p. 130 (autogr.).

Jesus the immortal God 82
And save for ever more.
Kenton, James.
MS. *Eng. poet. e. 20, p. 329 (autogr.).

83 Jesus the only thoughts of Thee
In Heaven with thee we may have place.
Gandy, Dr. Henry (?), translation of 'Jesus, dulcis memoria'.
MS. Rawl. D. 1253, fol. 325, in the hand of Dr. H. Gandy.

84 Jesus the soft and tender word
Nor slight the smallest grace.
Beddome, Benjamin.
MS. *Eng. misc. e. 227, fol. 173.

85 Jesus, the truth, the life, the way.
Blessings of grace and providence.
Kenton, James.
MS. *Eng. poet. e. 20, p. 388 (autogr.).

86 Jesus the truth, the life, the way
Now Lord! remember me.
Newton, John, 'Hymn'.
MS. Eng. poet. c. 51, p. 253.

87 Jesus th' eternal angel who
An everlasting rest to prove.
Kenton, James.
MS. *Eng. poet. e. 20, p. 177 (autogr.).

88 Jesus thou knowest my one desire
With Thee eternally to live.
Kenton, James.
MS. *Eng. poet. e. 20, p. 12 (autogr.).

89 Jesus thou Son of God
In yon bright world above.
Beddome, Benjamin.
MS. *Eng. misc. e. 227, fol. 82.

90 Jesus, thou source of endless bliss.
And let me then thy glory view.
Kenton, James.
MS. *Eng. poet. e. 20, p. 358 (autogr.).

91 Jesus thou spring of all my joys
Dear Jesus let me go.
Beddome, Benjamin, 'An Hymn'.
MS. *Eng. misc. e. 227, fol. 173$^{v}$.

92 Jesus, thou suffering dying lamb
In endless songs of love.
Kenton, James.
MS. *Eng. poet. e. 20, p. 241 (autogr.).

93 Jesus thy gracious aid I claim
And speak the word receive thy light.
Kenton, James.
MS. *Eng. poet. e. 20, p. 20 (autogr.).

94 Jesus Thy word fulfil
In all Thine image rise.
Kenton, James.
MS. *Eng. poet. e. 20, p. 76 (autogr.).

Jesus, Thy word receiving 95
To meet Thee in the skies.
Kenton, James.
MS. *Eng. poet. e. 20, p. 162 (autogr.).

Jesus to Israel's lost sheep first was sent 96
And by His sufferings we have health and ease.
MS. *Rawl. poet. 97, fol. 54 (autogr.).

Jesus to Thee my voice I raise 97
And all my life shall speak Thy praise.
Kenton, James.
MS. *Eng. poet. e. 20, p. 168 (autogr.).

Jesus when Thou hast fully wrought 98
Who saved and will forever save.
Kenton, James.
MS. *Eng. poet. e. 20, p. 206 (autogr.).

Jesus while He on earth remain'd, 99
Subjecting earthly to divine.
[Ken], Tho[mas], letter to one of the daughters of Thomas Thynne of Longleat, subscribed Tho: B and W.
MS. Add. C. 219, fol. 4 (autogr.).

Jesus who didst Thyself expose 100
And I am saved by grace alone.
Kenton, James.
MS. *Eng. poet. e. 20, p. 193 (autogr.).

Jesus, who died to buy the grace 101
So be it Lord, my heart replies.
Kenton, James.
MS. *Eng. poet. e. 20, p. 251 (autogr.).

Jesus with angry looks beholds 102
The faith which he oppos'd before.
Beddome, Benjamin.
MS. *Eng. misc. e. 227, fol. 49$^{v}$.

Jesus within the temple took survey 103
And giving that she gave her whole estate.
'Upon the poore widdow mite'.
MS. Rawl. poet. 116, fol. 127.

Jewels [being] lost are found again. This never: 104
'Tis but once lost: and once lost, lost for ever.
Couplet, 'On a maiden-head'.
MSS. Eng. poet. e. 97, p. 28; Rawl. poet. 153, fol. 22.

Joan and her maid to the counter were sent 105
For the wretched to day may be happy tomorrow.
MS. Eng. misc. b. 48, fol. 85.

Joane at the swan 106
And a touch-hole for the nose.
'On Joan Blake servant maid at the swan', not printed in *Modius salium*, 1751.
MS. Wood E. 32 (Modius salium), fol. 26$^{v}$.

107 **Job naked, with his children dead,**
**God's gracious will.**

[Ken], Tho[mas], letter to one of the daughters of Thomas Thynne of Longleat, subscribed Tho. B. and W.
MS. Add. C. 219, fol. 3 (autogr.).

108 **Jockey thy hornpipe's dull.**
**Us two to all the parish.**

Pr. Thomas Weelkes' *Ayeres or Phantasticke Spirites*, 1608, ii.
MSS. Mus. f. 7–10: f. 9, fol. 13.

109 **Jockey was a dowdy lad**
**And pipe a tune to please me.**

D'Urffey, Tho[mas], 'A Scotch songi n the Campagners. Set by Mr. Clerke'.
MS. Mus. Sch. C. 95, p. 132.

110 **Jockey was as brisk and blithe a lad**
**Mourning for the absence of my dear.**

'In the foole in fashion. Set by Mr. Clerke'.
MS. Mus. Sch. C. 95, p. 124.

111 **Jockey with Ginnye dancing**
**Ginny fell under and Jockie fell over.**

MS. CCC. 327, fol. 30.

112 **Jockye would be a gentleman**
**God grant all may be well, A.**

Song with refrain 'Disorder in many things', etc., *temp.* Charles I.
MS. Ashmole 38, p. 126.

113 **John Baptist he his head did lose**
**Now roasting in th' abyss.**

Tipping, William.
MS. *Rawl. poet. 101, fol. 74$^{v}$ (autogr.).

114 **John Bell Broken-Brow**
**Without mickle strife.**

'Att Farlam on the west Marches toward Scotland, neare Naworth Castle, this Epitaphe'.
Pr. Camden's *Remaines*, 1605, p. 59.
MSS. Ashmole, 38, p. 170; Eng. poet. e. 40, fol. 112.

115 **John Churchill did very ill**
**He is become most hateful.**

'On D: of Marlboroughs Entry [4 Aug.] 1714'.
MS. Rawl. poet. 155, p. 75.

116 **John Dryden enemies had three**
**He'd foil'd the Devil, and the Collier.**

'Upon Mr. Dryden'.
Pr. *Poems on Affairs of State*, iii, 1704, p. 379.
MS. Add. B. 105, fol. 6$^{v}$.

**John Grove grocer and dealer in tea** 117
**Plays the fiddle divinely, if I'm not mistaken.**

'Copied from a Board over the door of John Grove of White Waltham, Berks'.
MS. Eng. poet. c. 51, p. 1.

**John Hall is alive and lives in hope.** 118
**To live by the bell when thou shalt die by the rope.**

'Answre' to H854.
MS. Eng. poet. e. 14, fol. 89 rev.

**John London was condemned for selling [spoiling] wood** 119
**One sold his wood, the other bought a whore.**

Answer to 'Martin' (see l. 5), on the Bishops John Aylmer, said to have sold the elms at Fulham, and Richard Fletcher, who married the widow of Sir R. Baker as his second wife *c.* 1594/5.
MSS. CCC. 327, fol. 29; Tanner 306, two copies, fols. 189 and 190.

**John Nixon of this city alderman** 120
**A good fair copy for posterity.**

'On a Gravestone near the Pulpit', St. Mary's, Oxford.
MS. Top. Oxon. c. 299, fol. 81$^{v}$.

**John Palfreyman who lieth here** 121
**Also his father, when he dies.**

'On a Basket Maker at Grantham'.
MS. Ballard 47, fol. 43$^{v}$.

**John Payne did will when he was dead** 122
**And take the gift of your well-willer.**

'In sainte faythes under St. Paules for Mr. John Payne Esq. this'.
MSS. Ashmole 38, p. 198; Rawl. D. 859, fol. 91.

**John Smith why (shit on him) and then I think** 123
**My anagram will make his worship stink.**

'An Anagram on John Smyth'.
MSS. CCC. 328, fol. 26$^{v}$; Rawl. poet. 153, fol. 25; 160, fol. 175$^{v}$.

**John was the morning star that did fore-run** 124
**Jesus near cures: where John near made a wound.**

[Quarles, Francis], 'On John and Jesus'.
Pr. *Divine Fancies*, 1632, iv. 28.
MS. Rawl. poet. 117, fol. 170$^{v}$ rev.

**John whilom taught me to read Aristotle;** 125
**But witty speech full oft by them is shown . . . (incomplete).**

Boswell, James, 'An Imitation of Chaucer's stile'.
MS. *Douce 193, fol. 49$^{v}$ (autogr.).

126 Johnson! whose art instructs the poet's lyre
Whose blaze obscures the light their borrow'd beams bestow.
van Mildert, [William], 'Sonnet to Dr. Johnson'.
MS. Percy c. 8, fol. 152.

127 Join thy life-breathing lips to mine
On hills where precious spices grow.
Sand[y]s, George, translator, 'The Songe of Solomon'.
Pr. 1641.
MSS. e Mus. 201, fol. 1; Rawl. poet. 153, fol. 1.

128 Join verses all ye living souls
As now light dispels the dark.
[Milton, John], 'Chorus to Mr. Galliard's Hymn', from *Paradise Lost*, v, 197–208.
MSS. Mus. d. 8, fol. 75; d. 142, fol. 2.

129 Jolly (. . . incomplete . . .) wine
More then by his conquering sword.
'[ B]achanalians', incomplete song.
MS. Mus. e. 20, fol. 8$^{v}$.

130 Jolly Roger Twangdillo of Bloughden hill
'Twas she that brought down Twangdillo.
Amherst, Elizabeth, 'Jolly Roger Twangdillo of Bloughden Hill'.
MS. *Eng. poet. e. 109, p. 86.

131 Jolly true blues of the main, well skilled in heaving the log,
Who yields to proud Spain or vain France is a stranger to freedom and grog.
MS. Firth c. 18, fol. 198.

132 Joseph an aged man truly
Which thou hast bought so dear, so dear.
Dated '1654', cf. Edith Rickert, *Ancient English Christmas Carols*, 1910, p. 25 and p. 150 *n*.
MS. Eng. poet. b. 5, p. 118.

133 Joseph and Mary having three days past
He soon is lost, not so soon found again.
MS. *Rawl. poet. 97, fol. 45$^{v}$ (autogr.).

134 Joseph and Mary though amazed to see
Th' eternal God Christ's father true to be.
MS. *Rawl. poet. 97, fol. 47 (autogr.).

135 Jove, and his thunder-bolts, I can despise:
Received from those fountains of light, your eyes.
Morrice, John, 'A Copy of Verses written August the 4th 1707, at Mr. Cleiton's, of Church-Stretton'.
MS. *Rawl. poet. 114, fol. 17 (autogr.).

Jove heard my prayer Lyce thou art old 136
When they behold thy dark extinguished lamp.
W. A., translator, Horace, *Odes* IV. xiii.
MS. *Rawl. poet. 104, fol. 44$^{v}$ (autogr.).

Jove in distress, the goddess Thetis brings 137
Begets a son superior to his sire.
'Jove, Thetis, and Flora'.
MS. Rawl. poet. 172, fol. 141$^{v}$.

Jove in one mould ne'er framed each woman's mind 138
That Eden had a serpent she hath none.
'Symonides, of Woemen', translation *temp.* Queen Elizabeth.
MSS. Ashmole 36, 37, fol. 147.

Jove is as good as is my lady 139
Is as good as bawdy Jove.
MS. Rawl. poet. 120, fol. 33.

Jove reigns in Heaven but James doth reign on earth 140
The weeping day presageth future mirth.
'Divisum Imperium cum Jove Cæsar habet', couplet on the coronation of James II.
MS. Eng. poet. c. 25, fol. 78.

Joy and grief, once past are soon forgotten 141
And such is mortal man, when he is rotten.
Couplet.
MS. Rawl. poet. 66, fol. 54.

Joy and health, peace and wealth 142
On those that are needy.
'A wassaile song, to be sung at any time during Christmas to the tune of good your worship'.
MS. Eng. poet. b. 5, p. 67.

Joy, I did lock thee up but some bad man 143
Even God himself being pressed for my sake.
Herbert, George, 'The Bunch of Grapes'.
Pr. *The Temple*, 1633, p. 120.
MS. *Tanner 307, fol. 91$^{v}$.

Joy in the rising of our orient star 144
The child of man, the parent of a God.
Southwell, Robert, '[Meditation] of our Blessed Ladies nativitie'.
Pr. *Mæoniae*, 1595, p. 2.
MS. Eng. poet. b. 5, p. 76.

Joy to great Caesar 145
For none e'er can love, and be wise and rebel.
'Tune: Farinells ground' (not given).
MS. Mus. Sch. C. 95, p. 242.

146 Joy to my brother on this festive day
Crowned with fresh honours decked with greater fame.
Wynne, Charles Watkin Williams, 'Addressed to Sir W. W. Wynne [5th Baronet] on his coming of age, by his brother'. 1793.
MS. Top. Oxon. d. 163, fol. 76v.

147 Joy to my friend; may gentle fate
Nor add one word, except, Amen.
Jessop, William. 'Epithalamium on the marriage of Sir Richd Musgrove'.
MS. Percy b. 1, fol. 38v (autogr.).

148 Joy to the bridegroom and joy to the bride.
What they have provided to drink and to eat.
Williams, John, 'A Wedding Song'.
MS. *Rawl. poet. 192, fol. 138 (autogr.).

149 Joy to the widow and the bachelor
By you she should be overthrown.
Creswell, Robert, 'Epithal: To Mr. J. H. [of Gray's Inn] and Mrs. J. C.'
MS. *Eng. poet. f. 24, fol. 22 (autogr.).

150 Joy to your laurels, may Parnassus queen.
And mend at once the poet and the man.
'To Mr. Nahum Tate upon his being made Poet Laureat. 1693'.
MS. Don. c. 55, fol. 19.

151 Joyous may each revolving year
Such are the wishes of your friend.
Skinner, John, 'Another on the birthday of James. 1789'.
MS. *Eng. poet. d. 22, fol. 23.

152 Joys that are pure sincerely good
With love that's perfectly divine.
[Newburgh Hamilton, adapted from Milton], *Samson*, extract. Music by Handel.
MS. Mus. c. 107, fol. 65v.

153 Judah! thy praise thy brethren shall confe[ss]
God's people He gathers by Hea[ ].
Genesis xl. 8, from 'Paraphrased collection of some Prophecyes of the old Testamt. concerning Christ'.
MS. *Rawl. C. 113, fol. 2 (autogr.).

154 Judas 'gainst Christ harboured such enmity
Men might believe; He the Messias was.
MS. *Rawl. poet. 97, fol. 59 (autogr.).

155 Judas his malice more appears in this
Of death, sin; which Sathan on man did bring.
MS. *Rawl. poet. 97, fol. 59v (autogr.).

Jude by the Holy Ghost inspired did write 156
Prophets, Apostles, Christ the corner stone.
Clifford, Henry, Earl of Cumberland, 'Simon and Jude'.
MS. *Rawl. poet. 95, fol. 35v.

Judge and revenge my cause oh Lord, 157
Good Lord deliver me.
[Sternhold, Thomas], Psalm xliii.
MSS. Rawl. D. 886, fol. 12, with setting for 5 bells; Rawl. poet. 100, fol. 30v; 112, fol. 59 rev.

Judge me, oh God, and plead my cause 158
For health restored to thee.
Psalm xliii.
MS. *Montagu e. 10, fol. 63v.

Judge me oh God for all men partial are 159
Hope still in god to praise him still be bold.
Fairfax, Thomas, Lord, Psalm xliii.
MS. *Fairfax 40, p. 97 (autogr.).
MS. *Fairfax 38, p. 201.

Judge me, oh Lord, for I have walked 160
The living Lord I'll bless.
Psalm xxvi.
MS. *Montagu e. 10, fol. 17.

Judge not that field, because 'tis stubble 161
Judge not: their treasure is within.
[Quarles, Francis], 'On outward Shew'. Pr. *Divine Fancies*, 1632, i. 16.
MS. Rawl. poet. 90, fol. 60.

Judge not too fast: this tree that does appear 162
A Saule to day, may prove a Paule, the next.
[Quarles, Francis], 'On rash Judgment'. Pr. *Divine Fancies*, 1632, i. 57.
MS. Rawl. poet. 90, fol. 64.

Judge of all judge me 163
Sure aid, present comfort.
Sidney, Sir Philip, Psalm xliii.
MSS. *Rawl. poet. 24, p. 62; *25, fol. 36.

Judge (oh Lord) mine innocence 164
I will load, for oft salvations.
Jos: Br., Psalm xxvi.
MS. Rawl. poet. 61, fol. 31v.

Judgement and wit should sisters always be, 165
Or used as useless to eternal gain.
Williams, John, 'To Miss Betty (Ashe) upon her return from Bath, the Saturday before St. Simon and Jude. Ao. 1709'.
MS. *Rawl. poet. 191, fol. 102v (autogr.).

166 Judgement two syllables can make
While we live here we must provision make.
Flatman, [Thomas], 'A doomes-day thought'.
Pr. *Poems*, 1674, p. 103, dated 1659.
MSS. Rawl. poet. 84, fol. 112ᵛ rev.; 173, fol. 182, attr. to Mr. Flatman.

167 Judges were wont to ride on asses, yes
Or we like asses still be kept in law.
'In judices'.
MS. Don. d. 58, fol. 31.

168 Judicious reader, ere thou censurize
I hope shall relish our harsh-woven rhymes.
Barret, Robert, 'Proemium' to 'The Sacred Warr'.
MS. Add. C. 281, p. xxvi (autogr.).

169 Juggins had all the various powers of art
With equal skill to dress the feasts of gods.
[Bacon, Phanuel], 'The Praises of Tho. Juggins the Cook who dy'd at Oxford 1719'.
MS. Eng. poet. e. 45, fol. 61 (autogr.).

170 Jugurtha the Numidian king
Are sold, by traders of this court.
MS. Rawl. poet. 66, fol. 36.

171 Julia, if any curse did follow
Their lords away.
Fanshawe, Sir Richard, translator, 'To Julia', Horace, *Odes* II. viii.
MS. *Firth c. 1, p. 45.

172 Julia! you at your window sate
It proved a burning glass to me!
Parsons, William, 'To a Lady . . . often at her window'.
MS. *Don. d. 123, p. 153 (autogr.).

173 Julian how comes it that of late we see
The whores, rogues, bawds and rake-hells of Whitehall.
'Advice to Julian', Sir R. L'Estrange, 'Julian Secretary to the Muses'.
In B.M. MS. Harl. 7139, dated 1682.
MSS. Don. e. 24, p. 13; Firth c. 16, p. 10; Rawl. poet. 159, fol. 160ᵛ.

174 Julian with care peruse the lines I send
If managed well, may help thee yet in thine.
'To the Secretary of the Muses', Sir R. L'Estrange.
MS. Firth c. 16, p. 16.

175 Julian with Flora might compare
We must enjoy with her the regal feast.
On Mrs. Julian Crew.
MSS. Ashmole 36, 37, fol. 33ᵛ.

Juno was great the wife of powerful Jove 176
Then Juno, Pallas, or fair Venus are.
H. S.
MS. *Rawl. poet. 120, fol. 18 (autogr.).

Juno, we thank thee, and congratulate 177
With laurel, though his father wear it now.
'On Sir R[obert] Shirley's' [of Staunton Harold, Leics.] son [Seymour, b. 23 Jan. 1646/7].
MS. Eng. poet. e. 4, p. 71.

*Jure Divino* fills this grave 178
So say our laws: yet tyrants may.
Whig verses on James II.
MS. Rawl. poet. 159, fol. 137.

Just and fit actions Ptolemey (he saith 179
Shall never dare, do anything but fear.
[Jonson, Ben. (?)], 'A Speech out off Lucan', *Pharsalia*, viii. 484–95.
See W. D. Briggs in *Anglia*, xxxix, pp. 247–8, and *Ben Jonson*, ed. Herford and Simpson, xi, 1952, p. 164.
MS. Rawl. poet. 31, fol. 18.

Just as the amorous fly with fond desire 180
Or he who loves you, had had you before.
'A chast Wooer, to a marryed gentlewoman who was forsaken by her husband before he bedded her, and remayned foure years a widdow, wife and virgin'.
MS. Rawl. poet. 84, fol. 96 rev.

Just as the genuine eagle dares embrace 181
His hand is greased: a bribe commands his lip.
Southwell, Sir Robert, 'Deut. 16: 19. For a gift doth blind the eyes of the Wise'.
MS. *Eng. poet. f. 6, fol. 6 (autogr.).

Just as the lovely full-blown rose 182
I shall breathe my amorous prayer.
'Written in a very old cramped hand at the commencement of Baudoin's Emblems, Paris 1638'.
Pr. bk. 27980 e. 86, opp. p. viii.

Just come to age and to paternal wealth 183
'Twill be remembered he was born and died.
'On a certain Tradesman's son who lately gave a sumptuous entertainment to his acquaintance and Tradesmen on account of his coming of age'. Headed 'Mr. Stoughton'.
MS. Rawl. poet. 207, p. 183.

Just like a flower, that's but new blown. 184
Just in my state of innocence.
'Epitaph in Watford Church Yard in Hertfordshire . . . 1746'.
MS. Eng. poet. e. 40, fol. 150.

185 **Just like th'anointing oil**
**And ever spread its fragrance round.**
Beddome, Benjamin.
MS. *Eng. misc. e. 227, fol. 43[v].

186 **Just now the skies seemed clear, we then were glad,**
**'Tis greater now; behold! the barge at shore!**
Oldisworth, Giles or Robert, dialogue between [Robert Oldisworth] and [Gilbert Dethicke (?)] on a dangerous crossing of the Thames, 1637.
MS. *Rawl. C. 422, fol. 26, in the hand of Giles Oldisworth.

187 **Justice and love for want of sight**
**Will bring 'em there, and there they'll make 'em stay.**
Williams, John, 'Upon Justice and Love'.
MS. *Rawl. poet. 191, fol. 98[v] (autogr.).

188 **Justice incensed for vengeance calls**
**How much I to my Saviour owe.**
Beddome, Benjamin.
Pr. *Hymns . . . of B. Beddome,* 1818, no. 59.
MS. *Eng. misc. e. 227, fol. 83.

**Justice is here made up of might** 189
**By privilege of Parliament.**
Satire on the early years of the Long Parliament, [*c.* 1641–2].
MSS. Ashmole 36, 37, fol. 94; Douce 357, fol. 34; Malone 21, fol. 36; Tanner 306, fol. 298; see also I1230.

**Justice is pictured blind, and why? that she** 190
**So long as justice hath her sense of feeling.**
Robinson, Robert.
MS. *Rawl. poet. 218, p. 48 (autogr.).

**Justice of late hath lost her wits** 191
**She now is lapped up in a hide.**
On Sir Nicholas Hyde's becoming Lord Chief Justice, 5 Feb. 1627.
See Sir Simonds D'Ewes, *Autobiography,* ed. J. O. Halliwell, 1845, ii. 49.
MSS. Ashmole 38, p. 146; Eng. poet. e. 14, fol. 49; Malone 23, p. 119; Rawl. poet. 160, fol. 163[v].

# K

ENTRIES 1–103

1 Kate being pleased wished that her pleasure would
Or hath more scrapings or more dressings born.
Davies, [Sir] John, 'In Kattam'.
Pr. amongst 'Epigrames' with *Ovids Elegies*, translated C. M. [*c.* 1600].
MS. *Add. B. 97, fol. 42.

2 Kate, Ursey, Barbara these three virgins lie here
And friar Andrew, whom these three did bear.
Couplet.
MS. Firth d. 7, fol. 157.

3 Kate very eagerly doth still pursue
To have diurnal and nocturnal due.
'Epigram', couplet.
MS. Malone 19, p. 155.

4 Kate's teeth are white, Nell's black, the reason why,
Kate's are her own, but Nell her teeth did buy.
Couplet.
MS. Malone 19, p. 46.

5 Keep hid like serpent; lure with the dove
No treason is like that goes masked in love.
Couplet.
MS. Tanner 89, fol. 262.

6 Keep money still by thee in thine own hands.
Than if thou hadst put it into the bourse.
Robinson, Robert.
MS. *Rawl. poet. 218, p. 171 (autogr.).

7 Keep not thou silence, mighty God,
Enthroned in endless bliss.
Psalm lxxxiii.
MS. *Montagu e. 10, fol. 35.

8 Keep on your mask, and [yea] hide your eye
When life is done where shall I go.
Strode, William, 'Song'.
Pr. in *Poems of Pembroke and Ruddier*, 1660.
MS. *CCC. 325, fol. 70 (autogr.).
MSS. Rawl. poet. 153, fol. 19$^{v}$; 199, p. 84.

Keep station nature and rest heaven sure 9
And glory of our day set in his night.
King, Henry, 'On Prince Henry's Death'.
Pr. *Poems*, 1657, p. 95.
MSS. Eng. poet. e. 14, fol. 46; *e. 30, fol. 24; Malone 21, fol. 11; *22, fol. 15$^{v}$; Rawl. poet. 209, fol. 8$^{v}$.

Keep still an equal mind, not sunk 10
T'eternal banishment.
Fanshawe, Sir Richard, translator, 'To Delius'. Horace, *Odes* II. iii.
Pr. *Poems of Horace*, A. Brome, etc., 2nd ed., 1671, p. 56.
MSS. *Firth c. 1, p. 43; Rawl. D. 261, p. 14, attr. to Sir R. F.

Keep thy sight from vanity 11
With which men should rule their live.
'Quinque sensus externi . . . Ex. MS. . . . c. temp. Henry V'.
In B.M. MS. Harl. 1706, fol. 207$^{v}$.
MS. Eng. poet. e. 56, p. 118.

Keep thy tears reader and that softer sorrow 12
Be not as confused as the act was foul.
Prelude to an elegy on the murder of Thomas Scott, preacher, 1626, N381.
MS. Rawl. poet. 160, fol. 5.

Keep to the churches whilst you may 13
You may for ever vary.
'To th'Tune of Gather ye Rose Buds etc.'
Pr. *The Muses Farewel to Popery and Slavery*, 2nd ed., 1690, p. 169.
MSS. Don. e. 23, fol. 69$^{v}$; Firth c. 16, p. 230.

Keep well this sacred pawn thou bed of stone 14
The grave is but an usher to the skies.
Strode, William, 'An Epitaph', *c.* 1626.
MS. *CCC. 325, fol. 89$^{v}$ (autogr.).

Keep well your shop: so will your shop keep you: 15
Neglect your shop; oh then, goodman adieu.
Robinson, Robert, couplet.
MS. *Rawl. poet. 218, p. 59 (autogr.).

16 Keep your distance saucy swain
Sir Woodcock keep your distance.
Briggs, S[amson], 'Songe'.
MSS. Rawl. 147, p. 242 rev., attr. to S. Briggs; 210, fol. 62 rev.

17 Kendal is dead, and Cambridge riding post
What fitter sacrifice for Denham's ghost.
'Upon [Clarendon's] Grand Children', the children of James II and his first wife Anne *née* Hyde, May–June 1667. Couplet from the printed copy of 'Directions to a Painter', ed. 1667; *Advice-to-a-Painter Poems*, M. T. Osborne, 1949, no. 10.
MS. Don. e. 23, fol. 29.

18 Kept by Jehovah's power
Ye never can prevail.
Kenton, James.
MS. *Eng. poet. e. 20, p. 265 (autogr.).

19 Kilda! by thy winding shore
And headlong plunged into the roaring tide.
Richardson, William, Professor, 'The Death of Eira. an ode'.
Pr. *Poems chiefly Rural*, 1774, p. 17.
MS. Eng. misc. e. 241, fol. 55.

20 Kill me not every day
By way of imprest, all my future moan.
Herbert, George, 'Affliction'.
Pr. *The Temple*, 1633, p. 53.
MS. *Tanner 307, fol. 41v.

21 Kill not with your angry frown
For any service done to thee.
Burton, Francis.
MS. *Add. A. 267, fol. 150v (autogr.).

22 Kind advice I thankfully hear
I wish to be happy and wise.
Williams, John.
MS. *Rawl. poet. 184, fol. 89v (autogr.).

23 Kind and coming to all, she lays nets round about her
On design still steps forward, but never comes near.
Williams, John, 'Love-Characters'.
MS. *Rawl. poet. 184, fol. 93v (autogr.).

24 Kind companion of my youth
Rides the bark, which virtue steers.
[George Bubb,] 'Lord Melcombe to his Friend Dr. [Edward] Young', Oct. 1761. Transcript of copy sent to Young to be left 'among those of your papers which may possibly see the Light by a posthumous Publication'.
MS. Malone 26, fol. 161.

Kind countrymen, attention give, 25
Such coin throughout the world will pass.
'A Ready Cure for Uneasie Minds; for that their Money will not pass'.
MS. Firth d. 14, fol. 46.

Kind fate I do thank thee 26
And a fig for the clog of a wife.
Verses written *c.* 1666 (see fol. 36) on a blank page in collections of Joseph Meddus.
MS. Rawl. D. 929, fol. 9.

Kind Heaven assist our heir and banish strife 27
Send for your king, and let him crowned be.
'Might overcomes Right', Jacobite verses, acrostic on 'King James'.
MS. Rawl. C. 986, fol. 20.

Kind heaven has granted 28
But one, who like French, shall protect us.
'The Aldermans Guide, or a new Pattern for a Ld. Mayor, a Ballad . . . written by Dean Swift 1733'.
See Swift's *Poems*, ed. Williams, 1937, p. 1133.
MS. Ballard 50, fol. 106v.

Kind nature light this spark to show her worth 29
Which churlish Death as soon as seen put forth.
Inscription at Chester, couplet.
MS. Top. Cheshire c. 9, fol. 50.

Kind nature, to all her creatures gave 30
E'en the most mighty bend to love.
Skinner, John, translator, Anacreon, Ode ii.
MS. *Eng. poet. d. 22, fol. 27v.

Kind neighbour and countrymen, listen, I pray 31
I might be in danger of losing my nose.
'A Ballad of the Cutting Sr John Coventreys Nose', [1670].
MS. Don. b. 8, p. 246.

Kind pity chokes my spleen; brave scorn forbids 32
Power from God claimed, than God himself to trust.
Donne, John, 'Satyre'.
Pr. *Poems*, 1633.
MSS. *Eng. poet. e. 99, fol. 4v; *f. 9, p. 177.

Kind reader when you do peruse 33
Home again to plant his cabbage.
'A Touchstone for Tories', satire on George I and his family.
MS. Rawl. poet. 155, p. 163.

Kind spirit who dost thyself around disperse, 34
Which to demonstrate we did undertake.
'A Challenge to Vice and Atheism'.
MS. Rawl. poet. 173, fol. 178v.

35 King Agamemnon that he might repair
Can conquer earth, the heaven itself is yours.
Bacon, Sir Nicholas, 1623–66, translator, Boethius, *Consolations* IV. vii, 1664.
MS. Tanner 306, fol. 343 (autogr.).

36 King am I, Faith you lie
To them I trust. So you must.
'Soliloquy and Eccho', George I.
MS. Rawl. poet. 155, p. 32.

37 King Amon by his wicked servants slain
Such monstrous broods the people's rage devours.
'The Regicides'.
MS. Rawl. poet. 154, fol. 110.

38 King Asshuerus, 'mong a multitude
Are full of wisdom, merit highest praise!
MS. *Rawl. poet. 97, fol. 38 (autogr.).

39 King George by way of reformation
The Lord have mercy on the nation.
'An Extempore on the Speech and Proclamation', of George I.
MS. Rawl. poet. 155, p. 71.

40 King George's cause shall thrive when the sea burns
Knaves may in halters swing, that fools mayn't o'er us sway.
'The double Entendre'.
MS. Rawl. poet. 155, p. 99.

41*a* King Herod was a wicked King
Whose souls are in th'abyss.
Tipping, William.
MS. *Rawl. poet. 101, fol. 75 (autogr.).

41*b* King James made me to run for life from Dead Man's Riding
I ran to Goreil Gate, where death for me was biding.
On a stag killed by King James I, 26 Aug. 1608, at Ditchley.
MS. Hearne's diaries 67, p. 28.

42 King never proved more king in any thing,
Why (King) I see i'faith thou'lt needs be king.
On Humphrey King's *Halfe-penny worth of Wit*, 1613; transcribed from R. Heber's printed copy.
MS. Douce 190, fol. 9.

43 King of glory, King of peace,
To discharge what is behind.
Herbert, George, 'L'Envoy'.
Pr. *The Temple*, 1633, p. 192.
MS. *Tanner 307, fol. 147.

King of glory, King of peace 44*a*
To extol thee.
Herbert, George, 'Praise'.
Pr. *The Temple*, 1633, p. 140.
MS. *Tanner 307, fol. 106.

[King of grace, and full of pity] 44*b*
Christ us grant that it be so . . . (incomplete).
At end: 'Expliciunt quinquedecim Signa' [of Domesday].
See E.E.T.S., xxiv, 1895, p. 118.
MS. Tanner 407, fol. 45.

King of heaven, hell, sea, earth, whose thunders from 45
And one day suitably framedst by thy might.
J. F., 'The same Orpheus [the Thracian] to God'.
MS. *Eng. poet. f. 17, p. 54 (autogr.).

King of heaven we crave 46
By our enemies.
Translation of French verses on Edward II (?), dated 'xiij° Aug. 1593'.
MS. Tanner 306, fol. 187.

King Solomon so wise who wast 47
Great shame it should be told.
Tipping, William.
MS. *Rawl. poet. 101, fol. 68ᵛ (autogr.).

King Solomon, so wise who wast 48
I'll pay him honour too.
Tipping, William, 'Of Kinge Solomon'.
MS. *Rawl. poet. 101, fol. 98ᵛ (autogr.).

King William he had it behind 49
Enjoyed it with his Majesty.
'A Riddle'.
MS. Eng. poet. c. 51, p. 109.

King William pricked his sheriffs in council 50
All sheriffs' pricks are made to stand.
MS. Eng. poet. d. 152, fol. 83.

Kings and nobles, lords and slaves. 51
Are equal things, when in their graves.
Robinson, Robert, couplet.
MS. *Rawl. poet. 218, p. 92 (autogr.).

Kings and princes, great ones die: 52
Be they ne'er so strongly steeled.
Robinson, Robert.
MS. *Rawl. poet. 218, p. 166 (autogr.).

Kings are like gods on earth, when they redress 53
Their people's griefs, and save them in distress.
Couplet.
MS. Add. B. 8, fol. 67.

54 Kings guided by the star of wisdom must
Of all the gentiles who Christ's name do bear.
MS. *Rawl. poet. 97, fol. 39v (autogr.).

55 Kings, princes, lords, yea ladies fair,
See what come on't; at last the rich man's dead.
Robinson, Robert.
MS. *Rawl. poet. 218, p. 67 (autogr.).

56 Kings', queens', men's, judgement's [women's, virgin's] eyes
To show she was a woman.
'An Epitaphe on the Thrice Excellent Princes Queen Elizabeth'.
Pr. Camden's *Remaines*, 1637, p. 394.
MS. Ashmole 38, three copies, the second initialed N. B. [Nicholas Burghe], pp. 29, 36, and 167 in Burghe's hand; Don. d. 58, fol. 15; Eng. poet. c. 50, fol. 22v; e. 40, fol. 139; Rawl. poet. 26, fol. 88v.

57 Kings that do govern subjects only may
Their hearts as tribute to this female Kinge.
Beaumont, Thomas, 'On Mrs. Kinge'.
MS. *Malone 18, p. 48 (autogr.).

58 Kiss me oh kiss me with thy mouth for such
Or hart that o'er the spicy mountains go.
Fairfax, Thomas, Lord, [Songs of the old and New Testament:] 'The Songe of Solomon'.
MS. *Fairfax 40, p. 432 (autogr.).
MS. *Fairfax 38, p. 1.

59 Kiss me sweet and wary lover
What their number is bepined.
'Of kissing'.
MS. Eng. poet. e. 14, fol. 42; see also K61.

60 Kiss me sweet now we are here,
[So, so, so should lovers do].
'A songe'.
MS. Add. B. 97, fol. 17v.

61 Kiss me, sweet, the wary lover
What their number is bepined.
J[onson], B[en.], 'Catullus ad Lesbiam' [v]. 'The Forrest', vi.
MSS. Firth e. 4, p. 71, attr. to B. J.; Rawl. poet. 31, fol. 7; see also K59.

62 Kiss me sweet, with the kisses
So great a guest, is greatest gain.
Manisty, E[dward], translator, 'A Song of Songs'.
MSS. Rawl. D. 1327, fol. 3, attr. to E. Manisty; dedicated to Margarett Countesse of Manchester [1667–76]; Rawl. poet. 110, p. 1, attr. to E. Manisty, dated 1646, dedicated to Bernard Hide.

Kisses and favours are sweet things 63
But those have thorns, and these have stings.
Couplet, 'Sharpe sauce'.
From *Wits Recreations*. 1663, Ep. 653 (?).
MS. Eng. poet. d. 152, fol. 106v.

Kisses with warmth to give does love express 64
Too rashly love not nor suspect.
Williams, John, 'Of Love'.
MS. *Rawl. poet. 191, fol. 92v (autogr.).

Kisses you proems of succeeding woes 65
For if you rise to kiss you rise to fall.
'On kisses'.
MS. Eng. poet. f. 25, fol. 12v.

Kitty, a fair but frozen Maid 66
I'll kiss you, if you guess.
[Garrick, David], 'A Riddle'.
Pr. *Works*, 1785, ii. 5 07.
MS. Percy c. 8, fol. 19.

Kitty, think, though every grace 67
Love and beauty have their day.
Boswell, James, 'To Miss Kitty Colqhoun'.
Pr. *A Collection of Original Poems by Scotch Gentlemen*, ii, 1762, p. 81.
MS. *Douce 193, fol. 39 (autogr.).

Knavery upholds bravery, 68
And brings good men to slavery.
Robinson, Robert.
MS. *Rawl. poet. 218, p. 72 (autogr.).

Knaves are knave-wise, fools silly-precise: 69
And so their good counsels do wholly despise.
Robinson, Robert.
MS. *Rawl. poet. 218, p. 62 (autogr.).

Knaves fish for fools; they bait their hook and watch 'em. 70
And when they've fools; wise men can hardly match 'em.
Robinson, Robert.
MS. *Rawl. poet. 218, p. 163 (autogr.).

Knaves in them have great knowing parts; 71
But honest men have honest hearts.
Robinson, Robert, couplet.
MS. *Rawl. poet. 218, p. 123 (autogr.).

Knaves live by fools, to catch fools knaves do lurk 72
Nor fools, nor knaves? wise men would then want work.
Robinson, Robert, couplet.
MS. *Rawl. poet. 218, p. 3 (autogr.).

Knaves there are now, and fools (as heretofore) 73
And good men too, but oh their fashion's new.
Robinson, Robert.
MS. *Rawl. poet. 218, p. 32 (autogr.).

74 Kneller, by heaven and not a master taught,
Her works; and dying fears herself may die.

Pope, Alexander, on Sir Godfrey Kneller, 1723, Westminster Abbey.
See *Minor Poems*, ed. Norman Ault and John Butt, 1954, p. 312.
MSS. Top. gen. e. 32, fol. 53$^{v}$; Top. Oxon. c. 108, p. 47.

75 Kneller, with silence and surprise
Had drawn a George, or carved a Jove.

Addison, Joseph, 'To Sir Godfrey Kneller, on his picture of his sacred Majesty King George [I]'.
MS. Add. B. 106, fol. 50$^{v}$.

76 Knew I but the lad that writ
But whip him for his knavery.

[Jegon, John], answer to J20.
MS. Rawl. poet. 66, fol. 64.

77 Knewst thou whose these ashes were
Renew the letters with his tears.

'Mr. Washingtons epitaph' [Prince Charles's page, died in Spain 1623].
Pr. *Wits Recreations*, 1641, Sig. R6.
MSS. Eng. poet. c. 50, fol. 45; e. 14, fol. 91 rev.; Rawl. poet 26, fol. 76$^{v}$; 160, fol. 56$^{v}$, attr. to Lewis; see also K96.

78 Knit, and conformed by thy hand
Blot nor blush my face shall fill.

Herbert, Mary (*née* Sidney), Countess of Pembroke, Psalm cxix, 'K'.
MSS. *Rawl. poet. 24, p. 181; *25, fol. 122.

79 Know, Celia, since thou art so proud
Know her themselves through all her veils.

Carew, Thomas, 'Ingratefull beautie threatened'.
Pr. *Poems*, 1640.
MSS. *Don. b. 9, fol. 2$^{v}$; Rawl. poet. 206, p. 73.

80 Know coy disdain, I am above
Thy songs, in courting of a rock.

Shirley, James, 'To the proud Mistress'.
Pr. *Poems*, 1646.
MS. *Rawl. poet. 88, p. 63.

81 Know every christian man alive
I hereunto subscribe my name.

'A Receit for Sixpence . . . by Mr. Free Curate' of Great Woolford.
MS. Ballard 29, fol. 126.

82 Know faithless minion that within this breast
'Tis proof 'gainst beauty, and tongue-melting charms.

Ashmole, Elias.
MSS. Ashmole 36, 37, fol. 222$^{v}$ (autogr.).

Know lady that my life depends, 83
And your charity requited.

'To his m$^{irs}$.'
MSS. CCC. 328, fol. 82$^{v}$; Don c. 57, fol. 15, with music.

Know, little lock, first from my head, 84*a*
The drops of blood lost at thy fall.

Weaver, Thomas, 'Mauricia; to a lock of that hayre, which was Cut when she was wounded'. Mrs. Maurice of Llanbedr.
Pr. *Songs and Poems*, 1654.
MS. *Rawl. poet. 211, fol. 19$^{v}$ (autogr.).

Know passenger that there's interred 84*b*
Records the memory of worth or wit.

Fairfax, Thomas, Lord, 'On the Lady Barbara Bellasis', [*née* Cholmley, wife of Sir Thomas Belasyse, married *c.* 1600 (?)].
MS. *Fairfax 38, p. 493 (autogr.).

Know, that I falsehood, early could detest, 85
To nought inferior but the heavenly state.

Bate, Sally, 'To Mrs. Bate on her Marriage . . . 1768'.
MS. *Eng. poet. e. 28, p. 245.

Know this my brethren heaven is clear 86
And hay then up go we.

Quarles, Francis, 'The Tryumph of the Round-heads', etc., 1641.
Pr. *Distractions of our Times*, 1642; Quarles's *Shepherds Oracles*, 1646, Egl. xi; *Rump Songs*, 1662, Sig. B7$^{v}$.
MSS. Ashmole 36, 37, fol. 81; Don. c. 57, fol. 27$^{v}$, attr. to Fra. Quarles, with music; Rawl. poet. 26, fol. 133.

Know thou, oh stranger to the fame 87
A warmer heart death ne'er made cold.

[Burns, Robert], Epitaph 'For R. A. Esq.'
Pr. *Poems*, 1787, p. 341.
MSS. Engl. poet. e. 28, p. 351; Montagu e. 14, fol. 11$^{v}$, attr. to Burns.

Know thou that treadst on learned Smith inurned 88
We shall fall down and sleep with him in dust.

'On Mr. J. Smith of Magdalen College Oxon.'
In B.M. MS. Lansdowne 777, fol. 55, 'On Mr. John Smyth, Chaplayne to the Earl of Pembroke, 1624'.
MS. Eng. poet. e. 14, fol. 100$^{v}$ rev.

Know ye all wights that on my leaves do look 89
By day or by night.

Gough, Richard, 'In the first Page of the original Edition of Chaucer', 1764, with a corrected proof of a printed copy.
MS. *Eng. poet. c. 5, fol. 110 (autogr.).

90 **Know you (Fair) on what you look?**
**Of your white hand, they are mine.**
Crashaw, Richard, 'Upon Herberts Temple sent to a gentlewoman'.
MS. Tanner 465, fol. 48, attr. to R. Cr., and to Mr. Crashaw on fol. 1*a*.

91 **Know you mine hostess? she's the queen of sluts**
**Through queasiness would straight fall sick, and die.**
Oldisworth, Nicolas, 'On an uggly Wench'.
MS. *Don. c. 24, fol. 23[v] (autogr.).

92 **Know you this youth? he is a subtle dog.**
**That you his fault might thus in's neck verse read.**
Ashmole, Elias, 'Upon a Dog that had a Clog tyed to his Neck for worrying of Sheepe', March, 1642.
MSS. Ashmole 36, 37, fol. 222 (autogr.).

93 **Know you what he is you scorn?**
**Scorn, and bethorn eternity.**
Colman, Henry, 'On Christ crown'd with thornes'.
MS. *Rawl. poet. 204, fol. 8 (autogr.).

94 **Knowest thou not who send flowers in May,**
**To him all praises let us sing.**
Robinson, Robert.
MS. *Rawl. poet. 218, p. 170 (autogr.).

95 **Knowest thou this, soldier? 'tis a much chang'd plant, which yet**
**Roses for thorns?**
Crashaw, Richard, 'Upon the thornes taken downe from our Lords head bloody'.
MS. Tanner 465, fol. 36[v], attr. to Mr. Crashaw on fol. 1*a*.

96 **Knowest thou whose these ashes were**
**Renew the letters with his tears.**
'Upon the death of Mr. Thomas Washington who died in Spain', 1623.
MSS. Ashmole 38, p. 171; 47, fol. 60; Eng. poet. f. 10, fol. 116; see also K77.

**Knowing how much in absence lover lose** 97
**Think what the comfort is . . . (incomplete).**
Burton, Francis.
MS. *Add. A. 267, fol. 114 (autogr.).

**Knowing your love to th' state, and the politics** 98
**You may imagine, so I rest your friend.**
Reresby, Sir John, 'The Relation of the Plott (discovered in the year 1664) in mock-verse to my honoured Uncle Sr. Thamworth Reresby'.
MS. *Rawl. D. 204, fol. 104[v] rev. (autogr.).

**Knowledge a burden is, a burden known** 99
**Unless by him to others it be shown.**
Robinson, Robert, 'Scientia possessori onus, si non aliis eandem distribuat'.
MSS. Ashmole 826, fol. 110 (autogr.).; *Rawl. poet. 218, p. 106 (autogr.).

**Knowledge doth much in care of most content** 100
**Fair is his hap that such a face beholdeth.**
MS. Rawl. poet. 85, fol. 115.

**Knowledge like Phoebus, the vast globe surveys** 101
**And in affairs of trade, is just and wise.**
'Knowledge a Poem . . . to Mr. Auberry'.
MS. Top. Oxon. c. 220, p. 1.

**Knowledge who strives for to attain** 102
**Unless to him they bend.**
Verses used as a copy by Wiman Ramsey, *c.* 1595.
MS. Rawl. D. 649, fol. 35.

**Knowledge with poverty, a woeful thing.** 103
**Great wealth with ignorance a pow'rful king.**
Robinson, Robert, couplet.
MS. *Rawl. poet. 218, p. 173 (autogr.).

# L

ENTRIES 1–900

1 Labour in harvest with the ant
Old age thy joints will numb.
'Advice'.
MS. Rawl. poet. 90, fol. 103.

2 Labour in summer take pains with the ant
Else in the winter live cold and in want.
Couplet.
MS. Rawl. D. 954, fol. $19^v$.

Labour not to be rich . . . see D263.

3 Labour to get a friend, and then thy care
And no less praise here to preserve than gain.
Bulteel, John, 'De Amico'.
MS.* Rawl. poet. 159, fol. 212.

4 Laden with guilt oppressed with fear,
He will his saving grace afford.
Beddome, Benjamin.
Pr. *Hymns . . . of B. Beddome*, 1818, no. 381.
MS.* Eng. misc. e. 227, fol. $4^v$.

5 Laden with iniquities
Save me by Thy pitying love.
Kenton, James.
MS.* Eng. poet. e. 20, p. 260 (autogr.).

6 Ladies all glad 'e here comes doctor Paddye
So farewell bawdy doctors.
'Let Closestoole and Chamberpot Choose out a Doctor'.
MS. Rawl. poet. 160, fol. $183^v$; see also L14.

7 Ladies and gentlemen your most devoted
Ladies and gentlemen *votre serviteur*.
Boswell, James, Prologue.
MS. *Douce 193, fol. 95 (autogr.).

8 Ladies fair I most present you
For by the words there's nothing meant.
H. Sy.
MS. Rawl. poet. 116, fol. 61.

Ladies fly from love's smooth tale 9
That pity which you cast away.
[Carew, Thomas], 'Conquest by Flight'.
Pr. *Poems*, 1640; *Select Musicall Ayres and Dialogues*, 1653, i. 21; and *Poems of Pembroke and Ruddier*, 1660, p. 71.
MSS. Don. c. 57, fol. $68^v$, with music by H. Lawes; Rawl. poet. 160, fol. 106; see also Y428.

Ladies I beseech you blush not to see 10
I'll say no more until your hands plays tell.
Cavendish, Lady Jane, prologue to 'The Concealed Fancies'.
MS. *Rawl. poet. 16, p. 87.

Ladies I send you here a letter 11
For in this case the world is mum.
Samber, Robert, a letter inviting some ladies to a review in Hyde Park.
MS. *Rawl. poet. 134*b*, fol. 167 (autogr.).

Ladies I'm come an humble suitor to you all, 12
Till at the last his sense is stole away.
'An Epilogue to [Steele's] Tender Husband'.
MS. Montagu e. 13, fol. 126.

Ladies, I'm come to let you understand 13
The son retains the cash, the wife the breeches.
Prologue spoken by Geta before a performance of Terence's *Phormio*.
MSS. Eng. misc. e. 183, fol. 14; Eng. poet. f. 12, p. 74.

Ladies now glad ye, here comes Dr Paddye 14
And so farewell bawdy doctors.
'The Phisitions of London', probably *c.* 1607: cf. ref. on fol. 10 to Matthew Gwinne, first Gresham Professor of Physic, retired 1607.
MS. CCC. 327, fol. $8^v$; see also L6.

Ladies of London both wealthy and fair 15
Will make the best cuckolds of any.
MS. Mus. Sch. C. 95, p. 188.

16 Ladies, our author does by me declare,
No matter what the rest o'th' world do say.

[Killigrew, Sir William], Prologue to 'The Siege of Urbin'.

Pr. folio, 1666.

MS. Rawl. poet. 29 (autogr.).

17 Ladies that gild the glittering moon
Since Charles and Mary lost their beams.

'The Antiparode', on Y83, on the fall of Charles I.

MS. Ashmole 788, fol. 22.

18 Ladies that wear black cypress veils
Which lady's censured, which goes free.

Corbett, Richard, 'To the ladyes of the new dresse'. Answered by B378.

Pr. *Certain Elegant Poems*, 1647, p. 72; *Poetica Stromata*, 1648, p. 85; and *Wits Recreations*, 1640, no. 469.

MSS. Ashmole 36, 37, fol. 174, attr. to Dr. Corbet; 38, p. 65, attr. to Corbett; 47, fol. 111$^{v}$, attr. to Corbet; Eng. poet. c. 50, fol. 26; e. 14, fol. 78 rev., attr. to R. C.; e. 97, p. 29, attr. to Dr. Corbett Bishp. of Norwich; Malone 21, fol. 47, attr. to Dr. Corbett; Rawl. poet. 26, fol. 64$^{v}$; 117, fol. 177$^{v}$, attr. to Dr. Corbett; 206, p. 75, attr. to my L. of Norwidge; Tanner 465, fol. 58$^{v}$, attr. to Bp. Corbett.

19 Ladies there lives an aged hoary sage
If your applause shall sanctify our pains.

Cumberland, Mr., 'Epilogue'.

MS. Eng. poet. c. 51, p. 135*b*.

20 Ladies thus bowing low to you I come
The less our merit is, the more your praise.

'A Prologue to be spoken by Mr. Hind'.

MS. Eng. poet. c. 41, fol. 51.

21 Ladies, tonight we've trod an humble stage,
Which wit and beauty, like your own, inspire.

'The Epilogue—Spoken by Phormio' [Terence's play translated].

MSS. Eng. misc. e. 183, fol. 14; Eng. poet. f. 12, p. 77.

22 Ladies, when you to th' temple go
Their births begin, when others end.

Goff, Thomas, 'An Epitaph upon' [Henry King's wife Anne, *née* Berkeley, 1623/4].

MS. Rawl. D. 398, two copies, fols. 173 and 174.

Ladies, whose first stile is good 23
Though late, may you reach heaven at last.

Shirley, James, 'To th[e r]ight Ho$^{le}$. sisters the Ladie B[ishop] and Ladie Dia[na] Curs[on]'.

A different version, 'To the H[on.] Lady Dia[na] Curs[on] at his departure' printed in *Poems by James Shirley*, 1646, p. 38.

MS. *Rawl. poet. 88, p. 3.

Lady [chained] changed to Venus dove 24
If none stand stiff good morrow maid.

On the marriage of Lady Essex and the Earl of Somerset, 1613.

MSS. Don. c. 54, fol. 23; Eng. poet. e. 37, p. 62; Malone 23, p. 10, completed on p. 65; Rawl. poet. 26, fol. 18$^{v}$.

Lady Dorothy Drum sends her compliments 25
My lord she knows whose works and the shells for the grot.

MS. Eng. poet. e. 47, p. 90.

Lady I entreat you wear 26*a*
Turns the beholders into stone.

Herrick, Robert, 'One a Cherrie stone sent to the tip of Mrs Iemiammas Werldgraues eare on the one side a delicate face on the other side a deathes head'.

MS. Eng. poet. c. 50, two copies, fols. 37 and 94$^{v}$; Rawl. poet. 160, fol. 28, attr. to R. Herrick; 206, p. 66.

Lady in beauty and in favour rare 26*b*
And favour you may well both keep and give.

[Constable, Henry], sonnet, pr. *Diana*, 1592, Sig. C1$^{v}$.

MS. Ashmole 38, p. 53.

Lady my flame still burning 27
Yielding the fruit, that faithful love requireth.

Pr. John Farmer's *Madrigals*, 1599, no. iv.

MS. Mus. d. 8, fol. 67, copied by P. Hayes.

Lady, of beauties more than most divine 28
The life and counterfeit will so seem one.

Ch. M., Sonnett 13.

MS. Eng. misc. d. 239, fol. 9.

Lady reserved by the heavens to do pastor's company honour 29
And sorrows do require some respite unto the senses.

Sidney, Sir Philip, 'songe in exameter verse' from the *Arcadia*.

MS. *e Mus. 37, fol. 46; Rawl. poet. 85, fol. 22 (extracts).

Lady that hand of plenty 30
But still by fresh assaults quite to destroy me.

'A. 5. Voc. Lelio Bertani'.

Pr. *Musica Transalpina*, 1588, xxxviii.

MSS. Mus. f. 20–24: f. 20, fol. 33$^{v}$.

31 Lady we read that modesty began
Knowledge, you have it at your fingers' end.
Evans, Samuel, to Lady Elizabeth Poulett on her present of an embroidery to the University of Oxford, 9 July 1636.
MS. Bodl. 22, fol. 2.

32 Lady what's your face to me
We both lose yet win the field.
Shirley, James, 'To his Mrs. whom hee lov'd to enjoy her'.
Pr. *Poems*, 1646, p. 26.
MSS. Eng. poet. c. 50, fol. 110ᵛ; *Rawl. poet. 88, p. 13.

33 Lady, when I from you return
Of the best things you're one of those.
'Ode: To the Lady Ma: Wrath'.
MS. Don. b. 9, fol. 35ᵛ.

34 Lady why doth cares torment you
Oh no, no alas no.
Dialogue.
MS. Ashmole 38, p. 55.

35 Lady you'll wonder, when you see
Since there's no Helicon like love and thee.
[Brome, Alexander], 'To his Mistres'.
Pr. *Poems*, 1661, p. 8.
MS. Ashmole 47, fol. 141.

36 Laelius and Scipio, those great sons of fame,
Aloft the other springs, and to the clouds ascends.
'The Game of Goose. From the Gentleman's Magazine Decr. 1744'.
MS. Ballard 50, fol. 125.

37 Lais now old, that erst attempting lass
Nor dare she look upon her winter face.
Pr. Orlando Gibbons' *First Set of Madrigals*, 1612, xiii.
MSS. Mus. f. 20–24: f. 20, fol. 53ᵛ.

38 Lament ladies lament
Oh hone hone oh nea.
'A scottish song'.
MS. Ashmole 38, p. 124.

39 Lament lament; look look what thou hast done.
That in one hour didst mar, what heaven six days was making.
[Quarles, Francis], 'Adams fall'.
Pr. *Emblemes*, 1635, I. ii.
MS. Rawl. poet. 90, fol. 17ᵛ.

Lament lament you scholars all 40
But now we'll drink like doctors.
Randolph, Thomas, 'On the burninge of the signe of the miter in cham[bridge]'.
Pr. *Wit and Drollery*, 1656, p. 68; not in Randolph's *Poems*, 1638, 1640.
MSS. CCC. 328, fol. 45; Rawl. D. 108, fol. 110, attr. to Randolph; 1092, fol. 269, attr. to Tho. Randolph; Rawl. poet. 62, fol. 26ᵛ, attr. to Tho. Randolph of Trin. Coll.; 209, fol. 26.

Lament not Phoceus that thou art in love 41
The love to tender virgins waxeth cold.
W. A., translator, Horace, *Odes* II. iv.
MS. *Rawl. poet. 104, fol. 14 (autogr.).

Lament ye London dames, ye London wives, 42
That pious saint, her Arrabella sweet.
Spoure, Edmund, 'An Epitaph on Mrs Hester Spoure, late wife of Mr. Richard Spoure of Grey-Inn London'.
MS. *Eng. poet. c. 52, fol. 36 (autogr.).

Language thou art too narrow and too weak 43
Of grief; for all would waste a stoic's heart.
Donne, John, 'An Elegie on the death of Mrs Boulstred'.
MSS. *Eng. poet. f. 9, p. 60; Rawl. poet. 31, fol. 45.

Languish and despair my heart 44
Whose woes may make thee howl and die with grief.
MS. Mus. b. 1, fol. 24ᵛ, music by John Wilson.

Lash not thy stock out lavishly 45
Farewell the fruits of amity.
Verses used as a copy by Wiman Ramsey, *c.* 1595.
MS. Rawl. D. 649, fol. 36.

Last Easter I got married and that night we went to bed 46
Since the lowlands of Holland have parted my love and me.
'Lowlands of Holland'.
MS. Firth c. 18, fol. 152.

Last night a dream of dreams I had 47
Forced me to wake out of those dreams.
MS. Rawl. poet. 172, fol. 72.

Last night as the Devil skimmed over the wall 48
And are here holding truce with the angels of light.
Satire on Dr. John Robinson, Warden of Merton, 1750.
MS. Eng. misc. e. 241, fol. 107ᵛ.

49 Last night I heard the dogstar bark
Will fire the bush at his back.
'The second part to Tom of Bedlam', F544.
Pr. *Prince d'Amour*, 1660, p. 170.
MS. Mus. Sch. C. 96, fol. 49.

50 Last night I in my cups let slip,
One that remembreth what I prate.
'Ad Procillum', translation from Martial, *Epigrams* I. xxvii.
MS. Rawl. D. 1147, fol. 89v.

51 Last night when I to sleep my self had laid
They all concluded with an *Ave* Mary.
'The Vision of Toleration. 1687'.
Pr. *The Muses Farewell to Popery*, 1690, p. 25.
MSS. Firth c. 15, p. 263; c. 16, p. 152; Rawl. poet. 173, fol. 118v.

52 Last when I saw thee, thou dist sweetly play
A sweet faced creature with a double heart.
'To his Mrs'.
MS. Ashmole 47, fol. 104v; see also W1035.

53 Late as I lay with surging cares oppressed
All that I heard and saw to him was due.
Glean, Peter, 'A Dream upon the much lamented Death of William [Sancroft] late lord Bishop of Canterbury', 1693.
MS. Tanner 306, fol. 435v.

54 Late as I on my bed reposing lay,
I'd wink forever, be forever blind.
Oldham, [John], 'A Love Dream'.
MS. Rawl. poet. 173, fol. 77.

55 Late as I walked on the way
Wherefore I here do end.
Forman, Simon, in praise of Henry VIII and Queen Elizabeth, etc.; lacking one leaf.
MS. Ashmole 208, fol. 250 (autogr.).

56 Late eating and drinking I do forbear
I marvel th'art not now alive.
'The old L: Marques (beinge L: Thesaurer of th' age of 94) his sayinge', with 'The Answer'. [William Paulet, Marquess of Winchester, L. Treasurer 1549/50–1571/2].
MS. Rawl. poet. 148, fol. 110; cf. L61.

57 Late in a night
Now put an end to't.
'The Starry Vision'. Lines on the Restoration.
MS. Ashmole 47, fol. 164.

58 Late in rebellious rout did I disclaim
The life she gave me I'll give her again.
Burton, Francis.
MS. *Add. A. 367, fol. 138v (autogr.).

Late on a night as I lay sleeping 59
But when I waked she was away.
MS. Rawl. C. 813, fol. 48.

Late seriously revolving in my mind 60
Pray God I be the last shall lose his love.
Burton, Francis.
MS. *Add. A. 267, fol. 102v (autogr.).

Late suppers and wine I did forbear 61
And these be they that made me old.
'Gallen beynge asked howe he preserved his lyfe so longe Made thys aunswere'.
MS. Rawl. poet. 85, fol. 43v; see also L56.

Lately and late for late it was at night 62
That there is *signum* and signature both.
MS. Eng. poet. e. 14, fol. 24v.

Lately I thought, oh holy saint 63
Of bless'd connubial love.
'Corydon's Petition to St. Valentine'.
MS. *Eng. poet. d. 47, fol. 82.

Lately on yonder swelling bush 64
To wax more soft, her youth invades.
Waller, Edmund, 'The Bud'.
Pr. *Poems*, 1645, p. 149.
MS. *Don. d. 55, fol. 37.

Lately, the muses from their forked hill 65
Approved thy judgement in so sweet a choice.
On Humphrey King's *Halfe-penny worth of wit*, 1613. Transcribed from R. Heber's copy.
MS. Douce 190, fol. 12.

Laugh not fond fool 'cause I a face 66
Through fear and through desire.
MS. Mus. b. 1, fol. 132v, music by John Wilson.

Laugh ye profane, and swell and burst 67
And distant are our goals.
Watts, Isaac, ['The Atheists Mistake'].
Pr. *Horæ Lyricæ*.
MS. Rawl. D. 868, fol. 36v.

Laughs not the heart, when giants, big with pride 68
If reason's for me, God is for me too.
Churchill, Charles, 'The Apology Addressed to the Critical Reviewers'.
MS. *Eng. poet. d. 113, p. 36.

Launch forth brave barge; thou needst no danger dread, 69
If all; yet haste thou all in her, and more.
Ch. M., Sonnett 15.
MS. Eng. misc. d. 239, fol. 9v.

70 Launch forth my soul into a main of bliss
So oft they cried, these must be nailed for thee.
F. W., 'Sonnet 46'.
MS. *Rawl. C. 639, p. 217.

71 Launch out, great sovereign of the sea, and fight.
Sail safe, and bring you home the golden fleece.
Stapleton, Sir Robert.
MSS. Ashmole 36, 37, fol. 119, endorsed by Ashmole 'Sr. Robert Stapleton to the King 1666'; Firth c. 18, fol. 95.

72 Laura fair queen of love's despite, come grant me love in love's despite
Be as dark as hell to me.
Extract from R 167.
MS. Rawl. poet. 152, fol. 34.

73 Laura see the amorous vine
Then say, my fair! why should not we?
Parsons, William, '. . . in imitation of Anacreon'.
MS. *Don. d. 123, p. 62 (autogr.).

74 Laura! whom heavenly charms adorn,
You'll weep neglected youth!
Parsons, William.
MS. *Don. d. 123, p. 6 (autogr.).

75 Lavender blue and rosemary green
And you and I will keep the bed warm.
MS. Douce d. 59, fol. 48.

76 Lavinia glorious as May,
And winter took his former seat.
'Upon a gentlewoman walking forth'.
MS. Eng. misc. e. 13, fol. 19.

77 Lavish not wit in verse; to cast away
There is nor collect, nor collection.
Pestell, Thomas, 'To Fr. Noo:' i.e. Francis Noone of Walton in Leicestershire, 'Franc: Noone—1620', in Harvard Engl. MS. 228.
MS. *Malone 14, p. 29.

78 Law Chirurg[ry] and Divinity
. . . (incomplete) . . .
A fragment: the full text is in B.M. Add. MS. 28101, fol. 22.
MS. Rawl. poet. 26, fol. 161$^{v}$; see also L80.

79 Law is put down and conscience is slain
Most are undone all do complain.
Couplet.
MS. Eng. poet. c. 50, two copies, fols. 23$^{v}$ and 27.

80 Law, physic and divinity
They'll be ass ridden by all three.
'The triple plea betwixt the L:P:T.'
MSS. Add. B. 106, fol. 50; Rawl. poet. 172, fol. 165, dated 1681; 208, fol. 1$^{v}$; see also L78.

Laws like spiders' webs are wrought 81
Great flies escape, and small are caught.
Couplet, 'the poet compares the lawes to Cobwebs saying:' etc.
MS. Rawl. B. 14, fol. 53$^{v}$.

Lawyers aver the fault should be 82
If we live single past our time.
'On a Tax propos'd to be laid on Old Maids'.
MS. *Eng. poet. d. 47, fol. 51.

Lawyers do plead all cases, yet do thrive 83
Most by the dative and the ablative.
'On Lawiers', couplet.
MS. Rawl. poet. 153, fol. 22.

Lawyers of all men best esteem should have. 84
They good men honest keep and mend the knave.
Robinson, Robert, couplet.
MS. *Rawl. poet. 218, p. 23 (autogr.).

Lawyers themselves maintain, the common weal 85
And love, they want, not keeping amity.
'Upon the Prayse and Disprayse of Lawyers'; equivocal verses.
Pr. *Wit Restor'd*, 1658, p. 59.
MSS. Ashmole 38, p. 132; 47, fol. 52$^{v}$; Don. d. 58, fol. 37$^{v}$; Douce f. 5, fol. 13$^{v}$; Eng. poet. e. 14, fol. 87 rev.; e. 97, p. 96; f. 10, fol. 89$^{v}$; Malone 23, p. 221; Rawl. poet. 117, fol. 268 rev.

Lay by your pleading, law lies a bleeding 86
Thus have you seen me run my sword up to the hilts Sir.
[Jordan, Thomas].
Pr. *Merry Drollery*, 1661, p. 118, and *Rump*, 1662, i. 333. For attribution see notes in Bodl. pr. bk. Thorn-Drury d. 29, p. 252.
MSS. Rawl. B. 35, fol. 37; Rawl. poet. 37, p. 112.

Lay down thy lute Apollo: do not try 87
The case is left behind.
'Upon the death of Thomas Knowles Chorister of Westminster Abby'.
MS. Rawl. poet. 246, fol. 25.

Lay lightly, on her bosom, gentle earth 88
And, blighted by the chill of cold neglect Amelia died.
'Epitaph on Amelia, written, when at school at Reading and placed on her Tomb Stone', sent to Mrs. Horace Twiss.
MS. Don. d. 95, fol. 307 (autogr.).

89 Lay that sullen garland by me
Sleep will come sleep will cure.

Song.
Pr. *Select Musicall Ayres and Dialogues*, 1652, p. 22.
MSS. Eng. poet. b. 1, fol. 19; Mus. d. 8, fol. 43, music by John Taylor, copied by P. Hayes.

90 Lay thy lip to mine, my dear
But one eternal being.

In answer to I218.
MS. Rawl. poet. 37, p. 38.

91 Lazarus come forth: why could not Lazarus plead,
The voice that calls, gives, and gives then the power.

[Quarles, Francis], 'On Lazarus, the Damosell, and a Sinner'.
Pr. *Divine Fancies*, 1632, iii. 7.
MS. Rawl. poet. 90, fol. 71.

92 Lead me, ye fates, to Windsor's winding shore
Or heaven are they, or such as they live there!

Stukeley, William, 'Windsor. 7 Mar. 1755'.
MS. *Eng. misc. d. 450, fol. 22 (autogr.).

93 Lean, slender, gracil, wither'd, lank, and thin
Thy lusts are not the lusts of flesh, but spirit.

Oldisworth, Nicolas, 'To a Curtezan'.
MS. *Don. c. 24, fol. 72 (autogr.).

94 Learn, curious reader, ere you pass.
Whose heart could never yield.

On Sir Edward Denny, 1599, Waltham Abbey.
MS. Top. gen. e. 32, fol. 45$^{v}$.

95 Learn first one lesson well: When that you know,
Too much at once, the head remembers not.

Robinson, Robert.
MS. *Rawl. poet. 218, p. 149 (autogr.).

96 Learn hence, ye whigs, and act no more like fools,
For know, that you are clay, and they are brass.

'The Morall of the Fable', of the Pot and the Kettle, A1483.
MS. Rawl. poet. 173, fol. 120$^{v}$.

97 Learn to live well, if thou'dst die happily
And that thou mayst live happy, learn to die.

'A Happy Death'.
MS. Rawl. poet. 90, fol. 147$^{v}$.

98 Learn well thy trade, and labour hard:
Comest thou to beg, thou'lt find small giving.

Robinson, Robert.
MS. *Rawl. poet. 218, p. 140 (autogr.).

Learn your lesson first by leisure. 99
'Tis forgotten and comes to nought.

Robinson, Robert.
MS. *Rawl. poet. 218, p. 122 (autogr.).

Learn your lesson sure by heart, 100
What's loosely learn'd small time doth there remain.

Robinson, Robert.
MS. *Rawl. poet. 218, p. 156 (autogr.).

Learned Mæcenas, if you'll credit give 101
And deadly feuds destructive wars do breed.

B[rome], A[lexander], translator, Horace, *Epistles* I. xix.
Pr. *Poems of Horace*, A. Brome etc., 2nd ed., 1671, p. 354.
MS. Rawl. D. 261, p. 76.

Learning now doth fall a legging, 102
Art and science go a begging.

Robinson, Robert, couplet.
MS. *Rawl. poet. 218, p. 172 (autogr.).

Learning of late is fled the land 103
Physician weak, and lawyer false.

Creswell, Robert, 'The Dunces. To the tune of Petticoat-wag. Christmas, 1638. A Song'.
MS. Rawl. poet. 246, fol. 27$^{v}$.

Learning, worship, credit, patrimony 104
But that some go before, and some come after.

'Epitaph . . . at Rochester, on Thomas Penistone Esqr. Clarke of the Councell to Queen Elizabeth'.
MS. Eng. poet. e. 40, fol. 110.

Learning would I desire and knowledge crave 105
Though I were half sepulchred in my grave.

Couplet, translation from Latin.
MS. Rawl. D. 954, fol. 41.

Leave Cloris leave the woods 106
Than turtles suffer when they bill.

MS. Mus. b. 1, fol. 143$^{v}$, music by John Wilson.

Leave, leave; my mistress cries when I do kiss. 107
I'll leave the lips behind, but steal the bliss.

Ashmole, Elias, 'Kisse', 26 May 1648, couplet.
MSS. Ashmole 36, 37, fol. 230 (autogr.).

Leave me all other business, but tears. 108
Hymns to two mighty mercies God's and the King's.

[Paman], Cl[ement], Fil[ius]. 'The teares'.
MS. Rawl. poet. 62, fol. 10.

109 Leave me oh love which reachest but to dust
Eternal love maintain thy life in me.
[Sidney, Sir Philip], 'Splendidis Longum Valedico nugis'.
Pr. *Arcadia*, 1598.
MS. Eng. poet. d. 3, two copies, fols. 1 and 36.

110 Leave me shepherd leave me
And every word beguiles.
Song with a tune.
MS. Mus. Sch. G. 635, fol. 7.

111 Leave off dull Clelia strive in vain no more
All hearts are due to her not hers to you.
MS. Eng. poet. e. 31, fol. 153 rev., in the hand of Octavia Walsh.

112 Leave off fond hermit leave thy vow
A full crowned bowl first here's a health to thine.
[Brome, Alexander], 'To his Frend that had vow'd small Beare'.
Pr. *Poems*, 1661, p. 19.
MS. Ashmole 47, fol. 151.

113 Leave off, fond youth, leave off, these foolish toys!
For it shall never triumph over me.
Morrice, John, 'The Repuls', 3 Feb. 1707.
MS. *Rawl. poet. 114, fol. 58 (autogr.).

114 Leave off leave off fond foolish boy
She is not what she seems to be.
'A Songe'.
MS. Rawl. poet. 153, fol. 23v.

115 Leave off my sheep it is no time to feed
You bear no wool and loss is all my gain.
Sidney, Sir Philip, from the *Arcadia*; answer to F272.
MS. *e Mus. 37, fol. 72.

116 Leave off! No more with care thy soul disturb
Then to be happy and immortal too.
'The Halt'.
MS. Don. e. 19, fol. 29.

117 Leave off to muse my friends
And therewithal I waked.
Andrews, 'Swerdna his dreame'.
MS. *Rawl. poet. 92, fol. 21v.

118 Leave off to tell what soldiers do in Spaine
And to the trimming of her hair take heed.
W. A., translator, Horace, *Odes* II. ii.
MS. *Rawl. poet. 104, fol. 16v (autogr.).

Leave off, vain satirist, and do not think 119
His fiddlers bravely sing, but he recants.
[Saltmarsh, John, of Magdalene], 'Upon Mr. Cl[eveland] who made a Song against the D.Drs' i.e., 'the Mixed Assembly', F353, on the Westminster Assembly, 1643.
In B.M. MS. Harl. 6918, attr. to 'Saltmarsh of Magdalene'.
MS. Tanner 465, fol. 44.

Leave off with pain, the blackamore to scour, 120
Let reason rule, and do the thing thou may.
Whitney, Geoffrey, 'Æthiopem lavare'.
MS. *Rawl. poet. 56, fol. 31v.

Leave off your heavy trance 121
By keeping asunder.
'Grays Inn. Songs'.
MS. Rawl. poet. 117, fol. 248v rev.

Leave off your lying, flesh lies adying. 122
Where he doth, gently warm us.
'Tune, Law lyes a bleeding'.
MS. Rawl. poet. 37, p. 47.

Leave off your ogling Francis 123
And servant Roger Martin.
'Advice. Or an Heroic Epistle to Frank Villers . . . 1683'.
MSS. Firth c. 15, p. 151; c. 16, p. 40.

Leaving the close intrigues of state 124
Though paradise itself were lost.
MS. Don. e. 24, p. 33.

Lechery did consult with witchery 125
The lord and lady's lechery.
On the marriage of the Earl of Somerset and Lady Essex, 26 Dec. 1613.
MS. Rawl. D. 1048, fol. 64.

Led by my foolish vain desires 126
And nature's course by grace subdue.
Kenton, James.
MS. *Eng. poet. e. 20, p. 191 (autogr.).

Lee plays so well, we still should wish 127
To both I lend my aid.
Boswell, James, 'Mr. [John] Lee, The World and The Stage'.
MS. *Douce 193, fol. 42 (autogr.).

Lend words to a sad mourner's verse 128
My children do the like for me.
Darell, Sir Samson, 'On the death of the Lady Darell'.
MS. Rawl. poet. 210, fol. 56.

129 Lenten stuff is come to the town
And makes an end of lenten tide.
Elderton, W., 'A newe ballad entytuled Lenton stuff, for a lyttell muny ye maye have inowgh, to the tune of the Crampe'.
MS. Ashmole 48, fol. 115$^{v}$.

130 Lesbia let's live and love, and never weigh
Knowing that we have had so many kisses.
Imitation of Catullus, v, 'Vivamus, mea Lesbia. . .'.
MSS. Ashmole 36, 37, fol. 294.

131 Lesbia's smiles shall ne'er deceive me
Gentle love! resume thy throne.
'A Conflict between Love and Reason'.
MS. Rawl. poet. 116, fol. 112.

132 Less grateful to the traveller's thirst
Untouched, unpleased my soul.
Whaley, John, 'An Epistle to Mr. — at Cambridge. Poplar, Augt. 13: 1730'.
Pr. *Poems*, 1732, p. 164.
MS. Rawl. poet. 222, fol. 20$^{v}$.

133 Less hard it is, not to err our selves, than know
Trust not God conceiving men.
Fleming, Robert (?)
MS. Rawl. poet. 213, fol. 65$^{v}$, in Robert Fleming's hand.

134 Less learned bodies may have missed on't
She votes for 'the Exchequer' still.
'Epigram, Sibi constat', Cambridge.
MS. Eng. poet. c. 51, p. 101.

135 Less shall proud Rome her ancient trophies boast
And Anson's spoils, are from a tribute world.
'Britons Triumph (written Extempore, as the waggons loaded with Treasure pass'd thro' the City of London, taken by Admiral Anson)'. 1746.
MS. Montagu e. 13, fol. 92.

136 Lesser than I no God nor any greater
Jove only hath the name Cupid the power.
Song with music.
MS. Don. c. 57, fol. 45.

137 Lest our loves should part or sever,
Here's a rope to tie's together.
Couplet.
MS. Rawl. poet. 209, fol. 36$^{v}$.

138 Let able judges tell me by what name
To feed with meat and with hard words to kill.
Williams, John.
MS. *Rawl. poet. 191, fol. 103$^{v}$ (autogr.).

Let all in sweet accord 139
The King of Kings of all above.
[Sandys, George], Psalm xlvii, 3-part setting, [by W. Lawes].
Pr. *A paraphrase upon the Divine Poems*, 1638, and H. and W. Lawes, *Choice Psalmes*, 1648.
MS. Mus. Sch. E. 451, p. 46*a*.

Let all loyal subjects rejoice now amain 140
For this heavy tax he will freely take down.
'The Chimney-Men's Grief, or The poor Subjects Joyful Expectation of the Downfall of that Terrible Tax'.
MS. Firth d. 14, fol. 28.

Let all men know, a saving shrow 141
Of evils choose the lesser woe.
Robinson, Robert.
MS. *Rawl. poet. 218, p. 160 (autogr.).

Let all that hate thee Lord 'fore thee retire 142
Blest be our strength the god of Israel.
Fairfax, Thomas, Lord, Psalm lxviii.
MS. *Fairfax 40, p. 148 (autogr.).
MS. *Fairfax 38, p. 233.

Let all that putrifidean sect 143
Keep both itself, and state secure.
'A proper newe Ballett called the Summons to newe England to the Tune of the Townesmens cappe'.
Pr. *Merry Drollery*, 1661, ii. 103. Cf. L281.
MS. Tanner 306, fol. 286; see also L147.

Let all the blues with pious grief 144
The essence of good manners.
'Upon the Death of the Most Noble John Manners, Marquis of Granby, and Colonel of the Blues', died 18 Oct. 1770.
MS. Eng. poet. e. 28, p. 340.

Let all the common rout of books stand by 145
Had need of brazen lungs and forehead too.
Sprat, Thomas, 'Upon the Poems of the English Ovid, Anacreon, Pindar and Virgil Abraham Cowley in imitation of his own Pindarick Odes'. Written by Spratt in the copy of Cowley's works he presented to Wadham College, shelf-mark U. 16. 11.
MSS. Rawl. C. 556, fol. 35$^{v}$ rev.; Top. Oxon. e. 202, fol. 43, attr. to Dr. Spratt; see also L153.

Let all the earth with cheerful voice 146
And praise his sanctity.
Knollys, Fra., Psalm xcvii.
MS. *Rawl. poet. 60, p. 16 (autogr.).

147 Let all the fratrifidium sect
Keep both itself and state secure.
On the puritan immigrants to New England, *temp.* Charles I.
Pr. *Merry Drollery*, 1661, ii. 103, beginning 'Among the purifidian sect.' Cf. L281.
MS. Ashmole 38, fol. 225ᵛ; see also L143.

148 Let all the ingredients, from which art did draw
Let it be ready at thy utmost date.
'A guifte to the Lord Treasurer lord Weston . . . A seller of waters' with devices 'The meaning of which is that the giver wisheth all health' (July 1628—Feb. 1632/3).
MS. Ashmole 38, p. 77.

149 Let all the pretty names, that be
To pay her mite, in this poor song of mine.
'The Lilly of the Valleyes'.
MS. Eng. poet. e. 51, p. 57.

150 Let all the pris'ners stand forth to the bar
With Sathan in Hell's ever-burning fire.
Colman, Henry, 'The Sentence'.
MS. *Rawl. poet. 204, fol. 13ᵛ (autogr.).

151 Let all the ransomed nations sing
Glory be to God on high.
Kenton, James.
MS. *Eng. poet. e. 20, p. 90 (autogr.).

152 Let all the world in every corner sing.
My God and King.
Herbert, George, 'Antiphon'.
Pr. *The Temple*, 1633, p. 45.
MS. *Tanner 307, fol. 34ᵛ.

153 [Let all this meaner rout of books stand by]
Had need of brazen lungs and forehead too.
Sprat, Thomas, 'On the death and to the memory of Mr. Abraham Cowley', blank spaces left for verses 1 and 2.
Pr. Dryden's *Miscellany Poems*, 1716, iv. 296.
MS. Eng. poet. e. 4, p. 49; see also L145.

154 Let all with sweet accord
Sing praises with sacred mirth. Alleluja.
'A Hymn a 2 voc.'
MS. Mus. d. 10, fol. 39ᵛ.

155 Let ambition fire thy mind
Scorn thy crook and leave the plain.
[Congreve, William], song from *The Judgment of Paris.*
A different setting from the printed one by Eccles.
MSS. Mus. c. 107, fol. 10ᵛ; e. 20, fol. 14; Mus. Sch. C. 41, fol. 16.

Let April . . . see G126.

Let be wanton your business 156
Seeing that your best time is lame.
MS. Ashmole 176, fol. 98ᵛ.

Let beardless dolts Anacreontic 157*a*
And never more put rhyme to paper.
'The Poet'.
MS. Top. London e. 9, p. 77.

Let blessings Lord and mercy on us be shown 157*b*
And through earth's bounders all shall stand in fear.
Fairfax, Thomas, Lord, Psalm lxvii.
MS. *Fairfax 38, p. 232; see also O563.

Let Britain [Britons] now [a] her grateful homage pay. 158
And bind with Ormond's laurels James's crown.
'The Birth Day [of the old Pretender] June 10th 1715'. Cf. S88.
MSS. Eng. poet. e. 87, p. 110; Rawl. poet. 155, p. 21.

Let brutes, and vegetals that cannot think 159
Shows for my sake, what his bold hand would do.
Waller, Edmund, 'For the Drinckinge of Healths'.
Pr. *Poems*, 1645, p. 142.
MS. *Don. d. 55, fol. 24.

Let burgundy flow 160
And the whigs go to pot.
'An Answer to a Song of D'Urfey's'; see *Pills to Purge Melancholy*, 1719, ii. 43.
MS. Rawl. poet. 155, p. 112.

Let C. and G. do what they can, 161
Yet G. shall die like Doctor Lambe.
Couplet on Charles I and George, Duke of Buckingham.
MS. Tanner 465, fol. 100.

Let Charles so sw- 162
And Kate may be its mother.
Shepherd, [Fleetwood], Christ Church, Oxford, 'Burlesque', on Latin distich by Dr. Sebastian Smith of Christ Church.
MS. Eng. poet. e. 4, p. 202; see also L212.

Let cheerful smiles in every face 163
Shall echo back the praise.
'Hymn for Christmas Day—Collectn Poems'.
MS. Eng. poet. e. 39, p. 99.

Let commerce have her vast domain 164
Which never can decay.
Carter, William, of Manchester.
MS. Firth c. 18, fol. 43.

165 Let coward guilt with pallid fear
Of everlasting day.
Miss [Elizabeth] Carter, 'Written at Midnight in a Thunder-Storm'.
Pr. *Poems*, 1762, p. 36.
MS. Montagu e. 14, fol. 23.

166 Let cynics bark, and the stern stagyrite
Props of the church and pillars of the throne.
'The Paradox' on the seven Bishops, May 1688.
Pr. *A Collection of the Newest . . . Poems . . . against Popery*, 1689, p. 25.
MSS. Firth c. 16, p. 283; Rawl. poet. 152, fol. 187.

167 Let debauchees call matrimony dull
As the glad father will be proud to own.
'He Advises his Friend to Marry'. By 'M^r C. of K[ing's] C[ollege], C[ambridge]'.
MS. Rawl. poet. 222, fol. 2^v.

168 Let each one take his glass
Or live to betray one another.
'The Loyal Health', *temp.* Charles II.
MS. Rawl. poet. 159, fol. 162.

169 Let England rejoice with heart and with voice
Since crowds now come over with William and Mary.
'England's Congratulation'.
Dated 1690 in B.M. MS. Harl. 7315, fol. 184^v; 'Printed', as a broadside (?).
MS. Firth e. 6, fol. 25*a*.

170 Let England weep let Ireland roar
To welcome him that's far awa'.
Scotch song on the Old Pretender's birthday.
MS. Rawl. poet. 155, p. 143.

171 Let England's Church her sinking state deplore,
Give laws at will, and by the sword command.
'To the King's most excellent Ma^ty. . . . June 10th . . . Presented by the Secret Committee, and introduc'd by the Duke of Marlborough' [1715].
MSS. Eng. poet. e. 87, p. 112; Rawl. poet. 155, p. 121; 173, fol. 2^v; pr. bk. Firth b. 22, fol. 15.

172 Let Englishmen sit and consult at their ease
Too late you will say, then hang up the Scot.
'An Answer made to God a mercy good Scott'. Satire on the early proceedings of the Long Parliament, 1640.
Answer to Y394.
See C. H. H. Firth, *Scottish Historical Review*, 1906, p. 272.
MSS. Ashmole 36, 37, fol. 98; Douce 357, fol. 8^v; Rawl. poet. 26, fol. 96; 152, fol. 196; Tanner 306, fol. 292.

Let equipage and dress despair 173
Be only on Alpue.
[Etherege, Sir George], 'Song on Bassett'.
Pr. *Works*, 1704, p. 287.
MS. Firth c. 16, p. 55.

Let every heart and every eye, 174
Both light and knowledge dwell in me.
Beddome, Benjamin.
MS. *Eng. misc. e. 227, fol. 8.

Let fables speak and poets still invent 175
The sobbing sighs or move afflictive moans.
'Hell'.
MS. Rawl. poet. fol. 6^v.

Let Faux his [Faux's] powder-plot amaze no more; 176
Then when He made the devils hold their peace.
On the dissolution of Parliament, April 1653.
See King's *Poems*, ed. M. C. Crum, 1965, p. 253.
MSS. Rawl. D. 317, fol. 176*^v, in the hand of Bishop Henry King; Rawl. poet. 246, fol. 15.

Let female softness breathe the grateful strain 177
And the dark tomb to light eternal lead!
Seward, Anna, 'Inscription . . . in commemoration of the benefactors of the Female Society at Lichfield'.
Not in her *Poetical Works*, ed. Sir W. Scott, 1810.
MS. Eng. poet. c. 51, p. 76.

Let fickle fortune run 178
(torn away: v. 4, l. 4, 'by love to one'.)
[Southwell, Robert, 'From Fortunes reach'].
Pr. *St. Peters Complaint*, 1595, for G. Cawood.
MS. Eng. poet. b. 5, p. 53.

Let fighting fools commend the wars 179
And Venus' sacred rites from vulgar eyes conceal.
'Tutius est jacuisse foro, tenuisse puellam . . . Ovid'. 1735.
MS. Eng. misc. e. 240, p. 162.

Let folly praise, that fancy loves 180
Direct me when I die.
[Southwell, Robert], 'A Child my choyce'.
Pr. *St. Peters Complaint*, 1595.
MS. Eng. poet. b. 5, p. 91.

Let fools alone in their disguise. 181
Let thee and I learn to be wise.
Robinson, Robert.
MS. *Rawl. poet. 218, p. 71 (autogr.).

Let foreign nations of their language boast 182
We him in glory call, the son of man.
Herbert, George, 'The Sonne'.
Pr. *The Temple*, 1633, p. 162.
MS. *Tanner 307, fol. 123^v.

183 Let fragrant eastern breezes round thee play,
She had been constant then, and all my own.
'A Pastoral in Imitation of Mrs. Killegrew'.
MS. Montagu e. 13, fol. 160v.

184 Let god arise, and then his foes
Praised be god therefore.
[Sternhold Thomas], Psalm lxviii.
MS. Rawl. poet. 112, fol. 52v rev.

185 Let God arise, his enemies
Glory to him repeat.
Psalm lxviii.
MS. *Rawl. C. 113, fol. 48.

186 Let god but rise his foes shall quickly fall
And doth protect them all his name be blest.
Harington, Sir John, Psalm lxviii.
MS. *Douce 361, fol. 39.

187 Let God but rise, his very face shall cast
His force it is, in which their forces fight.
Herbert, Mary (*née* Sidney), Countess of Pembroke, Psalm lxviii.
MS. *Rawl. poet. 24, p. 94.

188 Let god the god of battle rise
So perish in his burning ire.
[Sandys, George], Psalm lxviii, 3-part setting by W. Lawes.
Pr. *Paraphrase upon the Divine Poems*, 1638, p. 80, and H. and W. Lawes, *Choice Psalmes*, 1648.
MS. Mus. Sch. E. 451, p. 67.

189 Let God the lord hear thee
When as to him our prayers do appear.
Sidney, Sir Philip, Psalm xx.
MSS. *Rawl. poet. 24, p. 24; *25, fol. 14v.

190 Let Greece have tales of thund'ring Joves
His canonizing yet may stay.
Pestell, Thomas, 'Song of King Locarus. 1636'. ['Locarus' = Carolus].
MS. *Malone 14, p. 45.

191 Let grief subside; 'tis fruitless to complain
Can Britons wish for more?
'Ode for the Prince of Wales's Birthday', 1751, music by William Boyce.
MS. Mus. Sch. D. 264, composer's autograph.

192 Let Harvey go round
He'd rather kiss Harvey's than theirs.
'Ballad on Lady Hervey. 1718'.
In B.M. MS. Harl. 7318, fol. 28, 'On Lord Townshend's refusing to drink Lady Harveys health'.
Pr. bk. Firth b. 22, fol. 29.

Let heaven rejoice triumphantly 193
Both now and evermore be done.
Huish, Alexander, 'Exultet caelum laudibus', translated 20. Oct. 1638.
MS. Eng. poet. e. 56, p. 53 (autogr.).

[Let, heavenly muse, enthusiastic fire] 194
Advanced to wed, not to subdue the main.
Blackmore, Sir Richard. Extract from *Eliza*, 1705.
MS. Rawl. D. 868, fol. 56v.

Let Hector Achilles and each brave commander 195
And if she but frown then down they all fall.
Duet by H. Purcell.
Pr. *Comes Amoris*, 1689, and *Banquet of Musick*, iv, 1690, p. 14. F. B. Zimmerman, *Purcell*, 1963, no. 501.
MS. Mus. Sch. C. 96, fol. 8v.

Let her be curded white, or as the moon 196
Value my self no Spaniard, for 'tis red.
James, Richard, 'A defence of red haire against a poeme apologeticall for a virginne whoe was proper of all things but a pale pocktretten face'.
MS. *James 35, p. 5 (autogr.).

Let her give her hand her glove 197
She is ever for the new.
Pr. *Academy of Complements*, 1646, p. 23. *Select Musicall Ayres and Dialogues*, 1652, ii. 26, music by W. Webbe.
MS. Don. c. 57, fol. 40, with music, not Webbe's setting.

Let her parents now confess 198
Where 'cause she is you mourn for her.
'Consolatorium ad parentes' of Mary Prideaux; continuation of S803.
MSS. CCC. 328, fol. 56v; Eng. poet. e. 97, p. 82.

Let higher thoughts to court aspire 199
To neither wished for nor abhorred death.
Song with music.
MS. Don. c. 57, fol. 22v.

Let him that is a David, in distress 200
To be God's gift as well as thought the best.
Williams, John, 'Of Insisting upon our own Integrity'.
MS. *Rawl. poet. 184, fol. 113 (autogr.).

Let him that will, ascend the tottering seat 201
But unacquainted with himself doth fall.
Hale, Sir Matthew, 'The Repose', translated from Seneca, *Thyestes*, 391–403.
Also attr. to Hale in B.M. MS. Add. 29921, fol. 68.
MSS. Rawl. poet. 90, fol. 133; 213, fol. 58v, attr. S. Matthew Hail; see also L203.

202 **Let him who from his tyrant mistress did**
**In either eye a tear each hand a verse.**
Carew, Thomas, 'An Elegie on the Death of the Lady Peniston sent to his Mrs out of France'. d. 14 Jan. 1619/20.
Pr. *Poems*, 1640, 'Lady Pen'.
MSS. Eng. poet. c. 50, fol. 67, attr. to T. C.; Rawl. poet. 160, fol. 54, attr. to Tho. Carew; 209, fol. $2^v$, attr. to T. C.

203 **Let him who will ascend the tott'ring seat**
**But unacquainted with himself doth fall.**
'Judge Hales [Sir Matthew]'s Paraphrase on' Seneca's *Thyestes*, 391–403.
MS. Rawl. poet. 173, fol. $58^v$; see also L201.

204 **Let hoary time's vast bowels be the grave**
**That the world's morning; this her midnight is.**
Crashaw, Richard, 'Upon the Frontispeace of Mr. Isaackson's Chronologie' [1633].
MS. Tanner 465, fol. $48^v$, attr. to R.Cr. and to Mr. Crashaw on fol. 1*a*.

205 **Let Homer sing of Ilium's queen**
**Unto the triple tree.**
Winnard, Thomas, 'Cheynel Cheyneliz'ed' [on Francis Cheynell, *c.* 1647–8].
MS. Eng. poet. e. 4, p. 146.

206 **Let honest tradesmen now attend,**
**Here's none but sorrows, grief, and care.**
'The Troubles of this World; or, Nothing Cheap but Poor Men's Labour'.
MS. Firth d. 14, fol. 56.

207*a* **Let infidels be hushed; fill high my glass;**
**To form so gay, so beautiful a toast.**
'The Toast'.
MSS. Ballard 50, fol. $105^v$; Eng. misc. e. 183, fol. 3.

207*b* **Let Ireland now no more cry Hitto,**
**Could do the like but Humphrey Hody.**
Translation in *Terrae Filius* speech of Hody's Latin verses on Queen Mary's death.
MS. Hearne's diaries 8, p. 179.

208 **Let it be so.**
**Seen by my faith, or understood.**
MSS. Rawl. poet. 66, fol. 2.

209 **Let it no longer be a forlorn hope**
**A black-faced house will love.**
Crashaw, Richard, 'Acts 8. Upon the Æthiopian'.
MS. Tanner 465, fol. 35, attr. to Mr. Crashaw on fol. 1*a*.

**Let it suffice a poor and humble debtor** 210
**To say and if he could it should be better.**
Couplet, subscribed 'Orla[ndo Furioso]' (cf. fol. $279^v$ rev.).
MS. Rawl. poet. 117, fol. 275 rev.

**Let it suffice, oh Lord, let it suffice** 211
**Is nearer, than when, we believed at first.**
MS. Rawl. poet. 66, fol. 57.

**Let Kate so thrive, and Charles so sw-** 212
**And Kate our country's mother.**
Shepherd, Fleetwood. Sancroft's note: 'In the Domiduca Oxoniensis on ye K[ing]'s Marriage [May 1661], Dr. [Sebastian] Smith of Christ Ch[urch] had this distich. 'Sic Katharina gerat, Carolus sic gignat; ut Illa Dicatur Patriae Mater, ut Ille pater'. Wch an unmannerly fellow thus English'd'.
MS. Sancroft 53, p. 39; see also L162.

**Let knaves dispute the rights of kings,** 213
**And drank good claret still.**
'A Bacchanalian Health'.
MS. Firth d. 13, fol. 42.

**Let Linus and Amphion's lute** 214
**They following had run away.**
[Randolph, Thomas], 'The song of discord'.
Pr. *Poems*, 1638.
MS. Eng. poet. c. 50, fol. $131^v$.

**Let longing lovers sit and pine** 215
**Nor lose my time on her that's coy.**
Ascribed to Henry Hughes in the index to Lawe's *Second Book of Ayres*, 1655.
MS. Rawl. poet. 65, fol. 27.

**Let love to love go kin[d]ly and soft** 216*a*
**The great god of love in the [tarna(?)] Johne.**
MS. Rawl. D. 913, fol. 6.

**Let man endeavour: God will sure provide:** 216*b*
**With all things wanting: no fit thing's denied.**
Robinson, Robert, 'Oret et laboret homo; Deus providebit et dabit'.
MS. *Rawl. poet. 218, p. 5 (autogr.).

**Let man's soul be a sphere, and then, in this** 217
**That thou mayst know me, and I'll turn my face.**
Donne, John, 'Goodfriday. 1613. Riding towards Wales'.
Pr. *Poems*. 1633.
MS. *Eng. poet. e. 99, fol. 54.

**Let me be called very bad** 218
**To have nothing at all.**
Lines on wealth and goodness, from a moral dialogue in prose.
MS. Rawl. D. 1092, fol. 34.

219 Let me but tell thee, what was wisely told
Excuse him whose wish is 'God give you joy'.
Oldisworth, Giles (?), 'verses once presented To Mrs. Andrewes on her marriage with Mr. Smith', but here applied to Mrs. Mary Overbury.
MS. *Rawl. C. 422, fol. 24v, in G. Oldisworth's hand.

220 Let me careless and unthoughtful lying
Silence the wanton boughs and birds that sing among.
Glee by Mr Thos. Linley.
MS. Mus. d. 177, fol. 71v.

221 Let me dear Jesus know thy Name
My night to endless day.
Beddome, Benjamin.
MS. *Eng. misc. e. 227, fol. 75v.

222 Let me enjoy you, for I fain would know
Till to your first you raise a second arch.
Pestell, Thomas, 'To my neighbour R. B. Archd: of Nott: now D. of Sarum': i.e. Richard Bailey, also President of St. John's College, Oxford.
MS. *Malone 14, p. 22.

223 Let me go to the wood says this pig
Kiss her to death says this pig.
'Song set to five Toes'.
MS. Douce d. 59, fol. 63.

224 Let me laugh, while others grieve.
Never in his journey's weary.
MS. Mus. b. 1, fol. 34v, music by John Wilson.

225 Let me, let me, hear no more
List and hear your cares away!
Parsons, William, 'Extempore at Bull's Library, Bath'. 1783.
MS. *Don. d. 123, p. 106 (autogr.).

226 Let me make one too, are you grown so stout,
Believe, if ever we have peace again, it must.
'A Speech to . . . General Monck and the Council of State, at Goldsmith's Hall', 10 April 1660.
MS. Firth c. 18, fol. 64.

227 Let me not hear what verdant fields be those
Keep close to God in Christ, and heaven is ours.
Cromwell, Edward, 'Lord show us thy way and it sufficeth', dated 'Jan. 23 1716–17'.
MS. *Rawl. poet. 165, fol. 38v (autogr.).

228 Let me not in confusion fall
Their end in shame and death.
Psalm lxxi.
MS. *Rawl. C. 113, fol. 51.

Let me not sigh my last, ere I bequeath 229
I give and grant my incapacity.
Sedley, Sir Charles, 'The Lover's Will'.
Not included in *Works*, ed. V. de S. Pinto, 1928.
MS. Rawl. poet. 222, fol. 33.

Let me oh Lord be quite released 230
That thy grace him maintains.
Arkwright's transcript of 'The French original of "Commandments tune" as given by Harper'.
MS. Mus. d. 195, fol. 16v rev.

Let me pour forth 231
Who e'er sighs most is cruellest, and hastes the other's death.
Donne, John, 'A Valediction'.
Pr. *Poems*, 1633.
MS. *Eng. poet. e. 99, fol. 120v; *f. 9, p. 21.

Let me see! bread and beer, tripe and dressing, hey day! 232
I pay for my doublet; pay you for your lining.
'A Taylor, on a Tavern-Bill'.
MS. Ballard 29, fol. 145.

Let me wander where I will 233
Laura haunts my fancy still.
Turnbull, G., song, 'Tune Lewie Gordon'.
MS. Eng. misc. e. 241, fol. 126v.

Let merchants trade to foreign lands 234
Come enter.
Endorsed 'The trade of whores from Mr. Franklin'.
MS. Eng. poet. c. 25, fol. 67.

Let mercy Lord to me extend 235
Praise please thee more than bullocks' blood.
Fairfax, Thomas, Lord, Psalm li.
MS. *Fairfax 40, p. 115 (autogr.); see also T2625*b*.

Let mother earth now deck her self with flowers 236
For Hymen will their coupled joys maintain.
Sidney, Sir Philip, from the *Arcadia*.
MS. *e Mus. 37, fol. 138.

Let no man ask, what foolish art, etc. 237
[Price, E.], scattered verses from translation of Ovid, *Epistulae ex Ponto*.
MS. *Douce 290, fol. 111 (autogr.).

Let no man think, that earth for him the best is, 238
But trust in Christ, in whom he'll find true rest is.
Robinson, Robert, couplet.
MS. *Rawl. poet. 218, p. 152 (autogr.).

239 Let no profane ignoble foot tread near
And want a mourner at his funeral.

King, Henry, 'An Epitaph uppon Richard Earl of Dorsett'.

Pr. *Poems*, 1657, p. 51; an inferior version pr. Corbett's *Poems*, 1647, p. 51.

MSS. Ashmole 38, p. 167, attr. to H.K.; CCC. 328, fol. 11$^v$; Eng. poet. c. 50, fol. 59$^v$; *e. 30, fol. 26; e. 97, p. 28, attr. to Dr. Corbet; Firth d. 7, fol. 169, attr. to Hen. King; *Malone 22, fol. 17; Rawl. poet. 209, fol. 9; Top. gen. e. 32, fol. 73, attr. to Richard Corbet.

240 Let noble Sir Positive lead the van
That his majesty lives at the Rose and the Crown.

'The Clubb Men of the House of Commons', 1694.

Pr. *Poems on Affairs of State*, iii, 1703, p. 330.

MSS. Eng. poet. c. 18, fols. 153$^v$, 152, 154–5; Locke c. 32, fol. 31.

241 Let none henceforth this wife for ever wed;
That horn'd her husband, then cut off his head.

'This was reported to bee made by the Lord of Castle-haven, when hee was beheaded, [14] May 1631, being accused by his wife, of rape, sodomy etc.'

MS. Rawl. poet. 26, fol. 21$^v$.

242 Let none suppose some foul disease
And be my white formality.

'On a student dying in the small pox'.

MS. Rawl. poet. 199, p. 57.

243 Let none suppose this relic of the just
Her alms, her praise, her soul, her body have.

Wither, George, 'An Epitaph on the Ladie Scott'.

MS. Ashmole 38, p. 179.

244 Let none with tears thy grave bedew
Of state broils or court faction.

'Uppon the translation of Sr John Walters (Cheife Barron)', 1630.

MS. Rawl. D. 398, fol. 181.

245 Let not a father be too venturous bold,
Children return to parents little back.

Robinson, Robert.

MS. *Rawl. poet. 218, p. 117 (autogr.).

246 Let not a fretting grudge
Save and deliver them, because in him they trust.

J. F., Psalm xxxvii.

MS. *Eng. poet. f. 17, p. 140 (autogr.).

247 Let not a gentle love displeasing
I'll go a-wooing in my boys.

Rundle, Dr. [Thomas, Bp. of Derry], 'A Song'.

MS. Eng. misc. f. 79, p. 85.

Let not a wife think scolding doth 248
If he's inclined to ill.

Robinson, Robert.

MS. *Rawl. poet. 218, p. 24 (autogr.).

Let not all discipline forsake the mind, 249
Secured, but others lie exposed to all.

Williams, John, 'He that has no Rule over his own Spirit, is like a City that is broken down, and without wall. Proverbs ye 25th'.

MS. *Rawl. poet. 191, fol. 62$^v$ (autogr.).

Let not man judge my future state 250
I'm not now in th' abyss.

Tipping, William.

MS. *Rawl. poet. 101, fol. 1$^v$ (autogr.).

Let not my confidence be ashamed, since 251
Then soul take strength the proud he slights as much.

Fairfax, Thomas, Lord, Psalm xxxi.

MS. *Fairfax 40, p. 64 (autogr.).

MS. *Fairfax 38, p. 167.

Let not my tender friends for me lament 252*a*
And I enjoy an everlasting peace.

'Epitaph'.

MS. Eng. poet. e. 39, p. 77.

Let not oh Lord a dumbness seize on Thee 252*b*
Jehovah 'alone most high on earth doth reign.

Fairfax, Thomas, Lord, Psalm lxxxiii.

MS. *Fairfax 40, p. 196 (autogr.).

MS. *Fairfax 38, p. 341.

Let not old age disgrace my high desire 253
Let not old age disgrace my high desire.

Sidney, Sir Philip, from the *Arcadia*.

MSS. *e Mus. 37, fol. 51$^v$; Rawl. poet. 172, fol. 6.

Let not the foul mouthed epicure blaspheme 254
For in two days before they had not ate.

'Upon the 7 loaves that fed 40000 pepill'.

MS. *Rawl. poet. 116, fol. 124$^v$.

Let not these lines have power at all 255
Who look with out, not inward eyes.

'Verses made by the La: G to G: Bucke:'

MS. Eng. poet. c. 50, fol. 58$^v$.

Let not these toys thine eyes offend 256
These next spare leaves to fill.

Introduction to a series of riddles.

MS. Rawl. poet. 217, fol. 71.

Let not this world your thoughts betray 257
But think upon your dying day.

Couplet.

MS. Rawl. D. 1334, fol. 26$^v$ rev.

258 **Let not thy sluggish sleep close up thy waking eye**
**Thus will I neither wail nor weep, but sing in godly wise.**
The first 2 verses pr. Byrd's *Psalmes, Songs, and Sonnets*, 1611.
MS. Gough Norfolk 43, fol. 37.

259 **Let Oliver ne'er be forgotten**
**Of honest good liquor reel home.**
'Oliver Redivivus', [i.e. James II].
Pr. *A Collection of 180 Loyal Songs*, 1685, p. 1, beginning 'Let Oliver now be forgotten'.
MS. Firth c. 16, p. 265.

260 **Let one soft word (sweet) cool the fire**
**Rain to this despised frame.**
Beaumont, Thomas, 'Sonnett'.
MS. *Malone 18, p. 73 (autogr.).

261 **Let other beauties boast in vain**
**So are her charms still new.**
MS. Rawl. poet. 196, fol. 43.

262 **Let other beauties have the power**
**But for my life can die no more.**
MSS. Ashmole 36, 37, fol. 194; Mus. b. 1, fol. 119v, with music by John Wilson.

263 **Let other buttocks have the power**
**But for my life can shit no more.**
Parody of L262, marked 'Dr. Wilson'.
MSS. Ashmole 36, 37, fol. 194.

264 **Let other poets martial deeds proclaim**
**Sacred to Brittain's royal George and you.**
Samber, Robert, lines to the second Earl of Dumbarton.
MS. *Rawl. poet. 134*b*, fol. 185 (autogr.).

265 **Let others call their sacred nine to aid,**
**But your victorious pen has forced the field.**
Farquhar, George, 'To the ingenious Ladye author of the Fatal Friendship A Tragedy, Design'd for a Recomendary Copy to her Play'. [Lost: *Greg Θ* 57].
MS. Rawl. poet. 172, fol. 132v, attr. to Mr. Farquhar.

266 **Let others go where Lowdore pours**
**To find sweet hope and comfort there.**
H[ofland,] [Mrs.] B., 'Lines inscribed to the Quarry Gill . . . Swinton, Yorkshire'.
MS. Montagu d. 4, fol. 257 (autogr.).

267 **Let others praise what likes them best**
**Chief friend to peace, chief port of ease.**
Watson, Thomas, 'A gratification unto Mr. John Case, for his learned Booke, lately made in the prayes of Musick', pr. Oxford, 1586.
MS. Rawl. poet. 148, fol. 100.

**Let others prepare for brisk wars and alarms** 268
**Their crowns and their sceptres they soon would despise.**
MS. Rawl. poet. 196, fol. 22.

**Let others rove to distant climes** 269
**My best resolves no longer blame / Nor . . . (incomplete).**
Gough, Richard.
MS. *Eng. poet. c. 5, fol. 192 (autogr.).

**Let others sing of heads, and some of caps** 270
**And Scaliger did thus outbrave the gout.**
Vintner, Henry, 'Upon a bile'.
MSS. Rawl. poet. 147, p. 7, attr. to Hen. Vintner; 210, fol. 50, attr. to Henry Vintner.

**Let other[s] weep for what they lost** 271
**Who loseth hope he loseth all.**
On the death of the infant prince, born 13 May 1629 (?).
MS. Ashmole 38, fol. 240v.

**Let poets prate of Hercules, of Theseus and Jason** 272
**The Acts of our Elisabeth so wondrous, and so rare.**
Howlet, Jo[hn], 'In Commendac'on of this Authoure', William Wodwall, on 'The Acts of Queen Elizabeth'.
MS. Eng. hist. e. 198, fol. 3.

**Let Rome no more her Peter's wonders tell** 273
**For wonders, Holland's Peter bears the bell.**
Couplet, translation of Latin epigram on Peter van Hoyn who 'met some stragling ships of the Plate-fleet, and brought them to the Texel'.
MS. Rawl. D. 1372, fol. 15v from end.

**Let royal James come over** 274
**Here's a health to the Lord's anointed.**
'The Loyal Health' to 'James III'.
MS. Rawl. poet. 155, p. 93.

**Let sceptic Momus cease to antedate** 275
**Terror but obligation when they come.**
E[dwards], T[homas], 'To one who bestowed a gratuity of 20li uppon St. John's Library', Oxford.
MS. Rawl. poet. 65, fol. 60v.

**Let scribblers brag no more, with pen endowed** 276
**The first commandment broke, and worshipped you.**
'To a Lady that presented the Ten Commandments cut out in Paperwork by her self to St. Johns Library Oxon'.
MS. Rawl. D. 390, fol. 86.

277 Let Seian or Theban or Epic inspire
Be you Pindar or Pope I must still be Concannon.
MS. Don. c. 81, fol. 161.

278 Let servile men with reigning vice comply
And killed the just, and he doth not resist you.
Williams, John, 'Against prevailing folly and mistake'.
MS. *Rawl. poet. 188, fol. 51^v^ (autogr.).

279 Let soft desires your heart engage
When discretion guides the choice.
[Motteux, Peter], 'In the Opera . . . the Island Princess . . . set by Mr. Leveridge'.
MS. Mus. Sch. C. 95, p. 129.

280 Let such as are of parents state possessed
Retain their virtue or resign their crest.
Couplet, on a page concerned with the Fairfax family.
MS. Top. Yorks. c. 26, fol. 174.

281 Let such as to new Ingland go
They are but that they may be pure.
Strode, William, 'An answer to the song against the New-Inglanders, made at the request for a well-wisher to that side; but in a sense Ambiguous'. Cf. L143, L147.
MS. *CCC. 325, fol. 111 (autogr.).

282 Let sullen sense with circling terrors big,
And all the fireside family of fun.
'Inest sua gratia parvis . . . ? if by Mr. [William] Crowe of N. Coll. or [William Lisle] Bowles of Trin . . .'.
MS. Eng. misc. e. 241, fol. 100.

283 Let that majestic pen that writes
And I with bread and cheese away, came rowndeley.
Davison, Francis, 'The Counterskuffle'.
MS. Don. c. 54, fol. 58.

284 Let the act against vagabonds chase the pretender
Which none will refuse but a whig or a rumper.
'An Health'.
MS. Rawl. poet. 155, p. 75; see also M250.

285 Let the Almighty God of war arise
That they may bless thy name for evermore.
Knollys, Fra., Psalm lxviii.
MS. *Rawl. poet. 60, p. 68 (autogr.).

286 Let the bowl pass free
We will prove so does every thing in't.
[Brome, Alexander], 'Copernicus'.
Pr. *Poems*, 1661, p. 61.
MS. Ashmole 47, fol. 152^v^.

Let the commons hunt their plots, with a hey 287
With a hey tranony, nony, nony no.
College, Stephen, 'A Satyrical Sonnet', 1678, on Charles II.
MS. Rawl. poet. 159, fol. 164^v^.

[Let the dreadful engines] . . . lightning flashes round 288
And so I fairly bid 'em and the world good night.
[D'Urfey, Thomas, song from *Don Quixote*.] F. B. Zimmerman, *Purcell*, 1963, no. 578(3).
MS. Mus. c. 28, fol. 12. Music by H. Purcell.

Let the dull brutish world that know not love 289
W'are like, alas, w'are like ourselves alone.
Philips, Katherine, 'Friendship'.
Pr. *Poems*, 1664, p. 158.
MSS. Rawl. poet. 90, fol. 9; 173, fol. 101^v^, attr. to Mrs. Phillips.

Let the dull miser hug his precious ore, 290
And giv'st 'em all a life of immortality.
Chatwin, John, 'There's no Solid joy but Vertue'.
MS. *Rawl. poet. 94, p. 106 (autogr.).

Let the main land and seagirt isles 291
Light is unto the righteous sown.
Psalm xcvii.
MS. *Rawl. C. 113, fol. 67*a*.

Let the rough soldiers arm when trumpets sound, 292
For one half flask, I'd quit the other three.
'A Bachinalian Rapture'.
MS. Rawl. D. 361, fol. 56^v^.

Let the shrill trumpet's loud alarms 293
Let all like Anna peaceful be.
Music in honour of Queen Anne by William Morley.
MSS. Mus. c. 6, fol. 23; Mus. Sch. C. 131.

Let the soft shepherd tune his oaten reed 294
And shake the dew drops from the lion's mane!
Parsons, William, 'Sonnet'.
MS. *Don. d. 123, p. 266 (autogr.).

Let the soldiers rejoice 295
A glorious morning.
[Betterton, Thomas (?)], song in *The Prophetess*, 1690, Act II, set by H. Purcell; F. B. Zimmerman, *Purcell*, 1963, no. 627(9b).
MSS. Mus. Sch. C. 95, p. 213; Rawl. poet. 196, fol. 28, subscribed M. N.

296 **Let the vast universe and therein every thing**
**Laud and adore the lord of light.**
[Howell, James (?)], 'A gradual hymn of a double cadence, tending to the honour of the holy name of God'.
Pr. Howell's *Familiar Letters* for 1 Aug. 1628.
MSS. Eng. poet. b. 5, p. 1; Tanner 466, fol. 7$^{v}$, copied from 'Fam. let. Sect. 5 p. 149' [2nd ed., 1650, i. 149].

297 **Let the vast universe, breathe forth its moan**
**That God, where our Queen Mary's gone before.**
Spoure, Edmund, 'An Elogie on . . . Queen Mary . . . 28th of December 1694'.
MS. *Eng. poet. c. 52, fol. 36$^{v}$ (autogr.).

298 **Let the voice of music breathe**
**And in his people's joy the monarch too be blest.**
[Whitehead, William], New Year Ode, 1768
Pr. *Poems*, 1790, ii. 92.
MS. Mus. Sch. D. 320, music by Boyce.

299 **Let the world go although it smiles**
**But in eternity sublime.**
Bromley, Henry, 'The Warning'.
MS. *Don. e. 19, fol. 4$^{v}$ (autogr.).

300 **Let the young in learning's toil**
**Flames the bright sun of steady joy.**
R. L., 'Ode, 1779'.
MS. *Eng. poet. e. 16, fol. 16.

301 **Let those soft poets, who have steeped your brains**
**Career dance to the music of the verse.**
Saltmarsh, Jo[hn], 'On Mr. [John] Russel's Battels of Leipsick, and Lutzen', [pr. Cambridge, 1634].
MS. Sancroft 53, p. 44.

302 **Let those wash their guts that have none in their brains**
**He soon will be rotten that drinks till he's mellow.**
Williams, John, 'Upon Goodfellowship'.
MS. *Rawl. poet. 192, fol. 81 (autogr.).

303 **Let those who meaner subjects dote upon**
**To praise the book, since I declare 'tis his.**
Southwell, Sir Robert, 'On the sacred Poems of my Ingenuous Freind Mr. Ed: Ellis:' [*Divine Poems with a Short Description of Christian Magnanimity*, 1658].
MS. *Eng. poet. f. 6, fol. 28 rev. (autogr.).

**Let us advance the good old cause** 304
**The clean contrary way.**
'A speech of a Noble Peer to the Mobily To the Tune of Hay then up go wee'; on the Whigs and the succession, 1679–81.
MS. Douce 357, fol. 124$^{v}$.

**Let us alone, ye mortals, and permit** 305
**It will be long, ere we do envy thee.**
Oldisworth, Nicolas, 'For a gentleman. On the embracing of his Friend'.
MS. *Don. c. 24, fol. 72$^{v}$ (autogr.).

**Let us be glad and clap our hands** 306
**With mercy and good will.**
Anthem.
MS. Rawl. poet. 23, p. 166, reference to setting by W. Bird.

**Let us consort with tempests; with earthquakes agree,** 307
**And fudle, and fudle, and fudle like men.**
'A Bachinalian Poem'.
MS. Eng. poet. d. 53, p. 35.

**Let us enjoy Philander the sweet peace** 308
**Ease for thy self and me in thine own mind.**
'Arcadia, the scene, Strephon and Philander, two of the most ancient Shepheards'.
MS. Malone 13, p. 87.

**Let us not raise dispute of God;** 309
**Oh let's presume no higher.**
Robinson, Robert.
MS. *Rawl. poet. 218, p. 76 (autogr.).

**Let us not treat of courts and kings** 310
**As happily as this begun.**
'Upon the Marriage of Mr. H. Jennings with Mrs. S-n K-t' dated 'Jan: 1: 1723/4'.
MS. Rawl. poet. 146, fol. 36*b*.

**Let us revel and roar** 311
**And we never takes care for the morrow.**
2-part song with music.
MS. Mus. e. 20, fol. 21.

**Let us this woman's praises sound** 312
**[Both now and still, whilst ages run].**
'Engl. Primer of our Ladie. 1631 . . . p. 38'.
MS. Eng. poet. e. 56, p. 60.

**Let us use time whilst we may** 313
**Love may return, but never lover.**
[Settle, Elkanah], song in translation of the 'Pastor Fido'.
MS. Rawl. poet. 8, fol. 18.

314 Let us with a gladsome mind
Ever faithful, ever sure.
Psalm xxxvi, 'J. Milton, poëm p. 13. done at 15 years old'; reference to Milton's *Poems*, 1645.
MS. Tanner 466, fol. 20$^v$.

315 Let us with loud and cheerful voice begin
Sing praise, to which heavens echo forth Amen.
Anthem.
MS. Rawl. poet. 23, p. 222, reference to setting by Thomas Ford.

316 Let voice [and] hand at once your joy express
All power on earth, his glory doth excel.
Fairfax, Thomas, Lord, Psalm xlvii.
MS. *Fairfax 40, p. 106 (autogr.).
MS. *Fairfax 38, p. 207.

317 Let warlike champions learn to suffer want
It cannot be that scotfree he should go.
W. A., translator, Horace, *Odes* III. ii.
MS. *Rawl. poet. 104, fol. 22 (autogr.).

318 Let whigs remember the fourth of November,
Yet we barter the church we own.
'Song', [1715] on the birthday and wedding day of William III, the birthday of James the Old Pretender, and the birthday and restoration of Charles II.
Pr. *A Collection of Loyal Songs, Poems, etc.*, 1750.
MSS. Eng. poet. e. 87, p. 75; Rawl. D. 400, fol. 95; Rawl. poet. 155, p. 77; pr. bk. Firth b. 22, fol. 17.

319 Let whoso will in icy state
And death with greatest grief doth own.
[Traherne, Thomas (?)], poem with Latin version.
MS. Lat. misc. f. 45, p. 203, in T. Traherne's hand.

320 Let wise men stand 'twixt knaves and fools,
Alas, it is no wonder.
Robinson, Robert.
MS. *Rawl. poet. 218, p. 94 (autogr.).

321 Let wits contest,
Of all God's mercies, is my posy still.
Herbert, George, 'The Posie'.
Pr. *The Temple*, 1633, p. 177.
MSS. Rawl. poet. 90, fol. 142$^v$; *Tanner 307, fol. 135.

322 Let wolves, and bears, be cruel in their kinds:
But women meek, and have relenting minds.
Couplet, 'of women'.
MS. Rawl. poet. 148, fol. 3.

Let worthless spirits fear unsteadfast love 323
Profit it self, in truth is but delight.
North, Dudley, 3rd Baron.
Pr. *A Forest of Varieties*, 1645.
MS. *North e. 41, fol. 52$^v$.

Let wrangling statesmen still debate 324
Would fill my little cot.
'The Little Cot . . . set . . . by E. McEwan'.
MS. Mus. e. 19, p. 87.

Let Zara ladies for the author plead 325
'Twill be to me a joyful resurrection.
Samber, Robert, epilogue to his tragedy *Orosmanes*, MS. Rawl. poet. 131, fol. 155.
MS. *Rawl. poet. 134*b*, fol. 161*b*$^v$ (autogr.).

Let's be jovial fill your glasses 326
And rates are fair and vestry's free.
'Verses on the new Rate at Windsor', endorsed 'The Election Song'.
MS. Eng. misc. b. 48, fol. 4.

Let's dance a dance upon the heath 327
We dance to th' echoes of our feet.
[Davenant, Sir William], witch's song, from *Macbeth*.
Pr. 1674, p. 27.
MSS. Ashmole 36, 37, fol. 69$^v$; see also L331.

Let's dance and sing and make good cheer 328
Take it in good part or else you do me wrong.
'A carroll for christmas'.
MS. Eng. poet. b. 5, p. 102.

Let's drink a health to the King, 329
By virtue of my protestation.
MS. Douce 357, fol. 7.

Let's drink disappointment to restless fanatics 330
That won't pledge the same.
'Dr. Sache[ve]rell's Health in a Catch. 1710', subscribed by the composer 'Wm Davis the 2d catch'.
MS. Mus. c. 16, fol. 125$^v$.

Let's have a dance upon the heath 331
We dance to th' echoes of our feet.
[Davenant, Sir William], song in *Macbeth*.
MS. Rawl. poet. 65, fol. 27$^v$; see also L327.

Let's live and let's love 332
And none are more happy than we.
Catch by Dr. P. Hayes.
MS. Mus. d. 177, fol. 13$^v$.

Let's live, my dearest Lesbia, and love, 333
And kiss a long eternity away.
'An Amorous Suit to Lesbia, from Catullus', *carm.* v.
MS. Rawl. poet. 173, fol. 52$^v$, attr. to Mr. Dryden.

334 Let's live my Lesbia, let us love
Lest we be envied for our pleasure.
Translation of Catullus', *carm.* v.
MS. Rawl. poet. 84, fol. 98 rev.

335 Let's not sigh single tempests, March seems here
Kisses the bleeding corpse. Then sighs and dies.
Proby, H[enry], 'The Dirge' on Sir Charles Lucas and Sir George Lisle, 1646.
MS. Rawl. poet. 62, fol. 20v.

336 Let's now compound, and for the present live,
When all is done, life's an incurable disease.
MS. Rawl. poet. 213, fol. 49v.

337 Let's see!
Or some spared bastard spring from old Hermogenes.
'Pindaricks to my much esteem'd Friend P[eter] C[ox] of Oxford, upon himselfe'.
MS. *Rawl. poet. 91, fol. 36 (autogr.).

338 Let's so front death as men may judge us past it
For good men but see death, the wicked taste it.
Couplet.
MS. Don. e. 6, fol. 16v.

339 Let's tipple, and drink up more sack,
Sing merrily huntsman wind thy horn.
Spoure, Edmund, 'A New song in praise of our English Wines, and other drinks' with 'A Little Concluding Catch'.
MS. *Eng. poet. c. 52, fols. 56, 62 (autogr.).

340 Let's worship God; oh let us him admire,
Lest he destroy us, who's a consuming fire.
Robinson, Robert, 'Deum admiremur, non de Deo curiose inquiramus'.
MS. *Rawl. poet. 218, p. 84 (autogr.).

341 Leuca in presence once a fart did let
My fart (quoth she) which did more laughter move.
Davies, [Sir] John, 'In Leucam'.
Pr. amongst 'Epigrames' with *Ovids Elegies*, transl. by C. M., [*c.* 1600].
MSS. *Add. B. 97, fol. 42v; Rawl. poet. 148, fol. 3v, attr. to D.

342 Levi the priest with patience still is mute
And she'll still bear or else she'll want her will.
'In Levi'.
MS. Don. d. 58, fol. 31v.

343 Levy the living genius fed
She pays her poets when they're dead.
'On the Richmond Grotto', 1735.
MS. Rawl. poet. 172, fol. 129v.

Lewellin, though physician to the king 344
No recipe is like a *mittimus*.
'The Doctor turn'd Justice', MS. added at end of Marvell's *Miscellany Poems*, 1681; pr. his *Works*, ed. E. Thompson, 1776, i, p. xlix.
MS. Eng. poet. d. 49, p. 265, attr. to Andrew Marvell.

Lewis now usurps the throne 345
The name of Lewis makes great Britain rue.
'On the Name of Lewis': George I was George Lewis.
MS. Rawl. poet. 155, p. 32.

Lewis of Feversham, see thou be wise 346
Then England's passing-bell is rung.
To Louis Duras, Earl of Feversham, 1688.
MS. Rawl. poet. 159, fol. 77.

Lewis, the wise, the brave, the great, 347
That ever her gods themselves are short of you.
'On the King of France Lewis 14th Civillity to King James'.
MS. Eng. misc. c. 116, fol. 8, initialed R. C.

Liber doth vaunt him chastely he hath lived 348
For a fifth sort I am sure thou canst not find.
Davies, [Sir] John, 'In Liberum'.
Pr. amongst 'Epigrames' with *Ovids Elegies*, translated by C. M., [*c.* 1600].
MS. *Add. B. 97, fol. 42.

Liber, thou joy of all thy friends, 349
Wisely doubles his short time.
Sedley, Sir Charles, 'To Liber. The Voluptuous Epicure'.
Paraphrase of Martial, *Epigrams* VIII. lxxvii.
MS. Rawl. poet. 173, fol. 157v.

Licoris was a coy young lass 350
Since this Licoris is unkind.
Mervall, Alphonso, subscribed 'Coridon'.
MS. *Rawl. poet. 166, p. 45 (autogr.).

Licus which lately is to Venice gone 351
Will not be bettered or increase a whit.
Davies, [Sir] John, 'In Licum'.
Pr. amongst 'Epigrames', with *Ovids Elegies*, translated by C. M., [*c.* 1600].
MSS. *Add. B. 97, fol. 46; *Rawl. poet. 212, fol. 65v rev.

Lidgate, Bawldwin, and many writers moe 352
Whenas he lies, this moan engraved would be.
Whetstone, George, 'A Remembraunce of Sir James Dier', d. 1582.
Pr. 1582, *S.T.C.* 25345.
MS. *Malone 6, fol. 17.

353 Lie still my dear
My infant joys or else I needs must perish.
'A song'.
Pr. in John Dowland's *Pilgrim's Solace*, 1612; *Academy of Complements*, 1646, p. 202. See Helen Gardner, *Donne: Elegies and Songs and Sonnets*, 1965, p. 245, and cf. A762, S1149.
MSS. Ashmole 47, fol. 73, attr. to Corbet; CCC. 328, fol. 47$^{v}$; Don. c. 57, fol. 29$^{v}$, with music; Rawl. poet. 214, fol. 81$^{v}$ rev.; see also T2851, T2871.

354 Life I am, yet must I die
Shall be one, in double heart.
E[des], D[r. Richard], Oxon., 'A Dialogue. Life, to Death'.
MS. Rawl. poet. 148, fol. 70.

355 Life is a crooked labyrinth and we
Those never clouded, nor that overcast.
King, Henry, 'The Labyrinth'.
Pr. *Poems*, 1657, p. 134.
MSS. *Eng. poet. e. 30, fol. 66; *Malone 22, fol. 41$^{v}$.

356 Life is a masque disguised and puffed with pleasures
We might have had a better pleasing show.
'Life and Death'.
MS. Rawl. poet. 26, fol. 13.

357 Life is a play at dice where chances fly
Sickness makes blots and death straight enter in.
'On life'.
MS. Eng. poet. f. 10, fol. 95.

358 Life is death's road, and death Heaven's gate must be
Heaven is Christ's throne, and Christ is life to me.
Couplet.
MS. Sancroft 59, p. 285 rev.; see also L360.

359 Life is the only time allowed
And live as we would wish to die.
Beddome, Benjamin.
MS. *Eng. misc. e. 227, fol. 85$^{v}$.

360 Life is the road to death
And Christ is life to me.
Inscription at St. Michael's, Bristol, on W. W. G., d. 20 June 1747.
MS. Rawl. D. 1090, fol. 189$^{v}$; see also L358.

361 Life is the way to death
Lord show me thy salvation.
'A Meditation upon . . . Life leads to death'.
MS. Rawl. poet. 90, fol. 127$^{v}$.

Life leads to death, so nature saith: 362
He that desires to live, must die.
'An Epitaph'. Cf. L361.
MS. Rawl. poet. 90, fol. 127$^{v}$.

Life of the world, immortal mind 363
My heart shall still repose on thee.
'A Hymn to the Eternal Providence'.
MS. Eng. poet. e. 47, p. 2.

Life only makes the body move about, 364
The body stirs not, when that life is out.
Robinson, Robert, couplet.
MS. *Rawl. poet. 218, p. 25 (autogr.).

Life steals away and our best hours are gone 365
It matters not from whom, but what we take.
MS. Add. B. 8, fol. 2 rev.

Life vital, food of hearts, a present Heaven! 366
Fountain of life! a sweeter stream is thine.
Madan, Spencer [Bp. of Peterborough (?) or 1758–1836], translator of Latin verses by Sir Philip Meadows in his Bible.
MS. Eng. poet. c. 51, p. 181.

Life with her is gone and I 367
Judging her the setting sun.
'Mrs. Departure'.
MS. Rawl. poet. 142, fol. 27$^{v}$.

Life's a lottery intermixed 368
Only peace of mind to gain.
Bate, Sally, 'A Song . . . 1767'.
MS. *Eng. poet. e. 28, p. 116.

Lift, lift your heads up oh ye gates! 369
Praises to God our King. Allelujah.
'A Hymne upon the Assention'.
MSS. Add. A. 301, fol. 25$^{v}$ rev.; Rawl. D. 361, fol. 330.

Lift up the heart, and voice too, high 370
Love Him as He hath loved thee.
Bromely, Henry.
MS. *Don. e. 19, fol. 15$^{v}$ (autogr.).

Lift up thy eyes behold the Trinity. 371
Of noble faithful friends for company.
F. W., 'Sonnet 6'.
MS. *Rawl. C. 639, p. 22.

Lift up your heads great gates and sing 372
Restore to them again and say, Alleluja.
Beaumont, Joseph, 'A Hymn, Ascension'.
MSS. Mus. d. 10, fol. 38, set for two voices; Rawl. poet. 62, fol. 17, attr. to Jos. Beaumont

373 Light cares can freely speak
Great cares heart rather break.
Couplet translating 'Curae leves loquntur, ingentes stupent' [Seneca, *Phaedra* 607].
MS. Rawl. D. 986, fol. 109ᵛ.

374 Light fingered wretch to keep his hands in ure
To steal such things as need must come to light.
'On a stealer of candells'.
MSS. Eng. poet. e. 14, fol. 86ᵛ rev.; Malone 19, p. 52.

375 Light gains do make a heavy purse,
Light gains are at a loss.
Robinson, Robert.
MS. *Rawl. poet. 218, p. 103 (autogr.).

376 Light is the shaft shot from Apollo's bow
Watch for thy death, death useth to surprise.
J. F. (?), 'Textor of the shortnesse of Life' [perhaps by Weaver (?)].
MS. *Eng. poet. f. 17, p. 2 (autogr.).

377 Light of the world descend
My way to Heaven pursue.
Kenton, James.
MS. *Eng. poet. e. 20, p. 348 (autogr.).

378 Lightly o'er the village green
Merry masons drink and sing.
Dyer, George, 'A Glee Sung at The Somerset House Lodge of Free Masons. Printed . . . Set to Music by R. Spofforth'.
Pr. *Poetics*, 1812, i. 123.
MS. *Eng. poet. c. 21, fol. 21.

379 Like a cold fatal sweat which ushers death
Whose influence may crown thy glorious war.
King, Henry, 'An Elegy. Upon the most victorious King of Sweden Gustavus Adolphus'.
Pr. *Swedish Intelligencer*, Third Part, 1633, and King's *Poems*, 1657, p. 104.
MSS. *Eng. poet. e. 30, fol. 58; Locke c. 32, fol. 3, attr. to Hen: King; *Malone 22, fol. 28ᵛ; Rawl. poet. 26, fol. 51, note at end 'Dr. Henry King fallor?'; 160, fol. 39ᵛ, attr. to Hen: King.

380 Like a cup without liquor, or a bottle *sans* ale,
I'd not marry myself till a thousand years old.
Barnes, Joseph, extempore 'Imitation and Contradiction' of L381.
MS. Hearne's diaries 11, p. 79.

Like a dog with a bottle [made] tied fast to his tail 381
Yet he lugs and he hugs it as a man does his wife.
Flatman, Thomas, '1670. Song set by —'.
Pr. *Poems*, 1686, p. 120.
MSS. *Firth d. 7, fol. 53; Rawl. poet. 84, fol. 22, attr. to T. Flatman; Sancroft 53, p. 27, attr. to Tho. Flatman.

Like a wandering ghost I appear 382
And fix them at last upon me.
'A Song'.
MS. Montagu e. 13, fol. 35.

Like as the damask rose you see 383
So man that dies shall live again.
As pr. *Crums of Comfort*: see L409–11. For a group of similar poems see J. Hannah, *Poems of H. King*, 1843, Appendix D, and Saintsbury's *Caroline Poets*, iii, 1921, p. 236.
MSS. Eng. poet. b. 5, p. 30; Malone 16, p. 54, incomplete; Rawl. D. 947, fol. 3.

Like as the doleful dove 384
Though these appear to wound.
Transcript of 4-part song by Tallis.
MS. Mus. d. 190, fol. 60.

Like as the dove which sealed up doth fly 385
More happy I might I in bondage bide.
Sidney, Sir Philip, from the *Arcadia*.
Pr. 1598, p. 477.
MSS. *e Mus. 37, fol. 237ᵛ; Rawl. poet. 148, fol. 86.

Like as the fountain of all light created 386
Which drew down God with such attractive love.
Alabaster, William, 'Son: 25. Incarnatio est maximum Dei donum'.
Pr. by B. Dobell, *Athenaeum* No. 3974, 26 Dec. 1903.
MS. *Eng. poet. e. 57, fol. 6ᵛ.

Like as the hand which hath been used to play 387
That something more than bodies us combine.
Strode, William, 'To a frinde'.
Pr. *Poems of Pembroke and Ruddier*, 1660, p. 108.
MS. *CCC. 325, fol. 75*a* (autogr.).

Like as the hart doth breath and bray 388
For health restored to thee.
[Hopkins, John], Psalm xlii.
MSS. Eng. misc. e. 478, p. 2; Rawl. poet. 112, fol. 59ᵛ rev.

Like as the hart that's hotly chased 389
His countenance shall give thee rest.
Fairfax, Thomas, Lord, Psalm xlii.
MS. *Fairfax 40, p. 93 (autogr.).
MS. *Fairfax 38, p. 183.

390 Like as the Julian eagle's drooping heart
Christ's spouse with her own feathers, heresies.
'Vt Aquila Imperialis, sic Ecclesia Christiana, Iam propriis configitur Alis'.
MS. *Rawl. poet. 97, fol. 78 (autogr.).

391 Like as the little frisking fly
Give me my love, and part the stake.
Lilliat, John, 'A welcome to Cupid'.
MS. Rawl. poet. 148, fol. 61 (autogr.).

392 Like as the morning star ushers the sun
Such was the flesh our saviour was clothed in.
Wentworth, Robert, 'Sainte John the Baptiste, the Morning Starre, or the Fore-runner of our blessed Lorde'.
MS. Rawl. poet. 201.

393 Like as the thirsty hart doth pant
For health restor'd to thee.
Psalm xlii.
MS. *Montagu e. 10, fol. 63.

394 Like as the trembling hare by hounds pursued
It is thy child, nature wills thee it cherish.
Sonnet, 'Canto 3' of sequence.
MS. *Add. B. 97, fol. 22.

395 Like as thy winged spirits always stand
Lo here I am, Lord whither wilt thou send me.
Alabaster, William, 'Son: 11. To Crist'.
MS. *Eng. poet. e. 57, fol. 2v.

396 Like attributes to those rehearsed above
That in his house Shiloh should raised be.
MS. *Rawl. poet. 97, fol. 20v (autogr.).

397 Like divers flowers whose divers beauties serve
You only yours too far beyond desert.
Sidney, Sir Philip, from the *Arcadia*.
MS. *e Mus. 37, fol. 114v.

398 Like gold, she still corrupts, who her adore,
Fierce, as the sun, and boundless as the air.
'Viscountess Vane' (d. 1788).
MS. Eng. poet. e. 28, p. 32.

399 Like oil and vinegar together blended
But all in vain she will be vinegar.
'An Allusion to Matrimony'.
MS. Percy c. 8, fol. 129.

400 Like one that hath a box o'er gilt with gold
Our joys deferred will prove our joy's increase.
H. S.
MS. *Rawl. poet. 120, fol. 21 (autogr.).

Like one who in her third widow-hood doth profess 401
But to know, that I love thee, and would be loved.
Donne, John, 'To Mr. Rowland Woodward'.
Pr. *Poems*, 1633.
MSS. *Eng. poet. e. 99, fol. 33; *f. 9, p. 82.

Like the men of great figure, unfurnished of sense 402
Fit to challenge esteem from all those that come near.
Williams, John, 'A Riddle. 'Tis a fine house that has nothing in it'.
MS. *Rawl. poet. 193, fol. 81v (autogr.).

Like the vain curlings of the watery maze 403
Troubling the waters, yearly mak'st them heal.
Marvell, Andrew, 'The first Anniversary of the Government Under his Highness the Lord Protector', MS. added in Marvell's *Miscellaneous Poems*, 1681, after p. 114.
Pr. *Works*, ed. E. Thompson, 1776, iii. 499; in *Poems on Affairs of State*, iv, 1707, attr. to Waller.
MS. *Eng. poet. d. 49, p. 115*e*; Eng. poet. e. 4, p. 78, attr. to Edmund Waller.

Like thee oh Sandys the filthy bird of night 404
You lost a knave, the court has gained a fool.
'Spoken extempore on seeing Mr. [Samuel] Sandys on the Treasury Bench in the House of Commons', 1742–3.
MS. Ballard 47, fol. 97.

Like those sick folks in whom strange humours flow 405
Sick to the death still loving my disease.
Sidney, Sir Philip, from the *Arcadia*.
MSS. *e Mus. 37, fol. 103v; Rawl. poet. 85, fol. 21v.

Like to a silent tone of unspoke speeches 406
To see such lines wrote on his epitaph.
'Pure Nonsense'.
Pr. *Wits Recreations*, 1641, Sig. Y4v; *Wit Restor'd*, 1658, p. 137.
MS. Eng. poet. e. 97, p. 166.

Like to an hermit poor in place obscure 407
To let in death when love and fortune will.
[Ralegh, Sir Walter].
Pr. *Britton's Bower of Delights*, 1591, p. 20; *Phoenix Nest*, 1593; Ferrabosco's *Ayres*, 1609; and attr. to Ralegh, in Sir Walter Rawleighs Farewell, 1644. See *T.L.S.*, 12 Dec. 1929, p. 1058.
MS. Rawl. poet. 85, fol. 25v.

408 Like to the casting of an eye
The news renewed and man new liv'd.
Strode, William, 'Song of Death and the Resurrection'.
MS. *CCC. 325, fol. 64$^v$ (autogr.); see also L415.

409–11 Like to the damask rose [ye] you see
So man that dies shall live again.
To one verse, ending 'The gourd consumes and man he dies', were added in F. Quarles' *Argalus and Parthenia*, 1629, one verse; in Simon Wastell's *Microbiblion*, 1629, four verses; and in *Crums of Comfort*, 10 ed., 1629, four verses and answer beg. 'Like to the seed . . .'.
MSS. Malone 19, p. 11, Wastell's version; Rawl. D. 859, fol. 158, *Crums of Comfort* version, subscribed by Hannibal Baskerville 'John Dun Anne Dun Undone'; Rawl. poet. 117, fol. 162 rev., Quarles' version; Top. gen. e. 32, fol. 74, one verse 'In Wandsworth Burying Ground Surry'; see also L383.

412 Like to the falling of a star;
The flight is past: and man forgot.
King, Henry, 'Sic Vita'.
Pr. *Poems*, 1657, p. 139; first pr. J. Fletcher's *Poems*, 1640.
MSS. *Eng. poet. e. 30, fol. 20$^v$; *Malone 22, fol. 14$^v$.

413 Like to the hand that hath been used to play
That somthing more than bodies us combine.
S[trode], W[illiam], 'To a friend'.
Pr. *Wits Recreations*, 1658, p. 101.
MSS. Ashmole 38, p. 68, attr. to Mr. Carew and pr. from this MS. as his, Wood's *Athenae*, ii. 659; CCC. 328, fol. 82$^v$; Eng. poet. e. 97, p. 162, attr. to W. S.

414 Like to the hundred merry tales
And so is Gondibert a bubble.
On Davenant's *Gondibert*.
MS. Rawl. poet. 152, fol. 204.

415 Like to the rolling of an eye
The news renewed and man new lived.
S[trode], W[illiam], 'On Death and Resurrection'.
MSS. Ashmole 47, fol. 43$^v$; CCC. 328, fol. 92; Eng. poet. c. 50, fol. 127$^v$; Malone 16, p. 53; Rawl. poet. 199, p. 94, attr. to W. S.

Like to the seed put in earth's womb . . . see L383, 409–11.

Like to the silent [thundering] tone of unspoke speeches 416
To see these lines set for his epitaph.
Corbett, Richard, 'nonsence'.
Pr. *Wits Recreations*, 1641, Sig. Y4$^v$, and *Wit Restor'd*, 1658, p. 137. Cf. *Poems*, ed. J. A. W. Bennett and H. R. Trevor-Roper, 1955, pp. 162–3.
MSS. Ashmole 36, 37, two copies, fols. 70 and 256, attr. to Dr. Corbet (pr. from this MS. by Gilchrist, 1807); CCC. 328, fol. 25; Rawl. poet. 117, fol. 186 rev., attr. to Dr. Corbett; 160, fol. 156; Tanner 465, fol. 83, attr. to Dr. Corbett.

Like to the weak estate of a poor friend 417
Deprives that glory from thy worthy verse.
W. B. [Dr. P. Simpson suggested William Barkstead], 'In Laudem Authoris' viz. F. Beaumont, 'Salmacis and Hermaphroditus'.
MS. Rawl. poet. 120, fol. 92$^v$.

Lilies and roses let them hang their head 418
Friends with their tears do make him spring again.
'In Eundem'. See D500.
MS. Don. d. 58, fol. 12$^v$.

Lincoln at once I sickened, my brain raved 419
I got just in to lie behind the door.
'On Mr William Ivye of Lincoln Colledge'.
MS. Don. d. 58, fol. 17.

Lions their nat'ral rage shall lay aside; 420
Rather than he'd prove false to you.
Morrice, John, 'Constancy Asserted'.
MS. *Rawl. poet. 114, fol. 189 (autogr.).

Liquid and watery pearls, love wept full kindly, 421
And into ashes turn me.
'A. 5. Voc Luca Marenzio'.
Pr. *Musica Transalpina*, 1588, xxxi.
MSS. Mus. f. 20–24: f. 20, fol. 29$^v$.

List passenger and you shall see 422
For shame forbear, now thou art dead to scold.
'Uppon a scoulde buried with hur husband'.
MS. Ashmole 38, p. 175*b*.

List you nobles, and attend, 423
For this time at the devil.
'Verses of the Queenes coming into England', May 1625.
MS. Rawl. C. 986, fol. 27.

424 Listen all I you pray
*Nisi bibit ad ostia stando.*
'A song in the prayse of sacke', macaronics. In B.M. MS. Harl. 3991, fol. 115$^{v}$, attr. to Francis Beaumont.
MSS. Ashmole 38, p. 125; Eng. poet. f. 10, fol. 99; Rawl. poet. 11, fol. 33.

425 Listen (decaying Ben) and counsel hear
Of this fat bellied person who these made.
'The Cuntrys Censure on Ben Iohnsons New Inn'.
MS. Ashmole 38, p. 79.

426 Listen fair ladies
As I could yet.
[Top line of title cropped by binder] 'forth her fall and miserable ende to the tune of Newe Hunt is upp Jane Shoare A Concubine to Edward the 4th'.
MS. Rawl. poet. 172, fol. 10.

427 Listen, gallants, to my words
See them when the sky doth fall.
Shirley, James, 'The Common Wealth of Birds'.
Pr. *Poems*, 1646, p. 34.
MS. *Rawl. poet. 88, p. 37.

428 Listen good friends to what I tell
Had been there.
Ballad, 'In Diabolum'.
MSS. Ashmole 36, 37, fol. 306.

429 Listen jolly gentlemen
And so an end I'll make.
Satire on King James I.
MSS. Malone 19, p. 87; 23, p. 19.

430 Listen, oh listen, how we hear of death,
Dying in Christ, with Christ we live forever.
Robinson, Robert.
MS. *Rawl. poet. 218, p. 148 (autogr.).

431 Listen sweet dove unto my song,
Unto his ancient and miraculous right.
Herbert, George, 'Whitsunday'.
Pr. *The Temple*, 1633, p. 51.
MS. *Tanner 307, fol. 39$^{v}$.

432 Listen ye lords and ladies all
And thus I make an end.
'The copye of an oration made and pronounced by Mr. [Thomas] Pownd of Lincolnes Inne with a Maske att the marriage of the earle of Sussex syster to Mr. Myldmay off Lyncolnes Inne, 1566'. Cf. *British Bibliographer*, ii, 1812, p. 612.
MS. Rawl. poet. 108, fol. 29$^{v}$.

Listen, ye sacred powers above 433
That we ourselves may live.
'On Serena indisposed'.
MS. *Eng. poet. d. 47, fol. 35.

Listening to the voice of nature 434
All a gracious God can give.
Kenton, James.
MS. *Eng. poet. e. 20, p. 22 (autogr.).

Listening to thy revelation 435
Ever with Thyself to reign.
Kenton, James.
MS. *Eng. poet. e. 20, p. 26 (autogr.).

Little and lazy, long and loud 436
Fair and foolish foul and proud.
'Discription of weomens qualities'.
MS. Don. c. 54, fol. 2.

Little Bow Peep has lost her sheep 437
Behind them. Fal la Fal la.
MS. Douce d. 59, fol. 64$^{v}$.

Little boys come out to play 438
And we'll have a pudding in half an hour.
MS. Douce d. 59, fol. 59$^{v}$.

Little-buzzing-wanton elf 439
A pretty Icarus hath undone.
'Upon a gnatt burnt in a candle'.
See L. C. Martin, *Works of Crashaw*, 1927, p. lxv.
MS. Tanner 465, fol. 44$^{v}$, attr. to Mr. Crashaw on fol. 1*a*; see also S483.

Little charm of placid mien 440
And the new fledged birds are singing.
'To Miss Georgiana Carteret, third Daughter to the Lord [John] Carteret [later Earl of Granville] August 10, 1725.
MS. Eng. poet. e. 40, fol. 65.

Little Dick if thou hast any wits 441
How many legs, a sheep hath, very well.
[Newman, Thomas], 'pret. Conceyts'.
MS. Top. Oxon. f. 39, fol. 23$^{v}$ (autogr.).

Little gets much, and much gets more, 442
And more doth gain a stock in store.
Robinson, Robert.
MS. *Rawl. poet. 218, p. 155 (autogr.).

Little I whilom deemed, my artless zeal 443
You deign to interweave this humble song.
Markham, Dr. [William (?)], 'On the Death of Prince Frederick', [spoken by (?)] Hon. David Lord Viscount Stormont, Christ Church', 1751.
MS. Top. Oxon. e. 172, fol. 54$^{v}$.

444 Little King Boggen he built a fine hall
And slated with pancakes, you ne'er saw the like.
MS. Douce d. 59, fol. 63.

445 Little lad little lad where wast thou born
Where they sup sour milk in a ram's horn.
MS. Douce d. 59, fol. 65v.

446 Little lute [tell the lout] when I am gone
To play on me, not th' instrument.
MSS. Ashmole 36, 37, fol. 143v; Eng. poet. e. 14, fol. 71, attr. to Dr. Cor.; see also I392, I407.

447 Little Miss Muffett
And frightened Miss Muffett away.
MS. Douce d. 59, fol. 53.

448 Little muses come and cry
Dem the weather dem the wind.
'A macaroni ode'.
MS. Eng. misc. e. 241, fol. 108.

449 Little Robin-Red-Breast sat upon a tree
Pussy-cat said mew and Robin jump'd away.
MS. Douce d. 59, fol. 53v.

450 Little their learning, less their sense
They'd bid astrology good-night.
'The same Folly', i.e. that of a Cunning Man—'farther expos'd'.
MS. Rawl. poet. 173, fol. 150.

451 Little think'st thou poor flower
As glad to have my body, as my mind.
Donne, John, 'The Blossome'.
Pr. *Poems*, 1633.
MS. *Eng. poet. e. 99, fol. 128.

452 Live as we have liv'd, still to each other new
'Tis good to know our age, not count our years.
'Ad uxorem: Ex Ausonio'.
MS. Don. d. 58, fol. 53.

453 Live ever, Felton, who hast brought to dust
Treason, ambition, pride, and filthy lust.
Couplet to the murderer of Buckingham, 1628.
MS. Tanner 465, fol. 102v.

454 Live Spencer ever, in thy Fairy Queene:
Well may the body die, but fame dies never.
Barnfield, Richard, 'A Remembrance of some English Poets', written in cipher.
MS. Ashmole 1153, fol. 138.

455 Live well Licinius safely steer
For fear of rending.
Sterrill, —, translator, Horace, *Odes* II. x.
MS. Ashmole 47, fol. 163.

Live with me, my love, in glee 456
It is to love and live with me.
H. S., 'A new Songe'.
MS. *Rawl. poet. 120, fol. 23v (autogr.).

Lives there a man, who does not feel, 457
Yours be the nobler task to raise them from the ground.
Dyer, George, 'The Race of Heroes'.
Pr. *Poetics*, 1812, i. 42.
MS. *Eng. poet. c. 21, fol. 55.

Living dying strived for life 458
For fear it cost the writer's head.
'A Poem on the death of Mary Queene of Scotts', ballad on the succession, *temp.* Elizabeth, marked 'xijd' by the copier.
MS. Willis 58, fol. 132.

Living not long, yet have I lived to see 459
He runs much faster then he did i' th' reins.
'In Circumpedem'.
MS. Don. d. 58, fol. 34.

Llewellin . . . see Lewellin.

Lo all that e'er I spent 460
That lost I.
Part of a memorial inscription in St. Peter's Church at St. Alban's, with the Latin, Quod expendi, habui. . . .
MS. Gough Herts. 3, fol. 91.

Lo! beauty grovelling instinct plainly warms, 461
Had Poll my tongue, how soon he'd say, I love.
'Spoken extempore, as a surly Parrot', 1735.
MS. Eng. misc. e. 240, p. 298.

Lo Burke by Bones, from Mary Hall expell'd 462
For dogs will go, where bones are to be had.
Burke, [Roland de, of St. Mary Hall, matric. 1776], 'Lines on his being expelled . . . by his Tutor Mr. Rawbone, Vice-Principal'.
MS. Top. Oxon. a. 29, fol. 73.

[Lo] Loo he that ys all holly yorz soo free 463
For my dere harte tyll þat my brethe me fayll.
Adapted from *Troilus and Criseyde*: cf. *Anglia*, xxxiv, 1911, p. 284.
MS. Rawl. C. 813, fol. 48v.

Lo! here a general metropolitan, 464
Who God's anointed and his church betray'd.
'On Dr. John Williams Abp. of York, and Ld. Keeper . . . He dy'd Mch. 25, 1649'.
MS. Ballard 29, fol. 145v.

465 Lo here a set of paper-pilgrims sent
Yet let the muses commit yours to fame.
'To the Incomparably vertuous Lady the Lady Harflette'.
MS. Firth e. 4, p. 1.

466 Lo here a strong man vanquished: death was stronger:
To morrow gone, perhaps this night's i'th' clay.
Robinson, Robert, 'Upon a stout and strongman, who sickned one day, and died the next. Mors omnia sternit'.
MS. *Rawl. poet. 218, p. 44 (autogr.).

467 Lo, here behold charactered to the eye
I only wish his brain were left behind.
Beaumont, Thomas, 'An epitaph on Sr J: B:' i.e. Sir John Beaumont, who died in 1627.
MS. *Malone 18, p. 44 (autogr.).

468 Lo here entombed virtue's divinest praise
Entombed lies enclosed in marble stone.
S[adleir], G[eorge], on Sir Thomas Bodley, 1613.
Pr. bk. Wood 460, after *Threnodia in obitum E. Lewkenor*, 1606 (autogr.).

469 Lo here he lies, that with one arm could more
That lost his own life for restoring thine.
On John Felton, murderer of Buckingham, 1628.
MS. Malone 23, p. 210.

470 Lo, here he lies, who long did death withstand
Who stoutly hath withstood death's utmost rage.
Fox, Richard, of King's School Sherborne, on the death of Robert Whetcombe, 'Antientest Governour of the King's Schoole of Sherebourne', 24 Oct. 1656.
MS. Gough Dorset 35(1), fol. 20*c*.

471 Lo here I am, Lord, whither wilt thou send me
Lord I am gone, oh give me thy commission.
Alabaster, William, 'Son: 12'.
MS. *Eng. poet. e. 57, fol. 3.

472 Lo here I find within this loathsome grave
The blessed fruits of a well governed life.
G. B., 'Epitaph 29' on Prince Henry, in 'Cestria Lugens', 1612.
MS. *Rawl. poet. 116, fol. 13.

473 Lo here I lie stretched out both hands and feet
My self a tombstone to my self will be.
'Ben Stone his Epitaph made by himselfe'.
MSS. Eng. poet. e. 14, fol. 98v, attr. to Stone; Malone 19, p. 60, attr. to Ben. Stone.

Lo here I stand the subject of all rhymes 474
When you are dust, I'm nature's ornament.
'Itter rockes oration in Commendation of himselfe'.
MS. Rawl. poet. 153, fol. 20v.

Lo here in earth my body lies 475
For nothing else, but Jesus sake.
Bollen, George, Dean of Lichfield, on himself, in Lichfield cathedral [d. Jan. 1602/3].
MS. Ashmole 853, fol. 50.

Lo here interr'd he lies, whose powerful will, 476
Cannot its owner always keep in breath.
Robinson, Robert, 'An Epitaph on a man of great power'.
MS. *Rawl. poet. 218, p. 9 (autogr.).

Lo! here lieth Thom. Nick's body 477
Whether fool's souls go to Heaven, or to Hell.
'An Epitaph on Thomas Nick'.
MS. Eng. poet. e. 40, fol. 109.

Lo here my lord by lady Pallas' lore 478
(In spite of Pes) to serve her majesty.
MS. Rawl. B. 88, fol. 10 rev. (autogr.).

Lo here my son a mirror vive and fair 479
How to become a perfect king indeed.
King James I, 'The Dedication of the booke. Sonnet'.
Pr., *Basilikon Doron*, 1599.
MSS. Douce 97, p. ix; Rawl. C. 744, fol. 36.

Lo! here she lies interred, who humbly gave 480
To mix his ashes, with her sacred dust.
'Epitaph. Collect. Poems'.
MS. Eng. poet. e. 39, p. 55.

Lo here the fair Chariclia, in whom strove 481
She shall appear true Æthiopian.
Cr[ashaw], R[ichard], 'Uppon the faire Æthiopian sent to a Gentlewoman'.
MS. Tanner 465, fol. 95v, attr. to R. Cr.

Lo here we lie, though turned to dust 482
And hope to rise even with the just.
Couplet on the tomb of Absolom and Elizabeth Leech at Kingston, *c.* 1693.
MS. Rawl. D. 682, fol. 77v.

Lo here, your Chaucer's pillar rectifies. 483
Dromus must pay their shares.
Lane, John, 'Comparatio'.
Pr., Chaucer Soc., 2nd ser., xxiii, xxvi, 1888–90, p. 236.
MS. Ashmole 53, fol. 80v.

484 Lo here's entombed the world's sweet rose not Rosimonde her name
Though scent be now quite altered and nothing suits the same.
Couplet, translation of Latin.
MS. Tanner 306, fol. 185ᵛ rev.

485 Lo how Soracte waxeth white with snow
From thy love's finger pull the ring held fast.
W. A., translator, Horace, *Odes* I. ix.
MS. *Rawl. poet. 104, fol. 4 (autogr.).

486 Lo, I the man whom fates have served on sops
Will draw your ears to vomit in your nose.
'A sonnett to cover myne Epistles taile peece'.
MSS. Ashmole 36, 37, fol. 140.

487 Lo! I who delighted with belles and with beaux
Each sister, that's pretty, with holy kiss greeting.
'The Quakers Meeting'.
MS. Top. London e. 9, p. 140.

488 Lo, I whose muse late sang of nuptial
Our house is almost buried with you twain.
P. F., 'Memoriae illustrissimae Rosamundae Darcye, charissimaeque Neptis suae P: ff. sic valedixit' (translation from Latin).
MS. Dodsworth 61, fol. 71.

489 Lo in this grave a maid doth lie
To marry her hath strook her dead.
Aldrich, Ed[ward], 'on Mris M: Aldrich'.
MS. Ashmole 38, fol. 240.

490 Lo, in this marble I entombed am,
That thou'lt believe two kings before a slave.
'On the D. of Buck'. 1628.
MS. CCC. 328, fol. 97; see also R32, R63.

491 Lo King Artor full manly and full wise
I made the psalter my mercy to fulfill.
Quatrains on Arthur, Charlemagne, and David.
MS. Tanner 407, fol. 32.

492 Lo, lady, thee this dial here I send:
Look on my face then, and thou canst not miss.
Ch. M., Sonnett 10.
MS. Eng. misc. d. 239, fol. 8.

493 Lo, laughing as I was at play
But rather laugh for company.
Oldisworth, Nicolas, 'An epitaph on litle Tho. Bacon, who dyed sodainly'.
MS. *Don. c. 24, fol. 31 (autogr.).

494 Lo, lo how from heaven like stars
To God be glory, Alleluia.
Pr. John Amner's *Sacred Hymns*, 1615, xxii.
MSS. Mus. f. 20–24: f. 20, fol. 72ᵛ.

Lo now the lingering hope is past, 495
Lest ye repent too late.
Broke or Brook, Thomas the younger, 'An Epitaphe declarying the lyfe and end of D. Edmund Boner'.
MS. Firth d. 14, fol. 84.

Lo on my neck this twist I bind 496
I hang and die in lingering pains.
Strode, William, Posy for 'A Necklace'.
MS. *CCC. 325, fol. 79ᵛ (autogr.).

Lo! on the foamy ocean 497
My soul it self in thoughts doth send.
Fleming, Robert, 'On my leaving England . . . to be Pastor of the English Church in Leyden . . . 1692'.
MS. *Rawl. poet. 202, fol. 5 (autogr.).

Lo: Richard Kilby lieth here 498–9
That they may leave good deeds behind.
On Richard Kilby, 1617. All Saints Church Derby.
MS. Ashmole 854, fol. 29.

Lo! sable clouds involve the skies 500
Prefer thee to the sweets of May!
Parsons, William, 'Ode . . . on Christmas Day'.
MS. *Don. d. 123, p. 23 (autogr.).

Lo! sable night ascends the dusky air, 501
And howl, exulting, through the dusky air.
Ralph, James, 'Night a Poem', in 4 books, dated at end 'Feb. 7 1726/7'. Printed 1728.
MS. Rawl. C. 778, fol. 5 (autogr.).

Lo! the rich casket's mimic dome, 502
With Bladud's healing streams.
Graves, Richard, 'The Cabinet . . . To Mr. Walker of Whitchurch in Oxfordshire [from] Claverton near Bath, 1750'.
Pr. Dodsley's *Collection of Poems*, iv, 1755, p. 330.
MS. Ballard 37, fol. 27 (autogr.).

Lo the year's final day! Nature performs 503
Strike those last clocks that knell th' expiring year!
Seward, Anna, 'Sonnet . . . Dec. 31st 1782'.
Pr. *Poetical Works*, ed. Sir W. Scott, 1810, iii. 163.
MS. Eng. poet. c. 51, p. 106.

Lo this noble and victor'ous conqueror 504
This noble king he reigned but twenty year.
Verses on the Kings of England, William I–Edward II.
MS. Digby 196, fol. 65.

505 Lo, Thomas Hamon here interred doth lie
Deserves a monument of memory.

Verses at Rye on the tomb of Thomas Hammon, d. 1607.
MS. Rawl. D. 682, fol. 49.

506 Lo we some antique hero's strength
When mountains heaped on mountains failed.

[Waller, Edmund], 'On the head of a Stagge'.
Pr. *Poems*, 1645, p. 65.
MS. Eng. poet. c. 50, fol. 122$^v$; see also S903.

507 Lo what delicious food
And sweet things sweeter still.

Beddome, Benjamin.
MS. *Eng. misc. e. 227, fol. 28$^v$.

508 Lo where he flies! Ye angels guide his flight
And join the triumphs of his native skies.

'On the Death of King George the Second'.
Pr. bk. Firth b. 22, fol. 62.

509 Lo; where he shineth yonder
So fair a star as Harry.

'Epitaph on prince Henry' 1612.
Pr. *Wits Recreations*, 1640, Epit. 102. In B.M. MS. Lansd. 777, fol. 66, attr. to Hugh Holland.
MS. Eng. poet. c. 50, two copies, fols. 23, 59.

510 Lo! where the rosy spring is seen
And weave from heavenly trees a never withering crown.

Dyer, George, 'Ode on the approaching Spring . . . on the banks of the Cam'.
Pr. *Poems*, 1792, p. 1.
MS. *Eng. poet. c. 21, fol. 13.

511 Lo, where this silent marble weeps
With life, with memory, with love.

MS. Eng. poet. c. 6, fol. 93.

512 Lo who for whom and whose I live
Who would not die to live in love with thee.

MS. Rawl. poet. 172, fol. 7.

513 Loaden with cares, oppressed with woe
Wilt 'venge, and answer Lord for me.

Colman, Henry, 'On my enemies unjust malice'.
MS. *Rawl. poet. 204, fol. 2$^v$ (autogr.).

514 Locked in death's frozen arms beneath is laid
Her sex's glory was Eliza S[avil].

'To a young Lady, who asked the Author what he would say of her, if she should die'.
MS. *Eng. poet. d. 47, fol. 129.

Locked in the arms of balmy sleep 515
That flash which melts the world.

Amherst, Elizabeth, 'A Sacred Lyric . . . on being awaken'd in the Night of Feb$^y$ 3. 1749–50 by a . . . storm'.
MSS. Eng. poet. e. 18, p. 24; *e. 109, p. 6.

London, a little world, within itself, 516
As bullies, canting priests, pimps, bawds and whores.

Spoure, Edmund, 'A Poeme on the famous citty of London'. 1695.
MS. *Eng. poet. c. 52, fol. 160$^v$ (autogr.).

[London bridge is fallen down] 517
With a gay lady.

'An addition to Londonbridge' *beg.* We'll build it up.
MS. Douce d. 59, fol. 50.

London is of great renown 518
Yet no man doth thereon co[m]plain.

MS. Rawl. D. 859, fol. 97$^v$.

London London sing and praise thy lord 519
Long live and reign our gracious queen.

'A proper new ballade wherein is plaine to be seen how god blesseth england for love of our Queene: Soung to the tune of tarletons caroll'. Initialed 'T.'
MS. Rawl. poet. 185, fol. 13.

Long annoys, and short contentings 520
Nightly breaks poor lovers' slumber.

MS. Mus. b. 1, fol. 57$^v$, music by John Wilson.

Long be the thread the fates have spun 521
Thy blessed Redeemer set thee free.

Vyse, William, Archdeacon of Salop., 'A Birthday Wish . . . to Sir Roger Newdigate June 1st 1767'.
MS. Eng. poet. c. 51, p. 92.

Long beards, heartless, 522
Makes England thriftless.

'Character of the English Men'.
Pr. *Fabyan's Chronicle*, 1516 (ed. Ellis, 1811, p. 440), the Scots satirizing the English in 1328; Puttenham's *Arte of English Poesie*, 1589, p. 144.
MSS. Eng. poet. e. 40, fol. 1, dated 1307; Malone 19, p. 151; Rawl. poet. 148, fol. 5$^v$, headed 'Edwardus Tertius'; 212, fol. 99$^v$.

Long days of absence, dear, I could endure 523
But naked every night let Nell unking thee.

MS. Don. b. 8, p. 504.

524 **Long did I muse ere I resolved to write**
**And me contentment in my widowhood.**
Burton, Francis.
MS. *Add. A. 267, fol. 61v (autogr.).

525 **Long did the churlish East detain**
**The power and will to bless.**
[Whitehead, William], Birthday Ode, 1771. Pr. *Poems*, 1790, ii. 105.
MS. Mus. Sch. D. 326. Music by Boyce.

526 **Long ere the morn did expect the return**
**And carouses to his career.**
'Adonis hunting' [Master Basse his Careere].
Cf. *Poetical Works of Basse*, ed. R. W. Bond, 1893, p. 127.
MS. Rawl. poet. 246, fol. 12.

527 **Long from our faithless and ingrateful isle**
**But him who has't innate Sophia's son.**
Roach, Richard, 'To K. George (the First), On His Thanks-Giving'.
MS. Rawl. D. 832, fol. 239 (autogr.).

528 **Long had bewailed Arabia's hapless swains**
**Alike for beauty, and for fame renowned.**
Lipscomb, William, 'On inoculation', prize verses, Oxford, 1772.
MSS. Add. A. 203, fol. 1, attr. to Mr. William Lipscomb of C.C.C.; Top. Oxon. c. 216, fol. 21, attr. to Lipscomb; d. 163, fol. 2, attr. to W. Lipscomb.

529 **Long had Hibernia viewed with envious eyes.**
**Hibernia's beauties were no beauties here.**
[Gough, Richard (?)], 'Enfield Assembly'.
MS. *Eng. poet. c. 5, fol. 224.

530 **Long had my pen lain dull and useless by,**
**I'd not despair, tho' I'd my father slain.**
'Satyr. 1688/9'.
MS. Firth c. 15, p. 311.

531 **Long had our happy isle enjoyed peace**
**Our monarch's royal head, or his sweet peace destroy.**
S[pinedge], A[nthony], 'On the Powderplot. A Pindarique Ode'.
MS. Tanner 306, fol. 383.

532 **Long had proud Carthage spurned the Roman state**
**And rivetted the monsters to their native earth.**
Browne, W[illiam], 'Scipio', lines written for the Election, June 1699 (?), at the Merchant Taylor's School.
Pr. bk. Vet. A3 c. 123, fol. 37.

**Long had St. Paul looked downward from the sky** 533
**And many copper-smiths shall do thee right.**
'Upon the Parliament's voting that the Cupolo of St. Paul's Church be cover'd with Copper'. [14 Feb. 1607/8].
MS. Lat. misc. e. 19, fol. 107v rev.

**Long had the famed imposter found success** 534
**And catch with greedy ears his dying breath.**
Oldham, John, 'Loyala's Will'. 'Satyrs upon the Jesuits', iii. Cf. L535.
MS. *Rawl. poet. 123, p. 164 (autogr.).

**Long had the reverend sham enjoyed success** 535
**I'th' conduct of their future villany.**
Oldham, John, 'Loyal's Will', draft of the 'Satyr upon the Jesuits', iii.
MS. *Rawl. poet. 123, p. 184 (autogr.).

**Long had usurping George in council sat** 536
**Flinch not a whit you'll but be damned at last.**
J. W., 'A Satyr on the Times . . . Dialogue between High-Dutch Illustrious and Low Dutch Glorious', the ghost of William III and George I.
MS. Rawl. poet. 155, p. 228.

**Long has Clarinda reigned queen of my heart,** 537
**'Twill prove my overthrow.**
Morrice, John, 'The Dilemma'. Feb. 4, 1707.
MS. *Rawl. poet. 114, fol. 65 (autogr.).

**Long has the husband here been ridiculed** 538
**Ye men will clap, and to your judgement stand.**
Prologue to 'The Lover's Strategem'.
MS. Rawl. poet. 18, p. xv.

**Long has the muse, pursuing higher themes** 539
**And tell the adventure round to every friend.**
Gough, Richard, 'The Adventure'. 1752.
MS. *Eng. poet. c. 5, fol. 43v (autogr.).

**Long hath it vexed our learned age to scan,** 540
**God make you wise, and me an honest man.**
'Who is a puritan'.
In B.M. Add. MS. 21433, fol. 83, subscribed D. H.
MS. Tanner 465, fol. 82.

**Long hath the French fleet with that of proud Spain** 541
**Success to our navy and god save our king.**
'New Song on the Victory over the Spanish Fleet by Admiral Jarvis' [Feb. 1797].
MS. Firth c. 18, fol. 58.

542 Long have I sought the wish of all
True happiness must die.
[Felltham, Owen], 'A discription of true happinesse'.
Pr. *Resolves*, 1661, 'Lusoria', p. 3.
MS. Rawl. poet. 90, fol. 32v.

543 Long have I sought to prove
In eternal sunshine reign.
Kenton, James.
MS. *Eng. poet. e. 20, p. 257 (autogr.).

544 Long have I studied for some mighty name
But faction rage remorse and endless care.
'On the Death of the Noble Wm. Gordon Vicount Kenmure who was made a Sacrifice to Usurpation and Whiggish Tyranny', 24 Feb. 1716.
MSS. Rawl. poet. 155, p. 251; 207, p. 84.

545 Long have I viewed long have I thought
Nor beg thy angle to sheath up his sword.
'The Resignation'.
MS. Rawl. D. 1095, fol. 152 rev.

546 Long have the sparks descried our *alma mater*
Yet female pride would turn that heaven to hell.
'A Satyre against the Cambridge Beauties'.
MS. Don. e. 24, p. 1.

547 Long I've neglected to the gods to pray,
For He that makes us rich, as soon can make us poor.
Warton, Thomas (1688(?)–1745), 'A Paraphrase on Hor:', *Odes* I. xxxiv, 1704.
MS. Don. c. 75, fol. 5 (autogr.).

548 Long lectures many go to hear:
They seem but as a sport.
Robinson, Robert.
MS. *Rawl. poet. 218, p. 60 (autogr.).

549 Long life to the queen and a prosperous reign
And he's a false brother who won't pledge the same.
'A new Health for the Fair Ladys att Tea or the Gentleman att Wine', 1710.
Pr. bk. Firth b. 21, fol. 73v.

550 Long lives the man that dies in lusty years,
Where now it reigns, and still shall live in rest.
Whetstone, George, 'Of the life etc. of Sir Phillip Sidney'.
Pr. 1587(?). *S.T.C.* 25349.
MS. *Malone 6, fol. 42.

551 Long lost in solitude of close retreat
And change time's transient joys for blest eternity.
Samber, Robert, 'On the Marriage of . . . the Lord Viscount Harcourt and his Lady', 1735.
MS. Rawl. poet. 11, fol. 4 (autogr.).

Long may this order flourish, and its fame 552
The parallel to old eternity.
Ashmole, Elias, on the Garter. 17 Feb. 1666/5.
MS. Ashmole 1744, opposite last printed page (autogr.).

Long on his lusts, he lackeyed, like a page 553
Till pleasures of his youth caused sorrows in his age.
Couplet.
MS. Rawl. poet. 66, fol. 21.

Long since fair Lucinda my passion did move 554
You will owe me so much as you never can pay.
MS. Rawl. D. 1006, fol. 2v.

Long since I poured my amorous moan 555
The prints of virtue and of reason!
Parsons, William, 'To Miss Hunter on her having set to Musick a song of mine'.
Pr. *Travelling Recreations*, 1807, ii. 143.
MS. *Don. d. 123, p. 195 (autogr.).

Long since thy worth (for which I much repent thee) 556
My self all thine, bid thee farewell, and rest, etc.
Glanvill, John, of Lincoln's Inn, 'Poeticall Astrologie', dedicated to Francis Kynnaston of Offeley in Shropshire, 18 February 1613.
MS. Ashmole 45(5).

Long since was Sands in heaven before he died 557
Sands had been greater and much better we.
Strode, William, translation of Latin verses on Sir Edwin Sandys and the last books of *Ecclesiastical Politie.*
MS. *CCC. 325, fol. 109 (autogr.).

Long since we lost thee did sad patience stay 558
Thou hast a garland here a crown above.
Beaumont, Thomas, 'A funeral elegie on Coll: Henry Grey slayne at A Victory obtayned by the english Protestants against the Irish Papists', 13 Nov. 1647.
MS. *Malone 18, p. 93 (autogr.).

Long time have I been a soldier 559
To bring home the King again.
'The Covenant Or, No King but the Old King's Son'.
MS. Firth c. 20, fol. 118.

Long time of the seas had old England been queen, 560
And health to each bold British tar.
'The Brave Tars of Old England'.
Pr. John Ashton, *Real Sailor Songs*, 1891, p. 24.
MS. Firth c. 18, fol. 21.

561 Long time plain-dealing in this haughty town
While knav'ry laughing, rung her passing bell.
'Plain-Dealing abandon'd'.
Pr. Rochester's *Poems*, 1685, p. 54.
MS. Rawl. poet. 173, fol. 159$^{v}$.

562 Long time the parcels of created glory
Oh model more than the university.
Alabaster, William, 'Son: 27. Christus recapitulatio omnium'.
MS. *Eng. poet. e. 57, fol. 7.

563 Longer I cannot hold and yet a fear
All robed in white sings lauds to him whom he denied.
Woodforde, Samuel, 'An Ode to the memory of . . . John, Lord Wilmot, Earl of Rochester'.
Pr. from this MS., J. Prinz, *Rochesteriana*, 1926, p. 59.
MS. Rawl. poet. 25, fol. 146 (autogr.).

564 Longer in length my life had gone
That man that made him souls at will.
'On a Cobler'.
MS. CCC. 328, fol. 30.

565 Look back Castara from thine eye
Till they prove innocent as mine.
[Habington, William], song with music for voice and theorbo.
Pr. *Castara*, 1634, i, p. 33.
MS. Don. c. 57, fol. 94.

566 Look back poor G—e and strictly search record
Your arms won't serve you, for your horse must fly.
'Respice et Cave'.
MS. Rawl. poet. 181, fol. 79$^{v}$.

567 Look Cloris in this fountain clear
But in a moment break.
MS. Mus. b. 1, fol. 103, music by John Wilson.

568 Look down bright goddess hear a virgin's prayer
Oh make him anything that I can't love.
Song with music.
MS. Mus. Sch. E. 397, p. 103 rev.

569 Look down oh God with pity look
Jesus shall make them good.
Beddome, Benjamin, 'An Hymn'.
MS. *Eng. misc. e. 227, fol. 58$^{v}$.

570 Look down thou guardian angels of our isle
Unless t'hear mass instead of common prayer.
'On the Queries upon the Tacking the late bill of occasionall Conformity to the land Tax bill', 1704–5.
MS. Eng. misc. c. 116, fol. 6, initialed R. C.

Look down triumphant god of war 571
Whom nothing can control.
'Song on Price Eugenes Victory over th' Turkes', Peterwarden, 5 Aug. 1716, or Belgrade 16 Aug. 1717.
MS. Rawl. poet. 152, fol. 168$^{v}$.

Look gracious Father pitying down 572
And fear thy wrath, and love thy grace.
'A Hymn by Mr. Turner for the Fast day on account of the Earthquake at Lisbon and an Aproching War with France'.
MS. Eng. misc. e. 227, fol. 29.

Look how the graces dance and sing 573
Nothing that may yield us joy.
Chatwin, John, 'In imitation of Anacreon's Odes', xlvi.
MS. *Rawl. poet. 94, p. 79 (autogr.).

Look how the panting winds obey 574
Her fan, her glove, or any thing.
Chatwin, John, 'On Aurelia's Fan'.
MS. *Rawl. poet. 94, p. 89 (autogr.).

Look how the russet morn exceeds the night 575
The eye of all the world loves to be grey.
Strode, William, 'The commendation of gray Eies'.
MS. *CCC. 325, fol. 94$^{v}$ (autogr.).
MSS. Ashmole 47, fol. 46$^{v}$; CCC. 328, fol. 79, attr. to Str.; Eng. poet. e. 97, p. 100; Malone 16, p. 13; Rawl. poet. 84, fol. 92$^{v}$ rev.

Look man before thee how thy death hasteth 576
Look man beneath thee, pains without rest.
'Godly admonition'.
Pr. Camden's *Remaines*, 1605, p. 49.
MSS. Ashmole 38, p. 177; Eng. poet. e. 40, fol. 121.

Look mistress mine within this hollow breast 577
Or pity me, and grant my sweet desire.
Pr. Pilkington's *First Book of Songs*, 1605, xii.
MSS. Mus. f. 7–10: f. 10, fol. 22.

Look my only dearest on my love-like heart 578
I die a martyr you an heretic.
[Carew, Thomas], 'To my dearest that is mistrustfull of her owne Beautie'.
Lines from 'To A. D. unreasonable distrustful, etc.', pr. *Poems*, 1640. Set by H. Lawes; see Dunlap, *Poems*, 1949, p. 255.
MS. Eng. poet. c. 50, fol. 121$^{v}$; see also F42.

579 Look not aloft on the spacious round.
United to eternal love.
Tune, 'If that there be a Phoenix in the world 'tis she'.
MS. Rawl. poet. 37, p. 67.

580 Look not, sad reader here to find
To find a king so far above a tomb.
Roe, [Sir] Thomas, 'Upon the death of the kinge of Sweden' 1632.
MS. Don. d. 58, fol. 19.

581 Look on a soldier that hath bravely served
That by desert the due of knighthood hold.
'Pasquils Mad-cappe'.
MS. Douce 280, fol. 122.

582 Look on me ever, though thine eye
Though all the world deny it.
MS. Malone 16, p. 29.

583 Look on this picture where you'll see,
For such a one was ne'er before.
Cavendish, Lady Jane, 'On my Sister Brackleys Picture'.
MS. *Rawl. poet. 16, p. 22.

584 Look out bright eyes and clear the air
Even the fetters that you wear.
MS. Mus. b. 1, fol. 40, music by John Wilson.

585 Look round about, and you will seldom find
A servant faithful, or a master kind.
Couplet.
MS. Sancroft 59, p. 269 rev.

586 Look round the habitable world, how few
But, when we have our wish, we wish undone?
MS. Eng. poet. c. 9, p. 49.

587 Look shepherds look, old Janus doth unfold
He, only he, is author of our peace.
Laniere, Nich[olas], 'A Pastorall Song, to the King on Newyeares day: Ano. Dni. 1663[/4]'.
Ll. 14–15, 16–23 taken from Jonson's *Underwood*, lxxix, 56–57, 58–65.
MSS. Ashmole 36, 37, fol. 166.

588 Look shepherds look? why? where?
God and men are reconciled.
Carol.
MSS. Ashmole 36, 37, fol. 255; Rawl. poet. 23, p. 151, reference to setting by Thomas Foord.

589 Look there be the fine [king] just landed at G[reenwich]
One guinea to drink a good health to royal K[ing Jimmy].
MS. Rawl. poet. 181, fol. 24.

Look Thyrsis, see the sun withdraws his light, 590
And there abide till the approach of morn.
Chatwin, John, 'A Pastoral Elegy on the Death of that Great Master of Poesie Mr. Edmond Spencer. Corydon and Thyrsis'.
MS. *Rawl. poet. 94, p. 273 (autogr.).

Look to me faith and look to my faith God 591
I were an angel singing what you were.
Donne, John, 'Another Elegie of the Prince [Henry, h]is death'.
Pr. *Poems*, 1633.
MS. Rawl. poet. 26, fol. 91[v].

Look to the east see the bright morning star 592
The earth her presents, Heaven his light doth bring.
Clifford, Henry, Earl of Cumberland, 'Epiphany'.
MS. *Rawl. poet. 95, fol. 32[v].

Look to your health in days canicular 593
From harder studies scholars excused are.
Barksdale, Clement, 'Health', distich.
MS. Autogr. c. 9, fol. 154 (autogr.).

Look towards the east and see a brighter ray 594
And thou, oh earth! drank up the crimson flood.
Walsh, Octavia.
MS. *Eng. poet. e. 31, fol. 30 (autogr.).

Look up and see, now Vines is gone 595
Lord perfect what thou hast begun!
Baxter, Richard.
Pr. *A Treatise of the . . . Sacrament of the Lords-Supper*, 1657, and in Baxter's *Poetical Fragments*, 1681, p. 124, with the date 18 Oct. 1656.
MSS. Rawl. C. 580, p. 317; Rawl. poet. 58, fol. 63[v].

Look up: And there, I see the fair abode 596
Nothing but objects of true love and wonder.
[Quarles, Francis], 'On a faire Prospect'.
Pr. *Divine Fancies*, 1632, iii. 93.
MSS. Rawl. poet. 90, fol. 72[v]; 213, fol. 54[v] rev.

Look up dejected soul, truth says thou mayst. 597
Living and dying let me still be thine.
D[arell], Sir S[amson], 'A sick mans Sabbath dayes journey'.
MS. Rawl. poet. 210, fol. 54 rev.

Look up fair lids the tresures of my heart 598
Till her eyes shine I live in darkest night.
Sidney, Sir Philip, from the *Arcadia*.
MSS. *e Mus. 37, fol. 115; Rawl. poet. 85, fol. 9, attr. to S. P. S.

599 Look up thou seed of envy and still bring
T'effect its feet, thou hast made thine own heart ache.
'On . . . Lord Weston Lo: high Treasurer . . . the day hee was made Earle of Portland [17. Feb. 1632/3] . . . By the True Louer of your Hon:[rs] Ben Johnson'.
Pr. *The Underwood*, lxxiii.
MS. Ashmole 38, p. 67.

600 Look what a little shred of earth it is
Now on you, do become you better far.
Oldisworth, Nicolas, 'To a gentle-woman that delighted too much in her garden'.
MS. *Don. c. 24, fol. 59$^{v}$.

601 Look yonder if thou hast an eye
Till her bright rays return.
Hillman, J[ohn, of Christ Church (?)], 'An Ode on Corinna walking in a Garden'.
MS. Rawl. D. 1092, fol. 270.

602 Looking and longing for deliverance
And all forbiddings of thy lips observe.
Herbert, Mary (*née* Sidney), Countess of Pembroke, Psalm cxix, 'L'.
MS. *Rawl. poet. 24, p. 182; *25, fol. 122$^{v}$.

603 Looking for pictures lately I was shown
For it looks just as if it would be burnt.
Walsh, William, 'Picture of Troy' [Greek Anthology].
MS. Malone 9, fol. 29$^{v}$ (autogr.).

604 Lord as the hart embossed with heat
And there his beauty see.
[Sandys, George], Psalm xlii, 3-part setting by W. Lawes.
Pr. *Divine Poems*, 1638, p. 52, and H. and W. Lawes, *Choice Psalmes*, 1648.
MS. Mus. Sch. E. 451, p. 67.

605 Lord be my judge and thou shalt see, my paths be right and plain
Wherefore to god, I will give praise, in all the people's sight.
[Hopkins, John], Psalm xxvi.
MS. Rawl. poet. 112, fol. 64$^{v}$ rev.

606 Lord! behold my helpless anguish
Despair at last I entertain.
Melton, Richard, 'A Complaint'.
MS. Rawl. poet. 65, fol. 96$^{v}$.

607 Lord bend to me thine ear
By Thee, by Thee my comfort wrought.
Herbert, Mary (*née* Sidney), Countess of Pembroke, Psalm lxxxvi, rejected version.
MS. *Rawl. poet. 25, fol. 81.

Lord blame me not when thou art wroth 608
To see the fruit of ghostly tilth.
The 3rd of 'Septem psalmi poenitentiales', Psalm xxxviii, Domine ne in furore tuo arguas.
MS. Ashmole 61, fol. 110$^{v}$.

Lord bless this labour the cursed earth restore 609
Or with its selfish magic bind my soul.
MS. *Don. f. 5, fol. 11$^{v}$.

Lord bless us! what a heavy bluster 610
And fairly throw my pen away.
'Comedy'.
MS. Top. London e. 9, p. 87.

Lord bow thine ear to my request and hear me by and by 611
And be ashamed because lord thou dost help and comfort me.
[Hopkins, John], Psalm lxxxvi.
MS. Rawl. poet. 112, fol. 45$^{v}$ rev.

Lord call to mind king David's trouble 612
I 'stablish shall his royal crown.
Harington, Sir John, Psalm cxxxii.
MS. *Douce 361, fol. 82$^{v}$.

Lord call to mind, lord keep in mind. 613
With fame, and glory rise.
Herbert, Mary (*née* Sidney), Countess of Pembroke, Psalm cxxxii.
MS. *Rawl. poet. 24, p. 198.

Lord chide me not in the tempestuous day 614
Oh haste to help my Saviour, oh my God.
Clifford, Henry, Earl of Cumberland, Psalm xxxviii.
MS. *Rawl. poet. 95, fol. 36$^{v}$.

Lord! cleanse our hearts which now are so obscene 615
Who, night and day, doth seek our overthrow.
[Corbet, W.], 'Med'.
MS. *Rawl. poet. 210, fol. 33.

Lord for thy promise sake defend 616
To thee ascend.
[Sandys, George], Psalm liv. 3-part setting by H. Lawes.
Pr. *Divine Poems*, 1638, p. 66, and H. and W. Lawes, *Choice Psalmes*, 1648.
MS. Mus. Sch. E. 451, p. 69.

Lord for us in danger's hour 617*a*
Shall more than conquer all.
Kenton, James.
MS. *Eng. poet. e. 20, p. 197 (autogr.).

Lord! furious in wrath do not correct 617*b*
Thou art my help, oh save me then with speed.
Fairfax, Thomas, Lord, Psalm xxxviii.
MS. *Fairfax 38, p. 195; see also L668.

618 Lord give me wisdom to direct my ways
To pick more manna, than will serve to day.
MSS. Mus. Sch. G. 632, fol. 1$^{v}$; Rawl. poet. 127, fol. 17$^{v}$.

619 Lord give our king and grant his princely son
That fills this earth with bliss, amen amen.
Harington, Sir John, Psalm lxxii.
MS. *Douce 361, fol. 42$^{v}$.

620 Lord give thy judgement to the King,
All by the seas embraced . . . (incomplete).
Psalm lxxii.
MS. *Rawl. C. 113, fol. 51$^{v}$.

621 Lord give thy judgements to the King
Amen amen say I.
[Hopkins, John], Psalm lxxii.
MSS. Mus. c. 1, fol. 18, with music 'by N. Haym London 1728'; Rawl. poet. 112, fol. 50$^{v}$ rev.

622 Lord, give thy judgements to the King,
Amen, amen, reply.
Psalm lxxii.
MS. *Montagu e. 10, fol. 22.

623 Lord give us grace to please thy righteous deity
Thy mercy Lord in Christ unto us show.
Robinson, Robert.
MS. *Rawl. poet. 218, p. 109 (autogr.).

624 Lord God, my health and hope of my salvation
Them from my sight me from their thought removed.
Harington, Sir John, Psalm lxxxviii.
MS. *Douce 361, fol. 53.

625 Lord god of health the hope and stay
Out of my sight are gone.
[Hopkins, John], Psalm lxxxviii.
MS. Rawl. poet. 112, fol. 45 rev.

626 Lord grant my just request oh hear my cry
And let thine eyes my righteousness behold.
'A Divine song Out of [George] Sandses translation' [pr. 1638], Psalm xvii, 'sett for three ladys' by Wm. Davis; composer's autograph.
MS. Mus. c. 16, fol. 98.

627 Lord greatly thy salvation
Will songs of praise accord.
Psalm xxi.
MS. *Rawl. C. 113, fol. 21.

628 Lord hear me that afflicted pray
No limitation know . . . (incomplete)
Psalm cii.
MS. *Rawl. C. 113, fol. 68.

Lord hear my knocking hark my cries 629
Have sought and found the bill.
'The souls access'.
MS. Rawl. poet. 58, fol. 39.

Lord hear my prayer and cry respect my ruth 630
Such foes as vex thy servant and annoy.
Harington, Sir John, Psalm cxliii.
MS. *Douce 361, fol. 88.

Lord hear my prayer, from enemies 631
His glory they declare.
Psalm lxiv.
MS. *Rawl. C. 113, fol. 46.

Lord hear my prayer hark the plaint 632
Thy servant am and shall.
[Norton, Thomas], Psalm cxliii.
MS. Rawl. poet. 112, fol. 30 rev.

Lord hear my prayer, hide not thyself 633
I will on God depend.
Psalm lv.
MS. *Rawl. C. 113, fol. 41.

Lord hear my prayer instantly. 634
And succour my distress.
Psalm cii. Byrd's 3-part setting.
Pr. *Songs of sundrie natures*, 1589, v.
MSS. Mus. f. 11–15: f. 11, fol. 4$^{v}$.

Lord hear my prayer, to thee exiled 635
Perform my vows with zeal.
Psalm lxi.
MS. *Rawl. C. 113, fol. 44$^{v}$.

Lord hear the prayer thou doest inspire, 636
Who these malicious dangers set.
Godolphin, S[idney], Psalm cxli.
MS. Malone 13, p. 1.

Lord hear the right, attention yield 637
Thy impress likeness grace.
Psalm xvii.
MS. *Rawl. C. 113, fol. 18.

Lord, hear the right, consider well 638
Awake with thy likeness.
Psalm xvii.
MS. *Montagu e. 10, fol. 6.

Lord help it is high time for me to call 639
Which if it last, woe to all simple hearts.
Sidney, Sir Philip, Psalm xii.
MSS. *Rawl. poet. 24, p. 14; *25, fol. 8$^{v}$.

Lord, hie Thee me to save 640
Lord make no long delay.
Herbert, Mary (*née* Sidney), Countess of Pembroke, Psalm lxx; rejected version.
MS. *Rawl. poet. 25, fol. 61.

641 Lord how are they increased
He gives 'em joy, and makes their fences strong.
Williams, John, Psalm iii.
MS. *Rawl. poet. 184, fol. 7v (autogr.).

642 Lord, how are they increased like floods who seek
Or those who now are vistors had been slaves.
Williams, John, Psalm iii.
MS. *Rawl. poet. 192, fol. 13 (autogr.).

643 Lord how can man preach thy eternal word?
And in the ear, not conscience ring.
Herbert, George, 'The Windowes.'
Pr. *The Temple*, 1633, p. 59.
MS. *Tanner 307, fol. 45v.

644 Lord how couldst thou so much appease
Reserving all for flesh again.
Herbert, George, 'Faith'.
Pr. *The Temple*, 1633, p. 41.
MS. *Tanner 307, fol. 32.

645 Lord how do they increase
His blessing he extendeth.
Sidney, Sir Philip, Psalm iii.
MSS. *Rawl. poet. 24, p. 2; *25, fol. 2.

646 Lord how he swells as if he had at least
He has a leash of churches in his belly.
[Quarles, Francis] 'On a Impropriator'.
Pr. *Divine Fancies*, 1632, iv. 73.
MS. Don. d. 58, fol. 39.

647 Lord, how I am all ague, when I seek,
Remember, that thou once didst write in stone.
Herbert, George, 'The Sinner'.
Pr. *The Temple*, 1633, p. 30.
MS. *Tanner 307, fol. 23v.

648 Lord how long, how long wilt thou,
My just hopes at his good pleasure.
Davison, Francis, Psalm xiii.
MSS. Rawl. D. 316, fol. 125v, dated at end 8 Aug. 1611; Rawl. poet. 61, fol. 14, attr. to Fr. Da.

649 Lord how reformed and quiet are we grown,
To oblige the town, the city, and the court.
'Prologue to Marriage Allamode. 1672. By Mr. [John] Dreiden'.
MS. Top. Oxon. e. 202, fol. 121.

650 Lord, how these troublers of my soul increase
'Tis he that blessings to his people gives.
Fairfax, Thomas, Lord, Psalm iii.
MS. *Fairfax 40, p. 4 (autogr.).
MS. *Fairfax 38, p. 117.

Lord I can suffer thy rebukes 651
And with confusion turn away. Hallelujah.
[Patrick, John], '4 voc.' Music by H. Purcell.
Pr. *A Century of Select Psalms*, 1684, no. vi, p. 5; F. B. Zimmerman, *Purcell*, 1963, no. 136.
MS. Mus. c. 28, fol. 111v.

Lord, I confess my sin is great: 652
Fractures well cured make us more strong.
Herbert, George, 'Repentance'.
Pr. *The Temple*, 1633, p. 40.
MSS. Rawl. poet. 90, fol. 135; *Tanner 307, fol. 31.

Lord I have done, and Lord I have misdone 653
Remember, th'art a Father, I, the child.
[Quarles, Francis], 'The Sinners Submission'.
Pr. *Emblemes*, 1635, III. vi.
MS. Rawl. poet. 90, fol. 23.

Lord I have left all, and my self behind 654
Desire possession, possession desire.
Alabaster, William, 'Son: 19'.
MS. *Eng. poet. e. 57, fol. 4v.

Lord I have sinned, and the black number swells 655
And then one drop, one drop of balsam will suffice.
Taylor, Jeremy, 'A Hymne'.
Pr. after the *Golden Grove*, 1655, p. 156.
MS. Rawl. poet. 90, fol. 163v.

Lord I should ingrate in highest nature prove 656
To David his anoint, whose race he'll own.
Fairfax, Thomas, Lord, Psalm xviii.
MS. *Fairfax 40, p. 33 (autogr.).
MS. *Fairfax 38, p. 145.

Lord I will mean and speak thy praise, 657
Both all my praise and more.
Herbert, George, 'Praise'.
Pr. *The Temple*, 1633, p. 151.
MS. *Tanner 307, fol. 115v.

Lord, I will praise thee with my heart and voice 658
Shall wear out of my heart this love of thine.
Knollys, Fra., Psalm xxx.
MS. *Rawl. poet. 60, p. 64 (autogr.).

Lord, if my grief were not opposed with joy 659
The more my heavenly affections be at rest.
[Quarles, Francis], 'On Greife, and Joy.'
Pr. *Divine Fancies*, 1632, iii. 65.
MS. Rawl. poet. 90, fol. 52.

Lord, if our days be few, why do we spend 660
Great God, we make them evil: Thou makest them few.
[Quarles, Francis], 'On the days of Man'.
Pr. *Divine Fancies*, 1632, ii. 69.
MS. Rawl. poet. 90, fol. 50v.

661 Lord if the genuine character
Christ by his Spirit dwells in me.
Kenton, James.
MS. *Eng. poet. e. 20, p. 38 (autogr.).

662 Lord if Thou shalt show me light
And crown me in the skies.
Kenton, James.
MS. *Eng. poet. e. 20, p. 188 (autogr.).

663 Lord, I'm in debt, and have not wherewithal
No debt is desperate, in respect of Thee.
[Quarles, Francis], 'On the Widowes Cruse'.
Pr. *Divine Fancies*, 1632, ii. 40.
MS. Rawl. poet. 90, fol. 68.

664 Lord in all generations
So shall our works be blest.
Psalm xc.
MS. *Rawl. C. 113, fol. 65v.

665 Lord in my silence, how do I despise
Planted in me.
Herbert, George, 'Frailty'.
Pr. *The Temple*, 1633, p. 62.
MS. *Tanner 307, fol. 48v.

666 Lord in the day of trouble hear
Thou glorious great I AM.
Kenton, James.
MS. *Eng. poet. e. 20, p. 221 (autogr.).

667 Lord, in the solemn shades of night
With rapture melts my soul.
'A Hymn. Collect. Poems'.
MS. Eng. poet. e. 39, p. 70.

668 Lord in thy furious wrath do not correct
Thou art my help oh save me Lord with speed.
Fairfax, Thomas, Lord, Psalm xxxviii.
MS. *Fairfax 40, p. 84 (autogr.); see also L617*b*.

669 Lord in thy Gospel we behold
The soul transporting sound.
Beddome, Benjamin.
MS. *Eng. misc. e. 227, fol. 10.

670 Lord in thy house who shall for ever bide
In holy hill unmoved shall dwell for ever.
Davison, Chr[istopher], Psalm xv.
MSS. Rawl. D. 316, fol. 126, attr. to Chr. Davison; Rawl. poet. 61, fol. 15; attr. to Chr. Da.

671 Lord in thy mansions who shall sojourn there
He's in a happy state that does these things.
Fairfax, Thomas, Lord, Psalm xv.
MS. *Fairfax 40, p. 28 (autogr.).
MS. *Fairfax 38, p. 141.

Lord in thy rage rebuke me not 672
Are troubled sore in me.
Psalm vi, 3-part setting.
Pr. Byrd's *Songs of sundry natures*, 1589, i.
MSS. Mus. f. 11–15: f. 11, fol. vv.

Lord in thy strength the king has much delight 673*a*
Be thou exalted, we will praise thy might.
Fairfax, Thomas, Lord, Psalm xxi.
MS. *Fairfax 38, p. 152; see also M535.

Lord! in thy tabernacle who shall dwell? 673*b*
He that lives thus, needs fear no punishment.
Morrice, John, Psalm xv, 'Jan. 15, 1707'.
MS. *Rawl. poet. 114, fol. 158 (autogr.).

Lord in thy truth and righteousness, 674
I may thy servant live.
Psalm cxliii.
MS. *Rawl. C. 113, fol. 100.

Lord in thy wrath correct me not, 675
For my most just desert.
Psalm xxxviii, 3-part setting.
Pr. Byrd's *Songs of Sundry natures*, 1589, iii.
MSS. Mus. f. 13–15: f. 11, fol. 2v.

Lord, in thy wrath rebuke me not, 676
So let them fly with shame, all who against me rise.
'The Penitential Psalms . . . newly Paraphras'd', Psalm vi.
MS. Rawl. poet. 90, fol. 151v.

Lord in thy wrath rebuke me not, 677
And still the more I sought, the more should lose my way.
Psalm xxxviii, 'newly Paraphras'd'.
MS. Rawl. poet. 90, fol. 153v.

Lord in thy wrath reprove me not 678
To their rebuke and shame.
[Sternhold, Thomas], Psalm vi.
MSS. Rawl. poet. 23, p. 132, two verses, with ref. to John Amner's setting; 112, fol. 70 rev.

Lord, in thy wrath reprove me not, 679
My safety and my stay.
Psalm xxxviii.
MS. *Montagu e. 10, fol. 59.

Lord incline to me thine ear 680
Thou'lt punish them thou'lt comfort me.
Fairfax, Thomas, Lord, Psalm lxxxvi.
MS. *Fairfax 40, p. 204 (autogr.); see also O597*a*.

Lord Jesu Cryst goddes sone on lyve 681
Have mercy on us for thy woundes fyve.
Couplet.
MS. Tanner 407, fol. 17v.

682 Lord Jesus Christ of man's soul the consolation
For thou for my sins hast made full sate.
Forman, Simon, 'Oratio', 1601.
MS. Ashmole 240, fol. 28$^{v}$ (autogr.).

683 Lord judge me and my case
Where congregations meet with thankfulness.
Sidney, Sir Philip, Psalm xxvi.
MSS. *Rawl. poet. 24, p. 33: *25, fol. 19$^{v}$.

684 Lord judge my cause, thy piercing eye
When I and all my hopes on thee rely.
[Sandys, George], Psalm xxvi, 3-part setting by H. Lawes.
Pr. *Paraphrase upon the Divine Poems*, 1638, and H. and W. Lawes, *Choice Psalmes*, 1648.
MS. Mus. Sch. E. 451, p. 32.

685 Lord keep me for I trust in thee, and do confess indeed
Of perfect joy are in thy face, and power for evermore.
[Sternhold, Thomas], Psalm xvi.
MS. Rawl. poet. 112, fol. 67$^{v}$ rev.

686 Lord, lend me tears, as conduits from mine eyes
Lest sin consume, both us, ours, and our city.
Lilliat, John, 'The Church complaynt'.
MS. Rawl. poet. 148, fol. 95$^{v}$ (autogr.).

687 Lord lend thine ear unto my prayer and crying
Shall see their seed established in thy sight.
Harington, Sir John, Psalm cii.
MS. *Douce 361, fol. 60$^{v}$.

688 Lord let not me a worm by thee be shent
Their shameful flying.
Sidney, Sir Philip, Psalm vi.
MSS. *Rawl. poet. 24, p. 6; *25, fol. 4.

689 Lord! let not worldly wisdom, make me wise
And in the want of all things, to abound.
MS. Rawl. poet. 66, fol. 7.

690 Lord let the angels praise thy name.
My God I mean my self.
Herbert, George, 'Misery'.
Pr. *The Temple*, 1633, p. 92.
MS. *Tanner 307, fol. 69$^{v}$.

691 Lord! let thine ear now listen to my muse
So shall my sorrows cease.
Corbet, W., 'In fallentes fratres.' Answered by Y480.
MS. *Rawl. poet. 210, fol. 3.

692 Lord let thy name my safety be
On my malicious foes.
Harington, Sir John, Psalm liv.
MS. *Douce 361, fol. 32.

Lord let thy name my saving succour be 693
Making me see, what I to see, delight.
Herbert, Mary (*née* Sidney), Countess of Pembroke, Psalm liv.
MSS. *Rawl. poet. 24, p. 77: *25, fol. 45$^{v}$.

Lord let thy spirit and thy grace 694
That leads to heaven that leads to thee.
Beddome, Benjamin
MS. *Eng. misc. e. 227, fol. 2$^{v}$.

Lord, like a beating pulse my faint soul goes 695
Panteth for the refreshing rivulet.
Southwell, Sir Robert, Psalm xli. 1.
MS. *Eng. poet. f. 6, fol. 7 (autogr.).

Lord Lofty on a sick bed lies, 696
Her Pug has broke a china jar.
Boswell, James 'Epigram'.
MS. *Douce 193, two copies, fols. 31 and 106$^{v}$ (autogr.).

Lord make me coy and tender to offend: 697
Yet use I not my foes, as I use Thee.
Herbert, George, 'Unkindness'.
Pr. *The Temple*, 1633, p. 86.
MS. *Tanner 307, fol. 64$^{v}$.

Lord make speed to deliver me, 698
Timely relief afford.
Psalm lxx.
MS. *Rawl. C. 113, fol. 50$^{v}$.

Lord my first fruits present themselves to thee; 699
Theirs, who shall hurt themselves, or me, refrain.
Herbert, George, 'The Dedication' of *The Temple*.
Pr. 1633, Sig. ¶4.
MS. *Tanner 307, fol. 1.

Lord my heart was glad when I 700*a*
I will freely spend my blood.
Fairfax, Ferdinando, 2nd Baron, Psalm cxxii.
MS. Fairfax 38, p. 478.

Lord now let my remaining days 700*b*
When this life's ended, to eternity.
Spoure, Edmund, 'Three Petitionary Penitentiall Anthems. 3'.
MS. *Eng. poet. c. 52, fol. 42 (autogr.).

Lord! now my sleep does me forsake 701
Praise father, son and holy Ghost.
[Ken, Thomas], 'A Midnight Hymn'.
A later version pr. *Winchester Manual of Prayers*, 1695, p. 148.
MS. Rawl. D. 361, fol. 326$^{v}$.

Lord of all in earth and heaven 702
Bow before his glorious throne.
Kenton, James.
MS. *Eng. poet. e. 20, p. 211 (autogr.).

703 Lord of hosts and king of glory
All my heart with love inspire.
Kenton, James.
MS. *Eng. poet. e. 20, p. 182 (autogr.).

704 Lord of my help! to thee I make my moan:
Pity might yield) and hid themselves out of my sight.
Knollys, Fra., Psalm lxxxviii.
MS. *Rawl. poet. 60, p. 22 (autogr.).

705 Lord of my life oh may thy praise
With gratitude, and praise.
'A Morning Hymn'.
MS. Eng. poet. e. 47, p. 36.

706 Lord of salvation I have cried
In dark oblivion lost.
Psalm lxxxviii.
MS. *Rawl. C. 113, fol. 62ᵛ.

707 Lord of sweet Helicon, celestial youth
Ulysses' consort has survived to fame.
Gough, Richard, [Epithalamion], incomplete: fair copy of beginning, rough draft of whole.
MS. *Eng. poet. c. 5, fol. 164 (autogr.).

708 Lord of the Sabbath, hear our vows
And sleep in death to rest with God.
Orton, —, 'A Hymn'.
MS. Eng. misc. e. 227, fol. 47.

709 Lord on thee my trust I lie
Thy face from them thou'lt never turn.
Fairfax, Thomas, Lord, Psalm xi.
MS. *Fairfax, 40, p. 23 (autogr.).; see also O596*b*.

710 Lord on thee my trust is grounded
Who this ill to me procure.
Herbert, Mary (*née* Sidney), Countess of Pembroke, Psalm lxxi.
MS. *Rawl. poet. 24, p. 100.

711 Lord open our dull sight, that we may see
Wherein we must repose our hope alone.
MS. *Rawl. poet. 97, fol. 28ᵛ (autogr.).

712 Lord our father's true relation
Mercy may from thrall redeem us.
Herbert, Mary (*née* Sidney), Countess of Pembroke, Psalm xliv.
MSS. *Rawl. poet. 24, p. 63; 117, fol. 265ᵛ rev.

713 Lord our God, how full of glory
All the earth throughout.
Jos. Br., Psalm viii.
MS. Rawl. poet. 61, fol. 12.

Lord Pam in the church (could you think it) kneel'd down, 714
Since God had no hand in his Lordship's promotion.
Swift, Jonathan, 'Epigram . . . On seeing a worthy Prelate [Dr. Hort Bp. of Kilmore] go out of Church . . . to wait on his Grace the D[uke] of D[orset]'.
Pr. *Miscellanies*, iii, 1732, p. 65.
MS. Eng. misc. f. 79, p. 91.

Lord plead my cause against my foes, 715
Sing laud and thanks always.
[Hopkins, John], Psalm xxxv.
MS. Rawl. poet. 112, fol. 62 rev.

Lord plead my cause with those that strive, 716
His praise shall never cease.
Psalm xxxv.
MS. *Rawl. C. 113, fol. 29.

Lord pride doth not exalt my horn 717
For e'er in God let Israel trust.
Fairfax, Thomas, Lord, Psalm cxxxi.
MS. *Fairfax 40, p. 343 (autogr.).
MS. *Fairfax 38, p. 159.

Lord rest not silent, unconcerned 718
Commands the universe.
Psalm lxxxiii.
MS. *Rawl. C. 113, fol. 59ᵛ.

Lord save me, floods o'erwhelm my soul, 719
His chosen may remain.
Psalm lxix.
MS. *Rawl. C. 113, fol. 49ᵛ.

Lord save me from my enemies 720
My zeal to bless the Lord.
Psalm lix.
MS. *Rawl. C 113, fol. 43ᵛ.

Lord save me from the evil man 721
The just shall dwell with thee evermore.
[Norton, Thomas], Psalm cxl.
MS. Rawl. poet. 112, fol. 30ᵛ rev.

Lord save me from those evil men 722
They in his presence dwell.
Psalm xl.
MS. *Rawl. C. 113, fol. 98ᵛ.

Lord save my soul whose settled resolution 723
The princely place of our perpetual pleasance.
Harington, Sir John, Psalm xvi.
MS. *Douce 361, fol. 8ᵛ.

724 Lord shower on us thy grace
May thee and thy salvation know.
[Sandys, George], Psalm lxvii. 3-part setting by H. Lawes.
Pr. *Paraphrase upon the Divine Poems*, 1638, and H. and W. Lawes, *Choice Psalmes*, 1648.
MS. Mus. Sch. E. 451, p. 42.

725 Lord, since I do perceive, how fast my soul
But both the talent and the increase thine.
Fleming, Robert, 'An ejaculation concerning time'.
Pr. *The Mirrour of Divine Love*, 1691, 'Poems', p. 44.
MS. Rawl. poet. 213, fol. 61v (autogr.).

726 Lord the quickening sense bestow
Centres in the Saviour's name.
Kenton, James.
MS. *Eng. poet. e. 20, p. 147 (autogr.).

727 Lord there is need of help and to bewail
The worst above the best of men are set.
Fairfax, Thomas, Lord, Psalm xii.
MS. *Fairfax 40, p. 25 (autogr.); see also W628*b*.

728 Lord, thou art mine, and I am thine,
Or rather make no Thine and mine.
Herbert, George, 'Clasping of hands'.
Pr. *The Temple*, 1633, p. 151.
MS. *Tanner 307, fol. 115.

729 Lord, thou seest to what a number
With thy chosen Israel.
Jos. Br., Psalm iii.
MS. Rawl. poet. 61, fol. 8.

730 Lord thou that in the heavens dost dwell
Their wives soon widows make.
Forman, Simon.
MS. Ashmole 802, fol. 127 (autogr.).

731 Lord thou wast before all time or thought
Stamped on our hearts sealed for thine own.
Fairfax, Thomas, Lord, Psalm xc.
MS. *Fairfax 40, p. 220 (autogr.); see also O647*a*.

732 Lord thou wilt love me; wilt thou not:
When he hath purged all mine ill.
[Harvey, Christopher], 'Resolutions and Assurance'.
Pr. *The Synagogue*, 1647, p. 12.
MS. Rawl. poet. 90, fol. 140.

733 Lord! though Thine indignation none can bear,
To lift themselves; He will in wrath consume.
MS. *Rawl. poet. 97, fol. 13v (autogr.).

Lord thy deserved wrath assuage 734
Before my fainting soul expire.
[Sandys, George], Psalm vi. 3-part setting by W. Lawes.
Pr. *Paraphrase upon the Divine Poems*, 1638, and H. and W. Lawes, *Choice Psalmes*, 1648.
MS. Mus. Sch. E. 451, p. 30.

Lord thy mysterious Providence 735
All gracious and divine.
Kenton, James.
MS. *Eng. poet. e. 20, p. 3 (autogr.).

Lord Thy warning I receive 736
All thy precepts to obey.
Kenton, James.
MS. *Eng. poet. e. 20, p. 174 (autogr.).

Lord to my suit incline thine ear 737
And out of straits thy servant take.
Fairfax, Thomas, Lord, Psalm cxliii.
MS. *Fairfax, 40, p. 369 (autogr.).
MS. *Fairfax 38, p. 449.

Lord to my weakness strength impart 738
In sweet fruition end.
Kenton, James.
MS. *Eng. poet. e. 20, p. 185 (autogr.).

Lord to thee I make my moan 739
Their confidence in him.
[Whittingham, William], Psalm cxxx.
MS. Rawl. poet. 112, fol. 32v rev.

Lord to thee, while I am living 740
When as I mourned.
Da[vison], Fr[ancis], Psalm xxx.
MS. Rawl. poet. 61, fol. 34.

Lord to thy flesh and blood when I repair 741
Reveal my sin and seal my pardon too.
Pestell, Thomas, 'On the Sacrament'.
Pr. *Sermons and Devotions*, 1659, p. 6.
MS. *Malone 14, p. 6.

Lord unto Sion turn thy face 742
Build up thy walls and love it still.
Anthem.
MSS. Mus. Sch. D. 212–16: D. 212, fol. 77v.

Lord Verulam is very lame, the gout of go-out feeling; 743
The hogshead that so late was broach'd, to run so near the lee.
'Sr. Fra. Bacon. L. Verulam. Vicount St. Albons. April 1621 . . . Thought to be done by Mr. [John] Hoskins of Hereford'.
Pr. from this MS., *Life*, etc., of Hoskyns, L. B. Osborn, 1937, p. 210.
MS. Rawl. B. 151, fol. 102v.

744 Lord we to us, no merits claim
But the just his praise shall ever sing.
Fairfax, Thomas, Lord, Psalm cxv.
MS. *Fairfax 40, p. 296 (autogr.); see also D260*a*.

745 Lord Wharton Sarum Hallifax is dead
Not fit for Heaven and too bad for hell.
'All together'.
MS. Rawl. poet. 155, p. 173.

746 Lord, what a sigh was there! Bless the king's ships
He sighs for th' sins he did, but cannot do.
Paman, Clement, 'The Old Courtyers sigh'.
MS. Rawl. poet. 147, p. 65.

747–8 Lord what endowments are inherent
To save Britannia's sinking state.
'The Magpyes', on George II, etc.
MS. Firth b. 4, fol. 49v.

749 Lord, what I once may be none knows, but Thou,
I wonder, I have strength to shiver; now!
'Giles Oldisworth his Ague'.
MS. *Rawl. C. 422, fol. 32 (autogr.).

750 Lord what is man, lost man,
That anthem here which once you sung above.
[Fuller, Bp. William]; Anthem by Purcell.
Pr. *Harmonia Sacra*, Playford, ii, 1693, fol. 1; cf. F. B. Zimmerman, *Purcell*, 1963, no. 192.
MS. Mus. c. 26, fol. 2.

751 Lord what thou hast done long since hath reached our ears
Arise Lord and save thou must do't or naught.
Fairfax, Thomas, Lord, Psalm xliv.
MS. *Fairfax 40, p. 98 (autogr.).
MS. *Fairfax 38, p. 202.

752 Lord what thy servants preach
And when I know approve.
Beddome, Benjamin.
MS. *Eng. misc. e. 227, fol. 46v.

753 Lord! what's come to my mother
Our Jane and our butler does know.
D'Urfey, Thomas, 'A Song in the Bath, or Western Lass, set by Mr. Jeremy Clarke'.
MS. Mus. Sch. C. 95, p. 70.

754 Lord when the sense of thy sweet grace
Dead to my self I live in Thee.
[Crashaw, Richard].
First pr. *Steps to the Temple*, 2nd ed., 1648.
MS. Don. c. 57, fol. 35v, with music.

755 Lord, when the wise men came from far
Then though we do not know we love.
Godolphin, Sidney.
MS. Malone 13, p. 85.

Lord! when thy justice into judgement turns 756
For God hath heard my cry, and granted me my will.
Psalm vi.
MS. Rawl. poet. 170, fol. 39.

Lord, when we leave the world and come to Thee, 757
The light-foot roebuck's not so swift as we.
[Quarles, Francis], 'Our backwardness to Good'.
Pr. *Emblemes*, 1635, I. xiii.
MS. Rawl. poet. 90, fol. 20v.

Lord! when we see the clouds do close 758
Least we go home by Weeping Cross.
Corbet, W.
MS. *Rawl. poet. 210, fol. 15.

Lord when with oppositions here I light 759
Who in thy servants good takes such delight.
Fairfax, Thomas, Lord, Psalm xxxv.
MS. *Fairfax 40, p. 74 (autogr.).
MS. *Fairfax 38, p. 174.

Lord, while I know Thee mine 760
That calls me up to Thee.
Kenton, James.
MS. *Eng. poet. e. 20, p. 239 (autogr.).

Lord while that thy rage doth bide 761
My salvation is in thee.
Sidney, Sir Philip, Psalm xxxviii.
MSS. *Rawl. poet. 24, p. 53; *25, fol. 31v.

Lord while thy just rage is biding 762
In all wretchedness.
Davison, Francis, Psalm vi.
MSS. Rawl. D. 316, fol. 126v, dated 13 July 1612; Rawl. poet. 61, fol. 9, attr. to Fr. Da.

Lord, whilst thy anger's fire, that wastes 763
To their loathed homes return.
J. F., Psalm vi.
MS. *Eng. poet. f. 17, p. 79 (autogr.).

Lord, whilst we travel earth, we in 764
Establish on us, yea establish thou it.
J. F., Psalm xc.
MS. *Eng. poet. f. 17, p. 34 (autogr.).

Lord, who createdst man in wealth and store, 765
Affliction shall advance the flight in me.
Herbert, George, 'Easter Wings'.
Pr. *The Temple*, 1633, p. 34.
MS. *Tanner 307, fol. 26v.

Lord who hast formed me out of mud, 766
That I may run, rise, rest with thee.
Herbert, George, 'Trinity-Sunday'.
Pr. *The Temple*, 1633, p. 59.
MS. *Tanner 307, fol. 46.

767 Lord who is he (which guides his steps so well)
Shall stand secure, and bravely bear the wrack.
Chatwin, John, Psalm xv.
MS. *Rawl. poet. 94, p. 155 (autogr.).

768 Lord who shall sojourn in thy holy place
And in thy sacred mount for ever rest.
Knollys, Fra., Psalm xv.
MS. *Rawl. poet. 60, p. 9 (autogr.).

769 Lord, who shall tread thy sacred courts
When sickening nature melts away.
B[urroughs, Benjamin, of Exeter College, Oxford], Psalm xv, dated 12 Sept. 1734.
MS. Eng. misc. e. 240, p. 29.

770 Lord with what bounty and rare clemency
Defrauding thee, who gavest two for one.
Herbert, George, 'Ungratefulnes'.
Pr. *The Temple*, 1633, p. 74.
MS. *Tanner 307, fol. 56v.

771 Lord with what care hast thou begirt us round?
One cunning bosom-sin blows quite away.
Herbert, George, 'Sinne'.
Pr. *The Temple*, 1633, p. 37.
MS. *Tanner 307, fol. 29.

772 Lord, with what glory wast thou served of old,
The note is sad, yet music for a king.
Herbert, George, 'Sion'.
Pr. *The Temple*, 1633, p. 99.
MS. *Tanner 307, fol. 74v.

773 Lord wouldst thou make my heart more fit
They shall be taught they are but men.
Fairfax, Thomas, Lord, Psalm ix.
MS. *Fairfax 40, p. 17 (autogr.).
MS. *Fairfax 38, p. 130.

774 [Lordings if ye] Lordyngges yff ye wyll herk and dwell
God ȝif us grace well to fare. Amen.
MS. Rawl. poet. 34, fol. 10v.

775 Lordly gallants tell me this
I shall be as brave as you.
[Wither, George].
Pr. *Faire-Virtue*, 1622, Sig. M8v.
MS. Eng. poet. c. 50, fol. 35v.

776 Lords of this land and makers of our laws
Or else his hoof will hurt both head and heart.
Two poems, first and last lines the same: I. 'An Admonition to the Parlament, 1588, made by a frantick foole to beware of Martin [Marprelate]'. II, 'An answere to the forsayd admotion and slaunderous lib[el] made agaynst Martyn. 1589', against Whitgift. The first pr. *Mar-Martine*, Bodl. 4° C 69 Th.
MS. Rawl. C. 849, fol. 396v.

Lorellus, by the law condemned to die, 777
Mean while Lorellus must to Tiburne range.
MS. Tanner 465, fol. 94v.

Lorn birds! whose simple minstrelsy the last 778
Alas too oft the cruel bosom lies!
Polwhele, [Richard], of Kenton, 'Sonnet 11 The Redbreasts'.
Pr. *Pictures from Nature*, Sonnet xv.
MS. Eng. misc. e. 241, fol. 115v.

Lorrain [he] you stole by fraud [he] you got Burgundy 779
Holland you bought my God you'll pay for't one day.
Couplet, translating Latin distich on Louis XIV.
MSS. Eng. poet. c. 25, fol. 75; Sancroft 53, p. 39, attr. to the E. of Rochester; Tanner 89, fol. 261v, attr. to the Earl of Rochester; see also Y292.

Lose no time nor youth but be 780
In thy sweet be gathered then.
Pr. *Mysteries of Love & Eloquence*, E[dward] P[hillips], 1658.
MSS. Don. c. 57, fol. 17v, music by John Wilson; Mus. b. 1, fol. 39v, music by Wilson.

Losing my way through darkness of the mist 781
Though he had Argus, and ten Argus eyes.
H.S.
MS. *Rawl. poet. 120, fol. 3v (autogr.).

Lost in a troubled sea of griefs I float 782
Where it for ever shall at anchor lie.
C[arew], T[homas], 'To his Mrs in absence. A Shipp'.
Pr. *Poems*, 1640.
MS. Eng. poet. c. 50, fol. 71v; see also T3295.

Lost is my love farewell adieu 783
Nay my love nay, farewell adieu.
MS. Ashmole 176, fol. 99.

Loud the glad triumphant strain 784
Dread foe to despot power, but champion of the laws.
Gray, Thomas, of New College, at the installation of the Duke of Portland as Chancellor, 4 July 1793.
MSS. Add. A. 272, fol. 39; Top. Oxon. d. 163, fol. 272v.

[Louis] Louys *le Grand,* for all his triumphs past 785
The monarch's a— is made the seat of war.
On Louis XIV, translation from Latin.
MS. Lat. misc. e. 19, fol. 123.

786 Lounging, sleeping, drinking, fiddling.
Thus he lives and thus he'll die. Farewell Neighbour Jerry.

'Jerry's Garland or two new songs to the tune of the Rakes of Mallow. Song the 1st by I.P. The Grammatical Poet'.
MS. Eng. poet. c. 41, fol. 75.

787 Love a thousand sweets distilling
Lest occasion slip away.

Shirley, James.
Pr. *Poems*, 1646, as the second verse of M278.
MS. *Rawl. poet. 88, p. 16.

788 Love acts on me a cruel wanton part.
Hymen my doctor be, the medicine you.

MS. Top. London. e. 9, p. 142.

789 Love and disdain dwells in my mistress' eyes
Will you not mourn at my sad obsequy.

Pr. John Wilson's *Cheerfull Ayres or Ballads*, 1660, p. 34.
MS. Mus. b. 1, fol. 42$^{v}$, music by Wilson.

790 Love and gay hope shall never part
Nor ought she to disdain it.

Middleton, Lady Elizabeth, song, music by W. Davis, composer's autograph.
MS. Mus. c. 16, fol. 115.

791 Love and obedience are a debt we owe
The heavens ever with thy praises fill.

Williams, John.
MS. *Rawl. poet. 184, fol. 1$^{v}$ (autogr.).

792 Love, any devil else but you
Racked carcasses make ill anatomies.

Donne, John.
Pr. *Poems*, 1633.
MS. *Eng. poet. e. 99, fol. 118$^{v}$; *f. 9, p. 101.

793 Love as 'tis said doth work with such strange tools,
Love with his toys, and tools, I shall despise.

'On [Love].'
Pr. *Wits Recreations*, 1663, Ep. 337.
MS. Eng. poet. d. 152, fol. 106$^{v}$.

794 Love at the first did fill the creation
In taking away that for which we had blame.

'An Hymne'.
MS. Rawl. poet. 37, p. 40.

795 Love bad me welcome, yet my soul drew back
So I did sit and eat.

Herbert, George, 'Love'.
Pr. *The Temple*, 1633, p. 182.
MS. *Tanner 307, fol. 139$^{v}$.

Love, brave virtue's younger brother 796
Love shall live, although he die.

Crashaw, Richard, 'Loves Horoscope'.
MS. Tanner 465, fol. 45, attr. to R.Cr.; attr. on fol. 1*a* to Mr. Crashaw.

Love bred of [on] glances, 'twixt amorous eyes 797
Angels are guests and dance at this blest wedding.

'Cant. 20'.
See Grierson's *Poems of Donne*, 1912, i. 450.
MS. Don. d. 58, fol. 27; *Eng. poet. f. 9, p. 8, attr. to J. D.; Mus. b. 1, fol. 86$^{v}$, with music by John Wilson; Rawl. poet. 117, fol. 222$^{v}$ rev., attr. to Dunne.

Love built a stately house, where Fortune came, 798
And built a braver palace then before.

Herbert, George, 'The World'.
Pr. *The Temple*, 1633, p. 76.
MS. *Tanner 307, fol. 58.

Love cease tormenting 799
Doth not enclose a heart of stone, or flinty.

Pr. Thomas Tomkin's *Songs*, 1622, vi.
MSS. Mus. f. 17–19: f. 19, fol. 6$^{v}$.

Love chilled with cold and missing in the skies 800
So soft is all of fire and ice composed.

In B.M. MS. Egerton 2013, fol. 25$^{v}$, with music by H. Lawes.
MSS. Don. c. 57, fol. 61, with music by H. Lawes; Eng. poet. c. 50, fol. 117$^{v}$.

Love compared to a game at tables; where the die 801
Do what you can they will be bearing men.

[Ayton, Sir Robert], 'Love compared to a game at tables'.
MS. Eng. poet. e. 14, fol. 89$^{v}$ rev.; see also L823, L880.

Love conquers sense and blinds the lover's eyes 802
But a blind error full of bitter pain.

'Eclog. the 1st Baptistae Mantuani. Love Describ'd'.
MS. *Rawl. poet. 197, fol. 10$^{v}$ (autogr.).

Love does transform a man and makes 803
And drop into th'abyss.

Tipping, William, 'Of Love. The Nature of Love'.
MS. *Rawl. poet. 101, fol. 30 (autogr.).

Love every man, owe no man grudge 804
Come come oh Christ come soon they say.

MS. Gough Norfolk 43, fol. 40$^{v}$.

Love fare thee well thy charms are o'er 805
To put his fetters on again.

'A Copy of Verses'.
MS. Montagu e. 13, fol. 142$^{v}$.

806 Love freely shows it self, unasked, unsought.
What comes unasked comes with a free good will.
Robinson, Robert.
MS. *Rawl. poet. 218, p. 110 (autogr.).

807 Love give me leave to serve thee and be wise
All other love is to your sex not you.
R[andolph], T[homas], 'A true Mrs.'
Pr. *Poems*, 1638, p. 51.
MSS. Ashmole 47, fol. 67ᵛ; Firth e. 4, p. 40, attr. to T. R.; Rawl. poet. 152, fol. 210; Tanner 306, fol. 425.

808 Love grown proud would govern me
I must joy in not removing.
MS. Mus. b. 1, fol. 18, music by John Wilson.

809 Love has some faults in fashion now
Values one star above a starred sky.
MS. Rawl. poet. 116, fol. 52ᵛ.

810 Love hath two divers wings, as lovers say;
Therefore the last, love, only use for me.
'On Love.'
Pr. *Wits Recreations*, 1663, Ep. 336.
MS. Eng. poet. d. 152, fol. 106ᵛ.

811 Love, how unequal are thy laws
And it's too late to leave it.
Sedley, Sir Charles, 'The perplexed Lover to his Cruel mistress'.
MS. Rawl. poet. 173, fol. 72.

812 Love I must tell thee, I'll no longer be
To free his neck from all prerogative,
[Brome, Alexander], 'Love's Anarchy'.
Pr. *Poems*, 1661, p. 12.
MS. Ashmole 47, fol. 140.

813 Love if a god thou art, then evermore
Heal me like her, or else wound her like me.
[Davison, Francis], Song.
Pr. *Poetical Rhapsody*, 1602, the first of the madrigals; Robert Jones, *First set of Madrigals*, 1607, v; and *Wits Recreations*, 1640, 467.
MS. Mus. Sch. F. 575, p. 4, with melody and lute accompaniment; Rawl. poet. 153, fol. 21ᵛ.

814 Love, if't would last it were a choice delight:
If not? 'tis so, if we'd forget it quite.
Ashmole, Elias, 'Love'. Couplet, 10 April 1648.
MSS. Ashmole 36, 37, fol. 229ᵛ (autogr.).

815 Love in thy youth fair maid be wise
And I too late shall sorrow.
Pr. W. Porter's *Madrigales and Ayres*, 1632, xix; and with music by William Webbe in *Catch that catch can*, 1652, p. 69.
MSS. Ashmole 38, p. 141; Mus. b. 1, fol. 33ᵛ, with music by John Wilson.

Love, into Chloe's chamber came 816
Oh!—oh!—who then would die a maid!
[Bacon, Phanuel], 'To [Chloe]—occasion'd by A Dream of Hers which she told to a Lady'.
MS. Eng. poet. e. 45, fol. 57 (autogr.).

Love is a bond (bring me that firm bond hither) 817
Of other ties there needs not any more.
Robinson, Robert.
MS. *Rawl. poet. 218, p. 171 (autogr.).

Love is a boy, and subject to the rod 818
But a mad brain's imaginary toy.
'Cupid'.
Pr. *Wits Recreations*, 1663, Ep. 346.
MS. Eng. poet. d. 152, fol. 106ᵛ.

Love is a boy by poets styled 819
Then spare the rod and spile the child.
Couplet.
MS. Rawl. poet. 153, fol. 30ᵛ.

Love is a fervent fancy in youth 820
In ancient dolts dotage.
[Price, E. (?) ], 'The description of love in yonge men, in men of myddell age, and in ould men'.
MS. Douce 290, fol. 91ᵛ, in E. Price's hand.

Love is a fiend, a fire, a heaven, a hell 821
Where pleasure, pain, grief, and repentance dwell.
'The definision of love', couplet.
MS. Eng. poet. e. 14, fol. 14.

Love is a fire, flies higher and higher 822
Till it be quenched with an equal desire.
Couplet.
MS. Rawl. poet. 153, fol. 20.

Love is a game at tables where the die 823
Do what you can they will be bearing men.
[Ayton, Sir Robert], 'On Love'.
Ascribed to Ayton in the two authoritative MSS., B.M. Add. 10308 and 28622; to Strode in B.M. MS. Harley 6931, fol. 35ᵛ (hence (?) also by Dobell). Pr. *Wits Interpreter*, 1655, Poems, p. 275.
MSS. CCC. 328, fol. 26ᵛ; Don. d. 58, fol. 37ᵛ; Rawl. poet. 206, p. 76; see also L801, L880.

Love is a mystery which no man can unfold 824
To be with one beloved, a man would choose to die.
Tipping, William, 'Of Love'.
MS. *Rawl. poet. 101, fol. 17 (autogr.).

Love is a senseless inclination 825
Never adored his beauty, but in hopes to make him kind.
Duet.
MS. Mus. Sch. C. 97, fol. 13 rev. at end.

826 Love is a sin love is a shame
But lust Sir Cutt shall feel his rod.
'Alas that ever Love was sinne: Cut: Halsall. writt in a window at Lichfield by severall persons'.
MS. Eng. poet. c. 50, fol. 36v.

827 Love is a spirit all compact of fire
Not dull to sink, but light and will aspire.
Couplet.
MS. Rawl. poet. 117, fol. 276v rev.

828 Love is in progress and his gifts doth lay
Abound all joys, there bides he during pleasure.
'Loves progresse'.
MS. Rawl. poet. 210, fol. 45v.

829 Love is like Justice represented blind,
Because it slights the things it should not mind.
Williams, John, couplet on 'Love is Blind'.
MS. *Rawl. poet. 191, fol. 98v (autogr.).

830 Love is lost nor can his mother
That though it shine, 'tis fire and will consume.
'Love's Hue and Cry'.
MS. Eng. poet. d. 152, fol. 98.

831 Love is now become a trade
A night a purchase for the poor.
Pr. *The Theater of Music*, i. 1685, music by H. Purcell. F. B. Zimmerman, *Purcell*, 1963, no. 393.
MS. Rawl. poet. 196, fol. 13.

832 Love is sickness full of woe
If not enjoyed, sighing cries, Hey, ho?
'Of love'.
MS. Eng. poet. e. 14, fol. 20.

833 Love is the balsam of the soul,
'Cause triumphs, raptures, ecstasies.
'The excellence of Divine Love'.
MS. *Don. f. 5, fol. 5.

834 Love is the fire that burns me,
Whose light should still relieve me.
Pr. Tho: Bateson's *Second Set of Madrigals*, 1618, i.
MSS. Mus. f. 17–19: f. 19, fol. 10v.

835 Love is the nimble gaoler of the mind
And then t'will prove our prison to be free.
Reresby, Sir John, 'A Song'.
MS. Rawl. D. 204, fol. 84 rev. (autogr.).

836 Love is the noblest passion of mind;
And think my winged charioteer was love.
Morrice, John, 'In laudem amoris'. *c.* 15 Aug. 1707.
MS. *Rawl. poet. 114, fol. 52 (autogr.).

Love is well known to be a grace. 837
Ne'er will go out no never.
Tipping, William.
MS. *Rawl. poet. 101, fol. 36v (autogr.).

Love justice honour here 838
Most renowned in their ends.
On Francis Fitzherbert, d. 13 Jan. 1619/20, Tissington Church, Derbyshire.
MS. Ashmole 854, fol. 54v.

Love led by faith, and fed with hope is able 839
Extremely heavy, love will make most light.
'A verse on divine Love.'
MS. Rawl. poet. 213, fol. 57v.

Love like a chemist can extract 840
Both run away if once they use their sight.
Reresby, Sir John, 'On Caelia's telling me of my faults a Sonnet.'
MS. Rawl. D. 204, fol. 97v rev. (autogr.).

Love looks not with the eyes but with the mind 841
And therefore is winged Cupid painted blind.
Couplet.
MS. Rawl. poet. 117, fol. 156v rev.

Love, love thou art best of human joys 842
Whate'er philosophers dispute.
Winchilsea, Anne, Lady.
Pr. *Miscellany Poems*, 1713, p. 270.
MS. Rawl. poet. 196, fol. 44v.

Love, Madam, is not yet so blind 843
But not of mine in love with you.
Williams, John, 'To a Lady saying Love is blind'.
MS. *Rawl. poet. 191, fol. 158 (autogr.).

Love me not for comely grace 844
To dote upon me ever.
Pr. John Wilbye's *Second Set of Madrigales*, 1609, xii.
MSS. Douce 280, fol. 66*a*; Eng. poet. e. 97, p. 156; see also L847.

Love, nature's plot, this great creation's soul, 845
A life, a fortune, all, to serve a friend.
[Philips, Katherine], 'A Friend'.
Pr. *Poems*, 1664, p. 189.
MSS. Rawl. poet. 90, fol. 7v; 173, fol. 102v.

Love! no, I am not such a foe 846
Laugh and drink sack with me.
[Jordan, Thomas], 'A song'. Subscribed 'In Gamball's Ayres' [and Dialogues, 1659].
Pr. Jordan's *Claraphil and Clarinda*, Sig. C8v.
MS. Rawl. poet. 84, fol. 43.

847 Love not me for comely grace
To dote upon me ever.
MS. Mus. b. 1, fol. 17, music by John Wilson; see also L844.

848 Love not that love that is a child and blind
That with your days your joys may multiply.
Davies, [Sir] John, 'Epithalamion . . . [15]95 Jan:' for William Stanley, Earl of Derby and the Lady Elisabeth de Vere, d. of Edward, 17th Earl of Oxford.
MS. *Add. B. 97, fol. 49.

849 Love now no fire hath left him
And so in mutual names of love burn both together.
MS. Mus. b. 1, fol. 138$^{v}$, music by John Wilson.

850 Love oft is taken for blind Cupid's game
So is all love that's only but in name.
Couplet.
MS. Rawl. poet. 172, fol. 8.

851 Love, or do not say you do
Will not lie unless with you.
'Of love.'
MS. Eng. poet. e. 14, fol. 82 rev.; see also S103.

852 Love, piety and sacred knowledge lie
His will appear the whitest soul of all.
On George Hatton, 2nd son of Sir Robert Hatton, d. 1630, buried at Hoginton. Pr. by G. C. Moore Smith, *Palaestra*, xlviii, 1925, p. 249, as possibly by T. Randolph.
MS. Top. Cambr. c. 1, three copies, fols. 107$^{v}$, 124, and 158.

853 Love quench this heat consuming
A heart of ice in breast of snow contained.
Madrigal.
Pr. *Musica Transalpina*, ii. 1597, music by Benedetto Palavacino
MSS. Mus. Sch. D. 233–6: D. 236, fol. 104 rev.

854 Love said to Reason 'know my power
I triumph in my turn.
Robinson, Mrs. [Mary], 'Lines'.
MS. Percy d. 9, fol. 16.

855 Love she inspires into all that see
But when she speaks, set all her lovers free.
Williams, John, 'Another . . . on a lady of an unpleasant conversation'. Couplet.
MS. *Rawl. poet. 191, fol. 6$^{v}$ (autogr.).

856 Love sick all o'er and little lack of dead
You only give not life, but keep back death.
MS. Eng. poet. c. 50, fol. 115$^{v}$.

Love, spite of honour's dictates, gave thee breath; 857
Honour, in spite of love, pronounc'd thy death.
Couplet on 'Bastard Child murdered by its Mother', with Latin distich.
MS. Top. gen. e. 32, fol. 48.

Love that great workman hath a new world made 858
But fruitless, though my spring be full of flowers.
E. M., 'A Lover Comparing himself to a world New-made done out of ffrench'.
Pr. *Poems of Pembroke and Ruddier*, 1660, p. 111.
MS. Rawl. poet. 160, fol. 103.

Love that long since hast to thy mighty power 859
Thence forth they plain, and make full piteous moan/Unto . . . (incomplete).
'An hymne in honour of love'.
MS. Ashmole 420, fol. 370 rev.

Love, the sweet sickness of the heart 860
And for a mistress hug a post.
Vyse, William, [Archd. of Salop (?)], 'A Valentine to a Physician'.
MS. Eng. poet. c. 51, p. 82.

Love thee? No shouldst thou fall into a trance 861
All, all but thee. 'Way fool and tempt no more.
'An Answere to the former Paper [I590], by Mr. Womack'.
MS. Rawl. poet. 147, p. 158.

Love thou hast forced me from all forms 862
Where hallelujahs, we do sing.
Headed, 'mackbeth . . . W. R.'
MS. Rawl. poet. 37, p. 15.

Love thy bright monarchy I now defy 863
They are false lights to me if not lik'd best.
MS. Mus. b. 1, fol. 129$^{v}$, music by John Wilson.

Love thy country, wish it well 864
Full perfection shall begin.
Bubb, George, Lord Melcombe, 'Ode'. Transcript of a copy sent to Dr. Young, 27 Oct. 1761, 'to be left among those of your Papers, which may possibly see the Light by a posthumous Publication'.
MS. Malone 26, fol. 161.

Love unreturned, how e'er the flame 865–6
The most wished monument.
Godolphin, S[idney], 'Constancye'.
MS. Malone 13, p. 5.

Love with the tresses of thy chestnut hair 867
Oh cruel stars which me such fortune gave.
Sonnet.
MS. Eng. poet. c. 50, fol. 84.

868 Love would discharge the duty of his heart
Bids silence sigh, that tongue cannot express.
Pr. Tho: Bateson's *First Set of Madrigals*, 1604, ii.
MSS. Mus. f. 17–19: f. 19, fol. 24v.

869 Loved I am, and yet complain of love
Let me be loved or else not loved be.
Sidney, Sir Philip, from the *Arcadia*.
MS. *e Mus. 37, fol. 64.

870 Lovely charmer, dearest creature
None could e'er be more beloved.
[Motteux, Peter], 'A Song in the Island Princess [1699, p. 12] set by Mr. Daniel Purcell'.
Pr. *Twelve New Songs*, 1699.
MSS. Mus. Sch. C. 95, p. 60, music by D. Purcell; E. 397, p. 91 rev., music by D. Purcell.

871 Lovely Delia, look and see
Charmer dear, if thou'lt be mine.
'The Invitation to a Lady in Town, On Valentine's Day, from a Gentleman in the Country'.
MS. *Eng. poet. d. 47, fol. 124.

872 Lover of scornful nymphs oh Faunus wild
And on the ground doth dance the careless clown.
W. A., translator, Horace, *Odes* III. xviii.
MS. *Rawl. poet. 104, fol. 30v (autogr.).

873 Love's a dream of mighty treasure,
Changing happy to be wise.
'Song.'
Pr. Gildon's *Miscellany Poems upon Several Occasions*, 1692, p. 68, headed 'Song: By Tho. Ch—, Esq.'
MSS. Firth c. 16, p. 253; Rawl. poet. 116, fol. 113.

874 Love's a gentle generous passion
Of the blissful state above.
MS. Eng. misc. b. 48, fol. 77.

875 Love's a tyrant, serious, grave,
But he that laughs may laugh at love.
'It is a certain rule that wit and passion are inconsistant. Hume's Essays'.
MS. Eng. misc. e. 240, fol. 62.

876 Love's a tyrant where it reigns
The other drives into despair.
'Song.'
MS. Rawl. poet. 152, fol. 165v.

877 Love's an affection has a thousand eyes
That love is blind though none so blind as they.
Williams, John, 'Upon Love is Blind'.
MS. *Rawl. poet. 191, fol. 97v (autogr.).

Love's arrows often do recoil 878
And virgins kissed it as they bled.
Palmer, Francis, of Christ Church, 'upon the death of [William] Cartwright, and his poems', 1643.
MS. Eng. misc. f. 49, fol. 52v rev.

Love's gentle sallies charm at first, but all 879
But briny waves pollute the amorous flood.
Morrice, John, 'Of Venus'. Owens's *Epigrams* I. xiii.
MS. *Rawl. poet. 114, fol. 163 (autogr.).

Love's like a game at tables where the die 880
Do what you can they will be bearing men.
[Ayton, Sir Robert], 'Of womens loves'.
MSS. Douce f. 5, fol. 9v; Eng. poet. e. 97, p. 54; f. 25, fol. 20v; Rawl. poet. 116, fol. 57; 117, fol. 32v; see also L801, L823.

Love's queen was conceived in the foamy froth 881
Hold the thing will away.
Mervall, Alphonso, 'Instructions for a servante'. Subscribed 'Tettix'.
MS. *Rawl. poet. 166, p. 41 (autogr.).

Love's tyrant power again I own 882
But who can love you more?
MS. Malone 41, fol. 50.

Loving, beloved, in all relations true, 883
The social virtues of this honest man.
On a tomb, 'Incerti . . . Alresford Hants'.
MS. Top. gen. e. 32, fol. 97v.

Low at thy feet oh God I fall 884
And bid a dying sinner live.
Beddome, Benjamin; cf. *Hymns . . . of B. Beddome*, 1818, no. 427.
MS. *Eng. misc. e. 227, fol. 54.

Lucas and Lisle! I see them both dubbed thrones 885
And levelling rebellion with the ground.
Proby, H[enry], 'On Sir Charles Lucas, and Sir George L'isle, murthered by the Rebells at Colchester', 28 August 1648.
MS. Rawl. poet. 62, fol. 19v.

Lucifer through pride fell from the sky 886
Is the way down, and not the way to mount.
Endorsed, 'Verses of my lord of essex first falt to the queene'.
MS. Rawl. poet. 170, fol. 1.

Lucina help nor are our clamours less 887
Give us a Venus, yet be Venus still.
Winnard, Thomas, fellow of St. John's College, Oxford, 1640–8, on the birth of Sir Robert Sherley's child, Seymour, b. 23 Jan. 1646/7.
MS. Rawl. poet. 65, fol. 54v.

888 Lucinda's all my soul's delight
She's ever new and never cloys.
'Song'.
MS. Rawl. poet. 152, fol. 143.

889 Lucretia blushed, and laid my book
Brutus be gone, she'll read.
Translation of Martial, *Epigrams* XI. xvi. 9, 10.
MS. Rawl. poet. 212, fol. 85.

890 Lucus long locks upon his shoulders wears
And why he dares not cut them off for his ears.
Couplet, 'upon Long hair'.
MS. CCC. 328, fol. 44.

891 Luke from the body's cure, the Lord translateth
As is the body by the soul surmounted.
Clifford, Henry, Earl of Cumberland, 'Saint Luke'.
MS. *Rawl. poet. 95, fol. 35v.

892 Lulla-babye, sleep be quiet
Lullaby baby lulla lulla by.
'A lullabye to Care'.
MS. Ashmole 38, p. 111.

893 Lure falconers lure
Then long too late we falconers cry, hey lo.
'A 5 Voc. Tho: Ravenscroft. . . Comedians modulation', a different version from that by John Bennet in Ravenscroft's *A Briefe Discourse* . . . 1614.
MSS. Mus. f. 11–15: f. 11, fol. 41v.

Luscus thy cock doth tread thy neighbour's hen. 894
But erelong they may prove cock o'th' game.
'In Gallinam Lusci uxorem.'
MS. Eng. poet. e. 14, fol. 64v.

Lust of a tree brought sin and death on all: 895
Of the Lords wisdom and His love to men.
MS. *Rawl. poet. 97, fol. 17v (autogr.).

Luxuriant with perennial green 896
And know a myrtle from a bramble.
Pye, —, of Farringdon, Berks., 1778, 'The myrtle and the bramble—a Fable. MS.'
MS. Eng. misc. e. 241, fol. 68v.

Lyce although she meets me in the park 897
For my desire is ne'er to see her more.
'Upon Lyce.'
MS. Malone 9, fol. 28v.

Lycus *see* Licus.

Lydgate *see* Lidgate.

Lydia, in heaven's name, 898–9
Should him to manly deeds betray?
Fanshawe, Sir Richard, translator, 'To Lydia', Horace, *Odes* III. vii.
MS. *Firth c. 1, p. 38.

Lying and cheating 900
Ungodly men to devour.
'The Dissenters Liberty of Conscience'.
MS. Rawl. poet. 197, fol. 4v (autogr. (?)).

# M

ENTRIES 1–985

1 *Ma chere Madame*
*Altoos gy qyt de best des verowan.*
Skinner, John, Macaronics to 'Madame de Veer a Noordwyk. July 2d 1789'.
MS. *Eng. poet. d. 22, fol. 25.

2 Mackay! what! that great, that noble name
Brave soldier, christian, subject, man and friend.
Fleming, Robert, 'An Elegy to the Memory of Lieutennant General Mackay . . . 1692'.
MS. *Rawl. poet. 202, fol. 5$^{v}$ (autogr.).

3 Macrinus, let this day appear,
To wash away night's lust.
Morrice, John, translator, part of the second satyr of Persius. 24 June 1705.
MS. *Rawl. poet. 114, fol. 152 (autogr.).

4 Mad paper stay; and grudge not here to burn
Would fain love him that shall be loved of her.
Donne, John.
Pr. *Poems*, 1633.
MS. *Eng. poet. f. 9, p. 114.

5 Madam, accept these voted flowers whose birth
And took this label from the mouth of fame.
Codrington, Robert, 'An Elegie to the Memory of Henry O'Bryen Earle of Thomond etc.', April 1639.
MS. Rawl. poet. 96, fol. 1$^{v}$.

6 Madam! although I cannot think my verse
But pray for him who with you here remains.
'To the Lady Naper Upon the death of her childe'.
MS. Rawl. poet. 84, fol. 97 rev.

*7a* Madam, although the sun's bright ray
Which you have made renowned.
Barnes, Joseph, 'The Canary-Bird's Song. Sept. 18. 1697'.
MS. Hearne's diaries 11, p. 139.

*7b* Madam, and friend, for truth must call you so
If look on virtue, truth, then look on you.
Cavendish, Lady Jane, 'On a Noble Lady'.
MS. *Rawl. poet. 16, p. 18.

Madam as in some climes the warmer sun 8
A dart as white, a ball of new fallen snow.
Waller, Edmund. Subscribed R. Waller.
Pr. *Poems*, 1645, p. 175, without subscription; 'From a Child' in *Poems*, 3rd ed., 1668, p. 89.
MS. *Don. d. 55, fol. 21$^{v}$.

Madam be cover'd why stand you bare 9
For open breast breeds secret horns.
'A song'.
MSS. Eng. poet. e. 14, fol. 19$^{v}$; Rawl. poet. 153, fol. 12; 160, fol 156$^{v}$.

Madam by us the genial gods do greet you 10
As the first day the marriage torch did burn.
'Verses spoken by the two daughters of the truly vertuous Mrs. Br: Sk: at the solemnization of the Annuall Nuptialls of the Right Noble Sr R. Cooke and his Lady Theophila'.
MS. Firth e. 4, p. 128.

Madam D'angloyse me tell you very true 11
A man in the world tat have so much shoye.
Dialogue between a Spaniard and an Englishwoman.
MS. Rawl. poet. 108, fol. 12.

Madam: due thanks are lodged within my breast 12
But may your heart keep Christmas all the year.
Strode, William, 'To the Lady Knighton'.
MS. *CCC. 325, fol. 80 (autogr.), incomplete.
MS. Eng. poet. e. 97, p. 139, attr. to W. S.

Madam! Forgive the zeal of him that dares 13
To a high place in Heaven and nigh to her.
'Verses Spoken to hir Royall Highness the Dutches of York in new Colledge Chappell. Oxon.' [by Francis Turner (?), 29 Sept. 1663]. See Wood, *Life and Times* ed. A. Clark, i, O.H.S. xix, 1891, p. 498.
MS. Rawl. poet. 19, fol. 87.

Madam, had all antiquity been lost 14
I' your self, all treasure lost before.
[Jonson, Ben.], [To Mary Lady Wroth], *Epigrammes*, cv.
MS. Don. e. 6, fol. 23$^{v}$.

15 **Madam I cannot but congratulate**
**There's no such thing as leading apes in hell.**
Lines on marriage.
MSS. Eng. misc. c. 292, fol. 110, single sheet addressed to Mrs. Susannah Hulett, dated Bristol, 19 Jan. 1732/3; Firth c. 15, p. 335.

16 **Madam I find (if fame believed may be)**
**As having caused a second Troy to burn.**
Walsh, William, 'Hiarbas to Dido'.
MS. Malone 9, fol. 12$^{v}$ (autogr.).

17 **Madam I here desire for to set forth**
**Think well of them 'cause they speak well of thee.**
'Praefatiuncula ad Amicam'.
MS. Rawl. poet. 194, fol. 29.

18 **Madam, I know you but as vulgars know**
**You when I now but view by deputy.**
Harvey, John, 'To the Lady Darell'.
MS. Rawl. poet. 210, fol. 58.

19–20 **Madam I loathe the censurers of the town**
**Is what knaves invent the fools believe.**
'Letter to my Lady Osborne 1688'.
MSS. Eng. poet. c. 18, fol. 65; e. 49, p. 36.

21 **Madam I once presumed to write**
**'Till he has sucked thy buttocks less.**
'The Ladys Case: Or a letter from an Injur'd Wife beyond sea to a Munster Crack . . . August 1721'.
MS. Eng. misc. c. 116, fol. 12$^{v}$, marked R. C.

22 **Madam, I pray give leave in this**
**Take him whose eyes speaks him not weak.**
Cavendish, Lady Jane, 'On a Noble Lady'.
MS. *Rawl. poet. 16, p. 18.

23 **Madam, I thank your bounty which thinks fit**
**And you will shirt me to eternity.**
Weaver, Thomas, 'To a Lady that promis'd him a winding-sheete'.
Pr. *Songs and Poems*, 1654.
MS. *Rawl. poet. 211, fol. 23$^{v}$ (autogr.).

24 **Madam I would but praise, not flatter, yet**
**I am the first drew truth to poetry.**
[Felltham, Owen], 'To his Mrs.'
Pr. *Resolves*, 1661, 'Lusoria', p. 5.
MS. Firth e. 4, p. 69, attr. to T. R.

25 **Madam, In vain you strive to cheat our sight,**
**And easier lay than represent the devil.**
Hall, Henry, Organist of Hereford Cathedral, 'To a Lady, that pretended to be a Ghost'.
MS. Eng. poet. f. 13, fol. 193.

**Madam intending to have tried** 26
**Nor that to one more noble write.**
Waller, Edmund, 'To a Ladie from whome hee receiv'd a Silver Penn'.
Pr. *Poems*, 1645, p. 62.
MSS. *Don. d. 55, fol. 5; Eng. poet. c. 50, fol. 124$^{v}$; *Rawl. poet. 174, p. 58.

**Madam, I've heard how surly knight,** 27
**I'll make the knight of Coventry look bluely.**
'Captain Charletons letter to Mrs. Palavicini upon Sr C. H. whiping her B.'.
Pr. *New Collection of Poems relating to State Affairs*, 1705, p. 567.
MSS. Tanner 306, fol. 480; Top. Oxon. c. 108, p. 33.

**Madam look out, your title is arraign'd** 28
**And restoration is the consequence.**
'To the Queen. 1710 (?)'.
Published 5 April, 1710, and in *Poems for and against Dr. Sacheverell*, 1710, iii. 22.
Pr. bk. Firth b. 21, fol. 72.

**Madam, new years may well expect to find** 29
**The princely burthen to the Gallick shore.**
Waller, Edmund, 'To the Lady Morton who carried away the Princesse [Henrietta Maria, 1646], sent her on New years day'.
First pr. as a broadside, 1661.
MSS. Locke e. 17, p. 78, attr. to Waller, with an extra couplet after line 32; Rawl. poet. 84, fol. 114 rev.

**Madam of all the sacred muse inspired** 30
**May guard us better, than from Carlisle's beams.**
Waller, Edmund, 'The Country to the Countess of Carlisle'.
Pr. *Poems*, 1645, p. 26.
MSS. *Don. d. 55, fol. 21, *Rawl. poet. 174, p. 28.

**Madam Olimpia rideth in her coach** 31
**By Eno's fair offspring till he be dead.**
Libel on Edward Coke and his second wife Lady Elizabeth Hatton, *c.* 1598.
MS. Don. c. 54, fol. 6$^{v}$.

**Madam, once more the obsequious muse,** 32
**Kind as the blessings you bestow.**
Poultney, [William, Earl of Bath (?)], 'To the Queen going to Bed'. Christ Church 26 Aug. 1702.
MS. Eng. poet. f. 13, fol. 183$^{v}$.

**Madam; or sure your soul is masculine** 33
**Yet then shall know that I do know them too.**
Pestell, Thomas, 'To the Lady Visc. Beaumont at Buxton' i.e. Bridget Monson, wife of Sapcot Beaumont.
MS. *Malone 14, p. 20.

34 **Madam, pray cast those glittering stones away,**
**More fit for your use, and yours for me.**
'To a Lady weareing Rich Pendants'.
MS. Add. A. 301, fol. 15[v] rev.

35 **Madam, since chance has so auspicious been**
**Yet what I cannot reach, I must admire.**
K. N. [or J. M.]: heading in code means 'Presenting a Gift to a Valentine'.
MS. Add. B. 106, fol. 28[v].

36 **Madam since fortune does design**
**Madam to you, the fairest maid of Kent.**
Spoure, Edmund, 'A Poem presented to my Vallentine Mrs. Elizabeth Henstridg a young Lady of Kent 1695'.
MS. *Eng. poet. c. 52, fol. 28[v] (autogr.).

37 **Madam so may my verses pleasing be**
**If I write truth, and make my subject you.**
[Beaumont, Francis], 'To the Countess of Rutland'.
Pr. as 'An Elegie by F. B.' in *Certain Elegies by sundrie excellent wits*, 1618.
MSS. Don. b. 9, fol. 56[v]; Eng. poet. c. 53, fol. 13; Rawl. poet. 31, fol. 37[v].

38 **Madam: they say, whene'er**
**With a clear joyful day.**
Oldisworth, Nicolas, 'To a Lady, looking out of a window'.
MS. *Don. c. 24, fol. 54 (autogr.).

39 **Madam to live is to enjoy**
**Privation only is.**
Chatwin, John. 'To a Lady who desir'd to know what Life was'.
MS. *Rawl. poet. 94, p. 264 (autogr.).

40 **Madam, to prove my debt you need not strive**
**To let your hand cure what your eyes have done.**
MS. Rawl. poet. 209, fol. 38.

41 **Madam to you alone I homage pay,**
**To meet the smiles in your propitious face.**
Chatwin, John, 'To the most incomparable of her Sex Mrs. E. J.'
MS. *Rawl. poet. 94, p. 110 (autogr.).

42 **Madam, were th' aged world now in his prime**
**And owe unto their heat as much as I.**
Williams, Richard, 'To the right vertuous Lady the Lady Weston'.
MS. Rawl. poet. 147, p. 234 rev.

43 **Madam what hast**
**Die if ye can; or if ye dare.**
[Roach, Richard], 'To a Lady Sick in Bed on her Birth Day'.
MS. Rawl. D. 832, fol. 243 (autogr.).

**Madam, when I began to honour you** 44
**I am converted now a statue speaks.**
Oldisworth, Nicolas, 'To an over-modest Ladie'.
MS. *Don. c. 24, fol. 68[v] (autogr.).

**Madam, when late your tenderness resigned** 45
**The powers of death than to relinquish you.**
Oldham, John, 'To Mrs Kingscot on the Death of her Daughter', 1675.
MS. *Rawl. poet. 123, p. 238 (autogr.).

**Madam, while on your golden locks I gaze** 46
**That vanquished Henry, Mars, and Jove.**
[Roach, Richard], 'The Golden Locks . . . This Poem was printed in one of the Public Papers: here Inserted with some Alteration'.
MS. Rawl. D. 832, fol. 186 (autogr.).

**Madam who understands you well, would swear** 47
**That you the life, and this your copy were.**
King, Henry, couplet 'To [a] Lady Upon Overburyes Wife'.
MS. *Malone 22, fol. 23.

**Madam; with so much wonder we are strook** 48
**And makes himself immortal in her fame.**
[Etherege, Sir George], 'On the Dutchess of Newcastle'; copied by Sancroft from *A Collection of Poems written on Several Occasions, By Several persons*, 1672, p. 58.
Pr. *A Collection of Poems, . . . upon several occasions*, 1673, p. 56; attr. to Etherege in *A Collection of Poems by Several Hands*, 1693, p. 173.
MS. Sancroft 53, p. 3.

**Madam, you are so happy, that you vex** 49
**She can maintain an everlasting spring.**
Oldisworth, Nicolas, 'To his aunt, the lady Litcott of Molesey'.
MS. *Don. c. 24, fol. 43[v] (autogr.).

**Madam you are so truly noble and so good** 50
**So make of objects, subjects, and your self a king.**
Cavendish, Lady Jane, 'On a Noble Lady'.
MS. *Rawl. poet. 16, p. 18.

**Madam your benefaction has been such** 51
**Longer, or interrupt him yours R double U.**
Whitehall, Robert, of Merton College, 'To the no less vertuous than ingenio[us] Mrs. Mary More; upon her sending Sr Thomas More's picture (of her own drawing) to the long Gallery at the publick Schools in Oxon. Xbris 26. 1674'.
Answered by J19. Pr. at Oxford, 1674. See F. Madan, *Oxford Books*, iii, 1931, 3029.
MSS. Rawl. B. 165, fol. 51; Rawl. D. 912, fol. 19.

52 Madam, your carriage did discover
But to be constant too, the devil.
Hammond, Antony, 'An Answer to a suppos'd Letter'.
MS. Rawl. D. 360, fol. 77 (autogr.).

53 Madam, your present of albifick paste
Of complements your very humble.
Hammond, Anthony, 'To the Lady M[arsham] Upon sending some Paste for my hands'.
Pr. *Miscellany of Original Poems*, 1720, p. 132.
MS. Rawl. D. 360, fol. 79 (autogr.).

54 Madam your work's all miracle, and you
I wish with joy you there may meet again.
Dalby, Edward, of New College, 'Uppon the Lady Paulet's Needleworke', given to Oxford University 9 July 1636.
MSS. Ashmole 47, fol. 120v; Bodl. 22, fol. 7, attr. to Edward Dalby B. Ar. No. Coll.

55 Madam, you're happy sure, you do the spring disclose
From whom such hopeful grafts do spring so fast.
'To Sir Robert Shirley [of Staunton Harold, Bart. his] Lady delivered of a Son on the Lords day', 23 Jan. 1646/7.
MS. Eng. poet. e. 4, p. 66.

56 Made of coarse and churlish clay
For curious china ne'er had such.
'On the duke of Buckinghams sonne', d. 16 March 1626/7.
MS. CCC. 328, fol. 63.

57 Made willing by Thy grace
Who loved and died for me.
Kenton, James.
MS. *Eng. poet. e. 20, p. 94 (autogr.).

58 Madge by no means immodest pranks abides
As to report of would appear too bawdy.
MS. Malone 19, p. 155.

59 Mador I am the son of Owen Gwynedd
My mind was whole to search the ocean seas.
Meredith, son of Rhesus, fl. *c.* 1477. Transcribed from the translation in Hakluyt's Voyages [1600], '3. Vol. p. 1'.
MS. Rawl. D. 398, fol. 17.

60 Maecenas, born of kings, my grace.
I'll touch the stars with my high brow.
Fanshawe, Sir Richard, translator, Horace, *Odes* I. i., 'To Maecenas'.
MS. *Firth c. 1, p. 31.

Maecenas in both tongues grown wonderous wise 61
And take thy pleasure for the present day.
W. A., translator, Horace, *Odes* III. viii.
MS. *Rawl. poet. 104, fol. 26v (autogr.).

Maecenas mention'd in my odes, to be 62
That is to say, unless his spleen abound.
F[anshawe], Sir R[ichard], translator, Horace, *Epistles* I. i.
Pr. *Poems of Horace*, A. Brome etc., 2nd ed., 1671, p. 300.
MS. Rawl. D. 261, p. 24.

Maecenas sprung from kingly race 63
Rejoicing in laborious toil.
Percy, Thomas, nephew to the Bp. of Dromore, translator, from Horace, *Odes* I. i.
MS. Percy c. 8, fol. 87 (autogr.).

Maecenas, Thuscan king's descent; 64
My lofty head shall knock the pole.
Fanshaw, Sir R[ichard], translator, 'to Maecenas', Horace, *Odes* I. i.
Pr. *Poems of Horace*, A. Brome etc., 1666, p. 1.
MS. Rawl. D. 261, p. 1.

Maecenas, whose descent old kings enhance 65
With my' head I'll knock the stars, and still look higher.
Sancroft, William, 'Translation Out of Horace', *Odes* I. i.
MS. *Sancroft 48, fol. 23 (autogr.).

Maecenas whose high lineage monarchs grace 66
My head sublime shall to the stars aspire.
Pike, J[ohn], 'Horace Lib. I Ode 1'.
MS. Eng. poet. c. 9, p. 74.

Maid, wife or widow, which bears the grave style 67
Oh tell me, where is he, why doth he not come.
Cavendish, Lady Jane. 'A Songe'.
MS. *Rawl. poet. 16, p. 13.

Maidens beware ye 68
To bear such a name.
'Advice to young Maidens A New Song'.
MS. Ballard 47, fol. 175.

Maidens fair come hear my ditty 69
She has jealous fears to smother.
Amherst, Elizabeth, 'Ballad on the same Miss M[onk]'.
MS. *Eng. poet. e. 109, p. 12.

Maids in your smocks 70
And good night with a pox.
MSS. Ashmole 36, 37, fol. 171v.

71 Maids see what you lack
Hath such dainty things to sell you.
[Pedlar's song].
MS. Eng. poet. f. 10, fol. 98v.

72 Maids, that would be wives, be wary:
To raise posterity upon.
'Of the choice of an Husband'.
MS. Rawl. poet. 26, fol. 81.

73 Maimed, weak, and faint, while Ahaziah lies
But if we come to God, we come at last.
'The Faire Warning'.
MS. Rawl. poet. 154, fol. 108.

74 Majestic beauty triumphs in your brow
Nor yet by matching too unequally.
'Marie Hatton. Anagram, I am a Throne'. Acrostic.
MSS. Ashmole 36, 37, fol. 52v.

75 Make hast I pray launch out your ships with speed
One you can blame in all the world it's he.
Satire on the Duke of Buckingham.
MS. Malone 23, p. 201.

76 Make joyful noise to God all lands
For ever bless the Lord.
Psalm lxvi.
MS. *Rawl. C. 113, fol. 47.

77 Make much of every moment of your time
Will bring his winding sheet and close his eyes.
MS. Mus. Sch. G. 632, fol. iv.

78 Make much of money, whilst you ha't,
Her courteous speech makes ev'ry man your friend.
Robinson, Robert.
MS. *Rawl. poet. 218, p. 131 (autogr.).

79 Make not too much of sorrow 'tis a guest
His judgement 'tis a sin not to believe.
H. B., 'To my worthy freind mr Samuell Clutterbuck on the death of his daughter Mrs Marg: Clutterbucke'.
MS. Ashmole 47, fol. 89.

80 Make, (oh my soul) the subject of thy song,
Praise him whose bands of time, no age can bind.
Herbert, Mary (*née* Sidney), Countess of Pembroke, Psalm civ.
MS. *Rawl. poet. 24, p. 150; *25, fol. 101v.

Make the great god thy fort and dwell 81
Enjoyed them long, save thee at last.
Carew, Thomas, Psalm xci.
MSS. Ashmole 38, p. 98, attr. to Mr. Thomas Carew; *Don. b. 9, fol. 9; Eng. poet. c. 50, fol. 52; Rawl. poet. 23, p. 125, ref. to setting by H. Lawes; 61, fol. 46v, attr. to Th. Carey; 160, fol. 77, attr. to Tho. Carewe.

Maker of all we thee entreat 82
Together with the holy Spirit.
'Engl. Primer of or Lady. 1631 . . . p. 337'.
MS. Eng. poet. 56, p. 21.

Maker of Heaven, and earth! make her to know 83
Severity'll deface the noblest mind.
Morrice, John, 'An other Acrostick' on Mary Davies. 3 Dec. 1707.
MS. *Rawl. poet. 114, fol. 134 (autogr.).

Malice is joined with madness: rage rules more 84
Of God's immediate hand, and providence.
MS. *Rawl. poet. 97, fol. 63 (autogr.).

Malicious tell-tale of approaching day, 85
And thy loathed carcass may no creature eat.
Chatwin, John, 'The Cock'.
MS. *Rawl. poet. 94, p. 221 (autogr.).

Malignus, like a sweeping pestilence 86
Both fit for the society of brutes.
Epigram, 1735.
MS. Eng. misc. e. 240, p. 269.

Mall at first motion no mankind endures 87
But make her drunk she is everlasting yours.
Couplet.
MS. Malone 19, p. 155.

'Mama'—'My dear'—'View well yon lordly thing 88
Then crush our tender limbs and greedily devour.
Samber, Robert, 'The Old Mouse and her Little One'.
MS. *Rawl. poet. 134*b*, fol. 175*b* (autogr.).

Man and wife are all one 89
And you see him no more 'till 'tis supper.
[Sheppard, Fleetwood (?)], 'A Description of a Hampton Court Life', 1689.
In B.M. MSS. Harl. 7315, fol. 166v, and Lansd. 852, fol. 98, attr. to Fleet. Shepheard.
MSS. Eng. poet. c. 18, fol. 68v; e. 49, p. 51; Firth c. 15, p. 307; e. 6, fol. 94v; Locke c. 32, fol. 25.

Man being made, by treading thus awry 90
Could not conceal his frailty from his God.
MS. *Rawl. poet. 97, fol. 5v (autogr.).

91 Man desires woman: woman longs for man:
What nature urgeth, who gainsay it can.
Robinson, Robert.
MS. *Rawl. poet. 218, p. 75 (autogr.).

92 Man doth a double birth inherit
Preserved so the church and prayer.
Corbett, Rich: Bish: of Norwich, 'Upon a Fonte'.
Not pr. among his poems.
MS. Eng. poet. e. 97, p. 12.

93 Man eat, and sinn'd, and fell. Vain shadow say
No more the land by numb'ring doth decrease.
'David's Plague'.
MS. Eng. poet. e. 4, p. 11.

94 Man gather wealth, get worldly power
What art thou then? Oh no man.
Robinson, Robert.
MS. *Rawl. poet. 218, p. 56 (autogr.).

95 Man his own shame, and ruin, does contrive;
We may adore the mystic Trinity.
Montagu, Charles, Earl of Halifax, 'On . . . the Spanish invasion An[o]: Dom[i]: 1588, . . . Gun-pow[der] Treason and this last plot' [1679]; verses sent to his mother.
MS. Montagu d. 1, fol. 78 (autogr.).

96 Man if thou know what did thy father when
I dare not say, it is so foully base.
James, Richard, 'An ep. of the same subject and person', i.e. Palladas on pride of men.
MS. *James 35, p. 18 (autogr.).

97 Man in a minute first is sown,
And then no more a man he's known.
Robinson, Robert.
MS. *Rawl. poet. 218, p. 102 (autogr.).

98 Man in what state so'ever thou be
*Ergo mortis memorare.*
'On a gravestone. Norleech chur[h]', copied by B. Willis from Wood.
MS. Willis 83, fol. 54.

99 Man is a foolish pamphlet, full of lies
Those never come, and these fly fast away.
MS. Rawl. poet. 84, inside cover.

100 Man is a little world the All's rhapsody
Prone, long square heads are beast[s] but round-heads men.
H. B., 'Roundheads'.
MS. Locke e. 17, p. 75.

Man is a lump, where all beasts kneaded be 101
Your friends find every day a mart of news.
Donne, John, 'To Sr Edward Herbert at Julyers'.
Pr. *Poems*, 1633.
MSS. *Eng. poet. e. 99, fol. 35; *f. 9, p. 108.

Man is a mixture both of good and evil: 102
Christ by his merits will in mercy save us.
Robinson, Robert.
MS. *Rawl. poet. 218, p. 96 (autogr.).

Man is a tree that hath no top in cares 103
Is given to no end but to have power to grieve.
MS. Rawl. poet. 206, p. 28.

Man is as a glass, life is as water 104
So runs the water out.
'On the frayltie of man'.
MS. Eng. poet. e. 14, fol. 89[v] rev.

Man is God's chiefest creature therefore must 105
Yet higher: doth anew them re-create.
MS. *Rawl. poet. 97, fol. 4 (autogr.).

Man is the world, and death the ocean 106
Of such a prey, and to his triumph add.
Donne, John, 'Elegye On the Lady Marckham'.
Pr. *Poems*, 1633.
MSS. *Eng. poet. e. 99, p. 24[v]; *f. 9, p. 124.

Man is to man his greatest earthly foe: 107
'Cause pride is high, and charity lies still.
Robinson, Robert.
MS. *Rawl. poet. 218, p. 75 (autogr.).

Man lived at first from tedious troubles free 108
Trouble, disease and care which haunt us still.
'Hesiod'.
MS. Don. d. 58, fol. 53.

Man look and see 109
Now intend for to amend.
'The saying of a dead man'.
MSS. Ashmole 378, fol. 12; Lat. th. d. 15, fol. 133.

Man love thy wife; thy husband, wife obey: 110
Wives are our heart, we should be head alway.
'Married folke'.
Pr. *Wits Recreations*, 1663, Ep. 657.
MS. Eng. poet. d. 152, fol. 103[v].

Man made the chief of all that made have been 111
When he his Lord's injunction doth despise.
MS. *Rawl. poet. 97, fol. 13 (autogr.).

Man moils and toils like a horse in a mill. 112
Yet all must die, yea th' happiest man alive.
Robinson, Robert.
MS. *Rawl. poet. 218, p. 83 (autogr.).

113 Man must again be born of quick'ning fire
One spirit, one baptism, and one faith make one.
'Idem' i.e. Richard Corbett on a font.
Not pr. among his poems.
MS. Eng. poet. e. 97, p. 12.

114 Man newly born is at full age to die,
Now heaven thee pulls, thou it, with violence.
Strode, William, 'An Epitaph'.
MS. *CCC. 325, fol. 96v (autogr.).

115 Man of terrestial creatures did the worst,
And drew on him the heavier punishment.
MS. *Rawl. poet. 97, fol. 13 (autogr.).

116 Man sprung from dust to dust returns again
And feels betimes the icy hand of death.
'Chapel le Frith Churchyard; [on] Samuel Kirk. 1764'.
MS. Top. Yorks. c. 2, fol. 4.

117 Man unkind
Lo here mine [heart].
MS. Tanner 407, fol. 52v.

118 Man! whosoe'er thou art that seekest Christ
Ye may be laid to sleep; believ't ye cannot die!
Wake, William, of Cambridge, translator, 'Aurelii Prudentii Hymnus de Epiphania Jesu'.
MS. Eng. misc. d. 1, fol. 24.

119 Man worse than worm, in blood first sprawling lies
And lost is rotten and forgotten dust.
Pestell, Thomas, 'On Man'.
MS. *Malone 14, p. 40.

120 Manhu, manhu, what thing is this
Pray we to god to grant us this.
Heskines, Peter, 'A Brefe discourse of the holy Eucharistе'.
MS. Rawl. poet. 219, fol. 14v.

121 Mankind that through the earth is spread
And his own high extract forsakes.
Hobart, John, translation of Boethius, *Consolations* III. vi, 1664.
MS. Tanner 306, fol. 333 (autogr.).

122 Mankind, whatsoe'er your clime
Pure, exact, inviolable.
J. F., Psalm c.
MS. *Eng. poet. f. 17, p. 170 (autogr.).

123 Mankind's composure passeth all compare
Him all his service cannot recompense.
MS. *Rawl. poet. 97, fol. 2v (autogr.).

124 Manna did fail the sons of Jacob when
Those most who in it most their food receive.
MS. *Rawl. poet. 97, fol. 21v (autogr.).

Manna from heaven unto the Hebrews sent 125
What will He for His saints in heaven provide?
MS. *Rawl. poet. 97, fol. 26v (autogr.).

Man's anxious earthly cares (oh 'tis not well) 126
Take off his spiritual thoughts of heaven and hell.
Robinson, Robert, couplet, 'Curae hominis terrenae cogitationes suas sprituales deripiunt'.
MS. *Rawl. poet. 218, p. 123 (autogr.).

Man's blindness, his obduracy is such 127
Which out of's love to man, He did sustain.
MS. *Rawl. poet. 97, fol. 23v (autogr.).

Man's body's like a house: his greater bones 128
Unsure at surest, and but short at longest.
Quarles, Francis, 'A description of Man'.
Pr. *Divine Fancies*, 1632, i. 42.
MS. Rawl. poet. 65, fol. 63v; 90, fol. 61v; 117, fol. 178v rev., attr. to Fran: Quarles; 213, fol. 53.

Man's but an earthen vessel, and he's found 129
And useless grown, it's then thrown out o'th' door.
Robinson, Robert, 'Homo vas fictile'.
MS. *Rawl. poet. 218, p. 25 (autogr.).

Man's disobedience heaped on him disdain 130
Can suffer; yet none can Thy presence shun!
MS. *Rawl. poet. 97, fol. 13 (autogr.).

Man's free redemption by our Saviour Christ 131
Why should we at men's faces be dismayed?
MS. *Rawl. poet. 97, fol. 26 (autogr.).

Man's heart and mind can not be tried 132
No friends can want within this land.
'A plain declaration of a just magistrate and true subject to his Countrey'.
MS. Rawl. B. 410, verso of last page (4 blank leaves, inserted by binder, follow).

Man's heart is this way, that way winding, 133
The thoughts thereof are past man's finding.
Robinson, Robert, couplet.
MS. *Rawl. poet. 218, p. 40 (autogr.).

Man's heart than which nothing to him more near 134
By Adam, is by us continued on.
MS. *Rawl. poet. 97, fol. 10 (autogr.).

Man's heart's by nature like a wilderness 135
Because we know not when the Lord will come.
Corbet, W., 'The Heart is deceitfull above all things, soe desperately wicked who can know it'. Jer: 17. 9.
MS. *Rawl. poet. 210, fol. 29.

136 Man's life, a travail, when we have weary been
After some sport it must at length be done.
'On man's life, disticks'.
MS. Eng. poet. e. 24, fol. 34; see also M143.

137 Man's life is like a shadow
To see God in his joys.
MS. Eng. poet. b. 5, p. 125.

138 Man's life is like a winter's day
He that goes soonest, has the least to pay.
'Epitaph . . . by a Cobler . . . in a Churchyard in Derbyshire'.
MS. Eng. poet. c. 51, p. 241.

139 Man's life is like an hour-glass, wherein
Our sins are finished, as our lives are done.
[Quarles, Francis], 'On an Hower-Glass'.
Pr. *Divine Fancies*, 1632, iv. 57.
MS. Rawl. poet. 90, two copies, fols. 74v and 101v.

140 Man's life is well compared to a feast
Comes death, and takes the table clean away.
'A Comparison of the Life of Man'.
MSS. Ashmole 1153, fol. 137v written in cipher, attr. to Richard Barnfield; Eng. poet. c. 50, fol. 33.

141 Man's life it is vain, for 'tis subject to pain
And angle and angle again.
'The Angler' endorsed 'Motto's inscribed on the Walls of Mr. Castle's House in Burford . . .'.
MS. Ballard 47, fol. 57v.

142 Man's life's a new tun'd cask of which they say
Takes what is left and turns the rest to ground.
'On the Death of a Butcher'.
MS. Ashmole 47, fol. 44.

143 Man's life's a travail, when we have wearied been,
After some sport it must at length be done.
'10 disticks of mans life and death . . . Mr. Sellers'.
MSS. Ashmole 36, 37, fol. 143; see also M136.

144 Man's like a glass filled full of water,
So soon is life run out.
'Mors ultima linea rerum'.
MS. Rawl. D. 954, fol. 44.

145 Man's memory is most strong, when 'tis most full.
More apt it is, and more and more it may.
Robinson, Robert.
MS. *Rawl. poet. 218, p. 144 (autogr.).

146 Man's mind uncertain is of fate:
It knoweth not at all.
MS. Rawl. poet. 66, fol. 53.

Man's plea to man, is that he never more 147
Makes his old gifts th' example of his new.
[Quarles, Francis], 'On Mans Plea'.
Pr. *Divine Fancies*, 1632, i. 45.
MS. Rawl. poet. 90, fol. 62.

Man's strength is weak, his pomp and glory vain 148
Let fall and broke, thrown out and trod upon.
Huish, Alexander, 'Cur mundus militat sub vanâ gloriâ. [Translated] Octob. 28, 1628'.
MS. Eng. poet. e. 56, p. 129 (autogr.).

Man's the creation's breviate the elect. 149
Volumes of praise.
'On the hand', incomplete (?).
MS. CCC. 328, fol. 80.

Many a maid have I gulled 150
Have I still though . . . missed.
Subscribed 'quoth: he that would if he coulde'.
MS. Rawl. poet. 85, fol. 46.

Many a time ev'n from my youth 151
Your labours may succeed.
Psalm cxxix.
MS. *Rawl. C. 113, fol. 93v.

Many blame me that I could do nothing 152
For had I not been slow she had been quick.
'On a chaste lover'.
MS. Don. d. 58, fol. 15v.

Many brave worthy men I've known to die: 153
Merry or sad, whether they laugh or cry.
Robinson, Robert.
MS. *Rawl. poet. 218, p. 123 (autogr.).

Many commend him, who hath wit or arts 154
But to befriend him none with money parts.
Robinson, Robert, couplet.
MS. *Rawl. poet. 218, p. 3 (autogr.).

Many condemn Gripe for his usury, 155
Of creatures, why should not a greater beast.
'On Gripe an usurer'.
MS. CCC. 328, fol. 35v.

Many desire but few or none deserve 156
Farewell the rest the soil will be disdained.
'Written to Mrs. A. V.', Anne Vavesor (?), cf. fol. 11.
MS. Rawl. poet. 85, fol. 116.

Many great strifes amongst us men, 157
Serve thee in peace and love.
Robinson, Robert.
MS. *Rawl. poet. 218, p. 148 (autogr.).

158 Many have been the vain attempts of wit
First get his son, then give him education.
[Sackville, Charles, Earl of Dorset], 'Epilogue to Tartuffe, spoken by himself'. Copied by Sancroft from *A Collection of Poems on Several Occasions, by several Persons*, 1672, p. 61.
Pr. *A Collection of Poems . . . upon several Occasions*, 1673, p. 59.
MS. Sancroft 53, p. 5.

159 Many healths do many destroy
And all these wishes crown.
Williams, John, 'A Health'.
MS. *Rawl. poet. 192, fol. 138 (autogr.).

160 Many man makes rhyme and looks to no reason
And looks to no reason.
Note by Professor F. P. Wilson: 'see Thomas (Fortescue), Lord Clermont, *History of the Family of Fortescue*, 2nd ed., 1880, pp. 263–5. Also the Bannatyne MS., ed. W. T. Ritchie, iii. 8–10, the Maitland Folio MS., ed. W. A. Craigie, i. 159–61, and the Commonplace-book of A. Melville, ed. W. Walker, pp. 21–25'.
MS. Digby 145, fol. 160v.

161 Many shall seek in Heaven to partake
With sweat and wounds obtained the victory.
Williams, John.
MS. *Rawl. poet. 191, fol. 2 (autogr.).

162 Many tongue-friends, false friends 'mongst men are known
But heart-friends, friends indeed are few or none.
Robinson, Robert, 'Multi sunt in lingua amici, in corde pauci', couplet.
MS. *Rawl. poet. 218, p. 51 (autogr.).

163 Many unjust grown rich, and pious poor
Riches from man to man uncertain pass.
[Stanley, Thomas, translator], 'On Ill gotten Wealth'.
In *The History of Philosophy*, 1655, p. 31, attr. to Solon.
MS. Rawl. poet. 90, fol. 60v.

164 Many when each hath little work to do
The hands engrave carve limn, and write.
MS. *Don. f. 5, fol. 11.

165 Many will ask the bell-man why
Say that the sun dispelled the dew.
'On Mrs. Dew that died on the death of her sonne'.
MSS. Ashmole 36, 37, fol. 145v.

Many will say, that cannot rise at all 166
As well as man cast head-long from the sky.
MS. Rawl. poet. 206, p. 29.

Many words have no meaning, 'tis not in my power 167
Now 'tis too soon, it then can't be too late.
Williams, John, 'Upon Mr. William Lowndes, Secretary to the Treasury . . . His Son William Lowndes, mr. John Shaw, and mr John Duncombe Junr. Commissioners for the Million and half Lottery ano 1709/10'.
MS. *Rawl. poet. 191, fol. 152 (autogr.).

Marble never wept for woman 168
Glory will wake in peace, now sleeping.
'An other Elegy', for Mistress R. L.
MS. Rawl. poet. 117, fol. 187 rev.

Marble piles, let no man raise 169
Both her mourner, and her tomb.
Browne, [William, of Tavistock], 'Epitaph uppon the Countess of Pembroke': the second verse of U59.
MSS. Rawl. poet. 117, fol. 268v rev.; 160, fol. 27, attr. to Browne.

Marble weep for thou dost cover 170
Earth thou hast not such another.
[Jonson, Ben.], 'On margaret Ratcliffe'. *Epigrammes*, xl.
MS. Ashmole 47, fol. 45v.

Marcella now grown old, hath broke her glass 171
Should show good countenance that conceiveth none.
MS. Eng. poet. f. 9, p. 18.

March forth my thoughts in love's high regiment 172
Sending bolts stronger then the bolts of Jove.
Adyn, Robert (?) (matr. March 1584/5, St. Alban's Hall), Acrostic on 'Margerie Williams'; cf. R152.
MS. Rawl. D. 1048, fol. 70v (autogr. (?)).

March! March! why the de'il dinna ye march? 173
Belt on your plaids and cock up your bonnet.
MS. Eng. poet. e. 8, fol. 4v.

March on sweet maidens all amort 174
To make with thee a heavenly quire.
Lilliat, John, 'A ditie upon the death of Dulcebell Porter, my scholler: whose Mother died the 20. of Nouember, 1598. and this her Daughter Januarii 20. 1598[/9]'.
MS. Rawl. poet. 148, fol. 93v (autogr.).

175 March with his wind hath struck a cedar tall
And yet sad May, must lose her flower of flowers.
'On Queen Anns Death', 2 March 1618/19, buried 13 May.
Pr. Camden's *Remaines*, 1637, p. 397.
MSS. Ashmole 38, p. 169; CCC. 328, fol. 75; Douce f. 5, fol. 31; Eng. poet. e. 14, fol. 87 rev.; e. 40, fol. 117; f. 10, fol. 92.

176 Marcus the miller held two mills to farm
Marcus hath done, his millstone be clean broken.
'Epigram'.
MS. Rawl. poet. 172, fol. 7v.

177 Marcus you came to me last night.
When one I would not lend?
'Translated from Martial', *Epigrams* IV. XV.
MS. Eng. poet. e. 28, p. 320.

178 Margery Mutton and Johnny Bopeep
He said kiss me and she said come.
MS. Douce d. 59, fol. 55v.

179 Maria thou persuadest me, be free
If so, eternally adieu to thee.
'To Miss Maria Aston a violent Whig', translation of Dr. Johnson's Latin.
MS. Eng. poet. c. 51, p. 16; see also p. 33.

180 Mark but the soaring kite: and she will read
And thou shalt find less mischief, and more mirth.
[Quarles, Francis], 'On the Kite'.
Pr. *Divine Fancies*, 1632, ii. 87.
MS. Rawl. poet. 90, fol. 71.

181 Mark but this flea, and mark in this
Will waste as this flea's death took life from thee.
Donne, John, 'The Flea'.
Pr. *Poems*, 1633.
MSS. CCC. 327, fol. 21v, attr. to J.D. (monogram); *Eng. poet. e. 99, fol. 121v; *f. 9, p. 29; Malone 19, p. 57, attr. to J. D.; Rawl. poet. 117, fol. 218 rev.; 172, fol. 74v, attr. to D[r.] D.

182 Mark here what figure stands for one, the right
Two silver fishes in his floods to swim.
Verses on mathematical figures and signs of the Zodiac.
MS. Rawl. poet. 206, p. 30.

183 Mark how that gliding star, that flaming tear
Who when he is most drowned is most preserved.
'Teares'.
MS. Rawl. poet. 246, fol. 34.

184 Mark how the bashful morn in vain
With open ears and with unfolded arms.
Carew, Thomas, 'The Marygold'.
Pr. *Poems*, 1640.
MSS. *Don. b. 9, fol. 27; Eng. poet. f. 25, fol. 20; Rawl. poet. 142, fol. 49v.

Mark how the drops do trickle down his face, 185
Could have made God in such a case have been.
Colman, Henry, 'On his sweate on Mount Olivet'.
MS. *Rawl. poet 204, fol. 8 (autogr.).

Mark, how the greedy rabble flock, to see 186
You'll want a midwife for the next pope Joane.
'On Mrs. Cellier in the pillory', 1680.
MS. Don. b. 8, p. 611.

Mark how the lanthorns cloud mine eyes 187
To see the rainbows wheelgun made of flax.
'A Non Sequitur by Dr. Corbet'.
MS. Rawl. poet. 142, fol. 39.

Mark how this polish'd eastern sheet 188
To fold up silks, may wrap up wit.
Carew, [Thomas], 'A Fancy'.
First pr. *Poems*, 1642.
Pr. bk. 27980 e. 86, p. 23.

Mark surly Thrasymed with stern grimace 189
The joys unspeakable of doing well.
Pike, John, 'The Contraste'.
MS. Eng. poet. c. 9, p. 72.

Mark that swift arrow how it cuts the air, 190
T'out-live Nestor in a day.
[Cowley, Abraham], 'Upon the shortness of Mans Life'.
Pr. *Sylva*, 1637, Ode vi.
MSS. Rawl. poet. 90, fol. 162; Rawl. poet. 213, fol. 2.

Mark this same smith, how with his bellows he 191
Then Venus sure would better favour me.
Oldisworth, Nicolas, 'For a Lover, standing by a Smith's Shoppe. An Ode'.
MS. *Don. c. 24, fol. 65v (autogr.).

Mark well the fruits, of drunkenness and play 192
And wisdom still, against such unthrifty cries.
[Whitney, Geoffrey], 'Ludus, Luctus, Luxus'.
MS. *Rawl. poet. 56, fol. 8v.

Mark well this stone it hides a precious treasure 193
In brief here lies embalmed with tears of love.
Sepulchral verse formerly in York minster, on Marmaduke Constable of Wassand in Holdernes Esq., d. 1607.
MS. Dodsworth 161, fol. 6v.

Mark what I say! and bear it well in mind 194
Yet we are safe; the fruit of God remains.
'The two Seeds'.
MS. Rawl. poet. 66, fol. 65.

195 Mark you the floor? that square and speckled stone
Could build so strong in a weak heart.
Herbert, George, 'The Church-floore'.
Pr. *The Temple*, 1633, p. 58.
MS. *Tanner 307, fol. 45.

196 Marriage and old age the same fate receive
But when we have them, then they make us grieve.
Walsh, William, translator, [Greek Anthology], 'p: 33: Vin'.
MS. Malone 9, fol. 27 (autogr.).

197 Marriage as old men say hath likened [hath often well compared] bin
And those that are within would fain come out.
Pr. *Wits Recreations*, 1640, no. 490.
MS. Eng. poet. f. 10, fol. 119; Rawl. poet. 206, p. 46; see also M202.

198 Marriage is a country dance,
Ending at last in back to back.
'On Matrimony'.
MS. *Eng. poet. d. 47, fol. 149.

199 Marriage is honourable they say in all
That gotten hath a lady and a whore.
On Bishop Fletcher, Feb. 1594/5.
MS. Tanner 306, fol. 188$^v$; see also M203.

200 Marriage is that sacred tie
Need a separation fear.
Colman, Henry, 'On Marriage'.
MS. *Rawl. poet. 204, fol. 18 (autogr.).

201 Marriage it seems is for better for worse
Through trembling and fear.
'J. S. Gentleman . . . set within the compasse of the fflute'.
Pr. *Wit and Mirth*, 1706, p. 39.
MS. Mus. Sch. C. 95, p. 128, with the *Wit and Mirth* tune.

202 Marriage (saith one) hath oft compared been
And those that are within would fain get out.
'Of Marriage', epigram.
MSS. Ashmole 36, 37, fol. 145$^v$; Malone 19, p. 44; see also M197.

203 Marriage they say is honourable in all
That gotten hath a lady and a whore.
On Bp. Richard Fletcher, 1594/5.
MS. Tanner 306, fol. 189; see also M199.

204 Marriage, thou state of jealousy and care,
The nauseous hospital must be endured.
Wilmot, John, Earl of Rochester.
Pr. *Remains*, 1718, p. 2.
MS. Rawl. poet. 173, fol. 95$^v$.

Married Sir Robert! Can the news be true? 205
Tell me if marriage proves so very sweet.
'A Dialogue between Sir Robert Howard and Coll: Titus'. 1692/3.
MSS. Eng. poet. c. 18, fol. 129$^v$; e. 49, p. 128.

Married wives may take and leave 206
Yet fain would do if that we durst.
'A maides Complaint'.
MS. Eng. poet. f. 25, fol. 12$^v$.

Marry and love thy Flavia, for she 207
For things in fashion every man will wear.
Donne, John, 'In Flaviam'. Elegy II.
Pr. *Poems*, 1633, p. 45.
MSS. Add. B. 97, fol. 55$^v$; Don. d. 58, fol. 48; Eng. poet. e. 14, fol. 29$^v$, attr. to Dr. Dun; e. 37, p. 31, attr. to J. D.; *e. 99, fol. 15$^v$; *f. 9, p. 116; Rawl. poet. 117, fol. 224 rev., attr. to Dunne; 160, fol. 104, attr. to J. D.

Mars, with thy wars 208
To dandle in my arms.
MS. Rawl. poet. 85, fol. 39*a*$^v$.

Martha was truly virtuous yet to blame 209
That lodged so chastely in her master's heart.
'Upon Martha and Mary'.
MS. Rawl. poet. 116, fol. 129.

Martha, with joy, received her blessed Lord. 210
Mary's to Thee: and Martha's to thy members.
[Quarles, Francis], 'On Martha and Mary'.
Pr. *Divine Fancies*, 1632, i. 47.
MS. Rawl. poet. 90, fol. 62$^v$.

Martyred in thought but martyred more in soul 211
To make those vows in vain, which you have pledge . . . (incomplete)
'The Lady Penelope Rich to S$^r$ Phillipe Sidney'; see I1073.
MS. Eng. poet. f. 9, p. 234.

Marvel not (reader) though the sun shine bright 212
I'd knock you soundly had I but bedstaves.
'On the sight of an old decayed patched bed with a pillow having T. R. as a marke on it'.
Pr. *Musarum Deliciae*, 1655, p. 59.
MS. Rawl. poet. 65, fol. 72$^v$.

Mary! I want a lyre with other strings; 213
And since thou owns't that praise I spare thee mine.
Cowper, William, 'Sonnet . . . address'd to his faithful friend Mrs. Unwin'.
Pr. *Life*, W. Hayley, 1803, ii. 43.
MS. Eng. poet. e. 28, p. 361.

214 Mary, incarnate virtue, soul and skin
Was a prime star of greatest clarity.
Strode, William, 'On [Sir William Strode's] Lady Marie'.
MS. *CCC. 325, fol. 40 (autogr.).

215*a* Mary the mistress that my heart admires
Whose love on blissful her can bliss bestow.
Barnes, Joshua, acrostic on Mary Westron.
MS. Hearne's diaries 11, p. 136.

215*b* Master's in the counting house
And pecked off her nose.
MS. Douce d. 59, fol. 55.

216 Mat Lewis was little, Mat Lewis was young
Should write not at all or should write common sense.
'The Old Hag in a Red Cloak . . . Inscribed to the Author of the "Grim White Woman"'.
MS. Percy c. 8, fol. 177ᵛ.

217 Mat: with his man late set on merriment,
To write, quoth's master, what my dog lays out.
MS. Tanner 465, fol. 94ᵛ.

218 Mated with grief a faithful shepherd sate
And farewell weeping I can wail no more.
'An Excellent Pastorall Dittye' by 'Sheepheard Montanus'.
MS. Douce 280, fol. 35ᵛ.

219 Matins were done; the morning fresh and fair,
Till N - n holds or C - r finds his tongue.
1724.
MS. Rawl. poet. 172, fol. 163*b*ᵛ.

220 Matthew by Christ called from the custom board
Be the disease, if more, it comes to us.
Clifford, Henry, Earl of Cumberland, 'Saint Mathew'.
MS. *Rawl. poet. 95, fol. 35.

221 Matthew Prior by your leave
But Nassau was the son of God.
'Occasioned by the foregoing Epitaph', C756, on Matthew Prior.
MS. Rawl. poet. 116, fol. 112.

222 Matt[hew] Wren is both grave and wise
And takes prince Rupert's place at night.
MS. Gough misc. antiq. 11, fol. 81ᵛ.

223 Mature for man the country damsel shares
And wisely chooses such a working wife.
'The Young Farmer's Choice for a Wife'.
MS. *Eng. poet. d. 47, fol. 16.

Maudlin oft tried with wine to wash off cares 224
But grief converted all the wine to tears.
Polwhele, John, 'Tibullus fol. 88 Elegia quinta'.
MS. *Eng. poet. f. 16, fol. 8 (autogr.).

Maurus his poisoned darts what needs the pure? 225
Or torrid sure I will not change my tone.
W. A., translator, Horace, *Odes* I. xxii.
MS. *Rawl. poet. 104, fol. 8 (autogr.).

May a performance more complete 226
Richer than those that do appear.
[Johnston, Nathaniel], acrostic on Martha Lister, wife of William Lister.
MS. Eng. poet. c. 25, fol. 35 (autogr.).

May all new years, and happiness, be so 227
Happy again, in your dear friends to see.
Cavendish, Lady Jane, 'On my Sister Brackley'.
MS. *Rawl. poet. 16, p. 28.

May all things that are worthy of desire 228
What's due to all, let none too long desire.
Williams, John, 'To Miss Ashe and Miss Betty'.
MS. *Rawl. poet. 184, fol. 53 (autogr.).

May all thy charms as do thy years increase 229
And blessing e'er wait thee through each year.
Gunning, John, to Lady Elizabeth Hamilton and Lady Coventry.
MS. Firth b. 4, fol. 52ᵛ.

May balmy peace and wreathed renown 230
Whose God and people are his care.
MS. Mus. c. 107, fol. 37ᵛ.

May every one what does best please him choose 231
Becomes a weak usurping woman's slave.
'Man's Folly further expos'd'.
MS. Rawl. poet. 173, fol. 165.

May fate with honour and with laurels crown 232
From the saved Neatherlands and conquered France.
'The Loyall Wish', *c.* 1695.
MS. Rawl. D. 361, fol. 221ᵛ.

May God an exemplary clergy send 233
So shall the people their bad lives amend.
Barksdale, Clement, 'Clergy', distich.
MS. Autogr. c. 9, fol. 154 (autogr.).

May God preserve the church and give her peace 234
And constant marks of love fraternal give.
Samber, Robert, 'The Bellman's prayer', from 'the Bellman's Verses'.
MS. *Rawl. poet. 134*b*, fol. 157ᵛ (autogr.).

235 May God, the father of mankind
My trembling soul convey.
Bate, Sally, 'To Lady Eliza Chaplin with the Dialogue of Amorett and Lisette'.
MS. *Eng. poet. e. 28, p. 124.

236 May I come in? The prompter bids me enter
And never wish for an Italian lover.
'Epilogue to the Tragedy of Julia', [by Robert Jephson], 1787, anon., to be spoken by Mrs. Siddons. The prologue printed in 1787 is by Malone, Epilogue by John Courtenay.
MS. Malone 41, fol. 30.

237 May I forth to meet the Czar?
Your bastard son and his whole idiot crew.
'The debate on George's Journey in MDCCXVI'.
MS. Rawl. poet. 207, p. 76.

238 May I, in an easy good old age
And never condescend to die.
Coley, Henry, translator, Horace, 'Dimidium facti, qui bene caepit'.
Pr. *Almanack*, 1694.
MS. Add. B. 8, fol. 73 (autogr.).

239 May I live to see William and Mary grow old
With bonfires and bells keep a glad funeral.
'The Loyal Wish', endorsed 1689.
MS. Rawl. poet. 159, two copies, fols. 78 and 82.

240 May I neither be observator nor trimmer
Nor write any longer then wise men will read.
MS. Eng. poet. d. 152, fol. 18.

241 May I not prosper, if I would not be
Four miles, and see you not, is too too much.
Sancroft, Archbishop William (?), translator, 'Martial ad Decianum,' *Epigrams* II. v.
MS. *Sancroft 48, fol. 26, in Sancroft's hand.

242 May I presume in humble lays
Then one may say the ball is ended.
'To a Lady who lov'd dancing'.
MS. Top. Oxon. b. 170, fol. 16v.

243 May it please your highness sovereign lady queen
Thy name be praised: and thus I end my speech.
Caradocke [Cradocke], Edward, 'A treatise touching the philosopher['s] stone ded. to Q. Elizabeth'. See I1266.
MS. Rawl. poet. 182, fol. 37.

244 May joy and harmony inspire
Our everlasting friend.
Kenton, James, 'A Wedding Song'.
MS. *Eng. poet. e. 20, p. 295 (autogr.).

May life be such, that death may bring a crown. 245*a*
This life's no more, when once our clock is down.
Robinson, Robert, couplet.
MS. *Rawl. poet. 218, p. 147 (autogr.).

May mirth and wine be still thy share 245*b*
A long lived father and a wicked wife.
In vol. 2 of 'Tacitus's Annals English 3 vols. 8vo. To the Hond L. B. C[alvert]', subscribed G . . . k.
MS. Hearne's diaries 66, p. 27.

May my dear ever have a cheerful heart 246
Even to him sing, all my remaining days.
Spoure, Edmund, 'An Acrostick on Mrs. Mary Spoure'.
MS. *Eng. poet. c. 52, fol. 4 (autogr.).

May never was so mild, as Grace was fair 247
But now are even by the grace of God.
'On one Grace Mild-may'.
MS. Rawl. poet. 206, p. 52.

May not an olive branch of peace? truth? love? 248
May all invite from brawls, to tranquil rest.
Lane, John, dedication of 'The Squiers Tale' to Queen Henrietta Maria (1630).
Pr. Chaucer Society, Ser. 2, xxiii, 1888, ed. F. J. Furnivall, p. 5.
MS. Ashmole 53, fol. iv.

May she for whom these lines are penned 249
The thoughts of him be first and last.
Montgomery, James, dedicatory verse for 'Rhapsody'.
MS. Eng. poet. d. 10, fol. 80v (autogr.).

May the act [laws] against vagrants close [soon reach] the Pretender 250
Which none will refuse but a whig or a rumper.
'Act against Vagrants', 1713. Jacobite verse.
MSS. Eng. misc. c. 116, fol. 7v; Eng. poet. e. 87, p. 14; see also L284.

May this good company 251
In joy and peace.
'A new Song to the Tune of God save the King'.
MS. Mus. e. 19, p. 91.

May this my small remembrance, have the bliss 252
Heaven shall repay them with eternity.
'On a paire of braceletts, with [a] Motto'.
MS. Rawl. poet. 153, fol. 21.

253 May those already curs'd Essexian plains
And is not dead but ceases to appear.
Waller, Edmund, 'Upon the deathe of my Ladie Rich', 24 Aug. 1638.
Pr. *Poems*, 1645, p. 108.
MSS. *Don. d. 55, fol. 32; Eng. misc. e. 262, fol. 40$^{v}$, attr. to Waller; *Rawl. poet. 174, p. 62.

254 May thou be blest with all that Heaven can send
And be thy latest gasp a sigh of love.
'To a Lady on her Birthday'.
MS. Top. London e. 9, p. 111.

255 May Venus glitter o'er the deep
And urge him not to lay his thunder down.
Horace, *Odes* I. iii, 'Occasion'd by a friends' Voyage to Barbados'.
MS. Top. London e. 9, p. 27.

256 May you have all that Heaven can give,
May answer to the wishes of your friend S. Bate.
'On my Birth Day by Miss Sally Bate Written by her at the Age of Thirteen'.
MS. *Eng. poet. e. 28, p. 43.

257 May you have all the joys of innocence
May you transfigured, not disfigured die.
'The happie wish, to Madam etc.'
MS. Rawl. A. 176, fol. 79.

258 May you spurn vice for ever from your feet,
And may religion be your constant friend.
'On Miss Aufrere's Birth Day by Miss S[ally] Bate made at the Age of Thirteen'.
MS. *Eng. poet. e. 28, p. 44.

259 May your abilities be shown
To punish rogues are never wanting.
'Counsellor Dansey and Mr. [Thomas (?)] Erskine; exchange of verses', 1796.
MS. Eng. poet. c. 51, p. 99.

260 Mazare a town of Sicily wherein
Has made him die as th'ill rich man.
Fairfax, Thomas, Lord, 'Elogie' on Cardinal Mazarin, translated from French.
MS. *Fairfax 40, p. 603 (autogr.).
MS. *Fairfax 38, p. 289.

261 Me, and some others, you are pleased to choose
Hereafter choose for that your enemies.
Hammond, Anthony, 'On a Friend who often troubled me with his Poetrie'.
MS. Rawl. D. 360, fol. 74$^{v}$ (autogr.).

Me Damon sends his amorous cause to plead, 262
This Damon begs, Orinda begs it too.
Farquhar, [George], 'Written [in] Orinda's Poems lent to a Lady in imitation of Ovid'.
MS. Rawl. poet. 172, fol. 132.

Me have of late been in England 263
And all *a mode de France.*
'A mock French song against the [Long] Parliam$^{t}$'.
MSS. Douce 357, fol. 35; Rawl. poet. 71, p. 23.

Me in all thy steps to tread 264
I meet my Lord in Heaven.
Kenton, James.
MS. *Eng. poet. e. 20, p. 73 (autogr.).

Me, may the mean not fear, nor great despise 265
Youth, age resembling, is a greater weight.
[Stanley, Thomas, translator, 'Advice' from Ausonius].
Pr. *The History of Philosophy*, 1655, p. 72.
MS. Rawl. poet. 90, fol. 104.

Me, who have lived so long amongst the great 266
The place's bounty here shall give you more.
Cowley, Abraham, translator, 'Prefering a Country-Life as many ways more Commodious than that of the City': Martial, *Epigrams* x. xcvi.
Pr. *Works*, 1668, 'Essays in Verse and Prose', p. 147.
MS. Rawl. poet. 173, fol. 55.

Me, whom each poet woos, in various strains 267
With flowers, while storms and winter are thy own!
MS. Don. c. 81, fol. 181.

Meander is not as he seems to be 268
Yet they that know him, know him for an ass.
Davies, [Sir John], of Gray's Inn, 'In Meandrum'.
MS. *Rawl. poet. 212, fol. 58 rev.

Meanwhile the queen fanning a secret fire 269
Which done, her whole life vanished into air.
Godolphin, S[idney, and Edmund Waller], translation of Virgil, *Æneid* iv.
Pr. *The Passion of Dido for Æneas*, translated by Edmund Waller and Sidney Godolphin, 1658. See *Poems of Godolphin*, ed. W. Dighton, 1931, p. xxxix.
MS. Malone 13, p. 291.

Meditating in thy law, 270
Till my God alone I love.
Kenton, James.
MS. *Eng. poet. e. 20, p. 104 (autogr.).

271 Meek and mild the artist you see
By whom he got so great riches.
'The Alchimysts Answere to Nature'; cf. A863.
MS. Ashmole 58, fol. 50.

272 Meek animal, though thou by cruel hand from skies
For my heart's thraldom and captivity.
Bampfield, J[ohn Codrington], 'A sonnet to Miss P-r's monkey . . . in the Morning Post'.
Not in *Poetical Works*, Routledge's British Poets, 1881.
MS. Eng. misc. e. 241, fol. 35.

273 Meek animal! whose sober mien
Is but at best to murmur and obey.
Crowe, [William], of New College, Oxford, 'Ode to an Ass'.
MS. Eng. misc. e. 241, fol. 73v.

274 Meek was her temper, modest was her life
Love the world less, and strive their souls to save.
Memorial in Gloucester Cathedral to Anne Hilton, d. 26 Feb. 1691/2.
Pr. Willis's *Cathedrals*, 1742, ii. 702.
MSS. Rawl. D. 1090, fol. 142; Willis 71, p. 293.

275 Meeting with time, slack thing, said I,
He doth not crave less time, but more.
Herbert, George, 'Time'.
Pr. *The Temple*, 1633, p. 115.
MSS. Rawl. poet. 90, fol. 139; *Tanner 307, fol. 87.

276 Meg and her husband Ned not long ago
'Cause he is cursed that parteth man and wife.
'Of a man and his wife fighting and on standing by would not part them his reason'.
MS. Malone 19, p. 10.

277 Megge lets her husband boast of rule and riches
But she rules all the roost and wears the breeches.
Couplet.
MS. Malone 19, p. 155.

278 Melancholy hence; and get
Make a springtide all the year.
Shirley, James, 'To a Gentlewoman Melancholy'.
Pr. *Poems*, 1646, with L787 as verse 2.
MS. *Rawl. poet. 88, p. 12.

279 Melodious Sir, could but my quill
Corant', Almaine and Sarabrand.
'To his much esteemed, Mr. Oliver Palmer [change ringer] in Bedford, these'. *c.* 1658.
MS. Rawl. D. 886, fol. 7v.

Melpomene, whom Jove our father deigns 280
Which to correct, or change, exceeds our might.
H[awkins], Sir T[homas], translator, Horace, *Odes* I. xxiv.
Pr. with attribution to Sir T[homas] H[awkins], *Poems of Horace*, A. Brome etc., 1666, p. 33. Lines 5 to end pr. *The Odes of Horace*, 1625, Sig. B4, and *Horace*, trd. Barten Holyday, 1652.
MS. Rawl. D. 261, p. 12.

Men all love money, but to several ends 281
Fools love to see 't, and play with 't, like Jack Dawe.
Robinson, Robert.
MS. *Rawl. poet. 218, p. 27 (autogr.).

Men are more eloquent then women made, 282
But women are more pow'ful to persuade.
Couplet, written by T. Hamond, 17th cent.
MS. Mus. f. 2, fol. 3.

Men are so selfish, they spoil one another; 283
And all to live one better then the other.
Robinson, Robert.
MS. *Rawl. poet. 218, p. 122 (autogr.).

Men call on God from day to day, 284
And run on to the devil.
Robinson, Robert.
MS. *Rawl. poet. 218, p. 116 (autogr.).

Men die, and human kind doth pass away 285
Yet care, that makes them die, doth ever stay.
'Of care', couplet.
MS. Eng. poet. e. 14, fol. 14.

Men for religion not dispute, 286
That, that is the thing intended.
Robinson, Robert.
MS. *Rawl. poet. 218, p. 4 (autogr.).

Men gather wealth, get worldly power, 287
What art thou then? Oh no man.
Robinson, Robert.
MS. *Rawl. poet. 218, p. 86 (autogr.).

Men get themselves great vast estates; 288
When death doth once defeat them.
Robinson, Robert.
MS. *Rawl. poet. 218, p. 134 (autogr.).

Men have many faults, women have but two 289
No good can they say nor good can they do.
'Of women', couplet.
MS. Douce f. 5, fol. 18v.

Men hoard up riches for themselves, 290
Here upon earth for ever.
Robinson, Robert.
MS. *Rawl. poet. 218, p. 48 (autogr.).

291 Men learned for relief do cringe,
Nor care to cherish arts.
Robinson, Robert.
MS. *Rawl. poet. 218, p. 172 (autogr.).

292*a* Men leave thee by obtaining, and straight flee
To which all soon return that travel out.
'On hope'.
MS. Rawl. poet. 213, fol. 66.

292*b* Men live (alas) as if life ne'er should fail
Or as hell were but an old woman's tale.
Couplet.
MS. Rawl. poet. 117, fol. 168$^{v}$ rev.

293 Men make religion mere dispute and strife
To show their wit, no rule to guide their life.
Robinson, Robert, couplet.
MS. *Rawl. poet. 218, p. 166 (autogr.).

294 Men match for love, for money too,
Great love to less will fall.
Robinson, Robert.
MS. *Rawl. poet. 218, p. 33 (autogr.).

295 Men may delighted be with springs
And that his Godhead in his works doth shine.
Traherne, Thomas, 'The Enquirie'.
MS. *Eng. poet. c. 42, fol. 9*b*$^{v}$ (autogr.).

296 Men may kiss our hands and gloves present
Their demi-gods our gifts salute your feet.
'Verses made upon a paire of slippers sent for a New yeares guifte 1631'.
MS. Ashmole 781, p. 165.

297 Men more do get, when wares they're selling,
Who gets by lying, gets by stealing.
Robinson, Robert.
MS. *Rawl. poet. 218, p. 120 (autogr.).

298 Men more for lust, than love do marry,
That thinks she's wise, yet nought doth know.
Robinson, Robert.
MS. *Rawl. poet. 218, p. 118 (autogr.).

299 Men never would their hellish hands imbrue
Upon the cup, Christ for man's scorn did drink?
MS. *Rawl. poet. 97, fol. 23$^{v}$ (autogr.).

300 Men of good parts, or skilled in rare arts
Through pride of their hearts, do lose their desarts.
Robinson, Robert, couplet.
MS. *Rawl. poet. 218, p. 89 (autogr.).

301 Men on this age sad grievance do heap
Who could have thought the world's at such a pass.
'The worlds at an End'.
MS. Rawl. D. 1095, fol. 146$^{v}$ rev.

Men post away, their motions violent 302
Of royal tears, yet all would fruitless be.
'An Elegie upon the Death of his Royal Highness Prince George of Denmark etc.', 1708.
MS. Rawl. poet. 114, fol. 175$^{v}$.

Men prate of faith of righteousness they chatter; 303
Money's the wheel, that turns the whole world round.
Robinson, Robert.
MS. *Rawl. poet. 218, p. 137 (autogr.).

Men preach, men fight, both to the self same end, 304
Whats'e'er by noise of tongue, they do pretend.
Robinson, Robert.
MS. *Rawl. poet. 218, p. 14 (autogr.).

Men rake and scrape and moil themselves, 305–6
Into the grave they're hurl'd.
Robinson, Robert.
MS. *Rawl. poet. 218, p. 16 (autogr.).

Men run and gape after this world, 307
Time from them all will snatch it.
Robinson, Robert.
MS. *Rawl. poet. 218, p. 77 (autogr.).

Men run up and down, men labour and plod, 308
And all to seek money their idol god.
Robinson, Robert, couplet.
MS. *Rawl. poet. 218, p. 113 (autogr.).

Men say dunder is a wonder 309
Our Baker his eloquence.
'On Robert Bolds baker to the Colledge neare Winton'.
MS. Malone 19, p. 8.

Men say it, and we often see it come to pass 310
Good turns in sand, shrewd turns are writ in brass.
Couplet.
MS. Rawl. poet. 117, fol. 274 rev.

Men say that honey's always guarded by 311
That thou had'st rather suck a pin than kiss.
'On a gentlewoman for putting a pin in her mouth to prevent kissing'.
MS. Rawl. poet. 199, p. 81.

Men say y'are fair; and fair ye are 'tis true, 312
But (hark!) we praise the painter now, not you.
Couplet, 'On a Painted Madam'.
Copied from *Wits Recreations*, 1663, Ep. 102 (?).
MS. Eng. poet. d. 152, fol. 104$^{v}$.

Men stand upon thorns to pull out your horns 313
When behind it gives them no pain boys.
MS. Rawl. B. 35, fol. 39 rev.

314 Men strive, who shall out-pride it who out-state it.
A lowly spirit's beneath them; oh they hate it.
Robinson, Robert, couplet.
MS. *Rawl. poet. 218, p. 175 (autogr.).

315 Men take the sacred seals of their salvation
Of all their mirth, remember Judas' sop.
[Quarles, Francis], 'On the receiving of the Lord's Supper'.
Pr. *Divine Fancies*, 1632, iii. 79.
MSS. Rawl. poet. 90, fol. 72; 117, fol. 170$^{v}$ rev.

316 Men talk of fears and none appearing,
Alas they are not worth the hearing.
Robinson, Robert, couplet.
MS. *Rawl. poet. 218, p. 58 (autogr.).

317 Men talk of God, of Christ of faith
Their works, their works would show.
Robinson, Robert.
MS. *Rawl. poet. 218, p. 9 (autogr.).

318 Men talk of heaven (indeed it is but talk)
And act for earth: as earthly men they walk.
Robinson, Robert, couplet.
MS. *Rawl. poet. 218, p. 116 (autogr.).

319 Men, that are low, have lofty thoughts:
Oh then they fear to fall.
Robinson, Robert.
MS. *Rawl. poet. 218, p. 21 (autogr.).

320 Men, that come learned from the schools
They'll make light darkness, darkness light of day.
Robinson, Robert.
MS. *Rawl. poet. 218, p. 76 (autogr.).

321 Men when they're under the power of the sword
Winter food then we must take, that's in season.
Robinson, Robert.
MS. *Rawl. poet. 218, p. 33 (autogr.).

322 Men, whilst they live upon poor worms tread,
Worms on men's flesh do feed, when men are dead.
Robinson, Robert, couplet.
MS. *Rawl. poet. 218, p. 3 (autogr.).

323 Men will thee deem or judge only to be
They'll find it then decked with divinity.
Anagram: 'Judith Gore Or Judge thee'.
MS. Rawl. poet. 117, fol. 33$^{v}$.

324 Men would fear sin, or not fear to confess't
If they like thee should make the world their priest.
Paman, Cl[ement], 'Epig. to Montaigne', couplet.
MS. Rawl. poet. 147, p. 47.

Mending their nets with draughts of fishes torn 325
But they that get a share in Christ, have more.
'The Call'.
MS. Rawl. poet. 154, fol. 111.

Merciful almighty Lord 326
And save me by Thy Grace.
Kenton, James.
MS. *Eng. poet. e. 20, p. 169 (autogr.).

Mercurial man enough before! 327
I'll do as you do, Sh - t a T - d.
'R. P. to J[ohn] L[umby]'.
MS. *Eng. poet. e. 42, fol. 89.

Mercury show'd Apollo Bartas' book; 328
Let me look to't, lest women wear the spurs.
Ward, N[athaniel (?)], 'On the Tenth Muse. (Anne Bradstreat's poëms, 1650)'.
MS. Sancroft 53, p. 38.

Mercy and grace shall be my song 329
To sing his praise above the sky.
Kenton, James.
MS. *Eng. poet. e. 20, p. 267 (autogr.).

Mercy and judgment to exalt 330
God's city and his land.
Psalm ci.
MS. *Rawl. C. 113, fol. 68.

Mercy dear lord, mercy oh saviour dear. 331
And save oh lord our sick Jerusalem.
'A 3. Voc. John Jenkins', transposed by T. Hamond.
MSS. Mus. f. 17–19: f. 19, fol. 25$^{v}$.

Mercy, oh Lord, there is with Thee 332
And bless me with thy light and love.
Kenton, James, Psalm cxxx.
MS. *Eng. poet. e. 20, p. 206 (autogr.).

Merely for death to grieve [pine] and mourn 333
Sleep, sleep, th'hast trod a weary race.
Strode, William, 'On the death of S$^{r}$ Thomas Pelham', 2 Dec. 1624.
MS. *CCC. 325, fol. 81$^{v}$ (autogr.).
MSS. Ashmole 47, two copies, fols. 41 and 51$^{v}$; CCC. 328, fol. 14, attr. to Stroud; Eng. poet. e. 97, p. 118, attr. to W. S.

Merling says in his book who will read right 334
And in the vale of Josaphat buried shall he be.
'The Prophesies of Merlinge . . . corrected [from] a very ancient manuscript' by Ashmole.
MS. Ashmole 1835, fol. 39$^{v}$.

335 Merrily my love and I
Of love's rich treasure.
Pr. Tho: Bateson's *First set of English Madrigales*, 1604, xxvii.
MSS. Mus. f. 20–24: f. 20, fol. 86$^{v}$.

336 Messiah, Lord of heaven and earth!
And all to Jesu's sceptre yield.
Kenton, James.
MS. *Eng. poet. e. 20, p. 378 (autogr.).

337 Methinks amid my heart I hear
Have power again raised to be.
Sidney, Sir Philip, Psalm xxxvi.
MSS. *Rawl. poet. 24, p. 49; *25, fol. 29.

338*a* Methinks death like one laughing lies
And for a trophy left her body dead.
Edward, Lord Herbert of Cherbury 'On Mrs. Boulstreed'. [July 1609].
Pr. *Occasional Verses*, 1665.
MSS. Eng. poet. f. 9, p. 207; Rawl. poet. 31, fol. 36$^{v}$, attr. to Sir Edw. Harbert.

338*b* [Methinks I could be intemperate in thy praise]
As well in giving out as taking in.
Oley, B., on *Hygiasticon*, Leonard Lessius, 1634, where it is pr.
MS. Eng. misc. e. 13, fol. 22$^{v}$.

339 Methinks I hear the ploughman all day long
Th'other, in great splendour, finds no peace at all.
'The contentment of a mean and great lot compared'.
MS. Rawl. poet. 213, fol. 53$^{v}$.

340 Methinks I see Britannia's genius here
And add new lustre to his father's crown.
'A Prologue . . . 9 Dec. 1745 . . . Theater Royal . . . Drury Lane, when the whole Receipt of the House was apply'd to . . . Giving . . . Soldiers . . . Flannel Waistcoats'.
MSS. Montagu e. 13, fol. 87$^{v}$; North b. 24, fol. 158.

341 Methinks I see our mighty monarch stand
To make way for the son to bring a whore.
'On Madam Lawson'.
Pr. *Poems on Affairs of State*, I. ii, 1703, p. 43.
See *Poems by [the] Earl of Rochester*, ed. V. de S. Pinto, 1953.
MSS. Don. b. 8, p. 646; Eng. poet. c. 18, fol. 20.

342 Methinks I see the nimble aged sire
Lord show me what it is, but never where.
'Pentelogia or the Quintessence of Meditation', in five sections, 'Mors tua', 'Mors Christi', 'Fraus Mundi', 'Gloria Coeli', 'Dolor Inferni'.
MS. Rawl. poet. 62, fol. 25.

Methinks I see you newly risen 343
The reins of government must break.
'The Looking-Glasse'.
See *Poems by [the] Earl of Rochester*, ed. V. de S. Pinto, 1953.
MS. Don. b. 8, p. 647.

Methinks, in this a mystery there lurks, 344
Why Johnson's Plays are now called Johnson's works.
'On B. Johnsons Book in fol.' 1616. Couplet, Answere dby A143*a*.
MSS. CCC. 309, fol. 25$^{v}$; 328, fol. 43$^{v}$.

Methinks that I have something for to say 345
Blest be those parents that have such a son.
L. F., 'Matertera Nepoti discedenti'.
MS. Rawl. poet. 194, fol. 41.

Methinks that reading these romances 346
The steps their predecessors led.
'Written in a Book of Novels' given to the copyist Wm. Parry by R. Hulse.
MS. Eng. misc. e. 183, fol. 80$^{v}$.

Methinks the hour is come, 347
In his dear bosom I lay down my head.
'Mr. [William] Mason's Poem on Death'.
MS. Rawl. poet. 173, fol. 152.

Methinks the poor town hath been troubled so long 348
To kill men by looking as if she would die.
[Sackville, Charles, Earl of Dorset].
Pr. *Works of Rochester, Rescommon, Dorset . . .* etc., 1721, p. 56.
MS. Rawl. B. 35, fol. 36$^{v}$ rev.

Methinks this word behold doth come to me 349
But with my saviour I shall live for ever.
Hooper, John, of Devon, 'Luke vii. 12, Behold there was a dead man carryed out, who was the only sonne of his Mother. A meditation uppon this text'.
MS. *Rawl. poet. 208, fol. 9 (autogr.).

Methinks those ancients did supinely err 350
Who in their potage have been used to drink.
'On an unjust parallel in the Night'.
MS. Rawl. poet. 210, fol. 62.

Methinks to night I cast my eyes around 351
And frequent visit here the loved remains.
'Prologue to the Play for erecting a Monument to Shakespear in Westminster Abbey by Mr. [Lewis] Theobald and spoke by Mr. Ryan, in Covent garden 10 April 1739'.
MS. Rawl. poet. 172, fol. 162.

352 Methinks with Lynus Kate deserves a place
Since to her music stones do move a pace.
Couplet.
MS. Eng. poet. e. 14, fol. 71.

353 Methought by God for mankind so unfit,
That his first blessing ruined it.
'On maidenhead'.
MS. Rawl. poet. 213, front cover.

354 Methought I saw the streams of fruitful Nile
So soon as you restored my life, my peace.
Mervall, Alphonso, 'To Cloris a dreame'. Subscribed 'Tettix'.
MS. *Rawl. poet. 166, p. 36 (autogr.).

355 Methought I walked in a dream
God help them, pray oh pray with me.
'Mr. [Serjeant John] Hoskins his Dreame in the Tower', July 1614–July 1615.
Pr. Wood's *Athenae*, ed. Bliss, ii, 1815, 627.
MSS. Ashmole 36, 37, fol. 213, attr. to Mr. Hoskins; 781, p. 129, attr. to Mr. Jo. Hoskins; Malone 19, p. 71, attr. to J. Hoskins; Rawl. B. 151, fol. 103, attr. to Mr. Hoskins; see also T1611.

356 Methoughts musing as I was laid
Praise to the King of Israel.
Carol with refrain, Nowell nowell, nowell, nowell Praise to the King of Israel.
MS. Eng. poet. b. 5, p. 31.

357 Michael with his good angels overcame
For Heaven hath lost, earth gained an enemy.
Clifford, Henry, Earl of Cumberland, 'Saint Michaell'.
MS. *Rawl. poet. 95, fol. 35$^{v}$.

358 Midas, a clown, by nature's hand designed
Thus truly told, and truly told of thee.
'Midas a Fable'. The date 1724 appears on the paper.
MS. Ballard 47, fol. 32.

359 'Midst a fair garden's various wild
And voles at once, and virtue lost.
Whaley, John, 'The Rose and the Butterfly; A Fable'.
Pr. *Poems*, 1732, p. 51.
MS. Rawl. poet. 222, fol. 10$^{v}$.

360 'Midst alabaster walls confin'd
And bears away the golden prize.
Rotheram, The Revd. —.
MS. Eng. poet. c. 51, p. 57.

361 'Midst blust'ring winds and swelling waves
Nor shall I trust and wait in vain.
Beddome, Benjamin.
MS. *Eng. misc. e. 227, fol. 7.

'Midst foes without and foes within 362
The victory's gained the conflict's o'er.
Beddome, Benjamin, 'An Hymn'.
Pr. *Hymns . . . of B. Beddome*, 1818, no. 541.
MS. *Eng. misc. e. 227, fol. 172$^{v}$.

'Midst largest heaps of untouched gold 363
Is squander'd by his lavish heirs.
Whaley, John, 'Minos and the Miser; A Fable'.
Pr. *Poems*, 1732, p. 127.
MS. Rawl. poet. 222, fol. 19.

'Midst thousand bleeding hearts, and sighing swains 364
He made the subject nations know their lord.
Whaley, John, 'To a Young Lady, on her Recovery From the Small Pox'.
Pr. *Poems*, 1732, p. 57.
MS. Rawl. poet. 222, fol. 6.

'Midst threat'ning danger threat'ning wants 365
The pity of thy heart.
Beddome, Benjamin.
MS. *Eng. misc. e. 227, fol. 72$^{v}$.

'Midst throngs of deep distress 366
Distant, look peace but hammer war.
J. F., Psalm cxx.
MS. *Eng. poet. f. 17, p. 119 (autogr.).

Might Heraclitus tears as some streams do 367
To heaven's theorbo, music of the sphere.
'All is Vanity'.
MS. Rawl. poet. 142, fol. 14.

Might I a wife choose pleasing to my mind 368
T'have lov'd so sweet an armful of content.
'The chusing of a wife'.
MS. Eng. poet. e. 14, fol. 74$^{v}$.

Might we ascend to excellence sublime 369
Above the reach of every dunce and drone.
'Omnibus et Singulis Ad quos presentes Literae perveniant . . .' copy-book verses (?), used as a cover to 'Peece Copies in Verse 1706/7', now missing.
MS. Rawl. D. 1028, fol. 1.

Mighty lord from this thy land 370
All go straight not one shall stray.
Herbert, Mary (*née* Sidney), Countess of Pembroke, Psalm lxxxv.
MSS. *Rawl. poet. 24, p. 126; *25, fol. 80$^{v}$.

Mighty ruler, God most true 371
Stir us all to worship thee.
'Primer Engl. and latine of K. Hen. 8 1546. The hymne for the third houre'.
MS. Eng. poet. e. 56, p. 69.

372 Mild as the evening of a summers' day
But charms like these make foibles be forgot.
Bate, Sally, 'Another Character, 1768. Miss Pearte'.
MS. *Eng. poet. e. 28, p. 227.

373 Mild mistress of my mournful muse so long
I pray that I may die in thy employment.
Burton, Francis.
MS. *Add. A. 267, fol. 105 (autogr.).

374 Mild peace is up in arms, and battles are
Can ne'er command, who cannot first obey.
Paman, Clement, 'St. Stephens feild'.
MS. Rawl. poet. 147, p. 66.

375 Militia boys, for my theme I now choose
And ever defend him from foreign alarms.
'A New Song in Praise of the Durham Militia', '1760'.
MS. Firth c. 20, fol. 35.

376 Milla, the glory of whose virtuous race
Blush'd, ran away, and scorn'd him ever after.
Copied by F. Douce from 'a ms. collection of poetry . . . time of Queen Elizabeth or James I'.
MSS. Douce e. 24, fol. 21; ending e. 25, fol. 1.

377 Milo lives long in France, and while he's there
His ground lacks ploughing up, so doth not she.
'In Milonem'. [Martial, *Epigrams* VII. ci]. Pr. F. Davison's *Poetical Rhapsody*, 1608.
MS. Don. d. 58, fol. 38.

378 Milo's from home, yet not withstanding this
His land's unploughed, his wife doth occupy.
'On a Cuckold . . . Turned out of the latten [of Martial] by D. D - st'. Martial, *Epigrams* VII. ci.
MS. Ashmole 38, p. 137.

379 Milton they say did learned Salmasius foil
But not one word of Bentley or of Boyle.
MS. Eng. poet. d. 152, fol. 18.

380 Mine, and the poet's plague consume you all,
And safer far by pimping get my bread.
'Julian's Farewell to the Muses. 1685'.
MSS. Firth c. 15, p. 169; c. 16, p. 52.

381 Mine be a cot beside the hill
And point with taper spire to Heav'n.
Rogers, Samuel, 'A Wish'.
MS. Percy d. 9, fol. 8v.

382 Mine eye bewrays
No friend except you will.
MS. Rawl. poet. 85, fol. 116v rev.

Mine eye through all my prospect round 383
Heaped on us by the proud.
J. F., Psalm cxxiii.
MS. *Eng. poet. f. 17, p. 101 (autogr.).

Mine eye why didst thou light 384*a*
For whom this grief I find.
Song in 4 parts, by Thomas Hamond, who notes 'The rest of the ditty is in my viole books'. 1st of 5 verses, which end 'with sorrow for relief' in B.M. Add. MS. 22583, fol. 92.
MSS. Mus. f. 7–10: f. 7, fol. 2.

Mine eye with all the deadly sins is fraught 384*b*
Wherefore my heart is damned in love's fire.
[Constable, Henry], sonnet, pr. *Diana*, 1592, Sig. C2.
MS. Ashmole 38, p. 53.

Mine eyes are open, yet perceive I nought 385
My tears with mercy, and my shame with grace.
Alabaster, William, Son. 38 'A morning meditatione'.
MS. *Eng. poet. e. 57, fol. 9v.

Mine eyes distressed with stormy winter's ire 386
Shed tears apace to quit their secret shame.
MS. Rawl. poet. 85, fol. 91.

Mine eyes I lift [unto] up to the hills 387
Mercy doth this, that hath no end.
Fairfax, Thomas, Lord, Psalm cxxi.
MS. *Fairfax 40, p. 327 (autogr.).
MS. *Fairfax 38, p. 425.

Mine eyes I would not sell for dross 388
Though Croesus wealth repaired my loss.
Couplet.
MSS. Rawl. D. 954, fol. 43; Rawl. poet. 209, fol. 31v.

Mine eyes leave off your weeping 389
That love should kill me.
MS. Rawl. poet. 85, fol. 45.

Mine eyes were once blessed with the sight 390
He'll languish, and turn shade again.
Mayne, Jasper, 'On Mris Anne King's Tablebook of Pictures'.
MSS. CCC. 309, fol. 60; 328, fol. 83; Eng. poet. c. 53, fol. 12; e. 97, p. 143, attr. to Jasper Mayne; Rawl. poet. 199, attr. to I. M.

Mine eyes with fervency of sprite 391
Which no man may come nigh.
5-part anthem.
MS. Mus. d. 12, fol. 12v.

392 Mine heart indites no slight or vulgar song
And all thy people praise thee now and ever.
Harington, Sir John, Psalm xlv.
MS. *Douce 361, fol. 27.

393 Mine own love Jesu most dulcet
Without end to govern alone.
'Jesu dulcissimus . . . Primer of Hen. 8. Engl. and Lat. 1536 . . . fol. 146'.
MS. Eng. poet. e. 56, p. 109.

394 Mira would twice in colours live
Attempt to draw you o'er again.
[Bacon, Phanuel], 'To Mira sitting twice for her Picture. To the Tune of The Play of Love, etc.'
MS. Eng. poet. e. 45, fol. 37 (autogr.).

395 Mira! your charms inspire my lays
And cause a lasting peace.
Motteux, Peter, 'Junr.', 'To Mira. A Song'.
MS. Eng. poet. c. 9, p. 129.

396 Mirror of poets, mirror of our age
And all we can imagine in mankind.
Waller, Edmund, 'Upon Ben: Johnson'.
Pr. *Poems*, 1645, p. 153.
MS. *Don. d. 55, fol. 38.

397 Misers distribute nothing while they live,
And spendthrifts when they die have nought to give.
Cowper, William, translator, from Owen, couplet 'On the Prodigal and the Covetous'.
Pr. from this MS., *Poetical Works*, ed. H. S. Milford, 4th ed., 1934, p. 666.
MS. Autogr. d. 21, fol. 192 (autogr.).

398 Misers! Say, can gold prolong
Gold, which I must leave behind.
'The Vanity of Riches. From Anacreon', xxiii.
MS. Ballard 29, fol. 134.

399 Miss Ashe's little thrush here lies
As this, pale corpse, poor bird be laid in dust.
Williams, John, 'An Epitaph upon Miss Ashe's thrush, written at her desire'.
MS. *Rawl. poet. 184, fol. 54v (autogr.).

400 Miss Betty, I say, Miss Betty I say
When you should read your Bible.
'Verses made by Miss Ashe'.
MS. *Rawl. poet. 191, fol. 105v.

401 Miss Betty Mr. Williams you here may find
Or else you'll not be of the self same mind.
'Item by her', i.e. Miss Ashe, 'in my [John Williams's] Chamber'.
MS. *Rawl. poet. 191, fol. 105v.

Miss Betty what are you in love 402
That I have cleared my self to night.
Sheppard, Elizabeth, 'to a person that [said] I was in love'.
MS. Top. Oxon. d. 287, fol. 47 (autogr.).

Miss Danae when fair and young 403
And clasp the padlock on her mind.
'The English Padlock'.
MS. Eng. poet. d. 152, fol. 28.

Miss Kitty, by her Mamma bred 404
Your doctrine is alluring.
'Miss Cadiere's Case a Song'. *Gentleman's Magazine*, i, 1731, p. 446.
MS. Ballard 50, fol. 111v.

Mistake me not I am not of that mind 405
And all for truth shall take it.
[Brome, Alexander], 'The Indifferent'.
Pr. *Poems*, 1661, p. 3.
MS. Ashmole 47, fol. 144v.

Mister and Mistress with all your guests 406
'Tis I must perform it for my name is Francis.
'Twelfe night merriment: an° 1602' at St. John's College, Oxford. Edited from this MS. by M. L. Lee, 1893.
MS. Rawl. poet. 212, fol. 81v rev.

Mr. Carpenter's dead, and gone up Jacob's ladder 407
If death would have spar'd him but a pissing while.
'One Mr. Carpenter that dyed of the stone'.
MS. Ashmole 38, p. 203.

Mr. Dolbin you've done well 408
And so Mr. Dolbin I wish you a good morning.
'The Bellman of De la Hay Wards, Address to Mr. Dolbin'. Tory verses on the impeachment of Sacheverell, 1710.
MS. Rawl. D. 383, fol. 61.

Mr. Fox, Mr. Fox. 409
Our Lear again may be king.
'Old Political Song . . . when the late Charles Fox proposed a Regency unrestricted. 1789'.
MS. Percy c. 8, fol. 150.

Mr. Permentor, stands at the centre 410
Like a man of war.
Hoskins, [John].
MS. Malone 19, p. 149.

Mrs. Battye hath her coats so high 411
And yet between them both a man was born.
[Taylor, John].
MS. Rawl. poet. 209, fol. 26v, attr. (?) to Spence; see also A1230, B102, F28.

412 Mrs. Holt that lusty colt
By letter of attorney.
4 lines on Sir Francis Prince, knighted 1611, and one Mrs. Holt.
MS. CCC. 327, fol. 31[v].

413 Mistress I court you with a golden mine
Where once he's lodged he'll never more depart.
'The Epistle', preface to a rhymed version of the *Song of Songs*.
MS. Rawl. poet. 64, fol. 1.

414 Mrs. Immerita [Marina] amongst some gossips sat
Prayed be it so, for that same sure was I.
'In Immeritam'.
MSS. Don. d. 58, fol. 33[v]; Tanner 465, fol. 94[v].

415 Mrs. Marina startles to see a frog
Yet fears she not what flesh can do unto her.
'On Mrs. Marina'.
MS. Eng. poet. e. 14, fol. 80 rev.

416 Mistress mine well may you fare
So so . . . true love should do.
MS. Don. d. 58, fol. 25[v].

417 Mistress Saturnia scorning long to brook
The servile swain that sells unsavoury breath.
'An other' i.e. Libel on Edward Coke and his second wife Lady Hatton, *c.* 1598.
MSS. Don. c. 54, fol. 7, doubtfully attr. to Sir John Haidon; Don. d. 58, fol. 46*a*[v]; Eng. hist. c. 308, fol. 100*a*.

418 Mistress to say you were untrue, were no
To all my former follies, warned by you.
'An Invictive agaynst his Mris. that proved false.'
MS. Ashmole 38, p. 60, attr. to 'Anthonye [Sawier (?)]', corrected to [Thomson (?)]; 47, fol. 76, attr. to J[ohn] C[oventry] (see fol. 75[v]).

419 Mocking old age is want of sense
Should bring you to the gallows young.
'Old Age honourable'.
MS. *Eng. poet. d. 47, fol. 139.

420 Modest [gentle] shentle when her [put] she
Pray send he word if her can love.
'A Welsh wooer'.
Pr. *Mysteries of Love and Eloquence*, E[dward] P[hilips], 1658, p. 140.
MSS. Ashmole 47, fol. 49; Rawl. poet. 84, fol. 40.

421 Modest humble, godly wise
Such she was, that now lies here.
'On a marble stone in the chancell of St. George Southwarke'.
MS. Sancroft 59, p. 293 rev.

Modest in speech, in garb, in act, in air, 422*a*
Norbourn's her name, and Stukely is her seat.
Barnes, Joshuah, 'Acrostick, on the name Mary Norbourn. Octob. 12 1703'.
MS. Hearne's diaries 11, p. 125.

Modest! When Christ home to thy house would go 422*b*
Not to thy house, into thy heart he'll come.
Sancroft, William, 'Lord I am not worthy thou shouldst come under my Roof', translation from Crashaw's *Epigrammata Sacra*, 1634.
MS. *Sancroft 48, fol. 12[v] (autogr.).

Moggy from Jockey she needs would depart, 423
But Moggy was jealous and that was enough.
MS. Firth c. 20, fol. 71.

Moist with one drop of thy blood, my dry soul 424
Salute the last, and everlasting day.
Donne, John, 'Holy Sonnetts. La Corona 6.' Pr. *Poems*, 1633.
MS. *Eng. poet. e. 99, fol. 42[v].

Mome, bark thy loudest and spare not (spiteful elf) 425
For know I care not, then thou'lt hang thy self.
Cheyney, William, 'To Momus', couplet.
MS. *Rawl. poet. 86, fol. 2.

Monarch of music verse and day 426
To rule and save mankind the power of kings was given.
[Cibber, Colley], 'Ode for His Majestys Birth Day Oct: 30 1735. Perform'd at Court on that Day by Dr. Maurice Greene.'
MSS. Mus. d. 33, in M. Greene's hand; d. 34.

Monarchs are men and every man must die 427
Did ever universal empire gain.
'Occasioned by the Death of King William . . . April 16th 1702'.
MS. Don. c. 55, fol. 25.

Monday I swear shall be a holiday 428
If he forswear himself but once a day.
Davies, [Sir] John, of Gray's Inn, 'In Mundayum'.
MS. *Rawl. poet. 212, fol. 57[v] rev.

Money comes and money goes, 429
Kindred, may have no friends; all turn their back.
Robinson, Robert.
MS. *Rawl. poet. 218, p. 14 (autogr.).

Money does all things in this world as king 430
And that's the cause they make such stir about thee.
MS. Rawl. poet. 196, fol. 11.

431 Money get, and be a man:
Pulls down princes, sets up slaves.
Robinson, Robert.,
MS. *Rawl. poet. 218, p. 145 (autogr.).

432 Money gets wealth, and wealth doth make rich men;
Oh to their earth they must return again.
Robinson, Robert.
MS. *Rawl. poet. 218, p. 168 (autogr.).

433 Money it self is good for naught:
Whereof we stand in need.
Robinson, Robert.
MS. *Rawl. poet. 218, p. 170 (autogr.).

434 Money makes a mighty man,
Thou welcome art, wheres'e'er thou dost appear.
Robinson, Robert.
MS. *Rawl. poet. 218, p. 93 (autogr.).

435 Money, this money doth all earthly things:
Of this vain world, whats'e'er the false tongue saith.
Robinson, Robert.
MS. *Rawl. poet. 218, p. 104 (autogr.).

436 Money, thou bane of bliss and source of woe
And while he digs out thee, falls in the ditch.
Herbert, George, 'Avarice'.
Pr. *The Temple*, 1633, p. 69.
MSS. Rawl. D. 924, fol. 341, attr. to Herbert; *Tanner 307, fol. 53.

437 Money, up and down that's hurled,
Though clothed all in plush.
Robinson, Robert.
MS. *Rawl. poet. 218, p. 17 (autogr.).

438 Money's a lady of a powerful awe,
But quite forsakes us, if we do abuse her.
Robinson, Robert.
MS. *Rawl. poet. 218, p. 169 (autogr.).

439 'Mongst all the ancient prophets can be found
Shall dwell in unknown light eternally.
'A Paraphrase on The History of the Prophet Jonas with some ejaculations intermixt', *c.* 1666.
MS. Rawl. poet. 170, fol. 64 (autogr.).

440 'Mongst all the glories here below,
And nought but air supplies their glorious place.
Chatwin, John, 'The Deceit'.
MS. *Rawl. poet. 94, p. 254 (autogr.).

441 'Mongst all the nauseous creatures of the town,
And from a stable thus they sally out.
Chatwin, John, 'The Cambridge Wit'.
MS. *Rawl. poet. 94, p. 53 (autogr.).

'Mongst all the plagues that torture poor mankind, 442
To find a medicine and the grief remove.
Chatwin, John, 'A Satyr against the Gout'.
MS. *Rawl. poet. 94, p. 153 (autogr.).

'Mongst all those precious juices 443
Drank old sack and called it nectar.
MS. Mus. f. 21, fol. 2.

'Mongst the learned in the law this opinion prevails 444
When at home ne'er was found one good one for me.
MS. Rawl. poet. 153, fol. 78.

'Mongst winding rocks (his swelling griefs t'allay) 445
Itself my coffin, monument, and grave.
'The Male-Content'.
MS. Rawl. poet. 90, fol. 120.

Monm[outh] the bunch is, fox am I 446
Fox shall turn goose, and learn to fly.
'Some verses on a Medal said to be presented by Mr. Hampden Junior [1653–1696] to the Countess of Monm— . . .'.
MS. Firth e. 6, fol. 119.

Monmouth's witty, Lauderdaile's pretty 447
And the king for a great politician.
MS. Don. b. 8, p. 568.

[Monsieur] Mounsier Mingo for quaffing doth pass 448–9
And dub me knight, Domingo.
'A. 4. Voc:. Orlando de Lassus'.
See F. W. Sternfeld 'Lasso's Music for Shakespeare's "Samingo"', *Shakespeare Quarterly* ix, 1958, p. 105.
MSS. Mus. f. 17–19: f. 19, fol. 50v.

Moon and stars covered shipmen wish for peace, 450
But only that the vulgar sort I hate.
W. A., translator, Horace, *Odes* II. xvi.
MS. *Rawl. poet. 104, fol. 19 (autogr.).

Mopsa I met and fain I would have kissed her 451
You have fair saint shall serve at our next meeting.
'In Mopsam'.
MS. Don. d. 58, fol. 33.

More anger yet . . . *see* More trouble yet . . .

More are undone by wicked lust and pride, 452
Then there are left in all the world beside.
Robinson, Robert, couplet.
MS. *Rawl. poet. 218, p. 88 (autogr.).

More clear than glass (Oh well! I will to morn 453
Whiles I of th'oak from whence thou flow'st do sing.
W. A., translator, Horace, *Odes* III. xiii.
MS. *Rawl. poet. 104, fol. 28v (autogr.).

454 More Cottons yet? What doth some envious fate
Sir Rowland was a living monument.
[Strode, William], 'Againe on the Death of Sr Rowland seconding that of Sir Robert Cotton'.
Pr. *Parentalia*, 1635, Sig. E3v.
MS. *CCC. 325, fol. 124 (autogr.).

455 More delightful are my woes
On my toils eternal rest.
'The Delights of Virtue'.
MS. Eng. poet. e. 47, p. 37.

456 More easy 'tis (though evil 'tis)
The blessings of this life.
Robinson, Robert, 'It is easier to sowe sedition, then to settle peace'.
MS. *Rawl. poet. 218, p. 114 (autogr.).

457 More glorious suns adorn fair London's pride
Than all rich England's continent beside.
Couplet.
MS. Rawl. poet. 117, fol. 274 rev.

458 More had I once, more would I have,
But rest upon him still.
'In Elingham Church near Bungey in Norfolk. Here lyeth buried. . . . More of Norwich Gentylman, who dyed. . .'.
MS. Ballard 29, fol. 60.

459 [More] precious then th'bewitching mines
That this My Real Hart shall so endure
Johnston, Nathaniel, '[Mar]tha Lyster. My Hart is real'.
MS. Eng. poet. c. 25, fol. 34v (autogr.).

460 More than a priest, he in the church might pass
More than philosopher, in all the rest.
MS. Rawl. poet. 66, fol. 28v.

461 More than content with what my labours gain
Or wear the cap and mask, on any stage.
'It is said that Mr. [David] Garrick sent the following lines to a Nobleman, who ask'd him if he did not intend being in Parliament. March . . 23rd 1761'.
MS. Montagu e. 13, fol. 169v.

462 More trouble yet? 'twas but an organist
Such idle anthems on a Holyday.
Holiday, Barten, 'answere to an organist', [William Meredith of New College (?)] on *the Marriage of the Arts*, 1621; cf. C229.
MSS. Eng. poet. f. 10, fol. 86v, attr. to Holyday; Malone 21, fol. 73; Rawl. D. 1092, fol. 270, attr. to B. Holliday.

More wealth, more wealth, you rich men say. 463
Mind less this world, think on eternity.
Robinson, Robert.
MS. *Rawl. poet. 218, p. 171 (autogr.).

Morpheus (thou turn-key to all human sense) 464
Reader, assure thy self, I'll spend a tear.
Q[uarles], J[ohn], 'Regale lectum Miseriae or A kingly Bed of Miserie . . . A Dreame', copied from 2nd ed., 1649.
MS. Rawl. B. 165, fol. 115.

Mortality, behold and fear 465
Yet to this shape all must be brought.
'Memento for Mortallitie. Taken from the veiwe of the sepulchres . . . In the Abbye of Westminster'.
Pr. *Help to Discourse*, W. B. and E. P., 1619; J. Freeman's *Ancient Funeral Monuments*, 1631; Beaumont's *Poems*, 1653, Sig. M2v; and a short version in *Wit's Recreations*, 1641, Sig. S2v.
MS. Ashmole 38, p. 175*c*.

Morus when bit by fleas puts out the light. 466
For now says he they cannot see to bite.
Walsh, William, translator, [Greek Anthology], '186', couplet.
MS. Malone 9, fol. 28 (autogr.).

Moses into a serpent turned his wand, 467
They'll share your treasure, thank your treasurer.
'The Parallel', on Godolphin, *c.* 1706.
MS. Smith 23, p. 115.

Moses' successour, and the son of Nun; 468
Happy he was; what need I more to say.
'Of valiant Joshua', no. 7 of 'Sacred Epigrams' sent to John Rhodes, Fellow of Trinity College Cambridge 1618–1649, by H. W.
MS. Tanner 466, fol. 98v.

Moses, the legislator 469
To my celestial home.
Kenton, James.
MS. *Eng. poet. e. 20, p. 305 (autogr.).

Most are transported with a fleshly mind 470
He will accept of no hypocrisies.
MS. *Rawl. poet. 97, fol. 23 (autogr.).

Most beautiful thou art in every feature 471
Ev'n had great Jove beheld he'd been your prize.
'An acrostick' on Mary Goose.
MS. Rawl. poet. 116, fol. 109.

Most blessed his 472
That shortly come, and come shall ne'er depart.
J. F., Psalm xxxii.
MS. *Eng. poet. f. 17, p. 29 (autogr.).

473 Most cruel Mors, hath killed the horse
Come you unto his burial.
'On the death of Mr. Murialls horse'. William Muryall, esquire bedell at Cambridge, 1555–6, 'servant and scholar' of Bishop Gardiner, master of Pembroke Hall.
MS. Malone 19, p. 150.

474 Most deal promoted by persons insentiate
To purchace grace and please god omnipotent.
Prognostication.
MS. Rawl. C. 813, fol. 151$^{v}$.

475 Most dearest love when as these rustic lines
As you shall prove: if you my love requite.
Corrected draft.
MS. Rawl. D. 864, fol. 235$^{v}$ (autogr.).

476 Most dogs can boast of collars bought
A dog's a cur that serves a slave.
'Mr. [William] Dawson [d. 1780] had a favorite Bull-dog who won the Collar at Wilmslow Wakes'.
MS. Top. Lancs. c. 3, p. 160.

477 Most famous university
For honours fosters art.
'Apoc. 5 [v. 2]', on the coat of arms of the University of Oxford.
MSS. Ashmole 36, 37, fol. 210.

478 Most glorious God that name of thine,
Now and for ever rendered be.
'A Psalm of praise for the promised glory'.
MS. Rawl. D. 1278, fol. 93$^{v}$.

479 Most glorious of th'immortals and almighty still
As mighty ever the common law to praise.
[Trail, Robert(?)], Cleanthes' Hymn, in the translator's own hand.
MS. Eng. misc. f. 79, p. 88*a*.

480 Most gracious and omnipotent
You cannot cast him out.
'On the Long Parliament'.
Pr. Cleveland's *Works*, 1687, p. 366.
MS. Rawl. poet. 173, fol. 105$^{v}$, attr. to Mr. Cleveland; see also M484.

481 Most gracious God, hear England's prayers
Shall well rewarded be.
Invective against William III.
MS. Rawl. D. 361, fol. 346.

482 Most gracious God pardon my sinful soul
Lord I believe, help thou my unbelief.
Dimock, Col. Cressy, 'A Penitential Confession'.
MS. Firth f. 1, fol. 50 (autogr. (?)).

Most gracious Lord, whose powerful goodness chose 483
As is most meet, all glorious praise inherit.
At end, 'Soli deo Gloria'.
MSS. Ashmole 36, 37, fol. 24.

Most gracious omnipotent 484
And surely pay your wages.
'A Panegirick . . . of the Par: att Westminstr. . .', 1647.
MSS. Douce 357, fol. 14$^{v}$; Tanner 466, fol. 60, attr. to Sir Henry Moody [Bart.], 'quondam Aul: Magd.'; see also M480.

Most gracious prince! undoubted sovereign queen 485
Doth Norwich live, whose hearts and goods are thine.
'Queen Elizabeth comeing in progresse unto Norwich . . . one . . . sung theis verses'.
Pr. *The joyfull Receyving of the Queene . . . Norwich* [1578]; see Nichols's *Progresses*, 1823, ii. 144.
MSS. Rawl. poet. 66, fol. 52; Top. Cheshire c.6, fol. 433.

Most gracious prince we from the country came 486
And craves this impress, Lord have mercy on us.
'Westmorelands petition to the king'.
MS. Rawl. poet. 71, p. 162.

Most horns for beauty serve or for defence 487
That by their horns they show some beast is near.
Williams, John, 'Upon Cuckolds horns'.
MS. *Rawl. poet. 191, fol. 118$^{v}$ (autogr.).

Most learned friend and reverend sir. 488
And take the little honest widow.
'R. P. Esqr. to J[ohn] L[umby], Sarum Nov. 11. 1733'.
MS. Eng. poet. e. 42, fol. 27.

Most maids resemble Eve, now in their lives 489
These oft have fruit ere they their husbands know.
[Davies, John, of Hereford], 'On Younge weomen.'
Pr. *Wits Bedlam*, 1617, Sig. I§1$^{v}$.
MSS. Ashmole 36, 37, fol. 176$^{v}$; 47, fol. 31; Eng. poet. f. 25, fol. 10.

Most merciful and righteous Lord 490
Thro' one eternal day.
Kenton, James, 'On the Death of . . . George the 2d', 25 Oct. 1760.
MS *Eng. poet. e. 19, p. 172 (autogr.).

491 Most modern wits such monstrous fools have shown
For no one fool is hunted from the herd.
[Dryden, John], 'Epilogue to Sr. Fopling Flutter, the play made by Mr. Etheridge'. Containing 2 lines not in the printed copies; see *R.E.S.*, July 1925.
MS. Don. b. 8, p. 558.

492 Most noble prince I am porter
Where of faith you shall find a sound built Rome.
Endorsed 'The queenes enterteinement at Wimbleton [15]99'; see Lyson's *Environs of London*, i, 1792, p. 521.
MS. Tanner 306, fol. 266.

493 Most noble Tucer under Ajax shield
If in the day of war thou wouldst go free.
'Anagram. Gervasius Cutlerus. [Regius Tucer Salvus (?)]'.
MS. Top. Yorks. c. 26, fol. 137.

494 Most on the first day of the new-born year
Out of my home-bred muse these verses sing.
Cheyney, William, 'The Preface'.
MS. *Rawl. poet. 86, fol. 3.

495 Most plainly lord, the frame of sky
(Of best things else) an end I see.
Herbert, Mary (*née* Sidney), Countess of Pembroke, Psalm cxix, 'M'.
MSS. *Rawl. poet. 24, p. 182; *25, fol. 106.

496 Most reverend grave judicious sirs,
If honest Tripos march to counter.
Avery, [John, of Corpus Christi, Cambridge (?)], 'Dns. Avery's Prologue to the Drs', and Epilogue, 1697(?).
MS. Rawl. D. 214, fol. 80.

497 Most reverend lords, the church's joy and wonder
The Squire of Newgate rock them on a sledge.
'Hudibras' [Sacheverell, George], ['on Calamy's Imprisonment, and Wild's Poetry. To the Bishops'].
Pr. as broadside, Wood 416 (97), dated by Wood, 1662[/3].
See *D.N.B.* under Wild for attribution.
MSS. Eng. poet. c. 25, fol. 58; Rawl. poet. 173, fol. 137, attr. to Mr. Butler.

498 Most reverend sir, whose love, whose liberal hand
Above all others you deserve great fame . . .
The first 4 lines of a translation of Latin verses addressed to Sir Thomas Vyner at Christ's Hospital, St. Matthew's day 1659.
MS. Rawl. D. 1041, fol. 122ᵛ.

Most sacred Majesty grant that we may have 499
You being yourself again, we will be yours.
'The Irish Petition . . . 1642'.
MS. Rawl. poet. 26, fol. 144ᵛ.

Most sacred Sir and best of human race 500
And this all tongues may justly speak of thee.
Cavendish, Jane, 'On his most sacred Ma:tie' (Charles I.).
MS. *Rawl. poet. 16, p. 9.

Most sad fatigues by plots on nations lies 501
Till th'earths last dark eclipse of no more sun.
Nalson, Robert, 'Of the Plott. 1683'.
MS. Top. Cheshire c. 6, fol. 14ᵛ (autogr.).

Most sins, at least, please sense; but this is treason 502
Not only 'gainst the crown of sense, but reason.
[Quarles, Francis], couplet, 'On Drunkennesse'.
Pr. *Divine Fancies*, 1632, iii. 21.
MS. Rawl. poet. 90, fol. 71ᵛ.

Most sweet content, how happy is his state 503
In summer's heat, and winter's freezing cold.
'Contentment'.
MS. Rawl. poet. 90, fol. 151.

Most true it is, I dare to say 504
He still might show his own.
'The Discovery: or The Squire turnd Ferret', on Mary Toft; copied from 2nd ed., 1727.
Pr. bks. Gough Surrey 15; 17, at end.

Most women have no characters at all 505
Sans teeth, sans eyes, sans taste, sans everything.
Parsons, William, Prologue.
MS. Don. c. 81, fol. 9 (autogr.).

Most worthy of admiration 506
Ample gratification.
'A Proposal of Marriage' and 'Answer'.
MS. Eng. poet. c. 51, p. 238.

Most worthy sirs, my wish and sole desire 507
And peace with mutual joys your lives attend.
Samber, Robert, 'To my Masters', from 'the Bellman's Verses'.
MS. *Rawl. poet. 134*b*, fol. 156 (autogr.).

Mother; my humble duty done, I crave 508
I rest, your loving son, George Buckingham.
'The copy of a letter written by the late deceased George Duke of Buckingham to his mother, since his death' 1628.
MS. Tanner 465, fol. 103ᵛ.

Mother of night, and all sad thoughts that love 509
Thaws cold despair and freezeth hot desire.
'Against melancholly'.
MS. Eng. poet. c. 50, fol. 80ᵛ.

510 Mother! when these unsteady lines
That she be loved, and I forgiven.
Opie, Mrs. Amelia, 'The dying Daughter. . .'.
MS. Percy d. 9, fol. 34.

511 Mount divine muse, with loyal wings and fly
And work your miracles by apprehension.
P. K., 'Carolismus. Or the Royall Patent On The Soveraigne touch'. Charles II.
MS. Tanner 306, fol. 387.

512 Mount, mount, my muse, climb, climb, with all thy force
Can buy this horse, this stable, or his manger.
'Ben. Stone on the white horse whence the vale is named'.
MS. Malone 19, p. 59.

513 Mount Sinai trembles, Israel shakes with fear
What e'er he saw or heard's ineffable.
Potenger, John, 'Doomsday'.
MS. *Eng. poet. d. 161, p. 111.

514 Mount up to paradise (my muse) and bring
By him's received an everlasting guest.
T. I., 'An Elegy upon the Death of the Countess of Clevelande.' Endorsed 'Mors in Olla'. Anne, daughter of Sir John Crofts of Saxham, d. 16 Jan. 1637/8.
MS. Eng. poet. c. 53, fol. 20.

515 Mounts, floods, meads, woods are sights to please the mind
He fails not in the soil but in the owner.
On Hornby, Yorkshire.
MS. Eng. poet. c. 25, fol. 61v.

516 Mourn all ye muses! All ye lovers mourn!
And her fixt sun shall with the Gods decline.
Chatwin, John, 'To the Memory of Madam Gwinn. A Pastoral. Daphnis and Amyntas'. 1687.
MS. *Rawl. poet. 94, p. 224 (autogr.).

517 Mourn all ye nymphs, that sit and sing
She first did love, but after change.
Morrice, John, 'An Acrostick, upon Mrs. M. D. [Mary Davies] Dec. 30, 1707'.
MS. *Rawl. poet. 114, fol. 133 (autogr.).

518 Mourn all ye nymphs with me lament your state
And brought new honour to great Tallbott's name.
'Satyr'.
MS. Firth c. 16, p. 67.

519 Mourn beauties all, and Cupids mourn
To seek to spoil my sweetheart's eyes.
A translation of Catullus, iii.
MS. Rawl. poet. 84, fol. 87.

Mourn forsaken Oxford 520
'Tis vain to hope for more.
'The end of Term'.
MS. Top. Oxon. b. 116, fol. 104.

Mourn hapless Caledonia mourn 521
Thy banish'd peace thy laurel torn.
'The tears of Scotland'.
MS. Montagu d. 26, fol. 4.

Mourn London mourn, 522
Hence came thy plagues, thence only pity floweth.
[Brome, Alexander], 'The Lamentation'.
Pr. *Poems*, 1661, p. 108, 'Written in 1648'.
MS. Ashmole 47, fol. 140v.

Mourn mourn, my pen and swell to signify 523
To make that ours which was his own last word, Amen.
Culpeper, Tho[mas], on John Clarke of University College.
MS. Malone 21, fol. 27.

Mourn not, my friend, the ills which mortals know 524
And angry surges sweep the bending skies . . . (incomplete)
MS. Top. Oxon. d. 315, fol. 14v.

Mourn not ye sisters, brothers, parents, friends 525
Heard all his prayers and snatched him for his own.
Smalbroke, Dr. Samuel, 'on Walter Horton Esq.', of Catton Hall.
MS. Eng. poet. c. 51, p. 18.

Mourn widowed Albion mourn great Anna's death 526
To change an earthly for a heavenly crown.
'On the Death of the Queen'. 1714.
MS. Rawl. poet. 152, fol. 190.

Mourned Judah's king when Abner fell 527
And crowned with everlasting joy.
Kenton, James, 'Monody . . on William Augustus Duke of Cumberland', 1765.
MS. *Eng. poet. e. 19, p. 206 (autogr.).

Mourners divine, admit a condolation 528
Her glory will be perfect ever more.
Gardner, Jo[hn], 'An Elegy on . . . Madm [Rose] Tanner, . . Daughter of . . John [Moore] Ld. Bishop (wife of . . Dr. John [*for* Thomas] Tanner Chancellor) of Norwich . . . d. March 15th 1706/7'.
MS. Tanner 306, fol. 472.

529 Move on thou floating trophy built to fame
With their own triumph, be crowned sovereign.
King, Henry, 'A Salutation of his Majestyes Shipp the Soveraigne'. 1637.
Pr. *Poems*, 1657, p. 49.
MSS. Ashmole 38, two copies, pp. 139 and 141, attr. to Dr. Henry King; *Eng. poet. e. 30, fol. 82; Jones 56, fol. 11, attr. to H. K.

530 Moves it your ire, sir, that you're fed
Lest ours should go for Calve's-Head Club.
Roach, Richard, 'To Dr. D—Philo-Medicus taking offence at his beeing Treated with Calves-Head'.
MS. Rawl. D. 833, fol. 133 (autogr.).

531 Much good is taught by age to youth:
Yet many old fables go for truth.
Robinson, Robert.
MS. *Rawl. poet. 218, p. 71 (autogr.).

532 Much had I heard of beauteous Anna's name,
A bright destruction, and a shining tomb.
'The Fatal Curiosity [on Miss] Nancy Brigantine or Brickenden'.
MS. Eng. poet. f. 12, p. 93.

533 Much have I seen in my few days.
Lord, Lord, for evermore.
Robinson, Robert.
MS. *Rawl. poet. 218, p. 39 (autogr.).

534 Much is revived was dead, not understood,
That may be excellent, if the whim be good.
Polwhele, John, 'Horace de arte poet.'.
MS. *Eng. poet. f. 16, fol. 10 (autogr.).

535 Much lord the king doth in thy strength delight
Be thou exalted Lord we'll praise thy might.
Fairfax, Thomas, Lord, Psalm xxi.
MS. *Fairfax 40, p. 42 (autogr.); see also L673*a*.

536 Much meat [breeds] doth gluttony procure
And roast meat in a pipe.
'On Tobacco'.
Pr. *Wits Recreations*, 1640, no. 131.
MSS. Ashmole 47, fol. 101; Douce f. 5, fol. 9ᵛ; Eng. poet. c. 50, fol. 126; e. 14, fol. 85ᵛ rev.; f. 10, fol. 94; Rawl. poet. 153, fol. 21ᵛ.

537*a* Much mischief shall be wrought, in the end of may
But ere all hallowtide men shall cry well-a-way.
Prophecy.
MS. Rawl. C. 813, fol. 155ᵛ.

537*b* Much sorrow in itself my love doth move
I have the pain, bear you the blame of it.
[Constable, Henry], sonnet, pr. *Diana*, 1592, Sig. C4.
MS. Ashmole 38, p. 54.

Much stirring business, cheerful morning air 538
Or if you have too much, give others more.
Williams, John, 'A Prescription for Melancholy'.
MS. *Rawl. poet. 193, on back end-cover (autogr.).

Much talk I hear of sects, and of a crew. 539
The goats, shall then, be severed from the sheep.
MS. Rawl. poet. 66, fol. 26.

Much talk's of faith: but few men do believe: 540
For want of money 'tis; 'tis not for sin.
Robinson, Robert.
MS. *Rawl. poet. 218, p. 120 (autogr.).

Much wine had passed, with much discourse 541
Cried candle's out, I'll do't and turned to whore.
'The Rose Tavern Clubb 1687'.
MSS. Eng. poet. c. 18, fol. 41; e. 49, p. 23; Firth c. 15, p. 260.

Much within small deal without, 542
Flashy wit not worth a pin.
Robinson, Robert.
MS. *Rawl. poet. 218, p. 133 (autogr.).

*Multum* and *malum* in English, translated 543
Is the man's name so generally hated.
'Much-ill', couplet on Sir Francis Mitchell, 1621.
MS. Rawl. B. 151, fol. 102ᵛ.

'Mun' Bonner when a bishop he should be 544*a*
He wedded hath a rich fat baker's wife.
On the Bishops Edmund Bonner and Richard Fletcher, Feb. 1594/5.
MS. Tanner 306, fol. 190.

Murray generous open free 544*b*
Handmaid to Diana chaste.
Boswell, James, 'Dunkeld Hermitage'. Incomplete (?).
MS. *Douce 193, fol. 56ᵛ,ʳ (autogr.).

Muse be a bride-maid, dost not hear 545
And drowsy nurse's lullaby.
R[andolph], T[homas], 'An Epithal: on his honored ffreind Mr. Hunt'.
Pr. *Poems*, 1638.
MS. Firth e. 4, p. 130.

Muse ere we part let witty Arnold know 546
They have their 'mends i' th'r hand at fingers' ends.
Pestell, Thomas, 'Replie to Mr Randolls Verses on the losse of his finger', A1402.
MS. *Malone 14, p. 32.

547a Muse get thee to a cell; and wont to sing
Where all do live; and elsewhere each thing dies.
Sir G. H.
Pr. *Poems of Pembroke and Ruddier*, 1660.
MS. Eng. poet. c. 50, fol. 69.

547b Muse go present these harmless lines, these many
Conceive my meaning and conceal it ever.
MS. Eng. poet. e. 14, fol. 32.

548 Muse let us change our style and live in peace
And peevish Jack will nev' write again.
'Utile Dulce'. 1681.
MSS. Douce 357, fol. $134^v$; Firth c. 15, p. 96.

549 Muse not my love, yet let my love still muse
All joys, no joys, what is cannot b' undone.
H.S.
MS. *Rawl. poet. 120, fol. $20^v$ (autogr.).

550 [Muse, now the servant of soft loves no more]
Poor beasts? a slow ox and a simple ass.
Crashaw, Richard, translator, 'Sospetto D'Herode'.
Pr. *Steps to the Temple*, 1646.
MSS. Eng. misc. e. 241, fol. 98; Tanner 466, two copies, fols. 154 and 164, the second attr. to R. C.

551 Muse, put on wings, and straight go muster all
An easy labour next to have no foes.
Taylor, William, of St. John's College, Oxford, on the birth of Sr R. Shirleys Childe', Seymour, b. 23 Jan. 1646/7.
MSS. Eng. poet. e. 4, p. 68; Rawl. poet. 65, fol. 53, attr. to Guil Taylor A. B. promus Joannensis.

552 Muses if more than nine come help relate
In that great warehouse of mortality.
Williams, Richard.
MS. Rawl. poet. 210, fol. $49^v$.

553 Muses in number nine in power great
Then good words lend it or good man Carper amend it.
Prologue to M677.
MS. Ashmole 38, p. 226.

554 Muses no more but mazes be your names
And humble faith on heavenly favour wait.
In B.M. Add. MS. 5495, fol. 28, 'Robert Earle of Essex against Sir Water Rawleigh'.
MS. Gough Norfolk 43, fol. $27^v$.

555 Muses wonder
Here lies under.
G.B. (?), on Prince Henry's death, 1612.
MS. *Rawl. poet. 116, fol. 3.

Music dear solace to my thoughts neglected 556
And to thy voice, her voice atone.
Music by Pilkington; pr. *First Book of Songs*, 1605, xix.
MSS. Mus. f. 7–10: f. 7, fol. 23.

Music the master of thy art is dead 557
Let's howl sad notes stolen from his own pure verse.
'In the Memory of my Freind John Tomkins', setting for 3 voices in the hand of W. Lawes.
MS. Mus. Sch. B. 2, p. 101.

Music, thou queen of souls! get up and string 558
Strike a sad note, and fix them trees again.
'Mr. Randolph in Comendation of Musick'.
Pr. Thomas Randolph's *Poems*, 1638.
MS. Don. e. 6, fol. $36^v$.

Music thou soft uniter of our hearts, 559
By whose almighty charms the heaven and earth were made.
Chatwin, John, 'An Ode'.
MS. *Rawl. poet. 94, p. 160 (autogr.).

Music thou soul of Heaven care-charming spell 560
As thou enchantest our ears.
[Herrick, Robert], 'Musicke'.
Pr. *Hesperides*, 1648.
MSS. Don. c. 57, fol. $52^v$, with music; Eng. poet. c. 50, fol. 65, with eight extra lines.

Music, tobacco, sack and sleep 561
The tides of sorrow backwards keep.
Couplet.
MS. Rawl. poet. 153, fol. $13^v$.

Musical sounds some calls harmonious charms 562
The spark of grief into a sable blaze.
'A Satyr on Musick'.
MS. Rawl. poet. 89, fol. 3.

Music's a crochet the sober think vain, 563
To please the dull fools that give money for wit.
'Against Musick'.
MS. Rawl. poet. 173, fol. 146.

Musing I lay with hopeless love oppress'd 564
Sleep loosed his bands, and I with trembling faintness waked.
Hammond, Anthony, 'A Dreame'.
Pr. *Miscellany of Original Poems*, 1720, p. 68.
MS. Rawl. D. 360, fol. $73^v$ (autogr.).

Musing in thoughtful solitude 565
That peace the world cannot destroy.
Skinner, John, Psalm cxx.
MS. *Eng. poet. d. 22, fol. 148.

566 Musing upon the mutability
That in short while after I caused him to die . . . (incomplete).
Historical events, 1443–6, written 'within the xx yere'.
MS. Rawl. C. 813, fol. 11.

567 Must Cromwell now, after concessions made
Lord no more fraud or mischiefs let us see.
Cromwell, Edward, '13 Nov. 1715', 2 lines from Ovid, *Metamorphoses* xiii, 'Englished and Paraphras'd thus'.
MS. *Eng. poet. 165, fol. 22 (autogr.).

568 Must he be ever dead? cannot we add
Which being his can therefore never die.
Herbert, Edward, Lord, of Cherbury, 'An Elegie uppon the Prince [Henry], his death', 1612.
Pr. Sylvester's *Lachrymae Lachrymarum*, 1613.
MS. Rawl. poet. 26, fol. 91, attr. to Sir Edward Herbert.

569 Must high born subjects innocently bleed
And from his temples wrest great James's Crown.
'An Alarm to the Drowsy'.
MS. Rawl. poet. 155, p. 136.

570 Must I, Actæon-like, be poet's play
That may his force, or crafty slights avoid.
Mervall, Alphonso, 'Dolores inferni circundederunt me; praeoccupauerunt me laquei Mortis. psal: 17°'. Subscribed 'Tettix'.
MS. *Rawl. poet. 166, p. 76 (autogr.).

571 Must I have patience still the din to hear
Bedlam's too little, half the nation's mad.
Lamb, Christopher, 'The Demi-Juror. A Satyre'.
MS. Rawl. poet. 181, fol. 33.

572 Must I then make the world incredulous
I may the bright Hesperian fruit enjoy.
Beaumont, Thomas, 'In Dulcias looks A double effect'.
MS. *Malone 18, p. 87 (autogr.).

573 Must I with patience ever silent sit
I would not be the men, to have their power.
[Wilmot, John, Earl of Rochester], Juvenal, Satire I, imitated.
Ascribed to Rochester in *Poems on Affairs of State*, i, 1703, ii. 32. Pr. *Works of Rochester and Roscommon*, 1707, p. 100.
MSS. Don. b. 8, p. 645; e. 24, p. 11; Douce 357, fol. 62.

Must she then languish and we sorrow thus 574
Convey into his hands thy golden dart.
C[arew], T[homas], 'Upon the Sicknes of E. S.'
Pr. *Poems*, 1640.
MS. Eng. poet. c. 50, fol. 68, attr. to T. C.; Eng. poet. f. 10, fol. 118ᵛ.

Must we depart then, and shall the heavens sole eye 575
Since only heaven can rule and death divide us.
'His Maᵗᵉ (Charles I] valediccon to the Queene at her departure'.
MS. Rawl. poet. 71, p. 1.

Must you be thought a judge of sense 576
Because your life's the farce you wrote.
'Supplemᵗ. to these Verses', T2269.
MS. Don. b. 8, p. 224.

Must you burn too? is not your master's fire 577
This of your hate cures that of my desire.
'On the burning of his lettres'.
MS. Rawl. poet. 199, p. 87.

Must your fair enflaming eye 578
That I must your martyr be.
'A sonnet to his Mʳˢ'.
MS. Ashmole 47, fol. 33.

Mute is my muse, that erst rang peals of joy 579
This world too vile, for such good men as he.
Lilliat, John, 'Doctor Goldingham his Ghoste'. [Dr. William Goldingham's will proved 1589].
MS. Rawl. poet. 148, fol. 61ᵛ (autogr.).

My able helpmate say what laws, 580
Then went to tea and coffee ready.
'A Handsell in return for a New Year's Gift', verses to J. Boswell.
MS. Douce 193, fol. 66.

My acts and conquests from a heptarchy 581
Wonder of all I reigned lived and died a maid.
Couplets on the Kings and Queens of England, Egbert to Queen Elizabeth.
MS. Add. D. 84, fol. 173ᵛ.

My beauty's gone; no Cupids bask 582
And set mankind on fire.
'A Reflection at the Toilette'.
MS. *Eng. poet. d. 47, fol. 5.

My bed's my grave, my grave's my bed 583
Presents death to my meditation.
Colman, Henry, 'on Death'.
MS. *Rawl. poet. 204, fol. 16 (autogr.).

584 My best dear friend, prithee now give o'er
Woes have their ebb as well as flood.
'A Perswasive against Grief'.
MS. Rawl. poet. 90, fol. 161v.

585 My best deserving friend but that I fear
'Twixt you and me to be a true love token.
Burton, Francis.
MS. *Add. A. 267, fol. 120 (autogr.).

586 My best esteemed friend how my poor heart
As to my self redoubling of thy kisses.
Burton, Francis,
'An Anagram {Elizabethe Gardner / Frauncis Burton}'.
MS. *Add. A. 267, fol. 120v (autogr.).

587 My best of friends: If in these worst of times
And that's the cause he writes himself below.
Wharton, George, verse letter, 11 Sept. 1648, signed 'George Lambert'.
MS. Ashmole 423, fol. 278 (autogr.).

588 My best of friends! what needs a chain to tie
Will period, though never crown, my hope.
King, Henry, 'An Acknowledgment'.
Pr. *Poems*, 1657, p. 64.
MSS. *Eng. poet. e. 30, fol. 45v; *Malone 22, fol. 39.

589 My blessed content desires but this
Nights undisturbed, days without strife.
P[roby], H[enry], 'Martialis Epigr.'
MS. Rawl. poet. 246, fol. 19.

590 My blunt friend Lollius, if I know thee right
Let me alone to get a quiet mind.
B[rome], A[lexander], translator, Horace, *Epistles* I. xviii.
Pr. *Poems of Horace*, A. Brome etc., 2nd ed., 1671, p. 348.
MS. Rawl. D. 261, p. 68.

591 My body being dead, my limbs unknown,
Get free, and so thou shalt even all admire.
Traherne, Thomas, 'The Preparative'.
MS. *Eng. poet. c. 42, fol. 4 (autogr.).

592 My body moulders but my soul
Amen, Amen, Amen.
Bradshaw, John, 'The clark's [Richard Marks of Bedford] Epitaph, as if made by himselfe, who was baptized Nov. 24, 1593, dyed March 7th 1668'.
MS. Tanner 466, fol. 113v.

593 My body resteth in the dust
And raise my body from the grave.
'Epitaph in Bray Church Yard in Berks'.
MS. Eng. poet. e. 40, fol. 138.

My body's small yet long and straight 594
But some their life-time me despise.
Riddle, 'A Tob[acco] pipe'.
MS. *Rawl. poet. 197, fol. 15 (autogr.).

My bold unthrifty eyes vent'ring to stray 595
For all to chaos had returned again.
Beaumont, Thomas, 'Of his first sight of his Mrs. at A window'.
MS. *Malone 18, p. 29 (autogr.).

My book yet thou art fair and like a maid 596
Continue so: let not a thought th . . . (incomplete).
'To this Booke'.
MS. Rawl. D. 316, fol. 122 (autogr.).

My bretheren all attend me 597
[You'll sink into perdition].
Satire on the Puritan emigrants, March 1638/9 (?).
See Firth, *Transanctions of Royal Hist. Soc.* Ser. 3, vi. 37. Pr. *Rump Songs*, 1662, sig. B1, 'The Zealous Puritan, 1639', and *Merry Drollery*, 1670, p. 95.
MSS. Ashmole 36, 37, fol. 100.

My bretheren beloved 598
And in praises eternally join.
Kenton, James.
MS. *Eng. poet. e. 20, p. 108 (autogr.).

My brother! and much more, hadst thou been mine 599
Or else this star a quarrel doth portend.
Corbett, Richard, 'to Mr. Alesbury upon the Comet . . . 1618'.
Pr. *Poems*, 1647, p. 31.
MSS. Ashmole 313, fol. 32v, attr. to Dr. Corbett; Smith 17, p. 140, attr. to Mr. Corbett, dated 9 Dec.; Tanner 306, fol. 251, dated 9 Dec. 1618, attr. to Dr. Corbet in Oxforde.

My calling is divine 600
Whilst my poor flock do starve.
'The Devine'.
From 'Yet other 12 wonders of the world', subscribed John Davys, F. Davison's *Poetical Rhapsody*, 2nd ed., 1608.
MS. Rawl. poet. 84, fol. 44.

My captive soul, it self bemoans 601
I'm coffined in sad garrison of rest.
Cavendish, Lady Jane, 'The Captive Buriall'.
MS. *Rawl. poet. 16, p. 20.

My Celia stay, why fliest thou so, 602
Or I am lost undone for ever.
'A Song'.
MS. Montagu e. 13, fol. 50v.

603 My censure, and my verdict, which you crave
Above to see bays, and a rochet under.
Oldisworth, Nicolas, 'To the worshipfull, Mrs. Strange of Summerford, a Poëtesse'.
MS. *Don. c. 24, fol. 36$^{v}$ (autogr.).

604 My charge it is, those breaches to repair
May boast himself the brightest thing that shines.
Waller, Edmund, 'The Apologie of Somnus for not approaching the Ladie whoe can doe any thing but sleepe when she pleaseth'.
Pr. *Poems*, 1645, p. 23.
MSS. *Don. d. 55, fol. 20$^{v}$; *Rawl. poet. 174, p. 23.

605 My children! of mine age, the only stay
Whenas the props, are plucked from the walls.
MS. Rawl. poet. 66, fol. 34.

606 My choice is made and I desire no change
My choice is made, and never will I change again.
Pr. Pilkington's *First Book of Songs*, 1605, ii.
MSS. Mus. f. 7–10: f. 7, fol. 15$^{v}$.

607 My comforts drop and melt away like snow:
Which they that know the rest, know more then I.
Herbert, George, 'The Answere'.
Pr. *The Temple*, 1633, p. 163.
MS. *Tanner 307, fol. 124.

608 My commons, and lords, I once hoped but in vain
That their money's all safe, betwixt me and my Queen.
'Vox et praeterea nihil . . . the King [George I]'s speech'.
MSS. Top. Oxon. b. 170, fol. 21; pr. bk. Firth b. 22, fol. 30, dated 1727.

609 My contemplation dazzles in the end
That while we all, we Him might comprehend.
Traherne, Thomas, 'The Anticipation'.
MS. *Eng. poet. c. 42, fol. 11$^{v}$ (autogr.).

610 My country dear I have forsook
And we have gained our ends.
[Weever, —], 'A New Court Ballad upon the Word Grudge, and the last part of his Ma$^{ties}$ first Speech to his Parliam$^{t}$' 20 March 1714/15'.
Pr. Hearne's *Collections*, ed. W. Rannie, O.H.S., xlii, 1901, p. 50, 'by Mr. Weever'.
MSS. Eng. poet. e. 87, p. 16; Hearne's diaries 53, p. 134; Rawl. C. 986, fol. 13; Rawl. poet. 155, p. 87; pr. bks. Firth b. 22, fol. 17; Linc. B 26. 75(7), attr. to Mr. Weaver.

My covenant with Thee my God 611
I'd loathe as much as fear.
Tipping, William, 'After Receiving the sacrament of the Lords Supper'. Dated July 5 1701.
MS. *Rawl. poet. 101, fol. 103 (autogr.).

My cross I do not bow unto 612
Our king a cross does wear.
MS. Rawl. poet. 101, fol. 4*b* (additional leaf in a different hand).

My cruel friend, too inconsiderate of my state 613
As faithful I love her, she may love me as well.
North, Dudley, 3rd Baron.
Pr. *A Forest of Varieties*, 1645.
MS. *North e. 41, fol. 28.

My Dady's a delver of dikes 614
That na body comes to woo.
'My Dady's a Delver of Dykes'.
MS. Eng. poet. e. 8, fol. 9.

My dam and I full twenty years 615
Rending the clouds asunder.
'A good husbands epitaph of his bad wife'.
MS. Malone 19, p. 155.

My dame behold a sailor brave! 616
Must haste to plough the ocean wave.
Dyer, George, 'Ode The Sailor'.
Pr. *Poems*, 1801, p. 179.
MS. *Eng. poet. c. 21, fol. 23.

My days have been so wondrous free 617
The mistress of my soul.
'To the tune of the Broom'.
MS. Eng. poet. e. 8, fol. 3$^{v}$.

My days were once so wondrous free 618
I cannot wish it less.
'Song by Dr. [Thomas] Parnel'.
Pr. *Gentleman's Magazine*, ix, 1739, p. 656, with music.
MS. Ballard 50, fol. 110.

My dear Alexis ah in vain 619
She spoke, and speaking quickly died!
'Delia to Alexis'.
MS. Eng. poet. c. 9, p. 91.

My dear and only love I pray 620
And ever love thee more.
[Graham, James, Marquis of Montrose]. See W. Chappell, *Old English Popular Music*, 1893, i. 193, and J. Hannah, *Poems of Sir Walter Raleigh*, etc., 1891, p. 203.
MS. Rawl. B. 35, fol. 46 rev.

621 My dear and only love take heed
But smiling sing thee to thy grave, and never [love thee more]

Pr. *Wit and Drollery*, 1661, p. 41; see W. Chappell, op. cit. in M620.
MS. Rawl. B. 35, fol. 58 rev.

622 My dear brother Ned,
For the South Carolina we've lost.

1782.
MS. Firth c. 18, fol. 93.

623 My dear companion and my faithful friend
On this great voyage to the world unknown.

Somervile, William, 'An Address to my Elbow Chair new Cloathed'. 1779.
Pr. Dodsley's *Collection of Poems*, iv, 1755, p. 302, and Somervile's *Poems*, 1779, (Johnson's Poets xlvii), p. 226.
MS. Ballard 47, fol. 22.

624 My dear Harry, I never saw anything like it since I was born
The sooner the better.

[Madan], Frederick (1742–1779), rhymed letter to Lady Hesketh (*née* Harriet Cowper).
MS. Eng. poet. c. 51, p. 117.

625 My dear, in merry mood, said Bob to Nan,
Quoth Nan, I cannot think upon my life.

'Epigram'.
MS. *Eng. poet. d. 47, fol. 31.

626 My dear little miss
Without this considering cap-a.

Lumby, John, 'To Miss A. L. to whom in a frolicksome Mood I had promis'd a Silk-Hatband . . . Sarum July 2 1731'.
MS. *Eng. poet. e. 42, fol. 15.

627 My dear little Molly I love thee so well,
May you both prove, the happiest pair in the nation.

'A Versaic Dialogue between Lord George Sutton and Mr. [Joshua] Peart written at Bugden, the 23d of Decr. 1767'.
MS. *Eng. poet. e. 28, p. 148.

628 My dear Lord Jesus! Oh! how sweet's the word!
Still will we cry, how long! My dear Lord Jesus!

'The Acrostick'.
MS. Eng. poet. e. 51, p. 46.

629 My dear Miss Ashe, great judgement all must own
Till mine for you can cease, or light the sun forsake.

Williams, John.
MS. *Rawl. poet. 191, fol. 84 (autogr.).

My dear Miss Ashe whose always charming mind 630
By heaven, so frequently, forbid to part.

Williams, John, 'To Miss Ashe and Miss Betty'.
MS. *Rawl. poet. 184, fol. 83.

My dear Molly Vyse 631
Prove free from all trouble and sorrow.

'Inge's 3 Close Jan$^{y}$ 2d 1789'.
MS. Eng. poet. c. 51, p. 70.

My dear, these lines my wished for place supply 632
Who long has been, and ever will remain.

'To Constantia'.
MS. Rawl. poet. 116, fol. 108.

My dear, thy beauty with thy virtue joined 633
Ere I will cease to love I'll cease to be.

'An acrostick' (Mary Goose).
MS. Rawl. poet. 116, fol. 109.

My dearest dear to heaven is gone 634
Mourn I shall till I die.

Tipping, William, 'Lamentation for my deere Hess'.
MS. *Rawl. poet. 101, fol. 12$^{v}$ (autogr.).

My dearest Dulcia and I 635
Want power or help to work their ends.

Beaumont, Thomas, 'Of A meetinge with his m$^{rs}$'.
MS. *Malone 18, p. 9 (autogr.).

My dearest friend that lovest me so 636
To show how wounded love may triumph over death.

'Ode In Imitation of Horace (1688)', *Odes* II. vi.
MSS. Eng. poet. e. 49, p. 43; Firth c. 15, p. 332.

My dearest God, let my prayer come to thee, 637
And have for them and theirs a post-eternity.

Psalm cii.
MS. Rawl. poet. 90, fol. 156.

My dearest hope vouchsafe to view the scroll 638
From whence receive a fool's, yet kind, farewell.

'A letter written to his revolted frynd K. H. by H.S.'
MS. *Rawl. poet. 120, fol. 25$^{v}$ (autogr.).

My dearest, if thou wilt agree 639
Join souls again in endless bliss.

Oldisworth, Nicolas, 'The country-gentleman's Wooing'.
MS. *Don. c. 24, fol. 22 (autogr.).

640 My dearest love! when thou and I must part
Am both testator thus, and legacy.
King, Henry, 'The Legacy'.
Pr. *Poems*, 1657, p. 26.
MSS. *Eng. poet. e. 30, fol. 64; *Malone 22, fol. 44v.

641 My dearest Molly, lovely maid,
Remember Tweedledee!
'A Mournful Ballad', by Tweedledee [G. Monro] 1780.
MS. Top. Oxon. e. 48, fol. 25.

642 My dearest Zara, little did I dream,
And make my plaint to thee in my misfortunes.
'Zara. A Tragedy'.
MS. Rawl. poet. 194, fol. 60.

643 My death is life to me my body dies
And thus I die to live, as you may see.
Shrimpton, John, translation of Latin verse on the Phoenix.
MS. Gough Herts. 3, fol. 34 (autogr.).

644 My death, the death of Christ, earth, heaven, and hell
Oh let me never have my Heaven here!
'Pentelogia'.
MS. *Eng. poet. e. 51, p. 58.

645 My earthly mould doth melt in watery tears
Thus doth my life within itself dissolve.
[Sidney, Sir Philip]. Extract from 1st Eclogue, pr. *Arcadia*, 1590.
MS. Rawl. poet. 85, fol. 65v.

646 My face! what then? shall that confine me so?
Than only what they knew and boasted of before.
'The Chamber. A Poem; To his timerous Countrymen complaining of his going forth, forst him to keepe his Chamber after his recovery from the small pox'.
MS. *Rawl. poet. 87, p. 20.

647 My fair is beautiful as love,
And music's on her tongue.
'Song'.
MS. Eng. poet. e. 39, p. 211.

648 My fair ye swains is gone astray
My Phillis my Phillis my lovely Phillis.
'Phillis. Set by Mr. Arne'.
MS. Mus. Sch. b. 8*, fol. 19v.

649 My falcon spirit shall not stoop
I well can lie alone.
MS. Don. d. 58, fol. 24.

My falsest mistress equally 650
Then jocund heart live ever free.
Beaumont, Thomas, 'on her Mariage'.
MS. *Malone 18, p. 22 (autogr.).

My fancy did I fix 651
I never served other saint nor idol other where . . . (incomplete).
Pr. Clement Robinson's *A Handefull of pleasant delites*, 1584.
MS. Ashmole 48, fol. 110v.

My fancy scorns to stoop in snow 652
Each its own interpreter.
MS. Rawl. poet. 142, fol. 26v.

My fancy you say does not reach very high 653
What need you be jealous, if Cloe's not fair?
'To Clarinda extempore', 1735.
MS. Eng. misc. e. 240, p. 155.

My father and I in foul and fair weather 654
Their rending and roaring changed to licking and fawning.
'A travilling song or my iter occidentale'. Tune, 'When the weather is colde and raw we etc.'
MS. Rawl. poet. 37, p. 62.

My father having moved his mind 655
To shield thee with his grace.
'The admonition of his Mother and her counsaile at his departing'.
MS. Rawl. poet. 185, fol. 6v.

My father is my son 656
And grandam to my brother.
'Dr. Bold Prebend: of Salisbury married the daughter of Tobie Sanford Dr. of Phisick . . . Tobie Sanford took to wife the daughter of Dr. Bold whereupon Tobie Sanford's daughter is brought in thus speaking:'
MSS. Ashmole 36, 37, fol. 143v.

My faults though great my Cynthia should forgive, 657
Then just to teach me—I can love but one.
'To Cynthia'.
MS. Montagu e. 13, fol. 92.

My first and second make combined 658
My whole (though strange) would suffer no decay.
'Charade'.
MS. Eng. poet. c. 51, p. 109.

My first glad fears and joyful tremblings past 659
Mecaenas purse strings strike the powerful rhyme.
Pestell, Thomas, 'Upon the Battaile, by [Thomas] Banc[roft].'
MS. *Malone 14, p. 31.

660 My first is a term intended and meant
If his neighbour is robb'd of his breath.
'Charade'.
MS. Eng. poet. c. 51, p. 110.

661 My first is a term that in Ireland is used
So they closed up its mouth with a seal.
'Charade'.
MS. Eng. poet. c. 51, p. 110.

662 My first love whom all beauty did adorn·
Each falling sparkling fit for any match.
Pr. Carew's *Poems*, 1640; Suckling's *Last Remains*, 1659.
Attr. to Walton Poole in B.M. MSS. Add. 33998, Egerton 2725.
MS. Malone 16, two copies, pp. 38, 56.

663 My flesh is consumed, there is but skin and bone
And grant them pardon of that they have offended.
'Howers of the B. virgin, Engl. and Latin ad usum Sarum. The 8 lesson for the Dirige'.
MS. Eng. poet. e. 56, p. 104.

664 My flesh shall slumber in the ground
And in my Saviour's image rise.
Memorial inscription on Thomas Plater, d. 1786, Baptist meeting house, Oxford.
MS. Top. Oxon. c. 300, fol. 76$^{v}$.

665 My foes prevail, my friends are fled
Amidst this sad captivity.
'Captivity', [Marie Antoinette].
MS. Eng. poet. c. 51, p. 276*b*.

666 My former later rhymes do not deprive
You two are one; that one, four deities.
Oldisworth, Robert or Giles, verses to 'Mrs Oldisworth'.
MS. *Rawl. C. 422, fol. 8, in the hand of Giles Oldisworth.

667 My former love was all confused and raw
I changed once never to change again.
Beaumont, Thomas, 'upon his change in affection'.
MS. *Malone 18, p. 30 (autogr.).

668 My fortune was the other day
Resolved to wed, resolved to trust.
North, Dudley, 3rd Baron.
Pr. *A Forest of Varieties*, 1645.
MS. *North e. 41, fol. 26.

669 My fortunes, and my joys this custom break
A last sick hour to syllables allow.
Donne, John, on Mrs. Boulstred.
Pr. *Poems*, 1635.
MSS. *Eng. poet. e. 99, fol. 116; *f. 9, p. 208; Rawl. poet. 31, fol. 41.

My fortunes are at your disposing set 670
Uncle, and father are in you both met.
Couplet.
MS. Rawl. poet. 117, fol. 276 rev.

My friend and I passing his shop did spy 671
Because he lives by nothing else but skin.
A. N. C., 'An Epigram on a Skinner'.
MS. Rawl. poet. 160, fol. 20$^{v}$.

My friend, I humbly thank you for the darts, 672
Who can write otherwise, with Cupid's darts.
Amherst, Elizabeth, 'On receiving a Fairing of a Bow and Arrows from a young Lady'.
MS. *Eng. poet. e. 109, p. 28.

My friend it behoveth thee to bear this in thy mind 673
So help me God and holy dame he died a poor man.
'In St. Peters Cornhill was this Old Inscription'.
MS. Rawl. D. 682, fol. 78.

My friend judge not me 674
Mercy I asked and mercy I found.
'Upon a Gentleman that brooke his necke falling from his Horse'.
Pr. Camden's *Remaines*, 1605, p. 55.
MSS. Ashmole 38, p. 177; Eng. poet. e. 40, fol. 123.

My friend, my banker, and my poet! 675
Oh Epicurus! lend thy sty!
Parsons, William, 'To Samuel Rogers. Imitation of Horace, [*Epistles* I. iv], 23 Apr. 1795'.
MS. *Don. d. 123, p. 253 (autogr.).

My friend my Celsus! that's most eloquent 676
Unfolded brings me both to food and rest.
Pestell, Thomas, 'To Mr. T. N[urse]: Physitian at Leicest:'
See *Poems*, ed. H. Buchan, 1940, p. 97.
MS. *Malone 14, p. 24.

My friend of late I have received your letter 677
A knave I found him and a knave I leave him.
'A question demaunded of a friend in a letter to know whether papist or puritane were better'.
MS. Ashmole 38, fol. 226.

My friend the life I lead at all 678
Of this my life early and late.
MS. Ashmole 48, fol. 25$^{v}$.

679 My friend, the man that's upright, just and pure,
Unto my lovely, smiling, lisping she.
Morrice, John, translator, Horace, *Odes* I. xxii.
MS. *Rawl. poet. 114, fol. 150 (autogr.).

680 My friend with sorrow hang not down thy head
Did bear to me great liking and affection.
W. A., translator, Horace, *Odes* I. xxxiii.
MS. *Rawl. poet. 104, fol. 11 (autogr.).

681 My friends exclaim, Clarus! Oh happy you!
'Gold you have none'. Why then she must love me.
'Pauperibus vates ego sum, quia pauper amavi. Ovid'. 1735.
MS. Eng. misc. e. 240, p. 315.

682 My friends go home and shed no tears
I must lie here till Christ appears.
Epitaph in Tottenham Church Yard, couplet.
MS. Eng. poet. e. 40, fol. 3.

683 My friends (good Lord) preserve
And no good man my foe.
MS. Rawl. poet. 148, two copies, fols. $2^v$ and 112.

684 My friends if you will understand
Like a great booby.
Song with tune.
MS. Rawl. poet. 152, fol. 208.

685 My friends whose kindness doth their judgements bind
I have no more to spend, and have not spent that.
Alabaster, William, 'Son:32'.
Pr. by B. Dobell, *Athenaeum*, No. 3974, 26 Dec. 1903.
MS. *Eng. poet. e. 57, fol. 8.

686 My friendship now is turn'd to love
My dearest Tunstal's wife.
Last verse of a poem sent to W. Tunstal in prison by 'Mrs. M. M.'
MS. Rawl. poet. 155, p. 254.

687 My God, a verse is not a crown
I am with thee, and most take all.
Herbert, George, 'The Quiddity'.
Pr. *The Temple*, 1633, p. 61.
MS. *Tanner 307, fol. 47.

688 My God and gold cannot possess one heart,
My God and I, or gold and I must part.
[Quarles, Francis], 'On God and Gold', couplet.
Pr. *Divine Fancies*, 1632, iv. 91.
MS. Rawl. poet. 90, fol. 53.

My God how wondrous is thy love 689
The object of my choice.
Beddome, Benjamin, Hymn.
MS. *Eng. misc. e. 227, fol. 55.

My God, I am wounded with my sin 690
The utmost smart, so Thou wilt cure.
MS. Rawl. poet. 23, p. 193, referring to setting by John Tomkins.

My God, I heard this day. 691
And both thy servants be.
Herbert, George, 'Man'.
Pr. *The Temple*, 1633, p. 83.
MS. *Tanner 307, fol. 63.

My God I read this day, 692
That thy bright beams may tame thy bow.
Herbert, George, 'Affliction'.
Pr. *The Temple*, 1633, p. 89.
MS. *Tanner 307, fol. 67.

My God I speak it from [with] a full assurance 693
And prisoner soul shall joy at jail delivery.
'Dr. [Edward] Latworth [or Lapworth] upon his death Bed'.
See *D.N.B.* for attribution.
MSS. Ashmole 781, p. 137, attr. to Dr. Latworth; Eng. poet. e. 57, fol. $12^v$, attr. to Dr. Lattworth; Rawl. poet. 26, fol. 13, attr. to Lattworth; see also O410.

My God, if writings may 694
Entered for both; far above their desert.
Herbert, George, 'Obedience'.
Pr. *The Temple*, 1633, p. 96.
MS. *Tanner 307, fol. $72^v$.

My God is all things unto me 695
Than with my self! Amen.
Shane, Samuel, 'God and the Soul . . . a Periphrase upon 1 Joh. 4:16', from a work called 'The Angelical Life'.
MS. Rawl. poet. 202, two copies, fols. $23^v$ and $33^v$.

My God, most glad to look, most prone to hear, 696
That it half spun, death may in sunder shear.
Herbert, Mary (*née* Sidney), Countess of Pembroke, Psalm lv.
MSS. *Rawl. poet. 24, p. 77; *25, fol. 46.

My God my God 697
The glory of this deed, and that he it did do.
J. F., Psalm xxii.
MS. *Eng. poet. f. 17, p. 125 (autogr.).

698 My God, my God; this broken heart; does break;
As well in this, as other gifts, like thee.
Oldisworth, Giles, 'Extasye . . . A Satyre against my-selfe presented to Mr. Busby (upon my birthday; 1638) Chiswick'.
MS. *Rawl. C. 422, fol. 43v (autogr.).

699 My God, my God! why hast thou me
His just and admired deeds.
Psalm xxii, 'The Passion of Christ, whereupon Gods kingdom is sett upp.'
MS. *Rawl. C. 113, two copies, fols. 3 (autogr.) and 21v.

700 My God, my God, why hast thou me forsaken,
His dooms one age shall to another send.
Sidney, Sir Philip, Psalm xxii.
MSS. *Rawl. poet. 24, p. 27; *25, fol. 16.

701 My God, my God, why leav'st thou me
Who shall his name confess.
Psalm xxii.
MS. *Montagu e. 10, fol. 12v.

702 My God my help my hope my joy
Then all shall to thy glory be.
Beddome, Benjamin.
MS. *Eng. misc. e. 227, fol. 71v.

703 My God my King thy laud
Give thanks both now and ever.
Harrington, Sir John, Psalm cxlv.
MS. *Douce 361, fol. 89v.

704 My God, my king, to lift thy praise,
While race you run of breathing days.
Herbert, Mary (*née* Sidney), Countess of Pembroke, Psalm cxlv.
MS. *Rawl. poet. 24, p. 214.

705 My God, my life, my all
And full salvation know.
Kenton, James.
MS. *Eng. poet. e. 20, p. 211 (autogr.).

706 My God, my lord, my help, my health,
As darkness they to me appear.
Herbert, Mary (*née* Sidney), Countess of Pembroke, Psalm lxxxviii.
MS. *Rawl. poet. 24, p. 129.

707 My God, my only safe-guard and delight
Give both desires and means of doing more.
Williams, John, 'A Prayer at giving a Charitable gift of any kind'.
MS. *Rawl. poet. 188, fol. 80v (autogr.).

708 My God my saviour thou alone
Till judgement ends in victory.
MS. *Don. f. 5, fol. 5v.

My God, oh why hast thou forsook 709
Yet wouldst not thou vouchsafe a look.
[Sandys, George], Psalm xxii. 3-part setting [by W. Lawes].
Pr. Sandys's *Paraphrase upon the Divine Poems*, 1638, p. 24, and H. and W. Lawes, *Choice Psalmes*, 1648.
MS. Mus. Sch. e. 451, p. 63.

My God, our heart by thy great might 710
And hear his humble prayer.
Williams, John, 'A Soliloquy at going to Church'.
MS. *Rawl. poet. 192, fol. 90 (autogr.).

My God to thee I dedicate 711
The glory be to thee.
'Amor ordinem nescit'.
MS. Rawl. C. 581, fol. 1.

My God, to thee my soul attract 712
My hope of bliss that has no end.
Williams, John, 'The Prayer'.
MS. *Rawl. poet. 192, fol. 1 (autogr.).

My God when I thy stars behold 713
To prize so small a treasure here, who hast so much above.
Earbery, Matthias, 'The true definition of a Man in a Paraphrase on psalm viii'.
MSS. Tanner 306, fol. 459, autogr., sent to Charles Trimnell when Bp. of Norwich, 1708–21; Rawl. D. 842, two copies, fols. 85v (autogr.) and 100.

My God! whose kind protecting hand 714
Nor vice, nor error, blot my plan!
Parsons, William, 'Hymn . . . at Bath for my mother on my Birthday 30 March 1783'.
MS. *Don. d. 123, p. 97 (autogr.).

My god why is thy presence thus retired 715
This he hath done shall be their song of praise.
Fairfax, Thomas, Lord, Psalm xxii.
MS. *Fairfax 40, p. 44 (autogr.).
MS. *Fairfax 38, p. 153.

My golden locks time hath to silver turned 716
To be your beadsman now, that was your knight.
'Certaine verses caus'd to bee songe to the Queens Matie by Sir Hen: Lea Kt when he yealded up his Helmit & launce to the Earle of Cumberland at the tilt yard An. do: 1590'.
Pr. Nichols's *Progresses of Q. Elizabeth*, 1823, iii. 49. See *Life and Minor Works of G. Peele*, D. H. Horne, 1952, p. 165.
MS. Eng. poet. c. 50, fol. 59; see also H1223

717 My good are excellent the candid say,
And without mercy censure all the rest.
Cowper, William, translator, from Owen, 'On his candid and uncandid readers'.
Pr. from this MS., *Poetical Works*, ed. H. S. Milford, 4th ed., 1934, p. 666.
MS. Autogr. d. 21, fol. 192 (autogr.).

718 My grandmother the only piece of good
Then in his life her nephews God should bless.
Cavendish, Lady Jane, 'On the Lady Ogle my deare Grandmother'.
MS. *Rawl. poet. 16, p. 30.

719 My gratitude obligeth me to pay
By these directions can your coffers fill.
Ashmole, Elias, 'To Mr. Nicholas Bowden Upon his giving me a Manuscript of the Philosophers stone'.
See MS. Ashmole 1459. i.
MSS. Ashmole 36, 37, fol. 232 (autogr.).

720 My gratitude thinks you are too kind,
For to beget, then 'tis to father be.
'An Injuction of Secrecye To . . . Lady H—, who was pleasd to command a Coppy of "Phaeton's sister"'.
MS. Add. A. 301, fol. 91v rev.

721 My head and my purse had a quarrel of late
But surely the head had a vacuum first.
'Epigram On a Rake'.
MS. Eng. poet. c. 9, p. 101.

722 My head and tail both equal are
Immediately to nothing change.
'A Riddle on the Figure 8'.
MS. Eng. poet. e. 40, fol. 134.

723 My heart and tongue shall yield thee thanks and praise
That they may know themselves to be but men.
Harington, Sir John, Psalm ix.
MS. *Douce 361, fol. 5.

724 My heart at first did stubborn prove
We catch but slime whilst we expect a star.
Chatwin, John, 'The Wandring heart'.
MS. *Rawl. poet. 94, p. 217 (autogr.).

725 My heart did heave; and there came forth, oh God
Thou dying daily, praise thee to thy loss.
Herbert, George, 'Affliction'.
Pr. *The Temple*, 1633, p. 64.
MS. *Tanner 307, fol. 50.

726 My heart doth joy and would draw near
And praised without end.
Forman, Simon, '. . . his thankesgyvinge . . . after his firste and second Troble'. 1579.
MS. Ashmole 802, fol. 121 (autogr.).

My heart doth take in hand, 727
For evermore oh lord.
[Hopkins, John], Psalm xlv.
MS. Rawl. poet. 112, fol. 58v rev.

My heart enflamed with zeal prepares 728
Shall praise ascribe to thee.
Psalm xlv.
MS. *Montagu e. 10, fol. 65.

My heart entire shall praise the Lord 729
His praises ever last.
Psalm cxi.
MS. *Rawl. C. 113, fol. 78.

My heart indites an argument of worth 730*a*
The world shall make no end of thanks to thee.
Herbert, Mary (*née* Sidney), Countess of Pembroke, Psalm xlv.
MSS. *Rawl. poet. 24, p. 66; *25, fol. 38v.

My heart indites; ('Tis subject of my thought) 730*b*
People shall praise Thee ever for the same.
Fairfax, Thomas, Lord, Psalm xlv.
MS. *Fairfax 38, p. 204; see also T1438.

My heart is even [a t]able plain of white 731
And inly pine and ever want the kissing.
Sonnet.
MS. Rawl. B. 88, fol. 32 (autogr.).

My heart is lened on the land 732
Give thine belevid on the land.
MS. Ashmole 48, fols. 111 (incomplete), 134.

My heart is sore but yet no force 733
I have not all my will.
MS. Rawl. C. 813, fol. 57v.

My heart it lies a bleeding for Carigfergus town 734
Ah! my lads says Elliot we'll show you warlike play.
MS. Firth c. 18, fol. 98.

My heart like Noah's harmless dove 735
To be confined again.
'To a Lady who allowed her Lover to be Inconstant'.
MS. Percy c. 8, fol. 129v.

My heart, Lord, applies all my gifts 736
To tread down enemies.
Psalm cviii.
MS. *Rawl. C. 113, fol. 76.

My heart, my heart alas why dost thou love thine enemy 737
Save most singular beauty and little pity.
'A. 5. Voc. Gironimo (*sic*) Conversi'.
Pr. *Musica Transalpina*, 1588, xxxix.
MSS. Mus. f. 20–24: f. 20, fol. 34v.

738 **My heart prepared, prepared is my heart**
**Shall lick the deadly dust.**
Herbert Mary (*née* Sidney), Countess of Pembroke, Psalm cviii, rejected version.
MS. *Rawl. poet. 25, fol. 110.

739 **My heart rejoiceth in the Lord**
**Of his annointed one.**
Fleming, Robert, '1 Samuel 2 Ch: Hannah's song. 1676'.
MS. Rawl. poet. 213, fol. 77 rev. (autogr.).

740 **My heart swells not with haughty pride**
**Upon the Lord depend.**
Psalm cxxxi.
MS. *Rawl. C. 113, fol. 94ᵛ, corrected by the author.

741*a* **My heart was set with true intent**
**Beware ye lovers of such treason.**
MS. Rawl. C. 813, fol. 14ᵛ.

741*b* **My heart was slain and none but you and I**
**Yet heaven will still have murder out at last.**
MS. Rawl. poet. 172, fol. 11.

742 **My heart was slain when none was by**
**Did do this wicked murder.**
[Heath, Robert, Clarastella's Indictment], verse 1.
Pr. *Clarastella*, 1650, p. 32.
MS. Mus. b. 1, fol. 127, with music by John Wilson.

743 **My heart with good thoughts does abound**
**Thy honour and high state.**
Psalm xlv.
MS. *Rawl. C. 113, fol. 35ᵛ.

744 **My heart within me leaps for joy**
**Invest with power and mighty strength.**
Fairfax, Thomas, Lord, ['Songs of the old and New Testament'] 'Hannah's Songe. 1. Sam: 2'.
MS. *Fairfax 40, p. 415 (autogr.).
MS. *Fairfax 38, p. 87.

745 **My heart's fair conqueress author of my grief**
**Or death, or you my love, to me more kind.**
North, Dudley, 3rd Baron.
Pr. *A Forest of Varieties*, 1645.
MS. *North e. 41, fol. 35.

746 **My heart's not haughty, neither are my eyes**
**Put thy hope aye.**
Fleming, Robert, Psalm cxxxi.
MS. Rawl. poet. 213, fol. 47 (autogr.).

747 **My honour, favour, life and all**
**A fatal knife did cut the string.**
Epitaph on the Duke of Buckingham, 1628.
MS. Tanner 465, fol. 102ᵛ.

**My honoured lord, since strange and foreign parts** 748
**Or speak my sorrow so my Lord farewell.**
'The Ladie Ger: to her Lord'.
MS. Eng. poet. c. 50, fol. 40ᵛ.

**My hopes are only raised by thy kind charms** 749
**Oh let me always hold thee in my arms.**
MS. Rawl. poet. 209, fol. 37ᵛ.

**[My] hopes rely on God, why should** 750
**His countenance approves.**
Psalm xi.
MS. *Rawl. C. 113, fol. 15ᵛ.

**My hovering thoughts would fly to heaven** 751
**Sell not thy soul for brittle joy.**
[Southwell, Robert], 'Mans cruell warre' [elsewhere 'civil'].
Pr. *Mæoniæ*, 1595.
MS. Eng. poet. b. 5, p. 15.

**My husband dear** 752
**And gloriously be crowned.**
'In Chapel Le Frith Church Yard, on John Bennet . . . 1671'.
MS. Top. Yorks c. 2, fol. 4.

**My journey late as I did take** 753
**That god may see a mean for John.**
Subscribed 'ffinis quoth harry sponare'.
MS. Ashmole 48, fol. 60.

**My joy, my life, my crown!** 754
**Oh could I love! and stops; God writeth, loved.**
Herbert, George, 'A true Hymne'.
Pr. *The Temple*, 1633, p. 162.
MSS. Rawl. poet. 60, p. 3; *Tanner 307, fol. 123ᵛ.

**My joyful soul, thy best affections raise** 755
**And more and more prevail.**
Williams, John, Psalm ciii.
MS. *Rawl. poet. 184, fol. 15ᵛ (autogr.).

**My Kebbell sweet in whom I trust** 756
**That keepeth fast my heart in hold.**
'John Manlon' partly rubbed out at end.
MS. Ashmole 48, fol. 119ᵛ.

**My king turned Æthiopian with the rays** 757
**Your bosom friend and bear you company.**
'To Mres A. D. who gave him Cheque mate'.
MS. Rawl. poet. 116, fol. 67 rev.

**My labouring soul no longer can sustain,** 758
**Sits down disconsolate, and starving dies.**
'The Disconsolate'.
MS. Rawl. poet. 90, fol. 116ᵛ.

**My lady hath forsaken me** 759
**She letteth him slip at length.**
MS. Ashmole 176, fol. 98.

760 My lady is a pretty one
That ever I saw.
Transcribed from B.M. Add. MS. 7578.
MS. Mus. d. 184, fol. 18.

761 My Lalage when I behold
And thou canst make us freeze beneath the line.
R[andolph], T[homas], 'A dialogue'.
Pr. *Poems*, 1638.
MS. Eng. poet. c. 50, fol. 105.

762 My Lesbia let us live and love
But kiss and unkiss till we die.
'Lesbia out of Catullus . . . English Songe' for the Oxford Act, 10 July 1680, not performed.
MS. Mus. Sch. C. 120.

763 My Lesbia swears she would Catullus wed,
And should be writ in air or running streams.
'Women's Fickleness; from Catullus', lxxii.
MS. Rawl. poet. 173, fol. 52ᵛ, attr. to Mr. Dryden.

764 My life shall sooner than affection end
To him, that is my real honest friend.
Southwell, Sir Robert, couplet.
MS. *Eng. poet. f. 6, fol. 53 (autogr.).

765 My life though long is gone and fled
And ever with the Lord remain.
'Epitaph in Hampstead Church Yard'.
MS. Eng. poet. e. 40, fol. 19.

766 My life to lose, my soul to save,
And be undressing for the grave.
Sepulchral verse on Francis Williamson, *Gentleman's Magazine*, Feb. 1800 (lxx. 116).
MS. Top. gen. e. 32, fol. 125.

767 My life was long yet wholly mixt with care
That do themselves from sin and evil keep.
Freind, John, 'Verses of my Grandmother Mary Tibbot who d. Nov. 19 1671'. Acrostic.
MS. Top. Oxon. f. 31, p. 307.

768 My light is god I need not darkness dread
And trust in him and trust to have no wrong.
Harington, Sir John, Psalm xxvii.
MS. *Douce 361, fol. 15.

769 My limbs were weary and my head opprest
Me thought I lay content though not at rest.
Morley, George, 'The Nightingale'.
Pr. *Musarum Deliciae*, 1656, p. 90.
MSS. Eng. poet. c. 50, fol. 133ᵛ; e. 97. p. 131, attr. to George Morley; Rawl. poet. 199, p. 49, attr. to G. M.

My little Ben now thou art young 770
Lest that as mine imprison thee.
'[John] Hoskins in the Tower to his little sonne Benjamin'.
MS. Rawl. poet. 117, fol. 16; see also S1026, S1365.

My little Lodge tease me no more 771
The charming Fanny Fielding.
'Horace Ode'. IV. i.
MS. Eng. poet. c. 18, fol. 200.

My little lord methinks it's strange, 772
When such as you fall down.
Lines to Abp. Laud, winter 1640–1.
MSS. Ashmole 36, 37, two copies, fols. 104 and 288; Douce 357, fol. 35ᵛ; Tanner 306, fol. 277.

My lodging is on the cold ground 773
She has another dear, oh no, etc.
'A Song', subscribed Mr. S. H.
MS. Rawl. poet. 214, fol. 83 rev.

My lodging it is on the cold ground 774
The cause of my misery.
[Davenant, Sir William], 'in the Rivals', [Act v].
MS. Rawl. poet. 65, fol. 31ᵛ.

My lord a diamond to me you sent 775
But that my ink was factious for this side.
'To my Ld. Chancellour Sr. ffr. Bacon'.
MSS. Rawl. poet. 26, fol. 48; 246, fol. 46ᵛ.

My Lord hath called for my son 776
Enough my Lord; now let me die.
Carey, Mary, 'Written . . . on the Death of my 4th and only Child, Robert Payler . . . Covent-Garden, Dec. 10th 1650'.
MS. Rawl. D. 1308, p. 178.

My lord! I do confess, at the first news 777
A man thrust out and a gay cloak left in.
Corbett, [Richard], 'on the guard dedicated to my Ld. Mordant'.
Pr. *Poetica Stromata*, 1648.
MSS. Ashmole 47, fol. 17, attr. to Dr. Corbit; Eng. poet. e. 97, p. 44, attr. to Dr. Corbett.

My lord; I humbly crave your help; what I 778
Like God, is to be like the Deity.
West, Rich[ard], 'A Postscript [to a panegyric on Lady Theophila Cooke] to . . . Lord Berkely'.
MS. Rawl. poet. 246, fol. 42ᵛ.

779 My lord is light and shineth bright
But threats his fatal end.
'Thomas ffairfax Anagram. ffax mea hosti ffera', by 'Mr. Ashmore in print', [*sc.* John Ashmore, but not pr. *Certain selected Odes of Horace*, 1621].
MS. Top. Yorks c. 26, fol. 175.

780 My lord, it is your absence, makes each see,
And as I hope for happiness, 'tis true.
Cavendish, Lady Jane, 'Passions Letter to my Lord my Father'.
MS. *Rawl. poet. 16, p. 1.

781 My lord it is your absence makes each see
I am a wit, but then pray, whisper't low.
Cavendish, Lady Jane. To the Earl of Newcastle.
MS. *Rawl. poet. 16, p. 84.

782 My lord my god in all distress,
That sought to work me ill.
[Hopkins, John], Psalm lxxi.
MS. Rawl. poet. 112, fol. 51 rev.

783 My lord the voice that did your sickness tell
And look as fresh, as when the spring appears.
Shirley, James, 'Upon the Lord of S[trafford] his recoverye'.
Pr. *Poems*, 1646, p. 32.
MS. *Rawl. poet. 88, p. 8.

784 My lord 'tis your virtue a great and a rare one
Good Harrie, brave Robbin and you noble Tommis.
Pestell, Thomas, 'To my Lord Cromwell Viscount le Cale'. Thomas, fourth Baron Cromwell, created Viscount Lecale 22 Nov. 1624. In the last line 'Harrie' is Henry Hastings, and 'Robbin' Robert Devereux.
MS. *Malone 14, p. 25.

785*a* My Lord unto my words give gracious ear
To shroud us with thy shadow like a shield.
Harington, Sir John, Psalm v.
MS. *Douce 361, fol. 2$^v$.

785*b* My lord when I your unsought glories viewed
Almost invisible, but still shined upon.
Flatman, Thomas, address to Sancroft, 1678(?).
Pr. *Life and Uncollected Poems*, dissertation, F. A. Child, Philadelphia, 1921.
MS. Tanner 306, fol. 389 (autogr.).

My lord, you may be called when you write 786
Suetonius: Tranquillus never while you fight.
Polwhele, John, couplet, 'An Epigram upon the Lord Broghills Romance Printed when in Arms againste the Kinge'. [Roger Boyle's *Parthenissa*, 1654–69].
MS. *Eng. poet. f. 16, fol. 58 (autogr.).

My lord your absence makes I cannot own, 787
Then am I crowned with height of bliss.
Brackley, Elizabeth, *née* Cavendish, to the Earl of Newcastle.
MS. *Rawl. poet. 16, p. 84.

My lord your picture spake you this, to be 788
That 'tis no fiction but a truth of thee.
Cavendish, Jane, 'The trueth of Pensell'.
MS. *Rawl. poet. 16, p. 4.

My lords and all you gentlemen 789
To your all wise opinion.
'K[ing]'s Speech Burlesqu'd'. 1692.
MSS. Eng. poet. c. 18, fol. 187$^v$; e. 50, p. 53.

My lords and gentlemen I greet ye 790
By my Lord keeper, so God b'wi' you.
'Kings Speech (1693)'.
MS. Eng. poet. e. 50, p. 57.

My lords and my commons 'tis my resolution 791
By send[ing] to old Nicholas me their second saviour.
'K[ing]'s Speech to the Parliament before his going to Ireland' 1690.
MSS. Eng. poet. e. 50, p. 47; Firth e. 6, fol. 31; Rawl. poet. 169, fol. 14$^v$.

My lords, I have received a letter 792
I'm for a war. Oh and I. and I.
'A Dialogue Between the K[ing William III], B[en]ting, and Sund[er]land, 1697'.
MS. Eng. poet. e. 50, p. 84.

My love and I for kisses played 793
Give me my stakes, take you your stakes again.
Pr. *Wits Recreations*, 1640, Sig. E3$^v$, and John Wilson's *Cheerfull Ayres or Ballads*, 1660, p. 144.
MSS. Ashmole 38, p. 149; 47, fol. 97; CCC. 328, fol. 81; Eng. poet. c. 50, fol. 131; d. 152, fol. 106$^v$; e. 97, p. 54; f. 10, fol. 103$^v$; Malone 19, p. 124; Mus. b. 1, fol. 16$^v$, music by John Wilson; Rawl. poet. 116, fol. 57; 199, p. 4, attr. to W. S.; Tanner 465, fol. 96; see also I55.

794 My love and I of late by chance
That with his blindness both our fondness tamed.
'Cupid discovered'.
MS. Rawl. poet. 172, fol. 5.

795 My love and I (the day being drest
Committed, where were none to see.
MSS. Ashmole 36, 37, fol. 194ᵛ.

796–7 My love doth fly with wings of fear
While she this love doth not disdain.
De Burgh [Richard, 4th (?)] Earl of Clanricard, 'Of the last Queene by the Earle of Clanricard'.
MS. Don. c. 54, fol. 7ᵛ.

798 My love he has ta'en on a bold sailor to be
Crying if I had but wings I would fly to my love.
MS. Firth c. 18, fol. 136.

799 My love is chaste without desire
Subservient still to honour's laws.
'To my dear Iris this discription of the little Passion which warms the heart of Aminta is sincerely Dedicated'.
MS. Montagu e. 13, fol. 133.

800 My love is made of nature's purest mould
But 't joys me most to think what is below.
'On a younge gentlewoman'.
MSS. Don. d. 58, fol. 43ᵛ; Douce f. 5, fol. 19; Eng. poet. e. 14, fol. 74; Hearne's diaries 30, p. 229.

801 My love is my dear one for dear she has cost me
For I should be sure to win.
Williams, John, 'Upon an Expensive Mistress'.
MS. *Rawl. poet. 191, fol. 97ᵛ (autogr.).

802 My love my thrice fair love I did behold
And there t'abide perhaps an hour or twain . . . (incomplete).
MS. Rawl. poet. 143, fol. 27.

803 My love rack'd thoughts obtained a short breathed truce
And only in dreams and death thou giv'st us joy.
Beaumont, Thomas, 'A Dreame'.
MS. *Malone 18, p. 69 (autogr.).

804 My love she does wait on a lady so fair,
Then you'll live as happy as Darby and Joan.
'The Sailor's Courtship to the Lady's Waiting Maid'.
MS. Firth c. 18, fol. 162.

My love to show her cold desire 805
Dimmed by the covering clouds he breeds.
North, Dudley, 3rd Baron, Song.
Pr. *A Forest of Varieties*, 1645, p. 46.
MSS. Don. c. 57, fol. 25, with music; *North e. 41, fol. 44.

My lovely fair one, my transporting joy, 806
And upon those dear lips would always stay.
Williams, John, 'Stand up and kiss me'.
MS. *Rawl. poet. 191, fol. 95 (autogr.).

My loving friend amorous bune 807
I would you were all beshitten.
'A lettere sende by on younge woman to a noder whiche aforetyme were ffelowes to geder'.
MS. Rawl C. 813, fol. 6ᵛ.

My loving friend whom eke I love 808
It was a thing of price.
'Riddle 36'.
MS. Rawl. poet. 217, fol. 77.

My lute within thy self thy tunes enclose 809
And lowest stops do yield the highest sound.
Sidney, Sir Philip, from the *Arcadia*.
MS. *e Mus. 37, fol. 121.

My Mamma, they say, 810
Spite of all she says?
Translation of French rhyme.
MS. Ballard 47, fol. 37ᵛ.

My masters all! 811
That now to tap high time it is.
[Bacon, Phanuel], 'Verses spoken over a Barrel of Ale by the Butler of Brazen-Nose, in the College Hall, according to the annual Custom'.
MS. Eng. poet. e. 45, fol. 52 (autogr.).

My masters you that read my rhyme 812
A turd in your teeth and there an end.
'Libell agaynst Bashe', or Basse, a squire of Stanstead, Herts.
MS. Rawl. poet. 85, fol. 66.

My masters you that undertake the game 813
None must do anything, but only say.
'To the lower house of Parliamt.,' endorsed 1640.
MSS. Ashmole 36, 37, fol. 87; Douce 357, fol. 6ᵛ; Rawl. poet. 26, fol. 95.

My mates, I give you here to understand 814
That he should worthy be to ask so much.
Oldisworth, Nicolas, 'To all his Acquaintance'.
MS. *Don. c. 24, fol. 66 (autogr.).

815 My mind craves not the Indian ore
Than Olympic games in Thessale fields.
Nalson, Robert, 'Mediis tranquillus in undis', 1672.
MS. Top. Cheshire c. 6, fol. 388$^{v}$ (autogr.).

816 My mind drawn up aloft by beauty's rays
Why you are sick; oh Sirs you must be well!
Ch. M., Sonnett 11.
MS. Eng. misc. d. 239, fol. 8$^{v}$.

817 My mind to me a kingdom is
No wealth is like a quiet mind.
Dyer, Sir Edward, 'sorte contentus abi'.
Pr. from MS. Rawl. poet. 85, *Oxford Book of 16th Century Verse.*
MSS. Eng. poet. f. 10, fol. 87; Rawl. poet. 85, fol. 19, attr. to E. Dier.

818 My mistress after service due, demanded
Who sets my love on such a peevish elf.
Pr. Tho. Bateson's *Second set of Madrigals*, 1618, ii.
MSS. Mus. f. 17–19: f. 19, fol. 11.

819 My mistress bids me still do what I will
Indeed for her I may do what I will.
MSS. Don. c. 57, fol. 23, with music; Rawl. poet. 142, fol. 49$^{v}$.

820 My mistress blushed and therewithal
And spent her spices there.
MS. Rawl. poet. 65, fol. 34.

821 My mistress bound me with a kiss
Kisses make men loath to go.
'Oscula sunt Veneris delectamenta'.
MS. Eng. poet. f. 25, fol. 15$^{v}$.

822 My mistress could not be content
That words are sins when deeds are not.
'On the word Jape in Chaucer'.
MS. Eng. poet. e. 97, p. 28, attr. to Jo. Donne.

823 My mistress frowns
And he that loves you best.
Burton, Francis.
MS. *Add. A. 267, fol. 145$^{v}$ (autogr.).

824 My mistress hath a precious eye
She is all sweet sir-reverence.
'In the praise of his Mris'.
MS. Eng. poet. e. 14, fol. 73.

825 My mistress I would have love's book
Making me mad for his self pity.
Cavendish, Lady Jane, song in 'The Concealed Fancies'.
MS. *Rawl. poet. 16, p. 102.

My mistress in her breast doth wear 826
And such a child as love.
MS. Rawl. poet. 85, fol. 76$^{v}$.

My mistress in two parts is singular, 827
That is the most beloved, and most untrue.
Beaumont, Thomas, 'Of his Mistresses two natures'.
MS. *Malone 18, p. 18 (autogr.).

My mistress is a lady 828
For the love of a standing pinnacle.
Preswicke, Tom, 'A Song'.
MS. Rawl. poet. 214, fol. 75.

My mistress is a paragon 829
A love, so fresh, so sweet, so white, so smooth, so soft as this.
'A. 5. Voc. Geo: Kirbye'.
MSS. Mus. f. 20–24: f. 20, fol. 23$^{v}$.

My mistress is a shuttle cock 830
She is a woman and a whore.
MS. Rawl. poet. 26, fol. 68.

My mistress is a tennis ball, 831
Her chiefest pride lies in her tail.
'On his Mris'.
MS. CCC. 328, fol. 90$^{v}$.

My mistress knows her beauty 832
All but her self disdaining.
'A Song'.
MS. Rawl. poet. 214, fol. 71$^{v}$.

My mistress loves no woodcock 833
And yet she loves my master.
'A Servingman on his Mrs.'
MSS. Ashmole 47, fol. 101$^{v}$; CCC. 328, two copies, fols. 37$^{v}$ and 87; Douce f. 5, fol. 7$^{v}$; Rawl. poet. 26, fol. 69.

My mistress lowers and saith I do not love 834
Choler adust is joyed in womankind.
Sidney, Sir Philip.
Pr. *Arcadia*, 1598, p. 478.
MS. *e Mus. 37, fol. 238.

My mother, when she was with child of me 835
Just as the Gods foretold, hanged, stabbed and drowned.
'Epigram on an hermaphrodite'.
MS. Ballard 29, two copies, fols. 114$^{v}$ and, attr. to Mr. Wilmot, 133$^{v}$; cf. fol. 118$^{v}$.

My mothers are all those that seek for and contrive, 836
The names they first have learnt continue to bestow.
Williams, John, 'The Explication' of T3469.
MS. *Rawl. poet. 184, fol. 89 (autogr.).

837 My motto is the treble; that you'll gather
They're th' base, of goodness, though so base they seem.
Cheyney, William, 'The strings untwine'd'. describing 'Tetrachordon Or a Knot of Foure Strings'.
MS. *Rawl. poet. 86, fol. 1v.

838 My mouth shall thanks and praises sing
And bless their habitation.
Harington, Sir John, Psalm xxxiv.
MS. *Douce 361, fol. 19.

839 My muse and I are drunk tonight
And France bring in another.
'The Game at Chess', on 'the Chits', *c.* 1679.
MSS. Douce 357, fol. 113; North b. 24, fol. 146.

840 My muse attend, inspire my pen to say
Yes calumny! they pray, rejoice and praise.
'On the Magdalen Charity really written by a Magdalen. A.D. 1789'.
MS. Montagu e. 14, fol. 58.

841 My muse in her ambitious flight
It must be Cloe's own.
'On a Lady Singing'.
MS. Eng. poet. e. 28, p. 321.

842 My muse in no sublime and lofty verse
And saves the robber and the ravisher.
'Whoredome Condemn'd'.
MS. Rawl. poet. 173, fol. 90.

843 My muse shall rehearse such blue-coats on horse-back
Who never fought men, but women and wine.
'On the Blew Guard etc.'
MS. Firth e. 6, fol. 130.

844 My muse to sing of various changes sought
Thus he approached his father's royal seat.
Moore, Thomas, translator, early 18th cent., 'P. Ovidij Nasonis Matamorphoseon Lib. I'.
MS. *Rawl. poet. 3, fol. 82 (autogr.).

845 My muse what ails this ardour
My life my death do count hers.
Sidney, Sir Philip, from the *Arcadia*: 'the burden [of Cleophila's] minde in Anacreon's kinde of verses'.
MS. *e Mus. 37, fol. 94.

846 My muse what makes thee to rehearse
But now full ripe, and only fit for God.
Spoure, Edmund, 'An Elogie in Memorie of Mrs. Grace Rodd'.
MS. *Eng. poet. c. 52, fol. 30 (autogr.).

My naked simple life was I. 847
Exalted there they ought to shine.
Traherne, Thomas, 'My Spirit'.
MS. *Eng. poet. c. 42, fol. 7 (autogr.).

My name anagrammized doth imply 848
Being dead to sin; with thee in Heav'n to live.
Daniell, Richard, 'Anagramma in nomen meum, i.e. { Richard Daniell, Rare child naild. }
MS. Rawl. poet. 97, fol. 77 (autogr.).

My name engraved herein 849
For dying men talk often so.
Donne, John, 'A Valediction. Of my name in the window'.
Pr. *Poems*, 1633.
MSS. *Eng. poet. e. 99, fol. 113; *f. 9, p. 96.

My name's Whitehall, god bless the poet 850
If I submit the king shall know it.
Couplet, 'Quoth Rob. Whitehall of Ch. Ch. to the Visitors an. 1648'.
Pr. *Modius salium*, 1751, p. 19.
MS. Wood E. 32 (Modius salium), fol. 14.

My nature Lord is vile, 851
That touch renew'd can never fail.
Beddome, Benjamin, 'An Hymn'.
MS. *Eng. misc. e. 227, fol. 6.

My numbers, once as my fresh honours gay 852
Too strong to fall, remains as fixed as fate.
'Verses . . . by a gentleman in Dublin upon the various changes of Fortune'.
MS. Eng. poet. c. 9, p. 79.

My occupation is 853
They boast what I have done.
'The Souldier'.
From 'Yet other 12 wonders of the world', subscribed John Davys, F. Davison's *Poetical Rhapsody*, 2nd ed. 1608.
MS. Rawl. poet. 84, fol. 44 rev.

My once dear love, hapless that I no more 854
As the divorced soul from her body parts.
King, Henry, 'An Elegy'.
Pr. *Poems*, 1657, p. 24.
MSS. *Eng. poet. e. 30, fol. 18; *Malone 22, fol. 11v; Rawl. poet. 172, fol. 83; Top. Oxon. e. 380, fol. 179.

My pains were eased, because her sickness did 855
A saint should lose her life to prove it true.
Oldisworth, Giles, 'Upon Mrs. Marg[ery] Apj[ohn]'.
MS. *Rawl. C. 422, fol. 30v (autogr.).

856 **My part is done, and you'll (I hope) excuse**
**To visit for the sins of lewd mankind.**
Oldham, John, 'Apology for the foregoing Verses', i.e. N463. See D. M. Vieth, *Attribution in Restoration Poetry*, 1963, p. 461.
MS. *Rawl. poet. 123, p. 16 (autogr.).
MS. Add. B. 106, fol. 38, attr. to Rochester.

857 **My passion is as mustard strong,**
**And mute as any fish.**
'A Simile of Proverbs upon Courtship'.
MS. Ballard 50, fol. 107ᵛ.

858 **My pen must be like to an angel's quill**
**From Living Earthly Mounted I'm Now Gone.**
Fleming, Robert 'An Acrostical Memorial, of [his father] the Reverend and Worthy Mr. Robert Fleming . . . 1694'.
MS. Rawl. poet. 202, fol. 14 (autogr.).

859 **My people to your law rehearsed**
**In height of all success.**
Psalm lxxviii.
MS. *Rawl. C. 113, fol. 55.

860 **My powers are all corrupt, corrupt my will,**
**By interposing earth 'twixt heaven and it.**
[Quarles, Francis], from *Job Militant*, 1624, Medn. 4.
MS. Rawl. poet. 127, fol. 13.

861 **My prayers are heard, oh Lyce, now**
**Now into colder ashes turn'd.**
Cartwright, William, translator, Horace, *Odes* IV. xiii.
Pr. *Comedies . . . with other Poems*, 1651, p. 256, and A. Brome's *Poems of Horace*, 1666, p. 148.
MSS. Don. e. 6, fol. 21, attr. to Gul. Cartwight ex aede christi; Rawl. poet 199, p. 6, attr. to W. C.

862 **My pretty, little, kind, endearing wife**
**With diligence, is yet the only true.**
Williams, John, 'To my Wife Miss Anne Gooddy upon her engagement to me upon St. Stephens day 1710. She being then about five years and a half old'.
MS. *Rawl. poet. 192, fol. 31 (autogr.).

863 **My prime of youth is but a frost of cares**
**And now I live and now my life is done.**
Tichbourne, Chidiock (?), 'The map of man'.
Pr. *Verses of Prayse and Joye . . . upon her Majesties preservation*, 1586.
MSS. Ashmole 47, fol. 52, copied from a defective MS.; 781, p. 138, attr. to Chidiock Tichborne; CCC. 328, fol. 74ᵛ; Eng. poet. e. 97, p. 215; f. 10, fol. 93; Malone 19, p. 54, attr. to Tychborne; Rawl. D. 859, fol. 143, attr. to Tichbourne; Rawl. poet. 172, fol. 7, attr. to Tichbourne; 208, fol. 2; Tanner 169, fol. 79, attr. to Tichborne, with a note by Sir Stephen Powle 'I have the originall written with his owne hande'; Wood 460, after *Threnodia in obitum E. Lewkenor*, 1606, initialed G[eorge] S[adleir] in his own hand.

**My promise is my word, the word I give** 864
**Thy stomach, till thou crawl'st upon my grave.**
'To his Credditors. S.R.', copied from a partly illegible original.
MS. Eng. poet. c. 53, fol. 11.

**My racking thoughts by no kind slumbers freed** 865
**But painful nights do joyful days succeed.**
'Mr. Hendal in Semele', Act III. Not part of Congreve's libretto.
MS. Mus. c. 107, fol. 69.

**My rebel ears I wond'red what they meant** 866
**For, my self did to you, not me, belong.**
Oldisworth, Nicolas, 'To the right Hoble. his Patron' [James Hay, first Earl of Carlisle].
MS. *Don. c. 24, fol. 11ᵛ (autogr.).

**My rock and strength oh Lord thou art** 867
**Happier God for their God embrace.**
Fairfax, Thomas, Lord, Psalm cxliv.
MS. *Fairfax 40, p. 372 (autogr.).
MS. *Fairfax 38, p. 451.

**My roving barge yet safe would leave the main** 868
**The port I'd fain have rid in.**
Verses containing anagrams of Anny *or* Anie. Hastinges.
MS. Eng. poet. f. 25, fol. 20ᵛ.

**My saint's the elixir of all beauty, she** 869
**Of their Pandora in my love.**
E[dwards], T[homas], 'Uppon his Mistress'.
MS. Rawl. poet. 65, fol. 60.

**My saviour's praises I will sing** 870
**Th' afflicted church, in thee who glory.**
Fairfax, Thomas, Lord, 'A Hymne to Christ the Mesiah'.
MS. *Fairfax 40, p. 519 (autogr.).
MS. *Fairfax 38, p. 51.

**My self I waste, to others shining bright** 871
**The candle's curst, that dies and gives no light.**
'Mr. Ashmore in print' with an emblem of a lighted candle, 'Luccem fferfax', and latin motto; [*sc.* John Ashmore, but not pr. *Certain selected Odes of Horace*, 1621].
MS. Top. Yorks. c. 26, fol. 175.

872 My senses do o'erflow with heat and passion
If to your selves we turn the Ignoramus.
'A modest and temperate reproofe of the schollers of Cambridge for slaundring Lawiers with that barbarous and gross title Ignoramus'.
See C. H. Cooper, *Annals of Cambridge*, iii, 1845, p. 88.
MSS. Don. c. 54, fol. 27v; Rawl. poet. 26, fol. 34v.

873 My servant shall prosper, Jehovah says
Their sight, and more considerate minds are clear[d].
'Isaiah 52 chaptr: 13 vers.'
MS. *Rawl. C. 113, fol. 8 (autogr.).

874 My sheep are thoughts which I both guide and serve
In you it is you must the judgement give.
Sidney, Sir Philip, from the *Arcadia*.
MS. *e Mus. 37, fol. 59v.

875 My shepherd is the living lord,
My dwelling place shall be.
S[ternhold], T[homas], Psalm xxiii.
MSS. Rawl. D. 886, fol. 11, with setting for hand-bells; Rawl. poet. 112, fol. 65 rev.

876 My ship, wherein I toss is grief, my mind
Save me in th' port, and take my ship a spoil.
Oldisworth, Giles, acrostic, with an emblem, a ship sailing: 'Once to my sister Fr. while shee fell sicke'.
MS. *Rawl. C. 422, fol. 25 (autogr.).

877 My sickly spouse, with many a sigh,
'Twas heav'ns will, to spare my wife.
'Epigram'.
MS. Eng. poet. c. 9, p. 109.

878 My silent soul aloud doth call
In every man his deeds.
Harington, Sir John, Psalm xlii.
MS. *Douce 361, fol. 36v.

879 My sins are like the hairs upon my head
Like twinkling stars before the rising sun.
Quarles, Francis, 'On Sins'.
Pr. *Argalus and Parthenia*, 1629, and *Divine Fancies*, 1632, ii. 67, 70, 73.
MSS. Don. c. 57, fol. 32v, with music; Rawl. poet. 90, fol. 69v; Rawl. poet. 117, fol. 161v rev., attr. to Fr. Quarles.

My sledge and hammer [both] lie reclined, 880
My nails are drove, my work is done.
'On a Grave-stone of a Blacksmith buried in Chester Church Yard'.
Pr. *Gentleman's Magazine*, iv, 1734, p. 387.
MSS. Ballard 50, fol. 105v; Eng. poet. e. 40, fol. 150; f. 12, p. 9.

My son, attentive hear the voice of truth 881
The soul shall soar sublime, and wing its way to heaven.
Fawkes, F[rancis], 'The Picture of old Age', Eccles. xii. 1–7.
MS. Eng. poet. e. 18, p. 22.

My son, I would not have you be 882
I may their full performance see.
Williams, John, 'To a Son'.
MS. *Rawl. poet. 192, fol. 34 (autogr.).

My son if that sulphur be absent away 883
And to God only thee commend.
'A Dialogue betwixt the Father and the Sonne'.
Pr. *Theatrum Chemicum Britannicum*, 1652, p. 365. Extra stanzas in MS.
MS. Ashmole 972, fol. 237*b*.

My son shall not a traveller become 884
Let this be's travel, to do good at home.
Barksdale, Clement, 'Travel'. distich.
MS. Autogr. c. 9, fol. 154 (autogr.).

My son the instruction that my words impart, 885
And fall where many mightier have been slain.
'An Hymn on the 7th Chapter of Proverbs'.
MS. Rawl. poet. 116, fol. 117.

My son whose good I earnestly desire, 886
The things they must desire to overthrow.
Williams, John, 'My Son Fear Thou the Lord and the King, and meddle not with them that are given to change'.
MS. *Rawl. poet. 189, fol. 35 (autogr.).

My son! Yes Lord, my only son, my Isaac, he 887
An aged faith the budding breast did line, . . . (incomplete)
'Abraham's Sacrifice'.
MS. Eng. poet. e. 4, p. 5.

My soul aspire to bless the Lord 888
And majesty record.
Psalm civ.
MS. *Rawl. C. 113, fol. 70v.

My soul desires the word 889
Not honey half so sweet.
Beddome, Benjamin.
Pr. *Hymns . . . of B. Beddome*, 1818, no. 688.
MS. *Eng. misc. e. 227, fol. 174v.

890 My soul doth magnify the lord
As 'twas, and, is, and must endure always.
'Magnificat translated by Sir T[homas] S[alusbury(?)];' Sir T. Salusbury's poems are mentioned on fol. 4.
MS. Eng. poet. c. 53, fol. 6ᵛ.

891 My soul doth magnify the Lord
He to his seed did prove.
Fleming, Robert, 'Luke Chap. I ver: 46. Marys song'.
MS. Rawl. poet. 213, fol. 67 (autogr.).

892 My soul exalt the Lord with hymns of praise
His praise (my soul) his praise shall be thy peace.
Wotton, [Sir] H[enry], Psalm civ 'translated to the Originall sense'. 'Opera [*Reliquiae*, 1651], p. 525 etc'.
MS. Tanner 466, fol. 16.

893 My soul get thee to thy rock
Though seen supports do fail.
'The Spiritual song'.
MS. Mus. Sch. G. 632, fols. 61ᵛ, 62ᵛ; G. 633, p. 78.

894 My soul give laud unto the Lord,
Praise ye also the same.
[Sternhold, Thomas], Psalm ciii.
MS. Rawl. poet. 112, fol. 41ᵛ rev.

895 My soul give thou unto the Lord
Do any thing for thee.
Dodsworth, Matheus, on his preservation from death in a fog, written at the end of a letter dated 7° [(?)] Decr. 1657.
MS. Rawl. D. 327, fol. 22ᵛ (autogr.).

896 My soul, hate fickle women: it's nothing strange
I'd hate her, as I hate Proserpina.
Oldisworth, Robert or Giles, 'Against miweing Mistresses'.
MS. *Rawl. C. 422, fol. 7ᵛ, in the hand of Giles Oldisworth.

897 My soul hath had a fever, a long while,
Thy blood must cure me, Jesus, or else none.
[Quarles, Francis], 'On a spirituall Feavour'.
Pr. *Divine Fancies*, 1632, ii. 26.
MS. Rawl. poet. 90, fol. 66ᵛ.

898 My soul how canst thou choose to sit upon
In God enjoy one bliss perpetual.
Fleming, Robert, 'Dissolution desirable; or A Soliloque', 'written Anno Domini 1684'.
MS. Rawl. poet. 213, fol. 56ᵛ rev. (autogr.).

My soul is full weary of this life that I lead 899
[And give them pardon where they have offended].
'Howers of the B. Virgin Eng. and Lat. ad usum Sarum. The 2 Lesson for the Dirige'.
MS. Eng. poet. e. 56, p. 98.

My soul is like a bird, my flesh the cage 900
Which now I waste in begging, in thy praise.
[Quarles, Francis], 'The Soule Compar'd to a Bird in a Cage'.
Pr. *Emblemes*, 1635, v. x.
MS. Rawl. poet. 90, fol. 28.

My soul is like to tinder, whereunto 901
Soon sets on fire every proffered match.
[Quarles, Francis], 'On a Tinder Box'.
Pr. *Divine Fancies*, 1632, ii. 20.
MS. Rawl. poet. 90, fol. 66.

My soul, my heart 902
Praises and thanks, spend on Jehova still.
Herbert, Mary (*née* Sidney) Countess of Pembroke, Psalm ciii.
MSS. *Rawl. poet. 24, p. 148; *25, fol. 100.

My soul oh lord doth now confess 903*a*
Thy blood from sin hath set me free.
'Confessio pia'.
MS. Rawl. poet. 112, two copies, fols. 23ᵛ rev. and 74 rev.

My soul (oh Lord) lifts up itself to Thee 903*b*
Out of all troubles let thine Israel come.
Fairfax, Thomas, Lord, Psalm xxv.
MS. *Fairfax 38, p. 160; see also I413.

My soul on God alone 904
And shrinks before his face.
Skinner, John, 'Mens acquiescit, etc.'
MS. *Eng. poet. d. 22, fol. 131.

My soul on God waits, only he 905
His mercy too is known.
Psalm lxii.
MS. *Rawl. C. 113, fol. 45.

My soul opprest with care and grief 906
Be eased of my pain.
5-part anthem.
MS. Mus. d. 12, fol. 14.

My soul praise God whose glorious majesty 907
Praise God my soul, my soul praise God.
Clifford, Henry, Earl of Cumberland, Psalm civ.
MS. *Rawl. poet. 95, fol. 6ᵛ.

My soul praise the lord speak good of his name 908
And say with the faithful praise the lord's name.
[Kethe, William], Psalm civ.
MS. Rawl. poet. 112, fol. 41 rev.

909 My soul praise thou the lord always
For ever to remain.
[Hopkins, John], Psalm cxlvi.
MS. Rawl. poet. 112, fol. 29 rev.

910 My soul the great god's praises sings
Then oh my soul the Lord adore.
Carew, Thomas, 'Psalme the 104'.
Pr. from MS. Don. b. 9, *Poems*, ed. R. Dunlap, 1949, p. 139.
MSS. Ashmole 38, p. 98*e*, attr. to Mr. Thomas Carew; *Don. b. 9, fol. 9ᵛ; Eng. poet. c. 50, fol. 52, attr. to T.C.; Rawl. poet. 160, fol. 77ᵛ, attr. to Tho. Carewe.

911 My soul the minutes haste away
How wilt thou be affected then . . . (incomplete).
Brown, S., 'A Thought on Sickness and Death'.
MS. Eng. poet. c. 9, p. 159.

912 My soul thy self from silence raise
Through ages all the heav'nly king.
Harington, Sir John, Psalm cxlvi.
MS. *Douce 361, fol. 90ᵛ.

913 My soul to god shall give good heed,
According to their deed.
[Hopkins, John], Psalm lxii.
MS. Rawl. poet. 112, fol. 53ᵛ rev.

914 My soul was racked with love's severest care
Died with remorse, lived in despair, yet loved.
'From The Vision, a Poem on Maria who stab'd herself'.
MS. Eng. poet. c. 9, p. 263.

915 My soul what aileth thee to be so sad
Transgression, sin, and all iniquity.
'Meditations upon the name of god set downe in the 34 chapt. of Exodus'.
MS. Gough Norfolk 43, fol. 31.

916 My soul what moveth thee to be sad
And make thy self ready, when he for thee send.
MS. Rawl. poet. 219, fol. 15ᵛ.

917 My soul: what's lighter than a feather: wind:
This bubble world: what, than the bubble: nought.
MS. Rawl. poet. 90, fol. 34ᵛ.

918 My soul, why art thou thus deject?
Sing Hallelujah at his birth.
A[ustin], W[illiam], '3rd Hymn for Christmas-day'.
Pr. *Certaine Devout . . . Meditations*, 1635, p. 53.
MS. Rawl. poet. 61, fol. 81.

My soul with all thy gifts and power 919
With them my soul accord.
Psalm ciii.
MS. *Rawl. C. 113, fol. 69ᵛ.

My soul's athirst, it weeps, it cries 920
What labour shall I spend . . . (incomplete).
MS. Rawl. D. 1372, fol. 70ᵛ.

My spirit, God wot, is weakened wondrous sore 921
[Have mercy on me, and heal thou my disease].
'Howers of the B. Virgin Engl. and Latin ad usum Sarum. The 7 lesson for the Dirige'.
MS. Eng. poet. e. 56, p. 103.

My stock lies dead, and no increase 922
Drop from above.
Herbert, George, 'Grace'.
Pr. *The Temple*, 1633, p. 52.
MS. *Tanner 307, fol. 40.

My strings can do what no man could 923
For time they fast in prison hold.
'On a watch-string'.
MS. CCC. 328, fol. 4ᵛ.

My study, wit, coin, hope, time, friends 924
To lease words of less cost.
Lilliat, John, translation from Latin.
MS. Rawl. poet. 148, fol. 88 (autogr.).

My suit is just, just Lord to my suit hark 925
I shall see thee in likeness shine.
Sidney, Sir Philip, Psalm xvii.
MSS. *Rawl. poet. 24, p. 18; *25, fol. 11.

My sweet Eliza now is far removed 926
Return Maria or Papa will die.
Gunning, John, on his daughters.
MS. Firth b. 4, fol. 52ᵛ.

My sweetest bird that art encaged here 927
Thou singing livest I singing die.
MS. Don. c. 57, fol. 66ᵛ, with music by H. Lawes.

My sweetheart and my lily flower 928
When your truelove he became.
MS. Rawl. C. 813, fol. 4.

My sword I'll hang up on the myrtle bough 929
'Twas yours your country's suffering rights to save.
Ogilvie, John, M.A., translation from Alcæus, from *Monthly Review*, Oct. 1762, p. 243.
MS. Eng. poet. c. 6, fol. 78.

930 My tap is run then, Baxter tell me why
Then let these lines be writ upon my tomb.
'The last will and Testament: of Anthony [Ashley Cooper] King of Poland'. At the end is written 'Here wants the Epitaph but when I get it shall send it'.
Printed as a broadsheet 1682, and in *A collection of 86 Loyal Poems*, 1685, p. 196.
MS. Eng. poet. c. 25, fol. 73.

931 My task is past, my care is but begun
My task is past and all my care is gone.
Guillim, John, 'To the generous reader'.
From the *Display of Heraldrie*, 1610, p. 282.
MS. Rawl. B. 20, fol. 34v.

932 My tears are now the ink wherewith I write,
For then in dolorous darkness my heart dies.
Burton, Francis.
MS. *Add. A. 267, fol. 79 (autogr.).

933 My thankful voice shall never cease
Palsied with fear, with trembling horror shook . . . (incomplete).
J. F., Psalm lxxvii.
MS. *Eng. poet. f. 17, p. 171 (autogr.).

934 My Theodora can those eyes
Since you an eye to him and me can lend.
[Brome, Alexander], 'To his Mistress'.
Pr. *Poems*, 1661, p. 17.
MS. Ashmole 47, fol. 156.

935 My Theodore to heaven is gone
Till us thou bring to Thee.
Tipping, William, 'Of my three Children who I trust in Christ Jesus . . . are in heaven'.
MS. *Rawl. poet. 101, fol. 84 (autogr.).

936 My thirsty soul betimes shall seek the [Thee] Lord
When their mouths are stopped that false liars are.
Fairfax, Thomas, Lord, Psalm lxiii.
MS. *Fairfax 40, p. 139 (autogr.).
MS. *Fairfax 38, p. 227.

937 My thoughts are winged with hopes, my hopes with love,
And love is sweetest, seasoned with suspect.
Pr. Dowland's *Songs or Ayres*, 1597, iii.
MSS. Mus. f. 7–10: f. 7, two copies, fols. 9 and 4v.

938 My thoughts how vain they are
Unless thou give the power.
Beddome, Benjamin
MS. *Eng. misc. e. 227, fol. 75.

My thoughts (I walking) wander 'mong the rest, 939
Wise man conceive this love may prove my death.
Oldisworth, Giles, 'The fallacy G.O. putt upon Mrs.Est', with an 'Honest interpretation'.
MS. *Rawl. C. 422, two copies, fols. 32v and 33v (autogr.).

My thoughts, my tongue, my pen, I do dispense 940
I change myself, but not my love alas.
Ch. M., Sonnett 4.
MS. Eng. misc. d. 239, fol. 6v.

My time, oh ye muses, was happily spent 941
Take heed, all ye swains, how ye love one so fair.
English verses [by John Byrom, from *Spectator* no. 603, 6 Oct. 1714], translated into Latin by G[eoffrey] Walmsley, Sid. Coll. Cambridge.
MSS. Ballard 50, fol. 121; Rawl. poet. 116, fol. 88.

My times of sorrow and of joy 942
Be thou my all in all.
Beddome, Benjamin.
Pr. *Hymns of B. Beddome*, 1818, no. 222.
MS. *Eng. misc. e. 227, fol. 78.

My tongue must be like to an angel's quill 943
Doing thy worst, thou helps him to the throne.
Fleming, Robert, 'An Achros[t]ick To the memory of the Reverend Master Robert Mackwood . . . Obijt May 26 1681'.
MS. Rawl. poet. 213, fol. 30v (autogr.).

My tongue to praise thine eyes I oft would strain 944
What though thou shalt be bit? I shall be kissed.
Ch. M., 'Sonnett 5'.
MS. Eng. misc. d. 239, fol. 7.

My trembling song, Awake! Arise! 945
Hosanna! Alleluiah to th'almighty king!
[Flatman, Thomas], 'Jan. 1. 1683/4. A New year's song. Before the King'.
Pr. *Poems*, 4th ed., 1686, p. 201, 'set by Dr. Blow . . . 1682/3'.
See *M. & L.*, xlvi, 1965, p. 108.
MS. Tanner 306, fol. 391 (autogr.).
MS. Mus. c. 26, fol. 124v, with music by Dr. John Blow, incomplete.

My troubled thoughts have waked my muse from sleep 946
He had as yet remained with us still.
Mills, Richard, 'In obitum clarissimi et Doctissimi viri Francisi Milles. qui obiit 1619'.
MS. Don. c. 54, fol. 2.

947 My true christian hearts of gold,
Brave boys, we'll fight for liberty.
'The Protestant Exhortation, Or. Verses of the Couragious Christian Collonel Walker, In London-Derry'.
MS. Firth d. 14, fol. 22.

948 My true love hath my heart and I have his
My true love hath my heart and I have his.
Sidney, Sir Philip, from the *Arcadia*.
MS. *e Mus. 37, fol. 109.

949 My various conflicts here
I shall thy fullness know.
Kenton, James.
MS. *Eng. poet. e. 20, p. 109 (autogr.).

950 My verse is gone I have all rhymes defied
Maypoles go first and then down goes the beacon.
'To Mr. Hammon of Beaudly. Dr. [Richard] Corbet'.
MS. Rawl. poet. 142, fol. 42.

951 [My verse is satire. Dorset lend your ear.]
The happy only are the truly great.
[Edward] 'Young's love of Fame'.
MS. Eng. poet. c. 9, p. 151.

952 My verses were commended thou dost say
Thy dirty brains; men see thy little worth.
'Ben Johnson, to his Detractor J[ohn] E[liot]' See Y501.
Pr. *Poems*, 1640.
MS. Ashmole 38, p. 82.

953 My vesture in the day is radiant white
And shall abide after it desolation.
Burton, Francis, 'An viij$^{th}$ [riddle] of the Heaven'.
MS. *Add. A. 267. fol. 7 (autogr.).

954 My visit at Eton renewed the old flame
When he knows that they come from your little make-weight.
'On A Captain's Lady'.
MS. Ballard 29, fol. 160.

955 My voice to god in cries I sent
Didst lead thy people as a flock.
Fairfax, Thomas, Lord, Psalm lxxvii.
MS. *Fairfax 40, p. 173 (autogr.).
MS. *Fairfax 38, p. 186.

956 My voice to thee it self extremely straining
Of godly men, will glory in thy glory.
Herbert, Mary (*née* Sidney), Countess of Pembroke, Psalm cxlii.
MS. *Rawl. poet. 24, p. 210.

My volume complete cries Sir Finical Fain 957
First solve me one question pray sir who will buy?
Boswell, James, 'Epigram'.
MS. *Douce 193, two copies, fols. 27 and 32 (autogr.).

My vows to god I mean to pay 958
Even so. Amen say I.
Forman, Simon, 'Repetition of the troble he had with the Doctors of Phisick in London and of his delivery in the plague 1592'.
MSS. Ashmole 240, fol. 25 (autogr.); 802, fol. 131 (autogr.).

My wanderer at last retreats 959
Who rules by nature's law.
Subscribed M[ary] N.
MS. Rawl. poet. 196, fol. 23$^{v}$.

My waning joys, my still increasing grief 960
Brings doubtful hope but dolour most assured.
MS. Rawl. poet. 85, fol. 18$^{v}$.

My wanton lines do treat of amorous love 961
A maiden smoothness seyreth (*sic*) half his limbs.
Beaumont, Francis, 'Salmacis and Hermaphroditus'. Dated 1634.
Pr. 1602.
MS. Rawl. poet. 120, fol. 95.

My warbling verse doth now begin to sail, 962
Discovered in god in highest degree.
F. W., 'Sonnet 29'.
MS. *Rawl. C. 639, p. 150.

My watchful eyes still thrown upon thy bower 963
That's all I crave in guerdon of my pain.
Andrews, —.
MS. *Rawl. poet. 92, fol. 14$^{v}$.

My weary pilgrimage at length is o'er 964
Bid all the troubles of the world farewell.
Inscription at St. Michael's, Bristol, on Anne Craven, d. 8 Feb. 1745.
MS. Rawl. D. 1090, fol. 190.

My weather-beaten soul long time has been 965
That, that would lay the storm of all my fears.
[Quarles, Francis], 'On the Soule'.
Pr. *Divine Fancies*, 1632, iv. 36.
MS. Rawl. poet. 90, two copies, fols. 52$^{v}$ and 76$^{v}$.

My whining lover, what needs all 966
For surfeits sooner, kill than fasts.
Suckling, Sir John.
Pr. *Fragmenta Aurea*, 1646, p. 28.
MSS. Ashmole 36, 37, fol. 134; Rawl. poet. 116, fol. 55$^{v}$, attr. to Sir John Suckline.

967 My wife and I full twenty years
Rending the clouds in sunder.
'A distick (*sic*) after the death of a Jealouse Scoldinge wife', subscribed 'Clitophon Lucippe'.
MS. Rawl. poet. 117, fol. 156 rev.

968 My winter's task, dear sir, has been to find
Good books, good horses, and you still my friend.
Potenger, John, 'The Second Letter [to C. H. Esqre.] in Verse'.
MS. *Eng. poet. d. 161, p. 50.

969 My wishes are but few all easy to fulfil
I make the limits of my power the bounds unto my will.
MS. Rawl. D. 954, fol. 44v.

970 My wishes greet the navy of the Dutch
True men may have their own now thieves fall out.
Equivocal verses on the Parliamentary and Dutch fleets, 1652–3.
MSS. Rawl. D. 317, fol. 200v; Rawl. poet. 246, fol. 15.

971 My wit's my wealth my learning is my land
Pens are my ploughs, my writings are my rents.
'A Scholler'.
MS. Eng. poet. f. 10, fol. 89.

972 My words and thoughts do both express this notion,
To gain at harvest an eternal treasure.
Herbert, George, 'Coloss. 3.3. Our Life is hid with Christ in God'.
Pr. *The Temple*, 1633, p. 77.
MSS. Rawl. poet. 90, fol. 137; *Tanner 307, fol. 58v.

973 My words in hope to blaze my steadfast mind
A woman's hand [with constant marble stone].
Sidney, Sir Philip, from the *Arcadia*.
MS. *e Mus. 37, fol. 62.

974 My wretched soul with sin oppressed
In heaven to have a dwelling place.
MS. Eng. poet. b. 5, two copies, pp. iii and 42.

975 Myrtilla like time is always a flying
For no prayers or vows can recall her again.
'Myrtilla flys Me'.
MS. Eng. poet. e. 40, fol. 33.

Myrtillo though my heart should break 976
Nor fear to lose but you.
MS. Rawl. poet. 172, fol. 110.

Myrtillo you were much to blame 977
And for that fault a victim fell.
'A Copy of Verses'.
MS. Montagu e. 13, fol. 135v.

Myself I hate when think I did 978
To all eternity.
Tipping, William, 'The Sincere Lover'.
MS. *Rawl. poet. 101, fol. 8 (autogr.).

Mysterious act! which dost at once put on 979
To live in death and while I live to die.
'Fasting'.
MS. Rawl. poet. 246, fol. 34.

Mysterious God of grace and love 980
And sing thy praise above.
Kenton, James.
MS. *Eng. poet. e. 20, p. 371 (autogr.).

Mysterious God unsearchable 981
For God is a consuming fire.
Kenton, James.
MS. *Eng. poet. e. 20, p. 161 (autogr.).

Mysterious riddle of the state 982
High misdemeanour but no treason.
'Clarendon's villanies unridled', Nov. 1667.
MSS. Add. A. 48, fol. 12v; Rawl. D. 924, fol. 312; Tanner 306, fol. 372, with 18 extra lines.

Mysterious signet! which on wax impress 983
Regain the seal, or I shall die with laughing.
Lumby, John, 'To Miss M. L[umby]', on the Loss of a seal.
MS. *Eng. poet. e. 42, fol. 48.

Mysterious words God sinking into man 984
Whate'er the Sybil's sacred page foretold!
Jones, Lewis, of Jesus College, Oxford, 'In Christi Nativitatem'.
MS. Top. Oxon. e. 167, two copies, fols. 27v and 33.

Mystical songs of love I sing 985
Never to part again.
'Epithalamia Sacra', lacking 4 leaves between pp. 130–1.
MS. Eng. poet. e. 51, p. 127.

# N

ENTRIES 1–615

1 Naibod in his mysterious arts
Rodolphus here prostrate doth lie.
Reynoldes, Lance., acrostic on Nicholas Culpeper.
MS. Ashmole 423, fol. 205 (autogr.).

2 Naked I came when I began to be
And slumber doth stark naked, he and I.
Flatman, Thomas, 'Nudus Redibo. June 15 1660. Set by Mr. Wm. Gregory'.
MSS. Add. B. 8, fol. 46v, attr. to T. F.; *Firth d. 7, fol. 22; Rawl. poet. 84, fol. 107 rev.

3 Naked she lay, clasped in my longing arms,
To do the wronged Corinna right for thee.
Wilmot, John, Earl of Rochester, 'The Imperfect Enjoyment'.
See Vieth, p. 381.
MS. Add. B. 106, fol. 39.

4 Name echo now whereon's religion grounded
Then keep the church and state fro' these lay men. Amen.
'An Eccho'.
MSS. Malone 21, fol. 30; Rawl. poet. 62, fol. 50; see also N470.

5 Names oft, and natures jump; so story tells
And Scipio, staff of age, his father's joy.
Sancroft, William, '*Φερώνυμος*'.
MS. *Sancroft 48, fol. 27v (autogr.).

6 Nan and Frank two quondam friends,
Betwixt the white staff knight, and lay of th' red nose.
'The Quarrel Between Frank and Nan. 1681'.
Pr. *Poems on Affairs of State*, 1703, ii. 122. 'Frank' glossed as Lord Newport; 'Nan' as Nan Capell, an orange woman.
MS. Firth c. 15, p. 111.

7 Nancy lies sick a bed
And a race of ginger.
MS. Douce d. 59, fol. 55v.

8 Nan's husband cares not for the people's chat
He by his gaining shows all wit withal.
MS. Malone 19, p. 156.

Narcissus loved and liked so his shape 9
For of self love, reproach and shame proceeds.
Whitney, Geoffrey, 'Amor sui'.
MS. *Rawl. poet. 56, fol. 97.

Narcissus loved his own feature 10
Himself to be the son of Jove.
Reynoldes, Lance., acrostic on Nicholas Culpeper.
MS. Ashmole 423, fol. 205v (autogr.).

Naso transformed shapes, loves and delight 11
What all have writ the moor-lands Dove is all.
Kynder, Philip (b. 1597), 'To Mr. Charles Cotton upon his Poems'.
MS. Ashmole 788, fol. 144.

Nassaw knight-errant of our church choose rather 12
By land; at sea strike to our faith's defender.
'The Loyall Protestnts. Responce', on William III.
MSS. Add. A. 301, fol. vi, attr. to Gerard [Cater (?)]; Rawl. D. 361, fol. 22v.

Nature a thousand ways complains, 13
And very small ones. ha, ha, he.
'Spoken on waking out of a Dream . . . London Mag: Jan. 1743'.
MS. Eng. poet. c. 9, p. 52.

Nature amidst the frenzy of her love 14
Reveal'd to Newton all her works above.
'On Sir Isaac Newton', couplet.
MS. Eng. poet. e. 40, fol. 71.

Nature and art at variance were 15
Now, boaster, tell me, who is thine?
'On a Lady'.
MS. Eng. poet. f. 12, p. 57.

Nature, and nature's laws, lay hid in night 16
God said, let Newton be, and all was light.
[Pope, Alexander], 'On . . . Sir Isaac Newton'. Couplet.
See *Minor Poems*, ed. N. Ault and J. Butt, 1954, p. 317.
MS. Eng. poet. e. 40, fol. 71.

17 Nature being old began
That no man cares to live now Harry's dead.
'Dr. Jaxons [William Juxon] verses on Prince Henrye his death', 1612.
MS. Ashmole 47, fol. 39; see also N43.

18 Nature bids you on this picture view
The world, and no such other to be found.
Cavendish, Lady Jane, 'On my Sister Fraunces Picture'.
MS. *Rawl. poet. 16, p. 22.

19 Nature brought forth, art taught him instantly
No farther I, farewell my friend for all.
Freind, Nathaniel, translator of George Royse's poem on John Freind, d. 1672.
MS. Top. Oxon. f. 31, p. 292 (autogr.).

20 Nature but once in love confess'd the flame
And Newton loving bravely told his name.
'On Sir Isaac Newton', couplet.
MS. Eng. poet. e. 40, fol. 71.

21 Nature canst find a name that can so well
Nature in him thou showedst thy greatest skill.
G. de Riv., 'Ivatt anag. Vitat'.
MS. *Rawl. poet. 104, fol. 62 (autogr.).

22 Nature courts happiness although it be
And all God's will can bear, can do, can choose.
Philips, K[atherine], O[rinda], 'Happiness'. Pr. *Poems*, 1664, p. 228.
MSS. Rawl. poet. 65, p. 10, attr. to K. P. O.; 90, fol. 6$^{v}$; 173, fol. 174$^{v}$, attr. to Mrs. Phillips.

23 Nature did well in giving poor men wit
That fools well moneyfied may pay for it.
Couplet.
MS. Rawl. poet. 153, fol. 28.

24 Nature does strangely female gifts dispense
Since even Skipworth brags he has success.
'Womans Wisdom 1683'.
MSS. Firth c. 16, p. 44; Rawl. poet. 159, fol. 79.

25 Nature festive blithe and gay
Full of jarring noise and strife.
Percy, Thomas, nephew to the Bishop of Dromore.
MS. Percy c. 8, fol. 70 (autogr.).

26 Nature gave the bull his horns
Active as light, unbounded as the air.
'Ἐις γυναῖκας', Anacreon, *Ode* ii.
MS. Add. D. 79, fol. 88 rev.

27 Nature has done her part do thou do thine
A witty sinner is the worst of fools.
'Lines to a young Gentleman'.
MS. Eng. letters d. 103, p. 138 rev.

Nature hath found a gem without compare 28
The ring the world is but you the jewel are.
'On a ring'.
MS. Eng. poet. e. 14, fol. 60.

Nature, how may this name be understood? 29
To take another, and forsake his way.
G. de Riv., 'Ivat anag. Vita'.
MS. *Rawl. poet. 104, fol 62 (autogr.).

Nature in all her virgin fancies seen 30
Let reason all enjoy without abuse.
Amherst, Elizabeth, 'Inscriptions intended for Newbold, 1771'.
MS. *Eng. poet. e. 109, p. 63.

Nature in pride her self for to excel 31
But fell beside herself, to mar it so.
E[des], D[r. Richard], on Lady Rich's having small pox, [1597].
MS. Rawl. poet. 148, fol. 69$^{v}$.

Nature in this [same] small volume [was] went about 32
Threw dust upon it and shut up the book.
[Browne, William, of Tavistock (?)], 'On the death of a young gentle woman'.
In B.M. MSS. Sloane 1446, fol. 65, on the daughter of Dr. [John] Prideaux; Lansdowne 777, fol. 60$^{v}$, on Anne Prideaux, died aged 6; Harl. 3910, fol. 4, 'Mrs. E. P.'. Pr. *Poems of W. Browne*, ed. G. Goodwin, 1894, ii. 287; also *Life*, etc., of J. Hoskyns, L. B. Osborn, 1937, p. 213.
MSS. CCC. 328, fol. 13$^{v}$; Eng. poet. c. 50, fol. 130$^{v}$; e. 14, fol. 100$^{v}$ rev.; e. 40, fol. 104; e. 97, p. 54, attr. to William Stroad; Firth e. 4, p. 110; Rawl. poet. 116, fol. 53; 199, p. 4; 206, p. 65.

Nature made all her creatures but this stone 33
A stone should speak then now no tears express.
MS. Eng. poet. e. 14, fol. 46$^{v}$.

Nature on earth a wonder to effect 34
That fortune is a sharer in my woe.
Beaumont, Thomas, 'On his M$^{rs}$ creation'.
MS. *Malone 18, p. 20 (autogr.).

Nature on th'Adrian waves saw Venice lie 35
You'll say that men built that, but this the gods.
Hutton, John, of New College, Oxford, 'In Urbem Venetia', with Sannazarius' epigram, I. xxxv, 'Viderat Adriacis Venetam Neptunus in undis'.
MS. Rawl. poet. 19, fol. 109.

36 Nature perceiving that her choicest piece
That straight their notes, in sem'breve sighs expired.
Ashmole, Elias.
MSS. Ashmole 36, 37, fol. 223$^{v}$ (autogr.).

37 Nature perversely to your wish has given
For misers only want what they possess.
'An Answer by the Hon: Thomas Harvey Esq$^{r}$ 2$^{d}$ son to the Earl of Bristol to Miss Morton'.
MS. Eng. poet. e. 40, fol. 6.

38 Nature surveying well her treasury
A sacrifice of admiration.
'On a gentle-womans eyes'.
MS. CCC. 328, fol. 25$^{v}$.

39 Nature that washed her hands in milk
Turn snow and silk and milk to dust.
[Ralegh, Sir Walter]. See *Poems*, ed. A. Latham, 1951, p. 119.
MSS. Eng. poet. c. 50, fol. 109; Mus. b. 1, fol. 77, with music by John Wilson.

40 Nature the bull with horns supplies
The fair, victorious where she goes.
[Philips, Ambrose, translator], 'The 2nd Ode [of Anacreon] On Women'.
Pr. *Pastorals*, etc., 1748, p. 140.
MS. Rawl. poet. 153, fol. 48.

41 Nature to every part assigns it's stage
When young will govern and when old would please.
'Epigram on the several Stages of Life'.
MS. Eng. misc. b. 48, fol. 52.

42 Nature took mighty pains in making you.
I, I anon.
MS. Rawl. poet. 152, fol. 246.

43 Nature waxing old began
That no man cares to live, now Henry's dead.
Juxon, William, 'On the death of prince Henry'.
MSS. CCC. 328, fol. 27$^{v}$; Douce f. 5, fol. 34$^{v}$, attr. to Dr. Juxton; Eng. poet. e. 14, fol. 99$^{v}$ rev., attr. to Dr. Juxon; Malone 21, fol. 3$^{v}$, attr. to Dr. Juxon; Rawl. poet. 212, fol. 151 rev.; see also N17.

44 Nature works wonderful effects 'tis true,
Subdue the country, and enslave the town.
Walsh, William, 'Elegy 26 In defence of Painting'.
MS. *Malone 9, fol. 46 (autogr.).

45 Nature's chief gifts unequally are carved
But all enjoy the common ill—a woman.
'Epigram'.
MS. Rawl. poet. 116, fol. 90.

Nature's confectioner (the bee) 46
That he committed parricide.
Cleveland, [John], 'Fuscara stunge or the Bee Errant'.
Pr. *Poems*, 1662, p. 4.
MS. Rawl. poet. 116, fol. 63.

Nature's great secretary's pen 47
You find a wither'd leaf, or a neglected brake.
Creswell, Robert, 'Spes Vigilantis somnius —of Hope . . . (Dithyramb)'.
MS. *Eng. poet. f. 24, fol. 35 (autogr.).

Nature's idea physic's rare perfection 48
The heavens by this time had been dyed black.
'On the praise of [Tobacco]'.
Pr. *Wits Recreations*, 1640, no. 134.
MSS. Eng. poet. e. 14, fol. 19; Rawl. poet. 84, fol. 73; Rawl. poet. 153, fol. 27$^{v}$.

Nature's lay idiot, I taught thee to love 49
And leave him then, being made a ready horse.
Donne, John, 'Elegye'.
Pr. *Poems*, 1633.
MSS. *Eng. poet. e. 99, fol. 22; *f. 9, p. 132; Malone 19, p. 80, attr. to J. D.; Rawl. poet. 117, fol. 207 rev., attr. to Dunne.

Nature's o'ercome by art (some artists say) 50
With many great rewards for's worthy parts.
Cheyney, William, 'Liberall artes. The Proeme'.
MS. *Rawl. poet. 86, fol. 25$^{v}$.

Naught can enough declare 51
That all false ways, quite out of love I cast.
Herbert, Mary (*née* Sidney), Countess of Pembroke, Psalm cxix, 'N'.
MSS. *Rawl. poet. 24, p. 183; *25, fol. 123.

Naught hinders man in all his life, 52
If bad, alas she doth undo him.
Robinson, Robert.
MS. *Rawl. poet. 218, p. 64 (autogr.).

Naught naught my Helicopis naught could move 53
May'st thou fulfil all th'ills of Booker's prophecy.
W. R., 'The Curse'.
MS. Rawl. poet. 199, p. 67.

Naught under heaven so strongly doth allure 54
Their harden'd heart enviourned with cruelty.
MS. Eng. poet. e. 14, fol. 14.

Naught vexes more proud rich men (can you blame them) 55
To their poor kindred they're so poorly free.
Robinson, Robert.
MS. *Rawl. poet. 218, p. 26 (autogr.).

56 Nauta was nominated for a whore
Being thus declined in what a case was she.
'The 6 cases attributed to Nauta'.
Pr. *Wits Recreations*, 1641, Sig. T4.
MSS. CCC. 328, fol. 47; Eng. misc. e. 183, fol. 71; Eng. poet. d. 152, fol. 104$^{v}$.

57 Navia six cups, Justina seven drink we
'Cause I have none come Somne be thou mine.
MS. Malone 19, p. 162.

58 Nay blackcoats, now look to 'it; you must away.
Ere long too they will dance o'th' rope.
Winnard, Thomas, 'An Owle at Athens. A Relation of the Earle of Pembrokes Entrance into Oxford. April 12, 1648'.
MS. Eng. poet. e. 4, p. 142.

59 Nay dry for shame those blubbered eyes
In your last love, you'll doubled find in me.
[Brome, Alexander], 'To a Widdow'.
Pr. *Poems*, 1661, p. 18.
MS. Ashmole 47, fol. 150$^{v}$.

60 Nay, faith! Clarinda you're not wise
'Twill raise my flame, and never damp the fire.
Chatwin, John, 'Ignorance'.
MS. *Rawl. poet. 94, p. 240 (autogr.).

61 Nay fie! Good sir! what do you mean,
Forget my practice of piety.
Clifton, Sir Clifford, 'upon Mr. Justice Charleton's wife, who dwelt at Nottingham'.
MSS. Ashmole 36, 37, fol. 204$^{v}$.

62 Nay fie, Platonics still adoring
As all must envy or admire.
[Brome, Alexander], 'Epithalamy'.
Pr. *Poems*, 1661, p. 25.
MS. Ashmole 47, fol. 156$^{v}$.

63 Nay, hear'st thou Will? 'tis time to look about,
Lest empty breeches hence away you carry.
Ashmole, Elias, 'Preparation for Groaning . . . To Mr. William Hutchinson . . . 30 May'.
MSS. Ashmole 36, 37, fol. 232$^{v}$ (autogr.).

64 Nay if our sins are grown so high of late,
Or Hell their fitter place.
Oldham, John, the second 'Satyr upon the Jesuits'.
Pr. *Works*, ed. Edward Thompson, 1770, i. 21.
MS. *Rawl. poet. 123, p. 190 (autogr.).; other drafts between pp. 174 and 293.

Nay let me weep, though others tears be spent 65
And lilies in their spring time hang their head.
Pr. Orlando Gibbons's *First Set of Madrigals*, 1612, xvii–xix.
MSS. Mus. f. 20–24: f. 20, fol. 50$^{v}$.

Nay, Madam, you may very well be seen 66
They fain would kill, though they dare strike no blows.
Oldisworth, Nicolas, 'To a yong Lady, that hadd the greene Sicknesse'.
MS. *Don. c. 24, fol. 38 (autogr.).

Nay painter, if thou darest design that fight 67
Kings are but cards in war, they're gods in peace.
'The Second Advice to the paynter for drawing the History of our Navall businesse in imitation of Mr. Waller'. See 'envoy', I1198.
Pr. *Poems on Affairs of State*, 1697, p. 24. See Denham's *Poetical Works*, ed. T.H. Banks, 1928, p. 327. *Advice-to-a-Painter Poems*, M. T. Osborne, 1949, no. 10.
MSS. Don. b. 8, p. 237, lacking 20 lines mistakenly transferred to next poem, attr. to Sir John Denham; e. 23, fol. 9, attr. to Sir John Denham; Eng. poet. d. 49, p. 157, attr. to Andrew Marvell; e. 4, p. 213; Locke e. 17, p. 160, attr. to Sir John Denham.

Nay pish nay fie nay out upon't 68
Since 'tis no more pray tickle me.
'A dalliing with a Lady'. Subscribed 'M$^{r}$. Marke D.'
MS. Rawl. poet. 214, fol. 73$^{v}$.

Nay pish, nay pue, nay faith, [away I pray] and will you fie; 69
And then at cards we better will agree.
'A mayds Denyall'.
Pr. Ritson's *Ancient Songs*, 1790, p. 104.
MSS. Ashmole 38, p. 150; 47, fol. 54; CCC. 328, fol. 87; Don. d. 58, fol. 44$b^{v}$; Eng. poet. e. 97, p. 185; Malone 19, p. 75; Rawl. poet. 85, fol. 4; 199, p. 10.

Nay prithee do, be coy and slight me 70
So I thy martyr am or never.
[Brome, Alexander], 'The Contrary'.
Pr. *Poems*, 1661, p. 14.
MS. Ashmole 47, fol. 147$^{v}$.

Nay prithee don't fly me 71
And that man has no worth that won't sometimes be mellow.
[Brome, Alexander], 'The Leveller'.
Pr. *Poems*, 1661, p. 72.
MS. Ashmole 47, fol. 161$^{v}$.

72 Nay prithee now be civil; hold thy hands
Now tell what thou and I have done.
P[aman], Cl[ement], 'Vernura and Celemon'.
MS. Rawl. poet. 147, p. 109.

73 Nay, Sam, don't say thy fate is bad,
The happy happy married man.
'An Epistle to a young Gentleman, who married his Bedmaker. In imitation of Horace', *Odes* II. iv. 1735.
MS. Eng. misc. e. 240, p. 298.

74 Nay start not (Sir) for know to you I came
Your servant Sir I must away. Good night.
'To a Freinde of Hir's in Love. Compos'd by M[rs]. B. P.'
MS. Rawl. poet. 84, fol. 2.

75 Nay Sylvia now you're cruel grown,
For rocks of diamonds I'll not kiss.
Chatwin, John, 'The Resolution'.
MS. *Rawl. poet. 94, p. 192 (autogr.).

76 Nay then farewell, if you must always be
Which melts his plumes to throw him down again.
'To Lorinda on the denyall of a kiss'.
MS. *Rawl. poet. 87, p. 57.

77 Nay, then the devil take all love! if I
And heaven knows what reward her teacher had!
Oldham, John, translator, Ovid, *Amores* II. v. 'To his M[rs]. that jilted him'.
MS. Rawl. poet. 173, fol. 45[v].

78 Ne gay attire, ne marble hall,
Mine house shall prove an hermitage.
[West, Gilbert], 'Father Francis his Prayer'.
Pr. Dodsley's *Collection of Poems*, iv, 1755, p. 265; cf. W. P. Courtney, *Dodsley's Collection*, 1910, p. 41. In B.M. MS. Sloane 4456, fol. 58[v], 'to St. Agnes'.
MS. Eng. poet. c. 41, fol. 25.

79 Near a country town
Which may spoil their devotion.
Gough, Richard, 'A Tale . . . On the Presbyterian Minister at Enfield 1772'.
MS. *Eng. poet. c. 5, fol. 218 (autogr.).

80 Near crystal springs and murmuring fountains
But with my dear would live and die.
'A Song'.
MS. Montagu e. 13, fol. 25.

81 Near Epsom at the king of Bantam's marriage
And that is all the amends that I desire.
'Upon a Gentlemans breaking a China bowl at a Wedding'.
Pr. *Poems on Affairs of State*, iii, 1698, p. 31.
MS. Eng. poet. c. 18, fol. 15[v].

Near his paternal seat, here buried lies, 82
And while they live, his name shall never die.
W[illiams], Sir C[harles] H[anbury], 'An Epitaph on the late Right Hon[b] Thomas Winnington Esq[r]' 1746.
MS. Montagu e. 13, fol. 156[v].

Near Holborn lies a park of great renown 83
Each duke for state may take a several post.
'A true, and perfect Relation of a bold, and Sawcy Beadle, being upon the watch . . . who was fairely kill'd by three Dukes'. [Feb. 1670/1].
Pr. *Poems on Affairs of State*, 1697, p. 147.
MSS. Don. b. 8, p. 207; Douce 357, fol. 110; Rawl. poet. 84, fol. 20[v].

Near the bear where there's a bawling 84
To send you another made of the same tune.
'Oxford verses . . . to the tune of the Pyramid', on Robert Pauling, Mayor of Oxford 1679–80.
MS. Eng. poet. c. 25, fol. 49.

Near to a murmuring fountain's purling head, 85–86
Who catch'd at Juno but embrac'd a cloud.
Chatwin, John, 'Dreaming of Her'.
MS. *Rawl. poet. 94, p. 132 (autogr.).

Near to a road where brewers live in state 87
Pray for your reformation when you're gone.
'Parochial Advice to a Proud B[isho]p who holds a fat living in Commendam . . . 1729/30'.
MS. Tanner 306, fol. 492.

Near to that sacred and immortal frame 88
Like other monarchs of the Steward line.
'A copy of Verses on the Statue of Queen Ann, in St. Pauls Churchyard'.
MS. Montagu e. 13, fol. 95[v].

Near to the rivers of proud Babylon 89
And with remorseless fury dash their brains against the stones.
Psalm cxxxvii.
MS. Don. c. 55, fol. 14[v].

Near to the town (as stories tell) 90
And country interest live for ever.
'The Virgin Dr.'
MS. Eng. poet. c. 41, fol. 70.

Near to this eglantine 91
With tears for him that Chloris wet her face.
Drummond, William, of Hawthornden. 'A Favourite Dog'.
Pr. *Poems*, 1616, 'Madrigals' xli.
MS. Top. gen. e. 32, fol. 73[v].

92 Near to this pillar there doth lie
To God and Christ the king of kings.
Inscription in Gloucester Cathedral to William Andrewes, d. 5 Aug. 1657.
Pr. Browne Willis, *Cathedrals*, 1742, ii. 700.
MSS. Rawl. D. 1090, fol. 143$^{v}$; Willis 71, p. 296.

93 Near to this place mix'd with the dust is laid
Desiring to be good, not minding to be great.
Inscription on monument in Gloucester Cathedral to Elizabeth Millechamp, d. 5 June 1700.
MS. Rawl. D. 1090, fol. 148$^{v}$.

94 Near unto this place doth lie
To as much virtue, as could live.
MS. Tanner 89, fol. 264$^{v}$.

95 Near [unto] Wilton sweet huge heaps of stones are found
She is the cause that all the rest I am.
Sidney, Sir Philip, 'The wondres of Ingland'. Pr. *Arcadia*, 1598, p. 481.
MSS. *e. Mus. 37, fol. 240; Rawl. poet. 85, fol. 102, subscribed 'Incertus author'.

96 Nebuchadnezzar king of kings complains
And now he can confess there is a God.
'The Paroxysme'.
MS. Rawl. poet. 154, fol. 110.

97 Necessity doth teach men wit,
Oh then their wit comes to 'em.
Robinson, Robert.
MS. *Rawl. poet. 218, p. 46 (autogr.).

98 Need, hard need, makes poor men thieves and beggars
'Cause covetous rich men are hard hearted baggers.
Robinson, Robert, couplet.
MS. *Rawl. poet. 218, p. 77 (autogr.).

99*a* Need makes the poor to work or else they're dead:
Penurious rich men do so poorly pay.
Robinson, Robert.
MS. *Rawl. poet. 218, p. 80 (autogr.).

99*b* Needs must I leave, and yet needs must I love
So beauty thou, beauty is not in thee.
[Constable, Henry], sonnet, pr. *Diana*, 1594, IV. i.
MS. Ashmole 38, p. 54.

100 Ne'er air was weaved of softer ray
Not to the throne but altar hies.
P[roby], H[enry], 'On the day of his majesties Coronation', Charles I, anniversary *temp.* civil war.
MS. Rawl. poet. 246, fol. 19.

Ne'er did Triptolemus in his chariot rise, 101
But steeds and wheels demand a spacious road.
[Cowper, William], translator, from Owen, 'Comfort for Walkers'. Pr. from this MS., *Poetical works*, ed. H. S. Milford, 4th ed., 1934, p. 665.
MS. Autogr. d. 21, fol. 191$^{v}$ (autogr.).

Ne'er think it strange to see good fortune fling 102
Who not pursues his day benights his fame.
Bulteel, John, 'Hanibal'.
MS. *Rawl. poet. 159, fol. 224$^{v}$.

Ne'er trouble thyself with the times nor their turnings 103
What fails us to day may befriend us tomorrow.
'Glee—Mat: Locke'.
MS. Mus. d. 177, fol. 67$^{v}$.

Neighbour Leycester by your leave 104
But all knows him that are wise.
Northamptonshire lampoon, early 17th cent.
MS. Carte 103, fol. 54$^{v}$.

Neither by law, nor gospel 'tis allowed; 105
That rich men should, much less poor men be proud.
Robinson, Robert, couplet.
MS. *Rawl. poet. 218, p. 44 (autogr.).

Nell's husband says she brought him nought but toys, 106
But yet without his help she brings him boys.
'Epigram', couplet.
MS. Malone 19, p. 155.

Neptune of whirling winds and huge waves terrible emperor 107
Ware the water water oft brings woe thrice woe to the waters.
Mills, Rob[ert], 'Ware the water . . . a certayne companye of youthes (schollars in Cambridge) rowing downe the ryver . . . the boote chaunced . . . to be torned ouer'.
MS. Rawl. poet. 85, fol. 78$^{v}$.

Never in Prince had subjects greater store 108
'Tis time to die, since dead is England's spring.
G. B., Epitaph 7 on Prince Henry in 'Cestria Lugens', 1612.
MS. *Rawl. poet. 116, fol. 6$^{v}$.

Never let a man take heavily 109
When she begins to scold do thou begin Twedle Twedle.
'A Sonett for a cursed wife', in a copy of *An Antidote Against Melancholy*. A similar verse printed, p. 68.
Pr. bk. Douce P 690, stuck on to the back cover.

110 Never more duly on his Cynthia's grace
And many prayers chaste thoughts doth disperse.
'An other [Sonnet] depending on' R22.
MS. Add. B. 97, fol. 19v.

111 Never more will I protest
Sells their freedom for a song.
Pr. Francis Beaumont's *Poems*, 1640, Sig. I3v.
MS. Rawl. poet. 116, fol. 53v.

112 Never poor slave so longed to be
That same bold desperate hand again should set me free.
'An Invective against Marriage with an ill Husband'.
MS. Rawl. poet. 90, fol. 166.

113 Never than now did death seem more a hag
Reaps greater wages, and for lesser pains.
'On the Death of Mr. Jo: Nelson who dyed of the small pox. 7br 20 [16]71'.
MS. Rawl. poet. 127, fol. 4v.

114 Never, till now, I thought that unread books
To bind each writer with a several chain.
Oldisworth, Nicolas, 'On his seeing the Study of Mr. Michael Oldisworth . . . once a fellow of Magdalen coll. in Ox.'
MS. *Don. c. 24, fol. 9v (autogr.).

115 Never was bargain better driven by fate
Th' espoused pair two realms, the sea, the ring.
Jonson, Ben., 'Upon the Union of England and Scotland', 1603.
MS. Don. c. 54, two copies, fols. 3v, and, attr. to Ben. Johnson, fol. 11; see also N117, W40, W1601.

116 Never was I less alone then being alone
I wish all my posterity they would ensue the same.
'Henry Lorde morley to his posteritye'. Subscribed 'Si ita Deo placet ita fiat. Wrytten over a chambar Dore wher he was wont to ly at Hollen Byery'.
Pr. *British Bibliographer*, Brydges and Haslewood, iv, 1814, p. 107, and E. Flügel, *Neuenglisches Lesebuch*, 1895, p. 37.
MS. Ashmole 48, fol. 9v.

117 Never was marriage better driven by fate
The married pair two realms, the sea the ring.
'Ben Johnson uppon kinge James his union of England and Scotland'.
MS. Rawl. poet. 117, fol. 164v rev; see also N115, W40, W1601.

Never weather-beaten sails more willing bent to shore 118
And take my soul to thee.
[Campion, Thomas].
Pr. *Two Bookes of Ayres*, [*c.* 1613], I. xi.
MS. Mus. Sch. G. 632, fol. 62, with Campion's music.

New joy, new joy unto our king 119
Thy power still be praised.
Sidney, Sir Philip, Psalm xxi.
MSS. *Rawl. poet. 24, fol. 25; *25, fol. 15.

New Mayor and new Recorder! the choice doubles 120
Let 'em go hang their calves plucks at their back.
'The Domestick Intelligence The Poets or Newes letter', dismissal of Nathaniel Bacon, recorder of Ipswich (?).
MS. Tanner 306, fol. 471.

News from a foreign country came, 121
A small and little thing.
Traherne, Thomas, 'On News', The Third Century, 26.
MS. Eng. th. e. 50, fol. 52 (autogr.).

News to expect from Houghton Hall 122
To one great being merciful and just.
'To the Ladies at Oxburgh'. In B.M. Add. MS. 31152, fol. 35, endorsed 'Sir Wm. Youngs verses on Sir Rt. Wall[pole's] seat and company'.
MS. Add. B. 105, fol. 94.

News would you have? here's news both old and new: 123
Oh would such news could ne'er be heard of more.
Robinson, Robert.
MS. *Rawl. poet. 218, p. 111 (autogr.).

Newton in transport seized on Nature's hand 124
The goddess blushing was at his command.
'On Sir Isaac Newton', couplet.
MS. Eng. poet. e. 40, fol. 71.

Newton with open mouth demands a stray 125
Till Carter speaks, or Newton holds his tongue!
'Dr. Carter, Provost of Oriel, admits a Gentleman from Hart-Hall, without a Discessit from Dr. Newton'.
MSS. Eng. poet. f. 13, fol. 15v; Hearne's diaries 105, p. 110; Top. London e. 9, p. 7.

Next after fervent pure and pious prayer 126
And those are mocked that ought to be supplied.
Williams, John, 'Of Good Advice ill given'.
MS. *Rawl. poet. 191, fol. 50v (autogr.).

127 **Next my advice, fair maidens, is to you**
**Alas! you cannot be for ever young.**
Samber, Robert, 'To the young Maids' from 'the Bellman's Verses'.
MS. *Rawl. poet. 134*b*, fol. 156$^{v}$ (autogr.).

128 **Next to the charming beauty of your stage**
**'Till when incognito he lurks in's bays.**
Farrar, Richard, 'A Letter to Sr. William Davenant, concerning my [i.e. John Bulteel's] Play Amorous Orontus [1665]'.
MS. Rawl. poet. 159, fol. 227.

129 **Nice honour by a private man**
**Is still a man of honour.**
'On the acquitting Lord B[y]ron', 1765.
MS. *Eng. poet. d. 47, fol. 165.

130 **Nicely the taste of ridicule to hit**
**Like Norfolk dumplin, and like Russian bear.**
[Gough, Richard (?)], 'Written extempore at C[orpus] C[hristi] C[ollege,] C[ambridge]'.
MS. Eng. poet. c. 5, fol. 99, in Gough's hand.

131 **Nicodemus a Jew, begged our Saviour when dead'**
**Is for carrying the tragedy further.**
'On the Dean of Westminster's [Dr. Zachary Pearce] endeavouring to destroy the New East Window of St. Margaret's Westminster . . . Extempore 1760'.
MS. *Eng. poet. d. 47, fol. 61.

132 **Nigh seated, where the river flows**
**Shall take, and dash against the stones.**
Herbert, Mary, *née* Sidney, Countess of Pembroke, Psalm cxxxvii.
MSS. Eng. poet. e. 57, fol. 14; *Rawl. poet. 24, p. 204.

133 **Nigh the mournful period drew**
**Reign with our exalted head.**
Kenton, James.
MS. *Eng. poet. e. 20, p. 64 (autogr.).

134 **Nigh to the banks of Avon, where the stream**
**So great a triumph, when a stag did fall.**
'Suley [near Wansford, Northants.], Bowling greene'. Translation of printed Latin verses dedicated to Charles, Earl of Westmorland.
MS. Eng. misc. d. 1, fol. 45.

135*a* **Night being come away thou must**
**Raising thy soul, thy face to see.**
Reynoldes, Lance., acrostic on Nicholas Culpeper.
MS. Ashmole 423, fol. 206 (autogr.).

**Night had her sable curtain drawn** 135*b*
**Sweat, shivered, shit and died.**
'Holmes's Ghost to The Tune of Babes in the wood', on Dr. Cary Butt of Lichfield.
MS. Top. Staffs. c. 1, fol. 75$^{v}$.

**Night nurse of mortals from her quiet breast** 136
**Beauty doth fade gold rusts and pleasure spends.**
Burton, Francis, 'A Newe yeares guifte to Mr. Nathaniell Fulwer upon this Theame Miscentur gaudia luctu' [N. F. possibly of Magdalen Hall and Grays Inn, b. *c.* 1562].
MS. *Add. A. 267, fol. 8 (autogr.).

**Night's dismal shades once more are fled,** 137
**My tongue his constant praise.**
'Morning hymn. Gent. Mag. July 1735'.
MS. Eng. poet. c. 9, p. 106.

**Nimble boy in thy warm flight** 138
**Lo here lies Cupid blest in death.**
[Habington, William], Song.
Pr. *Castara*, 1634, p. 29.
MS. Don. c. 57, fol. 60, with music.

**Nimbly labour: be not dull** 139
**Thou must surely pay that score.**
Robinson, Robert.
MS. *Rawl. poet. 218, p. 150 (autogr.).

**Nine days are past and yet the wonders new** 140
**Than the demands for hackneys though they tire.**
'Verses not upon Edgerly the Carier's Wife but Edgerlay's wife the Carier'.
MSS. Eng. poet. e. 14, fol. 76; f. 10, fol. 93$^{v}$.

**Nine tailors make a man, the proverb says** 141*a*
**A tailor, now becomes a complete man.**
'On the Victory att Erxdorff. 1760'.
Pr. bk. Firth b. 22, fol. 59.

**Niobe once did stand** 141*b*
**So she might tread on me.**
Barnes, Joshua, translator, Anacreon 'Od. 20. v. 303'.
MS. Hearne's diaries 11, p. 100.

**No airy shadow does my soul pursue** 142
**And one's far absence you shall know the whole.**
Samber, Robert.
MS. *Rawl. poet. 134*b*, fol. 173*b* (autogr.).

**No amorous style affects my pen** 143
**Sore kicked by true nobility.**
Sherley, Henry, 'The Battaile the Combattantes, Sr. Ambrose Vaux Knight; and Glascott the Bayley of Southwarke'.
MS. Ashmole 38, p. 75.

144 No annals shall be writ but what relate
If they make martyrs, we may make a saint.
'An Elegy upon the death of the Archbishop of Canterburie beheaded A° 1644 written by a learned hand att Oxon.'
MS. Top. Cheshire c. 6, fol. 240ᵛ.

145 No art, no ribbon does there need to grace
Since all you seek falls short of what you have.
Amherst, Elizabeth, 'Lines slipt into a young Lady's ribbon Box who was fond of Dress', Miss Monk.
MS. *Eng. poet. e. 109, p. 21.

146 No beauty Salust is upon the gold
Yet it in heart reject, contemn, despise.
W. A., translator, Horace, *Odes* II. ii.
MS. *Rawl. poet. 104, fol. 13ᵛ (autogr.).

147 No beauty spots should ladies wear
That would be held a maid of honour.
Fairfax, Thomas, Lord, 'Upon a Patch Face'.
MS. *Fairfax 40, p. 570 (autogr.).
MS. *Fairfax 38, p. 317.

148 No beauty with the helps of art
Than this is to the mind.
MS. Rawl. poet. 116, fol. 42.

149 No bondage worse doth man enslave,
Then to a good wife to be bound.
Robinson, Robert.
MS. *Rawl. poet. 218, p. 79 (autogr.).

150 No coranto news I undertake
And so the commencement grows new.
Cleveland, John, 'A Song. On the New Commencement'.
Pr. *Poems*, 1653.
MS. Rawl. poet. 147, p. 48, attr. to Cleveland; Tanner 465, fol. 83, attr. to Mr. Cleveland St. John. Coll.

151 No critic scorning, sharp and terse,
Bears in its chime, a magic spell.
Temple, R. G., to W. Parsons.
MS. Don. c. 81, fol. 138 (autogr.).

152 No cure on earth can make an old man sound:
All glory be to thee our heavenly King.
Robinson, Robert.
MS. *Rawl. poet. 218, p. 175 (autogr.).

153 No curious notions whilst our hand is still
To show thy praise and all Thy foes withstand.
Williams, John, 'The Diligent hand makes Rich'.
MS. *Rawl. poet. 191, fol. 124 (autogr.).

No daisies enamel the plains, 154
And longs to behold them again!
Parsons, William, 'A Pastoral Ballad'.
MS. *Don. d. 123, p. 38 (autogr.).

No day so clear, but brings at length dark night 155
And all estates an end of life must make.
MS. Ashmole 51, fol. 6.

No diet in the kitchen drest, 156
Maintains and holds up all.
Robinson, Robert.
MS. *Rawl. poet. 218, p. 45 (autogr.).

No doubt the task is far beyond compare 157
Because 'twas order'd by a hand so fair.
Williams, John, 'Upon some Pigeon which Miss Betty broild, made at her desire'. Couplet.
MS. *Rawl. poet. 191, fol. 105 (autogr.).

No doubt with real sincerity 158
That I eternally may live.
Kenton, James.
MS. *Eng. poet. e. 20, p. 8 (autogr.).

No earthly thing doth truly grieve me more, 159
Than to behold fools rich and wise men poor.
Robinson, Robert, couplet.
MS. *Rawl. poet. 218, p. 65 (autogr.).

No epitaphs need make the just man famed 160
The good are praised, when they are only named.
Couplet, 'On Mr. Thomas Allen'.
Pr. *Wits Recreations*, 1641, Epitaph 22.
MSS. Sancroft 53, p. 44; 59, p. 292 rev.

No eye, nor ear nor lip nor knee, 161
And do thy holy will.
Beddome, Benjamin.
MS. *Eng. misc. e. 227, fol. 7.

No fragrant flower hath half so sweet a smell; 162
It charms my soul, and scents the ambient air.
Morrice, John, 'On Clarinda's breath . . . Jan. 10, 1707'.
MS. *Rawl. poet. 114, fol. 140 (autogr.).

No friend have I, in all this world 163
Should I be there without him.
Tipping, William.
MS. *Rawl. poet. 101, fol. 78ᵛ (autogr.).

No fruitful field am I, no blessed wheat, 164
To sin, yet, Lord, reduce me to thy fold.
4 lines translating Latin distich.
MS. Rawl. D. 954, fol. 40ᵛ.

165 No glory I covet, no riches I want,
Is what all, if they will, may enjoy.
'On Contentment'.
MSS. Ballard 50, fol. 108; *Eng. poet. d. 47, fol. 144; Mus. e. 20, fol. 17v, set by Mr. Abiel W[illiams].

166 No greater blessing in this life
Than a cross wife that scolds and brawls.
Robinson, Robert.
MS. *Rawl. poet. 218, p. 79 (autogr.).

167 No house I living found, but dead a grave
I'm clothed and covered that in life went naked.
'Uppon a Beggar', translating Latin epitaph.
MS. Ashmole 38, p. 173.

168 No ivy green with me, no gilded wood
And put his breathless corpse in fertile soil.
W. A., translator, Horace, *Odes* II. xviii.
MS. *Rawl. poet. 104, fol. 19v (autogr.).

169 No Jesuit ever took in hand
Which, had they wanted gold, they still had wanted.
'Hudibras unprinted'.
MS. Aubrey 6, fol. 115.

170 No joys of sense, like conscious goodness please
A life of rapture from the wound of death.
'On Virtue'.
MS. Eng. poet. e. 47, p. 30.

171 No latin at this time; for, Peter's tide
To leave Bar-jonas, and, with Peter, rest.
Oldisworth, Giles, 'my holy-daye verses for St. Peters-day', as a Westminster boy, 29 June 1638.
MS. *Rawl. C. 422, fol. 1 (autogr.).

172 No letter that we write but mourns in black
Saints, like Eumorphë, never live till death.
Oldisworth, Robert or Giles, 'Upon Mrs. M[argery] A[pjohn]'.
MS. *Rawl. C. 422, fol. 30v, in the hand of Giles Oldisworth.

173 No letters so full and expressive can be
The second to peerage, to pension, to Pitt.
Williams (?), 'On the late Lord Chatham'.
MS. *Eng. poet. e. 7, fol. 18v (autogr.).

174 No longer blame those on the banks of Nile
If you ne'er seek me out, I'll think you wise.
'A Riddle'.
Pr. *Poems on Affairs of State*, iii, 1698, p. 268.
MSS. Eng. poet. c. 18, fol. 29; d. 152, fol. 58v; Rawl. poet. 173, fol. 142.

No love, to love of man and wife 175
For all, is one; and one, is all.
Eedes, Dr. [Richard], 'Of Man and Wife'.
MS. Rawl. poet. 148, fol. 62.

No lover saith I love, nor any other 176
Love-slain, lo here I lie.
[Donne, John].
Pr. *Poems*, 1633.
MS. Rawl. poet. 31, fol. 21.

No lute, or lover durst contend with thee 177
Hadst added to thy love but charity.
P[aman], C[lement], 'To Tho: Carew', couplet.
MS. Rawl. poet. 147, p. 108.

No man is sorry for poor Joseph's woe; 178
Who will with tears of sorrow wash Christ's feet.
H. W., 'The affliction of Joseph', sent to John Rhodes, fellow of Trinity College, Cambridge, 1618–1649.
MS. Tanner 466, fol. 98v.

No man loves fiery passion, can approve 179
His courage is as little as his wit.
[Ayton, Sir Robert], stanzas from 'There is no wordly pleasure here below'.
MSS. Ashmole 36, 37, fol. 192, with a tune, stanzas 3–5, interpolated stanza, 7, 9–10; Rawl. poet. 65, fol. 31, stanzas 3, 5, 9, 10.

No man was e'er so blest as I, 180
But fancy was the only bride.
Chatwin, John, 'On his finding Aurelia's Globe'.
MS. *Rawl. poet. 94, p. 130 (autogr.).

No man with dirt likes to be spatter'd, 181
But children and fools love to be flatter'd.
Robinson, Robert, couplet.
MS. *Rawl. poet. 218, p. 153 (autogr.).

No man's condition is so base as his: 182
Be added to the hate of God and man.
[Quarles, Francis], 'The Hypocrite'.
Pr. *Divine Fancies*, 1632, i. 23.
MS. Rawl. poet. 90, fol. 42.

No marvel, if the flocks, do err and stray, 183
Whose guides cannot agree upon the way.
Couplet.
MS. Rawl. poet. 66, fol. 60.

No marvel if the sun's bright eye 184
Might feel a dart by touching you.
Strode, William, 'To a Gentlewoman for a Frinde'.
MS. *CCC. 325, fol. 71v (autogr.).
MS. CCC. 328, fol. 78v, attr. to Str.

185 No marvel that lawyers are rich
Th'other takes to give.
'Of Lawyers and Poets'.
MS. Douce f. 5, fol. 9.

186 No marvel then that Helicon
The fountain of our store.
MS. Tanner 306, fol. 117.

187 No marvel, thou great monarch did'st complain
H'as grief enough, that finds no world but this.
[Quarles, Francis], 'On Alexander'.
Pr. *Divine Fancies*, 1632, i. 56.
MS. Rawl. poet. 90, fol. 51.

188 No marvel, though the sun do hide his head
Doth only satisfy it self, not us.
[John] 'Lilliat his Lenvoy, or Lacrime of this great rayne, and rage of Weather'.
MS. Rawl. poet. 148, fol. 114 (autogr.).

189 No money! Pox on you!
Or if out of the treaty I leave you.
'An angry Message to the Citty Anno 1696', as from William III.
MS. Rawl. D. 361, fol. 215v.

190 No more
The glory of whose face shall all thy griefs discuss.
J. F., Psalm xlii.
MS. *Eng. poet. f. 17, p. 155 (autogr.).

191 No more can I describe each sacred breast,
Extremely good, beyond expression sweet.
Chatwin, John, 'On Lisonia's Breasts'.
MS. *Rawl. poet. 94, p. 49 (autogr.).

192 No more Clarinda shall thy charms
Love is not always true.
A version in B.M. MS. Harl. 2127 fol. 31r is headed 'Prudence Draper her songe. 1648'. Answered by B358.
MS. Rawl. poet. 116, fol. 40v; see also N201.

193 No more Clemena glance no more
Killed by those eyes whose looks first made me love.
MS. Rawl. poet. 196, fol. 26v.

194 No more, dear Alderman, thy thoughts perplex
For thou wilt find 'em both of doubtful gender.
'To the Senior Alderman of S—'.
MS. Ballard 47, fol. 37.

195 No more dear Smith the hackneyed tale renew
And leave you liberty to do so too.
Chatterton, Thomas, 'The Defence. Dec. 25. 1769'.
MS. Eng. poet. e. 6, fol. 2 at end (autogr.).

No more do flattering visions of the night 196
Our daughters honest youths, like you, engage.
'By a Gentleman upon his return to his Wife'.
MS. Rawl. poet. 116, fol. 100v.

No more fond man no more thy praise bestow 197
With thee, my Saviour, I may find a place.
'Te Deum'.
MS. Rawl. poet. 170, fol. 70.

No more I will thy love importune 198
Since I can never hope, I never may desire.
Pr. Thomas Tomkins's *Songs*, 1622, ii.
MSS. Mus. f. 17–19: f. 19, fol. 5*a*v.

No more I'll break my head to teach my tongue 199
The running hand, and sermon is the best.
Creswell, Robert, 'On Short-Hand'.
MS. *Eng. poet. f. 24, fol. 36 (autogr.).

No more I'll buy empty impertinent fame 200
Nor buy it most wisely of I cannot tell who.
Williams, John, 'The 3ds. [i.e., third words in each line] are—I'le never give it'.
MS. *Rawl. poet. 184, fol. 52v (autogr.).

No more Laurenda shall thy charms 201
Since love's of such a mind.
MS. Rawl. poet. 65, two copies, fols. 23v, 24v; see also N192.

No more let dark December lower 202
Thy youth meet love, thine age respect.
Parsons, William, 'To a Lady on her Birthday. 19 Dec. 1778'.
Pr. *Travelling Recreations*, 1807, i. 11.
MS. *Don. d. 123, p. 40 (autogr.).

No more let impious faction rule the day 203
Dispels our griefs, and scatters all our fears.
On Charles II, 1660.
MS. Add. B. 8, fol. 70v.

No more let Italy, with scornful pride 204
And spread thy lustre o'er thy native land.
Hawkins, Sir John, 'Daily Advr . . . Feb: 21: 1741: To Mr. John Stanley'.
MS. Eng. poet. c. 9, p. 69.

No more loved partner of my soul 205
With never fading joy.
'The Wifes Consolation to her Husband under Affliction'.
MS. Eng. poet. e. 47, p. 79.

No more marble let him have, 206
To say his tomb were rich, not he.
Shirley, James, 'Epitaph' [On a Parson] inscribed in a small piece of Marble'.
Pr. *Works*, ed. A. Dyce, 1833, vi. 502, from this MS.
MS. *Rawl. poet. 88, p. 36.

207 No more my muse! of aweless fop or fool
Close up the text, or we shall ne'er ha' done.
'The Heroe'. William III's expedition to Landen, etc., 1693.
MS. Rawl. D. 361, fol. 44.

208 No more, no more
And let our pains be less our power more.
[Brome, Alexander], 'The Riddle'.
Pr. *Poems*, 1661, p. 110, 'Written in 1644'.
MS. Ashmole 47, fol. 141$^{v}$.

209 [No more of courts, of triumphs, or of arms]
And sing His praise, who gave me power to sing.
Blackmore, Sir Richard, 'Hymn to the Creator of the World'.
Extract from *The Creation*, vii. 687.
MS. Eng. poet. e. 39, p. 15.

210 No more of Jack for reasons (not of state)
Read but that rhyme it speaks the reasons from yours, etc.
'To Mr. J[ohn] B[ulteel] with' T1899.
MS. Rawl. poet. 159, fol. 206.

211 No more of tears I have not left in store
Melt thy white snow, and turn to fire like me.
Pr. with music by H. Lawes in *Select Ayres and Dialogues*, ii, 1669, p. 37.
MS. Mus. b. 1, fol. 127$^{v}$, music by John Wilson.

212 No more of this ear-lechery! lay by
There is no music like consort in love.
Polwhele, John, 'To Mrs. M. E. who sange to her Lute'.
MS. *Eng. poet. f. 16, fol. 1$^{v}$ (autogr.).

213 No more of your admired year
And Lewis lead you by the nose.
'The Pacquet returned', on the situation between England, France and Holland, Spring 1688.
MS. Douce 357, fol. 154.

214 No more presumptuous man thy God abuse
And prove too weak their mischiefs to avoid.
Williams, John, 'Against Common Swearing and Cursing'.
MS. *Rawl. poet. 193, fol. 65 (autogr.).

215 No more shall mirth my bosom swell
When I am in the tomb!
Ireland, William Henry, 'Lines from Rinaldo'.
MS. Percy d. 9, fol. 23$^{v}$.

216 No more the gratulating strain
Her life enfeebled spare.
R. L., 'Ode—occasioned by the confinement of the Lady . . . 1780'.
MS. *Eng. poet. e. 16, fol. 20.

No more, thou little winged archer, now no more 217
It once again.
'A Songe'.
MSS. Rawl. poet. 153, fol. 24$^{v}$; 199, p. 62.

No more unto my thoughts appear 218
Too weak to be your shrine.
Godolphin, S[idney].
MS. Malone 13, p. 65.

No more, ye tools of Pit, resound 219
The Jews are in despair.
Jessop, William, epigram, 1789.
MS. Percy b. 1, fol. 63 (autogr.).

No more, you sages, cry 'tis long ago 220
For 'twas but t'other day the great Hough died.
'On the Death of Dr. Jon. Hough late Bp. of Worcester. Magdalen College Oxon. May 9th 1743'.
MS. Ballard 50, fol. 191$^{v}$.

No mother like the hen preserves her young 221
Then to me sinner show thyself a mother.
Pr. *Parthenia Sacra*, ed. I. Fletcher, 1633, p. 183.
MS. Eng. poet. b. 5, p. 108.

No motto, virtues, arts or complete arms 222
When angels shrillest trumps sound last alarms.
Cheyney, William, 'An Epitaph'.
MS. *Rawl. poet. 86, fol. 35$^{v}$.

No muse but one true Sir? No poet but you sir? 223
Oh Papa, oh paw, paw, oh Po-pe, oh puppy.
[Roach, Richard], 'Odoenus Redivivus. To Mr. Pope on his Dunciad'.
MS. Rawl. D. 833, fol. 138 (autogr.).

No music ever was 224
Should hold a full bottle.
'A Catch'.
MS. Rawl. poet. 214, fol. 77$^{v}$.

No, my old friend, your scorn has quenched 225
Kill it or in exchange your own impart.
Creswell, Robert, 'Love Revolted'.
MS. *Eng. poet. f. 24, fols. 12, 11$^{v}$ (autogr.).

No, never I swear, in the course of my life! 226
A walking excuse for the bill of a snipe!
Maitland, Miss, 'Extempore'.
MS. Eng. poet. c. 51, p. 288.

No news? not yet? How lingering are the feet 227
To meet thee in Elizium. Thus it follows.
Ashmole, Elias, 'Wanting an account of [undeciphered ideograph] journey by water, 18th June, 1646'. Probably addressed to Helen Thornborough (Lady Thornborough).
MSS. Ashmole 36, 37, fol. 249 (autogr.).

228 No night did ever me such pleasure bring.
I'll wish that it like this may have no end.
Beaumont, Thomas, 'Of A ring he tooke from hir'.
MS. *Malone 18, p. 62 (autogr.).

229 No, no, he's gone, I hear'd the angels sing
And's death baptize the waters with his name.
P[aman], Cl[ement], 'On his Death', i.e. Edward King's.
MS. Rawl. poet. 147, p. 147.

230 No no I tell thee no
Ne'er to part from my dear dear delight.
Pr. John Wilson's *Cheerfull Ayres or Ballads*, 1660, p. 84.
MS. Don. c. 57, fol. 78, music by Nic. Lanier.

231 No no I will sooner trust the wind
Dies his own martyr and not thine.
[Stanley, Thomas].
Pr. J. Gamble's *Ayres and Dialogues*, 1656, p. 32, and in Stanley's *Poems*, 1647, p. 46.
MS. Mus. b. 1, fol. 142$^{v}$, music by John Wilson.

232 No, no; I'll ne'er believe the soul's confined
And triumph in our loss.
Baynes, John, [of Balliol Coll., Oxford (matric. 1717) (?)], 'Upon the Death of the Reverend Mr. Fletcher', i.e. Richard, son of William F. of Aston, Yorks. [*c.* 1718 (?)].
MS. Lister 10, fol. 1$^{v}$, in John Baynes' hand.

233 No no! it cannot be for whoe'er set
As wrestlers, thus you must be naked too.
C[artwright], W[illiam], 'Beauty and deniall'.
Pr. *Poems*, 1651, p. 217.
MS. Rawl. poet. 199, p. 8, attr. to W. C.

234*a* No no, my dear I never thought
At a most dev'lish price they're sold.
Boswell, James, 'Epigram'.
MS. *Douce 193, fol. 27$^{v}$ (autogr.).

234*b* [No no no no I cannot hate my foe]
Can not complain, No no etc.
Sidney, Sir Philip, 'To the tune of a Neapolitan song'.
Pr. *Arcadia*, 1598, p. 485.
MS. *e Mus. 37, fol. 242.

235 No, no unfaithful world thou hast
Than either Greek or Roman ever could before.
P[hilips], K[atherine], O[rinda], 'Upon Mr. Abraham Cowleys Retirement. Ode 1'.
Pr. *Poems*, 1667, p. 122.
MSS. Rawl. poet. 65, fol. 16$^{v}$, attr. to K. P. O.; Rawl. poet. 90, fol. 5$^{v}$.

No noble acts of Hector I 236
Good Lord deliver me.
'A Relation of this Combate: Composed . . . before Trypoly, Aug. 31, 1675'.
See the *Diary of Henry Teonge*, 1675–9, ed. 1825, p. 65.
MS. Firth c. 18, fol. 24.

No not a quack sad poets doubt you 237*a*
Punish your fingers for your brains.
Corbett, [Richard], 'in exhortacion to the universitie concerning their printed poetry more especiallie at the queens death', Queen Anne, 1618.
Pr. *Poetica Stromata*, 1648.
MSS. Douce f. 5, fol. 12$^{v}$; Eng. poet. e. 97, p. 77, attr. to Dr. Corbett.

No organist nor fiddler nor yet fool 237*b*
They'll scarce be known from *ignes fatui*.
On 'The Marriage of the Arts', 1621.
MS. Malone 21, fol. 73.

No other gift can we bestow 238
Together mixed in one heroic lyre.
May, Thomas, 'A new yeares gift to her Maiestye'.
MS. Rawl. poet. 116, fol. 48$^{v}$.

No other Gods create but me 239
Covet not what's thy neighbour's due.
'The Decalogue English'd'.
MS. Rawl. poet. 153, fol. 40.

No passion's rooted deeper or extends 240
So ugly outward, but a sink of sin.
Fairfax, Thomas, Lord, 'Of Anger'.
MS. *Fairfax 40, p. 574 (autogr.).
MS. *Fairfax 38, p. 262.

No peace is had, where parties stand 241
There nothing is amiss.
Robinson, Robert.
MS. *Rawl. poet. 218, p. 112 (autogr.).

No peace is had, where priests do strive 242
Mad palfreys kick and wince.
Robinson, Robert.
MS. *Rawl. poet. 218, p. 130 (autogr.).

No pedigrees nor [or] progenies [prodigies, projects] 243
And new coin the commonwealth.
'The Generation of vipers', *c.* 1642.
MSS. Ashmole 36, 37, fol. 159; 38, fol. 228; Douce 357, fol. 31; Rawl. poet. 26, fol. 143$^{v}$; 61, fol. 48; 71, p. 154.

244–5 **No pimping here, nor fornication**
**The old proverb's true that God's in Glo'ster.**
'From Gloucestershire'. [Dec. 1733–Jan. 1735 (?)].
MS. Ballard 47, fol. 69v.

246 **No pompous show, no vain parade**
**That God whom highest heavens adore.**
Kenton, James.
MS. *Eng. poet. e. 20, p. 25 (autogr.).

247*a* **No poor Dutch peasant winged with all his fear**
**We'll boldly back and say the price is raised.**
[Dryden, John], 'Epilogue', for Jonson's *Silent Woman* at Oxford 1673.
Pr. *Miscellany Poems,* 1684.
MS. Rawl. poet. 19, fol. 152.

247*b* **No power lends immortality to men**
**When sublime piles and monuments do fail.**
MS. Rawl. poet. 117, fol. 165v rev.

248 **No praise it is that he whom Python slew**
**Let us to reason fellow-servants be.**
R[udyerd, Sir Benjamin].
Pr. *Poems of Pembroke and Ruddier,* 1660, p. 7.
MS. Rawl. poet. 31, fol. 31v.

249 **No pyramis, nor carved tomb compliment**
**Is to himself a long lived marble shrine.**
King, John, 'Epitaph: Non hic Pyramides etc.', translation of Latin, MS. Rawl. D. 398, fol. 195, on Bishop John King, d. 1621.
See *B.Q.R.*, v, 1929, p. 329, and *B.L.R.* iv, 1953, p. 208.
MS. Rawl. D. 317, fol. 171 (autogr.).

250 **No rarer thing that you can find**
**If you have content you need no more.**
'An Antidote of Rare Physick, 6 June 1685'.
Pr. *Roxburghe Ballads*, vi, ed. J. Woodfall Ebsworth, 1889, p. 354.
MS. Firth c. 20, fol. 65.

251 **No respite from my tortures can I have**
**And the same music ev'ry hour renew.**
[Beckingham, Charles], 'Sarah the Quaker to Lothario', [Spencer Cowper].
Answered by A1289. See T. Whincop, 'List of . . . Dramatic Authors', pr. in his *Scanderbeg*, 1747.
MS. Eng. poet. e. 40, fol. 77.

252 **No right or power on earth thou sayest is given**
**And spare the rogue, because we scorn the fool.**
'Verses made upon Mr. Batty's sermon preach'd at Oxon.' *Gentleman's Magazine*, i, 1731, p. 367.
MS. Ballard 50, fol. 110.

**No rout we save poor western knave!** 253
**Oh hone! oh hone!**
'Mr. P's Lamentation 1642'.
MS. Rawl. poet. 26, fol. 145v.

**No, sacred pages, never more repine** 254
**But, like the furnace, flash upon thy foes.**
'An Elegy on the burning of the *Memorial* [*of the Church of England*, by James Drake] by order of the Court at the Old Bailey upon the presentation of a very Whiggish Grand Jury. Sep. 4. 1705'.
Pr. *Poems on Affairs of State*, iv, 1707, p. 34. Reprinted as on 'Dr. Sac[hevere]ll's Sermon', *Tory Pills* . . . 1715, ii. 21.
MSS. Eng. poet. e. 87, p. 48; Rawl. poet. 173, fol. 1; Tanner 306, fol. 470.

**No sad thought his soul affright** 255
**In this world befall a man.**
MS. Don. c. 57, two copies, fol. 18 with music, fol. 28.

**No shame, my friend, that Jenny's charms** 256
**One who has past his fortieth year.**
'To Mr. L-ngf-rd on his marrying his Bedmaker, in imitation of Horace' *Odes* II. iv. 1735.
MS. Eng. misc. e. 240, pp. 281–2 and 290.

**No, she shall ne'er escape, if gods there be,** 257
**But so be damn'd of mere necessity.**
Oldham, John, 'On a Woman, who by her Falshood and Scorn was the Death of my Friend . . . 1678'.
MS. *Rawl. poet. 123, p. 54 (autogr.).

**No sin's too great for mercy; nor no faith so small** 258
**But may lay hold on Christ. That's all in all.**
Couplet.
MS. Rawl. poet. 66, fol. 63.

**No songs of joy but sighs and sad complaints** 259
**I wish this wretch to speed if he scape the halter.**
H. S.
MS. *Rawl. poet. 120, fol. 14 (autogr.).

**No sooner comes a country clown** 260
**And proves a downright modish prig.**
'The Black Joak', song with tune.
MS. Mus. Sch. G. 636, fol. 12v.

**No sooner had the royal senate met,** 261
**The crown the bridegroom and the church the bride.**
Blount, Charles, 'A Supplement to the Opening of the Sessions', 1691.
MSS. Eng. poet. c. 18, fol. 117v, attr. to Cha: Blount; e. 49, p. 120, attr. to Cha: Blount.

262 No sooner old Bell
And his mace again got.
Ballad on the Bedell of Oxford University, John Bell, superior Bedell of Arts 1605–36; see MS. Wood E. 5, fols. 127v and 128v.
MSS. Jones 27*, fol. 18v; Tanner 306, fol. 302.

263 No sooner old Dennis
That so he may scape the gallows.
'On those that canvassed for [Dennis] Edward's place the Vergerer', Oxford University, 1642–3; see Wood, *Life and Times*, ed. A. Clark, ii, O.H.S. xxi, 1892, pp. 75 and 86.
MSS. Eng. poet. e. 97, p. 175; Tanner 306, fol. 302v, attr. to J. E.; 466, fol. 65v.

264 No sooner out, but grumble: is the brick
Bow to strange Gods, till Israel was forbid.
[Quarles, Francis], 'On the grumbling Israelites'.
Pr. *Divine Fancies*, 1632, i. 87.
MS. Rawl. poet. 90, fol. 65.

265 No sooner peeped in the world came out the womb
Your joys to mine are a parenthesis.
Sepulchral inscription on Miles Clent, d. 7th June 1658, Gloucester Cathedral.
Pr. Browne Willis, *Cathedrals*, 1742, ii. 713.
MSS. Rawl. D. 1090, fol. 132v; Willis 71, p. 276.

266 No sooner see the world but hence he must;
I shall make haste to come and dwell with thee.
Corbet, W., 'on the Death of My deare Grandchild Barnard Corbet, 3 years and 2 [months] old'.
MS. *Rawl. poet. 210, fol. 43.

267 No spring nor summer beauty hath such grace
I shall ebb on with them that homeward go?
Donne, John, 'Elegye Autumnall'.
Pr. *Poems*, 1633.
MSS. Eng. poet. e. 14, fol. 38, attr. to Dr. Dun; *e. 99, fol. 114v; *f. 9, p. 38; Rawl. poet. 117, fol. 220 rev., attr. to Mr. Dunne; 160, fol. 103v, attr. to J. D.

268 No state so sure, no seat within this life
And Nero oft, in Numa's clothing goes.
Whitney, Geoffrey, 'Nusquam tuta fides'.
MS. *Rawl. poet. 56, fol. 98v.

No strength of flesh is able to withstand 269
But to his faithful soul, the spoils must yield.
Rid[eout (?)], W[illiam (?)] of King's School Sherborne, on the death of Robert Whetcombe, 'Antientest Governour of the King's Schoole of Sherebourne', 24 Oct. 1656. For attribution cf. fol. 39.
MS. Gough Dorset 35(1), fol. 20*d*.

No strong entangling chains, can blessed Peter hold 270
[Through ages infinite, beyond the count of days].
'Engl. Primer of our Lady. 1631. p. 25'.
MS. Eng. poet. e. 56, p. 49.

No sullen cloud with frowning seek 271
[The year is all spring when she is in prime].
Strode, William.
A fragment on fol. 130, beg. Her breath is Incense, is apparently connected with this poem.
MS. *CCC. 325, fol. 122v (autogr.).

No Sylvia 'tis not your disdain 272
Either begin my bliss, or end my pain.
Weaver, Thomas, 'To Sylvia frowning'.
Pr. *Songs and Poems*, 1654.
MS. *Rawl. poet. 211, fol. 3v (autogr.).

No, th'art a fool, I'll swear, if e'en thou grant: 273
If once he loose the sting he grows a drone.
Mr. [Abraham] Cowley, 'Against enjoyment'.
Pr. *Works*, 1668, 'The Mistress', p. 32.
MS. Rawl. poet. 173, fol. 98.

No, thou shalt ne'er escape from vengeance free 274
Would make through all their night new blushes dawn.
Oldham, John, draft for 'A Satyr upon a Woman'.
MS. *Rawl. poet. 123, p. 99 (autogr.).

No time is mine, but that, that's now at hand 275
Do't now, anon perhaps will be too late.
Robinson, Robert, 'Quod facis, fac cito'.
MS. *Rawl. poet. 218, p. 15 (autogr.).

No tongue can his perfections tell 276
Raised by him, that immortal is.
Reynoldes, Lance., acrostic on Nicholas Culpeper.
MS. Ashmole 423, fol. 204v.

No two men ever shalt thou meet or find 277
So several spirits have their diff'rent graces.
Robinson, Robert.
MS. *Rawl. poet. 218, p. 135 (autogr.).

278 No Venus, no your force will not prevail
And what you cannot separate, approve.
I[reland, George of Exeter Coll. Oxf.], 'Sept. 2 1734'.
MS. Eng. misc. e. 240, p. 19.

279 No wanton muse does dictate this in spite
My ears I hazard to secure your head.
At end, 'Scripsit solus'; addressed to Queen Anne (?).
MS. Rawl. D. 383, fol. 89.

280 No way unworthy of his fair descent
Not move thy tears, but warm thee with like flame.
Godolphin, S[idney], 'On Sr. F. Carew', i.e. Sir Ferdinando Carey (d. 1638).
MS. Malone 13, p. 102.

281 No weak partiality
Thus the promis'd crown obtain.
Kenton, James.
MS. *Eng. poet. e. 20, p. 60 (autogr.).

282 No woman born, as Stanhope dares to hint
Her eyes to God to prove their fire on man.
M. M.
MS. Eng. misc. e. 241, fol. 3$^v$.

283 No wonder, death so soon, as with one dart
Whom love so join'd, death could no longer part.
Lines on the deaths of three daughters of Sir Charles Scarburgh, 1706–7, in Acton church.
MS. Rawl. D. 896, fol. 16.

284 No wonder I am never free from fear
Since thee to please, henceforth I'll make my care.
Tipping, William, 'Friday morn: June 8. Contempl.'
MS. *Rawl. poet. 101, fol. 106 (autogr.).

285 No wonder Powis, Finch and Shoar
Or else that thou art mad.
'A Lampoon 1701'.
MS. Rawl. D. 361, fol. 54.

286 No wonder sleep from careful lovers flies
And for another joy, suspend her sleep.
[Waller, Edmund], 'Of the Ladie whoe cann Sleepe when shee Pleaseth'.
Pr. *Poems*, 1645, p. 45.
MSS. *Don. d. 55, fol. 6$^v$; Eng. poet. c. 50, fol. 125; *Rawl. poet. 174, p. 25.

287 No wonder storms more dreadful are by far
Burn but the witch and all things will do well.
'From Lansborough's MS. A Satyr', against the Duchess of Marlborough.
In B.M. MS. Harl. 6914, dated 1703.
MS. Malone 30, fol. 102$^v$; see also N291.

No wonder that I make so little show 288
See him! and live! and stand on holy ground!
Bromley, Henry, 'Psalm 119. 32'.
MS. *Don. e. 19, fol. 17 (autogr.).

No wonder that such swarms of beggars lurk 289
If at my death, thou'lt give me but a crown.
[Quarles, Francis], 'On Beggars'.
Pr. *Divine Fancies*, 1632, ii. 29.
MS. Rawl. poet. 90, fol. 66$^v$.

No wonder, that your dog turds oft doth eat 290
To a tongue that licks your lips a turd's sweet meat.
'Martiall the Roman Satyrist on a whore'. [*Epigrams* I. lxxxiii]. Couplet.
MS. Ashmole 38, p. 33.

No wonder winds [and storms] more dreadful [terrible] are by far 291
And we no more should murmur at the vine.
'On the great storm, 26 Nov. 1703', on the Duchess of Marlborough.
MSS. Eng. poet. e. 50, p. 11; Rawl. C. 986, fol. 15$^v$; Rawl. D. 383, fol. 89; Rawl. poet. 173, fol. 129$^v$; Smith 23, p. 132; pr. bk. Firth b. 21, fol. 57$^v$; see also N287.

No words can impart 292
Since we're made of the nobler ingredients.
Homer, Philip Bracebridge, 'To Stella in answer'.
MS. *Add. C. 282, p. 64.

No worldly science can so much advance 293
Their fame, long since with them had perished.
MS. *Rawl. poet. 97, fol. 27$^v$ (autogr.).

[N]o worldly wight can her attain 294
Be honour laud and praise.
'The death of Sir John Eland of Eland in old Rithm'.
See *Historical Manuscripts Commission*, 3rd Report, Appendix p. 293, item xii, for description of another copy.
MS. Top. Yorks. c. 25, fol. 184.

No youthful blood, nor blushing vein 295
His epithalme; and epitaph; So old etc. (incomplete (?)).
'A Nubtiall-Funerall, upon old Flemminge, of Stanmore who aged 82, was marryed There. Octob. 12 1635'.
MS. Rawl. poet. 117, fol. 181$^v$ rev.

Nobility's too great to be 296
But know, thy baseness saves thy hide.
'The Ass and the Lion'.
MS. *Eng. poet. d. 47, fol. 140.

297 Noble, generous, great and good
And who e'er takes it, takes a tartar.
'Hue and Cry after a Stray Heart'.
MS. Eng. poet. e. 40, fol. 27.

298 Noble I am, and chief of all my kind
Many quaint devices by me thou mayst out find.
'Riddle'.
MS. Rawl. poet. 217, fol. 76.

299 Noble king Lud
His ending although his beginning.
Pr. *Description of Love*, 2nd ed., 1620, Sig. E2; *Windsor Drollery*, 1672; and *Pills to Purge Melancholy*, 1714.
MS. Eng. poet. c. 50, fol. 43ᵛ.

300 Nobles all come mourn with me
For which the spaniards chafe in thought oh hone . . . (incomplete).
Lament for the Earl of Essex after his execution 25 Feb. 1600/1.
MS. Rawl. A. 122, fol. 13ᵛ.

301*a* Nobles and poets by your leave
Let Bourbon and Nassaw go higher.
Epitaph for Prior's tomb in Westminster Abbey, 'said to be done by himself', from Mist's Journal, 4 July 1724.
MS. Hearne's diaries 104, p. 28.

301*b* Noctivagus walking in the evening sad
That I am sure I married with the devil.
Pr. *The Description of Love*, 2nd ed., 1620, Sig. B8ᵛ.
MS. Eng. poet. c. 50, fol. 34.

302 Noisy nothing! stalking shade!
From the circle here of love.
'On honour'.
MS. Rawl. poet. 213, fol. 3.

303 None but a vicious rich man will defy
The low estate of pious poverty.
[Jordan, Thomas], 'On Pious Poverty', couplet.
Pr. *Divinity and Morality*, Sig. §§§6.
MS. Rawl. poet. 90, fol. 84ᵛ.

304 None but my self knows where my strait shoe wrings me,
Nor can you know when, where or how love stings me.
Ashmole, Elias, '30 July 1748. 45 minutes after noon', couplet.
MSS. Ashmole 36, 37, fol. 231 (autogr.).

305 None could unless first sworn plead public cause
Fallax would do it rather then his gown lose.
Translation of Latin verses: 'In Fallacem Leguleium'.
MS. Rawl. poet. 152, fol. 35.

None hates learning but these harmers 306
Catchpoles, userers, fools and farmers.
Couplet.
MS. Rawl. poet. 117, fol. 272 rev.

None in the species are more void of sense 307
Refusing labour, but to die, or starve.
'To an Indolent fellow who relied on Miracles'.
MS. Percy c. 8, fol. 126ᵛ, 126ʳ.

None like peevish Edentula is to be found 308
Or lament much the loss of a troublesome life.
Williams, John, 'The Picture of an old favourite'.
MS. *Rawl. poet. 191, fol. 119 (autogr.).

None loathes the world ye [*sic*] much, and loves to scoff it 309
But gold and grace will make him surfeit of it.
Couplet.
MS. Rawl. poet. 206, p. 28.

None look as I, and can conceal their flame, 310
To sign my pardon if I say amiss.
D[arell], Sir S[amson], 'To the Lady Coke'.
MS. Rawl. poet. 210, fol. 55ᵛ.

None to another friend can be 311
These are a poor company.
Fairfax, Thomas, Lord, 'Vulgar Proverbs'.
MS. *Fairfax 40, p. 613 (autogr.).
MS. *Fairfax 38, p. 291.

None will rejoice on this unhappy day 312
They in their guiltiness may read their doom.
On the death of Queen Anne, 1 Aug. 1714.
MS. Rawl. poet. 155, p. 134.

None without hope, e'er loved the brightest fair 313
He is half cured who wishes for a cure.
Lyttelton, [George, 1st Baron], 'Maxims in Love'.
Pr. Dodsley's *Collection of Poems*, ii, 1748, p. 61.
MS. Percy d. 9, fol. 13ᵛ.

Nor Adam's sin, nor all that Sathan can 314
Turns to the author's own confusion.
MS. *Rawl. poet. 97, fol. 15ᵛ (autogr.).

Nor can religion be a garment fit to cover it, 315
Your beams they'll scatter at such a royal heat.
Saltmarsh, James, 'To the Kinge', fragment; on the Scotch risings, 1639–40 (?).
MS. Ashmole 47, fol. 103.

316 Nor court, nor shop-crafts were thine arts but those
The body may, and must: arts cannot die.
Stonehouse, Walter, 'On John Tradescante the elder, deceased', copy for printer of *Museum Tradescantianum*, 1656.
MS. Ashmole 826, fol. 34.

317 Nor dead, nor living, sleeping nor awake
Ne monarch I, above the monarchs sit.
G. B., 'Epitaph. 30', on Prince Henry, in 'Cestria Lugens', 1612.
MS. *Rawl. poet. 116, fol. 13$^{v}$.

318 Nor did I well nor thought I did amiss
Such was the heedless heat of youthful pleasure.
C[otton], A[ndrew], 'Versa pagina Eiusdem Domini A: C:' 2 lines copied by Ashmole from the back of the leaf on which he found I557.
MSS. Ashmole 36, 37, fol. 35$^{v}$.

319 Nor faith, nor hope whate'er their source,
The knowledge of her God.
Hayl[e]y, [William], 'A Hymn written for Sunday Schools'.
MS. Montagu e. 14, fol. 41$^{v}$.

320 Nor go not sit, nor stand the cripple cries
What says he then if he says true, he lies.
'On a beggar and cripple'.
MS. Douce f. 5, fol. 5; see also I51, I85, I92, T444.

321 Nor hardest rock, deep den, nor hollow cave
Man must come forth, and take his doom for all.
MS. *Rawl. poet. 97, fol. 14 (autogr.).

322 Nor horse nor man e'er turned home
Aught bettered by the sight of Rome.
Couplet.
MS. Ashmole 48, fol. 136.

323 Nor is it grieved (grave youth) the memory
Bring better notes or choose a meaner text.
[Corbett, Richard], on Dr. Daniel Price.
Pr. *Poetica Stromata*, 1648; *Parmassus Biceps*, 1656.
MS. Malone 19, p. 101.

324 Nor let soft slumbers close your eye
To lead to virtue and to God.
'Lines of advice given by Pythagoras'.
MS. Percy d. 9, fol. 24$^{v}$.

325 Nor love nor fate [can me, dare I] do I accuse
But only that I lived and died.
'A song' in Richard Brome's *Northerne Lasse*, 1632, II. vi.
MSS. Ashmole 47, fol. 71; Don. d. 58, fol. 27$^{v}$; Eng. poet. e. 97, p. 144; f. 16, fol. 3, with reference to 'Mr. Brooms playe'; Rawl. poet. 153, fol. 19; see also N377.

Nor love thy life, nor hate; but what thou liv'st 326
And patiently attend thy dissolution.
Motto adapted from Milton, *Paradise Lost*, xi. 551, for collection of epitaphs, late 18th cent.
MS. Top. gen. e. 32, inside front cover.

Nor morning red nor blushing fair 327
Ere Adam wore a beard she was in her prime.
[Davenant, Sir William], song in *Love and Honour*, IV. i.
MS. Rawl. poet. 62, fol. 33.

Nor must he fall, nor shall his merits lie 328
Let me be hanged for so fell stout Montrosse.
'On the death of The Marquesse of montrose, executed at Edinburgh', 21 May, 1650.
MS. Rawl. poet. 84, fol. 109.

Nor rich nor poor, but in proportion 329
Means to his mind give Richard Egerton.
Couplet, 'Richarde Egertons. Anagram. Regarde not riches. Lorde'.
MS. Malone 16, p. 45.

Nor riches I covet, nor glory I want; 330
Contribute to gladden my heart.
'Song'.
MS. Eng. misc. f. 79, p. 62.

[Nor 'scapes he so: our dinner was so good] 331
He would have liv'd only to save his meat.
Cleveland, [John, 'Upon a Miser that made a feast, and the next day dyed for griefe'.]
Pr. *Poems, by J. C.*, 1651, Sig. A5$^{v}$.
MS. Eng. poet. f. 24, fol. 31.

Nor sordid wealth I ask, nor wide domain 332
And live to all but happiness alone!
Holloway, William, 'A Fragment . . . E. India House, May 4 1799'.
MS. Montagu c. 5, fol. 41.

Nor this contented thee—thou, bent to save 333
For each, his lot, his talents, manners, race.
Cowper, William.
Pr. from this MS., *Poetical works*, ed. H. S. Milford, 4th ed., 1934, p. 667.
MS. Autogr. d. 21, fol. 191 (autogr.).

Nor time, nor tide, for any person stays 334
'Mongst angels praising God eternally.
Spoure, Edmund, 'A Motto for a Clock. Ut hora, sic fugit vita'.
MS. *Eng. poet. c. 52, fol. 62 (autogr.).

Nor yet the crude materials of the earth 335
Shall be the lofty theme of my aspiring muse.
'On the Creation: Collectn. Poems'.
MS. Eng. poet. e. 39, p. 78.

336 Norfolk's proud villas now were left
But Morden was on earth her name.
'The Norwich Assembly, or The Decent of Venus'.
MS. Rawl. poet. 222, fol. 11$^{v}$.

337 Northampton happier in his choice
Worn out of date have chill'd my wearied muse.
MS. Douce 357, fol. 146$^{v}$.

338 Nose, nose, jolly red nose,
And they gave me that jolly red nose.
MS. Douce d. 59, fol. 52.

339 Not a few men (I have been told)
To talk and prate they are so bold.
Robinson, Robert.
MS. *Rawl. poet. 218, p. 143 (autogr.).

340 Not a hard bed i'th' country to procure?
And so I bid thee farewell, hait-gee-ho.
'Iter Boreale [Robert Wild] his Countrey Clowne, 1665'.
MS. Don. b. 8, p. 430.

341 Not aged only subject are to death,
Not wealth, not greatness can keep in the breath.
Robinson, Robert.
MS. *Rawl. poet. 218, p. 23 (autogr.).

342 Not all men wise or honest be,
So long as death the world endure.
Robinson, Robert.
MS. *Rawl. poet. 218, p. 60 (autogr.).

343 Not all that parent earth can give,
Give me! Oh give me happiness.
'Seeking for Happiness'.
MS. Eng. poet. e. 40, fol. 143.

344 Not all the popular rage, and rude
Whilst you the secrets of the Gods relate.
'A Paraphrase on Horace', *Odes* III. iii.
MS. Malone 15, p. 56.

345 Not all the threats or favours of a crown
Who love fierce drivers and a looser rein.
[Montagu, Charles, Earl of Halifax], 'The Man of Honour occasioned by the postscript of Penn's letter', 1687.
Pr. *A Collection of the Newest . . . Poems . . . against Popery*, 1689, i. 1; *The Muses Farewel to Popery and Slavery*, 1689, p. 1; and *Works and Life of . . . Halifax*, 1715, p. 10.
MSS. Firth c. 16, p. 147; Don. e. 23, fol. 49; e. 24, p. 41; Douce 357, fol. 148$^{v}$.

Not as one flesh, my dear I love 346
Yet must not with her die.
Tipping, William, 'Of my deare Hess'.
MS. *Rawl. poet. 101, fol. 19 (autogr.).

Not as the godly faithful race 347
They flee before the God of Heaven.
Kenton, James.
MS. *Eng. poet. e. 20, p. 273 (autogr.).

Not as to one that's proud have I this sent 348
That thou art both beloved of Gods and men.
Burton, Francis, 'An Anagram. Dorothie Stapleforde. The Lords a foe to pride'.
MS. *Add. A. 267, fol. 107$^{v}$ (autogr.).

Not asking or expecting aught 349
And truly sets the world on fire.
'Imitations of Ovid: I. A Poem, occasioned by the Hangings in the Castle of Dublin, in which the Story of Phaeton is expressed'.
Ascribed by Malone to Swift.
MS. Malone 30, fol. 95.

Not beauty could have had more lasting charms 350
True as my grief and flowing as my eyes.
MS. Malone 9, fol. 58.

Not because thy face is fair 351
Troth I love you cause I do.
Tatham, John, 'Ostella asking, why I loved her '
Pr. *Ostella*, 1650, p. 23.
Pr. bk. 27980 e. 86, before p. 57.

Not born, not dead, not christened, not begot, 352
Which while thou seemest to read, thou readest Nott.
'Uppon Pegg Nott a whore'.
MSS. Ashmole 38, p. 173; CCC. 328, fol. 43$^{v}$; Rawl. poet. 206, p. 61; see also N356.

Not caring to observe the wind 353
The coldest breast, the rudest tame.
Waller, Edmund, 'Of lovinge att the first sight'.
Pr. *Poems*, 1645, p. 81.
MSS. *Don. d. 55, fol. 25; *Rawl. poet. 174, p. 66.

Not, Chloe, that I better am, 354
'Tis easy to be true.
MS. Eng. misc. b. 48, fol. 79.

Not crowns nor kingdoms I desire, 355
God is my only happiness.
Beddome, Benjamin.
MS. *Eng. misc. e. 227, fol. 6$^{v}$.

356 Not dead; not born, not christened, not begot
Which whilst thou readest, yet thou readest not.
Epitaph on a woman named 'Not'.
MSS. Ashmole 36, 37, fol. 218; Don. c. 55, fol. 2v; Douce f. 5, fol. 34; Eng. poet. e. 14, fol. 87v rev.; Firth e. 4, p. 6; Rawl. poet. 26, fol. 62v; 117, fol. 22v; 160, fol. 27; Smith 17, p. 119*a*; see also N352.

357 Not Elen here alone, but in this grave
Crown of flowers and gems immortal places.
On Elen Thomas of the parish of St. Clement Danes, buried there 16 April 1619.
MS. Ashmole 38, p. 196.

358 Not eyed, not white, nor over old,
That cheese is over good.
'Of Cheese', translation of Latin couplet, 'Non Argus, Gehezi, Mathusalem Magdaleneve, / Non Esau, Lazarus: caseus ille bonus'.
MS. Rawl. poet. 26, fol. 61.

359 Not far from Christ-Church, as you pass the street
I'd choose to walk afoot, or on an Oxford hack.
Holland, Thomas, of Jesus Coll. Oxford, 'The Soldiers Wooden Horse; 1715'.
MS. Ballard 29, fol. 145v.

360 Not for her sake, but for our own we grieve
And undefaced an endless date maintain.
'On Mrs. Martha Fitz-Herbert'.
MS. Eng. misc. e. 183, fol. 17.

361 Not for in colour, it was like thy hair
Because 'tis cordial would 'twere at thy heart.
Donne, [John], 'To a gentlewoman'.
MS. Rawl. poet. 117, fol. 225v rev., attr. to Dunne; see also N397.

362 Not for our sakes doth God forgive
Till not a spot remain.
Beddome, Benjamin.
MS. *Eng. misc. e. 227, fol. 46.

363 Not for our selves, alone we are create,
Undoeth their heir, and quite decayeth their name.
Whitney, Geoffrey, 'Quae ante pedes'.
MS. *Rawl. poet. 56, fol. 36.

364 Not for their worth, but for thy worthiness,
Thy beauty's record, thine shall be the glory.
North, Dudley, 3rd Baron, Sonnet 2.
Pr. *A Forest of Varieties*, 1645.
MS. *North e. 41, fol. 7v.

Not full asleep nor full awaking 365
With a mantle of everlasting brightness.
'The Visione'.
MS. Rawl. poet. 121, fol. 71.

Not he, who soars to height of power 366
And ever with my Jesus reign.
Kenton, James.
MS. *Eng. poet. e. 20, p. 304 (autogr.).

Not hear my message! but the bearer shun! 367
And I fall downward from this rolling sky.
Sedley, Sir Charles [?], 'Upon a Gentle-woman's Refusal of a Letter From one she was Engag'd to'.
From Sedley's *Works*, 1722. Pr. *Poetical Recreations*, 1688, attr. to Sir C. S.
MS. Rawl. poet. 222, fol. 30.

Not ill enough to say I'm sick 368
If 'tis not love, say what disease?
'Amare et sapere vix Deo conceditur', 1735.
MS. Eng. misc. e. 240, p. 264.

Not in a bare and empty sound 369
By telling me his name was love.
Kenton, James.
MS. *Eng. poet. e. 20, p. 116 (autogr.).

Not in rich furniture, or fine array 370
And leave th'earth to their food.
Herbert, George, 'The H. Communion'.
Pr. *The Temple*, 1633, p. 43.
MS. *Tanner 307, fol. 33v.

Not in thy wrath against me rise 371
Thy hand upon me lies.
[Sandys, George], Psalm xxxviii, 3-part setting by H. Lawes.
Pr. *Paraphrase upon the Divine Poems*, 1638, and with music by H. Lawes in *Choice Psalmes*, 1648.
MS. Mus. Sch. E. 451, p. 40.

Not kiss? By Jove I must and make impression 372
So it were warm, and soft, and could but move.
'A Paradoxe of a Painted face'.
See Donne's *Poems*, ed. Grierson, 1912, i. 456. Pr. *Poems of Pembroke and Ruddier*, 1660.
MSS. CCC. 327, fol. 15v; 328, fol. 32, attr. to Sherly; Eng. poet. e. 14, fol. 83 rev., attr. to Dr. Dun; Malone 21, fol. 74; 117, fol. 29v, attr. to Mr. Wm. Baker.

Not like the diamond and gold 373
Nor is ev'rything gold, that may glisten.
'A Riddle', with verses headed 'solv'd by a young Lady'.
MS. Eng. poet. e. 40, fol. 146.

374 Not long ago I spied a lad
And afterwards looks back.
Spoure, Edmund, 'A Poem on . . . once being in company with a Clergyman . . . habited in Gay apparrell'.
MS. *Eng. poet. c. 52, fol. 48 (autogr.).

375 Not long time since I saw a cow
As he held up her tail.
'A Representation of the states of the Low Countries under the govermt. of the Prince of Orange'.
MS. Rawl. poet. 160, fol. 163$^{v}$.

376 Not love alas which makes me moil in woe
And hope for hap all though it be in pain.
Swerdna, i.e. Andrews, —.
MS. *Rawl. poet. 92, fol. 16.

377 Not love nor fate do I accuse
For which offence I fall and die.
'A Song'.
MS. Eng. poet. e. 14, fol. 84$^{v}$ rev.; see also N325.

378 Not many moons have from their silver bows
To kill this lion that thus tears Christendom.
'The lamentable cries of at least 1500 Christians: (now Prisoners in Argiers under the Turkes). With a Petition' (incomplete); *temp.* James I.
MS. Rawl. poet. 152, fol. 36.

379 Not monumental stones preserves thy fame
Stanlye for whom this stands shall stand in heaven.
'An epitaph'.
MS. Rawl. poet. 117, fol. 269 rev.

380 Not more inconstant is the wind,
Three thousand that for having none.
'The Curate, Tradesmen and the Bishop'.
MS. *Eng. poet. d. 47, fol. 73.

381 Not more lamented for so hard a fate
As Alexander did the Gordian.
'A distracted Elegie upon that most execrable murther of Thomas Scott Preacher whoe was kild by an English soldier in a Church-Porch at Utrecht', 18 June 1626.
MS. Rawl. poet. 160, fol. 5.

382 Not of th' importance you suppose,
That more important fleas may feed.
'The Reflection which the little Flea makes upon Pride'. cf. Pope's *Essay on Man*, Ep. 1, ll. 131 et seq.
MS. Ballard 50, fol. 108.

Not Paul who first did thither pass 383
And went not downwards to the sky.
Fleming, Robert.
MS. Rawl. poet. 213, fol. 49$^{v}$ (autogr.).

Not Rome in all its splendour could compare 384
And Mrs. Stafford yield to Ballock Hall . . . *cetera desunt.*
'Nobilitas sola, atque unica virtus', Spring 1680.
Pr. *Poems on Affairs of State*, 1, 1703, ii. 33.
MSS. Don. b. 8, p. 657; Firth c. 15, p. 36.

Not roses couch'd within a lily bed 385
And envy's paleness got thy white and red.
Pr. John Wilson's *Cheerfull Ayres or Ballads*, 1660, p. 132, and E. P[hillips], *The Mysteries of Love and Eloquence*, 1658.
MS. Mus. b. 1, fol. 30, music by John Wilson.

Not sick in body, but in mind most free 386
(Of this my will) I make executor.
Colman, Henry, 'My last will, and Testament'.
MS. *Rawl. poet. 204, fol. 22 (autogr.).

Not so the ravish'd grateful bard admires 387
Unless our lost Urania soon return.
'To Urania just leaving the Countrey. Occasion'd by her having committed a Copy of Verses to his perusal'.
MS. *Rawl. poet. 91, fol. 12 (autogr.).

Not that he needed monument of stone 388
When brass and marble monuments shall fall.
On John Heigham, 'Marshall of the Hall of Kinge James and Kinge Charles', d. 20 May 1632. Stanford-in-the-Vale, Berks.
MSS. Rawl. D. 1480, fol. 90; Sancroft 59, p. 286 rev.

Not that I am a king's house, or that I 389
Could you but hence see two things; hell, and air.
Oldisworth, Nicolas, 'Hampton-court here speaketh'.
MS. *Don. c. 24, fol. 29.

Not that I my mistress wish 390
To cry her wit, will sell her ware . . . (incomplete).
'On the Choyce of his Mrs'.
MS. Eng. poet. e. 14, fol. 67$^{v}$; see also N394.

Not that I think fair friend that these my rhymes 391
I shall my being and my birthday curse.
Burton, Francis.
MS. *Add. A. 267, fol. 101$^{v}$ (autogr.).

392 Not that I think my humble verse can frame
The sole relief of an uneasy mind.
'The Presentation' of a translation of Cicero, *De Amicitia*.
MS. Eng. misc. b. 21, fol. 7.

393 Not that I want a faithful post to her
At its last gasp but this, kiss, kiss and die.
MS. Eng. poet. c. 50, fol. 74$^{v}$.

394 Not that I wish my mistress
And pleasant but are nought for food.
'Description of a wisht mistris'.
Pr. *Poems of Pembroke and Ruddier*, 1660, p. 79.
MSS. Rawl. poet. 116, fol. 54$^{v}$; 117, fol. 182 rev.; see also N390.

395 Not that I would be counted coy
His lady's lips with kisses sweet.
Briggs, S[amson], 'A Choice'.
MS. Rawl. poet. 147, p. 245 rev.

396 Not that I would instruct or tutor you
What your self are, what other wives should be.
King, Henry, 'To A. R.' on Overbury's *Wife*.
Pr. *Poems*, 1657, p. 8.
MSS. *Eng. poet. e. 30, fol. 36$^{v}$; *Malone 22, fol. 23$^{v}$.

397 Not that in colour it was like thy hair
Because 'tis cordial I would 'twere at thy heart.
Donne, John, 'The Chayne'.
Pr. *Poems*, 1635, p. 89.
MSS. Ashmole 36, 37, fol. 61$^{v}$, attr. to J. Done; CCC. 327, fol. 5, attr. to Donne; Don. c. 54, fol. 24$^{v}$; Eng. poet. e. 14, fol. 30$^{v}$, attr. to D. Dun; *Eng. poet. e. 99, fol. 13; *f. 9, pp. 209–13, 44; Rawl. poet. 160, fol. 171$^{v}$, attr. to J. Done; 212, fol. 152$^{v}$ rev.; see also N361.

398 Not that my pockets lack what on my head
Like Hopkins psalm for ever and for aye (incomplete).
Bulteel, John, 'To some Fe-malecontents. Apology'.
MS. *Rawl. poet. 159, fol. 207$^{v}$.

399 Not that thy trees of Penshurst groan
Redeem the rest from endless care.
Waller, Edmund, 'To my Lord of Leicester'.
Pr. *Poems*, 1645, p. 42.
MSS. *Don. d. 55, fol. 11; *Rawl. poet. 174, p. 34.

400 Not the fine silver, nor pure gold
It was, it is, it will be so.
Robinson, Robert, 'Mors est inevitabilis'.
MS. *Rawl. poet. 218, p. 9 (autogr.).

Not the high flights romantic poets feign 401
And wish your self a subject for her sake.
J. W., 'On Mrs. Jane Bowdler occasioned by her seeing of King Ja[mes III]'s Picture'.
MS. Rawl. poet. 155, p. 66.

Not the parched Ethiop, nor they 402
And only burn the dross.
'After his Recovery from a Feaver . . . M[artin] Llewellin. poëm. p. 111'. [*Men-Miracles*, etc., 1656].
MS. Tanner 466, fol. 6$^{v}$.

Not thou with greater joy dost meet 403
Good b' wi' t' ye.
Evans, A., 'Mr. P[erci]val's Answer' to B352. Latin on fol. 154.
MS. Lat. misc. e. 19, fol. 175.

Not to acknowledge good received, 404*a*
Oh that's a thing is hateful.
Robinson, Robert.
MS. *Rawl. poet. 218, p. 176 (autogr.).

[Not to be wrought by malice, gain or pride] 404*b*
And the dead conquered, whilst the living slew.
Cartwright, [William], lines used in inscription on a monumental column to Sir Bevil Granvil, d. 5 July, 1643, by his grandson G. Granville, Lord Lansdown.
Pr. 1643, and in *Poems*, 1651, p. 303. See John Collinson's *History of Somerset*, 1791, i. 158.
Gough Maps 44, fol. 149.

Not to commend, or censure thee, or thine 405
May find the bigger, not the better books . . . (incomplete).
J. B., 'On the merry Beggars', commendatory verse prefixed to *A Joviall Crew* by Richard Brome, 1652.
MS. Sancroft 53, p. 48.

[Not to know vice at all, and keep true state] 406
You may securely sin but safely never.
Jonson, Ben, *The Forrest*, xi, last couplet only.
MS. Rawl. poet. 117, fol. 276$^{v}$ rev.

Not to the hills where cedars move 407
On earth! 'tis thither, thither would I go.
Flatman, Thomas, 'A Wish . . . Sept. 10, 1659 . . . Set by Capt. S. Taylor'.
MSS. *Firth d. 7, fol. 20; Rawl. poet. 84, fol. 107$^{v}$ rev.

Not twice two years of age, a weary breath 408
Loseth some days of rest, but more of sorrow.
Sepulchral verses, St. Saviour's, Southwark.
MS. Sancroft 59, p. 293 rev.

409 Not unto us belongs the claim
Who is for ever magnified.
Psalm cxv.
MS. *Rawl. C. 113, fol. 79$^{v}$.

410 Not unto us lord not to us
Praise ye the lord I say.
[Norton, Thomas], Psalm cxv.
MS. Rawl. poet. 112, fol. 37$^{v}$ rev.

411 Not us I say, not us,
Will now, and still oh praise the lord.
Herbert, Mary (*née* Sidney), Countess of Pembroke, Psalm cxv.
MSS. *Rawl. poet. 24, p. 169; *25, fol. 114$^{v}$.

412 Not want of heart, but scant of art
Nor is't nor shall be scant.
'A New-yeares gift'.
MSS. Douce f. 5, fol. 18$^{v}$; Eng. poet. f. 10, fol. 94$^{v}$.

413 Not willing terror does his image move;
Than thorns, and thistles, springing from the curse.
Waller, Edmund, 'The Love of God declar'd in Man's Redemption'.
Pr. *Divine Poems*, 1685, canto iii.
MS. Eng. poet. e. 39, p. 36.

414 Not with the glarish pageantry
Shall king of kings forever reign.
Kenton, James.
MS. *Eng. poet. e. 20, p. 88 (autogr.).

415 Not without cause the olive tree is slow
Messias in her womb's anointed Christ.
Pr. *Parthenia Sacra*, ed. I. Fletcher, 1633, p. 135.
MS. Eng. poet. b. 5, p. 106.

416–17 Not words, but money fills the bag.
But money is the best desert.
Robinson, Robert.
MS. *Rawl. poet. 218, p. 80 (autogr.).

418 Nothing applied to common use
Is pressed with all his might.
Howard, Henry, Earl of Northampton, translator, 'Verses from Ovid', in the dedication to Lady Katharine Barkley of his philosophical treatise.
MSS. Add. B. 83, fol. 6; Bodl. 616, fol. 11.

419 Nothing desire that you can't enjoy,
Disgrace I seek for when I stoop to pride.
Williams, John, 'The 2$^{nds}$ [second words] are, I will do as you desire'.
MS. *Rawl. poet. 191, fol. 13$^{v}$ (autogr.).

420 Nothing doth more infatuate our wit
More eagerly; to bring us to his will.
MS. *Rawl. poet. 97, fol. 9 (autogr.).

Nothing hath a motive been, 421
That something hath some savour.
Verses on 'Something' [*temp.* Charles II].
MS. Rawl. D. 1459, fol. 67.

Nothing is more certain than death 422
Then must we leave this world of earth.
MS. Rawl. D. 1334, fol. 28 rev.

Nothing lasts always, which the earth forth brings 423
Labour and age wear out all earthly things.
Robinson, Robert, couplet.
MS. *Rawl. poet. 218, p. 99 (autogr.).

Nothing lies hid from radiant eyes, 424
The heart she gets returns no more.
Waller, Edmund, 'To Madam Stewart [Duchess of Richmond 1622 (?)–85] upon hir Returning a lost letter to E: W.'
Pr. *Poems*, 1668, p. 230.
MSS. Rawl. poet. 19, fol. 79; 84, fol. 28$^{v}$, on 'Madame Stuart now Duchess of Richmond'.

Nothing like God's most holy will, esteem; 425
Who here God's praise; and all men's good, intend.
Williams, John, 'To Miss Ashe'.
MS. *Rawl. poet. 191, fol. 6 (autogr.).

Nothing more sharper than low things 426
Like those that rise of nought.
MS. Rawl. poet. 148, fol. 1.

Nothing seemed hard to his courage, wit or pride 427
Success still following as he changed his side.
'Alcibiades', couplet.
MS. Rawl. D. 1372, fol. 47 from end.

Nothing that needful is to feed the mind 428
Without a scare-crow and no guts within.
Williams, John, 'Upon a certain dissenting preacher'.
MS. *Rawl. poet. 192, fol. 81 (autogr.).

Nothing that's plain 429
But may be witty if thou hast the vein.
Two lines.
MS. Don. e. 6, fol. 16$^{v}$.

Nothing, thou elder brother even to [of the] shade, 430
Flow swiftly into thee, and in thee ever end.
Wilmot, John, Earl of Rochester, 'Upon Nothing, or Somewhat of Nothing'.
See Vieth, p. 399.
MSS. Add. B. 106, fol. 19$^{v}$, attr. to Rochester; Don. b. 8, p. 654, attr. to Rochester; Locke c. 32, fol. 12; Rawl. poet. 90, fol. 106; 173, fol. 151$^{v}$, attr. to Ld. Roch$^{tr}$; Sancroft 53, p. 68, attr. to E. R.; Tanner 306, fol. 410.

431 Nothing to owe and wish no more
And not be poor.
MS. Rawl. poet. 66, fol. 29.

432 Nothing upon the world's great stage
As living but to die.
'An Imitation of Simonides on human Life'.
MS. *Eng. poet. d. 47, fol. 151.

433 Nothing venture, nothing have:
What he gets he may put in his shoes.
Robinson, Robert.
MS. *Rawl. poet. 218, p. 168 (autogr.).

434 Nothing we fear or hate without a cause
A stranger drake, his little duck shall tread.
'The poore mans meditation upon the Lawyer's problem'.
MS. Rawl. poet. 212, fol. 55v.

435 Nourished with sighs and fright and formed with fears
As when the sun vouchsafes to gild a shower.
'To my Lord Francis Villiers', posthumous son of the murdered Duke of Buckingham.
MS. Rawl. poet. 26, fol. 38.

436 *Noverint universi per praesentes*
*Valedixit Dominus.*
Macaronics.
MS. Malone 19, p. 99.

437 Now
Through whose means thou and I might both be jointly blest?
Oldisworth, Nicolas, 'An Ode, of 12 kindes of Verses'.
MS. *Don. c. 24, fol. 37 (autogr.).

438 Now a botch take thee, Tom: where hast thou been
That you can, when you list, behold the king.
Oldisworth, Nicolas, 'An eglogue betweene a Carter and a sheapard, made on Mr. Mic. Oldisworth's Comming into the country'.
MS. *Don. c. 24, fol. 41v (autogr.).

439 Now Æolus calls his northern winds to rest
A life which all shall wish but few shall find.
Sidney, William, 'To the honourable Philip York . . . on his happy Marriage'.
MS. *Rawl. poet. 70, fol. 10 (autogr.).

440 Now after all this catalogue abroad
And so a long farewell, farewell to thee.
Spoure, Edmund, 'A Regumdare'.
MS. *Eng. poet. c. 52, fol. 136v (autogr.).

Now aid me ye muses in loftiest verse 441
Conducted us safely to West Cowes at last.
Account of an excursion to the Isle of Wight sent by W. Edgcombe to Miss Carter, Goatby, Lincs., 1791. The second page is missing.
MS. Don. e. 11, fol. 83.

Now alas! it must be so; 442
Shout thy all-redeeming love.
Kenton, James, 'On the Death of Miss Deborah Harley (the 2d)', *d.* in her fourth year, 17 Aug. 1761.
MS. *Eng. poet. e. 19, p. 191 (autogr.).

Now all the news upon the Exchange, is of the golden lady 443
If this be so there's many moe, besides us will be merry.
On the return of Prince Charles and the Duke of Buckingham from Spain, October 1623.
MS. Tanner 306, fol. 258.

Now all to Albion see them wafted o'er 444
Conferred by Hamilton of Coventry.
Beginning of 'a long Poem of 119 lines address'd to Lord Harrington'.
MS. Firth b. 4, fol. 52.

Now all you British hearts of gold 445
Who've pulled the French pride down.
'A New Song Made upon the Engagement fought in the West Indies, when the La Blanche . . . commanded by Capt. Faulkner, beat the French ship, La Pare'. 1795.
MS. Firth c. 18, fol. 19.

Now ancient English melody is banished out of doors 446
But we shan't see the like again.
''Twas merry in hall'.
MS. Eng. misc. e. 241, fol. 50v.

Now (as I live) I love thee much 447
It might be more.
[Felltham, Owen], 'A Song'.
Pr. *Resolves*, 1661, 'Lusoria', p. 31.
MS. Rawl. D. 737, fol. 17 rev.

Now at the last the riddle is expounded 448
Or else they threaten, kings shall reign no more.
'A Ballad on the late Addresse', 1680.
MSS. Don. b. 8, p. 681; Douce 357, fol. 84; Rawl. poet. 152, fol. 1.

Now at the supper of the Lamb, 449
And th' holy Ghost, beyond all days.
'Engl. Primer of our Ladie. 1631 . . . p. 14'.
MS. Eng. poet. e. 56, p. 37; extra verses by Alexander Huish (autogr.), p. 40.

450 Now Bess we are married and now let me say
The summer of love shall repose in my heart!
Wolcot, Dr. John, 'Corin's profession'.
MS. Percy d. 9, fol. 19v.

451 Now by my knighthood I am proud
My brains I now would fain be d[ ].
Speed, Samuel (1683–1731 (?)), 'Don Quixote', verses written at the Merchant Taylor's School, for the Election 1699 (?).
Pr. bk. Vet. A3 c. 123, fol. 9 (autogr.).

452 Now Cambridge is a merry town
Each other to disgrace.
'A . . . ballade of Cambridge', on Ruggle's *Ignoramus*.
Pr. by H. Huth, *Inedited Poetical Miscellanies*, 1870, Sig. H8.
MSS. Firth d. 7, fol. 70; Malone 19, p. 133.

453 Now cease my song the plaintive strain.
Nor tracing back the child forget that I am man.
Dyer, George, 'Ode written in the cloisters of Christ's-Hospital in London'.
Pr. *Poems*, 1801, p. 9.
MS. *Eng. poet. c. 21, fol. 15.

454 Now Charles his offspring bought with frequent prayers
As near in goodness as in majesty.
Strode, William, 'On the Star which appear at Prince Charles his Birth', May, 1630.
MS. *CCC. 325, fol. 51v (autogr.).

455 Now Chloris laughs and swears how she affects me
Women can weep and laugh both with a wind.
Pr. Michael East's *Second Set of Madrigales*, 1606, xvii–xviii.
MS. Douce 280, fol. 69v.

456 Now Christ his time of private living past
Alone Christ wrought out man's redemption.
MS. *Rawl. poet. 97, fol. 58v (autogr.).

457 Now [Christ] Chrecht me save
And so adieu.
A version of 'The Irsh Beggar', I397.
MSS. Ashmole 38, p. 114, subscribed J. Shancke; CCC. 328, fol. 95; Rawl. D. 398, fol. 242.

458 Now civil wars a second age consume
To point good men to a safe land.
Fanshawe, Sir Richard, translator, 'To the People of Rome', Horace, *Epodes* xvi.
MS. *Firth c. 1, p. 69.

Now comedies goodnight, for since the age 459
When knave or fool appears, that's I, that's I.
Endorsed 'Prologue to a play'.
MS. Eng. poet. c. 25, fol. 71.

Now comes in the glorious year 460
Which he too well remembers.
Song with tune.
MS. Mus. Sch. G. 636, fol. 15v.

Now Cupid or never 461
What Turnus must do.
[Northman, —]. From *Camilla*, music by M. A. Bononcini.
MS. Mus. c. 107, fol. 1.

Now curses on ye all! ye womankind! 462
And bear't to Hell in triumph with a dismal howl.
Chatwin, John, 'Against A Woman who by her inconstancy was the Death of his Friend'.
MS. *Rawl. poet. 94, p. 177 (autogr.).

Now curses on you all! ye virtuous fools, 463
And acted somewhat, which might merit more than Hell.
[Oldham, John], 'Pindarique' [A Satyr Against Vertue].
Pr. *Works*, ed. Edward Thompson, 1770, i. 76. See D. M. Vieth, *Attribution in Restoration Poetry*, 1963, p. 458.
MS. *Rawl. poet. 123, p. 3 (autogr.).
MSS. Add. B. 106, fol. 34, attr. to Roch.; Rawl. D. 1480, fol. 201, attr. to Oldham.

Now Davis for a bird is in 464
But yet it is but for a Martin.
[Sir John] 'Davi[e]s being committed to prison for a quarrell betweene him and Martin, wrote as ensueth', couplet.
MS. Rawl. poet. 148, fol. 4.

Now deign my muse, inspire thy poet's lays, 465
And blest with them how happy I could live.
Percy, Thomas, nephew of the Bp. of Dromore, 'Ode to Contemplation . . . In Feb. 1777'.
MS. Percy c. 8, two copies, fols. 50 (autogr.), and 94.

Now did the saffron morn her beams display 466
Ending the funeral with a solemn feast.
Congreve, William, 'The Lamentations of Hecuba, Andromache, and Helen over the dead Body of Hector . . . from the Greek . . . Iliad. ω'.
Pr. Dryden's *Examen Poeticum*, 1693, p. 215.
MS. Add. B. 105, fol. 42.

467 Now does the glorious day appear
And make heav'ns mighty concave ring.
[Shadwell, Thomas], 'An Ode written for the Birthday of Queen Mary . . . music by Hen. Purcell' [1689 (?)].
F. B. Zimmerman, *Purcell*, 1963, no. 332.
Pr. *The Muses Farewell to Popery*, 1690, p. 223.
MS. Mus. c. 28, fol. 19.

468 Now each creature joys the other
Hath her bosom decked with flowers.
[Daniel, Samuel], 'Madrigal the 2[d]'. Copied by P. Hayes from John Farmer's *Madrigals*, 1599.
MS. Mus. d. 8, fol. 9.

469 Now each flowery bank of May
Whose love is life, whose hate is death.
Pr. Orlando Gibbons's *First set of Madrigals*, 1612, xii.
MSS. Mus. f. 11–15: f. 11, fol. 33[v].

470 Now echo on what's religion grounded? Roundhead
Then god keep king and state from those same men. Amen.
'The Eccho'.
Pr. *The Prologue and Epilogue . . . by Francis Cole* [Abraham Cowley], 1642.
MS. Douce 357, fol. 41[v]; see also N4.

471 Now even on dry land doth the sailor rest.
Which seemed embalmed with pitch before he died.
'An Epitaph on a Saylour'.
MS. CCC. 328, fol. 58[v].

472 Now every place fresh pleasures yields
Loudly in echoes shall rejoice.
MS. Rawl. poet. 196, fol. 12[v].

473 Now falsehood's masks so common grow
Cries out I cannot cannot bear it.
Boswell, James, 'Epigram'.
MS. *Douce 193, fol. 25[v] (autogr.).

474 Now farewell good Christmas
My carol here ends.
'A caroll for twelfth day'.
Pr. *New Christmas Carols*, 1661, Sig. B1[v].
MS. Eng. poet. b. 5, p. 60.

475 Now farewell summer's fervid sky
Shall pencil woods and groves, and streams and purple skies.
Dyer, George, 'Written at the close of Autumn after rambling through Cambridgeshire and Essex'.
Pr. *Poems*, 1801, p. 119.
MS. *Eng. poet. c. 21, fol. 18.

Now fie upon him what is man 476
Think on thy coffin, not thy bridal bed.
Flatman, Thomas, 'Song. 1671. Set by R. Hill'.
MSS. *Firth d. 7, fol. 52; Rawl. D. 260, fol. 36[v]; Rawl. poet. 173, fol. 85[v], attr. to Mr. Flatman.

Now fie upon the peevish sect 477
Than either saint or murderess.
Weaver, Thomas, 'Song'.
Pr. *Songs and Poems*, 1654.
MS. *Rawl. poet. 211, fol. 34 (autogr.).

Now, fie upon't, quoth Flattery 478
Said every thing I meant to say.
Dormer Stanhope, Philip, 4th Earl of Chesterfield (?), 'Truth at Court . . . 1761'.
Not. pr. in his *Miscellaneous Works*, iii, 1778.
MS. Lat. misc. e. 53, p. 52, attr. to Ld. Chesterfield.

Now first I mark the magic foot of spring 479
Which gives thee life, can bring no joy to me.
'Absence'.
MS. Percy d. 9, fol. 10.

Now flaming charioteer of love aproach 480
All plenty, peace, and fair prosperity.
Hodnett, Will., 'Epithalamie to George Mountagu and Elizabeth Irby'.
MS. Rawl. poet. 116, fol. 75.

Now for a night of jollity and mirth 481
Thus favoured by the smiles of Jove.
'A Burletta of Errors founded on the fable of Jupiter and Alcmena'.
MS. Eng. poet. c. 11, fol. 27.

[N]ow for dispensing power, himself doth show 482
[Spill blood and treason(?)] till it tumble down.
Fragment.
MS. Rawl. D. 864, fol. 200.

Now for good St. Stephen's sake 483
We will loiter but a little.
'[Carol] for St. Ste[phen's] day to the tune of derry, derry, downe'.
MS. Eng. poet. b. 5, p. 64.

Now for some ages had the pride of Spain 484
With Laurel in his hand, and half Peru.
Waller, Edmund, 'Of our present warr with Spain, and first victory at Sea', 8 Sept. 1656.
Pr. broadside, and by S. Carrington, *History of the Life and Death of Oliver, Late Lord Protector*, 1659.
MS. Rawl. poet. 147, p. 170.

485 Now forth the kingly banners go.
Hath saved, do thou for ever guide.
'Engl. Primer of our Ladie. 1631 . . . p. 13'.
MS. Eng. poet. e. 56, p. 36.

486 Now from fair Thetis' bed brisk Phoebus rose
He said, and wavered on the fatal tree.
Parsons, William.
MS. *Don. d. 123, p. 8 (autogr.).

487 Now glorious heavens we shall not need to fear
Thy praise shall ever in men's mouths be found.
Stephenson, John, 'Upon the Ephemerides of the profoundlie lerned Astrologer Mr. William Lilly'.
MS. Ashmole 423, fol. 144 (autogr. (?)).

488 Now god above that never wrought amiss
That first devised the leather bottell.
MS. Locke b. 7, fol. 171$^{v}$.

489 Now God and his good angels guard me; when
A greater sin than lust to think on thee.
W. R., 'To an ugly woman tempting him'.
MS. Rawl. poet. 199, p. 76.

490 Now God preserve, as you well do deserve
Oh but log was too heavy to dance it.
'Ben Johnsons Maske before the Kinge', extract from *The Masque of Christmas*, 1616.
MS. Rawl. poet. 160, fol. 173.

491 Now God preserve our realm
From every such pitiful poet.
'Peru. Or a new Ballad . . .' on Sir William Davenant's *Cruelty of the Spaniards in Peru*, 1658.
MSS. Ashmole 36, 37, fol. 163.

492 Now good my friend conform you to the rest
Let not your wings be greater than your nest.
Couplet.
MS. Rawl. poet. 117, fol. 275 rev.

493 Now grant (great god of love) that I may still
That I desire in such assaults to die.
'Contented Love'; the opening lines on fol. 69$^{r}$ rev. are wrongly headed 'On Dr. Price Being Vice-chancellour'.
MS. Rawl. poet. 84, fol. 69$^{r, v}$ rev.

494 Now had his highness bid farewell to Spain
One link dissolved, the whole creation ends.
Waller, Edmund, 'Of the Danger his Majesty (being Prince) escaped att the Rode att Saint Andrews'.
Pr. *Poems*, 1645, p. 1.
MSS. *Don. d. 55, fol. 12; *Rawl. poet. 174, p. 12.

Now had the coal-black steeds of pitchy night 495
At sight hereof, forthwith I did awake.
Barnfield, Richard, 'The Combat, between Conscience and Covetousnesse, in the mind of Man', written in cipher.
MS. Ashmole 1153, fol. 129.

Now had the sun sunk down to's liquid bed 496
They all awakened in St. James Square.
'The taking of Namure. Lt. Generall Rumney [16]95'.
MS. Locke c. 32, fol. 36.

Now have I lost at the dice and tablery 497
For daily it cometh.
Prophecy.
MS. Rawl. C. 813, fol. 152$^{v}$.

Now hoary winter grasps his icy wand 498
Of what we offer—the object your applause.
Skinner, John, 'Prologue to the Play of the Drummer acted at Claverton by the family in the Christmas Hollidays 1795'.
MS. *Eng. poet. d. 22, fol. 43.

Now hot and cold I am, how all my veins 499
Plague us poor lovers and we must obey.
MS. Rawl. D. 396, fol. 159.

Now I despise, what I too rashly prized 500
Will them admire whom kinder thoughts adore.
Williams, John.
MS. *Rawl. poet. 184, fol. 52 (autogr.).

Now I have found the reasons why 501
So we in love and pity both shall die.
'Second part' of I141.
MS. Mus. b. 1, fol. 166$^{v}$, music by John Wilson.

Now I have found thee, I will ever more 502
Lord, so I am if here my thoughts might rest.
Alabaster, William, 'Son: 13. uppon the Crucifix.'
MS. *Eng. poet. e. 57, fol. 3.

Now I see thy looks were feigned 503
[Cupid plague thee for thy treason].
[Lodge, Thomas], Song, copied from Thomas Ford's *Musicke of Sundrie Kindes*, 1607, iv.
MS. Mus. d. 8, fol. 14$^{v}$.

Now I with generous Cowley see 504
With Charles they'd leave their empires for a cell.
'Solitude . . . Ap. 8, 1684', presented by M. A. to William Sancroft, 1689.
MS. Rawl. poet. 154, fol. 55$^{v}$.

505 Now if some envious madam that for no man
So let her; That's her humour, this is mine.
Bulteel, John, on Mrs. Mabella Tynte, *temp.* Commonwealth.
MS. *Rawl. poet. 159, fol. 223v.

506 Now if the sons of Jacob being to go
Who receive Christ, receive the Holy Ghost.
MS. *Rawl. poet. 97, fol. 25v.

507 Now I'll enjoy my long neglected ease,
At sixty she new offers may receive.
Williams, John, 'the 2ds [second words] are. I'le give but sixty'.
MS. *Rawl. poet. 184, fol. 52 (autogr.).

508 Now I'm prepared against my Lord doth come
Lord I'm ready call me then away.
Cavendish, Lady Jane, 'Hope's preparation'.
MS. *Rawl. poet. 16, p. 39.

509 Now in my humble, but obscure retreat
I'd laugh with you, and with Squire C. be grave.
Potenger, John, 'A Letter'.
MS. *Eng. poet. d. 161, p. 126.

510 [Now in the dead of night his passion keeps]
[But he, his only Eve, could only love].
Hammond, Anthony, 'A Midnight Thought. to Amynta', lines 6–22.
Pr. *Miscellany of Original Poems*, 1720, p. 6.
MS. Rawl. D. 360, fol 76 (autogr.).

511 Now in the spring of life, bright, learned and gay
Which, wither'd once, can charm the sense no more.
Williams (?), —, 'Imitation of Horace', *Odes* IV. x.
Pr. *British Magazine*, 1765, subscribed A. B.
MS. *Eng. poet. e. 7, fol. 15 (autogr.).

512 Now is it true earth moves, and Heaven stands still,
Turns to the antipodes.
MS. Rawl. poet. 206, p. 28.

513 Now is my time Sir since you can desert
Lays bags of yellow boys by reverend side.
Gough, Richard, 'On the Presbyterian Minister at Enfield. 1772'.
MS. *Eng. poet. c. 5, fol. 213 (autogr.).

514 Now is the welcome night addressed
For so true love is tried.
'An Epithilamion'.
MSS. Ashmole 38, p. 155; Eng. poet. f. 25, fol. 8.

515 Now is the winter gone, the earth hath lost
June in her eyes in her heart January.
[Carew, Thomas], 'On the spring'.
Pr. *Poems*, 1640.
MS. CCC. 328, fol. 19v; see also N563.

Now Israel may say and that truly 516
His name hath saved us from those wicked men.
[Whittingham, William], Psalm cxxiv.
MS. Rawl. poet. 112, fol. 33v rev.

Now Israel may say and truly say 517
To him made heaven and earth be praise for ay.
Harington, Sir John, Psalm cxxiv.
MS. *Douce 361, fol. 80.

Now it is time to drink now time to dance 518
And under Caesar not a captive go.
W. A., translator, Horace, *Odes* I. xxxvii.
MS. *Rawl. poet. 104, fol. 12 (autogr.).

Now Joan we are married and now let me say 519
The summer of love shall reside in my heart.
'Corin to Joan'.
MS. Eng. poet. c. 51, p. 308.

Now Jove at length hath sent enough sharp hail 520
But beat them back with a revenging host.
W. A., translator, Horace, *Odes* I. ii.
MS. *Rawl. poet. 104, fol. 1v (autogr.).

Now ladies you would take it ill I doubt 521
I do not care, for I am a married man.
Walbank, ['Harriacus', matr. 1677/8], of Trinity College Oxford, 'The Epilogue' to the Music speech, 1684.
MS. Top. Oxon. e. 280, p. 660.

Now lent is gone and past 522
For ever satisfied.
MS. Rawl. poet. 37, p. 93.

Now let her change and spare not 523
Love is not had where none is.
[Campion, Thomas], song.
Pr. Pilkington's *First Book of Songs*, 1605, viii; also set by Campion, pr. *Third book of Ayres*, n.d. ii, and by Robert Jones, pr. *Ultimum Vale*, 1608, xvii.
MSS. Mus. f. 7–10: f. 10, fol. 20, music by Pilkington.

Now let my tears like rivers flow 524
Thy mercies greater are.
Beddome, Benjamin, 'An Hymn'.
MS. *Eng. misc. e. 227, fol. 59.

Now let them vote, declare, contrive 525
But the next sea voyage shall be theirs.
'Upon the meeting of the King and Queene upon Edge-hill', 13 July 1643.
MSS. Ashmole 36, 37, fol. 1.

Now let th' impetuous winds arise 526
Detain the fair Susanna here!
Parsons, William, 'Song'.
MS. *Don. d. 123, p. 27 (autogr.).

527 Now lettest thou oh Lord
Of thine own Israel.
'The Song of Simeon or nunc dimittis'.
MS. Eng. poet. e. 51, p. 177.

528 Now listen brave Oxonians, listen to our verse
And received in her ladyship's stead.
'On Dr. Price Being Vice-chancelour', William Piers (Peirs, Pearce), Vice-chancellor 1621–3, afterwards Bp. of Peterborough and of Bath and Wells.
MS. Rawl. poet. 84, fol. 69 rev.

529 Now Lord Hood is sailed with his valiant crew,
Then peace and felicity again will abound.
'Success to the Grand Fleet; Or, the Honest Briton's Prayer'.
MS. Firth c. 18, fol. 57.

530 Now Lord I beg of thee before I pray,
That in Christ's blood, to bathe me purely white.
Cavendish, Lady Jane.
MS. *Rawl. poet. 16, p. 40.

531 Now, Lord, or never they'll believe on thee
Thou to their teeth hast proved thy deity.
Crashaw, Richard, 'On the miracle of the Loaves'.
Pr. *Steps to the Temple*, 1646.
MSS. Eng. misc. e. 241, fol. 96$^v$; Rawl. poet. 90, fol. 105$^v$; Tanner 465, fol. 33$^v$, attr. to Mr. Crashaw on fol. 1*a*.

532 Now mark ye well and I shall tell
*Puer natus est nobis.*
'A carroll'.
MS. Eng. poet. b. 5, p. 73.

533 Now may I see the time hath been in vain
A lamentable hey ho.
Song with music.
MS. Don. c. 57, fol. 33.

534*a* Now may thy servants still record
The heaven and earth's large architect.
Beaumont, Thomas, 'The 124th Psalme'.
MS. *Malone 18, p. 101 (autogr.).

534*b* Now, muse, a loftier strain invites thy pen,
And still let beauty with good letters join.
Barnes, Joshuah, 'On Major Phil. Prime's Sister, 1703'.
MS. Hearne's diaries 11, p. 123.

535 Now my freedom's regained
Only envied by him that is plagued with a wife.
'A song sett by Mr. Willis'.
MS. Mus. Sch. C. 95, p. 69.

Now my glad thoughts perceive the blind boy's quiver. 536
His joys that loves and is beloved again.
Beaumont, Thomas, 'Of his happines in Love'.
MS. *Malone 18, two autogr. drafts, pp. 8 and 36.

Now my year's rent is paid, but that you'll say 537
Since they're the circumcision of the heart.
Cf. T1968, fol. 33$^v$.
MS. Rawl. poet. 246, fol. 34$^v$.

Now now I see though earth and hell conspire 538
And let us all *una voce* say Amen.
A. N., 'The Gunne powder Conspiracie Anagrammatized Nowe God can preserve the Prince'. 1629.
MS. Rawl. poet. 160, fol. 34.

Now now Lucatia now make haste 539
And now they call away away.
Birkenhead, Sir John, song, music by H. Lawes; pr. *The Second Book of Ayres and Dialogues*, 1655, p. 3.
MS. Mus. Sch. F. 572, p. 86.

Now now the fight's done and the great God of war 540
That Cupet in saddle sits bending his bow.
MS. Mus. Sch. G. 640, fol. 39 rev., with a tune.

Now now's the time so oft by truth 541
Two, like two ripe shacks of corn.
[Herrick, Robert, Epithalamie to Sir Thomas Southwell and his Ladie, 1618].
Pr. *Hesperides*, 1648.
MS. Eng. poet. c. 50, fol. 84.

Now, oh now I needs must part 542
Who both lived and died true.
Song, pr. John Dowland's *Songs or Ayres*, 1597, vi.
MSS. Ashmole 38, p. 128; Mus. f. 7–10: f. 10, fol. 6$^v$, with Dowland's music.

Now our Athenian olive spreads. To you 543
True fruit from you to pay you thus with leaves.
[Locke, John], 'Verses to A[lexander] P[opham]'.
MS. Locke c. 32, fol. 10 (autogr.).

Now peep bo peep, thrice happy blest mine eyes 544
[Phillis awakes and I must leave my love].
Pr. Pilkington's *First Book of Songs*, 1605, i.
MSS. Mus. f. 7–10: f. 7, fol. 24.

545 Now Phoebus did the world with frowns survey
And Cardiff's cliffs obscured Ramillies field.
'Asgill's lamentation for the losse of Mr. Harley. From the Greek of Homer left imperfect by Mr. Walsh', 11 Feb. 1708.
MSS. Ballard 47, fol. 85; Top. Oxon. c. 108, p. 69.

546 Now, prithee gentle ghost, let me request
Straight I must run the gauntlet fare-you-well.
F. T., 'A Translation' of Horace, *Satires* II. v, 'the Speakers (instead of Tiresias and Ulysses,) Hugh Peters'es Ghost, and The Discontented Colonel'.
MS. Rawl. poet. 19, fol. 7.

547 Now really it is very cross
Where stood a cross before.
'A remonstrance on behalf of the Yarmouth Cross—by a Nondestructive'.
MS. Eng. poet. d. 10, fol. 76.

548 Now reformation
Would cry down the king.
D'Urfey, Thomas, 'A Song in the Campaigner . . . Tune of Mr. Henry Purcell's'.
Cf. *Purcell*, F. B. Zimmerman, 1963, 611(7).
MS. Mus. Sch. C. 95, p. 137.

549 Now reigns King George the second of the name
Peace, from which fountain riches always flow.
Samber, Robert, 'On the King', from 'the Bellman's Verses'.
MS. *Rawl. poet. 134*b*, fol. 155 (autogr.).

550 Now sable night concludes the day,
But ever live, and wake and sing.
'Evening Hymn', [pr. in *Gentleman's Magazine*, v, July 1735].
MS. Eng. poet. c. 9, p. 110.

551 Now saucy whigs ye'd [you'd] best take heed,
To heirs begot 'twixt him and Benting.
'Epitaph on ABC or Elegy on M[ary] P[rincess of] O[range].'
MS. Rawl. poet. 181, two versions, fols. 16, 17v.

552 Now seldom wooers at thy windows knock
And casts thee withered in cold Hebrus' groves.
W. A., translator, Horace, *Odes* I. xxv.
MS. *Rawl. poet. 104, fol. 9 (autogr.).

553 Now shall Christ's weary pilgrimage be ended
Death made thee way to life, and Hell to Heaven.
Clifford, Henry, Earl of Cumberland, 'Ascension'.
MS. *Rawl. poet. 95, fol. 34.

Now she burns as well as I 554
So shalt thou quench her fire and mine.
[Carew, Thomas], 'To her againe shee burneing in a feavor'.
Pr. *Poems*, 1640.
MS. *Don. b. 9, fol. 23.

Now since your excellence hath thought it fit 555
We're totally condemned, for to night.
Cavendish, Lady Jane, Epilogue to 'The Concealed Fancies', addressed to the Earl of Newcastle.
MS. *Rawl. poet. 16, p. 156.

Now Sir the sun or earth hath circled round 556
Which disagree go dig down Mauborne hills.
James, Richard, 'An Anniversarie of marridge to Mr Philip Woodhouse'.
MS. *James 35, p. 19 (autogr.).

Now Sol's proud chariot towards the sea declines. 557
And that at greater joys we would aspire.
Walsh, Octavia, 'Evening'.
MS. *Eng. poet. e. 31, fol. 4 (autogr.).

Now thanked be the great god Pan 558
What then must I that keep the knave.
Sidney, Sir Philip, from the *Arcadia*.
MS. *e Mus. 37, fol. 29v.

Now that I want a faithful post . . . see N393.

Now that the daystar doth arise 559
May in silence sing God's praise.
[Cosin, John], 'Iam lucis orto sydere, Collection of private devotions . . . 1627. p. 46'.
MS. Eng. poet. e. 56, p. 66.

Now that the mid day heat doth scorch my shame 560
Oh where was I, that was not where I am.
Alabaster, William, 'So: 8. Ego sum vitis'.
MS. *Eng. poet. e. 57, fol. 2.

Now that the night doth her black wings 561
To live with thee in light of bliss.
Huish, Alexander, 'Nox atra rerum contegit', translated 30 Jan. 1634/5.
MS. Eng. poet. e. 56, p. 142 (autogr.).

Now that the twinkling stars essay 562
For the world's monarchy forgo?
Tate, [Nahum], 'The Midnight Thought', lines 1–25.
Pr. *Poems*, 1677, p. 111.
MS. Rawl. D. 868, fol. 55.

Now that the winter's gone, the earth hath lost 563
A face of June but heart of January.
[Carew, Thomas], 'Upon the springe'.
Pr. *Poems*, 1640.
MSS. Eng. poet. f. 25, fol. 13v; Malone 21, fol. 45; see also N515.

564 Now the bright morning star
And welcome thee, and wish thee long.
Milton, John, 'Ode to May', Mus. Bac. exercise of Joseph Harris, 1773, composed 1765.
MS. Mus. Sch. Ex. b. 11.

565 Now the captain did require
Such good men there is but few.
*The Female Sailor's Garland* (Douce PP 183), part iii.
MS. Firth c. 18, fol. 146.

566 Now the cheerful day doth spring
Glory to God we may sing.
'Primer English and Latine of K. Hen. 8. 1546. The hymne for Matyns'.
MS. Eng. poet. e. 56, p. 66.

567 Now the cold winter's gone
Equal though we live for ever.
MS. Rawl. poet. 196, fol. 34.

568 Now the declining sun gan downward bend
Struck with a virtuous emulation.
Strode, William, 'A Translation of the Nightingale out of Strada', [*Prolusions* II. vi].
MS. *CCC. 325, fol. 74$^{v}$ (autogr.).
MSS. Eng. poet. 50, fol. 61; Rawl. poet. 160, fol. 51$^{v}$; 199, p. 50, attr. to W. Strode.

569 Now the declining sun his height had past
So much even little souls desire t' excel.
['Betwixt a Lutanist and a Nightingall . . . Translated by two ffrendes'], 'The second Translation': the first is N568.
MS. Eng. poet. c. 50, fol. 62.

570 Now the great Jehova reigns
That he will pull them down.
'Wm. Snelling had these verses given him the 1 of Sept. 1650 by the Spirit. Robert Snelling is the younger Brother'.
MS. Rawl. D. 864, fol. 233$^{v}$.

571 Now the impetuous sons of France
The paper first and then the fire.
Parsons, William, 'To Mr. Weston on his advising me to publish . . . poems'. Apr. 1795.
MS. *Don. d. 123, p. 248 (autogr.).

572 Now the tenant trots to town
Letting me a lease for life.
Burton, Francis, 'A Sonnet alluding to Michaelmas day'.
MS. *Add. A. 267, fol. 141 (autogr.).

Now the veil is pulled off and this pitiful nation 573
And there in despite he shall reign.
Jacobite song.
MS. Rawl. poet. 169, fol. 16.

[Now] the world hath shut his light 574
Sleeping, waking, not forsake thee.
MS. Eng. poet. c. 50, fol. 55.

Now thou art dead I write, when breath is gone 575
The knowing to remember thee and write.
L. de C. (?), 'An Elegie upon the death of Dr. Donne'.
MS. Rawl. poet. 160, fol. 43.

Now thou, dear Will, and every friend's withdrawn, 576
By representing, to relieve his pains.
W. S., 'An Epistle to Mr. W— Fellow of Trinity College in Cambridge. In praise of an University Life'.
MS. Rawl. poet. 173, fol. 167$^{v}$.

Now thou hast loved me one whole day 577
For by tomorrow I may think so too.
Donne, John.
Pr. *Poems*, 1633, p. 197.
MSS. CCC. 327, fol. 7$^{v}$; *Eng. poet. e. 99, fol. 104$^{v}$; *f. 9, p. 105.

Now thou hast seen aspiring Dudley's son 578
O'erwhelm both him and all the bastard brood.
'An Epilogue to the Lady Jane Grey [by Nicholas Rowe, pr. 1715]. Address'd to the Prince of Mum' i.e. the Prince of Wales, afterwards George II.
MSS. Rawl. poet. 155, p. 119; 207, p. 21.

Now thou my heart hast wounded my heart take 579
Amends that's made for an heart [killing(?)] thief.
MS. Top. Yorks. c. 26, fol. 140.

Now time would be, no more 580
You can this time restore.
Couplet, translating 'Iam fuerit nec post unquam revocare licebit'.
MS. Rawl. D. 986, fol. 110.

Now 'tis my lot to be in love 581*a*
That you my new year's gift will be.
Creswell, Robert, 'A Newyears gift (a Je ne scay quoy)'. Answered by C730.
MS. *Eng. poet. f. 24, fol. 33 (autogr.).

Now to that Lord whose power is celestial 581*b*
With deadly voice as though his heart would break.
Cavendish, Thomas, cancelled prologue to 'Elegiacall Poems upon sundry persons . . . times of Henry VIII, Edward VI and Queen Mary'.
MS. Dugdale 28, fol. 228$^{v}$.

582 Now to the utmost southern goal
Or walk the academic shade.
'For the Winter Solstice. Decr. 11th 1740. By M. A.'
MS. Eng. misc. f. 79, p. 78.

583 Now treasons haunt the throne
To work a thorough reformation.
'Medly on the Association', with music [*temp.* Charles II].
MS. Mus. Sch. C. 95, p. 194.

584 Now tune it again
For if ever we lose this the next will be Babell.
'Oxford verses' on the journey of the City's representatives to London to protest against the payment of dues to the University on St. Scolastica's day. 1681.
See Wood's *Life and Times*, ed. A. Clark, ii. O.H.S. xxi, 1892, p. 512.
MS. Eng. poet. c. 25, fol. 49.

585 Now Venus yields me sweet delight
Which all men's minds oftimes do please.
'Solons verses on himself'. Translation in North's Plutarch, Life of Solon (folio 1603, p. 99).
MS. Rawl. D. 1372, fol. 26v from end.

586 Now wand'ring wight sailing to heavenly land
A paradise that heart cannot comprise.
F. W., 'Sonnet. 24'.
MS. *Rawl. C. 639, p. 123.

587 Now war is all the world about
To be imbrued.
Fanshawe, Sir Richard, 'An Ode upon . . . His Ma'ties Proclamation . . . 1630 Com'anding the Gentrie to . . . the Countrie'.
MS. *Firth c. 1, p. 82.

588 Now wars dissensions, want and taxes cease,
Since crowds now come over with William and Mary.
'Englands Congratulation . . . 1690'.
MSS. Eng. poet. c. 18, fol. 90; e. 49, p. 84.

589 Now was our heavenly vault, deprived of the light
Unarmed alas unwarned, to take a man asleep.
Sidney, Sir Philip, from the *Arcadia.*
MS. *e Mus. 37, fol. 187v.

590 Now was the time when winter's wrath seemed calm
To write withal . . .
G. B. 'Epitaph 34' on Prince Henry in 'Cestria Lugens', 1612.
MS. *Rawl. poet. 116, fol. 15.

Now we are in conjunction 591
[That one heart all divine].
'The union of Christ and his beloved spouse. Tune: when the stormy winds do blow'.
MS. Rawl. poet. 37, p. 84.

Now we are met let's merry be 592
Let's laugh and sing our belly's full.
'Glee 4 voc. Simon Ives', (probably taken from *The Musical Companion*, 1673), with added parts.
MS. Mus. d. 8, two copies, fols. 26v, 27.

Now we perceive why mortals have two eyes 593
And when they once were two, then they were none.
Oldisworth, Nicolas, 'On the death of both Mris. Summer and her Childe'.
MS. *Don. c. 24, fol. 53v (autogr.).

Now westward Sol had spent the richest beams 594
(That lived so sweetly) dead so sweet a grave!
Crashaw, Richard, 'Fidicinis, and Philomelae—Bellum Musicum'. [Strada, *Prolusions* II. vi].
MS. Tanner 465, fol. 46, attr. to R. Cr.; attr. to Mr. Crashaw on fol. 1*a*.

Now, where art thou St. Taffy, 595
And so retrieve your glory.
'On the 1st . . . March 1714/15 being the Birth Day of The Princess, and celebrated by the Welch-Men in honour of St. David and the P. of Wales'.
MS. Eng. poet. e. 87, p. 6.

Now while slow hours do feed the time's delay 596
So may you fight with age, and conquer kind.
'The Night songe going to their Bedd'.
MS. Ashmole 38, p. 109.

Now, while the moon, full-orbed, serenely bright, 597
Too proud to beg, too rich to be a slave.
Taylor, Edward, 'On the Origin, Utility, and Powers of Poetry'.
MS. Eng. poet. c. 11, fol. 73.

Now whilst Whitehall wears black and men do fear 598
Grief will dissolve them, no Protector need.
Wild, Robert, 'Upon the Death of Dennis Bond Esqr. Who died at Westminster 4 dayes before the Lord Protector', 30 Aug. 1658.
MS. Barlow 54, fol. 56.

599 Now who says poets don't in blood delight
If you're but good when pleas'd, e'en so's the devil.
'Epilogue Spoken by Mrs. Mary Lee'.
MS. Rawl. poet. 152, fol. 130ᵛ.

600 Now will we never wonder, though we meet
Robbed all her fellows of whate'er is sweet.
Oldisworth, Nicolas, 'On Mris. Katharine Bacon'.
MS. *Don. c. 24, fol. 27ᵛ (autogr.).

601 Now, ye livery of London, give ear to my song,
And our moon shall shine forth in a glorious full orb.
'An Equivalent for the Man in the Moon' on Sir John Salter's election as Lord Mayor in preference to Sir Robert Godschall, 1740.
MS. Eng. misc. b. 48, fol. 8.

602 Now you have Lesbos, and fair Samos seen
And what we no where find, have everywhere.
S. W., translator, Horace, *Epistles* I. xi.
Pr. *Poems of Horace*, A. Brome etc., 2nd ed. 1671, p. 333.
MS. Rawl. D. 261, p. 51.

603 Now you must imagine first
And well betrusted bees sweet bag.
'The Fayrie Kings diet'.
Pr. '*A Description Of the King and Queene of Fayries*, by R. S., 1635.
MS. Rawl. poet. 142, fol. 45.

604 Now young-eyed spring, on gentle breezes born
And gild existence in her dim decline.
Seward, Anna, 'Sonnet', 1787.
MS. *Pigott d. 12, fol. 11ᵛ (autogr.).

605 Now you've taken off my case
Ticking brother watch and pray.
'An Address from the Watch to the Reader'.
MS. Eng. misc. e. 227, fol. 50ᵛ.

606 Now's the feast of Valentine:
Till their mother earth shall die.
Robinson, Robert, 'Upon Valentine day'.
MS. *Rawl. poet. 218, p. 54 (autogr.).

607 Noy's flood is past, the Banckes appear
The Heath's burnt up, the Finch chirps there.
'Uppon his Ma.ᵗˡˢ two Lord Cheyff Iustices of the Common pleas and his two Atturneys', Aug., Sept., 1634.
MSS. Ashmole 38, p. 87; Tanner 466, fol. 66ᵛ.

*Nullus Francisco tumulus nullusque Philip[p]o* 608
For Christopher hath all the room.
'Epitaphs of Sir Francis Walsingham and Sir Philip Sidney'. 'Christopher' is Sir Christopher Hatton.
MS. Firth d. 7, fol. 155; see also P148.

Numantiae's wars my friend tell not at all 609
Now sweetly kissing which before did frown.
W. A., translator, Horace, *Odes* II. xii.
MS. *Rawl. poet. 104, fol. 17 (autogr.).

Number the days the cloudy and the clear, 610
Doth penance daily yet sins all his life.
Translation from Latin distich.
Pr. *The Academy of Complements*, 1650, p. 131.
MS. Rawl. D. 954, fol. 41ᵛ.

Numicius to admire nothing at all, 611
If not, I pray, make use of these with me.
B[rome], A[lexander], translator, Horace, *Epistles* I. vi.
Pr. *Poems of Horace*, A. Brome etc., 2nd ed., 1671, p. 314.
MS. Rawl. D. 261, p. 36.

Nymph of my soul forgive my sighs 612
In love with innocence and thee.
'A Song' by 'Dr. [John] Woolcott I believe'.
MS. Eng. misc. c. 241, fol. 69.

Nymph of the grot, those sacred springs I keep 613
And drink in silence or in silence lave.
Pope, [Alexander], translation of Latin.
See *Minor Poems*, ed. N. Ault and J. Butt, 1954, p. 248.
MS. Eng. misc. e. 241, fol. 111.

Nymphs and fairies sweetly sing 614
To this blessed deity, fa la la.
'A 5. Voc. Tho: Ravenscroft . . . Hipo Micolidian cum Hipo Phrigian'.
MSS. Mus. f. 11–15: f. 11, fol. 39ᵛ.

Nymphs and shepherds come away 615
Can never know such bliss.
[Shadwell, Thomas], from *The Libertine*: music by Purcell, 1692 (?). Cf. *Purcell*, by F. B. Zimmerman, 1963, no. 600(1b).
MS. Mus. d. 3, fol. 2.

PRINTED IN GREAT BRITAIN
AT THE UNIVERSITY PRESS, OXFORD
BY VIVIAN RIDLER
PRINTER TO THE UNIVERSITY